CASES AND MATERIALS

NONPROFIT ORGANIZATIONS

FOURTH EDITION

by

JAMES J. FISHMAN
Professor of Law,
Pace University School of Law

STEPHEN SCHWARZ
Professor of Law Emeritus,
University of California, Hastings College of the Law

FOUNDATION PRESS
2010

THOMSON REUTERS

© 1995, 2000 FOUNDATION PRESS

© 2006 THOMSON REUTERS/FOUNDATION PRESS

© 2010 By THOMSON REUTERS/FOUNDATION PRESS

     1 New York Plaza, 34th Floor

     New York, NY 10004

     Phone Toll Free 1–877–888–1330

     Fax (646)424–5201

     foundation–press.com

Printed in the United States of America

ISBN 978–1–59941–665–6

Mat #40853344

To Liz, Lisi, Diana, and Sophie

JJF

To F.K.G.

SS

PREFACE

Nonprofit organizations have been influential in American society since colonial times. They wield considerable economic power, contributing more than five percent of the nation's gross domestic product and employing nearly ten percent of its workforce. Only within the past few decades, however, has the unique body of law affecting nonprofits attracted the broader attention of legal scholars and practitioners. In introducing its "Developments in the Law" issue devoted to nonprofit corporations almost 20 years ago, the Harvard Law Review capsulized this emergence of the nonprofit sector as a discrete field of study:

> For many years, only tax specialists and a few cognoscenti appreciated the unique legal issues related to nonprofit corporations. Only recently has the rest of the bar come to recognize that representing nonprofit corporations constitutes a separate legal discipline. A number of professional working groups now focus on various aspects of nonprofit corporation law; for example, the American Bar Association recently promulgated a model nonprofit corporation statute. The academic literature in the field has mushroomed, and law schools have begun to integrate the field into their curricula.

Developments in the Law—Nonprofit Corporations, 105 Harv.L.Rev. 1578 (1992).

This book—the first comprehensive law school text in the field—was another step in this evolution. Before publication of the first edition in 1995, some law schools offered courses in nonprofit organizations, ranging from global surveys to more specialized tax offerings, but instructors and curricular growth were hindered by a dearth of published teaching materials. Our goal was to help fill the void by crafting a book to ease the burden on experienced teachers and entice newcomers to teach, study and practice in this fascinating and dynamic area. Today, the maturity of this field of study is reflected in the increasing number of law schools offering nonprofit organizations courses as well as the publication of several other casebooks. The field has appeal to students and teachers with interests in wide-ranging areas such as corporations, taxation, estate planning, constitutional law, antitrust, law and economics, environmental law, health law, and public interest law. These legal issues are increasingly of interest, we think, because so many lawyers and law students become involved with nonprofit organizations as directors, trustees, members, and volunteers, and in those capacities they are frequently called upon for advice.

With an expanding body of law and such a potentially diverse constituency, each new edition presents a challenge of covering those topics of greatest importance and yet preserving flexibility for instructors with different emphasis and expertise, all while keeping the book to a manageable length. To that end, we have attempted to maintain an up-to-date teaching text that is adaptable to a two or three-unit survey course, a policy-oriented seminar, or a more specialized J.D. or LL.M tax-exempt organizations class. The state law and federal tax materials are separate, self-standing units of the book, but important tax concepts are previewed in Chapter 1 and, as relevant, in subsequent chapters that focus primarily on state law. And within the tax chapters, we selectively employ a "two track" approach to accommodate the more global classes where students and instructors may prefer a policy-oriented overview while still offering the additional detailed coverage that is suitable for a graduate tax course.

The book includes a wide variety of materials—edited cases, legislative history, excerpts from scholarly articles and books, writings from other disciplines, and authoritative IRS administrative materials. For most topics, it provides extensive authors' text, notes, questions, bibliographic references for further reading, and problems for class discussion. To enliven the coverage, the notes and questions frequently refer to the rich array of real world controversies and news reports, offering an opportunity for students to evaluate critically the increasingly publicized underside of the nonprofit sector.

This Fourth Edition incorporates many new developments occurring during the four-year shelf life of its predecessor, most notably the enactment of the Pension Protection Act of 2006, the most comprehensive legislation affecting charitable nonprofits since 1969. The IRS also has been busy, ratcheting up its scrutiny of hospitals and universities, redesigning the Form 990 information return, issuing new regulations on the public support tests that enable charities to avoid private foundation status, and expanding its jurisdiction over governance matters that traditionally have been a prerogative of the states. The Fourth Edition also reflects several recent state law developments, such as the almost universal adoption of the Uniform Prudent Management of Institutional Funds Act (just in time for the economic downturn and its devastating impact on charitable endowments) and new case law on donor standing, as well the American Bar Association's major revision of its Model Nonprofit Corporation Act and the steady progress of the American Law Institute's project on Principles of the Law of Nonprofit Organizations.

This edition is more than just an update. Concerned that the barrage of new developments and the authors' voracious appetites were causing the book to gain far too much weight, we revisited every chapter with the goal of pruning wherever possible. Some of the longer cases and notes have been edited, and dated or redundant materials were removed. Although the Fourth Edition still may have too many details for some (and not enough for others), it is almost 100 pages shorter than its predecessor—no small feat given the long-winded proclivities of the legal and academic professions.

Turning to the specifics of organization and coverage, the Fourth Edition consists of five parts. Part One (Chapter 1), an introduction, describes the universe of nonprofits, addresses the principal theoretical rationales for the nonprofit sector and introduces the tax treatment of charities, which are the dominant presence in the sector. If the study of nonprofit organizations has serious academic merit, as we believe it does, theoretical questions such as why the nonprofit sector exists should be addressed at an early point and revisited frequently. To that end, the introductory chapter provides a history of nonprofit organizations in the United States and offers a balanced perspective on the role of the nonprofit sector in the economy and society, both domestic and international.

Part Two (Chapters 2–4) looks at nonprofit organizations from the state perspective. Chapter 2 covers formation, including choice of form, the practical aspects of formation, basic state statutory approaches to the nonprofit entity, and the purposes and powers of nonprofit corporations and charitable trusts. Since the choice of legal form by an organization's founders may have profound ramifications if it dissolves or seeks to modify its purposes, Chapter 2 also addresses dissolution issues, including the doctrines of cy pres and deviation, and the legal questions confronting a nonprofit organization that seeks to restructure its operations or convert to a for-profit form.

Chapter 3 explores operation and governance, beginning with an overview of the legal responsibilities and role of the governing board, and then turning to the shifting standards of fiduciary obligations relating to the duty of care, the duty of loyalty and conflicts of interest, the duty of obedience, investment responsibility, and state enforcement of fiduciary obligations. Chapter 4 concludes the state law coverage by examining the regulation of charitable solicitation, including constitutional obstacles confronted by state regulators and proposals for a federal regulatory scheme.

Part Three (Chapters 5–8) is devoted to the tax treatment of charitable organizations. The emphasis in Chapter 5 is on the affirmative requirements and operational limitations faced by organizations seeking tax-exempt status as charities under § 501(c)(3), with more abbreviated coverage of state and local tax exemption issues. This edition incorporates a number of important new qualification developments, including the evolving definition of charity, the increasing scrutiny of hospitals and universities by Congress and the IRS, and continuing concerns over excessive compensation and political activities.

Chapter 6 addresses the dynamic issue of commercial activities—their impact on qualification for tax exemption; the unrelated business income tax; and the special challenges and planning opportunities presented by complex structures such as taxable subsidiaries and joint ventures. Chapter 7 turns to the distinction between private foundations and public charities, first describing the universe of private foundations and grantmaking alternatives, such as donor-advised funds and supporting organizations. It goes on to identify strategies to avoid private foundation status and surveys the regulatory challenges facing organizations unable to escape the private foundation regulatory regime. Chapter 8, which is devoted to law and philanthropy from the perspective of donors and fundraisers, includes a variety of basic and advanced materials on the charitable contributions deduction and planned giving opportunities. All these chapters employ, more or less, the "two track" approach mentioned earlier, beginning with an overview, then turning to basic tax principles, and concluding with more advanced and often technical material. This organization allows instructors to pick and choose the depth of their tax coverage.

Part Four shifts the focus to mutual benefit and membership organizations. Chapter 9 is an overview of the tax exemption requirements affecting mutual benefit organizations such as trade associations, labor unions and social clubs. Chapter 10 is devoted to the special problems of private membership associations, including important constitutional questions revolving around freedom of association.

Part Five (Chapter 11) considers other legal issues that did not comfortably fit elsewhere. For now, it is confined to the application of antitrust law to nonprofits, with particular emphasis on the health care and education sectors.

To complement the casebook, we have prepared a separate and completely updated softbound Supplement (Nonprofit Organizations: Statutes, Regulations and Forms), which contains excerpts from the ABA's recently published "third edition" of the Model Nonprofit Corporation Act, the nonprofit corporation laws of several leading jurisdictions, the Uniform Prudent Investor Act, the Uniform Prudent Management of Institutional Funds Act, and selected sections of the Restatements of Trusts and other statutes. The Supplement also includes all relevant sections of the Internal Revenue Code and Treasury Regulations; important IRS forms, such as the redesigned Form 990 information return and the Form 1023 application for § 501(c)(3) exemption; sample articles and bylaws for a nonprofit corporation; a simple charitable trust instrument; and a sample conflict of interest policy. Suggested assignments to Statutes, Regulations and Forms are provided in bold type at the beginning of most sections of the casebook.

As for other matters of style and format, we have edited cases and other original sources freely to make them more accessible to students. Citations and internal cross references in excerpted materials have been deleted without so indicating. Textual omissions are indicated by asterisks, and editorial additions are in brackets. Many footnotes from original sources have been omitted without renumbering those that remain. Our goal was to make the text gender neutral, and we have tried to alternate between masculine and feminine pronouns to represent both sexes. Coverage in this edition is current through May 1, 2010.

We are indebted to many people for their help and guidance during the gestation period of this text. This has been a collaborative effort in the best sense, and many who teach, write and practice in the field have graciously offered their advice and encouragement. We owe special thanks to John Simon, who has done so much to nurture the field, for his many helpful insights during the preparation of the First Edition; to Harvey Dale, the founder and director of the National Center on Philanthropy and the Law at New York University School of Law, who has encouraged this project from its incubation stage and offered us the unique opportunity to present our work-in-progress to leading scholars and practitioners at an invitational conference at NYU; and to Bill Hutton, who generously allowed us to adapt problems and colorful characters that he developed and refined over many years. We also are grateful to the other participants in the NYU conference: Bob Boisture, Laura Chisolm, Marion Fremont–Smith, Harvey Goldschmid, Carlyn McCaffrey, Jill Manny, and Peter Swords. And thanks too to Rob Atkinson, whose views on the appropriate model for a law school nonprofits course greatly stimulated our thinking; to Miriam Galston for her meticulous editing and valuable substantive comments; and to John Colombo, Mike Klausner, Evelyn Brody and Ellen Aprill for their scholarly contributions to the field and thoughtful suggestions on coverage and content. Any errors or other transgressions, of course, remain those of the authors.

Professor Fishman also wishes to thank the Brooklyn and Pace University Schools of Law, which provided research support; NYU School of Law's National Center on Philanthropy and the Law, which provided access to its philanthropy library; and Kate Fitzpatrick, Brooklyn Law School class of 2009 and Alexandra Campbell–Ferrari, Pace Law School class of 2012, who served as a research assistants during the preparation of this edition. Professor Schwarz extends thanks to Hastings College of the Law for its ongoing institutional support; Adele Dorison and Barbara Rosen, for their invaluable assistance as research assistants and editors on earlier editions; and the students in his classes over many years at the University of Florida, NYU, Arizona State, and Hastings (particularly the spring 2010 class), who endured rough early drafts and later helped to improve many of the problems and other materials.

And last but hardly least, we are grateful for the support of our families, friends, and colleagues, and for their understanding of the demands of producing a first edition and keeping it current.

JAMES J. FISHMAN
STEPHEN SCHWARZ

June 2010

ACKNOWLEDGEMENTS

With appreciation, the authors acknowledge the following authors, publishers, and other copyright holders who gave permission to reprint excerpts from their works:

American Bar Association, Business Law Section, Lizabeth A. Moody, Foreword to Model Nonprofit Corporation Act xxiv-xxix (3rd ed. 2008). Copyright © 2008 by the American Bar Association. Reprinted with permission. This information or any portion thereof may not be copied or disseminated in any form or by any means or stored in an electronic database or retrieval system without the express written consent of the American Bar Association.

William D. Andrews, Personal Deductions in an Ideal Income Tax, 86 Harvard Law Review 309, 344–348, 356–358, 371–372, 374–375 (1972). Copyright © 1972 by the Harvard Law Review Association.

Boris I. Bittker and George K. Rahdert, The Exemption of Nonprofit Organizations from Federal Income Taxation, 85 Yale Law Journal 299, 307–316, 348–357 (1976), reprinted with permission of the Yale Law Journal Company and Fred B. Rothman & Co.

Zechariah Chafee, The Internal Affairs of Associations Not for Profit, 93 Harvard Law Review 993, 993–995 (1930). Copyright © 1930 by the Harvard Law Review Association.

John A. Edie, First Steps in Starting a Foundation 6–10, 25–27 (3d ed.). Copyright © 1993 by The Council on Foundations, Inc.

Ira Mark Ellman, Driven from the Tribunal: Judicial Resolution of Internal Church Disputes, 69 California Law Review 1378, 1382–1389, 1397–1400 (1981).

David F. Freeman and The Council on Foundations, The Handbook on Private Foundations 1–9, 248–253 (rev. ed. 1991). Copyright © 1991 by The Council on Foundations, Inc.

Barry R. Furrow, Sandra H. Johnson, Timothy S. Jost & Robert L. Schwartz, The Law of Health Care Organization and Finance 448–452 (1991). Reprinted with permission of the West Publishing Company.

John W. Gardner, The Independent Sector, in America's Voluntary Spirit xiii-xv (Brian O'Connell ed., The Foundation Center, 1983). Copyright © 1983 by Brian O'Connell.

Henry Hansmann, The Rationale for Exempting Nonprofit Organizations from Corporate Income Taxation, 91 Yale Law Journal 54, 72–75

(1981), reprinted by permission of the Yale Law Journal Company and Fred B. Rothman & Co.

Henry Hansmann, Reforming Nonprofit Corporation Law, 129 University of Pennsylvania Law Review 497, 504–509 (1981), with permission of Fred B. Rothman & Co. Copyright © 1981 by Henry B. Hansmann.

Kenneth L. Karst, The Efficiency of the Charitable Dollar, 73 Harvard Law Review 433, 445–449 (1960). Copyright © 1960 by the Harvard Law Review Association, Inc.

Bevis Longstreth, Modern Investment Management and the Prudent Man Rule 3–6 (1986). Copyright © 1986 by Bevis Longstreth. Published by Oxford Press.

New York University School of Law, Program on Philanthropy and the Law, Ellen Harris, Lynn S. Holley, Christopher J. McCaffrey, Fundraising Into the 1990s: State Regulation of Charitable Solicitation After *Riley*.

Note, State Power and Discrimination by Private Clubs: First Amendment Protection for Nonexpressive Associations, 104 Harvard Law Review 1835, 1838–1839 (1991). Copyright © 1991 by the Harvard Law Review Association.

Teresa Odendahl, Charity Begins at Home: Generosity and Self–Interest Among the Philanthropic Elite 3–5, 232–240 (1990). Copyright © 1990 by Basic Books, Inc. Reprinted by permission of Basic Books, a division of HarperCollins Publishers, Inc.

Lester M. Salamon, The Nonprofit Sector: A Primer 11–13, (2d ed. 1999). Copyright © 1999 by Lester M. Salamon. Published by The Foundation Center, 79 Fifth Avenue, New York, N.Y. 10003.

Lester A. Salamon, The Rise of the Nonprofit Sector, Foreign Affairs, July/August 1994. Reprinted by permission of Foreign Affairs. Copyright © 1994 by the Council on Foreign Relations, Inc.

John Simon, Harvey Dale & Laura Chisolm, The Federal Tax Treatment of Charitable Organizations, in The Nonprofit Sector: A Research Handbook (Walter W. Powell & Richard Steinberg, eds., 2d ed. 2006), Yale University Press. Copyright © 2006 by Yale University.

Burton A. Weisbrod, To Profit or Not to Profit: The Commercial Transformation of the Nonprofit Sector 1–4 (1999). Reprinted with the permission of Cambridge University Press and Burton A. Weisbrod.

SUMMARY OF CONTENTS

TABLE OF CONTENTS

TABLE OF CASES

Principal cases are in bold type. Non-principal cases are in roman type. References are to Pages.

TABLE OF STATUTES

TABLE OF TREASURY REGULATIONS

TABLE OF REVENUE RULINGS

TABLE OF MISCELLANEOUS RULINGS

TABLE OF AUTHORITIES

References are to Pages.

Wing, Kenneth T., Thomas Pollak & Amy Blackwood, The Nonprofit Almanac (Urban Institute Press, 2008), 13, 71

Wirtschafter, Nathan, Note, Fourth Quarter Choke: How the IRS Blew the Corporate Sponsorship Game, 27 Loy. L.A. L. Rev. 1465 (1994), 631.

Witte, Brian, Catholic Diocese of Wilmington files bankruptcy, Wash. Post, Oct. 18, 2009, 121.

Wright, Carolyn D., Christian Coalition Fails to Obtain Tax–Exempt Status, 25 Exempt Org. Tax Rev. 9 (1999), 544.

Wright, Carolyn D., UCC, IRS Settle Decade–Long Exemption Dispute: 501(c)(3) Status Revoked for Three Years, 28 Exempt Org. Tax Rev. 189 (2000), 460.

Wyatt, Edward, Smithsonian–Showtime Deal Raises Concerns, N.Y. Times, March 31, 2006, 670.

Young, David & Steven W. Tigges, Into the Religious Thicket—Constitutional Limits on Civil Court Jurisdiction Over Ecclesiastical Disputes, 47 Ohio St. L.J. 475 (1986), 1010.

Young, Gary J. et al., Community Control and Pricing Patterns of Nonprofit Hospitals: An Antitrust Analysis, 25 J.Health Pol., Pol'y & L., 1051 (2000), 1032.

*

CASES AND MATERIALS

NONPROFIT ORGANIZATIONS

INTRODUCTION

CHAPTER 1

AN OVERVIEW OF THE NONPROFIT SECTOR

A. INTRODUCTION

Model Nonprofit Corporation Act (3d ed.) § 6.40.

Cal. Corp. Code § 5410.

The vast array of organizations in the United States that share the designation "nonprofit" are said to inhabit a "sector" of American society—commonly referred to as "the nonprofit sector" and also variously labeled as the "third," "independent," "charitable," "voluntary," "philanthropic," "civil society," and "tax-exempt" sector. The operative assumption is that nonprofits play a societal role that is distinct from that of government and the private, for-profit sector, but much of this terminology is misleading or incomplete. Far from being independent, many nonprofit organizations have a close programmatic and financial relationship with government or private business. Not all nonprofits are charitable or rely on volunteers, nor do all charities derive the bulk of their support from private philanthropy. And nonprofits may and often do earn a profit.

The diversity of the nonprofit sector is evident from this list of familiar and obscure organizations culled from the Internal Revenue Service's list of charitable nonprofits eligible to receive tax-deductible contributions: American Acupuncture and Herbs Research Institute, Phillips Exeter Academy, Girl Scouts of America, the International Society of Talking Clock Collectors, Talmudic Research Institute, Museum of Neon Art (Los Angeles), Meditation Center of Michigan, Polynesian Cultural Center, Mothers Club of Grosse Point South High School, The Sassafras Foundation, Lincoln Center for the Performing Arts, Planned Parenthood, Church of Scientology International, and Renegade Rollergirls of Oregon.

The nonprofit form of organization extends well beyond the charitable, religious, and educational organizations in the above list. Nonprofits include labor unions, fraternal lodges, social clubs, college fraternities, trade associations, and even professional sports leagues. They range from modest entities such as a three-person dance company or a neighborhood free medical clinic, to substantial institutions such as Harvard University, the Bill and Melinda Gates Foundation or the Mayo Clinic, with revenues and assets in the billions.

Uniting this diverse population and distinguishing most nonprofits from for-profit entities is one defining characteristic: the "nondistribution constraint." As explained by Professor Henry Hansmann:

A nonprofit organization is, in essence, an organization that is barred from distributing its net earnings, if any, to individuals who exercise control over it, such as members, officers, directors, or trustees. By "net earnings" I mean here pure profits—that is, earnings in excess of the amount needed to pay for services rendered to the organization; in general, a nonprofit is free to pay reasonable compensation to any person for labor or capital that he provides, whether or not that person exercises some control over the organization. It should be noted that a nonprofit organization is not barred from earning a profit. Many nonprofits in fact consistently show an annual accounting surplus. It is only the distribution of the profits that is prohibited. Net earnings, if any, must be retained and devoted in their entirety to financing further production of the services that the organization was formed to provide. Since a good deal of the discussion that follows will focus upon this prohibition on the distribution of profits, it will be helpful to have a term for it; I shall call it the "nondistributional constraint."

Most nonprofits of any significance are incorporated. For these organizations, the nondistribution constraint is imposed, either explicitly or implicitly, as a condition under which the organization receives its corporate charter. Thus a nonprofit corporation is distinguished from a for-profit (or "business") corporation primarily by the absence of stock or other indicia of ownership that give their owner a simultaneous share in both profits and control.

In the corporation law of some states, the nondistribution constraint is accompanied or replaced by a simple statement to the effect that the organization must not be formed or operated for the purpose of pecuniary gain. Often such a condition as applied is equivalent to the nondistribution constraint. Occasionally, however, it is interpreted more restrictively to mean that an organization may not be incorporated as a nonprofit even if it is intended to assist in the pursuit of pecuniary gain in a more indirect manner.

* * *

Sometimes nonprofit organizations are formed as charitable trusts without being incorporated, although for operating nonprofits this approach is uncommon in the United States. In such cases, control over the organization lies with the trustees, and the nondistribution constraint is imposed by the law of trusts, which prohibits trustees from taking from the trust anything beyond reasonable compensation for services rendered.

Henry Hansmann, The Role of Nonprofit Enterprise, 89 Yale L.J. 837, 840 (1980).

This introductory chapter marks the boundaries of the nonprofit sector, describes its inhabitants and history, explains its widespread presence in our society, and previews the distinctive state and federal legal regimes that govern and regulate nonprofit organizations in the United States.

John W. Gardner, The Independent Sector

in America's Voluntary Spirit ix, xiii—xv (Brian O'Connell ed., 1983).

In a totalitarian state, most organized activity is governmental—and the little that is not is heavily controlled or influenced by government. Almost everything is bureaucratized and subject to central goal-setting and rule-making.

In the nations that the world thinks of as democracies, there is, in contrast, a large area of activity outside of government. The United States probably outstrips all others in the size and autonomy of its nongovernmental sector. The major portion of our private sector consists of activities designed for profit; a smaller portion consists of nonprofit activities. Both profit and nonprofit segments have many dealings with government, but both recognize that their vitality depends in part on their success in holding themselves free of central bureaucratic definition of goals.

Our subject here is the nonprofit segment. It has been variously labelled the voluntary sector, the third sector or—more recently—the independent sector.

In its diversity and strength the voluntary sector is uniquely American—not in the fact of its existence, because it exists elsewhere, but in its extraordinary richness and variety. It encompasses a remarkable array of American institutions—libraries, museums, religious organizations, schools and colleges, organizations concerned with health and welfare, citizen action groups, neighborhood organizations and countless other groups such as Alcoholics Anonymous, the Urban League, the 4H Clubs, the Women's Political Caucus, the Salvation Army, and the United Way. * * *

Attributes of the Sector

It is worth reviewing some of the characteristics of the independent sector that make it a powerfully positive force in American life. There is no point in comparing it favorably or unfavorably with other sectors of the society. Each has its function.

Perhaps the most striking feature of the sector is its relative freedom from constraints and its resulting pluralism. Within the bounds of the law, all kinds of people can pursue any idea or program they wish. Unlike government, an independent sector group need not ascertain that its idea or philosophy is supported by some large constituency, and unlike the business sector, they do not need to pursue only those ideas which will be profitable. If a handful of people want to back a new idea, they need seek no larger consensus.

Americans have always believed in pluralism—the idea that a free nation should be hospitable to many sources of initiative, many kinds of institutions, many conflicting beliefs, and many competing economic units. Our pluralism allows individuals and groups to pursue goals that they themselves formulate, and out of that pluralism has come virtually all of our creativity.

Every institution in the independent sector is not innovative, but the sector provides a hospitable environment for innovation. Ideas for doing things in a different, and possibly better, way spring up constantly. If they do not fill a need, they quickly fall by the wayside. What remains are the few ideas and innovations that have long-term value. New ideas and new ways of doing things test the validity of accepted practice and build an inventory of possible alternative solutions which can be used if circumstances change.

Government bureaucracies are simply not constructed to permit the emergence of countless new ideas, and even less suited to the winnowing out of bad ideas. An idea that is controversial, unpopular, or "strange" has little chance in either the commercial or the political marketplace. In the nonprofit sector, someone with a new idea or program may very well find the few followers necessary to help nurse it to maturity. Virtually every significant social idea of the past century in this country has been nurtured in the nonprofit sector.

The sector is the natural home of nonmajoritarian impulses, movements, and values. It comfortably harbors innovators, maverick movements, groups which feel that they must fight for their place in the sun, and critics of both liberal and conservative persuasion.

Institutions of the nonprofit sector are in a position to serve as the guardians of intellectual and artistic freedom. Both the commercial and political marketplaces are subject to leveling forces that may threaten standards of excellence. In the nonprofit sector, the fiercest champions of excellence may have their say. So may the champions of liberty and justice.

The sector preserves individual initiative and responsibility. As in the for-profit sector, there are innumerable opportunities for the resourceful—to initiate, explore, grow, cooperate, lead, make a difference. At a time in history when individuality is threatened by the impersonality of large-scale social organization, the sector's emphasis on individual initiative is a priceless counterweight.

To deal effectively with the ailments of our society today, individual initiative isn't enough, there has to be some way of linking the individual with the community. In the independent sector, such linkages are easily forged. Citizens banding together can tackle a small neighborhood problem or a great national issue.

The past century has seen a more or less steady deterioration of American communities as coherent entities with the morale and binding values that hold people together. Our sense of community has been badly battered, and every social philosopher emphasizes the need to restore it.

What is at stake is the individual's sense of responsibility for something beyond the self. A spirit of concern for one's fellows is virtually impossible to sustain in a vast, impersonal, featureless society. Only in coherent human groupings (the neighborhood, the family, the community) can we keep alive our shared values and preserve the simple human awareness that we need one another. We must recreate a society that has its social and spiritual roots firmly planted in such groupings—so firmly planted that those roots cannot be ripped out by the winds of change, nor by the dehumanizing, automatizing forces of the contemporary world.

This is not to express a sentimental aversion to large-scale organization or national action. Many of the forces acting upon us can only be dealt with by large-scale organizations, national in scope, including a vigorous government. But if we intend that the overarching governmental organizations we create be our servants and not our masters, we must have vital communities.

The Great Shared Task

My observations about the positive aspects of the sector are not intended to gloss over the flaws that are evident in its institutions and organizations. Some nonprofit institutions are far gone in decay. Some are so badly managed as to make a mockery of every good intention they might have had. There is fraud, mediocrity, and silliness. In short, the human and institutional failures that afflict government and business are also present in the voluntary sector. Beyond that, it is the essence of pluralism (in the society as a whole as well as in this sector) that no particular observer will approve of everything that goes on. If you can't find a nonprofit institution that you can honestly disrespect, then something has gone wrong with our pluralism.

But these considerations are trivial compared to the attributes that make the independent sector a source of deep and positive meaning in our national life. If it were to disappear from our national life, we would be less distinctly American. The sector enhances our creativity, enlivens our communities, nurtures individual responsibility, stirs life at the grassroots, and reminds us that we were born free. Its vitality is rooted in good soil—civic pride, compassion, a philanthropic tradition, a strong problem-solving impulse, a sense of individual responsibility and, despite what cynics may say, an irrepressible commitment to the great shared task of improving our life together.

NOTE: THE UNDERSIDE OF THE NONPROFIT SECTOR

John Gardner's uplifting testimonial is one side to the story that is about to unfold. Gardner is an optimist, eloquently accentuating the virtues of nonprofit organizations and their abundant contributions to society. He dismisses as "trivial" the "underside" of the nonprofit sector despite that darker side's profound influence on the development of the law you are about to study. This Note rounds out the picture.

Previous editions of this text included an excerpt, now somewhat dated, from a book authored in the early 1990s by two reporters for the Philadelphia Inquirer.[1] This self-styled expose was the culmination of a pathbreaking series of investigative reports about the role played by nonprofit organizations in the American economy. The series shed light on the vast amounts of tax-exempt wealth in certain segments of the sector; the dramatic growth of nonprofit business ventures; the dearth of any "charity" in many nonprofit hospitals and universities; the rise of gaudy compensation packages; and the power wielded by private foundations, characterized by the authors as "warehouses of wealth." In the tradition of much modern investigative journalism, some of these revelations were merely anecdotal, and the reports overstated the breadth of nonprofit sector wealth. Only a relative handful of charities, mostly foundations, elite universities and major religious denominations, have vast amounts of untaxed income or property. Many more are small organizations, with lowly compensated staff and volunteers doing good works. But the Philadelphia Inquirer series made a major impact, inspiring more journalists and even a few scholars to investigate and report on the underside of the sector. In so doing, they captured the attention of legislators, regulators and the general public. Major newspapers began to assign reporters to cover charities and philanthropy with a critical eye, and the print media emerged as an influential watchdog of nonprofit sector behavior.[2] These efforts over many years have exposed serious diversions of charitable assets, excessive trustee and executive compensation, failure to adhere to appropriate norms of fiduciary duty, creeping commercialism, abuses relating to charitable contributions of noncash property, and the use of charities as tax shelter facilitators and even financiers of terrorism. A few highly selective examples (most of which, along with many more, are discussed in the text) include:

- In 1995, the Wall Street Journal was the first to report that the Foundation for New Era Philanthropy, a Pennsylvania charity that promised to double the money of donors and charities who entrusted New Era with millions of dollars, was a classic Ponzi scheme. The organization ultimately went bankrupt, resulting in serious losses to some charities, and its chief executive was sentenced to 12 years in prison. In 2008, it was deja vu all over again and then some when many large and small charities learned that their investments with Bernard Madoff had been lost in the largest Ponzi scheme in American history.

- Spurred by reports first published by the Star–Bulletin in Honolulu in the late 1990s and later expanded in the Wall Street Journal, the Bishop Estate, a charitable trust and Hawaii's largest landowner, became the focus of federal and state investigations for excessive compensation paid to trustees and financial mismanagement. Facing

---

1. Gilbert M. Gaul & Neill A. Borowski, Free Ride: The Tax–Exempt Economy (1993).

2. Whether or not this level of investigative print journalism will continue in the future is in some doubt as for-profit newspapers struggle to survive.

a loss of tax-exempt status and criminal convictions, the Bishop Estate's five trustees resigned and a large civil settlement was paid in exchange for major changes in its governance.

- In 2003, the Washington Post published a series of articles raising questions about various policies and practices of the Nature Conservancy, one of the oldest and largest U.S. conservation organizations. Allegations of impropriety included questionable transactions with insiders, valuation abuses on gifts of conservation easements, inept stewardship, and inappropriate practices. The series triggered an IRS audit and an extensive investigation and report by the Senate Finance Committee.

- In 2005, the Los Angeles Times reported financial irregularities at the Getty Museum, one of the world's largest cultural institutions, leading to an investigation by the California attorney general and the resignation of the museum's president and curator of antiquities.

- The Wall Street Journal, the New York Times, and the Chronicle of Philanthropy all exposed abuses of "supporting organizations," a type of tax-favored public charity that some donors have used to circumvent the more rigorous federal regulation imposed on private foundations.

- The Atlantic Monthly chronicled the increasing commercialism of American higher education, such as lucrative research alliances and licensing deals with for-profit companies, sales of naming rights for professorships, buildings and athletic facilities, and forays into distance learning and other "dot com" businesses.

- Various news reports revealed that some donors claiming tax deductions vastly overstated the value of their noncash gifts to charities. Some of the more blatant abuses were with lifetime gifts of fractional interests in works of art that continue to hang on the donor's wall, mounts of dead animals contributed to fake museums, conservation easements, and more prosaic assets such as used cars and old clothes.

- The venerable Smithsonian Institution was found to have a dysfunctional governing board structure that contributed to ill-advised business ventures, overpaid executives, and various other indicia of "mission drift."

- Some prominent politicians and their enablers used "educational" charities to raise tax-deductible funds to support their causes and campaigns, often in violation of both tax and federal election law.

- The broad concepts of charity have been called into question by a gradual commercialization of nonprofit hospitals, universities and museums, causing policy makers and the public to call for a new definition of charity and more refined criteria for tax and other governmental benefits.

As will become apparent in the chapters to follow, these and many other reports of abuse, mission drift, and even fraud created the perception of widespread misbehavior by charities and their trusted fiduciaries and inept enforcement by state and local governments. Although there is a measure of validity to this perception, wrongdoing is not as pervasive as the media hype would suggest[3] and it has not reached the level of an epidemic. The steady flow of negative publicity nonetheless captured the attention of Congress, leading to an ongoing dialogue between the congressional tax-writing committees, nonprofit sector representatives, the IRS, some state attorneys general, and academics from many disciplines. This is not a new phenomenon. It has occurred before, most notably in 1950, when Congress decided to tax the unrelated business income of otherwise tax-exempt nonprofits, and again in 1969 when private foundations were singled out for heightened regulation. The most recent wave of scrutiny was launched in 2004 by the Senate Finance Committee, under the leadership of Senators Charles Grassley (R–Iowa) and Max Baucus (D–Mont.), when it issued a 19–page Discussion Draft containing a sweeping set of reform proposals and best practices for tax-exempt organizations.[4] Many of the recommendations focused on improving transparency and governance and increasing funds for federal and state enforcement. The Discussion Draft was comprehensive in scope. It suggested reforms for tax exemption qualification standards, self-dealing and compensation of nonprofit board members and other insiders, private foundation grantmaking and administrative expenses, federal and state enforcement, information reporting and disclosure, and nonprofit governance. An impetus for some of these proposals was the American Competitiveness and Corporate Accountability Act of 2002, commonly known as "Sarbanes–Oxley," which was enacted in the wake of the Enron and Worldcom corporate accounting scandals and applies primarily to publicly traded for-profit corporations and had a ripple effect on charities.

Tax-exempt organizations also were a major target in a voluminous Joint Committee on Taxation report issued in early 2005 to explore options for improving tax compliance and eliminate costly "tax expenditures."[5] At about the same time, the House Ways and Means Committee entered the fray with hearings on oversight and compliance in the tax-exempt sector

---

3. See, e.g., Marion R. Fremont–Smith & Andras Kosaras, Wrongdoing by Officers and Directors of Charities: A Survey of Press Reports 1992–2002, 42 Exempt Org. Tax Rev. 25 (2003), which found only 152 incidents of reported civil and criminal misconduct during the 10–year period covered by the study. It is likely that many acts went unreported.

4. See Senate Finance Comm. Staff Discussion Draft, June 22, 2004, available at finance.senate.gov/hearings/testimony/2004 test/062204stfdis.pdf (hereinafter "Discussion Draft"). A background document prepared by the Joint Committee on Taxation in conjunction with the June 2004 hearings summarizes the law and includes extensive statistical data on tax-exempt organizations. See Joint Committee on Taxation, Description of Present Law Relating to Charitable and Other Exempt Organizations and Statistical Information Regarding Growth and Oversight of the Tax–Exempt Sector (JCX–44–04), June 22, 2004, available at www.house.gov/jct/x-44–04.pdf.

5. Joint Committee on Taxation, Options to Improve Tax Compliance and Reform Tax Expenditures (JCS–02–05), January 27, 2005, available at www.house.gov/jct/s-2–05.pdf.

and specific issues affecting nonprofit hospitals and other health care organizations.[6] Two distinct areas of concern emerged from these deliberations. The Senate Finance Committee focused primarily on improving transparency and governance and correcting systemic problems in specific areas, all of which are discussed in later chapters. Good governance facilitates well-run charities, and dissuades improper behavior. Transparency sheds light on an organization's practices, which in turn should enhance ethical and effective operations and facilitate oversight. Both are essential elements in assuring that charities operate with integrity and effectiveness in meeting their missions.[7] If fully embraced, and to some extent it has been, the Senate Finance Committee's approach would elevate the role of the federal government vis a vis the states as the principal regulator of good governance, accountability, and transparency.

The questions raised and later abandoned by the House Ways and Means Committee were broader and ultimately more challenging. The 2005 Ways and Means Committee Hearings examined the legal history of the tax-exempt sector; its size, scope and impact on the economy; and the need for better oversight from Congress and the IRS. A particular focus was the elusive definition of "charitable" in § 501(c)(3) and the need for more coherent tax exemption qualification standards. This largely theoretical inquiry addressed the rationale for and scope of tax-exempt status—asking questions (as we do later in this text) about what kind of activities § 501(c)(3) should encompass?[8] The House hearings sought to reexamine some of the fundamental principles of current law against the background of the historical development of federal tax exemption. A threshold question was the extent to which charities are providing services to the public commensurate with their favored tax status. Among the other issues raised were: Should criteria for granting exempt status be reconsidered? Should some categories of exempt entities be eliminated? What governance standards should apply? Is there sufficient transparency in general and specifically in setting the compensation packages of executives? How much lobbying and political campaign activity should be permitted? And when nonprofit and for-profit entities such as hospitals engage in similar activities, are the nonprofits providing sufficiently distinct services to justify their exemption? Most of these questions are covered in depth in Chapters 3 and 5.

The shock waves emanating from this heightened congressional scrutiny led to the most extensive self-examination by the nonprofit sector in

---

6. The House Hearings were informed by a comprehensive document describing the history and present law of tax exemption. See Joint Committee on Taxation, Historical Development and Present Law of the Federal Tax Exemption for Charities and Other Tax–Exempt Organizations (JCX–29–05), April 29, 2005, available at www.house.gov/jct/x–29–05. pdf. Witness statements for the House hearings are available at waysandmeans.house/gov/hearings.asp (hereinafter "2005 House Hearings").

7. See generally 2005 House Hearings, supra note 6, Statement of Hon. David M. Walker, Comptroller General, U.S. Government Accountability Office.

8. See Chapter 5B, infra, at pp. 297–314, for coverage of the rationale for charitable tax exemptions.

many decades. Leading this mobilization was Independent Sector, an association of over 500 charities, which convened a Panel on the Nonprofit Sector at the encouragement of the Senate Finance Committee. In June 2005, the Panel issued its Final Report, which includes eight "overarching principles" (some critics saw them as self-serving platitudes) to guide its more than 120 specific recommendations. The principles emphasize the importance of a vibrant and independent charitable sector, the responsibility of the sector to ensure its integrity and credibility through self-regulation and education, and the need for balanced government oversight.[9] In April 2006, the Panel issued a Supplemental Report addressing nine additional areas related to transparency and accountability.[10] Some of the Panel's more significant recommendations will be mentioned in later chapters in connection with the topics to which they relate, as will several major law reform projects.

As the temperature rose, mainstream nonprofit representatives moderated their resistance to some of the suggested reforms, agreeing on the need for improved self-regulation. A consensus emerged on some statutory changes to address the most egregious abuses and the need for greater nonprofit transparency and accountability. Many nonprofit organizations, particularly the more established and prestigious, rushed to reform themselves by adopting some of the Senate proposals, particularly Sarbanes–Oxley-like certification of financial results by senior executives and implementation of internal financial controls.[11] At the same time, a few of the more radical proposals met with opposition, particularly any restrictions on the charitable contributions tax deduction, caps on nonprofit executive compensation, a complete ban on any self-dealing transaction between public charities and their insiders, federally prescribed rules on the size of nonprofit boards or other governance policies, and a new federal agency independent from the IRS to assume responsibility for oversight of charities.

As the debate continues, the Internal Revenue Service has taken steps to address the most serious systemic problems. Historically, the Service has suffered from inadequate staffing, diminished resources and an inability to analyze and use the data collected on exempt organizations. From 1995 to 2003, despite a 40 percent increase in the number of tax returns filed by exempt organizations, IRS staffing in the exempt organizations division steadily declined.[12] But beginning in 2003, staffing has increased as have examinations,[13] and the Form 990 information was redesigned to offer

---

9. Panel on the Nonprofit Sector, Strengthening Transparency, Governance, Accountability of Charitable Organizations: A Final Report to Congress and the Nonprofit Sector 20–22 (June 2005), available at www.nonprofitpanel.org/final (hereinafter "Final Report").

10. Panel on the Nonprofit Sector, Strengthening Transparency, Governance, Accountability of Charitable Organizations: A Supplement to the Final Report (April 2006), available at www.nonprofitpanel.org/supplement.

11. See Michael M. Phillips, Big Charities Pursue Certification to Quell Fears of Funding Abuses, Wall Street J., Mar. 9, 2005, at A1.

12. See 2005 Senate Hearings, available at finance.senate.gov/sitepages/hearing030505.htm, Statement of Mark W. Everson, at 2.

13. Id. at 14.

more detail and transparency. The Service has targeted for audits selected areas where abuses have been alleged or more data is needed, such as hospitals and universities; executive compensation; the use of charities as tax shelter facilitators; and political campaign activity.

As for Congress, just a few weeks after the previous edition of this text was published, it enacted the most significant nonprofit tax legislation in decades as part of the Pension Protection Act of 2006.[14] The 2006 legislation included a few carrots and many more sticks, including a handful of charitable giving incentives most of which have since expired along with stiff new rules to regulate real and perceived abuses. Since then, politics as usual has resumed and interest in pursuing nonprofit tax reforms has abated in favor of gridlock. Inevitably, however, with the demand for increased revenue at the federal and state levels, pressure will increase on at least the wealthier nonprofits to make their activities more transparent and to justify why they are deserving of tax and other governmental benefits.

B.   DIMENSIONS OF THE NONPROFIT SECTOR

The dimensions of the nonprofit sector are constantly being measured. Bean counting abounds on the number and categories of nonprofits, their sources of support, income, expenses, employees, and share of the gross national product. Independent Sector estimated that there were approximately 1.9 million nonprofit organizations in the United States as of 2008. If one counts local chapters of regional or national groups, the number grows to over 6 million. As of the last authoritative report, in 2005 nonprofits had 12.9 million paid employees, representing 9.7 percent of the U.S. economy, and an additional 4.7 million full-time equivalent volunteer workers were employed by charitable institutions.

The nonprofit sector is a growth industry. An IRS study reported that during the 20–year period from 1975 to 1995, the real assets and revenues of tax-exempt organizations filing information returns tripled, compared to real growth in gross domestic product during the same period of 74 percent. Joint Committee on Taxation, Description of Present Law Relating to Charitable and Other Exempt Organizations and Statistical Information Regarding Growth and Oversight of the Tax–Exempt Sector (JCX–44–04), June 22, 2004. Nonprofit organizations accounted for five percent of the gross domestic product in 2006. As of 2009, nonprofit organizations filing information returns with the IRS reported $4.24 trillion in assets and $1.97 trillion in total revenue—and these figures do not include churches, which are not required to file with the IRS. Molly F. Sherlock & Jane G. Gravelle, An Overview of the Nonprofit and Charitable Sector 12 (Congressional Research Service, Nov. 17, 2009).

---

14. But have no fear—the provisions of the Pension Protection Act to be studied here have nothing to do with pensions.

NOTE: WHERE THE MONEY COMES FROM—SOURCES OF FUNDING OF THE CHARITABLE SECTOR

It may come as a surprise, but the major sources of funds derived by what we will come to know as charitable (or public benefit) organizations are fees, dues, and charges for services provided. As reflected in Table 1.1, below, in 2005 private contributions accounted for only 12 percent of revenue compared to 49 percent from fees for services and 29 percent from government.

Table 1.1

Sources of Nonprofit Sector's Funds 2005

Source	Amount (in Billions) of Dollars	Percentage of Total
Dues Fees & Charges	590.0	49
Contributions	143.8	12
Government	351.1	29
Investment Income	80.9	7
Other	30.4	3
TOTAL	$1,196.2	100%

Source: Kenneth T. Wing, Thomas Pollak & Amy Blackwood, The Nonprofit Almanac (Urban Institute Press, 2008). Some dollar figures are rounded.

- *Fees, service charges, and other commercial income.* The major source of support of America's nonprofit, public-benefit, service organizations are fees, service charges, and other commercial income. Included here are college tuition payments, charges for hospital care not covered by government health insurance, other direct payments for services, and income from investments and sales of products. This source alone accounts for over half of all nonprofit service-organization revenues.

- *Government.* The second most important source of income of nonprofit, public-benefit, service organizations is government. Government grants, contracts, and reimbursements account for 29 percent of nonprofit service-organization income. This reflects a widespread pattern of partnership between government and the nonprofit sector in carrying out public purposes, from the delivery of health care to the provision of education.

- *Private Giving.* The 12 percent of total income that nonprofits receive from private giving makes this the third largest source of nonprofit service-organization income.

As summarized in Tables 1.2 and 1.3, individuals were the major source of charitable giving, and most of those gifts were made to churches. The $307.65 billion in 2008 charitable giving was two percent less than total giving in the previous year—the first decline in giving since 1987 and only the second since 1956. Table 1.3 ranks the recipients of charitable gifts, with religious organizations at the top with 35 percent of total gifts in 2008, up from 33 percent in 2007 but down from 43.6 percent in 1998.

Table 1.2

Sources of Charitable Giving, 2008

Source	Amount (in Billions) of Dollars	Percentage of Total
Individuals	$229.28	74.5
Foundations	41.21	13.4
Bequests	22.66	7.3
Corporations	14.5	4.7
TOTAL	$307.65	100%

Source: American Association of Fund–Raising Counsel, Giving USA 2009: The Annual Report on Philanthropy for the year 2008 (2009). A summary of the data is available at http://www.aafrc.org.

Table 1.3

Recipients of Charitable Giving, 2008

Recipient	Amount (in Billions) of Dollars	Percentage of Total
Religion	$106.89	35
Education	40.94	13
Foundations	32.65	11
Health	21.64	7
Human services	25.88	9
Public/society benefit	23.88	8
Arts, culture, humanities	12.79	4
Environment, animals	6.58	2
International affairs	13.30	4
Foundation grants to individuals	3.71	1
Unallocated giving	19.39	6
TOTAL	$307.65	100%

Source: American Association of Fund–Raising Counsel, Giving USA 2009: The Annual Report on Philanthropy for the Year 2008 (2009).

Lester M. Salamon, The Rise of the Nonprofit Sector

For. Aff. 109 (July/Aug. 1994).

A striking upsurge is under way around the globe in organized voluntary activity and the creation of private, nonprofit or nongovernmental organizations. From the developed countries of North America, Europe and Asia to the developing societies of Africa, Latin America and the former Soviet bloc, people are forming associations, foundations and similar institutions to deliver human services, promote grass-roots economic development, prevent environmental degradation, protect civil rights and pursue a thousand other objectives formerly unattended or left to the state. * * *

In the developed countries, for example, a significant expansion of citizen activism has been evident for several decades. A 1982 survey of nonprofit human service organizations in 16 American communities showed that 65 percent had been created since 1960. The number of private associations has similarly skyrocketed in France, with more than 54,000 formed in 1987 alone, compared to about 11,000 per year in the 1960s. Recent estimates record some 275,000 charities in the United Kingdom, with income approaching five percent of gross national product. In Italy, research conducted in 1985 showed that 40 percent of the organizations had been formed since 1977.

This phenomenon is even more dramatic in the developing world, where some 4,600 Western voluntary organizations are now active, providing support to approximately 20,000 indigenous nongovernmental organizations. In India, the Village Awakening Movement, which grew out of the Gandhian tradition, is active in thousands of villages. Bangladesh boasts approximately 10,000 registered nongovernmental organizations. In Sri Lanka, the Sarvodala Shramadana movement has organized more than 8,000 villages to produce small-scale improvement projects. Elsewhere, some 21,000 nonprofit organizations have formed in the Philippines; nearly 100,000 Christian Base Communities built on local action groups now dot the Brazilian countryside; some 27,000 nonprofit organizations are now reported in Chile and 2,000 in Argentina; and recent estimates indicate that 30 percent of Kenya's capital development since the 1970s has come from the Harambee movement, which has led local communities to initiate a wide variety of development projects.

Similar developments have also been evident in Eastern Europe and the former Soviet Union. Well before the dramatic political events that captured world attention in 1989, important changes were taking place beneath the surface of East European society, and voluntary organizations were very much at the center of them. Indeed, a veritable "second society" had come into existence, consisting of thousands, perhaps millions, of networks of people who provided each other mutual aid to cope with the economy of scarcity in which they lived. By the late 1970s, these networks were already acquiring political significance.

This process has only accelerated since the overthrow of the communist governments. As of 1992, several thousand foundations were registered with governmental authorities in Poland. In Hungary, 6,000 foundations and 11,000 associations had been registered by mid–1992. A Foundation Forum was established in Bulgaria in 1991, linking close to 30 newly created private groups. Although slower in the former Soviet Union, this process has recently accelerated there as well. A Foundation for Social Innovations was formed in 1986, in the second year of perestroika, as a way to translate citizen initiatives into effective social action. Since then dozens of other foundations and nonprofit organizations have been created into assist gifted and talented children, to protest the Chernobyl nuclear disaster, to call attention to the disappearance of the Aral Sea, to encourage cultural heterogeneity, and for dozens of other purposes.

How can we explain the extraordinary growth and pervasiveness of this phenomenon? Pressures to expand the voluntary sector seem to be coming from at least three different sources: from "below" in the form of spontaneous grass-roots energies, from the "outside" through the actions of various public and private institutions, and from "above" in the form of government policies. * * *

Why has this flourishing of third-sector activity occurred now? Four crises and two revolutionary changes have converged both to diminish the hold of the state and to open the way for this increase in organized voluntary action.

The first of these impulses is the perceived crisis of the modern welfare state. Over the past decade or so the system of governmental protection against old age and economic misfortune that had taken shape by the 1950s in the developed West no longer appeared to be working. * * *

Accompanying the crisis of the welfare state has been a crisis of development. The oil shocks of the 1970s and the recession of the early 1980s dramatically changed the outlook for developing countries. In sub-Saharan Africa, Western Asia and parts of Latin America average per capita incomes began to fall. * * *

A global environmental crisis has also stimulated greater private initiative. The continuing poverty of developing countries has led the poor to degrade their immediate surroundings in order to survive. * * *

Finally, a fourth crisis—that of socialism—has also contributed to the rise of the third sector. * * *

Beyond these four crises, two further developments also explain the recent surge of third-sector organizing. The first is the dramatic revolution in communications that took place during the 1970s and 1980s. * * *

The combined expansion of literacy and communications has made it far easier for people to organize and mobilize.

The final factor critical to the growth of the third sector was the considerable global economic growth that occurred during the 1960s and early 1970s, and the bourgeois revolution that it brought with it. * * *

NOTE: RESTRICTIONS ON NGOS IN NEW DEMOCRACIES

Nonprofit organizations, which are described as symbols of democratic society in the above excerpt, have been perceived as threats by some governments. A Russian law governing nonprofits that took effect in April 2006 gives the authorities the power to monitor domestic and foreign nongovernmental organizations and to arbitrarily shut them down. The legislation has been criticized because it forced some foreign organizations to terminate their activities, threatened domestic NGOs, and made it more difficult for foundations to make grants to their counterparts abroad.

Under the legislation, Russian nonprofit organizations must report all money received from outside Russia. The legislation also allows authorities to shut down foreign charities that threaten Russia's "political independence," "unique character," "cultural heritage," or "national interests." See Suzanne Perry, Russia's New Charity Law is Controversial, Chron. Philanthropy, Feb. 9, 2006, at 31, and Suzanne Perry, American Charities Protest Plan to Restrict Foreign Groups in Russia, Chron. Philanthropy, Dec. 8, 2005, at 39. For the approach in the United States to hostile interests and prevention of nonprofit organizations from serving as fronts for terrorism, see the excerpt below and Chapter 8B1b, infra, at p. 833.

NOTE: INTERNATIONAL CHARITIES AND TERRORIST ACTIVITY

We normally think of charities as reflecting the highest motives of human impulse and generosity. But nonprofits have also been used as covers for illicit activities. Investigations in the aftermath of September 11th have revealed the frequent use of Muslim charitable organizations to funnel money, aid, and material for terrorist uses. The Benevolence International Foundation of Illinois, which operated in Bosnia, has been accused of financing Osama Bin Laden and the Al Qaeda terrorist network. Several Saudi Arabian charities are alleged to have supported terrorist activities. This is a nondenominational problem. For instance, when the gang of organized crime boss John Gotti moved from Brooklyn to Queens, N.Y., it incorporated itself as a mutual benefit organization, the Bergin Hunting and Fishing Association.[1] As early as 1996, groups such as Hamas, a radical Islamic organization; Kahane Chai, a right wing Jewish group; the Liberation Tigers of Tamil Eelam, a Sri Lankan terrorist organization; and the Provisional Irish Republican Army were known to have engaged in fundraising in the United States through purported charitable organizations. William Patton, Preventing Terrorist Fundraising in the United States, 30 Geo. Wash. J.Int'l L & Econ. 127, 129 (1996). Charitable organizations have been used to launder drug money and as a front for arms purchases. In response to these problems, the United States and other governments have attempted to freeze the assets of such groups. Separating "bad dollars" from "good dollars" can be difficult. Some charities, not engaged in funding terrorist activities, have claimed they have been victims of ethnic profiling or guilt by a similar-sounding name. See Glenn R. Simpson & Robert Block, Politics & Policy: U.S. Moves to Stop Terror Funding Pose Risks With Allies, Wall St.J., Oct. 9, 2001, at A24; Glenn R. Simpson, Hesitant Agents: Why the FBI Took Nine Years to Shut Group It Tied to Terror, Wall St. J. Feb. 27, 2002, at A1.

---

1. The gang could shoot but not spell straight. It was named for the street of its former venue, Bergan Avenue. Selwyn Raab, "John Gotti Dies in Prison at 61," N.Y. Times, June 11, 2002, at A1.

NOTES

1. *The National Taxonomy of Exempt Entities*. Given the diversity of the nonprofit sector in the United States, it should surprise that until recently there has been no generally accepted classification or taxonomy of its members or even an agreed upon definition of nonprofit. The most complete statistical profile can be found in the publication, Nonprofit Almanac: Dimensions of the Independent Sector, which is published periodically by Independent Sector in partnership with the Urban Institute. The Nonprofit Almanac examines the nonprofit sector in relation to other sectors of the economy from a variety of perspectives.

The National Center for Charitable Statistics (NCCS) at Independent Sector has developed a classification system for tax-exempt organizations known as the National Taxonomy of Exempt Entities. Since 1987, the NCCS in cooperation with the Statistics of Income Division of the Internal Revenue Service has completed the initial classification of over 1.1 million tax-exempt organizations. The NTEE System identifies organizations by primary purpose, major program, type of governance, area of service, and clientele, beneficiaries or members served. There are 26 major groups in the NTEE system, ranging from arts, culture, and humanities to mutual/membership benefit organizations. A second level of analysis focuses on the major mission or the major areas in which the organization operates. A third level of the taxonomy identifies the governance of the organization, whether the ownership or affiliation is private nonsectarian, religious, or governmental. The fourth level of the taxonomy identifies specific characteristics of the organization's target population-gender, age, racial or ethnic characteristics, defined groups—and geographical area of service or impact. See Virginia Ann Hodgkinson, Murray S. Weitzman, John A. Abrahams, Eric A. Crutchfield and David R. Stevenson, Nonprofit Almanac 1996–1997, ch. 5; App. A (1996); Virginia A. Hodgkinson, Mapping the Nonprofit Sector in the United States: Implications for Research, 1 Voluntas 6 (1990).

For a criticism of the NTEE see Sarah E. Turner, Thomas I. Nygren & William G. Bowen, The NTEE Classification System: Tests of Reliability/Validity in the Field of Higher Education, 4 Voluntas 73–94 (1993) (the New York Shakespeare *Festival* is classified as a "fair, county, other"; the "Southern California–Southern Nevada End *Stage* Renal Disease Network" and the Association of Professional Ball *Players* of America are classified as "theatres." Id. at 86).

2. *An International Taxonomy*. Problems of definition are even greater from a global perspective because of the patterns of differentiation of societies, levels of developments, differing legal systems, historical factors and other traditions. Lester M. Salamon & Helmut K. Anheier, In Search of the Nonprofit Sector I: The Question of Definitions (Johns Hopkins Comparative Nonprofit Sector Project, Working Paper No. 1, 1992). On the international level, the Johns Hopkins Comparative Nonprofit Sector Project is attempting to understand the scope, structure, and role of the nonprofit sector by developing a common framework and approach. This project adopts a structural/operational definition which

identifies a broad range of organizations by five characteristics: formally constituted; nongovernmental in basic nature; self-governing; non-profit distributing; and voluntary to some meaningful extent. Salamon and Anheier developed an International Classification of Nonprofit Organizations (ICNPO) drawing on Standard Industrial Classification (SIC) systems embodied in national income accounting around the world, but modified to accommodate key components of the nonprofit sector overlooked in SIC. This classification scheme identifies twelve broad groups of organizations: culture and recreation; education and research; health; social services; environment; development and housing; law, advocacy, and politics; philanthropic intermediaries and volunteerism promotion; international; religion; business, professional associations, unions; and not elsewhere classified. Lester M. Salamon & Helmut K. Anheier, In Search of the Nonprofit Sector II: The Problem of Classification (Johns Hopkins Comparative Nonprofit Sector Project, Working Paper No. 3, 1992).

3. *Tracking International Developments.* The International Journal of Civil Society Law, under the editorship of Professor Karla Simon of Catholic University School of Law, tracks developments in law affecting society and nongovernmental organizations around the world. The Journal is available on line at http://www.iccsl.org/pubs/index-journal.html.

4. *For Further Reading.* Mark Sidel, States, Markets and the Nonprofit Sector in South Asia, 78 Tul. L. Rev. 1611 (2004); Lester M. Salamon, S. Wojciech Sokolowski et al., Global Civil Society: An Overview (Johns Hopkins University Institute for Policy Studies, 2 vols., 2001 & 2004); The State of Nonprofit America (Lester M. Salamon ed., 2002); Michael O'Neill, Non Profit Nation (2002); Helmut K. Anheier & Kusuma Cunningham, Internationalization of the Nonprofit Sector, in The Jossey–Bass Handbook of Nonprofit Leadership and Management (Robert D. Herman ed., 1994); William G. Bowen, Thomas I. Nygren, Sarah E. Turner, & Elizabeth A. Duffy, The Charitable Nonprofits (1994); The Nonprofit Sector in the Mixed Economy (Avner Ben–Ner & Benedetto Gui eds., 1993); America's Voluntary Spirit: A Book of Readings (Brian O'Connell ed., 1983); Virginia A. Hodgkinson & Richard W. Lyman, The Future of the Nonprofit Sector: Challenges, Changes and Policy Considerations (1989); The Nonprofit Sector in International Perspective: Studies in Comparative Culture and Policy (Estelle James ed., 1989); Kathleen D. McCarthy, Virginia A. Hodgkinson, Russy D. Sumariwalla et al., The Nonprofit Sector in the Global Community (1992); The Emergence of the Nonprofit Sector in the United States (1989); The Nonprofit Sector: A Research Handbook (Walter W. Powell & Richard Steinberg, eds., 2d ed. 2006); Research Papers Sponsored by the [Filer] Commission on Private Philanthropy and Public Needs (1977).

C. CHARITY, PHILANTHROPY AND NONPROFIT ORGANIZATIONS: A HISTORICAL INTRODUCTION

An attitude favorable to philanthropy existed from the beginning of settlement in the new world. Colonists were accustomed to the traditional support and enforcement of charities in England. Churches, which exerted a significant influence within colonial society, were favorably disposed to philanthropic endeavors. As the excerpt below by Robert Bremner indicates, despite disagreement on other matters the various churches in the colonies "all shared the traditional Protestant emphasis upon the individual's responsibility for the spiritual material welfare of the community, and accordingly supported a variety of charitable institutions." Howard S. Miller, The Legal Foundations of American Philanthropy 1776–1844 at x (1961).

Robert H. Bremner, American Philanthropy

5–18 (2d ed. 1988).

The earliest American philanthropists, as far as European records go, were those gentle Indians of the Bahama Islands who greeted Columbus at his first landfall in the New World. In view of the cruelty and exploitation these natives were to suffer at the hands of white men there is something ominous in Columbus's report that they were "ingenuous and free" with all they had, gave away anything that was asked of them, and bestowed each gift "with as much love as if their hearts went with it."

From other Indians pioneer white settlers obtained a wealth of practical assistance in the difficult task of adjusting to life in an alien land. The names of most of these benefactors are forgotten, but one at least is familiar to every schoolboy. Squanto, who had once been kidnapped by an Englishman and carried off to be sold into slavery, escaped from bondage and returned to New England. There, during the starving time at Plymouth in the winter of 1620–21, Squanto proved "a special instrument sent of God" for the good of the enfeebled, bewildered Pilgrims. He taught them, in the words of William Bradford, "how to set their corn, where to take fish, and to procure other commodities, and was also their pilot to bring them to unknown places for their profit, and never left them till he died." * * *

Philanthropy is philanthropy wherever and by whomever practiced. * * * All we can lay claim to on the score of uniqueness is that philanthropy *in* America took such a firm root and grew so prodigiously that it early assumed a stature and significance all its own.

To understand why this happened we must remember, first, that the age of colonization coincided with one of the great periods of European philanthropy. The seventeenth century saw the launching of heroic missionary enterprises, a revival of interest in charitable works, the development in England of a system of tax-supported poor relief, and the organization of a host of associations for specialized philanthropic purposes. America inspired some of these undertakings and benefited directly or indirectly from nearly all of them, for the discovery of the New World affected the conscience as well as the cupidity of the Old. Almost every effort at colonization had, or claimed to have, a philanthropic motivation: there were natives to be converted to Christianity, poor men to be provided with land and work, and a wilderness to be supplied with the institutions of civilization. It is not too much to say that many Europeans regarded the American continent mainly as a vastly expanded field for the exercise of benevolence.

The real founders of American philanthropy, however, were men and women who crossed the Atlantic to establish communities that would be *better* than, instead of like or different from, the ones they had known at home. The Puritan leader John Winthrop (1588–1649) forthrightly stated their purpose in the lay sermon, "A Model of Christian Charity," which he preached on the ship "Arbella" to "the great company of religious people" voyaging from old to New England in the year 1630. Winthrop used "Charity" as a synonym for love rather than in the modern sense of aid to the poor; and the "Model" he proposed was not a new scheme of benevolence but a code of conduct for a company of Christians who had entered into a covenant with God. The Puritans' God permitted no breach of contract but demanded strict performance of each article in the covenant. Therefore, as Winthrop said, "in this duty of love we must love brotherly without dissimulation, we must love one another with a pure heart fervently, we must bear one another's burdens, we must not look only on our own things but also on the things of our brethren. Neither must we think that the Lord will bear with such failings at our hands as He doth from those among whom we have lived. * * * "

Like later philanthropists, Winthrop justified disparities in wealth and condition as divinely ordained. * * * Differences in condition existed, not to separate and alienate men from one another, but to make them have more need of each other, and to bind them closer together "in the bond of brotherly affection." And those differences, important and essential though Winthrop believed them to be, seemed less significant to him than "our community as members of the same body." * * *

Winthrop's vision of a community united and exalted by religious dedication was not to be realized even in Puritan New England. * * * Competition, individualism, and self-interest proved too strong to be suppressed, and what Roger Williams, in a letter to Winthrop's son, called "the common trinity of the world—Profit, Preferment, Pleasure"—soon made their appearance. Even so, Winthrop's ideal was never entirely forsaken. The forces of disunity, although they could not be held down, did not quite prevail; and, not only in the colonial period, but in later eras as well, Americans continued to feel under a special obligation to bring the duty of neighborly and brotherly love, everywhere professed, into "familiar and constant practice."

Half a century after Winthrop and the Puritans started to build their city upon a hill in New England, William Penn (1644–1718) began his holy experiment in Pennsylvania. * * * To Penn and the Quakers * * * mending the world was to be accomplished by employing the rewards of diligence and frugality for benevolent and humanitarian purposes—not casually and incidentally, but wholeheartedly—as the major business of life. * * *

Assumptions of social superiority and inferiority, however, were typical of seventeenth-century thought rather than peculiar to the Quakers. Penn himself emphasized the responsibilities rather than the privileges that went with rank. He took the doctrine of stewardship both seriously and literally, believing that men were indebted to God not only for their wealth but for their very being, and accountable to Him for the way they spent their lives as well as their fortunes. His concept of stewardship was free of the condescension with which it is so often associated because, in his case, the doctrine of stewardship was joined to an equally serious and literal belief in the brotherhood of man. Penn was, after all, one of "The People called Friends," and, like other Quakers, he rejected the Calvinistic notion of the Elect. Whatever the differences in material conditions among men, all men were children of God, carriers of His seed, and spiritually equal in His sight.

Penn anticipated Benjamin Franklin in admiration for industry, thrift, and the other economic virtues that are now attributed to the middle class. Practical man that he was, Penn certainly had an appreciation for the value of money, but he believed that God gave men wealth to use rather than to love or hoard. Of all the vices, avarice struck him as worst. * * *

Next to avarice Penn abhorred waste, display, and the pursuit of pleasure. Here again Penn's puritanical attitude expressed his social conscience: if all the money wasted on luxury and extravagance were put to public use, the wants of the poor would be well satisfied. To be sure, mortal man required diversion; but (or so Penn said), "The best recreation is to do good." There will be time enough for making merry "when the pale faces are more commiserated, the pinched bellies relieved and naked backs clothed, when the famished poor, the distressed widow, and the helpless orphan * * * are provided for."

Cotton Mather (1663–1728), unfortunately better remembered today for his part in the witchcraft trials than for his benevolent activities, is one of the commanding figures in the history of American philanthropy. The son of a president of Harvard, and himself one of the founders of Yale, Mather was the most prolific and conspicuously learned writer of the colonial period. Of the approximately four hundred and fifty works he is known to have published, one of the least pretentious, *Bonifacius*, or as it is usually known, *Essays To Do Good* (1710), enjoyed the greatest and longest popularity. In it Mather proposed that men and women, acting either as individuals or as members of voluntary associations, should engage in "a perpetual endeavor to do good in the world." Such advice, coming from a son of the Puritans, was hardly novel. It was the method Mather outlined rather than the objective that was new. And it was this individualistic, voluntary method * * * that was destined to characterize American philanthropy for many years to come.

Mather regarded the performance of good works as an obligation owed to God rather than as a means of salvation; yet, as a constant expounder of the doctrine of stewardship, he had no doubt that God would punish the unfaithful steward. Moreover, as he was frank enough to admit and bold enough to proclaim, doing good was a reward in itself. To help the unfortunate was an honor, a privilege, "an incomparable pleasure." * * * Mather took pains to point out, doing good was sound policy, a mild but effective instrument of social control. Pious example, moral leadership, voluntary effort, and private charity were the means by which competing and conflicting interests in society might be brought into harmony.

To Mather charity emphatically did begin at home; for he believed that each man must start his career of doing good by correcting whatever was amiss in his own heart and life. Yet for all the emphasis on personal reform, Mather's was a social gospel. Keep a list of the needy in your neighborhood, he urged his readers; be on the lookout for persons who may require help, and seize each opportunity to be useful with "rapturous assiduity." Always bear in mind that "charity to the *souls* of men" is the highest form of benevolence. Send preachers, Bibles, and other books of piety to heathens at home and abroad; support the church, and keep a watchful eye on the spiritual health of the community. Very often, he said, the poor need "admonitions of piety" quite as much as alms. "Cannot you contrive to mingle a spiritual charity with your temporal bounty?"

Mather's own charitable gifts were sufficient to make him a one-man relief and aid society. But Mather's real contribution to the practice of philanthropy lay in his recognition of the need for enlisting the support of others in benevolent enterprises. He was a tireless promoter of associations for distributing tracts, supporting missions, relieving needy clergymen, and building churches in poor communities. At the same time, in sermons and private conversations, he called the attention of the rich to the needs, physical as well as spiritual, of the poor. From personal experience he learned that the recompense of the charitable was multiplication of occasions to be serviceable. "Those who devote themselves to good devices," he drily observed, "usually find a wonderful increase of their opportunities." In a beautiful simile he likened a good deed to "a stone falling into a pool—one circle and service will produce another, till they extend—who can tell how far?"

Despite, or as Mather would have said, because of his sincere concern for the poor, he advocated extreme care in the bestowal of alms. "Let us try to do good with as much application of mind as wicked men employ in doing evil," was his motto. Giving wisely was therefore an even greater obligation than giving generously; and withholding alms from the undeserving as needful and essentially benevolent as bestowing them on the deserving.

The most famous tribute to the Essays To Do Good came from an unlikely source. In youth—actually boyhood—Benjamin Franklin (1706–90) had been an enemy of the Mathers, and the pseudonym adopted in his earliest published work, Silence Dogood, was an unkind thrust at Cotton Mather. In old age, however, Franklin advised Samuel Mather, Cotton's son, that the *Essays* had influenced his conduct throughout life. "I have always set a greater value on the character of a *doer of good*, than on any other kind of reputation," he wrote, "and if I have been * * * a useful citizen, the public owes the advantage of it to that book." * * *

In addition to numerous similarities, there was a significant difference between Franklin's views and those of Penn and Mather. Penn demanded that money, instead of being hoarded or spent on impious luxuries, should be used for comforting the poor. Mather dreamed of a city in which each house would have an alms-box bearing the message *"Think on the Poor."* Franklin, however, conceived of a society in which there would be no poor and little need for relief or charity. He sprang from a different class and addressed himself to a different audience than Penn or Mather. Far from forgetting his humble origin, he traded on it throughout life. * * *

Franklin was above all a man of the eighteenth century and it is not wise to insist too strongly on the modernity of his approach to social problems. In much that he did or suggested, however, it is possible to recognize principles that later came to be recognized as characteristic of both enlightened public policy and of constructive philanthropy. Preventing poverty always impressed him as a more sensible course than relieving it. In calling for repeal of the poor laws on the ground that public provision for the needy had an even greater tendency than almsgiving to pauperize the poor, Franklin went beyond Mather, who had warned of the abuses of private charity, and foreshadowed the scientific philanthropists and reformers of the nineteenth century. * * *

Franklin's philanthropic activities, although varied, followed a consistent pattern. Starting in 1727 with the Junto, a club for the mutual improvement of its members, and the library (1731) which was the Junto's first offshoot, Franklin proceeded to organize or assist in organizing a host of civic projects. He founded a volunteer fire company, developed schemes for paving, cleaning, and lighting the streets of Philadelphia, and sponsored a plan for policing the city. His political talents were never better displayed than in his ability to unite public and private support behind municipal improvements. He played a leading part in the establishment of both the Pennsylvania Hospital (1751) and the academy which became the University of Pennsylvania. Funds provided in his will made possible the founding, more than a century after his death, of a technical institute in Boston. His interest in "improving the common Stock of Knowledge" led to the formation in 1743 of the American Philosophical Society, the first and for many years the foremost American institution for promoting research in the natural and social sciences.

Franklin demonstrated that the sovereign remedy of self-help, so often prescribed for individuals, could be applied with equally beneficial results to society. He did not invent the principle of improving social conditions through voluntary associations, but more than any American before him he showed the availability, usefulness, and appropriateness of that method to American conditions. The voluntary method, as Franklin's success with it suggested, and as later events were to prove, was precisely suited to the inclinations of his countrymen.

NOTE: THE DEVELOPMENT OF NONPROFIT LAW IN THE UNITED STATES

The immediate stimulus for the benevolent atmosphere to charity in the new world was the pressing need for the establishment of public facilities such as hospitals, churches, and schools: "[The colonists] did not debate the question of public versus private responsibility * * * public and private philanthropy were so completely intertwined as to become almost indistinguishable. The law itself reflected a pragmatic approach to the solving of social problems through philanthropy. Colonial assemblies went out of their way to remove obstacles in the way of charities. The courts valuing social betterment above legal technicalities, asserted a permissive charity doctrine that supported donors' benevolent intentions, even when the formulation of their plans was clearly imperfect." Howard S. Miller, The Legal Foundations of American Philanthropy 1776–1844, at xi (1961).

Philanthropic approaches in Colonial America were not uniform. From the beginning, public and private philanthropy coexisted. In Boston and other Massachusetts towns, public spending for poverty relief combined with private contributions and legacies. The typical vehicle for private philanthropic efforts was the English charitable use, which enjoyed universal approval.

In the immediate post–Revolutionary period, the favorable attitude toward charity continued. The law relating to charities reflected the general uncertainty and transition that characterized all American law in the post–Revolutionary period. Miller, supra, at 15. Cf. William Nelson, Americanization of the Common Law: The Impact of Legal Change on Massachusetts Society 1760–1830, at 68 (1975). Each state utilized an approach reflective of its local needs and customs. Most state constitutions were silent about philanthropy. The Massachusetts constitution of 1780, however, provided: "It shall be the duty of legislatures and magistrates, in all future periods of this Commonwealth * * * to countenance and inculcate the principles of humanity and general benevolence, public and private charity * * * and all social affections, and generous sentiments among the people."

Pennsylvania, Vermont, and New Hampshire also gave constitutional protection to charities. Other states passed statutes facilitating and reaffirming the benefits of charities to the community. In part, the retention of prior statutes and practices resulted from the general continuation of English law and precedent in the first years following Independence.

In England the charitable trust rather than the corporation has been the predominant form of organization for charitable activities. The reason was that the state historically was the source of power to create corporations whereas the creator of the charitable trust was afforded greater freedom. Marion Fremont–Smith, Foundations and Government 34–35 (1965). The charitable trust has had a more uncertain use in the United States because of quirks of our history and early ignorance as to its origins. In the aftermath of the Revolution, many states repealed all British statutes. Several states refused to uphold the validity of charitable trusts. Courts in those jurisdictions mistakenly concluded that since the Statute of Charitable Uses was no longer in effect, trusts could not be upheld because equitable powers for their enforcement did not exist at common law and were not exercised by Chancellors prior to 1601. Though this historical error was corrected in Vidal v. Girard's Executors, 43 U.S. (2 How.) 127, 11 L.Ed. 205 (1844), throughout the nineteenth century charitable trusts remained under a cloud and were construed strictly in several jurisdictions. In their place the charitable corporation was used for eleemosynary organizations.

Another reason the charitable corporation was favored over the charitable trust was the power of the legislature or executive of a state to dictate the terms of corporate privilege. Regulation of that privilege was thought to provide the state with greater control over charitable activities than the charitable trust, control of which would be exercised by an equity court. Cf. Levy v. Levy, 33 N.Y. 97, 112 (1865); Dallin Oaks, Trust Doctrines in Church Controversies, 1981 B.Y.U.L. Rev. 805, 858–60.

As early as the 17th century, the corporation was used in the New World as an organizational form for charitable activities. Almost all colonial corporations had charitable purposes. They were churches, charities, educational institutions, or municipal corporations. Lawrence M. Friedman, A History of American Law at 188 (2d ed. 1985). The practice of executive or legislative branches in the colonies from the beginning of the eighteenth century was to confer upon owners or inhabitants of political divisions or organizations with political or governmental functions the attribute of legal personality, the essence of corporateness. This line of reasoning led to the incorporation of religious societies. At the beginning of the eighteenth century several colonies, borrowing from an English 1597 statute, 39 Eliz., ch. 5 (1597), which allowed for the automatic incorporation of hospitals and houses of correction, provided for self-incorporation of some religious, charitable or municipal institutions.

The early colonial corporations were of two kinds. The first was the public corporation-municipal corporations chartered by the towns or a few administrative boards charged with the oversight of public education, charity, and the like on behalf of local units of government. The second kind, private corporations, included ecclesiastical, educational, charitable, and business corporations. The most numerous in this second category were corporations concerned with religious worship. Next in numerical size were those formed for charitable or educational purposes, although they still might have a religious nature. Business corporations were few and of little importance. Many of the colonial business corporations would be considered cooperatives or quasi-philanthropic today. They were incorporated for the purpose of erecting bridges, building or repairing roads, or promoting ends of general public utility.

From the first years of the Republic, most states actively encouraged the incorporation of private associations that performed vital public services. Robert Seavoy, The Origins of the American Business Corporation

1784–1855, 255 (1982). Upon Independence, several state legislatures passed statutes permitting general incorporation of charitable organizations such as churches, schools, and literary societies.

The rationale motivating the passage of early general incorporation acts included advantage to the public if such incorporations were increased; convenience to individuals desiring to incorporate; relief of legislative workload; and promotion of freedom of religion. Incorporation also enabled the trustees of a charitable organization to receive legacies and bequests, and it provided cheap legal process at the local level to ensure property was held in the corporate name, thus enabling title in such property to be defended at law in the name of the corporation. The local public service function of early American corporations distinguished them from their English counterparts and led to their legislative encouragement. By the second decade of the nineteenth century, general incorporation statutes existed in New York for educational institutions, libraries, agricultural societies, medical societies, and Bible and common prayer organizations. Other charitable and benevolent organizations were readily granted incorporation by special legislative charter. Whenever a class of benevolent organizations was recognized as being essentially nonpolitical and noncontroversial, a general incorporation law for that activity was readily passed.

Despite the encouragement of corporateness, legislatures retained a tight control over corporate purposes and activities. The New York general incorporation statute of 1784 for the incorporation of religious societies had limitations upon the amount of an estate these bodies could accumulate and required trustees to render stated accounts to the Chancellor. All of the early general incorporation statutes contained limitations upon the amounts of revenue to be held by such organizations and the purposes for which such revenue was to be applied and requirements for furnishing inventories and reporting any excess property to the legislature. The legislative policy was to enforce within certain limits the accumulation of property.

New York, which interpreted charitable trusts strictly, developed a broad legislative scheme for public charities through the medium of corporate bodies. Beginning in 1790 the New York legislature, concurrently with the general incorporation statutes, incorporated by special charters societies for a variety of religious, literary, scientific, benevolent, and charitable purposes. The corporate body thus was kept under tight legislative control and supervision.

In 1840 the New York legislature passed an act authorizing gifts of real and personal property to any incorporated college or other charitable institution. In 1848 the legislature passed a general incorporation statute for all classes of charitable organizations. 1848 N.Y. Laws 19. A similar movement toward the consolidation of charitable corporations into one general incorporation statute occurred in other states in the middle of the nineteenth century.

Other states' charitable corporation statutes evolved similarly. In California in 1850, the first legislature enacted an "Act Concerning Corporations" which specifically allowed charitable organizations to incorporate. 1850 Cal. Stat. §§ 175–84. Thereafter, a variety of piecemeal legislation was passed expanding the types of organizations that could incorporate. California nonprofit legislation was generally skeletal, outlining purposes specifically permitted, elections of directors, bylaw provisions, and the requirements for the holding and mortgaging of property. In 1931, California enacted a General Nonprofit Corporation Law, Cal. Civ. Code, Title 12, Art. I (1931), based largely upon an Ohio act, which in turn had been drafted on the basis of the nonprofit statutes of New York, Maryland, Illinois and Michigan. 1 H.W. Ballantine & R. Sterling, California Corporation Laws 529 (1949). The General Nonprofit Corporation Law abandoned many of the restrictions on charitable corporations, and gave nonprofit corporations greater flexibility in internal affairs. Nonprofit corporations were, however, also bound by the General Corporation Law, thereby carrying into nonprofit corporation law an undefined body of business corporate law. In other areas, such as the law relating to standards of conduct of directors, trust principles governed. The General Nonprofit Corporation Law was largely incorporated into the Corporation Code of 1947. In 1980, the current Nonprofit Corporation Law became effective and for the first time treated California nonprofit corporation law as a coherent whole. The American Bar Association's Revised Model Nonprofit Corporation Act, completed in 1987, largely is based on the California statute. A "Third Edition" of the Model Nonprofit Corporation Act was adopted in 2008 by a task force appointed by the Business Law Section of the American Bar Association.

For Further Reading. Marion R. Fremont–Smith, Governing Nonprofit Organizations 19–115 (2004); Henry Hansmann, The Evolving Law of Nonprofit Organizations: Do Current Trends Make Good Policy?, 39 Case W.Res.L.Rev. 807 (1988); F. Emerson Andrews, Philanthropy in the United States (1974); Robert H. Bremner, American Philanthropy (2d ed. 1988); Merle Curti, American Philanthropy and the National Character, 10 American Quarterly 420–437 (Winter, 1958) reprinted in America's Voluntary Spirit (Brian O'Connell ed., 1983); James J. Fishman, The Development of Nonprofit Corporation Law and an Agenda for Reform, 34 Emory L.J. 619 (1985); Peter Dobkin Hall, Historical Perspectives on Nonprofit Organizations, in The Jossey–Bass Handbook of Nonprofit Leadership and Management (Robert D. Herman ed., 1994); Peter Dobkin Hall, A Historical Overview of the Private Nonprofit Sector, in The Nonprofit Sector: A Research Handbook (Walter W. Powell ed., 1987); Howard S. Miller, The Legal Foundations of American Philanthropy 1776–1844 (1961).

NOTE: SOCIAL ENTERPRISE ORGANIZATIONS

Social enterprise organizations are for-profit firms committed to philanthropic activity. They have been characterized as "for-benefit corporations," falling between traditional businesses and charities, and are said to inhabit a "fourth sector" of society composed of organizations driven by social purposes and financial promise.[1] A recent catalyst for social enterprise investment was the announcement in 2006 that the Google Corporation would commit one percent of the company's stock worth $1 billion, and one percent of its annual profits over the next twenty years to invest in businesses with a social purpose.[2] Initially, Google established a traditional private foundation and contributed $90 million to it. The second philanthropic vehicle, Google.org, to which most of the support is being given, is a for-profit entity. Other businesses and entrepreneurs, such as private equity funds, have also formed large pools of capital for social purposes outside of charitable tax exempt structures.[3] What are the legal differences between traditional charities and social enterprise organizations?

The social enterprise movement is based upon the belief that market forces offer a more flexible, efficient and effective approach to promoting the public good than traditional charitable nonprofits, such as private foundations, which are subject to a restrictive regulatory regime.[4] Social enterprise corporations harken back to the cooperative movements in England and the United States in the nineteenth century. Social enterprise organizations are unconcerned with the tax issues that envelope traditional charitable activity. They are fully taxable, can issue shares of stock and return profits to investors. Their proponents argue that private sector interests will be encouraged to invest in social enterprises because they will derive a financial return while providing a public benefit.

Vermont became the first state to enact legislation that recognizes a social enterprise firm as a separate legal form of organization. See 11 Vt. Stat. Ann. § 3001(23) (2008). The "low profit limited liability company," or "L3C," is organized for a business purpose but: (1) significantly furthers the accomplishment of one or more charitable or educational purposes within the meaning of § 170(c)(2)(B) of the Internal Revenue Code, (2) might not have been formed but for the L3C's relationship to the accomplishment of charitable or educational purposes, and (3) no significant purpose of which is the production of income or the appreciation of property. If a company later fails to satisfy any of these requirements, it ceases to be an L3C and exists as a regular limited liability company. Similar legislation has been enacted in Michigan, Wyoming, North Dakota, Utah, and Illinois, and L3C bills are pending in several other states. For a discussion of these approaches, see Michael D. Gottesman, From Cobblestones to Pavement, The Legal Road Forward for the Creation of Hybrid

---

1. Stephanie Strom, Make Money, Save the World, Businesses and Nonprofits are Spawning Corporate Hybrids, N.Y. Times, May 6, 2007, § 3, at 1. The other three are the government, private and nonprofit sectors.

2. Nicole Wallace, Blending Business and Charity, Chron. Philanthropy, Sept. 28, 2006, at 14; Katie Hafner, Philanthropy Google's Way: Not the Usual, N.Y. Times, Sept. 14, 2006, at A1.

3. See Stephanie Strom, What's Wrong With Profit, N.Y. Times, Nov. 13, 2006, at F1; Jenny Anderson, A Hedge Fund With High Returns and High Reaching Goals, N.Y. Times, Nov. 13, 2006, at F14.

4. See Chapter 7, infra, at pp. 703–704.

Social Organizations, 26 Yale L. & Pol'y Rev. 345 (2007); Dana Brakman Reiser, For-profit Philanthropy, 77 Fordham L. Rev. 2437 (2009).

A major purpose of the L3C structure is to permit private foundations to become co-owners or lenders by making what are known as "program-related investments" ("PRIs"). PRIs count as qualified distributions for purposes of the five percent payout requirement imposed on private foundations and they are exempted from certain penalties on imprudent investments.

For-profit public benefit ventures raise several questions. Does the creation of such hybrid forms of organization serve to blur the line between for-profit and nonprofit entities? See Chapter 6B, infra, at pp. 570–591. Are they charities? Are they more efficient and effective than traditional charities?[5] Are social enterprises permanent entities or merely reflections of transitory stock market success or rising earnings? Should they receive tax benefits? If so, under what circumstances?[6]

D. RATIONALES FOR THE NONPROFIT SECTOR

1. THE ROLE OF NONPROFIT ENTERPRISE

What explains the existence of the nonprofit sector? Why does the legal system confer special treatment, such as tax exemptions and other benefits, on nonprofit organizations? In addressing these threshold questions, Lester Salamon has suggested that at least five major considerations are involved:

1. *Historical.* The nonprofit sector's existence can be explained by historical factors, such as the growth of voluntary organizations in the American colonies that predated government.

2. *Market Failure.* As elaborated in the excerpts below, nonprofit organizations exist in response to certain inherent limitations of the American market economy.

3. *Government Failure.* A vibrant nonprofit sector springs from the failure of government to provide collective goods because much government action requires majority support. Nonprofit organizations are formed by smaller groups of people to address needs that government is unwilling or unable to support.

---

5. The advantages of social enterprise firms compared to traditional charities and the structuring options are discussed in Robert A. Wexler, Social Enterprise: A Legal Context, 54 Exempt Org. Tax Rev. 233 (2006) and Robert A. Wexler, Effective Social Enterprise–A Menu of Legal Structures, 63 Exempt Org. Tax Rev. 565 (2009). For a criticism of social enterprise for nonprofits, see Ben Casselman, Why "Social Enterprise" Rarely Works, Wall St. J., June 1, 2007, at W3.

6. For an argument that for-profit entities should receive the same tax advantages as nonprofits, see Eric Posner & Anup Malani, The Case for For–Profit Charities, 93 Va.L.Rev. 2017 (2007) (there is no good argument for making those tax subsidies available only to charities that adopt the nonprofit form). For a criticism of Posner and Malani, see Brian Galle, Keep Charity Charitable, 88 Texas L.Rev. 1213 (2010).

4. *Pluralism/Freedom*. As demonstrated by the many reforms in American society that originated in the nonprofit sector, nonprofit organizations play a valuable role in promoting the values of pluralism and freedom.

5. *Solidarity*. The nonprofit sector is a mechanism through which an individualistic democratic society can express solidarity through joint action.

The excerpts below elaborate on the questions—what is the nonprofit sector and why do we have it?

Lester M. Salamon, America's Nonprofit Sector: A Primer

11–13 (2d ed. 1999).

The Rationale: Why Do We Have a Nonprofit Sector?

Why does the nonprofit sector exist in the United States, or any other country? Why did such organizations come into existence, and why do we give these organizations special tax and other advantages? * * *

Market Failure

[T]he creation of nonprofit organizations has been motivated by certain inherent limitations of the market system that dominates the American economy. Economists refer to these as *market failures*. Essentially, the problem is this: The market is excellent for handling those things we consume individually, such as shoes, cars, clothing, food. For such items, consumer choices in the marketplace send signals to producers about the prices that consumers are willing to pay and the quantities that can be sold at those prices. By contrast, the market does not handle very well those things that can only be consumed collectively, such as clean air, national defense, or safe neighborhoods. These so-called public goods involve a serious "free-rider" problem because, once they are produced, everyone can benefit from them even if they have not shared in the cost. Therefore, it is to each individual's advantage to let his or her neighbor bear the cost of these public goods because each individual will be able to enjoy them whether he or she pays for them or not. The inevitable result, however, will be to produce far less of these collective goods than people really want and thus to leave everyone worse off.

To correct for this, some form of nonmarket mechanism is needed. One such mechanism is government. By imposing taxes on individuals, government can compel everyone to share in the cost of collective goods. Indeed, in classical economic theory the problem of providing collective goods is the major rationale for the existence of government.

But in a democracy government will only supply those collective goods desired by a majority. Where such support is lacking, another mechanism is needed, and one such mechanism is the nonprofit sector. Nonprofit organizations allow groups of individuals to pool their resources to produce collective goods they mutually desire but cannot convince a majority of their countrymen to support. This can happen, for example, when particular subgroups share certain cultural, social, or economic characteristics or interests not shared by all or most citizens of a country. Through nonprofit organizations such subgroups can provide the kinds and levels of collective goods they desire. The greater the heterogeneity of the population, therefore, the larger the nonprofit sector is likely to be.

A slightly different kind of market failure occurs where information asymmetries exist, e.g., where the purchasers of services are not the same as the consumers, a situation economists refer to as *contract failure*. This is the case, for example, with nursing homes, where the consumers are often elderly people with limited consumer choice or ability to discriminate among products and the purchasers are their children. In such situations, the purchasers, unable to assess the adequacy of services themselves, seek some substitute for the market mechanism, some provider they can trust. Because nonprofits do not exist principally to earn profits, they often are preferred providers in such situations.

Government Failure

Since the existence of "market failures"—of inherent limitations of the market system—serves, in classical economic theory, as the justification for reliance on government, it is clear that market failures alone cannot explain the existence of a nonprofit sector. Also important are "government failures," inherent limitations of government that help to explain why nonprofit organizations are needed. In the first place, even in a democracy it is often difficult to get government to act to correct "market failures" because government action requires majority support. By forming nonprofit organizations, smaller groupings of people can begin addressing needs that they have not yet convinced others to support. In short, it is not market failure alone that leads to a demand for nonprofit organizations. Rather, it is the failure of *both* the market and the state to supply collective goods desired by a segment of the population, but not by enough to trigger a governmental response.

Even when majority support exists, however, there is still often a preference for some nongovernmental mechanism to deliver services and respond to public needs because of the cumbersomeness, unresponsiveness, and bureaucratization that often accompanies government action. This is particularly true in the United States because of a strong cultural resistance to the expansion of government. Even when government financing is viewed as essential, therefore, it is often the case that private, nonprofit organizations are utilized to deliver the services that government finances. The result * * * is a complex pattern of cooperation between government and the nonprofit sector.

Henry Hansmann, Reforming Nonprofit Corporation Law

129 U.Pa.L.Rev. 497, 504–509 (1981).

B.   The Role of Nonprofit Organizations

To understand the unique functions served by the nonprofit form of organization, it is helpful to compare the role of nonprofits with that of profit-seeking (or "for-profit" or "business") organizations.

Like for-profit organizations, virtually all nonprofit organizations are, in a sense, engaged in the sale of services. This is, of course, true by definition for commercial nonprofits. Yet donative nonprofits, too, "sell" their services—and it is the donors who are the purchasers. For example, when an individual makes a contribution to the American Red Cross, or to the Metropolitan Opera, it is not quite a pure gift in the sense that the directors of the organization are free to do anything that they wish with the money. Rather, the contribution is a payment made with the understanding that it is to be devoted entirely to assisting disaster victims, or to presenting more and better opera productions. That is, such contributions are essentially efforts to "buy" disaster relief, or opera, and this is what the organizations in question exist to provide and "sell."

Why is it necessary that organizations such as these be nonprofit? In particular, why could not a for-profit firm provide the same services? The reason, in most cases, appears to be that either the nature of the service in question, or the circumstances under which it is provided, render ordinary contractual devices inadequate to provide the purchaser of the service with sufficient assurance that the service was in fact performed as desired. The advantage of the nonprofit form in such circumstances is that it makes the producer a fiduciary for its purchasers, and thus gives them greater assurance that the services they desire will in fact be performed as they wish.

1.   Clarifying Examples

Some examples may help to make this clear.

a.   Third Party Payment

Consider, initially, those donative nonprofits, such as CARE, the Salvation Army, and the American Red Cross, that collect contributions with which to provide relief to the poor and distressed. Why is it necessary that these organizations be nonprofit? Could not profit-seeking firms instead provide the same service—whether dried milk for hungry children in Africa, or bandages for disaster victims, or food for derelicts—in return for payments from philanthropically included individuals?

The answer, in considerable part, apparently lies in the fact that the individuals who receive the services in question have no connection with the individuals who pay for them. Thus, for example, suppose that a profit-seeking counterpart to CARE were to promise to provide one hundred pounds of dried milk to hungry children in Africa in return for a payment of ten dollars. Because the patron has no contact with the intended recipients, he or she would have no simple way of knowing whether the promised service was ever performed, much less performed well. Consequently, the owners of the firm would have both the incentive and the opportunity to provide inadequate service and to divert the money thus saved to themselves.

The advantage of the nonprofit form in such circumstances is that, because the nondistribution constraint prohibits those who control the organization from distributing to themselves out of the organization's income anything beyond reasonable compensation for services they render to the organization, they have less opportunity and incentive than would the managers of a for-profit firm to use the organization's patrons intend it to be used for. In these circumstances, therefore, an individual would presumably much prefer to patronize a nonprofit organization than a for-profit organization. Consequently, it is not surprising that such redistributive services are provided almost exclusively by nonprofit firms.

b.   Public Goods

Similar reasoning applies to the provision of what economists term a "public good"—that is, a good or service such that (1) the cost of providing the good to many persons is not appreciably more than the cost of providing it to one; and (2) once the good has been provided to one person, it is difficult to prevent others by enjoying it as well.[7] Typical examples are noncommercial broadcasting, public monuments, and scientific research.

Even if individual consumers are willing to contribute to the cost of such services, rather than yielding to the incentive to be "free-riders" on the contributions of others, it is likely that they will do so only if the services are provided by a nonprofit. The reason for this is simply that, owing to the indivisible nature of the service involved, the consumer generally has no simple means of observing whether his or her contribution has increased the level of the service provided. Rather, the consumer must take the producer's word that the contribution will be used to purchase more of the good, rather than simply going into someone's pocket. Such a promise will be easier to believe if the producing firm is subject to the nondistribution constraint. Thus, listener-supported radio, tax reform lobbying, and heart research are all typically financed through nonprofit organizations.

c.   Complex Personal Services

Those organizations—most of which we would classify as commercial nonprofits—that provide complex and vital personal services, such as nursing care, day care, education, and hospital care, offer yet another example. The patients at a nursing home, for example, are often too feeble or ill to be competent judges of the care they receive. Likewise, hospital patients and consumers of day care, owing to the difficulty of making an

---

7. Public goods, because of these characteristics, are often, but need not be, provided by the government. See generally E. Mansfield, Microeconomics 470–94 (3d ed. 1979).

accurate personal appraisal of the kind and quality of services they need and receive, must necessarily entrust a great deal of discretion to the suppliers of those services. The nondistribution constraint reduces a nonprofit supplier's incentive to abuse that discretion, and, consequently, consumers might reasonably prefer to obtain these services from a nonprofit firm.

2.   "Contract Failure"

In short, nonprofit firms serve particularly well in situations characterized by what I shall refer to, for simplicity, as "contract failure"—that is, situations in which, owing either to the nature of the service in question or to the circumstances under which it is produced and consumed, ordinary contractual devices in themselves do not provide consumers with adequate means for policing the performance of producers. In such situations, the nonprofit form offers consumers the protection of another, broader "contract"—namely, the organization's commitment, through its nonprofit charter, to devote all of its income to the services it was formed to provide.

It follows that the charter of a nonprofit corporation serves a rather different purpose than does the charter of a business corporation. In a business corporation, the charter, and the statutory and decisional law in which it is embedded, serves primarily to protect the interests of the corporation's shareholders from invasion by those immediately in control of the corporation, including management and other shareholders. In a nonprofit corporation, on the other hand, the restrictions imposed on controlling individuals by the charter and the law are primarily for the benefit of the organization's patrons. As a consequence, business corporation law is often a poor model for nonprofit corporation law. * * *

3.   Countervailing Considerations

The nonprofit form brings with it costs as well as benefits. The curtailment of the profit motive that results from the nondistribution constraint can reduce incentives for cost efficiency, for responsiveness to consumers, and for expansion or creation of new firms in the presence of increasing demand. Moreover, the inability of nonprofits to raise equity capital through the issuance of stock can severely hamper their ability to meet needs for new capital. Only when contract failure is relatively severe is it likely that the advantages of nonprofits as fiduciaries will clearly outweigh these corresponding disadvantages, and thus give the nonprofit firm a net advantage over its for-profit counterpart.

Further, the nondistribution constraint is obviously not airtight. Indeed, as will be emphasized below, the constraint is often poorly policed and even, in many cases, poorly defined. As a consequence, the managers of nonprofits often find, and take advantage of, the opportunity to profit at the expense of the organization. Such behavior, of course, further reduces the advantages offered to patrons by nonprofit as opposed to for-profit firms in situations of contract failure.

In the case of services for the needy, public goods, and other services commonly provided by donative nonprofits, the need for a fiduciary organization is so obvious that for-profit firms are virtually unheard of. On the other hand, contract failure is not so obviously a critical problem for many consumers of the services that are often provided by commercial nonprofits, such as day care, nursing care, hospital care, and education. As a consequence, these services are commonly provided by for-profit as well as nonprofit firms.

D. Summary

In sum, I am suggesting that the essential role of the nonprofit organization is to serve as a fiduciary for its patrons in situations of contract failure. This statement, it should be emphasized, has both a positive (descriptive) and a normative aspect. Taken descriptively, it is an assertion that nonprofit organizations tend to arise in situations in which there is evidence of contract failure and not in cases in which contract failure is absent. Casual empiricism appears to support this conclusion, at least in its broad contours. More important for the purposes at hand, however, is the normative aspect of this analysis—namely, the assertion that the fiduciary role described here is the *appropriate* role for nonprofit organizations.

NOTES AND QUESTIONS

1. *Contract Failure.* Does contract failure fully explain the origins and development of the nonprofit sector? How do we explain that some nonprofits, such as hospitals, nursing homes and some educational institutions, coexist as for-profit, nonprofit, and government entities? What is the relationship of government to the nonprofit sector? Doesn't the government often serve the role of intervening when there is contract failure? Are there incentives for managers of nonprofits to cheat by avoiding the nondistribution constraint?

2. *Another View of the Governmental Role.* Economic theories of market and contract failure assume that nonprofit organizations fill a gap between the business and government sectors. However, government has turned more of the responsibilities for delivery of publicly financed services over to nonprofit organizations than it has retained for itself. In the process government is the most important source of income for most social service agencies. Lester M. Salamon, Partners in Public Service: The Scope and Theory of Government–Nonprofit Relations, in The Nonprofit Sector: A Research Handbook 99, 100 (Walter W. Powell, ed. 1987). Thus, one may view government and the nonprofit sector as a partnership or independent contractor relationship. Professor Salamon has suggested that rather than view the voluntary sector as a residual response to the failures of the market and government, it is the preferred mechanism for providing collective goods. Id. at 111. From this perspective the government is the residual provider when the voluntary sector is unable or unwilling to carry the burden. In theory the government provides a steady stream of financial

support, sets priorities based on political consensus, and distributes benefits more equitably than the private sector. Voluntary organizations, however, can operate more efficiently and personally on a smaller scale than
government. Salamon notes that the partnership may not work so well in
practice as voluntary agencies may lose their independence, or could distort
their missions by going where the money is, or become bureaucratized. Id.
at 114–116.

3. *Responses to Hansmann.* Hansmann's work has been enormously
influential. For critiques see Rob Atkinson, Altruism in Nonprofit Organi-
zations, 31 B.C.L. Rev. 501 (1990); Ira Mark Ellman, Another Theory of
Nonprofit Corporations, 80 Mich. L. Rev. 999 (1982); Richard Steinberg &
Bradford Gray, 'The Role of Nonprofit Enterprise' in 1992: Hansmann
Revisited, 22 Nonprofit & Voluntary Sector Q. 297–317 (1993).

4. *For Further Reading.* To Profit or Not to Profit: The Commercial
Transformation of the Nonprofit Sector (Burton A. Weisbrod ed., 1998);
Avner Ben–Ner, Nonprofit Organizations: Why Do They Exist in Market
Economies?, in The Economics of Nonprofit Institutions: Studies in Struc-
ture and Policy (Susan Rose–Ackerman, ed. 1986); William J. Baumol &
William G. Bowen, Performing Arts—The Economic Dilemma 378–386
(1966); Richard Steinberg, Economic Theories of Nonprofit Organization,
in The Nonprofit Sector: A Research Handbook 117–139 (Walter W. Powell
& Richard Steinberg eds., 2d ed. 2006); Estelle James & Susan Rose–
Ackerman, The Nonprofit Enterprise in Market Economics (1986); The
Economics of Nonprofit Institutions: Studies in Structure and Policy (Susan Rose–Ackerman ed., 1986); Burton A. Weisbrod, The Voluntary Non-
profit Sector: An Economic Analysis (1977); and Burton A. Weisbrod, The
Nonprofit Economy (1988).

2.   POLITICAL AND SOCIAL THEORIES

Economists have more easily generated theories that attempt to account for the development of nonprofits than have political and social
theorists. James Douglas has written: "The task of devising a political
analogue to market failure bristles with difficulties. At a fundamental level
economists have a common criterion or measuring rod—that of 'utility' for
judging the desirability of a form of organization." Economists can claim
that market failure occurs when pursuit by individuals of their own utility
is calculated not to result in maximum utility for society. No similar
unifying measure can be applied to political institutions. Political Theories
of Nonprofit Organization, in The Nonprofit Sector: A Research Handbook
43 (Walter W. Powell ed., 1987).

Yet economic theories are not free of criticism. They neglect the role of
government and government policy by assuming that government policymakers merely implement the demand of the people for collective goods and
have no independent role to play in shaping the nonprofit sector. Steven
Rathgeb Smith & Michael Lipsky, Nonprofits for Hire 31–32 (1993). Economic theories underestimate the fact that our voluntary sector has

emerged because of historical and political factors as well as economic needs.

Political and social theorists attempt to answer such questions as: given the wealth of services provided by government at all levels why do we need nonprofits at all, particularly those that carry out a public function or coexist with governmental organizations that provide the same services? Why does government provide direct subsidies to many nonprofit organizations in the form of grants plus indirect assistance through tax exemption? Do nonprofits play a particular role in our democratic system?

Political theory offers several justifications for the emergence and roles of nonprofits in democratic societies. Government action is bounded by political feasibility whereas private organizations need not heed the majority's will. Nonprofits can engage in experimentation and innovative projects for which government would need to build a certain level of support among the electorate. Additionally, governmental benefits must be distributed equitably which can have a confining effect on their supply. For instance, if the public voted regularly to provide funds for AIDS research, would the same level of assistance be provided? Thus, governments tend to be more constrained, bureaucratic, and less innovative than nonprofits. As John Stuart Mill noted: "Government operations tend to be everywhere alike. With individuals and voluntary associations, on the contrary, there are varied experiments, and endless diversity of experience." On Liberty 135 (Oxford: World Classics ed. 1912) (1859).

The nonprofit sector is also a force for democracy. It promotes a diversity of views and support, complementing government efforts in some areas and filling gaps in others. Nonprofits play a crucial role in promoting the values of freedom and pluralism, by encouraging individual initiatives for the public good. Lester Salamon, America's Nonprofit Sector: A Primer 14 (2d ed. 1999). Nonprofits are also manifestations of community. As Alexis DeTocqueville and others have noted, voluntary associations mediate between the bureaucratic institutions of government and the individual. See Peter L. Berger & Richard J. Neuhaus, To Empower People: The Role of Mediating Structures in Public Policy (1977).

NOTE

For Further Reading. Elisabeth F. Clemens, The Constitution of Citizens: Political Theories of Nonprofit Organizations, in The Nonprofit Sector: A Research Handbook 207 (Walter W. Powell & Richard Steinberg, eds., 2d ed. 2006); Miriam Galston, Civic Renewal & The Regulation of Nonprofits, 13 Cornell J.L. & Pub. Pol'y 289 (2004); Barbara K. Bucholtz, Reflections on the Role of Nonprofit Associations in a Representative Democracy, 7 Cornell J. Law & Pub. Policy 555, 571–583 (1998); James Douglas, Why Charity?: The Case for a Third Sector (1983); Waldemar A. Nielsen, The Endangered Sector (1979); Lester M. Salamon, Partners in Public Service, in The Nonprofit Sector: A Research Handbook 99 (Walter W. Powell ed., 1987).

E.   THE LEGAL FRAMEWORK

Like their for-profit counterparts, nonprofit organizations are governed by a variety of legal regimes. These evolving bodies of law can be broadly (and rather arbitrarily) divided into three categories: organization and governance, taxation, and other regulatory law. The legal rules often vary depending on whether a nonprofit organization is a charity, broadly defined, or in the less favored category often referred to as mutual benefit organizations.

Organization and governance of a nonprofit entity, the principal topic of Part Two of this text (Chapters 2–4), are primarily matters of state law. Many states have enacted distinct nonprofit corporation statutes that address the mechanics of forming a nonprofit corporation, operational issues, fiduciary obligations and liabilities of officers and directors, structural changes such as mergers and conversions to for-profit status, dissolution, and the oversight role of the state attorney general. Among the goals of modern nonprofit corporation statutes is to recognize the unique and diverse nature of nonprofits, to promote ease of formation and operation, to provide practical answers to everyday problems faced by nonprofit organizations and their managers, and to recognize the different roles played by nonprofit corporations. Part Two also addresses attempts by the states to regulate charitable solicitation, and the significant constitutional obstacles to those efforts.

Part Three (Chapters 5–8) turns to the distinctive tax treatment of charitable organizations. Charities, whether they are formed as nonprofit corporations or charitable trusts, have long enjoyed exemptions from income, real property, sales, and other more specialized taxes. They also are eligible to receive tax-deductible contributions for income, gift and estate tax purposes. Table 1.4, below, is a list of the categories of nonprofit organizations eligible for exemption from federal income tax and the number of organizations registered with the Internal Revenue Service in each category. The excerpt following Table 1.4 previews the Internal Revenue Code's intricate classification scheme and provides an overview of the federal tax treatment of charities. The influence of this large and complex body of "fiscal law" is considerable, often shaping a charity's organizational structure, the compensation paid to its officers and employees, its ability to engage in commercial or political advocacy activities, and its fundraising practices. The less stringent tax exemption requirements for mutual benefit and other noncharitable organizations, as well as other special legal problems of private membership associations, are addressed in Part Four (Chapters 9 and 10).

Apart from taxes, nonprofit organizations are subject to various other forms of regulation that bear on their relationships with private parties other than donors, officers, or members. These regulatory regimes include the laws of tort, contract, bankruptcy, labor and employment, securities, and antitrust. The most dynamic field of regulatory law affecting nonprofits is antitrust, which is examined in Part Five (Chapter 11).

Table 1.4

Tax–Exempt Organizations Registered With the IRS

		2008	2009
Section 501(c) by subsection:			
(1)	Corporations organized under act of Congress	142	162
(2)	Title-holding companies	7,131	7,170
(3)	Religious, charitable, and similar organizations	1,186,915	1,238,201
(4)	Social welfare organizations	135,494	137,276
(5)	Labor and agricultural organizations	60,291	62,462
(6)	Business leagues	89,409	90,908
(7)	Social and recreation clubs	73,173	76,243
(8)	Fraternal beneficiary societies	63,194	63,097
(9)	Voluntary employees' beneficiary associations	11,996	11,867
(10)	Domestic fraternal beneficiary societies	20,964	21,279
(12)	Benevolent life insurance associations	6,836	6,878
(13)	Cemetery companies	11,401	11,720
(14)	State-chartered credit unions	3,532	3,443
(15)	Mutual insurance companies	2,005	1,915
(17)	Supplemental unemployment benefit trusts	434	424
(19)	War veterans' organizations	36,306	37,878
(25)	Holding companies for pensions and other entities	1,239	1,171
Other 501(c) subsections		105	135
Section 501(d) Religious and apostolic associations		164	205
Section 501(e) Cooperative hospital service organizations		36	35
Section 501(f) Cooperative service organizations of operating educational organizations		1	1
Section 501(k) Child care organizations		14	14
Section 501(n) Charitable risk pools		1	1
Nonexempt charitable trusts		144,284	140,210
Total tax-exempt organizations and other entities		1,855,067	1,912,695

Source: IRS Data Book, 2009.

John Simon, Harvey Dale & Laura Chisolm, The Tax Treatment of Charitable Organizations

in The Nonprofit Sector: A Research Handbook (Walter W. Powell & Richard Steinberg, eds., 2d ed., 2006).

AN OVERVIEW OF THE FEDERAL TAX TREATMENT OF CHARITABLE ORGANIZATIONS

A Federal Tax Taxonomy

The tax treatment of charitable organization can best be understood by looking at the big picture—the larger universe of nonprofit entities of which the charitable sector is a major part. Viewing the nonprofit sector as a whole, one realizes that there is not a single federal tax treatment but instead many separate treatments. With some minor exceptions, however, what all of the inhabitants of this sector have in common is, first, the "nondistribution constraint": they are entitled to make profits but are forbidden to distribute these profits to any person or entity (other than another nonprofit organization)—they have, in conventional terms, no "owners"—and, second, exemption from the federal income tax imposed on non-nonprofit corporations, unincorporated associations, or trusts under the principal exemption statute, § 501 of the Internal Revenue Code of 1986, as amended (which we will usually refer to simply as "the 'code' "). There are two major sets of nonprofit organizations:

(1) What we will refer to as "charitable organizations" or "charities"—organizations described in § 501(c)(3) as "organized and operated exclusively for religious, charitable, scientific, testing for public safety, literary, or educational purposes." The shorthand "charitable" or "charity" is used for these groups, even though it is only one of several adjectives used in § 501(c)(3), partly because "charitable" is the residual category used to classify these groups when they do not fit under any of the other adjectives, and partly because the Supreme Court has held that all § 501(c)(3) groups must conform to certain fundamental common-law charitable criteria. (Bob Jones University v. United States, 461 U.S. 574 (1983)). In that case, "charity" as used in § 501(c)(3) or in the legal argot, it may be noted, does not correspond with the usages of yesteryear, when the word had a meaning largely confined to aid for the poor and the sick.

(2) What we will refer to as "noncharitable nonprofits"—organizations listed in §§ 501(c)(4)–(25). Here we have social welfare organizations, social clubs, veterans' organizations, labor unions, burial societies, chambers of commerce, marketing cooperatives, and other associations that may roughly be described as carrying forward the private interests of the members.

The distinctions between these two sets of exempt organizations have been expressed not only in the shorthand terms "charitable" and "noncharitable" but also (1) by describing the (c)(3)s as "public benefit" organizations and the other exempt groups as "mutual benefit" entities or

(2) by stating that the (c)(3)s tend, more than the other exempt groups, to provide "collective goods" (Weisbrod 1980), often referred to as "public goods"—goods and services whose benefits cannot be captured by any one individual to the exclusion of others. Each of these generalizations is largely accurate, but none is error-free. Thus, many (c)(4) "social welfare" groups would easily meet a "charitable," "public benefit," or "public goods" test but fail to qualify for (c)(3) status for other reasons. And many (c)(3)s fail to meet lay understandings of "charity" (opera companies, for example, that charge $50 for the cheapest seats), act very much like "mutual benefit" organizations (the most exclusive prep schools, for example, or churches that conduct largely social "retreats"), or appear to produce few public goods (very expensive nursing homes, for example).

We find, within the charitable set, two major subsets that are distinctly—one might say dramatically—different legal species: the private foundations and the charities that are not private foundations. Among professionals in the nonprofit field, private foundations are often referred to as "foundations" and the nonfoundations as "public charities"—usages we will follow in this chapter. The foundations are further divided, as we shall see, into the "operating" and "nonoperating" categories.

Before proceeding with our account of these § 501(c) sets and subsets, we must note that it is somewhat reductionist. There are several tax-exempt species that lie outside the § 501(c) categories (e.g., pension funds, consumer and farmer cooperatives, and political organizations of various kinds). Moreover, each of the categories contains some outliers—organizations (e.g., churches) subject to rules that partly differ from the rules applicable to other entities in the same category. In addition, there are entities—community foundations—that resemble nonoperating foundations but are treated as public charities, and other entities—"exempt operating foundations"—that seem like operating foundations but are subject to different (and lighter) rules. Finally, the expression "federal tax treatment" masks the fact that there are four principal federal taxes—individual income tax, corporate income tax, estate tax, and gift tax—whose provisions relating to the nonprofit sector do not fully overlap.

Consequences of Charitable vs. Noncharitable Status

Focusing on the § 501(c) categories, we first consider the consequences of charitable versus noncharitable status. The most celebrated result has to do with deductibility. While all § 501(c) organizations are exempt from taxation on their income, there is a dramatic difference in their eligibility for contributions that are deductible by the donors. Contributions of cash or property (but not services) to § 501(c)(3) charities generally are deductible by individuals and corporations for income tax purposes (§ 170) and also are deductible for estate and gift tax purposes (§§ 2055, 2522). Gifts to noncharitable nonprofits generally are not deductible, except for contributions to veterans' groups, nonprofit cemetery companies, and fraternal benefit organizations that use the gifts for charitable purposes (§ 170(c)).

An organization's charitable-versus-noncharitable status also determines the regime of regulatory, equity, and border patrol rules to which the organization will be subject. In general, the noncharitable groups are not constrained by a number of the provisions that apply to charities. On the other hand, charities enjoy other benefits not available to the other nonprofits. Some relate to eligibility for various forms of favorable federal tax treatment other than exemption and deductibility. Thus, charities can create retirement plans and make payments into them that are tax-sheltered for the employees—without the elaborate and expensive apparatus of a "qualified pension plan" (§ 403(b)); charities have a greater capacity to derive capital from municipal bond financing (§ 145(a)(1)); and only charities are exempt from the Federal Unemployment Tax Act (§§ 3301–11) and the federal gambling tax (§ 4421(2)(b)).

Other favorable consequences of a group's charitable status relate to federal nontax provisions. Although preferential nonprofit postal rates are not expressly based on an organization's nonprofit tax status, the postal regulations use criteria so similar to the nonprofit tax criteria (39 C.F.R. § 111.1 [1990]) that one can safely say that these preferential rates are available to charities but not to the other nonprofits. In addition, the charitable groups—but not the other nonprofits—are exempt from involuntary bankruptcy proceedings (11 U.S.C. § 303(a) [1988]), from buyer liability under the Robinson–Patman Act (15 U.S.C. § 13c), and, for most purposes, from the securities regulation laws (15 U.S. §§ 77c(a)(4), 80a–3(c)(10) [1988]).

Distinctions within the Charitable World

Starting in 1954, and more ambitiously in 1969, Congress made distinctions—created a class system, some would say—within the § 501(c)(3) charitable world. The charity world was first divided into two parts referred to earlier: the private foundations and the public charities. The private foundations were defined as constituting all groups that flunked certain tests set up by § 509 of the code. To pass these tests, a group must be a school, a church, a hospital (or hospital-related research entity), a state college or university support entity, a group that meets one of two alternative (and fairly complicated) definitions of a "publicly supported" organization, or an entity that qualifies (under one of three alternative tests) as a "supporting organization" of a public charity. Organizations meeting these tests (and certain variations upon them) obtain public charity classification. This subdivision was meant to separate donor-controlled or otherwise "closely held" grant-making organizations (e.g., the Ford Foundation and lesser dispensers) from operating charities with relatively broad-based donor or beneficiary constituencies—and to accord preferred treatment to the latter group, the public charities. It was in the foundation camp that more fiscal abuses were thought to lie, more political activism, and more "unaccountable" wealth; in any event, it was thought that dollars given to grant-making foundations entered the stream of active charitable use more slowly than gifts to operating charities.

In the midst of the 1969 congressional deliberations, however, it was discovered that the private foundation category, as pending legislation defined it, included all kinds of non-grant-making bodies that did not happen to be schools, churches, hospitals, or publicly supported organizations. Many research institutions, social action groups, museums, and other nonprofits would fall outside the public charity definitions. Congress could have moved them into public charity status, but instead it subdivided the foundation world into the operating foundations and the nonoperating foundations (the grant-making ones). Probably the most important legal feature of the operating foundation is that it spends 85 percent of its income on the active conduct of its charitable program, as opposed to grant making (§ 4942(j)(3) and related regulations).

Foundations are charity's least-favored branch. Under each of the four functions of nonprofit tax law—support, equity, regulatory, and border patrol—the tax code (largely as a result of the Tax Reform Act of 1969) disadvantages private foundations as compared with other § 501(c)(3) entities. This difference in treatment under the code has been generally accepted by the foundation and legal communities. Over the years since 1969 there have been efforts, usually successful, to achieve congressional or administrative moderation of some features of the overall regime. Congress enacted partial—in some cases gossamer—reductions of the tax on investment income, of the payout requirements, of the excess business holdings deadlines, and of the self-dealing provisions. And the IRS "provided a mild form of interpretive deregulation" of the antilobbying and jeopardizing investment rules. But the basic framework remains intact and—although criticized by some academic commentators—has not been seriously questioned by the foundations or their legal or associational representatives.

———

This legal framework governing nonprofits brings with it benefits, such as tax exemptions, and burdens, such as the nondistribution constraint. In meeting with the founders of a new enterprise that might qualify for nonprofit status, a lawyer must inquire about their purposes and goals, proposed activities, the sources of funding, and the desired relationship of the founders and others to the organization. The problem below offers an opportunity to address some of these pre-formation issues.

For Further Reading. Bazil Facchina, Evan Showell & Jan E. Stone, Privileges and Exemptions Enjoyed by Nonprofit Organizations: A Catalog and Some Thoughts on Nonprofit Policymaking (N.Y.U. School of Law Program on Philanthropy and the Law, 1993); Thomas Silk, The Legal Framework of the Nonprofit Sector in the United States, in The Jossey–Bass Handbook of Nonprofit Leadership and Management (Robert D. Herman ed., 1994); Developments in the Law–Nonprofit Corporations, 105 Harv.L.Rev. 1578 (1992).

INTRODUCTORY PROBLEM

The purpose of this introductory problem is to launch a general discussion of some preliminary considerations relating to the decision whether to form an organization as a for-profit business or a nonprofit entity and, if nonprofit, to consider options on choice of organizational form (corporation, trust, unincorporated association) and tax-exempt status (§ 501(c)(3) or some other section of the Code).

Leona Read and Tom O'Brien, both full-time law professors with considerable practical experience, are interested in forming and operating an entity that will conduct continuing legal education programs to attorneys in your state. The impetus is the continuing education mandated by the local state bar for all lawyers. For now, Leona and Tom intend to remain as full-time faculty members, but ultimately they may devote more time to continuing education if it proves to be successful.

Leona and Tom are seeking some general advice as to what factors should be considered in deciding whether to conduct their continuing education activity as a for-profit business or a nonprofit educational organization, and any legal issues related to choosing a name for their new entity. In Chapter 2, you will have the opportunity to provide advice on the appropriate legal form on the assumption they choose to form a nonprofit entity and the formal organizational steps required under your jurisdiction's law.

PART TWO

ORGANIZATION AND OPERATION OF NONPROFIT ORGANIZATIONS—THE STATE PERSPECTIVE

CHAPTER 2

FORMATION, DISSOLUTION AND RESTRUCTURING

A. CHOICE OF THE LEGAL FORM OF A NONPROFIT ORGANIZATION

A threshold decision for the founders of a nonprofit entity is the legal structure the organization will adopt. Both tax and non-tax considerations must be evaluated. Tax considerations include: the appropriate type of federal tax exemption, the organization's classification as a public charity or private foundation, the forms of organization permitted under the Internal Revenue Code, and the consequences of each type.[1] Non-tax factors include the speed with which one needs to establish the organization, concerns with limited liability, the sophistication and goals of the organizers, financial resources, and the type and scale of activities to be conducted. Among other considerations are the capacity to own property and contract, the capacity to sue and be sued, liabilities to third parties, the permanence of the organization and ease of dissolution, and governance requirements.[2]

Assuming that the entity will apply for some type of federal income tax exemption, it must choose from the organizational forms recognized by the Internal Revenue Code. To obtain exempt status under § 501(c)(3), the most desirable exempt status because the organization is eligible to receive tax-deductible contributions, a nonprofit entity must be a corporation, trust, or unincorporated association. Section 501(c)(3) refers to a "corporation, community chest, fund or foundation," but does not specify how any of those organizations must be formed. It has long been established that trusts, though not mentioned in the statute, are included in the terms "fund" or "foundation".[3] Most exempt organizations are corporations and a few are unincorporated associations.[4] It is not possible to operate an

---

1. These issues are considered in Chapter 5, infra.

2. See generally Cherie L. Evans & Patrick B. Sternal, Choice of Entity Considerations, in Advising California Nonprofit Corporations, ch. 2 (California Continuing Education of the Bar, 3d ed. 2009); Nancy Melhlman & Lisa Watts, Nonprofit Organizations: A Guide to Choosing Form (National Center on Philanthropy and the Law), available at http://www1.law.nyu.edu/ncpl/pdfs/Monograph/Nonprofit_Organizations_Final.pdf.

3. Fifth–Third Union Trust Co. v. Commissioner, 56 F.2d 767 (6th Cir.1932); G.C.M. 15778, XIV–2 C.B. 118 (1935).

4. For federal tax purposes, the corporate form includes unincorporated associations which are taxed as corporations under I.R.C. § 7701(a)(3).

exempt organization as an individual[5] or as a partnership,[6] but a limited liability company with two or more members that are charities or governmental entities can qualify for § 501(c)(3) tax exemption if various conditions are met.[7]

1. UNINCORPORATED ASSOCIATIONS

Revised Uniform Unincorporated Association Act.

Many smaller nonprofits are unincorporated associations, a form that involves nothing more than two or more persons organized for a common purpose. The most prominent and substantial unincorporated associations are labor unions and political organizations. For many years, the American Bar Association was an unincorporated association. More typically, the unincorporated association is used by newly created entities or those commencing the incorporation process. This form may be suitable for fledgling organizations with uncertain prospects, a limited expected duration, or founders who are unlikely to bring the activity or project to fruition.

The advantages of unincorporated associations are their informality and flexibility. Unlike a nonprofit corporation, no governmental approvals must be obtained in order to form or dissolve unincorporated associations. They can obtain recognition of federal tax exemption under § 501(c)(3) and are required to follow the filing requirements binding exempt entities.[8] An unincorporated association needs neither a constitution nor bylaws except if it seeks recognition of exempt status under § 501(c)(3).[9]

The disadvantages of unincorporated association status outweigh the benefits. Few statutory rules govern or guide unincorporated associations, and there is little case law. The law of agency governs most legal relationships. Unincorporated associations have no separate legal existence apart

---

5. I.R.S. Exempt Orgs. Handbook, § 321.1 (1977).

6. Emerson Inst. v. United States, 356 F.2d 824 (D.C.Cir.1966).

7. See Richard A. McCray & Ward L. Thomas, Limited Liability Companies as Exempt Organizations—Update, IRS Exempt Organizations Continuing Professional Education Text for FY 2001, available at http://www.irs.gov/co. A single-member LLC whose sole member is a tax-exempt charity is treated as a division of that member for tax purposes, but it may elect to be treated as a separate entity and, if it does, it must separately apply for exemption. I.R.S. Ann. 99–102, 1999–43 I.R.B. 545.

8. Under I.R.C. § 7701, associations generally are treated as corporations for purposes of § 501(c)(3). The Internal Revenue Service tends to look more closely at applications from unincorporated associations. The organizing documents must be signed by a minimum of two people associated under its terms. I.R.S. Exempt Orgs. Handbook § 321.5 (1985). If the unincorporated association has received recognition of exemption and later incorporates, it must file a new application for recognition of exemption. Bruce R. Hopkins, The Law of Tax Exempt Organizations § 24.1(b) (9th ed. 2007).

9. "A formless aggregation of individuals without some organizing instrument, governing rules, and regularly chosen officers would not be a tax exempt charitable entity for purposes of § 501(c)(3)." IRS Exempt Organizations Handbook § 321.4. The written articles of association must include a clause that provides that upon dissolution, the organization's assets will be transferred to another exempt organization. Treas. Reg. § 1.501(c)(3)–1(b)(4).

from their members, and individual members may be found personally liable. Absent an enabling statute, an unincorporated association cannot receive or hold property in the association's name. The organization has no perpetual duration, nor can it contract in its own name or hold title to property. Upon dissolution, members are entitled to their pro rata share of assets unless the articles of association provide otherwise. Since an unincorporated association is not a separate legal entity, all members are parties defendant of an alleged liability of the association. A majority of jurisdictions have passed legislation treating the unincorporated association as an entity for legal purposes such as capacity to sue or be sued. A final disadvantage is that banks, creditors, and other vendors, which all are more accustomed to dealing with corporations, may be reluctant to conduct business with an unincorporated association.

A Uniform Unincorporated Nonprofit Association Act was approved by the Commissioners on Uniform State Laws in 1992 but it has been adopted by only twelve states. A Revised Uniform Unincorporated Nonprofit Association Act ("RUUNAA") received approval in 2008, but it has been adopted only by Nevada. The new Act attempts to draft away some of the major disabilities of nonprofit unincorporated associational status and fulfill the expectations of their participants. RUUNAA offers a template to small informal organizations, which are unlikely to have legal advice, and provides solutions to certain problems created by common law treatment.

RUUNAA parts ways with the common law by recognizing an unincorporated nonprofit association as a legal entity with the ability to hold and dispose of property, to sue in its own name and be sued, and to be the beneficiary of a trust or contract. An unincorporated association's contract and tort liability will be distinct from its members and managers. It will have perpetual existence unless the association's governing principles specify otherwise and may engage in profit making activities, so long as it adheres to the nondistribution constraint.

Many of the governing principles are adopted from partnership or limited liability company law. The Act provides limited liability of sorts to members and managers, similar to nonprofit corporations. Unincorporated nonprofit association members are neither agents nor fiduciaries solely by reason of membership. The governance structure resembles partnerships or corporations. Managers have a fiduciary duty to the association. In short, the RUUNAA offers a holding pattern for informal associations until its members or managers decide to incorporate.

2.   CHARITABLE TRUSTS

Sample Form of Charitable Trust.

The oldest type of nonprofit entity is the charitable trust, whose existence has been traced prior to the Statute of Uses of 1601.[10] A

---

10. 43 Eliz. ch. 4. In England, charitable trusts were enforced long before the seventeenth century. Prior to the fifteenth century, when the Chancellor first began to enforce uses

charitable trust is a fiduciary relationship with respect to property arising from a manifestation of the grantor's intention to create it. The person holding the trust property (the trustee) is subjected to equitable duties to deal with the property for a charitable purpose in accordance with the terms of the trust and applicable law. Restatement (Third) of Trusts §§ 2, 76. Charitable trusts differ from private trusts in several ways. Their object is to benefit the community rather than private individuals. Assets of a charitable trust must be irrevocably dedicated to the purposes of that trust. Therefore, no disposition of property for an otherwise valid purpose will be invalid because of the indefiniteness, lack of existence or capacity, or uncertainty of the beneficiaries. Charitable trusts are enforced by the attorney general rather than by the trust's beneficiaries, and they can be of unlimited duration unhindered by the rule against perpetuities. 5 Austin Wakeman Scott & Mark L. Ascher, Scott & Ascher on Trusts § 37.1 (5th ed. 2009) (hereinafter "Scott & Ascher on Trusts").

Although still the predominant form of charitable organization in England, the charitable trust had a more checkered existence in certain areas of the United States in the nineteenth century. Charitable trusts are suitable for holding property for charitable purposes and often are used for private foundations that are engaged solely in making grants. The charitable trust form offers: ease and swiftness of formation, administration with fewer formalities than the corporate form, fewer housekeeping requirements, perpetual or indefinite period of existence, and the possibility of continuing control by the grantor. Charitable trusts may be less expensive to maintain than a nonprofit corporation.

A charitable trust instrument names the trustees, states the charitable purpose, establishes policies for administration, distribution of assets and dissolution, names successor trustees or method of selection, and states the duration of the trust.[11] Management of the charitable trust rests in the trustees.[12] They may be selected by the settlor, by a court in certain circumstances, and may be self-perpetuating if the trust instrument so provides.

Where time is of the essence for the receipt of assets, a trust is easily and quickly formed. Unlike the corporation there is no need for prior approval to create a trust. The requisites for effective formation of a charitable trust are essentially the same as those applicable to private trusts except there is no requirement of identifiable beneficiaries. The settlor must only describe with definiteness a purpose which is legally charitable. The naming or describing of individuals or classes of persons is

---

and trusts, both inter vivos and testamentary gifts for charitable purposes received some protection in courts of law. 5 Scott & Ascher on Trusts § 37.1.1. Organizations such as churches existed far back into antiquity.

11. Charitable trusts can be indefinite in duration unless the grantor has reserved a right of revocation or power to modify. 5 Scott & Ascher on Trusts, §§ 37.4.1, 37.4.2.

12. A trustee has comprehensive powers to manage the trust and to carry out its terms and purposes. All powers must be exercised in accordance with the trustee's fiduciary obligations. Restatement (Third) Trusts § 70.

merely to show the conduit through which the benefit is to flow.[13] A trust may be created by the declaration of the settlor, by conveyance, by deed or will to a trustee, or by making a contract by the settlor in favor of a trustee.

3.   NONPROFIT CORPORATIONS

Model Nonprofit Corp. Act (3d ed.) §§ 1.40(3), (5), (8), (37); 2.02. N.Y. Not-for-Profit Corp. L. § 201.

The predominant form of exempt organization in the United States is the nonprofit corporation. As mentioned previously, its primary distinction from the business corporation is the nondistribution constraint.[14] This does not preclude nonprofit corporations from earning a profit; it only prevents them from distributing any net profit to their members, who are the nonprofit equivalent of corporate shareholders. A particular advantage of the nonprofit corporate form is that the governing statutes are comparable to state corporate law. This similarity offers a familiar model to a nonprofit corporation's legal counsel as well as a body of analogous case law that often can be transported to the nonprofit context.

Compared to the unincorporated association or charitable trust, the charitable corporation must conform to more formalities in its creation and dissolution, but internal governance normally is more flexible, making it easier to react to changed circumstances such as the resignation or death of a director. A corporation can hold new elections while a change in trustee may require application to a court. It can easily amend corporate governing instruments.[15] The corporation is an artificial entity that can sue and be sued, contract, and hold property in its own name. It has an indefinite existence, and a centralized management known as the board of directors. Directors of a nonprofit corporation are held to a lower standard of care than charitable trustees. Directors also enjoy the advantage of limited

---

13. The theory is that in the case of the charitable trust, the beneficial property interest is devoted to the accomplishment of purposes that are beneficial or supposed to be beneficial to the community. Therefore the persons receiving such benefits need not be designated. 6 Scott & Ascher on Trusts, § 38.8.

14. Consumer cooperatives, a specialized breed of nonprofit, do permit dividend distributions to their members. Cooperative corporation statutes typically limit the purposes for which such corporations can be formed to agricultural, housing, or medical activities. See N.Y. Coop. Corp. Law § 13; Mo. Ann. Stat. § 357.010; Henry B. Hansmann, Reforming Nonprofit Corporation Law, 129 U.Pa. L.Rev. 497, 595–596 (1981).

15. However, corporate flexibility is not unlimited. In Alco Gravure, Inc. v. Knapp Foundation, 64 N.Y.2d 458, 490 N.Y.S.2d 116, 479 N.E.2d 752 (1985), the court held that directors of a not-for-profit corporation did not have unlimited power of amendment as to how assets were to be administered or to effectuate a transfer of assets on dissolution of a nonprofit corporation where amendment would have changed the purpose for which funds were given to the corporation. Many features of corporate flexibility such as the ability to delegate to officers and agents and amending rules of procedure can be incorporated in a trust by carefully drafted powers in the governing trust instrument. Carolyn C. Clark & Glenn M. Trost, Forming a Foundation: Trust vs. Corporation, 3 Prob. & Prop. Rev. 32 (May/June 1989).

liability. The corporation offers more established patterns than the trust for determining the legal consequences of engaging in multiple operations (consolidations and mergers, reorganizations).

The circumstances under which proceedings by which creditors can reach property differ. If a charitable corporation incurs a liability in contract or tort, an action at law lies against the corporation, while it is in equity, if at all, that a creditor can reach trust property.[16]

When property is conveyed to a charitable corporation, the organization usually has full ownership rights in the property. However, a charitable corporation does not hold property beneficially in the same sense as a business corporation, because the Attorney General can sue to prevent a diversion of property from the purposes for which it was given.[17] When property is left by will to a charitable corporation or property is conveyed to a corporation by an executor, the corporation is not thereafter bound to account as if it were a testamentary trustee.

B.   BASIC STATUTORY APPROACHES TO THE NONPROFIT CORPORATION

1.   IN GENERAL

Model Nonprofit Corp. Act § 4 (1964).

Cal. Corp. Code §§ 5111, 5130, 5410.

Ill. Comp. Stat. ch. 805, § 105/103.05.

N.Y. Not-for-Profit Corp. L. §§ 201–02, 204–05, 404–06, 508, 515.

Model Nonprofit Corp. Act (3d ed.) §§ 3.01–03.

States have adopted widely differing approaches in their statutory treatment of nonprofit corporations. A decreasing number still follow in whole or in part the original Model Nonprofit Corporation Act, which was adopted in 1952 and revised in 1957 and 1964.[1] Those states having no separate statute for nonprofits often subsume them under the general corporate law, in a section for nonstock corporations.[2] New York and

---

16.   5 Scott & Ascher on Trusts, at § 37.1.1 at 2357 n. 9.

17.   Id. But see Lefkowitz v. Lebensfeld, 68 A.D.2d 488, 417 N.Y.S.2d 715 (1979), aff'd 51 N.Y.2d 442, 415 N.E.2d 919, 434 N.Y.S.2d 929 (1980), where the attorney general, purporting to represent the ultimate beneficiaries of charities which had received an unrestricted gift of corporate stock, sued the corporation that issued the stock to compel the declaration and payment of dividends and payment of the market value of the shares which had been purchased from the charities at a price below market value. The court dismissed the action, because the attorney general did not have standing to sue third parties who allegedly were liable to the charitable organizations.

1.   See 1 Marilyn E. Phelan, Nonprofit Enterprises §§ 1:12–1:63 (2000 & Supp. 2009) for a description of state nonprofit statutes. See also Marion R. Fremont–Smith, Governing Nonprofit Organizations, ch. 3 (2004).

2.   Del. Code Ann. tit. 8, § 102(a)(4); Kansas Stat. Ann. § 17–6002(a)(4); Md. Code Ann. Corps. & Ass'ns §§ 5–201 to 5–209, Okla. Gen. Corp. Act. § 1002.

California have their own very different statutes, particularly as to how nonprofits should be classified. Many jurisdictions adopted the Revised Model Nonprofit Corporation Act (RMNCA), which was approved by the American Bar Association in 1987. The Revised Model Act's classification of nonprofits, based upon the California approach,[3] attracted less favor than has the remainder of the statute.[4] The recently adopted Model Nonprofit Corporation Act (3rd ed.), which closely follows the ABA's Revised Model Business Corporation Act, has done away with the Revised Model Act's tripartite division of nonprofit organizations.[5]

Some jurisdictions have separate provisions for specific types of nonprofits. For example, religious corporations or hospital service institutions utilize the general nonprofit statute only for matters dealing with internal governance or corporate housekeeping.[6] Several states limit the purposes for which nonprofit corporations may be formed.[7] Others allow incorporation for any lawful purpose, limited only by the nondistribution constraint.[8] The trend is in favor of liberalization of purposes.[9]

A leading treatise summarizes some of the other differences in approach:

> While the states have some common themes in their nonprofit corporate statutes, there are many differences. All the state statutes prohibit the payment of dividends. Most prohibit the issuance of stock; however, some do permit it.[10] State statutes do not prohibit the making of a profit by a nonprofit corporation. Most provide for the payment of a reasonable compensation to officers and directors, and for the payment of other non cash benefits to their members.[11] In addition some

---

3.   Compare RMNCA § 3.01 with Cal. Corp. Code §§ 5111, 7111, 9111.

4.   See introduction to Revised Model Act at xx; Texas has adopted the Revised Model Act's standards for directors. Tex. Bus. Orgs. Code § 22.201. Idaho and Mississippi have adopted the Revised Model Act but did not incorporate the provisions that differentiated between mutual and public benefit corporations. Jurisdictions adopting the Revised Model Act include: Idaho (Idaho Code §§ 30–3–1 to 30–3–145); Mississippi (Miss. Code Ann. §§ 79–11–31 to 79–11–661); Montana (Mont. Code Ann. §§ 35–2–113 to 35–2–1402); Oregon (Or. Rev. Stat. §§ 65.001 to 65.990); Tennessee (Tenn. Code Ann. §§ 48–51–101 to 48–68–105); and Wyoming (Wyo. Stat. §§ 17–19–101 to 17–19–1807).

5.   Lizabeth A. Moody, Foreword to the Model Nonprofit Corporation Act (3d ed.), infra p. 58. The "Third Edition" of the Model Act was adopted by a task force appointed by the ABA Business Law Section's Committee on Nonprofit Organizations in August 2008 and was published by the Section in 2009.

6.   See N.Y. Not-for-Profit Corp. L. § 201(b); N.Y. Relig. Corp. L. § 2(b).

7.   See Alaska Stat. § 10.20.005; Fla. Stat. Ann. § 617.0301; 805 Ill. Comp. Stat. Ann. § 105/103.05.

8.   Thus, Indiana provides: "A corporation incorporated under this article [Nonprofit Corporations] has the purpose of engaging in any lawful activity unless a more limited purpose is set forth in the articles of incorporation." Ind. Code Ann. § 23–17–4–1–(a) (West 1998); see also Ohio Rev. Code Ann. § 1702.03 (West 1998); Wis. Stat. Ann. § 181.0301 (West 1998).

9.   Henry Hansmann, Reforming Nonprofit Corporation Law, 129 U.Pa.L. Rev. 497, 510 (1981). The MNCA (§ 3.01(a)) also adopts the permissive approach.

10.   See, e.g., Pa. Stat. Ann. Tit. 15, § 572.

11.   See D.C. Code Ann. § 527.

states permit distribution of the assets to the members upon liquidation or upon final dissolution, except for charitable organizations.[12] Some states classify nonprofit corporations into categories, whereas most do not. Some states provide standards of conduct for the officers and directors; others do not. The newer state statutes provide for member derivative actions,[13] whereas many of the states do not have such a provision.

Marilyn Phelan, 1 Nonprofit Enterprises § 1:11 at 32–33 (2000 & Supp. 2009) (footnotes renumbered).

2.   FORMING A NONPROFIT CORPORATION

Model Nonprofit Corp. Act (3d ed.) §§ 2.01–2.06.

Sample Certificate of Incorporation and Bylaws.

If the decision has been made to incorporate, the next step is to select the state of incorporation. That typically will be the jurisdiction in which the organization intends to conduct its activities.[1] The law of the state of incorporation normally governs internal organizational affairs. After the state of incorporation has been selected, the corporation then must be formally organized. The first stage of the organization process is to prepare a "certificate of incorporation" or "articles of incorporation" or "charter" (the statutory language differs from state to state but the phrase means the same thing). The certificate of incorporation is eventually filed with the appropriate state official, usually the secretary of state. Though the requirements differ somewhat by jurisdiction, the nonprofit statutes generally require the certificate to contain the name of the organization,[2] a statement and description of the purposes of the organization, the name of an agent for service of process, and the names and addresses of the original incorporators or directors. If the organization will be a public benefit corporation there will be a provision stating that upon dissolution the organization will distribute its assets to other public benefit organizations to meet the requirements of § 501(c)(3) of the Internal Revenue Code, and if the nonprofit is a private foundation it will act or refrain from acting so

---

12.   See, e.g., Ariz. Rev. Stat. Ann. §§ 10–1026, 10–1046.

13.   See, e.g., the New York Not-for-Profit Corporation Law of 1970, N.Y. Not-for-Profit Corp. Law § 623; Calif. Nonprofit Corporation Law of 1980, Cal. Corp. Code §§ 5710; 7710; 9912.

1.   There may be occasions where speed of incorporation is critical. In some states, such as New York, the incorporators must obtain a consent or waiver of consent by specified authority that the proposed organization is or is not a particular activity such as a school or hospital. N.Y. Not-for-Profit Corp. L. § 404. In that situation the incorporation takes some time. Delaware, which has no separate nonprofit corporate statute, may be a viable alternative. Incorporation in Delaware can be accomplished virtually overnight, and the organization then may apply for authority to do business in the home jurisdiction as a registered foreign corporation.

2.   Statutes often require specific language, such as "association," "club," "foundation," or words that cannot be used absent approvals from the appropriate bodies. See Cal. Corp. Code § 5122; N.Y. Not-for-Profit Corp. L. § 301.

as not to subject itself to various excise taxes. If the corporation has members, a provision relating thereto may be in the certificate. Several jurisdictions permit limitation of the liability of unpaid directors of the organization if the corporation places this limitation in the certificate.[3] Additionally, there are any number of optional provisions that may be included.

After the articles of incorporation have been drafted, the nonprofit corporation may be required to obtain certain consents for particular types of organizations such as hospitals, educational organizations, or a particular type of nonprofit. After the consents are obtained, and in certain jurisdictions after the attorney general is notified, the certificate is filed with the secretary of state and the organization's corporate existence commences.

A nonprofit corporation also requires a set of bylaws, which are the procedures or internal rules governing the entity. The bylaws generally are a more detailed and flexible document than the articles of incorporation, and they may contain any provision not inconsistent with the corporate law of the jurisdiction. Typically, bylaws contain notice requirements for special and annual meetings, definitions of members if a membership corporation, the date of the annual meeting, quorum requirements for conducting business, member tenure, election procedures, removal and filling vacancies of directors. The bylaws will also specify the number and responsibilities of officers, the fiscal year, committees of the board, indemnification provisions, whether informal actions by the board or members are permitted, and procedures for amendment. See Barbara L. Kirschten, Nonprofit Corporation Forms Handbook (2009). Though most of the clauses in the articles of association and bylaws are standardized "boilerplate" provisions, careful drafting is important, particularly if the organization's charitable purposes come under challenge. See Matter of Troy, 364 Mass. 15, 57, 306 N.E.2d 203, 227 (1973), where the mere fact that a corporation was formed under a nonprofit statute did not by itself establish it was a charitable corporation. A court must consider language of constitution, articles of organization, bylaws, purposes and actual work performed.

After the articles of association have been accepted by the appropriate state official, an organizational meeting is held. The initial board of directors is elected, officers are appointed, the bylaws are approved, authorization to open a bank account is granted, and a federal tax identification number is obtained from the Internal Revenue Service. The corporation then should apply for recognition of exemption from federal income taxation by the IRS. When recognition of exemption and the category of exemption is received by the organization, the exemption letter relates back to the founding date of the organization if the application was filed within 15 months (or, in some cases, 27 months) after the end of the month in which it was formed. See Chapter 5C2, infra, at pp. 317–319. Some

---

3.   See Va. Code Ann. § 13.1–870.1.

jurisdictions also require a separate application in order to obtain state income and property tax exemptions.

3.   CATEGORIES OF NONPROFIT ORGANIZATIONS: PUBLIC BENEFIT AND MUTUAL BENEFIT

In studying the law of nonprofit organizations, a useful distinction can be made between "public benefit" and "mutual benefit" organizations. These categories, though not universally accepted, have been adopted by the California Nonprofit Corporations Code and other jurisdictions and are used by scholars in the field.[1] A public benefit organization can be defined as a group serving what may loosely be called a public or charitable purpose—to do good works, benefit society or improve the human condition. In contrast, a distinctive characteristic of mutual benefit organizations is that they are formed primarily to further the common goals of their members rather than for profit or a public or religious purpose. Many of these groups exist to serve rather narrow interests. The bond may be economic, as with chambers of commerce and labor unions, or social, as with country clubs and fraternal lodges. The public benefit vs. mutual benefit dichotomy will be used frequently in this text to distinguish between these two broad categories of nonprofits.

Public Benefit Corporations. The public benefit category embraces what are known for tax purposes as § 501(c)(3) public charities (including charitable, religious, educational and other organizations that derive their support from the general public) and private foundations, which also derive their exempt status from § 501(c)(3) of the Internal Revenue Code but are subject to special regulatory controls and sanctions. Also included are § 501(c)(4) social welfare organizations which are tax-exempt but, unlike § 501(c)(3) charities, are not eligible to receive tax-deductible charitable contributions or bequests. See Chapter 9B, infra, at pp. 828–834.

One general rule applicable to public benefit corporations is that their members, if any, and other stakeholders, unlike shareholders in business corporations, can have no ownership interest in the corporation. The assets of a public benefit corporation are held for public or charitable purposes and not to benefit members, directors, officers or controlling persons. The assets may not be distributed to members, directors or officers either while the public benefit corporation is operating or upon its dissolution. A membership, unlike a security, cannot be sold or otherwise transferred. A public benefit corporation may not purchase any of its memberships or rights arising from them and even if a member resigns or his or her

---

1. Each of these Codes also includes "religious corporations" as a separate category. The American Bar Association's recently superseded Revised Model Nonprofit Corporation Act adopted the tripartite approach. § 1.40. In general, rules applicable to public benefit corporations also apply to religious corporations, but religious corporations, in recognition of their special constitutional status, are afforded more flexibility and are subject to less governmental oversight. The 2008 Model Nonprofit Corporation Act dropped this distinction.

interest is terminated, a public benefit corporation cannot make a payment to the member for the membership.[2]

Most public benefit corporations have no members and are governed by self-perpetuating boards of directors. A membership organization refers to the legal rights of members to elect directors and to vote on important matters such as mergers, dissolutions or bylaw changes. The legal meaning of membership should be distinguished from its common usage in the nonprofit sector, which typically refers to free admission, discounts on purchases, or receipt of informational newsletters. Generally, public benefit corporations are more strictly regulated by the state than mutual benefit corporations.

Mutual Benefit Corporations. Mutual benefit corporations hold themselves out as benefitting, representing and serving a group of individuals or entities. In theory, the members of these organizations have pooled their resources to do what they might have chosen to do separately without additional tax consequences. As such, they are not appropriate objects of taxation. In practice, of course, mutual benefit organizations may do much more. The conduct of a business with non-members and investment in securities or real estate are familiar examples of extracurricular behavior.

Members may have an economic interest in mutual benefit corporations. They may not receive distributions while a mutual benefit corporation is operating, but their membership interests may be sold or transferred to the corporation or third parties, and they may receive distributions when the corporation dissolves. Members of mutual benefit corporations have broad rights to vote on bylaw amendments to protect their economic and other interests. If they do not approve of the manner in which their corporation is operating, they may elect new directors or take other action to protect their position as members. Because the members form a countervailing force roughly equivalent to shareholders, there is little need to give the attorney general, who has primary state authority over public benefit corporations, broad jurisdiction over the activities of mutual benefit corporations.[3]

Lizabeth A. Moody, Foreword to the Model Nonprofit Corporation Act (Third Edition)

American Bar Association, pp. xix–xxii (2008).

The Third Edition of The Model Nonprofit Corporation Act marks a significant development in the evolution of The Model Nonprofit Corporation Act ("the MNCA"). * * *

The original MNCA was prepared by the Committee on Corporate Laws of the Section of Corporation, Banking, and Business Law (now the

---

2. Michael C. Hone, American Bar Association, Introduction to American Bar Association Revised Model Nonprofit Corporation Act xxv (1988).

3. Id. at xxvii.

Section on Business Law) of the American Bar Association in 1952. Until promulgated with the 1952 Act, most "non business" organizations, if they chose to incorporate, used devices such as "nonstock" provisions found within the state's general corporation law, or, as was the case with most churches, petitioned the state legislature for a charter. Amendments to the original MNCA by the Committee on Corporate Laws took place in 1957 and 1964.

In the Foreword to the 1952 Act, the Committee stated: "It [the Model Nonprofit Corporation Act] is a companion to the Model Business Corporation Act prepared by the Committee. In organization, style and procedures, the Model Nonprofit Corporation Act follows the Model Business Corporation Act as closely as the subject matter permits."

In 1979, the Committee on Nonprofit Corporations (as it was then called) of the [Business Law Section] accepted a charge to revise the MNCA. A drafting committee was appointed and met regularly over the next eight years. The completed revision was approved in 1987 * * * and published as the Revised Model Nonprofit Corporation Act.

The fundamental policy decisions for the Revised MNCA were as follows: The Revised MNCA was to supersede the earlier versions of the MNCA and would be a single integrated statute covering all nonprofit corporations. Further, "[t]he Revised Act was to attempt to provide a framework in which an organization could be structured by its creators to implement their goals and allow them flexibility in operation and design." As with the first act, the Revised Model Act was to follow the Model Business Corporation Act, "as closely as the subject matter permits." * * *

The Revised MNCA adopted a scheme of classifying nonprofit corporations into public benefit corporations, mutual benefit corporations, and religious corporations as a result of legislative developments in two states. New York had adopted a nonprofit corporation statute totally different from the MNCA that divided nonprofit corporations into four distinct classifications: Type A (mutual corporations), Type B (charitable organizations), Type C (business-like organizations), and Type D (miscellaneous). Each classification had differing rules and a different regulatory pattern. In the late 1970s, California, after passing a revolutionary business corporation statute, passed an equally revolutionary nonprofit statute in 1980. The California statute was unrelated to the new California business corporation statute. Somewhat following New York's lead, California adopted a classification system where nonprofit corporations were divided into three parts: Public Benefit, Mutual Benefit, and Religious. The California statute essentially was to become the pattern for the Revised MNCA.

Following the adoption of the Revised MNCA in 1987, there was no further action with respect to the MNCA until 2000. In the meantime, the Model Business Corporation Act (MBCA) was continually reviewed and amended by the [Business Law Section's] Committee on Corporate Laws. Although between 1988 and 2000, many states adopted new nonprofit corporation legislation, relatively few used the Revised MNCA in its entirety. Very few adopted the classification system for nonprofit corporations that had been built into the Revised MNCA. The [Business Law Section's] Committee on Nonprofit Corporations * * * decided to undertake a general revision of the Revised MNCA.

* * *

SIGNIFICANT ASPECTS OF THE THIRD EDITION

Initial decisions made by the drafting committee at the beginning of its deliberations on preparing the Third Edition were to: (1) follow the Model Business Corporation Act provisions to the extent possible, considering certain differences that distinguish nonprofit corporations from for profit corporations; (2) eliminate the classification scheme included in the Revised MNCA; and (3) make the provisions pertaining to the role of the attorney general optional, if desired, with a suggestion to adopting states that provisions regarding the supervision of nonprofit organizations would be better located in a different place in a state's statutory scheme. Other significant changes involve fundamental transactions, the use of alternative governance arrangements, and the elimination of cumulative voting.

1. Classification of Nonprofit Corporations

In the earlier versions of the MNCA, prior to adoption of the Revised MNCA in 1987, all types of nonprofit corporations were defined as "a corporation no part of the income or profit of which is distributable to its member directors or officer," with special provisions where needed. The major differences between the three categories of corporations introduced in the Revised MNCA related to distributions; the repurchase of memberships from members or controlling persons; the standards for conflict of interest transactions; indemnification; and the powers of supervision vested in the attorney general of the state of incorporation. Except in those areas, all nonprofit organizations were treated alike under the statute.

Despite the insistence on the inclusion of the classification system when the Revised MNCA was adopted, the classification system became the most disputed part of the Revised MNCA after its adoption. Many of the states that adopted the Revised MNCA did not incorporate the classification provisions. Often for those that did, problems arose out of incorrect selection. The fact that the classifications did not mirror those of the Internal Revenue Service with respect to tax-exempt organizations turned the choice into a trap for the, unwary.

Although the Third Edition has eliminated the classification system, it still recognizes the special position of certain nonprofit corporations; for example, it includes two important restrictions that apply to charities. One of those restrictions provides that a fundamental transaction property held in trust or otherwise dedicated to a charitable purpose may not be diverted from that purpose without an appropriate order. The other restriction prohibits private inurement in transactions such as mergers.

2. Role of the Attorney General

The decision of the drafting committee to mark as optional the provisions relating to the role of the attorney general was based on the fact that charitable organizations may not necessarily be structured as a corporation, with the result that supervisory provisions for them might be inadvertently omitted from a state's statutory scheme. Charities may be organized as unincorporated nonprofit associations or, under the law of some states, as limited liability companies, and to cover some other forms of entities requires a statute with broader scope. Critics have also characterized powers granted to the attorney generals as ineffective, and perhaps unconstitutional, under the U.S. Constitution, with respect to certain religious organizations.

3.   Fundamental Transactions

Following the pattern of the MBCA, a series of transactions derived from the Model Entity Transactions Act (META) have been included in the Third Edition, including domestications,[1] conversions to another form of entity, and cross-entity mergers.

4.   Alternative Governance Arrangements

The Third Edition contains a series of provisions dealing with the concept of a "designated body." That concept was included in the Revised MNCA, but in a way that was relatively opaque and not well understood. The Third Edition defines a "designated body" as "a person or group, other than a committee of the board of directors, that has been vested by the articles of incorporation or bylaws with powers that, if not vested by the articles or bylaws in that person or group, would be required by this [act] to be exercised by the board or the members." Its effect is to allow "some, but less than all" the powers of the board of directors to be exercised by a designated body, in which case the rules applicable to the board of directors apply to the designated body and the actual directors are relieved from their duties and liabilities to the extent they have been replaced by the designated body.

5.   Elimination of Cumulative Voting[2]

Although the Revised MNCA provided that a corporation could hold elections of directors by cumulative voting if the articles of incorporation so provided, the Third Edition has eliminated cumulative voting (subject to a transitional provision applicable to corporations with cumulative voting at

---

1. "Domestication" is a process that permits a corporation to change its state of incorporation, allowing a nonprofit corporation in a particular jurisdiction to become incorporated in another as a "foreign" nonprofit corporation or vice versa. Eds.

2. Cumulative voting allows members of a nonprofit organization to cast all of their votes for a single nominee for the board of directors when an organization has multiple openings on its board. In contrast, in "regular" or "straight" voting, members may not give more than one vote per share to any single nominee. Cumulative voting increases the ability of a minority group of members to secure representation on the board of directors. For example, if the election is for three directors and a member has three votes, one for each board opening, under the regular or straight voting method the member could vote only one for each

the time the Third Edition is enacted) as inappropriate for nonprofit corporations because the voting power of members should not be tied to their economic investment and because a nonprofit director is often chosen for reasons other than the betterment of the economic results of the corporation.

THE FUTURE OF NONPROFIT CORPORATION LAW

The Third Edition of the MNCA undoubtedly will not be the last word on what has become a dynamic area of law. The [ABA Business Law Section] has committed to a continual review of the MNCA and a procedure to effect amendments appropriate to the time and society.

NOTE: CRITICISM OF THE MODEL NONPROFIT CORPORATION ACT (THIRD EDITION)

If it is embraced by state legislatures, the new Model Act will have enormous influence in the internal structuring and operating procedures of nonprofit corporations, but it has been criticized by several respected nonprofit law scholars and prominent practitioners. Although the drafting committee solicited comments from interested parties, critics expressed concern that there was insufficient time to respond. A major substantive objection was that the close alignment with the Model Business Corporation Act will undermine the legal differences between for-profit and nonprofit corporations. The Model Act also abandons the useful distinction between public benefit and mutual benefit organizations and fails to take into account other recent reform projects of great importance to charities, such as the Uniform Prudent Management of Institutional Funds Act, the Uniform Trust Code, and the American Law Institute's Principles of the Law of Nonprofit Organizations.

Another objection was that the Model Act fails to reflect adequately three overarching federal tax concerns: the requirements of the organizational test under § 501(c)(3) of the Internal Revenue Code, the role of regulators and the courts in protecting charitable assets following fundamental structural change (critics say the Act confuses the role of the attorney general), and the need to coordinate state and federal tax law relating to compliance with the federal tax rules that impose monetary penalties on insiders who engage in "excess benefit" transactions and the organization managers who knowingly approve such transactions.

For a summary of these criticisms, see Evelyn Brody & Marion R. Fremont–Smith, Draft Model Nonprofit Corp. Act Needs Coordination with Tax Code, 119 Tax Notes 617 (May 12, 2008).

PROBLEMS

1. Review the introductory problem in Chapter 1E, supra, at p. 45. Assume that Leona and Tom have decided to form a nonprofit rather than

---

candidate. With cumulative voting, the member could choose to vote all three votes for one candidate, or otherwise divide the votes whichever way the member wanted. Eds.

a for-profit organization. They would like you provide some advice as to the appropriate form for their entity and the formal organizational steps required under your jurisdiction's law. For some appropriate forms to implement your organizational choice, see the Statutes, Regulations and Forms Supplement.

2. In the following problems, consider which form of charitable entity would best assist your client. You also may wish to begin considering issues of federal tax exemption. See I.R.C. § 501(c)(3) and Chapter 5C, infra, at pp. 315–323.

(a) In November, Marissa Scoville was informed by her financial advisor, Petra Lynch, that she faced a substantial income tax liability for that year because of large capital gains from stock sales. Lynch recommended that Ms. Scoville should increase her charitable contributions to reduce her overall tax bill. Ms. Scoville thought that was a splendid idea. She was greatly concerned for the plight of the llama, a four-footed animal from South America known for its warm fur, surefootedness, and ability to spit. Lynch warned her that she needed to make her contribution by the end of the year. Ms. Scoville knew of no charities that focused on llamas, but she wanted to control the charitable efforts in any case.

(b) Anthony Trollope was a Victorian novelist who has a devoted following today. Septimus Harding desires to found the Northern Chemung County Trollope Society, which will be a literary discussion group of Trollope devotees. Four of his friends also are interested in participating. Harding hopes to receive grants from the State Council on the Humanities and from private foundations and individuals.

(c) A group of parents in West Dudleytown, dissatisfied with the quality of day care in their community, decide to establish their own nonprofit child care center. What is the best way to organize a nonprofit day care center under the laws of your jurisdiction?

(d) Mycroft Holmes, a recent alumnus of Sturdley Law School, is distressed with the lack of leisure time activities at the school. He decides to establish the Sturdley Law School Cricket Association and Leisure Time Center. An acquaintance of his, a wealthy English sportsman, Sir Marmaduke Stein, offers to donate $100,000 to the Sturdley Cricket Association and Leisure Time Center. Space would be made available at Sturdley Law School. The Center could be used by alumni and students, but it would be a completely separate entity and not under law school control.

C. PURPOSES AND POWERS OF NONPROFIT CORPORATIONS

1. LAWFUL PURPOSE AND PUBLIC POLICY

At one time most jurisdictions strictly limited the purposes for which a nonprofit organization could incorporate. Nonprofit statutes sometimes would restrict the allowable categories to those found in the text of § 501(c)(3) of the Internal Revenue Code or its predecessor, or create a list of permissible functions based upon the organization's activities or the economic relationship between the organization and its members.[1] In at least twenty-two states,[2] including New York as late as 1993, state officials such as a judge, the attorney general, the secretary of state, and in Mississippi, the governor[3] had substantial discretion to review and reject a nonprofit organization's charter.[4] This authority sometimes was used to deny corporate status as against the public policy of the state, but the real reason often was that the organization offended the sensibilities of those involved.[5] Professor Norman Silber suggests there was a greater scrutiny of nonprofit access to corporate status than for business corporations, because of the consequences to the tax rolls, the strains that nonprofits would put on community resources and generosity, the complementary activities to governmental functions, and the social status of the incorporators, who would reflect beneficially or adversely on the values of the community.[6]

There were few objections to judges or officials determining whether applicants for charitable corporate status would be engaging in appropriate activities or public usefulness. Although courts appeared best adapted to the task of sorting out worthy and unworthy purposes, and useful and worthless causes, by exercising a broad discretion under general grants of authority, jurists determined which organizations would be socially beneficial and rejected others according to their view of community morality.[7] Such an approach meant that organizations that went beyond community norms or represented unpopular or feared causes would not pass the gatekeeper's scrutiny and would be denied incorporation. While judicial discretion may have reflected the will of the majority, it also discriminated against foreigners,[8] cultural diversity,[9] controversial causes,[10] persons of

---

1. Note: Permissible Purposes for Nonprofit Corporations, 51 Colum. L. Rev. 889, 890 (1951).

2. Norman I. Silber, A Corporate Form of Freedom 66–67 n. 2 (2001).

3. Miss. Code Ann. § 5310 (1942), *overturned* in Smith v. Ladner, 288 F.Supp. 66 (S.D.Miss.1968).

4. The rationale for such oversight was that the incorporated status was a privilege initially granted by the legislature by special act rather than a right. Later, incorporation became available for corporations with specified purposes, but the legislature retained some control over chartering nonprofit groups which they vested in a state official or judge. Note: Judicial Approval as a Prerequisite to Incorporation of Non-profit Organizations in New York and Pennsylvania, 55 Colum. L. Rev. 380, 382 (1955).

5. Henry Hansmann, Reforming Nonprofit Corporation Law, 129 U. Pa.L.Rev. 497, 526, n. 70 (1981).

6. Silber, supra note 2, at 24.

7. Id. at 32.

8. In re Agudath Hakehiloth, 18 Misc. 717, 42 N.Y.S. 985 (1896) (immigrant Jewish group denied incorporation by former Confederate general, Justice Roger Pryor, because meetings would occur on Sunday, the Lord's—at least the Christian Lord's—day.)

9. Application of Catalonian Nationalist Club, 112 Misc. 207, 184 N.Y.S. 132 (Sup. Ct. 1920).

10. In re Lithuanian Workers' Literature Soc'y, 196 A.D. 262, 187 N.Y.S. 612 (App. Div. 1921); In re General Von Steuben Bund, 159 Misc. 231, 287 N.Y.S. 527 (Sup. Ct. 1936).

low income and labor unions[11] and persons of color.[12]

By the mid-twentieth century, statutory and judicial developments imposed constraints on judicial and administrative discretion in reviewing applications for nonprofit corporation status. State officials' roles became ministerial. If articles of incorporation were drafted in proper legal form, they were to be accepted. Another approach, increasingly used today, permits incorporation for any "proper" purpose so long as the organization is not operated for personal pecuniary profit and adheres to the nondistribution constraint.[13] It is difficult to discern from reading the statutes just what purposes are improper. Clearly an organization desiring to incorporate for an activity that is illegal is an improper purpose.[14] At the other end of the continuum, organizations adhering to the nondistribution constraint and engaging in traditional charitable activities such as free medical services would be proper purposes. Difficulties arise at the margins: an ostensibly charitable organization's activities are completely commercial, such as a nonprofit hospital that provides absolutely no charitable care and differs in no substantial way from a for-profit hospital or a nonprofit gas station where the manager is paid a salary but all profits are donated to a Little League.[15]

There still remained a reluctance to approve the articles of incorporation of controversial organizations. In 1975, the Ohio Supreme Court upheld the Secretary of State's refusal to accept the articles of incorporation of the Greater Cincinnati Gay Society because "homosexuality as a valid life style" was contrary to the public policy of the state, even though Ohio had decriminalized all private activity between consenting adults. State ex rel. Grant v. Brown, 39 Ohio St.2d 112, 313 N.E.2d 847, appeal dismissed and cert. denied sub nom. Duggan v. Brown, 420 U.S. 916, 95 S.Ct. 1110 (1975).

---

11. In re Rox Athletic Ass'n, 318 Pa. 258, 178 A. 464, 465 (1935); People ex rel. Padila v. Hughes, 296 Ill.App. 587, 16 N.E.2d 922 (1938).

12. Benevolent & Protective Order of Elks v. Improved Benevolent & Protective Order of Elks of the World, 205 N.Y. 459, 98 N.E. 756 (1912) (African American order's use of name so similar to white order as to provide confusion); NAACP v. Patterson, 353 U.S. 972, 77 S.Ct. 1056 (1957) (Texas attorney general permanently enjoins activities of NAACP instate; Louisiana banned local unincorporated chapters of NAACP; Alabama attorney general sued in equity to prevent NAACP and related affiliates from operating in state).

13. Cf. Cal. Corp. Code § 5111; N.Y. Not-for-Profit Corp. L. § 102(a)(5); see generally Henry Hansmann, Reforming Nonprofit Corporation Law, supra note 5, at 509–538.

14. State ex rel. Church v. Brown, 165 Ohio St. 31, 133 N.E.2d 333 (1956) (secretary of state's refusal to accept articles of incorporation held to be proper where formation of nonprofit corporation to provide facilities to practice coed nudism violated statute prohibiting anyone 18 years or over from wilfully exposing his private parts in presence of two or more persons of the opposite sex).

15. Cf. Hansmann, supra note 5, at 515–519 (nonprofit shoe store).

NOTES

1. *Lawful Purposes and the Power of Governmental and Judicial Officials to Refuse to Accept Certificates of Incorporation.* The statutes and decisions have moved away from administrative discretion to grant or deny corporate charters absent a failure to follow mandatory incorporation requirements. State ex rel. Grant v. Brown would not be followed in most jurisdictions today. In Owles v. Lomenzo, 38 A.D.2d 981, 329 N.Y.S.2d 181 (3d Dept.1972), aff'd sub nom. Gay Activists Alliance v. Lomenzo, 31 N.Y.2d 965, 293 N.E.2d 255, 341 N.Y.S.2d 108 (1973), the New York Secretary of State rejected the incorporation of the Gay Activists Alliance on the grounds that the name was inappropriate and the proposed corporate purposes raised serious questions as to whether the organization would promote activities contrary to public policy and to the penal law. The Supreme Court dismissed the incorporators' appeal, but that decision was reversed by the appellate tribunals. Since the formal requirements of the statute were complied with and the corporate purposes (which included promotion of an understanding and tolerance, instillation of self respect and safeguarding and fostering of equal rights for homosexuals) offended no law, the Secretary of State lacked the authority to label those purposes violative of "public policy." 31 N.Y.2d at 966.

2. *Public Policy.* Permissible "public policy" differs from lawful charitable purpose. A trust or charitable organization cannot be created for a purpose that is illegal. A purpose is illegal if the trust or charity's object is in violation of the criminal law, tends to induce the commission of a crime, or if the accomplishment of the purpose violates public policy. See 6 Scott & Ascher on Trusts, supra, § 38.11. "Public policy" is not a lodestar but evolves over time, place, and circumstances as society's standards change. Restatement (Third) of Trusts § 28 com. a. In Association for the Preservation of Freedom of Choice v. Shapiro, 9 N.Y.2d 376, 174 N.E.2d 487, 214 N.Y.S.2d 388 (1961), petitioners sought to incorporate an organization whose purposes were to further segregation and to "encourage, promote, and aid in scientific research into problems engendered by a multicultural society, into problems of intergroup relations, in areas of ethnic characteristics and patterns, and into the implications and effects of such problems on freedom of choice and association, and to publish and to encourage, promote, aid and assist in publication of the results of such research in suitable scholarly periodicals and other publications * * *." The lower courts denied the application because the objects and purposes of the proposed corporation were not in accord with public policy and were injurious to the community. The New York Court of Appeals reversed, since the public policy of the state was not violated by purposes which were not unlawful. The Court limited the discretion of the exercise of judicial power to ascertain whether the proposed corporation was for lawful purposes, a function which could not be handily carried out by the legislature or readily left to ministerial officers such as the secretary of state, "hence it was committed to the judiciary, but only that and nothing more so far as the language of the statute is concerned." Two judges dissented. Questions of

lawful purpose and public policy also have arisen in connection with the qualification for recognition of federal tax-exempt status of racially discriminatory schools under § 501(c)(3) of the Internal Revenue Code. See Bob Jones University v. United States, Chapter 5C4, infra, at pp. 370–389.

2. COMMERCIAL PURPOSES

Model Nonprofit Corp. Act (3d ed.) § 3.02.

N.Y. Not-for-Profit Corp. L. § 204.

Nonprofit organizations may conduct activities or businesses for pecuniary gain so long as the profit is used for the organization's exempt purposes and there is no distribution of profits to members, nor exploitation of the organization for direct monetary gain. While profits may not directly inure to members, as the next case demonstrates, members may receive intangible benefits incidental to the exempt activities of the organization.

People ex rel. Groman v. Sinai Temple

California Court of Appeal, 1971.
20 Cal.App.3d 614, 99 Cal.Rptr. 603.

■ FILES, PRESIDING JUSTICE.

[The Sinai Temple was incorporated in 1908 as a religious corporation and not for the object of any pecuniary profit. In 1963 it purchased the Forest Lawn Cemetery Association, which included 82 acres of cemetery property and undeveloped land in the Hollywood hills near Los Angeles. The investment proved very profitable. After certain private parties complained, the attorney general brought a quo warranto suit, contending that a nonprofit corporation may not engage in a commercial, competitive, profit-making business as one of its primary intended activities; that Sinai Temple was operating its cemetery as a profit-making business, competing in the market with other cemeteries and making a profit which was being used to pay off the purchase price of its cemetery property; and that the members of the congregation benefited, because they received a discount on the price of cemetery land, which was not given to nonmember customers, and this constituted a distribution to members. Eds.]

Plaintiff's main contention is simply that a corporation organized in nonprofit form may not engage in commercial, competitive, profit-making business as one of its main intended activities. We are of the opinion that the activities of defendant, as set forth in the complaint, are not in excess of the powers authorized by Corporations Code section 9200, and that the history of the nonprofit corporation statutes confirms this interpretation of the present statute. [The court then quoted the applicable statute. Eds.]

The defendant's purposes—religious and cemetery—are expressly recognized in the statute as lawful purposes. The statute does not expressly prohibit the earning or accumulation of profits by the corporation. Instead, the statute requires that the purposes "do not contemplate the distribution of gains, profits, or dividends to the members." The use of the word "distribution" indicates that the accrual of gains is not thereby prohibited.

* * *

Other Contentions of Plaintiff

Plaintiff argues that the last sentence of Corporations Code section 9200 implies that the corporations therein referred to may not seek profits from their main-purpose activities. That sentence reads: "Carrying on business at a profit as an incident to the main purposes of the corporation and the distribution of assets to members on dissolution are not forbidden to nonprofit corporations, but no corporation formed or existing under this part shall distribute any gains, profits, or dividends to any of its members as such except upon dissolution or winding up."

The argument is that this sentence, explicitly authorizing "business at a profit as an incident," would be meaningless unless business at a profit for the main purpose was forbidden. We do not believe that language was intended to carry that implication. The sentence gives recognition that corporations formed under section 9200 which do not ordinarily make profits (e.g., religious, social, charitable or educational corporations) may lawfully carry on incidental businesses which do.[3] * * *

* * *

In interpreting the statute it is necessary to distinguish between the inurement of benefits and the distribution of profits.

Many corporations organized under section 9200, and particularly religious corporations, benefit their members, even though the corporations are strictly nonprofit in nature. It is common knowledge that such corporations often receive endowments, bequests and substantial gifts from members and interested nonmembers which make it possible for the organization to provide benefits costing more than the recipients pay by way of dues or contributions. We do not understand plaintiff to argue that a corporation organized under section 9200 may not lawfully benefit its members except upon a strict quid pro quo basis. The furnishing of benefits to members, without charge or without receiving full cash value in return, is not per se the payment of a dividend, gain or profit by a corporation organized under section 9200.

* * *

---

3. For some examples of incidental profit-making businesses conducted by nonprofit charitable corporations, see Cedars of Lebanon Hosp. v. County of L.A., 35 Cal.2d 729, 745, 221 P.2d 31 (1950) (thrift shop in a hospital), and Y.M.C.A. v. County of L.A. 35 Cal.2d 760, 772, 221 P.2d 47 (1950) (restaurant, barbershop, valet shop and gym store in Y.M.C.A.). Those cases deal with whether the buildings so used were exempt from property taxation, but the power of the nonprofit corporations to carry on these activities was not questioned.

Here the profits accrue from the pursuit of defendant's cemetery purpose, which purpose is expressly authorized by the governing statute and by defendant's articles of incorporation.

The judgment is affirmed.

■ JEFFERSON AND DUNN, JJ., concur.

■ Hearing denied; WRIGHT, C.J., and MOSK, J., dissenting.

NOTE: COMMERCIAL PURPOSES AND PROPERTY TAX EXEMPTIONS

At one time, many states saw an impenetrable barrier between business and charitable activities. For example, New York's Membership Corporations Law, the predecessor to its Not-for-Profit Corporation Law, did not permit organizations involved in business-type activities to incorporate as a charity. As the business/charity boundary became more ambiguous with the emergence of nonprofit enterprise in new areas such as housing and economic development, the law responded. New York created a special category of nonprofit corporation that engaged in business or quasi-business activities.[1] Other states reached an expansive view of nonprofit activity through judicial decision, but later in reaction to pressures on their tax base retreated from this position and challenged nonprofits' qualifications for state property tax exemptions.

States are conflicted over nonprofits' commercial activities that may attract business, create jobs and lessen the need for public support, but reduce needed tax revenue. Minnesota demonstrates this ambivalence. The University of Minnesota and several for-profit corporations formed the North Star Development Corporation to engage in applied research for the benefit of the Twin Cities area and to attract smaller companies. This would stimulate the local economy and provide access to a research center for companies too small to support one on their own. The University was concerned about the amount of applied research, as distinguished from basic research conducted by faculty and students and believed that North Star would relax pressure on it by fulfilling the needs of local industry for applied research. North Star engaged in a broad variety of research projects for government clients and private industry.

The issue arose whether North Star was a business conducted for profit or a purely public charity. If the latter, its property would be exempt from property taxation. Initially, the Supreme Court of Minnesota, with two judges dissenting, held North Star's for-profit incorporators had conducted only a minor amount of business with it, and control of the corporation rested with the University of Minnesota's board of regents, so it was eligible for property tax exemption. The majority reserved judgment whether North Star was a purely public charity. State v. North Star Research and Development Institute, 294 Minn. 56, 200 N.W.2d 410 (1972).

---

1. N.Y. Not-for-Profit Corp. L. § 201 * * * "Type C—A not-for-profit corporation of this type may be formed for any lawful business purpose to achieve a lawful public or quasi-public objective."

The Court revisited its decision three years later in North Star Research Institute v. Hennepin County, 306 Minn. 1, 236 N.W.2d 754 (Minn. 1975) and narrowed the original holding. The Court defined the issue: is a nonprofit corporation engaged in applied research which to a significant degree makes its services available to private enterprises, who pay for the research defined and requested by them on a cost-plus basis and acquire ownership of the information developed as a result of the undertaking, entitled to tax-exempt status? Minnesota decisions used a six-pronged test, though each prong was not mandatory, to determine whether organizations in Minnesota were eligible for state tax exemption.[2] The Court concluded that North Star was not entitled to tax exemption as a "purely public charity" within meaning of the state constitution and statutes, despite fact that substantial part of research was done for governmental agencies, federal and state.

Then, in Under the Rainbow Child Care Center, Inc. v. County of Goodhue, 741 N.W.2d 880 (Minn. 2007), the Minnesota Supreme Court further narrowed the availability of property tax exemptions for charities. The case involved a licensed day care center that lost money every year. Rainbow charged market rates to all who sent their children to the day care facility. Its weekly rates were higher than both of the other child care centers in Red Wing, Minnesota for infants, toddlers, and preschool children, who constituted 55 of Rainbow's 70–child licensed capacity. The court held that: (1) a day care organization that does not provide goods or services free or at considerably reduced rates as a substantial part of its operations is not exempt from payment of real property taxes as an institution of purely public charity; (2) the child care center did not satisfy the exemption; and (3) payments made by a governmental entity for goods or services provided to one of its citizens are not considered "donations" for purposes of determining whether the entity providing the goods or services is an institution of purely public charity. In mentioning the six-part test, the court stated that these are not necessarily the only relevant factors, but in all cases one factor must be present—the recipients of the "charity" must receive the services on a subsidized basis. Rainbow did not provide scholarships to needy families, and its argument that some families received a 20 percent discount through government funding was insufficient. Rainbow could not count the government's "charity" as its own.

Reaction to the Rainbow Child Care Center decision was swift. In May 2009, legislation was enacted to clarify the "purely public charity" defini-

---

2. The test was: (1) whether the stated purpose of the undertaking is to be helpful to others without immediate expectation of material reward; (2) whether the entity involved is supported by donations and gifts in whole or in part; (3) whether the recipients of the "charity" are required to pay for the assistance received in whole or in part; (4) whether the income received from gifts and donations and charges to users produces a profit to the charitable institution; (5) whether the beneficiaries of the 'charity' are restricted or unrestricted and, if restricted, whether the class of persons to whom the charity is made available is one having a reasonable relationship to the charitable objectives; and (6) whether dividends, in form or substance, or assets upon dissolution are available to private interests. North Star Research Institute, 236 N.W.2d at 757.

tion by setting forth specific legal criteria derived from the Minnesota Supreme Court's *North Star* decision. In addition to one of the requirements that a material number of the charity's recipients received benefits or services at reduced cost, tax assessors should consider whether the organization provided services to the public that alleviated burdens or responsibilities that would otherwise be borne by the government. Thus, Rainbow and similarly situated charities could qualify as purely public charities even if they charged for services. Minn. Stat. § 272.02(7)(a) (2009). Similar issues are played out in almost every jurisdiction.

NOTES AND QUESTIONS

1. *Scope of Nonprofit Commercial Activities.* Many nonprofits engaged in commercial-type activities can and do earn a profit. According to the most recently available data, in 2005 public benefit organizations had a total estimated revenue of $1.1 trillion (and expenses about the same) of which 70.4 percent, or $774 billion, came from fees for services from government and private sources. Kenneth T. Wing, Thomas H. Pollak & Amy Blackwood, Nonprofit Almanac 2008, Summary, available at http://www.urban.org/books/nonprofit_almanac/. Because of the nondistribution constraint, however, a nonprofit may not declare dividends or pay excessive salaries. If an organization competes in an industry where there are for-profit or government-run counterparts, does that confer an unfair competitive advantage to the nonprofit firms? What would be the probable response of economists who adhere to the market or contract failure theory to this situation? See Chapter 6C2, infra, at pp. 596–603, for a discussion of these questions from the perspective of federal tax policy.

2. *State Tax Concerns: In General.* The issues of commercial activity of nonprofits raised in *Groman* have been of concern to financially pressed states seeking additional sources of tax revenue. State exemptions from income taxation are similar to federal exemption under § 501(c)(3) of the Internal Revenue Code. Some states automatically grant exempt status to organizations that obtain a federal § 501(c)(3) exemption. Others reach the same result by statute. Additionally, in varying degrees all states grant tax exemptions for property owned by nonprofit organizations and used in their charitable and other exempt activities. See E.C. Lashbrooke, Tax–Exempt Organizations 86–119 (1985); Property Tax Exemption for Charities: Mapping the Battlefield (Evelyn Brody ed., 2002), and Chapter 5C8, infra, at pp. 440–445.

3. *State Property Tax Exemptions.* The terms "charitable" and "educational" have been construed much more narrowly when nonprofit organizations, even those with recognition of federal § 501(c)(3) status, have applied for a property tax exemption under state law. Courts have required organizations to do more than serve the public interest or be educational in nature to qualify for exemption. For example, in Michigan United Conservation Clubs v. Township of Lansing, 423 Mich. 661, 378 N.W.2d 737 (1985), the court affirmed denial of an educational exemption for a conservation organization that *inter alia* promoted conservation education, because the organization neither fit into the general scheme of education

provided by the state, nor substantially contributed to relief of the burden of government. The organization was not "charitable" because, taken as a whole, its activities were not for the benefit of the general public without restriction nor did they benefit an indefinite number of persons, and its property generally was unavailable to non-members.

In determining whether a party qualifies for exemption from the property tax, the property at issue must be owned and used by the claimant who is exempt, and the property must be used solely for the exempt purposes for which the claimant was organized. Fraternities at the University of South Dakota which were state and federally reorganized tax-exempt nonprofit corporations were denied state property tax exemption on the ground that the property was not used exclusively for benevolent and charitable purposes. Alpha Gamma Zeta House Ass'n v. Clay County Board of Equalization, 583 N.W.2d 167 (S.D.1998).

4. *Nonprofit Hospitals.* Nowhere has the dispute over state tax exemptions been more rancorous than with nonprofit hospitals. Historically, hospitals were considered charitable institutions. Although they accepted money from paying patients, they also treated the poor free of charge. See Chapter 5C3b, infra, at pp. 323–329. With the advent of third party payment through medicare and medicaid and the transformation of American medicine, the charitable role of hospitals has diminished. State tax collectors and some commentators have argued that hospitals that do not provide a substantial level of service to the poor are no different than their for-profit counterparts and should lose their exemption.

Many of these issues came to a head in Utah County v. Intermountain Health Care, 709 P.2d 265 (Utah 1985), where a divided Utah Supreme Court affirmed a county board of equalization's denial of exempt status from the property tax exemption for two nonprofit hospitals because they had not sufficiently demonstrated that they met the court's criteria for being a charity. Id. at 269–270. Thereafter tax authorities in several other states revoked the exempt status of nonprofit hospitals but often were reversed by state courts. The hostilities continue. For additional discussion of state property tax exemptions for hospitals, see Chapter 5C3b, infra, at pp. 337–339.

PROBLEM

Edward Jackson, a mechanic, wishes to open a nonprofit gas station. He will charge less than competitors, pay himself a salary commensurate with that of other mechanics, and will use all profits to build and maintain fields for the local Little League baseball program. Could he incorporate the gas station as a nonprofit organization?

3.   Charitable Purposes

Restatement (Third) Trusts § 28.

From time immemorial societies have granted certain activities exemption from taxation. For just as long, tensions have existed over the scope of this privilege. The view that charitable status is a special entitlement requiring justification in social terms has historic antecedents in English and American law. Chauncey Belknap, The Federal Income Tax Exemption of Charitable Organizations: Its History and Underlying Policy, IV Research Papers Sponsored by the [Filer] Commission on Private Philanthropy and Public Needs 2027 (1977). In a political context English restrictions on what was "charitable" evolved from a desire to restrict gifts to churches. Charitable organizations and trusts use social resources in the form of foregone tax revenues. Despite any value to individual beneficiaries or evidence of a settlor's moral qualities, they must justify themselves on some level that society is benefiting from the philanthropic entity's operation and that the activity fulfills some legal or intrinsic notion of charity. Miriam Galston, Public Policy Constraints on Charitable Organizations, 3 Va. Tax Rev. 291, 303 (1984).

The ordinary meaning of the term "charitable" is relief of the poor. However, the legal definition, far broader and distinct from the usual usage of the word, means a function to promote the general welfare that is not violative of public policy. See generally Bruce R. Hopkins, The Law of Tax Exempt Organizations §§ 6.1–6.3 (9th ed. 2007). Thus, purposes other than relief of poverty are recognized as charitable. The courts have used several approaches as they have wrestled with the definition of charity. Certain religious institutions have always been exempt from taxation ("Also we certify you, that touching any of the priests and Levites, singers, porters, Nethinim, or Ministers of this House of God, it shall not be lawful to impose toll, tribute, or customs upon them."—Ezra 7:24). One way to distinguish charitable from noncharitable activity has been to utilize a taxonomic approach, creating categories of activities that are presumably charitable, derived from the statutes and cases. The Restatement (Third) of Trusts § 28 lists six such categories: relief of poverty, advancement of education; advancement of religion; promotion of health; governmental or municipal purposes; and other purposes beneficial to the community. These categories, however, are not exclusive. Additional purposes which are of benefit to the community have also been considered charitable. The excerpt below traces the development of the legal definition of charity in England which has had enormous influence in the United States. For the application of these principles under the federal tax laws, see Chapter 5C3, infra, at pp. 319–323.

Preamble to the Statute of Charitable Uses
43 Eliz., ch. 4 (1601).

> Whereas lands, tenements, rents, annuities, profits, hereditaments, goods, chattels, money and stocks of money have been heretofore given, limited, appointed, and assigned as well by the Queen's most excellent Majesty, and her most noble progenitors, as by sundry other well-disposed persons; some for relief of aged, impotent and poor people, some for maintenance of sick and maimed soldiers and mariners, schools of learning, free schools and scholars in universities, some for

repair of bridges, ports, havens, causeways, churches, sea-banks, and highways, some for education and preferment of orphans, some for or towards relief, stock or maintenance for houses of correction, some for marriages of poor maids, some for supportation, aid and help of young tradesmen, handicraftsmen, and persons decayed; and others for relief or redemption of prisoners or captives, and for aid or ease of any poor inhabitants concerning payments of fifteens, setting out of soldiers and other taxes; * * *

NOTE: THE STATUTE OF CHARITABLE USES AND THE MEANING OF CHARITY

Although gifts had been made for so called "pious causes" for centuries before, the modern law of charity commenced in 1601 when Parliament enacted the Statute of Charitable Uses, 43 Eliz. ch. 4, officially titled "An Act to Redress Misemployment of Lands, Goods and Stocks of Money Heretofore Given to Charitable Uses." The Statute had two main objectives: the first was to reform the administration of charity by establishing commissions in each English county to inquire into the misapplication of trusts established for charitable purposes. The second, and historically most important, was fulfilled in the statute's preamble: the specification of those purposes which were considered charitable and therefore within the jurisdiction of the commissions. The categories of charitable uses were never regarded as exclusive but as typical of the kinds of philanthropic activities which the state wished to encourage. Public benefit was the key to the statute, and the relief of poverty its principal manifestation. Gareth Jones, History of the Law of Charity 1532–1827 26–27 (1969). Other uses, principally religious, fell outside the preamble but also were considered charitable. Id. at 56–57.

Over the intervening centuries a number of broad categories of activities have been recognized as charitable, including the relief of poverty, the advancement of education, religion and science, the promotion of health, and lessening the burdens of government. The common law origins of charity have had a lasting influence on the evolution of "charitable" activities under corporate and tax codes. As these materials will demonstrate, charity is an evolving concept constantly changing to meet the needs of society. This flexibility has been recognized by the courts and the Internal Revenue Service. See Chapter 5C3a, infra, at pp. 319–323.

John P. Persons, John J. Osborne, Jr., & Charles F. Feldman, Criteria for Exemption Under Section 501(c)(3)—The Development of the Legal Definition of Charity in England

IV Research Papers Sponsored by the [Filer] Commission on Private Philanthropy and Public Needs 1909, 1912–1916 (1977).

The English Statute of Charitable Uses, enacted in 1601 near the end of the reign of Elizabeth I, contained the first comprehensive definition of charitable purposes. The Statute is generally regarded as the starting-point of the modern law of charity. However, for many centuries prior to 1601 Englishmen had been making gifts and bequests for so-called "pious causes." During the Middle Ages the Roman Catholic Church, through its ecclesiastical courts, had exclusive jurisdiction over all testamentary dispositions and expected its members to leave a portion of their wealth to the church in order to insure their salvation. Scholars who have studied the wills of this period report a heavy emphasis upon this theme of "salvation at a price." The pious causes that were customarily selected included the saying of masses and prayers for the dead, the maintenance of lamps and tapers before alters, the establishment of chantries, the provision of alms for the poor, and the building and endowment of churches—generally "anything of a holy nature to keep away the devils which were supposed to surround the dying and the dead."

[As the Middle Ages came to a close, the pious bequests included in wills became more secular. Around 1362 appeared William Langland's *The Vision of Piers the Plowman,* which in one part advised the wealthy to save their souls by using their fortunes for a number of enumerated charitable purposes. The poem was enormously influential on social thinking of the period that followed it, and when the Statute of Charitable Uses was enacted more than 200 years later, it was natural for the draftsmen to formulate the statutory definition of charity in terms strikingly similar to those found in Langland's poem. Eds.]

While this preamble is commonly referred to as a definition, it is in reality an enumeration of purposes which were at the time regarded as charitable. This enumeration was not intended to be all inclusive. The preamble "did not attempt to mark out the limits of legal charity or condemn as non-charitable those uses with were outside its letter and equity." One area that was given only token attention in the preamble was religion. The omission of all religious purposes (except the repair of churches) was intentional. England had only recently completed its Reformation, and as a consequence the crown had dissolved the monasteries, taken over the religious foundations, and confiscated the assets of numerous trusts which had theretofore been established for religious purposes "might infect by association other charitable uses, whose endowments the Crown could then appropriate." * * *

A history of the period states that "[p]ublic benefit was the key to the statute, and the relief of poverty its principal manifestation." The 1601 Statute was enacted as a supplement to the comprehensive system of poor laws adopted by Parliament in 1597 and restated in 1601. Professor W.K. Jordan states that this system "was essentially prudential, having been drafted and passed by a government which liked to be fore-armed against all emergencies and which had been seriously frightened by the distress and the attendant disorders just prior to the convention of Parliament in 1597." * * *

For over a century after the enactment of the 1601 Statute of Charitable Uses, the task of defining charity did not present a difficult problem for the English judiciary. The character of philanthropy did not depart significantly from the categories of charitable activity comprehensively listed in the preamble, which was liberally construed in accordance with its basic intent.

However, by 1736 a reaction had set in against the steady increase in charitable land holdings. Parliament passed in that year a Mortmain Act which voided devises of land to charity and vested the property so devised in the testator's heirs or next-of-kin. The motivation behind the Act was anti-clerical, but the impact of the statute was not restricted to ecclesiastical charities. * * *

Under the 1736 Act, by classifying a devise of land as charitable, the judges could insure that the land would not pass to charity but to the testator's heirs, thus effectuating the intent of the Act. On the other hand, because the 1736 Act applied only to devises of land and not to bequests of personalty, in cases of the latter type the courts could protect the testator's heirs only by holding that the bequest was not charitable. The conflicting decisions that resulted from this situation introduced uncertainty and confusion into the English law of charity, which had not previously been seriously troubled by the problem of definition.

In 1805 more confusion was generated by the decision in *Morice v. Bishop of Durham*. There, the Chancellor, Lord Eldon, held that only purposes set forth in the 1601 Statute of Charitable Uses, or purposes analogous thereto, were charitable in the eyes of the law. This was a retreat from the earlier view that the 1601 Statute was not an exclusive touchstone of legal charity but merely an enumeration of the types of activities that were at that time considered charitable. The effect of Lord Eldon's decision was to make "charity" a word of art whose meaning could be discovered only by reference, or analogy, to the "chart" set forth in the 1601 Statute. However, the decision failed to give succeeding English judges a clear policy as to how they were to use this chart in the resolution of new cases.

An effort at achieving an orderly synthesis of the decisions was made in 1891 by Lord Macnaghten in the following famous passage from *Commissioners of Income Tax v. Pemsel*:[22]

"Charity" in its legal sense comprises four principal divisions: trusts for the relief of poverty; trusts for the advancement of education; trusts for the advancement of religion; and trusts for other purposes beneficial to the community, not falling under any of the preceding heads. * * * The Trusts last referred to are not the less charitable in the eye of the law, because incidentally they benefit the rich as well as the poor, as indeed, every charity that deserves the name must do either directly or indirectly.

Although this passage is more of a classification than a definition, it does contain the unifying concept of "other purposes beneficial to the community." However, this did not succeed in resolving the problems of

---

22.   22 Q.B.D. 296 (1891); A.C. 531 (1891).

the judiciary, as indicated by the following statement by Lord Sterndale 30 years later:

I * * * am unable to find any principle which will guide one easily, and safely, through the tangle of cases as to what is and what is not a charitable gift. If it is possible I hope sincerely that at some future time or other a principle will be laid down. The whole subject is in an artificial atmosphere altogether. A large number of gifts are held charitable which would not be called charitable in the ordinary acceptance of the term, and when one takes gifts which have been held to be charitable, and compares them with gifts which have been held not to be charitable, it is very difficult to see what the principle is on which the distinction rests.

[With the Charities Act of 2006, England finally freed itself from the parameters of the Statute of Charitable Uses and the *Pemsel* case by expanding the definition of charity, moving beyond common law precedents, and bringing the definition into the twenty-first century. The Charities Act presents an expanded list of thirteen charitable purposes, ending with a catchall clause that would includes charitable activities that serve a public benefit. Charities Act, ch. 50, §§ 1–2. A charity must serve a public benefit. The contours of that phase are determined by guidance published by the Charity Commission. Eds.]

Jackson v. Phillips

Supreme Court of Massachusetts, 1867.
96 Mass. (14 Allen) 539, 556.

■ GRAY, J.

A charity in a legal sense, may be more fully defined as a gift, to be applied consistently with existing laws, for the benefit of an indefinite number of persons, either by bringing their hearts under the influence of education or religion, by relieving their bodies from disease, suffering or constraint, by assisting them to establish themselves in life, or by erecting or maintaining public buildings or works or otherwise lessening the burdens of government. It is immaterial whether the purpose is called charitable in the gift itself, if it is so described to show that it is charitable in its nature.

NOTES

1. *State Definitions of Charity.* Statutes in a number of states either define the term "charity" or list a number of purposes deemed to be charitable. See Code Ga. Ann. §§ 53–12–110; Okla. Stat. Ann. tit. 60 § 601, George Gleason Bogert & George Taylor Bogert, The Law of Trusts and Trustees § 361 at 4–5 (rev. 2d ed. 1991 & 2009 Supp.). Some state statutes define "charitable" more broadly than § 501(c)(3) of the Internal Revenue Code. See, e.g., Fla. Stat. ch. 496.404 (1991) (" 'Charitable organization' means any person who is or holds himself out to be established for any

benevolent, educational, philanthropic, humane, scientific, artistic, patriotic, social welfare or advocacy, public health, environmental conservation, civic, or other eleemosynary purpose"). See Marion R. Fremont–Smith, Governing Nonprofit Organizations 4849, 117–133 (2004); Developments in the Law–Nonprofit Corporations, 105 Harv. L. Rev. 1578, 1634 n.1 (1992).

Most state cases arise over the issue of exemption from property taxes. Courts are called upon to construe the meaning of a particular charitable purpose to determine whether it refers to the activities of the organization seeking exemption. Courts have generally been expansive in their definitions, moving beyond the view of Justice Gray in Jackson v. Phillips. For example, in United Church of Christ v. Town of West Hartford, 206 Conn. 711, 539 A.2d 573, 578 (1988), a property tax exemption case, the court "recognized that the 'definition of charitable uses and purposes has expanded with the advancement of civilization and the daily increasing needs of man' * * * It no longer is restricted to mere relief of the destitute or the giving of alms but comprehends activities, not in themselves self-supporting, which are intended to improve the physical, mental and moral condition of the recipients and make it more likely that they will become useful citizens." See generally Bogert & Bogert, supra § 361 at 5–11. However, a trial court in Pennsylvania took a more restrictive view, denying a property tax exemption to a private college on the ground that it was not an "institution of purely public charity" within the meaning of the Pennsylvania Constitution, but this position was reversed on appeal. See City of Washington v. Board of Assessment, 550 Pa. 175, 704 A.2d 120 (1997). See Chapter 5C8, infra, at pp. 442–444.

2. *"Charitable" in the Internal Revenue Code.* Congress has never defined the term "charitable". Section 501(c)(3) of the Code lists eight purposes enabling an organization to qualify for what is commonly known as a "charitable" exemption. Treas. Reg. § 1.501(c)(3)–1(d)(2) refers to the term's "generally accepted legal sense" and is "within the broad outlines of 'charity' as developed by judicial decisions." The language of the regulations closely reflects the Statute of Charitable Uses. See Chapter 5C3a, infra, at pp. 319–323.

3. *The Scope of Charity.* Sometimes an activity is conclusively charitable; at other times it is merely a rebuttable presumption. Miriam Galston, Public Policy Restraints on Charitable Organizations, 3 Va. Tax Rev. 291, 305 (1984). Thus, a charitable trust or corporation whose purpose is to provide scholarships for needy children to attend the School of the American Ballet Theater obviously would be charitable, but a trust for a dancing school for springer spaniels would not. Cf. In re Hummeltenberg, 1 Ch. 237, 242 (1923). A fund to establish a museum to house the work of the celebrated American artist Jasper Johns would clearly be in furtherance of charitable purposes, and just as certainly a trust or foundation to establish a museum to exhibit the meritless doodles of the casebook editors would not. Cf. Medical Soc'y of South Carolina v. South Carolina Bank of Charleston, 197 S.C. 96, 14 S.E.2d 577 (1941). Between these extremes, how should courts draw lines?

In the principal case below and those discussed in the Note that follows, is there any consistent thread in the court's definition of charity? Is there a fixed standard to define what is charitable or must it be defined on a case by case basis? Does the concept of "charitable" necessarily remain subjective? Is it dependent upon time and circumstance?

De Costa v. De Paz

Chancery, 1754.
2 Swans 487.

The questions in this case arose upon the will of one Elias de Paz, who thereby directed his executors to invest a sum of £1200 in some government or other security; and directed that the revenue arising therefrom should be applied for ever in the maintenance of a *Jesiba*, or assembly for daily reading the Jewish law, and for advancing and propagating their holy religion; and directed that his executors, during their respective lives, should have the management of the assembly, and appointed A. B. and C. his residuary legatees; and the bill was to have this £1200 laid out according to the will.

The Lord Chancellor upon the opening asked, if there had ever been a case where such a charity as this had been established, for it being against the Christian religion, which is part of the law of the land, he thought he could not decree it.

Mr. Clark said, that no cases could be found antecedent to the act of toleration (1 W. & M. c. 18), where a bequest of this kind had been established; yet since that act, by which sects differing from the established religion are by law tolerated, there may be some instances; but the present case is of a sect that can only be said to be connived at; that it may therefore become material to consider whether this bequest will not come within the statute of Edward the 6th, of superstitious uses (1 Ed. 6, c. 14), and whether there are not some vesting clauses in the statutes concerning superstitious uses, that may give this legacy to the crown.

Ryder, Attorney General. The Act of Toleration gave no new right to sectaries, but only took away the effect of the penal laws, and gave people liberty of worshipping God their own way. Before the Revolution there were cases that have not been received since, particularly Baxter's case. (1 Vern. 248, revised after the Revolution, 2 Vern. 105.) (See 7 Ves. 76). How is the present case? It is only for propagating and reading that law which is allowed in our church, and which is the foundation of the Christian religion. By the toleration a liberty was at last given to these people. By the statute of Edward the 6th, superstitious devises of lands and personal estate are not made void, but come to the crown, and this court has considered the statute as making a gift to the crown; and therefore that might be the foundation of the first determination in *Baxter's* case: there could be no other ground for it.

Mr. Noel, for the residuary devisees, insists that this bequest is absolutely void; as being in opposition to the Christian religion, and for establishing the Jewish; and that it cannot take effect to vest in the crown as a devise to a superstitious use, because it is not so; and therefore as it is part of the will that cannot be performed, it falls into the residuum, and must go to the devisees of that.

The cases before the revolution where the crown interposed, were a great strain on the power of the crown, and not approved by the court, and could be on no other foundation than as vested in the crown as a bequest to a superstitious use.

Ld. Hardwicke, Chancellor. This case requires two considerations; 1st. Whether the legacy in question is good, and such as this Court can or ought to establish? and, 2dly, If not, whether it is void absolutely, or only to the particular intent, so as to leave it a general legacy, and such as the crown may dispose of? As to the first, I am of opinion that it is not a good legacy, and ought not to be established, no such instance being found. Nobody [is] more against laying penalties or hardships upon persons for the exercise of their particular religion than I am; but there is a great difference between doing this and establishing them by acts of the Court. The cases of dissenting ministers before the Toleration were different; particularly *Baxter*'s case, was not of an illegal bequest, but was a bequest for poor ejected ministers; and even as to this case of the Jewish religion, it would be for a different consideration, were it for the support of poor persons of that religion. Orders are made by me and the Master of the Rolls, every year, upon petitions for their support, as poor people. But this is a bequest for the propagation of the Jewish religion; and though it is said, that this is a part of our religion, yet the intent of this bequest must be taken to be in contradiction to the Christian religion, which is a part of the law of the land, which is so laid down by Lord Hale and Lord Raymond, and it undoubtedly is so, for the constitution and policy of this nation is founded thereon. As to the Act of Toleration no new right is given by that, but only an exemption from the penal laws. The Toleration act recites the penal laws, and then not only exempts from those penal laws, but puts the religion of the dissenters under certain regulations and tests. This renders those religions legal, which is not the case of the Jewish religion, that is not taken notice of by any law, but is barely connived at by the legislature.

But the second question is more doubtful, as to what will be the consequence of my opinion upon the first? The objection is, that this is a superstitious use, and so that the bequest must go to the crown; but in answer to this it is said, that can only be in cases that are within the statute of Edward 6. But the cases have gone further; and in *Baxter*'s case it is said, that the Court hath taken in charities in *eodem genere*, and though this decree was reversed, yet it was on the general point that the bequest was not illegal. (7 Ves. 76.) And there is another case to this purpose, which is, the Attorney General and Guise (2 Vern. 266), where the case of one Combes is mentioned, which was before the Toleration Act; and there such bequest was held not void. But if this is to be considered as a superstitious use, it would be a proper consideration for a court of revenue; for I do not think the crown is obliged to apply a bequest to a superstitious use to a charity. If it be an illegal bequest, then it is another consideration, and the Court may direct the application. Therefore, upon this part of the case I have great doubt, and all I shall do at present is, to direct the money to be paid into the bank, and shall reserve the determination as to the disposition of it for further consideration.—Mr. Coxe's MSS.

As to the said legacy of £1200 given by the said will towards the establishing a Jesiba, or assembly for reading and improving the Jewish law, his Lordship declared that he was of opinion, that the same was not good in law, and ought not to be decreed or established by this Court; but doth reserve the consideration, whether the said sum of £1200 ought to fall and accrue to the residue of the said testator's personal estate, or be applied to any other, and what use, & c. 6th December 1743, Reg. Lib. As 1743, fol. 94.

NOTES

1. *The Rationale of the Decision.* Charitable trusts existed before the Reformation. Initially, they were supervised by ecclesiastical courts and then by Chancery. The Statute of Charitable Uses of 1601, 43 Eliz.I, c.4. gave them statutory backing. See Gareth Jones, History of the Law of Charity, 1532–1827 5–11, 16–23 (hereinafter "Jones"). Charitable trusts enjoyed three privileges: "the privilege of exemption from the rule against perpetuities, the privilege of being a valid or 'good' trust even if the testamentary disposition to charity was in imprecise terms (in which case precise terms would be laid down by the Court); and the privilege of obtaining fresh objects if those laid down by the founder were at the outset, or became incapable of execution." Owen Tudor, Charities 142–143 (5th ed. 1929).

Because De Paz's bequest had a religious object, it did not fail as a charitable trust even though its purposes were impermissible. His next of kin thus were not entitled to the fund. The cy pres doctrine allowed a court or the king to specify a new object as near as possible to the testator's original intention. See Section D2 of this chapter, infra, at pp. 90–95, for a discussion of the cy pres doctrine. Lord Chancellor Hardwicke held that the matter of disposition of the money should be referred to the king for disposition. The king, under the sign manual[1], applied the bequest to an Anglican foundling hospital for the support of preachers and the instruction of children in that institution in the Christian religion![2]

---

1. The sign manual was a direction of the crown under the king's signature and at the suggestion of the attorney general. Ronald Chester, George Gleason Bogert & George Taylor Bogert, The Law of Trusts and Trustees § 432 (3d ed. 2005 & 2009 Supp.) (hereinafter "The Law of Trusts and Trustees").

2. The case is discussed in 6 Scott & Ascher on Trusts § 39.5.1. n. 4; Jones, supra p. 81, at 143.

How could such a result be justified? Not only was De Paz denied the purpose of his bequest, his next of kin were disinherited for a charitable purpose that probably was repugnant to the testator. In a later case[3] Chief Justice Wilmot, who thought that the trust in De Costa v. De Paz should have failed, offered a rationale for the decision:

> The donation was considered as proceeding from a general principle of piety in the testator. Charity was an expiation of sin and to be rewarded in another state; and therefore, if political reasons negatived the particular charity given, this Court thought the merits of the charity ought not to be lost to the testator, nor to the public, and that they were carrying on his general pious intention; and they proceeded upon a presumption, that the principle, which produced one charity, would have been equally active in producing another, in case the testator had been told the particular charity he meditated could not take place. The Court thought one kind of charity would embalm his memory as well as another, and being equally meritorious, would entitle him to the same reward.

Bequests for other religions were also diverted. Trusts for the maintenance of non-Anglican religions existed, but they lurked behind the anonymity of innocently sounding absolute gifts.[4]

2. *The Alphabet Trust.* The critic, novelist and playwright George Bernard Shaw created a testamentary trust, which would support the development of a new English alphabet consisting of at least forty letters, in place of the official alphabet of twenty-six letters. The trust would translate Shaw's play, *Androcles and the Lion*, into the new alphabet and finance studies into how much time could be saved by writing with the new alphabet. The income from Shaw's estate—copyrights and royalties—would be devoted to the alphabet project for twenty-one years and then go to the British Museum, the Royal Academy of Dramatic Art and the Irish National Gallery. The first two residuary legatees challenged the alphabet trust as void, because it was for an object rather than a person. The court, which seemed to assume Shaw was joking, held that the trust was not educational, because there was no element of teaching or education involved. Nor did the trust involve the fourth *Pemsel* category (supra p. 76), "trusts for other purposes beneficial to the community." The court concluded the alphabet trust was analogous to trusts for political purposes, which were not considered charitable. In Re Shaw (deceased) Public Trustee v. Day & Others, 1 All E.R. 745 (1957). Under the court's analysis, would a trust or foundation to support research in theoretical physics or the possibilities of life in other galaxies be upheld? Could Shaw's trust be structured to circumvent the court's objectives but validate the testator's wishes?

3. *"Educational" Organizations and Property Tax Exemptions.* Courts have applied as restrictive a definition of "educational" as the court in *Re Shaw* to charities seeking exemption from the property tax even

---

3. Attorney–General v. Downing, Wilm. 1, 32, Amb 549 (1767).

4. Jones, supra p. 81, at 143.

when they have received recognition of exemption under § 501(c)(3) of the Internal Revenue Code. In American Association of Cereal Chemists v. County of Dakota, 454 N.W.2d 912 (Minn.1990), organizations that published technical literature, held meetings for presentation and discussion of research papers and reports, and presented short courses to train science graduates and college teachers in new areas of science and lab techniques were denied a property tax exemption, because they did not offer a curriculum which embraced a sufficient variety of academic subjects to provide a general education nor was the training readily assimilated into general education. See also Ladies Literary Club v. City of Grand Rapids, 409 Mich. 748, 298 N.W.2d 422 (1980) (§ 501(c)(3) organization that promoted trips to see museums and plays, sponsored lectures on antiques, music and poetry, and provided a library for public use did not sufficiently relieve the government's educational burden or fit into the general scheme of education); New Canaan Academy, Inc. v. Town of Canaan, 122 N.H. 134, 441 A.2d 1174 (1982) (school for instruction in meditative arts, which consisted principally of sitting meditation, instruction in Tai Chi, and course entitled Zen Basketball was not "educational institution;" in determining exemption from taxation, courts should consider whether institution is organized to develop faculties and powers and expansion of knowledge through systematic course of instruction or schooling, as distinguished from mere communication of facts or ideas).

4. *Miss Manners's Trust*. Shaw's wife, Charlotte, created a trust for a chair or professorship in Ireland to teach the Irish people "self control, elocution, oratory, and deportment in the acts of personal contact of social intercourse" and good manners. The court upheld the trust, describing it as a finishing school for the Irish people and education, though "of a somewhat pedantic and precious type." The court added though "[e]ducation was not always successful in improving the characters and capabilities of those who are subject to it, but such is its aim and purpose." In re Shaw's Will Trusts v. National City Bank, [1952] Ch. 163, [1952] 1 All E.R. 49, [1951] W.N. 617.

5. *Soul Man*. In 1946 James Kidd wrote a holographic will and placed it in a safe deposit box. A few years later Kidd disappeared without a trace. Not until 1964 was his will discovered and offered for probate. Kidd's will provided: " * * * money to go in a research or some scientific proof of a soul of the human body which leaves at death I think in time their [sic] can be a Photograph of soul leaving the human at death." The trial court found that even though the words "trust" or "trustee" were not used, a valid charitable trust had been created with a corpus of $175,000 and ordered the money given to a neurological institute engaged in research into normal and abnormal functioning of the nervous system. There were 102 claimants to the trust of which six joined an appeal, including one claiming that she saw her soul leave during a volunteer experiment in Stuttgart, Germany in 1937.

The Arizona Supreme Court reversed and directed the trial court to determine which of the other claimants, including a physical research organization, a foundation engaged in research as to whether some aspect of man's nature survives, an individual who asserted he had some scientific proof of soul and wished to do further research, and an individual engaged in pursuit of scientific knowledge of phenomena including manifestations of human soul, were deemed qualified to receive and carry out the trust. In re Estate of Kidd, 106 Ariz. 554, 479 P.2d 697 (1971). But see In Matter of Carpenter, 163 Misc. 474, 297 N.Y.S. 649 (1937) (trust created by the will of a Theosophist to pay the income to such highly evolved individuals with much occult knowledge who are ceaselessly working for the advancement of the race and the alleviation of the sufferings of humanity as the trustee might deem worthy not charitable.)

6. *The Scope of Charitable Purpose Revisited.* What criteria should be applied to determine that a purpose is charitable and serves a public benefit? Who should decide? The validity of a charitable entity depends upon its objective effects, that is to what extent society objectively benefits from the charity's existence. If the activity falls within one of the traditional classifications of charity, there is a rebuttable presumption that it is valid. If the activity does not fall within one of the traditional categories, courts examine whether rational persons in general might reasonably believe that public advantages might accrue. Galston, supra p. 73, at 306. This may protect charitable activities from the tyranny of the majority or the personal beliefs of the court. In an Irish case, In re Cranston, 1 I.R. 431, 446–447 (1898), upholding a trust to promote vegetarianism, the Court said:

> What is the tribunal which is to decide whether the object is a beneficent one? It cannot be the individual mind of a Judge, for he may disagree, *toto coelo*, from the testator as to what is or is not beneficial. On the other hand, it cannot be the *vox populi*, for charities have been upheld for the benefit of insignificant sects, and of peculiar people. It occurs to me that the answer must be—that the benefit must be the one which *the founder* believes to be of public advantage, and his belief must be at least rational, and not contrary either to the general law of the land, or to the principles of morality. A gift of such a character, dictated by benevolence, believed to be beneficent, devoted to an appreciably important object, and neither *contra bonos mores* nor *contra legem*, will, in my opinion, be charitable in the eye of the law, as settled by decisions which bind us. It is not for us to say that these have gone too far.

7. *Are "Benevolent" and "Charitable" and "Philanthropic" Synonymous?* Bequests and donations are often made for "benevolent" and "charitable" or "philanthropic" purposes. Are the words synonymous? If so, it is unnecessary to use all the words. English cases have held that the words do not mean the same thing. An example of an object that might be considered benevolent but not charitable was a trust to provide a pennyworth of sweets for all boys and girls under the age of fourteen within a certain parish. In re Pleasants, 39 T.L.R. 675 (1923). In some cases trusts using the words "benevolent" have been treated as noncharitable because

they permitted an application of trust property to purposes having no public benefit. The Law of Trusts & Trustees, § 370 at 86. In the United States the majority rule considers the terms as synonymous and upholds the disposition for charitable purposes. Many jurisdictions have adopted statutes utilizing the word synonymously. But some courts have construed "benevolent" as insufficient to limit the purposes to those of a charitable level. One approach has been to apply a subjective test to a determination of "benevolent" but to determine a charitable purpose from an objective perspective. 6 Scott & Ascher on Trusts, § 39.4.1.

PROBLEMS

Determine whether the proposed purposes in the following alternatives would be considered charitable:

(a) A trust directing an income of $100 per week to the "oldest respectable inhabitant of Biloxi."

(b) A legacy to the Francis Bacon Society, whose main purpose is to encourage the study of the evidence in favor of Francis Bacon's authorship of the plays commonly ascribed to Shakespeare. The purpose of the legacy is to find Bacon–Shakespeare manuscripts.

(c) The Flat Earth Society, an English organization whose members do not believe the earth is a sphere, desires to establish an American branch and to seek tax exemption.

(d) John Macmuffin is a law professor who writes novels and short stories in the summer. None have been published, and he desires to establish a foundation or trust to promote and publish his writings.

(e) Skinheads form a charitable organization, Breaking Heads Inc., to further its goal of driving non-aryans out of the United States.

(f) Several law professors desire to incorporate National Educators for Repeal of Drug Statutes ("NERDS") as a public benefit organization to advocate legalization of drug use.

D. DISSOLUTION AND DISTRIBUTION OF ASSETS

1. PUBLIC BENEFIT VS. MUTUAL BENEFIT

In this section we examine some of the issues involving dissolution and distribution of assets, comparing the treatment of public benefit and mutual benefit organizations. Nonprofit organizations may outlive their purposes, utility to society, or the support of their members. Financial difficulties may threaten their survival. They may be formed for a limited duration or for a specific task, or merge with another organization. A study by William Bowen and others on the disappearance of nonprofit organizations differentiated between two types of closure: the inability of an entity to satisfy its creditors, and a decision by the board either to merge or to voluntarily liquidate the assets. William G. Bowen, Thomas I. Nygren, Sarah E. Turner, & Elizabeth A. Duffy, The Charitable Nonprofits 96 (1994). Bowen et. al. advance two hypotheses on nonprofit survival which illustrate some differences between nonprofit and for-profit dissolutions. First, nonprofits are more likely to resist closure and simply hold on in the face of economic setbacks than for-profits, which may see economic and tax benefits in combinations or liquidations. Second, nonprofits with substantial assets are less likely to close than other nonprofits. Id. at 99. There may be greater pressures to keep nonprofits in existence than for profit-seeking entities. Many nonprofits survive too long, drawing down their resources to finance annual deficits, or they stay alive on the basis of faded but still useful reputations. Boards may be embarrassed to close or to seek a merger with a stronger organization.

Dissolution is a legal procedure regulated by statute.[1] If assets remain after the nonprofit dissolves, where should they go? Can the organization's board or members distribute them to themselves? The answer depends upon the particular jurisdiction, the form of the nonprofit, and whether the organization's assets are owned outright or held in trust.

NOTES

1. *Public Benefit or Mutual Benefit?* The Los Angeles County Pioneer Society was founded in 1897 as an unincorporated association of pioneers living in Los Angeles County, with about 600 members. The articles of incorporation provided: "That the purpose for which this corporation is formed is to cultivate social intercourse and friendship among its members, to collect and preserve data touching the early history of Los Angeles County and the State of California, to collect and preserve articles, specimens and material things illustrative or demonstrative of the customs, modes and habits of the aforesaid times in said State; to perpetuate the memory of those who, by their labors and heroism, contributed to make the history of said County and State; and in furtherance of said purpose (to do all acts) necessary and convenient for the promotion of the aforesaid purpose; and to exist as a social corporation under the provisions of the laws of the State of California, covering such corporations, and not for pecuniary profit." In 1910, the members incorporated as a non-profit corporation. Over the years membership decreased until in 1941 there were fewer than 100 members. In that year and later years, Mrs. Emma Stoltenberg, a member of Pioneer, made substantial gifts to the Society, and on her death in 1946 she left additional sums to Pioneer by will. The membership continued to decrease. In 1948 the Society amended its bylaws to close its membership and provide that existing members had a proprietary interest in its assets, and then decided to dissolve the corporation, distribute the assets among the members, and continue the organization as an unincorporated association to carry out the purposes of the articles of

---

1. See Model Nonprofit Corp. Act (3d ed.) Ch. 14; N.Y. Not-for-Profit Corp. L. Arts. 10–11, Cal. Corp. Code Pt. 2, Chs. 15–17; Pt. 3, Chs. 15–17. 805 Ill. Comp. Stat. Article 12.

incorporation. Pioneer contended that the gifts of Mrs. Stoltenberg were for the benefit of the members of Pioneer personally and were not received for charitable purposes, and petitioned for judicial supervision of the dissolution. Several members objected and the attorney general intervened.

The California Supreme Court, in a decision by Justice Roger Traynor, held that Pioneer's activities were recognized charitable purposes, and a successor trustee should be appointed to carry out the charitable intent of the donor. The court concluded that the attempt to distribute the assets to the private benefit of Pioneer's members was an improper diversion of assets. Two judges dissented on grounds that the Pioneer Society was a social club and educational benefits of the society were for the members, rather than the public. In Re Los Angeles County Pioneer Society, 40 Cal.2d 852, 257 P.2d 1 (1953).

In re Pioneer Society reflects the general rule that public benefit organizations must transfer their assets on dissolution to charitable or similar uses,[1] while mutual benefit organizations may distribute their assets to members upon dissolution or in accordance with such other plan provided for in the certificate of incorporation or bylaws.[2] Many jurisdictions[3] have based their dissolution provisions on § 46(c) of the original Model Nonprofit Act, which has been criticized for placing no meaningful restrictions on distributions in dissolution beyond the ambiguous requirement that assets "held by the corporation subject to limitations permitting their use only for charitable * * * or similar purposes" must be transferred to other organizations "engaged in activities substantially similar to those of the dissolving corporation."[4]

2. *Dissolution Requirements under § 501(c)(3).* In order to qualify for federal recognition of tax-exempt status under § 501(c)(3), an organization must be organized and operated exclusively for charitable or other exempt

---

1. See, e.g., Model Nonprofit Corp. Act (3d ed.) § 14.05(c), providing that property dedicated to a charitable purpose may not be diverted from its purpose by the dissolution of a nonprofit corporation unless the corporation obtains an order from a court of the attorney general and Model Nonprofit Corp. Act (3d ed.) § 14.05(d), providing that, except for reasonable compensation, members of a nonprofit corporation and other affiliated persons may not receive any financial benefit in connection with the dissolution unless the person is an entity with a charitable purpose. See also Cal. Corp. Code § 5410 (no corporation shall make any distribution); N.Y. Not–For–Profit Corp. L. § 1005(a)(3)(A) ("[a]ssets received and held by the corporation for a purpose specified as Type B * * * shall be distributed to one or more domestic or foreign corporations or other organizations engaged in activities substantially similar to those of the dissolved corporation * * * ").

2. See Model Nonprofit Corp. Act (3d ed.) § 14.05 (a)(7) (a dissolved nonprofit corporation continues its existence to wind up and liquidate its affairs, including distributing its remaining property as required by law and its governing documents and otherwise as approved or among its members per capita); Cal. Corp. Code § 8717(b) ("If the articles or bylaws do not provide the manner of disposition, the assets shall be distributed among the members in accordance with their respective rights therein"); N.Y. Not-for–Profit Corp. L. § 1005(a)(3)(B).

3. 805 Ill. Comp. Stat. Ann. § 105/112.16; Ore. Rev. Stat. Ann. § 65.637.

4. Henry Hansmann, Reforming Nonprofit Corporation Law, 129 U.Pa. L.Rev. 497, 575–579 (1981).

purposes. See Chapter 5C1, infra, at pp. 315–317. This "organizational test" is met if the organization's articles require that on dissolution the assets must be distributed for an exempt purpose or would be distributed by a court to another organization to be used in a manner that would best accomplish the general purposes for which the dissolved organization was organized. Treas. Reg. § 1.501(c)(3)–1(b)(4). The organizational test is not met if the articles or applicable state law provide that the organization's assets would be distributed on dissolution to its members or shareholders.

3. *Voluntary and Involuntary Dissolution.* Nonprofit corporations may dissolve voluntarily or involuntarily by judicial order. Voluntary dissolution may occur upon the happening of certain contingencies such as: (1) bankruptcy; (2) disposition of all corporate assets; (3) failure to conduct an activity for a statutorily specified period (see e.g., Cal. Corp. Code §§ 6610, 8610); (4) the loss of all the corporation's members; (5) the loss or surrender of a corporate charter by a subordinate chapter to its head corporation; or (6) duration in the charter was limited by a specific event or date which occurred. A statutorily specified number of members, directors, or the attorney general can petition for voluntary dissolution.

Among the reasons provided in the statutes for involuntary dissolution are: (1) abandonment of activity; (2) insufficient assets to discharge liabilities; (3) board deadlock; (4) internal dissension by members; (5) fraudulent mismanagement, or abuse of the corporate privilege; (6) failure to carry out corporate purposes; (7) waste of corporate assets; (8) failure to pay creditors as liabilities become due; (9) failure to carry out corporate purposes; (10) violation of statutes, corporate privileges or powers; or (11) failure to pay appropriate taxes or adhere to filing or recordkeeping requirements (Model Nonprofit Corp. Act (3d ed.) § 14.30; N.Y. Tax L. § 203–a(1)). Under the federal bankruptcy code, a nonprofit organization, unlike a for-profit entity, cannot be forced into involuntary liquidation or reorganization. 11 U.S.C.A. § 303(a). Creditors are left to follow the applicable state statutes. But a nonprofit can voluntarily seek liquidation under the federal bankruptcy code.

4. *Procedure for Dissolution.* Although the procedures differ depending upon the jurisdiction, the process of dissolution typically involves a resolution by the board of directors and a plan of dissolution, which must be approved by an appropriate vote of the membership (typically two-thirds of votes cast). In corporations without members, the board will adopt the dissolution plan by resolution. Dissolution requires notice to creditors and involves payment of liabilities and distribution of remaining assets. If the organization is a public benefit corporation, the plan will specify the distributees. In those cases the attorney general is notified and the plan is submitted to a court for approval. If a regulatory agency has approved the formation of the organization, it will be notified and must approve the dissolution. Mutual benefit corporations are subject to less supervision by the attorney general than public benefit corporations. Upon the dissolution of a mutual benefit corporation, the assets remaining after creditors have been paid normally will be distributed to the members.

In determining whether to approve a plan of distribution proposed by a corporation's board, a court will consider: (1) the source of the funds to be distributed, whether received through public subscription or under the trust provision of a will or other investment; (2) the purposes and powers of the corporation as enumerated in its charter; (3) the activities in fact carried out and services actually provided by the corporation; (4) the relationship of the activities and purposes of the proposed distributee(s) to those of the dissolving corporation; and (5) the bases for the distribution recommended by the board. Matter of Multiple Sclerosis Service Organization, 68 N.Y.2d 32, 35, 505 N.Y.S.2d 841, 842, 496 N.E.2d 861, 862 (1986). If the organization is a mutual benefit corporation, the plan of dissolution and distribution of assets must be submitted to a vote of the members. A certificate of dissolution is filed with the secretary of state.

After dissolution, the corporation carries on no activities except winding up of its affairs, preserving and protecting assets, minimizing liabilities, discharging existing liabilities, disposing of properties that will not be distributed in kind, and paying liabilities and distributing corporation assets in accordance with the specifications of the dissolution plan. If the organization has insufficient assets to cover its liabilities, the court may appoint a receiver to preserve the assets.

PROBLEMS

1. In the following problems, consider what steps would be required to dissolve the organizations previously formed in the problem set at p. 63 under the law of your jurisdiction:

(a) It is five years since your client, Ms. Scoville, began assisting llamas, and they are thriving. Others have rallied to the cause. Ms. Scoville has another charitable interest to which she would like to devote her time and resources—saving the double-breasted seersucker. The National Bird Association has a Save the Seersucker project. How can Ms. Scoville engineer a change in her charitable efforts?

(b) Unfortunately for Harding and his friends in the Northern Chemung County Trollope Society, local residents would rather read Stephen King and John Grisham. Funding sources also are unsympathetic. The Trollope Society decides to dissolve. It has $115 in assets in a bank account.

(c) Assume the day care center, named Runamuck Child Care Center, has been a success but financing has been an ongoing problem, and the children of the founders are now in law school. Runamuck has $100,000 in assets. The directors decide to go out of business and dissolve.

(d) Neither Sturdley law students nor alumni have any interest in cricket or any other form of leisure. The Leisure Time Center has been unable to attract additional funds. The organization's board decides to dissolve.

2.　The articles of incorporation of a charitable organization state that it was formed: (1) "to promote, foster, encourage and sponsor activities for the character building of youth, and to advance the educational, vocational, civic, social, commercial and economic interest in and about West Duckburg, and (2) to promote sociability and friendship among its members; to manage and conduct entertainments, excursions, social meetings and such activities as hiking, swimming, crafts, to unite the members in the bonds of friendship, and to provide a forum for full and fair discussion." The organization collected dues and owned a campground and lodge. It offered potluck suppers, hiking, craft studies, and parties for its members. The organization solicited some contributions and accepted some donations. It did not seek local tax exemption. The members of the organization have voted to dissolve, and they seek to distribute the assets of the corporation among themselves after creditors have been paid. Is this possible? What factors would you examine in reaching a conclusion?

3.　A nonprofit corporation operated a hospital from 1927 to 1971. The articles of incorporation provide: " * * * the corporation was formed to maintain and operate a hospital as well as to perform acts of charity among the sick." In the event of liquidation or dissolution the articles named two hospitals and the Archbishop of Los Angeles as successors. The board of directors decides to abandon the operation of the hospital in favor of neighborhood outpatient clinics. Would the proposed changes be permitted under the nonprofit statute of your jurisdiction or the Model Nonprofit Corporation Act?

2.　Charitable Trusts: The Doctrine of Cy Pres

Principles of the Law of Nonprofit Organizations § 460(b).

Restatement (Third) of Trusts § 67.

A charity must comply with the terms contained in a trust or gift instrument. Unanticipated circumstances can arise. The passage of time may make the gift or trust impossible or impracticable to comply with its terms. What can the charity do? The gift or trust instrument may contain language that addresses the possibility of a change in circumstances. If the donor is still alive the charity may seek a modification or a release of a restriction. Many larger charities will have gift policies that phase out restrictions upon passage of a specific amount of time, the occurrence of an event, certain circumstances, or in the good faith judgment of the recipient. Principles of the Law of Nonprofit Organizations, § 430 cmt. 3.[1] If the

---

1.　As this edition of the text went to press in early 2010, the various completed drafts of the American Law Institute's Principles of the Law of Nonprofit Organizations project were either "tentative" or "preliminary." Tentative Drafts of the provisions on governance (§§ 300–380) and the treatment of gifts (§§ 400–490) have been approved by the ALI membership. Chapters on the relationship between the charity and the state, and supervision and enforcement, are in the preliminary draft state and have not yet been considered by the membership.

donor is deceased or refuses to release the restriction, it is absolute and the charity must go to court to seek a modification under the cy pres or deviation doctrines.

The law favors charitable trusts, and courts will use their equitable powers to save a trust from failure or to reform it so as to accomplish its general purposes by applying the doctrine of cy pres (pronounced "see pray"). The theory of cy pres is that when a charitable purpose becomes impossible, inexpedient, or impracticable of fulfillment or already accomplished, equity will permit the trustee to substitute another charitable object which reasonably approaches the designated purpose as closely as possible. The Law of Trusts & Trustees, § 431. The doctrine of cy pres, therefore, is a saving device that permits a court to direct the application of charitable trust property to a charitable purpose different from that designed in the trust instrument. Cy pres is recognized in nearly all American jurisdictions. 6 Scott & Ascher on Trusts, § 39.5, n. 2.

Thus, equity will modify a charitable trust to meet unexpected contingencies where the settlor had a general charitable intent. However, the power of modification is strictly construed and closely circumscribed. The degree of frustration must be relatively great; the donor must at least have implicitly consented to the change; and the degree of change must be relatively small. Restatement (Third) of Trusts § 67. Traditionally, in modifying a trust's purpose, the court would follow the donor's original purpose as closely as possible or *cy pres comme possible*—Norman french for "as near as possible." The Law of Trusts & Trustees, § 431.

Most courts apply a three-part test derived from the Restatement of Trusts to determine whether a cy pres modification is proper. The applicant must show: 1) a valid charitable trust exists; 2) the settlor's specific charitable obligation is frustrated, necessitating cy pres modification to carry out the settlor's wishes; and 3) the settlor had a general charitable intent not restricted to the precise purpose identified in the trust instrument. Though courts apply the doctrine conservatively, cy pres has been applied in a wide variety of contexts.

NOTES AND QUESTIONS

1. *Accomplishment of Purpose.* In Jackson v. Phillips, 96 Mass. 539 (1867), the testator, who died in 1861, gave a $10,000 bequest "for the preparation and circulation of books, newspapers, the delivery of speeches, lectures and other means as in their judgment will create a public sentiment that will put an end to negro slavery in this country," and a $2,000 bequest "for the benefit of fugitive slaves who may escape from the slaveholding states of this infamous Union from time to time." The Thirteenth Amendment abolishing slavery was ratified in 1865. The court held that the charitable bequests did not fail but were to be applied to carry out the intentions of the testator as nearly as possible. The first bequest was to be paid by the trustees periodically to an association, already established, to promote the education, support and interests of former

slaves. The second bequest, of which only a small amount remained, was to be used for needy black residents of Boston and the surrounding area.

2. *Insufficient Funds to Accomplish Purpose.* A testatrix bequeathed $2,000 to found a home for cats, but the funds were insufficient to establish a cat house. The court ordered the money to be given to the Connecticut Humane Society, which cared for abandoned animals. Shannon v. Eno, 120 Conn. 77, 179 A. 479 (1935).

3. *Avoidance of Unconstitutional or Illegal Conditions.* When charitable trusts contain provisions that violate constitutional or statutory norms, courts may reform the offending clause. Trustees of University of Del. v. Gebelein, 420 A.2d 1191 (Del.Ch.1980) (trust for scholarship for white females in state university amended cy pres to eliminate "white" but not female); Wooten v. Fitz–Gerald, 440 S.W.2d 719 (Tex.Civ.App.1969) (court eliminated "white" from trust to be used for "aged white men."). See generally, 6 Scott & Ascher on Trusts, § 39.5.5; Restatement (Third) of Trusts § 28 cmt. f; cf. Bob Jones Univ. v. United States, 461 U.S. 574, 103 S.Ct. 2017 (1983) (racial discrimination in admission of students incompatible with charitable status), Chapter 5C4, infra, at p. 369. When courts attempt to apply the cy pres doctrine to impermissible restrictions they must find that a general charitable intent on the part of the testator outweighs the impermissible provision in order to preserve the trust. In situations where societal values, policies, and constitutional norms have changed, courts occasionally exercise breathtaking powers of interpretation to save the charitable trust. Thus, in Ebitz v. Pioneer Nat. Bank, 372 Mass. 207, 361 N.E.2d 225 (1977), where a will directed the establishment of a public charitable trust "to aid and assist worthy and ambitious young men to acquire a legal education," the court construed "men" in its generic sense to include women. A study of 40 cases challenging restrictive charitable trusts found that courts applied the cy pres doctrine in 29 cases to reform the trust. In all but four, the court found the testator had a general charitable intent and removed the offending clause. David Luria, Prying Loose the Dead Hand of the Past: How Courts Apply Cy Pres to Race, Gender, and Religiously Restricted Trusts, 21 U.S.F. L. Rev. 41, 42–44 (1986).

Courts have been less inclined to apply the cy pres doctrine to cases of gender discrimination than race discrimination. Absent state action, courts are unwilling to apply cy pres to religiously restrictive charitable trusts. When courts have eliminated gender restraints, they have found state action and used cy pres to reform the offending phrase. For example, in In re Certain Scholarship Funds, 133 N.H. 227, 575 A.2d 1325 (1990), a school district's participation in the administration of a gender-based discriminatory charitable trust that provided tuition for "one worthy protestant boy who was a scholar at Keene High School" constituted state action within the ambit of the state's constitution and equal protection clause. The court changed the words "Protestant Boy" to "student." Other courts have reformed trusts to eliminate the state action, thereby permitting the discriminatory purpose to remain. In re Estate of Wilson, 59 N.Y.2d 461, 465 N.Y.S.2d 900, 452 N.E.2d 1228 (1983).

If a donor would have preferred to allow the trust to fail rather than continue free of the impermissible restriction, or if the restriction is illegal, the property may go to another charity or the residuary, or a court may refuse to apply cy pres. Evans v. Abney, 224 Ga. 826, 165 S.E.2d 160 (1968), aff'd, 396 U.S. 435, 90 S.Ct. 628 (1970) (because language of will negated general charitable intent, cy pres did not apply); Connecticut Bank & Trust Co. v. Cyril and Julia C. Johnson Memorial Hospital, 30 Conn. Supp. 1, 294 A.2d 586 (1972).

4. *Where Legatee Refuses to Accept Gift Subject to Restriction.* If a legatee refuses to accept a donation because of a restriction, courts may remove the offending provision to validate the gift, hold it for another institution, or give it to the testator's next of kin. In Howard Savings Institution v. Peep, 34 N.J. 494, 170 A.2d 39 (1961), a testator donated scholarships to Amherst College for "deserving American born, Protestant, Gentile boys of good moral repute, not given to gambling, smoking, drinking or similar acts." Because the religious restrictions were contrary to its charter, Amherst refused to accept the bequest unless the restriction was lifted. The court held the doctrine of cy pres applied because the basic intention of the donor was to give the gift to Amherst.

5. *The Buck Trust.* In 1975 Beryl H. Buck left her estate, valued between $7–10 million, to a charitable trust to provide "care for the needy in Marin County and for other nonprofit charitable, religious or educational purposes in that County." At the time the population of Marin County was 220,000. It had the highest per capita income of any California county and the second highest of any over–50,000 person county in the nation. Its unemployment rate was 3.2% in 1986, the lowest of all the Bay area counties. The trust was administered by the San Francisco Foundation.

By 1985, after the sale of greatly appreciated oil stock in its endowment, the trust's assets had grown to $380–$400 million, generating over $23 million each year for distribution. The San Francisco Foundation had difficulty spending the income efficiently and deciding where it would do the most good. The Buck Trust assisted various Marin governmental social service agencies and made some controversial grants for bicycle paths and jogging tracks in affluent areas, and $195,000 to a homeowners' association to maintain a clubhouse and pool. A high school theater group received $165,000.

In 1984 the San Francisco Foundation petitioned to modify the trust under an expansive interpretation of the cy pres doctrine. It sought to relax the geographical limits to enable the trust to make grants in the four neighboring Bay Area counties. In re Estate of Buck, No. 23259 (Cal. Super. Ct., Marin County, Aug. 15, 1986) (reprinted in full 21 U.S.F.L. Rev. 691 (1987)). The Foundation argued that the unanticipated growth in the corpus rendered the express provisions meaningless as a reflection of true intent. Therefore, the Foundation urged the court to assume the disposition of a reasonable executor. The Foundation equated reasonableness with an efficiency standard and argued that trust income remaining after Marin County's legitimate needs were satisfied should be spread across the Bay Area, offering a more efficient and effective solution.

The attorney general initially supported the Foundation but later switched sides. Citizens and groups from Marin County also opposed the modification. The court found that cy pres was inapplicable and denied the petition for modification. It added that ineffective philanthropy, inefficiency or relative inefficiency do not constitute impracticability under the cy pres doctrine. Cy pres may not be invoked on the grounds that it would be more fair, equitable or efficient to spend the trust funds in a manner different from that specified by the testator. In June 1986, the case was settled out of court with the Marin County limitation intact, and The San Francisco Foundation was removed as a trustee.

Should charitable inefficiency be grounds for the application of cy pres? Does the public have an interest in preventing charitable inefficiency? How should charitable efficiency be balanced against the intent of the donor? In such a balancing would the donor's intent be submerged? If the court had modified the Buck Trust, would other donors hesitate to create charitable trusts? If the efficiency standard was adopted, who should determine it? The trustee? A court? The Foundation, claiming surprise resulting from the greatly increased corpus of the trust, argued that it was seeking to avoid charitable waste. Do the circumstances surrounding Mrs. Buck's gift differ from the situation where a trust is found to have an impermissibly restrictive purpose and courts go out of their way to generalize a testator's intent to reform the trust?

Can one assume Mrs. Buck's intent would remain the same with the knowledge that her trust would produce $30 million per year rather than the $750,000 annually she expected for Marin County? If there had been a modification of the Buck Trust why should it have stopped at the boundaries of the five county Bay Area? Why not the world? Would Mrs. Buck have entrusted her fortune to The San Francisco Foundation, or would she have established her own foundation? Should there be a rule against perpetuities for enforceability of a charitable trust or restrictions on a charitable gift? Would application of § 67 of the Restatement (Third) of Trusts or § 460(b) of the ALI's Principles of the Law of Nonprofit Organizations lead to a different result?

6. *A Dog's Life*. Leona Helmsley, widow of a real estate mogul, famously said: "We don't pay taxes. Only the little people pay taxes," a practice that led to her serving eighteen months in federal prison. When she was released she got a dog, a Maltese named Trouble. Ms. Helmsley died in 2007. She left a $12 million trust to care for Trouble, who was her biggest beneficiary. This brought death threats against the dog. Her estate, estimated at the time between $4 and $8 billion, was left to the Leona M. and Harry B. Helmsley Charitable Trust. The mission statement of the trust was for "purposes related to the provision of care for dogs." With the support of the New York Attorney General, the trustees petitioned the Manhattan Surrogate's Court to determine if the trust could be used for

more than dog-related purposes. The court ruled that the trustees could apply the trust's funds for such charitable purposes and in such amounts as they in their sole discretion determined. The mission statement, which also allowed the trustees to give to other charitable activities, was found to be merely precatory. The body of the trust instrument, which did not contain a restriction for dogs, had the legal effect. In another proceeding, Trouble's trust was reduced to a mere $2 million.[1] See Mike Spector, Crisis on Wall Street: Helmsley Fortune Ruled Not for Dogs Only, Wall St.J., Feb. 26, 2009, at C3. When the Trust announced its first round of grants amounting to $136 million, animals received leftovers—only $1 million. Was the court's decision correct? Is this the same situation as the Buck Trust? Should idiosyncratic purposes be upheld so long as they are lawful? Should there be limits on how much one can give to charity and receive a tax deduction?

7. *Strict Impossibility Not Required.* In United States v. Cerio, 831 F.Supp. 530 (E.D.Va.1993), an alumnus of the Coast Guard Academy devised a charitable trust for the Academy for purposes of establishing a trust fund, the annual income of which was to be awarded each year to the graduating cadet who attained the highest grade point average in chemistry and physics. Based on the size of the trust corpus, the proposed cadet award would range from $65,000 to $130,000. The Coast Guard claimed that unless the trust was modified in a cy pres proceeding, it would refuse the gift on the grounds that the trust as written was impossible to perform; it would seriously disrupt the Academy's operations and interfere with the attainment of its goals such as a commitment to teamwork. The court exercised the cy pres power, finding that the testator primarily desired to foster academic excellence and the particular manner in which the trust was to be performed was secondary. The court held that use of cy pres did not require literal impossibility but essential impracticability, and it modified the trust to provide for more modest awards as well as science fellowships and visitorships.

8. *Cy Pres without Judicial Review.* Section 6(d) of the Uniform Prudent Management of Institutional Funds Act (see Chapter 3C5, infra, at page 208), which regulates funds held by charities, permits a charitable organization to modify a restriction on its own without court approval for small funds (less than $25,000 or another amount as determined by the enacting jurisdiction) that have existed for more than 20 years (or another time period as determined by the enacting jurisdiction), after giving 60 days notice (or another notice period as determined by the enacting jurisdiction) to the attorney general. The attorney general may then take action if the proposed modification appears inappropriate. The provision is meant to permit a charitable organization to lift a restriction that may no longer make sense where the cost of a judicial *cy pres* proceeding would be so great as to be prohibitive.

---

1. Section 408 of the Uniform Trust Code provides that a trust may be created to provide for the care of an animal alive during the settlor's lifetime, except to the extent a court determines that the value of the trust property exceeds the amount required for intended use.

3.   THE DOCTRINE OF DEVIATION

Principles of the Law of Nonprofit Organizations § 460(a), (d).

Restatement (Third) of Trusts § 66.

Related to cy pres is the doctrine of deviation under which a court may alter the administrative or distributive provisions of a trust. The deviation doctrine will be applied when it appears to the court that compliance is impossible or illegal, or that owing to circumstances unanticipated by the settlor compliance would defeat or substantially impair the accomplishment of the purposes of the trust. Restatement (Third) of Trusts § 66(1). Courts have been more willing to allow modifications for administrative reasons than for changes in purpose. Deviation is more readily available upon showing that, in light of unanticipated circumstances, a modification would assist in carrying out the settlor's or donor's purpose. Cy pres applies to the modification of the trust's purposes and deviation to its administration, but the distinction sometimes is difficult to draw. Strictly speaking, in applying the doctrine of deviation a court cannot change the original charitable objective of the settlor or divert the bequest to an entity with a purpose different from the purpose set forth in the trust instrument. Restatement (Third) of Trusts § 66, cmt. a. Deviation can be used where a term of a trust is illegal, changed circumstances have occurred, or to escape investment restrictions on the sale of property even though such sales are unauthorized or forbidden by the terms of the trust. 5 Scott & Ascher on Trusts, § 37.3.3.

In re the Barnes Foundation

Pennsylvania Court of Common Pleas, 2004.
24 Fiduc. Rep.2d 94.

■ OTT, J.

[Dr. Albert Barnes amassed a priceless collection of impressionist and post-impressionist art, which included 69 Cezannes, 60 Matisses, 44 Picassos and 180 Renoirs. A combative, opinionated, rigid person for whom every straw was the last, Barnes developed idiosyncratic views of aesthetics, psychology and their relation to art appreciation, which were scorned by the art establishment. He established a school to promote his views and a created a foundation to house his collection in Lower Merion, Pennsylvania, an affluent suburb of Philadelphia. An indenture creating the Barnes Foundation specified that it was an educational institution rather than a museum, restricted public access, and stated that its terms could not be changed. Since Dr. Barnes' death in an automobile accident in 1951, the Barnes Foundation has been involved in litigation involving public access to its collection, requests by the Foundation for deviation from the indenture, and suits alleging mismanagement. Facing possible bankruptcy because of its precarious finances, the Foundation accepted an offer from three wealthy Pennsylvania foundations to help raise funds to move its collection from Lower Merion to a more accessible location in Philadelphia. The offer was conditioned on the Foundation's receiving court approval of a new governance structure that would expand its board and reduce the influence of Lincoln University, a historically black college that had been granted authority by Dr. Barnes to nominate four of the five board members. In this deviation suit, which was supported by the Pennsylvania attorney general, the Foundation sought to expand its board and relocate its art collection to Philadelphia. Eds.]

* * *

Dr. Barnes and The Foundation entered into a trust indenture under date of December 6, 1922, whereby Dr. Barnes donated his artwork to the Foundation to accomplish its charitable purposes. The collection amassed by Dr. Barnes during his lifetime, which is housed at the Lower Merion gallery is large and virtually priceless. Dr. Barnes also funded The Foundation with an initial endowment of approximately six million dollars. The Foundation's bylaws incorporate the December 6, 1922 indenture, as amended, in its entirety.

In the instant petition, The Foundation sets forth its current financial state as follows. Dr. Barnes' initial endowment has been depleted. The Foundation is unable to cover its general operating expenses and to meet its needs in areas such as professional staffing, conservation treatment, fund-raising, collection assessment, facilities care, and public relations. The Foundation's ability to generate revenue from visitors to or fund-raising activities at the Merion gallery is limited by the existing zoning restrictions in Lower Merion Township, The Foundation's ability to raise revenue is also limited by the small size of its Board of Trustees.

The Foundation states that its "current fiscal situation is dire, puts at risk The Foundation's ability to fulfill its primary purpose, and threatens The Foundation's survival." In the hopes of ensuring its ability to continue its purpose in the future and to improve its finances, The Foundation struck an agreement with two of Philadelphia's leading philanthropic institutions, the Pew Charitable Trusts (hereinafter "Pew") and the Lenfest Foundation (hereinafter "Lenfest,") whereby Pew and Lenfest promised to help The Foundation raise approximately $150 million. It is the conditions attached to this promise that have catapulted The Foundation back into court. The fund-raising assistance from Pew and Lenfest is predicated upon the relocation of The Foundation's art collection from Merion to a new site to be built in Philadelphia, and upon the expansion of the number of trustees on The Foundation's Board. Both of these proposals run afoul of Dr, Barnes' indenture and The Foundation's charter and bylaws. Accordingly, The Foundation now seeks to amend these documents.

* * *

The least controversial of the matters presently before us is the proposed change in the size of the Foundation's Board of Trustees. Dr. Barnes' indenture provided for five trustees. The initial Board consisted of Dr. Barnes, his wife, and three other individuals. After the deaths of Dr. and Mrs. Barnes, vacancies in the office of trustee were filled as follows:

Girard Trust Company (now Mellon Bank) nominated one trustee, and Lincoln University nominated the other four. The indenture specified that: "no Trustee shall be a member of the faculty or Board of Trustees or Directors of the University of Pennsylvania, Temple University, Bryn Mawr, Haverford or Swarthmore Colleges, or Pennsylvania Academy of the Fine Arts" (Indenture, as amended, ¶ 17).

Under the changes now being proposed by The Foundation, the Board would consist of fifteen members. Lincoln University would nominate five persons for election. Mellon would no longer be involved. Upon approval of the changes, the current five trustees would immediately elect three additional trustees and Lincoln would immediately nominate three new names for election. A nominating committee chosen from these trustees would then recommend the remaining nominees for election to the Board. For the election of these final trustees on the initial expanded Board, Pew and Lenfest would jointly have the power to approve the nominations, however, the two institutions would have no authority in the nomination or election of trustees thereafter. The petition asserts that a larger Board is necessary because modern nonprofit corporations require larger governing boards consisting of "members who have access to a variety of communities and resources and who can provide governance expertise."

In light of the testimony summarized supra, we find ample support for the proposal that the Board of Trustees of The Foundation should be expanded. It is clear that the stewardship of a modern-day nonprofit must rest on many shoulders. It is imperative that the trustees have wide-ranging experience, expertise, and contacts, and the ability to attract donors of substance. A board of only five trustees, no matter how talented and dedicated the individuals may be, cannot meet the enormous responsibility of carrying The Foundation into the twenty-first century.

The legal authority for amending Dr. Barnes' indenture on this issue can be found in the doctrine of deviation. This doctrine has played a part in much of the recent litigation involving The Foundation. This court and the Pennsylvania Superior Court examined the doctrine in connection with certain changes to Violette de Mazia's testamentary trust that were being proposed to carry out a settlement agreement between the de Mazia trust and The Foundation. The undersigned determined that the changes were substantive, not administrative, and that the doctrine was inapplicable. In its opinion reversing this decision, the Superior Court stated:

The doctrine of deviation has been summarized in the Restatement (Second) of Trusts:

> [A] court will direct or permit the trustee of a charitable trust to deviate from a term of the trust if it appears to the court that compliance is impossible or illegal, or that owing to circumstances not known to the settlor and not anticipated by him compliance would defeat or substantially impair the accomplishment of the purposes of the trust. Restatement (Second) of Trusts § 381 (1959). Those terms subject to deviation are limited to administrative provisions of the trust, i.e., "the details of administration which the settlor has pre-

scribed in order to secure the more important result of obtaining for the beneficiaries the advantages which the settlor stated he wished them to have." § 561 Bogert, The Law of Trust and Trustees, at 27.

In order to permit deviation from the administrative provisions of a trust, courts generally require the presence of two elements: "(1) unforeseen and unforeseeable change in circumstances, and (2) a frustration of the settlor's main objectives by this change, if strict obedience to the settlor [sic] directions were required." Bogert supra at 230. It must be emphasized that the relief afforded by deviation is not based on mere convenience, but on the necessity of effecting a change in a situation where compliance with the terms of the trust "would defeat or substantially impair the accomplishment of the purposes of the trust," Colin McK. Grant Home v. Medlock, 292 S.C. 466, 472, 349 S.E.2d 655, 659 (1986).

The doctrine of deviation also played a role in another proceeding wherein The Foundation sought permission 1) to hold fundraising events at its Merion facility, and 2) to increase the admission fee to the gallery to $10 and 3) to open the gallery to the public six days a week. The undersigned denied the first request on the grounds that it ran afoul of language in Dr. Barnes' indenture and The Foundation had failed to prove that, because it was impossible to raise adequate funds otherwise, deviation was necessary. This court approved an increase in the admission price to $5 and agreed that the gallery could be open one additional day per week. On appeal by The Foundation, the Superior Count reversed us on the fundraising issue, on the grounds that the events contemplated by The Foundation fell outside the ambit of prohibited activities in Dr. Barnes' indenture, and, as a result, deviation was not an issue. That Court upheld the undersigned on the other two issues, agreeing that The Foundation had failed to show that deviations from the terms of the indenture were necessary.

* * *

With this authority in mind, we believe it appropriate to permit deviation on this issue. We determine that the provisions in the indenture concerning the structure of the Board of Trustees of The Foundation are administrative in nature. We agree that Dr. Barnes could have foreseen neither the complicated, competitive, and sophisticated world in which nonprofit now operate, nor the range of expertise and influence the members of their governing bodies must now possess, We conclude that maintaining the status quo in this regard would substantially impair the accomplishment of the Foundation's charitable purposes, and that approving the expansion of its Board of Trustees is therefore necessary.

The second major issue before us—relocating the art collection to Philadelphia—is far more complex.

[The court then described the pertinent provisions of the December 6, 1922 indenture between Dr. Barnes and the Barnes Foundation. At Dr. Barnes' death the collection would be closed. No additional works of art could be purchased. No buildings for any purpose could be erected on the property and all the paintings would remain in exactly the same places as they were at the time of Barnes' and his wife's death. No paintings could be loaned or sold. Should the collection be destroyed or otherwise become impossible to administer, then the property and funds contributed by Dr. Barnes would be applied to an object as near as possible in connection with an existing institution and organized in Philadelphia or its suburbs. Eds.]

* * *

Except for those years when The Foundation has enjoyed these non-recurring infusions of cash, The Foundation has been operating in the red over the past decade. The deficits can be traced, in large part, to the incredibly expensive and lengthy litigation in which The Foundation was embroiled in the 1990s. In addition to obtaining permission to send some of the collection on tour, the previous administration attempted to increase revenues by increasing public admission to the gallery. This effort was stymied by the limits imposed by Lower Merion Township, to wit, the gallery can be open only on Fridays, Saturdays and Sundays, and only 1200 visitors are allowed per week. The admission price remains at five dollars ($5) as per the decree of this court. [The Foundation's endowment was constrained by Dr. Barnes' insistence that it be invested only in tax-exempt bonds or securities on the legal list of approved investments of the state of New York. Eds.]

* * *

The Foundation suggests that it has laid the groundwork for invoking the doctrine of deviation on the issue of relocating the collection. We have set forth the basic concepts of this doctrine, including the language of the Restatement (Second) of Trusts, supra. Our Superior Court has cited to Corpus Juris Secundum for the proposition that the party seeking the deviation (here The Foundation) has the burden of proof. We too quote therefrom as follows:

> In exercising its jurisdiction to modify or alter, the court should . . . be exceedingly cautious. Courts will exercise such power only when it clearly appears to be necessary and only in extreme cases.

90 C.J.S. Trusts, § 97 (2002 ed.) This language sets forth a "clear and convincing" standard of evidence in deviation matters. Furthermore, if the court is convinced that deviation is appropriate, it must choose the least drastic modification.

* * *

Dr. Barnes' indenture does not specifically state that the gallery must be maintained in Merion or cease to exist. Nevertheless, it is difficult to dismiss Dr. Barnes' choice of venue as a minor detail. Dr. and Mrs. Barnes lived on the site, in the administration building adjacent to the gallery. Dr. Barnes' indenture provided for the administration building to be used as classrooms for the art education program after his and Mrs. Barnes' deaths. The focus of the education program is the ensembles of art in the gallery.

The arboretum on the grounds is also an integral part of the educational work that was the goal of Dr. Barnes' experiment.

[The court concluded that a financial exigency existed but ordered the Foundation to present additional information that a move was the only recourse available, and that sale of the Foundation's other assets would not solve the financial problems. After presentation of the evidence requested and subsequent hearings, the court issued a second opinion. Eds.]

In re the Barnes Foundation

Pennsylvania Court of Common Pleas, 2004.
2004 WL 2903655, 25 Fiduc. Rep. 2d 39.

■ OTT, J.

In this opinion, we consider the evidence presented at the second round of hearings on The Barnes Foundation's second amended petition to amend its charter and bylaws. * * * We felt that The Foundation needed to show more than the adumbration of proposed changes that was presented at the December hearings, and after conferences in camera following the issuance of our January 29, 2004 opinion, the open areas of inquiry were distilled into three questions: 1) Can The Foundation raise enough money through the sale of its non-gallery assets to keep the collection in Merion and achieve fiscal stability; and are there ethical and/or legal constraints on such a sale of assets? 2) Can the facility envisioned in Philadelphia be constructed on the proposed $100,000,000 budget? and 3) Is The Foundation's three-campus model—the new facility housing the art education and public gallery functions, Merion as the site of the administrative offices and the horticulture program, and Ker–Feal, the Chester County farmhouse on 137+ acres, operating as a living museum—feasible?

[The Court then presented a summary of the evidence. Eds.]

* * *

In view of the foregoing, we find that The Foundation showed clearly and convincingly the need to deviate from the terms of Dr. Barnes' indenture; and we find that the three-campus model represents the least drastic modification necessary to preserve the organization. By many interested observers, permitting the gallery to move to Philadelphia will be viewed as an outrageous violation of the donor's trust. However, some of the archival materials introduced at the hearings led us to think otherwise. Contained therein were signals that Dr. Barnes expected the collection to have much greater public exposure after his death. To the court's thinking, these clues make the decision—that there is no viable alternative—easily reconcilable with the law of charitable trusts. When we add this revelation to The Foundation's absolute guarantee that Dr. Barnes' primary mission—the formal education programs—will be preserved and, indeed, enhanced as a result of these changes, we can sanction this bold new venture with a clear conscience.

Our conclusion that The Foundation should prevail does not mean all doubts about the viability of its plans have been allayed. Of serious concern are its fundraising goals. While Mr. Callahan was on the stand, we commented on his contagious optimism. It is clear The Foundation's Board will have to catch it. Mr. Callahan was only one of the many witnesses who acknowledged that The Foundation is raising the bar enormously above both its own fundraising abilities in the past and those of non-profits in general. "Ambitious" and "aggressive" were among the adjectives we heard to describe the target levels on which the Deloitte report is based. There is a real possibility that the development projections will not be realized, perhaps not in the first few years, but later on, when the interest and excitement about the new venture have faded. If that occurs, or the admissions do not meet expectations, or any of the other components of the Deloitte model do not reach their targets, something will have to give. We will not speculate about the nature of future petitions that might come before this court; however, we are mindful of the vehement protestations, not so long ago, that The Foundation would never seek to move the gallery to Philadelphia, and, as a result, nothing could surprise us.

We make a final observation about finances and the plans now being approved. The capital cost analysis prepared by Perks Reutter Associates contemplates renovations to the Merion facility to the tune of $1,600,000. In excess of $12,000,000 was spent upgrading the gallery during the world tour of some of The Foundation's works in 1993 and 1994. The irony of converting a state-of-the-art gallery into perhaps the most expensive administration building in the history of non-profits is not lost to us. Looking to the future, it is of the utmost importance that that Board of Trustees steer The Foundation so that another such irony does not surface ten or fifteen years hence.

In light of the foregoing, by separate decree entered *eo die*, The Foundation's second amended petition to amend is granted.

NOTE AND QUESTIONS

1. *Barnes and the Buck Trust.* Is the Barnes Foundation situation the same as the Buck Trust (supra, p. 93) but with a different result? Or is there something more?

2. *Donor Intent.* Should donor intent, so long as it is lawful, always be respected? Did the deviation turn a primarily educational institution into a more traditional art museum?

3. *The Restatement of Trusts and the Deviation Doctrine.* The court cited Restatement (Second) of Trusts § 381 as justification for permitting deviation from Barnes' indenture. Comment e to that section states:

> e. Where sale of land forbidden by terms of trust. If a testator devises land for the purpose of maintaining a school or other charitable institution upon the land, and owing to a change of circumstances it becomes impracticable to maintain the institution on the land, the

court may direct or permit the trustee to sell the land and devote the proceeds to the erection and maintenance of the institution on other land, even though the testator in specific words directed that the land should not be sold and that the institution should not be maintained in any other place.

If, however, the testator provided that if the institution should not be maintained upon the land devised the charitable trust should cease, the trustee will not be directed or permitted to maintain the institution on other land. See § 401.

If the maintenance of the institution on the land devised was an essential part of the testator's purpose, the court also will not direct or permit the trustee to maintain the institution on other land. See § 399.
Did the court apply the Restatement section correctly?

4. *Liberalizing the Granting of Relief.* In recent years there has been an increased willingness to grant relief and modify restrictions. In Niemann v. Vaughn Community Church, 154 Wash.2d 365, 113 P.3d 463 (2005), the court considered whether an alleged restrictive covenant on the alienation of church property from one church to another prevented the receiving church from selling the original church property in order to relocate to a larger, nearby property. The court classified the restriction on the sale of property as an administrative provision and granted relief on the basis of equitable deviation and discussed the differing approaches of the second and third restatements for applying deviation:

> The Restatement (Second) standard provides a relatively narrow standard for applying deviation:

>> The court will direct or permit the trustee of a charitable trust to deviate from a term of the trust if it appears to the court that compliance is impossible or illegal, or that owing to circumstances not known to the settlor and not anticipated by him compliance would defeat or substantially impair the accomplishment of the purposes of the trust.

> Restatement (Second) of Trusts § 381. * * * For a court to allow deviation under this standard, compliance with the trust terms must "defeat" or "substantially impair" the trust's primary purpose.

> The Restatement's most recent rendition of the rule grants courts broader discretion to permit deviation, providing that "[t]he court may modify an administrative or distributive provision of a trust, or direct or permit the trustee to deviate from an administrative or distributive provision, if because of circumstances not anticipated by the settlor the modification or deviation will further the purposes of the trust." Restatement (Third) of Trusts § 66(1). While the first prong of the most recent version is substantially similar to the Restatement (Second), the second prong requires only that "modification or deviation will further the purposes of the trust." Id. By requiring a lower threshold finding for equitable relief, this standard gives courts broader discretion in permitting deviation. * * *

The commentary accompanying the Restatements also provides insight into court's application of equitable deviation. It is important to recognize that the objective of equitable deviation is not to disregard the intention of the settlor, but rather to "give effect to what the settlor's intent probably would have been had the circumstances in question been anticipated." See Restatement (Third) of Trusts § 66 cmt. (deviation may be allowed with regards to the "provisions governing the management or administration of the trust estate." *Id.* at cmt. b). Both versions contemplate deviation from express terms either directing or forbidding the sale of certain properties. See also Restatement (Second) of Trusts § 381 cmts. d, e.

The ALI Principles (§ 460) also liberalize this doctrine.

5. *Deviation or Cy Pres.* In Trustees of Dartmouth College v. City of Quincy, 357 Mass. 521, 258 N.E.2d 745 (1970), the language of a charitable trust created under a testator's will established a school "for the education of females * * * who are native born, born, I wish it to be understood, in the town of Quincy, and none other than these." The school was established, but eventually the funds from the trust were inadequate to cover the operating costs. Because of the requirement that only Quincy girls could matriculate, attendance declined and financial difficulties affected accreditation. The trustees formulated a proposal to allow non-Quincy born girls to attend only to fill unused space, while restricting trust money for girls eligible under the testator's will. The issue was whether the Court had power to approve the variations of the testator's plan or to modify the trust's express language. If not, then a gift over to Dartmouth College, the residuary legatee, would take effect.

Applying the doctrine of deviation, the court allowed the admission of non-Quincy girls. Because the gift had not yet failed entirely or become impossible of execution strictly in accordance with the terms of the will, the court found cy pres inapplicable. The court found that the trustees' proposals were secondary to the general intention of establishing a school. The clause stating that the school was for the education of native-born Quincy females referred only to the use of the testator's gift, was a subordinate detail, and could be disregarded if changed circumstances rendered it obstructive or inappropriate to the accomplishment of the primary charitable purpose. See also Wigglesworth v. Cowles, 38 Mass.App. Ct. 420, 648 N.E.2d 1289 (1995).

PROBLEMS

In the following problems consider whether a court upon application would apply the doctrines of cy pres or deviation.

1. Marianna Ortiz created a charitable trust for the Sturdley Library. The trust instrument requires that the corpus be invested in the bonds of the Amalgamated Widget Corporation. A public market for the bonds no longer exists because Amalgamated Widget merged into another corporation.

2. In 1923 Phillipe Glebov established a trust to provide assistance to White Russian emigrees who fled Bolshevik persecution. The last of these emigrees died in 1993.

3. Wanda Pudnick bequeathed 17 paintings to the Pudnick trust for exhibition in the Crawford Museum. Her will provided, however, that if a satisfactory art gallery was ever to exist in the city of North Caanan, the paintings were to be exhibited there. The Crawford Museum possesses all 17 paintings but exhibits only three of them. The others remain in storage, but are available to scholars for research purposes. No gallery exists in North Caanan. The Pudnick Trust desires to sell the paintings.

4. Same facts as in Problem 3, above, except the Pudnick Trust proposes to sell two of the 14 paintings in storage and use the funds to build a new gallery in North Caanan.

5. Dorothy Mancino executed a trust to distribute a portion of her estate to: "St. Michael's Medical Center, Xenia, Ohio for use among the sick-poor in accordance with the hospital's mission." The money was distributed to the hospital shortly after Dorothy's death in 1990. In 1992 the hospital was sold to an unrelated for-profit health care institution. The trustee sought to award the funds to another hospital in Xenia. The former hospital trustees urge that the money be awarded to a St. Michael's hospital in Bippus, Indiana.

4. DISTRIBUTION OF ASSETS TO PUBLIC BENEFIT CORPORATIONS

When a public benefit—i.e., "charitable"—organization receives a donation of property, does it hold the donated property in trust as a charitable trustee or does it possess full ownership rights? Do the fiduciary requirements applicable to charitable trustees also apply to directors of a charitable corporation? The answers to these questions may affect how the property can be used by the charitable corporation as well as its disposition on dissolution. Scott and Ascher on Trusts states: "The truth is that, in some senses, a charitable corporation is a trustee, and in other senses, it is not. The question in each case is whether a rule that applies to trustees also applies to a charitable corporation" The treatise then concludes rather equivocally:

> Ordinarily, 'the rules' that apply to charitable trusts apply as well to charitable corporations, though some do not. It is probably more misleading to say that a charitable corporation is not a trust than to say that it is, but one must understand that any such statement is subject to various qualifications.

5 Scott & Ascher on Trusts, § 37.1.1. The ambiguity is reflected when a gift containing restrictions or conditions is made to a charitable corporation. The Restatement (Third) of Trusts § 28, cmt. a provides that while an unrestricted gift to a corporate charity does not create a trust, a gift made for a specific purpose does. The ALI's Principles of the Law of Nonprofit Organizations § 400(a), cmt. a, rejects the position that every conditional

or restricted or conditional gift becomes a trust for all purposes. State jurisdictions differ on the issue.

Some nonprofit statutes provide that a charitable corporation holds full ownership rights in donated property and is not deemed a trustee. See N.Y. Not-for-Profit Corp. L. § 513. Where a donor makes an unrestricted gift to a charitable corporation, the corporation may use the donated property for any of its charitable purposes. Alumnae Assn. of Newport Hosp. School of Nursing v. DeSimone, 106 R.I. 196, 258 A.2d 80 (1969); Y.M.C.A. v. Morgan, 281 N.C. 485, 189 S.E.2d 169 (1972).

California cases support the proposition that a corporation organized exclusively for charitable purposes holds its assets in trust for the purposes enumerated in its articles of incorporation even if the assets were not expressly earmarked for charitable trust purposes when the corporation acquired them. Lynch v. Spilman, 67 Cal.2d 251, 263, 62 Cal.Rptr. 12, 20, 431 P.2d 636, 644 (1967). But there is an ambiguity in this position. When a bequest, devise, or donation is made to a public benefit corporation, the organization holds that property with an absolute interest but is expected to apply it to the charitable purposes in its articles of incorporation. Queen of Angels Hospital v. Younger, 66 Cal.App.3d 359, 368, 136 Cal.Rptr. 36, 41 (1977). Thereafter, if the organization decides to dissolve, the remaining assets are held in trust so that they are sure to be conveyed to another public benefit corporation.

However, when property is given to a charitable corporation for specific purposes or with restrictions or conditions are placed upon its use, the weight of authority holds that it can only be used for that particular purpose. For example, in St. Joseph's Hospital v. Bennett, 281 N.Y. 115, 22 N.E.2d 305 (1939), the testator devised an endowment fund, the income of which was used for the ordinary maintenance expenses of a hospital. The hospital brought an action seeking to apply the fund in partial payment of a $175,000 mortgage debt or in its judgment to use the principal for purposes within its corporate powers other than ordinary maintenance. The attorney general opposed on the ground that the bequest was a gift in trust. Finding that the bequest did not create a trust but an absolute gift, the lower courts held that the hospital need not maintain the gift. The Court of Appeals reversed. It found that technically no trust arose from a gift to a charitable corporation with express directions to apply the gift in a specific manner to corporate purposes, and it conceded that a nonprofit corporation is not bound by all the rules and limitations applicable to charitable trustees. The majority nonetheless held, over two dissents, that a charitable corporation may not receive a gift for one purpose and use it for another unless the alternative use was authorized by a court applying the cy pres doctrine.

While the doctrines of cy pres and deviation are remedies used with charitable trusts, the cy pres power also applies to absolute gifts to charitable corporations. As illustrated by the *Multiple Sclerosis* case below, the standard governing distribution of assets of a dissolving corporation is less strict than the cy pres doctrine of charitable trust law.

Matter of Multiple Sclerosis Service Organization of New York, Inc.

New York Court of Appeals, 1986.
68 N.Y.2d 32, 496 N.E.2d 861, 505 N.Y.S.2d 841.

■ MEYER, JUDGE:

[The Multiple Sclerosis Service Organization (MSSO) was formed in 1965 by a group of volunteers affiliated with a local chapter of the National Multiple Sclerosis Society who withdrew from the local chapter to focus primarily upon rehabilitation—helping MS sufferers to function in society to their maximum potential—while the national society focused primarily upon research. For seventeen years MSSO operated a recreational center for those with multiple sclerosis and provided transportation, specialized equipment, and furnished counseling services relating to their condition. Dwindling finances and the advancing age of its members resulted in the determination that MSSO could no longer continue its activities. The board of directors resolved to sell its principal asset, the service center; pay its debts; and select recognized charities to receive any remaining assets. The sale of the service center was approved by a supreme court justice. A committee was then appointed to find distributees engaged in substantially similar activities. Four organizations were selected, primarily because of their emphasis upon on-site care and service to clients suffering from irreversible and chronic medical conditions requiring extensive long-term treatment, albeit not multiple sclerosis. After the board adopted a resolution providing for distribution to the four organizations, a petition seeking supreme court approval of the proposed distribution was filed and notice was given as required by the New York Not-for-Profit Corporation Law to the attorney general. The New York City chapter of the National Multiple Sclerosis Society sought leave to intervene, asserting that its activities were "more akin" to those of MSSO than the four distributees selected, and that the proposed distribution would be an improper diversion if distributed to other than MS-oriented charities. The Special Term found that the distributees were engaged in activities substantially similar to those of MSSO "in that each rendered services to permanently disabled people which enabled them to function to their potential" and approved the proposed distribution. The Appellate Division unanimously reversed. The Court of Appeals reversed the Appellate Division and remitted to the Supreme Court for a hearing. Eds.]

* * *

The question before us is not whether principles of a cy pres nature apply to the distribution of the assets of a dissolving charitable corporation but what the governing principle is. There is no question that the common-law cy pres standard was "as near as possible," that being the literal translation of the Anglo–French from which the words were taken (Bogert, Trusts and Trustees 431, at 490 [2d ed. rev.]; 4 Scott, Trusts 399, at 3084 [3d ed.]). * * *

A

* * *

Apparent from [the N.Y. Not-for-Profit Corporation Law] provisions is the Legislature's intention to require that assets given to a charitable corporation for a particular purpose be used by the corporation while it is in existence for the purpose specified by the donor, unless the restriction is released by the donor or by a court (NPCL § 522) or, circumstances having so changed as to make impracticable or impossible the literal carrying out of the purpose, a court (with the consent of the donor if living) permits otherwise (EPTL § 8–1.1[c]). But it is also apparent, for the reasons hereafter set forth, that the Legislature did not intend the stringent "as near as possible" standard of the common law to govern distribution of assets of a dissolving charitable corporation received other than through a will or other limiting instrument, but rather provided for distribution to corporations or organizations engaged in substantially similar activities and left it to the board of directors in the first instance to determine to whom distribution should be made.

B

The common-law cy pres doctrine, or "ancient doctrine of approximation" as it has been termed, embodies the English concept that when a donor parts with his property for a charitable purpose it shall be forever devoted to that purpose, whether or not the particular donee continues to exist. If the donee ceases to exist, the property may be devoted to a kindred charity; one that is, "as near as may be" to the charity contemplated by the donor (see also, Matter of Goehringer, 69 Misc.2d 145, 146–147, 329 N.Y.S.2d 516; Restatement [Second] of Trusts § 399 comment a, at 297–298). The purpose of the doctrine was to prevent the failure of a charitable trust. * * *

[The court then discussed the development of the cy pres doctrine in New York. Eds.]

* * *

It is, thus, apparent that for more than half a century the criterion governing distribution or dissolution has been not that the particular purpose of the donor be carried out "as near as possible," but that the general purpose of the donor, or for which the corporation was organized or the fund collected be "most effectively [or best] accomplish[ed] * * * free from any express or implied restriction" and that the same standard has governed distribution of both the unexpended funds received for a charitable purpose by a membership corporation about to be dissolved, and the unexpended funds raised by a voluntary association through public subscription for a charitable purpose which has been accomplished.

C

The most immediately noticeable difference between N–PCL § 1005(a)(3)(A) and the statutes we have so far considered is the changed standard governing distribution. The revision from "best accomplish the general purposes" to "engaged in activities substantially similar to those of the dissolved corporation" is not discussed in the legislative history of the N–PCL, but in light of the almost uniform standard of the various statutes discussed above and the provision of the Membership Corporations Law that distribution was to be "free from any express or implied restriction" imposed on the dissolving corporation, it is apparent that the "codification of the 'cy-pres' doctrine" to which the Joint Legislative Committee Memorandum referred was to the doctrine as spelled out in the Membership Corporations Law (and other statutes referred to above) rather than to the common law "as near as possible" principle. But beyond that the change to "substantially similar activities" from "best accomplishes" or "most effectively accomplishes" cannot be ignored, for, as the words are commonly understood, "substantially similar" is broader in scope and less limiting than "most effectively accomplishes" (cf. Matter of Falk, 110 Misc.2d 104, 110, 441 N.Y.S.2d 785).

Of importance also is the fact that whereas the common-law rule was phrased in terms of the original purpose of the testator, grantor or donor (Bogert, op. cit. § 431, at 490; Restatement [Second] of Trusts § 399 comment b; 4 Scott, Trusts, op. cit. § 399, at 3084), as were all of the statutes referred to above, it is not the "purposes" but the "activities" of the dissolving corporation which under N–PCL § 1005(a)(3)(A) governs the choice of recipient charities. Of course, that does not mean that a charitable corporation is not limited by the statement of purposes set forth in its charter (Alco Gravure, Inc. v. Knapp Found., 64 N.Y.2d 458, 490 N.Y.S.2d 116, 479 N.E.2d 752); rather it means that to the extent that its activities have been more limited than the statement in its charter, the latter rather than the former must be taken into consideration in determining whether a proposed distributee meets the statutory test.

Nor does respondents' argument that the Joint Legislative Committee's statement that section 1005 "makes very important innovations with respect to the distribution of corporate assets upon dissolution by adopting a 'cy-pres' provision to regulate the distribution" establish the Legislature's intent to adopt the common-law standard. As noted above, that standard in modified form had been applicable to membership corporations engaged in charitable pursuits as well as to voluntary associations since 1948 or earlier. Thus the innovation was not that for the first time cy pres became applicable but that the standard to be applied to property other than particular purpose assets of a type B not-for-profit corporation was whether the recipient charities were "engaged in activities substantially similar" rather than the modified common-law standard—"best accomplish the general purposes."

It follows that, as was held in Matter of Goehringer, 69 Misc.2d, at pp. 146–147, 329 N.Y.S.2d 516, supra, statutes under which the assets of charitable corporations are distributed upon dissolution, such as NPCL § 1005(a)(3)(A) and Education Law § 220, are not quite like cy pres statutes such as EPTL 8–1.1 in that "[i]n ordering distribution under the dissolution statutes, the Supreme Court is not concerned with the directions or intentions of the creator or testator but only that the funds be transferred to a charitable recipient having similar purposes to the dissolved charitable corporation." Although a cy pres concept is involved, it is not the strict standard of the common law that applies to distribution of the assets of a corporation being dissolved under the NPCL, but a "quasi cy pres" standard. * * *

III

* * *

[W]e note the further substantial change made by the N–PCL in according the board of the dissolving charitable corporation a substantial role in the selection of the corporations or organizations to which distribution is to be made. At common law, framing the scheme for application or distribution of the property was a matter for the court, which could apply cy pres and frame a scheme to which the trustees did not consent, although the court would usually give weight to the wishes of the trustees (Restatement [Second] of Trusts § 399 comment f). And under Personal Property Law § 12 and Real Property Law § 113, that was true not only where a trust existed but also as to property held by a charitable corporation. "Over such gifts it [the court] is given general control and while it is said the court may make such an order 'on the application of the trustee or the person or corporation having the custody of the property' the language should not be construed as limiting the power of the court to act only when application is so made. It may act on information by the state. It may act on its own motion." But, as already noted, under N–PCL § 1005(a)(3)(A), it is the board of directors which adopts the plan of distribution pursuant to which the successor corporation or organization will receive the property and the plan is not submitted to the court for approval until after it has been submitted to and approved by the members entitled to vote.

The approval of the court is not under the statute to be perfunctory, but in enacting N–PCL article 10, the Legislature "substantially revise[d] the existing law governing membership corporations" * * * "require[d] a board resolution recommending the plan" * * * and that "the plan of distribution * * * be approved by a justice of the supreme court." It intended also that not-for-profit corporations have "a strong board of directors". * * * Although a court, asked to approve a plan of distribution, acts in a discretionary capacity, so likewise does the board in carrying out its more formal role in devising a plan which the NPCL has given it. Therefore, its choice of acquiring organizations and corporations should not be lightly set aside.

* * *

A further factor to be considered in assessing the propriety of the plan is how the funds, of which the moneys now in the hands of the board are the residue, were acquired. [T]here is no record evidence of any "particular purpose" gifts by will or other instrument.[5] There are in the record letters and petitions addressed to the Attorney General or the New York City Chapter stating the signers' belief that distribution should be to the chapter, but nothing to establish that any limitation other than the MSSO charter applied to their gifts when made. Was a public solicitation made and, if so, what was said about use of the funds by MSSO or by the donor? (Cf. NPCL § 102[a][14].) Absent an express or implied representation by MSSO, no "particular purpose" is established, and it will be assumed that contributions made voluntarily and without restriction are general gifts for use by the charitable corporation for any of its general corporate purposes. A "particular purpose" may also be established by the donor but it will usually be the case that, as noted in Loch v. Mayer, 50 Misc. 442, 448, 100 N.Y.S. 837, dealing with a disaster relief fund solicited by a church, "[f]ew donations were accompanied with writings of any kind, and no such writing, so far as the evidence shows, states with any attempt at precision the terms of the trust." As to any contribution found to have been made for a restricted purpose, it will also be of importance whether it has been fully expended.

Relevant also, as already noted, will be the activities of the corporation in fact carried out under its charter, and to a lesser extent the corporate purposes stated in the charter. Specifically, in terms of the present case has the emphasis of MSSO as shown by its creation and its activities been on the disease or on service? Both are specifically mentioned in its name and both are referred to in the statement of its purposes contained in its amended certificate of incorporation.

For the foregoing reasons, the judgment appealed from and the order of the Appellate Division brought up for review should be reversed, with costs to appellants, and the matter remitted to Supreme Court, Kings County, for further proceedings in accordance with this opinion.

■ WACHTLER, C.J., and SIMONS, KAYE, ALEXANDER and HANCOCK, JJ., concur.

■ TITONE, J., taking no part.

NOTES AND QUESTIONS

1. *Extent of Divergence from Original Purposes.* How far can a court diverge from an organization's original purposes in the distribution of a charitable corporation's assets? The corporate statutes are not helpful. See 805 Ill. Comp. Stat. 105/112.16 (assets shall be transferred or conveyed to

---

5.   Assets legally required to be used for a particular purpose are those received pursuant to a will or other instrument limiting the purpose for which the assets may be used. N–PCL § 513 provides that although a type B corporation holds full ownership rights in property received in trust for, or with direction to apply the same to, a purpose specified in its certificate of incorporation, it "shall not be deemed" a trustee of an express trust of such assets (§ 513[a]) but is required to "apply all assets thus received to the purposes specified in the gift instrument" (§ 513[b]) except as permitted by EPTL article 8 or N–PCL § 522. The record does not indicate that MSSO holds any "particular purpose" assets. [This footnote has been moved from its original placement. Eds.]

one or more domestic or foreign corporations, societies or organizations engaged in activities "substantially similar to those of the dissolving corporation.") The standard seems even less stringent in California. See Cal. Rev. & Tax Code § 214(a)(6). ("upon liquidation, dissolution, or abandonment of the owner [of property] will not [accrue] to the benefit of any private person except a fund, foundation or corporation organized for religious, hospital, scientific or charitable purposes".) Suppose a nonprofit health maintenance organization providing family care converts to for-profit status and creates a charitable foundation to receive the assets from the sale. Could it use the funds to create endowed chairs in health studies at three universities, two of which are out of state? Should it be required to serve general purposes similar to those served by the HMO-provision of health care at affordable costs? If your answer is yes, would the donation of assets to another nonprofit HMO lead to charges by for-profit health care providers of unfair competition? See Michelle Meldin & Jane Perkins, HMO Conversions: How to Distribute the Charitable Assets, 21 Clearinghouse Rev. 467, 468 (1968).

2. *Property Given for a Specific Purpose and the Corporation Dissolves or Changes Its Purposes.* If property is given for a particular charitable purpose and the corporation dissolves or changes its purposes, the particularized gift or bequest will not automatically pass to a successor corporation. The more restrictive common law cy pres or deviation doctrines will apply and the property will pass to a charitable corporation that meets those stricter standards. Daloia v. Franciscan Health System, 79 Ohio St.3d 98, 679 N.E.2d 1084 (1997); Matter of Goehringer, 69 Misc.2d 145, 147–148, 329 N.Y.S.2d 516 (1972). In Attorney General v. Hahnemann Hosp., 397 Mass. 820, 494 N.E.2d 1011 (1986), the board of trustees of a nonprofit hospital expanded the hospital's purposes in its articles of incorporation to include participation in any activity that promoted the health of the general public. A trust had contributed funds to the hospital for more narrow purposes than those provided in the restated articles. The board voted to sell all of the hospital's assets. The court forbade the hospital from applying the previously donated restricted funds to its newly amended purposes but not those given free of restrictions. It commented: "those who give to a home for animals do not anticipate a future board amending the charity's purpose to become research vivisectionists." *Id.* at 836 n. 18. If the donor manifests an intention that property revert upon dissolution, courts will so order.

3. *Quasi–Cy Pres or Deviation?* In Matter of Othmer, 185 Misc.2d 122, 710 N.Y.S.2d 848 (Surr. Ct. 2000) the court purportedly applied cy pres to allow a hospital to use enough principal of an income-only fund as security for a new multi-billion dollar debt in order to carry out a strategic plan for capital projects and additional working capital, noting significant developments in the health care industry and that operating or financial failure of the hospital would frustrate donors' charitable objectives. Didn't the court apply the doctrine of deviation?

4. *Dissolution of Local Chapters of National Organizations.* What if MSSO originally had been a chapter of the National Multiple Sclerosis

organization and later withdrew from it? Could its property be retained by the organization or would it vest in the parent? The answer depends upon the extent of dependence by the local organization on the parent, not whether it is an integral part of the parent. 6 Scott & Ascher on Trusts § 39.3.3. See New Jersey Ass'n for Children with Learning Disabilities v. Burlington County Ass'n for Children with Learning Disabilities, 163 N.J.Super. 199, 394 A.2d 406 (Super. Ch. 1978) (local charitable organization which is integral part of larger state or national organization may not secede from state or national organization and take organizational property with it); Phillips v. Perrin, 253 Or. 540, 450 P.2d 767 (1969) (local union which seceded from old international union did not have the right to take assets with it in the face of specific constitutional provisions of international union to the contrary); National Grange v. O'Sullivan Grange, 35 Wash.App. 444, 667 P.2d 1105 (1983) (local chapter had no authority to convey property without consent of executive of state chapter; provision in bylaw that gave national organization reversionary interest in property was not unreasonable).

5. *Disputes over Church Property.* Disputes over church assets often occur when a local church withdraws from a parent body. Where churches have a congregational government, the property belongs to the local church, which can dispose of it as it sees fit upon dissolution. In Metropolitan Baptist Church of Richmond v. Younger, 48 Cal.App.3d 850, 121 Cal.Rptr. 899 (1975), the members of the congregation voted to dissolve the church corporation and to liquidate and distribute its assets to local churches, a theological seminary, a serviceman's center, and to a Baptist Church in another state. The church's articles of incorporation recited that its purpose was the founding and conducting of a Baptist Church in Richmond, Contra Costa County, California. Other evidence indicated the founders' purposes to preach and teach the Scriptures in that county in essential accord with the beliefs of fundamental Baptist Churches. There were no other churches in the county. The court held that the church's assets would not be distributed as recommended by the membership but in accordance with the church's purposes in the articles of incorporation. The court applied the cy pres doctrine to direct the assets to be divided wholly between two Baptist Churches in neighboring counties because they would most closely carry out the original purposes for which the church was created and were geographically near the City of Richmond. The church argued that its proposed distribution of property was an ecclesiastical decision. Why didn't the First Amendment prohibit the court from interceding? See Chapter 10F2, infra.

E. CONVERSION FROM A NONPROFIT ORGANIZATION TO A FOR-PROFIT ENTITY

Model Nonprofit Corp. Act (3d ed.) §§ 9.01–9.03, 9.30–9.31, 9.33.

A nonprofit organization usually dissolves and distributes its assets in an atmosphere of difficulty caused by financial or other problems. In this section we examine another scenario: the organization has such economic potential that investors wish to operate the activity as a profit-seeking venture, distributing its earnings to the owners. From an economic perspective, market failure no longer exists, and the particular industry may not need the benefits of tax exemption. This type of transformation has occurred most frequently in the health care industry, with nonprofit health maintenance organizations, hospitals, and Blue Cross insurance plans. It could conceivably occur with any nonprofit whose assets or activities present greater value as a profit-seeking entity. As a for-profit, the organization will be better equipped to raise needed capital through the sale of securities.

HMO Conversions. Health maintenance organizations (HMOs) offer comprehensive primary health care through physicians who are employees or partners or through arrangements with groups of physicians on a cost efficient basis to subscriber members on a prepaid fee contract.[1] Though prepaid medical services have existed since the 18th century, in the second half of the 20th century their use widened because HMOs were seen as devices to hold down the ever-increasing cost of medical care. Physicians originally founded HMOs, but they came to be controlled and managed by professional managers. Because of the availability of federal assistance, nonprofit HMOs dominated the industry. Through the Health Maintenance Act of 1973, 42 U.S.C.A. §§ 300e–300e–14, the federal government served as a venture capitalist to the industry, providing loans and financing guarantees for nonprofit HMOs. In 1983 the federal loan programs ceased, and HMOs with growing capital needs began to convert to for-profit status. Conversions provided access to capital through the public sale of securities. Most HMOs are now profit-seeking entities, compared to fewer than 20 percent in 1981.[2]

Hospital Conversions. In the mid 1990s, conversions of nonprofit hospitals to for-profit status dramatically increased as investor-owned hospital chains such as Columbia/HCA continued consolidation of the hospital industry by targeting nonprofit hospitals.[3] The impetus for hospital mergers and conversion of hospitals was for economic synergies and easier access to capital.[4] Other factors created enormous temptations for local hospitals to convert. Too many hospital beds for too few patients engendered competition between hospitals. Increasing capital requirements

---

1. See Mich. Comp. Laws § 333.21005; N.Y. Pub. Health § 4401(1).

2. Douglas M. Mancino & Robert C. Louthian, Taxation of Hospitals & Health Care Organizations § 21.01 (rev. ed. 2009).

3. In 1995, Columbia acquired 33 formerly tax-exempt hospitals. In 1996, 17 of its 28 acquisitions or joint ventures involved tax-exempt hospitals with an additional 14 acquisitions pending. Bruce Japsen, Another Record Year for Dealmaking: Activity Among Medium–Size Companies—Fuels Continued Drive Toward Consolidation, Mod. Healthcare, Dec. 23, 1996, at 37. In 1995, 48 nonprofit hospitals had converted or planned to convert to for-profit status, but this trend slowed in 1996 as only 63 hospitals accounting for 8 percent of the hospitals that merged converted to for-profit status. Demise of the Not-for-Profit Has Been Greatly Exaggerated, Mod. Healthcare, Dec. 23, 1996, at p. 35.

4. Mancino & Louthian, supra note 2.

for new equipment to attract patient business placed many nonprofit hospitals at a competitive disadvantage. For-profit chains using economies of scale and instituting administrative efficiencies were able to provide services for less than their nonprofit counterparts. Many community hospital boards faced with a perilous financial situation were induced by what seemed to be huge sums to sell their hospitals to for-profit hospital chains too quickly, at too low a value and with little community input. After 2000, conversions declined substantially.

Blue Cross Conversions. Hospitals established nonprofit Blue Cross plans in the 1930s to ensure that patients would have the means to pay for care. For years, the "Blues" enjoyed regulatory and tax exemptions because of their social mission. Competitive pressures caused by the growth of managed care plans drastically increased capital needs and the loss of tax exemption[5] led to waves of mergers and attempted conversions to for-profit status.[6]

The primary issue in Blue Cross conversions has been how much money do Blues, which received benefits from tax exemption when they operated as nonprofits, owe to their communities and what are these assets worth? Should the charitable assets in these conversions be valued at the current value of the benefit of the state tax exemption or the total value of the assets converted? The results are mixed.[7]

Structuring the Conversion Transaction. Several approaches have been used to structure conversion transactions. They include a conversion in place, a sale of assets, a merger into a for-profit, and a drop-down conversion.

In a conversion in place, the board recommends an amendment to the corporation's articles of incorporation that removes its nonprofit aspects and adds for-profit powers. The newly converted for-profit corporation is empowered to issue stock, to conduct all lawful business and to pay dividends. The legal entity remains in existence. The "XYZ charitable corporation" merely becomes the "XYZ business corporation." Existing contractual relationships remain. The conversion in place, which is permitted only in a few jurisdictions, such as Arizona and California, is favored by HMOs.

In an asset sale, the nonprofit sells its operating assets to a for-profit corporation for fair market value. Unlike a conversion in place, an asset sale will require the for-profit to obtain appropriate state licenses. After the

---

5. Blue Cross lost its federal tax exemption in 1986. I.R.C. § 501(m).

6. Louise Kertesz, Not Your Father's Blue Cross, Mod. Healthcare, October 14, 1996, at 14. Liz Runge, "The Blues are Learning Some New Tunes," 97 Best's Rev. Life–Health Insur. ed. 60 (Mar. 1997), available in LEXIS, News Library, BRLIFE file.

7. In Georgia and Missouri, courts concluded Blues had no charitable obligation or transfer of assets required as they were not organized for charitable purposes. In other jurisdictions there have been difficult negotiations over price. In New York, the charitable assets of Empire Blue Cross were used by the state to give raises to hospital workers, with very little going into a private foundation. New York's approach was upheld in Consumers Union v. State of New York, 5 N.Y.3d 327, 806 N.Y.S.2d 99, 840 N.E.2d 68 (2005).

sale, the for-profit corporation owns the business assets formerly owned by the charitable corporation, which may receive stock, notes, or other property in addition to cash as consideration. This is a typical transaction structure for the purchase of a nonprofit hospital by a for-profit acquirer. Federal and state laws require that the proceeds of sale continue to be held in the charitable stream and used for charitable purposes.[8] Foundations are usually the post-conversion holder of these charitable assets.

In a merger, the charity typically forms a new for-profit corporation to which it contributes its assets in exchange for cash, notes, and stock. The nonprofit corporation then merges into the for-profit corporation. Merger of a nonprofit into a business corporation is permitted in a few states. A foundation or nonprofit corporation is created to receive the stock of the surviving corporation or cash. After the conversion, there are ordinarily two organizations: the for-profit corporation and a private foundation.

The drop-down conversion involves the transfer of some or all of the operating assets and liabilities of a hospital, HMO or Blue Cross to a wholly or partially owned subsidiary in exchange for stock and/or notes. This approach was used by Blue Cross of California when it transferred a substantial percentage of its assets to Wellpoint Healthcare, a wholly owned for-profit subsidiary. After the transaction is completed, the for-profit subsidiary may go into the equity markets with an initial public offering. In a drop-down conversion, the original owner of assets usually retains a substantial percentage of equity in the newly formed corporation. After the conversion, there may be three organizations. In addition to the for-profit corporation and a § 501(c)(3) private foundation, a § 501(c)(4) organization may be created to receive and hold the stock for later sale. The § 501(c)(4) organization remits the proceeds of stock sales to the foundation.[9]

Abuses. For many years conversions proceeded stealth-like under the radar of state and federal regulators. Serious breaches of fiduciary responsibility often occurred. For example, the Family Health Program (FHP), founded as a nonprofit in 1961 and led by Dr. Robert Gumbiner offered prepaid medical and dental care through a network of 22 company operated clinics in Southern California, Utah, and Guam as well as contractual arrangements with physicians in Arizona and New Mexico. When FHP first applied for conversion to for-profit status in February, 1985, it valued its assets at approximately $13.5 million. Gumbiner and seventeen other investors founded HMO Health Group, Inc. as the for-profit purchaser of FHP's assets. Gumbiner owned 50.5 percent of HMO Health Group. The Department of Corporations rejected the $13.5 million figure and proposed $47 million as the fair market value. The Department and FHP then negotiated a $38.5 million price which included $7.2 million in cash, and the rest paid over ten years. Eight months after the conversion, HMO

---

8.   Treas. Reg. § 1.501(c)(3)–1(b)(4).

9.   See Mancino & Louthian, supra note 2, ch. 21; Thomas Silk, Conversions of Tax Exempt Nonprofit Organizations: Federal Tax Law and State Charitable Law Issues, 13 Exempt Org. Tax Rev. 745 (1996).

Health Group made a public offering of stock with a market value of $150 million dollars. Approximately $25.3 million went to HMO Health Group and just under $10.6 million went to the FHP Foundation, established as part of the conversion. The former managers, including Dr. Gumbiner continued to hold a 75.9 percent stake in the for-profit company worth $114 million.

Particularly criticized were golden parachutes (lucrative severance agreements) and rich employment contracts for nonprofit executives and trustees handling the conversion. For example, when Columbia/HCA attempted to purchase Blue Cross of Ohio, the initial agreement provided that four Blues executives including outside counsel were to receive $19 million in consulting and non-compete fees as part of the transaction and $3 million was to be paid to seven former trustees. The Ohio Department of Insurance rejected the transaction.

Reactions Against Conversions. Increased publicity of conversion transactions, which highlighted the inadequacy of state conversion procedures, encouraged many jurisdictions, including Arizona, California, Colorado, Georgia, Nebraska, Ohio, and Washington, to enact legislation that brought greater state oversight, required public hearings, mandated fair market valuation, and enhanced the authority of the attorney general.[10]

The New Foundations. When a nonprofit sells its assets or converts to a for-profit entity, the sales proceeds must remain in the charitable stream. There have been several approaches to handling the consideration generated by conversion transactions: creation or affiliation with a public charity; distribution of assets to other tax-exempt charities; deposit of the resulting assets in the state treasury; and the most common, creation of a new private foundation.

Since 1990, 197 foundations have been formed through conversions. More than 75 percent were created in the 1990–1999 period. Some of the new foundations are immense, as the two foundations created from the conversion of California Blue Cross demonstrate. Based on the latest data available at the end of 2008, the California Healthcare Foundation has assets of $913 million, and the California Endowment has assets of $4.65 billion. The California Wellness Foundation, formed in 1992 from conversion of Health Net, an HMO, has assets of $723 million (down from $1.3 billion the previous year!). The Rose Foundation in Denver, formed in the

---

10. California's statute requires the conversion price to be at fair market value, the assets resulting from the conversion to be held by an independent foundation, and the converting organization to have in place policies prohibiting conflicts of interest. See Cal. Health & Safety Code §§ 1399.70; Vincenzo Stampone, Note, Nonprofit Hospital Conversions Spur Legislation, 22 Seton Hall Legis. J. 627 (1998). Nebraska's Nonprofit Hospital Sale Act requires the attorney general to consider whether the hospital exercised due diligence in deciding to sell, selecting a purchaser, and negotiating the terms and conditions of sale; whether conflicts of interest were disclosed and expert assistance was used; whether the seller will receive fair value and the sale proceeds will be used for appropriate charitable health care purposes. For a criticism of increased attorney general activism see, Thomas L. Greaney & Kathleen M. Boozang, Mission, Margin, and Trust in the Nonprofit Health Care Enterprise, 5 Yale J. Health 1 (2005).

aftermath of the sale of Rose Hospital, has assets of over $200 million. At the end of 2004 organizations created from conversions held $18 billion in assets.[11]

The foundation solution to the charitable assets resulting from conversion has not been trouble-free. The formation of the foundation comes well after conversion has been finalized, almost as an afterthought. The community and public are not involved.

Do the new foundations have continuing responsibilities for health care? Or can they broaden their mission? Under traditional cy pres analysis, if there was a hospital conversion, the assets would have to be used for the delivery of primary health care as provided by a hospital, e.g., health care for poor.[12] Some foundations moved far away from the illness side, i.e., direct medical care.[13]

Instead of creating a foundation, Professor John Colombo has proposed an exit tax on nonprofit conversion transactions which, he believes, will enhance regulatory interest in conversion transactions, provide greater flexibility in addressing community needs than traditional cy pres doctrine, and offer a structured framework for governmental economic interests in conversion transactions.[14] How would you set the level of taxation? Could participants evade the tax by structuring the transaction as a joint venture? Will an exit tax have an adverse effect on the market for conversion transactions? Finally, is placing assets that were in the charitable stream into the maw of the state treasury likely to remove them from the charitable stream completely?

Reform Proposals. The Senate Finance Committee staff, in its 2004 Discussion Draft proposing charitable reform legislation, and the Joint Committee on Taxation, in its 2005 report on revenue-raising options, both proposed that the IRS conduct pre-transaction review of contemplated conversions to ensure they were in the public interest. Under the Joint Committee proposal, the IRS would have the opportunity to participate in state conversion proceedings and no conversion could be completed unless the IRS approved or failed to disapprove within one year of seeking approval. The proposal also would impose a transaction tax on conversions

---

11. Grantmakers in Health, A Profile of Foundations Created from Health Care Conversions 1 (2009); Grantmakers in Health, The Business of Giving: Governance and Asset Management, in Foundations Formed from Health-care Conversions (2005), available at http://www.gih.org. Forty-six percent of these organizations are private foundations, 50 percent are public charities, and 4 percent social welfare organizations. Id.

12. Attorney Gen. v. Hahnemann Hospital, 397 Mass. 820, 830–833, 494 N.E.2d 1011, 1018–1020 (1986).

13. In Los Gatos, California, 20 percent of Valley Foundation's $2 million in grants went to the arts. The Jackson Foundation, born of the sale of Regional Medical Center in Dickson, Tennessee, considered financing a sports-training complex, an arts center, and a foreign language program. It provided two airplanes and made pilot training a free elective at the local high school. Tamar Lewin & Martin Gottlieb, In Hospital Sales, An Overlooked Side Effect, N.Y. Times, Apr. 27, 1997, at 1.

14. A Proposal for an Exit Tax on Nonprofit Conversion Transactions, 23 J. Corp. L. 779, 794 (1998).

and liquidations of charities equal to the excess of the value of the terminating charity's net assets over the value of net assets that remain dedicated to charitable purposes after the transaction. It would expand the § 4958 intermediate sanctions rules to patrol against inflated valuations and compensation that benefit the acquirer and its officers and directors. See Senate Finance Comm. Staff Discussion Draft, June 12, 2004, at 6–7; Joint Committee on Taxation, Options to Improve Tax Compliance and Reform Tax Expenditures (JCX–02–05), Jan. 27, 2005, at 230–246.

In its 2006 Supplemental Report, the Panel on the Nonprofit Sector opposed any expanded IRS role, believing that state charity officials were in the best position to evaluate the impact of a conversion on a local community and to perform pre-transaction reviews more quickly. The Panel recommended that all states should have review procedures in place and urged the development of a model nonprofit conversion act.[15]

What are the best ways to deal with these problems? Should it be through increased state scrutiny of nonprofit dissolutions, or should the Internal Revenue Service patrol the abuses by enforcing the prohibitions against inurement of private gain and private benefit? If the latter, are questions of federalism raised? Some of these issues are discussed in Chapter 5D, infra, at pp. 445–461.

F.   OTHER NONPROFIT RESTRUCTURING

1. *Corporate Reorganizations.* Nonprofit hospitals have come under increasing financial pressures because of changes in medical care financing and delivery of services, increased competition, and rigorous cost control efforts. Many have responded by reorganizing their corporate structures in an attempt to gain operational flexibility in the face of increased regulation; implement innovative approaches and improving balance sheets; attracting doctors and patients; and delivering better health care more efficiently. Melvin Horowitz, Corporate Reorganization: The Last Gasp or Last Clear Chance for the Tax–Exempt, Nonprofit Hospital?, 13 Am. J. L. & Med. 527, 543 (1988). The most common form of restructuring is a parent-subsidiary holding company model whereby a parent company is organized under the nonprofit statute of the state of incorporation. The nonprofit hospital becomes a subsidiary or subdivision of the parent. The parent holding company may have several nonprofit and profit-seeking subsidiary organizations in addition to the hospital including home health agencies, long term care facilities, renal dialysis centers, imaging equipment leasing, real estate development and management, data processing, computer programming and billing for health providers, commercial cleaning, catering, day care centers and motels for ambulatory surgical or convalescing patients. See Dana Brakman Reiser, Decision-makers Without Duties: Defining the Duties of Parent Corporations Acting as Sole Corporate Members in

---

15. Supplemental Report 18–20 (2006), available at http://www.nonprofitpanel.org/supplement.

Nonprofit Healthcare Systems, 53 Rutgers L.Rev. 979 (2001). The reorganization process includes a private letter ruling from the Internal Revenue Service to assure continuation of nonprofit status. The holding company then controls the hospital-subsidiary's board.

2. *Whole Hospital Joint Ventures.* As resistance grew to nonprofit hospital conversions, investor-owned chains resorted to a consolation prize by entering into joint ventures with nonprofit hospitals. Under a common structure, a joint venture entity (usually a limited liability company) is created to which the nonprofit hospital transfers ownership of one or more hospitals, which is usually the nonprofit's principal operating asset. The joint venture then contracts with a for-profit chain to manage the hospital. The for-profit often contributes one of its hospitals or other assets to the joint venture. If the nonprofit's contribution of assets is valued more highly than the for-profit's, the latter may make a cash contribution to the nonprofit so that each party's investment is the same. Part of the cash received will be used to redeem existing debt. The joint venture agreement typically provides that any distribution of earnings will be proportional to equity interests and that the nonprofit and for-profit partners will be equally represented on the venture's governing board.[1] After entering into the agreement, the nonprofit no longer is directly engaged in the delivery of health care services and usually becomes a grantmaking foundation. These transactions are attractive to community hospitals faced with market pressures resulting from industry-wide consolidation.

The arguments in favor of hospital joint ventures are that they afford survival advantages to community hospitals through integration in a growing network. By giving the for-profit company day-to-day control over the formerly nonprofit hospital, the joint venture allows for full integration into the economies of scale of the network. Representation on the joint venture board, combined with community benefit mandates in the joint venture agreement, assure that community benefit considerations remain central to the hospital's operations.[2] Additionally, the nonprofit receives from the for-profit partner a substantial cash payment that can be used for fund grantmaking or direct charitable activities. The hospital now owned by the for-profit joint venture is back on the tax rolls increasing local tax revenues.

The benefits to the for-profit partner include practical operating control of the nonprofit's assets purchased at from 50–80 percent of the full appraised value; economies of scale; operating synergies; and increased market share.[3] The for-profit also will cause the joint venture entity to contract with it for a variety of services that will yield substantial fees.

---

1.   See, e.g., Robert A. Boisture & Albert G. Lauber, Jr., Comment Letter to IRS on Whole Hospital Joint Ventures, 16 Exempt Org. Tax Rev. 650, 652–653 (1997).

2.   Cain Brothers, Focus on Joint Venture Arrangements, 12 Strategies in Capital Finance 2 (Spring 1995).

3.   Boisture & Lauder, supra note 1, at 653.

Critics of whole hospital joint ventures point to the attenuated control over the hospital's operations (the nonprofit's control often is reduced to veto power rather than a proactive authority); a diminution in responsiveness and loyalty to the nonprofit board representatives as the profit imperative moves to the fore; a diminution in the hospital's charitable and community focus; the subordinate role of nonprofit representatives to the joint venture's board; concerns over whether the nonprofit receives fair market value for its assets because of the "confidentiality" and "no shop" provisions that surround negotiations; threats to the nonprofit's exempt status because the assets contributed to the joint venture may be used for private rather than community benefit; and the fact that economic benefits derived by the for-profit partner are far more than incidental in relation to the community benefits.

Joint ventures raise significant federal tax issues, including the question whether the nonprofit partner continues to qualify for tax exemption. For coverage of the tax issues, see Chapter 6H2, infra, at pp. 667–690.

3. *Charities in Bankruptcy*. The end of the road for nonprofit organizations in financial difficulty may be bankruptcy. The great recession has battered nonprofits with particular severity as donors, foundations, government and endowment portfolios have been affected. Nonprofit bankruptcy has come out of the shadows, because more institutions cannot meet financial obligations or finance their debt, and must turn to the courts for protection, reorganization or dissolution. Performing arts organizations have been particularly hard hit, but bankruptcy has become a last resort for museums, nonprofit housing developers and social services organizations, and dioceses. One of the largest bankruptcies has been that of the National Heritage Foundation, a manager of donor advised funds that ran into problems in promoting controversial and illegal giving techniques. Other charities have examined mergers to survive the recession.[4]

When a charitable organization files for bankruptcy, a conflict ensues between two public policies: the desire to preserve assets for the public purposes for which they were donated and federal bankruptcy law's goal of maximizing assets for distribution to creditors.[5] Unlike other entities

---

4. See See Shelly Banjo & Mitra Kalita, Mergers, Closings Plague Charities, Wall St. J., Feb. 1, 2010, at A1; Stephanie Strom, Bankruptcy Now Touching Nonprofits, N.Y. Times, Feb. 20, 2009, at A17; Nicole Wallace, One in Five Charities Considering Mergers to Help Survive Hard Economic Times, Chron. Phil., Mar. 12, 2009, available at http://philanthropy.com/ premium/articles/v21/i10/10002702.htm. The clergy abuse scandal has pushed seven American Catholic dioceses into bankruptcy. Brian Witte, Catholic Diocese of Wilmington files bankruptcy, Wash. Post, Oct. 18, 2009, available at http://www.washingtonpost.com/wp-dyn/content/ article/2009/10/18/AR2009101802500_pf.html.

5. For an excellent overview of these issues, see Evelyn Brody, The Charity in Bankruptcy and Ghosts of Donors Past, Present and Future, 29 Seton Hall Legis.J. 471 (2005) and Shalom L. Kohn, Patrick J. Whaley & Paul J. Dostart, Section of Taxation Fall Meeting (Chicago, Sept. 12, 2003), available in LEXIS, Legal Library, ABA Section of Taxation, ABA Section of Taxation Meeting, Materials File. The sexual abuse scandals in the Catholic Church demonstrate the drastic consequences of bankruptcy. Seven dioceses, including Portland (Oregon), Spokane, and Tucson, have gone into bankruptcy. The dioceses had argued that each parish was a separate legal person that owned its own property and the legal estate of the

nonprofit corporations can only be the subject of a voluntary bankruptcy.[6] When an organization files for bankruptcy, an estate is created that includes all of the assets of the organization.[7] Federal bankruptcy law determines what property interests of the debtor nonprofit are included. An automatic stay takes effect and protects the organization and its property from certain creditors' actions to allow an orderly case administration.

Ideally, the charity will be able to formulate a plan to reorganize, which will outline how it will satisfy its creditors and enable it to emerge from bankruptcy. The plan must be fair and equitable to the creditors. During this time the organization remains in possession of its assets and continues to operate. A trustee may be appointed with the consent of the organization or for cause, if there has been fraud or mismanagement. The plan must be accepted by a number or an amount of debt as specified in the Bankruptcy Code.[8] After the plan is confirmed and the creditors paid off, the organization emerges from bankruptcy. If the organization's financial situation is so dire that it cannot continue to exist, it will be wound up and dissolved.

Important issues for charities in bankruptcy are what assets go in the bankrupt estate, how are restricted funds treated, and whether the organization can make distributions from endowed funds to assist the organization in difficult times. An unrestricted gift is part of the bankruptcy estate and will be eventually distributed to creditors. Restricted gifts are kept out of the estate, but if the income from the gift was used prior to filing the bankruptcy petition to pay general expenses, such income will be applied to the organization's debts.[9] Assets given or placed in trust are not part of the bankruptcy estate. If legal title is held by an independent third party trustee, the asset will not constitute property of the bankrupt estate. When the charity serves as its own trustee, the issue is closer. If the charity cannot reorganize and continue, the restricted charitable assets that survive the bankruptcy will be subject to a cy pres proceeding in a state court.[10]

---

diocese was limited to the chancellery buildings. In the Portland and Spokane cases, the bankruptcy court ruled that all parishes and church buildings were part of the bankrupt estate. In re Catholic Bishop of Spokane, 329 B.R. 304 (Bank. E.D. Wash. 2005); In re Roman Catholic Archbishop of Portland, 335 B.R. 868 (Bankr. D. Or. 2005).

6. Several jurisdictions allow for involuntary dissolution of a public benefit nonprofit and appointment of a receiver. See Cal. Corp. Code §§ 6510, 6513.

7. 11 U.S.C. § 541(a).

8. 11 U.S.C.A. § 1126(a).

9. In re Winsted Memorial Hospital, 249 B.R. 588 (Bankr. D.Conn.2000).

10. A trust provision expressing the settlor's own choice of an alternative charitable purpose will be carried out, obviating the cy pres proceeding. Restatement (Third) of Trusts § 67, cmt. b.

CHAPTER 3

OPERATION AND GOVERNANCE

A. INTRODUCTION

This chapter examines the functions, powers and duties of those who govern nonprofit organizations and the problems associated with enforcing those obligations. These operational and governance questions are influenced by the legal form that the organization adopts to conduct its activities.

In an unincorporated association the governance structure is determined by the organization's articles of association, constitution or bylaws. Members in good standing have the right to participate in association activities, receive notice of and attend meetings, and participate in group decisions. The lines of authority, however, are vague and governed by agency principles. Harry G. Henn & Michael George Pfeiffer, Nonprofit Groups: Factors Influencing Choice of Form, 11 Wake Forest L.Rev. 181, 194 (1975).

Charitable trusts are governed by trustees who have the legal authority to do all things necessary to administer the trust. The specific powers of a charitable trustee are determined by the terms of the trust instrument and the governing statute. They consist of such powers as are necessary or appropriate for the carrying out of the purposes of the trust and which are not forbidden by the terms of the trust or the law. Austin W. Scott & Mark L. Ascher, Scott & Ascher on Trusts, §§ 18.1, 37.3.2 (5th ed. 2009) (hereinafter "Scott & Ascher on Trusts"); Unif. Trust Code §§ 815, 816. Trustees generally are held to stricter fiduciary norms of oversight than directors of nonprofit corporations. Although there are differing legal standards for trustees of charitable trusts and directors of nonprofit corporations, the terms "trustee" and "director" often are used interchangeably. One should be aware that the degree of legal accountability will depend upon the choice of form rather than the name by which those responsible are called. Unless the trust instrument provides otherwise, trustees are typically self-perpetuating but may be removed by court order and need not bother with membership meetings, elections, quorums, and the governance and suffrage issues found in the corporation. Title to trust property resides in the trustee. Trustees have the authority to contract with third parties in administering the trust, but the trustees are bound unless a clear exclusion is stipulated.

If a nonprofit organization is incorporated, a board of directors exercises its corporate powers and directs the management of its activities. The governance structures of nonprofit corporations resemble their profit-seeking counterparts, and the substantial body of legal precedent in the business corporate area is a helpful referent. The ABA Business Law Section's Model Nonprofit Corporation Act consciously parallels its its counterpart, the Model Business Corporation Act. Internal governance procedures, filing provisions, formation of corporations, requirements for corporate officers and agents, corporate powers and fundamental transactions, such as mergers and dissolutions, all conform to their respective for-profit counterparts. This approach makes life easier for corporate lawyers, who presumably are familiar with their state's corporate statute. But it should not be assumed that all nonprofit corporate problems fit neatly into the business corporate paradigm.

NOTE: GOOD GOVERNANCE AND ETHICAL PRACTICES

Examples of poor judgment, ethical lapses and outright fraud course throughout these materials. Nothing so tarnishes the nonprofit sector's halo than wrongdoing by charities. More often than not, these actions indicate inadequate corporate governance procedures and a lack of transparency of the organization's activities. Good governance is the implementation of certain principles and policies that should protect the organization from misconduct. Many law reform projects, associations of nonprofits, charity watchdog groups, experts, attorneys general and the Internal Revenue Service have promoted good governance and accountability practices through the issuance of guidebooks, principles and reports.[1] Among the most recognized guidelines are the 33 recommendations of the Independent Sector's Panel on the Nonprofit Sector, Principles for Good Governance and Ethical Practices, available at http://www.nonprofitpanel.org/report /principles/Principles_Guide.pdf. The American Law Institute's ongoing project on Principles of the Law of Nonprofit Organizations is another influential effort to formulate governance standards within the framework of nonprofit law to assist organizations in adopting legal and ethical practices of good behavior and policy.

Ultimately, a nonprofit's governance structure is the result of a decision by its governing board as to the policies and practices that will guide it. A charitable organization has no choice but to comply with all applicable federal and state laws and regulations, but governance decisions are usually matters of choice. Some aspects of good governance are obvious: regular board meetings with agendas, annual elections of directors, minutes of meetings, directors' access to books and records, the delegation of responsibility to board committees (executive, audit, finance, and development) or delegation in appropriate situations to outside experts (investment management, legal affairs).

Good governance policies encourage a charity's board to approve and review the organization's mission, annual budget and financial transactions; determine staff compensation practices and policies; and evaluate senior employees. A governing body should assure that information systems

---

1. For a comprehensive listing of such publications, see American Law Institute, Principles of the Law of Nonprofit Organizations, Part II, Introduction, pp. 10–16 (Tentative Draft No. 1, 2008).

are in place to protect the organization's assets and to keep accurate and complete financial records. The board should implement policies and procedures to manage conflicts of interest between individuals and the organization and establish ethical fundraising practices.

It is one thing to have rules and structures in the organization's bylaws, such as notice requirements for meetings or the establishment of committees. It is quite another to actually engage in practices that ensure the board monitors the organization's activities, and puts in place systems that keep it informed while enabling officers and staff to manage the charity's affairs. As good governance demands have increased, additional burdens have been placed on governing board members.

A disconnect sometimes exists between the principles of good nonprofit governance and the mandates of state nonprofit law. For example, with very few exceptions, state nonprofit corporation statutes do not require an organization to have a conflict of interest policy.[2] Under state law, whether an organization adopts a such a policy is within the discretion and judgment of the governing board. Nonprofit corporate statutes deal with conflicts of interest, but the focus is upon who has the burden of proof to show the transaction was fair to the organization at the time it was approved.[3]

Nonprofit corporate law, like its for-profit analogue, is a kind of constitutional law in that its dominant functions are to regulate the manner in which a nonprofit corporation is constituted, define the relative rights and duties of those participating in the organization and delimit the powers of the organization in relation to the external world.[4] Modern nonprofit corporate statutes are enabling acts, which make it easy for individuals to organize and operate an organization whether it is large or small. While some corporate statutory requirements are mandatory: "after the corporate existence has begun, an organizational meeting ... shall be held ..."[5]—for example, many more sections are supplementary or gap-fillers, meaning they apply only if internal corporate documents fail to determine certain rules. Thus, a quorum for a members' meeting is a majority of the total votes entitled to be cast, unless the organization selects a higher or lesser number.[6] Beyond certain fundamental requirements, state nonprofit statutes do not prescribe specific corporate governance practices.

---

2. One exception is Arizona, which requires a nonprofit corporation to have a conflict of interest policy. Ariz. Rev. Stat. § 10–3864. A few jurisdictions require health care organizations or other specialized organizations to have conflict of interest policies. See Ark. C. § 20–46–304 (community health centers); R.I. § 27–19.2–4 (nonprofit hospitals in accord with IRS guidelines); Ct. Gen. Stat. § 36A–454b (credit unions).

3. See Cal. Corp. Code § 5233; N.Y. Not-for-Profit Corp. L. § 715; Model Nonprofit Corp. Act (3d ed.) § 8.60.

4. Cf. Melvin Aron Eisenberg, The Structure of the Corporation 1 (1976).

5. See N.Y. Not-for-Profit Corp. L. § 405 Model Nonprofit Corp. Act (3d ed.) § 2.05(a).

6. See Model Nonprofit Corp. Act (3d ed.) § 7.26. N.Y. Not-for-Profit Corp. L. § 608. A reduction in the quorum requirement is limited to not less than one hundred votes or one-tenth of the total number of votes entitled to be cast, whichever is lesser. Id. at § 608(b).

In most jurisdictions, nonprofit governance procedures are matters of internal organizational decision.[7] The articles of association, the bylaws or resolutions create other rules that have been determined by the members or the governing body as appropriate for that particular organization. This approach promotes flexibility, so that differing organizations can create structures, most useful and efficient for their particular activities.[8] Good governance initiatives proceed from a different vantage point: the organization's actual practices rather than its formal structures.

The assumption of good governance mandates is they will improve a charity's performance and assist in the attainment of the organization's mission. There is no empirical data that confirms such assumptions. Nevertheless, the pressures on boards are unrelenting and will not relax until such time as no charities engage in wrongdoing.

B. Boards of Directors and Trustees

1. Responsibilities of the Board

Model Nonprofit Corp. Act (3d ed.) § 8.01.

Cal. Corp. Code § 5210.

Principles of the Law of Nonprofit Organizations §§ 320, 325.

The board of directors as a body is ultimately responsible for the oversight of a nonprofit corporation. Although single directors have little

---

7. New Hampshire offers the broadest prescriptions for governance structure. A charitable nonprofit corporation must have at least five voting members, who are not of the same immediate family or related by blood or marriage. No employee of a charitable nonprofit corporation shall hold the position of chairperson or presiding officer of the board. N.H. Rev. Stat. Ann. § 292:6–a. Maine and California require a majority of a nonprofit corporation's directors to be financially disinterested. Cal. Corp. Code § 5227; Me. Rev. Stat. Ann. Tit. 13–B, § 713–a(2). A few states have adopted certain Sarbanes–Oxley type provisions, typically the requirement of an audit committee if the organization reaches a certain level of revenues. See Wash. Rev. Code. § 19.09.540. California requires charities with gross revenues of $2 million or more to conduct independent audits and establish and maintain an audit committee (charitable trusts are not subject to the audit committee requirement). Cal. Govt. Code § 12586(e)(1), (e)(2). Executive compensation must be reviewed and approved by the governing board to ensure the payment is "just and reasonable." Cal. Govt. Code § 12586(g); The Model Nonprofit Corporation Act (§§ 16.01, 16.20–21) requires keeping of corporate records, such as minutes of meetings and appropriate accounting records, but does not require an audited financial statement.

8. In the words of Professor Ira Ellman: "... a corporate code [is] a means by which to facilitate activity ... Even though it may have a number of mandatory rules, therefore, the corporation code is not regulatory in its essential purpose. Instead, we use the code to create a legal structure that is useful as a vehicle for a particular type of legitimate activity ... [E]very group of individuals pursuing a lawful activity should be able to find a form of organization that meets its needs: an organization whose defining rules fit the group's *raison d'etre,* whose gap-filling rules tend to meet the participants' expectations, and whose value-based rules help to protect both the participants and third parties from abuses of the organizational form." Ira Mark Ellman, Another Theory of Nonprofit Corporations, 80 Mich.L.Rev. 999, 1004 (1982).

authority in their individual capacities, they are legally accountable and have certain rights and obligations flowing from their office. Because most public benefit corporations have no members, the board is the sole policy making authority and is self-perpetuating. In mutual benefit nonprofits, members may play an organizational role similar to shareholders in a business corporation. The role of the board will usually remain the same in both types of nonprofits, except that members will have powers of ratification for important changes, such as merger (Model Nonprofit Corp. Act (3d ed.) § 11.04), dissolution (Model Nonprofit Corp. Act (3d ed.) § 14.02(b)(2)), election of directors (Model Nonprofit Corp. Act (3d ed.) § 8.04), and certain other rights and privileges. Nonprofit directors and trustees are selected for many reasons: they represent constituent groups, have special skills, are sources of funding, bring recognition to the organization through their prominence, or represent the community or sources of support. They must be responsive to several constituencies: the one that elected or appointed them, the constituency the organization serves, and the constituency of legal accountability. ABA Section of Business Law, Guidebook for Directors of Nonprofit Corporations 8–10 (George W. Overton & Jeannie Carmadelle Fry eds., 2d ed. 2002).

William G. Bowen, a former president of Princeton University, has written that at the most basic level, all boards, for-profit and nonprofit, serve six principal functions: (1) to select, encourage, advise, evaluate and, if need be, replace the chief executive officer; (2) to review and adopt long-term strategic directions and to approve specific objectives, financial and other, such as reviewing the basic mission of the organization in light of changed circumstances; (3) to ensure to the extent possible that the necessary resources, including human resources, will be available to pursue the strategies and achieve the organization's objectives; (4) to monitor the performance of management; (5) to ensure that the organization operates responsibly as well as effectively; and (6) to nominate suitable candidates for election to the board, and to establish and carry out an effective system of governance at the board level, including evaluation of board performance. Inside the Boardroom: Governance by Directors and Trustees 18–20 (1994). In the appropriate situation profit-seeking and nonprofit boards also may initiate and adopt corporate plans, commitments and actions; initiate and adopt changes in accounting principles and practices; provide advice and counsel to principal executives; instruct any committees, senior executives or other officers and review their actions; and manage the organization and direct as to all other corporate matters as needed. See Principles of the Law of Nonprofit Organizations § 320.

Despite the parallels, there are significant differences between the boards of profit-seeking and nonprofit corporations. For-profit boards concentrate on developing and carrying out board strategies for enhancing shareholder value while nonprofit boards are more committed to the organization's mission. While a business board may have an obligation to divest itself of unprofitable activities, a nonprofit board has a greater duty to stay the course if it is to be true to its mission. Corporate boards devote much more time to reviews of performance than the typical nonprofit. The bottom line, the talisman of profit-seeking activity, is easier to measure than nonprofit effectiveness. Some nonprofit boards with significant endowments or other monetary assets oversee more directly than their corporate counterparts the investment of funds entrusted to the institution. Bowen, supra, at 20–24. Some external functions of the board are unique to nonprofit organizations, such as fundraising, representing the organization to the outside community and mobilizing and caring for volunteers. Fundraising responsibilities may include personal contributions, soliciting direct gifts from board members or other individuals; facilitating government, corporate, and foundation funding; or obtaining needed goods and services at lower than market price. Board members may represent the nonprofit to the public or resolve problems with governmental agencies, donors or beneficiaries of the organization's programs.

Management of nonprofit organizations normally is vested in its senior employees. A basic function of the board is to select these executives and to oversee their performance. The model that an organization adopts will depend upon the size and scope of the nonprofit's activities, its needs and characteristics, and the board environment. Nonprofit boards will interpret their roles in different ways. In the words of one commentator: "Most of the problems that befall * * * groups stem from the fact that boards have, over the years, translated [their] mandate with as much variety as husbands and wives interpret their vows to love, honor, and obey," Carole Saline, quoted in Melissa Middleton, Nonprofit Boards of Directors Beyond the Governance Function, in The Nonprofit Sector: A Research Handbook 141 (Walter W. Powell, ed. (1987)). Board decisionmaking processes are as varied as the nonprofit sector, and they often differ from the ideal legal model of the board. Decisions often are made on the basis of incomplete information, under rushed circumstances, or on the basis of gut feelings or experiences rather than the formalized method of decisionmaking that the legal model suggests.

Many of the board's activities are more prosaic than the legal model of board responsibility would indicate. It has been suggested that a board's most important judgment is the content of its agenda, that is, the decision as to what it will tend to and how it will allocate the limited resources and time available. See Bayless Manning, The Business Judgment Rule and the Director's Duty of Attention: Time for Reality, 39 Bus. Law. 1477, 1484 (1984). Usually management rather than the board sets the agenda for board consideration. Thus, the board is more often reactive than initiatory. The larger the nonprofit organization, the more complex and diverse will be its activities and the less likely a board will become involved in a particular decision. Formal board decisions are but a small part of a board's activities. An enormous amount of board meeting time deals with ongoing housekeeping functions which require neither deliberation nor formal decision. These include routine approvals, listening to reports from management and tending to procedural matters. Despite the diversity in nonprofit board environments, there are minimal responsibilities and levels of attention that the law requires of all board members.

2.   LIMITATIONS ON BOARD POWERS

Rev. Model Nonprofit Corp. Act § 6.21.

Cal. Corp. Code § 5056.

If a nonprofit organization has a membership structure, the members have certain rights, principally to elect or remove the directors, to amend the bylaws, and to approve organic changes initiated by the board, such as dissolution or merger. In dealing with an organization's members, the board must act fairly. It can curtail or abolish certain members' rights or even decide to convert the nonprofit into a non-membership organization, but the membership must have adequate notice, information, and the right to vote upon such changes. The corporation may not subvert corporate democracy to perpetuate itself in office.

Fitzgerald v. National Rifle Association

United States District Court, District of New Jersey, 1974.
383 F.Supp. 162.

■ WHIPPLE, CHIEF JUDGE.

Plaintiffs have petitioned this Court for an Order requiring the defendant, National Rifle Association of America, (NRA), to publish certain advertising in The American Rifleman, NRA's official journal. On behalf of Fitzgerald, plaintiffs submitted an advertisement concerning Fitzgerald's candidacy for the NRA's Board of Directors, which defendants refused to publish.

The 75 member Board consists of, and is elected by, so-called "life members" of the NRA. There are approximately 146,000 members in this category, while "annual members" number more than 800,000. Annual members are not eligible to vote for the Board of Directors, but may make recommendations to a "Nominating Committee" which selects candidates for the election.

The Nominating Committee is selected by the president of the NRA, who is elected by the members of the Board of Directors. As noted above, this Committee, which is comprised of life members, engages in the process of nominating candidates for the Directors' election. NRA By-laws also provide for a written ballot in this election.

In an effort to gain nomination, plaintiff Fitzgerald first became a life member by paying the necessary fee. He then sought support from the membership by means of an advertisement in The American Rifleman.

Upon receipt of the proffered ad, with which proper payment was tendered, the NRA advised that the material was unsuitable for publication. On its advertising rate card, the NRA states that it "reserves the right to reject or discontinue any advertisement and to edit all copy."

The defendant justifies its refusal to publish the plaintiffs' advertisement by citing an impressive list of precedents upholding the right of a newspaper or magazine to refuse to accept for publication any advertisement submitted to it by a prospective advertiser. The discretion afforded publishers to deny space to those seeking to buy it is premised on the characterization of newspapers as private enterprises, rather than as businesses clothed with a public interest.

Accordingly, a newspaper publisher is generally free to contract and deal with whomever he chooses in the same manner as other businessmen. This Court has no quarrel with this principle and recognizes the general right of a newspaper or magazine to decide what advertisements it will and will not accept. It is the Court's view, however, that this rule is not absolute in all circumstances. Like the vast majority of legal rights and privileges, the right here in question must yield when its exercise would result in the curtailment of another right of even greater social importance. * * *

In the instant case, this Court must decide whether the publisher's right must give way when balanced against the fiduciary duty of corporate directors to insure fair and open corporate elections. This duty of course extends only to the association membership. Plaintiffs Fitzgerald and Abelman are members in good standing of the NRA and thus qualify to bring this issue to the Court's attention. The third plaintiff, NRA Members for a Better NRA, is not now, nor has it ever been, affiliated with the NRA in any way. As to this plaintiff, therefore, all relief is denied. All future references to plaintiffs in this Opinion apply only to Messrs. Fitzgerald and Abelman.

At the outset it is important to note that The American Rifleman is the official journal of the NRA. As such it is neither published for, nor circulated to, the general reading public. The Court takes judicial notice that the Rifleman is available only to NRA members. It is not sold at newsstands, nor are subscriptions accepted from non-NRA members. The magazine's publishing costs are met through NRA membership dues, as well as through the acceptance of advertising. In addition to containing articles of general interest to gun enthusiasts, the Rifleman is used to acquaint NRA members with the policies and activities of the association.

Finally, it should be pointed out that the Rifleman is an integral part of the NRA's election process. Once the nominating committee has selected its list of candidates for office, the list is published in the Rifleman. Voters then must refer to the Rifleman in order to exercise their franchise.

This special relationship between the NRA and The American Rifleman indicates that the Rifleman is closer in form to a corporate newsletter than to a traditionally commercial publication such as Time or Newsweek. Indeed in the instant case, traditional distinctions between a publisher and an advertiser become blurred, since the plaintiffs may justifiably claim an ownership interest in the American Rifleman. Plaintiffs are members in good standing of the association which publishes the magazine and their dues go in part to meet the magazine's printing costs.

The NRA itself is organized under the laws of the State of New York pursuant to that state's Not–For–Profit Corporation Law § 101, et seq. Like all corporate directors and officers, the management of the NRA owes a fiduciary duty to its stockholders (in this case the association's membership) to conduct the NRA's affairs in a good faith effort to promote the best interests of the association. In the case of the NRA, this common law duty is augmented by Section 717(a) of the N.P.C.L., which provides in part:

Directors and officers shall discharge the duties of their respective positions in good faith * * *

Because of the special relationship between the NRA and The American Rifleman, it is this Court's view that the fiduciary obligations of the association's directors and officers applies with equal vigor to the operation of The American Rifleman.

As part of their overall fiduciary relationship with the stockholders, it is well established that the directors and officers cannot manipulate the affairs of the corporation primarily with the intent of securing control of the corporation to one faction of stockholders or of excluding another. Justice Douglas speaking for the Court in Pepper v. Litton, 308 U.S. 295, 311, 60 S.Ct. 238, 247, 84 L.Ed. 281 (1939), firmly restated this principle in the following language:

He who is in such a fiduciary position cannot serve himself first and his cestuis second. He cannot manipulate the affairs of his corporation to their detriment and in disregard of the standard of common decency and honesty. * * * He cannot use his power for his own personal advantage and to the detriment of the stockholders and creditors no matter how absolute in terms that power may be and no matter how meticulous he is to satisfy technical requirements. For that power is at all times subject to the equitable limitations that it may not be exercised for the aggrandisement, preference, or advantage of the fiduciary to the exclusion or detriment of the cestuis.

The principles enunciated above make it clear that officers and directors cannot utilize corporate instrumentalities such as The American Rifleman to perpetuate themselves in office. If the concepts of fiduciary duty and corporate democracy are to exist as something more than pious frauds, dissident stockholders must have the opportunity to alert fellow stockholders to alternative policies and programs. Corporate elections become hollow mockeries if candidates are unable to bring their candidacies and platforms to the attention of the stockholders at large.

In the instant case, plaintiffs Fitzgerald and Abelman have been thwarted in every attempt to place their viewpoint and Fitzgerald's candidacy before the general membership. Plaintiffs first sought a list of NRA members (to which they were entitled by virtue of N.P.C.L. § 621(b)) and were refused access. Defendant justified its refusal on the ground that the cost of a private mailing to the more than 1,000,000 NRA members would be prohibitive. The plaintiffs then sought to place an advertisement in The American Rifleman, announcing Fitzgerald's platform and candidacy, and asking for contributions. Although the advertisement was tendered along with proper payment, it too was denied.

In the Court's view, this series of events raises the spectre of management bad faith. At the very least, a great potential exists for the self-perpetuation of the incumbent NRA hierarchy.

The only justification defendant offers for refusing plaintiffs' advertisement is to point out that the defendant's magazine publishes as part of its advertising information a notice that it "reserves the right to reject or discontinue any advertisement and to edit all copy."

This explanation does not satisfy the heavy burden placed on directors and officers to justify their dealings with corporate shareholders. As was noted in the case of In re Brunner Air Compressor Corp., 287 F.Supp. 256, 263 (N.D.N.Y.1968):

> (A director's) dealings with the corporation are subjected to rigorous scrutiny and where any of their contracts or engagements with the corporation is challenged the burden is on the director * * * not only to prove the good faith of the transaction but also to show its inherent fairness from the viewpoint of the corporation and those interested therein.

In view of the "equitable limitations" of decency and fair dealings imposed on defendant's management, and the special status of The American Rifleman as the corporate publication of the NRA and an integral part of its election process, it is this Court's opinion that the traditional right of a magazine to refuse publication of an advertisement must give way. * * *

The defendant raises the additional argument that the relief sought by plaintiffs violates the First Amendment guarantee of a free press.

In the instant case, the Court has found that the defendant's refusal to publish plaintiffs' advertisement, at the very least, creates the potential for the violation of defendant's corporate trust. The Court has already noted the unusual nature of The American Rifleman and its special relationship to the NRA and to the plaintiffs. The guarantees of the First Amendment cannot serve as the justification for improper utilization of a corporate publication such as The American Rifleman. The First Amendment cannot be used as a pretext for denying stockholders their right to participate in corporate affairs.

In the instant case, the claims of constitutional deprivation are particularly ill founded. No effort is being made here to shackle The American Rifleman by forbidding it to espouse any editorial policies or to report any news events. Under normal circumstances, The American Rifleman would be the most convenient forum for reaching the membership at the NRA. However, following defendant's refusal to supply the plaintiffs with a membership list, the Rifleman becomes the only forum for reaching the membership. It is not an abridgement of anyone's First Amendment rights to require the NRA's management to live up to its obligations to deal fairly and honestly with the association's membership, and to maintain a viable corporate democracy in the only manner possible given the circumstances the management itself has created.

To conclude, it is this Court's opinion that it is the duty of the NRA's directors and officers to take all necessary steps to insure an informed electorate and fair corporate elections. The Court does not believe, however, that the defendant should be required to do more than is absolutely necessary to provide this insurance.

The Court believes that the maintenance of a viable corporate democracy in this case requires that the plaintiffs be permitted to alert their fellow NRA members to their policy positions and to Fitzgerald's candidacy. It does not believe that corporate democracy requires the defendant to allow plaintiffs the opportunity to solicit campaign contributions through the pages of The American Rifleman.

It is therefore, on this 23rd day of September, 1974

ORDERED that upon tender of proper payment The American Rifleman accept and publish the advertisement originally submitted by the plaintiffs, except for the following lines:

"Is your gun worth a buck?" * * * "And your contributions to his campaign".

Plaintiffs shall submit an appropriate Order, consented to, at least as to form, by the defendant.

NOTES

1. *Equal Time?* Why did the court exclude "Is your gun worth a buck?" * * * "And your contributions to his campaign?" Must the American Rifleman provide equal time to an NRA member who believes in gun control?

2. *Elimination of Voting Rights of Members.* Directors of a corporation have a fiduciary duty of fair dealing with the membership in situations where corporate action is being proposed which may affect one or more shareholders adversely. In Ferry v. San Diego Museum of Art, 180 Cal. App.3d 35, 225 Cal.Rptr. 258 (1986), the museum decided to amend its bylaws to eliminate members' voting rights and called a special meeting of the members to approve the changes. The plaintiff-members alleged that the trustees and officers had engaged in a course of conduct to revise the bylaws secretly without informing the membership of their activities and the significance of the revision. The notice to the membership to revise the bylaws did not mention that members' voting rights would be eliminated. The plaintiff sought to review the proposed bylaws but was limited to ten minutes, was not offered a copy of the old bylaws for comparison purposes, and was denied access to the recent minutes of the board of trustees.

Fearing the revision would lose, the board cancelled the special meeting and decided to solicit proxies at the annual meeting. The proxy materials minimized the significance of the bylaw changes and provided that the members could examine the bylaws in the rotunda of the museum. The California Corporations Code § 5341 requires a fair and reasonable procedure for the termination of membership rights conducted in good faith.

The court held that fair and reasonable election procedures were fundamental to the proper governance of nonprofit corporations. The museum's technical compliance with bylaw amendment procedures did not mean that the procedure was fair and reasonable. Summary judgment for the museum was reversed. See also Braude v. Havenner, 38 Cal.App.3d 526, 113 Cal.Rptr. 386 (1974).

3. *Practice Note: The Perils of Democracy.* Counsel drafting election procedures need to balance between rules that entrench incumbents through their control of the electoral process and those that too easily allow insurgents to oust the board, which can cause instability for the organization. The problems for an organization with a too democratic board election process are demonstrated by the challenge faced by the Sierra Club's national board from an insurgent slate of anti-immigrant animal rights activists. Under the Sierra Club's procedures all 744,000 members in its 64 chapters are eligible to vote for the national board. Anyone who garners 360 club members' signatures can become a board candidate. A low electoral turnout plus an effort to get issue supporters to join the Sierra Club for purposes of the election made the organization vulnerable to a hostile takeover. The insurgents were defeated. National organizations typically retain more control over board nominations. See Felicity Barringer, Established Candidates Defeat Challengers in Sierra Club Voting, N.Y. Times, Apr. 22, 2004, at 18; Stephen G. Greene, Hostile Takeover or Rescue, Chron. Philanthropy, Apr. 12, 2004. The policy issues about whether or not to have voting members are discussed in Dana Brakman Reiser, Dismembering Civil Society: The Social Cost of Internally Undemocratic Nonprofits, 82 Or. L. Rev. 829 (2003).

C.   FIDUCIARY OBLIGATIONS

1.   THE FIDUCIARY CONCEPT

Few legal concepts combine the power and pervasiveness of fiduciary obligation. The fiduciary concept arises in the study of corporations and torts, and it also is a fundamental principle in agency relationships in nonprofit organizations. Fiduciaries are, in many different ways, obliged to act unselfishly and to give other persons or institutions the advantage of their knowledge and skill. The fiduciary obligation thus presupposes that persons subject to it are capable, at least in defined circumstances, of renouncing the immediate pursuit of self-interest.

The fiduciary obligation is notably elusive as a concept. The particular duties it imposes vary in different contexts, as does the justification for imposing the obligation itself. However illusory, the obligation unifies disparate types of legal relationships, including agency, intra-corporate, attorney-client relationships; relations between directors, officers and an organization's members or the public; and between employees, and managers and the organization.

The word "fiduciary" comes from the Latin word "*fiducia*," meaning trust. The term entered English law reports in the mid-nineteenth century, and was descriptive of relationships similar to that between a trustee and *cestui que trust* (beneficiary). "Fiduciary" replaced "trust," which in the same era came to have a precise technical meaning, namely that B had settled legal ownership of property on A to be used on behalf of B or others. "Trust" earlier meant more broadly or imprecisely that B reposed confidence in A. The fiduciary obligation came to have a life of its own in the English chancery courts which historically were a separate court system of equity. See Deborah A. DeMott, Fiduciary Obligation, Agency and Partnership 12 (1991).

Because of the generality and imprecision of many fiduciary norms, the vulnerability of many beneficiaries to misconduct by fiduciaries, and the difficulty of applying such standards to concrete guides for behavior, judicial opinions interpreting and applying fiduciary rules sound like sermons. A good example is the oft-cited words of Judge Cardozo in Meinhard v. Salmon, 249 N.Y. 458, 464, 164 N.E. 545, 547 (1928):

> Joint adventurers, like copartners, owe to one another, while the enterprise continues, the duty of the finest loyalty. Many forms of conduct permissible in a workaday world for those acting at arm's length, are forbidden to those bound by fiduciary ties. A trustee is held to something stricter than the morals of the marketplace. Not honesty alone, but the punctilio of an honor the most sensitive, is then the standard of behavior.

This elevated language provides little concrete guidance to a director of an organization.

Breaches of fiduciary duty occur with unsettling frequency in the nonprofit world, as illustrated by these two contemporary examples:

- In 2008 Dr. Harold J. Raveche, the president of the Stevens Institute of Technology of Hoboken, New Jersey, earned a salary and bonus of $1,089,780. His compensation had tripled in a decade and was among the highest paid to presidents of private research institutions, more than the presidents of Harvard, Princeton or MIT. Since 1988 he had received $1.8 million in loans at below market rates to purchase two vacation homes. Approximately half of the loans were forgiven in a 2007 employment agreement. Dr. Raveche's administration spent more than the board-approved spending rates, used gifts and bequests to pay operating expenses, invaded restricted assets and collateralized the endowment. Commencing in 1999, annual financial reports to the public and board of directors misstated the school's assets during certain years. The university's independent accountants regularly warned school officials about deficiencies in management and financial policies. In 2005 the accounting firm fired the school as a client. The successor auditor repeatedly found internal control deficiencies. In 2008 Stevens paid the Internal Revenue

Service $750,000 in penalties and unpaid taxes owed by taxable technology subsidiaries. According to a complaint filed by the New Jersey Attorney General, former trustees told investigators that the board was not informed about key financial information, the financial status of the endowment or compensation matters.[1]

- In a celebrated case to be studied later in the chapter, Adelphi University placed its insurance business with a firm controlled by one of its trustees, who never disclosed the fee arrangement or terms of coverage to the other board members, and implied it was free. The trustee used her position to unfair advantage in obtaining the account.[2]

There are two breaches of fiduciary obligations by the board members in the above examples, but the nature of the fiduciary breach differs. In the first, the failure of the board to know the size of the president's compensation or the college's financial situation was a breach of the duty of care. The board did not conduct its responsibilities with the necessary diligence or make informed decisions about important matters. In the second, the board member was guilty of a conflict of interest or a breach of the duty of loyalty. She improperly used her position to obtain a benefit for herself at the expense of the organization.

There are very few reported judicial decisions involving breaches of fiduciary duty by nonprofit directors. When such abuses are uncovered, either through an investigation by a state attorney general or a journalistic exposé, the matter usually is settled quickly. The impact of such notoriety can be devastating to an organization, cutting off donor support even after the problems are rectified.

Fiduciary principles in the law of nonprofit organizations have been applied with neither consistency nor coherence. As the following materials demonstrate, courts have used different standards in determining the duty of care and loyalty expected from directors of nonprofit corporations. When reading these cases, determine what standard the court applies and consider whether it is appropriate.

2. THE DUTY OF CARE

Model Nonprofit Corp. Act (3d ed.) §§ 8.30, 8.33, 8.41–42.

Cal. Corp. Code §§ 5230–31.

N.Y. Not-for-Profit Corp. L. §§ 717, 719.

Principles of the Law of Nonprofit Organizations §§ 310, 315.

The duty of care concerns the standard of conduct applied to directors in the discharge of their responsibilities. Directors must exercise their

---

1. See Brian Whitl & Chris Megerian, *AG Alleges Improper Spending at Stevens, Lawsuit Seeks to Force Ouster of President and Top Trustee,* Newark Star Ledger, Sept. 18, 2009, at 1; Sam Dillon, *College is Beset by Accusations in New Jersey,* N.Y. Times, Dec. 22, 2009, at A1.

2. Committee to Save Adelphi v. Diamondopolous, see infra p. 178.

responsibilities in good faith and with a certain degree of diligence, attention, care, and skill. Broadly stated, a director can fail to discharge her duty in two ways: by failing to supervise the corporation (the duty of attention) or even if the director is disinterested, independent and acts in good faith, by failing to make an informed decision about a matter that comes before the board for action.

The significance of the duty of care and its complement, the business judgment rule, is that they relate to a process of decisionmaking. If a director acts in good faith, with the requisite degree of care, and within her authority, a court will not review the action, even if it proves disastrous to the organization. Thus, the duty of care focuses upon the manner in which directors exercise their responsibilities, rather than the correctness of the decision.

The duty of care raises two fundamental inquiries. The first is of process: did the directors act with sufficient care in reaching their decision? The second question is substantive: was the decision so rash as to warrant being set aside or imposing personal liability on the directors? If the response to the questions are affirmative, the director is protected by the business judgment rule, or more precisely in the nonprofit context, the best judgment rule. The business judgment rule provides that directors shall not be liable for harm to the corporation for exercise of their judgment so long as they exercised care. The protection of the business judgment rule only applies in the absence of fraud, illegality, or a disabling conflict of interest.

As the cases in this section demonstrate, the degree of care expected from nonprofit directors has varied. Courts and legislatures are cognizant that most directors are unpaid and serve out of a sense of civic duty. One cannot make the position of director so legally burdensome that people will not join boards or will refuse to allow the organization to undertake risks. Nonetheless, there is a tension between the desire to encourage competent and energetic people to serve and the need that directors be accountable for the activities of organizations whose rationale is to serve the community in the case of public benefit nonprofits and the membership in mutual benefit associations.

a. THE ABSENCE OF A STANDARD OF CARE

George Pepperdine Foundation v. Pepperdine

California Court of Appeal, Second District, Division 2, 1954.
126 Cal.App.2d 154, 271 P.2d 600.

■ MOORE, PRESIDING JUSTICE.

Appeal from judgment of dismissal after demurrers, general and special, had been sustained and plaintiff had declined to amend its second amended complaint, herein referred to as complaint.

The complaint is by a nonprofit, charitable corporation against its former directors for damages resulting from "dissipation of its assets through illegal and speculative transactions and mismanagement of its affairs" by defendants during their incumbencies. It alleges a loss in eleven years of $3,000,000 of assets and the unlawfully incurring of indebtedness in the sum of $525,000. It demands judgment against the several directors.

* * *

The complaint is in 16 counts and is grounded on "two basic theories of liability" says its author; "the first theory of liability will be referred to as the note theory and is grounded upon the actions of defendants in causing plaintiff to issue to the public some $551,300 in promissory notes without first obtaining a permit * * * and for considerations of no value or of less value than the principal amounts of the notes involved."

The second theory of liability is "mismanagement" which is grounded upon the acts of defendants in dissipating all the assets of plaintiff over a period of years in speculative transactions and by making gifts of its assets after it became insolvent.

[The complaint also alleged that George Pepperdine, the founding donor, carried out transactions with the consent and approval of the other directors that caused the foundation to become insolvent. Its precarious financial condition was concealed by the board. Even though the directors other than Mr. Pepperdine did not participate in the transactions leading to the insolvency, the complaint alleged that they were negligent in failing to stop them. Eds.]

* * *

It is alleged that at the time of plaintiff's incorporation on April 18, 1931, George Pepperdine was possessed of considerable personal fortune, was widely known in California as one interested in and a supporter of charitable, educational and religious work and religious organizations. After 1937 he was widely known in connection with Pepperdine College in Los Angeles, which college was well known as the results of its educational and athletic activities and which was believed to hold and own properties of great value and investments of the character suitable for substantial, charitable institutions.

The pleading makes the affirmative declaration that Mr. Pepperdine endowed the foundation and the college with his own private fortune in the amount of not less than $3,000,000. From the time of its incorporation, he dominated and controlled it and "at no time did any of said other defendant directors and officers attempt to exercise any control over said George Pepperdine or in any way direct or restrict his complete domination of plaintiff or exercise any independent judgment or make any independent investigation with respect to any of the transactions entered into by defendant George Pepperdine or in any way direct or restrict his complete domination of plaintiff or exercise any independent judgment." As a rule, there were only three trustees. They held few and infrequent meetings at which a quorum was seldom present, and at such meetings nothing was done except to vote approval of the inter-meeting transactions of President

Pepperdine who was also treasurer and general factotum; in other words, the corporation was George Pepperdine's other self.

From the text of the complaint, it is observed that between December 31, 1939 and December 1948 plaintiff's assets "continually diminished by reason of losses through bad investments and other transactions, with the result that, not later than December of 1948, plaintiff was insolvent and without moneys or assets readily convertible into money with which to meet its obligations as they became due or with which to make further investments."

The pleading proceeds to allege plaintiff's entry into transactions, to wit, the sale of its promissory notes to the public to raise money or to purchase securities of foreign corporations. It describes the manner of selling such notes as violative of the corporate securities act, the payment of commissions, no permit having been obtained. It recites the negligent acquisition of assets of no value or of little value while plaintiff's promissory notes found their ways into the hands of innocent holders for value. The result was the dissipation of the $3,000,000 and the incurring of a debt of $551,300 for which it had received property worth no more than $120,900. A regrettable situation! but is it one that requires a burnt offering or that demands the swinging of human forms from the gibbet to gratify the rancor of intimate observers? The instant action is a new demonstration of a familiar social phenomenon: when a tragic loss occurs, find a victim to throw to the lions. The perspicacity of the trial court was not overtaxed to discern the weakness of plaintiff's position and thrice registered disapproval. While its counsel has brilliantly unraveled the mysteries of a pleading and argued well for the certainty of causes not united and separately stated, yet he has not woven a pattern of justice out of the materials at hand whereby to adjudicate liability on the part of respondents.

Plaintiff is a nonprofit corporation. Its creative statute and, impliedly, its articles permit it to invest and reinvest its funds and properties. It was an enterprise created by the brain and brawn of one only George Pepperdine. He had the vision, the industry, the thrift and the charitable instincts to accumulate a fortune and to dedicate it to the public good and his services to its expansion and increment and to the disbursement of its revenues and corpus to deserving charitable, benevolent or religious institutions. Had he confined his investments to his own field in which he accumulated his millions, or had he with wizard-like precision so invested the corpus of the trust as to reap more millions for the public benefit through his very own corporation, he would now walk in a wilderness of praises of himself and of the foundation's memorials unto his saint-like character. But now, after he and his friends have without promise or hope of reward unsuccessfully attempted to steer the institution of his creation to a harbor of safety and properly to dispense its charities to worthy causes, the current directorate seek to reduce them all to penury for ill-conceived plans, unwisely pondered and hastily executed. Each director sought only the public good. Not a chirp in the voluminous pleading intimates that a corrupt motive marred the character or inspired the acts of one of them.

Aside from President Pepperdine, all directors were evidently devoting their time to the enterprise primarily for the purpose of acquiring an intimacy with the institution and of gaining knowledge of methods of dispensing charity. Inasmuch as the foundation was the progeny of the president's imagination, they naturally deferred to his judgment or his wishes in weighing the merits of proposals submitted to the board. With the exception of a financial genius who might arise, how could one of his appointees resist his conclusion upon facts pertaining to the art of investing wealth for gain? He had been educated in the university of hard knocks[3] and by virtue thereof, and of his success as a man of practical affairs, it was protocol to defer to his judgments. Now, an adverse judgment entered against such directors would operate a gross injustice for no crime but nonfeasance or neglect.

Assuming that the alleged losses were due to the alleged egregious blunders of the board under the leadership of President Pepperdine, and to have been the result of his negligence and of the lack of zealous interest on the part of the others, why should he be now required to restore to his corporation what he once gave from his bounty and which was lost solely by reason of his ignorant or careless reckoning? Although a director of such a corporation is held to the highest degree of honor and integrity, he is not personally liable for mistake of judgment. Graham Bros. Co. v. Galloway, Woman's College, 190 Ark. 692, 81 S.W.2d 837, 840. President Pepperdine could not have purposed to sabotage his own enterprise, so stupendous and magnificent as to extend its influence into the far reaches of many necessitous fields of human endeavor. His inclinations, inferred from the allegations, were such as naturally to incline him to foster and prosper an institution of his own creation. His ambition to propagate the Christian system, to spread the influence of religion, and to widen the paths of learning was a girding support for his scheme to make the Foundation a success.

He and his associates are now sued for damages in enormous sums of money for neglect, for delicts, for erroneous judgments in the government and management of the Foundation. If Mr. Pepperdine had never organized the Foundation, but had set himself up to bestow his fortune on deserving charities and had at the same time continued to "invest and reinvest" his own moneys and properties and finally by miscalculations have lost it all, would any one be so crazy and cruel as to assert a claim against him for his carelessness in not holding intact the fortune which he intended to bestow on others? Who is "Foundation" otherwise than the shadow of George Pepperdine, if not his alter ego? If he as an individual could not be sued for negligently investing his own moneys intended for charitable uses, why should his own "Foundation" under the management of strangers prosecute an action to recover from the original donor and his friends what, through negligence, they lost for the Foundation?

---

3. The pleading is verbose in relating how widely and well he was known for his religious and benevolent activities, but not a word about his learning.

The only rational explanation of Mr. Pepperdine's failure in steering the course of plaintiff is that he was lost in the new sphere into which his charities brought him or he suffered an internal change. It is no uncommon thing for a man of the practical business world to fail as a statesman or philosopher. For illustration, it is a far cry from the daily grind of operating a line of ocean steamers, farming extensive acres, drilling oil wells, mining, or of buying, sorting, storing and distributing merchandise, to the experience of a man sitting on a plush chair and choosing the field in which to invest his wealth and selecting the groups on which to bestow it.

Or Mr. Pepperdine could have experienced a deterioration of his mental processes with advancing years, or a change of occupation could have frustrated his talents. If any of such misfortunes encompassed him and deprived him of his erstwhile powers, should he and his patriotic associates now be plundered of their personal possessions to fill the never-to-be gratified maw of charity? If Mr. Pepperdine experienced either a breakdown of his intellectual powers or a transmutation of his intelligence in his new world of disbursing charity, he should not be further victimized by an action at law initiated by the very agency he created to serve mankind. In his zeal to conserve the status quo he caused securities of the foundation to be issued without having obtained a permit, but even by doing this forbidden act he sought no personal gain. His aim was not to impair the peace or welfare of the state, but to enhance its dignity and enlarge its welfare by increasing the opportunities of its citizens for a richer life. The losses to the Foundation thereby entailed are the product of impoverished thought or inaccurate calculation and are on a parity with his improvident, ill-conceived investments. But whatever they are, it does not properly lie with appellant to accept and retain the fruits of them and then denounce them as bases for recovery on account of the negligence of respondent.

Reason, justice, equity and law stand aghast at the judgment proposed by the second amended complaint.

Moreover, appellant is without capacity to prosecute the instant action. The assets of a charitable corporation, in the final analysis, belong to the state and a suit for their recovery can be maintained only by the officer designated by law.

If the beneficiaries of the Foundation had been specified by name and were capable of receiving, holding and using the gift in the manner intended, they could prosecute an action on their own account to recover the corpus of the trust. Larkin v. Wikoff, 75 N.J.Eq. 462, 72 A. 98, 79 A. 365. But the Pepperdine Foundation is a purely benevolent, public, charitable trust whose beneficiaries are of an indefinite class of persons. Consequently, the only person qualified to maintain an action on behalf of the Foundation is the Attorney General.

* * *

[The court then affirmed the dismissal of the complaint on the ground that it was poorly drafted. Eds.]

■ Fox, J., concurs.

■ McComb, J., concurs in the judgment.

NOTES

1. *Standard of Care.* What makes *Pepperdine* unique is the court's explicit holding that because of the voluntary nature of a director's service on a nonprofit board, the standard of care should be lower than the trust or corporate standard. Though the case was overruled, Holt v. College of Osteopathic Physicians & Surgeons, 61 Cal.2d 750, 757, 394 P.2d 932, 937, 40 Cal.Rptr. 244, 249 (1964); Cal. Corp. Code § 5230(6) (West Supp.1993), the approach reflects a widespread attitude that nonprofit directors are essentially volunteers, and aggressive attempts to enforce their responsibilities are inappropriate and will discourage individuals from board service. Thus, courts and attorneys general tend to be overly solicitous of directors, which may explain why so few cases reach trial. Typically, when a duty of care violation manifests itself and is reported by the press, the publicity hastens settlement of any actions brought by the attorney general. In recent years many jurisdictions have lowered the standard of care or have given additional protection to directors who serve without compensation. See Cal. Corp. Code § 5047.5 (West 1998); Minn. Stat. Ann. § 317A.257 (West 1998); N.Y. Not–For–Profit Corp. L. § 720a (McKinney 1999) for examples.

2. *Duty to Uncover Wrongdoing?* The complaint alleged that Mr. Pepperdine concealed from the board that assets of the foundation were being dissipated. Do the other directors today have a responsibility to uncover wrongdoing? See Principles of the Law of Nonprofit Organizations § 350 cmt. b(4); Model Nonprofit Corp. Act (3d ed.) § 8.30(b) cmt. 2.

b.   THE TRUST STANDARD

Lynch v. John M. Redfield Foundation

California Court of Appeal, Second District, 1970.
9 Cal.App.3d 293, 88 Cal.Rptr. 86.

■ SCHWEITZER, ACTING PRESIDING JUSTICE.

[The Redfield Foundation arranged that dividends earned on securities be sent to a bank for deposit in the Foundation's checking account. The money was then distributed periodically by the directors to various donees. Serious disagreements arose between the directors as to donees and as to management. One of the directors refused to attend meetings called by the other directors and called a meeting to elect two other directors. Because of the controversies, the bank would not order drafts on the Foundation's account unless all directors concurred in the action. The bank continued to receive dividend income and deposited it in the Foundation's checking account, which earned no interest. The attorney general alleged misman-agement by the directors for permitting cash to accumulate for approximately five years, in failing to manage the assets of the Foundation in a businesslike manner, and in failing to carry out the Foundation's charitable purposes. Eds.]

* * *

Assets of a charitable corporation are impressed with a trust. Members of the board of directors of such corporation are essentially trustees. In making investments of trust funds the trustee of a charitable trust is under a duty similar to that of the trustee of a private trust.

From the standpoint of sound legal practice the only technique to be employed by the directors of a charitable corporation in California in the performance of their duties is that of compliance with strict trust principles. It should be noted that, while directors of charitable corporations are exempt from personal liability for the debts, liabilities or obligations of the corporation, they are not immune from personal liability for their own fraud, bad faith, negligent acts or other breaches of duty. * * *

* * * Ordinarily it is the duty of the trustee to invest funds so that they will be productive of income. The trustee can properly take a reasonable amount of time in looking out for proper trust investments, and is not liable for failure to make the property productive during such time. If, however, he delays for an unreasonable length of time before making investments, he commits a breach of trust. Whether his delay in making investments is unreasonable depends upon all the circumstances.

In determining whether there has been a breach of duty, the standard of care is * * * commonly referred to as the prudent man investment rule: "In investing, reinvesting, purchasing, acquiring, exchanging, selling and managing property for the benefit of another, a trustee shall exercise the judgment and care, under the circumstances then prevailing, which men of prudence, discretion and intelligence exercise in the management of their own affairs, not in regard to speculation, but in regard to the permanent disposition of their funds, considering the probable income, as well as the probable safety of their capital. * * *"

Turning to the instant case, our question is whether defendant directors, under the circumstances existent during the years 1961 through 1966, complied with the prudent man investment rule by allowing trust income to accumulate in a non-interest-bearing account for approximately five years. In deciding this question we note that cases involving the obligations and duties of executors and administrators furnish little assistance; unlike a trustee who is charged with a duty to invest, the executor's primary obligation is to safeguard assets. We also note that although most of the authorities cited with respect to a trustee's duty to invest pertain to the investment of principal, we see no reason why the principle is not equally applicable to the duty to invest accumulated income; no authority has been found that makes or discusses such a distinction * * *.

The trial court held that under the circumstances five years was not an unreasonable length of time to hold the income in a non-interest-bearing account * * *.

In the instant case the directors apparently concede that the retention of income in a non-interest-bearing account for a five-year period would normally not meet the standards of the prudent man investment rule, but argue that under the circumstances they should be excused. They mention the cause, a dispute among themselves; the effect, the "blocking" of the bank account; the remedy, a costly lawsuit; the fact that they served without compensation; and the fact that during the period of inaction, the corpus gained approximately 100 per cent in value. Two of the directors strenuously argue that if there be a finding of negligence which caused a loss, they be exonerated because they acted in good faith, and that the fault rested exclusively with director Heaver.

We are satisfied from the authorities heretofore cited that the directors failed to meet the standards of the prudent man investment rule, and that none of the circumstances exonerate them from liability. The "blocking" of the bank account and the possibility of litigation were merely results of their dispute. Thus the primary cause of the loss of income was fault on the part of one or more directors. * * *

Most of the evidence at trial related to the dispute between the directors, the action of the dissident director, and the apparent good faith efforts of the other two to settle their differences and to carry out their obligations to the Foundation and the beneficiaries. There is substantial evidence of good faith and the trial court so found. But good faith is no defense in an action against trustees based on negligence. * * * Each trustee is liable for damages caused by the negligent acts of a cotrustee; liability of trustees for negligence is joint and several. Thus, evidence of good faith on the part of some of the directors, and evidence attempting to place fault on the part of one of the directors was irrelevant and immaterial to the issues tendered by the complaint; * * *.

We conclude as a matter of law under the undisputed facts of this case that the directors breached the prudent man investment rule by failing to invest the income during the five-year period. * * *

NOTE

In Matter of Donner, 82 N.Y.2d 574, 626 N.E.2d 922, 606 N.Y.S.2d 137 (1993), a trustee held in violation of the duty of care was subjected to draconian liability. The decedent left an estate of more than $12.5 million. The major assets were in inter vivos trusts consisting of interest sensitive securities. The executors were the longtime counsel and the financial advisor to the decedent. Before and after the decedent's death the value of the securities in the trusts declined precipitously. There were more than $786,000 in losses from the sale of assets in the estate. The court limited the co-executors to a single commission, ordered some repayments of commissions and other expenses, and ordered the co-executors to pay the estate the actual investment losses from the date of death until the assets were sold and collected. One of the co-executors argued that the trustees opted to retain the assets during an eighteen month period of adverse market conditions to avail a more advantageous time to sell at higher prices. The court found that the attorney-executor was aware of the losses caused by the investment decisions of his co-fiduciary but did not act with the prudence required by the circumstances. Therefore, the co-executors did not fulfill their duty of care which arose from their unique status vis-à-vis decedent to preserve the assets of the estate. The Court of Appeals affirmed. For further reading see Ronald Chester, The Lawyer as Charitable Fiduciary: Public Trust or Private Gain?, 25 Pac. L.J. 1353 (1994). Compare Restatement (Third) of Trusts § 81 cmt. b.

c. THE CORPORATE STANDARD

Stern v. Lucy Webb Hayes National Training School for Deaconesses

United States District Court, District of Columbia, 1974.
381 F.Supp. 1003.

■ GESELL, DISTRICT JUDGE.

This is a class action which was tried to the Court without a jury. Plaintiffs were certified as a class under Rule 23(b)(2) of the Federal Rules of Civil Procedure and represent patients of Sibley Memorial Hospital, a District of Columbia non-profit charitable corporation organized under D.C.Code 29–1001 et seq. They challenge various aspects of the Hospital's fiscal management. The amended complaint named as defendants nine members of the Hospital's Board of Trustees,[1] six financial institutions, and the Hospital itself. Four trustees and one financial institution were dropped by plaintiffs prior to trial, and the Court dismissed the complaint as to the remaining financial institutions at the close of plaintiffs' case.

Several different causes of action were initially alleged. Some were rejected after hearing pretrial motions. Others were dismissed at the close of plaintiffs' evidence and still others are now awaiting determination following completion of the record. The most significant pretrial rulings have been fully covered in a prior opinion, Stern v. Lucy Webb Hayes Nat. Train. Sch. for Deacon. & M., 367 F.Supp. 536 (D.D.C.1973). This Memorandum Opinion will set forth the basis of the Court's determinations made at the close of plaintiffs' case and will, in addition, resolve the remaining issues which went to full trial. All of these matters have been fully briefed and argued and proposed findings of fact have been submitted, all of which the Court has carefully considered. The record consists of 1,169 pages of transcript and 137 exhibits.

The two principal contentions in the complaint are that the defendant trustees conspired to enrich themselves and certain financial institutions with which they were affiliated by favoring those institutions in financial

---

1. The directors of the Hospital are termed "trustees" under the by-laws. However, the use of the term by the Court does not imply a legal conclusion as to the duty they owe the Hospital and its patients.

dealings with the Hospital, and that they breached their fiduciary duties of care and loyalty in the management of Sibley's funds. The defendant financial institutions are said to have joined in the alleged conspiracy and to have knowingly benefited from the alleged breaches of duty. The Hospital is named as a nominal defendant for the purpose of facilitating relief.

I. Corporate History.

The Lucy Webb Hayes National Training School for Deaconesses and Missionaries was established in 1891 by the Methodist Women's Home Missionary Society for the purpose, in part, of providing health care services to the poor of the Washington area. The School was incorporated under the laws of the District of Columbia as a charitable, benevolent and educational institution by instrument dated August 8, 1894. During the following year, the School built the Sibley Memorial Hospital on North Capitol Street to facilitate its charitable work. Over the years, operation of the Hospital has become the School's principal concern, so that the two institutions have been referred to synonymously by all parties and will be so treated in this Opinion. As increasing demands were made upon Sibley's facilities, the Hospital was renovated several times. Finally, in the mid–1950's, it was decided to move the Hospital to a new location on Loughboro Road in Northwest Washington. The nearby Hahnemann Hospital, another Methodist charity, was merged with Sibley in 1956 in anticipation of this move. The new Sibley Memorial Hospital was dedicated on June 17, 1962.

In 1960, shortly after ground was broken for the new building, the Sibley Board of Trustees revised the corporate by-laws in preparation for an expected increase in [t]he volume and complexity of Hospital business following the move. Under the new by-laws, the Board was to consist of from 25 to 35 trustees, who were to meet at least twice each year. Between such meetings, an Executive Committee was to represent the Board, and was authorized, inter alia, to open checking and savings accounts, approve the Hospital budget, renew mortgages, and enter into contracts. A Finance Committee was created to review the budget and to report regularly on the amount of cash available for investment. Management of those investments was to be supervised by an Investment Committee, which was to work closely with the Finance Committee in such matters.

In fact, management of the Hospital from the early 1950's until 1968 was handled almost exclusively by two trustee officers: Dr. Orem, the Hospital Administrator, and Mr. Ernst, the Treasurer. Unlike most of their fellow trustees, to whom membership on the Sibley Board was a charitable service incidental to their principal vocations, Orem and Ernst were continuously involved on almost a daily basis in the affairs of Sibley. They dominated the Board and its Executive Committee, which routinely accepted their recommendations and ratified their actions. Even more significantly, neither the Finance Committee nor the Investment Committee ever met or conducted business from the date of their creation until 1971, three years after the death of Dr. Orem. As a result, budgetary and investment decisions during this period, like most other management decisions affecting the Hospital's finances, were handled by Orem and Ernst, receiving only cursory supervision from the Executive Committee and the full Board.

Dr. Orem's death on April 5, 1968, obliged some of the other trustees to play a more active role in running the Hospital. The Executive Committee, and particularly defendant Stacy Reed (as Chairman of the Board, President of the Hospital, and ex officio member of the Executive Committee), became more deeply involved in the day-to-day management of the Hospital while efforts were made to find a new Administrator. The man who was eventually selected for that office, Dr. Jarvis, had little managerial experience and his performance was not entirely satisfactory. Mr. Ernst still made most of the financial and investment decisions for Sibley, but his actions and failures to act came slowly under increasing scrutiny by several of the other trustees, particularly after a series of disagreements between Ernst and the Hospital Comptroller which led to the discharge of the latter early in 1971.

Prompted by these difficulties, Mr. Reed decided to activate the Finance and Investment Committee in the Fall of 1971.[3] However, as Chairman of the Finance Committee and member of the Investment Committee as well as Treasurer, Mr. Ernst continued to exercise dominant control over investment decisions and, on several occasions, discouraged and flatly refused to respond to inquiries by other trustees into such matters. It has only been since the death of Mr. Ernst on October 30, 1972, that the other trustees appear to have assumed an identifiable supervisory role over investment policy and Hospital fiscal management in general.

Against this background, the basic claims will be examined.

[The conspiracy and self-dealing claims are discussed in Section C3b of this chapter, infra, at pp. 171–178. Eds.]

* * *

III. Breach of Duty.

Plaintiffs' second contention is that, even if the facts do not establish a conspiracy, they do reveal serious breaches of duty on the part of the defendant trustees and the knowing acceptance of benefits from those breaches by the defendant banks and savings and loan associations.

A. The Trustees.

Basically, the trustees are charged with mismanagement, nonmanagement and self-dealing. The applicable law is unsettled. The charitable corporation is a relatively new legal entity which does not fit neatly into the established common law categories of corporation and trust. As the discussion below indicates, however, the modern trend is to apply corporate

---

3. Although the committees had never met prior to 1971, the Board had duly elected trustees to serve on them every year since their creation in 1960. The by-laws were simply ignored.

rather than trust principles in determining the liability of the directors of charitable corporations, because their functions are virtually indistinguishable from those of their "pure" corporate counterparts.

1. Mismanagement

Both trustees and corporate directors are liable for losses occasioned by their negligent mismanagement of investments. However, the degree of care required appears to differ in many jurisdictions. A trustee is uniformly held to a high standard of care and will be held liable for simple negligence, while a director must often have committed "gross negligence" or otherwise be guilty of more than mere mistakes of judgment.

This distinction may amount to little more than a recognition of the fact that corporate directors have many areas of responsibility, while the traditional trustee is often charged only with the management of the trust funds and can therefore be expected to devote more time and expertise to that task. Since the board members of most large charitable corporations fall within the corporate rather than the trust model, being charged with the operation of ongoing businesses, it has been said that they should only be held to the less stringent corporate standard of care. More specifically, directors of charitable corporations are required to exercise ordinary and reasonable care in the performance of their duties, exhibiting honesty and good faith.

2. Nonmanagement

Plaintiffs allege that the individual defendants failed to supervise the management of Hospital investments or even to attend meetings of the committees charged with such supervision. Trustees are particularly vulnerable to such a charge, because they not only have an affirmative duty to "maximize the trust income by prudent investment," Blankenship v. Boyle, 329 F.Supp. 1089, 1096 (D.D.C.1971), but they may not delegate that duty, even to a committee of their fellow trustees. Restatement (Second) of Trusts 171, at 375 (1959). A corporate director, on the other hand, may delegate his investment responsibility to fellow directors, corporate officers, or even outsiders, but he must continue to exercise general supervision over the activities of his delegates. Once again, the rule for charitable corporations is closer to the traditional corporate rule: directors should at least be permitted to delegate investment decisions to a committee of board members, so long as all directors assume the responsibility for supervising such committees by periodically scrutinizing their work. Restatement (Second) of Trusts 379, comment b (1959).

Total abdication of the supervisory role, however, is improper even under traditional corporate principles. A director who fails to acquire the information necessary to supervise investment policy or consistently fails even to attend the meetings at which such policies are considered has violated his fiduciary duty to the corporation. While a director is, of course, permitted to rely upon the expertise of those to whom he has delegated investment responsibility, such reliance is a tool for interpreting the delegate's reports, not an excuse for dispensing with or ignoring such reports. A director whose failure to supervise permits negligent mismanagement by others to go unchecked has committed an independent wrong against the corporation; he is not merely an accessory under an attenuated theory of respondent superior or constructive notice.

* * *

Having surveyed the authorities as outlined above and weighed the briefs, arguments and evidence submitted by counsel, the Court holds that a director or so-called trustee of a charitable hospital organized under the Non–Profit Corporation Act of the District of Columbia (D.C.Code 29–1001 et seq.) is in default of his fiduciary duty to manage the fiscal and investment affairs of the hospital if it has been shown by a preponderance of the evidence that:

(1) while assigned to a particular committee of the Board having general financial or investment responsibility under the by-laws of the corporation, he has failed to use due diligence in supervising the actions of those officers, employees or outside experts to whom the responsibility for making day-to-day financial or investment decisions has been delegated; or

(2) he knowingly permitted the hospital to enter into a business transaction with himself or with any corporation, partnership or association in which he then had a substantial interest or held a position as trustee, director, general manager or principal officer without having previously informed the persons charged with approving that transaction of his interest or position and of any significant reasons, unknown to or not fully appreciated by such persons, why the transaction might not be in the best interests of the hospital; or

(3) except as required by the preceding paragraph, he actively participated in or voted in favor of a decision by the Board or any committee or subcommittee thereof to transact business with himself or with any corporation, partnership or association in which he then had a substantial interest or held a position as trustee, director, general manager or principal officer; or

(4) he otherwise failed to perform his duties honestly, in good faith, and with a reasonable amount of diligence and care.

Applying these standards to the facts in the record, the Court finds that each of the defendant trustees has breached his fiduciary duty to supervise the management of Sibley's investments. All except Mr. Jones were duly and repeatedly elected to the Investment Committee without ever bothering to object when no meetings were called for more than ten years. Mr. Jones was a member of the equally inactive Finance Committee, the failure of which to report on the existence of investable funds was cited by several other defendants as a reason for not convening the Investment Committee. In addition, Reed, Jones and Smith were, for varying periods of time, also members of the Executive Committee, which was charged with acquiring at least enough information to vote intelligently on the opening of new bank accounts. By their own testimony, it is clear that they failed to do so. And all of the individual defendants ignored the investment sections of the yearly audits which were made available to them as members of the Board. In short, these men have in the past failed to exercise even the most cursory supervision over the handling of Hospital funds and failed to establish and carry out a defined policy.

The record is unclear on the degree to which full disclosure preceded the frequent self-dealing which occurred during the period under consideration. It is reasonable to assume that the Board was generally aware of the various bank affiliations of the defendant trustees, but there is no indication that these conflicting interests were brought home to the relevant committees when they voted to approve particular transactions. Similarly, while plaintiffs have shown no active misrepresentation on defendants' part, they have established instances in which an interested trustee failed to alert the responsible officials to better terms known to be available elsewhere.

It is clear that all of the defendant trustees have, at one time or another, affirmatively approved self-dealing transactions. Most of these incidents were of relatively minor significance: one interested trustee would join a dozen disinterested fellow members of the Executive Committee in unanimously approving the opening of a bank account; two or three interested trustees would support a similarly large group in voting to give or renew the mortgage. Others cannot be so easily disregarded. Defendant Ferris' advice and vote in the relatively small Investment Committee to recommend approval of the investment contract with Ferris & Co. may have been crucial to that transaction. Defendant Reed assumed principal responsibility for account levels between 1969 and 1971, during which period the Security checking account grew to more than a million dollars. And defendant Smith, in his capacity as President of Jefferson Federal, personally negotiated the interest rates on a $230,000 certificate account with the Hospital.

That the Hospital has suffered no measurable injury from many of these transactions—including the mortgage and the investment contract— and that the excessive deposits which were the real source of harm were caused primarily by the uniform failure to supervise rather than the occasional self-dealing vote are both facts that the Court must take into account in fashioning relief, but they do not alter the principle that the trustee of a charitable hospital should always avoid active participation in a transaction in which he or a corporation with which he is associated has a significant interest.

[The relief ordered is discussed in Section C3b of this chapter, infra, at pp. 175–178. Eds.]

NOTES AND QUESTIONS

1. *Corporate Standard.* The corporate standard adopted in Stern v. Lucy Webb, also known as the *Sibley Hospital* case, has become the

predominant standard for the duty of care. According to Marion Fremont–Smith, 43 states have adopted duty of care provisions in nonprofit statutes (Governing Nonprofit Organizations 208 (2004)), as has the Model Nonprofit Corporation Act (§ 8.30).

2. *What's the Standard?* Just what is the real difference in the standard of care imposed in Lynch v. Redfield and Stern v. Lucy Webb? Would the directors of the hospital have been liable under a trust standard? Courts distinguish between simple negligence as violation of the trust standard and the gross negligence necessary for a corporate standard. Is this a real distinction that provides any useful guidance for a board of directors? Baron Rolfe once defined gross negligence as the same thing as ordinary negligence "with the addition of a vituperative epithet." Williamson v. Brett, 152 Eng. Rep. 737 (1843). Does the difficulty of differentiation merely invite counsel to claim all breaches are gross negligence?

3. *Components of the Duty of Care.* Nonprofit statutes typically provide that a director shall perform her duties in good faith and with that degree of diligence, care and skill which ordinarily prudent persons would exercise under similar circumstances in like positions. N.Y. Not-for-Profit Corp. L. § 717; Cal. Corp. Code §§ 5231, 7231. However, they do not offer specific guidance as to how the director should execute her responsibilities. The vague generalities enunciating standards of conduct for the duty of care provide outside boundaries for board behavior. Broadly stated, a director can fail to discharge her duty of care in two ways: by failing to properly manage or supervise the corporate entity (the duty of attention), or by failing to make an informed decision about an important transaction or fundamental change in the way the corporate entity operates (the duty of informed decision making). The duty of care also presupposes that directors are acting in good faith and without a disabling conflict of interest. The degree of skill required in the statutes is the tort standard of the ordinary prudent person in contrast to a standard that calls for a degree of expertise. This focuses upon basic directorial attributes of common sense, practical wisdom and informed judgment. Section 8.30 of the Model Nonprofit Corporation Act replaces the "ordinary prudent person" with a "person in like position," attempting to move away from the concept of negligence as a standard. Id. at cmt. 2.

The phrase "In like position * * * under similar circumstances" recognizes that the nature and extent of responsibilities of directors vary depending upon the nature of the organization and obliquely recognizes that the directors of most nonprofits are volunteers. In order to find liability, the breach of duty must have brought about the loss to the nonprofit organization.

a. *The Duty of Attention.* The duty of attention requires the director to actively participate in the organization's activities and operations. Elements of such active participation include regular attendance at board meetings, review of minutes and written materials disseminated to directors prior to or at meetings, periodic meeting with senior management, access to and review of the organizations's books and records, careful review of financial statements, and access to and the opportunity to ask questions of outside experts such as accountants or attorneys. Cf. Charles Hansen, The Duty of Care, The Business Judgment Rule, and the American Law Institute Corporate Governance Project, 48 Bus. Law. 1355, 1359–60 (1991); American Bar Association Section of Business Law, Guidebook for Directors of Nonprofit Corporations 19–20 (2d ed. 2002) (hereinafter "Guidebook for Directors"). A director needs an adequate source of information which generally is supplied by the staff. The process by which a director informs herself will vary depending upon the organization and the director, but the duty of care requires that every director take steps to become knowledgeable about background facts and circumstances before taking action on the matter at hand. The obligation to initiate or cause an inquiry occurs only when the circumstances would alert a reasonable director or officer to such a need. Model Nonprofit Corp. Act (3d ed.) § 8.30(b), cmt. 2.

b. *Informed Decisionmaking*. The informed decision requirement focuses upon the preparedness of the director or officer in making the decision as opposed to the quality of the decision itself. Elements of informed decisionmaking would include opportunities to hear a presentation by management accompanied by written materials explaining the rationale for the decision, to hear the advice and recommendation of outside experts, to debate and deliberate upon a proposal; where appropriate, to gather information from comparable institutions; and the opportunity to request any additional information deemed relevant by a director from management or outside experts as well as time to consider that additional information. All these elements depend upon the size and scope of the organization's activities.

c. *Delegation*. Directors do not manage the nonprofit organization on a day-to-day basis. Thus, they delegate management responsibilities but in so doing should set policies and oversee corporate agents. There are limits to delegation. Directors are not personally liable for actions or omissions of their agents so long as the persons have been prudently selected and the principal delegation is made to the chief executive officer of the organization. Guidebook for Directors, supra, pp. 23–25.

d. *Reliance*. Directors and officers may rely upon information, opinions, reports or statements, including financial statements and other financial data prepared by employees, counsel, accountants or other knowledgeable and competent persons or by a committee of the board on which the director does not serve. Cf. N.Y. Not-for-Profit Corp. L. § 717(b); Model Nonprofit Corp. Act (3d ed.) § 8.30(d)–(f). In order to rely on a report, the director must read and evaluate it, reasonably believe the contents to be accurate, and honestly assume that the agents presenting such reports are within their professional or expert competence.

4. *The Best Judgment Rule*. The business judgment rule—more appropriately known in the nonprofit context as the best judgment rule—provides that if a director has made a decision by informing herself in good faith without a disabling conflict of interest, there will be neither judicial

inquiry nor liability even if the action was unfortunate for the organization or its membership. This safe harbor does not encompass breaches involving bad faith, criminal activity, fraud, or willful and wanton misconduct. Basically, the best judgment rule says that courts will not second guess the actions of directors even if in hindsight they turn out to be unwise. While the rule is well established in corporate law, it applies as well to nonprofit directors, and the standards utilized by the courts in nonprofit cases are derived from the corporate context. See Janssen v. Best & Flanagan, 662 N.W.2d 876, 883 (Minn. 2003); Mahan v. Avera St. Luke's, 621 N.W.2d 150, 154 (S.D. 2001); Beard v. Achenbach Memorial Hospital, 170 F.2d 859 (10th Cir. 1948).

In Scheuer Family Foundation, Inc. v. 61 Assocs., 179 A.D.2d 65, 582 N.Y.S.2d 662 (1st Dept.1992), a member and director of a charitable corporation brought a derivative action against directors of the foundation, the foundation's asset manager and investment advisor which were controlled by the defendant directors. The complaint alleged that the defendants negligently invested the foundation's assets, engaged in self-dealing transactions, and withheld information concerning these activities from other directors. The court concluded that the defendant directors' interest in the foundation and in the investment advisor and asset manager was "precisely the type of dual interest and potential for self-interest which would create an exception to the shield provided by the business judgment rule and render open to judicial scrutiny allegations of the improprieties by the board * * *." Id. at 69, 582 N.Y.S.2d at 664. As a result, the defendants' actions would be evaluated under the duty of care standard. The business judgment rule also does not shield directors from liabilities for decisions, actions or the lack thereof which violate specific laws such as tax or environmental statutes, or from claims not based upon a director's duty to the corporation such as discrimination or defamation.

5. *Why Such a Low Standard of Review?* The standard of review applied to duty of care violations by courts is quite low as compared to the legal standard of conduct, and statutory developments have made liability improbable except in the most egregious cases such as improper loans or distribution of corporate assets. N.Y. Not-for-Profit Corp. L. § 719; Model Nonprofit Corp. Act (3d ed.) § 8.33; Cal. Corp. Code §§ 5237, 7236, 9245; 805 Ill. Comp. Stat. Ann. 105/108.65. What is the rationale for such a low standard of care?

6. *Monitoring Nonprofit Boards.* Are nonprofit boards easier or more difficult to monitor than their corporate counterparts? Why might nonprofit boards be so susceptible to breaches in the duty of care? Daniel Kurtz, a New York attorney who was head of the Charities Bureau of the New York Attorney General's Office, has said, "probing questions by charity board members have been viewed as simply bad manners." Felicity Barringer, Charity Boards Learn to be Skeptical, N.Y. Times, Apr. 19, 1992, at 10. Many nonprofit board memberships confer social status. Robin Pogrebin, Trustees Find Cultural Board Seats are Still Highly Coveted Luxury Items, N.Y. Times, Apr. 3, 2010, at C1. Powerful group dynamics constrain the

willingness of directors to voice concern or dissent, discouraging them from openly questioning or contradicting management except in extraordinary circumstances. Developments in the Law—Corporations and Society, 117 Harv. L.Rev. 2181, 2186 (2004), citing Jay W. Lorsch with Elizabeth MacIver, Pawns or Potentates: The Reality of America's Corporate Boards 84–86 (1989). An active or investigative approach may be considered out of place in the genteel world of many nonprofit boards. Is there something about the make-up of nonprofit boards that makes active oversight difficult? The common business professional, social and economic background of business corporate directors has been well documented. See Lisa M. Fairfax, The Bottom Line on Board Diversity: A Cost Benefit Analysis of the Business Rationale for Diversity on Corporate Boards, 2005 Wis. L.Rev. 795, 832–834 (2005); Marleen O'Connor, The Enron Board: The Perils of Group Think, 71 U Cin. L. Rev. 1233, 1245 (2003).

7. *Inattentive Directors*. Nonprofit executives often have difficulty in encouraging board members to become active and involved in the organization. Directors who do not direct are a common problem in the nonprofit world. If a socialite, financier, or movie star sits on a board, can the organization's chief executive be expected to criticize them for lack of attention or devotion to the organization? Is there a solution to the conflict between the need to obtain prominent people for boards which gives recognition to the organization and assists fundraising and the desire to have an active and involved board?

The Smithsonian Institution, one of the nation's iconic nonprofits, is federally chartered. The composition of its board of regents is determined by congressional legislation mandating membership for certain designated notables, including the Vice President and Chief Justice of the United States, six members of Congress, and nine others. The Smithsonian board had three business meetings a year and presided over 19 museums, 9 research centers and the National Zoo. Some of the designated board members rarely attended. The Smithsonian came under criticism from Congress and the press for overly generous compensation and benefits paid to its executives, inadequate controls and a declining financial situation. According to the Smithsonian's Inspector General, the board was unaware of compensation practices and the Institution's other problems. Can a board as structured possibly oversee such a vast institution, even if its prominent members had the time and desire to do so?

In June 2007, a report by an independent review committee appointed by the Smithsonian's Regents found that its former CEO, Lawrence Small, who resigned under pressure earlier in the year, received excessive compensation some of which was disguised as a housing allowance for mortgage payments even though he had owned his own home for many years, had no mortgage, and did not use the home extensively for Smithsonian functions. The review committee found that Small and his chief deputy took off 950 days over seven years, with much of this "leave" used to serve on corporate boards where Small earned an additional $5.7 million. The report also concluded that Small's fundraising prowess was exaggerated when compared to his predecessor, and that the Regents did nothing to make him accountable for personal expenses. A second report by the Smithsonian's Governance Committee recommended far-reaching changes to make the Regents more active and responsible fiduciaries, the Smithsonian more transparent, and the creation of systems to enable senior officials to have direct access to the Regents. Both reports are available on the Smithsonian's web site.

8. *Meddlesome Directors.* The American Red Cross, chartered by Congress in 1905, has been criticized in recent years for its response to 9/11 and Hurricane Katrina. It manages the nation's blood supply, a $1 billion business, and has paid over $5 million in fines for safety lapses. Congressional legislation in 1947 provided that the President of the United States appoint seven cabinet secretaries to the 50 person board. The designated members rarely attended meetings, and had no influence on the organization. Thirty-five board members were elected by the 800 local chapters, and they control the board. The congressional legislation designated the chairman of the board as the "principal officer." The result of the governance structure was constant meddling by the board into Red Cross operations, leading to five presidents or acting presidents in five years. The organization has been secretive about its finances and governance, essentially accountable to no one. Because it is federally chartered, the Red Cross is exempt from state filing requirements, and the Ninth Circuit Court of Appeals held the organization exempt from the federal Freedom of Information Act. Irwin Memorial Blood Bank v. American National Red Cross, 640 F.2d 1051 (9th Cir. 1981).

In October 2006, the Board recommended changes to the Congressional charter, the bylaws and other governing documents, which would bring the governance structure more in line with other organizations. In May 2007, the American National Red Cross Governance Modernization Act was signed into law. Pub.L. 110–26, 121 Stat. 103. It reduces the board of governors to 20 but not until 2012. All governors are elected by the board. The designated directors become part of an advisory board that meets with the governing board once each year. The responsibilities of the board are to focus on long term strategic planning, monitoring the organizations management and traditional governance concerns. The statute (36 U.S.C. § 300112) creates an office of the ombudsman, which must submit to the appropriate Congressional committees an annual report concerning any trends and systematic matters that the ombudsman has identified as confronting the organization. The findings specify that the Red Cross is a charity but also an instrumentality of the United States.

9. *Overcommitted Directors.* A common problem for nonprofit organizations is that some directors, particularly those with "trophy" names, like to stack boards—that is, they serve on too many to be effective. Corporate governance experts have decried the overcommitment of star directors on corporate boards. The National Association of Corporate Directors has recommended that directors serve on no more than five boards. In May 1999, the United Way of Santa Clara went bankrupt. The board had little

knowledge of the financial crisis and was unaware that when the executive director dismissed 32 staff members, she gave them a severance package at a total cost of $1 million. The Chairman, a San Jose beer distributor, served on 34 other charity and civic boards. David Cay Johnston, In the Wealthy Silicon Valley, a United Way Runs Dry, N.Y. Times, May 16, 1999, at 28. Board service consists not only of attendance at meetings, but sitting on committees of the board and preparing for meetings. Individuals who sit on multiple boards may not be able to commit the time necessary to effectively perform their board duties. If a problem arises with an organization on whose board an overcommitted director serves, can she defend herself on the grounds that she was a courtesy or inactive director? See Francis v. United Jersey Bank, 87 N.J. 15, 432 A.2d 814 (1981); Stern v. Lucy Webb Hayes, 381 F.Supp. 1003 (D.D.C.1974). For a discussion of these issues, see Principles of the Law of Nonprofit Corporations § 320 cmt. b.

One solution to this problem proposed by Michael Klausner and Jonathan Small is that the law recognize a bifurcated board made up of governing and non-governing board members. They maintain that all directors should not be asked or expected to govern, and the analogy to for-profit boards is misplaced because nonprofit directors are often called upon to perform specific functions or provide special expertise—fundraising, links to the community etc. The authors suggest that directors could choose to govern one year and not govern another, depending on their interest and availability. Failing to Govern? The Disconnect Between Theory and Reality in Nonprofit Boards, and How to Fix It, 3 Stan. Soc. Innovation Rev. 42 (Spring 2005). Do you see any problems with such an approach? Or would it be preferable to provide some individuals with an honorary title rather than formal board member status? See Marion R. Fremont–Smith, Governing Nonprofit Organizations 433 (2004).

10. *A Shifting Standard of Care.* The corporate standard of care is hardly a difficult test to meet. Is it sufficiently high to be used for all board decisions no matter how trivial or significant to the organization? Dual standards occasionally have been applied under corporate law principles. At common law the directors of banking and financial corporations had to exercise a higher degree of care and skill than directors of other corporations. See Greenfield Sav. Bank v. Abercrombie, 211 Mass. 252, 255, 97 N.E. 897, 899 (1912) (the bank is designed to help the poorer members of society and directors have a higher responsibility). A higher standard has been included legislatively for trustees of ERISA pension funds. Employee Retirement Income Security Program, 29 U.S.C.A. § 1104(a)(1)(B) (1974).

When business corporations are faced with an organic change, such as a change in control or tender offer, boards have been held to more rigorous standards in reaching decisions than in ordinary matters and have had to satisfy more demanding requirements that they had reasonable grounds for their decision. See Unocal v. Mesa Petroleum, 493 A.2d 946, 955 (Del.1985); Revlon, Inc. v. MacAndrews & Forbes Holdings, Inc., 506 A.2d 173 (Del. 1985); Smith v. Van Gorkom, 488 A.2d 858 (Del.1985).

Should there be a distinction in the standard of care of nonprofit directors depending upon whether the matter for consideration is ministerial, involving day-to-day operations, or a decision relating to the organization's core functions, exempt purposes or future? Should a trust standard apply to matters of particular importance to the organization and to the community, such as organic changes (dissolutions, mergers, a change of purpose), an exodus from the community served, or a conversion to for-profit status?

Some examples where a higher standard might be used include: a nonprofit hospital historically serving the poor in a community decides to move to an affluent suburb in order to increase revenues for profitable activities; a museum desires to change its collecting emphasis from modern art to classical art or to deaccession one collection to concentrate and strengthen other areas;[1] or a nonprofit public television station or hospital decides to dissolve and sell its assets to a for-profit equivalent. Would a dual standard create difficulty for boards in determining their responsibilities in a particular situation? Would it deter nonprofits from engaging in entrepreneurial risk?

PROBLEMS

Consider in the following problems whether there has been a breach of the duty of care, and if so, what damages if any would be imposed upon the directors.

(a) Eugenia Vandergelt, a well-known interior designer, philanthropist, and socialite, is invited to join the board of the Peoria Mission, a nonprofit organization that provides food and shelter to the homeless. Ms. Vandergelt agrees to join the board on the understanding that she will not be expected to attend board meetings. Her name will bring recognition to the organization from other potential donors, and she has agreed to host an annual cocktail party for contributors. The other board members agree with the terms of this appointment.

(b) General Hospital has been saddled with a $4 million deficit. It hires George Jones as its chief executive officer to pare the deficit by $200,000 per year. The trustees have not received annual audits and when they questioned Jones about how the plan was progressing, he responded: "Things are going okay." In fact, in two years the deficit had grown to $10 million dollars.

---

1. See Carol Vogel, New York Public Library to Sell Major Art Works to Raise Funds, N.Y. Times, April 11, 2005, at A1 (nineteen works included a Gilbert Stuart portrait of George Washington, which did not sell); Metropolitan Museum of Art, Report on Art Transactions, 1971–1973 (1973) reprinted in 2 Law, Ethics & The Visual Arts, 7–114 to 7–154 (1979) (deaccession of valuable collection of ancient coins); Rowan v. Pasadena Art Museum, Case No. C322817 (Calif. Superior Court, County of Los Angeles), filed Sept. 22, 1981; Failing, Is the Norton Simon Museum Mismanaged, Art News, Oct. 19, 1990, at 136 (change of focus of museum from modern to classical art in return for financial support).

(c) United Public Radio (UPR), an umbrella organization of public radio stations, is in perpetual financial difficulty. After substantial discussion, the board votes to create *Tune In*, a radio magazine and program guide. The start-up costs are defrayed through a grant from a private foundation. UPR's premise is that its affluent listenership would attract advertising, and with lower postal costs the venture would become profitable. The board commissioned no market research on the interest in such a magazine. In fact UPR's projections were unrealistic to begin with, and the publication became a financial drain losing $6 million in two years and threatening UPR's existence. The establishment of a magazine is in every instance a risky endeavor. According to the Magazine Publishers Association, nine out of ten new magazines fail within 18 months of their first issue, a fact unknown to the board at the time it approved the decision to publish.

(d) Assume that in (c), above, the board retained a magazine consulting firm listed on the magazine association website to assist it in reaching its decision. In fact, the firm's principal partners misrepresented their qualifications and had never worked in the magazine industry and several had criminal records.

(e) The Internal Revenue Service found the Tammy Lee Foundation to be in violation of § 4941 of the Internal Revenue Code, which imposes severe excise tax penalties on various self-dealing transactions between private foundations and insiders such as foundation managers. The foundation's executive director had received interest-free loans in the amount of $50,000. The executive resigned. Five years later, the Service again finds the Foundation in violation because several employees' children have received summer travel grants from the foundation's "Global Understanding Project."

d.   CHARITABLE IMMUNITY, LIMITATION OF DIRECTORS' LIABILITY AND INDEMNIFICATION

Model Nonprofit Corp. Act (3d ed.) §§ 2.02(b)(8), (c); 8.50–8.58.

Cal. Corp. Code §§ 5047.5, 5238, 5239, 7231.5.

Ill. Comp. Stat., ch. 805, § 105/108.70.

N.Y. Not–for–Profit Corp. L. § 720–a.

Principles of the Law of Nonprofit Organizations § 380.

Volunteer Protection Act of 1997.

1. *Charitable Immunity*. Charitable immunity, the principle that charities are not liable for the consequences of the torts of their members, employees, or directors, entered American law in the nineteenth century as a misinterpretation of dicta from two already overruled English cases. John R. Feather, Comment, The Immunity of Charitable Institutions from Tort Liability, 11 Baylor L. Rev. 86, 86–89 (1959); Note, The Quality of Mercy: "Charitable Torts" and Their Continuing Immunity, 100 Harv. L. Rev.

1382, 1383–84 (1987) (hereinafter, "Charitable Torts"). Adopted by the majority of American jurisdictions, charitable immunity was justified on several different grounds. One was the trust fund theory: charitable expenditures were limited by the intent of the donor. To apply charitable assets to damages would divert them to a completely different purpose than intended. A second rationale was that the doctrine of respondeat superior, which holds employers liable for the torts of their employees and agents committed within the scope of their employment, did not apply to charities because they did not profit from their employees' work. Another justification was public policy. A fourth was implied waiver of liability: since charitable beneficiaries paid no consideration for services received, they assumed all risks of negligence. Charitable Torts, supra, at 1384.

Beginning with President of Georgetown College v. Hughes, 130 F.2d 810 (D.C.Cir.1942), which rejected the charitable immunity of a hospital sued by a nurse injured negligently by a hospital employee acting in the course of duty, the doctrine, never unanimously accepted, eroded. Rumors of its demise were exaggerated, however, and it reemerged in the 1980's. The doctrine's decline was checked by the expansion of potential liability faced by nonprofits; several well-publicized recoveries against charities, and an insurance crisis in the 1980s that caused nonprofits to face greatly increased premiums for insurance and shrinking coverage within policies. See Developments in the Law–Nonprofit Corporations, 105 Harv.L.Rev. 1578, 1682 (1992) (hereinafter "Developments"). Many nonprofits were financially unable to purchase any insurance at all even if they could find a liability policy.

Historically, the number of lawsuits filed against nonprofit organizations was small. Disincentives to litigation included restrictions to members' rights to sue, the relatively few charitable nonprofits with members, and the lack of standing of patrons, beneficiaries or the public. See Section D of this chapter, infra, at pp. 221–240. As nonprofits themselves proved financially unable to meet liability demands, litigation against individuals, particularly directors, increased. Charles R. Tremper, Are Nonprofit Board Members Indecently Exposed?, 22 U.S.F.L.Rev. 857 (1988). One response was risk pooling, where charities joined together and improved their risk management techniques. States reacted to the decline of charitable immunity and the insurance crisis by creating new limitations on the liability of charitable actors. The new legislation attempts to balance the concern of unlimited liabilities on volunteers against a blanket immunity which would deny all compensation to a class of victims. Most states protect some volunteers from liability for negligent acts while allowing recovery for more flagrant wrongdoing. A few jurisdictions predicate protection of volunteers on the sponsoring organization maintaining adequate liability insurance or meeting some other standard. Other jurisdictions retain limited versions of charitable immunity or impose damage caps on recovery, limit recovery to the amount of their available insurance or protect certain assets of charitable organizations from judgment. Charles R. Tremper, Compensation for Harm from Charitable Activity, 76 Cornell L. Rev. 401, 411–412 (1991).

What are the arguments for and against charitable immunity? Does charitable immunity matter for poverty stricken charities? Are there shielding techniques common to the business world that nonprofits could engage in to limit their liability?

2. *Limitation of Directors' Liability.* The common law doctrine of charitable immunity shielded only organizations. Developments, supra at 1685. The decline in charitable immunity made directors reluctant to serve even though they rarely were found liable for the torts of their charities. Protection of individuals affiliated with nonprofits has been through statute. Almost every state has passed legislation that limits the liability of individuals involved with nonprofit or charitable organizations. The type and extent of liability varies widely. For a survey of state approaches, see Jill R. Horwitz & Joseph Mead, Letting Good Deeds Go Unpunished: Volunteer Immunity Laws and Tort Deterrence, Appendix, 6 J. Empirical Legal Studies 535 (2009). The new statutes typically do not exempt intentionally harmful behavior, reckless or grossly negligent acts, or situations where the individual does not proceed in good faith. Most of these statutes cover directors, officers, and unpaid board members. Approximately one-half of the states protect all uncompensated volunteers regardless of their position. The laws are ambiguous, complex, and they have little case law to clarify them.

3. *Federal Volunteer Protection Act.* Congress enacted the Volunteer Protection Act of 1997, Pub. L. 105–19, 111 Stat. 26 (codified at 42 U.S.C. § 14501) to limit the liability of volunteers of nonprofit and governmental entities for harm caused to others if they met the following criteria: (1) the volunteer was acting within the scope of her responsibilities at the time of the act or omission; (2) the volunteer was properly licensed, certified, or authorized by the appropriate authorities for the activities or practice in the state where the harm occurred; (3) the harm was not caused by willful or criminal misconduct, gross negligence, reckless misconduct, or a conscious, flagrant indifference to the rights or safety of the individual harmed by the volunteer; and (4) the harm was not caused by the volunteer operating a motor vehicle, vessel, aircraft or other vehicle for which the state required an operators license and insurance.

The Volunteer Protection Act preempts state laws to the extent of any inconsistency with it, except where the state law provides additional protection from liability. It does not protect the volunteer from lawsuits, but provides a complete defense when a suit is brought by a third party. The Act also does not protect a volunteer against an action brought by the organization against the volunteer. Five specific categories of behavior, including hate crimes and crimes of violence, are not protected by the Act. The Act preempts state immunity laws unless they provide greater protection and limits the award of punitive damages. Presumably, the Act does not limit recovery for economic loss. Immunity statutes become important during responses to public health and disaster emergencies. Volunteer health responders are protected but in only a few jurisdictions does the immunity extend to entities such as hospitals. See James G Hodge, Jr.,

Stephanie H. Cálves, Lance A. Gable, Elizabeth Meltzer, & Sara Kraner, Risk Management in the Wake of hurricanes and Other Disasters: Hospital Civil Liability Arising From the Use of Volunteer health Professionals During Emergencies, 10 Mich. St. U. J. Med. & L. 57, 77–78 (2005).

4. *Indemnification.* Indemnification is the payment by an organization of a director's legal costs, judgments, settlements and other expenses arising out of litigation and theoretical legal action from a director's service to the corporation. The purpose of indemnification is to provide financial protection to directors and officers against expenses of litigation. Daniel Kurtz, Board Liability 102 (1988). Directors' and officers' insurance policies complement indemnification.

The modern source of indemnification is statutory. At common law there was uncertainty as to the extent to which corporations could indemnify their directors and officers against personal liabilities. Some cases held that there was no right to indemnification in the absence of a statute. Texas Society v. Fort Bend Chapter, 590 S.W.2d 156 (Tex.Civ.App.1979). Indemnification reflects a compromise between the desire not to reward directors and officers for acts which are harmful to the organization and the reality that directors would not serve without indemnification.

If a director is sued and successfully defends the action, the corporation must indemnify the director for litigation expenses unless limited by the articles of incorporation. Model Nonprofit Corp. Act (3d ed.) § 8.52. A corporation may indemnify a director if the individual acted in good faith, reasonably believed the conduct was in the corporations's best interest or acted in a manner that was not opposed to the corporation's best interests, and in the case of a criminal proceeding, had no reasonable belief that the conduct was unlawful. Id. at § 8.51(a). Generally, indemnification will not lie for a director found liable to a corporation in a derivative action brought on behalf of the corporation. Most jurisdictions allow the corporation to advance litigation expenses. A director or officer successful on the merits or unsuccessful in defense but feeling entitled to reimbursement can seek court ordered indemnification.

5. *For Further Reading.* Jill R. Horwitz & Joseph Mead, Letting Good Deeds Go Unpunished: Volunteer Immunity Laws and Tort Deterrence, 6 J. Empirical Legal Studies 535 (2009); Sharona Hoffman, Responders' Responsibility: Liability and Immunity in Public Health Emergencies, 96 Geo.L.J. 1913 (2008); Kenneth W. Biedzynski, The Federal Volunteer Protection Act: Does Congress Want to Play Ball?, 23 Seton Hall Legis. J. 319, 349 (1999); David Barrett, A Call for More Lenient Director Liability Standards for Small, Charitable Nonprofit Corporations, 71 Ind. L. J. 697, 1000 (2000); Developments in the Law–Nonprofit Corporations, 105 Harv. L. Rev. 1578, 1678–1699 (1992); Note, The Quality of Mercy: "Charitable Torts" and Their Continuing Immunity, 100 Harv. L. Rev. 1382 (1987); John F. Olson & Josiah O. Hatch III, Director and Officer Liability: Indemnification and Insurance (2004); Charles R. Tremper, Compensation for Harm from Charitable Activity, 76 Cornell L. Rev. 401 (1991); Charles

R. Tremper, Reconsidering Legal Liability and Insurance for Nonprofit Organizations (1989).

e.   PIERCING THE CORPORATE VEIL

When a nonprofit organization is incorporated, the corporate entity becomes distinct from its members, officers, directors, employees and creditors. Corporate status provides limited liability for those involved with the organization. This means individuals are not responsible for corporate debts, and creditors can only levy against corporate assets. If the corporate form is merely a shield for individual activity, a device to engage in fraud or avoid legal obligations, or the organization ignores corporate formalities or intentionally engages in activity with a lack of adequate capitalization, a court may ignore the corporate form and use the equitable doctrine of "piercing the corporate veil" to hold individuals or another corporation liable.

This is an area of metaphor and name calling. Courts will use words such as "instrumentality", "device" or "alter ego" which means another aspect of oneself. If an individual influences and so dominates an entity that there is a unity of interest and ownership so that the individual and the nonprofit cannot be separated and to respect the corporate status would work as a fraud, a court will disregard the corporate entity. There are analogous doctrines in federal tax law of private inurement and private benefit that if applied, may result in revocation of an organization's tax exempt status. See Chapter 5D, infra, at pp. 445–461. Piercing decisions are fact intensive, and it is difficult to come up with a consistent principled rule, but there are usually two factors present: the rules relating to corporate status have been violated, and it would be unjust to allow individuals to hide behind the corporate structure.

Adherence to corporate formalities is important. A failure to hold meetings, elect directors, maintain separate books or engage in the other incidents of corporate governance are indicia courts consider. For example, in HOK Sport, Inc. v. FC Des Moines, FC, 495 F.3d 927 (8th Cir. 2007), Kyle Krause established a nonprofit organization, TSF, to construct a soccer stadium that would be owned by the city of Urbandale, Iowa and used by his soccer team. Krause was the president, only officer, and member of the board of directors. The nonprofit lacked separate books or capital, incurred unpaid expenses of over $700,000, shifted funds between the nonprofit and Krause's for-profit corporations, never held a board meeting and hired Krause's wife as its only full-time employee. The court found such a unity of interest and ownership that the corporate entity could not be separated from Krause and held him personally liable for TSF's debts.

Reverse piercing occurs where a creditor seeks the assets of the nonprofit to satisfy a debt of an individual. In this scenario, the organization and individuals are "alter egos". In Towe Antique Ford Foundation v. Internal Revenue Service, 999 F.2d 1387 (9th Cir. 1993), the Service levied on the foundation's 91 classic automobiles to satisfy the delinquent income tax liabilities of Edward Towe and his wife. Applying Montana law, the court found that the cars were improperly conveyed to the foundation, which was a mere instrument of Towe, who was the sole officer and controlled day-to-day operations, commingled his own affairs and that of his family and transferred the cars to the foundation in anticipation of federal tax liabilities. The court permitted a levy on the corporation's automobiles to satisfy the Towes' indebtedness.

3.   THE DUTY OF LOYALTY

a.   INTRODUCTION

Model Nonprofit Corp. Act (3d ed.) §§ 8.31, 8.33, 8.60, 8.70.

Cal. Corp. Code §§ 5227, 5233–37, 7233, 7236.

N.Y. Not-for-Profit Corp. L. §§ 715–16.

Principles of the Law of Nonprofit Organizations §§ 310, 330.

Directors owe a duty of loyalty to the corporation on whose board they serve. This duty requires them to act in a manner that does not harm the corporation. It further requires directors to avoid using their position to obtain improperly a personal benefit or advantages which might more properly belong to the corporation. The fact that a director had an interest in a transaction is less significant than whether it was fair to the corporation at the time the decision was made and whether the decision was reached in an impartial board environment. The duty of loyalty requires directors to place the interests of the corporation ahead of their personal gain. A director is expected to make decisions objectively, to refrain from participation, and to obtain approval from the corporation where there is a relationship which impairs the director's objectivity. Principles of Nonprofit Organizations § 330(b). In a conflict of interest situation, directors receive more favorable financial benefits than they would gain in an open market or they enjoy priority over open market competitors.

Conflicts of interest, divided loyalties, and transactions among directors, officers, and charitable corporations abound in the nonprofit sector. Breaches of loyalty are not only much easier to identify than breaches of care, they are more prevalent. Patterns of interested transactions parallel business corporate practices and are bounded only by human ingenuity. Some common forms of interested transactions include:

1.   The use of an organization's property or assets on a more favorable basis than available to outsiders:

> Boswell, a director of the El Paso Opera Company, uses the opera house for his daughter's wedding. Normally the opera rents its building for outside use at a cost of $15,000. Boswell only pays $1,000, the direct costs of opening the opera house.

See Harding Hosp. v. United States, 505 F.2d 1068 (6th Cir.1974) (preferential lease for office space); Gilbert M. Gaul & Neill A. Borowski, Warehouses of Wealth: The Tax–Free Economy, Phila. Inquirer, April 22, 1993, at A1 (low interest and no interest loans to executives). Directors are expected to pay fair value for more than the de minimis use of an organization's property. See Joe Stephens & David Ottaway, Nonprofit Sells Scenic Acreage to Allies at a Loss, Wash. Post, May 6, 2003, at A1 (Nature Conservancy resold donated land with development restrictions at loss to trustee or supporter, followed by a charitable contribution to make up the difference in value, allowing buyer to take charitable deduction).

2.   Usurpation of a corporate opportunity:

In 1977, a nonprofit broadcasting network established a cable TV programming subsidiary (The Family Channel) financed in large part by the charitable donations of viewers. The nonprofit decided to divest the subsidiary in 1989, because its family entertainment format became so lucrative that the tax-exempt status of the parent was jeopardized. The televangelist chairman of the parent and his son formed a for-profit company with other investors, including the nonprofit broadcasting network and a major cable television operator as minority shareholders. The for-profit company purchased the programming subsidiary from the nonprofit for $250 million dollars, a price set by an independent appraisal. Most of the purchase was debt-financed. The televangelist and his family acquired a controlling voting interest in the for-profit buyer for a total cash investment of $183,000. In 1992, the for-profit company went public at $15 per share and the televangelist's investment became worth $90 million and it increased in value to $108 million by 1994. The televangelist, who remained chairman of the nonprofit broadcasting network, received $390,611 in salary from the for-profit in 1992; his son earned $465,731. In 1997, the televangelist's for-profit company was sold to media baron Rupert Murdoch's News Corporation for $1.7 billion. The original opportunity to go public belonged to the nonprofit.

See 139 Cong. Rec. E 3057 (daily ed. Nov. 24, 1993) (statement of Rep. Stark); Brett D. Fromson, Stock Sale to Multiply Robertsons' Riches, Wash. Post, April 14, 1992, at D1; Benjamin Weiser, An Empire on Exemptions? Televangelist Pat Robertson Gained Fortune, and Critics, in Sale of His Cable Network, reprinted in 9 Exempt Org. Tax Rev. 747 (April, 1994); Geraldine Fabrikant, Murdoch Set to Buy Family Cable Concern, N.Y. Times, June 12, 1997, at D1.

3.   The use of material nonpublic organizational information or position:

Sheridan, a dealer in federal period furniture, sits on the board of and is a member of the acquisitions committee of the Summerthur Museum, which has a major collection of American furniture. At a meeting of the acquisitions committee, he learns that Mr. and Mrs. Phyfe, owners of a major collection of federal furniture, are considering disposing of their collection. The museum would attempt to get the Phyfes to donate their collection, but does not know whether that is a possibility. A few months later, Sheridan purchases the Phyfe collection for $1 million.

The director has used material nonpublic information for his benefit. He has not usurped a corporate opportunity, because there is no indication the museum would have had the opportunity to obtain the collection, but the information he has gathered belonged to the museum.

4. Insider advantages and corporate waste:

At a time when the Marbury Library has incurred annual deficits of $200,000, the board of directors votes itself salaries amounting to $100,000 per year which are paid from proceeds of sales of items from the collection.

See People Ex Rel. Scott v. Silverstein, 86 Ill.App.3d 605, 41 Ill.Dec. 821, 408 N.E.2d 243 (1980). This constitutes corporate waste and the directors will be required to restore the funds received.

5. Competing with the organization:

A Condominium Unit Owner's Association provides cable television service to its members for a fee and is about to obtain cable television. A director of the association upgrades the existing television reception system and charges members for the service.

See Kirtley v. McClelland, 562 N.E.2d 27 (Ind.Ct.App.1990); Mile–O–Mo Fishing Club, Inc. v. Noble, 62 Ill.App.2d 50, 210 N.E.2d 12 (1965) (former president and director of a nonprofit corporation breached his fiduciary obligations in purchasing property that he knew the corporation desired to purchase). A director breaches her fiduciary duty by competing with the organization on whose board she serves.

In many situations, interested transactions are a healthy necessity. They may provide access to resources unavailable from the marketplace. The financial status of the nonprofit organization may be so poor that market sources of credit, supplies, or services are unattainable. A loan of money, goods, or services may be obtainable only from a director, an individual concerned with the organization's welfare. In other situations the interested transaction may be unethical or illegal and, therefore, violates the director's duty of loyalty to the corporation and to the public.

In analyzing conflicts of interest, one should focus upon both the procedural aspects of the transaction and upon its substantive nature. The procedural aspects of a transaction relate to the process by which the transaction is approved for the corporation by the board of directors. The procedural inquiries include whether corporate procedures for interested transactions have been established and whether they were followed in the particular transaction; whether the board environment was impartial and objective at the time the decision was made; whether the information relating to the transaction was fully disclosed by the interested director to the relevant decisionmakers; and whether the interest of the director was disclosed to the relevant decisionmakers. Substantive factors in conflict of interest transactions involve the fairness of the transaction to the corporation in terms of what the corporation received, the frequency of interested transactions between directors and the organization, and the overall financial status of the organization in relation to the transaction.

Whether an interested transaction should be permitted or not depends greatly on its facts and circumstances and the director's motivations for entering the transaction. A type of transaction which may be perfectly proper in one context may be inappropriate under slightly different circumstances. For example, nonprofit organizations have been formed as successors to proprietary corporations, typically schools, hospitals, and nursing homes. The shareholder directors of the proprietary organization become the directors of the nonprofit corporation. If the successor organization pays the proprietary organization a fair rental value for its property or reasonable compensation for the proprietary's assets, the interested transaction should be permitted. If the nonprofit successor serves the directors own interests, assumes for-profit liabilities in a bailout context, or overpays the rental costs or purchases the assets at an inflated price, the transaction is impermissible self-dealing. Cf. Rev. Rul. 76–441, 1976–2 C.B. 147; Bruce R. Hopkins, The Law of Tax–Exempt Organizations § 31.7(b) (9th ed. 2007).

b.   INTERESTED TRANSACTIONS

Nixon v. Lichtenstein

Missouri Court of Appeals, 1997.
959 S.W.2d 854.

■ Hoff, Judge.

Allene Lichtenstein and Arlene Frazier (collectively referred to as "Appellants") appeal from a civil judgment against them which ordered their removal as board members of the Lichtenstein Foundation (the Corporation) and reimbursement of approximately $300,000 to the Corporation. We affirm.

* * *

The David B. Lichtenstein Foundation (the Foundation) was a charitable foundation created by an indenture for trust (trust indenture) executed by David B. Lichtenstein, Sr. in December 1947. The Foundation board consisted of five directors, including David B. Lichtenstein, Sr., all of whom served without compensation. The Foundation had no paid staff. In 1986 David B. Lichtenstein, Sr. died. Thereafter, Mr. Lichtenstein's sons, including Daniel Lichtenstein, ran the Foundation.

On July 15, 1987, Daniel Lichtenstein and his daughter filed a petition against Boatmen's Bank challenging the administration of David B. Lichtenstein, Sr.'s estate (Boatmen's Litigation). The Foundation was a plaintiff in the lawsuit and paid all legal fees for Daniel Lichtenstein and his daughter. On May 18, 1989, the probate court dismissed the Foundation as a plaintiff finding that it did not have an interest in the litigation. However, the Foundation continued to pay all legal fees and expenses for Daniel Lichtenstein and his daughter in the Boatmen's Litigation.

In 1990, Daniel Lichtenstein's wife, Allene Lichtenstein, was appointed to the board of the Foundation. After Allene Lichtenstein joined the board, the directors began paying themselves $12,000 each as an annual salary, the board was expanded from five members to nine members, and over $700,000 was charged to the Foundation for the purchases of personal property.

In December 1991, in accordance with the original trust indenture, Daniel Lichtenstein dissolved the Foundation and poured the assets into a nonprofit corporation, the Corporation. The Corporation's articles of incorporation retained the provisions and restrictions contained in the original trust, including restrictions prohibiting self-dealing by board members and placing a cap on their compensation of five percent of the Corporation's gross income. The Corporation continued to pay Daniel Lichtenstein and his daughter's expenses in the Boatmen's Litigation.

In 1992, Allene Lichtenstein's sister, Arlene Frazier, served on the Corporation's board of directors and was appointed as an administrative assistant of the Corporation. Initially, Arlene Frazier was paid $10,400 annually, but her compensation soon increased to $52,000 per year.

On January 20, 1993, Allene Lichtenstein was designated first vice president/director and was paid $120,000 per year. Soon after, a raise moved her salary to $125,000 per year. Also in 1993, at the Corporation's expense, Allene Lichtenstein installed a telephone in every room in her house so that she could work at home while caring for her ill husband, Daniel Lichtenstein.

After conducting an audit of the Foundation's taxes for the years 1989, 1990, and 1991, the Internal Revenue Service (IRS) sent a letter dated September 21, 1993, to the Corporation suggesting certain changes that needed to be made in order for the Corporation to retain its tax exempt status. Specifically, the IRS letter made reference to the Boatmen's Litigation, stating:

> It appears that the Foundation was making payments for 100% of the legal expense[s]. The disbursements made by the Foundation for legal expenses were not the Foundations [sic] legal obligation. The Foundation was dismissed as being a petitioner and was not considered an interested party. Any payment of legal expenses should have been made by the legal petitioners Daniel Lichtenstein and [his daughter] * * * Correction will need to be made. Correction will be accomplished when Daniel Lichtenstein and [his daughter] repay the Foundation all legal expenses paid for them during the years under audit.

In January 1994, Daniel Lichtenstein died. Allene Lichtenstein was the primary beneficiary of Daniel Lichtenstein's personal trust and estate. After her husband's death, Allene Lichtenstein assumed the position of president and chief executive officer of the Corporation. No legal expenses stemming from the Boatmen's Litigation were ever reimbursed to the Corporation by Daniel Lichtenstein's personal trust, his estate, or his daughter.

On February 28, 1995, the Attorney General of Missouri filed a petition for trust accounting and a request for a temporary restraining order against the Corporation and [nine] Corporation board members. The Corporation consented to the accounting. As a result of such accounting, the Attorney General filed the underlying petition alleging the Corporation board member defendants engaged in self-dealing and breached their fiduciary duties to the Corporation by: (1) paying and receiving compensation which was in excess of the five percent cap; (2) paying and receiving compensation in excess of the fair market value, if any, of services provided; (3) purchasing personal property with Corporation funds; (4) failing to collect for the Corporation Boatmen's Litigation expenses from former Corporation board members; (5) paying for personal travel with Corporation funds; (6) installing a personal phone system with Corporation funds; and (7) attempting to conceal improper personal property purchases. Seven of the nine board members entered into a settlement agreement with the Attorney General. They agreed to resign and reimburse the Corporation for fees they received in excess of the five percent cap the original trust indenture and the Corporation's articles of incorporation established.

* * *

In extensive Findings of Fact and Conclusions of Law filed on September 17, 1996, the trial court found Allene Lichtenstein and Arlene Frazier had engaged in acts of self-dealing, wasted assets, misused assets, and acted in a manner inconsistent with the best interests of the Corporation. The trial court also found the attorneys' fees in the Boatmen's Litigation totaled $79,787, and it was "inappropriate" for the Foundation to have paid those fees. The trial court removed Appellants as directors and officers of the Corporation, appointed three of David B. Lichtenstein, Sr.'s other relatives to the board, and ordered Appellants to reimburse the Corporation for various improper expenses. This appeal followed.

TRUST LAW VERSUS THE BUSINESS JUDGMENT RULE

In their first point on appeal, Appellants contend the trial court erred in applying trust law principles, rather than corporate law principles, in assessing Appellants' duties to the Corporation; in concluding Appellants breached their fiduciary duties; and in denying Appellants' motion for new trial. Appellants assert the Foundation was legitimately converted into a corporation, and corporate rather than trust standards should apply. Appellants argue that applying corporate law principles, specifically the business judgment rule, would better suit their roles in the Corporation because directors of public benefit corporations have more varied responsibilities than trustees. Additionally, Appellants urge that applying the business judgment rule would effectuate the intent of David B. Lichtenstein, Sr. because he provided for the incorporation within the trust indenture. Last, Appellants contend that applying trust law sets poor precedent because it would "open the door" to applying trust law principles to any corporation that was once a trust.

"The business judgment rule protects the directors and officers of a corporation from liability for intra vires decisions within their authority made in good faith, uninfluenced by any other consideration than the honest belief that the action subserves the best interests of the corporation." When a corporate director or officer's decision falls within the business judgment rule, the court will not interfere with that decision.

The trial court considered this issue and determined that the stricter standard imposed on trustees is applicable here rather than the less restrictive standard under the business judgment rule. The trial court reasoned, "the fiduciary duties imposed by law on those responsible for management of property held in trust are not diminished by the transfer of those assets to a charitable corporation" (all letters in original text capitalized). We agree.

Contrary to Appellants' assertions, Missouri courts have not permitted directors of charitable foundations to manage charitable assets less responsibly than trustees of a charitable trust. Upon creation of a corporation from a trust provided for in a will, the corporation becomes the alter ego of the trustees and as such, the propriety of the corporate directors' acts must be determined in light of the will and must be controlled by the provisions of the decedent's will.

In this case, the Corporation's articles of incorporation retained the provisions and restrictions set forth in the trust indenture, including the prohibition against self-dealing by board members and the five percent gross income cap on board members' compensation. The trust indenture did not expressly impose a lesser fiduciary duty on the Corporation's directors. Because of these circumstances, we find no error in the trial court's application of trust law instead of the business judgment rule. We find the trial court did not err in finding that Appellants have engaged in self-dealing and have not acted in good faith or in the best interests of the Corporation. Point denied.

* * *

REMOVAL OF APPELLANTS FROM BOARD OF DIRECTORS

* * *

[The court found no error in the trial court's order removing the appellants as directors of the Corporation. Eds.]

APPOINTMENT OF DIRECTORS TO BOARD

Next, Appellants contend the trial court erred in appointing David Lichtenstein, Jr., Doris Lichtenstein, and Gayle Lichtenstein to the Corporation's board of directors, and in holding that three interim directors should continue to serve as directors. Appellants assert the trial court had no authority to make such appointments because it did not follow section 355.361 RSMo 1994, which sets forth the method for appointing directors of a not-for-profit corporation.

Section 355.361 RSMo 1994 states that the directors remaining on a corporate board may fill board vacancies by the vote of a quorum and, if fewer than a quorum exists, by a majority vote of the remaining directors. At the time the trial court entered judgment, no directors remained on the Corporation's board. Out of the original nine directors, seven had resigned upon settlement of the Attorney General's claims against them. Appellants were the remaining two directors who were removed from the board by the trial court's order. Thus, section 355.361 RSMo 1994 is not dispositive.

Section 355.726.1(2)(e) RSMo 1994 permits a trial court to dissolve a public benefit corporation when the corporation "is no longer able to carry out its purposes." Because there were no remaining directors, the Corporation was clearly unable to carry out its purposes because three directors are needed at all times. Section 355.321 RSMo 1994. However, "[p]rior to dissolving a corporation, the court shall consider whether * * * [t]here are reasonable alternatives to dissolution." Section 355.726.2(1) RSMo 1994.

In Whan v. Whan, 542 S.W.2d 7 (Mo.App. E.D.1976), this Court reviewed the trial court appointment of trustees when no trustees remained to administer a trust. This Court concluded that

> [a] trust will not be permitted to fail because the trustee named in the instrument creating it cannot administer the trust. A court of equity will appoint a new trustee. Having found that the agreement created a trust and that the trustees must be removed, the court was under an obligation to appoint a new trustee to avoid the failure of the trust.

Id. at 12 (citation omitted).

Because the Corporation was formed from a charitable trust, and the trial court has the responsibility of considering reasonable alternatives to the dissolution of a corporation, we find the trial court did not err in appointing three Lichtenstein family members to serve as directors and retaining three interim directors who had been appointed to serve while there were no directors. Point denied.

[The court affirmed the trial court's findings that Allene Lichtenstein was liable for repaying $79,787 in legal fees plus interest for the Boatman's litigation and that the expenditure of $10,000 for the installation of a telephone system in the Lichtenstein home was a breach of her fiduciary duty to the corporation. Eds.]

Judgment affirmed.

NOTES

1. *Abuses in Family Foundations.* As demonstrated in the principal case, family foundations have been a frequent source of fiduciary wrongdoing, often by members of the donor's family. The Massachusetts attorney general forced Paul Cabot, the scion of one of New England's oldest families, to repay a family foundation more than $4 million that he had used for personal expenses and compensation. An investigation in the Boston Globe uncovered that Cabot received $7.5 million over nine years

from the foundation, including paying himself $1 million (raised to $1.4 million in 2001) because he said he needed the extra money to pay for his daughter's wedding; yachting and golf club bills; and the expenses related to two houses. Cabot agreed to sell both houses and give the proceeds to the foundation and to be barred from serving as an officer of the foundation. See Walter V. Robinson & Michael Rezendes, Foundation Chief Agrees to Repay Over $4m, Boston Globe, Dec. 16, 2004, at A1.

In June 2004, a Texas jury ordered two former executives of the Carl B. and Florence E. King Foundation to repay $7.5 million they had taken in excessive salaries, credit card charges and lucrative retirement packages, which were not approved by the board. The jury also imposed $14 million in punitive damages. The award was confirmed. Abbott v. Yeckel, 2004 WL 2676213 (Tex. Prob. 2004).

2. *Reform Proposals*. Because of the extent of abuses among family foundations, the office of the then New York attorney general Eliot Spitzer asked Congress in 2003 to consider banning any private foundations with less than $20 million in assets. See Grant Williams, Making Philanthropy Accountable, Chron. Philanthropy, June 26, 2003, at 23. In its 2004 Discussion Draft of charitable reform proposals, the Senate Finance Committee staff proposed either to forbid any compensation to private foundation directors or trustees or to limit board compensation to a prescribed de minimis amount and impose limits on compensation of other foundation insiders. See Senate Finance Comm. Staff Discussion Draft, June 22, 2004, at 5, available at http://finance.senate.gov/hearings/testimony/2004test/062204stfdis.pdf. For more coverage of state and federal regulation of trustee and executive compensation, see Chapter 5D1, infra, at pp. 454–458, and Chapter 7D2, infra, at p. 769.

Stern v. Lucy Webb Hayes National Training School for Deaconesses

United States District Court, District of Columbia, 1974.
381 F.Supp. 1003.

[The facts appear supra at p. 145]

II. Conspiracy.

Plaintiffs first contend that the five defendant trustees and the five defendant financial institutions were involved in a conspiracy to enrich themselves at the expense of the Hospital. They point to the fact that each named trustee held positions of responsibility with one or more of the defendant institutions as evidence that the trustees had both motive and opportunity to carry out such a conspiracy.

* * *

Plaintiffs further contend that the defendants accomplished the alleged conspiracy by arranging to have Sibley maintain unnecessarily large amounts of money on deposit with the defendant banks and savings and loan associations, drawing inadequate or no interest * * * [t]he Hospital in fact maintained much of its liquid assets in savings and checking accounts rather than in Treasury bonds or investment securities, at least until the investment review instituted by Mr. Reed late in 1971. In that year, for example, more than one-third of the nearly four million dollars available for investment was deposited in checking accounts, as compared to only about $135,000 in securities and $311,000 in Treasury bills. Although substantial sums were used to purchase certificates of deposit, which produce at least a moderate amount of income, the Hospital occasionally purchased a certificate yielding lower interest rates than were available at other institutions.

It is also undisputed that most of these funds were deposited in the defendant financial institutions. A single checking account, drawing no interest whatever and maintained alternately at Riggs National Bank and Security National Bank, usually contained more than $250,000 and on one occasion grew to nearly $1,000,000.

Defendants were able to offer no adequate justification for this utilization of the Hospital's liquid assets. By the same token, however, plaintiffs failed to establish that it was the result of a conscious direction on the part of the named defendants. As mentioned above, it was Mr. Ernst alone rather than any of the defendant trustees who maintained almost exclusive control over the Hospital's investments until his death in 1972. As Treasurer, he could shift money between banks or accounts within banks and purchase or sell securities without consulting any other trustee. Since the Investment and Finance Committees never met, only Dr. Orem and a few of the other officers apparently were aware of Mr. Ernst's investment policies. While it is true that a yearly audit was made available to the Board and that the Executive Committee had to approve the opening of new accounts, these matters were treated as mere formalities. All of the defendant trustees testified that they approved Ernst's recommendations as a matter of course, rarely if ever read the relevant details of audits critically, and generally left investment decisions to the presumed expertise of Mr. Ernst. Several also commented that the Treasurer regarded their suggestions as "interference" in these matters and none forced the issue.

Mr. Ernst's own reasons for pursuing this conservative investment policy are not altogether clear. It has been suggested that his experience in the Depression was an important contributing factor. That same experience undoubtedly helps explain his belief that Sibley should maintain close relationships with a few local banks and his evident decision to favor those banks which held a mortgage on the Hospital and which had interlocking directorships with the Sibley Board.

There is no evidence that the defendant trustees reached a mutual agreement to direct or even to encourage Ernst in such favoritism. It is true that the trustees frequently approved transactions which benefited institutions with which they were affiliated and that occasionally a particular trustee would even seek out such an arrangement, but plaintiffs have not shown that any of these decisions derived from a conspiratorial agreement. Moreover, when the Board's own investigations brought the inadequacy of Mr. Ernst's policies home to the Board, the trustees moved toward a more realistic investment program in a manner that negates existence of a prior agreement. Significant reductions in bank deposits have been made, and the newly elected Treasurer is attempting—with mixed success—to hold demand deposits below $500,000, a level which he deems adequate for the operation of the Hospital.

Plaintiffs also attempted to bolster the conspiracy theory by pointing to two other Hospital transactions: the continuation of a mortgage with the defendant financial institutions and the signing of an investment advisory agreement with Ferris & Co. The mortgage in question dates back to the late 1950's, when the Sibley Board began negotiations with various local banks to obtain a loan to finance construction of the new hospital building. When these negotiations fell through, the Board obtained an adequate loan commitment from a Texas bank. Although local banks had earlier refused to assist the Hospital, several of the trustees then organized a syndicate of Washington banks willing to provide the loan on equally favorable terms to the Texas proposal and persuaded the Board to accept the local offer. As a result, the syndicate agreed in 1959 to lend Sibley $3,000,000, secured by a mortgage on the hospital. This sum was increased to $3,500,000 in 1961.

The loan was renewed in 1969 and is still partially outstanding. Although Sibley probably had sufficient funds to pay off the loan without totally impairing its ability to meet obligations as they become due, the Executive Committee voted instead for renewal. The cash flow would have put operations on a tight basis and the trustees had in mind that available money might well be needed for the renovation of certain property owned by Sibley.

The terms of this loan were entirely fair to Sibley at all times. There is no indication that the Board could have received better terms elsewhere or that it failed diligently to seek an optimum arrangement at the time of the original loan. The renewal in 1969 also appears to have been a reasonable, good-faith business decision. There is no indication that either decision was motivated by a desire to benefit the banks involved at the Hospital's expense.

The idea of employing an investment service was raised by Mr. Jones at the meeting of Sibley's Investment Committee. It was decided that Mr. Ferris, a member of that committee, should present a proposal from Ferris & Co., of which Mr. Ferris was Chairman of the Board and principal stockholder, for the provision of continuing investment advisory services to Sibley. Mr. Ferris presented such a proposal on April 12, 1971, and the committee voted to recommend approval. Mr. Ferris urged and may have voted in favor of that recommendation at an informal session of the Investment Committee, but thereafter he resigned from the Investment Committee to avoid further possible conflicts of interest. For a short time he then served as Acting Treasurer over the objection of some trustees. Upon formal approval by the Hospital's counsel and the Executive Committee, of which Ferris was not a member, Sibley entered into the "Investment

Advisory Agreement" with Ferris & Co., which written contract is still in effect today. Plaintiffs concede, and the Court finds, that Ferris & Co.'s fee for investment service was fair and equitable. Plaintiffs concede that Ferris & Co. did a good job, although shifts in market prices resulted in some losses in the account which, incidentally, would not have occurred if the Hospital had kept the money in certificates of deposit. No conspiratorial inference can be drawn from this course of dealing.

[The Court concluded that a conspiracy could not be implied merely from the fact that the hospital did considerable business with financial institutions that had some interlocking ties to the Board of Trustees. Eds.]

3. Self–Dealing

Under District of Columbia Law, neither trustees nor corporate directors are absolutely barred from placing funds under their control into a bank having an interlocking directorship with their own institution. In both cases, however, such transactions will be subjected to the closest scrutiny to determine whether or not the duty of loyalty has been violated. A deliberate conspiracy among trustees or Board members to enrich the interlocking bank at the expense of the trust or corporation would, for example, constitute such a breach and render the conspirators liable for any losses. In the absence of clear evidence of wrongdoing, however, the courts appear to have used different standards to determine whether or not relief is appropriate, depending again on the legal relationship involved. Trustees may be found guilty of a breach of trust even for mere negligence in the maintenance of accounts in banks with which they are associated, while corporate directors are generally only required to show "entire fairness" to the corporation and "full disclosure" of the potential conflict of interest to the Board.

Most courts apply the less stringent corporate rule to charitable corporations in this area as well. It is, however, occasionally added that a director should not only disclose his interlocking responsibilities but also refrain from voting on or otherwise influencing a corporate decision to transact business with a company in which he has a significant interest or control.

Although defendants have argued against the imposition of even these limitations on self-dealing by the Sibley trustees, the Hospital Board recently adopted a new by-law, based upon guidelines issued by the American Hospital Association, which essentially imposes the modified corporate rule described above:

Article XXVIII, Conflicts of Interests Section 1. Any duality of interest or possible conflict of interest on the part of any governing board member shall be disclosed to the other members of the board and made a matter of record through an annual procedure and also when the interest becomes a matter of board action. Section 2. Any governing board member having a duality of interest or possible conflict of interest on any matter shall not vote or use his personal influence on the matter, and he shall not be counted in determining the quorum for the meeting, even where permitted by law. The minutes of the meeting shall reflect that a disclosure was made, the abstention from voting, and the quorum situation. Section 3. The foregoing requirements shall not be construed as preventing the governing board member from briefly stating his position in the matter, nor from answering pertinent questions of other board members since his knowledge may be of great assistance. Section 4. Any new member of the board will be advised of this policy upon entering on the duties of his office.

* * *

B. The Financial Institutions.

While it is thus established that the named trustees acted in breach of fiduciary duty, the institutional defendants are not liable simply because they benefited from those breaches. Under the prevailing rule of law, a bank or other financial institution is only liable for losses sustained by a trust by reason of its dealings with a trustee if the institution had actual or constructive knowledge that the transaction was in breach of the trustee's fiduciary duty. This principle applies to dealings with corporate fiduciaries as well as trustees, and to situations in which, as here, the alleged breach entails the maintenance of excessive demand deposits in the defendant bank.

Actual knowledge of a breach of fiduciary duty can, of course, be inferred from the sheer size and inactivity of some accounts in question, the number and significance of interlocking relationships, and a history of questionable investment transactions with the fiduciary. In addition, constructive knowledge may be found where an interlocking officer or director has actual knowledge of the excessive nature of the deposits and participates, on behalf of the bank, in the bank's decision to accept those deposits.
* * *

Under those principles, the Court finds that the institutional defendants are not liable for any loss of income that may have been suffered by the Hospital. Each bank and savings and loan association was aware only of its own accounts, and no single institution maintained Sibley deposits so large that it should have investigated the fidelity of the Hospital Board. Plaintiffs have failed to demonstrate that any of the transactions in question would have alerted a reasonable bank officer to breaches of fiduciary duty, so actual knowledge of such breaches cannot be found. Nor was there constructive knowledge, because the interlocking trustees were themselves ignorant—however wrongfully—of Ernst's imprudent investment policies. Only an agent's actual knowledge can be imputed to his principal.

IV. Relief.

The foregoing constitutes the Court's findings of fact and conclusions of law * * * It must now consider the appropriate relief in light of its finding that the defendant trustees have breached their fiduciary duties of care and loyalty to the Hospital.

In addition to a declaration defining the duties and obligations of the trustees in the disputed area of the Hospital's fiscal management, plaintiffs press for injunctive relief. Among other things, they urge that defendant trustees be removed and disqualified, that the Hospital be barred from transacting business with any firm if an officer, director, partner or substantial shareholder of that firm is a Hospital trustee, that an accounting be ordered, and that damages be assessed against the defendant trustees. In short, plaintiffs approach this matter as though each trustee of the Hospital were individually responsible for an abuse of fiduciary duty under an express trust which has made the Hospital's patients beneficiaries. Were such the case, application of very strict sanctions would be necessary. However, the trustees here stand in a different status, as the Court's analysis shows, and the proof does not in any way necessitate sanctions as harsh as those suggested.

The function of equity is not to punish but merely to take such action as the Court in its discretion deems necessary to prevent the recurrence of improper conduct * * * Where voluntary action has been taken in good faith to minimize such recurrence, even though under the pressure of litigation, this is a factor which the Court can take into account in formulating relief * * *

In attempting to balance the equities under the circumstances shown by the record, there are a number of factors which lead the Court to feel that intervention by injunction should be limited. First, the defendant trustees in this case constitute but a small minority of the full Sibley Board. Yet, in several respects, the responsibility for past failures adequately to supervise the handling of Hospital funds rests equally on all Board members. Second, it is clear that the practices criticized by plaintiffs have, to a considerable extent, been corrected and that the employees and trustees who were principally responsible for lax handling of funds have died or have been dismissed. Third, there is no indication that any of the named trustees were involved in fraudulent practices or profited personally by lapses in proper fiscal supervision, and, indeed, the overall operation of the Hospital in terms of low costs, efficient services and quality patient care has been superior. Finally, this case is in a sense one of first impression, since it brings into judicial focus for the first time in this jurisdiction the nature and scope of trustee obligations in a nonprofit, non-member charitable institution incorporated under D.C.Code 29–1001 et seq.

The Court is well aware that it must take proper steps to insure a clean break between the past and the future. Personnel changes and a recent greater awareness of past laxity are encouraging, as is the addition of Article XXVIII to the Hospital's by-laws, but good intentions expressed post-litem must be accompanied by concrete action. Accordingly, it is desirable to require by injunction that the appropriate committees and officers of the Hospital present to the full Board a written policy statement governing investments and the use of idle cash in the Hospital's bank accounts and other funds, and establish a procedure for the periodic reexamination of existing investments and other financial arrangements to insure compliance with Board policies. No existing financial relationships should be continued unless consistent with established policy and found by disinterested members of the Board to be in the Hospital's best interests. In addition, each trustee should fully disclose his affiliation with banks, savings and loan associations and investment firms now doing business with the Hospital.

Removal of the defendant trustees from the Sibley Board would be unduly harsh, and this will not be ordered. These trustees are now completing long years of service and they will soon become less active in the day-to-day affairs of the Hospital because of age or illness. It would unduly disrupt the affairs of the Hospital abruptly to terminate their relationship with that institution. Others must soon take over their roles in carrying forward the Hospital's affairs, and it is therefore unnecessary to interfere by order of removal or disqualification with a transition that is necessarily already taking place due to other immutable factors.

The management of a non-profit charitable hospital imposes a severe obligation upon its trustees. A hospital such as Sibley is not closely regulated by any public authority, it has no responsibility to file financial reports, and its Board is self-perpetuating. The interests of its patients are funnelled primarily through large group insurers who pay the patients' bills, and the patients lack meaningful participation in the Hospital's affairs. It is obvious that, in due course, new trustees must come to the Board of this Hospital, some of whom will be affiliated with banks, savings and loan associations and other financial institutions. The tendency of representatives of such institutions is often to seek business in return for advice and assistance rendered as trustees. It must be made absolutely clear that Board membership carries no right to preferential treatment in the placement or handling of the Hospital's investments and business accounts. The Hospital would be well advised to restrict membership on its Board to the representatives of financial institutions which have no substantial business relationship with the Hospital. The best way to avoid potential conflicts of interest and to be assured of objective advice is to avoid the possibility of such conflicts at the time new trustees are selected.

As an additional safeguard, the Court will require that each newly-elected trustee read this Opinion and the attached Order. Compliance with this requirement must appear in a document signed by the new trustee or in the minutes of the Sibley Board. In view of the circumstances disclosed by the record it will be desirable, in addition, to require public disclosure which will further insure that the Board's recently-avowed good intentions are faithfully carried out. To this end, the Court will direct that prior to each meeting of the full Board the members of the Board shall receive, at least one week in advance, a formal written statement prepared by the Hospital's Treasurer or Comptroller disclosing in detail the full extent of all business done by the Hospital since the last Board meeting with any bank, savings and loan association, investment service or other financial institution with which any trustee or officer of the Hospital is affiliated as a trustee, director, principal officer, partner, general manager or substantial shareholder. Moreover, all such dealings shall be summarized by the Hospital's auditors in their annual audit and a copy of the annual audit shall be made available on request for inspection by any patient of the Hospital at the Hospital's offices during business hours. Such arrangements should continue for a period of five years.

For the reasons set forth in its Memorandum and Order of November 30, 1973, and at various pretrial hearings, the Court declines to award damages incident to the injunctive and declaratory relief appropriate under Rule 23(b)(2) of the Federal Rules of Civil Procedure or to reconsider the denial of certification under Rule 23(b)(1) and (3). No accounting will be ordered, and all other relief requested by plaintiffs is denied. Since plaintiffs do not press their claim for attorneys' fees at this time, the Court will postpone action on that issue until such time as it is raised and briefed by the parties.

* * *

The Committee to Save Adelphi v. Diamandopoulos

Board of Regents of the University of the State of New York, 1997.
http://hdl.handle.net/10244/502.

[As the *Sibley Hospital* case demonstrates, it is rare to have a duty of care violation that does not include impermissible conflicts of interest. In February, 1997, the New York State Board of Regents removed 18 of the 19 trustees of Adelphi University for dereliction of duty in overseeing the university and the actions of its president as well as the breach by several trustees of their duty of loyalty through business dealings undisclosed to the full board. Adelphi is located on Long Island, New York. When Peter Diamandopoulos became president in 1985, the university had 7,000 students, an endowment of $4 million, a decaying capital plant, and a declining student pool. Diamandopoulos hoped to double the size of the student body, create an honors college with a rigorous core curriculum, and increase the endowment. Although the president, if not the rising stock market, did increase the endowment to $48 million and the campus was renovated, the student body declined 40 percent to 4,300 as did selectivity and academic reputation. Along the way Diamandopoulos lost the support of all campus constituencies except the trustees, most of whom he appointed. A decisive moment in Diamandopoulos's administration came in the fall of 1995, when the Chronicle of Higher Education revealed that he was the nation's second highest paid college president. A Committee to Save Adelphi was formed and brought allegations to the New York Board of Regents, accusing the governing board and president of misappropriation of funds, conflicts of interest, and lavish expenditures by the president. See William H. Honan, Campus in Turmoil: A Special Report; Adelphi, a Little University with Big Ideas, N.Y. Times, Feb. 5, 1997, at B1.

The New York Board of Regents is an independent body, appointed by the state legislature to five-year terms, and it possesses the authority to regulate all aspects of education in New York State. Pursuant to the New York Education Law, educational institutions must receive the Regents' consent to be incorporated or grant degrees. New York Education Law § 226(4) grants the Regents the power to remove trustees for neglect of duty, an action which has been exercised only four times in 80 years. The New York Not-for-Profit Corporation Law regulates corporate governance and fiduciary obligations of educational corporations.

Among other reasons for the removal of Adelphi's trustees were excessive compensation paid to the university's president, a failure to review his job performance, refusal to abide by the University's bylaws relating to faculty governance, as well as board misconduct, neglect of duties and impermissible conflicts of interest. The board as a whole was uninformed of the President's compensation and expenses, which reached $837,113 in 1995–96. His salary package included an option to purchase a University-owned luxury apartment in Manhattan, a rent-free President's home on campus, an $82,000 Mercedes, and reimbursed expenses such as cognac at $150 a glass. The following part of the decision deals with the interested transactions of the board. Eds.]

III. The Conflicts of Interest.

In addition to the fiduciary duty of care, trustees of not-for-profit institutions also owe a fiduciary duty of loyalty to the corporation. The duty of loyalty:

> [R]equires a director to have an undivided allegiance to the organization's mission—when using either the power of his position or information he possesses concerning the organization or its property. And it bars a director from using his position or information concerning the organization and its property in a manner that allows him to secure a pecuniary benefit for himself. * * * [T]he director's conduct, at all times, must further the organization's goals and not his own interests. As fiduciaries with a duty of loyalty to the corporation, board members "may not profit improperly at the expense of the corporation."

A. Adelphi's Insurance Coverage.

In 1985, Alexander and Alexander was Adelphi's insurance brokerage firm, Chubb, Inc., its primary carrier ("Chubb"), and LRF, its risk management consultant firm. In 1986, instability in the insurance industry jeopardized Adelphi's coverage. In the spring of that year, LRF warned that Adelphi's premiums were likely to increase by as much as $400,000. Chairman Byrne thus appointed an ad hoc committee to evaluate Adelphi's insurance predicament and report back to the board. The committee, comprised of trustees Jay Raddock, Gerald Guterman and Ernesta Procope, was chaired by Procope because of her expertise in insurance and was formed as a subcommittee of the finance committee. According to Procope, the committee's charge was to review the current program and determine its adequacy. The ad hoc committee in turn assigned this task to E.G. Bowman, Inc. ("Bowman"), an insurance brokerage firm wholly owned and run by Procope. Bowman is in the business of designing insurance coverage programs for its clients and obtaining coverage from carriers. * * *

There is no dispute that, as of October 1986, Chubb was threatening to cancel Adelphi's coverage. Adelphi gave Treiber–Salerno, a brokerage firm, a broker of record letter authorizing it to explore alternative coverage on behalf of Adelphi.* * * Procope suggested to Diamandopoulos that Adelphi move its insurance from the Long Island office of Chubb, to the Manhattan office of Chubb, where Bowman had relationships upon which it would capitalize to retain the Chubb coverage. Diamandopoulos issued a broker of record letter to Bowman in December 1986 for this purpose.

Adelphi subsequently received an insurance proposal from Treiber–Salerno on or about January 14, 1987. The proposal was analyzed for Adelphi by Bowman, which, because it also held a broker of record letter, could fairly be characterized as Treiber–Salerno's competition for Adelphi's business. In a January 29, 1987 letter to Adelphi's vice president of administration, George Osborne (copied to Diamandopoulos), Bowman advised against the Treiber–Salerno proposal because it did not contain sufficient information to allow Bowman to properly compare the coverages offered with those currently in effect. Bowman indicated that it "needed specimen policies, a C.I.G.N.A. quotation letter, and a description of the proposed safety group" to thoroughly analyze the proposal. Bowman also expressed a concern about penalties Adelphi might incur if it changed carriers midterm. LRF shared this concern. Bowman closed by seeming to solicit Adelphi's business for a fee:

> As you are aware, we are presently performing these necessary services without compensation. This is primarily the result of our respect and consideration of your president, Dr. Diamandopoulos. We *look forward to the evolution of a mutually rewarding long-term business relationship.*

(emphasis supplied). Procope admitted under oath that this "looks like a pitch" for Adelphi's business.

Diamandopoulos discussed the letter with Osborne and Adelphi treasurer Hennessy, and directed Bowman to move the Chubb policy to the Manhattan office. Diamandopoulos then rejected the Treiber–Salerno proposal, without requesting the missing information Bowman said it would need to analyze the proposal. LRF was dismissed as a risk manager on February 17, 1987, and Alexander and Alexander's termination followed.

Up until this point, the board believed that Bowman was acting purely as an advisor to the ad hoc committee. Then, at the February 27, 1987 meeting of the finance and investment committee, Diamandopoulos reported for the first time that Bowman would actually be handling the University's insurance work for fiscal year 1986–1987. He said that the work was being undertaken "free of charge."

In fact, 1986–1987 is the only year in which Bowman earned no fee for its work for Adelphi. Bowman ultimately earned a commission for the 1987–1988 successful renewal with Chubb. Bowman then continued to handle all of the university's insurance work, and currently handles all aspects of the Adelphi account—for a fee. As Bowman had hoped for in its January 1987 letter, its consulting role blossomed into a "long term business relationship," the material terms of which neither Procope nor Diamandopoulos ever disclosed to the board. Those terms include the issuance of broker of record letters and Bowman's receipt of fees since 1987 in the approximate amount of $1,227,949. These fees represent a 10–15% commission taken against policy premiums. The only "free" service Bowman provides to Adelphi is the risk management service formerly provided by LRF.

In our judgment, Procope and Diamandopoulos neglected their fiduciary duties to Adelphi in several respects. First, Procope failed to disclose the material terms of the relationship between Bowman and the University. The record shows that, while the board members knew of Procope's relationship to Bowman, they believed Bowman was providing its services to the University free of charge. Indeed, both Diamandopoulos and Hennessy had expressly told the board so, and neither Procope nor Diamandopoulos ever said anything to correct this misimpression. Even when Procope filed her first conflict of interest statement in March 1996, she revealed nothing about the fee arrangement: "My firm, E.G. Bowman, Co., Inc., serves as a broker (insurance) for Adelphi University". The failure of Procope and Diamandopoulos to disclose these material terms to the board prevented the board from making an informed choice of brokers and assessing whether there was any potential conflict between Procope's role as trustee and her business interests.

Moreover, Procope appears to have used her position as a trustee to give Bowman an unfair advantage in obtaining the Adelphi account. The facts show that the free consulting services originally provided by Bowman turned into a business relationship for which other brokers were blocked from competing. The only other broker that Adelphi even considered—Treiber–Salerno—was eliminated by Diamandopoulos when it failed to provide sufficient information in its proposal. Ironically, that proposal was assessed as inadequate by *Bowman*, Treiber–Salerno's sole competitor. Moreover, neither Diamandopoulos nor Procope ever asked Treiber–Salerno for the information needed to thoroughly evaluate the proposal. Indeed, Procope—in a graphic illustration of the confusion between her dual roles—testified that *she* made no attempt to obtain the information, because it "was not *Bowman's* responsibility" to do so. We believe that it was Procope's responsibility, as the *trustee* with insurance expertise upon whom the board was relying for advice, to ask for that information on *Adelphi's* behalf, and to ensure that the competition for Adelphi's business was broad, open and fair. Instead, Procope's conduct ensured the elimination of all competition, securing to Bowman the Adelphi account. This is precisely the "evolution" Bowman had hoped for when it first "pitched" Adelphi's business in January 1987.

Based upon the record, we also find that Diamandopoulos' actions were not consistent with his duties of undivided loyalty and care to Adelphi. Had

Diamandopoulos been acting solely in Adelphi's interest or as a reasonably prudent trustee, he would have seriously considered other brokers, obtained additional information from Treiber–Salerno to permit a critical evaluation of its proposal, ensured an independent analysis of Treiber–Salerno's offer, and investigated whether anticipated short-term penalties could be mitigated. Under the circumstances, Diamandopoulos' actions can reasonably be interpreted as intended to curry favor with Procope—who has played a key role in setting his compensation every year since 1986—by guaranteeing the Adelphi account to her company for at least as long as she remained a trustee.

The trustees went to considerable lengths at the hearing and in their post-hearing brief to prove that the arrangement between Bowman and Adelphi was "fair", i.e., economically advantageous, to Adelphi. They seem to rely on N–PCL § 715 for the proposition that if the deal were fair, then Procope has no conflict of interest for which she can be removed. We think this too expansive a reading of § 715. Section 715 speaks only to the circumstances under which a corporation by legal action may void a contract where a conflict of interest is found to exist. It does not stand for the proposition that if the contract is ultimately found to be fair, the conflict never existed and the interested trustee is absolved of any wrongdoing. To the contrary, while fairness to the corporation may somewhat relax the conflict of interest constraints, the director's conduct must, at all times, further the organization's goals and not his or her own interests. Based upon the record before us, we cannot find that Procope's actions at all times furthered Adelphi's goals and not her own interests. Indeed, the magnitude of the commissions earned by her wholly-owned company ($1,227,949), the obvious and intentional solicitation of Adelphi's business, the failure to ensure a level playing field of competitors—all demonstrate that Procope acted in self-interest. Because of her conflicted roles, we will never know whether or not Adelphi obtained the lowest cost coverage best suited to its needs, or whether another broker would have been a better choice.

Under these facts, we recommend the removal from the board of Diamandopoulos and Procope for neglect of their duties of due care and loyalty.

B.   The Lois Advertising Campaign.

Trustee George Lois ("Lois") is a creator of advertisements and owner of LOIS/USA, an advertising agency. Lois was recruited to the board in 1993 by Diamandopoulos because of Lois' advertising expertise. Throughout his trusteeship, Lois has been the chair of the Institutional Advancement Committee, the purpose of which is to advance the "imagery and perception" of Adelphi. Trustee Hilton Kramer also served on that committee.

When Lois joined the board Adelphi had another advertising agency under contract. Shortly into his tenure, Lois decided that Adelphi needed a different approach to marketing. Lois met with Diamandopoulos and proposed a new and creative advertising campaign centered around the idea of teachers as mentors. At the December 1994 meeting of the board, Lois presented his proposal to the full board. On a motion by Diamandopoulos, seconded by Procope, the board unanimously approved the campaign, with Lois apparently failing to recuse himself from the vote. Before acting, neither the committee nor the full board established an advertising budget, discussed Lois' fees, reviewed the projected cost of the advertising, or solicited proposals from other advertising agencies. Once the Lois campaign was approved, Adelphi dismissed its then advertising agency. On March 8, 1995, Lois reported to the full board on the progress of his work. At the conclusion of Lois' presentation, Diamandopoulos thanked Lois for "giving his services, *free of charge*, to the University." (Emphasis added).

From December 1994 until June 1996, the board thus proceeded under the mistaken belief that Lois was not being paid for his work for Adelphi. In reality, while Lois had donated valuable creative services to the university, he had also received approximately $155,000 in commissions from advertisements placed on Adelphi's behalf, and was paid costs for producing recruitment brochures for Adelphi. Neither Lois nor Diamandopoulos disclosed these material facts to the board, until Lois was required to file his financial disclosure statement in June 1996. In it he acknowledged for the first time that, beginning in "April 1995 payments were made by Adelphi *for production of advertisements and placement of ads*. All charges for creative work * * * have been waived." (Emphasis added).

On this record, we find that Lois neglected both his duties of due care and undivided loyalty to Adelphi. The Institutional Advancement Committee, with Lois as chair, was charged with promoting Adelphi's public image. Implicit in this charge was the obligation to select the advertising agency and campaign best suited to Adelphi's needs. Instead, Lois' committee sought no proposals and considered no ideas other than those advanced by Lois, its chairman. Under these circumstances, Lois' dual roles as vendor and client prevented him from faithfully and objectively discharging his fiduciary obligation to advance only Adelphi's goals and not his own interests.

Lois also violated his fiduciary duty by failing to disclose to the board that LOIS/USA was, indeed, being paid for services rendered to Adelphi. A fiduciary has a duty to fully disclose to his board all the material terms of any transaction that might present a conflict of interest, including any terms of compensation. In this case, full and fair disclosure would have enabled the board to make an informed choice of advertisers and assess whether Adelphi's relationship with LOIS/USA was beneficial to Adelphi. Instead, Lois let stand the board's false impression that his services were given free of charge, effectively eliminating any competition for the Adelphi advertising account.

We further find that Diamandopoulos neglected his fiduciary duty to Adelphi by misrepresenting the terms of LOIS/USA's relationship with Adelphi. The record shows that Diamandopoulos knew that Adelphi was compensating Lois for production work and the placement of ads, yet

Diamandopoulos told the board that the services were being provided "free of charge." Diamandopoulos had a fiduciary duty to tell the board the truth about Lois' fees and apprise the board of any potential conflict of interest. Instead, Diamandopoulos told no one.

On this record, we recommend the removal of trustees Diamandopoulos and Lois for neglect of their fiduciary duties of due care and loyalty.

C. The Board's Failure to Protect Adelphi From Interested Trustee Transactions.

We further find that the full board of trustees neglected its duty of due care to Adelphi by failing to take appropriate action once it learned of Procope's and Lois' potential conflicts.

In 1995, the board of trustees finally adopted the 1993 recommendation of its auditors, Deloitte and Touche, that all trustees file written statements disclosing any potential conflicts of interest. As noted above, Procope filed her statement in March 1996, confirming for the first time that "my firm, E.G. Bowman, Inc., serves as a broker (insurance) for Adelphi University," and raising the possibility of a conflict between Procope role as trustee and businesswoman. In our view, this revelation should have raised serious questions among prudent trustees about the propriety of the Bowman/Adelphi relationship. At a minimum, the board should have fully reviewed the circumstances that gave rise to the Bowman/Adelphi relationship, carefully examined the financial terms of the relationship and how they were established, solicited and fairly considered other insurance brokerage firms and proposals, and considered action against Diamandopoulos and Procope for neglecting their fiduciary duties to Adelphi as described above. There is no evidence in the record before us that the board took any action to protect the University's interests.

As in the case of Adelphi's insurance, we find that, once the board learned in June 1996 that a company owned by Lois was being paid for services provided to Adelphi it was the board's responsibility to review the terms of LOIS/USA's compensation, solicit and review other advertising proposals, and consider action against Diamandopoulos and Lois for breach of their fiduciary duties to the University. The failure of the full board to take any action based upon the information it learned from Lois' financial disclosure form constitutes a neglect of duty.

On these facts, we recommend the removal of trustees Diamandopoulos, Procope, Burke, Byrne, Calabrese, Carlino, Contominas, Damadian, Friedman, Goulandris, Kramer, Krasnoff, Kulukundis, Lois, Riggio, Samios, Silber and Silveri for neglect of their duty of care.

NOTES AND QUESTIONS

1. *The Impact of Adelphi.* Were the actions of the Adelphi board illegal or unethical? See N.Y. Not-for-Profit Corp. L. § 715. Was it reasonable for the board to believe that Adelphi's advertising campaign was for free? For a critical view of the Adelphi decision see Roger Kimball, The

Third Degree–Adelphi University's Faculty–Trustee Dispute, Nat'l. Rev. May 10, 1997, at 31 ("[t]he case was built on a tissue of irrelevancies, groundless allegations, and the resentment of a few disenchanted faculty members * * * a labor dispute masquerading as a battle over educational principle").

2. *The Role of the Attorney General.* In most jurisdictions, the attorney general is responsible for governmental supervision of charitable organizations including colleges and universities. After the Regents' decision, the New York State attorney general brought an action in restitution against the former trustees and Diamandopoulos, who was removed from his position by the new board. Vacco v. Diamandopoulos, 185 Misc.2d 724, 715 N.Y.S.2d 269 (1998).

In Massachusetts, the attorney general interceded and compelled a change in governance procedures at Boston University and required the then-president John Silber to return a bonus from the trustees for selling a university-owned biotechnology company. The university had filed a false report relating to the transaction. The president also received low or no-interest loans which he used to purchase university-owned housing at below market rates. Trustees, including members of a five-person executive committee on compensation that voted on the president's salary and benefits, were alleged to have received lucrative business contracts with the university. Dr. Silber was one of the Adelphi trustees removed.

3. *Remedies for Breaches of Fiduciary Duty.* For breaches of the duty of care by a fiduciary involving inattention or inaction in the absence of self-dealing, courts have applied remedies short of fines and removal from office. For instance, as Judge Gesell observed in *Stern v. Lucy Webb*, the "function of equity is not to punish but merely to take such action as the Court in its discretion seems necessary to prevent the recurrence of improper conduct." There the court required newly elected trustees to read the decision. Other courts have subjected fiduciaries to equitable sanctions, such as removal or injunctions to stop the inappropriate behavior.

Breaches of the duty of loyalty stand on a different footing. Courts have employed civil and criminal penalties, and attempted to recapture improper gains or even imposed punitive damages. In a settlement of the attorney general's lawsuit the ousted Adelphi trustees paid the university $1.23 million from their personal funds and assumed an additional $400,000 in legal fees. Adelphi received an additional $1.45 million from the board's directors' and officers' liability insurance policy. Dr. Diamandopoulos refunded nearly $650,000 to the University, paid more than $100,000 in rent for the University's Manhattan apartment, and dropped claims for an additional $767,000. David M. Halbfinger, Lawsuits Over Ouster of Adelphi Chief Are Settled, N.Y. Times, Nov. 18, 1998, at B1.

In another case, Harry John, an officer, director and trustee of a nonprofit corporation engaged in a variety of self-dealing conduct including: direct stock sales from his personal securities account to the corporation which allowed him to cash out of a falling market, false expenses and travel vouchers, securities and tax fraud, waste of corporate assets and other misuse of funds. The court removed John from all of his positions, denied indemnification by the organization, and ordered restitution of $1.7 million. John v. John, 153 Wis.2d 343, 450 N.W.2d 795 (App.1989). The televangelists Jim and Tammy Faye Bakker and a chief associate were required to return several million dollars in excessive salaries and misused funds of the PTL Club. In re Heritage Village Church and Missionary Fellowship, 92 B.R. 1000 (Bankr. D.S.C. 1988). In other situations constructive trusts for the nonprofit have been created. See, Mile–O–Mo Fishing Club v. Noble, 62 Ill.App.2d 50, 210 N.E.2d 12 (1965).

4. *Interested Transactions Statutes.* As of January 2003, forty-eight states had codified the duty of loyalty in their nonprofit corporation act or through their business corporation statutes. Marion R. Fremont–Smith, Governing Nonprofit Organizations 218 & Appendix, Table 3 (2004). These statutes or case law provide a procedure for legitimizing certain interested transactions between fiduciaries and a nonprofit organization. Others incorporate by reference the interested transaction provision of the general corporate code, as did Judge Gesell in Stern v. Lucy Webb Hayes. Generally, the key to validation of a conflict of interest provided by the statutes is disclosure of the material facts of the transaction and of the fiduciary's interest; approval of the transaction by a disinterested board, board committee, or appropriate authority within the organization; or in the case of mutual benefit corporations, approval by the members. If there is no such disclosure or if the vote of interested directors is necessary, the organization can void the contract unless it is established by the parties with the conflict of interest that the transaction was fair to the organization at the time it was authorized.

The real impact of interested directors statutes goes to the procedural question of who has the burden of proof. Following the procedures outlined in the statutes places that burden upon the party challenging the transaction. If independent, disinterested directors acting in good faith approve the transaction, the interested directors' action will be shielded by the business judgment rule. If the statute's procedures are not followed, the interested fiduciaries will have the burden of proving the transaction was fair and reasonable.

5. *Absolute Prohibitions.* Certain interested transactions, such as loans and guarantees to directors, are absolutely prohibited. See, e.g., Model Nonprofit Corp. Act (3d ed.) § 8.32 (optional provision); Ill. Rev. Stat. ch. 805 ¶ 108.80; N.Y. Not-for-Profit Corp. L. § 716. Aren't there ever reasons to grant low-interest loans to officers or staff, such as home mortgage relief or encouraging medical staff to work in a low income area?

6. *Attorney General Approval.* The California Corporations Code § 5233(d)(1) provides that the attorney general or a court in an action in which the attorney general is a party can approve an interested transaction before or after it is consummated. Does this clause provide business efficacy? Will an attorney general respond in sufficiently timely fashion? Should the strained resources of the attorney general be devoted to essentially internal governance matters in a context other than a judicial

proceeding? Does this involve the attorney general too deeply in the ordinary affairs of nonprofits?

7. *Self–Dealing in the Health Care Area.* Self-dealing frequently has occurred in the conversion of nonprofit health provider facilities to profit seeking entities. The managers of the nonprofit who accept the sale price are usually shareholders of the for-profit who have an interest in the lowest possible price. See Chapter 2E, supra, at pp. 114–119.

8. *Conflict of Interest Policies.* Although statutes establish procedures for approving interested transactions, they usually do not require organizations to have conflict of interest policies. Only Arizona requires nonprofit corporations which have assets with a book value of more than $10 million or revenues greater than $2 million to adopt a conflict of interest policy regarding transactions between the corporation and interested persons. "Interested person" refers to an officer or director of the nonprofit but not an employee. Ariz. Rev. Stat. § 10–3864 (West 1999). New Hampshire requires interested transactions over $5,000 between directors, officers or trustees and a charitable trust to be published in a newspaper of general circulation in the community in which the charitable trust's principal New Hampshire office is located or in a newspaper of general circulation throughout the state. N.H. Stat. Ann. § 7:19–a (1999).

The Panel on the Nonprofit Sector's Principles for Good Governance and Ethical Practice recommends that a charity should adopt and implement policies and procedures to ensure that all conflicts of interest or their appearance are managed through disclosure, recusal of interested parties from decisionmaking or other means. Of even greater influence is the IRS's revised Form 990 annual information return (see Section D2 of this chapter, infra, at p. 224), which inquires whether the organization has a conflict of interest policy, if the organization monitors and enforces compliance with the policy, and further requests a description of the policy. their own standard approval procedures. Many organizations have conflict of interest policies that go beyond statutory mandates in that they require disclosure of *all* conflicts of interest rather than those which are material. One approach is for board members to complete a conflict of interest questionnaire annually, and sign a statement that they have read the organization's conflict of interest policy and are in compliance with it. Board members who acquire a conflict must report it to the appropriate office or official and must refrain from consideration (which the statutes do not prohibit) or voting on the interested matter.

9. *Planning.* You are general counsel of Sturdley College. Several members of the board of trustees have business interests with the college. Trustee Virginia Graham's firm, Graham Construction, usually is the general contractor when Sturdley constructs a new facility. Winfield Philpot of Philpot Investments handles the college's endowment funds. Sturdley uses Consolidated Bank, where trustee Clive Gretsky is Senior Vice President, for its banking and payroll needs. After reading the Adelphi decision, what advice would you offer to the Board of Trustees with respect to these relationships?

NOTE: TROUBLE IN PARADISE—THE BISHOP ESTATE

Federal and state regulators forced the removal of the trustees of Hawaii's Bishop Estate, one of the nation's most affluent charitable trusts on grounds of financial improprieties, excessive compensation, and conflicts of interest. In May 1999 a state probate judge removed four of the trustees and accepted the resignation of the fifth to forestall the IRS's threatened revocation of the Estate's federal tax exempt status. In a separate action brought by two of the trustees, another state court judge permanently removed a third trustee for mismanagement and interference in the operation of the Estate's school.

The Bishop Estate was created in 1884 by the bequest of Princess Bernice Pauahi Bishop, the last direct descendant of King Kamehameha I, who unified the Hawaiian Islands into one kingdom. Her will specified that upon her death 434,300 acres of the royal lands would be deposited into a charitable trust to be used for the benefit of the Kamehameha School for native Hawaiians. It further provided that the Bishop Estate shall be governed by five trustees appointed by the sitting justices of the Hawaii Supreme Court. The trustees were compensated generously. In the five years ending in 1998, each earned over $800,000 annually. Compensation was based upon two percent of the trust's tax-free revenue plus commissions on some of the taxable profits. The board divided up its responsibilities into a lead trustee system so that one trustee provided oversight in areas such as asset management or educational affairs, frequently exercising unilateral authority, with no board oversight or deliberation. In terms of board governance, are there any consequences to such compensation largess or the management culture?

The Bishop Estate's activities had been shrouded in secrecy. Although certain controversial practices were known for years, the Hawaiian community shielded the Estate from censure. This immunity began to erode in 1995 when the Estate, citing a financial squeeze and a desire to consolidate its mission, eliminated community education outreach programs that assisted 10,000 people annually, including children and young parents in largely native Hawaiian areas. Additionally, one of the trustees interfered unilaterally in the Kamehameha School's operations. For the first time, the Estate's beneficiaries offered public criticism. After a report ("Broken Trust") was published by five prominent Hawaiians, including a law professor at the University of Hawaii, the governor ordered the attorney general to commence an inquiry.

An IRS audit commenced in 1996 focused upon excessive compensation of the trustees, use of charitable funds for personal purposes, conflicts of interest and self-dealing, and impermissible lobbying. The IRS would not agree to resolve the problems raised in the audit unless the incumbent trustees were removed because it believed the Estate's assets were at risk. In a separate investigation, state regulators had uncovered instances of excessive compensation; concentration of immense sums on an international investment portfolio rather than expanding the school and its services; trustee conflicts of interest including personal investing in projects in which the Bishop Estate also invested; use of Estate employees to do personal work; and micromanagement of the educational institution. One of the trustees negotiated *on behalf of* a group purchasing an asset from the Estate. The state proceeding was settled in 2000 when the Estate agreed to pay $25 million, all covered by insurance. See Stephen G. Greene, Insurer to Pay $25–Million to Settle Dispute in Hawaii, Chron. Philanthropy, Oct. 5, 2000, at 42.

The Bishop Estate entered into a closing agreement (a form of settlement contract) with the IRS that gave the Service extraordinary oversight of the Estate for five years and required extensive corporate governance reforms. The Estate retained its tax-exempt status by paying more than $9 million to settle a tax liability, and each trustee reportedly was assessed with an excise tax of approximately $40,000. See Stephen G. Greene, Bishop Estate to Pay IRS $9–Million But Retain its Tax–Exempt Status, Chron. Philanthropy, Jan. 13, 2000, at 50. The agreement required a reorganized governance structure placing day-to-day management in the hands of a chief executive officer. In contrast to the past, the trustees now exercise a more traditional policymaking and general oversight role and along with senior executives are subject to a conflict of interest policy.

The Bishop Estate closing agreement is reported in 27 Exempt Org. Tax Rev. 174 (2000) and is available on the Estate's web site at http://www.ksbe.edu.newsroom/legal.html. For a comprehensive history and analysis of the Bishop Estate saga, see Samuel P. King & Randall W. Roth, Broken Trust: Greed, Mismanagement, and Political Manipulation at America's Largest Charitable Trust (2006).

c. BUSINESS OPPORTUNITIES

A "business" or "corporate opportunity" means the chance to engage in an activity of which a director, or officer, or employee becomes aware: a) in connection with the performance of her functions that reasonably should lead the individual to believe that the person offering the opportunity expects it to be offered to the nonprofit organization; or b) through the use of the organization's information or property and the individual should reasonably be expected to believe the activity would be of interest to the organization; or c) any opportunity to engage in an activity of which a director, officer, or employee becomes aware of and knows is closely related to an activity in which the nonprofit is engaged or expects to engage. Cf. American Law Institute, Principles of Corporate Governance § 5.05(b) (1994). The common law doctrine of "corporate opportunity" is a core part of the director's duty of loyalty. Once a new project is deemed to be a corporate opportunity, a fiduciary may not appropriate it without first offering it to the nonprofit and disclosing any conflict of interest. Pursuit of the project in the absence of full disclosure or without proper rejection from the nonprofit organization constitutes a breach of fiduciary duty. Cf. Eric Talley, Turning Servile Opportunities to Gold: A Strategic Analysis of the Corporate Opportunities Doctrine, 108 Yale L.J. 277, 279 (1998). As with so many other rules of law, the principle is easy to state but difficult to apply.

The following case involves a § 501(c)(7) social club, but it offers an excellent discussion of the corporate opportunity doctrine.

Northeast Harbor Golf Club, Inc. v. Nancy Harris

Supreme Judicial Court of Maine, 1995.
661 A.2d 1146.

■ ROBERTS, JUSTICE.

Northeast Harbor Golf Club, Inc., appeals from a judgment entered in the Superior Court (Hancock County, Atwood, J.) following a nonjury trial. The Club maintains that the trial court erred in finding that Nancy Harris did not breach her fiduciary duty as president of the Club by purchasing and developing property abutting the golf course. Because we today adopt principles different from those applied by the trial court in determining that Harris's activities did not constitute a breach of the corporate opportunity doctrine, we vacate the judgment.

I.

The Facts

Nancy Harris was the president of the Northeast Harbor Golf Club, a Maine corporation, from 1971 until she was asked to resign in 1990. The Club also had a board of directors that was responsible for making or approving significant policy decisions. The Club's only major asset was a golf course in Mount Desert. During Harris's tenure as president, the board occasionally discussed the possibility of developing some of the Club's real estate in order to raise money. Although Harris was generally in favor of tasteful development, the board always "shied away" from that type of activity.

In 1979, Robert Suminsby informed Harris that he was the listing broker for the Gilpin property, which comprised three noncontiguous parcels located among the fairways of the golf course. The property included an unused right-of-way on which the Club's parking lot and clubhouse were located. It was also encumbered by an easement in favor of the Club allowing foot traffic from the green of one hole to the next tee. Suminsby testified that he contacted Harris because she was the president of the Club and he believed that the Club would be interested in buying the property in order to prevent development.

Harris immediately agreed to purchase the Gilpin property in her own name for the asking price of $45,000. She did not disclose her plans to purchase the property to the Club's board prior to the purchase. She informed the board at its annual August meeting that she had purchased the property, that she intended to hold it in her own name, and that the Club would be "protected." The board took no action in response to the Harris purchase. She testified that at the time of the purchase she had no plans to develop the property and that no such plans took shape until 1988.

In 1984, while playing golf with the postmaster of Northeast Harbor, Harris learned that a parcel of land owned by the heirs of the Smallidge family might be available for purchase. The Smallidge parcel was surrounded on three sides by the golf course and on the fourth side by a house lot. It had no access to the road. With the ultimate goal of acquiring the property, Harris instructed her lawyer to locate the Smallidge heirs. Harris testified that she told a number of individual board members about her attempt to acquire the Smallidge parcel. At a board meeting in August 1985, Harris formally disclosed to the board that she had purchased the Smallidge property. The minutes of that meeting show that she told the board she had no present plans to develop the Smallidge parcel. Harris testified that at the time of the purchase of the Smallidge property she nonetheless thought it might be nice to have some houses there. Again, the board took no formal action as a result of Harris's purchase. Harris acquired the Smallidge property from ten heirs, paying a total of $60,000. In 1990, Harris paid $275,000 for the lot and building separating the Smallidge parcel from the road in order to gain access to the otherwise landlocked parcel.

The trial court expressly found that the Club would have been unable to purchase either the Gilpin or Smallidge properties for itself, relying on testimony that the Club continually experienced financial difficulties, operated annually at a deficit, and depended on contributions from the directors to pay its bills. On the other hand, there was evidence that the Club had occasionally engaged in successful fund-raising, including a two-year period shortly after the Gilpin purchase during which the Club raised $115,000. The Club had $90,000 in a capital investment fund at the time of the Smallidge purchase.

In 1987 or 1988, Harris divided the real estate into 41 small lots, 14 on the Smallidge property and 27 on the Gilpin property. Apparently as part of her estate plan, Harris conveyed noncontiguous lots among the 41 to her children and retained others for herself. In 1991, Harris and her children exchanged deeds to reassemble the small lots into larger parcels. At the time the Club filed this suit, the property was divided into 11 lots, some owned by Harris and others by her children who are also defendants in this case. Harris estimated the value of all the real estate at the time of the trial to be $1,550,000.

In 1988, Harris, who was still president of the Club, and her children began the process of obtaining approval for a five-lot subdivision known as Bushwood on the lower Gilpin property. Even when the board learned of the proposed subdivision, a majority failed to take any action. A group of directors formed a separate organization in order to oppose the subdivision on the basis that it violated the local zoning ordinance. After Harris's resignation as president, the Club also sought unsuccessfully to challenge the subdivision. Plans of Harris and her family for development of the other parcels are unclear, but the local zoning ordinance would permit construction of up to 11 houses on the land as currently divided.

After Harris's plans to develop Bushwood became apparent, the board grew increasingly divided concerning the propriety of development near the golf course. At least two directors, Henri Agnese and Nick Ludington, testified that they trusted Harris to act in the best interests of the Club and that they had no problem with the development plans for Bushwood. Other directors disagreed.

In particular, John Schafer, a Washington, D.C., lawyer and long-time member of the board, took issue with Harris's conduct. He testified that he had relied on Harris's representations at the time she acquired the properties that she would not develop them. According to Schafer, matters came to a head in August 1990 when a number of directors concluded that Harris's development plans irreconcilably conflicted with the Club's interests. As a result, Schafer and two other directors asked Harris to resign as president. In April 1991, after a substantial change in the board's membership, the board authorized the instant lawsuit against Harris for the breach of her fiduciary duty to act in the best interests of the corporation. The board simultaneously resolved that the proposed housing development was contrary to the best interests of the corporation.

[T]he complaint alleged that during her term as president Harris breached her fiduciary duty by purchasing the lots without providing notice and an opportunity for the Club to purchase the property and by subdividing the lots for future development. The Club sought an injunction to prevent development and also sought to impose a constructive trust on the property in question for the benefit of the Club.

The trial court found that Harris had not usurped a corporate opportunity because the acquisition of real estate was not in the Club's line of business. Moreover, it found that the corporation lacked the financial ability to purchase the real estate at issue. Finally, the court placed great emphasis on Harris's good faith. It noted her long and dedicated history of service to the Club, her personal oversight of the Club's growth, and her frequent financial contributions to the Club. The court found that her development activities were "generally * * * compatible with the corporation's business." This appeal followed.

II.

The Corporate Opportunity Doctrine

Corporate officers and directors bear a duty of loyalty to the corporations they serve. As Justice Cardozo explained the fiduciary duty in Meinhard v. Salmon, 249 N.Y. 458, 164 N.E. 545, 546 (1928):

> A trustee is held to something stricter than the morals of the marketplace. Not honesty alone, but the punctilio of an honor the most sensitive, is then the standard of behavior. As to this there has developed a tradition that is unbending and inveterate.

Maine has embraced this "unbending and inveterate" tradition. Corporate fiduciaries in Maine must discharge their duties in good faith with a view toward furthering the interests of the corporation. They must disclose and not withhold relevant information concerning any potential conflict of interest with the corporation, and they must refrain from using their position, influence, or knowledge of the affairs of the corporation to gain personal advantage.

Despite the general acceptance of the proposition that corporate fiduciaries owe a duty of loyalty to their corporations, there has been much confusion about the specific extent of that duty when, as here, it is contended that a fiduciary takes for herself a corporate opportunity.* * * This case requires us for the first time to define the scope of the corporate opportunity doctrine in Maine.

Various courts have embraced different versions of the corporate opportunity doctrine. The test applied by the trial court and embraced by Harris is generally known as the "line of business" test. The seminal case applying the line of business test is Guth v. Loft, Inc., 5 A.2d 503 (Del.1939). In Guth, the Delaware Supreme Court adopted an intensely factual test stated in general terms as follows:

> [I]f there is presented to a corporate officer or director a business opportunity which the corporation is financially able to undertake, is, from its nature, in the line of the corporation's business and is of practical advantage to it, is one in which the corporation has an interest or a reasonable expectancy, and, by embracing the opportunity, the self-interest of the officer or director will be brought into conflict with that of his corporation, the law will not permit him to seize the opportunity for himself.

Id. at 511. The "real issue" under this test is whether the opportunity "was so closely associated with the existing business activities * * * as to bring the transaction within that class of cases where the acquisition of the property would throw the corporate officer purchasing it into competition with his company." The Delaware court described that inquiry as "a factual question to be decided by reasonable inferences from objective facts."

The line of business test suffers from some significant weaknesses. First, the question whether a particular activity is within a corporation's line of business is conceptually difficult to answer. The facts of the instant case demonstrate that difficulty. The Club is in the business of running a golf course. It is not in the business of developing real estate. In the traditional sense, therefore, the trial court correctly observed that the opportunity in this case was not a corporate opportunity within the meaning of the Guth test. Nevertheless, the record would support a finding that the Club had made the policy judgment that development of surrounding real estate was detrimental to the best interests of the Club. The acquisition of land adjacent to the golf course for the purpose of preventing future development would have enhanced the ability of the Club to implement that policy. The record also shows that the Club had occasionally considered reversing that policy and expanding its operations to include the development of surrounding real estate. Harris's activities effectively foreclosed the Club from pursuing that option with respect to prime locations adjacent to the golf course.

Second, the Guth test includes as an element the financial ability of the corporation to take advantage of the opportunity. The court in this case relied on the Club's supposed financial incapacity as a basis for excusing Harris's conduct. Often, the injection of financial ability into the equation will unduly favor the inside director or executive who has command of the facts relating to the finances of the corporation. Reliance on financial ability will also act as a disincentive to corporate executives to solve corporate financing and other problems. In addition, the Club could have prevented development without spending $275,000 to acquire the property Harris needed to obtain access to the road.

The Massachusetts Supreme Judicial Court adopted a different test in Durfee v. Durfee & Canning, Inc., 323 Mass. 187, 80 N.E.2d 522 (1948). The Durfee test has since come to be known as the "fairness test." According to Durfee, the true basis of governing doctrine rests on the unfairness in the particular circumstances of a director, whose relation to the corporation is fiduciary, taking advantage of an opportunity [for her personal profit] when the interest of the corporation justly call[s] for protection. This calls for application of ethical standards of what is fair and equitable * * * in particular sets of facts.

As with the Guth test, the Durfee test calls for a broad-ranging, intensely factual inquiry. The Durfee test suffers even more than the Guth test from a lack of principled content. It provides little or no practical guidance to the corporate officer or director seeking to measure her obligations.

The Minnesota Supreme Court elected "to combine the 'line of business' test with the 'fairness' test." Miller v. Miller, 301 Minn. 207, 222 N.W.2d 71, 81 (1974). It engaged in a two-step analysis, first determining whether a particular opportunity was within the corporation's line of business, then scrutinizing "the equitable considerations existing prior to, at the time of, and following the officer's acquisition." The Miller court hoped by adopting this approach "to ameliorate the often-expressed criticism that the [corporate opportunity] doctrine is vague and subjects today's corporate management to the danger of unpredictable liability." In fact, the test adopted in Miller merely piles the uncertainty and vagueness of the fairness test on top of the weaknesses in the line of business test.

Despite the weaknesses of each of these approaches to the corporate opportunity doctrine, they nonetheless rest on a single fundamental policy. At bottom, the corporate opportunity doctrine recognizes that a corporate fiduciary should not serve both corporate and personal interests at the same time. * * *

III.

* * *

[The court then discussed the approach of the American Law Institute's Principles of Corporate Governance § 5.05, which prohibits a director or senior officer from taking a corporate opportunity unless the individual offers the opportunity to the corporation, makes full disclosure of any conflict of interest and of the details of the opportunity. The director or senior executive must obtain the organization's informed rejection following such disclosure, and the rejection must be fair to the corporation. Normally such approval must be obtained in advance, but defective disclosure can be ratified in certain circumstances. Eds.]

Under the ALI standard, once the Club shows that the opportunity is a corporate opportunity, it must show either that Harris did not offer the opportunity to the Club or that the Club did not reject it properly. If the Club shows that the board did not reject the opportunity by a vote of the disinterested directors after full disclosure, then Harris may defend her actions on the basis that the taking of the opportunity was fair to the corporation. If Harris failed to offer the opportunity at all, however, then she may not defend on the basis that the failure to offer the opportunity was fair.

[T]oday we follow the ALI test. The disclosure-oriented approach provides a clear procedure whereby a corporate officer may insulate herself through prompt and complete disclosure from the possibility of a legal challenge. The requirement of disclosure recognizes the paramount importance of the corporate fiduciary's duty of loyalty. At the same time it protects the fiduciary's ability pursuant to the proper procedure to pursue her own business ventures free from the possibility of a lawsuit.

The importance of disclosure is familiar to the law of corporations in Maine. Pursuant to 13–A M.R.S.A. § 717 (1981), a corporate officer or director may enter into a transaction with the corporation in which she has a personal or adverse interest only if she discloses her interest in the transaction and secures ratification by a majority of the disinterested directors or shareholders.

IV.

Conclusion

The question remains how our adoption of the rule affects the result in the instant case. The trial court made a number of factual findings based on an extensive record. The court made those findings, however, in the light of legal principles that are different from the principles that we today announce. Similarly, the parties did not have the opportunity to develop the record in this case with knowledge of the applicable legal standard. In these circumstances, fairness requires that we remand the case for further proceedings. Those further proceedings may include, at the trial court's discretion, the taking of further evidence.

NOTES AND QUESTIONS

1. *Business Opportunities at Charities. Harris* involved a mutual benefit organization, but the corporate opportunity doctrine also arises in

public benefit organizations. American Baptist Churches v. Galloway, 271 A.D.2d 92, 710 N.Y.S.2d 12 (2000) involved the misappropriation of a business opportunity by an officer of a nonprofit, who had been hired to help the charity develop an aids care facility. The officer seized control of the project for himself by forming another nonprofit corporation, which then purchased the site for the proposed facility. The court found that an agent could not divert or exploit for his own benefit an opportunity that was an asset of his principal, or use the principal's resources to organize a competing business. Two other defendants, who were directors of the corporation formed to usurp the opportunity, were denied immunity even though they were uncompensated directors, because their conduct towards the plaintiff was harmful and grossly negligent. See also Mid–List Press v. Nora, 275 F.Supp.2d 997 (D. Minn. 2003) (officer of nonprofit press misappropriated corporate trade name and ISBN for personal benefit).

2. *Model Nonprofit Corporation Act and ALI Principles Approaches.* Section 8.70 of the Model Act employs the broader notion of "business opportunity" that encompasses any opportunity, without regard to whether it would come within the judicial definition of a "corporate opportunity" as it may have been developed by courts in a jurisdiction. By action of the board of directors or members of a nonprofit corporation, a director can receive a disclaimer of corporate interest in the matter before proceeding with such involvement. In the alternative, the corporation may (i) decline to disclaim its interest, (ii) delay a decision respecting granting a disclaimer pending receipt from the director of additional information (or for any other reason), or (iii) attach conditions to the disclaimer it grants. The American Law Institute's Principles of the Law of Nonprofit Organizations adopt the approach of the Model Act. See § 330 cmt. (c)(1). A director who is found by a court to have violated the duty of loyalty or the business opportunity doctrine is subject to damages or an array of equitable remedies, including injunction, disgorgement or the imposition of a constructive trust in favor of the organization.

d. PROPOSALS FOR REFORM

Under state law, transactions between a public benefit nonprofit corporation and its directors are neither void nor voidable so long as the conflict of interest is disclosed and the transaction is approved by disinterested directors or the organization's members, or the transaction is fair to the corporation.

Marion Fremont–Smith has summarized the principal shortcomings of state standards in failing to impose meaningful penalties for noncompliance, which has the effect of undermining enforcement efforts. They include: (1) permitting self-dealing transactions to be ratified after the fact without a showing of fairness; (2) applying the business judgment rule to excuse all but extreme gross negligence; and (3) condoning broad indemnification, backed by insurance paid for by the corporation even in some circumstances in which there was bad faith. Marion R. Fremont–Smith,

Governing Nonprofit Organizations 435 (2004). The wide range of proposals to reform the duty of loyalty are discussed below.

1. *Prohibiting Self–Dealing.* Professor Henry Hansmann has urged a flat prohibition against all self-dealing transactions involving controlling persons or any other organizations in which such an organization has a financial interest except on the same terms available to others. Reforming Nonprofit Corporation Law, 129 U. of Pa. L. Rev. 497, 567–572 (1981). See also Deborah A. DeMott, Self–Dealing Transactions in Nonprofit Corporations, 59 Brook. L.Rev. 131 (1993). Professor Hansmann would reinstitute the trust law standard. A trustee ordinarily is subject to "a strict prohibition against engaging in transactions that involve self-dealing or that otherwise involve or create a conflict between the trustee's fiduciary duties and personal interests." Restatement (Third) of Trusts § 78(2) (2007).

On the federal level the private inurement proscription of federal tax law serves to prevent insiders from siphoning off a charity's name or assets for financial gain, and the intermediate sanctions regime imposes monetary penalties on any excess benefit transactions between "disqualified persons" and the organization. See I.R.C. § 4958 and Chapter 5D, infra, at pp. 445–474.

A strict prohibition against any interested transactions by a director of a nonprofit corporation offers the advantages of predictability and ease of application. The *in terrorem* penalty that fair as well as unfair transactions can be rescinded provides a sure deterrent to self-dealing. A supposed but not empirically verified benefit of the absolute prohibition would be a lessening of burdens on the courts and attorneys general. A total prohibition of all interested transactions would reinforce the fiduciary concept and help ensure that the "public" purpose of the organization is achieved.

2. *Arguments in Favor of Some Self–Dealing.* Would not a total prohibition against any conflicts of interest by nonprofits be too severe, by carrying in its swath useful interested transactions that nonprofits, particularly smaller ones, need to survive? An absolute ban ignores the reality of much of the charitable sector. Many nonprofit organizations benefit from engaging in transactions with board members. Generally, few people have as much interest in the welfare of the nonprofit or understand it better than its directors. Self-dealing transactions can be efficient for the organization. The transaction costs are low. Interested directors may be able to lend money or provide services or do business with a nonprofit at a lower rate, because they know the organization best. Because the organization may not be able to obtain equivalent goods in the marketplace, these benign interested transactions may be the only source. A nonprofit would often lose advantageous opportunities otherwise available to it if it were completely barred from entering into any transactions with its directors or any entity in which the directors have an interest.

Despite the predictability and mechanical attractiveness of a prohibition on all self-dealing, a complete ban would fail, because directors intent on misdeeds would conceal their conduct. Note, The Fiduciary Duties of Loyalty and Care Associated with Directors and Trustees of Charitable

Organizations, 64 Va. L. Rev. 449, 460 (1978). The detection burden would be the same. Finally, as nonprofit organizations become more complex and professionally managed, there may be greater need for individuals who happen to be interested directors. A nonprofit needs patron directors more than the patron directors need the nonprofit.

3. *A Middle Road.* Professor Harvey Goldschmid has suggested that an interested transaction be fair to the corporation and that a court review of transactions be governed under "loyalty standards" rather than the business judgment rule. Harvey J. Goldschmid, The Fiduciary Duties of Nonprofit Directors and Officers: Paradoxes, Problems, and Proposed Reforms, 23 J. Corp. L. 631, 651 (1998). Marion Fremont–Smith would repeal statutes that prevent directors from voiding an approved self-dealing transaction if it is subsequently found to be unfair to the corporation. Fremont–Smith, supra, at 436. Presumably, even without a statute, a court exercising its equitable powers could unwind such a transaction.

PROBLEMS

In the following problems determine whether there is a conflict of interest and, if so, consider whether the transaction can be sanitized under the Revised Model Nonprofit Corporation Act.

(a) Oaklawn Hospital is seeking land to build an outpatient facility. Sandra Brown, a director, is the sole stockholder of Burbank Realty Corporation, which owns a plot of land that would be suitable for the facility. Ms. Brown causes a real estate broker to offer the plot to Oaklawn Hospital, but the broker fails to disclose Brown's ownership of Burbank. Oaklawn Hospital's board agrees to approve the purchase of the property for a fair price. One month later the hospital learns of Brown's interest in Burbank.

(b) Same as (a), above, except that, prior to the vote on the acquisition, Ms. Brown discloses to the hospital board her interest in Burbank but fails to mention that the site may contain underground water that makes construction difficult.

(c) Same as (a) above, except that Burbank doesn't own the plot but has recently purchased an adjoining property which Brown expects to increase greatly in value if the hospital purchases the property. Brown recommends that the hospital purchase the property next to hers without disclosing her interest.

(d) Family Aid, an organization that provides temporary housing to homeless families, is potentially in the market for a small apartment building. Mark Smith, Family Aid's executive director, recently inherited a run-down, partially rented building with 24 apartments. Smith has no experience in real estate, but he is convinced that with $1 million in renovations the building will be worth $6 million. Smith has offered the building to a number of sophisticated real estate investors who have responded with counteroffers in the $2 million range. Smith listed the property with a commercial real estate broker for six months at a price of $4 million, but received no offers. Smith then offers the building to Family Aid for $4 million, making full disclosure and arguing that this was a good price. A, B and C, who are disinterested directors, consult a real estate expert who advises that the building might be worth $4 million, but this was a very high price and the expert would not pay it. The Board accepts Smith's offer.

(e) Joan Costeau, a curator in the Department of Oceanic Art at the Pacific Museum, collects oceanic art herself. She purchases several items for the museum from Lee Berton, a dealer in Oceanic Art, who gives her a courtesy 50 percent discount on her own purchases.

(f) Native American Crafts operates programs to manufacture and distribute products of Native Americans who reside on reservations. The products are marketed through a group of independent distributors. A majority of the directors organize the Y Corporation as a separate marketing organization to replace the independent distributors. Y Corporation is at least as profitable to Native American Crafts as the independent distributors.

(g) Tracy Murray, a curator in the rare book collection of the Plano Library, learns of the availability of a collection of first editions of Mrs. Afra Behn, a seventeenth century novelist and playwright, from a visitor to the rare book room. Murray purchases the collection for himself. The library has a collection of first editions of nineteenth and twentieth century American and twentieth century British writers but no seventeenth century English authors.

(h) Same facts as (g), above, except Murray learns of the collection's availability while browsing at a book fair while on vacation.

4. THE DUTY OF OBEDIENCE

Another somewhat less recognized duty of board members is to carry out the purposes of the organization as expressed in the articles of association or certificate of incorporation. The duty of obedience resembles the trustee's duty to administer a trust in a manner faithful to the wishes of the creator. 1 Scott & Ascher on Trusts § 2.2.4. Unless allowed by the law, nonprofit directors may not deviate in any substantial way from the duty to fulfill the particular purposes for which the organization was created. Daniel L. Kurtz, Board Liability 84–85 (1989). In a sense the duty of obedience requires the directors to refrain from transactions and activities that are *ultra vires*, i.e., beyond the corporation's powers and purposes as expressed in its certificate of incorporation. The ultra vires doctrine has been emasculated in corporate law, but a director may be subject to suit if a corporation has entered into or completed an ultra vires transaction. Model Nonprofit Corp. Act (3d ed.) § 3.04(c). Thus, the director has a duty to follow the purposes and powers as expressed in the governing legal documents.

Matter of the Manhattan Eye, Ear & Throat Hospital v. Spitzer

Supreme Court, New York County, 1999.
186 Misc.2d 126, 715 N.Y.S.2d 575.

■ FRIED, J.

[Manhattan Eye Ear & Throat Hospital (Meeth), a nonprofit specialty care hospital, sought authorization from the Supreme Court to close the hospital and sell substantially all of its real estate assets to another hospital and to a commercial developer. The transaction was subject to § 511 of the New York Not-for-Profit Corporation Law, which requires that the court be satisfied that the "condition and the terms of the transaction are fair and reasonable" and that the "purposes of the corporation ... will be furthered." The court concluded that the proposed sale was not fair and reasonable to the corporation and did not promote the purposes of the corporation as required for court approval. In the course of the decision, the court discussed the duty of obedience. Eds.]

* * *

It is axiomatic that the Board of Directors is charged with the duty to ensure that the mission of the charitable corporation is carried out. This duty has been referred to as the "duty of obedience." It requires the director of a not-for-profit corporation to "be faithful to the purposes and goals of the organization," since "[u]nlike business corporations, whose ultimate objective is to make money, nonprofit corporations are defined by their specific objectives: perpetuation of particular activities are central to the raison d'être of the organization." Analysis of the duties of charitable directors more commonly arises in an action brought by the A[ttorney] G[eneral] alleging breach of the duties owed to the corporation under N–PCL §§ 112 and 720, and does not appear to have been discussed in any reported decision under section 511. But the duty of obedience, perforce, must inform the question of whether a proposed transaction to sell all or substantially all of a charity's assets promotes the purposes of the charitable corporation when analyzed under section 511.

NOTES

1. *Change of Organization Purpose.* When a nonprofit board desires to alter the fundamental objectives of an organization, it must amend its articles of association and bylaws after notice to the appropriate state officials. Model Nonprofit Corp. Act (3d ed.) §§ 10.01, 10.30. Thus, in Attorney General v. Hahnemann Hospital, 397 Mass. 820, 494 N.E.2d 1011 (1986), a hospital sought to sell its assets to become a grant-making institution for hospitals and convalescent homes. The attorney general

sought to prevent the sale on the ground that such a transfer was beyond the authority of the hospital's board of trustees because it was a closing of the hospital's affairs and could only be conducted through the statutory procedures for dissolution. The trustees amended the articles of organization to authorize sale of all assets of the hospital, and the court upheld the sale.

The court noted that, in the absence of an amendment of the articles of organization, the trustees would have violated their fiduciary duty if they had attempted to use the proceeds from the sale of assets. The attorney general argued unsuccessfully that an organization could only amend its articles of organization so as to further the dominant charitable purposes to ensure that donations were used for the purposes the donors contended. The court noted the legislation did not so attempt to limit the right of amendment.

In Brown v. Memorial National Home, 162 Cal.App.2d 513, 329 P.2d 118 (1958), the attorney general brought an action for declaratory relief as to conflicting claims to the assets of charitable trusts created for a patriotic organization. The evidence sustained a finding that the corporation, which had acquired funds in trust for the benefit of needy members of the organization and for the benefit of needy parents of servicemen who were World War II victims, could not repudiate the trusts by attempting to dedicate the property to different uses and exclusion of the patriotic organization. The diversion of the funds to unauthorized purposes afforded grounds for removal of the trustee.

Directors violated their duty of obedience to an organization's purposes when they voted to close a hospital in favor of neighborhood clinics. Although various clauses of the articles of incorporation referred to plural purposes, the essential framework of the purposes clauses was the operation of a hospital. Queen of Angels Hospital v. Younger, 66 Cal.App.3d 359, 136 Cal.Rptr. 36 (1977).

2. *The Duty to Obey the Law*. A nonprofit corporation and its directors and officers have the responsibility to comply with the law. In the *Adelphi* case, supra p. 178, the New York State Board of Regents also found that by omitting the president's salary from the annual federal informational tax return, Form 990, Adelphi University failed to comply with Internal Revenue Code reporting requirements. The University was fined, audited, and threatened with revocation of tax-exempt status for repeated failure to file. This was a duty of law compliance violation. The Regents also determined that Adelphi's board of directors had countenanced an almost complete breakdown of the University's governance structure as evidenced in its Articles of Governance, a duty of obedience violation.

Nonprofits are subject to a bewildering array of statutes ranging from federal and state tax laws, civil rights statutes, and antitrust laws which affect all organizations. See Bazil Facchina, Evan Showell, & Jan E. Stone, Privileges & Exemptions Enjoyed By Nonprofit Organizations: A Catalog and Some Thoughts on Nonprofit Policymaking (NYU Prog. Philanthropy & The Law, 1993). Other statutes are applicable to specific types of organizations such as private foundations. See Chapters 7, 10 and 11, infra. A director, officer or trustee can be held responsible for a violation of the law. For example, a director or officer is liable for a corporation's failure to pay taxes if she meets the Internal Revenue Code's definition of "responsible person" and the failure to pay has been "willful". I.R.C. § 6672.

Directors involved in day-to-day administration of the organization in matters related to taxes and financial records are "responsible persons." Although directors are responsible for compliance with legal requirements in areas of obvious significance, such as payment of taxes, they are not responsible for technical compliance with every aspect of a regulatory regime.

3. *The Tax Context.* The duty of obedience often arises in the tax context. Organizations exempt from taxation under § 501(c)(3) of the Internal Revenue Code must be organized and operated exclusively for certain approved purposes. No part of their "net earnings" may inure to the benefit of any shareholder or individual. There are restrictions on lobbying activities and a prohibition on intervention in political campaigns. See Chapters 5D and 5E, infra, at pp. 445–458 and 474–545. If an organization is operated for non-exempt purposes, the directors have violated their duty of obedience. In *Adelphi*, the Regents found the failure to file required tax documents was the president's responsibility, acting in his capacity as chief executive officer rather than as a trustee. Directors should have in place procedures and systems that are likely to assure compliance and enable them to monitor compliance appropriately.

4. *Is There a Duty of Obedience?* Critics argue that there is no duty of obedience to the organization or its donors because it could conflict with the duty of loyalty to current and future charitable beneficiaries. Under this formulation, directors and trustees have a duty to keep the purposes of a charity current to meet contemporary needs. The concern is that requiring obedience to an organization's original mission even if it no longer makes any sense will result in the inefficient use of charitable assets. See, e.g., Marion R. Fremont–Smith, Governing Nonprofit Organizations 225–226 (2004); Henry Hansmann, The Ownership of Enterprise 295–296 (1996). The duty of obedience has received recent scholarly support. See Rob E. Atkinson, Obedience as the Foundation of Fiduciary Duty, 34 J. Corp. Law 43 (2008); Jeremy Benjamin, Note: Reinvigorating Nonprofit Directors' Duty of Obedience, 30 Cardozo L. Rev. 1677 (2009) and Linda Sugin, Resisting the Corporatization of Nonprofit Governance: Transforming Obedience into Fidelity, 76 Fordham L. Rev. 893 (2007).

5. INVESTMENT RESPONSIBILITY

Charitable organizations such as hospitals, universities, private foundations, and churches control huge amounts of wealth that must be invested to provide annual operating support for the organization. These assets are set aside in permanent funds known as endowments. How a nonprofit's endowment is to be invested and by whom has long created legal and practical challenges for nonprofit directors and trustees. Given the complexity of financial markets, only the most trained fiduciaries reasonably could be expected to make investment decisions themselves. Trust and corporate law allows a governing board to delegate to committees, officers or employees of the institution the authority to act in place of the board in investment and reinvestment of an organization's funds or to contract with independent investment advisors, investment counsel, or managers, banks or trust companies, and it authorizes the payment of compensation for investment advisory or management services. Uniform Prudent Management of Institutional Funds Act § 5; Restatement (Third) Trusts § 171. Delegation is a matter of fiduciary judgment and discretion. In administering a trust or overseeing an organization's investment activities, a fiduciary has the power and may have a duty to delegate such functions in such a manner as a prudent investor would delegate under the circumstances. Restatement (Third) Trusts § 227, com. j. When a governing board or a trustee seeks professional advice, its responsibility is at least to define the institution's investment objectives and approve investment strategies and programs. The law historically has created boundaries as to the type of financial instruments that are appropriate for trust or charitable investment. In recent years theories of appropriate portfolio management have outdistanced the legal doctrines. This section examines the evolution of legal restrictions on investments.

a.   THE PRUDENT PERSON

Restatement (Second) Trusts § 227, 228.

Uniform Prudent Management of Institutional Funds Act.

Employee Retirement Income Security Act of 1974 ("ERISA") § 404.

U.S. Dept. of Labor Reg. 29 C.F.R. § 2550.404A–1 (1992).

Internal Revenue Code § 4944.

Restatement (Third), Trusts (Prudent Investor Rule) §§ 171, 210, 211, 213, 227, 228, 379, 389.

Uniform Prudent Investor Act.

Cal. Corp. Code §§ 5240–41.

N.Y. Not-for-Profit Corp. L. §§ 512–514.

The prudent person of trust law, like his sibling the reasonable person of tort law, is a relatively recent figure in Anglo–American jurisprudence.[1] The roots of the fiduciary relation toward a fund of money known as a trusteeship is several centuries old, but the legal fiction of the "prudent person" did not appear until 1830 with Harvard College v. Amory. Prior to that case the duty of a trustee in regard to the investment of trust funds

---

1. The reasonable person test first appeared in Vaughan v. Menlove, 3 Bing. N.C. 468, 132 Eng. Rep. 490 (1837). See W. Page Keeton et al., Prosser & Keeton on Torts 174, 592 (5th ed. 1984 & 2005 Supp.)

was to follow a "court list" developed by the English Court of Chancery of presumptively safe investments that principally directed trustees to invest in government securities.[2]

In *Harvard College v. Amory*, the trustees were directed by the terms of a $50,000 testamentary trust of John M'Lean to "loan the same upon ample and sufficient security or to invest the same in safe and productive stock either in the public funds, bank shares of other stock, according to their best judgment and discretion * * *," paying the income to the testator's wife for her lifetime and thereafter to deliver the principal to Harvard College and Massachusetts General Hospital in equal shares to be held by them and used to further their charitable purposes.[3]

The trustees invested in several bank and insurance stocks as well as those of two manufacturing companies which declined in value. The two charitable remaindermen, Harvard and Mass. General, sought to surcharge the trustees for the reduction in value of the insurance and manufacturing stocks, which declined from $41,000 to $29,000, on the ground that they were not proper trust investments. This was the English rule at the time.

Justice Putnam, who delivered the opinion of the court, rejected the reasoning behind the English rule as having "very little or no application" to American trust law, because American government securities were both exceedingly limited in amount compared to the amount of trust funds to be invested and in any event not necessarily a safe investment. Additionally, investments in private corporations were subject to suit by law whereas the government could only be supplicated.[4]

Pointing out that other supposedly "safe" investments such as mortgage lending and real estate ownership were also subject to fluctuation, Justice Putnam concluded with some timeless investment wisdom: "Do what you will, the capital is at hazard."[5] He then pronounced what came to be called the prudent person rule:

> All that can be required of a trustee to invest, is, that he shall conduct himself faithfully and exercise a sound discretion. He is to observe how men of prudence, discretion and intelligence manage their own affairs, not in regard to speculation, but in regard to the permanent disposition of their funds, considering the probable income, as well as the probable safety of the capital to be invested.[6]

The court concluded that the trustees acted according to their best skill and discretion.

---

2.   Bevis Longstreth, Modern Investment Management and the Prudent Man Rule 11 (1986).

3.   26 Mass. (9 Pick.) 446, 447 (1830).

4.   Id. at 460.

5.   Id. at 461.

6.   Id.

Bevis Longstreth, Modern Investment Management and the Prudent Man Rule

3–6 (1986).

In recent years the field of finance has exploded with innovation. New investment products and services abound. New investment techniques are constantly being tested and applied. The risks of inflation, the volatility of interest rates, the deregulation of financial intermediaries, and the unbundling of financial services have combined to present investment managers with challenges and opportunities far greater than have existed in the past. Recent experience shows how difficult it is to beat the averages. For managers subject to the prudent man rule in one form or another— fiduciaries we will call them—the task of meeting the challenges and exploiting the opportunities is much more difficult. They must measure their investment decisions against constrained interpretations of a legal standard that have lagged far behind changes in investment theory and in the market place. Nothing in the origins of the prudent man rule would have predicted its present condition. * * *

Much of the flexibility of the original Harvard College standard was diminished by later cases and commentary, and those encrustations have been slow to change. As interpreted by courts, the rule has looked to established practices to determine prudence. Innovators are suspect precisely because they are ahead of the crowd. As the rate of change in portfolio management increases, so too must the rate at which the prudence standard adjusts to these new realities. Yet this process of adjustment lags. * * *

Options and futures, short-selling, repurchase agreements, securities lending, currency hedging, venture capital, use of nonproductive assets such as precious metals, leverage through margin accounts or second mortgages (in contrast to the often greater leverage acquired through ownership of common stock) are suspect to varying degrees under such traditional statements of prudence as can be found in the late Professor Austin Wakeman Scott's time-honored treatise on trusts and the American Law Institute's venerable Restatement of Trusts, for which the same preeminent scholar served as the Reporter. * * *

The prudent man rule of the Treatise and the Restatement only applies directly to trustees for private trusts, and then only in the absence of directions to vary from this standard, which may be included in the trust instrument. Moreover, recently various legislative and regulatory efforts have been made explicitly to depart from the traditional prudence standard in defining the duties of fiduciaries outside the province of private trusteeship. Examples include the Uniform Management of Institutional Funds Act of 1972 (UMIFA), applicable to charitable organizations, the regulations under Section 4944 of the Internal Revenue Code, applicable to private foundations, and the Employee Retirement Income Security Act of 1974 (ERISA) and its regulations, applicable to pension funds. In 1985, the law changed for California trustees of private trusts when that state enacted a new and substantially more flexible version of the prudent man rule. * * *

Traditional interpretations of the prudent man rule define "prudence" negatively as the absence of "speculation" and then label particular products and techniques as speculative for all time and purposes. These interpretations suggest that the prudence of each investment should be judged in isolation, without particular reference to its intended function in the overall design of the portfolio. They also suggest that, while fiduciaries should preserve the nominal value of their funds, they need not seek to increase that value, even when inflation makes the steady erosion of purchasing power a near certainty.

* * *

Another problem arises out of the special vocabulary associated with some of the new products. On the futures markets, one is either a "hedger" or a "speculator," but never an investor. For those reared with the traditional notion that prudent money managers must not speculate, this terminology may give pause. So too may the use of the term "margin" to describe the initial good faith deposit made on acquiring a futures position. And it is the customary use of "naked" to describe the writer of puts (even when written against cash) that worries fiduciaries who have only recently grown accustomed to "covered" call writing.

Widely accepted lessons of modern economics push hard against these constraining notions of prudence. Indeed, it would not be an exaggeration to observe that today the prudent man rule as elaborated in the Treatise, the Restatement, and much of the case law would virtually compel a fiduciary to act imprudently in terms of economic reality.

The Modern Paradigm of Prudence

[T]he traditional legal doctrine of prudence and the economic assumptions on which that doctrine rests stand irreconcilably opposed to notions of prudence drawn from the marketplace and financial theory. The law's prudent man bears little resemblance to prudent men and women engaged in the real world of investment, even those engaged in "safeguarding the property of others." * * *

A modern paradigm for prudence, then, would shift the focus from the disembodied investment to the fiduciary, the portfolio, and its purpose. In light of the overarching principle, reaffirmed by the most soundly reasoned cases and recent legislative and administrative developments, that prudence is a test of conduct and not performance, the soundest vehicle for accomplishing that shift is a paradigm of prudence based above all on process. Neither the overall performance of the portfolio nor the performance of individual investments should be viewed as central to the inquiry. Prudence should be measured principally by the process through which investment strategies and tactics are developed, adopted, implemented, and monitored. Prudence is demonstrated by the process through which risk is managed rather than by the labeling of specific investment risks as either prudent or imprudent. Investment products and techniques are essentially neutral; none should be classified prudent or imprudent per se. It is the way in which they are used, and how decisions as to their use are made, that should be examined to determine whether the prudence standard has been met.

More specifically, for any investment product or technique employed by a fiduciary or any delegate selected by the fiduciary in connection with such employment (including pooled investment vehicles), the test of prudence is the care, diligence, and skill demonstrated by the fiduciary in considering all relevant factors bearing on that decision. If particular investment products or techniques are not imprudent per se, neither are they per se prudent for all purposes and at all times. Their use, without more, will not suffice. Prudence is not self-evident. Nor will it be enough to point to their use by other fiduciaries. What matters is not that others have used the product or technique (for whatever reasons), but the basis for its use by the fiduciary in question.

Among the relevant factors to be considered are at least the following:

1. The role the investment product or technique is intended to play in the total portfolio.

2. Whether that role is reasonably designed, as part of the total portfolio, to serve the purposes for which the portfolio is being held and invested, taking into account the risk of loss and opportunity for gain associated with the investment product or technique (including such factors as tax effects and informational costs of initiation, monitoring, and termination), the composition of the portfolio in terms of its diversification and systemic risk, and the minimum projected cash flows from income and capital gain over future periods compared with the maximum projected cash demands on the portfolio over those periods.

3. The competence of the fiduciary or the delegates selected by him to employ the product or technique.

4. If delegates are involved, the reasonableness of the terms and conditions of such delegation, taking into account the compensation structure, monitoring mechanisms, and provisions for termination.

If the test of prudence is to be found in the process by which investment choice is exercised, it follows that documents must be kept to record that process for future use in the event of challenge.

Judging the prudence of a fiduciary's investments according to the quality of the surrounding decision-making process in no way disables one from concluding in any particular case that an investment was, in essence, "too risky." * * * In examining the prudence of a fiduciary's investment record, a court may be expected to scrutinize the substantive elements of the decision-making process, not to substitute its judgments for those of the fiduciary, but to assure that some rational basis for the fiduciary's judgments existed.

————

b.   THE UNIFORM PRUDENT MANAGEMENT OF INSTITUTIONAL FUNDS ACT

As the excerpt by Longstreth notes, the promise of flexibility conveyed by the prudent man standard failed in application because interpretations rendered by judges and commentators were more receptive to the legal principle of stare decisis than to the evolving economic principles that inform investment management. Modern portfolio management demanded a new paradigm of prudence which embraced modern economic theory. Bevis Longstreth, Modern Investment Management and the Prudent Man Rule 152–157 (1986). There also were concerns about the legal liabilities of trustees. In a Ford Foundation study in the late 1960s, William L. Cary and Craig B. Bright found that there was little developed law restricting the power of trustees to invest endowment funds to achieve growth and that the impediments to such freedom of action were more legendary than real. The Law and Lore of Endowment Funds 60 (1969). However, the lack of constraining legal precedent was insufficient for institutional trustees to ignore prudence and the conservatism inherent in trust law principles. See Edward C. Halbach, Jr., Trust Investment Law in the Third Restatement, 77 Iowa L. Rev. 1151, 1153–1154 (1992); Jeffrey N. Gordon, The Puzzling Persistence of the Constrained Prudent Man Rule, 62 N.Y.U. L. Rev. 52 (1987); Longstreth, supra, at 125–194.

Concern over the uncertain standards governing directors of nonprofit corporations in managing and investing endowments and other charitable funds led in 1972 to the adoption of the Uniform Management of Institutional Funds Act (UMIFA). It was eventually adopted by 48 states. UMIFA was modernized in 2006 when the National Conference of Commissioners on Uniform State Laws approved the Uniform Prudent Management of Institutional Funds Act (UPMIFA) and recommended it for enactment by state legislatures. As this edition went to press, UPMIFA had been adopted by 44 states and the District of Columbia and introduced in the legislatures of four others. UPMIFA provides a modern articulation of the prudence standards for the management and investment of charitable funds and endowment spending, and it incorporates certain recent revisions with respect to charitable trusts, as set forth in the Uniform Prudent Investor Act (UPIA). See infra p. 211.

UPMIFA applies to charitable "institutions," a category that includes incorporated or unincorporated organizations operated exclusively for educational, religious, charitable, or other eleemosynary purposes, or government entities to the extent they hold funds exclusively for those purposes. § 2(4). It also applies to trusts managed by a charity. The revisers' goal was that standards for managing and investing institutional funds should be the same regardless of whether a charity is organized as a trust, corporation or some other entity. The rules do not apply, however, to funds of wholly charitable or split-interest trusts (such as charitable remainder trusts) managed by a corporate or individual trustee. But in most states, those types of charitable trusts are subject to comparable rules under modern prudent investor statutes.

Standard of Conduct in Managing and Investing Institutional Funds (§ 3). Section 3 of UPMIFA specifically authorizes governing boards to invest in a wide range of personal and real property and sets forth many of the factors a charity should take into account in making a prudent investment decision. Section 3 incorporates the general duty to diversify investments and consider the risk and return objectives of the fund.

UPMIFA's standard of care is derived from the Internal Revenue Code's private foundation regulations dealing with investment responsibility of managers of private foundations. Treas. Reg. § 53.4944–1(a)(2). Section 4944 of the Code imposes excise taxes if a private foundation engages in investments that jeopardize its exempt purposes and seems to adopt a corporate standard of care. Treas. Reg. 53.4944–1(a)(2)(i). See Chapter 7D5, infra, at pp. 794–795. UPMIFA requires governing boards to exercise "ordinary business care and prudence" under the facts and circumstances prevailing at the time of the action or decision. Boards may consider the long and short term needs of the institution in carrying out its exempt purposes, its present and anticipated financial requirements, expected total return on its investments, price level trends, and general economic conditions. The commissioners' comment to the section states that the standard of care is comparable to the business corporate director rather than a private trustee. Section 5 clarifies the right of nonprofit fiduciaries to delegate and to contract with independent financial advisors.

Elimination of Historic Dollar Value (§ 4). Under UMIFA, a charitable corporation could only spend amounts above "historic dollar value" that it determined to be prudent. Historic dollar value is defined as all contributions to an endowment fund valued at the time of contribution. Over a long period of time historic dollar value can become meaningless. For example, if a donor provides for a bequest in her will, the date of valuation will likely be the donor's date of death. The determination of historic dollar value could vary significantly depending upon when in the market cycle the donor died. A fund actually could be below historic dollar value at the time the charity receives a bequest if the asset had declined between the donor's death and the distribution of the asset from the estate. National Conference of Commissioners on Uniform State Laws, Uniform Prudent Management of Institutional Funds Act, Prefatory Note (2006).

UPMIFA abandoned the historic dollar value limitation on endowment fund spending and replaced it with a broader standard of prudence that offers greater flexibility to directors. Subject to the intent of a donor expressed in a gift instrument, a charitable organization may spend any amount that is prudent, consistent with the purposes of the fund, relevant economic factors and the donor's intent that the fund should continue in perpetuity (or for a period specified in the gift instrument). The elimination of the historic dollar value limitation is motivated by the view that a donor's intent to create a fund of long duration that preserves its value is not always best served by a strict adherence to maintaining historic dollar value and, under certain circumstances, dipping below historic dollar value can, in the long-run, better serve such donor intent.

The elimination of the historic dollar value limitation becomes significant during an economic downturn, such as the financial crisis that began in 2008. The sharp decline in equities left many charitable endowments under their historic dollar values. This accelerated efforts by states to enact UPMIFA. The Act permits a charitable organization, subject to donor intent, to "appropriate for expenditure or accumulate so much of an endowment fund as the institution determines to be prudent for the uses, benefits, purposes and duration for which the endowment fund is established." Seven criteria guide the institution in such decisions: "1) duration and preservation of the endowment fund; 2) the purposes of the institution and the endowment fund; 3) general economic conditions; 4) the effect of inflation or deflation; 5) the expected total return from income and the appreciation of investments; 6) other resources of the institution; and, 7) the investment policy of the institution."

For jurisdictions that have not adopted UPMIFA, such as New York, the organization can seek donor permission to release or modify an endowment restriction. Generally, heirs would not have authority to give consent unless they have been designated to do so in the gift instrument. If the donor is deceased, the organization could seek judicial release of an endowment restriction. In New York the attorney general is a necessary party, and relief is only granted if the organization can establish that, without it, the organization will fail or be so diminished it will be substantially different. The relief is treated as a borrowing. The New York City Opera was in such serious financial straits that the attorney general gave approval and a court agreed for the Opera to "borrow" $23.5 million of its total endowment of $33 million to pay off debts and to meet payroll and other needs. See Daniel Wakin, City Opera Taps Into Endowment, N.Y. Times, April 18, 2009, at C2.

Donor Intent (§ 4). UPMIFA improves the protection of donor intent with respect to expenditures from endowments. When a donor expresses clear intent in a written instrument, the Act requires that the charity follow the donor's instructions. When a donor's intent is not so expressed, UPMIFA directs the charity to spend an amount that is prudent consistent with the purposes of the fund, relevant economic factors and the donor's intent that the fund continue in perpetuity.

Section 4(c) provides rules of construction to assist charitable organizations in interpreting donor intent. It states that terms in a gift instrument designating a gift as an endowment, or a direction/authorization in the gift instrument to use only "income," "interest," "dividends," or "rents, issues or profits," or "to preserve the principal intact," or similar words create an endowment fund of permanent duration (unless there is additional language limiting duration) but do not otherwise limit spending authority.

Under UPMIFA, these rules of construction will be applied retroactively to funds already in existence.

Optional Presumption of Imprudence (§ 4(d)). UPMIFA includes as a provision to be included at the enacting jurisdiction's option a presumption of imprudence if a charitable organization spends more than seven percent of an endowment fund in any one year. The presumption is meant to protect against spending an endowment too quickly. The comments to § 4 of UPMIFA also include an optional provision requiring notice to the attorney general for small charitable organizations invading historic dollar value. The provision is meant to curb imprudent spending by small, unsophisticated charitable organizations. In particular, the provision would: (1) apply only to charitable organizations with endowment funds valued, in the aggregate, at less than $2 million (or another amount established by the enacting jurisdiction); and (2) require such organizations to notify the attorney general (but not obtain its consent) before spending below historic dollar value. The attorney general would then have the opportunity to review the organization and its spending decision, educate the organization on prudent decision-making for endowment funds and intervene if the AG determines the spending would be imprudent. For an excellent discussion of the interaction of UMIFA, UPMIFA and the Uniform Prudent Investor Act, see Susan N. Gary, Charities, Endowments, and Donor Intent: The Uniform Prudent Management of Institutional Funds Act, 41 Ga. L. Rev. 1277 (2007).

NOTE: OTHER REVISIONS OF THE TRADITIONAL PRUDENT PERSON RULE

ERISA. In addition to UPMIFA, many jurisdictions have begun to enact modern prudent investor statutes applicable more generally to fiduciaries. See, e.g., Cal. Prob. Code § 16045 et seq.; Fla. Stat. § 518.11; Ill. Comp. Stat. ch. 760 § 55 (1993); N.Y. E.P.T.L. § 11–23; Va. Code Ann. § 26–45.1. Other currents of change have included the Employee Retirement Income Security Act of 1974 (ERISA), which utilizes the corporate standard of care and prudence, § 404(a)(1)(B), 29 U.S.C.A. § 1104(a)(1)(B). Under ERISA, a fiduciary is expected to diversify the investments in the plan to minimize the risk of large losses, § 404(a)(1)(C), 29 U.S.C.A. § 1104(a)(1)(C). The Internal Revenue Service's private foundation regulations relating to jeopardy investments suggest that the fiduciary meets the standard of care by scrutinizing the portfolio as a whole. Treas. Reg. § 53.4944–1(a)(2)(i). Most importantly, The Restatement (Third) of Trusts, § 227 (the prudent person rule) reformulates the traditional rule, not only making it gender neutral but also reflecting principles of modern portfolio management.

Restatement (Third) of Trusts. The Uniform Prudent Investor Act (UPIA), which has been adopted in whole or part by 44 states, regulates the investment responsibilities of trustees of charitable trusts, among others. Building on the Restatement (Third) of Trusts and existing prudent investor statutes and reflecting current principles of modern portfolio theory, the UPIA makes five fundamental alterations in criteria for prudent investing: (1) the standard of prudence is applied to any investment as part of the total portfolio, rather than to individual investments (§ 2(b)); (2) the trade-off in all investing between risk and return is the fiduciary's central consideration (§ 2(b)); (3) categorical restrictions on types of investments are abrogated; the trustee can invest in anything that plays an appropriate role in achieving the risk/return objectives of prudent investing (§ 2(e)); (4) diversification of investments is part of the definition of prudent investing; and (5) delegation of investment and management functions is specifically permitted (§ 9). These statutes provide clearer guidance to fiduciaries of standards of care and powers of delegation in funds investment, and reflect current notions of prudent investment.

Under this new prudent person rule, no investments or investment techniques are *per se* imprudent. Sound diversification is fundamental to risk management and ordinarily is required of trustees. Risk and return are so directly related that trustees have a duty to analyze and make conscious decisions concerning levels of risk appropriate to the purposes and circumstances of the endowment invested.[1] The standard of care "is to be applied to investments not in isolation but in the context of the trust portfolio and as a part of an overall investment strategy * * *." Restatement (Third) Trusts § 227(a). The trustee has a duty to diversify the investments of the trust unless under the circumstances it is prudent not to do so. Id. § 227(b). The prudent investor rule seeks to restore the generality and flexibility of the original rule. The question of prudent behavior focuses upon the *process* by which investment strategies are selected, implemented, and monitored. See John H. Langbein, The Uniform Prudent Investor Act and the Future of Trust Investing, 81 Iowa L.Rev. 641 (1996).

PROBLEM

Franklin Wood donated $750,000 to Sturdley College to endow a full tuition scholarship for modern language study. The gift was invested as a restricted fund with Sturdley's endowment. For many years the income from the fund more than covered the full tuition for the scholarship. Sturdley's spend rate from its endowment is 4.5 percent. As a result of a steep drop in stock prices, the Wood Fund has declined to $600,000. To maintain the level of expenditure necessary to cover full tuition, the Wood Fund would have to spend 8.5 percent of its principal.

(a) If Sturdley is in a jurisdiction that has adopted UPMIFA, what can it do to maintain the full tuition?

(b) What result if Sturdley is in a jurisdiction in which UMIFA governs?

---

1. As it is used in economic literature, the term "risk" refers to the volatility of return. All investments involve risk. Thus, a fiduciary must manage risk by focusing upon a particular endowment fund's risk tolerance, i.e. its tolerance for volatility. Restatement (Third) Trusts, § 227, com. e.

c.   MODERN ENDOWMENT INVESTMENT STRATEGIES: RISKS AND REWARDS

Most charities of any size have endowments, which provide a stream of income and maintenance of the corpus in perpetuity.[1] Colleges and universities with large endowments finance a significant part of their operations through the return received from the investment of this capital. Private foundations typically are funded through a gift of assets that becomes an endowment, and grants are paid out of the earnings generated.[2] An endowment allows an organization to provide intergenerational equity, so that tomorrow's students, scientists, patients, or parishioners will receive the same or greater benefits taking into account the effects of inflation as today's beneficiaries. The size of endowments of charitable institutions in the United States is immense.[3] In the early and mid 2000s higher education endowments grew annually by double digit figures, led by Harvard's which ballooned from a little over $5 billion in 1993 to $36.6 billion at the end of the fiscal year ending June 30, 2008. Yale's grew from $3.1 billion to $22.9 billion in that period. However, higher education endowments averaged only 3 percent returns in a difficult environment in fiscal 2008. Then, the bottom dropped out as the financial crisis wreaked havoc on endowment portfolios.

At the end of the 2009 fiscal year, Harvard's endowment was $25.7 billion, (down 36.6 percent from the previous year); followed by Yale at $16.3 billion (down 28.6 percent) and Stanford at $12.6 billion (down 26.7

1.   Endowment gifts are distinguishable from a gift for current use. An endowment fund is an institutional fund or part thereof, not expendable by the institution on a current basis under the terms of the applicable gift investment. UPMIFA § 1(2). Quasi-endowment is a term that describes unrestricted capital gifts which the charitable institution has decided to treat as endowment. Endowment funds are contrasted to funds, such as tuition revenues, which are held for a very short term and are likely to be invested in treasury bills or commercial paper. Joel C. Dobris, Return Modern Portfolio Theory, and College, University Foundation Decisions, on Annual Spending from Endowments: A Visit to the World of Spending Rules, 28 Real Prop. Prob. & Tr. J. 49, 51 n. 4 (1993) (hereinafter Dobris).

2.   I.R.C. § 4942(e)(1) requires private foundations to spend at least five percent of their current investment asset value for charitable purposes. See Chapter 7C3, infra. A similar payout requirement has been proposed for donor-advised funds maintained by public charities. See Chapter 7A4b, infra, at p. 735. Early in 2008, Senators Baucus and Grassley of the Senate Finance Committee sent letters to over 100 colleges urging them to increase their endowment payout rate from the 4.6 percent average and use some of that golden horde for tuition relief. Despite the declining economic environment, Senator Grassley has not retreated from this issue. "Contrary to what colleges might argue, the weak economy makes a strong case for more endowment spending on student aid. If an endowment is a rainy-day fund, it's pouring. Colleges' smart saving and investing could really help students right now." See John Hechinger, College Endowments Plunge, Wall St. J., Jan. 27, 2009, at D3.

3.   A 2009 survey by the National Association of College and University Business Officers reported that 52 educational institutions held $1 billion or more in assets at the end of their 2009 fiscal years. A summary of the survey is available at www.nacubo.org. See also Goldie Blumenstyk, Average Return on Endowment Investments Is Worst in Almost 40 Years, Chron. Higher Educ., Jan. 10, 2010, available at http://Chronicle.com.

percent).[4] On average a survey of over 800 higher education institutions showed loses on average of 18.7 percent, the worst rate of return since the Great Depression. Universities with the largest endowments (over $1 billion) lost more on average (20.5 percent) than smaller ones. Endowments of foundations, healthcare, social service, and cultural institutions were similarly affected. Looking only at this one-year period, institutions with larger endowments tended to decline the most because of their concentration in investment strategies such as private equity and real estate, which involve more short-term risk, but these larger endowments tended to outperform more conventional portfolios when measured over a longer time horizon.

As the Longstreth excerpt, supra p. 205, discusses, endowment funds historically were invested and spent quite conservatively. The "income" (e.g., dividends and interest) generated by an endowment could be currently expended, but the "principal" of the fund remained inviolate. Beginning in the 1970s, nonprofits were faced with inflation; government cutbacks in support; limitations on tuition increases; and in some sectors of education, a decline in demand. These developments necessitated new endowment investment strategies.[5] The adoption of UMIFA and its successor and the influence of modern portfolio theory encouraged spending rules and investment decisions no longer based on arcane trust accounting concepts such as "income" and "principal" but on the concept of total return, which includes both traditional income as well as the market appreciation of the endowment portfolio. Responsible charities typically leave in the endowment an amount equal to the inflation rate to preserve the purchasing power of the fund and assure intergenerational equity, but UPMIFA now permits them to spend the remainder of the income plus a prudent portion of the portfolio's appreciation. Most institutions determine their current spending rate by applying a percentage to the average value of the endowment over several preceding years.[6]

Total return investing allowed charities with endowments to spend more for current needs. Institutions whose endowments had been wholly invested in bonds or preferred stock offering a reliable income stream diversified their portfolios by allocating more to domestic and international equities and a wide range of alternative investments.[7] For many years the

---

4. Tamar Lewin, Investment Losses Cause Steep Dip in University Endowments, Study Finds, N.Y. Times, Jan. 28, 2010, at A14. Although the declines are the greatest since the Depression, these endowments have only fallen to their 2005 levels, and they had positive returns over the ten years ending June 30, 2009.

5. Henry Hansmann, Why Do Universities Have Endowments? 19 J. Legal Studies 3, 10 (1990).

6. Dobris, supra note 1, at 56–60. In 2009, the average endowment spending rate was 4.4 percent, up from 4.3 percent the previous year. The spend rate is calculated by dividing the amount of endowment funds spent by the value of the endowment at the beginning of the fiscal year. The increase in spend rate does not reflect a decision to spend more, but a decline in the value of the endowment. Blumenstyk, supra, note 3.

7. According to a study of 842 colleges and universities by the National Association of College and University Business Officers, in the fiscal year ending June 30, 2009, the average allocation for survey participants was: 19 percent in U.S. stocks, 13 percent in fixed income, 12 percent in international equities, 5 percent in cash and 51 percent in alternative investments. See http://www.nacubo.org.

highest returns were earned by the largest endowments, which had access to the most sophisticated money managers and the in-house expertise to evaluate a complex mix of alternative investments.[8] Less affluent institutions were unable to achieve such high returns, because they lacked the capital to invest in the higher risk, higher reward alternative asset classes and were reluctant to distort their asset allocation by placing too great a percentage of their endowment in high risk investments. Instead they utilized investment pools such as Commonfund (www.commonfund.org), which manages the endowments of 1,600 institutions in a variety of funds of differing risk, or The Investment Fund for Foundations (www.tiff.org), which offers private foundations access to a diverse group of asset classes at relatively low cost. When the markets turned, the largest endowments with riskiest, illiquid investments were hurt the worst.

Larger endowment institutions often fund 35 percent or more of their operating budget through the endowment payout. In response to the declines, colleges, museums and other charities froze or delayed construction and expansion projects, cut operating budgets, drew on cash reserves, implemented hiring and salary freezes, ordered layoffs, and a few sued their financial advisors. Many colleges are struggling to preserve financial aid. Several institutions have issued bonds to raise money for expenses or to allow them to hold on to illiquid assets until their price rises. Rating services have cut university credit ratings. On top of this, charitable giving declined 57 percent on an inflation adjusted basis in 2008 compared to the previous year, the largest percentage drop in 50 years, and in fiscal 2009 giving to colleges dropped 11.9 percent.[9]

Harvard, which in recent history has competed with Yale and Stanford for first place in the endowment derby, offers a cautionary tale of the dangers of excessive risk and illiquidity. Harvard invested a huge amount in swaps, financial instruments to lock in interest rates, in expectation that rates would rise in the future when the University would borrow heavily to build its new Alston campus. When financial markets unexpectedly collapsed in 2007, central banks reduced some bank lending rates to zero. This meant the value of the swaps declined, and Harvard had to post approximately $1 billion in collateral. Other schools to a lesser extent were in the same position. At the same time, the endowment and the university's cash account were declining sharply. Harvard did what individuals do when they

---

8. Alternative investments include hedge funds, which traditionally were pools of capital used to purchase securities on both sides of a market risk. Today, the term connotes any lightly regulated investment pool that engages in a wide range of investment strategies, some of which are high-risk, which seek to generate superior long-term returns by exploiting market inefficiencies. Alternative investments also include private equity, such as venture capital and leveraged buyout funds, which take stakes in start-up businesses or buy firms primarily with borrowed money in the hope of cashing out at a later time when the firm is acquired by another company or goes public. The largest endowments also achieve diversification by investing in real assets, such as real estate, oil and gas and timber.

9. Kathryn Masterson, Private Giving to Colleges Dropped Sharply in 2009, Chron. Higher Educ., Feb, 4, 2010; Stephanie Strom, Charitable Giving Declines, a New Report Finds, N.Y. Times, June 10, 2009, at A16; Matthew Kaminski, The Age of Diminishing Endowments, Wall St. J., June 6–7, 2009, at A11.

need cash—they borrowed—$2.5 billion of which nearly $500 million was used to terminate the swaps agreements. Harvard's problems were exacerbated by the percentage of endowment allocated to illiquid assets. Even the cash account, normally invested conservatively in short-term commercial paper and money market funds, had been invested along with the endowment, an extremely risky move. The impact on the university was substantial. Capital spending was halved, and the building of the new campus postponed. There were layoffs, closure of libraries, pay freezes and budget cuts, an end to students' hot breakfasts, and perhaps most unthinkable— no more cookies at faculty meetings.[10]

NOTES

1. *Failure to Understand and Monitor Investments.* Although UPMI-FA and the Restatement (Third) of Trusts encourage a delegation of investment management, a nonprofit board cannot thereafter abdicate its responsibility to monitor the delegates and understand the nature of the investment strategy. The University of Minnesota System and the University of Minnesota Foundation reached an out-of-court settlement with a money management firm because the firm failed to inform officials at the University of the risks involved in trading derivative instruments invested on the University's behalf. Kim Strosnider, Settlement Reached at University of Minnesota, Chron. Higher Education, Nov. 28, 1997, at A42. De-Pauw University sued an investment advisory firm and its principals alleging that they failed to thoroughly investigate the hedge funds they recommended and misrepresented facts about them. The university had invested $3.25 million in one of the Bayou Group's hedge funds. Bayou fabricated its returns and collapsed in 2005. See Ian McDonald, Clients Are Suing Hennessee Group Over Bayou Advice, Wall St. J., Oct. 15–16, 2005, at B6. The 2008 financial crisis has led to litigation from charities claiming they were misled into investing into vehicles that were much riskier than imagined or illiquid.

2. *Doubling Your Money in Six Months.* The Foundation for New Era Philanthropy (New Era) made an offer few financially hard-pressed charities could refuse. Charities loaning money to New Era were promised that they could double their "investment" in six months thanks to the generosi-

---

10. See Michael McDonald, John Lauerman and Gillian Wee, Harvard Swaps Are So Toxic Even Summers Won't Explain, Bloomberg, December 18, 2009, available at Bloomberg.org.; Beth Healy, Harvard ignored warnings about investments, Boston Globe, Nov. 29, 2009, available at http://boston.com; Stephanie Strom, Nonprofits Paying Price For Gamble on Finances, N.Y. Times, Sept. 24, 2009 at 16. Other large endowment institutions have been similarly affected. Stanford intended to sell $5 billion of illiquid assets to raise cash but later pulled back because the markets improved or the offers were too low. Yale reduced staff, froze salaries for deans and officers, reduced the number of graduate students and turned down the heat to 68 degrees in order to close a $150 million budget deficit. Cornell laid off 150 staff and another 432 took early retirement. Princeton eliminated 43 positions in order to reduce its operating budget by $170 million over two years. Lisa W. Foderaro, Yale, With $150 Million Deficit, Plans Staff and Research Cuts, N.Y. Times, Feb.4, 2010, at A28; Craig Karmin and Peter Lattman, Stanford Pulls Asset Sales Off Auction Block, Wall St. J., Dec. 15, 2009, at C1.

ty of anonymous benefactors who would match the amounts placed with New Era. The anonymous donors relied on New Era to research and monitor worthy beneficiaries. New Era's head, John G. Bennett, Jr., a former drug abuse counselor, persuaded hundreds of charities and prominent donors to "deposit" money with the organization. Charities were told they could participate for three years. The justification for placing money under New Era's control was to assure that the funds would be used only for new projects and to allow the "foundation" to make use of the float, i.e., the interest earned from investment of deposits in treasury bills. New Era was a "ponzi" scheme. The anonymous donors never existed. Returns were paid to earlier investors from the loans or gifts of subsequent contributors until the scheme collapsed. When the crash came, New Era had $31 million in assets, over $350 million in liabilities, and more than 250 embarrassed charities and donors trailing in its wake, including such prominent philanthropists and experienced investors as Laurence E. Rockefeller and William E. Simon, and institutions such as the University of Pennsylvania, the Nature Conservancy, and many religious organizations. If anyone had investigated, they would have discovered that from 1981 to 1983 several federal and state tax and judgment liens had been filed against Bennett or organizations with which he was associated.

A creative settlement was reached by the trustee in bankruptcy. Groups that profited from the New Era scheme—the earlier investors—returned a total of $39 million of the money they received over their contributions to repay organizations that lost money. Prudential Securities, which handled New Era's funds, agreed to pay $18 million to settle charges that it aided the fraud. Charities received approximately 65 percent of what they placed with New Era. Bennett was sentenced to twelve years in jail. Charity Chief Sentenced for Part on Ponzi Scheme, N.Y. Times, Sept. 23, 1997, at A23.

A few years after New Era, five members of a Florida evangelical group, Greater Ministries International, were convicted of fraud and money laundering in a pyramid scheme reminiscent of New Era. Greater Ministries International received $448 million from 18,000 investors solicited through lists of church congregations after having promised doubling the investors' money within 17 months. The investors were told their funds would be invested in silver, diamond, and gold mines and at high-interest foreign debt. The investments failed or never existed. Payments to earlier investors were made from funds contributed by later participants. See Chuck Fager, Jury Convicts Greater Ministries of Fraud, Christianity Today, April 23, 2001, available at http://www.ct.library.com/6581. These two schemes were mere hors d'ouevres for what was to come later.

3. *The Biggest Sure Thing: Madoff.* The largest and longest running Ponzi scheme ever was created by Bernard Madoff, who collected an estimated $65 billion over thirty years before the inevitable collapse. Madoff's "innovation" was not to promise extraordinary profits—double your money in six months—but steady returns of 10–12 percent. The Foundation for New Era Philanthropy and Greater Ministries International

Ponzis preyed on Christian religious organizations and individuals. Madoff stole from many Jewish foundations and organizations and their wealthy benefactors, who invested based on social contacts.

The victims included colleges and universities (Yeshiva to the tune of $110 million; New York Law School; Brandeis; Tufts); philanthropists; charities; and over 100 private foundations (including Steven Spielberg's and Elie Weisel's). Most of the private foundations were family foundations, established by wealthy heirs or entrepreneurs. Several were wiped out and required to close. Others scaled back their grants with obvious impact on their beneficiary charities. Charities that focused on human rights, criminal justice and reproductive health were particularly affected. In three cases the bankruptcy trustee has sued to "claw back," that is, retrieve from foundations or their creators, funds invested and later redeemed with appreciation from Madoff. Some nonprofits (New York University, for example) invested with hedge funds that fed money into Madoff funds. These "feeder" funds received referral fees for funneling this money, but the charities allege they did not know their investments would wind up with Madoff.

How could this happen? Constant returns over time are impossible. There was a lack of transparency of Madoff's investment approach. He was unwilling to disclose his investment strategy. The size of Madoff's fund exceeded the total trading in the securities his investors purportedly owned. In fact, Madoff never traded at all. His auditor was a two partner accounting firm located in a suburban strip mall. Who is to blame for so many charities investing in this scheme? For a sampling of the extensive press coverage, see Diane B. Henriques et al., Madoff Scheme Kept Rippling Outward, Crossing Borders, N.Y. Times, Dec. 20, 2008, at 1; Eleanor Laise & Dennis K. Berman, The Madoff Fraud Case: Impact on Jewish Charities Is Catastrophic–Programs for Bone–Marrow Transplants and Human–Rights Campaigns Find Themselves in Peril, Wall Street J., Dec. 16, 2008, at A20; Ben Gose, Charities Calculate Losses in Alleged Ponzi Scheme, Chron. Philanthropy, Dec. 16, 2008, available at http://philanthropy.com/news/updates/index.php?id=6582; Amir Efrati, Criminal Probe Expands to High–Profile Investors Who Say They Were Stung, Wall St. J., May 18, 2009, at A1. For a list of the foundations that invested with Madoff, see Nicholas Kristoff, Madoff and America's (Poorer) Foundations, N.Y. Times, Jan. 29, 2009, available at http://kristof.blogs.nytimes.com/2009/01/29/madoff-and-americas-poorer-foundations/?scp=1–b&sq=&st=nyt.

The downturn in the financial markets revealed other Ponzi schemes and fraudulent investments in which charities had invested. Even before the Madoff exposure, the Bayou Hedge funds collapsed ensnaring the Christian Brothers School of Nashville, which had invested $1.2 million. The bankruptcy trustee was successful in clawing back the redemption of that investment, because the school was on notice when it redeemed that something was wrong at the fund. In re Bayou Group, LLC, 396 B.R. 810 (Bkrtcy.S.D.N.Y. 2008). The University of Pittsburgh and Carnegie Mellon lost the $114 million they invested in Westridge Capital Management, a firm run by two individuals accused of using the firm as a personal piggy bank. The universities had relied on the recommendation of an outside investment consultant and were lured by the promise of big returns on alternative investments, an unregulated category that includes hedge funds and sometimes risky investment strategies. See Paul Fain, 2 Universities Seek Answers After $114–Million Vanishes in an Alleged Swindle, Chron. Higher Educ. Mar. 5, 2009, available at http://chronicle.com/daily/2009/03/122990n.htm.

4. *Failure to Diversify*. Is it a breach of the duty of care if a board fails to diversify its investments? For a period of ten years Boston University invested a total of $120 million in a biotechnology company, Seragen, and owned 57 percent of the company before it was taken over by another company for pennies on the dollar. At the time the university purchased its original $25 million investment, its total endowment was $175 million. Are there duty of care violations here? Would your answer change if members of the university board of trustees also invested in the company?

5. *Socially Responsible Investing*. Charities by definition are created for the public good. Do fiduciaries have a corresponding responsibility to invest a charity's funds in assets or firms that are socially responsible? Socially responsible investing is the systematic incorporation of social and ethical values in addition to financial criteria in making investment decisions. Can a trustee or director legally invest in socially responsible investments or is this a violation of the prudent person rule?

Socially responsible investing is not a new concept. In the seventeenth and eighteenth centuries, the Society of Friends chose not to invest in the slave trade or the munitions industry. In the early twentieth century some churches refused to invest their endowments in alcohol or tobacco. More recently, many institutions divested securities of companies that conducted business in South Africa during the period of apartheid. Empirically, relatively few charitable organizations have adopted social investment policies. See generally Lewis D. Solomon & Karen C. Coe, Social Investments by Nonprofits: A Legal and Business Primer for Foundation Managers and Other Nonprofit Fiduciaries, 66 U.M.K.C. L. Rev. 213 (1997); Michael S. Knoll, Ethical Screening in Modern Financial Markets: The Conflicting Claims Underlying Socially Responsible Investment, 57 Bus. Law. 681 (2002).

Private foundations may engage in program-related investments, which are investments the primary purpose of which is to accomplish one or more charitable purposes described in § 170(c)(2)(B) and no significant purpose of which is the production of income or the appreciation of property. I.R.C. § 4944(c). See Chapter 7D5, infra, at p. 794. A loan to a business in a geographic area that is economically depressed is an example of a program related investment. However, most foundation endowments are traditionally invested.

Several mutual funds and institutional investors have pursued social investing. Government pension funds, particularly those of state employees, frequently have engaged in strategically targeted investing in their communities. When an asset manager develops a socially responsible portfolio it must identify certain characteristics that will distinguish the socially-screened portfolio from a more typical diversified portfolio. The investment or portfolio manager will utilize a double bottom line approach combining traditional financial analysis with a screening approach to identify profitable and socially responsible companies. Solomon and Coe, supra, at 234. Investments that would be avoided might include traditional "sin securities"—tobacco, alcohol and gambling; weapons and defense contractors; nuclear power; companies that have violated labor statutes or have invested in countries that violate human rights. Social investors might target profitable companies in certain sectors—environmentally sensitive companies, good corporate citizens, or firms with the appropriate attitude toward consumers, women, minorities, preservation of natural resources, or international corporate citizenship. Id. Because of the screening criteria, some social-oriented mutual funds are composed of investments of common stock in smaller or mid-sized companies rather than larger "blue chips." Holdings of a social portfolio also may be more volatile than a traditional portfolio. Whether social investing returns correlate to other portfolios is a matter of some dispute.

PROBLEM

Congratulations. You have become general counsel of Sturdley College. Brandy Alexander, Sturdley's president, comes to your office to ask your advice. She says: "The College's biggest donor over the years has been the Chevas Riegal Foundation, a $40 million family foundation founded by Chevas and Shirley Riegal. I serve on the Foundation's Board, along with Chevas, Shirley and their two adult children. The Foundation has no separate investment committee and no written investment or asset allocation policy. Chevas oversees the Foundation's investments. In 2003, based largely on advice from one of his wealthy friends and a fellow country club member, Chevas unilaterally decided to invest 90 percent of the Foundation's assets with B. Madoff & Co., which provided a 2–page summary of its investment strategies and consistent 8 to 10 percent returns over the prior ten years. On December 15, 2008, the Foundation learned that the entire investment with Madoff was worthless. Do I and the Foundation's directors have anything to worry about?" Before answering, consider the following additional questions:

(a) Have the Foundation's directors breached their duty of care? What additional facts do you need to know? If there is a breach, what are the legal ramifications?

(b) Assume that Chevas is also the chair of the finance committee of Sturdley's Board of Trustees, though the committee doesn't meet much. He is considered an investment guru, and the Board always followed his advice. In 2003, Chevas recommended that Sturdley invest $10 million with Bernard Madoff & Co. The Board was informed of the investment, and no one objected. The Madoff investment represents 10 percent of the Sturdley College's endowment's assets. Does the Board have any legal problems?

D.   Enforcement of Fiduciary Obligations

Many more external constraints exist for publicly held business corporations than for nonprofits. They include: the need to raise money in the capital markets; shareholder demands for increasing profitability and a rising stock price; the market for corporate control; and the scrutiny of investment analysts. External curbs play a lesser role for nonprofits, allowing them greater freedom to pursue their objectives without the concern that decisions will be criticized or revised by market forces. Because nonprofit outcomes may be harder to measure than for-profit counterparts, organizations may go on for years unobserved, undistinguished, unaccomplished, and largely unregulated.[1] Peter Swords has distinguished between two types of nonprofit accountability: "negative accountability" which refers to failures that allow self-dealing or quasi-looting; that is, the diversion of organizational funds from its exempt purpose, and "positive accountability" which alludes to the organization's effectiveness in executing its mission.[2] Though positive accountability is more important for it is a measure for all nonprofits, it is more difficult to gauge. The primary monitor of a public benefit nonprofit's performance is the state, but the degree of state scrutiny varies widely lying along a continuum. Hospitals, health care providers, and educational institutions are heavily regulated. Mutual benefit nonprofits and certain public charities are virtually self-regulated. Through its corporate governance initiative, the IRS has become important in influencing enforcement of fiduciary obligations. This section examines methods of enforcing a charitable organization's fiduciary obligations.

1.   Self-Regulation: Norms, Best Practices, and Principles

Fiduciary accountability presents a paradox. The number of nonprofit organizations has expanded enormously. At the same time enforcement efforts by regulators have declined, and there is little chance of legal sanction for violations.[3] Increasing publicity about charitable scandals may

---

1. William G. Bowen, Inside the Boardroom: Governance by Directors and Trustees 4–10 (1994).

2. The Form 990 As An Accountability Tool for 501(c)(3) Nonprofits, 51 Tax Law. 571, 574 (1998).

3. Staffing problems and a relative lack of interest in monitoring nonprofits makes attorney general oversight more theoretical than deterrent. See Marion R. Fremont–Smith, Governing Nonprofit Organizations 443–447 (2004). The number of exempt organization returns examined by the IRS declined from 12,589 in 1993 to 5,754 in 2003. See Joint Committee on Taxation, Description of Present Law Relating to Charitable and Other Exempt Organizations and Statistical Information Regarding Growth and Oversight of the Tax–Exempt Sector 37–40 (JCX–44–04), June 22, 2004, available at www.house.gov/jct/x–44–04.pdf.

give the impression that wrongdoing is widespread, yet most organizations and trustees abide by the rules, adhere to good practices and demonstrate fidelity to the organization's mission and the eleemosynary ideal. Why is the level of fidelity so high? Why do most fiduciaries do what's right? The answer may be that most charitable fiduciaries have internalized the norms of appropriate behavior, or adhere to principles and practices promulgated by professional associations.

Norms are informal social regularities that individuals feel obligated to follow because of an internalized sense of duty or a fear of external non-legal sanctions.[4] Norms can transform the abstract mandates of the statutory fiduciary requirements into practice guides. Many nonprofit associations have guidelines that to which their members adhere. Good governance, professional associations, and nonprofit rating organizations have published best practices. The American Law Institute's project on Principles of the Law of Nonprofit Organizations also is formulating both legal principles and best practices.

Independent Sector has compiled nearly one hundred standards of practice, codes and principles developed by charity watchdog groups, nonprofit and foundation associations, the IRS,[5] professional associations and individual organizations. See http://www.independent sector.org/issues/accountabilitystand2.html. These standards of practice and ethical codes, organized by type of organization or mission served, region, or type of nonprofit assist board members and staff to develop norms and practices that are accountable, evaluative and ethical. The Panel on the Nonprofit Sector has issued Principles for Good Governance and Ethical Practice: A Guide for Charities and Foundations to assist board members, staff, and advisers of nonprofit organizations.[6]

Since 2003, staffing has increased as have examinations. In fiscal year 2008, the IRS examined 7,861 returns of exempt organizations. 2008 IRS Data Book, Table 13 (2009).

4.   Richard H. McAdams, The Origin, Development and Regulation of Norms, 96 Michigan Law Review 338, 340 (1997) (hereinafter McAdams). Judge Posner has described a norm as "a rule that is neither promulgated by an official source, such as a court or a legislature, nor enforced by the threat of legal sanctions, yet is regularly complied with." Richard A Posner, Social Norms and the Law: An Economic Approach, 87 Am. Econ. Rev., Papers and Proc. of the Hundred and Ninth Ann. Meeting of the Am. Econ. Ass'n., May 1993, at 365, 365–369.

5.   The IRS has published a paper "Governance and Related Topics–501(c)(3) Organizations" in its Life Cycle of a Public Charity educational outreach. The paper addresses mission, organizational documents, governing body, governance and management policies, financial statements and Form 990 reporting and transparency and accountability. The paper attempts to help charities ensure that directors understand their roles and responsibilities and actively promote good governance policies. This is both an effort to encourage organizations to "regulate" themselves and reaffirms that the oversight of fiduciary abuse has moved to the federal level. The document is available at http://www.irs.gov/pub/irs-tege/governance_practices.pdf.

6.   The principles are a useful checklist of best practices and are accompanied by background commentary and explanations of the rationale for each principle. They are available at http://www.nonprofitpanel.org/ Report/principles/Principles_Reference.pdf.

2. RECORDKEEPING AND FILING REQUIREMENTS

Model Nonprofit Corp. Act (3d ed.) §§ 16.01–16.07; 16.20–16.21.

Cal. Corp. Code §§ 6215–16, 6320–23, 6330, 6333–34, 6811–14, 8320.

N.Y. Not-for-Profit L. §§ 513, 519–522, 621.

California Nonprofit Integrity Act of 2004.

To encourage accountability, most jurisdictions have created ongoing disclosure regimes requiring charitable organizations to maintain specified records and to file financial and other documents with appropriate governmental authorities on an annual basis. Initially, when an organization seeks exemption from state taxation or seeks to incorporate, it will file its certificate of incorporation or articles of association with the appropriate agency. Typically, these are public documents.

Organizational Records. The Model Nonprofit Corporation Act requires a public benefit organization to maintain various corporate records: minutes of meetings and records of deliberations if taken without a meeting; appropriate accounting records; and membership lists. Model Nonprofit Corp. Act (3d ed.) § 16.01. Cf. Cal. Corp. Code § 6320; N.Y. Not-for-Profit Corp. L. § 621. An organization must prepare an annual report or financial statement. Model Nonprofit Corp. Act (3d ed.) § 16.22; Cal. Corp. Code § 6321; N.Y. Not-for-Profit Corp. L. § 519. Members have a right to inspect and copy an organization's records such as a membership list when such request is made in good faith and for a proper purpose. Members also have a right to receive an annual financial statement, and directors have a right to inspect books and records. Model Nonprofit Corp. Act (3d ed.) §§ 16.02–03, 16.05, 16.20; Cal. Corp. Code §§ 6330, 6336.

State Registration and Filing Requirements. State filing requirements differ and can become quite complex. Generally, organizations may have to register with the attorney general or another agency, and file annual financial reports. Cal. Govt. Code § 12584; N.Y. E.P.T.L. § 8–1.4. If a nonprofit intends to solicit funds from the public, over 45 states require the organization to register, file financial reports, and in some cases register professional fundraisers. See Chapter 4A, infra, at pp. 243–259. Any oversight is likely to come from the public, for the documents submitted typically are not reviewed by the state authorities until and unless there has been a failure to file or allegations of wrongdoing.

New York illustrates the filing burdens on nonprofits. All New York nonprofit organizations (except churches) which hold property or receive income to be used for charitable purposes must register with the Charities, Trusts and Estates Bureau of the New York State Law Department (the attorney general's office) within six months after they receive such property or income. N.Y. E.P.T.L. § 8–1.4. Thereafter, the organization must file an annual report with the attorney general within six months after the close of the fiscal year if at any time during the year its assets exceed

$25,000.[1] Organizations with unrelated business income must file an Unrelated Business Income Tax Report with the New York State Department of Taxation and Finance. Annual financial reports and very detailed information concerning solicitation and the use of professional fundraisers also must be filed with the attorney general. There also may be filings with local authorities. Organizations of any size will need the assistance of an accountant.

Federal Filing Requirements. Organizations that have obtained recognition of exempt status from the Internal Revenue Service must file annual information returns on Form 990. I.R.C. § 6033.[2] The form must be filed by the 15th day of the fifth calendar month following the close of the period for which the return is required. Treas. Reg. § 1.6033–2(e). An organization must file a Form 990 even before it is recognized by the IRS as exempt. Private foundations with assets of $5,000 or more must file an annual Form 990–PF information return. Organizations with $1,000 or more of gross income from an unrelated trade or business must file Form 990T. I.R.C. 6043(b). Form 990 is a public document. The filing requirements and related public disclosure rules are discussed in more detail in Chapter 5H2, infra, at pp. 548–551.

Form 990 also has become a major disclosure tool at the state level as the result of the cooperation between the IRS, the National Association of State Charity Officials and the National Association of Attorneys General. At the state level the Form 990 is acceptable to state officials for purposes of filing an annual report in most states requiring such a filing. The Pension Protection Act of 2006 increased the level of cooperation and disclosure between state charity regulators and the Service. State regulators now can request tax information to enable them to prosecute wrongdoing without undertaking initial investigations that might strain the state's limited resources.[3]

---

1. Filing requirements differ depending on the income of the organization and whether professional fundraisers are used.

2. There are exceptions for churches, schools, certain other organizations, and "small charities" other than private foundations, that normally (i.e, over a three-year measuring period) have gross receipts of less than $25,000 (to be raised to $50,000 beginning in 2010 tax years). I.R.C. § 6033(a)(3). Most small charities are now required to electronically submit Form 990–N, also known as the e-Postcard, unless they choose to file a complete Form 990 or Form 990–EZ. I.R.C. § 6033(i). The postcard, which contains eight simple questions, provides notice of their existence to the IRS. A charity that fails to file for three consecutive years will lose its exemption unless it can show "reasonable cause" for its delinquency. I.R.C. § 6033(j).

3. See I.R.C. § 6103(p)(4), which section provides that upon written request by an appropriate state officer, the Secretary of the Treasury may disclose: a notice of a proposed refusal to recognize an organization as exempt under § 501(c)(3); a notice of a proposed revocation of tax exemption of a § 501(c)(3) organization; the issuance of a proposed deficiency the tax imposed under I.R.C. § 507 for certain terminations of exempt status; the names, addresses, and taxpayer identification numbers of organizations that have applied for § 501(c)(3) exemption; and returns and return information disclosed in the process of seeking or losing exemption. The items disclosed may be used in civil administrative and civil judicial proceedings pertaining to the administration of state laws regulating tax exempt status, charitable trusts, charitable solicitation and fraud. There are limitations on use of this

Sarbanes–Oxley for Nonprofits. In the aftermath of the collapses of Enron, Worldcom and Arthur Andersen, Congress passed the American Competitiveness and Corporate Accountability Act of 2002, known as the Sarbanes–Oxley Act ("SOX"), which requires chief executives and chief financial officers of publicly listed companies to personally certify the validity of their corporation's financial statements and that they validly represent the financial condition of the company. The legislation requires corporate boards to have audit committees consisting of independent directors and mandates the creation of effective financial reporting systems.

The California Nonprofit Integrity Act of 2004, which took effect on January 1, 2005, adopted SOX-type requirements. Charities that are required to register with the California Attorney General and have gross revenues of $2 million or more in a fiscal year must prepare audited financial statements and make them publicly available in the same way as the annual Form 990 information return. If organized in corporate form, the board of these charities must appoint an audit committee. The audit committee may include persons who are not members of the governing board, but paid staff, including top management or any person with a material financial interest in any entity doing business with the charitable corporation, are ineligible, as are the president and chief financial officer even if not paid. Additionally, the boards or appropriate committee (or trustee if a trust) of all registered charities of any size must review and approve the compensation, including benefits, of the chief executive officer and the chief financial officer of the organization. The approving body must determine that the compensation is "just and reasonable." These reviews must occur when the officer is hired, the term is renewed or extended or when the compensation package is modified. The Act also contains provisions giving charitable organizations greater control over fundraising activities and commercial fundraising contracts.

Several states introduced but few enacted SOX legislation. The Panel on the Independent Sector's project on Principles for Good Governance and Ethical Practice has incorporated some SOX-type recommendations.[4] Surprisingly, many charities have implemented SOX principles voluntarily. Whether SOX should be adopted by charities has raised enormous scholarly interest, with the majority of commentators opposed.

---

information and penalties for unauthorized use. See Staff of the Joint Committee on Taxation, General Explanation of Tax Legislation Enacted in the 109th Congress 621–623 (JCS–1–00, Jan. 17, 2007).

4. Principles for Good Governance and Ethical Practice: A Guide for Charities and Foundations, Appendix 5; Board Source & Independent Sector, The Sarbanes–Oxley Act and Implications for Nonprofit Organizations, 2003.

3. THE ROLE OF THE ATTORNEY GENERAL

Model Nonprofit Corp. Act (3d ed.) §§ 1.53, 1.7, 3.04, 14.30–14.31.

Cal. Corp. Code §§ 5142, 5250, 6511, 9230.

N.Y. Not-for-Profit Corp. L. § 112.

The attorney general usually has the responsibility of supervision and oversight of charitable trusts and corporations and may maintain such actions as appropriate to protect the public interest. In a few jurisdictions, this role is performed by the district or county attorney. Even before the enactment of the Statute of Charitable Uses in 1601, suits were brought by the attorney general to enforce charitable trusts. 5 Scott & Ascher on Trusts § 37.3.10. Unlike a private trust, the beneficial interest in a charitable trust does not reside in individual beneficiaries but in the community, an indefinite class. The property is devoted to the accomplishment of purposes beneficial to the community at large. By definition the objective of the public benefit corporation is to further the public interest. The attorney general represents the public in enforcing the purposes of the trust or corporation. The common law duties of the attorney general reflected the expectations of society: that there should be a single evolving duty to carry out the charitable purposes of the trust, that it was necessary to keep trust property productive, and that trustees should be prohibited from diverting charitable funds for improper purposes or self-dealing. Marion R. Fremont–Smith, Governing Nonprofit Organizations 305–314, 324 (2004). The common law principles asserted by the attorney general were carried over to America during the Colonial period. See generally Office of the Ohio Attorney General, The Status of State Regulation of Charitable Trusts, Foundations, and Solicitations, in V Research Papers Sponsored by the [Filer] Commission on Private Philanthropy and Public Needs 2705, 2710 (1977). These precepts have been supplemented by statute in most jurisdictions.

Today, the attorney general represents the state and the public, promoting accountability by charities and fiduciaries. He has an enforcement or supervisory interest in property or income devoted to charitable uses, estates or trusts in which there is a charitable interest; may maintain registries of charitable trusts and trustees; and is an interested party in all proceedings affecting charitable trusts, uses and estates. The attorney general can institute appropriate proceedings in situations involving the state or public interest and to secure compliance with statutory norms or ensure proper administration of trusts. Brown v. Memorial Nat. Home Fdn., 162 Cal.App.2d 513, 537–538, 329 P.2d 118, 132–133 (1958). The attorney general's jurisdiction extends to suits to protect charities where an attack is made on the organization's property, or to protect against self-dealing, waste and diversion of funds. See Mary Grace Blasko, Curt S. Crossley, David Lloyd, Standing to Sue in the Charitable Sector, 28 U.S.F.L. Rev. 37, 45–47 (1993).

Specific Powers of the Attorney General. The attorney general has the power to investigate, subpoena witnesses, and require production of books and records. In civil actions he can annul the corporate existence, dissolve corporations that have acted ultra vires or restrain them from carrying out unauthorized activities. He may remove directors or trustees; dissolve corporations under applicable state procedures; enforce the rights of members, directors or officers; bring proceedings and accounts for the assets of corporations upon dissolution; supervise indemnification awards; and investigate transactions and relationships of directors and trustees to determine whether property held or used by them has been allocated to charitable purposes. The attorney general may maintain an action against a plaintiff seeking a declaratory judgment; can bring a *quo warranto* proceeding to assure that absolute gifts to charitable corporations are applied according to the terms of gift (St. Joseph's Hospital v. Bennett, 281 N.Y. 115, 22 N.E.2d 305 (1939)); must receive notice when suit is instituted by others, Model Nonprofit Corp. Act (3d ed.) § 1.70; and is a necessary party to settlement of litigation where charitable beneficiaries are affected, where there is a sale of assets, or a change of use of assets are considered. Minn. Stat. Ann. § 501B.01(5) Sub. 4; Mass. Gen. L. ch. 180, § 8A. While the attorney general must receive notice of cases concerning a charity, there is no need to make him a party. The option to intervene lies with the attorney general. Bertram v. Berger, 1 Ill.App.3d 743, 274 N.E.2d 667, 670 (1971).

Information Gathering Responsibilities. In many jurisdictions the attorney general has been given statutory authority for gathering information about charities and trustees. Charitable trusts and nonprofit corporations must register and file reports with his office. The Uniform Supervision of Trustees for Charitable Purposes Act, 7B U.L.A. 727 (1978) has been adopted in whole or part in many jurisdictions. This statute requires registration of charitable trusts and charitable corporations with the attorney general, periodic reports to the attorney general who may institute appropriate proceedings, investigate, supervise, and subpoena. A Revised Oversight of Charitable Assets Act is in the drafting process. Professor Laura Chisolm is the Reporter.

While religious corporations and certain other charities may be excluded from filing requirements, the attorney general can subpoena religious groups suspected of fraudulent behavior. Abrams v. Temple of the Lost Sheep, 148 Misc.2d 825, 562 N.Y.S.2d 322 (1990). Other responsibilities of the attorney general typically include maintenance of a registry of all public benefit organizations, oversight of periodic filing requirements, and monitoring financial filing requirements.

Oversight of Charitable Solicitation. In most jurisdictions the attorney general is responsible for the oversight and enforcement of regulations dealing with charitable solicitation. This has become a major area of attorney general focus. Statutes have conferred upon the attorney general broad authority to protect the public and donors from deceptive and fraudulent solicitation practices or diversion or waste of donated funds so as to ensure the proper use of contributed funds for the beneficiaries' benefit. Typically this includes monitoring and enforcement powers over registration requirements for charities and professional fundraisers. See Chapter 4B, infra.

NOTES

1. *Obstacles to Enforcement.* Staffing problems and a relative lack of interest in monitoring nonprofits makes attorney general oversight more theoretical than deterrent in most jurisdictions. Surveys have indicated the paucity of resources of state attorneys general offices devoted to the oversight of charities. The most recent study, conducted through telephone interviews by Professor Gary Jenkins of the Ohio State University School of Law, found that states have dedicated a median of one full-time equivalent attorney to charity oversight. Seventy-four percent of the states responding had one or fewer full-time equivalent attorneys working on nonprofit oversight, with seventeen states reporting no such lawyers at all.[1] However, this does not mean that offices without full-time charities bureaus do no enforcement. Enforcement is often episodic, though some jurisdictions—California, New York and Massachusetts are good examples displayed renewed vigor, particularly in correcting abuses involving fraudulent charitable solicitation and charitable trusts.[2]

2. *Limitations on Attorney General Authority.* Despite the authority to supervise charities, the attorney general does not have the power to manage charities in their everyday affairs. In re Horton's Estate, 11 Cal.App.3d 680, 90 Cal.Rptr. 66, 68 (1970). Thus, courts have prohibited the attorney general from intervening in suits contesting wills involving charities, Commonwealth ex rel. Ferguson v. Gardner, 327 S.W.2d 947 (Ky.1959), In re Roberts' Estate, 190 Kan. 248, 373 P.2d 165 (1962); to order deviations from trust provisions, Midkiff v. Kobayashi, 54 Hawaii 299, 507 P.2d 724, 745 (1973); or to enforce obligations owing to charities. In Lefkowitz v. Lebensfeld, 51 N.Y.2d 442, 434 N.Y.S.2d 929, 415 N.E.2d 919 (1980) the New York attorney general sought to compel a charitable corporation to which stock had been given without designation of a particular charitable purpose to sue the issuing corporation to force payment of dividends. The New York Court of Appeals held that the attorney general had no standing without first making a demand upon the charitable corporation to sue the issuer of the stock. The court concluded that to give standing in this situation would be to grant the attorney general all but unlimited power to act as the alter ego of the charitable corporation. Thus, the attorney general lacked authority to bring an action against third parties allegedly liable to the charitable organization.

---

1. Garry W. Jenkins, Incorporation Choice, Uniformity, and the Reform of Nonprofit State Law, 41 Ga. L. Rev. 1113, 1128–1129 (2007).

2. For a recent article about proactive use of attorneys general powers, see, Ashley L. Taylor, Jr., Anthony F. Troy, Katherine W. Tanner Smith, State Attorneys General: The Robust Use of Previously Ignored State Powers 40 Urb. Law. 507 (2008).

3. *Lack of Standing for Others*. Other than the attorney general only persons with a special and definite interest, such as directors, have standing to institute a legal action. The general public lacks such interest. If any member of the public could initiate suit, a director or trustee would frequently be subjected to unreasonable and vexatious litigation. See George S. Bogert & George T. Bogert, The Law of Trusts and Trustees § 411 (Ronald Chester, ed., 3d ed. 2005); Rob Atkinson, Unsettled Standing: Who (Else) Should Enforce the Duties of Charitable Fiduciaries?, 23 J.Corp.L. 655 (1998).

4. *Reform Proposals: A State Board of Charities*. Over the years there have been various proposals to deal with the dearth of enforcement efforts by state attorneys general and to improve the enforcement mechanisms to assure a higher level of performance by nonprofits. Professor Kenneth Karst suggested the creation of a new agency at the state level, a state board of private charities which would have primary responsibility for supervising private charities and for administering the various state controls over their operation. Kenneth Karst, The Efficiency of the Charitable Dollar, 73 Harv. L. Rev. 433, 476–483 (1960). This new agency would replace the attorney general and would consolidate the collection of information which is currently distributed among a number of departments in many states. Professor Karst assumes that a new state agency will have the capacity to audit the reports that are filed. Is it likely that such a new agency could obtain sufficient funds? Is the nonprofit sector too broad to be supervised by one "charities" agency?

5. *Use of Relators*. Another suggestion has been to expand the use of relators to complement attorney general enforcement. A relator is a party who may or may not have a direct interest in a transaction, but is permitted to institute a proceeding in the name of the people when that right to sue resides solely in the attorney general. Expanded use of relators would avoid the dangers of broadened standing. Usually a relator must have a direct interest in the matter of the proceeding. Jurisdictions differ regarding whether a relator must seek permission of a court in order to bring suit and the formal status the relator occupies as a party to the litigation. Some jurisdictions complement the state regulation of charities by allowing relators to file with the attorney general informations alleging abuses by charitable organizations. In this situation, the suit may be brought by the attorney general or on relation of a third person, who need not have a direct interest in the matter. The attorney general, rather than the relator, has control over the conduct of the lawsuit, but the relator is liable for costs, which otherwise would have to be paid by the state. Relator status has been granted in the nonprofit context to bar associations, People ex rel. L.A. Bar Assoc. v. California Protective Corp., 76 Cal.App. 354, 244 P. 1089 (1926); taxpayers, People v. Thompson, 101 Ill.App.2d 104, 242 N.E.2d 49 (1968); cemetery plot holders, State ex rel. Londerholm v. Anderson, 195 Kan. 649, 408 P.2d 864 (1965); directors of other state departments, People ex rel. Brown v. Illinois State Troopers Lodge No. 41, 7 Ill.App.3d 98, 286 N.E.2d 524 (1972); and members of a social club, State ex rel. Van Aartsen v. Barton, 93 So.2d 388 (Fla.1957).

6. *Expanded Standing Because of Attorney General Conflicts.* The limited resources available to attorneys general force them to selectively intervene in cases. Attorneys general are also creatures of politics, and their political interests may conflict with and guide their case agenda. Commentators and a few courts have taken cognizance that political factors often play a role in determining whether that office will intervene in a particular matter and have allowed other interested parties standing. See In re Milton Hershey School, 867 A.2d 674, 687 (2005), appeal granted, 586 Pa. 717, 889 A.2d 1219 (2005); Jonathan Klick & Robert H. Sitkoff, Agency Costs, Charitable Trusts, and Corporate Control: Evidence From Hershey's Kiss–Off, 108 Colum. L. Rev. 749 (2008) (Pennsylvania attorney general's intervention in the proposed Hershey Trust sale, instead of improving the welfare of the needy children who were the Trust's main beneficiaries, preserved charitable trust agency costs of $850 million and destroyed roughly $2.7 billion in shareholder wealth that resulted when the Trust was exposed to the takeover market); Evelyn Brody, Whose Public? Parochialism and Paternalism in State Charity Law Enforcement, 79 Ind. L.J. 937 (2004); Marion R. Fremont–Smith, Governing Nonprofit Organizations 327–328, 446 (2004); Mark Sidel, The Struggle for Hershey: Community Accountability and the Law in Modern American Philanthropy, 65 U. Pitt. L. Rev. 1 (2003); and David Villar Patton, The Queen, The Attorney General, and the Modern Charitable Fiduciary: A Historical Perspective on Charitable Enforcement Reform, 11 U. Fla. J.L. & Pub. Pol'y 131 (2000).

In Consumers Union v. State, 5 N.Y.3d 327, 806 N.Y.S.2d 99, 840 N.E.2d 68 (2005), which involved the conversion of New York's Empire Blue Cross into a for-profit corporation, a statute authorizing the transaction had to be defended by the attorney general. The board of Blue Cross lacked any incentives to jeopardize the conversion. For purposes of protecting Empire's nonprofit assets, the court granted standing to the plaintiffs, who were purchasers of Blue Cross health insurance.

4. TRUSTEES/DIRECTORS

The Attorney General does not have exclusive power to enforce a charitable trust or corporation. A trustee or director or other person having sufficient special interest may also bring an action for this purpose even against other trustees or directors to enforce a charitable trust or on behalf of a charitable corporation. Model Nonprofit Corp. Act (3d ed.) § 13.02.

In Holt v. College of Osteopathic Physicians and Surgeons, 61 Cal.2d 750, 394 P.2d 932, 40 Cal.Rptr. 244 (1964), minority trustees of a charitable corporation sought standing to sue to enjoin the majority of trustees from wrongfully diverting corporate assets. The majority of trustees claimed that only the attorney general, who had declined to intervene, could bring such an action. Justice Roger Traynor, citing the prevailing view of American jurisdictions that the attorney general does not have exclusive power to intervene, allowed the minority trustees standing. He noted the attorney general may not have notice of wrongdoing, may not be in a position to become aware, and there was no rule or policy against supplanting the attorney general's power of enforcement by allowing other responsible individuals to sue on behalf of the nonprofit. The attorney general would be a necessary party to the litigation and represent the public interest.

NOTE

Honorary Titles. The phrases "board of directors" or "board of trustees" refer to that collective body who are charged with the responsibility for conducting the affairs of a nonprofit corporation or a charitable trust. Model Nonprofit Corp. Act (3d ed.) § 8.01(b). Nonprofit organizations frequently create positions or bodies which may seem to have the attributes of directors or trustees, but in fact are honorific. These positions, sometimes called boards of advisors, honorary directors or life trustee, can not exercise the powers of board members, nor do they possess the statutory or common law rights of standing of a director or trustee. See Steeneck v. University of Bridgeport, 235 Conn. 572, 668 A.2d 688 (1995).

5.   DONORS

Kenneth L. Karst, The Efficiency of the Charitable Dollar

73 Harv. L. Rev. 433, 445–449 (1960).

It is not unnatural for a charity's founder to be interested in its administration even though he decides not to take an active part as a trustee or officer. Yet nearly all of the modern American decisions hold that neither the settlor of a charitable trust nor his successors may sue to enforce the trust. These decisions have been applauded, and contrary decisions criticized, on the ground that the law should not "permit a sentimental interest to be sufficient basis for enlisting the aid of the court."

Sentiment aside, there is of course a better reason for allowing the founder to enforce a charitable trust. He is likely to be the one person other than the fiduciaries themselves who knows and cares the most about the charity's operations. Permitting him to sue does not expose the charity to multiple suits by members of the general public any more than would a suit by cotrustees.

The same considerations obviously apply to the founder of a charitable corporation, but the law has been equally reluctant to give him standing to enforce the terms of his donation.[49] As a substitute, the founder was permitted from an early time to reserve the power of visitation, which was a power to direct the corporate charity in certain aspects of its management.[50] Although the practice of reserving such a power has fallen into disuse in the United States, there are cases of surprising modernity

---

49.   See Note, The Charitable Corporation, 64 Harv. L. Rev. 1168, 1177 (1951).

50.   See Tudor, Charitable Trusts, 194, 199–206 (5th ed. 1929).

recognizing the doctrine. It has been described as a "relic of earlier times," and indeed there seems to be no present-day justification for it. The early cases based the doctrine on "the power every one has to dispose, direct, and regulate his own property," but we now recognize that property given by a donor to charity is no longer "his own" in any sense which allows him to dispose of it as he pleases. A far more serious objection to the visitorial power is that it undercuts the responsibilities of charitable fiduciaries. We cannot expect effective and responsible management from directors who are not permitted to direct. The doctrine of visitation should be given a swift statutory burial.

If we permit the founder of a charity to sue to enforce the duties of the charity's managers, we must then decide whether to allow the same standing to one who is not a founder but is a substantial donor. The doctrine of visitation was occasionally so extended by the terms of the charter because the justification for the power was essentially the same in both cases. The modern justification for permitting the founder to enforce these duties is also applicable to the substantial donor; he, too, is ordinarily greatly interested in the charity's proper operation. But giving the substantial donor these enforcement powers creates a correlative administrative problem. Certainly no one would argue that the man who contributes five dollars to the Red Cross should be permitted to bring suit against its officers for violation of their duty; such a rule would be the practical equivalent of conferring standing on the entire population. For this reason it is universally held that contributors to public charities have no standing to enforce the duties of their fiduciaries.

NOTE: CARL J. HERZOG FOUNDATION, INC. v. UNIVERSITY OF BRIDGEPORT

At common law, a donor who made a completed charitable contribution, whether as an absolute gift or in trust, had no standing to bring an action to enforce the terms of the gift or trust unless the donor had expressly reserved the right to do so. Carl J. Herzog Foundation, Inc. v. University of Bridgeport, 243 Conn. 1, 699 A.2d 995 (Ct. 1997) exemplifies the common law rule. In *Herzog* the issue was whether Connecticut's adoption of UMIFA established donor standing. The foundation had given matching grants of $250,000 to provide need-based merit scholarships to disadvantaged students in Bridgeport's nursing program. A few years later it learned that the university had closed the nursing school. The foundation sued on the ground that the funds were no longer being used for their specified purpose. It requested a temporary and permanent injunction, ordering the defendant to segregate from its general funds matching grants totaling $250,000, an accounting for the use of the fund, and a reestablishment of the fund in accordance with the purposes outlined in the gift instrument. In the event that those purposes could not be fulfilled, the foundation requested the court to redirect the funds to the Bridgeport Area Foundation, which was prepared to administer them in accordance with the original agreement. The university moved to dismiss on the ground that the plaintiff lacked standing.

The court concluded that Connecticut's version of UMIFA did not establish a new class of litigants, namely donors, who gained standing to enforce an unreserved restriction in a completed charitable gift. UMIFA authorized the governing board to obtain the acquiescence of the donor to a release of restrictions and, in the absence of the donor, to petition the appropriate court for relief in appropriate cases. Thus, the donor had no right to enforce the restriction, no interest in the fund and no power to change the eleemosynary beneficiary of the fund. It could only acquiesce in a lessening of a restriction already in effect.[1]

NOTES AND QUESTIONS

1. *Disputes over Restricted Gifts.* In recent years conflicts between donors or their families and charities over donor-restricted gifts have increased. As *Herzog* demonstrates, it can be difficult for disgruntled donors to enforce the terms of the restriction. Charities are usually responsive to a donor's complaint for fear of the chilling effect of publicity of the discontent or other benefactors. In times of economic crisis, many charities, particularly educational institutions, may attempt to use restricted funds for economic relief. Some donors become angry when colleges and universities attempt to monetize gifts and broaden the use of restricted assets. This has led to threats of litigation or actual lawsuits and unpleasant publicity for the institution. A notorious recent example was the unilateral decision of Brandeis University's trustees to close its Rose Art Museum and sell the masterpieces from its collection. After the predictable uproar, the university backed off from selling the collection but announced its intent to convert the museum into an educational center. See John Hechinger, New Unrest on Campus as Donors Rebel, Wall St. J., April 23, 2009, at A1. For an overview of some of the legal issues, see Neil T. Kawashima, Art for Donor's Sake, Chron. Phil., Feb. 12, 2009, available at http://philanthropy.com/premium/articles/ v21/i08/08003201.htm.

Many disputes arise years after the contribution, when original donors are in the ground and their descendants, some with time on their hands, believe the gift restrictions have not been upheld. Sometimes the charity does not live up to the conditions. Often circumstances change or the organization lacks the resources to live up to the terms of the gift. In other

---

1.   Granting donors control over their gift property after the completion of the gift may create potential adverse tax consequences. Pursuant to § 170(a) of the Internal Revenue Code and § 1.170A–1(c) of the Treasury Regulations, an income tax deduction for a charitable contribution is disallowed, unless the taxpayer has permanently surrendered "dominion and control" over the property or funds in question. Where there is a possibility not "so remote as to be negligible" that the charitable gift subject to a condition might fail, the tax deduction is disallowed. See also I.R.C. § 2055; Treas. Reg. § 20.2055–2(b) (similar provisions for estate tax deductions). In retaining the common law rule, the drafters of UMIFA assured that the donor would not be so not be so tethered to the charitable gift through the control of restrictions that she would not be entitled to claim a federal charitable contribution deduction for the gift.

situations, a contribution is given to a charitable entity which thereafter amends its purposes, such as when a scholarship fund is donated to a single sex school, and the school later becomes coeducational. Or a gift instrument contains a precatory instruction without a specific restriction but an understanding has been reached and is later violated, as when a donor gives a collection of artworks to a museum and is verbally promised that the collection will never be sold but years later it is "deaccessioned." For a discussion of deaccessioning issues, such as the Metropolitan Museum of Art's sale of the collection of Adelaide de Groot and disposal of art works by other museums because of the financial crisis or other reasons, see Derek Fincham, Deaccession of Art and the Public Trust (Jan. 25, 2010), available at http://ssrn.com/abstract=1470211. How might a donor ensure that her restricted gift is used for its intended purpose? For a thorough study of the issues of donor's rights, see Evelyn Brody, From the Dead Hand to the Living Dead: The Conundrum of Charitable Donor Standing, 41 Ga. L. Rev. 1183 (2007).

2. *Heirs of Donors' Rights.* Perhaps the most notorious and certainly the most expensive dispute involving heirs occurred between the Robertson Family and Princeton University. In 1961, Charles and Marie Robertson gave $35 million to Princeton University to train graduate students in its Woodrow Wilson School of Public and International Affairs to serve in the federal government, particularly in foreign relations. The gift, which had grown to $650 million, was administered by a foundation under a seven-person board, four chosen by the school and three selected by the family. See I.R.C. § 509(a)(3) and Chapter 7C4, infra, at pp. 751–763, for the tax treatment of such supporting organizations. In 2000, three children of the donors and another relative filed suit against Princeton, alleging that an estimated $200 million had not been used for the intended purposes authorized by the donors. The heirs claimed standing as trustees of the foundation, and they sought to allow the heirs to use the gift money independently from Princeton and demand the university reimburse all allegedly diverted funds.

Shortly before trial the Robertson family and Princeton settled their dispute. The legal fees had reached $80 million! Under the settlement Princeton retains full control of the endowment associated with the Robertson Foundation. The Robertson Foundation eventually will be dissolved and its assets transferred to the University to create an endowed fund. Over a three year period Robertson Foundation funds will be used to reimburse a Robertson family foundation, the Banbury Fund, for the $40 million in legal fees that were paid by the Fund over the course of the litigation. Commencing in 2012, the Robertson Foundation will provide $50 million in funding over ten years for a new foundation to prepare students for careers in government service. Who won?

Robertson raised but failed to answer some common questions about restricted gifts, such as—should donor standing extend beyond the living donor, and did the heirs have standing? The answers were unclear because the plaintiffs were on the board of the Robertson Foundation, a supporting organization of Princeton whose sole objective was the support of the graduate program at the University. How can a charity deal with circumstances that have changed since the time a restricted gift was given, but the changes do not reach a level warranting traditional cy pres relief? What sorts of self-help can beneficiaries such as Princeton exercise? For a detailed description of the case, see Iris J. Goodwin, Ask Not What Your Charity Can Do for You: Robertson v. Princeton Provides Liberal–Democratic Insights into the Dilemma of Cy Pres Reform, 51 Ariz. L. Rev. 75 (2009).

In Smithers v. St. Luke's–Roosevelt Hospital Center, 281 A.D.2d 127, 723 N.Y.S.2d 426 (Sup. Ct. App. Div. 2001), the widow of the donor of a charitable gift that established an alcoholism treatment center run by the defendant hospital was granted standing to sue to enforce the terms of the contribution. In 1971, R. Brinkley Smithers, a recovering alcoholic, pledged $10 million for the establishment of the Smithers Alcoholism Treatment Center. With the first $1 million, the hospital purchased a mansion in Manhattan to house the rehabilitation program. Smithers remained involved in the management and affairs of the program, and though the relationship was sometimes strained he completed his pledge. Smithers died in 1994, and one year later the hospital announced its plans to move the center into a hospital ward and sell the mansion. In 1995, Mrs. Smithers discovered the hospital had transferred funds from the Smithers Endowment to its general fund in violation of the gift. The widow, appointed special testatrix of the Smithers estate for the purpose of pursuing the claim, sought to enjoin the sale of the building and to obtain an accounting. Although two successive administrations of attorneys general entered certificate of discontinuances with the hospital, the court held that though the attorney general represented ultimate charitable beneficiaries, it was not the exclusive representative of donors of charitable gifts. One judge dissented.

Other protesting heirs of donors have not been so deep-pocketed nor successful, yet the lawsuits keep coming. In 1886, Josephine Newcomb donated $100,000 to Tulane University in memory of her deceased daughter, H. Sophie Newcomb, for the establishment of a separate women's college within the University. In the aftermath of Hurricane Katrina, Tulane merged Newcomb College into a coeducational undergraduate division pursuant to a post-Katrina renewal plan. Two of Ms. Newcomb's great-great nieces sued Tulane to enjoin Newcomb's closing and consolidation. The Louisiana Code of Civil Procedure is based on the Code Napoleon, which gives donors, their heirs and successors-in-interest standing to sue for revocation of a donation for non-performance of a condition and a corollary right to enforce the terms of the gift. After the case wended its way up and down the Louisiana court system, the plaintiffs were denied standing, because they could not show that they were successors in interest, which would give them standing, rather than mere descendents, which would not. Howard v. Administrators of the Tulane Educational Fund, 986 So.2d 47 (La. 2008).

3. *Boola Boola, No Moola Moola.* In 1995 Yale University returned a $20 million gift from Lee Bass for Western Civilization studies after the donor became dissatisfied with the implementation of the program. What are the tax consequences to Mr. Bass upon return of the gift? See I.R.C. § 111.

4. *Naming Rights Disputes.* Suppose one of the conditions of a major gift is the naming of a building after the donor or his family. After a period of time—assume 40 years—the building has become outmoded and is in need of a major renovation. A new donor makes an even larger gift to completely renovate the facility, and the charity agrees to rename it, leaving perhaps a small plaque in the lobby to recognize the earlier donor— e.g., Jones Gym becomes the Smith Pavilion. Should the Jones family have any legal rights to enjoin the renaming of the facility? What if there were no renovation but Mr. Jones had been convicted of a felony and the university wished to remove his name from the building?

The family of Avery Fisher, after whom Avery Fisher Hall at Lincoln Center for the Performing Arts was named, has disputed Lincoln Center's renovation plan that would have changed the Hall's name to acknowledge a new donor. See Robin Pogrebin, Avery Fisher Hall Forever, Heirs Say, N.Y. Times, May 13, 2002, at E1; Robin Pogrebin, Philharmonic to Give Home a New Interior, N.Y. Times, May 20, 2004, at A1. For a scholarly survey of legal issues related to naming gifts, see John K. Eason, Private Motive and Perpetual Conditions in Charitable Naming Gifts: When Good Names Go Bad, 38 U.C. Davis L. Rev. 375 (2005).

5. *Cy Pres and Restricted Gifts.* One way for the institution to trump the efforts of donors to force a gift to be used for other purposes is for the charitable organization to apply to a court under the cy pres doctrine to change the charitable object of the gift (see Chapter 2D2, supra, p. 90). The Uniform Trust Code § 413(a) and the Restatement (Third) of Trusts § 67 offer the possibility of an expansion of traditional cy pres standards, adding "wasteful" to the traditional trilogy of "impossibility, impracticability and illegality." The cy pres doctrine may be applied without the consent of the donor.

6. *Restricted Gifts to Nonprofit Healthcare Providers.* If a nonprofit hospital merges or converts to for-profit status, there may be hundreds of restricted gifts of varying size. When hospitals primarily were institutions for the poor, it was common for affluent individuals to endow a bed which would assure their servants of medical care. When a merger or conversion is announced, a due diligence team of the law firm representing the hospital in the transaction will examine all restricted gifts, attempt to communicate with living donors, contact the attorney general, and commence a proceeding under the relevant state UPMIFA statute or under cy pres.

7. *Other Recent Developments.* The Commissioners on Uniform States Laws has adopted a Uniform Trust Code, all or parts of which has been adopted by 22 states and the District of Columbia at last count in 2009. Among other things, the UTC expands donor standing rights by giving

settlors of charitable trusts a statutory right to sue to enforce the terms of their charitable gifts in trust. Uniform Trust Code § 405(c), 7 C.U.L.A. 61 (2000). The UTC also permits a settlor of a trust to initiate a cy pres proceeding. Id. at § 410(b).

Some courts recently have been applying contract law to permit donor lawsuits despite the traditional view that restricted gifts are not contracts. See, e.g., Glenn v. University of Southern California, 2002 WL 31022068 (Cal. App. 2002) (unpublished), which involved a dispute over the administration of an endowed professorship. After the case was remanded to consider the donor's breach of contract claim, the parties reportedly settled.

6.   THE RIGHTS OF MEMBERS TO SUE

Model Nonprofit Corp. Act (3d ed.) §§ 13.02, 16.02–04.

N.Y. Not-for-Profit Corp. L. § 519.

Members of a nonprofit organization may have standing to sue.[1] Some courts have held that members of nonprofit corporations may bring derivative suits, viewing the members as analogous to shareholders in business corporations.[2] Members also may sue to enjoin an ultra vires act[3] or sue former directors or officers of a charity. In Cross v. Midtown Club, Inc.,[4] members of a nonprofit luncheon club had standing to sue the organization over its refusal to admit women as members and guests in violation of the charter. Members have been given the statutory right to inspect the nonprofit's records and may sue to enforce that right.[5] However, many nonprofits are non-membership organizations with self-perpetuating

---

1. Model Nonprofit Corp. Act (3d ed.) § 13.02 (member or members having five percent or more or by fifty members, whichever is less); see Cal. Corp. Code §§ 5420, 7420, 7710; N.Y. Not–For–Profit Corp. Law §§ 623(a), 720(b)(3); Henry Hansmann, Reforming Nonprofit Corporation Law, 129 U. of Pa. L.Rev. 497, 606 (while most statutes are silent on standing questions, they generally adopt charitable trust rules). Some state courts have given standing to members; See Bourne v. Williams, 633 S.W.2d 469 (Tenn.App.1981); Brenner v. Powers, 584 N.E.2d 569 (Ind.App.1992); Jackson v. Stuhlfire, 28 Mass.App.Ct. 924, 547 N.E.2d 1146 (1990); Morgan v. Robertson, 271 Ark. 461, 609 S.W.2d 662 (App.1980) (members can bring derivative suit); Governing Bd. Dar House v. Pannill, 561 S.W.2d 517 (Tex.Civ.App.— Texarkana, 1977); Leeds v. Harrison, 7 N.J.Super. 558, 72 A.2d 371 (1950). Other courts have refused to grant members standing to sue. Basich v. Board of Pensions Evangelical Church, 493 N.W.2d 293 (Minn.App.1992) (congregationalists of church not members); Voelker v. Saint Louis Mercantile Library Ass'n., 359 S.W.2d 689 (Mo.1962).

2. Bourne v. Williams, 633 S.W.2d 469, 473 (Tenn.Ct.App.1981). The Model Nonprofit Corporation Act (3d ed.) provides for derivative suits by members having five percent of the vote or fifty in number, whichever is less. § 13.02(a). Several jurisdictions permit such suits, Ill. Ann. Stat. ch. 805 § 107.80; Mich. Comp. Laws Ann. §§ 450.2491–450.2493.

3. Model Nonprofit Corp. Act (3d ed.) § 3.04.

4. 33 Conn.Supp. 150, 365 A.2d 1227 (1976).

5. Stueve v. Northern Lights, 118 Idaho 422, 797 P.2d 130 (1990) (member of nonprofit rural electric cooperative granted access to cooperative records); Bourgeois v. Landrum, 396 So.2d 1275 (La.1981) (voting church members granted examination rights of corporate records pursuant to Louisiana nonprofit statute).

boards. For this latter sort of organization, normally only the attorney general or a director has standing to sue.[6]

Under trust and corporate principles, the public has no standing to sue absent a specific statutory grant. The rationale is that property is devoted to the accomplishment of purposes which are beneficial to the community at large, rather than to a specific person.[7] Even a specific beneficiary of a charity is but an intermediary through whom the public advantage is achieved. Therefore, enforcement of charitable purposes is undertaken by the attorney general on behalf of the public.[8] A more practical reason for denying the public standing is that the persons benefited by charities are usually members of a large and shifting class of the public. If any member of that class had standing, the charity would be subjected to much unnecessary litigation.[9]

7. BENEFICIARIES AND SPECIAL INTERESTS

Beneficiaries of charitable trusts and other plaintiffs, including corporations, occasionally have been granted standing to sue if they can show some special interest beyond being a mere member of the public or the attorney general is unwilling or unable to intervene. Standing has been granted to certain beneficiaries of trusts, plaintiffs suing governmental entities to enforce the terms of a gift, or a class claiming they are directly affected by some action.

A general survey of courts' willingness to allow private parties to sue for the enforcement of charitable obligations found the following elements of importance: (1) the extraordinary nature of the acts complained of and the remedy sought by the plaintiff; (2) the presence of fraud or misconduct on the part of the charity or its directors; (3) the state attorney general's availability or effectiveness; (4) the nature of the benefited class and its relationship to the charity; and (5) the subjective and case-specific factual circumstances. Mary G. Blasko, Curt S. Crossley, & David Lloyd, Standing to Sue in the Charitable Sector, 28 U.S.F.L. Rev. 37, 61–78 (1993).

A review of standing cases between 1980 and 2001 by Marion Fremont–Smith found that of thirty-seven cases, the right to bring suit was granted to private individuals in twelve, denied in twenty-four and remanded to determine whether a public interest was involved in one. Governing Nonprofit Organizations 330–336 (2004). The general rule, however, remains that, absent a statutory right, there is no private enforcement of a charitable trust, a nonprofit trust, or a nonprofit corporation.

---

6. Model Nonprofit Corp. Act (3d ed.) §§ 1.70, 13.02.

7. 5 Scott & Ascher on Trusts § 37.3.10; Mark Tushnet, The New Law of Standing, 62 Cornell L. Rev. 663, 675 (1977).

8. Bogert & Bogert, The Law of Trusts and Trustees § 54 (quoting In re Pruner's Estate, 390 Pa. 529, 136 A.2d 107 (1957)).

9. Id. at § 411.

NOTES

1. *Student Plaintiffs*. Courts generally have denied standing to student plaintiffs. The Barnes Foundation litigation, see Chapter 2D3, supra, at p. 96, raised a standing issue. A student enrolled in the Foundation's educational programs sought intervener status, which was denied. The Pennsylvania Supreme Court held that this failure foreclosed the student's ability to file an appeal. In re the Barnes Foundation, 582 Pa. 370, 871 A.2d 792 (2005). Accord: In Associated Students of Univer. Ore. v. Oregon Inv. Council, 82 Or.App. 145, 728 P.2d 30 (1986); Beukas v. Trustees Fairleigh Dickinson, 255 N.J.Super. 552, 605 A.2d 776 (1991); State ex rel. Central Institute for the Deaf v. Burger, 949 S.W.2d 126 (Mo.App.1997).

2. *Matters of Public Importance*. Traditional standing limitations occasionally have been relaxed in matters of public importance that relate to charities or where the plaintiffs have a special interest.[1] In an earlier decision in Stern v. Lucy Webb Hayes Nat'l Training School for Deaconesses and Missionaries, Judge Gesell held that patients of the hospital certified as a class under Fed. R. Civ. P. 23(b)(2) for purposes of seeking injunctive relief in advance of damages to be paid into hospital funds. Certification was denied however under Fed. R. Civ. P. 23(b)(3), which might entitle patients to receive monetary recovery. 367 F.Supp. 536, 540 (D.D.C.1973). See also Consumers Union v. State, 5 N.Y.3d 327, 806 N.Y.S.2d 99, 840 N.E.2d 68 (2005) (health care subscribers given standing to challenge use of exempt assets in conversion); Romero v. Northwest Area Foundation, 129 Fed. Appx. 337 (9th Cir. 2005) (plaintiff farm workers, residents of Yakima County, granted standing to pursue a promissory estoppel claim against the Northwest Area Foundation for allegedly reneging on promise to reimburse for time spent in the planning process for an aborted project to reduce poverty.)

---

1. See Alco Gravure, Inc. v. Knapp Fdn., 64 N.Y.2d 458, 479 N.E.2d 752, 490 N.Y.S.2d 116 (1985) (beneficiary employees of nonprofit corporation had standing to challenge trustees dissolution of nonprofit corporation and transfer of its assets); Fitzgerald v. Baxter State Park, 385 A.2d 189 (Me.1978) (land was conveyed to the state as a trust for a state park; park authority and attorney general as members of former trustees were to carry out the purposes of the trust; plaintiffs as Maine citizens and users of park were given standing to sue); Gordon v. City of Baltimore, 258 Md. 682, 267 A.2d 98 (1970) (taxpayer had standing to sue to prevent transfer by charitable corporation of its library to another corporation so that city of Baltimore would support library); Parsons v. Walker, 28 Ill.App.3d 517, 328 N.E.2d 920 (1975) (citizens have standing to oppose deviation of gift of land made to state university for park); Paterson v. Paterson General Hospital, 97 N.J.Super. 514, 235 A.2d 487 (1967) (residents of city and taxpayers had standing to sue to prevent relocation of hospital); YMCA v. Covington, 484 A.2d 589 (D.C.App.1984) (members of YMCA had standing to sue YMCA for breach of duty). But see Simon v. Eastern Ky. Welfare Rights Org., 426 U.S. 26, 96 S.Ct. 1917 (1976) (indigents had no standing to maintain an action against the Secretary of the Treasury and Internal Revenue Service in order to set aside a ruling that a nonprofit hospital was exempt from taxation even though it did not provide free or below-cost services to the poor); Christiansen v. National Savings and Trust Co., 683 F.2d 520 (D.C.Cir.1982) (subscribers of health plan did not have standing to enforce director's fiduciary duties).

PROBLEMS

In the following problems determine whether the plaintiffs would be granted standing.

1.   Bob Barker made a $1 million donation to Humble Library to computerize its card catalog. He believes the funds have been misspent and sues to force the directors to give an accounting.

2.   A group of alumni of Fenster College has alleged waste of the college's assets and challenged the actions of the board of trustees, who have sold a substantial portion of the college's land to a religious organization.

3.   Some members of an art museum, a public benefit non-membership corporation, filed suit against the trustees of the museum, accusing them of disposing of artworks for inadequate or no consideration, or failing to maintain adequate records of acquisition, and favoring certain individuals by giving them long-term loans of artwork.

4.   Trustees of a home for elderly indigents sought to close the home and merge it with a nursing home and hospice. Four residents of the home sought to intervene to protest the closing.

5.   Donald J. Trump, the real estate titan, helped create a little-known state park in Northern Westchester County, New York, donating the land for public use after a failed attempt to gain permission to build a golf course on the site. Not surprisingly, the park is named after Mr. Trump. The Donald J. Trump State Park was placed on a list of 58 parks and historic sites that New York plans to close because of a budget crisis. When Mr. Trump heard of this, his response was: "If they're going to close it, I'll take the land back." Assume Mr. Trump seeks your legal advice. Does he have standing to sue? See Corey Kilgannon, Park Bearing Name of Trump Gets Fired, He Isn't Pleased, N.Y. Times, March 4, 2010, at A33.

CULMINATING PROBLEM

Sturdley Children's Hospital operates a world renowned nonprofit research and teaching hospital for children's diseases. It provides outpatient and in-patient medical services. According to its Certificate of Incorporation, Sturdley's corporate purposes are to:

> establish, provide, conduct, operate and maintain a hospital in the City, County and State of Atlantis for the general treatment of children suffering from acute illnesses; perform plastic surgery; treat and maintain a school for post graduate instruction in the treatment of children's illnesses; and conduct associated and basic research.

In recent years there have been significant advances in medical technology, and an upheaval in the dynamics and economics of healthcare. The impact of these changes has not escaped specialty hospitals, such as Sturdley. Inpatient censuses have been drastically decreasing, reducing hospital revenues, a trend which is expected to continue, if not accelerate, with the ongoing shifts to ambulatory surgery.

To cope with these changes and to boost revenue, Sturdley opened two community based Children's Diagnostic and Treatment Centers (CDTC) in poorer sections of Sturdley City. The hospital's financial condition continued to worsen. Sturdley's board of directors met and appointed a strategic committee to review: (1) whether Sturdley can survive in today's medical and economic environment as an independent hospital; (2) what are the strategic options available; and (3) how should Sturdley respond to a possible offer from other hospitals?

Sturdley then entered into a written retention agreement with the investment banking firm of Lebron, Bryant, Inc. to assist the strategic committee in evaluating its strategic options. The retainer agreement also authorized Lebron, Bryant to seek out parties "interested in entering into a transaction with the Hospital." The "transaction" referred to was defined in the retention agreement as "any merger, consolidation, reorganization, recapitalization, sale, business combination or other transaction pursuant to which the Hospital and/or any assets of the Hospital are involved in acquiring, being acquired by or combining with a third party." Sturdley agreed to pay Lebron, Marbury a retainer fee of $100,000, and agreed that "[u]pon the closing of a Transaction," it would pay a "Transaction Fee" of one percent (1%) of the "Aggregate Transaction Value." The agreement was executed by the chairman of Sturdley's board and a representative of Lebron, Bryant A few months later Lebron, Bryant issued a report that concluded the hospital business had no value, that Sturdley could not remain independent, but the real estate had considerable value and the board should consider it a valuable asset.

After reviewing the report, the strategic committee concluded that the hospital had no future, but that CDTCs might allow Sturdley to evolve into another type of health services provider. It recommended that Sturdley close the hospital, sell its real estate assets and use the proceeds to move forward with a new mission. At the next board meeting after a short discussion, the board unanimously voted to close the hospital and sell the real estate to the highest bidder.

When news that Sturdley might close became public, the medical staff formed "Friends of Sturdley" and sued to stop the closure. Parents of chronically ill children who used the hospital also opposed the proposed closing because there would be a greater burden on the parents in taking their children to more distant, less distinguished hospitals. They retained counsel to oppose the decision.

Unexpectedly, a member of Sturdley's board, Donald Schlump, a local real estate developer, said his firm had long desired to build in Sturdley's neighborhood, and would be interested in purchasing the hospital buildings for $45 million. It would demolish the existing buildings and construct the Schlump Excesso, a forty story condominium.

The board voted to accept Schlump's proposal if Lebron, Bryant issued an opinion that the price was fair. Schlump participated in the meeting and voted in favor of the transaction. Lebron, Bryant concluded that the price was fair. Sturdley and the Schlump Organization signed an agreement, with a sixty day no-shop clause, which meant Sturdley could not solicit other bids. The board then commissioned a business plan in support of CDTCs, for which Sturdley expected to use the money from the real estate.

Thereafter, Sturdley received an unsolicited offer from North Sturdley Children's Hospital to either combine with it, which would keep the hospital open as a subsidiary of North Sturdley, or to sell the real estate to it for $27 million for use for health care services, but not limited to children. Lebron, Marbury advised against accepting the offer, because it said Sturdley as a hospital had no business value.

Under the Atlantis nonprofit statute, the sale, lease, exchange or other disposition of all or substantially all the assets of a nonprofit must be approved by a county court judge. The standard applied is whether the consideration and terms of the transaction as a whole are fair and reasonable at the time the contract was entered into and whether the seller's use of the sale proceeds will promote the corporation's purposes in light of the conditions prevailing when presented to the court.

This problem raises many of the legal issues discussed in this chapter. Assume you are an attorney representing Sturdley Hospital. What legal arguments would be raised by opponents to the hospital's plans? What are their chances of success? How would you counter them? How would you advise your client to avoid some of the legal objections and complications to its plans?

CHAPTER 4

REGULATION OF CHARITABLE SOLICITATION

A. INTRODUCTION

Abuses by some nonprofits in soliciting funds from the public have been the most persistent problem facing state attorneys general in their regulation of charities. As the following examples illustrate, solicitation practices range from questionable use of funds to outright fraud.

- A well known fundraiser for political causes switches to solicitations on behalf of advocacy groups for the aged. Using modern techniques of direct-mail fundraising, tens of millions of direct mail appeals generate millions of dollars in contributions. Virtually all of the contributions go to the fundraiser's firm for fees and to generate more mailings. The exempt organization's directors and executives consist entirely of direct mail experts and former employees of the fundraiser. See Erik Eckholm, Alarmed by Fund–Raiser, The Elderly Give Millions, N.Y. Times, Nov. 12, 1992, at A1.

- In 2008, paid solicitors in California passed along to charities only 44 percent of funds raised; in New York 39.5 percent; and Massachusetts 41 percent. These figures mark a modest improvement in recent years in the amounts that charities received from fundraising campaigns. In 2003, charities in California, Colorado, Massachusetts and New York on average received a little over one-third of the money raised on their behalf by professional telemarketers. In Massachusetts, telemarketers kept on average 71 cents of every dollar raised; New York 66 cents; California 62 cents; and Colorado, 41 cents. Leah Kerkman, Paid Fund Raisers Earn Mixed Results for Nonprofit Groups, Chron. Philanthropy, Feb. 9, 2006, at 26; Sharnell Bryan, Percentage of Funds Pocketed by Charity Telemarketers Varies by State, Chron. Philanthropy, Jan. 20, 2005, at 19.

- A reporter sponsored a girl from Mali through the Save the Children Federation and decided to visit the child. The sponsored child had been dead for four years, and letters to donors purportedly from children were written by the organization. See Lisa Anderson, The Miracle Merchants, Chic. Tribune, Mar. 15, 1998, at 1.

Charitable giving is a $308 billion annual industry.[1] As in any business, its participants are faced with competition, and abuses by some industry

---

1. According to the Giving USA Foundation, in 2008 donations to charitable causes reached $307.65 billion, a 2 percent drop in current dollars from 2007. Giving USA Founda-

members occur. When a charitable contribution has been made, there often is no discernible outcome to the donor. A contribution is usually an act of faith that money donated is put to its promised use.[2] Indisputably, some fraud in charitable solicitation exists. Misuse of monies raised for charitable purposes is not only a fraud upon the donor, it can be a diversion of tax dollars from state or federal treasuries. Courts have long concluded that the state could use its police powers to limit and regulate charitable solicitation to ensure that dollars raised are efficiently spent and public benefit maximized. This power of regulation, however, is limited by constitutionally imposed boundaries.

In response to the problems created by unscrupulous charitable solicitors, a majority of states have developed elaborate registration and filing systems requiring charities and fundraising solicitors to register, file annual reports, and notify the state of any changes in their status. For charities, solicitation provides not only an opportunity to raise funds but also to communicate a message and to educate or engage the public in debate on policies or programs.[3] Charities have challenged these attempts to regulate solicitation, arguing that the efforts are constitutionally overbroad, give state officials too much discretion, and are unduly burdensome, particularly for smaller charities.

The state regulatory schemes share three common elements. First, they provide for mandatory disclosure through state and local registration and licensing requirements that make financial and operational information available to the public. Second, the statutes make unlawful any fraudulent solicitation activities carried on by groups purporting to represent charities, by charitable groups, or by professional solicitors. Penalties range from cancellation of registration to criminal sanctions. Third, states unsuccessfully have included provisions controlling the costs of solicitation and administration so as to increase the percentage of funds directly spent on the exempt purposes of the organization.[4] As the excerpt below indicates, the most vexing problem for state regulators is the low percentage of donated dollars that actually reach the designated charity.

---

tion, U.S. charitable giving estimated to be $307.65 billion in 2008 (2009), available at http://www.philanthropy.iupui.edu/News/2009/docs/GivingReaches300billion_06102009.pdf.

2. See Henry Hansmann, Reforming Nonprofit Corporation Law, 129 U.Pa.L.Rev. 497, 505 (1981).

3. Ellen Harris, Lynn S. Holley, Christopher J. McCaffrey, N.Y.U. Program on Philanthropy and the Law, Fundraising into the 1990s: State Regulation of Charitable Solicitation After *Riley*, 24 U.S.F.L.Rev. 571, 572 (1990).

4. Karen S. Quandt, The Regulation of Charitable Fundraising and Spending Activities, 1975, Wis. L. Rev. 1158, 1160 (1975).

Ellen Harris, Lynn S. Holley, Christopher J. McCaffrey, N.Y.U. Program on Philanthropy and the Law, Fundraising into the 1990's: State Regulation of Charitable Solicitation After Riley

24 U.S.F.L.Rev. 571, 577–584, 588–589 (1990).

II. The Role of States Vis-a-Vis Charities

A. State Support of Charitable Solicitation Laws

State regulation of charitable solicitation is arguably a natural and necessary outgrowth of states' interests vis-a-vis charities. State regulation of charitable solicitation, while reflecting a recently growing concern with the scope of fundraising, is indicative of the historically close relationship between the states and charities. The states have long acted in a role of "parens patriae" to ensure the integrity and public service character of charities. This role dates as far back as the Statute of Charitable Uses in England, enacted in 1601. This statute not only delineated the specific organizational purposes deemed to be charitable, it also set up commissions with broad powers to investigate and redress the misapplication of charitable funds.

Currently, the states' role vis-a-vis charities is multifaceted. States may act to "protect" or to "regulate" charities, providing a substitute for the market mechanisms that influence for-profit organizations. Charitable solicitation laws may act to regulate the "charitable environment," thereby encouraging charitable giving. These laws may also work to protect the interests of the general public, including both those who donate to charities and those who receive charitable benefits.

A state may argue that through charitable solicitation legislation, it "protects" charities from abuse by those who provide high cost solicitation services. Such legislation is often described as "pro-charity" because it is designed, at least in part, to ensure that charities receive the maximum funds to which they are entitled. For example, limits on fees which professional solicitors may receive protect charities from being overcharged for these services. Licensing and registration requirements protect charities against fraudulent professionals. Thus, regulators may argue that charitable solicitation laws aim to decrease charities' vulnerability to fraud.

State solicitation regulations limiting fees paid to fundraisers also may protect charities against their own corruptive self-interest. For instance, in hiring a professional solicitor, a charity generally bears no financial risk. The solicitor will raise all of the money she can, take a share of the money collected on either a percentage basis or by deducting her expenses, and turn the remainder over to the charity.[41] Hence, the charity is able to make

---

41. Under professional solicitation contracts, charities generally have very little to do with the fundraising. During a typical telephone solicitation campaign:

A solicitation firm agrees to rent office space, install the phones, hire the callers, make the calls and collect the money pledged. With few exceptions, this method of fundraising involves selling tickets to an entertainment event and/or the sale of advertising space in a

a profit without incurring any costs. According to the Commonwealth of Massachusetts, "when a solicitor offers to run the whole fundraising campaign for a percentage, the charity may view this as 'found money' * * * ". In such cases, a charity may think it is getting the best of deals— "something for nothing." Charitable solicitation regulations may reflect a state's opinion that the appeal of "easy money" may leave charities unable to evaluate objectively the benefits and risks of undertaking a solicitation campaign.

States may also assert that their solicitation laws act as "economic regulation" of the big business of charitable solicitation. Charitable solicitation laws may be necessary to compensate for the lack of economic disincentive available to discourage charities from utilizing costly fundraising services. The conduct of trustees and directors of charities is subject neither to the traditional profit and loss constraints of the marketplace nor to the scrutiny of shareholders or investors. Those who run charities may be volunteers, not professional managers, and may lack the expertise to choose the best fundraising alternatives. States may argue that state-imposed limits on solicitation fees ensure that charities are reasonably managed, and that money raised is not applied to wasteful, inefficient fundraising schemes.

Charitable solicitation laws also serve to regulate the "charitable environment" by promoting the public's perception of the integrity and efficiency of charities. These laws may represent a state's response to a perceived "growing public perception that charitable donations are used only to solicit more charitable donations in seemingly endless waves of unwelcome 'junk mail.' " Donors may react to information about high solicitation fees by discontinuing their support of a charity. Growing public cynicism might endanger the future marketability of a charity's good name. States may thus argue that solicitation laws attempt to guard against public cynicism concerning charitable giving much in the same way that political contribution laws attempt to protect against the erosion of public confidence in the political arena. In political contribution cases, the Supreme Court has noted that states have a valid interest not only in guarding against the appearance of corruption.

States may also argue that they have a substantial interest in maintaining a good "charitable environment" because charities generally provide many vital services to state citizens. * * * Money donated to an inefficient or wasteful charity may detract from the total amount of funds available to all charities through public contribution. Consequently, chari-

---

program book, journal or other publication. Again, the arrangements are handled by the soliciting firm including printing, renting a location or the show, obtaining insurance, and booking and paying for performers. For this, the organization hiring the solicitor agrees to accept a percentage of the funds raised or a fixed dollar amount.

"Paid Telephone Soliciting in Connecticut During 1987 for Charitable, Civic, Police and Firefighter Organizations" (a report to Mary M. Heslin, Commissioner of Consumer Protection, and Joseph I. Lieberman, Attorney General; prepared by The Public Charities Unit, a joint program of the Dep't. of Consumer Protections, the Office of the Attorney General)(April 8, 1988) at 1.

table organizations are able to assume less of the burden of providing services to the community. Hence, states may assert that they have an important interest in encouraging "charity and charitable contribution and to maximize the funds which flow to the charity."[51]

Charitable solicitation laws also reflect the states' historic role as parens patriae, or protector of the public interest. As the State of Maryland has argued, "[c]ontracts between charitable organizations and charitable fund-raisers are thus not merely bilateral, rather they establish a triangular relationship with the public as a third party whose interests must be protected." The "general public" consists of two groups of individuals— those who donate to charity and those who benefit from it. (Of course, these two groups may overlap.) Donors may benefit from limitations on fundraising costs, which protect their expectations that their contributions will go primarily to a charitable purpose. Also beneficial may be the dissemination of information concerning fundraising costs, which allows potential donors "intelligently [to] decide between the competing claims of charities." Perhaps most importantly, state solicitation laws protect the ultimate beneficiaries of charitable services, who are often poor, elderly, handicapped, or disadvantaged. These groups generally have neither the resources nor the legal know-how to ensure that charitable donations are properly spent on charitable purposes. If, as regulators assume, the universe of the "charitable dollar" is finite, solicitation laws prohibiting high solicitation fees prevent funds, which would very likely be used to provide charitable services, from being diverted to pay for fundraising services.[56]

States have often guarded the interests of citizens under the banner of their police powers, and have used this power to protect the general public from unwanted solicitation and intrusion. Generally, the tasks of discouraging the visits of unwanted callers falls on the shoulders of individual homeowners. However, there are reasonable measures a state may take to supplement the individual's efforts. These measures are generally based on one of several broad bodies of legal history. In addition to their reliance on the laws of fraud, regulators have based their use of the police powers on (1) the general arena of nuisance law; and (2) the law covering nonfraudulent criminal activity, such as burglary. Under nuisance laws, a state may try to pass regulations restricting the time, place, and manner in which solicitors can call on people's homes in an attempt to maintain public order and peace, and to protect the citizens from nocturnal disturbances. A state may also regulate solicitation in order to prevent criminal activity, particu-

---

51.   Id. In an important early article entitled, The Efficiency of the Charitable Dollar: An Unfulfilled State Responsibility, Professor Kenneth Karst argued that "[t]he greatest possible portion of the wealth donated to private charity must be conserved and used to further the charitable, public purpose; waste must be minimized and diversion of funds for private gain is intolerable." Kenneth Karst, The Efficiency of the Charitable Dollar: An Unfulfilled State Responsibility, 73 Harv. L. Rev. 433, 434 (1960).

56.   But cf. Steinberg, Should Donors Care About Fundraising? in The Economics of Nonprofit Institutions 347 (S. Rose–Ackerman ed., 1986) (charitable solicitation always is beneficial to charities because even a 99% contingent fundraising fee necessarily increases the amount of money going to charitable purposes).

larly crimes such as burglary. This theory is based on the idea that burglars and other criminal intruders frequently pose as door-to-door solicitors in order to conduct surveillance on potential targets for future criminal conduct. This reasoning has been used to justify registration requirements that act to keep police apprised of the identity of those traveling the neighborhood and going door-to-door. It has also been used, unsuccessfully, to justify denying door-to-door solicitation permits to people with prior felony records.

States thus may have varied interests in regulating charitable solicitation. Through solicitation laws, states act to protect both charities and donors from fraud. This protection may extend to ensuring that charities, lured by "easy money," make sound financial judgments. States also protect charitable beneficiaries, by making sure that as much money as possible goes to realize charitable goals and not to enrich professional fundraisers. Through their police powers, states protect their citizens against the nuisance and criminal activity that may accompany door-to-door fundraising. Charitable solicitation laws act to regulate charities in place of the market mechanisms that serve to regulate for-profit businesses. These regulations serve to maintain the "charitable environment" necessary for charities to continue their provision of public services in an age of government cutbacks. Fundraising regulations ensure that donors' expectations of charitable giving are fulfilled, thus encouraging the public's continued charitable support.

B.   Charities' Perspectives on Solicitation Laws

Charities have criticized recent solicitation laws as antithetical to their interests because these laws often unduly burden a charity's ability to freely communicate ideas. Many charities also argue that solicitation laws may reflect an inaccurate and inappropriate conceptualization of the states' interests in the operation of charities, and unduly infringe upon the charity's autonomy and ability to operate. Arguments for state regulation, derived from historical precedents, may no longer be relevant due to the changing nature of charities. * * * Today's charities, however, include many public interest, educational, religious, and advocacy groups. * * *

Charitable solicitation laws, although designed as economic regulation, frequently impinge upon charities' free speech interests. Many charities utilize fundraising for the purpose of advocating ideas and disseminating information, as well as for soliciting funds. Thus, any regulation of solicitation campaigns will necessarily implicate free speech concerns. The Constitution accords free speech, a "fundamental right," the "highest degree of protection." Decisions concerning which beliefs to espouse and how to expend public support lie at the very heart of the constitutional guarantee of free speech. Consequently, a charity may argue that if it regards a solicitation campaign as necessary to "spread its message," it should be able to contract for such a campaign no matter what the cost. Independent Sector, a group representing the interests of over 450 volunteer groups, has argued that "an organization should be free to pursue stubbornly an unpopular but legitimate charitable objective, free from second-guessing by state authorities."

Thus, it is impossible to view charitable solicitation laws solely in terms of "economic regulation" as distinct from regulation-of-speech interests. Financial decisions relating to how much a charity will spend on fundraising are "inextricably related to policies and objectives." In the eyes of some, percentage limitations on a solicitor's fee are particularly offensive. Such limitations prohibit charities from choosing "the activity they deem best to promote their views and information, since they must choose the activity with the lowest cost-to-funds-raised ratio." Disclosure laws that make successful solicitation very difficult, if not impossible, may also add to the impracticability of a charities' ability to use professional solicitation services.

* * *

Charities thus often have mixed views of state solicitation efforts. Fundraising regulations may reflect a conception of the states' role vis-a-vis charities that is outdated and often insensitive to the varied interests and needs of charities. Solicitation laws, while under the guise of "economic regulation," may be unduly burdensome of charities' free speech interests. As charities provide an important means of expression of the value of pluralism, charitable solicitation laws must be carefully drawn to avoid hampering the continued vitality of charities. Many charities support and have been active in the development of fair standards of accountability, recognizing the need to address state and individual concerns with the integrity of charitable fundraising.

C. States' Concerns Regarding Charitable Solicitation

The primary state concern regarding charitable solicitation campaigns is the low percentage of contributions often received by a charity. Fundraising, which previously had been largely conducted by unpaid volunteers, has become much more sophisticated and complex. Consequently, a majority of funds raised often goes to pay the expenses of costly professional campaigns. * * * As solicitors generally exert a great deal of control over the operation of a campaign, it may be difficult for the charity or the state to monitor solicitation expenses. Hence, it is asserted that fundraisers, unbeknownst to the contributing public, have purchased, in effect, a charity's good name and charitable reputation in order to take advantage of the public's charitable generosity.

United Cancer Council, Inc. v. Commissioner

United States Court of Appeals, Seventh Circuit, 1999.
165 F.3d 1173.

■ POSNER, CHIEF JUDGE.

The United Cancer Council is a charity that seeks, through affiliated local cancer societies, to encourage preventive and ameliorative approaches to cancer, as distinct from searching for a cure, which has been the emphasis of the older and better-known American Cancer Society, of which UCC is a splinter. The Internal Revenue Service revoked UCC's charitable exemption and the Tax Court upheld the revocation, precipitating this appeal.

So far as relates to this case, a charity, in order to be entitled to the charitable exemption from federal income tax, and to be eligible to receive tax-exempt donations, must be "organized and operated exclusively for * * * [charitable] purposes" and "no part of the net earnings of [the charity may] inure[ ] to the benefit of any private shareholder or individual." The IRS claims that UCC (which is defunct) was not operated exclusively for charitable purposes, but rather was operated for, or also for, the private benefit of the fundraising company that UCC had hired, Watson & Hughey Company (W & H). The Service also claims that part of the charity's net earnings had inured to the benefit of a private shareholder or individual—W & H again. The Tax Court upheld the Service's second ground for revoking UCC's exemption—inurement—and did not reach the first ground, private benefit. The only issue before us is whether the court clearly erred in finding that a part of UCC's net earnings inured to the benefit of a private shareholder or individual.

It is important to understand what the IRS does not contend. It does not contend that any part of UCC's earnings found its way into the pockets of any members of the charity's board; the board members, who were medical professionals, lawyers, judges, and bankers, served without compensation. It does not contend that any members of the board were owners, managers, or employees of W & H, or relatives or even friends of any of W & H's owners, managers, or employees. It does not contend that the fundraiser was involved either directly or indirectly in the creation of UCC, or selected UCC's charitable goals. It concedes that the contract between charity and fundraiser was negotiated at an arm's length basis. But it contends that the contract was so advantageous to W & H and so disadvantageous to UCC that the charity must be deemed to have surrendered the control of its operations and earnings to the noncharitable enterprise that it had hired to raise money for it.

The facts are undisputed. In 1984, UCC was a tiny organization. It had an annual operating budget of only $35,000, and it was on the brink of bankruptcy because several of its larger member societies had defected to its rival, the American Cancer Society. A committee of the board picked W & H, a specialist in raising funds for charities, as the best prospect for raising the funds essential for UCC's survival. Another committee of the board was created to negotiate the contract. Because of UCC's perilous financial condition, the committee wanted W & H to "front" all the expenses of the fundraising campaign, though it would be reimbursed by UCC as soon as the campaign generated sufficient donations to cover those expenses. W & H agreed. But it demanded in return that it be made UCC's exclusive fundraiser during the five-year term of the contract, that it be given co-ownership of the list of prospective donors generated by its fundraising efforts, and that UCC be forbidden, both during the term of the contract and after it expired, to sell or lease the list, although it would be free to use it to solicit repeat donations. There was no restriction on W & H's use of the list. UCC agreed to these terms and the contract went into effect.

Over the five-year term of the contract, W & H mailed 80 million letters soliciting contributions to UCC. Each letter contained advice about preventing cancer, as well as a pitch for donations; 70 percent of the letters also offered the recipient a chance to win a sweepstake. The text of all the letters was reviewed and approved by UCC. As a result of these mailings, UCC raised an enormous amount of money (by its standards)—$28.8 million. But its expenses—that is, the costs borne by W & H for postage, printing, and mailing the letters soliciting donations, costs reimbursed by UCC according to the terms of the contract—were also enormous—$26.5 million. The balance, $2.3 million, the net proceeds of the direct-mail campaign, was spent by UCC for services to cancer patients and on research for the prevention and treatment of cancer. The charity was permitted by the relevant accounting conventions to classify $12.2 million of its fundraising expenses as educational expenditures because of the cancer information contained in the fundraising letters.

Although UCC considered its experience with W & H successful, it did not renew the contract when it expired by its terms in 1989. Instead, it hired another fundraising organization—with disastrous results. The following year, UCC declared bankruptcy, and within months the IRS revoked its tax exemption retroactively to the date on which UCC had signed the contract with W & H. The effect was to make the IRS a major creditor of UCC in the bankruptcy proceeding. The retroactive revocation did not, however, affect the charitable deduction that donors to UCC since 1984 had taken on their income tax returns.

The term "any private shareholder or individual" in the inurement clause of section 501(c)(3) of the Internal Revenue Code has been interpreted to mean an insider of the charity. A charity is not to siphon its earnings to its founder, or the members of its board, or their families, or anyone else fairly to be described as an insider, that is, as the equivalent of an owner or manager. The test is functional. It looks to the reality of control rather than to the insider's place in a formal table of organization. The insider could be a "mere" employee—or even a nominal outsider, such as a physician with hospital privileges in a charitable hospital, or for that matter a fundraiser, National Foundation, Inc. v. United States, 13 Cl.Ct. 486, 494–95 (1987)—though the court in that case rejected the argument that the fundraiser controlled the charity.

The Tax Court's classification of W & H as an insider of UCC was based on the fundraising contract. Such contracts are common. Fundraising has become a specialized professional activity and many charities hire specialists in it. If the charity's contract with the fundraiser makes the latter an insider, triggering the inurement clause of section 501(c)(3) and so destroying the charity's tax exemption, the charity sector of the economy is in trouble. The IRS does not take the position that every such contract has this effect. What troubles it are the particular terms and circumstances of UCC's contract. It argues that since at the inception of the contract the charity had no money to speak of, and since, therefore, at least at the beginning, all the expenses of the fundraising campaign were borne by W & H, the latter was like a founder, or rather refounder (UCC was created in 1963), of the charity. The IRS points out that 90 percent of the contributions received by UCC during the term of the contract were paid to W & H to defray the cost of the fundraising campaign that brought in those contributions, and so argues that W & H was the real recipient of the contributions. It argues that because W & H was UCC's only fundraiser, the charity was totally at W & H's mercy during the five-year term of the contract—giving W & H effective control over the charity. UCC even surrendered the right to rent out the list of names of donors that the fundraising campaign generated. The terms of the contract were more favorable to the fundraiser than the terms of the average fundraising contract are.

Singly and together, these points bear no relation that we can see to the inurement provision. The provision is designed to prevent the siphoning of charitable receipts to insiders of the charity, not to empower the IRS to monitor the terms of arm's length contracts made by charitable organizations with the firms that supply them with essential inputs, whether premises, paper, computers, legal advice, or fundraising services.

Take the Service's first point, that W & H defrayed such a large fraction of the charity's total expenses in the early stages of the contract that it was the equivalent of a founder. Pushed to its logical extreme, this argument would deny the charitable tax exemption to any new or small charity that wanted to grow by soliciting donations, since it would have to get the cash to pay for the solicitations from an outside source, logically a fundraising organization. We can't see what this has to do with inurement. The argument is connected to another of the Service's points, that W & H was UCC's only fundraiser during the period of the contract. If UCC had hired ten fundraisers, the Service couldn't argue that any of them was so large a recipient of the charity's expenditures that it must be deemed to have controlled the charity. Yet in terms of the purposes of the inurement clause, it makes no difference how many fundraisers a charity employs. W & H obtained an exclusive contract, and thus was the sole fundraiser, not because it sought to control UCC and suck it dry, but because it was taking a risk; the exclusive contract lent assurance that if the venture succeeded, UCC wouldn't hire other fundraisers to reap where W & H had sown.

And it was only at the beginning of the contract period that W & H was funding UCC. As donations poured into the charity's coffers as a result of the success of the fundraising campaign, the charity began paying for the subsequent stages of the campaign out of its own revenues. True, to guarantee recoupment, the contract with W & H required UCC to place these funds in an escrow account, from which they could be withdrawn for UCC's charitable purposes only after W & H recovered the expenses of the fundraising campaign. But this is a detail; the important point is that UCC did not receive repeated infusions of capital from W & H. All the advances that W & H had made to UCC to fund the fundraising campaign were repaid. Indeed, it is an essential part of the government's case that W & H profited from the contract.

The other point that the Service makes about the exclusivity provision in the contract—that it put the charity at the mercy of the fundraiser, since if W & H stopped its fundraising efforts UCC would be barred from hiring another fundraiser until the contract with W & H expired—merely demonstrates the Service's ignorance of contract law. When a firm is granted an exclusive contract, the law reads into it an obligation that the firm use its best efforts to promote the contract's objectives. If W & H folded its tent and walked away, it would be in breach of this implied term of the contract and UCC would be free to terminate the contract without liability.

The Service also misses the significance of the contract's asymmetrical treatment of the parties' rights in the donor list. The charitable-fundraising community distinguishes between "prospect files" and "housefiles." A prospect file is a list of people who have not given to the charity in question but are thought sufficiently likely to do so to be placed on the list of addressees of a direct-mail fundraising campaign. If the prospect responds with a donation, his or her name is transferred to the housefile, that is, the list of people who have made a donation to the charity. A housefile is very valuable, because people who have already donated to a particular charity are more likely to donate to it again than mere prospects are likely to donate to it for the first time. The housefile's value to the charity is thus as a list of people who are good prospects to respond favorably to future solicitations. Its value to the fundraiser is quite different. The fundraiser is not a charity. The value to it of a housefile that it has created is the possibility of marketing it (as a prospect file—but as a prospect file in which all the prospects are charitable donors rather than a mere cross-section of potential donors) to another charity that hires it. So it made perfect sense for the contract to give the fundraiser the exclusive right to use the UCC housefile that it created in raising money for other charities, while reserving to UCC the right to use the housefile to solicit repeat donations to itself.

The Service's point that has the most intuitive appeal is the high ratio of fundraising expenses, all of which went to W & H because it was UCC's only fundraiser during the term of the contract, to net charitable proceeds. Of the $28–odd million that came in, $26–plus million went right back out, to W & H. These figures are deceptive, because UCC got a charitable "bang" from the mailings themselves, which contained educational materials (somewhat meager, to be sure) in direct support of the charity's central charitable goal. A charity whose entire goal was to publish educational materials would spend all or most of its revenues on publishing, but this would be in support rather than in derogation of its charitable purposes.

Even if this point is ignored, the ratio of expenses to net charitable receipts is unrelated to the issue of inurement. For one thing, it is a ratio of apples to oranges: the gross expenses of the fundraiser to the net receipts of the charity. For all that appears, while UCC derived a net benefit from the contract equal to the difference between donations and expenses plus the educational value of the mailings, W & H derived only a modest profit; for we know what UCC paid it, but not what its expenses were. The record does contain a table showing that W & H incurred postage and printing expenses of $12.5 million, but there is nothing on its total expenses.

To the extent that the ratio of net charitable proceeds to the cost to the charity of generating those proceeds has any relevance, it is to a different issue, one not presented by this appeal, which is whether charities should be denied a tax exemption if their operating expenses are a very high percentage of the total charitable donations that they receive. To see that it's a different issue, just imagine that UCC had spent $26 million to raise $28 million but that the $26 million had been scattered among a host of suppliers rather than concentrated on one. There would be no issue of inurement, because the Service would have no basis for singling out one of these suppliers as being in "control" of UCC (or the suppliers as a group, unless they were acting in concert). But there might still be a concern either that the charity was mismanaged or that charitable enterprises that generate so little net contribution to their charitable goals do not deserve the encouragement that a tax exemption provides. Recall that most of UCC's fundraising appeals offered the recipient of the appeal a chance to win a sweepstake, a form of charitable appeal that, we are told, is frowned upon. There may even be a question of how reputable W & H is (or was). But these points go to UCC's sound judgment, not to whether W & H succeeded in wresting control over UCC from the charity's board.

UCC's low net yield is no doubt related to the terms of the fundraising contract, which were more favorable to the fundraiser than the average such contract. But so far as appears, they were favorable to W & H not because UCC's board was disloyal and mysteriously wanted to shower charity on a fundraiser with which it had no affiliation or overlapping membership or common ownership or control, but because UCC was desperate. The charity drove (so far as the record shows) the best bargain that it could, but it was not a good bargain. Maybe desperate charities should be encouraged to fold rather than to embark on expensive campaigns to raise funds. But that too is a separate issue from inurement. W & H did not, by reason of being able to drive a hard bargain, become an insider of UCC. If W & H was calling the shots, why did UCC refuse to renew the contract when it expired, and instead switch to another fundraiser?

We can find nothing in the facts to support the IRS's theory and the Tax Court's finding that W & H seized control of UCC and by doing so became an insider, triggering the inurement provision and destroying the exemption. There is nothing that corporate or agency law would recognize as control. A creditor of UCC could not seek the satisfaction of his claim from W & H on the ground that the charity was merely a cat's paw or alter ego of W & H, as in Pepper v. Litton, 308 U.S. 295, 311–12, 60 S.Ct. 238, 84

L.Ed. 281 (1939), or Freeman v. Complex Computing Co., 119 F.3d 1044, 1051–53 (2d Cir.1997). The Service and the Tax Court are using "control" in a special sense not used elsewhere, so far as we can determine, in the law, including federal tax law. It is a sense which, as the amicus curiae briefs filed in support of UCC point out, threatens to unsettle the charitable sector by empowering the IRS to yank a charity's tax exemption simply because the Service thinks the charity's contract with its major fundraiser too one-sided in favor of the fundraiser, even though the charity has not been found to have violated any duty of faithful and careful management that the law of nonprofit corporations may have laid upon it. The resulting uncertainty about the charity's ability to retain its tax exemption—and receive tax-exempt donations—would be a particular deterrent to anyone contemplating a donation, loan, or other financial contribution to a new or small charity. That is the type most likely to be found by the IRS to have surrendered control over its destiny to a fundraiser or other supplier, because it is the type of charity that is most likely to have to pay a high price for fundraising services. It is hard enough for new, small, weak, or marginal charities to survive, because they are likely to have a high expense ratio, and many potential donors will be put off by that. The Tax Court's decision if sustained would make the survival of such charities even more dubious, by enveloping them in doubt about their tax exemption.

We were not reassured when the government's lawyer, in response to a question from the bench as to what standard he was advocating to guide decision in this area, said that it was the "facts and circumstances" of each case. That is no standard at all, and makes the tax status of charitable organizations and their donors a matter of the whim of the IRS.

There was no diversion of charitable revenues to an insider here, nothing that smacks of self-dealing, disloyalty, breach of fiduciary obligation or other misconduct of the type aimed at by a provision of law that forbids a charity to divert its earnings to members of the board or other insiders. What there may have been was imprudence on the part of UCC's board of directors in hiring W & H and negotiating the contract that it did. Maybe the only prudent course in the circumstances that confronted UCC in 1984 was to dissolve. Charitable organizations are plagued by incentive problems. Nobody owns the right to the profits and therefore no one has the spur to efficient performance that the lure of profits creates. Donors are like corporate shareholders in the sense of being the principal source of the charity's funds, but they do not have a profit incentive to monitor the care with which the charity's funds are used. Maybe the lack of a profit motive made UCC's board too lax. Maybe the board did not negotiate as favorable a contract with W & H as the board of a profitmaking firm would have done. And maybe tax law has a role to play in assuring the prudent management of charities. Remember the IRS's alternative basis for yanking UCC's exemption? It is that as a result of the contract's terms, UCC was not really operated exclusively for charitable purposes, but rather for the private benefit of W & H as well. Suppose that UCC was so irresponsibly managed that it paid W & H twice as much for fundraising services as W & H would have been happy to accept for those services, so that of UCC's $26 million in fundraising expense $13 million was the equivalent of a gift to the fundraiser. Then it could be argued that UCC was in fact being operated to a significant degree for the private benefit of W & H, though not because it was the latter's creature. That then would be a route for using tax law to deal with the problem of improvident or extravagant expenditures by a charitable organization that do not, however, inure to the benefit of insiders.

That in fact is the IRS's alternative ground for revoking the exemption, the one the Tax Court gave a bye to. It would have been better had the court resolved that ground as well as the inurement ground, so that the case could be definitively resolved in one appeal. But it did not, and so the case must be remanded to enable the court to consider it. We shall not prejudge the proceedings on remand. The usual "private benefit" case is one in which the charity has dual public and private goals, and that is not involved here. However, the board of a charity has a duty of care, just like the board of an ordinary business corporation, and a violation of that duty which involved the dissipation of the charity's assets might (we need not decide whether it would—we leave that issue to the Tax Court in the first instance) support a finding that the charity was conferring a private benefit, even if the contracting party did not control, or exercise undue influence over, the charity. This, for all we know, may be such a case.

REVERSED AND REMANDED.

NOTES AND QUESTIONS

1. *United Cancer Council Settlement.* On remand, the Tax Court was deprived of the opportunity to reconsider the case when the IRS and UCC settled their longstanding exemption dispute. UCC, which had filed for bankruptcy, conceded that it was not entitled to exemption under § 501(c)(3) for the years 1986–1989, and the IRS restored UCC's exemption from 1990 forward. As a condition to the settlement, UCC agreed to stop raising funds from the general public and to limit its activities to accepting charitable bequests and transmitting them to local cancer councils for direct care of patients. For discussion of the private inurement and private benefit issues, see Chapter 5D, infra, at pp. 445–461.

2. *The Rationale of Regulation.* The theory behind mandatory disclosure is that an informed, potential donor will be able to make a reasoned decision based upon the facts disclosed, which will prevent fraud. Telco Communications v. Carbaugh, 885 F.2d 1225, 1231–32 (4th Cir.1989).

All disclosure requirements assume that donors really care about how the money they contribute will be used. Is that necessarily so? Donors contribute for a variety of reasons; ensuring that their dollars are efficiently spent is but one of the motivations. To some extent giving is like voting. One reason people participate in elections is that it is an extremely inexpensive mechanism for self-definition. The vote costs nothing because the probability an individual's vote will be decisive in a particular election approaches zero (except in Florida). Dwight R. Lee, Politics, Ideology and the Power of Public Choice, 74 Va. L. Rev. 191, 193 (1988). Voting is an inexpensive way for people to feel patriotic, self-righteous and altruistic. Some charitable giving may be explained by the fact that the *feeling* of altruism is more important than the object of the gift. The biblical maxim that "it is better to give than receive" may be grounded in psychological behavior. See generally Rob Atkinson, Altruism in Nonprofit Organizations, 31 B.C.L. Rev. 501 (1990). Other less altruistic reasons may be tangible benefits: tax deductions, benefit dinners and balls, fear of social disapproval at work or in the community, or desire to please the solicitor, who may be a friend, a girl scout, or more likely, the scout's parent. Does the statutory structure adopt a one dimensional view of why people donate?

3. *Exemptions from Registration.* Many statutes provide exemptions from the registration and reporting requirements. For instance, religious organizations often are exempt from the filing and other requirements because of fears of First Amendment entanglements. While most of these exemptions are understandable on grounds of avoiding constitutional problems or promoting administrative husbandry, recent events demonstrate that some religious organizations are no less likely to engage in improper fundraising than other nonprofits.

Some states have exempted membership organizations from the registration requirements. See, e.g., N.Y. Exec. L. § 172–a2(b), Cal. Bus. & Prof. Code § 17510.3. The justification is that the interest of the State is to protect the general public from fraud. When membership organizations solicit their own constituency, it is appropriate to regard such solicitations as private and beyond the purposes of state regulation. National Foundation v. City of Fort Worth, 415 F.2d 41, 48 (5th Cir.1969), cert. denied, 396 U.S. 1040, 90 S.Ct. 688 (1970); Bruce R. Hopkins, Charity Under Siege 90 (1980). The membership exemption allows a state's limited resources to be focused on public solicitations. Athornia Steele, Regulation of Charitable Solicitation: A Review and Proposal, 13 J. Legis. 149, 181 (1986). Does this exemption make sense if the purpose of charitable registration is to curtail violations in fundraising? Do members have an even greater interest than the public?

Occasionally, the membership and religious exemptions collide. In Heritage Village Church and Missionary Fellowship v. State, 299 N.C. 399, 263 S.E.2d 726, aff'g 40 N.C.App. 429, 253 S.E.2d 473 (1979), the court declared unconstitutional a statute exempting religious organizations from a licensing requirement provided the organization's budget was derived primarily from membership contributions. Religious organizations soliciting beyond their flock had to obtain a license, but no similar exemption was provided to non-religious organizations. The court rejected the underlying statutory assumption that funds solicited within the organization would not be solicited or expended in a fraudulent manner, while funds solicited outside of the organization could be subject to fraud. It also dismissed the idea that the membership would keep closer tabs upon organizational officials in contrast to organizations which solicited outside the general public. Id. at 411–412, 263 S.E.2d at 733.

Similarly, in Larson v. Valente, 456 U.S. 228, 102 S.Ct. 1673 (1982), the Supreme Court found unconstitutional a Minnesota statute which exempted religious organizations if more than half of their contributions were received from members, parent or affiliated organizations. The court rejected the premise that members of a religious organization can and will exercise supervision and control over the organization's solicitations when contributions from members exceed 50 percent, that membership control is an adequate safeguard, and the need for public disclosure rises in proportion with the percentage of non-member contributors. Id. at 248–249. In contrast to the assumptions of the legislation, membership monitoring might be an adequate safeguard if the organization had to file the same information as other exempt organizations. The statutes in *Heritage* and *Larson* faced an additional difficulty because they exempted some religious organizations from the burdens of the registration while less traditional religions which had to obtain support outside of the membership had to comply with the statutory obligation. This was violative of the establishment clause. Steele, supra at 179–180, 190.

Another common exemption is based upon organizational size. Smaller charities, determined by the amount raised or annual budget, are exempt from filing requirements. See, N.Y. Exec. L. § 172–a2(d) (organizations receiving under $25,000 not required to register). This exemption is justified because it would be cost inefficient for smaller organizations to comply with the statute and for regulators to enforce compliance. Is there any direct correlation between smallness and probity?

Many statutes exempt educational institutions, libraries, hospitals or other institutions because they are closely regulated by other state agencies. However, these other state agencies are usually interested in outputs (the quality of product delivered) rather than inputs (how funds are solicited from the public). Contributors may not realize that they have to contact other agencies for information about certain kinds of organizations.

4. *Implications of Barriers to Regulation of Contingent Fee Fundraising*. Are there consequences to the nonprofit sector as a whole if barriers to contingent fee fundraising are lowered?

5. *Overregulation of an Unimportant Problem?* Charitable fraud is not insubstantial. Some scams are nationwide and elicit millions of dollars, but state attorneys general have many competing demands on their resources. In the overall picture of state enforcement, how important is charitable fraud compared to other issues of crime and defalcation or other matters of importance to the state? How much of an additional burden do we want to place upon law abiding charities if we build an efficient monitoring and enforcement system? In the context of society's other problems, how important is this issue?

The scale of the registration and disclosure framework seems immense given the scope of the voluntary sector compared to the resources available for enforcement. Much of the regulation is really registration and reporting. The paucity of staff means in reality there is no true monitoring of activity. Richard Steinberg has commented that mandatory disclosure appears unnecessary but harmless. Economic Perspectives on Regulation of Charitable Solicitation, 39 Case West. Res. L. Rev. 775, 794 (1988–89). Is the mandatory disclosure system an expensive edifice that is unused by the public, increases agency costs for the charitable sector, and does relatively little to thwart abuses?

B.   CONSTITUTIONAL RESTRICTIONS ON REGULATION

Schaumburg v. Citizens for a Better Environment
Supreme Court of the United States, 1980.
444 U.S. 620, 100 S.Ct. 826.

■ MR. JUSTICE WHITE delivered the opinion of the Court.

[The Village of Schaumburg, a suburb of Chicago, enacted an ordinance prohibiting door-to-door or on-street charitable solicitations by organizations that did not use at least 75 percent of their receipts for "charitable purposes." Those purposes were defined to exclude solicitation expenses, salaries, overhead, and other administrative expenses. After being denied a solicitation permit, Citizens for a Better Environment, a nonprofit environmental organization, challenged the ordinance on constitutional grounds. The Supreme Court, with one dissent (Chief Justice Rehnquist), held that the ordinance was unconstitutionally overbroad, in violation of the First and Fourteenth Amendments. Justice White traced the Court's prior treatment of the law relating to solicitations by charitable organizations. Eds.]

It is urged that the ordinance should be sustained because it deals only with solicitation and because any charity is free to propagate its views from door to door in the Village without a permit as long as it refrains from soliciting money. But this represents a far too limited view of our prior cases relevant to canvassing and soliciting by religious and charitable organizations.

In Schneider v. State, 308 U.S. 147, 60 S.Ct. 146, 84 L.Ed. 155 (1939), a canvasser for a religious society, who passed out booklets from door to door and asked for contributions, was arrested and convicted under an ordinance which prohibited canvassing, soliciting, or distribution of circulars from house to house without a permit, the issuance of which rested much in the discretion of public officials. The state courts construed the ordinance as aimed mainly at house-to-house canvassing and solicitation. This distinguished the case from Lovell v. Griffin, 303 U.S. 444 (1938), which had invalidated on its face and on First Amendment grounds an ordinance criminalizing the distribution of any handbill at any time or place without a permit. Because the canvasser's conduct "amounted to the solicitation * * * of money contributions without a permit" Schneider, supra, at 159, and because the ordinance was thought to be valid as a protection against fraudulent solicitations, the conviction was sustained.

This Court disagreed, noting that the ordinance applied not only to religious canvassers but also to "one who wishes to present his views on political, social or economic questions," 308 U.S., at 163, and holding that the city could not, in the name of preventing fraudulent appeals, subject door-to-door advocacy and the communication of views to the discretionary permit requirement. The Court pointed out that the ordinance was not limited to those "who canvass for private profit," ibid., and reserved the question whether "commercial soliciting and canvassing" could be validly subjected to such controls. Id., at 165.

Cantwell v. Connecticut, 310 U.S. 296, 60 S.Ct. 900, 84 L.Ed. 1213 (1940), involved a state statute forbidding the solicitation of contributions of anything of value by religious, charitable, or philanthropic causes without obtaining official approval. Three members of a religious group were convicted under the statute for selling books, distributing pamphlets, and soliciting contributions or donations. Their convictions were affirmed in the state courts on the ground that they were soliciting funds and that the statute was valid as an attempt to protect the public from fraud. This Court set aside the convictions, holding that although a "general regulation, in the public interest, of solicitation, which does not involve any religious test and does not unreasonably obstruct or delay the collection of funds, is not open to any constitutional objection," id., at 305, to "condition the solicitation of aid for the perpetuation of religious views or systems upon a license, the grant of which rests in the exercise of a determination by state authority as to what is a religious cause," id., at 307, was considered to be an invalid prior restraint on the free exercise of religion. Although Cantwell turned on the free exercise clause, the Court has subsequently understood Cantwell to have implied that soliciting funds involves interests protected by the First Amendment's guarantee of freedom of speech. Virginia Pharmacy Board v. Virginia Citizens Consumer Council, 425 U.S. 748, 761 (1976); Bates v. State Bar of Arizona, 433 U.S. 350, 363 (1977).

In Valentine v. Chrestensen, 316 U.S. 52 (1942), an arrest was made for distributing on the public streets a commercial advertisement in violation of an ordinance forbidding this distribution. Addressing the question left open in *Schneider*, the Court recognized that while municipalities may not unduly restrict the right of communicating information in the public streets, the "Constitution imposes no such restraint on government as respects purely commercial advertising." 316 U.S., at 54. The Court reasoned that unlike speech "communicating information and disseminating opinion" commercial advertising implicated only the solicitor's interest in pursuing "a gainful occupation." Ibid.

The following Term in Jamison v. Texas, 318 U.S. 413 (1943), the Court, without dissent, and with the agreement of the author of the Chrestensen opinion, held that although purely commercial leaflets could be banned from the streets, a State could not "prohibit the distribution of handbills in the pursuit of a clearly religious activity merely because the handbills invite the purchase of books for the improved understanding of the religion or because the handbills seek in a lawful fashion to promote the raising of funds for religious purposes." 318 U.S., at 417. The Court reaffirmed what it deemed to be an identical holding in *Schneider*, as well as the ruling in *Cantwell* that "a state might not prevent the collection of funds for a religious purpose by unreasonably obstructing or delaying their collection." 318 U.S., at 417. See also Largent v. Texas, 318 U.S. 418 (1943).

In the course of striking down a tax on the sale of religious literature, the majority opinion in Murdock v. Pennsylvania, 319 U.S. 105 (1943), reiterated the holding in *Jamison* that the distribution of handbills was not transformed into an unprotected commercial activity by the solicitation of funds. Recognizing that drawing the line between purely commercial ventures and protected distributions of written material was a difficult task, the Court went on to hold that the sale of religious literature by itinerant evangelists in the course of spreading their doctrine was not a commercial enterprise beyond the protection of the First Amendment.

On the same day, the Court invalidated a municipal ordinance that forbade the door-to-door distribution of handbills, circulars, or other advertisements. None of the justifications for the general prohibition was deemed sufficient; the right of the individual resident to warn off such solicitors was deemed sufficient protection for the privacy of the citizen. Martin v. Struthers, 319 U.S. 141 (1943). On its facts, the case did not involve the solicitation of funds or the sale of literature.

Thomas v. Collins, 323 U.S. 516 (1945), held that the First Amendment barred enforcement of a state statute requiring a permit before soliciting membership in any labor organization. Solicitation and speech were deemed to be so intertwined that a prior permit could not be required. The Court also recognized that "espousal of the cause of labor is entitled to no higher constitutional protection than the espousal of any other lawful cause." Id., at 538, 65 S.Ct., at 326. The Court rejected the notion that First Amendment claims could be dismissed merely by urging "that an organization for which the rights of free speech and free assembly are claimed is one 'engaged in business activities' or that the individual who leads it in exercising these rights receives compensation for doing so." Id., at 531. Concededly, the "collection of funds" might be subject to reasonable regulation, but the Court ruled that such regulation "must be done, and the restriction applied, in such a manner as not to intrude upon the rights of free speech and free assembly." Id., at 540–541.

In 1951, Breard v. Alexandria, 341 U.S. 622 was decided. That case involved an ordinance making it criminal to enter premises without an invitation to sell goods, wares, and merchandise. The ordinance was sustained as applied to door-to-door solicitation of magazine subscriptions. The Court held that the sale of literature introduced "a commercial feature," id., at 642, and that the householder's interest in privacy outweighed any rights of the publisher to distribute magazines by uninvited entry on private property. The Court's opinion, however, did not indicate that the solicitation of gifts or contributions by religious or charitable organizations should be deemed commercial activities, nor did the facts of Breard involve the sale of religious literature or similar materials. Martin v. Struthers, supra, was distinguished but not overruled.

Hynes v. Mayor of Oradell, 425 U.S. 610 (1976), dealt with a city ordinance requiring an identification permit for canvassing or soliciting from house to house for charitable or political purposes. Based on its review of prior cases, the Court held that soliciting and canvassing from door to door were subject to reasonable regulation so as to protect the citizen against crime and undue annoyance, but that the First Amendment required such controls to be drawn with " 'narrow specificity.' " Id., at 620. The ordinance was invalidated as unacceptably vague.

Prior authorities, therefore, clearly establish that charitable appeals for funds, on the street or door to door, involve a variety of speech interests— communication of information, the dissemination and propagation of views and ideas, and the advocacy of causes—that are within the protection of the First Amendment. Soliciting financial support is undoubtedly subject to reasonable regulation but the latter must be undertaken with due regard for the reality that solicitation is characteristically intertwined with informative and perhaps persuasive speech seeking support for particular causes or for particular views on economic, political, or social issues, and for the reality that without solicitation the flow of such information and advocacy would likely cease. Canvassers in such contexts are necessarily more than solicitors for money. Furthermore, because charitable solicitation does more than inform private economic decisions and is not primarily concerned with providing information about the characteristics and costs of goods and services, it has not been dealt with in our cases as a variety of purely commercial speech.

NOTE: WATCHTOWER BIBLE & TRACT SOCIETY v. VILLAGE OF STRATTON

In Watchtower Bible & Tract Society v. Village of Stratton, 536 U.S. 150, 122 S.Ct. 2080 (2002), the Supreme Court struck down a local ordinance that made it a misdemeanor for canvassers who promoted any cause without first obtaining a permit from the mayor's office by completing and signing a registration form. In an 8–1 decision, the Court, reaffirming a long line of cases, held the regulation violated the First Amendment because it was overbroad as it applied to religious proselytizing, anonymous speech and the distribution of handbills. The decision offers scarce comfort to door-to-door fundraisers, for the court said in dictum:

> The text of the Village's ordinance prohibits 'canvassers' from going on private property for the purpose of explaining or promoting any 'cause' unless they receive a permit and the residents visited have not opted for a 'no solicitation' sign. Had this provision been construed to apply only to commercial activities and the solicitation of funds, arguably the ordinance would have been tailored to the Village's interest in protecting the privacy of its residents and protecting fraud. Id. at 2089.

Riley v. National Federation of the Blind

Supreme Court of the United States, 1988.
487 U.S. 781, 108 S.Ct. 2667.

■ JUSTICE BRENNAN delivered the opinion of the Court.

[The North Carolina Charitable Solicitations Act defined the prima facie "reasonable fee" that a professional fundraiser could charge according to a three-tiered schedule. A fee up to 20 percent of receipts collected was deemed reasonable; a fee between 20 and 35 percent was deemed unreasonable upon a showing that the solicitation at issue did not involve the dissemination of information, discussion, or advocacy relating to public issues as directed by the charitable organization that benefitted from the solicitation; and a fee exceeding 35 percent was presumed unreasonable, but the fundraiser could rebut the presumption by showing that the fee was necessary either because the solicitation involved the dissemination of information or advocacy on public issues directed by the charity, or because otherwise the charity's ability to raise money or communicate would be significantly diminished. The Act also provided that a professional fundraiser must disclose to potential donors the average percentage of gross receipts actually turned over to charities by the fundraiser for all charitable solicitations conducted in the state within the previous 12 months. Finally, the Act provided that professional fundraisers could not solicit without an approved license, whereas volunteer fundraisers could solicit immediately upon submitting a license application. A coalition of professional fundraisers, charitable organizations, and potential donors challenged the legislation. The district court ruled that the challenged provisions on their face unconstitutionally infringed upon freedom of speech and enjoined their enforcement. The United States Court of Appeals for the Fourth Circuit affirmed. Eds.]

II

We turn first to the "reasonable fee" provision. In deciding this issue, we do not write on a blank slate; the Court has heretofore twice considered laws regulating the financial aspects of charitable solicitations. We first examined such a law in Schaumburg v. Citizens for a Better Environment, 444 U.S. 620, 100 S.Ct. 826, 63 L.Ed.2d 73 (1980). There we invalidated a local ordinance requiring charitable solicitors to use, for charitable purposes (defined to exclude funds used toward administrative expenses and the costs of conducting the solicitation), 75% of the funds solicited. We began our analysis by categorizing the type of speech at issue. The village argued that charitable solicitation is akin to a business proposition, and therefore constitutes merely commercial speech. We rejected that approach and squarely held, on the basis of considerable precedent, that charitable solicitations "involve a variety of speech interests * * * that are within the protection of the First Amendment," and therefore have not been dealt with as "purely commercial speech." Applying standard First Amendment analysis, we determined that the ordinance was not narrowly tailored to achieve the village's principal asserted interest: the prevention of fraud. We concluded that some charities, especially those formed primarily to advocate, collect, or disseminate information, would of necessity need to expend more than 25% of the funds collected on administration or fundraising expenses. Yet such an eventuality would not render a solicitation by these charities fraudulent. In short, the prevention of fraud was only "peripherally promoted by the 75–percent requirement and could be sufficiently served by measures less destructive of First Amendment interests." We also observed that the village was free to enforce its already existing fraud laws and to require charities to file financial disclosure reports.

We revisited the charitable solicitation field four years later in Secretary of State of Maryland v. Joseph H. Munson Co., 467 U.S. 947, 104 S.Ct. 2839, 81 L.Ed.2d 786 (1984), a case closer to the present one in that the statute directly regulated contracts between charities and professional fundraisers. Specifically, the statute in question forbade such contracts if, after allowing for a deduction of many of the costs associated with the solicitation, the fundraiser retained more than 25% of the money collected. Although the Secretary was empowered to waive this limitation where it would effectively prevent the charitable organization from raising contributions, we held the law unconstitutional under the force of *Schaumburg*. We rejected the State's argument that restraints on the relationship between the charity and the fundraiser were mere "economic regulations" free of First Amendment implication. Rather, we viewed the law as "a direct restriction on the amount of money a charity can spend on fundraising activity," and therefore "a direct restriction on protected First Amendment activity." 467 U.S., at 967, and n. 16, 104 S.Ct., at 2852–2853, and n. 16. Consequently, we subjected the State's statute to exacting First Amendment scrutiny. Again, the State asserted the prevention of fraud as its principal interest, and again we held that the use of a percentage-based test was not narrowly tailored to achieve that goal. In fact, we found that if the statute actually prevented fraud in some cases it would be "little more than fortuitous." An "equally likely" result would be that the law would "restrict First Amendment activity that results in high costs but is itself a part of the charity's goal or that is simply attributable to the fact that the charity's cause proves to be unpopular." Id., at 966–967, 104 S.Ct., at 2852.

As in *Schaumburg* and *Munson*, we are unpersuaded by the State's argument here that its three-tiered, percentage-based definition of "unreasonable" passes constitutional muster. Our prior cases teach that the solicitation of charitable contributions is protected speech, and that using percentages to decide the legality of the fundraiser's fee is not narrowly tailored to the State's interest in preventing fraud.[5] That much established, unless the State can meaningfully distinguish its statute from those dis-

---

5. The dissent suggests that the State's regulation is merely economic, having only an indirect effect on protected speech. However, as we demonstrate, the burden here is hardly incidental to speech. Far from the completely incidental impact of, for example, a minimum wage law, a statute regulating how a speaker may speak directly affects that speech. See Meyer v. Grant, 486 U.S. 414, 421–423, and n. 5, 108 S.Ct. 1886, 1892, and n. 5, 100 L.Ed.2d 425 (1988). Here, the desired and intended effect of the statute is to encourage some forms of solicitation and discourage others.

cussed in our precedents, its statute must fall. The State offers two distinctions. First, it asserts a motivating interest not expressed in *Schaumburg* or *Munson*: ensuring that the maximum amount of funds reach the charity or, somewhat relatedly, to guarantee that the fee charged charities is not "unreasonable." Second, the State contends that the Act's flexibility more narrowly tailors it to the State's asserted interests than the laws considered in our prior cases. We find both arguments unavailing.

The State's additional interest in regulating the fairness of the fee may rest on either of two premises (or both): (1) that charitable organizations are economically unable to negotiate fair or reasonable contracts without governmental assistance; or (2) that charities are incapable of deciding for themselves the most effective way to exercise their First Amendment rights. Accordingly, the State claims the power to establish a single transcendent criterion by which it can bind the charities' speaking decisions. We reject both premises.

The first premise, notwithstanding the State's almost talismanic reliance on the mere assertion of it, amounts to little more than a variation of the argument rejected in *Schaumburg* and *Munson* that this provision is simply an economic regulation with no First Amendment implication, and therefore must be tested only for rationality. We again reject that argument; this regulation burdens speech, and must be considered accordingly. There is no reason to believe that charities have been thwarted in their attempts to speak or that they consider the contracts in which they enter to be anything less than equitable. Even if such a showing could be made, the State's solution stands in sharp conflict with the First Amendment's command that government regulation of speech must be measured in minimums, not maximums.

The State's remaining justification—the paternalistic premise that charities' speech must be regulated for their own benefit—is equally unsound. The First Amendment mandates that we presume that speakers, not the government, know best both what they want to say and how to say it. * * *

The foregoing discussion demonstrates that the State's additional interest cannot justify the regulation. But, alternatively, there are several legitimate reasons why a charity might reject the State's overarching measure of a fundraising drive's legitimacy—the percentage of gross receipts remitted to the charity. For example, a charity might choose a particular type of fundraising drive, or a particular solicitor, expecting to receive a large sum as measured by total dollars rather than the percentage of dollars remitted. Or, a solicitation may be designed to sacrifice short-term gains in order to achieve long-term, collateral, or noncash benefits. To illustrate, a charity may choose to engage in the advocacy or dissemination of information during a solicitation, or may seek the introduction of the charity's officers to the philanthropic community during a special event (e.g., an awards dinner). Consequently, even if the State had a valid interest in protecting charities from their own naivete or economic weakness, the Act would not be narrowly tailored to achieve it.

The second distinguishing feature the State offers is the flexibility it has built into its Act. The State describes the second of its three-tiered definition of "unreasonable" and "excessive" as imposing no presumption one way or the other as to the reasonableness of the fee, although unreasonableness may be demonstrated by a showing that the solicitation does not involve the advocacy or dissemination of information on the charity's behalf and at the charity's direction. The State points out that even the third tier's presumption of unreasonableness may be rebutted.

It is important to clarify, though, what we mean by "reasonableness" at this juncture. As we have just demonstrated, * * * the State's generalized interest in unilaterally imposing its notions of fairness on the fundraising contract is both constitutionally invalid and insufficiently related to a percentage-based test. Consequently, what remains is the more particularized interest in guaranteeing that the fundraiser's fee be "reasonable" in the sense that it not be fraudulent. The interest in protecting charities (and the public) from fraud is, of course, a sufficiently substantial interest to justify a narrowly tailored regulation. The question, then, is whether the added flexibility of this regulation is sufficient to tailor the law to this remaining interest. We conclude that it is not.

Despite our clear holding in *Munson* that there is no nexus between the percentage of funds retained by the fundraiser and the likelihood that the solicitation is fraudulent, the State defines, prima facie, an "unreasonable" and "excessive" fee according to the percentage of total revenues collected. Indeed, the State's test is even more attenuated than the one held invalid in *Munson*, which at least excluded costs and expenses of solicitation from the fee definition. Permitting rebuttal cannot supply the missing nexus between the percentages and the State's interest.[7]

But this statute suffers from a more fundamental flaw. Even if we agreed that some form of a percentage-based measure could be used, in part, to test for fraud, we could not agree to a measure that requires the speaker to prove "reasonableness" case by case based upon what is at best a loose inference that the fee might be too high. Under the Act, once a prima facie showing of unreasonableness is made, the fundraiser must rebut the showing. Proof that the solicitation involved the advocacy or dissemination of information is not alone sufficient; it is merely a factor that is added to the calculus submitted to the factfinder, who may still decide that the costs incurred or the fundraiser's profit were excessive. Similarly, the Act is impermissibly insensitive to the realities faced by small or unpopular charities, which must often pay more than 35% of the gross receipts collected to the fundraiser due to the difficulty of attracting donors. Again, the burden is placed on the fundraiser in such cases to rebut the presumption of unreasonableness.

According to the State, we need not worry over this burden, as standards for determining "[r]easonable fundraising fees will be judicially

---

7. Even if percentages are not completely irrelevant to the question of fraud, their relationship to the question is at best tenuous, as *Schaumburg* and *Munson* demonstrate.

defined over the years." Speakers, however, cannot be made to wait for "years" before being able to speak with a measure of security. In the interim, fundraisers will be faced with the knowledge that every campaign incurring fees in excess of 35%, and many campaigns with fees between 20% and 35%, will subject them to potential litigation over the "reasonableness" of the fee. And, of course, in every such case the fundraiser must bear the costs of litigation and the risk of a mistaken adverse finding by the factfinder, even if the fundraiser and the charity believe that the fee was in fact fair. This scheme must necessarily chill speech in direct contravention of the First Amendment's dictates.

This chill and uncertainty might well drive professional fundraisers out of North Carolina, or at least encourage them to cease engaging in certain types of fundraising (such as solicitations combined with the advocacy and dissemination of information) or representing certain charities (primarily small or unpopular ones), all of which will ultimately "reduc[e] the quantity of expression." Whether one views this as a restriction of the charities' ability to speak, or a restriction of the professional fundraisers' ability to speak, the restriction is undoubtedly one on speech, and cannot be countenanced here.

In striking down this portion of the Act, we do not suggest that States must sit idly by and allow their citizens to be defrauded. North Carolina has an antifraud law, and we presume that law enforcement officers are ready and able to enforce it. Further North Carolina may constitutionally require fundraisers to disclose certain financial information to the State, as it has since 1981. If this is not the most efficient means of preventing fraud, we reaffirm simply and emphatically that the First Amendment does not permit the State to sacrifice speech for efficiency.

III

We turn next to the requirement that professional fundraisers disclose to potential donors, before an appeal for funds, the percentage of charitable contributions collected during the previous 12 months that were actually turned over to charity. Mandating speech that a speaker would not otherwise make necessarily alters the content of the speech. We therefore consider the Act as a content-based regulation of speech. See Miami Herald Publishing Co. v. Tornillo, 418 U.S. 241, 256, 94 S.Ct. 2831, 2839, 41 L.Ed.2d 730 (1974)(statute compelling newspaper to print an editorial reply "exacts a penalty on the basis of the content of a newspaper").

The State argues that even if charitable solicitations generally are fully protected, this portion of the Act regulates only commercial speech because it relates only to the professional fundraiser's profit from the solicited contribution. Therefore, the State asks us to apply our more deferential commercial speech principles here. See generally Virginia Pharmacy Bd. v. Virginia Citizens Consumer Council, Inc., 425 U.S. 748, 96 S.Ct. 1817, 48 L.Ed.2d 346 (1976).

It is not clear that a professional's speech is necessarily commercial whenever it relates to that person's financial motivation for speaking. Cf.

Bigelow v. Virginia, 421 U.S. 809, 826, 95 S.Ct. 2222, 2235, 44 L.Ed.2d 600 (1975)(state labels cannot be dispositive of degree of First Amendment protection). But even assuming, without deciding, that such speech in the abstract is indeed merely "commercial," we do not believe that the speech retains its commercial character when it is inextricably intertwined with otherwise fully protected speech. Our lodestars in deciding what level of scrutiny to apply to a compelled statement must be the nature of the speech taken as a whole and the effect of the compelled statement thereon. This is the teaching of *Schaumburg* and *Munson*, in which we refused to separate the component parts of charitable solicitations from the fully protected whole. Regulation of a solicitation "must be undertaken with due regard for the reality that solicitation is characteristically intertwined with informative and perhaps persuasive speech * * *, and for the reality that without solicitation the flow of such information and advocacy would likely cease." *Schaumburg*, supra, 444 U.S., at 632, 100 S.Ct., at 834, quoted in *Munson*, 467 U.S., at 959–960, 104 S.Ct., at 2848. Thus, where, as here, the component parts of a single speech are inextricably intertwined, we cannot parcel out the speech, applying one test to one phrase and another test to another phrase. Such an endeavor would be both artificial and impractical. Therefore, we apply our test for fully protected expression.

North Carolina asserts that, even so, the First Amendment interest in compelled speech is different than the interest in compelled silence; the State accordingly asks that we apply a deferential test to this part of the Act. There is certainly some difference between compelled speech and compelled silence, but in the context of protected speech, the difference is without constitutional significance, for the First Amendment guarantees "freedom of speech," a term necessarily comprising the decision of both what to say and what not to say.

The constitutional equivalence of compelled speech and compelled silence in the context of fully protected expression was established in *Miami Herald Publishing Co. v. Tornillo, supra.* There, the Court considered a Florida statute requiring newspapers to give equal reply space to those they editorially criticize. We unanimously held the law unconstitutional as content regulation of the press, expressly noting the identity between the Florida law and a direct prohibition of speech. "The Florida statute operates as a command in the same sense as a statute or regulation forbidding appellant to publish a specified matter. Governmental restraint on publishing need not fall into familiar or traditional patterns to be subject to constitutional limitations on governmental powers." Id., 418 U.S., at 256, 94 S.Ct., at 2839. That rule did not rely on the fact that Florida restrained the press, and has been applied to cases involving expression generally. For example, in Wooley v. Maynard, 430 U.S. 705, 714, 97 S.Ct. 1428, 1435, 51 L.Ed.2d 752 (1977), we held that a person could not be compelled to display the slogan "Live Free or Die." In reaching our conclusion, we relied on the principle that "[t]he right to speak and the right to refrain from speaking are complementary components of the broader concept of 'individual freedom of mind,' " as illustrated in *Tornillo.* 430 U.S., at 714, 97 S.Ct., at 1435 (quoting West Virginia

Board of Education v. Barnette, 319 U.S. 624, 637, 63 S.Ct. 1178, 1185, 87 L.Ed. 1628 (1943)).

These cases cannot be distinguished simply because they involved compelled statements of opinion while here we deal with compelled statements of "fact": either form of compulsion burdens protected speech. * * *

We believe, therefore, that North Carolina's content-based regulation is subject to exacting First Amendment scrutiny. The State asserts as its interest the importance of informing donors how the money they contribute is spent in order to dispel the alleged misperception that the money they give to professional fundraisers goes in greater-than-actual proportion to benefit charity. To achieve this goal, the State has adopted a prophylactic rule of compelled speech, applicable to all professional solicitations. We conclude that this interest is not as weighty as the State asserts, and that the means chosen to accomplish it are unduly burdensome and not narrowly tailored.

Although we do not wish to denigrate the State's interest in full disclosure, the danger the State posits is not as great as might initially appear. First, the State presumes that the charity derives no benefit from funds collected but not turned over to it. Yet this is not necessarily so. For example, as we have already discussed in greater detail, where the solicitation is combined with the advocacy and dissemination of information, the charity reaps a substantial benefit from the act of solicitation itself. See *Munson*, supra, 467 U.S., at 963, 104 S.Ct., at 2850; *Schaumburg*, 444 U.S., at 635, 100 S.Ct., at 835. Thus, a significant portion of the fundraiser's "fee" may well go toward achieving the charity's objectives even though it is not remitted to the charity in cash.[10] Second, an unchallenged portion of the disclosure law requires professional fundraisers to disclose their professional status to potential donors, thereby giving notice that at least a portion of the money contributed will be retained.[11] Donors are also undoubtedly aware that solicitations incur costs, to which part of their donation might apply. And, of course, a donor is free to inquire how much of the contribution will be turned over to the charity. Under another North Carolina statute, also unchallenged, fundraisers must disclose this information upon request. N.C.Gen.Stat. § 131C–16 (1986). Even were that not so, if the solicitor refuses to give the requested information, the potential donor may (and probably would) refuse to donate.

Moreover, the compelled disclosure will almost certainly hamper the legitimate efforts of professional fundraisers to raise money for the chari-

---

10. In addition, the net "fee" itself benefits the charity in the same way that an attorney's fee benefits the charity, or the purchase of any other professional service benefits the charity. That the fundraiser's fee does not first pass through the charity's hands is of small import.

11. The Act, as written, requires the fundraiser to disclose his or her employer's name and address. Arguably, this may not clearly convey to the donor that the solicitor is employed by a for-profit organization, for example, where the employer's name is "Charitable Fundraisers of America." However, nothing in this opinion should be taken to suggest that the State may not require a fundraiser to disclose unambiguously his or her professional status. On the contrary, such a narrowly tailored requirement would withstand First Amendment scrutiny.

ties they represent. First, this provision necessarily discriminates against small or unpopular charities, which must usually rely on professional fundraisers. Campaigns with high costs and expenses carried out by professional fundraisers must make unfavorable disclosures, with the predictable result that such solicitations will prove unsuccessful. Yet the identical solicitation with its high costs and expenses, if carried out by the employees of a charity or volunteers, results in no compelled disclosure, and therefore greater success. Second, in the context of a verbal solicitation, if the potential donor is unhappy with the disclosed percentage, the fundraiser will not likely be given a chance to explain the figure; the disclosure will be the last words spoken as the donor closes the door or hangs up the phone.[12] Again, the predictable result is that professional fundraisers will be encouraged to quit the State or refrain from engaging in solicitations that result in an unfavorable disclosure.

In contrast to the prophylactic, imprecise, and unduly burdensome rule the State has adopted to reduce its alleged donor misperception, more benign and narrowly tailored options are available. For example, as a general rule, the State may itself publish the detailed financial disclosure forms it requires professional fundraisers to file. This procedure would communicate the desired information to the public without burdening a speaker with unwanted speech during the course of a solicitation. Alternatively, the State may vigorously enforce its antifraud laws to prohibit professional fundraisers from obtaining money on false pretenses or by making false statements. These more narrowly tailored rules are in keeping with the First Amendment directive that government not dictate the content of speech absent compelling necessity, and then, only by means precisely tailored. "Broad prophylactic rules in the area of free expression are suspect. Precision of regulation must be the touchstone in an area so closely touching our most precious freedoms." NAACP v. Button, 371 U.S. 415, 438, 83 S.Ct. 328, 340 (1963) (citations omitted).

IV

Finally, we address the licensing requirement. This provision requires professional fundraisers to await a determination regarding their license application before engaging in solicitation, while volunteer fundraisers, or those employed by the charity, may solicit immediately upon submitting an application.

---

12. The figure chosen by the State for disclosure is curious. First, it concerns unrelated past solicitations without regard for whether they are similar to the solicitation occurring at the time of disclosure. Thus, the high percentage of retained fees for past dinner-dance fundraisers must be disclosed to potential contributors during a less expensive door-to-door solicitation. Second, the figure does not separate out the costs and expenses of prior solicitations, such as printing, even though these expenses must also be borne by charities not subject to the disclosure requirement (i.e., those engaging in employee or volunteer staffed campaigns). The use of the "gross" percentage is even more curious in light of the fact that most contracts between the solicitor and the charity provide for a fee based on the percentage of "net" funds collected (i.e., the gross funds collected less costs), making this more relevant figure far easier to come by.

Given our previous discussion and precedent, it will not do simply to ignore the First Amendment interest of professional fundraisers in speaking. It is well settled that a speaker's rights are not lost merely because compensation is received; a speaker is no less a speaker because he or she is paid to speak. And the State's asserted power to license professional fundraisers carries with it (unless properly constrained) the power directly and substantially to affect the speech they utter. Consequently, the statute is subject to First Amendment scrutiny. See Lakewood v. Plain Dealer Publishing Co., 486 U.S. 750, 755–756 (when a State enacts a statute requiring periodic licensing of speakers, at least when the law is directly aimed at speech, it is subject to First Amendment scrutiny to ensure that the licensor's discretion is suitably confined).[13]

Generally, speakers need not obtain a license to speak. However, that rule is not absolute. For example, States may impose valid time, place, or manner restrictions. See Cox v. New Hampshire, 312 U.S. 569, 61 S.Ct. 762, 85 L.Ed. 1049 (1941). North Carolina seeks to come within the exception by alleging a heightened interest in regulating those who solicit money. Even assuming that the State's interest does justify requiring fundraisers to obtain a license before soliciting, such a regulation must provide that the licensor "will, within a specified brief period, either issue a license or go to court." Freedman v. Maryland, 380 U.S. 51, 59, 85 S.Ct. 734, 739, 13 L.Ed.2d 649 (1965). That requirement is not met here, for the Charitable Solicitations Act (as amended) permits a delay without limit. The statute on its face does not purport to require when a determination must be made, nor is there an administrative regulation or interpretation doing so. The State argues, though, that its history of issuing licenses quickly constitutes a practice effectively constraining the licensor's discretion. We cannot agree. The history to which the State refers relates to the period before the 1985 amendments, at which time professional fundraisers were permitted to solicit as soon as their applications were filed. Then, delay permitted the speaker's speech; now, delay compels the speaker's silence. Under these circumstances, the licensing provision cannot stand.

V

We hold that the North Carolina Charitable Solicitations Act is unconstitutional in the three respects before us. Accordingly, the judgment of the Court of Appeals is

---

13.   Even were we to focus only on the charities' First Amendment interest here, we still could not adopt the dissent's reasoning, for its logic in that regard necessarily depends on the premise that professional fundraisers are interchangeable from the charities' vantage. There is no reason to believe that is so. Fundraisers may become associated with particular clients or causes. Regulating these fundraisers with the heavy hand that unbridled discretion allows affects the speech of the clients or causes with which they are associated. Nor are we persuaded by the dissent's assertion that this statute merely licenses a profession, and therefore is subject only to rationality review. Although Justice Jackson did express his view that solicitors could be licensed, a proposition not before us, he never intimated that the licensure was devoid of all First Amendment implication. Thomas v. Collins, 323 U.S. 516, 544–545, 65 S.Ct. 315, 329, 89 L.Ed. 430 (1945)(Jackson, J., concurring).

Affirmed.

■ [The opinions of JUSTICE SCALIA, concurring in part and concurring in judgment, and of JUSTICE STEVENS, concurring in part and dissenting in part, are omitted. CHIEF JUSTICE REHNQUIST, with whom JUSTICE O'CONNOR joined, dissented. The dissent distinguished between the actions of the solicitors in earlier cases such as *Schaumburg*, which involved religious solicitation and incidental fundraising, and the activities of professional "for-profit fundraisers" in *Munson* and *Riley*. Among the other points made in the dissent were: (1) charitable solicitation when pursued by professional fundraisers deserved no more protection than other forms of commercial speech; (2) the North Carolina statute was less burdensome than the Maryland statute in *Munson* and more carefully tailored to the state's interest in regulating fundraising fees; (3) on the record of the case, since the burden on speech was remote and incidental, there was no reason to apply the "heightened scrutiny" standard; (4) in contrast to *Munson*, the North Carolina statute was narrowly tailored to serve the states' interest in combating fraud; (5) disclosure by the professional fundraiser of true facts was not such a burden on speech as to require strict scrutiny; and (6) the licensing provisions that differentiated between professional and volunteer or in-house fundraisers related to the states' interest in protecting the public and charities and was but an incidental burden. Eds.]

NOTES AND QUESTIONS

1. *Cost of Fundraising Ratios*. A high ratio of expenses to funds raised, though controversial, does not of itself indicate that a nonprofit is mismanaged, corrupt, or inefficient. Cost of fundraising ratios (CFRs) are but one piece of data used to evaluate a charity. A nonprofit's CFR may be high for a number of reasons, such as: it is a nascent organization with an unfamiliar mission; it has undertaken a campaign to recruit new donors; the primary purpose of the solicitation is educational; or the average contribution received is small. Other factors such as salaries and administrative costs, quantitative measures of mission attainment, and the number of people actually served by the charity compared to other organizations in the same field are just as important. Nor does a low CFR of itself indicate the ethical high ground of reasonable costs. Fundraising cost ratios can be minimized (disguised?) by allocating expenses into categories such as public education, program services, general expenses or administration instead of fundraising.

Assume a charity signs a contract with a professional fundraiser providing that any funds received by the charity will be after expenses and costs have been taken out by the fundraiser. Can the charity validly claim that it has no fundraising costs? Several studies have found a substantial percentage of charities report on their Form 990 annual informational tax return that they incurred no fundraising costs while state filing records revealed that in fact the organization spent substantial amounts on fundraising.

A study examining 2000 tax year data by the Urban Institute's Center on Nonprofit and Philanthropy and the Center on Philanthropy at Indiana University found that more than a third of nonprofit groups that collected $50,000 or more claimed on their Form 990 that they spent nothing on fundraising, even though that was often not true. The study examined the tax returns of more 125,000 nonprofit groups, and conducted surveys of overhead costs and accounting practices at 1,500 of them. The researchers concluded that many groups that receive the best ratings from watchdog groups are not as efficient as they seem, and that many charities lack the capacity to track such costs accurately. The report is available at www.nccs-coststudy.org. Why do so many charities willfully fail to report fundraising expenses?

Because the rules for determining overhead costs are vague and every charity interprets them differently, some charity watchdogs have criticized the emphasis on overhead ratios or cost of fundraising, and suggest donors should focus on the charity's effectiveness, measured by impact of the organization on its beneficiaries. See http://www.philanthropyaction.com/documents/Worst_Way_to_Pick_A_Charity_Dec_1_2009.pdf. For example, Charity Navigator, which rates charities, has deemphasized overhead. State attorneys general seem unaware of these developments.

2. *Post–Riley Cases.* In the wake of *Riley*, states attempted to preserve regulatory options which did not contravene the First Amendment. Percentage limitations on fundraising costs are clearly impermissible. The courts have continued to wrestle with the countervailing interests of states' needs to regulate charitable solicitation effectively and the requirements of the Constitution. In Telco Communications v. Carbaugh, 885 F.2d 1225 (4th Cir.1989), the Fourth Circuit upheld a section of Virginia's solicitation code which required professional solicitors to disclose in writing at the time of solicitation that a financial statement for the last fiscal year was available. The court found that the section of the code which informed the public about the availability of financial information on solicitors from the state office of consumer affairs prevented fraud and promoted substantial state interests not inherently incompatible with the First Amendment. See also Nebraska v. Kelley, 249 Neb. 99, 541 N.W.2d 645 (1996) (statute which required certification in letter of approval from county attorney before charitable solicitation was permitted outside organization's home county constituted unconstitutional prior restraint, overbreadth and vagueness); and Independent Charities of America v. Minnesota, 82 F.3d 791 (8th Cir.1996), cert. denied, 519 U.S. 993, 117 S.Ct. 482 (1996) (statute restricting participants in state employees annual fund drive to organizations incorporated in state or headquartered in the service area in which charitable campaign took place did not violate free speech rights of charities or implicate commerce clause; government workplace was non-public forum and law was rationally related to legitimate governmental objectives of decreasing disruption to workplace and rendering campaign more manageable and relevant to state employees.)

A Texas statute required companies that solicited and resold donations of clothing and other household items on behalf of charities to disclose the amount of money received by the charities and specify whether the sum was a set percentage or a flat fee. The receptacles for donations were not staffed, and the solicitors rarely disclosed their names but used the name of a charity. In National Federation of Blind of Texas, Inc. v. Abbott, 682 F.Supp.2d 700 (N.D. Tex. 2010), the court found the statute was not narrowly tailored and was an unconstitutional restriction on speech.

3. *Registration Requirements.* Statutes that require fundraisers to receive licenses and give officials discretion in granting them have been found unconstitutionally vague. Hynes v. Mayor of Oradell, 425 U.S. 610, 620, 96 S.Ct. 1755, 1760 (1976). But registration requirements for professional fundraisers are permissible. Id. at 616–619. Registration requirements and mandatory public disclosure of financial information at a central repository have become the most common forms of regulation. Leslie G. Espinoza, Straining the Quality of Mercy: Abandoning the Quest for Informed Charitable Giving, 64 Calif. L. Rev. 605, 699 (1991). So long as the required information is objective, and state officials have little discretion in rejecting or delaying a charity's solicitation campaign, a registration requirement will be upheld. Fundraising into the 1990s, supra at 61. Could a state require a charity to disclose information that would be unconstitutional as pre-solicitation disclosure, after the solicitation had been made?

In Famine Relief Fund v. West Va., 905 F.2d 747 (4th Cir.1990), the court upheld a statutory requirement that charities file with the state their contracts with professional solicitors or statements summarizing the terms of such contracts. Since state regulations could constitutionally require the filing of financial statements, the filing of contracts provided only greater detail and description to information already disclosed on the expense side of the charity's income statement. However, the enforcement procedures under the West Virginia statute did not afford charities sufficient due process before imposing a prior restraint on its speech because the state refused to license a charity to solicit funds in the state while the charity was awaiting judicial determination of the administrative denial of its registration.

Some states have horrifyingly elaborate filing requirements. See N.Y. Exec. L. §§ 171a–177. How much information can the state require? Could it require information on the disbursement of all of the charity's funds? For charities that solicit nationally, the registration requirements can be an expensive burden. Thirty-six of the 39 states that require charities to register before commencing a solicitation in the state have adopted a common registration form, the Uniform Registration Statement. See Statutory Supplement. The form was developed by a unique partnership of the National Association of State Charities Officials, the National Association of Attorneys General and the Multi–State Filer Program, a consortium of nonprofit organizations. Additionally, Form 990 requires reporting of fundraising expenses.

4. *Professional Fundraisers' Bonding Requirements.* Can states have different regulations and fees for organizations that hire professional fundraisers from those who utilize volunteers or have in-house employee fundraisers? Some jurisdictions require professional fundraisers to post a bond before commencing a solicitation on behalf of a charity. In contrast, volunteer solicitors may have a lower rate or receive complete exemption from posting a bond. Such a distinction was upheld in Heritage Publishing v. Fishman, 634 F.Supp. 1489 (D.Minn.1986).

In American Target Advertising v. Giani, 199 F.3d 1241 (10th Cir. 2000), cert. denied, 531 U.S. 811, 121 S.Ct. 34 (2000), the Tenth Circuit struck down several provisions of Utah's Charitable Solicitations Act but upheld other sections including registration and annual fee requirements, and disclosure mandates. American Target offered fundraising services to nonprofit organizations and entered into a contract with a nonprofit, Judicial Watch, to manage its national direct mail campaign. By virtue of this contract, American Target was classified as a professional fundraising consultant under the Utah Charitable Solicitations Act, which required all such consultants to register with the state, obtain a permit, pay an annual fee of $250 and post a bond or letter of credit in the amount of $25,000.

American Target challenged the Solicitations Act as an impermissible abridgement of protected speech, an unconstitutional prior restraint, and maintained it had insufficient unpledged collateral on hand to secure the bond. The court found that the registration and disclosure provisions clearly targeted fraud and enabled Utah citizens to make informed decisions concerning their charitable donations. The bond requirement, however, was found to support a different state interest, providing a victim relief fund for those injured through violations of the Act which only peripherally supported the recognized interest in regulatory oversight. The court held the bond provision unnecessarily interfered with First Amendment freedoms and only peripherally supported the state interest in regulatory oversight.

5. *Disclosure of Professional Status.* In *Riley*, the Court said in dictum that " * * * nothing in this opinion should be taken to suggest that the State may not require a fundraiser to disclose unambiguously his or her professional status. On the contrary, such a narrowly tailored requirement would withstand First Amendment scrutiny." 478 U.S. at 799 n. 7, 106 S.Ct. at 3226 n. 7. The Court suggested more benign and narrowly tailored options. It gave as an example that the State may itself publish the detailed financial disclosure forms it requires professional solicitors to file which would communicate the desired information to the public without burdening a speaker with unwanted speech in the course of his solicitation. Publication might be of help to investigative reporters or foundations or corporations considering a sizable grant, but unless such requests somehow become commonplace will publication assist the typical prospective donor any more than the right to request a copy of the organization's latest annual report? See N.Y. Exec. Law § 174–b. Could a state require the

solicitor to declare at the point of solicitation the fee arrangement between the professional solicitor and the client charity?

Is the majority in *Riley* correct in footnote 11 that the requirement that a state mandates a fundraiser to disclose unambiguously his or her professional status is narrowly tailored to prevent fraud? Isn't such a prophylactic rule violative of the First Amendment, particularly when no misleading statements are made? Does your answer depend upon whether the solicitor was a professional, an in-house employee, or a volunteer?

Justice Scalia in his concurrence in *Riley* stated that he could not see how requiring a professional solicitor to disclose his professional status was narrowly tailored to prevent fraud. He assumed that donors were aware that a portion of their donations might go to solicitation or other administrative expenses and voluntary solicitors would announce their status as a selling point. He concluded: "... it is safer to assume that the people are smart enough to get the information they need than to assume that the government is wise or impartial enough to make the judgment for them."

6. *Donor Inquiries.* The Supreme Court noted: "Donors are also undoubtedly aware that solicitations incur costs, to which part of their donation might apply. And, of course a donor is free to inquire how much of the contribution will be turned over to the charity." 487 U.S. at 799, 108 S.Ct. at 2679. Another North Carolina statute required fundraisers to disclose this information on request. The court pointed out that if the solicitor refused to give the requested information, the potential donor may (and probably would) refuse to donate. Id. What if the solicitor lies? Will the donor discern the truth? Is it likely that a donor who asked for such information would contribute?

7. *Enforcement of Antifraud Statutes. Riley* suggested that the state should vigorously enforce its anti-fraud laws to prohibit professional fundraisers from obtaining money by false pretenses or by making false statements. The Illinois attorney general sued a professional fundraiser for fraud, contending that the fundraiser knowingly misrepresented to donors that a significant amount of each dollar donated would be paid over to charity when in fact the fundraiser would retain 85 percent of the gross receipts raised. The Illinois Supreme Court dismissed the complaint, concluding that the state attempted to regulate the fundraiser's ability to engage in protected activity based upon a percentage-rate limitation, the regulatory principle rejected in *Riley*.

In Illinois ex rel. Madigan v. Telemarketing Associates, 538 U.S. 600, 123 S.Ct. 1829 (2003), the Supreme Court unanimously reversed. Treating the case as a fraud action, the Court held that fraudulent charitable solicitation is unprotected speech, and the states may maintain fraud actions when fundraisers make false or misleading misrepresentations designed to deceive donors about how their donations will be used. The Court distinguished fraud actions, which focus on representations made in individual cases, from statutes that categorically ban solicitations when fundraising costs run high. In *Riley*, the statute did not depend on whether the fundraiser made fraudulent representations to potential donors. The

First Amendment, stated the Court in *Telemarketing Associates*, did not require a blanket exemption from fraud liability for a fundraiser who intentionally misled in its appeal for donations. The Court noted, however, that high fundraising costs by themselves or mere failure to voluntarily disclose the fundraiser's fee when contacting a potential donor do not, without more, establish fraud. Why don't state officials just prosecute fraudulent fundraisers under existing criminal statutes?

8. *Local Regulations.* Local ordinances regulating solicitation are an additional burden for fundraisers. In Gospel Missions of America v. Bennett, 951 F.Supp. 1429 (C.D.Cal.1997), a federal district court held that 60–year old Los Angeles City and County ordinances regulating charitable solicitation were unconstitutionally vague and overbroad. Although the city and county ordinances differed slightly, they required, among other things, solicitors to file a notice of intention to solicit information specified in the ordinances and additional information that the city could require in its discretion. Soliciting organizations had to disclose detailed financial information and to report personal information about board members and to file statements with "sufficient information" of any agreements made with professional fundraisers or solicitors. Solicitation was prohibited unless an information card, which included mandated language conveying the city's opinion as to the nature and worthiness of the solicitation, was presented to a potential contributor. The city retained the right to revoke the card upon receipt of additional information rendering any information set forth in the card incorrect. The ordinance also mandated that the city verify "good character" and "sufficient financial resources" of an applicant for a professional fundraiser license and required payment of a $55 fee and a $5,000 bond. The ordinances exempted solicitations made solely for evangelical, missionary, or religious purposes. Thousands of municipalities have similar regulations.

The court held that the requirement that an information card be given or exhibited to solicited persons was not facially invalid under the First Amendment. However, the other provisions as drafted were unconstitutional, because they were overbroad and so vague that persons of common intelligence could only guess at their meaning. Several provisions placed unbridled discretion in the hands of officials and constituted a prior restraint on speech. The exemption for solicitation for religious and related purposes violated the Establishment Clause. The provisions for disclosure of the soliciting organization's internal operations opened them to public scrutiny and were unrelated to any legitimate governmental interest. The fee and the bond were not narrowly tailored to meet the city's interests.

In another victory for fundraisers, a federal court struck down a county fundraising regulation. Pinellas County, Florida required fundraising consultants to register with the county before performing services for their clients, charities soliciting within the county. The ordinance also prohibited a charity from soliciting if it had a contract with a professional solicitor, before that person had been issued the required permit.[1] In American Charities for Reasonable Fundraising Regulation v. Pinellas County, 189 F. Supp. 2d 1319 (M.D. Fla. 2001), the court held that professional fundraising consultants assisting charities that sent material to the general public had insufficient contacts with the county to permit it to assert legislative jurisdiction. Application of the ordinance violated due process rights.

9. *Accountability and the American National Red Cross.* Does a donor in the aftermath of a disaster have the right to expect her contribution will be used for relief of victims of the incident that generated the contribution? Can an organization raise funds for x but actually use the funds for x + 1 or other activities within the organization's exempt purposes? In the aftermath of the World Trade Center attacks, over $2 billion was contributed to assist victims and their families. The American National Red Cross received nearly $1 billion. To the dismay of donors, victims and the public, the disaster relief organization initially indicated that it was holding back $200 million of the total raised to enable it to improve the delivery of its disaster services and expand into new programs of aid for future terrorist attacks. While this may have made administrative sense, it became a public relations disaster. The Red Cross reversed itself in response to widespread criticism and faced federal and state calls for more financial scrutiny and government oversight of its operations. See Stephanie Strom, Red Cross Pressed to Open Its Books, N.Y. Times, June 5, 2002, at A7.

Young v. New York City Transit Authority

United States Court of Appeals, Second Circuit, 1990.
903 F.2d 146, cert. denied, 498 U.S. 984, 111 S.Ct. 516 (1990).

[Is there any distinction between regulating the activities of professional solicitors and homeless people begging for money? Is there a constitutional distinction between the words "Give me liberty or give me death!" and "Give me a dime"? In Young v. New York City Transit Authority, the issue was whether the prohibition of begging and panhandling in the New York City subway system violated the First Amendment.

The regulations in question prohibited solicitations for any purpose but permitted certain non-commercial activities such as: "public speaking, distribution of written materials; solicitation for charitable, religious or political causes; and artistic performances including the acceptance of donations". N.Y. Comp. Codes R. & Regs. tit. 21 § 1050.6(c). The non-commercial uses were subject to certain place restrictions—not on subway cars or within 25 feet of a token booth. Id. at 1050.6(c)(1). The district court concluded that begging constituted a type of speech that merited the

---

1. Fundraising consultants are persons or corporations retained by a charity for a fixed fee to plan, advise, consult or prepare material for solicitation, but do not manage or conduct or carry on any fundraising activities. In contrast, professional solicitors perform for compensation any service in connection with contributions, which will be solicited by the compensated persons.

full protection of the First Amendment and permanently enjoined the enforcement of the ban on panhandling. It was unable to distinguish charitable solicitation and begging on the basis of the diminished communicative content of begging, the differences between the relative intents of the two types of solicitors or the historical treatment of begging.

The Second Circuit, in a decision by Judge Altimari, reversed. The court held that the regulation was justified by governmental interests that were content neutral and unrelated to the suppression of free speech. Id. at 148. It concluded that begging was much more conduct than speech. In determining whether the conduct possessed sufficient communicative elements and an intent to convey a particularized message that was likely to be understood by those who viewed it, the court concluded that most beggars did not intend to convey any social or political message. Rather, the court found, "they beg to collect money," and thus speech was not the essence of the act. Id. at 153. Would the result be the same if the individual was soliciting for or was a representative of the Coalition for the Homeless? As to the distinction between begging and the charitable solicitation cases commencing with *Schaumburg*, the Court continued:]

On this appeal the plaintiffs also argue that there is no meaningful distinction between begging and other types of charitable solicitation. The contention is an echo of the district court's finding that "a meaningful distinction cannot be drawn for First Amendment purposes between solicitations for charity and begging." The district court based its finding on three Supreme Court cases: Schaumburg, supra; Secretary of State of Maryland v. Joseph H. Munson Co., Inc., 467 U.S. 947, 104 S.Ct. 2839, 81 L.Ed.2d 786 (1984); and Riley v. National Federation of The Blind of North Carolina, Inc., 487 U.S. 781. In these cases the Supreme Court considered laws regulating solicitations by organized charities, and held that such solicitation constituted a type of speech protected by the First Amendment. At a loss to detect a distinction between such solicitation and begging, the district court reasoned that begging must also enjoy constitutional protection. The district court apparently assumed that the outcome of the three Supreme Court cases would have been the same if, instead of involving door-to-door solicitation by organized charities, they had involved begging and panhandling in the subway. We think that the district court misconstrued the line of reasoning that underpins the trilogy * * *.

[N]either Schaumburg nor its progeny stand for the proposition that begging and panhandling are protected speech under the First Amendment. Rather, these cases hold that there is a sufficient nexus between solicitation by organized charities and a "variety of speech interests" to invoke protection under the First Amendment.

Consistent with the Schaumburg reasoning, the TA [Transit Authority] amended 21 N.Y.C.R.R. § 1050.6 to allow for solicitation by organized charities in certain areas of the subway system, while totally prohibiting begging and panhandling. Despite the district court's inability to draw a distinction between begging and solicitation by organized charities, the amended regulation reflects the TA's ability to do so. Before the district court was evidence that subway passengers experience begging as intimidating, harassing and threatening. Moreover, the passengers perceive that beggars and panhandlers pervade the system. Indeed, such conduct has been reported in virtually every part of the system. Nowhere in the record is there any indication that passengers felt intimidated by organized charities. In amending the regulation based on its experience, the TA drew a distinction between the harmful effects caused by individual begging and the First Amendment interests associated with solicitation by organized charities. Further, the TA obviously made a judgment that while solicitation by organized charities could be contained to certain areas of the system, the problems posed by begging and panhandling could be addressed by nothing less than the enforcement of a total ban. We think that the amendment of the regulation reflects the TA's concerns to respect the First Amendment in accordance with Schaumburg and at the same time to protect its patrons from being accosted. We find no reason to quarrel with these legitimate concerns.

Both the reasoning of Schaumburg and the experience of the TA point to the difference between begging and solicitation by organized charities. In the instant case, the difference must be examined not from the imaginary heights of Mount Olympus but from the very real context of the New York City subway. While organized charities serve community interests by enhancing communication and disseminating ideas, the conduct of begging and panhandling in the subway amounts to nothing less than a menace to the common good. See Members of the City Council of the City of Los Angeles v. Taxpayers for Vincent, 466 U.S. 789, 805, 104 S.Ct. 2118, 2128, 80 L.Ed.2d 772 (1984)(The government may "protect its citizens from unwanted exposure to certain methods of expression which may legitimately be deemed a public nuisance."). The lone dissent in *Schaumburg* recognized this difference stating: "[N]othing in the United States Constitution should prevent residents of a community from making the collective judgment that certain worthy charities may solicit * * * while at the same time insulating themselves against panhandlers, profiteers, and peddlers." *Schaumburg*, 444 U.S. at 644, 100 S.Ct. at 840 (Rehnquist, J., dissenting).

The district court attempted to discredit this difference by suggesting that historically begging has not been considered a *malum in se*. Similarly, the plaintiffs warn that the prohibition of begging is "a stark departure * * * from our Judeo–Christian tradition." We are not unaware that the giving of alms has long been considered virtuous in our Western tradition. In antiquity the humanist and jurist, Cicero, said of Caesar: "Of all thy virtues none is more marvelous and graceful than charity." Some centuries later the Christian thinker, Augustine of Hippo, observed that it is essential to the virtue that "charity obeys reason, so that charity is vouchsafed in such a way that justice is safeguarded, when we give to the needy." In Medieval times the Jewish philosopher, Moses Maimonides, espoused a charity such that "no contribution should be made without the donor feeling confident that the administration is honest, prudent and capable of management." The district court itself stated that "[i]n early English common law, begging by those able to work was prohibited, but beggars who were unable to work were licensed and restricted to specific areas." Thus, while there can be no doubt that giving alms is virtuous, in the Western tradition there is also no doubt that the virtue is best served when it reflects an "ordered charity." It does not seem to us that the TA's regulation of solicitation and ban on begging are inconsistent with the concept. Although this discussion is certainly not determinative of the legal issues now before us, we mention it here only because both the plaintiffs and the district court have attributed a fair amount of weight to it. We take this opportunity, therefore, to suggest that it is not the role of this court to resolve all the problems of the homeless, as sympathetic as we may be. We must fulfill the more modest task of determining whether the TA may properly ban conduct that it finds to be inherently harmful in the subway system.

* * *

CONCLUSION

We hold that 21 N.Y.C.R.R. § 1050.6 does not violate the First Amendment, and consequently, we reverse and vacate the district court's judgment permanently enjoining the various defendants from enforcing a prohibition against begging in their respective public transit facilities. In addition, we vacate the district court's judgment declaring that N.Y. Penal Law § 240.35(1) violates the New York State Constitution.

■ MESKILL, CIRCUIT JUDGE, concurring in part and dissenting in part:

I concur with the majority opinion insofar as it vacates the district court's invalidation of N.Y. Penal L. § 240.35(1) (McKinney 1989). With respect to the First Amendment issues, however, the difficult question for me is whether any legally justifiable distinction can be drawn between begging for one's self and solicitation by organized charities. I am unable to do so, and therefore I respectfully dissent from the Court's disposition of these claims.

According to the majority, common sense tells us that begging enjoys no First Amendment protection because it is conduct unassociated with any particularized message and because begging, unlike "charitable solicitation," is mere solicitation for money with a diminished communicative content. I agree that common sense and everyday experience should inform our decision. Their true teaching, however, is that both beggars and organized charities who send representatives into the subway have one primary goal: in the words of the majority, "the transfer of money." Nevertheless, in Village of Schaumburg v. Citizens for a Better Environment, 444 U.S. 620, 100 S.Ct. 826, 63 L.Ed.2d 73 (1980), the Supreme Court saw fit to extend First Amendment protection to the fundraising efforts of organized charities. In my opinion, beggars deserve that same protection.

In *Schaumburg*, the Court held that charitable solicitation is protected because it "is characteristically intertwined with * * * speech seeking support for particular causes or for particular views on economic, political, or social issues.'' 444 U.S. at 632, 100 S.Ct. at 834. Notably, the Court did not suggest that charitable solicitation is protected expression because it is always accompanied by speech on social issues. If that were the test, then it is doubtful that any organized charity soliciting contributions in the New York subway would be engaged in protected expression. Those charities receive countless donations without engaging in any discussion whatsoever with the typical donor rushing to catch a train. Rather, the *Schaumburg* Court held that First Amendment protection attaches to all charitable solicitation, whether or not any speech incident to the solicitation actually takes place, because a sufficient nexus exists between a charity's expression of ideas and its fundraising. That is, a charity's representatives often explain the purpose of the charity's work to potential donors and perhaps engage in a discussion regarding social issues. In addition, the receipt of donations is essential to the continued existence of a charity. The record in the present case, as well as the common experience of those who ride the New York subways, indicates that begging is protected expression for exactly the same reasons.

Plaintiffs Young, Walley and Gilmore all state in their affidavits that they often speak with potential donors about subjects such as the problems of the homeless and poor, the perceived inefficiency of the social service system in New York and the dangerous nature of the public shelters in which they sometimes sleep. The speech and association inherent in these encounters is without doubt protected by the First Amendment. See, e.g., Connick v. Myers, 461 U.S. 138, 145, 103 S.Ct. 1684, 1689, 75 L.Ed.2d 708 (1983). Similarly, a beggar who holds a sign saying ''Help the Homeless'' or ''I am hungry'' is engaged in First Amendment activity. See Cohen v. California, 403 U.S. 15, 18–19, 91 S.Ct. 1780, 1784–85, 29 L.Ed.2d 284 (1971)(person wearing jacket with anti-war slogan engaged in protected expression of views). Any attempt to distinguish between beggars who hold signs or engage in discussions and those who simply ask for money would be unrealistic. Accordingly, if First Amendment protection extends to charitable solicitation unaccompanied by speech, as it apparently does, it must extend to begging as well. See Riley v. National Federation of the Blind, Inc., 487 U.S. 781, 108 S.Ct. 2667, 2677, 101 L.Ed.2d 669 (1988) (*Schaumburg* ''refused to separate the component parts of charitable solicitations from the fully protected whole''); see also Virginia State Board of Pharmacy v. Virginia Citizens Consumer Council, Inc., 425 U.S. 748, 764–65, 96 S.Ct. 1817, 1827, 48 L.Ed.2d 346 (1976)(holding commercial speech to be protected although ''not all commercial messages contain the same or even a very great public interest element'').

The majority suggests that plaintiffs are free to engage in First Amendment activity in the subway provided that they do not request donations. This is precisely the argument that was rejected in *Schaumburg* as ''represent[ing] a far too limited view of [the] * * * cases relevant to canvassing and soliciting by religious and charitable organizations.'' The rationale for the Supreme Court's rejection of this argument was that charitable organizations would be unable to continue their advocacy and dissemination of ideas without the ability to solicit donations. The majority acknowledges the importance of contributions to a charitable organization's work, but fails to recognize that a beggar's First Amendment activity is no less dependent on his requests for money. In the seclusion of a judge's chambers, it is tempting to assume that beggars could obtain jobs and spend their free time distributing leaflets or buttonholing passersby in the subway to further the cause of the homeless and poor. The record in this case, however, permits no such speculation. Plaintiff Young states in his affidavit, for example, that he solicits money in the subway so that he can buy food, medicine and other essentials, and take the subway to the Bronx, where he sometimes earns enough money unloading trucks to rent a room for the night. He receives no public assistance. Plaintiff Walley, who is fifty years old, states that he solicits donations because he is unable to find work. If he sleeps in a shelter, he receives reduced public assistance of $21.50 every two weeks. Plaintiff Gilmore's solicitation also is the result of her need for food and medical treatment. To suggest that these individuals, who are obviously struggling to survive, are free to engage in First Amendment activity in their spare time ignores the harsh reality of the life of the urban poor.

Because begging is speech protected by the First Amendment, it is necessary to determine whether the TA regulations withstand the proper level of scrutiny. I agree with the majority that the TA's regulation is content-neutral. Defendants have offered substantial evidence to support their claim that the regulations are aimed at the secondary effects of begging such as increased crime and traffic congestion, rather than at any message conveyed by the beggars. See City of Renton v. Playtime Theatres, Inc., 475 U.S. 41, 48, 106 S.Ct. 925, 929, 89 L.Ed.2d 29 (1986)(zoning restriction applicable to adult movie theaters content-neutral because aimed at secondary effects of such theaters); * * * The protected expression in this case is the beggars' speech incident to their solicitation of alms, not symbolic conduct.

NOTES

1. *Begging Statutes and the First Amendment.* If you support the minority in *Young*, is your view influenced by the fact that at least eight of the fourteen states then in the Union prohibited begging when the First Amendment was ratified? Loper v. N.Y. City Police Dep't., 766 F.Supp. 1280, 1287 (S.D.N.Y.1991), aff'd, 999 F.2d 699 (2d Cir.1993).

2. *Comparison with Charitable Solicitation.* Some courts have concluded that no distinction of constitutional dimension exists between soliciting funds for oneself and for charities. These courts have held that beggars inform the public about societal conditions and that begging is thus protected speech. Blair v. Shanahan, 775 F.Supp. 1315 (N.D.Cal.1991), mod., 38 F.3d 1514 (9th Cir.1994); Loper v. N.Y. City Police Dep't., supra.

3. *Southern California Panhandling.* Harry Perry, a roller-skating performance artist, and Robert "Jingles" Newman, an animal rights activist who solicited donations on behalf of the "Animal Freedom Fighters"

and sold literature and other items regarding animal rights, challenged a Los Angeles ordinance that prohibited sales and solicitations of donations along the boardwalk of Venice Beach, a mecca for the unconventional and a virtual carnival for vendors, performers and solicitors of all kinds. The ordinance contained two exceptions to the prohibitions: the sale of periodicals and the solicitation of donations and sale of merchandise by a nonprofit organization. The Ninth Circuit held that the ordinance, though content neutral for purposes of the First Amendment, was not narrowly tailored to serve governmental interests of protecting local merchants and aiding free traffic flow. Perry v. Los Angeles Police Dept., 121 F.3d 1365 (9th Cir.1997). The court concluded there was no justification for eliminating only those individuals without a nonprofit affiliation because there was no evidence that those without nonprofit status were any more cumbersome upon fair competition than those with nonprofit status. Los Angeles countered with a regulation prohibiting aggressive solicitation. Los Angeles Municipal Code, Ch. IV, Art. I, § 41.59 (1997). A federal district court enjoined enforcement of that regulation pending resolution of a lawsuit challenging it. Los Angeles Alliance for Survival v. City of Los Angeles, 987 F.Supp. 819 (C.D.Cal.1997)

NOTE: SOLICITATION OVER THE INTERNET

The Charleston Principles: Guidelines on Charitable Solicitation Over the Internet.

The development of the Internet presents fascinating questions concerning regulation of charitable solicitation in cyberspace. The Internet provides a less costly opportunity to engage in a national quasi-telemarketing or mail campaign. Nonprofits have taken advantage of the Internet to provide information on how to make contributions as well as the opportunity to do so. Online donations to the nation's largest charities have grown substantially. A Chronicle of Philanthropy survey of 203 large charities found that they raised a total of $1.4 billion in 2008 online. Although the rate of online giving growth declined, it still grew a median of 22 percent from the previous year's survey. Noelle Barton & Paula Wasley, Online Giving Slows, Chron. Philanthropy, May 7, 2009, available at http://philanthropy.com/article/Online–Giving–Slows/57595/.

Several Internet sites act as a clearinghouse for nonprofits by providing information about the organization, serving as a repository for contributions and the forwarding of money raised minus a fee to the designated charity. Other sites operate in ways similar to affinity credit cards which forward a small percentage of the amount charged to a designated cause. "Shop-for-a-cause" web sites promise to send a percentage of money to either causes listed on the site or in some cases designated by customers. Some charities have been listed on sites without their permission. The flow of dollars to the charity has not been seamless or regular, and many of the sites have minimum thresholds before contributions are forwarded. Are the clearinghouses and the shopping sites engaged in professional solicitation requiring registration in the states where they sell goods or individuals contribute? See Reed Abelson, Pitfalls for Internet Shoppers with Charitable Bent, N.Y. Times, March 31, 1999, at A1.

The courts have begun to wrestle with the jurisdictional and constitutional issues relating to Internet transactions. See, e.g., Reno v. A.C.L.U., 521 U.S. 844, 117 S.Ct. 2329 (1997). Assume a nonprofit organization maintains a web site which may be accessed by the residents of a particular state where the organization has no other contacts. May that state assert personal jurisdiction over the organization in order to require the nonprofit to register under that state's charitable solicitation legislation, to enjoin a solicitation, impose fines or prosecute an action on the basis of fraud? Is there a difference between the posting of a web page which must be accessed by the viewer and the transmission of an e-mail message actively sent by the solicitor?

A posting over the Internet requesting a contribution would seem to be a solicitation under the law of many jurisdictions and would subject the organization to the registration and filing requirements of those states. For instance, New York defines "solicit" * * * to directly or indirectly make a request, whether express or implied through any medium. N.Y. Exec. L. § 171–a(9). In California, solicitation for charitable purposes means "any request, plea, entreaty, demand, or invitation, or attempt thereof, to give money or property, in connection with which: (1) any appeal is made for charitable purposes; * * * " Cal. Bus. & Prof. Code § 17510.2(a)(1). The Uniform Registration Statement specifies that the "operative terms 'charitable' and 'solicitation' are defined very broadly and may even include, for example, an Internet posting by an environmental organization inviting contributions from the public."

The National Association of Attorneys General (NAAG) and the National Association of State Charity Officials (NASCO) issued The Charleston Principles: Guidelines on Charitable Solicitations Using the Internet, a series of nonbinding guidelines for state regulators concerning regulation of charitable solicitations over the Internet. The Principles assume that existing registration statutes apply to and encompass Internet solicitations and would require a charity or fundraiser that uses the Internet to solicit to register in its home state if that jurisdiction has a registration requirement. An entity not domiciled in a particular state would have to register in that state if its non-Internet activities alone would be sufficient to require registration; or if it specifically targets persons physically located in the state for solicitation; receives contributions from the state on a repeated and ongoing basis or a substantial basis; or sends e-mail messages or contacts them in other ways to promote its web site.

For a state to assert personal jurisdiction over a non-resident defendant without violating due process there must be a showing that the defendant purposefully established "minimum contacts" with the state and that the maintenance of the suit would not offend "traditional notions of fair play and substantial justice." International Shoe Co. v. Washington, 326 U.S. 310, 316, 66 S.Ct. 154, 158 (1945). Where these requirements are met, jurisdiction cannot be avoided merely on the basis that the defendant did not physically enter the state. Burger King v. Rudzewicz, 471 U.S. 462, 105 S.Ct. 2174 (1985).

The mere existence of a web site seems insufficient by itself to establish jurisdiction. There must be "something more to indicate that the defendant purposely (albeit electronically) directed his activity in a substantial way to the forum state." Cybersell, Inc. v. Cybersell, Inc., 130 F.3d 414, 417 (9th Cir.1997). In Zippo Manufacturing Co. v. Zippo Dot Com, Inc., 952 F.Supp. 1119, 1124 (W.D.Pa.1997), the court reviewed Internet jurisdiction cases and found that "[t]he likelihood that personal jurisdiction can be constitutionally exercised is directly proportionate to the nature and quality of commercial activity that an entity conducts over the Internet." The *Zippo* court used a sliding scale to determine whether or not jurisdiction could be exercised by examining the level or interactivity and the consensual nature of exchange of information that occurred on the Web site. Id. at 1124. Other courts have rejected the sliding scale approach. For instance, in GTE New Media Services, Inc. v. BellSouth, 199 F.3d 1343 (D.C.Cir.2000), the court held that the use of the web sites were unilateral acts by the individuals themselves rather than purposeful activity in the forum on the part of the web site's operators. Therefore, jurisdiction did not lie. This line of cases reflects a move toward more traditional jurisdictional principles of "intended effects" and "minimum contacts" analysis rather than the interactive nature of the web site itself. F. Lawrence Street & Mark Grant, Law of the Internet §§ 3.01[1], 3.03[3][5] (2009).

One treatise comments that "[t]here is no consensus as to what factors are relevant—or how they should be weighed—in determining whether or not there is sufficiently 'something more' upon which to base personal jurisdiction. Kent D. Stuckey, Internet and Online Law § 10.02 (2005). In Millennium Enterprises, Inc. v. Millennium Music, LP, 33 F. Supp.2d 907, 928 (D.Or.1999) the court observed, '[c]ourts have reached differing conclusions with respect to those cases falling into the middle "interactive" category identified in Zippo.... In these cases, some courts find that an interactive Website alone is sufficient to establish minimum contacts. Others find minimum contacts through additional non-Internet activity in the forum, regardless of whether the activity is related to the underlying claim. Finally, some courts require additional conduct in the forum that is related to the plaintiff's cause of action.' "

Thus, a first question with charitable solicitation is whether it is closely related to commercial activity? Other issues are the level of "interactivity" on the website and the presence of additional forum-related activity such as citizens of a jurisdiction contributing money to a nonprofit organization. Cf. Developments in the Law—The Law of Cyberspace, 112 Harv. L. Rev. 1574, 1699 (1999).

It seems clear that if someone pledges $100,000 to a charity over the Internet, the charity could sue the pledgee if she reneged on the promise. Restatement 2d Contracts § 90(2) (a charitable subscription * * * is binding without proof that the promise induced action or forbearance). If the charity reneged on its promise to name a building after the donor in return for the contribution, the contributor would have standing to sue. It would make little difference if the pledge was by mail, telephone, e-mail or Internet. Jurisdictionally, an Internet transaction should be no different from any other contract. Cf. CompuServe v. Patterson, 89 F.3d 1257 (6th Cir.1996). If the charity was a sham and used the contribution for non-exempt purposes, would the attorney general of the state where the contribution was made have jurisdiction? Or if an organization has solicited residents of a particular state and residents of that state have made contributions to the charity, it seems that state's attorney general would have standing to sue the charity locally and to force it to register. The Charleston Principles put aside jurisdictional principles by declaring that states will enforce the law against any entity whose Internet solicitations mislead or defraud persons within the particular state without regard to whether that entity is domiciled or required to register in that state. *Principles*, Art. II.

In Heroes, Inc. v. Heroes Foundation, 958 F.Supp. 1 (D.D.C.1996), the plaintiff, a charity located in the District of Columbia, sued the Boomer Esiason Hero's Benevolent Fund for trademark infringement. The defendant, a New York charitable corporation which solicited funds to support the survivors of police officers and firefighters killed in the line of duty and to find a cure for cystic fibrosis, moved to dismiss for lack of personal jurisdiction. The plaintiff was required to show that the defendant met the requirements of the District's long-arm statute. The court held that it could exercise personal jurisdiction because the defendant had purposefully availed itself of the privilege of conducting activities in the District of Columbia by soliciting donations on its web site and in the Washington Post:

> Because the defendant's home page is not the only contact before the Court, * * * the Court need not decide whether the defendant's home page by itself subjects the defendant to personal jurisdiction in the District. In weighing the importance of this particular contact, however, the Court notes that the defendant's home page explicitly solicits contributions, and provides a toll-free telephone number for that purpose. The home page also contains the defendant's allegedly infringing trademark and logo, the subject of the plaintiff's underlying claims. And the home page is certainly a sustained contact with the District; it has been possible for a District resident to gain access to it at any time since it was first posted.

Id. at 13–14. See also Carefirst of Md. Inc. v. Carefirst Pregnancy Ctrs. Inc., 334 F.3d 390 (4th Cir. 2003) ("semi-interactive" website insufficient to find minimum contacts where only concrete exchange with Maryland residents was single donation); MADD v. DAMMADD, Inc., 2003 WL 292162 (N.D.Tex.) (suit by Texas nonprofit against New York nonprofit for trade infringement dismissed; site's activities, though allowing interaction and exchanges with Texas residents, were no more than "attenuated contacts" where with regards to donations, there were no more than five donors with contributions amounting to only two percent of organization's annual contributions); Obermaier v. Kenneth Copeland Evangelistic Associations, 208 F.Supp.2d 1288 (M.D.Fla. 2002) (personal jurisdiction on Texas organization existed in suit for fraudulent transfers to individuals/organizations in Florida where active solicitation over Internet site). For the tax consequences of Internet charitable giving, see Chapter 8B6, infra, at pp. 864–865.

NOTE: EMBEDDED GIVING

"If you purchase this casebook, the authors will donate one dollar to the Sturdley Home for Decrepit Law Professors." This common marketing tool is called "embedded giving," the practice of building a donation into the purchase of an item.[1] It has moved to the Internet, where search engines such as GoodSearch.com and web sites donate a percentage of the revenue received to charities. Several legal issues may arise. Some sites allow only registered nonprofits to participate in the program, but others allow the donor to name the cause, which may not be tax exempt at all.[2] Donors cannot be certain their money is going to the supposed beneficiary. Some programs fail to disclose what part of the transaction will go to charity. Charities occasionally are unaware that they are to receive these donations, and have not given permission to use their names. Who gets the charitable deduction—the donor or the manufacturer? What if the manufacturer or sponsor doesn't turn over the promised percentage to the charity?

Twenty-two states have enacted commercial co-venturer laws to deal with these issues.[3] These statutes generally require state registration, filing of contracts between the charity and manufacturer/sponsor before the inauguration of the program, the terms of the agreement, reporting requirements, and mandatory disclosures to consumers.[4] The problem with state efforts is that enforcement is minimal.

PROBLEMS

1. You are an assistant attorney general in a state that does not regulate charitable solicitation. The Attorney General has asked you to

---

1. Stephanie Strom, Charity's Share From Shopping Raises Concern, N.Y. Times, Dec. 13, 2007, at A1; Kerri Murphy, "Embedded Giving": How Do You Know Where "A Portion of the Proceeds" Are *Really* Going? (2008), paper on file with authors. This approach, also called cause-related marketing, originated in the 1980s with an American Express campaign to restore the Statue of Liberty and Ellis Island.

2. Igive.com specifies that the user can designate his or her favorite cause in the United States or Canada as the recipient of funds donated by merchants after the user makes a purchase.

3. New York defines a commercial co-venturer as "[a]ny person who for profit is regularly and primarily engaged in trade or commerce other than in connection with the raising of funds or any other thing of value for a charitable organization and who advertises that the purchase or use of goods, services, entertainment, or any other thing of value will benefit a charitable organization." N.Y. Exec. L § 171–a.

4. See Cal. Bus. & Prof. Code §§ 17510.3–17510.4 (2009).

propose legislation to deal with the problems caused by the organizations described below. What would you advise?

(a) Save Social Security for Seniors (SSSS) is an exempt organization that advocates protection of existing social security payments to senior citizens. It has raised millions of dollars through mass mailings but 98 percent has been paid over to ABC Direct Mail Services Company, a direct mail fundraising firm. Under its standard contract, ABC receives a flat monthly consulting fee, plus a per-piece charge for mail. Apart from letters to potential donors, SSSS has engaged in almost no public advocacy in support of existing levels of social security. Two of the seven directors of SSSS are present or former employees of the direct mail company.

(b) Support the Tuna, Inc. is a new charitable organization whose members believe that the tuna is a direct ancestor of humans and to eat tuna fish is a form of cannibalism and injurious to health. They have used ABC to raise money as well as the consciousness of the public to make them tuna friendly. Approximately 95 percent of the money raised has gone to ABC.

(c) Profaid is a nonprofit organization that assists retired law professors. It relies on contributions and sales of handicrafts made by emeritus professors. Profaid uses a web page to solicit contributions. For a contribution of $100, it promises to send a key ring made by Professor Roscoe Sturdley. Several residents of the state have complained to the attorney general's office that they have sent contributions but have not received the key rings. Can the attorney general do anything about Profaid?

2. Analyze whether the following statutes are constitutional and, if not, why do they fail?

(a) A state statute forbids police and fire organizations from employing professional solicitors.

(b) A county ordinance prohibits solicitation on roadways or highways of the county.

(c) A city ordinance regulates the sale of merchandise on the public streets of Metropolis, a small city. The Local Chapter of the Committee of Solidarity with the People of Fredonia operates a booth. Under the ordinance merchandisers must apply to the police department for a permit. Some of the merchandise sold contains political, religious, philosophical or ideological messages.

C. PROPOSALS FOR REFORM: FEDERAL REGULATION OF CHARITABLE SOLICITATION

Regulation of charitable solicitation has been largely a state concern and responsibility. As this chapter demonstrates, state efforts at regulation have met uncertain results when challenged for First Amendment intrusions. In the past two decades there have been increasing calls for federalizing oversight of fundraising practices. Arguments in favor of federal regulation include recognition that today many charities operate across state lines; the Supreme Court's grant of constitutional protection for solicitors; the increased compliance costs to charities from proliferation of state regulation of charities with different forms; and the increase in donor confidence engendered by federal regulation. See Developments In the Law: Nonprofit Corporations, 105 Harv. L. Rev. 1578, 1647–48 (1992) (hereinafter "Developments"). Contingent fee fundraising has been a particular concern. Over the past 20 years, several bills have been introduced in Congress focusing on contingent fee fundraising practices where a substantial part of the proceeds are used to compensate a professional fundraiser. None has been enacted.

1. *The Internal Revenue Code as Regulator*. A starting point for federal oversight of nonprofit fundraising is the Internal Revenue Code. The Internal Revenue Service requires exempt organizations to list the amount of professional fundraising fees paid to outside fundraisers for solicitation campaigns on their annual Form 990 information returns.

As demonstrated by the *United Cancer Council* case, an exempt organization using most of its funds raised to pay the costs of professional fundraisers may jeopardize its tax-exempt status. Organizations seeking to qualify for charitable exemption under § 501(c)(3) must be operated exclusively for one or more exempt purposes. Treas. Reg. § 1.501(c)(3)–1(c)(1). An organization that principally raises funds for exempt purposes must carry on "a charitable program commensurate in scope with its financial resources" and may not confer an impermissible private benefit. See Rev. Rul. 64–182, 1964–1 C.B. 186 and Chapter 5D2, infra, at pp. 458–461.

Section 4958 of the Internal Revenue Code, known as the intermediate sanctions legislation, imposes an excise tax on disqualified persons (i.e., "insiders") who receive excess financial benefits from engaging in transactions with § 501(c)(3) public charities or § 501(c)(4) social welfare organizations. A high cost of fundraising ratio could be an excess benefit transaction, and a professional fundraiser could become an "insider" if the fundraiser is "in a position to exercise substantial influence over the affairs of the organization." I.R.C. § 4958(f)(1)(A). For a discussion of intermediate sanctions see Chapter 5D3, infra, at pp. 461–474.

2. *Charitable Solicitation as an Unfair Trade Practice*. Legislation was introduced in 1990 to include nonprofit organizations within the jurisdiction of the Federal Trade Commission and impose federal disclosure and reporting requirements on charitable solicitation efforts. The bill would have applied to all nonprofits except political parties and preempted inconsistent state statutes. H.R. 3964, 101st Cong. 2d Sess. (1990). The Federal Trade Commission Act prohibits: "unfair methods of competition . . . and unfair or deceptive acts or practices." 15 U.S.C.A. § 45(a)(1). Section 13b of the FTC Act authorizes the Federal Trade Commission (FTC) to obtain preliminary and permanent injunctions to prevent unfair trade practices.

Deceptive charitable fundraising would have become a deceptive trade practice.

More recently the FTC has focused on telemarketing fraud which has included charities seeking donations. The Telemarketing and Consumer Fraud Abuse Prevention Act of 1994, Pub. L. No. 103–297, 108 Stat. 1545 (codified in sections of 7 & 26 U.S.C.), which became effective in 1995, authorizes the FTC to prescribe rules prohibiting deceptive telemarketing acts or practices and presumably could be used to regulate charitable solicitation. Id. § 3. The statute also empowers state attorneys general to bring action in federal district court to enforce the rules of the Commission if residents of their state have been affected by deceptive telemarketing but does not supersede existing authority of state officials from action under state laws. The statute clearly gives the Commission the authority to regulate charitable telephone solicitations.

3. *Crimes Against Charitable Americans.* In the aftermath of September 11th, 2001, Congress passed and the President signed the USA Patriot Act, which in § 1011, called "Crimes Against Charitable Americans," amended the Telemarketing and Consumer Fraud and Abuse Prevention Act, 15 U.S.C. § 6101 et seq. to include fraudulent charitable solicitations, which were exempted from the original sales call rules. Congress expected the enormous charitable response in the aftermath of 9/11 to be accompanied by a corresponding increase in fraudulent fundraising. This did not occur. The rules require solicitors to promptly and clearly state the purpose of their call and the name and address of the charity. USA Patriot Act, Pub. L. No. 107–56, § 1011 (2001).

4. *Unconstitutional Conditions.* Is a condition of tax exemption that requires disclosure (in other words, forcing a nonprofit organization to speak) constitutional? In a line of decisions, the Supreme Court has held that the government may not condition a benefit on the beneficiary's surrendering a constitutional right, even if the government may withhold that benefit altogether. See Kathleen Sullivan, Unconstitutional Conditions, 102 Harv. L. Rev. 1413 (1989). Professor Sullivan has pointed out that while much of this unconstitutional conditions doctrine developed in the context of outright government grants, the Supreme Court has expressly treated tax exemptions and tax deductions identically with cash subsidies for unconstitutional conditions purposes. In Speiser v. Randall, 357 U.S. 513, 78 S.Ct. 1332 (1958), the Court held that a veteran otherwise entitled to a property tax exemption may not be denied that benefit for failure to take a loyalty oath. Courts have treated cash subsidies and exemptions differently in the establishment clause area, upholding exemptions for churches, Walz v. Tax Commission, 397 U.S. 664, 90 S.Ct. 1409 (1970) but striking down grants to religious schools, Lemon v. Kurtzman, 403 U.S. 602, 91 S.Ct. 2105 (1971).

5. *Restrictive Conditions on Tax Benefits and the First Amendment.* A further issue is whether selective denial of tax benefits violates the First Amendment. The Supreme Court cases are split on whether speech restrictive conditions on tax benefits violate the First Amendment. *Compare*

Regan v. Taxation with Representation, 461 U.S. 540, 103 S.Ct. 1997 (1983), in Chapter 5F3, infra, at pp. 489–496, (federal tax law can deny tax exemption and eligibility to receive deductible contributions to organizations that engage in substantial lobbying activities while excepting veterans organizations) and Rust v. Sullivan, 500 U.S. 173, 111 S.Ct. 1759 (1991) (5–4 decision upheld administrative regulations prohibiting recipients of federally funded family planning programs from providing abortion counseling and referral advocating abortion), *with* Arkansas Writers' Project, Inc. v. Ragland, 481 U.S. 221, 107 S.Ct. 1722 (1987) (Arkansas statute that imposed a state sales tax on general interest magazines but not on newspapers and religious, professional, trade, and sports journals struck down because of its subject-matter distinction between general interest magazines and other special interest kinds), and Finley v. NEA, 795 F.Supp. 1457 (C.D.Cal.1992) (National Endowment of the Arts denial of four artists' proposals because of controversial political and social contact of works violated First Amendment). After *Rust*, would legislation requiring disclosure at the point of solicitation be an unconstitutional condition to receiving exemption from taxation?

Taxation of Charitable Organizations

CHAPTER 5

TAX EXEMPTION: CHARITABLE ORGANIZATIONS

A. INTRODUCTION

Part Two of this text considered the organization, operation, dissolution, restructuring, and regulation of nonprofit organizations from the state perspective—issues of internal governance, fiduciary obligations and duties, and the special problem of regulating charitable solicitation. Part Three shifts the focus to the federal tax treatment of charitable organizations. The Internal Revenue Code long ago emerged as a significant regulator of nonprofit activity. The requirements for obtaining federal tax exempt status, the Code's elaborate system of classifying nonprofits, and the accompanying maze of charitable deduction rules are a constant presence for nonprofit directors, managers, fundraisers, philanthropists—and scholars. As Professor John Simon has so aptly put it, "[c]harity seems destined to be enmeshed in tax policy debate not only because so is everything in our society but also because, over the years, we have come to entrust to the tax system a central role in the nourishment and regulation of the nonprofit sector." John G. Simon, The Tax Treatment of Nonprofit Organizations: A Review of Federal and State Policies, in The Nonprofit Sector: A Research Handbook 68 (Walter W. Powell ed., 1987).

Tax benefits for nonprofit organizations have a venerable history, perhaps as old as civilization itself.[1] As chronicled in the Bible, "Joseph made it a law over the land of Egypt unto this day, that Pharaoh should have the fifth part; except the land of the priests only, which became not Pharaohs * * *." Genesis 47:26. Historical studies have reported that religious institutions were not taxed in ancient civilizations because they were thought to be owned by the gods themselves and thus beyond the reach of mortal taxing authorities. Although for a time churches were subject to taxation in England and church property was confiscated during the Reformation, the practice of granting tax exemptions ultimately spread to secular charities, culminating with the British Statute of Charitable

---

1. Much of this discussion of the history of tax exemptions is derived from Chauncey Belknap, The Federal Income Tax Exemption of Charitable Organizations: Its History and Underlying Policy, in IV Research Papers Sponsored by the [Filer] Commission on Private Philanthropy and Public Needs 2025 (1977). See also Marion R. Fremont–Smith, Governing Nonprofit Organizations 56–67 (2004); John D. Colombo & Mark A. Hall, The Charitable Tax Exemption (1995).

Uses of 1601. Long regarded as the model for what was to come in America, the 1601 Statute was the first codification of charitable trust law, offering in its preamble one of the earliest lists of charitable purposes and relaxing the technical conveyancing rules of the common law to facilitate charitable transfers.[2]

The American colonists adopted the European tradition of providing tax exemptions for church property. Most of the colonies extended these benefits to higher education, with Rhode Island going so far as to exempt all the properties of the professors of Brown University from taxation. Federal income tax exemptions made their debut in 1894 with the enactment of the first corporate income tax, which included an explicit exemption for " * * * corporations, companies, or associations organized and conducted solely for charitable, religious or educational purposes * * * [and] stocks, shares, funds or securities held by any fiduciary or trustee for charitable, religious, or educational purposes * * *." Revenue Act of 1894, ch. 349, 32, 28 Stat. 556. A comparable provision has been included in every subsequent federal income tax act. The deduction for charitable contributions, proposed but rejected in 1913, was adopted in 1917 (with a limit of 15 percent of income) in response to the fear that higher tax rates would cause philanthropy to decline. It since has become one of the most entrenched features of our federal tax system.[3]

The early history of the law of tax-exempt organizations is relatively uninformative. Congress, courts, and the tax collectors paid scant attention to the nonprofit sector, preferring to concentrate on profit-seeking individuals and entities whose activities offered a more promising source of revenue. As Professor Boris Bittker observed, in the early days of the income tax law "all nonprofit organizations were lumped together and exempted from tax as though fungible members of an undifferentiated mass." Boris I. Bittker & Lawrence Lokken, 4A Federal Taxation of Income, Estates and Gifts ¶ 100.1.1 (3d ed. 2003). Beginning after World War II and continuing to the end of the 20th century and beyond, however, nonprofit organizations, particularly charities, have come under increasing scrutiny. As nonprofits gained wealth and influence, the wisdom of unbridled tax exemption and the accountability of the sector have become recurring subjects of controversy. Chapter 1 provided an introductory aerial view of these developments and the federal tax treatment of charities.[4] This and later chapters in Part Three follow up with the details.

---

2.   See Chapter 1C, supra, at pp. 25–26, and Chapter 2C3, supra, at pp. 72–77.

3.   The background and policy aspects of the charitable deduction are discussed in Chapter 8A, infra, at pp. 807–828.

4.   See excerpt from John Simon, Harvey Dale & Laura Chisolm, The Federal Tax Treatment of Charitable Organizations, in The Nonprofit Sector: A Research Handbook (Walter W. Powell & Richard Steinberg, eds., 2d ed. 2006), in Chapter 1E, supra, at pp. 41–44. See also Joint Committee on Taxation, Historical Development and Present Law of the Federal Tax Exemption for Charities and Other Tax–Exempt Organizations (JCX–29–05), April 19, 2005.

NOTES

1. *The Role of the Tax System.* In surveying the policies that shape the tax treatment of charitable nonprofits, Professors John Simon, Harvey Dale and Laura Chisolm have identified four essential functions that are useful reference points for the material to come. They are: support, equity, regulatory, and border patrol. See John Simon, Harvey Dale & Laura Chisolm, The Federal Tax Treatment of Nonprofit Organizations, in The Nonprofit Sector: A Research Handbook 267 (Walter W. Powell & Richard Steinberg eds., 2d ed., 2006).

The support function encourages the continuation and expansion of the nonprofit sector through relief from tax. As discussed in the next section of this chapter and again in Chapter 8 in regard to charitable contributions, a central policy issue is whether tax exemptions and charitable deductions are subsidies and, if so, whether this type of support is justified and appropriately provided by the tax system.

The equity function, with its goal of redistributing resources and opportunities, has its roots in the history of charity. The debate here is over the extent to which tax benefits should depend upon an organization's redistributional mission. For example, should exempt status be conditioned on service to the poor and disadvantaged? What is the appropriate degree of private benefit that may be derived by donors, and how much influence may donors wield?

The tax system exercises its regulatory function by policing the fiduciary behavior of a nonprofit's trustees, managers and donors. At the outset, this raises a recurring jurisdictional puzzle: is the federal tax system, which is intended primarily to collect revenue, the most appropriate regulator? Why shouldn't the states play a more active role? The Internal Revenue Service's dominant regulatory role pervades the law of exempt organizations, most prominently in the special regime governing private foundations.

Finally, the border patrol function shapes what nonprofits may and may not do if they wish to secure and maintain their exempt status. The constraints on lobbying and political campaign activity, for example, limit the involvement of § 501(c)(3) charities in various aspects of the political process, while the restrictions on commercial activity and the unrelated business income tax patrol the nonprofit-business border.

These four functions have profoundly influenced the behavior of the nonprofit sector. The challenge for students and scholars is to discern a coherent rationale for these policies.

2. *For Further Reading.* The leading treatises on taxation of exempt organizations are Frances R. Hill & Douglas M. Mancino, Taxation of Exempt Organizations (2002 with current Supp.) and Bruce R. Hopkins, The Law of Tax–Exempt Organizations (9th ed. 2007). An excellent survey of the area also can be found in Boris I. Bittker & Lawrence Lokken, 4A Federal Taxation of Income, Estates and Gifts, chs. 100–104 (3d ed. 2003 with current Supp.). Until 2004, the Internal Revenue Service's perspective

on substantive and procedural issues affecting exempt organizations was periodically revealed in the Service's Exempt Organizations Continuing Professional Education Technical Instruction Program textbook, which is available on line at www.irs.gov/charities/index.html. Encyclopedic coverage of current developments is provided by The Exempt Organizations Tax Review, published monthly by Tax Analysts.

————

THE ROAD AHEAD

The remainder of this chapter considers in detail the federal tax exemption standards under § 501(c)(3) for charitable organizations, which also are known as public benefit organizations under the laws of some states. Chapter 6 addresses the commercial activities of charities (and some other nonprofit organizations), including their impact on exempt status and the unrelated business income tax—the principal statutory watchdog patrolling the nonprofit-business border. Chapter 7 turns to the special tax issues raised by the distinction between public charities and private foundations. Chapter 8 concludes Part Three with a survey of the charitable contributions deduction. Issues of state and local taxation, which were previewed in Chapter 2, are addressed selectively. Mutual benefit and other noncharitable nonprofit organizations are the principal subject of Part Four (Chapters 9 and 10).

B.   THE RATIONALE FOR CHARITABLE TAX EXEMPTIONS

Virtually all charities derive their tax-exempt status under § 501(c)(3) of the Internal Revenue Code, which encompasses organizations "organized and operated exclusively for religious, charitable, scientific, testing for public safety, literary, or educational purposes, or to foster national or international amateur sports competition * * * or for the prevention of cruelty to children or animals * * *" provided that: (1) no part of the net earnings of the organization inures to the benefit of any private shareholder or individual, (2) no substantial part of its activities may consist of certain activities aimed at influencing legislation, and (3) the organization does not participate or intervene in any political campaign on behalf of any candidate for public office.

Exemption under § 501(c)(3) brings with it a wide range of additional tax benefits and exemptions from other forms of government regulation. Most importantly, virtually all § 501(c)(3) organizations qualify to receive tax-deductible contributions for income, estate and gift tax purposes. I.R.C. §§ 170; 2055; 2522. With very few exceptions, other exempt organizations are not eligible to receive tax-deductible gifts. Section 501(c)(3) charities also may be eligible to issue tax-exempt bonds to finance some of their activities (I.R.C. § 145), are exempt from federal unemployment taxes (I.R.C. § 3306(c)(8)), enjoy preferred postal rates (39 C.F.R. § 111.1

(1990)), qualify to provide special tax-deferred retirement plans for their employees (I.R.C. § 403(b)), are likely to qualify for exemption from various state and local taxes, and may be entitled to exemption under antitrust, securities, labor, bankruptcy, and other regulatory regimes.[1]

What is the rationale for all this largesse? Are tax exemptions equivalent to a government "subsidy" to the benefited groups and, if so, what makes nonprofits worthy of this government support? If it is appropriate to subsidize nonprofits, why should the support come from the tax system? What are the implications of accepting or rejecting a particular rationale for exemption? These questions are not wholly theoretical. Advisors to exempt organizations and their donors often must defend the tax benefits enjoyed by their clients. And as we shall discover shortly, the resolution of exemption qualification controversies and even some constitutional questions often turns on the perceived rationale for exempt status. It is thus appropriate to introduce the policy dimension at the outset and revisit these normative questions frequently in studying the taxation of nonprofit organizations.

1.   Traditional Public Benefit Subsidy Theories

The early history of the charitable tax exemption in the United States is surprisingly uninformative. Congress, preoccupied with the wisdom and constitutionality of an income tax, appears to have been acting based on some intuitive sense that it was simply not appropriate as a matter of history or tax policy to tax charitable organizations.[2] Courts and commentators, when called upon to explain tax exemptions, developed what is variously referred to as the "public benefit" theory, justifying charitable tax exemptions on the basis of the public benefits conferred by the organizations-benefits which relieve the burdens of government by providing goods or services that society or government is unable or unwilling to provide.[3] A variation of this traditional "quid pro quo" theory emphasizes the secondary community benefits offered by nonprofit organizations by their contributions to a robust and pluralistic American society and their role as innovators and efficient providers of public benefits.

The brief excerpt that follows represents one classic articulation of the conventional wisdom. It was prepared in 1954 for the Rockefeller Foundation by its legal counsel and later published by The Commission on Private Philanthropy and Public Needs (the Filer Commission), a panel of prominent citizens formed in 1973 to study private philanthropy.

---

1.   For a comprehensive catalog of the privileges and benefits accorded nonprofit organizations by federal, state, and local governments, see Bazil Facchina, Evan Showell & Jan E. Stone, Privileges and Exemptions Enjoyed by Nonprofit Organizations: A Catalog and Some Thoughts on Nonprofit Policymaking (N.Y.U. School of Law, Prog. on Philanthropy and the Law, 1993).

2.   See H.R. Rep. No. 1860, 75th Cong., 3d Sess. 19 (1938); James J. McGovern, The Exemption Provisions of Subchapter F, 29 Tax Lawyer 523 (1976).

3.   See, e.g., Trinidad v. Sagrada Orden de Predicadores, 263 U.S. 578, 44 S.Ct. 204 (1924).

Chauncey Belknap, The Federal Income Tax Exemption of Charitable Organizations: Its History and Underlying Policy

IV Research Papers Sponsored by the [Filer] Commission on Private Philanthropy and Public Needs 2025, 2039 (1977).

Since medieval times, certain activities rating high in the scale of contemporary values have been accorded tax exemption. From the time when old world culture was first transplanted to America, charitable activities have been granted various forms of tax favors. The basic motive for these tax favors has been a wish to encourage activities that were recognized as inherently meritorious and conducive to the general welfare. In some cases it was also true that the exempted organizations performed activities that government would otherwise be forced to undertake, but it is believed that governmental saving has not been the decisive factor influencing the exemption of charitable activities from tax.

Some of these activities, as a matter of law and tradition, fall outside the scope of government action. Others, although within the area where government action would be permissible, are regarded as better left in private hands, for two reasons. The first reason is that private enterprise and diversity of action are believed to do the specific job better. The second reason is that the preservation of the American policies of individual initiative and of decentralization is deemed vital in itself.

The co-ordinate privileges of tax exemption and deductibility for tax purposes of gifts to tax-exempt organizations are remarkably well-conceived devices by which government can aid and stimulate private charitable enterprise, without subjecting it to control.

The essence of the advantage of this system is that it is automatic. The government does not control the flow of funds to the various organizations; the receipts of each organization are determined by the values and the choices of private givers. The donors determine the direction of their own funds, and the distribution of "tax savings" as well. The income of each individual organization is a product of donations it receives and the investment wisdom of its managers. Since all of these operations are out of the hands of government under the exemption and deduction statutes, the beneficiary organizations receive their governmental aid without having to petition for it. They are, therefore, in [Harvard] President Eliot's words " * * * untrammelled in their action, and untempted to unworthy acts or mean compliances."

Similarly, under the automatic system of tax exemptions and deductions, private bodies, and not government, determine the application of the funds. Private conviction and inspiration, in all of their diversity, are free to inquire, to experiment, and to take action. Effort may be wasted, mistakes may be made, agencies may even work at cross-purposes; but in the long run the well-being of mankind is thus fostered. The basic premise of the system is that progress comes through freedom.

NOTES AND QUESTIONS

1. *Tax Expenditures*. Under traditional theory, tax exemptions and charitable deductions are viewed as government subsidies to the organizations and their donors. This form of financial support has been called a "tax expenditure" in modern tax policy parlance. As first defined by the Congressional Budget and Impoundment Control Act of 1974, P.L. 93–344, "tax expenditures" are "revenue losses attributable to exclusion, exemption, or deduction from gross income or which provide a special credit, a preferential rate of tax, or a deferral of tax liability." Id. at § 3.3. Proponents of this mode of analysis contend that tax expenditures are analogous to direct outlay programs and thus are an alternative means by which the government spends its money.

Tax expenditures are distinguished from "structural" provisions of an income tax system. Implicit in our normative structure, for example, is that a tax will be imposed on a proper yet practical concept of net income. The Internal Revenue Code thus permits taxpayers to deduct ordinary and necessary business expenses and excludes from the tax base a variety of economic benefits (e.g., certain fringe benefits) that would be impractical to include in the tax base. But many deductions, exclusions and other preferences are not compelled by structural or practical considerations. Rather, they are designed to encourage certain economic behavior or to reduce the tax liabilities of taxpayers in special circumstances. These are "tax expenditures." Familiar examples include the deductions for home mortgage interest, state and local income and property taxes, accelerated depreciation, and the exclusion from gross income for interest on state and local municipal bonds.

Harvard President Charles William Eliot, who is quoted in Belknap's excerpt above, questioned the notion of tax expenditures as far back as 1874. "It has been often asserted," Eliot said, "that to exempt an institution from taxation is the same thing as to grant it money directly from the public treasury. This statement is sophistical and fallacious." Contrasting tax exemptions with direct government grants, Eliot added:

> The exemption method is comprehensive, simple and automatic; the grant method, as it has been exhibited in this country, requires special legislation of a peculiarly dangerous sort, a legislation which inflames religious quarrels, gives occasion for acrimonious debates, and tempts to jobbery. The exemption method leaves the trustees of the institutions fostered untrammelled in their action, and untempted to unworthy acts or mean compliances.

> The exemption method is emphatically an encouragement to public benefactions. On the contrary, the grant method extinguishes public spirit. No private person thinks of contributing to the support of an institution which has once got firmly saddled on the public treasury. The exemption method fosters the public virtues of self-respect and reliance; the grant method leads straight to an abject dependence upon that superior power–Government. The proximate effects of the two

methods of state action are as different as well-being from pauperism, as republicanism from communism. It depends upon the form which the action of the State takes, and upon the means which must be used to secure its favor, whether the action of the State be on the whole wholesome or pernicious. The exemption is wholesome while the direct grant is, in the long run, pernicious.

Charles William Eliot, Views Respecting Present Exemption from Taxation of Property Used for Religious, Educational and Charitable Purposes 392 (1874), quoted in Chauncey Belknap, The Federal Income Tax Exemption of Charitable Organizations: Its History and Underlying Policy, in IV Research Papers Sponsored by the [Filer] Commission on Private Philanthropy and Public Needs 2025, 2038–2039 (1977).

As part of the budget process, the Joint Committee on Taxation and the Treasury Department prepare annual reports estimating tax expenditures. Under the Joint Committee's methodology, charitable tax exemptions are not classified as tax expenditures because "the nonbusiness activities of [such] organizations generally must predominate and * * * [i]n general, the imputed income derived from nonbusiness activities conducted by individuals or collectively by certain nonprofit organizations is outside the normal income tax base." Joint Committee on Taxation, Estimates of Federal Tax Expenditures for Fiscal Years 2009–2013, 10 (JCS–1–10) Jan. 11, 2010. This view is not universally shared by tax expenditure purists. The charitable deduction, however, is classified as a tax expenditure (see Chapter 8A2, infra, at pp. 824–825), as is the exclusion from income available to holders of tax-exempt bonds issued by § 501(c)(3) organizations.

2. *Why a Subsidy?* If tax exemptions are subsidies, what justifies the support? Would a system of direct grants be preferable? One frequently articulated justification for tax exemptions is that the benefited organizations relieve government from burdens that it otherwise would have to bear. Is that explanation underinclusive? Does § 501(c)(3) confer exempt status on organizations conducting activities that government is not obligated to undertake? Another justification is that tax exemptions support activities that provide a community benefit. Is this overinclusive? What is a "community benefit" and what agency of government is best equipped to make that determination? Do nonprofits that charge for their services, such as hospitals, theaters, and many private schools, provide a community benefit?

3. *Equitable Considerations.* When viewed as a subsidy, tax benefits for charities are challenged on equitable grounds because the economic benefit derived by donors increases proportionally to their marginal tax bracket. Under classical tax expenditure theory, the government "spends" more for charitable gifts by high-bracket taxpayers and provides little or no subsidy for gifts by low-income taxpayers, many of whom do not even itemize deductions. Put differently, the government adds proportionately more of the subsidy to a high-income taxpayer's giving and proportionately less to the low-income taxpayer's contribution. So viewed, the charitable deduction is said to have an "upside-down" effect. See, e.g., Giving in

America: Toward a Stronger Voluntary Sector, Report of the [Filer] Commission on Private Philanthropy and Public Needs 109 (1975). Do these concerns apply with equal force to the § 501(c)(3) income tax exemption and the charitable deduction? For additional discussion of the rationale for the charitable deduction, see Chapter 8A2, infra, at pp. 808–828.

2. INCOME MEASUREMENT THEORY

Beginning in the 1970s, legal scholars began rethinking the traditional rationale for charitable tax exemptions. In a seminal article, Boris Bittker and George Rahdert took issue with the mainstream subsidy theory, arguing that the exemption for public benefit nonprofits is simply a natural outgrowth of a taxing system aimed at measuring income. Under this income measurement or tax base theory, public benefit organizations are exempt because there is no reasonable way to measure their net income under established principles developed for taxing nonprofit entities. As a result, they are inappropriate objects of income taxation. If public benefit organizations were not exempt, the authors asked, how would they be taxed? Would contributions to a church or school be income? Would church property be eligible for the depreciation allowance? Would expenditures for social services be deductible as ordinary and necessary business expenses? And would it be possible to devise an appropriate tax rate? Historically, charitable tax exemptions often were justified by tax base theories—e.g., an early rationale for federal tax exemption appears to be that charities had no income. Is this historical justification still valid? The excerpt below summarizes Bittker and Rahdert's modern income measurement theory.

Boris I. Bittker and George K. Rahdert, The Exemption of Nonprofit Organizations from Federal Income Taxation

85 Yale L.J. 299, 307–316 (1976).

A. Measuring the "Income" of Public Service Organizations

Though differing in form and in the boundaries of their permissible activity, all exempt organizations engaged in public service activities share one common feature: if they were deprived of their exempt status and treated as taxable entities, computing their "net income" would be a conceptually difficult, if not self-contradictory task. From its inception, the federal income tax has been imposed not on gross receipts or gross income, but on an adjusted net amount—roughly speaking, gross income less business expenses. As a guide in computing "net" or "taxable" income, an extensive body of legal and accounting principles derived from business and financial practice has been developed. But these principles rest on the premise that the organization seeks to maximize its profit, and hence are not a satisfactory way of measuring the success of organizations that reject this basic premise. When the familiar methods of income measurement prescribed by the Internal Revenue Code, the accounting profession, or administrative practice are applied to nonprofit organizations, these methods must be stretched to, or beyond, the breaking point.

This result can be readily illustrated by a simple example. Assume that a charitable organization's receipts and disbursements for the year are as follows:

Receipts:		*(thousands)*
1.	Interest from endowment	$100
2.	Membership dues	25
3.	Gifts and bequests	75
4.	Total receipts	200

Disbursements:		
5.	Salaries of staff	$ 25
6.	Medical welfare programs for indigent persons	125
7.	Total disbursements	$150

Net:		
8.	Receipts less disbursements (line 4 minus line 7)	$ 50

The first step in computing the organization's hypothetical taxable income is to take account of its endowment income (line 1), but nothing else is this simple. Should the dues paid by its members (line 2) be treated as gifts to the organization and excluded from gross income under § 102, which provides that gifts and bequests are not taxable? Or are dues the functional equivalent of business income because the organization has obtained them by advertising its activities, promising to apply the funds to its announced charitable purposes, and allowing the members to participate in its affairs in the manner specified by its charter and by-laws? Similarly, do the gifts and bequests (line 5) qualify for exclusion from the organization's gross income under § 102, or should that provision be restricted to gifts and bequests received by individuals in a personal context, and not applied to amounts received by an organization as a result of its systematic solicitation of contributions? To the extent that dues, gifts, and bequests are used to increase the organization's endowment, should they be treated as contributions to capital, excluded from gross income under § 118?

At a more fundamental level, in view of the organization's duty to use contributions for its charitable purposes, should it be regarded as a mere conduit through which the funds move from the donor to the ultimate recipients, without creating any tax consequences for the intermediary? If an individual puts funds into a separate bank account to be used by him for charitable purposes, the deposit itself (as distinguished from interest thereon) could hardly be regarded as creating income. Should the dues and contributions received by a charitable organization be seen as a series of such individual deposits, which do not become taxable income simply because they are jointly administered by, or for, the benefactors? Or should the organization be treated as having a life of its own, separate from its contributors, and thus as having "income" when it collects funds that will be disbursed in a significantly different manner, given the natural evolution of bureaucracies, from the way the individuals would have spent their own funds if acting independently.

Once these puzzles in the definition of the organization's gross income have been solved, we must then decide which expenses may be deducted to arrive at net income. Do staff salaries (line 5) constitute "ordinary and necessary business expenses" under § 162, when paid by an organization that does not seek profits? Individuals who engage in such benevolent activities as giving money to needy relatives, acquaintances, or beggars cannot deduct their contributions, let alone any expenses for travel, advice, or bookkeeping incurred in distributing their largesse, no matter how extensive and systematic their generosity may be. Is this the proper analogy in deciding whether a charity can deduct its expenses, or should it instead be treated as an enterprise whose "business" is benevolence? The answer to these questions will bear on the proper classification of the medical and welfare program (line 6). If the salaries paid to the organization's staff are deductible business expenses because the charity's "business" is charity, then the funds given by it to the indigent should also be treated as business expenses.

The Internal Revenue Service has persistently asserted, with substantial success in the litigated cases, that expenditures not motivated by the desire for profit cannot be deducted as business expenses under § 162. For example, the taxpayer is allowed to offset any receipts generated by his "hobbies" against his related expenditures, but cannot deduct the loss if expenditures exceed receipts. If applied to non-profit organizations, this interpretation of § 162 would lead to a bizarre result, which can be illustrated by a simple example. Assume two retirement homes for the poor, each of which is operated by a nonprofit (but nonexempt) corporation and has 100 guests whose maintenance costs $3,000 per year each. If the first home operates at the breakeven point because it charges each guest $3,000 annually, it will, like the hobby farmer operating a breakeven farm, have neither income nor loss. If the second home has an endowment of $3 million, producing $300,000 interest per year, and is hence able to open its doors to guests who cannot afford to pay at all, it will have $300,000 of gross income but no deductible expenditures, because its maintenance charges do not arise in a profit-seeking venture. It will, therefore, be subject to a corporate tax of $138,500 (at current rates), or more than 45 percent of gross income, even though its guests are wholly indigent, while the other institution, whose guests may have been better off to begin with, will have no taxes to pay.

At first blush, the comparison may seem incomplete, since the personal tax status of the paying guests of the first institution has not been taken into account. Is the tax on the free institution simply a substitute for the income taxes paid by the paying guests of the first institution on their personal income, so that their $3,000 annual fees are after-tax amounts, while the expenditures of the free institution are also after-tax amounts? The trouble with this effort to reconcile the two cases is that the paying guests may be below the taxable income level, or derive their $3,000 fees from exempt social security benefits, gifts from members of their families, or other exempt sources. And even if their income had been fully taxed, their effective rate would not have been comparable to the 45 percent tax imposed on the free institution (and hence indirectly on its guests) unless they came from the upper reaches of the income ladder—$75,000 or above. Moreover, this way of analyzing the two cases suggests that the endowment income of the free institution should be imputed to the guests it supports, and this in turn implies that if they are below, or even substantially above, the poverty level, they are being grossly overtaxed.

In an effort to avoid this unpalatable dilemma, it might be argued that the concept of "business expenses" should be enlarged, by statutory amendment if necessary, to permit nonprofit institutions to deduct all amounts expended to advance their charitable or other nonprofit objectives. This would achieve substantially the same result as tax exemption, save for amounts earned in one year and either accumulated for future expenditure or spent on buildings and equipment. Since these accumulations and capital outlays are irrevocably dedicated to the institution's nonprofit objectives, however, we do not regard this alternative mode of computing a nonprofit organization's income as very appealing; nor can we see that it has any economic or social advantages over a regime of complete exemption.

If, as we believe, any attempt to treat charitable activity as a "business" is self-contradictory, can the income of a charitable organization be computed by treating its disbursements as charitable contributions, to be deducted under the rules applicable to other philanthropically inclined taxpayers? Although this approach seems more promising at the outset as a method of computing income than the § 162 route just examined, it proves on further analysis hardly more satisfactory.

To begin with, if the charity must rely on the current statutory provision (§ 170) for its right to deduct charitable contributions, it would encounter the obstacle that § 170 permits contributions to be deducted only if they are channeled by the taxpayer claiming the deduction through a nonprofit organization. Natural persons and business organizations cannot deduct charitable contributions made directly to needy individuals; and since philanthropic organizations are themselves tax-exempt, there has heretofore been no need to allow them to deduct such benefactions. If they had to rely on § 170, and it could be twisted to allow a deduction for direct grants to needy persons when paid by a charitable organization, another obstacle is encountered: taxpayers are allowed to deduct charitable contributions only up to specified percentages of their adjusted gross or taxable income—five percent [now ten percent, Ed.], in the case of corporations. If charitable organizations were subject to these percentage restrictions, they would no doubt consistently report higher profit margins on their gross receipts than the nation's most successful business corporations. A charity with $100,000 of income, for example, could deduct only $5,000 of charitable contributions if the five percent limit of § 170(c) applied, leaving 95 percent of its income as taxable "profit" even if the entire amount was spent to advance its eleemosynary objectives. Yet removal of the percentage limit for charities would mean that charities using all of their receipts for charitable purposes would be "unprofitable" as judged by Internal Revenue Code standards, while, conversely, those making the smallest current contributions would be the most "profitable," even though the retained funds were allocated for charitable expenditures in the immediate future.

* * *

So far, we have not complicated the problem of measuring a nonprofit organization's income by assuming any expenditures for nondeductible capital outlays, but the effect of such investments must be examined. If the Church of the Gospel spends all of its receipts to support missionaries who live in tents, does it have less "net income" than the Church of the Adoration, which uses some of its receipts to construct a basilica (with an estimated useful life of 50 years) and to purchase a reliquary whose useful life cannot be predicted, at least not by the secular engineering methods with which the Internal Revenue Service is conversant? If both churches were ordinary business enterprises, the former could deduct all of its expenses currently, and hence would have no net income, while the latter would have to report income currently, because it could neither deduct nor depreciate the cost of the reliquary and could depreciate only a small fraction of the cost of the basilica. No doubt a church with reliquaries and buildings is "rich" in certain senses; Savanarola might denounce its possessions as an affront to the Almighty and Sotheby's could sell them on the auction block. But in the more modest framework of an income tax system, much can be said for treating both churches alike, even if equality is not compelled by the establishment clause of the First Amendment.

Depending, then, on the answers to these riddles, and depending also on such statutory clarification as might be forthcoming, the "net income" or "loss" of our hypothetical charity is one of a dozen different amounts. By itself, this possibility, though exasperating, is not unprecedented; "income" is a vaguer concept than the layman imagines. But our excursion has taken us through several unusually murky caverns, leaving—in our view—no escape from the conclusion that the very concept of "taxable income" for charitable or other public service organizations is an exotic subject more suited to academic speculation than to practical administration.

B.   The Appropriate Tax Rate for Public Service Organizations

If despite these conceptual difficulties a satisfactory measure of the income of a charitable organization can be found, or if the difficulties are simply overridden by legislative fiat in favor of an arbitrary formula, we then face the problem of prescribing a suitable tax rate. This should not be plucked from the sky, nor should the rates prescribed for other taxpayers be applied to public service organizations unless their circumstances are comparable. Contemporary tax theorists would want a rate schedule that was consonant with either the "benefit" or the "ability to pay" theories of taxation. Though vague and malleable, these efforts to match the burden with the taxpayer's circumstances are less arbitrary than any alternative standard.

Ideally, since the economic burden of the tax will fall on the organization's ultimate beneficiaries (unless the tax prompts the benefactors to increase their gifts), the organization's income should be imputed to these recipients so it can be taxed at each one's personal tax rate. The difficulty with this approach, of course, is that the identity of the beneficiaries will rarely be known when the income is received by the organization; in this respect, they resemble the beneficiaries of a "sprinkling" trust. Recognizing that the beneficiaries of a charitable organization are usually too widely dispersed to allow an accurate imputation of the association's income, Congress might tax the entity itself, as a surrogate for its beneficiaries, at the estimated average rate at which the income would be taxed to the individuals if an imputation were feasible. As an alternative, Congress might conclude that justice would be better served by foregoing any tax on the entity's income, lest the estimated rate be higher than an accurate imputation would have produced. This decision would draw strength from the fact than an average rate, even if low, is bound to overtax the most needy beneficiaries of most philanthropic organizations.

The fact that recipients of gifts, whether they benefit from personal generosity or institutional philanthropy, are allowed by § 102 of the Internal Revenue Code to exclude these receipts from their gross income provides independent support for a decision to exempt charitable organizations. Since direct gifts from the original donor to the ultimate recipients would be excluded from their gross income, it would not be inappropriate to allow the same amount to pass untaxed through the organization, viewing it as a conduit to convey gifts from donors to their beneficiaries, rather than as an entity with independent taxpaying ability. Moreover, the benefits of a vast range of government services are received tax-free by citizens; this state of affairs has long been accepted as unavoidable, because it is simply not feasible to measure and impute the value of these benefits to the recipients in order to tax each person at an appropriate marginal rate. The largesse of public service organizations is not much different, and this analogy argues for exempting their income from taxation, thus allowing their resources to pass intact to the beneficiaries.

QUESTIONS

1. Does the income measurement theory provide an acceptable normative standard for charitable tax exemptions? Does it tell us anything about what makes charities worthy of preferred treatment or why tax exemptions are an appropriate reward? Or would Bittker and Rahdert say that these questions are irrelevant?

2. Is it accurate to say that all charitable organizations have no measurable income? What about a hospital that derives most of its revenue from fees, a school that relies primarily on tuition, or other "commercial"

nonprofits that derive substantially all their income from sales of goods or services that they produce?

3. Is the income measurement theory limited to explaining the income tax exemption for nonprofits? Does it also justify other tax benefits, such as eligibility to receive deductible contributions and real property tax exemptions? To be acceptable, should a rationale explain all the privileges and exemptions enjoyed by nonprofits?

4. As a technical and practical matter, would it be such an insurmountable task to tax nonprofit organizations?

3.   Capital Subsidy Theory

Bittker and Rahdert's attempt to articulate a more rigorous theory to justify charitable income tax exemptions went largely unnoticed beyond a small segment of the academic community. Those who absorbed it were stimulated but left dissatisfied. Professor Bittker's Yale Law School colleague, Henry Hansmann, was one of the first scholars to argue that Bittker and Rahdert had overstated the difficulties of determining the appropriate tax base for a nonprofit. For those organizations deriving all or nearly all of their revenue from the sale of goods or services, Hansmann argued, it would be no great task to import conventional tax concepts and come up with a meaningful net earnings figure. Even for nonprofits that relied on donations for their support, traditional tax concepts might be adapted by treating donations as includable in gross income and allowing deductions for the expenses of providing services related to the organization's exempt purposes. To be sure, there would be unique issues and some difficulties, but Hansmann argued persuasively that it would be possible to construct a definition of taxable income for all types of nonprofits that was consistent with the concepts employed in defining taxable income for business entities.

In a pioneering series of articles, Professor Hansmann employed law and economics methodology, first to explain the existence of nonprofit enterprises and then to examine the rationale for exemption. As previewed in Chapter 1, Hansmann concluded that nonprofit firms typically arise as the most efficient providers of goods and services in situations where, because of the circumstances under which goods or services are purchased or consumed or the nature of the service itself, consumers have difficulty evaluating the quantity or quality of the product or service. In these "contract failure" situations, for-profit firms may have an incentive and opportunity to exploit consumers, while nonprofits are viewed as more trustworthy because the nondistribution constraint prevents their founders, managers or members from diverting profits for personal use. See Chapter 1D1, supra, at pp. 33–37. Hansmann links the contract failure theory to the rationale for tax exemptions by arguing that income tax exemptions are a necessary tool to compensate nonprofits for the constraints they face in gaining access to capital markets by virtue of their inability to offer profit shares to private investors and their inadequate access to debt financing. Tax exemptions thus act as a capital formation subsidy, enabling nonprofits to finance growth through retained earnings, and they enhance the ability of nonprofits to borrow. Hansmann's theory is summarized in the following excerpt.

Henry Hansmann, The Rationale for Exempting Nonprofit Organizations From Corporate Income Taxation

91 Yale L.J. 54, 72–75 (1981).

There is an efficiency rationale for the exemption that is more appealing than [the public benefit and income measurement rationales], although it seems never to have been expressly offered before. That rationale is that the exemption serves to compensate for difficulties that nonprofits have in raising capital, and that such a capital subsidy can promote efficiency when employed in those industries in which nonprofit firms serve consumers better than their for-profit counterparts.

Nonprofit organizations lack access to equity capital since, by virtue of the nondistribution constraint [the rule that prohibits nonprofits from distributing their earnings to shareholders, Eds.], they cannot issue ownership shares that give their holders a simultaneous right to participate in both net earnings and control. Consequently, in raising capital, nonprofits are limited to three sources: debt, donations, and retained earnings. These three sources may, in many cases, prove inadequate to provide a nonprofit with all of the capital that it needs.

Donations are commonly an uncertain source of capital for nonprofits, and an inadequate one as well. Free-rider incentives presumably keep the flow of contributions to donative nonprofits—many of which provide public goods—well below the socially optimal level, and commercial nonprofits, by definition, receive few gifts of any sort. Debt, too, has distinct limits as a source of capital for most nonprofits. Lenders are commonly unwilling to provide anything near 100% of the capital needs even of proprietary firms, and are evidently even more conservative in lending to nonprofit firms. One reason for this is that, as debt comes to account for something close to 100% of a nonprofit's capital, it becomes increasingly unlikely that the organization's assets will provide adequate security for the debt. Of course, such a lack of security need not rule out debt financing. Debt, like equity, can be used as an instrument for risky investments; one need simply run up the interest rate on loans and bonds as they come to account for a larger fraction of the organization's capital. However, the transaction costs of using debt instruments for capital financing under conditions of substantial risk are high, and presumably prohibitive beyond some point well short of 100% debt financing.

As a consequence of these restrictions on external financing, a nonprofit organization's ability to accumulate retained earnings is of substantial importance as a means of capital expansion. The reason for this is twofold. First, accumulated earnings can be used directly to finance capital improvements. Second, the amount of debt financing that a nonprofit can obtain is proportional to some extent on the amount of revenue it can derive from retained earnings, since capital purchased with such earnings provides an extra margin of security for the debt, and since the cash flow from such earnings is evidence to lenders that interest payments on the debt can be covered. To be sure, retained earnings, even when added to the sources of external financing available to nonprofits, are likely to prove an inadequate source of capital where the need for expansion is strong. But at least such earnings have the advantage that they are likely to be proportional to the degree to which demand for the organization's services exceed its ability to supply them, since excess demand will generally permit the organization to raise its prices (or attract larger donations).

A case therefore can be made against an income tax on nonprofits on the ground that such a tax would (at current corporate rates) cut retained earnings roughly in half, and hence would further cripple a group of organizations that is already capital-constrained. Or, put differently, the exemption can be understood as a subsidy to capital formation.

Of course, the mere fact that nonprofits as a class have difficulty raising adequate amounts of capital does not in itself constitute a justification for providing them with a capital subsidy. Quite the contrary: if the only thing distinguishing nonprofit from for-profit providers of a given service is that the nonprofits have difficulty raising adequate amounts of capital, then a capital subsidy to the nonprofits would simply be wasteful; the industry should be left to the for-profit firms. Indeed, presumably the reason why most sectors of our economy are dominated by for-profit firms is that they constitute, overall, the most efficient means of mobilizing productive resources—including, in particular, capital.

The problem, however, is that often nonprofits are, aside from problems of capital formation, more efficient than their for-profit counterparts in providing those services characterized by contract failure. For such services, the cost of capital subsidy provided by corporate tax exemption may be more than compensated for by the efficiency gains deriving from the expansion of nonprofit producers that the subsidy encourages.

Thus, the need for capital subsidies provides some justification for exempting nonprofits from corporate income taxation in those industries in which, owing to contract failure, nonprofits have important efficiency advantages over for-profits. And this, it appears, is the strongest argument that can be offered for the current policy of exempting many, but not all, nonprofits from taxation.

This argument is not without difficulties. For one thing, as already noted, it is not obvious that the exemption as currently administered is confined to those industries characterized by contract failure. This objection could be met, however, by redefining the contours of the exemption as suggested below.

More importantly, an exemption from income taxation is a crude mechanism for subsidizing capital formation in the nonprofit sector. The extent to which nonprofit firms are capital constrained evidently varies considerably from one industry to another, and, even within industries, from one firm to another. Although direct evidence of the degree of under- or over-investment among nonprofit firms is largely lacking, there is strong indirect evidence suggesting that nonprofit firms in rapidly growing service industries, such as nursing care, have had their growth noticeably hampered by an inadequate supply of capital. At the same time, there is good reason to believe that in many cases nonprofit firms are substantially overcapitalized; this often seems to be the case today, for example, with nonprofit hospitals. Simply granting or denying income tax exemption will obviously fail to eliminate all such disparity in access to capital among nonprofit firms. The exemption alone can only ameliorate, not eliminate, severe cases of capital constraint, while, in turn, denial of the exemption will in itself be inadequate to insure that a nonprofit does not accumulate capital far in excess of the efficient level of investment.

NOTES AND QUESTIONS

1. *A Crude Subsidy?* Some critics contend that Hansmann's capital subsidy theory is flawed because it is not sensitive to differences in capital needs among different deserving types of nonprofits. A more direct and efficient method for subsidizing capital formation, so the argument goes, exists through direct grants or the issuance of tax-exempt bonds. See, e.g., Mark A. Hall & John D. Colombo, The Charitable Status of Nonprofit Hospitals: Toward a Donative Theory of Tax Exemption, 66 Wash.L.Rev. 307, 388 (1991). Why aren't consumers naturally drawn to nonprofits in contract failure situations even without a tax subsidy? Hansmann concedes that tax exemptions may be a crude mechanism for subsidizing certain "industries" within the charitable sector, such as some hospitals and nursing homes that operate in a manner similar to for-profit firms. His answer is that the tax laws "may simply be a problem of an uncritical overextension of the exemption" and he invites policymakers to consider whether the standards for § 501(c)(3) exemption, as currently interpreted, are too permissive.

2. *The Donative Theory.* Another suggested rationale is based on the premise that charitable tax exemptions should be limited to those organizations capable of attracting a substantial level of donative support from the general public. Under this "donative theory," tax exemption overcomes the funding shortfall resulting to these organizations because non-donors "free ride" on services that are provided to their charitable beneficiaries. Professors Mark Hall and John Colombo first advanced the donative theory in the context of nonprofit hospitals. Mark A. Hall & John D. Colombo, The Charitable Status of Nonprofit Hospitals: Toward a Donative Theory of Tax Exemption, 66 Wash. L. Rev. 307, 390 (1991). In a second article, they elaborated on the donative theory and described how it might be implemented. See Mark A. Hall & John D. Colombo, The Donative Theory of the Charitable Tax Exemption, 52 Ohio St. L.J. 1379, 1381 (1991); John D. Colombo & Mark A. Hall, the Charitable Tax Exemption (1995).

Implementation of the donative theory raises a host of practical questions. For example, against what base is donative support measured? What percentage of that base must come from donations for an organization to qualify as charitable? What donations count? Is it sufficient if they all come from one person or family, or must donative support be from the general public? Who is the public? Acknowledging that the appropriate threshold is a value judgment that ultimately must be resolved in the political arena, Hall and Colombo generally concluded that one-third of an organization's gross revenues should come from public donations over a four-year measuring period. They were willing to relax the one-third threshold to 10 or 20 percent for certain categories of historically exempt organizations, such as schools or hospitals. Why is one-third the magic number? Would it be more appropriate to condition exempt status on the number of donors? In the last analysis, is the donative theory inherently arbitrary or imprecise? Hall and Colombo defend the one-third test as consistent with historical experience. For example, in Chapter 7 we will see that a one-third threshold is consistent with several tests used to determine whether a § 501(c)(3) organization qualifies as a "public charity," thus avoiding private foundation status. See I.R.C. §§ 509(a)(1), (2); 170(b)(1)(A)(vi); Treas. Reg. § 1.170A–9T(f)(2). But the private foundation regulations also permit an organization to qualify as a public charity with only 10 percent public support if it engages in active fundraising and has other attributes that ensure accountability to the public. Treas. Reg. § 1.170A–9T(f)(3).

To resolve other practical implementation issues, Hall and Colombo would import many of the other rules used to determine if a § 501(c)(3) organization qualifies as a public charity. For example, they would include donations from any one source in the "good support" numerator only to the extent they did not exceed two percent of the organization's annual gross revenue and exclude one-time "unusual grants" from both the top and bottom of the support fraction, at least if the gift was from a source unrelated to the organization's management or founder. See John D. Colombo & Mark A. Hall, The Charitable Tax Exemption 193–224 (1995). How would traditional charities, such as churches, private schools, health care organizations, and cultural organizations fare under the donative theory?

3. *And What About Altruism?* Professor Hansmann's rationale for tax exemptions is grounded in notions of economic efficiency. Is this perspective too narrow? Professor Rob Atkinson challenged Hansmann's "emerging orthodoxy" by arguing that tax exemptions are justified as an appropriate subsidy rewarding the altruistic decision by a nonprofit's founders to forego profits. Rob Atkinson, Altruism in Nonprofit Organizations, 31 B.C.L.Rev. 501 (1990). Atkinson defines altruistic organizations as all nonprofits other than "mutual commercial" nonprofits (such as parent-controlled day care centers where the founders directly benefit from the organization's production). Under his altruism theory, any nonprofit organization whose income is being used to subsidize consumption by someone other than those who control the organization would be entitled to a tax exemption without any inquiry into the merits of the consumption or the

public benefits flowing from it. "The metabenefit of altruistic production would suffice." Id. at 619. As long as the organization remains nonprofit, Atkinson argues, this element of altruism remains, even if all other factors of production must be purchased at market prices. Atkinson's theory has the virtue of certainty and it would be relatively easy to administer, but it is far more expansive than the other theories.

Does altruism adequately explain why the founders of an organization choose to adopt the nonprofit form? Should any nonprofit organization be entitled to tax-exempt status simply because it agrees, by adopting the nonprofit form, to refrain from distributing any profits to private individuals? Or should there be some more limiting principle? If so, is the appropriate criterion related to the nature of the organization's activities, the sources of its financial support, or other factors?

4. *Or is it Pluralism?* Other commentators and nonprofit sector advocates argue that the desire to encourage and foster pluralism in American society is at the heart of the rationale for tax exemption. See, e.g., Bruce R. Hopkins, The Law of Tax–Exempt Organizations § 1.4 (9th ed. 2007). If so, are there any limits to the concept of pluralism that inform the qualification criteria for tax benefits to charity?

5. *Other Theories.* A variety of other theories have been advanced, primarily by academic commentators, to explain charitable tax exemptions. See, e.g., Rob Atkinson, Theories of Federal Tax Exemption for Charities: Thesis, Antithesis, and Syntheses, in Rationales for Federal Income Tax Exemption (National Center on Philanthropy & the Law, 1991), available at www.law.nyu/ncpl/libframe.html; Evelyn Brody, Of Sovereignty and Subsidy: Conceptualizing the Charity Tax Exemption, 23 J. Corp. L. 585 (1998) (viewing the charitable sector as a quasi-sovereign, which causes the system to refrain from taxing charities but also imposes limitations so that the sector does not become too powerful); Nina J. Crimm, An Explanation of the Federal Tax Exemption for Charitable Organizations: A Theory of Risk Compensation, 50 Fla. L. Rev. 419 (1998) (tax exemptions provide a government-financed risk premium to compensate nonprofits for providing public goods that will not produce an economic return); Johnny Rex Buckles, The Community Income Theory of the Charitable Contributions Deduction, 80 Ind. L. J. 947 (2005) (since government exists to promote the welfare of the community and charities are agents to benefit the community, the income of the community and its agents should be exempt from tax).

4. PROPERTY TAX EXEMPTIONS

Many nonprofits do not earn a significant net profit or rely on charitable contributions as a major source of their support. State and local tax exemptions may be the most significant governmental benefit for these organizations, especially if they own real property. Property tax exemptions historically received less scrutiny than federal income tax exemptions, but they have assumed greater importance as state and local governments seek new sources of revenue. Like income tax exemptions, property tax exemptions are justified as appropriate government subsidies to support and encourage the public benefits and service provided by the nonprofit sector. Critics emphasize the inroads from tax-exempt property into the tax base of a local municipality and the lack of any corresponding return benefits from many nonprofits to the community bearing the exempt burden. Others stress the need for all nonprofits to pay their "fair share" for essential state and local government services.

Defenders of property tax exemptions have challenged the notion of a subsidy and attempted to explain the exemption based on a "tax base defining" rationale. In a leading study, Professor Thomas Heller proposed five alternatives to the conventional wisdom: (1) if property taxes are an indirect charge for government benefits, nonprofits are exempt because it is not clear that they are substantial consumers of those benefits; (2) property taxes serve to correct deficiencies in the federal income tax, such as the failure to tax imputed income from owner-occupied housing, and no such correction is needed for nonprofit organizations; (3) property taxes are a tool of land use planning, forcing owners to convert their property toward market preferred uses—a regulatory policy that is inappropriate when applied to nonprofit landowners; (4) the property tax is a wealth tax based on redistributional principles that do not apply to nonprofit organizations; and (5) the property tax, as customarily defined, is a vestige of history without any normative principles and, under this "customary definition," nonprofits do not belong in the tax base. See, e.g., Thomas C. Heller, Is the Charitable Exemption from Property Taxation an Easy Case? General Concerns About Legal Economics and Jurisprudence, in Essays on the Law and Economics of Local Government 183 (D. Rubinfeld ed., 1979).

In a landmark study of property tax exemptions in New York, Peter Swords has argued that the incidence of property tax must fall either on an exempt organization's beneficiaries or its donors. Since beneficiaries tend to be poor, imposing taxes on nonprofit property would not pass muster under an "ability to pay" criterion. Swords also points to various secondary benefits, such as the economic efficiency that flows from the ability of nonprofits to supply public goods that otherwise would not be produced in sufficient quantities. See Peter L. Swords, Charitable Property Tax Exemptions in New York State 191–209 (1981).

For further discussion of state tax issues, see Chapter 2C2, supra, at pp. 69–71, and Section C8 of this chapter, infra, at pp. 440–445.

For Further Reading: Property Tax Exemption for Charities: Mapping the Battlefield (Evelyn Brody ed. 2002); L. Richard Gabler & John F. Shannon, The Exemption of Religious, Educational, and Charitable Institutions from Property Taxation, in IV Research Papers Sponsored by the [Filer] Commission on Private Philanthropy and Public Needs 2535 (1977); Rebecca S. Rudnick, State and Local Taxes on Nonprofit Organizations, 22 Cap.U.L.Rev. 321 (1993); William R. Ginsberg, The Real Property Tax Exemption of Nonprofit Organizations: A Perspective, 53 Temple L.Q. 291 (1980); Robert T. Bennett, Real Property Tax Exemptions of Non–Profit Organizations, 16 Clev.–Mar.L.Rev. 150 (1967).

C.   AFFIRMATIVE REQUIREMENTS FOR CHARITABLE TAX EXEMPTION

1.   ORGANIZATIONAL AND OPERATIONAL TESTS

Internal Revenue Code: § 501(c)(3).

Treasury Regulations: § 1.501(c)(3)–1(a), (b)(1)–(4), (c)(1)–(2).

As previewed earlier, the "charitable nonprofits"—those that derive their exemption from § 501(c)(3)—are by far the most important category within the nonprofit sector. They include churches, schools, hospitals, arts and environmental groups, and the broad array of other organizations that fall under the rubric of "charity." To qualify for exempt status under § 501(c)(3), an organization must meet the following requirements:

1.   It must be organized as a nonprofit corporation, or as a "community chest, fund, or foundation." "Corporation," for this purpose, is construed to include unincorporated associations, and "fund or foundation" includes wholly charitable trusts.

2.   It must be organized and operated exclusively for religious, charitable, scientific, testing for public safety, literary, or educational purposes, to foster national or international amateur sports competition (as long as the activity does not involve the furnishing of athletic facilities or equipment), or to prevent cruelty to children or animals.

3.   No part of its "net earnings" may inure to the benefit of any private shareholder or individual.

4.   No "substantial part" of the organization's activities may consist of certain lobbying activities, with substantiality being measured either by a vague balancing standard or, for eligible electing charities, by more objective expenditure tests.

5.   The organization may not participate or intervene in any political campaign on behalf of or in opposition to any candidate for public office.

The Treasury Regulations expand upon these requirements, providing that an organization must satisfy a formalistic "organizational test" and an objective "operational test." Treas. Reg. § 1.501(c)(3)–1. Although these regulations have largely been overshadowed by an increasingly developed body of case law, they are the obligatory starting point for a study of the requirements for exemption under § 501(c)(3).

The Organizational Test. The organizational test relates solely to the language used in the organization's governing document (e.g., trust instrument, articles of incorporation or association, charter; including the language only in the bylaws is insufficient), which must (1) limit the purposes of the organization to one or more exempt purposes described in

§ 501(c)(3), and (2) not expressly empower the organization to engage (except to an insubstantial degree) in any activities which do not further one or more exempt purposes. Treas. Reg. § 1.501(c)(3)–1(b)(1)(i).

The organization's purposes as stated in its governing document may be as broad as the statute itself ("formed for charitable and educational purposes within the meaning of § 501(c)(3) of the Code"), or more limiting ("formed to operate a school for adult education"), but may not be overly broad ("to promote the health and welfare of the human race") or authorize non-exempt activities ("to engage in the operation of a social club"). Treas. Reg. § 1.501(c)(3)–1(b)(1)(ii) & (iii). Nor may the articles empower the organization to engage in any impermissible activities, such as more than an insubstantial amount of lobbying or any participation in political campaigns. Treas. Reg. § 1.501(c)(3)–1(b)(3). Indeed, a properly drafted governing document should expressly prohibit the organization from engaging in impermissible political activities.

The regulations are principally concerned with the magic language in the articles of organization. Under the organizational test, it is not enough to show that an organization is actually operated for exempt purposes (Treas. Reg. § 1.501(c)(3)–1(b)(1)(iv)), although a few cases have permitted extrinsic evidence to help an organization cure a technical foot fault and preserve its exempt status (see, e.g., Blake v. Commissioner, 30 T.C.M. 781 (1971)).

Another critical element of the organizational test looks to the distribution of assets on dissolution. Either in its charter or under applicable state law, the organization must expressly dedicate its assets to one or more exempt purposes in the event of dissolution. The required dedication does not exist if assets may be distributed to the organization's members. This requirement is easily met by providing that upon dissolution the assets will be distributed to another § 501(c)(3) organization in furtherance of an exempt purpose. Treas. Reg. § 1.501(c)(3)–1(b)(4). Even if the charter is not explicit on this point, the test is met if state law requires that the organization's assets must be dedicated to a charitable purpose on dissolution. The Service has published a list of states that provide for the distribution of a nonprofit's assets by operation of law in a manner that satisfies the organizational test. See Rev. Proc. 82–2, 1982–1 C.B. 367. It also has stated that the following language will satisfy the dissolution requirement of the organizational test:

> Upon dissolution of [this organization], assets shall be distributed for one or more exempt purposes within the meaning of Section 501(c)(3) of the Internal Revenue Code, or corresponding section of any future Federal tax code, or shall be distributed to the Federal government or to a state or local government, for a public purpose.

Rev. Proc. 82–2, supra, § 2.05. See also I.R.S. Publication 557 (rev. June 2008) at 69–72 for sample organizational documents for nonprofit corporations and charitable trusts.

The Operational Test. The operational test requires the organization to engage "primarily in activities that accomplish one or more of [the] exempt purposes specified in section 501(c)(3)." Treas. Reg. § 1.501(c)(3)–1(c)(1). This test is not met if "more than an insubstantial part of [the organization's] activities is not in furtherance of an exempt purpose." Id. Examples of impermissible conduct include inurement of net earnings to private individuals and operating as an "action organization"—i.e., engaging in the substantial lobbying or political campaign activities proscribed by the Code. Treas. Reg. § 1.501(c)(3)–1(c)(2) & (3).

The operational test does little more than paraphrase the statute. Far more instructive are the evolving definitions of the "exempt" purposes specified in § 501(c)(3), as applied to fact patterns illustrated in the materials that follow, and the interpretations of the inurement and political activity prohibitions also covered later in this chapter. The "operational test" regulations, however, make one notable concession. In focusing on an organization's "primary" activities and suggesting that an "insubstantial" part of those activities may further a non-exempt purpose, they confirm that operated "exclusively" means operated "primarily" for exempt purposes. Treas. Reg. § 1.501(c)(3)–1(c)(1). Insubstantial non-exempt operations have long been tolerated by the Service, despite the seeming inflexibility of the term "exclusively." See Better Business Bureau v. United States, 326 U.S. 279, 66 S.Ct. 112 (1945). For example, a § 501(c)(3) organization may engage in some business activities unrelated to its exempt purposes without risking loss of exemption, but the net income from any such business is potentially subject to the unrelated business income tax. See I.R.C. § 511 et seq. and Chapter 6, infra.

2.   APPLICATION FOR § 501(c)(3) EXEMPTION

Internal Revenue Code: § 508(a)–(c).

Treasury Regulations: § 1.508–1(a)(1), (2)(i), (3)(i).

The Notice Requirement. Most nonprofit organizations seeking recognition as tax-exempt charities under § 501(c)(3) and as eligible recipients of tax-deductible contributions under § 170 must "notify" the Internal Revenue Service that they are applying for exemption and obtain a favorable determination of their exempt status. These requirements apply to all aspiring § 501(c)(3) organizations formed after October 9, 1969, except for churches, their integrated auxiliaries, conventions and associations of churches, and organizations other than private foundations that normally have gross receipts of $5,000 or less. I.R.C. § 508(a), (c)(1); Treas. Reg. 1.508–1(a)(3).[1] Organizations covered by a group exemption letter also are exempt from filing. A group exemption letter is a ruling issued to a central organization recognizing the exemption of a group of "subordinate" organi-

---

1. An organization's annual gross receipts are "normally" less than $5,000 if they do not exceed $7,500 for its first taxable year, an aggregate of $12,000 for its first two taxable years, and $15,000 for its first three years. Treas. Reg. § 1.508–1(a)(3)(ii).

zations—for example, Boy or Girl Scout chapters, local church parishes, and the like. Treas. Reg. 1.508–1(a)(3)(i)(C).

The notice requirement also applies to § 501(c)(3) organizations (other than churches) that seek to avoid private foundation status. See I.R.C. § 509(a). In general, any § 501(c)(3) organization formed after October 9, 1969 is presumed to be a private foundation unless it notifies the IRS that it is not a private foundation. I.R.C. § 508(b); Treas. Reg. § 1.508–1(b). The substantive rules and procedures for avoiding private foundation status are discussed in Chapter 6, infra.

Form 1023. A § 501(c)(3) organization meets the notice requirement by filing an Application for Recognition of Exemption on IRS Form 1023 within 15 months from the end of the month in which it was organized. Treas. Reg. § 1.508–1(a)(2)(i).[2] Preparing Form 1023 can be a daunting experience. Applicants must provide a narrative description of their past, present and planned future activities; detailed financial data, including a proposed 3–year budget for new organizations; and answers to a long list of questions relating to the organization's governing body, its relationship to other organizations, compensation and other financial arrangements with officers, directors, trustees and employees, and its actual and proposed fund raising activities. Certain organizations, such as churches, schools, hospitals, homes for the aged, child care providers, and successors to for-profit organizations, must provide additional information on special schedules. The exemption application was revised extensively in 2004 and now includes questions about the applicant's adherence to "best practices," such as conflict of interest and compensation policies, which are recommended but not yet legally required to obtain exemption. Even more detailed information is requested from organizations seeking to avoid private foundation status. Form 1023 also requires the organization to submit numerous attachments, including a conformed copy of its articles of organization or other enabling documents and its by-laws. Complete copies of Form 1023 and its instructions are included in the Statutes, Regulations and Forms Supplement and are available on the IRS's web site at http://www.irs.gov.

Completed exemption applications must be submitted to the IRS office in Covington, Kentucky. If an application raises unique or unsettled issues, the case may be referred to the IRS National Office in Washington, D.C. The application must be accompanied by a "user fee," which as of 2010 is $400 for organizations with annual gross receipts averaging not more than $10,000 during the preceding four years and for new organizations that anticipate not more than $10,000 gross receipts over their first four years. The fee for all other applicants is $850, except that beginning in 2010 the user fee for applications prepared using the IRS's Cyber Assistant software is $200. The user fee for group exemption requests is $3,000.

---

2. Organizations automatically may extend the filing period to 27 months if they file a completed application within the extended period and indicate that the form is being filed pursuant to Rev. Proc. 92–85, 1992–2 C.B. 490. An additional extension may be granted for good cause. Id.

An organization that files its application for exemption within the required notice period (including extensions) and receives a favorable determination letter from the IRS will be recognized as exempt from the date of its creation. The organization's donors then will be assured that gifts made from the date of creation are tax-deductible, and the organization's name will be added to IRS Publication 78, a bulky multi-volume "cumulative list" of all organizations recognized as eligible to receive charitable contributions under § 170. Publication 78's list of eligible donees also can be found on the IRS's web site and is available through several other on-line services. If the IRS requires an organization to alter its activities or organizational documents during the application process, its exemption will be effective as of the date specified in the favorable determination letter. If the application was untimely but the organization qualifies for exemption, the IRS's normal practice is to grant § 501(c)(4) exempt status up to the date when the application was filed and § 501(c)(3) status thereafter. See Rev. Rul. 80–108, 1980–1 C.B. 119. In that event contributions made before the application was filed are not tax-deductible. I.R.C. § 508(d)(2)(B).

An organization that receives an adverse determination letter will be advised of its right to file a protest with the IRS Appeals Office. Filing the protest invokes the usual IRS appeals procedures, including the right to a conference and the ability to request "technical advice" from the National Office. An organization that anticipates difficulties in obtaining a favorable determination should make its best and most complete case during this administrative process. As discussed below, exhaustion of all administrative remedies is essential to set the stage for a judicial determination through the declaratory judgment procedure authorized by § 7428 of the Code.

For other procedural issues, see Section F of this chapter, infra, at pp. 545–566.

3. THE MEANING AND SCOPE OF CHARITY

a. INTRODUCTION

Treasury Regulations: § 1.501(c)(3)–1(d)(1) & (2).

To qualify for exemption under § 501(c)(3), an organization must be organized and operated exclusively for one or more of the exempt purposes specified in the Internal Revenue Code. Treas. Reg. § 1.501(c)(3)–1(d)(1). The term "charitable" is the broadest of those purposes. Although Congress has never specifically defined the term, the regulations—borrowing principles from charitable trust law—expansively construe it in its "generally accepted legal sense" by providing that charity includes a wide range of activities that go well beyond relief of the poor. The concept of "charitable" has expanded over the years to meet changing societal needs. This evolution was well described by the Joint Committee on Taxation in the following excerpt from its 2005 report prepared for hearings convened by the House Ways and Means Committee to examine the legal history of the tax-exempt sector, its impact on the economy, and the need for more coherent tax exemption qualification standards.

Excerpt from Historical Development and Present Law of the Federal Tax Exemption for Charitable and Other Tax–Exempt Organizations

Staff of Joint Committee on Taxation, April 19, 2005 (JCX–29–05) 61–68.

C. Exempt Purposes of Section 501(c)(3) Organizations

In general

The Code lists the exempt purposes that may qualify an organization for exemption as a charitable organization, including religious, charitable, scientific, literary, or educational purposes. The meaning of such purposes is left to Treasury regulations, other administrative guidance, and court decisions. In general, none of the exempt purposes listed in section 501(c)(3) has a precise meaning. Over time, the IRS and the courts have struggled to provide meaning to the terms in the context of actual organizations, and, in general, the meanings have expanded rather than contracted.

Since the inception of the exemption for charitable organizations, issues have arisen as to the meaning of the term charitable. In general, there are two definitions of charity, the ordinary and popular sense and the legal sense. As described below, these two definitions of charity are significantly different and, depending on which is used, point to a narrowly defined or expansive charitable sector. As the law has developed, charitable has been construed in its legal sense and not in its ordinary sense.

The meaning of charity—present law

Legal versus ordinary sense

As noted above, there are two approaches to the meaning of the term charitable—the legal sense and the ordinary and popular sense. The legal definition is derived from the law of charitable trusts and is broader than the ordinary sense of the term, which generally means the relief of the poor and distressed. Since 1959, Treasury regulations have defined the term "charitable" in the legal sense, as follows:

> The term "charitable" is used in section 501(c)(3) in its generally accepted legal sense and is, therefore, not to be construed as limited by the separate enumeration in section 501(c)(3) of other tax-exempt purposes which may fall within the broad outlines of "charity" as developed by judicial decisions. Such terms includes: Relief of the poor and distressed or of the underprivileged; advancement of religion; advancement of education or science; erection or maintenance of public buildings, monuments, or works; lessening of the burdens of Government; and promotion of social welfare by organizations designed to accomplish any of the above purposes, or (i) to lessen neighborhood tensions; (ii) to eliminate prejudice and discrimination, (iii) to defend

human and civil rights secured by law; or (iv) to combat community deterioration and juvenile delinquency.

The definition is broad, encompassing several ideas that would not generally be considered as charitable in the ordinary sense. For example, the "erection or maintenance of public buildings" is not grounded in helping the poor or distressed but is directed more to the provision of a public good. The "promotion of social welfare" indicates that an activity is charitable if it aids the public at large, through community benefit programs, or by advocating ideals such as human and civil rights, even if no particular needy person is directly benefited by the activity. Thus, in general, the legal definition of charitable is best understood as including activities that are intended to benefit the general welfare or public interest (including charitable activities in the ordinary sense of the term), which itself can be construed broadly or narrowly and which will expand and contract over time to reflect changing notions of the public interest.

Public policy requirement

In addition to meeting the regulatory definition of charitable, an organization described in section 501(c)(3) is not organized and operated for exempt purposes if a purpose of the organization is against public policy or is illegal. The leading example of violation of the public policy doctrine is Bob Jones University v. United States. *Bob Jones University* concerned whether schools with racially discriminatory admissions policies qualified for exemption under section 501(c)(3). The Supreme Court concluded that Congress intended that the definition of charity be based on the common law with the result that the purpose of a charitable organization "may not be illegal or violate established public policy." [The public policy limitation is discussed in Section C4 of this chapter, infra, at pp. 370–398. Eds.]

Common law principles—charitable class and community benefit

Consistent with the Court's conclusion in *Bob Jones University* that "charity" is based on the common law, common law principles in addition to the public policy requirement inform the Federal tax law definition of charity. The charitable class requirement provides that an organization be organized to benefit a sufficiently large or indefinite class of people. The IRS has applied this rule in many cases, for example denying exemption because the class of beneficiaries served by an organization was so small as not to provide a public benefit.

The community benefit doctrine permits exemption as a charitable organization if the result of an activity inures to the benefit of the community, even though a private person is the immediate beneficiary of the activity. Through the community benefit doctrine, the IRS has recognized the exemption of an organization that gave financial assistance to legal interns, ruling that although the interns received an incidental private benefit, the purpose of the payments were to assist residents of a depressed community through the provision of free legal services.

Charity is an evolving concept, as its definition depends upon contemporary standards. In many cases, the IRS has changed the standard for charitable as conditions in society have changed. For example, until 1969 charitable hospitals were required to provide some patient care for low or no cost. This standard was changed to a community benefit standard in 1969. [The tax exemption requirements for hospitals and other aspects of the community benefit standard are discussed in Section C3b of this chapter, infra, at pp. 323–344. Eds.]

* * *

NOTES AND QUESTIONS

1. *The Evolving Definition of Charity*. As the Joint Committee excerpt describes, the tax concept of charity has evolved considerably from its earliest English origins. Proposed Treasury regulations issued in 1956, following the Service's historically restrictive interpretation, employed a "relief of the poor" concept, providing that "[o]rganizations formed and operated exclusively for charitable purposes include generally organizations for the relief of poverty, distress, or other conditions of similar public concern." Prop. Treas. Reg. § 1.501(c)(3)–1(b), 21 Fed. Reg. 460, 463 (1956). When final regulations were issued in 1969, however, the Service adopted the more expansive "community benefit" standard that owes its origins to Lord MacNaghten's venerable articulation in the 1891 case of Special Commissioners of Income Tax v. Pemsel, 22 Q.B.D. 296, A.C. 532. See Treas. Reg. § 1.501(c)(3)–1(d)(2) and Chapter 2C3, supra, at pp. 72–79.

2. *Redefining Charity*. In 2005, the House Ways and Means Committee held hearings to begin reexamining some of the fundamental principles of current law against the historical background of federal tax exemptions. A threshold question was whether charities are providing services to the public commensurate with their favored tax status. Among the other global issues raised were whether it was time to reconsider the criteria for exempt status and whether some categories of exempt entities should be eliminated.

Testimony from two law professors illustrated the difficulty of these fundamental questions. One perspective was offered by Professor John Colombo of the University of Illinois, one of the proponents of the donative theory discussed earlier in this chapter, who argued that only organizations substantially dependent on donations from the public for their operating revenue are worthy of exemption. Under Professor Colombo's theory, donations are a signal that an organization is doing something worthwhile and is not otherwise sufficiently funded by the private market or by the government.

Professor Frances Hill of the University of Miami testified that tax exemptions should be granted only to those charities that affirmatively demonstrate a public benefit to an appropriate class of beneficiaries. Noting that current administrative efforts focus largely on preventing impermissible private benefit, she argued that the absence of private benefit does not necessarily show that an organization serves a public benefit. Would the adoption of Professor Hill's affirmative benefit requirement give state and federal authorities undue authority in determining whether an organization provides a public benefit? Will this approach impose a governmentally approved conformity on the nonprofit sector? Does every exempt organization provide a tangible public benefit? See Hearings Before the House Committee on Ways and Means, April 20, 2005. Complete witness statements are available at http://waysandmeans.house/gov/hearings/asp. See also Stephanie Strom, What is Charity?, N.Y. Times, Nov. 14, 2005, at E1 (discussing the public debate over whether the nonprofit sector has drifted from the core notions of charity).

b.   HOSPITALS AND OTHER HEALTH CARE ORGANIZATIONS

Measured by assets and revenue, health care organizations are the largest component of the charitable sector. According to a recent reliable count, hospitals held 38 percent of the total assets and earned 57 percent of total revenues in the sector. Molly F. Sherlock & Jane G. Gravelle, An Overview of the Nonprofit and Charitable Sector 10 (Cong. Research Service, Nov. 17, 2009). The health care sector includes hospitals, clinics, health maintenance organizations, home health care agencies, medical research organizations, homes for the aged, and a myriad of other service providers. Health care is big business, and the legal structures have become complex. The growth of private and employer-provided health insurance, and the introduction in 1965 of government programs such as Medicare and Medicaid, altered the economics of the health care sector and transformed the American hospital, as well as the standards for federal tax exemption. More recently, the convergence of practices between for-profit and nonprofit hospitals has made it increasingly difficult to differentiate for-profit from nonprofit health care providers and to explain why nonprofit hospitals are deserving of tax exemption.

The promotion of health has long been regarded as a charitable purpose, and most nonprofit health care organizations easily qualify for exemption under § 501(c)(3) if they are organized and operated for "charitable" purposes. But what does current law require for a hospital to be charitable? The answer to that question has changed over the years as federal and state tax regulators and the courts have struggled (some would say, failed) to articulate and apply a coherent exemption qualification standard to a vast and dynamic sub-sector that appears to be drifting away from the core concept of charity.

When § 501(c)(3) was first enacted, most nonprofit hospitals operated like traditional charities by treating indigent patients and relying on volunteer labor. The Service's first articulation of a standard for hospital tax exemptions was consistent with this traditional concept. In a 1956 ruling, the Service relied on "relief of poverty" as the underlying rationale for exemption and required a tax-exempt hospital to treat indigent patients without regard to their ability to pay. Rev. Rul. 56–185, 1956–1 C.B. 202.

The ruling also required tax-exempt hospitals to adopt an "open staff" policy. In 1969, the Service replaced the charity care requirement with a community benefit standard that mirrored the concept of charitable in the treasury regulations. These and later developments are surveyed in the materials that follow.

Revenue Ruling 69–545

1969–2 Cum.Bull. 117.

Advice has been requested whether the two nonprofit hospitals described below qualify for exemption from Federal income tax under section 501(c)(3) of the Internal Revenue Code of 1954. * * *

Situation 1. Hospital A is a 250–bed community hospital. Its board of trustees is composed of prominent citizens in the community. Medical staff privileges in the hospital are available to all qualified physicians in the area, consistent with the size and nature of its facilities. The hospital has 150 doctors on its active staff and 200 doctors on its courtesy staff. It also owns a medical office building on its premises with space for 60 doctors. Any member of its active medical staff has the privilege of leasing available office space. Rents are set at rates comparable to those of other commercial buildings in the area.

The hospital operates a full time emergency room and no one requiring emergency care is denied treatment. The hospital otherwise ordinarily limits admissions to those who can pay the cost of their hospitalization, either themselves, or through private health insurance, or with the aid of public programs such as Medicare. Patients who cannot meet the financial requirements for admission are ordinarily referred to another hospital in the community that does serve indigent patients.

The hospital usually ends each year with an excess of operating receipts over operating disbursements from its hospital operations. Excess funds are generally applied to expansion and replacement of existing facilities and equipment, amortization of indebtedness, improvement in patient care, and medical training, education, and research.

Situation 2. Hospital B is a 60–bed general hospital which was originally owned by five doctors. The owners formed a nonprofit organization and sold their interests in the hospital to the organization at fair market value. The board of trustees of the organization consists of the five doctors, their accountant, and their lawyer. The five doctors also comprise the hospital's medical committee and thereby control the selection and the admission of other doctors to the medical staff. During its first five years of operations, only four other doctors have been granted staff privileges at the hospital. The applications of a number of qualified doctors in the community have been rejected.

Hospital admission is restricted to patients of doctors holding staff privileges. Patients of the five original physicians have accounted for a large majority of all hospital admissions over the years. The hospital maintains an emergency room, but on a relatively inactive basis, and primarily for the convenience of the patients of the staff doctors. The local ambulance services have been instructed by the hospital to take emergency cases to other hospitals in the area. The hospital follows the policy of ordinarily limiting admissions to those who can pay the cost of the services rendered. The five doctors comprising the original medical staff have continued to maintain their offices in the hospital since its sale to the nonprofit organization. The rental paid is less than that of comparable office space in the vicinity. No office space is available for any of the other staff members.

Section 501(c)(3) of the Code provides for exemption from Federal income tax or organizations organized and operated exclusively for charitable, scientific, or educational purposes, no part of the net earnings of which inures to the benefit of any private shareholder or individual.

Section 1.501(c)(3)–1(d)(1)(ii) of the regulations provides that an organization is not organized or operated exclusively for any purpose set forth in section 501(c)(3) of the Code unless it serves a public rather than a private interest.

Section 1.501(c)(3)–1(d)(2) of the regulations states that the term "charitable" is used in section 501(c)(3) of the Code in its generally accepted legal sense.

To qualify for exemption from Federal income tax under section 501(c)(3) of the Code, a nonprofit hospital must be organized and operated exclusively in furtherance of some purpose considered "charitable" in the generally accepted legal sense of that term, and the hospital may not be operated, directly or indirectly, for the benefit of private interests.

In the general law of charity, the promotion of health is considered to be a charitable purpose. Restatement (Second), Trusts, sec. 368 and sec. 372; IV Scott on Trusts (3d ed. 1967), sec. 368 and sec. 372. A nonprofit organization whose purpose and activity are providing hospital care is promoting health and may, therefore, qualify as organized and operated in furtherance of a charitable purpose. If it meets the other requirements of section 501(c)(3) of the Code, it will qualify for exemption from Federal income tax under section 501(a).

Since the purpose and activity of Hospital A, apart from its related educational and research activities and purposes, are providing hospital care on a nonprofit basis for members of its community, it is organized and operated in furtherance of a purpose considered "charitable" in the generally accepted legal sense of that term. The promotion of health, like the relief of poverty and the advancement of education and religion, is one of the purposes in the general law of charity that is deemed beneficial to the community as a whole even though the class of beneficiaries eligible to receive a direct benefit from its activities does not include all members of the community, such as indigent members of the community, provided that the class is not so small that its relief is not of benefit to the community. Restatement (Second), Trusts, sec. 368, comment (b) and sec. 372, comments (b) and (c); IV Scott on Trusts (3d ed. 1967), sec. 368 and sec. 372.2. By operating an emergency room open to all persons and by providing hospital care for all those persons in the community able to pay the cost thereof either directly or through third party reimbursement, Hospital A is promoting the health of a class of persons that is broad enough to benefit the community.

The fact that Hospital A operates at an annual surplus of receipts over disbursements does not preclude its exemption. By using its surplus funds to improve the quality of patient care, expand its facilities, and advance its medical training, education, and research programs, the hospital is operating in furtherance of its exempt purposes.

Furthermore, Hospital A is operated to serve a public rather than a private interest. Control of the hospital rests with its board of trustees, which is composed of independent civic leaders. The hospital maintains an open medical staff, with privileges available to all qualified physicians. Members of its active medical staff have the privilege of leasing available space in its medical building. It operates an active and generally accessible emergency room. These factors indicate that the use and control of Hospital A are for the benefit of the public and that no part of the income of the organization is inuring to the benefit of any private individual nor is any private interest being served.

Accordingly, it is held that Hospital A is exempt from Federal income tax under section 501(c)(3) of the Code.

Hospital B is also providing hospital care. However, in order to qualify under section 501(c)(3) of the Code, an organization must be organized and operated exclusively for one or more of the purposes set forth in that section. Hospital B was initially established as a proprietary institution operated for the benefit of its owners. Although its ownership has been transferred to a nonprofit organization, the hospital has continued to operate for the private benefit of its original owners who exercise control over the hospital through the board of trustees and the medical committee. They have used their control to restrict the number of doctors admitted to the medical staff, to enter into favorable rental agreements with the hospital, and to limit emergency room care and hospital admission substantially to their own patients. These facts indicate that the hospital is operated for the private benefit of its original owners, rather than for the exclusive benefit of the public. See Sonora Community Hospital v. Commissioner, 46 T.C. 519 (1966), aff'd. 397 F.2d 814 (1968).

Accordingly, it is held that Hospital B does not qualify for exemption from Federal income tax under section 501(c)(3) of the Code. In considering whether a nonprofit hospital claiming such exemption is operated to serve a private benefit, the Service will weigh all of the relevant facts and circumstances in each case. The absence of particular factors set forth above or the presence of other factors will not necessary be determinative.

NOTES AND QUESTIONS

1. *The Community Benefit Standard: Early Origins.* Revenue Ruling 69–545 was the IRS's first major articulation of the community benefit standard. The ruling was not based on any thoughtful public policy debate but rather was the result of a successful lobbying effort by nonprofit hospitals. They argued that the arrival of Medicare and Medicaid and the growth of private insurance would eliminate demand for charity care, rendering the traditional relief of the poor standard anachronistic. For the definitive critical history of the ruling, see Daniel M. Fox & Daniel C. Schaffer, Tax Administration as Health Policy: Hospitals, the Internal Revenue Service, and the Courts, 16 J. Health Pol., Pol'y & Law 251 (1991).

2. *An Unsuccessful Challenge.* The validity of Revenue Ruling 69–545 was challenged by a group of health and welfare organizations, poverty rights advocates, and private individuals. This coalition found a sympathetic audience in the federal district court, which held that Congress had intended to define the term charitable narrowly, granting exemptions only to those hospitals serving the poor. On appeal, the D.C. Circuit reversed, upholding the ruling and its much broader definition of charitable. The appeals court noted that the ruling did not necessarily dispense with the "relief of the poor" standard but provided an alternative method under which a nonprofit hospital could qualify as charitable. The Supreme Court granted certiorari but held that the plaintiffs lacked standing and never reached the merits of the community benefit standard. Eastern Kentucky Welfare Rights Org. v. Shultz, 370 F.Supp. 325 (D.D.C. 1973), rev'd, 506 F.2d 1278 (D.C. Cir. 1974), vacated on other grounds, 426 U.S. 26, 96 S.Ct. 1917 (1976).

The plaintiffs in *Eastern Kentucky Welfare Rights* were urging the IRS to adhere to the traditional view of charity. Inherent in this position was that the benefit of charitable tax exemptions should only be enjoyed by charities serving society's least advantaged members—what Professor John Simon has called the "equity function" of charitable tax exemptions. See Section A of this chapter, supra, at p. 296. Is this insistence on a redistributive ethic—e.g., serving the poor—as a condition to tax exemption consistent with a modern concept of charity that seeks to promote a wider range of societal goals, such as promotion of arts and culture, higher education and pluralism?

3. *Emergency Rooms.* In Revenue Ruling 69–545, the Service ruled that a tax-exempt hospital must maintain an emergency room that is open to all persons regardless of ability to pay. What if a hospital does not operate an emergency room because state health officials have determined that such facilities would duplicate emergency services and facilities that are adequately provided by another medical institution in the community? Certain specialized hospitals, such as eye and cancer facilities, offer medical care limited to special conditions that are unlikely to necessitate emergency care and thus do not, as a practical matter, operate emergency rooms. In Revenue Ruling 83–157, 1983–2 C.B. 94, the Service ruled that these

specialized hospitals qualify for § 501(c)(3) exemption despite their lack of emergency facilities. The ruling requires other "significant factors," however, that evidence the hospital's commitment to community health care. These may include a broad-based board of directors, an open medical staff policy, treatment of medicare and medicaid patients, and the application of any operating surplus to improving facilities, equipment, patient care and medical research.

4. *Health Insurance Providers.* At one time, nonprofit health insurance providers qualified for tax exemption as § 501(c)(4) social welfare organizations. The Service's longstanding policy gave shelter to organizations such as Blue Cross and Blue Shield and their affiliates. In 1986, Congress intervened by enacting § 501(m), which disqualifies an organization from exemption under either § 501(c)(3) or § 501(c)(4) if a "substantial part of its activities consists of providing commercial-type insurance." I.R.C. § 501(m)(1). An "insubstantial" commercial insurance activity will not cause a loss of exemption, but any net revenue will be subject to the unrelated business income tax.

5. *Health Maintenance Organizations.* Revenue Ruling 69–545 can be interpreted as saying that nonprofit hospitals have no obligation to provide any charity care other than having an open emergency room. Should it be enough simply to be organized as a nonprofit corporation and provide access to health care to the "general community" or is something more required for § 501(c)(3) tax exemption? How broad must the benefited community be for a health care provider to be "charitable?" As new forms of health care providers emerged, the IRS began to confront these issues. In doing so, it appears to have retreated from the permissive standard suggested by Revenue Ruling 69–545 and contributed to a confused state of the law.

The first signs of a retreat came with the IRS's early challenges to health maintenance organizations. HMOs provide medical care to subscribers through networks of physicians, hospitals, clinics and other providers who enter into contractual arrangements with the HMO. HMOs come in many forms, but two common characteristics have troubled the Service: a membership structure (excessive private benefit?), and the resemblance of HMOs to insurance programs (substantial nonexempt purpose?). The early HMOs were group practice plans providing comprehensive health care services to members for a prepaid fee using salaried in-house staff. The Service ruled that this type of HMO was relegated to less favored tax-exempt status as a § 501(c)(4) social welfare organization. The principal rationale for denying exemption under § 501(c)(3) was that HMOs, as membership organizations, did not serve a sufficiently broad community.

In Sound Health Ass'n v. Commissioner, 71 T.C. 158 (1978), the Tax Court rejected the Service's position, but the unique "staff model" HMO in *Sound Health* was a poor test case for denial of exemption. Sound Health provided health services at a clinic facility using primarily a salaried staff. It was open both to its subscribers, who paid a fixed premium, and also to nonmembers on a fee-for-service basis. Emergency cases were handled without regard to a patient's membership status, and free or reduced rate care was provided to a limited number of indigent patients. All members of the community who could pay the premiums were eligible for membership, and a subsidized dues program accommodated some low-income patients. Sound Health also had an educational and research program. The Tax Court concluded that Sound Health made at least as strong a case of community benefit as the IRS-blessed "Hospital A" in Revenue Ruling 69–545. It also held that the prepayment feature was a valid risk-spreading device that was similar to insurance but did not result in any impermissible private benefit.

The Service ultimately acquiesced to the result in *Sound Health,* but it remained hostile to any HMO that failed to meet a 14–factor test including criteria such as actual delivery of health care services, free care and reduced rates for indigent patients, a meaningful subsidized dues program, a broad community board, and health education programs open to the entire community. G.C.M. 39828 (Sept. 30, 1987). Particularly targeted were contract model HMOs that arranged for the delivery of health care through agreements with physicians or other entities but did not actually provide medical services using their own staff. The Service's position was accepted by the Third Circuit, which held that a Pennsylvania nonprofit HMO serving a predominantly rural population of paying subscribers did not qualify for exemption under § 501(c)(3). Geisinger Health Plan v. Commissioner, 985 F.2d 1210 (3d Cir.1993). The court found that the Geisinger Health Plan (GHP), which contracted with a network of § 501(c)(3) affiliates (a clinic and two hospitals) to provide physician and hospital services to its subscribers, did no more than arrange for its paying subscribers to receive health care services. A small subsidized dues program for low-income members was not enough to establish the requisite community benefit. Despite the fact that GHP enhanced health care in an underserved rural area, the court concluded that it primarily benefited itself rather than the community. In so holding, the Third Circuit stated that the IRS did not completely eliminate a charity care requirement for nonprofit hospitals.

If one accepts the community benefit standard as articulated in Revenue Ruling 69–545, the result in *Geisinger Health Plan* seems strange because the organizational structure of the Geisinger system was mandated by state licensing requirements. As an integrated unit, GHP and its affiliates satisfied most of the Service's criteria for community benefit, but the Third Circuit was unwilling to grant exempt status to a stand-alone entity that was not an actual provider of health care. The best that can be gleaned from this muddled controversy is that the Service's current concept of community benefit requires more than simply providing health care services to paying customers, and that the tax law is having difficulty keeping up with the transformation of the health care sector.

The *IHC* case, which follows, is another court's attempt to require "something more" to establish community benefit.

IHC Health Plans, Inc. v. Commissioner

United States Court of Appeals, Tenth Circuit, 2003.
325 F.3d 1188.

■ Tacha, Chief Circuit Judge.

[Intermountain Health Care, Inc. ("IHC") was formed in 1970 as a Utah nonprofit corporation by the Church of Jesus Christ of Latter Day Saints ("the Church"). IHC assumed ownership and control of fifteen hospitals previously owned by the Church. In the early 1980s, as part of a reorganization plan, IHC formed IHC Health Services, Inc. ("Health Services"), transferring all the hospitals and related operating assets. IHC was the sole corporate member of Health Services. By the end of 1999, Health Services operated 22 hospitals in Utah and Idaho and employed approximately 520 physicians. All the hospitals participated in the Medicare and Medicaid programs. Between 1997 and 1999, Health Services provided nearly $1.2 billion in unreimbursed health-care services to patients covered by Medicare, Medicaid, and other governmental programs and furnished more than $91 million in free health care services to indigent patients. Both IHC and Health Services were recognized by the IRS as tax-exempt § 501(c)(3) organizations and were not parties to this case.

This case involved three other subsidiaries of IHC—IHC Health Plans, Inc. ("Health Plans"), IHC Care, Inc. ("Care") and IHC Group, Inc. ("Group")—that were formed by IHC to operate as health maintenance organizations within what is known as an integrated delivery system. IHC controlled the three HMOs, while Health Services provided them with centralized management services, such as human resources.

IHC's formation of three separate HMOs was largely driven by state and federal regulatory considerations, and each HMO served different constituencies. Health Plans was a state-licensed HMO and preferred provider organization. It served large and small employer groups and individuals, including Medicaid recipients. In 1999, Health Plans enrolled about 20 percent of the total population of the state of Utah, and its members included 50 percent of Utah's total Medicaid population. Care was a "direct-contract" HMO offering federally qualified health plans. Federal law required the use of a separate entity. Group was a different model of federally qualified HMO.

The IRS determined that none of the three IHC HMOs qualified as charitable. It retroactively revoked the § 501(c)(3) exemption of Health Plans and denied exemption to Care and Group. All three organizations filed a declaratory judgment suit in the Tax Court, which affirmed the IRS's determination. Eds.]

II.   Discussion

* * *

B.   Overview of Applicable Law

"Our analysis must start from the proposition that exemptions from income tax are a matter of legislative grace." * * * Thus, we must narrowly construe exemptions from taxation. * * * In this case, petitioners seek exemption under 26 U.S.C. § 501(c)(3). * * * [T]he sole question we must consider is whether Health Plans, Care, and Group operated exclusively for exempt purposes within the meaning of section 501(c)(3).

C.   Whether Health Plans, Care, and Group Operated for a Charitable Purpose

This inquiry requires us to address two basic questions. First, we must consider whether the purpose proffered by petitioners qualifies as a "charitable" purpose under section 501(c)(3). "The term 'charitable' is used in section 501(c)(3) in its generally accepted legal sense and is ... not to be construed as limited by the separate enumeration in section 501(c)(3)." 26 C.F.R. § 1.501(c)(3)–1(d)(2). An organization will not be considered charitable, however, "unless it serves a *public rather than a private interest*." 26 C.F.R. § 1.501(c)(3)–1(d)(1)(ii) (emphasis added).

Second, we must determine whether petitioners in fact operated *primarily* for this purpose. * * *

In this case, the Tax Court concluded that "the promotion of health for the benefit of the community is a charitable purpose," but found that neither Health Plans, Care, nor Group operated primarily to benefit the community. For the reasons set forth below, we agree.

1.   The promotion of health as a charitable purpose

In defining "charitable," our analysis must focus on whether petitioners' activities conferred a *public* benefit. 26 C.F.R. § 1.501(c)(3)–1(d)(1)(ii) ("An organization is not organized or operated exclusively for [an exempt purpose] ... unless it serves a public rather than a private interest."). The public-benefit requirement highlights the *quid pro quo* nature of tax exemptions: the public is willing to relieve an organization from the burden of taxation in exchange for the public benefit it provides. * * * As the Supreme Court has recognized, "[c]haritable exemptions are justified on the basis that the exempt entity confers a public benefit—a benefit which the society or the community may not itself choose or be able to provide, or which supplements and advances the work of public institutions already supported by tax revenues." Bob Jones Univ. v. United States, 461 U.S. 574, 591 (1983) (emphasis added).

a.   Evolution of the "community benefit" standard

The IRS has long recognized that nonprofit hospitals may be exempt as "charitable" entities under section 501(c)(3). See generally John D. Colombo, Health Care Reform and Federal Tax Exemption: Rethinking the Issues, 29 Wake Forest L. Rev. 215, 218 (1994). "Exemption for hospitals, in fact, is so ingrained in the lore of taxation that today about half the states specifically enumerate hospitals as exempt entities, alongside such traditional exemption bulwarks as churches and educational institutions." Id. at 215. Early on, the touchstone for exemption was the provision of free or below-cost care. Id. at 217. In 1956, the IRS published Rev. Rul. 56–185, which provided that a hospital "must be operated to the extent of its financial ability for those not able to pay for the services rendered and not exclusively for those who are able and expected to pay."

By the last part of the twentieth century, however, with the advent of Medicare and Medicaid and the increased prevalence of private insurance, nonprofit hospitals moved away from this "relief of poverty" function. Colombo, supra, at 218. "The financing of their services evolved in parallel, from primary dependence on the generosity of religious orders and charitable donors, to almost exclusive reliance on payments for services rendered." M. Gregg Bloche, Health Policy Below the Waterline: Medical Care and the Charitable Exemption, 80 Minn. L. Rev. 299, 300 (1995).

[The court then summarized the history of the IRS's published rulings interpreting the community benefit standard. Eds.] Thus, under the IRS's interpretation of section 501(c)(3), in the context of health-care providers, we must determine whether the taxpayer operates primarily for the benefit of the community. And while the concept of "community benefit" is somewhat amorphous, we agree with the IRS, the Tax Court, and the Third Circuit that it provides a workable standard for determining tax exemption under section 501(c)(3).

b.   Defining "community benefit"

In giving form to the community-benefit standard, we stress that "not every activity that promotes health supports tax exemption under § 501(c)(3). For example, selling prescription pharmaceuticals certainly promotes health, but pharmacies cannot qualify for ... exemption under § 501(c)(3) on that basis alone." Rev. Rul. 98–15. In other words, engaging in an activity that promotes health, *standing alone,* offers an insufficient indicium of an organization's purpose. Numerous for-profit enterprises offer products or services that promote health.

Similarly, the IRS rulings in 69–545 and 83–157 demonstrate that an organization cannot satisfy the community-benefit requirement based solely on the fact that it offers health-care services to all in the community[17] in exchange for a fee.[18] Although providing health-care products or services to all in the community is necessary under those rulings, it is insufficient, standing alone, to qualify for tax exemption under section 501(c)(3). Rather, the organization must provide some additional "plus."

This plus is perhaps best characterized as "a benefit which the society or the community may not itself choose or be able to provide, or which

---

17.   We recognize that certain health-care entities provide specialized services, which are not required by "all" in the community, and we do not mean to foreclose the possibility that such entities may qualify as "charitable" under section 501(c)(3). * * *

18.   At least where the fee is above cost. We express no opinion on whether an enterprise that sold health-promoting products or services entirely at or below cost would qualify for tax exemption under 501(c)(3).

supplements and advances the work of public institutions already supported by tax revenues." Bob Jones Univ., 461 U.S. at 591. Concerning the former, the IRS rulings provide a number of examples: providing free or below-cost services, see Rev. Rul. 56–185; maintaining an emergency room open to all, regardless of ability to pay, see Rev. Rul. 69–545; and devoting surpluses to research, education, and medical training, see Rev. Rul. 83–157. These services fall under the general umbrella of "positive externalities" or "public goods." Bloche, supra, at 312.[19] Concerning the latter, the primary way in which health-care providers advance government-funded endeavors is the servicing of the Medicaid and Medicare populations.

c.   Quantifying "community benefit"

Difficulties will inevitably arise in quantifying the required community benefit. The governing statutory language, however, provides some guidance. Under section 501(c)(3), an organization is not entitled to tax exemption unless it operates for a charitable purpose. Thus, the existence of some incidental community benefit is insufficient. Rather, the magnitude of the community benefit conferred must be sufficient to give rise to a strong inference that the organization operates *primarily for the purpose of benefitting the community*. Geisinger I, 985 F.2d at 1219.

Thus, our inquiry turns "not [on] the nature of the activity, but [on] the *purpose* accomplished thereby." Bethel Conservative Mennonite Church v. C.I.R., 746 F.2d 388, 391 (7th Cir.1984) (emphasis added). Of course, because of the inherent difficulty in determining a corporate entity's subjective purpose, we necessarily rely on objective indicia in conducting our analysis. In determining an organization's purpose, we primarily consider the manner in which the entity carries on its activities.

d.   The resulting test

In summary, under section 501(c)(3), a health-care provider must make its services available to all in the community *plus* provide additional community or public benefits. The benefit must either further the function of government-funded institutions or provide a service that would not likely be provided within the community but for the subsidy. Further, the additional public benefit conferred must be sufficient to give rise to a strong inference that the public benefit is the *primary purpose* for which the organization operates. In conducting this inquiry, we consider the totality of the circumstances. With these principles in mind, we proceed to review the Tax Court's decision in the present case.

---

19.   Under the Treasury Department's view, for-profit enterprises are unlikely to provide such services since " 'market prices . . . do not reflect the benefit [these services] confer on the community as a whole.' " Bloche, supra, at 312 (quoting Tax–Exempt Status of Hospitals, and Establishment of Charity Care Standards: Hearing before the House Comm. on Ways and Means, 102d Cong., 1st Sess. 34–37 (1991) (statement of Michael J. Graetz, Deputy Assistant Secretary for Tax Policy, U.S. Dep't of the Treasury)). Thus, the provision of such "public goods"—at least when conducted on a sufficiently large scale—arguably supports an inference that the enterprise is responding to some inducement that is not market-based. Cf. id.

2.   The Tax Court correctly defined "charitable" and applied the appropriate legal test under 501(c)(3)

Petitioners first contend that the Tax Court erred in its conclusion regarding the applicable law. Based upon our discussion supra, we disagree. The Tax Court correctly recognized the "promotion of health for the benefit of the community" as a charitable purpose. Health Plans, 82 T.C.M. at 602 ("[I]t is now well settled that the promotion of health for the benefit of the community is a charitable purpose."). Further, the Tax Court considered the community-benefit requirement based on the totality of the circumstances.[21] Id. at 604 ("The community benefit test requires consideration of a variety of factors that indicate whether an organization is involved in the charitable activity of promoting health on a communitywide basis.... Considering all the facts and circumstances ... we conclude that petitioner did not provide a meaningful community benefit."). Thus, the Tax Court did not err in determining the applicable law.

3.   The Tax Court correctly concluded that petitioners do not operate primarily to promote health for the benefit of the community

Petitioners next argue that the Tax Court erred in concluding that petitioners did not operate primarily for the benefit of the community. We disagree.

a.   Nature of the product or service and the character of the transaction

In this case, we deal with organizations that do not provide health-care services directly. Rather, petitioners furnish group insurance entitling enrollees to services of participating hospitals and physicians. [The court then discussed how the IHC group determined premiums based on the risk assumed and cited cases where the commercial nature of an activity cast doubt as to an entity's charitable purpose. Eds.]

b.   Free or below-cost products or services

The fact that an activity is normally undertaken by commercial for-profit entities does not necessarily preclude tax exemption, particularly where the entity offers its services at or below-cost. Cf. Bloche, supra, at 311 n. 31. But petitioners provide virtually no free or below-cost health-care services. All enrollees must pay a premium in order to receive benefits. As the Eighth Circuit has recognized, "[a]n organization which does not extend some of its benefits to individuals financially unable to make the required payments [generally] reflects a commercial activity rather than a charitable one." Federation Pharmacy Servs., Inc. v. C.I.R., 625 F.2d 804, 807 (8th Cir.1980). Further, the fact that petitioners in no way subsidize dues for those who cannot afford subscribership distinguishes this case from the HMOs in Sound Health Ass'n v. C.I.R., 71 T.C. 158 (1978), and Geisinger I, 985 F.2d at 1219.

---

21. Because the community-benefit requirement is considered under a totality-of-the-circumstances test, we reject petitioners' challenge to the Tax Court's reliance on any one of the numerous factors cited in support of its conclusion.

We acknowledge, as did the Tax Court, that petitioners' "adjusted community rating system likely allowed its enrollees to obtain medical care at a lower cost than might otherwise have been available." Care, 82 T.C.M. at 625; Group, 82 T.C.M. at 615. Again, however, selling services at a discount tells us little about the petitioners' *purpose.* "Many profitmaking organizations sell at a discount." Federation Pharmacy, 72 T.C. at 692, aff'd 625 F.2d 804 (8th Cir.1980). In considering price as it relates to an organization's purpose, there is a qualitative difference between selling at a discount and selling below cost.

In sum, petitioners sole activity is arranging for health-care services in exchange for a fee. To elevate the attendant health benefit over the character of the transaction would pervert Congress' intent in providing for charitable tax exemptions under section 501(c)(3). Contrary to petitioners' insinuation, the Tax Court did not accord dispositive weight to the absence of free care. Neither do we. Rather, it is yet another factor that belies petitioners' professions of a charitable purpose.[27]

c. Research and educational programs

Nothing in the record indicates that petitioners conducted research or offered free educational programs to the public. This bolsters our conclusion that petitioners did not operate for the purpose of promoting health for the benefit of the community.

d. The class eligible to benefit

(1) Health Plans

As the Tax Court noted, "[Health Plans] offered its [coverage] to a broad cross-section of the community including individuals, the employees of both large and small employers, and individuals eligible for Medicaid benefits." Health Plans, 82 T.C.M. at 604. In fact, in 1999, Health Plans' enrollees represented twenty percent of Utah's total population and fifty percent of Utah residents eligible for Medicaid benefits.[29]

Nevertheless, even though almost all Utahans were potentially eligible to enroll for Health Plans coverage, the self-imposed requirement of membership tells us something about Health Plans' operation. As the Third Circuit noted in Geisinger I:

The community benefitted is, in fact, limited to those who belong to [the HMO] since the requirement of subscribership remains a condition precedent to any service. Absent any additional indicia of a

---

27. As the Eighth Circuit has noted, "a 'charitable' hospital may impose charges or fees for services rendered, and indeed its charity record may be comparatively low depending upon all the facts ... but a serious question is raised where its charitable operation is virtually inconsequential." Federation Pharmacy, 625 F.2d at 807 (8th Cir.1980) (quoting Sonora Cmty. Hosp. v. C.I.R., 46 T.C. 519, 526 (1966)) (internal quotation marks omitted).

29. We acknowledge that Health Plans' service to Utah's Medicaid community provides some community benefit. The relevant inquiry, however, is not "whether [petitioner] benefitted the community at all ... [but] whether it primarily benefitted the community, as an entity must in order to qualify for tax-exempt status." Geisinger I, 985 F.2d at 1219.

charitable purpose, this self-imposed precondition suggests that [the HMO] is primarily benefitting itself (and, perhaps, secondarily benefitting the community) by promoting subscribership throughout the areas it serves.

985 F.2d at 1219. Further, while the absence of a large class of potential beneficiaries may preclude tax-exempt status, its presence standing alone provides little insight into the organization's purpose. Offering products and services to a broad segment of the population is as consistent with self promotion and profit maximization as it is with any "charitable" purpose.

(2) Care and Group

Neither Care nor Group offered their health plans to the general public. Rather, both Care and Group limited their enrollment to employees of large employers (employers with 100 or more employees). Thus, as the Tax Court found, "[Care and Group] operate[d] in a manner that substantially limit[ed] [the] universe of potential enrollees." Care, 82 T.C.M. at 625; Group, 82 T.C.M. at 615. Based on this finding, the Tax Court correctly concluded that neither Care nor Group promoted health for the benefit of the community.

e. Community board of trustees

Finally, we consider petitioners' board composition. Prior to 1996, Health Plans' bylaws provided that "[a] plurality of Board members shall represent the buyer-employer community and an approximately equal number of physicians and hospitals representatives shall be appointed." As the IRS noted, Health Plans' pre–1996 bylaws skewed control towards subscribers, rather than the community at large. In 1996, however, Health Plans amended its bylaws to require that a majority of board members be disinterested and broadly representative of the community.

It makes little difference whether we consider petitioners' board prior to 1996 or following the amendments. Even if we were to conclude petitioners' board broadly represents the community, the dearth of any actual community benefit in this case rebuts any inference we might otherwise draw.

4. Conclusion

For the above reasons, we agree with the Tax Court's conclusion that petitioners, standing alone, do not qualify for tax exemption under section 501(c)(3).

[The court then considered the taxpayers' alternative argument that they qualified for exemption based on the fact that their activities were an "integral part" of Health Services and essential to Health Services in accomplishing its tax-exempt purpose. Under the "integral part doctrine," if an organization's sole activity is an "integral part" of an exempt affiliate's activities, the organization may derive its exemption vicariously from the affiliate. The court rejected any application of this doctrine insofar as it rested on a derivative theory of exemption. But it accepted an interpretation that, based on the totality of facts and circumstances, recognized that the performance of a particular activity that is not inherently charitable may nonetheless further a charitable purpose. See Treas. Reg. § 1.502–1(b), in which a subsidiary operated for the sole purpose of providing electric power to its clearly tax-exempt parent was itself recognized as exempt. The court concluded that the requisite nexus between the taxpayers and their affiliate, Health Services, was lacking here because they contracted approximately 80 percent of physician services from independent physicians with no direct link to Health Services. As a result, it held that the taxpayers did not function solely to further Health Services' performance of its exempt activities. Eds.]

III. Conclusion

Based on the foregoing, we AFFIRM the Tax Court's decision denying petitioners tax-exempt status under 26 U.S.C. § 501(c)(3).

NOTES

1. *The Integral Part Doctrine.* In the *Geisinger Health Plans* litigation, the courts also considered an alternative argument for exemption based on the integral part doctrine. See Treas. Reg. § 1.502–1(b). In *Geisinger*, the Tax Court held on remand that GHP did not meet this test because the court was unable to determine whether GHP had performed substantial services for individuals who were not patients of its tax-exempt affiliates. It thus found that GHP failed to prove that its activities would not have been considered an unrelated trade or business if they had been carried on by the related entities. Geisinger Health Plan v. Commissioner, 100 T.C. 394 (1993).

The Third Circuit affirmed on a different theory, finding that GHP's relationship to its affiliates did not enhance its own charitable character so as to give it a "boost" toward exemption, as (supposedly) required by the regulations, because the affiliation did nothing to increase the portion of the community for which the GHP system promoted health. Geisinger Health Plan v. Commissioner, 30 F.3d 494 (3d Cir.1994).

2. *State Property Tax Exemptions.* The abandonment of charity care as the proper standard for hospital tax exemptions has been questioned. In one of the first such cases, the Utah Supreme Court upheld the denial of a state property tax exemption to two nonprofit hospitals that failed to provide any significant care to indigent patients. Utah County ex rel. County Board of Equalization v. Intermountain Health Care, Inc., 709 P.2d 265 (Utah 1985). The Utah Tax Commission subsequently added a requirement that nonprofit hospitals must provide an annual "gift to the community" that exceeds the value of its property tax exemption. The "gift" must be quantifiable—e.g., the reasonable value of unreimbursed care to indigent patients or of volunteer and community service. See Utah State Tax Commission, Property Tax Division, Standards of Practice, available at http://propertytax.utah.gov/standards/standards02.pdf.

In response to *Intermountain Health Care*, several other states reconsidered their tax exemption standards for nonprofit hospitals. Some enacted legislation requiring hospitals to conduct and report community benefit needs assessments or meet highly specific community benefit standards to qualify for state tax exemptions. For example, Pennsylvania's Purely Public Charity Act (10 Pa. Cons. Stat. §§ 371–85 (1999)) includes a list of criteria and requires charities to provide a minimum amount of community services based on one of seven specified standards—e.g., providing uncompensated goods or services equal to five percent of costs. Id. In 1993, Texas enacted legislation specifying the percentage of revenues or tax benefits received that must be dedicated to charity care in order for a hospital to qualify for property tax exemption. Tex. Tax Code Ann. § 11.1801(a) (Vernon 2001) (generally, four percent of net patient revenue or 100 percent of tax benefits received).

The most influential recent property tax dispute involved Provena–Covenant Medical Center, a Catholic health care facility in Urbana, Illinois. Provena's stated policy was to accept all patients regardless of ability to pay, but it did not widely advertise the policy and referred its few uninsured nonpaying patients to collection agencies. The Illinois Department of Revenue denied a property tax exemption to Provena on the ground that the hospital property, technically owned by Provena's corporate parent, was not owned by an "institution of public charity" and not used exclusively for charitable purposes, as required by the Illinois law. In denying the exemption, the Department of Revenue pointed to a lack of charity care and Provena's aggressive billing and collection practices for uninsured patients. A state trial judge reinstated Provena's exemption, but the Illinois Fourth District Court of Appeals reversed, finding that significant charity care was an essential prerequisite for hospital property tax exemptions in Illinois.

On a further appeal by the hospital, the Illinois Supreme Court upheld denial of the exemption. Provena Covenant Medical Center v. Department of Revenue, 925 N.E.2d 1131 (Ill. 2010). All five justices hearing the appeal (two justices recused themselves) concurred in the judgment on the ground that the record was inadequate on the question of whether the property was owned by an "institution of public charity." The hospital had failed to introduce sufficient evidence on the charitable character of Provena's corporate parent, which held legal title. That would have been enough to resolve the case, but the justices chose to engage in a spirited exchange of views on the substantive standard to be applied in determining if the property was used exclusively for charitable purposes. Three of the five justices—not enough for a binding precedent on a seven-person court—found that use of the hospital property was not "charitable" primarily because Provena's charity care, as the court chose to define it, was only about 0.7 percent of the hospital's revenue. The plurality construed the concept of charity under Illinois law to require a "gift" element; activities that provided a community benefit, such as education and other programs to promote health, were not "charitable." In this context, the requisite "gift" had to be free or below-cost service to patients without an ability to pay through insurance or otherwise. But the court left undefined the precise amount of free or discounted care that was required. In reaching these conclusions, the plurality reasoned that admitting a patient who is unable to pay and then billing at the highest rates and writing off the charge as a bad debt after aggressive collection efforts is not charity care, nor are contractual discounts with payers such as Medicare and Medicaid or an open emergency room. The court also rejected Provena's alternative argument that it qualified for exemption as a religious organization. The two dissenting justices rejected the plurality's "quantum of charity care" requirement, characterizing it as judicial legislation, and instead embraced the more permissive community benefit test. For a description and analysis of the Illinois Supreme Court's opinion, see John D. Colombo, Provena Covenant: The (Sort of) Final Chapter, 65 Exempt Org. Tax Rev. 489 (2010).

A few other state courts or legislatures have not followed the trend toward resurrecting a charity care standard. See, e.g., Medical Center Hosp. of Vt., Inc. v. City of Burlington, 152 Vt. 611, 566 A.2d 1352 (1989); Downtown Hosp. Ass'n v. Tennessee State Bd. of Equalization, 760 S.W.2d 954 (Tenn.Ct.App. 1988).

For more general discussion of state property tax exemptions, see Chapter 2C2, supra, at pp. 69–71.

3. *Congressional and IRS Scrutiny.* Congress periodically revisits the tax exemption standards for nonprofit hospitals but it rarely reaches any new consensus. In the early 1990s, bills were introduced that would have denied § 501(c)(3) status and certain other tax benefits for hospitals not meeting a more stringent standard. One proposal would have required hospitals to provide adequate emergency medical services (e.g., a full-time emergency room open to all members of the public regardless of ability to pay), service to Medicaid patients, and a certain level of charity care or other community benefits. Sanctions would have included loss of exempt status, ineligibility to receive tax-deductible contributions but, in some situations, an interim monetary penalty would be imposed before exemption was stripped. An effort in 1994 to enact a charity care standard for nonprofit health care providers as part of comprehensive health care reform legislation also was unsuccessful.

In 2005, Congress launched a new inquiry into the actual practices of nonprofit hospitals and the longstanding community benefit standard for charitable tax exemption. Senate Finance Committee chair Charles Grassley asked ten large hospital systems to provide detailed information about issues such as their charity care and community benefit activities, patient billing, and joint ventures with for-profit firms. Senator Grassley's first "big picture" question set the stage by asking:

How does your organization define charity care? What types of activities or programs does your organization include in its definition or determination of charity care? Which of these activities or programs would your organization not incur, at all or to the same extent, if you were organized and operated as a for-profit hospital? Does your organization maintain a charity policy? If so, please describe the policy or provide a copy of such policy? Does this policy require that certain types and amounts of charity care are provided?

Forty-five additional questions probed the details of every facet of the targeted hospitals' operations. See Senate Finance Committee Press Release, Grassley Asks Non-profit Hospitals to Account for Activities Related to Their Tax–Exempt Status, available at finance.senate.gov/press/Gpress/2005/prg052505.pdf. The House Ways and Means Committee also got into the act, inviting testimony from government officials, academics and industry representatives. For witness statements, see http://waysandmeans.house.gov/hearings.asp.

Prodded by Congress, the IRS ratcheted up its scrutiny of nonprofit hospitals. In 2007, it released an interim report of its findings on the community benefit practices of nonprofit hospitals. based on responses to questionnaires received from 500 hospitals. Not surprisingly, virtually all the hospitals surveyed reported that they provided some community benefits. The largest category was "uncompensated care," but questions remain about what that really means. The interim report was characterized as inconclusive by the IRS because of inconsistent reporting practices and unclear definitions. An executive summary is available at http://www.irs.gov/pub/irs_tege/eo_interim_hospital_report_execsummary_072007.pdf. Further analysis of the data will be made before any final report.

Senator Grassley simultaneously released a discussion draft of proposed tax reforms including, among other things, a requirement that § 501(c)(3) hospitals establish written charity care policies; use 5 percent of operating expenses or revenues for charity care; conduct periodic community needs assessments; and control all joint ventures with for-profit partners. The discussion draft is available at http://www.senate.gov/~finance/press/Gpress/2007/prg071907a.pdf. In April 2007, Senator Grassley asked the GAO to prepare a report on community benefits provided by nonprofit hospitals and their executive and board compensation. The GAO's report concluded that hospitals had great latitude in determining what activities and programs helped them meet the community benefit standard and that, although some states had attempted to fill the gap by imposing community benefit requirements, their standard differed substantially. A particular point of contention is whether unpaid amounts billed to patients without adequate insurance and written off by the hospital as bad debts should be considered community benefit. The American Hospital Association says yes but others say no. Similarly, the GAO report noted a lack of consensus on whether costs billed but not reimbursed by Medicare should be considered community benefit. The report is available at http://www.gao.gov/new.items/do8880.pdf.

The drumbeat continued in 2009 when the IRS released its 191–page final report, which reached these conclusions:

- Nonprofit hospitals vary widely in the amount and type of charitable benefits they provide. Fewer than one-fifth of the hospitals surveyed accounted for 78 percent of the aggregate community benefit expenditures.

- The 500 hospitals surveyed reported spending an average of 9 percent of total revenues on providing "community benefits," such as free care, education and research. Rural hospitals spent less than urban medical centers.

- Most hospitals follow proper procedures in establishing compensation for their executives. The average and median total compensation paid to top officials were $490,000 and $377,000, respectively, with hospitals in high population areas paying the most (the average was $1.4 million in 20 hospitals with the highest compensation).

- The community benefit and reasonable compensation standards have proved difficult for the IRS to administer because they involve application of imprecise legal standards to complex, varied and evolving fact patterns. For example, the IRS conceded that a major limitation of the report was the difference in how hospitals define uncompensated care, with some including Medicare shortfalls (i.e., the difference between the hospital's stated costs and the government reimbursement) and others providing data based on inflated "rack rate" charges rather than actual costs.

The report is available at http://www.irs.gov/charities/article/0,id= 203109,00.html.

4. *Form* 990. The IRS has begun to collect more information from nonprofit hospitals through new detailed schedules that have been included on the revised Form 990 information return. Schedule H asks hospitals whether they have a charity care policy ("yes" or "no"). If the answer is yes, a list of questions follows about who is eligible, whether charity care is factored into the hospital's budget, and whether an annual community benefit report is prepared and made available to the public. Form 990 also requires hospitals to complete detailed schedules on charity care programs, community building activities, and bad debt, medicare and collection practices. The IRS hopes that the new Schedule H will result in more consistent measurement and reporting of community benefit expenditures and, as a result, will provide greater insight into whether the standard should be refined or replaced by a brighter line test.

5. *New Qualification Requirements for Hospitals.* On March 23, 2010, President Obama signed the Patient Protection and Affordable Care Act, which included among its many "reforms" additional § 501(c)(3) tax exemption requirements for charitable hospitals. Although no specific charity care mandate was enacted, the new rules move in that direction, with an emphasis on process. For tax years beginning after March 23, 2012, every "hospital facility" must conduct a community needs assessment at least once every three years and adopt an implementation strategy to meet the needs identified by the assessment. The assessment must take into account input from persons who represent the broad interests of the community served by the facility and must be made widely available to the public.

I.R.C. § 501(r)(1)(A), (r)(3). Noncompliance will trigger a $50,000 penalty and possibly loss of exemption. I.R.C. § 4959. The hospital also must disclose in its annual Form 990 how it is addressing the needs identified in the assessment or why those needs have not been addressed, and make audited financial statements widely available (I.R.C. § 6033(b)(15)). The Act directs the IRS to review information submitted by hospitals about their community benefit activities at least once every three years. (H.R. 3590, § 9007(c)).

Additional provisions require hospitals to: (1) adopt, implement and widely publicize a written financial assistance policy that includes eligibility criteria, the basis for calculating amounts charged to clients, and the methods for applying for financial assistance (I.R.C. § 501(r)(1)(B), (r)(4)(A)); (2) adopt policies for providing emergency medical treatment in a manner that does not discriminate against individuals who qualify for financial assistance under the hospital's policy or government programs (I.R.C. § 501(r)(4)(B)); and (3) bill patients who qualify for financial assistance no more than the amount the is generally charged to patients with insurance, not the inflated "rack rates" that are often billed to uninsured patients (I.R.C. § 501(r)(1)(C), (r)(5)). Finally, the legislation prohibits hospitals from undertaking extraordinary collection actions against patients without first making reasonable efforts to determine whether a patient is eligible for financial assistance. I.R.C. § 501(r)(1)(D), (r)(6).

6. *Policy Issues.* In critically evaluating the tax exemption standard for nonprofit hospitals, an appropriate question is: how do modern nonprofit hospitals differ from for-profit hospitals and are the differences sufficient to justify tax benefits for the nonprofits? Many private nonprofit hospitals seem very much like their for-profit counterparts, and it has been suggested that they are so similar that a patient would not be able to identify any meaningful differences.

A study by Professor Jill Horwitz of the University of Michigan argues that there are qualitative differences in that for-profit hospitals are more likely to offer the most profitable services, such as open heart surgery, and less likely than either nonprofit or government hospitals to offer valuable, essential but unprofitable services, such as psychiatric emergency care, AIDS treatment, trauma services, and obstetric care. She also found that for-profit hospitals respond more quickly to changes in financial incentives, illustrating the point with data showing how for-profits moved quickly to increase their offerings of home health care when it was profitable and were much quicker to exit that market when profit margins declined. Professor Horwitz concludes that nonprofit hospitals are more willing than for-profits to offer services even though they happen to be unprofitable and they thus make a valuable contribution to the mix of medical services available in a community. Although she argues that charity care is important, Professor Horwitz's main point is that other unique features of nonprofit hospitals—e.g., their services, quality and innovation—benefit all members of society and justify continued tax benefits. See Jill R. Horwitz, Why We Need the Independent Sector: The Behavior, Law, and Ethics of

Not-for-Profit Hospitals, 50 UCLA L.Rev. 1345 (2003); Hearings Before the House Ways and Means Committee, Statement of Jill R. Horwitz, May 26, 2005, available at waysandmeans.house.gov/hearings.asp.

Other studies, focusing primarily on financial behavior, found fewer differences to justify tax exemption. Similarities between for-profit and nonprofit hospitals were found in their costs, sources of capital, exercise of market power, and use of technology. For-profits were able to pay higher compensation, but nonprofits have increasingly used performance-based pay and entered into joint ventures with for-profit providers or formed taxable subsidiaries to increase revenue and offer financial incentives to physicians and managers. See, e.g., Frank A. Sloan, Commercialism in Nonprofit Hospitals, in To Profit or Not to Profit: The Commercial Transformation of the Nonprofit Sector 151 (Burton Weisbrod ed., 1998); M. Gregg Bloche, Health Policy Below the Waterline: Medical Care and the Charitable Exemption, 80 Minn. L.Rev. 299 (1995); John D. Colombo, The Failure of Community Benefit, 15 Health Matrix: Journal of Law–Medicine 29, 44–51 (2005) and sources cited therein. See also Chapter 11B for discussion of the antitrust issues related to health care organizations.

7. *Other Exemption Qualification Issues.* The health care sector raises a variety of other federal tax issues, beginning with the basic exemption standards considered here. Health care providers do not qualify for exempt status under § 501(c)(3) if any part of their net earnings inures to the benefit of "insiders" such as officers, trustees, and influential physicians, or if they provide a substantial private benefit to noninsiders. Insiders and organization managers also may be subject to intermediate sanctions in the form of an excise tax under § 4958 if they receive or authorize excess economic benefits as a result of their position with the organization. Revenue from activities that are not substantially related to a health care provider's charitable or other exempt purposes may be subject to the unrelated business income tax. Inurement and private benefit issues are discussed in Section D of this chapter, infra, at pp. 445–461. The unrelated business income tax and joint ventures are covered in Chapter 6.

8. *For Further Reading.* John M. Quirk, Turning Back the Clock on the Health Care Organization Standard for Federal Tax Exemption, 43 Willamette L.Rev. 69 (2007); John D. Colombo, The IHC Cases: A Catch–22 for Integral Part Doctrine, A Requiem for Rev. Rul. 69–545, 34 Exempt Org. Tax Rev. 401 (2001); Douglas Mancino, Income Tax Exemption of the Contemporary Nonprofit Hospital, 32 St. Louis U.L.J. 1015 (1988); Robert C. Clark, Does the Nonprofit Form Fit the Hospital Industry, 93 Harv. L. Rev. 1417 (1980); John D. Colombo, Health Care Reform and Federal Tax Exemption: Rethinking the Issues, 29 Wake F. Law Rev. 215 (1994); Nina J. Crimm, Evolutionary Forces: Changes to For–Profit and Non-for-Profit Health Care Delivery Structures: A Regeneration of Tax Exemption Standards, 37 B.C. L. Rev. 1 (1995).

PROBLEMS

Keeping in mind the competing views on the rationale for tax exemption discussed earlier in the text, consider under the standards of current law (such as they are) and from a policy standpoint whether the following organizations qualify for federal tax exemption under § 501(c)(3):

(a) Suburban General Hospital ("Hospital") is a 500–bed nonprofit regional facility, with a broad community-based board of directors and medical staff privileges open to all qualified physicians but no teaching or research program. Hospital only accepts patients who can pay for their health care, either directly or through private insurance or Medicare. Hospital has an open emergency room, but it routinely diverts non-emergency patients to a nearby county hospital. Its primary mission is to offer the most profitable medical services, such as acute care and surgery, and it avoids less profitable areas.

(b) Same as (a), above, except that in addition to its several very profitable departments Hospital also provides services such as psychiatric emergency and obstetric care that operate at a deficit but are cross-subsidized by the profitable departments.

(c) Same as (a), above, except Hospital acquired its assets at fair market value from a for-profit partnership operated by a group of physicians. Physician services at Hospital are provided by an exclusive contract with a for-profit group practice consisting primarily of the doctors who owned the facility before it was acquired by Hospital. These doctors represent 40 percent of the Hospital's board of trustees.

(d) Community Drug Store, a nonprofit pharmacy not affiliated with a hospital or clinic, sells prescription drugs, orthopedic shoes, walkers and other medical products at cost to elderly and handicapped persons near a large urban low-income housing development.

c. PUBLIC INTEREST LAW FIRMS AND OTHER LEGAL SERVICES

Traditional legal aid organizations qualify as charitable because they provide free services to low-income individuals or charge modest fees based on a client's ability to pay. See Rev. Rul. 69–161, 1969–1 C.B. 149, amplified by Rev. Rul. 78–428, 1978–2 C.B. 177. The more controversial question considered in this section is whether organizations that engage in "public interest" litigation are charitable and, if so, what constitutes the "public interest." In the early 1970's, the Service announced that it was "studying" whether public interest law firms would continue to qualify for exempt status under § 501(c)(3). The public interest bar viewed the announcement as a veiled threat and, after a firestorm of protest, the Service gradually retreated.[1] The rulings that follow articulate the current policy.

---

1. For a comprehensive survey of these developments, see A.M. Wiggins, Jr. & Bert W. Hunt, Tax Policy Relating to Environmental Activities and Public Interest Litigation, in IV Research Papers Sponsored by the [Filer] Commission on Private Philanthropy and Public Needs 2045 (1977).

Revenue Ruling 75–74

1975–1 Cum. Bull. 152.

Advice has been requested whether the nonprofit organization described below, which otherwise qualifies for exemption from Federal income tax under section 501(c)(3) of the Internal Revenue Code of 1954, is operated exclusively for charitable purposes.

The organization is organized and operated as a public interest law firm in accordance with the guidelines set forth in Rev. Proc. 71–39, 1971–2 C.B. 575 and Rev. Proc. 75–13. The organization represents clients in court and in proceedings before administrative agencies. The organization has engaged in "public interest" litigation in areas such as environmental protection, urban renewal, prison reform, freedom of information, injunction suits challenging governmental and private action or inaction, and "test" cases of significance to the public.

Under its articles of incorporation and by-laws, the overall management of the organization is vested in a board of governors, the majority of whom are attorneys. The members of the board are prominent attorneys, law professors, and leaders of public interest organizations.

Several members of the board of governors comprise a litigation committee, whose function is to determine, for each proposed case, whether the case meets certain criteria for selection. The criteria of the Committee include: whether the case involves a matter of important public interest; whether the individuals or groups involved cannot afford competent private legal counsel; whether the case affords opportunities for participation by law students; and whether the organization's resources are adequate in view of the complexity of the case.

The organization does not accept cases in which private persons have a sufficient economic interest in the outcome of the litigation to justify the retention of private counsel. The organization's financial support is derived from grants and contributions. Section 501(c)(3) of the Code provides for the exemption from Federal income tax of organizations organized and operated exclusively for charitable purposes.

Section 1.501(c)(3)–1(d)(2) of the Income Tax Regulations provides that the term "charitable" is used in section 501(c)(3) of the Code in its generally accepted legal sense.

In Rev. Proc. 71–39, 1971–2 C.B. 575, the Internal Revenue Service announced guidelines pursuant to which it would recognize public interest law firms as exempt from the Federal income tax as organizations described in section 501(c)(3) of the Code.

Organizations meeting the guidelines of Rev. Proc. 71–39 are recognized as charities because they provide a service which is of benefit to the community as a whole. They provide legal representation on issues of significant public interest where such representation is not ordinarily provided by traditional private law firms. In this way, the courts and administrative agencies are afforded the opportunity to review issues of significant public interest and to identify and adjudicate that interest.

Charitability rests not upon the particular positions advocated by the firm, but upon the provision of a facility for the resolution of issues of broad public importance. For this reason, section 3.05 of Rev. Proc. 71–39 recognizes that it is for the public interest law firm itself, through a board or committee representative of the public interest, to select the cases in which representation is warranted.

Charitability is also dependent upon the fact that the service provided by public interest law firms is distinguishable from that which is commercially available. It is a general rule of charity law that the providing of an ordinary commercial service to the members of a community, even if done on a not-for-profit basis, is not regarded as charitable.

It is generally recognized that public interest representation is not ordinarily provided on a continuing basis by private law firms. Although a number of reasons have been given for the inability of private firms to provide sufficient representation of this type, it is primarily due to the fact that this type of representation is not economically feasible for private firms. In the typical public interest case, no individual plaintiff has a sufficient economic interest to warrant his bearing the cost of retaining private counsel. Even if the community as a whole has a significant cumulative economic interest, individual interests are generally so varied and diffused that it is not practical to rely upon collective financing of such cases.

This lack of economic feasibility in public interest cases is an essential characteristic distinguishing the work of public interest law firms from that of private firms and is a prerequisite of charitable recognition. For this reason section 3.01 of Rev. Proc. 71–39 provides that the activity of public interest law firms would not normally extend to direct representation of litigants in actions between private persons where their financial interests at stake would warrant representation from private legal sources.

The above described organization, which otherwise qualifies for exemption and which is operated in conformity with the guidelines of Rev. Proc. 71–39, provides representation in cases of important public interest that are not economically feasible for private firms. Accordingly, it is operated exclusively for charitable purposes and qualifies for exemption under section 501(c)(3) of the Code. * * *

Revenue Procedure 92–59

1992–2 Cum. Bull. 411.

SEC. 1.   PURPOSE

The purpose of this revenue procedure is to supersede Rev. Proc. 71–39, 1971–2 C.B. 575, to modify and supersede Rev. Proc. 75–13, 1975–1 C.B. 662, to revoke Rev. Rul. 75–75, 1975–1 C.B. 154, and to amplify Rev. Rul.

75–76, 1975–1 C.B. 154, by setting forth guidelines for public interest law firms, including procedures under which a public interest law firm may accept fees for its services. The Internal Revenue Service will issue rulings and determinations regarding exemption to new public interest law firms and test the charitable character of such organizations already holding such rulings based on the guidelines set forth in this revenue procedure. These guidelines are not inflexible and an organization will be given the opportunity to demonstrate that under the facts and circumstances of its particular program, adherence to the guidelines is not required in certain respects in order to ensure that the operations are totally charitable.

SEC. 2.   BACKGROUND

.01 In Rev. Proc. 71–39, the Service announced guidelines pursuant to which it would recognize public interest law firms as exempt from federal income tax under section 501(c)(3) of the Internal Revenue Code. Section 3.02 of Rev. Proc. 71–39 provides that the public interest law firm does not accept fees for its services except in accordance with procedures approved by the Service.

* * *

.05 Rev. Proc. 75–13 sets forth procedures under which a public interest law firm may accept fees for its services. Under these procedures, the organization may not receive or request fees from its clients for the provision of legal services. Attorney fees paid by opposing parties, however, are permissible if awarded by a court or administrative agency in a case or settlement agreement.

.06 The procedures of Rev. Proc. 75–13 were published to eliminate the possibility that a decision to litigate might rest on the payment the firm receives instead of the economic feasibility or the litigants and thus render a public interest law firm's practice indistinguishable from a private firm's. The Service has reconsidered these procedures and concluded that safeguards sufficient to distinguish a public interest law firm's practice from the private practice of law can be implemented without absolutely prohibiting public interest law firms from receiving client-paid fees.

.07 Section 3 below sets forth general guidelines under which the Service will determine whether a public interest law firm meets the test of being exclusively charitable and thus is entitled to recognition of exemption as an organization described in section 501(c)(3) of the Code. Section 4 below sets forth approved procedures for the acceptance of court awarded attorneys' fees. Section 5 below sets forth additional procedures to apply in the case of client-paid fees to assure that the public interest law firm that accepts client-paid fees remains distinguishable from a private law firm. The procedures in Section 5 are not applicable to out-of-pocket costs incurred in litigation.

SEC. 3.   GENERAL GUIDELINES

.01 The engagement of the organization in litigation can reasonably be said to be in representation of a broad public interest rather than a private interest. Litigation will be considered to be in representation of a broad public interest if it is designed to present a position on behalf of the public at large on matters of public interest. Typical of such litigation may be class actions in which the resolution of the dispute is in the public interest; suits for injunction against action by government or private interests broadly affecting the public; similar representation before administrative boards and agencies; test suits where the private interest is small; and the like.

.02 The litigation activity does not normally extend to direct representation of litigants in actions between private persons where the financial interests at stake would warrant representation from private legal sources. In such cases, however, where the issue in litigation affects a broad public interest or will have an impact on the broad public interest, the organization may serve as a friend of the court.

.03 The organization does not attempt to achieve its objectives through a program of disruption of the judicial system, illegal activity, or violation of applicable canons of ethics.

.04 The organization files with its annual information return a description of cases litigated and the rationale for the determination that they would benefit the public generally.

.05 The policies and programs of the organization (including compensation arrangements) are the responsibility of a board or committee representative of the public interest, which is not controlled by employees or persons who litigate on behalf of the organization nor by any organization that is not itself an organization described in section 501(c)(3) of the Code.

.06 The organization is not operated, through sharing of office space or otherwise, in a manner so as to create identification or confusion with a particular private law firm.

.07 There is no arrangement to provide, directly or indirectly, a deduction for the cost of litigation that is for the private benefit of the donor.

.08 The organization does not accept fees for its service except in accordance with the procedures set forth in Sections 4 and 5 below.

.09 The organization must otherwise comply with the provisions of section 501(c)(3) of the Code, that is, it may not participate in, or intervene in, any political campaign on behalf of (or in opposition to) any candidate for public office, no part of its net earnings may inure to the benefit of any private shareholder or individual, and no substantial part of its activities may consist of carrying on propaganda or otherwise attempting to influence legislation, (except as otherwise provided in section 501(h)).

.10 A public interest law firm may accept reimbursement from clients or from opposing parties for direct out-of-pocket expenses incurred in the litigation. Courts have traditionally distinguished out-of-pocket costs such as filing fees, travel expenses, and expert witness fees from attorneys' fees.

These expenses are usually nominal in comparison to the amount of attorneys' fees.

SEC. 4. ACCEPTANCE OF ATTORNEYS' FEES

.01 The organization may accept attorneys' fees in public interest cases if such fees are paid by opposing parties and are awarded by a court or administrative agency or approved by such a body in a settlement agreement.

.02 The organization may accept attorneys' fees in public interest cases if such fees are paid directly by its clients provided it adopts additional procedures as set forth in Section 5 of this revenue procedure.

.03 The likelihood or probability of a fee, whether court awarded or client-paid, may not be a consideration in the organization's selection of cases. The selection of cases should be made in accordance with the procedures set forth in Section 3 of this revenue procedure.

.04 Cases in which a court awarded or client-paid fee is possible may not be accepted if the organization believes the litigants have a sufficient commercial or financial interest in the outcome of the litigation to justify retention of a private law firm. The organization may, in cases of sufficient broad public interest, represent the public interest as amicus curiae or intervenor in such cases.

.05 The total amount of all attorneys' fees (court awarded and received from clients) must not exceed 50 percent of the total cost of operation of the organization's legal functions. This percentage will be calculated over a five-year period, including the taxable year in which any fees are received and the four preceding taxable years (or any lesser period of existence). Costs of legal functions include: attorneys' salaries, nonprofessional salaries, overhead, and other costs directly attributable to the performance of the organization's legal functions. An organization may submit a ruling request where an exception to the above 50 percent limitation appears warranted.

.06 The organization will not seek or accept attorneys' fees in any circumstances that would result in a conflict with state statutes or professional canons of ethics.

.07 All attorneys' fees will be paid to the organization, rather than to individual staff attorneys. All staff attorneys and other employees will be compensated on a straight salary basis, not exceeding reasonable salary levels and not established by reference to any fees received in connection with the cases they have handled.

.08 In addition to the information required by Section 3.04 of this revenue procedure, the organization will file with its annual information return a report of all attorneys' fees sought and recovered in each case.

SEC. 5. ADDITIONAL RULES APPLICABLE TO CLIENT–PAID FEES

.01 Client-paid fees may not exceed the actual cost incurred in each case, viz., the salaries, overhead, and other costs fairly allocable to the litigation in question. Costs may be charged against a retainer, with any balance remaining after the conclusion of the litigation refunded to the litigant.

.02 Once having undertaken a representation, a public interest law firm may not withdraw from the case because the litigant is unable to pay the contemplated fee.

* * *

PROBLEMS

Consider whether the following organizations qualify for exemption under § 501(c)(3):

(a) The Free Market Legal Foundation, a nonprofit organization established by wealthy individuals and private foundations to counter the impact of "liberal" public interest law firms. Its programs include litigation of precedent-setting cases, research, and public education. The Foundation is dedicated to the principles of free enterprise, private property rights, limited government, free speech, and reform of the civil and criminal justice systems. Its recent litigation has included: a suit to challenge several Environmental Protection Agency regulations regarding strip mining in the West; a suit to challenge on constitutional grounds a minority scholarship program at a state university; an action on behalf of a Georgia factory owner who refused to allow an OSHA inspector into his plant without a search warrant; defense of a state initiative ending bilingual education; representation of students at various major universities who have been charged with violation of "hate speech" codes; and defense of a constitutional challenge to a state law prohibiting same-sex marriages.

(b) Middle Class Legal Services ("MCLS"), a nonprofit organization formed by five recent law school graduates to provide routine legal services in areas such as family law, bankruptcy, landlord-tenant, probate and simple tax controversies, to individuals and small businesses who are able to pay below-market fees ranging from $65 to $150 per hour. The stated purpose of MCLS is to provide services to those who are not poor enough to qualify for traditional legal services organizations and yet are unable to pay the prevailing rates charged by law firms and sole practitioners in the community.

(c) The Local Bar Association ("LBA"), a voluntary membership organization formed to promote the interests of the legal profession in a major American city. LBA's primary activity is the operation of a lawyer referral service that provides low and middle income persons with an opportunity to obtain representation from a panel of participating attorneys on matters such as divorce, probate, bankruptcy, landlord-tenant, and employment law matters. Other activities include the maintenance of a public law library, continuing legal education seminars and a tribunal to inquire into complaints of ethical and unauthorized practices and to report violations to the state bar association.

d.   COMMUNITY DEVELOPMENT AND LOW–INCOME HOUSING

The charitable sector includes many organizations seeking to ameliorate the problems of urban poverty through community economic development and affordable housing projects. Organizations operated for "[r]elief of the poor and distressed or of the underprivileged" have long qualified as "charitable" under § 501(c)(3). The more difficult questions are whether charitable status extends to nonprofit organizations that form effective economic partnerships with the private sector. Beginning in the early 1970s, the Service recognized that arresting urban problems through philanthropic venture capital could be a charitable purpose even if it might involve some incidental private benefit extending beyond the charitable class. The rulings below illustrate the Service's general approach in these areas, and the subsequent problems provide an opportunity to apply these broad guidelines to some typical fact patterns.

Revenue Ruling 74–587

1974–2 Cum. Bull. 162.

Advice has been requested whether a nonprofit organization formed and operated in the manner described below is exempt from Federal income tax under section 501(c)(3) of the Internal Revenue Code of 1954.

The organization's charter provides that it is organized exclusively for charitable purposes and restricts its activities to those not proscribed by section 501(c)(3) or other related provisions of the Code. The declared objectives of the organization are the relief of poverty, the elimination of prejudice, the lessening of neighborhood tensions, and the combating of community deterioration in certain economically depressed areas through a program of financial assistance and other aid designed to improve economic conditions and economic opportunities in these areas.

In furtherance of such objectives the organization devotes its resources to programs designed to stimulate economic development in high density urban areas inhabited mainly by low-income minority or other disadvantaged groups. Because of the lack of capital for development, the limited entrepreneurial skills of the owners, the social unrest and instability of the area, and the depressed market within which they operate, many of the businesses located in these high density urban areas have declined or fallen into disrepair, and others have ceased to operate.

The organization undertakes to combat such conditions by providing funds and working capital to corporations or individual proprietors who are not able to obtain funds from conventional commercial sources because of the poor financial risks involved in establishing and operating enterprises in these communities or because of their membership in minority or other disadvantaged groups. The program is designed to enable the recipient of funds or capital to start a new business or to acquire or improve an existing business. Depending upon the circumstances, the financial assistance may be in the form of low-cost or long-term loans or the purchase of equity interests in the various enterprises. The terms of any loan will be reasonably related to the needs of the particular business. Where the financial assistance takes the form of acquiring an equity interest, the organization disposes of such interest as soon as the success of the business is reasonably assured.

In selecting recipients for aid, the organization consults with other nonprofit and governmental organizations operating anti-poverty and anti-discrimination programs to identify particular undertakings that will fill a community need and offer the greatest potential community benefit. Preference is given to businesses that will provide training and employment opportunities for the unemployed or under-employed residents of the area. In selecting a recipient for financial assistance, the organization considers the applicant's motivation, education, experience, and prior participation in management and job training programs. It also considers recommendations from other organizations conducting rehabilitation and training programs.

The organization does not actively participate in the day-to-day operation of the businesses to which it provides financial assistance; however, it does review their progress periodically to assure that the funds are used for the organization's purposes. In addition, when appropriate, the organization provides technical assistance and counseling.

The facts relating to the financial activities undertaken by the organization in carrying out this program established that these loans and purchases of equity interest are not undertaken for purpose of profit or gain but for the purpose of advancing the charitable goals of the organization and are not investments for profit in any conventional business sense.

The organization is financed by grants from foundations and by public contributions.

Section 501(c)(3) of the Code provides for the exemption from Federal income tax of organizations organized and operated exclusively for charitable purposes.

Section 1.501(c)(3)–1(a) of the Income Tax Regulations provides that in order to be exempt as an organization described in section 501(c)(3) of the Code, the organization must be one that is both organized and operated exclusively for one or more of the purposes specified in that section. An organization that fails to meet either the organizational or the operational test is not exempt.

Section 1.501(c)(3)–1(d)(2) of the regulations defines the term "charitable" as including the promotion of social welfare by organizations designed to relieve the poor and distressed or the underprivileged, to lessen neighborhood tensions, to eliminate prejudice and discrimination, or to combat community deterioration.

The corporate charter declares the purposes of the organization to be exclusively charitable and contains appropriate restrictions against engaging in any activities proscribed under section 501(c)(3) or related provisions of the Code. To that extent, therefore, the organization meets the organizational requirements of the applicable regulations provisions.

To satisfy the "operational test" the organization's resources must be devoted to programs that qualify as exclusively charitable within the meaning of section 501(c)(3) of the Code and applicable regulations.

Through its program of financial assistance, the organization is devoting its resources to uses that benefit the community in a way that the law regards as charitable. Such conclusion follows from the fact that the organization's described program of aiding minority-owned businesses promotes the social welfare of the community, since it helps to lessen prejudice and discrimination against minority groups by demonstrating that the disadvantaged residents of an impoverished area can operate businesses successfully if given the opportunity and proper guidance. It also helps to relieve poverty, while at the same time lessening neighborhood tensions and dissatisfaction arising from the lack of employment opportunities by assisting local businesses that will provide a means of livelihood and expanded job opportunities for unemployed or underemployed area residents. Finally, it combats community deterioration by helping to establish businesses in the area and by rehabilitating existing businesses that have deteriorated.

Although some of the individuals receiving financial assistance in their business endeavors under the organization's program may not themselves qualify for charitable assistance as such, that fact does not detract from the charitable character of the organization's program. The recipients of loans and working capital in such cases are merely the instruments by which the charitable purposes are sought to be accomplished.

Accordingly, the organization is exempt from Federal income tax under section 501(c)(3) of the Code.

Revenue Ruling 70–585

1970–2 Cum.Bull. 115.

Advice has been requested whether nonprofit organizations created to provide housing for low or moderate income families under Federal and State programs qualify for exemption from Federal income tax as charitable organizations described in section 501(c)(3) of the Internal Revenue Code of 1954.

Section 501(c)(3) of the Code provides for the exemption from Federal income tax of organizations organized and operated exclusively for charitable purposes.

Section 1.501(c)(3)–1(d)(2) of the Income Tax Regulations defines the term "charitable" as including the relief of the poor and distressed or of the underprivileged, and the promotion of social welfare by organizations designed to lessen neighborhood tensions, to eliminate prejudice and discrimination, or to combat community deterioration.

It is held generally that where an organization is formed for charitable purposes and accomplishes its charitable purposes through a program of providing housing for low and, in certain circumstances, moderate income families, it is entitled to exemption under section 501(c)(3) of the Code. The fact that an organization receives public funds under State or Federal programs for housing is not determinative; qualification is based on whether or not the organization is charitable within the meaning of section 501(c)(3).

The following situations are illustrative of the foregoing principle.

Situation 1.   An Organization Formed to Aid Low Income Families

An organization was formed to develop a program for new home construction and the renovation of existing homes for sale to low income families on long-term, low-payment plans. It purchases homes for renovation and lots for building new homes throughout the city in which it is located. It builds new homes for sale to low income families who qualify for loans under a Federal housing program and who cannot obtain financing through conventional channels. It also aids financially those families eligible for the loans who do not have the necessary down payment. Rehabilitated homes are made available to families who cannot qualify for any type of mortgage loan. The cost of these homes is recovered, if possible, through very small periodic payments. The organization derives its operating funds through Federal loans and contributions from the general public. Where possible, renovations are made with volunteer help.

By providing homes for low income families who otherwise could not afford them, the organization is relieving the poor and distressed. Thus, it is held that this organization is organized and operated exclusively for charitable purposes, and it is exempt from Federal income tax under section 501(c)(3) of the Code. The determination of what constitutes low income is a factual question based on all of the surrounding circumstances.

Situation 2.   An Organization Formed to Eliminate Prejudice and Discrimination

An organization was formed to ameliorate the housing needs of minority groups by building housing units for sale to persons of low and moderate income on an open occupancy basis. It constructs new housing that is available to members of minority groups with low and moderate income who are unable to obtain adequate housing because of local discrimination. These housing units are so located as to help reduce racial and ethnic imbalances in the community. They are sold at or below cost to low or moderate income families or rented, with options to purchase, to families who cannot presently afford to purchase. Preference is to be given to families previously located in ghetto areas. The organization also informs the public regarding integrated housing as a means of minimizing potential misunderstanding and stabilizing integrated neighborhoods. It is financed by contributions from the general public and by funds obtained under Federal and State housing programs.

As the organization's activities are designed to eliminate prejudice and discrimination and to lessen neighborhood tensions, it is engaged in charitable activities within the meaning of section 501(c)(3) of the Code. See Rev. Rul. 68–655, C.B. 1968–2, 213. Accordingly, it is held that this organization is exempt from Federal income tax under section 501(c)(3) of the Code.

Situation 3. An Organization Formed to Combat Community Deterioration

An organization was formed to formulate plans for the renewal and rehabilitation of a particular area in a city as a residential community. Studies of the area showed that the median income level in the area is lower than in other sections of the city and the housing located in the area is generally old and badly deteriorated.

The organization's membership is composed of the residents, businesses, and community organizations in the area. The organization cooperates with the local redevelopment authority in providing residents of the area with decent, safe, and sanitary housing without relocating them outside the area. The organization has developed an overall plan for the rehabilitation of the area; it sponsors a renewal project in which the residents themselves take the initiative; and it arranges monthly meetings to involve residents in the planning for the renewal of the area. As part of the renewal project, it purchased an apartment house that it plans to rehabilitate and rent at cost to low and moderate income families with preference given to residents of the area. The organization is supported by Federal funds, membership fees, and contributions.

Since the organization's purposes and activities combat community deterioration by assisting in the rehabilitation of an old and run-down residential area, they are charitable within the meaning of section 501(c)(3) of the Code. Thus, it is held that the organization is exempt from Federal income tax under section 501(c)(3) of the Code.

Situation 4. An Organization Formed to Provide Moderate Income Families With Housing in a Particular Community

An organization was formed to build new housing facilities for the purpose of helping families to secure decent, safe, and sanitary housing at prices they can afford. Its membership is composed of community organizations that are concerned with the growing housing shortage in the community. A study of the area shows that because of the high cost of land, increased interest rates, and the growing population, there is a shortage of housing for moderate income families in the community. The organization plans to erect housing that it to be rented at cost to moderate income families. The organization is financed by mortgage money obtained under Federal and State programs and by contributions from the general public.

Since the organization's program is not designed to provide relief to the poor or to carry out any other charitable purpose within the meaning of the regulations applicable to section 501(c)(3) of the Code, it is held that it is not entitled to exemption from Federal income tax under section 501(c)(3) of the Code.

* * *

NOTES

1. *The Age of Specialization.* Community development and low-income housing have become highly technical sub-specialties, requiring expertise in sources of government funding, debt financing techniques, partnership tax, and the real estate development process—all areas going well beyond the scope of this text. Particularly important is the low-income housing tax credit, which helps for-profit and nonprofit developers raise equity to purchase, rehabilitate, and construct affordable housing. See I.R.C. 42. In introducing this topic, a leading treatise has warned:

> Nonprofit developers should be aware that this [low-income housing tax credit] program is extremely complicated and rife with land mines for those uninitiated in this type of financing. Early in the development process, sponsors who are seriously considering a tax credit project should retain tax counsel experienced in the low-income housing tax credit. Bennett L. Hecht, Developing Affordable Housing: A Practical Guide for Nonprofit Organizations 148 (1994).

2. *Low–Income Housing Safe Harbor.* In Rev. Proc. 96–32, 1996–1 C.B. 717, the Service clarified the standards for low-income housing organizations seeking to qualify for exemption under § 501(c)(3). The revenue procedure was issued in response to the emergence of new models of affordable housing, such as mixed-income developments that did not exclusively serve the very poor but rather sought to promote social and economic integration of low and moderate income residents. The revenue procedure includes a bright line test providing that an organization will qualify for exemption if at least 75 percent of its units are occupied by families who are low-income (80 percent of the areas's median income) under federal housing guidelines. At least 20 percent of those units must be occupied by residents who are "very-low income" (50 percent of the areas's median), or 40 percent must be occupied by residents whose incomes do not exceed 120 percent of the areas's very low-income limit. If the safe harbor is met, a limited number of housing units may be occupied by residents with income above governmentally prescribed income limits. The safe harbor requires that the housing must be "affordable" to its charitable beneficiaries but permits an organization to evict tenants for failure to pay rent or misconduct. Any organization unable to meet the safe harbor may rely on a facts and circumstances test that looks to other factors demonstrating the organization's charitable purposes. Finally, the revenue procedure warns that the Service will carefully scrutinize situations where arrangements

involving private developers or management companies may result in impermissible inurement or private benefit.

3. *For Further Reading.* Michael L. Sanders, Joint Ventures Involving Tax–Exempt Organizations, ch. 13 (3d ed. 2007); Bradley Myers, The Low–Income Housing Credit: A Proposal to Address IRS Concerns Regarding Partnerships Between Non–Profit and For–Profit Entities, 60 Tax Law. 415 (2007).

PROBLEMS

Consider whether each of following nonprofit organizations qualify for exemption under § 501(c)(3) and, if not, what structural and operational changes would improve its chances:

(a) Urban Renewal, Inc. ("URI") was formed to increase business patronage in a ten square mile section of South Central Gotham City, an inner-city neighborhood that is primarily inhabited by African Americans and Korean Americans. URI accomplishes its purposes by: presenting television and radio advertisements describing the advantages of shopping in the area, informing news media on the area's problems and potentials, operating a telephone service to provide information to prospective shoppers on transportation in the area, and providing financial assistance through low-interest loans and the purchase of equity interests in business enterprises in the area. The organization is run by a board of directors consisting of five members of the Gotham City business community (three are white, one is Korean American and one is Latino). Two members of the board own businesses in South Central Gotham City.

(b) Affordable Housing, Inc., which was formed to develop a program for new home construction and the renovation of existing homes for sale to low-income families. The organization purchases and renovates existing homes and builds new homes for sale to low-income families who qualify for loans under various federal housing assistance programs.

(c) Same as (b), above, except that the organization was formed to assist moderate-income families to secure decent, safe and sanitary housing at an affordable price. The organization will construct housing and rent it at cost to qualifying families.

e. PROTECTION OF THE ENVIRONMENT

Environmental organizations qualify for § 501(c)(3) exemption as charitable, educational, or scientific. In the early days of the environmental movement, there was some doubt as to whether activities to preserve and protect the natural environment were "charitable" or whether an environmental organization needed to base its exemption application on narrower grounds, such as public education or scientific research. Rulings issued in the 1970s made it clear that the IRS had come to recognize protection of the environment as a charitable purpose.

Revenue Ruling 76–204

1976–1 Cum. Bull. 152.

Advice has been requested whether the nonprofit organization described below, which otherwise qualifies for exemption from Federal income tax under section 501(c)(3) of the Internal Revenue Code of 1954, is operated exclusively for charitable purposes.

The organization was formed by scientists, educators, conservationists, and representatives of the community-at-large for the purpose of preserving the natural environment. It accomplishes this purpose by acquiring and maintaining ecologically significant undeveloped land such as swamps, marshes, forests, wilderness tracts, and other natural areas. The organization acquires the land either as a recipient of a charitable gift or bequest, or as a purchaser. In order to be constantly aware of the availability of significant undeveloped areas, the organization works closely with Federal, state, and local government agencies, and private organizations concerned with environmental conservation.

Some of the land is maintained by the organization itself for the purpose of preserving it in its natural state. Generally, public access to such land is limited so that the delicate balance of the ecosystem remains undisturbed. In these situations the organization will allow educational and scientific research or study as long as such use will not disrupt the particular ecosystem.

Other tracts of land are merely held and preserved by the organization until arrangements can be made to transfer title to the land to a government conservation agency. This usually occurs when the agency is presently unable to acquire the land itself, but where the parcel is particularly suited for inclusion into a new or existing park, wilderness area, or wildlife preserve. Depending upon the circumstances surrounding the organization's initial acquisition of the land, and the restrictions on the particular government agency involved, the organization either makes an outright gift of the land to the agency, or is reimbursed by the agency for the cost of the land. Aside from this occasional reimbursement, the organization does not regularly receive any support from the government, but receives most of its funding from the general public.

Section 501(c)(3) of the Code provides for the exemption from Federal income tax of organizations organized and operated exclusively for charitable purposes.

Section 1.501(c)(3)–1(d)(2) of the Income Tax Regulations states that the term "charitable" is used in section 501(c)(3) of the Code in its generally accepted legal sense and includes the advancement of education and science.

It is generally recognized that efforts to preserve and protect the natural environment for the benefit of the public serve a charitable purpose. Restatement (Second) of Trusts § 375 (1959). In Noice v. Schnell, 101 N.J. Eq. 252, 137 A. 582 (E. & A. 1927), the court held that a bequest, in trust, to preserve and protect from commercial development the Palisades along the Hudson River was a valid charitable trust. In addition, in President and Fellows of Middlebury College v. Central Power Corporation of Vermont, 101 Vt. 325, 143 A. 384 (1928), the court found that a devise of land to preserve a specimen of original Vermont forest was a charitable bequest. Similar charitable bequests have been upheld in other cases dealing with environmental preservation. See, e.g., Richardson v. Essex Institute, 208 Mass. 311, 94 N.E. 262 (Mass.1911); Cresson's Appeal, 30 Pa. 437 (1858); and Staines v. Burton, 17 Utah 331, 53 P. 1015 (Utah 1898).

Several published Revenue Rulings have also recognized the charitable and educational nature of organizations designed to preserve and promote the natural environment. For example, Rev. Rul. 70–186, 1970–1 C.B. 128, holds that an organization formed to preserve a lake as a public recreational facility and to improve the condition of the water in the lake to enhance its recreational features qualifies for exemption under section 501(c)(3) of the Code. In addition, Rev. Rul. 67–292, 1967–2 C.B. 184, holds that an organization formed for the purpose of purchasing and maintaining a sanctuary for wild birds and animals for the benefit of the public may qualify as exempt from Federal income tax under section 501(c)(3).

Furthermore, the promotion of conservation and protection of natural resources has been recognized by Congress as serving a broad public benefit. For example, Congress declared in the National Environmental Policy Act of 1969, 42 U.S.C.A. 4321 (1969), that the prevention and elimination of damage to the environment stimulates the health and welfare of man and enriches the understanding of ecological systems and natural resources important to the nation.

The benefit to the public from environmental conservation derives not merely from the current educational, scientific, and recreational uses that are made of our natural resources, but from their preservation as well. Only through preservation will future generations be guaranteed the ability to enjoy the natural environment. A national policy of preserving unique aspects of the natural environment for future generations is clearly mandated in the Congressional declarations of purpose and policy in numerous Federal conservation laws. See, e.g., Wilderness Act, 16 U.S.C.A. § 1131 (1964)(wilderness areas); Estuarine Areas Act, 16 U.S.C.A. § 1221 (1968)(estuaries); Wild and Scenic Rivers Act, 16 U.S.C.A. § 1271 (1968)(rivers); Water Bank Act, 16 U.S.C.A. § 1301 (1970)(wetlands). While the public benefits from environmental conservation are clearly recognized and measurable, an equally important public purpose is served by preserving natural resources for future generations.

In this case, by acquiring and preserving (whether by self-maintenance or through transfer to a governmental agency) ecologically significant undeveloped land, the organization is enhancing the accomplishment of the express national policy of conserving the nation's unique natural resources. In this sense, the organization is advancing education and science and is benefiting the public in a manner that the law regards as charitable. The restrictions on current access to the lands maintained by the organization are essential to the preservation of their natural state, and are therefore essential to the fulfillment of the organization's charitable purpose. A similar principle is set forth in Rev. Rul. 75–207, 1975–1 C.B. 361, which holds that the value of an island, owned by a private foundation dedicated to preserve the natural ecosystems on the island to which access is limited to invited public and private researchers, may be excluded from the foundation's minimum investment return under section 4942(e) of the Code.

Accordingly, the organization is operated exclusively for charitable purposes and qualifies for exemption from Federal income tax under section 501(c)(3) of the Code.

* * *

Revenue Ruling 78–384

1978–2 Cum.Bull. 174.

Advice has been requested whether the nonprofit organization described below is operated exclusively for charitable purposes, and thus qualifies for exemption from federal income tax under section 501(c)(3) of the Internal Revenue Code of 1954.

The organization is a nonprofit corporation that owns farm land. It restricts the use of its farm land to farming or such other uses as the organization deems ecologically suitable for the land. The organization states that it benefits the public by restricting its land to uses compatible with the ecology of the area.

Section 501(c)(3) of the Code provides for the exemption from federal income tax of organizations organized and operated exclusively for charitable purposes.

Section 1.501(c)(3)–1(d)(2) of the Income Tax Regulations states that the term "charitable" is used in section 501(c)(3) of the Code in its generally accepted legal sense.

Rev. Rul. 76–204, 1976–1 C.B. 152, holds that an organization preserving ecologically significant land for the benefit of the public is operated exclusively for charitable purposes under section 501(c)(3) of the Code.

Although the organization described above restricts its land to uses that do not change the environment, it is not preserving land that has any distinctive ecological significance within the meaning of Rev. Rul. 76–204. In addition, any benefit to the public from this organization's self-imposed restriction on its own land is too indirect and insignificant to establish that the organization serves a charitable purpose within the meaning of section 1.501(c)(3)–1(d)(2) of the regulations.

Accordingly, because the organization does not preserve ecologically significant land and has not otherwise established that it serves a charitable purpose, it is not operated exclusively for charitable purposes, and thus does not qualify for exemption from federal income tax under section 501(c)(3) of the Code.

Rev. Rul. 76–204 is distinguished.

NOTES

1. *Land Trusts*. Nonprofit nature conservancies, often known as land trusts, have emerged as a popular conservation vehicle. Proponents of land trusts point to their flexibility and ability to act more quickly than government agencies and negotiate more discretely with landowners. Donations of real property and conservation easements to land trusts typically entitle donors to substantial tax savings. See Chapter 8C6, infra, at p. 882. Local property tax benefits also may be available. A leading guidebook in the field describes a land trust as follows:

Land trusts are local, state, or regional nonprofit organizations directly involved in protecting land for its natural, recreational, scenic, historical, or productive value. Most land trusts are private, nonprofit corporations. There are also a few governmental or quasi-governmental bodies called land trusts that operate with the freedom and flexibility of a private trust, some of which have a private board or the ability to use private funds. Land trusts are not "trusts" in the legal sense, and may also be called "conservancies," "foundations," or any number of other names descriptive of their purposes.

Land trusts are distinguished by their first-hand involvement in land transactions or management. This involvement can take many forms. Some land trusts purchase or accept donations of land or of conservation easements (permanent, binding agreements that restrict the uses of a piece of land to protect its conservation resources). Some manage land owned by others or advise landowners on how to preserve their land. Some land trusts help negotiate conservation transactions in which they play no other role. Land trusts often work cooperatively with government agencies by acquiring or managing land, researching open space needs and priorities, and assisting in the development of open space plans. They also may work with other non-profit organizations and sometimes with developers. A land trust may do one, several, or all of these things.

Some land trusts are organized to protect a single piece of property, but the more active trusts have a larger land protection agenda. They may focus their efforts in a community, in a region, on a particular type of resource, or on a protection project. Some operate statewide and work cooperatively with local land trusts in addition to conducting their own land conservation projects. Resources protected by land trusts include forests, prairie grasslands, islands, urban gardens, river corridors, farmland, watersheds, parklands, marshes, ranchland, scenic vistas, cultural landscapes, Civil War battlefields, and hiking trails.

Land Trust Alliance, Starting a Land Trust: A Guide to Forming a Land Conservation Organization (2000).

2. *For Further Reading.* Elizabeth Byers & Karin Marchetti Ponte, The Conservation Easement Handbook (rev. ed. 2005); Stephen J. Small, Federal Tax Law of Conservation Easements (4th ed. 1997 & current Supp.). Other resources are available from the Land Trust Alliance at http://www.landtrustalliance.org/conserv.

PROBLEMS

Consider whether the following organizations qualify for tax exemption under § 501(c)(3):

(a) The Mt. Sutro Preservation League, an organization formed by property owners in a residential area to acquire and hold about 100 acres of undeveloped woods adjoining their homes. The League seeks to prevent further commercial development of the area and to support a lawsuit enjoining the construction of a hospital building by a nearby medical center.

(b) The Martinez Agricultural Trust, an organization that owns and operates 500 acres of Kansas farmland as a demonstration conservation project. The Trust tests experimental farming methods and soil restoration techniques, and develops new strains of crops. Results of its research are made available to area farmers. The land has no significant environmental attributes and is adjacent to a larger property owned by the Martinez family, who donated the farmland to the Trust and control its board of directors.

(c) The Hardscrabble County Land Conservancy, an organization empowered to acquire, hold, manage, and dispose of land in a manner designed to preserve and enhance farms and ranches and protect them against conversion to nonagricultural uses. The Conservancy's programs are designed to advance clearly delineated federal and state land conservation policies. The Conservancy intends to acquire, through charitable donations and purchases from farmers and other landowners, easements that restrict the use of the affected property to exclusively agricultural land.

f. DISASTER RELIEF

The enormous outpouring of philanthropy following the September 11, 2001 terrorist attacks raised questions about the legal requirements for a disaster relief organization to qualify as "charitable" under § 501(c)(3) and the tax consequences for individuals and businesses receiving financial assistance. These issues remained in the forefront in the wake of the relief efforts following the Tsunami disaster of December 2004, devastating Gulf

Coast hurricanes, floods and tornados in the Midwest, and the 2010 earthquakes in Haiti and Chile.

Some of these issues had been addressed by the IRS in response to earlier disasters,[1] and the Treasury regulations have long provided that the concept of "charitable" includes "relief of the poor and distressed or of the under privileged . . ." Treas. Reg. § 1.501(c)(3)–1(d)(2). Within a week after September 11, 2001, the IRS elaborated by releasing the advance text of a publication, clarifying its view of the rules for existing organizations and new charities formed in response to the World Trade Center attacks. Legislation enacted by Congress in early 2002 further clarified and liberalized the rules. This discussion highlights some of the major issues.

Disaster Relief as a Charitable Purpose. The IRS disaster relief publication begins by stating the obvious: providing aid to relieve distress caused by a natural or civil disaster (e.g., fire, flood, hurricane, earthquake, riot and the like) or emergency hardship "is charity in its most basic form." IRS Publication 3833, Disaster Relief: Providing Assistance Through Charitable Organizations (July 2009) ("Publication 3833"). Disaster relief can include loans, grants of money, or providing basic necessities such as food, clothing, housing, medical assistance and psychological counseling. Immediately following a disaster, providing these types of essential aid is considered charitable regardless of a recipient's financial resources, but long-term assistance only can be provided to persons who are "appropriate recipients of charity." Publication 3833, at 11–12.

In determining those who may properly receive assistance from a charitable organization, the critical question narrows to what constitutes a "charitable class" of beneficiaries. A charitable class must be large or indefinite enough that providing aid to its members benefits the community as a whole. For that reason, a disaster-relief organization does not qualify as charitable if its benefits are limited to a very few specified individuals or families, and in theory donors may not earmark contributions for a particular victim.[2] The following examples from the IRS publication are instructive:

> **Example 1:** Linda's baby, Todd, suffers a severe burn from a fire requiring costly treatment that Linda cannot afford. Linda's friends and co-workers form the Todd Foundation to raise funds from fellow workers, family members, and the general public to meet Todd's expenses. Since the organization is formed to assist a particular individual, it would not qualify as a charitable organization.

---

1. In 1999, for example, the Service published an article in its annual training manual on the subject. See Ruth Rivera Huetter & Marvin Friedlander, Disaster Relief and Emergency Hardship Programs, Exempt Organizations Continuing Professional Education Technical Instruction Program for FY 1999, at 219.

2. We say "in theory" because, in practice, earmarking is not uncommon—e.g., "send your donation to the Jane Doe Trust Fund at XYZ Bank (clearly not tax-deductible), or to the Jane Doe Relief Fund at Community Foundation (technically, the wrong way to solicit, but donors often get a receipt telling them their gift is tax-deductible)".

Consider this alternative case: Linda's friends and co-workers form an organization to raise funds to meet the expenses of an open-ended group consisting of all children in the community injured by disasters where financial help is needed. Neither Linda nor members of Linda's family control the charitable organization. The organization controls the selection of aid recipients and determines whether any assistance for Todd is appropriate. Potential donors are advised that, while funds may be used to assist Todd, their contributions might well be used for other children who have similar needs. The organization does not accept contributions specifically earmarked for Todd or any other individual. The organization, formed and operated to assist an indefinite number of persons, qualifies as a charitable organization.

* * *

Example 2: A hurricane causes widespread damage to property and loss of life in several counties of a coastal state. Over 100,000 homes are damaged or destroyed by high winds and floods. The group of people affected by the disaster is large enough so that providing aid to this group benefits the public as a whole. Therefore, a charitable organization can be formed to assist persons in this group since the eligible recipients comprise a charitable class.

Example 3: A hurricane causes widespread damage to property and loss of life in several counties of a coastal state. In one of the affected counties, an existing charitable organization has an ongoing program that provides emergency assistance to residents of the county. A small number of residents of this county suffered significant injury or property damage as a result of the storm. The organization provided assistance to some of these individuals. The organization's assistance was provided to a charitable class because the group of potential recipients is indefinite in that it is open-ended to include other victims of future disasters in the county.

Publication 3833, at 10–11.

Needy or Distressed Test. One of the more sensitive questions to arise out of the September 11th attacks was the extent to which a victim or victim's family must demonstrate financial need to become part of an appropriate charitable class. Some victims of the World Trade Center disaster were quite affluent, and others had ample life insurance or were covered by generous employee benefit programs. The IRS initially expressed serious concern that organizations disbursing funds to victims of the attacks would risk their charitable status if distributions were made without regard to the victims' financial need. See Diana B. Henriques & David Barstow, Victims' Funds May Violate U.S. Tax Law, N.Y. Times, Nov. 12, 2001, at B1. The Service's traditional view was that disaster victims need not be totally destitute to be needy and they can qualify as "distressed" even if they are not poor. But an outright transfer of funds based solely on an individual's involvement in a disaster without regard to the individual's particular needs or distress was viewed as impermissible private benefit. After a disaster, need or distress often depends on timing and context—e.g., a charity distributing short-term assistance in the few days or weeks following a disaster, such as housing, food, or crisis counseling would require far less documentation of financial need than an organization distributing longer-term aid. See Publication 1833, at 12–13.

In response to concerns raised by New York City's Twin Towers Fund and other large charities, the IRS reconsidered and shifted to a very permissive stance, announcing that it would treat relief payments from charities as related to the organization's exempt purposes if "made in good faith using objective standards." IRS Notice 2001–78, 2001–50 I.R.B. 1. See also David Barstow & Diana B. Henriques, I.R.S. Makes An Exception on Terror Aid, N.Y. Times, Nov. 17, 2001, at B1. Was the Service's change of its long-held position a compassionate response to the September 11th tragedy, or a capitulation to public pressure that distorts the concept of charity and creates serious inequities? Should the change of position apply to all future disasters?

Employer–Related Assistance. Special problems are raised by organizations formed by a particular employer to provide relief for employees and their families. Consider, for example, a financial services firm at the World Trade Center with 1,000 employees many of whom died in the attack. May the company establish a charitable organization (or use an existing corporate foundation) to provide financial assistance to families of employees, or would this result in impermissible private benefit? Does it matter if the organization is a public charity or a private foundation? And do the benefits provided constitute taxable compensation? The IRS has developed criteria to be weighed in determining whether employer-related assistance programs were charitable. Employment must be merely a "qualifying factor" for relief (it gets you in the door) and a sufficiently large or "indefinite" charitable class must exist (e.g., small companies with only a few employees couldn't qualify). In the case of employer-sponsored public charities, payments made to employees for employer-sponsored disaster relief will be considered consistent with charitable purposes if: (1) the class of beneficiaries is large or indefinite (i.e., a "charitable class"), and (2) the recipients are selected based on an objective determination of need by an independent committee controlled by individuals who are not in a position to exercise substantial influence over the employee's affairs. If these requirements are met, any financial assistance received by employees or their families are presumed to be made for charitable purposes and are excluded from the recipient's gross income as gifts. Publication 1833, at 18–19.

Private Foundations: Special Problems. Private foundations are subject to a stricter regulatory regime than public charities. For a brief discussion of the special problems faced by private foundations providing disaster relief, see Chapter 7D2, infra, at p. 771.

Assistance to Businesses. Many businesses near the World Trade Center, large and small, suffered severe economic dislocation as a result of the terrorist attacks. Are grants or loans (e.g., to meet payroll or relocate) to these businesses consistent with the concept of charity, or do they result in impermissible private benefit? Put more succinctly, can a business be an appropriate object of charity? Prior to September 11, 2001, the Service's view was that, apart from helping a business owner meet the most basic needs, any more general financial assistance was inconsistent with the concept of charity. After receiving submissions from the American Bar Association Tax Section and others, however, the Service moderated this restrictive view and announced that affected businesses could treat grants from charitable organizations as tax-free gifts if the charity had donative intent and was not expecting anything of value in return. See Letter from Lewis J. Fernandez, Deputy Associate Chief Counsel, Internal Revenue Service to Richard M. Lipton, Chair, ABA Section of Taxation, April 15, 2002, reprinted in 36 Exempt Org. Tax Rev. 522 (2002). The IRS's current position is that disaster assistance may be provided to businesses "to aid individual business owners who are financially needy or otherwise distressed" or for other charitable purposes, such as to combat community deterioration. But once a business has been restored to viability or a newly-attracted business is self-supporting, further charitable assistance is no longer appropriate. Publication 1833, at 7–8.

Legislation. Congress resolved some of the issues with which the IRS was grappling by enacting the Victims of Terrorism Tax Relief Act, P.L. 107–134 in 2002. This legislation provides tax relief exclusively for victims of the September 11th terrorist attacks and the anthrax bioterrorism in late 2001. The legislation clarified that payments made by § 501(c)(3) charities as a result of these two terrorist events would be considered as made for exempt purposes even without a specific assessment of financial need if the payments are made in good faith under an objective formula consistently applied.

Congress also enacted § 139 of the Internal Revenue Code, which provides that "qualified disaster relief payments" received from any payor (a charity, an employer or a third party) by individuals for personal, family, living or funeral expenses, and for repair or replacement of items lost in a disaster, are excluded from gross income. Thus, for example, payments made by commercial airlines to families of passengers killed as a result of a qualified disaster would be excluded from gross income. A "qualified disaster" is a disaster that results from terrorist or military actions or an accident involving a common carrier, or is a Presidentially declared disaster or an event that the Secretary of the Treasury determines to be of a "catastrophic" nature. I.R.C. § 139(c).

Temporary targeted legislation is occasionally enacted for major disasters, such as Hurricanes Katrina and Rita, which ravaged the Gulf Coast in the fall of 2005, and the 2010 earthquakes in Haiti and Chile. For example, the Katrina Emergency Tax Relief Act of 2005 included provisions that temporarily expanded charitable contribution deductions by individuals and corporations, increased charity-related mileage deductions, and gave tax assistance for rebuilding homes affected by the hurricanes. Contributors to Haitian relief funds in early 2010 who itemize deductions were permitted to elect to deduct their gifts on their 2009 returns to accelerate the tax benefit.

For Further Reading. Ellen P. Aprill & Richard L. Schmalbeck, Post–Disaster Tax Legislation: A Series of Unfortunate Events, 56 Duke L.J. 51 (2006); Robert A. Katz, A Pig in a Python: How the Charitable Response to September 11 Overwhelmed the Law of Disaster Relief, 36 Ind.L.Rev. 252 (2003); Betsy Buchalter Adler & Barbara A. Rosen, Disaster! Practices and Procedures for Charities Providing Relief After 9/11: A Case Study, 96 J. Tax'n 297 (May 2002). For a discussion of the theft, fraud and waste that occurs in the disaster relief context, see Hema V. Shenoi, Compassion without Competence, Mandating a Financial Oversight Committee in New Disaster Relief Nonprofit Organizations, 74 Brook.L.Rev. 1253 (2009). For a description of the charitable response to 9/11, see Michael F. Melcher with Alex Mandl, The Philanthropic Response to 9/11 (2003).

PROBLEMS

A devastating series of storms, tornados and resulting floods have caused widespread death and destruction to Three Rivers, a regional high-tech center with an economically diverse population of 800,000. The disaster has caused 1,500 deaths; 30,000 residents have lost their homes; and 50,000 others, many in the region's wealthiest neighborhoods, have been temporarily displaced. Among those affected are employees of TR Technologies ("TRT"), the region's largest employer, with a workforce of 30,000.

Numerous efforts are underway to provide relief to victims of the disaster through the local chapter of the American Red Cross and other local civic and religious groups; the Three Rivers Community Foundation (a public charity); and the TRT Foundation, a private foundation created ten years ago by TRT.

As part of your law firm's pro bono practice, you have been asked to consider and resolve the following questions:

(a) In general, what options do donors have in providing financial assistance to victims of the disaster? Do the tax consequences differ depending on whether donors provide assistance directly to a victim or through an existing or newly formed charity?

(b) To what extent must charities providing disaster relief consider a victim's financial need? Is it permissible, for example, to provide assistance to upper middle-class families with adequate insurance if they have been displaced from their home or lost the family's sole source of support?

(c) In general, will the TRT Foundation jeopardize its § 501(c)(3) exemption if it provides financial assistance to TRT employees and their families who are disaster victims? To what extent, if any, are the relief payments received by these victims included in the recipient's gross income?

g.   CREDIT COUNSELING ORGANIZATIONS

Internal Revenue Code: § 501(q)

Credit counseling organizations (CCOs) assist people in financial distress to gain control over their finances. At their best, they provide free or low-cost education on financial management, advise individuals how to reduce debt and avoid bankruptcy, and help negotiate and structure debt repayment plans. At their worst, CCOs use deceptive advertising, engage in fraudulent business practices, pay excessive salaries, and exploit vulnerable consumers. The earliest nonprofit CCOs were sponsored by an odd coalition of credit card companies, government, private philanthropy and labor unions. They initially limited their services to low-income clients, eventually broadening their client base to the general public.

CCOs were first granted tax-exempt status as § 501(c)(4) social welfare organizations. Rev. Rul. 65–299, 1965–2 C.B. 165. Those that engaged in public education and provided counseling to low-income clients achieved § 501(c)(3) exemption as charitable or educational organizations. Rev. Rul. 69–441, 1969–2 C.B. 115. The IRS denied charitable exemptions to CCOs that did not restrict their services to the poor or charged fees but, after losing several court cases, it retreated and began approving § 501(c)(3) exemption to CCOs that provided free public education even if they served the general public and charged nominal fees for debt management plans. See, e.g., Consumer Credit Counseling Services of Alabama, Inc. v. United States, 44 AFTR 2d (RIA) 5122 (D.D.C. 1978).

Nonprofit CCOs began to proliferate in the 1990s as a result of the American culture of excessive debt and stricter new consumer protection laws from which nonprofits were exempted. Although they were hard to distinguish from for-profit businesses, most of these new breed CCOs obtained tax-exempt status despite their high fees, excessive salaries, shady relationships with for-profit affiliates, and little or no public education or service to the poor. The IRS and other regulators gradually took notice, as did the New York Times, which highlighted industry abuses in a front-page expose. Jennifer Bayot, Not-for-Profit Credit Counselors Are Targets of an I.R.S. Inquiry, N.Y.Times, Oct. 14, 2003, at A1. These developments, along with changes to the Bankruptcy Code requiring individuals seeking debt protection to certify that they received counseling from an approved nonprofit CCO, spurred Congress to conduct its own investigation on several fronts.

The pivotal policy questions were whether the IRS already had sufficient tools to deny or revoke exemption to abusive CCOs; whether problems were better addressed outside the tax code by consumer protection legislation; or, as proposed by the Senate Finance Committee staff in its 2004 "discussion draft" of exempt organization tax reforms, whether § 501(c)(3) exemption standards should be tightened. The Panel on the Nonprofit Sector strongly opposed any attempt "to narrow the broad range of missions embraced by charitable organizations or mandate the methods or programs that may be used to further exempt purposes." Panel on the

Nonprofit Sector, Strengthening Transparency, Governance, Accountability of Charitable Organizations: A Supplement to the Final Report (April 2006), at 25. Although the Panel was quick to condemn CCOs that had no charitable or educational mission, it feared the ripple effect ramifications of micro-managing tax exemption standards to correct a problem that it believed was better handled outside the tax law. Congress disagreed, however, and in 2006 it enacted detailed statutory requirements that CCOs must satisfy (in addition to prior law) to qualify for exemption under either § 501(c)(3) or § 501(c)(4). I.R.C. § 501(q).

An organization that provides credit counseling services as a substantial purpose generally will be eligible for exemption under § 501(c)(3) or § 501(c)(4) only if it provides credit counseling services tailored to the specific needs and circumstances of consumers and meets seven other requirements. For example, it may not refuse to provide services to a consumer because of inability to pay. It also must establish a reasonable fee policy, have an independent governing board, and minimize affiliations with for-profit businesses in the lending and debt management industries. I.R.C. § 501(q)(1).

And there's more—such as additional requirements for CCOs seeking to qualify as either charities or social welfare organizations. Section 501(c)(3) status will be granted only to CCOs that do not solicit contributions from consumers during the initial counseling process or when the consumer is receiving services from the organization; and the organization's aggregate revenue from creditors that is attributable to debt management plan services does not exceed 50 percent of total revenues, with higher percentages during a three-year transition period. I.R.C. § 501(q)(2). CCOs seeking exemption as a § 501(c)(4) social welfare organization must apply for exemption under the same "notice" rules in § 508 generally applicable to charities. I.R.C. § 501(q)(3).

These new rules could serve as a model for more wide-ranging refinements of charitable tax exemption standards for other sub-sectors, such as health care and education, if and when Congress desires to act. The legislative history suggests that some of the new requirements for CCOs affect "core issues," such as providing services without regard to ability to pay and having an independent board, that should be relevant in evaluating qualification of other organizations for tax exemption. Joint Committee on Taxation, General Explanation of Tax Legislation Enacted in the 109th Congress 612, n. 858 (2007).

4. THE PUBLIC POLICY LIMITATION

A distinct aspect of the meaning of "charity" is a loosely defined public policy limitation that is superimposed over the list of exempt purposes in § 501(c)(3). An outgrowth of the common law of charitable trusts, this broader concept of "charitable" requires a § 501(c)(3) organization to serve a public purpose and disqualifies any organization that is operated for illegal purposes or engages in activities contrary to a clearly established public policy. The Supreme Court first applied the public policy standard to deny exemption to a racially discriminatory religious school in the celebrated *Bob Jones University* case. As illustrated by the case and the materials following it, it remains uncertain to what extent this limitation extends beyond racial discrimination in education.

Bob Jones University v. United States

Supreme Court of the United States, 1983.
461 U.S. 574, 103 S.Ct. 2017.

■ CHIEF JUSTICE BURGER delivered the opinion of the Court.

We granted certiorari to decide whether petitioners, nonprofit private schools that prescribe and enforce racially discriminatory admissions standards on the basis of religious doctrine, qualify as tax-exempt organizations under § 501(c)(3) of the Internal Revenue Code of 1954.

I

A

* * *

[Even after the Supreme Court's landmark decision in Brown v. Board of Education, the Internal Revenue Service routinely granted exempt status under § 501(c)(3) to private schools, without regard to their racial admissions policies. That policy began to shift in 1967, when the Service announced that it would deny tax exemptions to racially discriminatory private schools that received state aid. Two years later, parents of black public school children in Mississippi sued to enjoin the Service from granting exemptions or allowing charitable contributions to any discriminatory school within that state. In the midst of the litigation, the Service announced that it could no longer justify granting tax-exempt status to discriminatory schools, whether or not they received state aid or were church-related. But the case had become complicated by the intervention of parents and children who supported or attended private segregated Mississippi schools. It proceeded to a three-judge district court, which held in Green v. Connally, 330 F.Supp. 1150 (D.D.C.1971), aff'd mem. sub nom. Coit v. Green, 404 U.S. 997, 92 S.Ct. 564, 30 L.Ed.2d 550 (1971) that racially discriminatory schools in Mississippi did not qualify for exempt status because they violated a sharply defined federal policy against discrimination in education. In Rev. Rul. 71–447, 1971–2 C.B. 230, the Service extended the policy nationwide, basing its position on the common law requirement that the purpose of a charitable trust may not be illegal or contrary to public policy.

Following the mandate in *Green*, the Service issued guidelines aimed at enforcing the nondiscriminatory policy and extending it even to church-related schools that claimed their discriminatory policies were motivated by sincere religious beliefs. See Rev. Rul. 75–231, 1975–1 C.B. 159. In the early 1970's, the Service revoked the exemption of Bob Jones University, a fundamentalist Christian institution that had admitted a few black students but prohibited interracial dating and marriage, and denied exempt status to Goldsboro Christian Schools, which refused to admit blacks on religious grounds. Bob Jones filed suit seeking to enjoin the Service's revocation. The case wended its way up to the Supreme Court, which held in Bob Jones University v. Simon, 416 U.S. 725, 94 S.Ct. 2038, 40 L.Ed.2d 496 (1974) that the Anti–Injunction Act (§ 7421(a) of the Internal Revenue Code) prohibited the University from obtaining judicial review of the Service's action before the assessment or collection of any tax. As a result, Bob Jones regrouped, challenging the revocation in a suit for refund of federal unemployment taxes paid with respect to its employees. Goldsboro Christian Schools initiated its action with a similar refund suit. At the time these cases were commenced, exempt organizations generally were unable to obtain a declaratory judgment with respect to adverse IRS determinations and were forced to await a specific tax deficiency and then sue for a refund. As discussed in Section F1 of this chapter, infra, at pp. 545–548, § 7428 now eases the path to judicial review of adverse IRS exemption rulings. Eds.]

B

No. 81–3, Bob Jones University v. United States

Bob Jones University is a nonprofit corporation located in Greenville, South Carolina. Its purpose is "to conduct an institution of learning * * * giving special emphasis to the Christian religion and the ethics revealed in the Holy Scriptures." The corporation operates a school with an enrollment of approximately 5,000 students, from kindergarten through college and graduate school. Bob Jones University is not affiliated with any religious denomination, but is dedicated to the teaching and propagation of its fundamentalist Christian religious beliefs. It is both a religious and educational institution. Its teachers are required to be devout Christians, and all courses at the University are taught according to the Bible. Entering students are screened as to their religious beliefs, and their public and private conduct is strictly regulated by standards promulgated by University authorities.

The sponsors of the University genuinely believe that the Bible forbids interracial dating and marriage. To effectuate these views, Negroes were completely excluded until 1971. From 1971 to May 1975, the University accepted no applications from unmarried Negroes,[5] but did accept applications from Negroes married within their race.

Following the decision of the United States Court of Appeals for the Fourth Circuit in McCrary v. Runyon, prohibiting racial exclusion from private schools, the University revised its policy. Since May 29, 1975, the University has permitted unmarried Negroes to enroll; but a disciplinary rule prohibits interracial dating and marriage. That rule reads:

---

5. Beginning in 1973, Bob Jones University instituted an exception to this rule, allowing applications from unmarried Negroes who had been members of the University staff for four years or more.

"There is to be no interracial dating.

"1. Students who are partners in an interracial marriage will be expelled.

"2. Students who are members of or affiliated with any group or organization which holds as one of its goals or advocates interracial marriage will be expelled.

"3. Students who date outside their own race will be expelled.

"4. Students who espouse, promote, or encourage others to violate the University's dating rules and regulations will be expelled."

The University continues to deny admission to applicants engaged in an interracial marriage or known to advocate interracial marriage or dating.

Until 1970, the IRS extended tax-exempt status to Bob Jones University under § 501(c)(3). By the letter of November 30, 1970, that followed the injunction issued in Green v. Kennedy, the IRS formally notified the University of the change in IRS policy, and announced its intention to challenge the tax-exempt status of private schools practicing racial discrimination in their admissions policies.

* * *

Thereafter, on April 16, 1975, the IRS notified the University of the proposed revocation of its tax-exempt status. On January 19, 1976, the IRS officially revoked the University's tax-exempt status, effective as of December 1, 1970, the day after the University was formally notified of the change in IRS policy. * * *

The United States District Court for the District of South Carolina held that revocation of the University's tax-exempt status exceeded the delegated powers of the IRS, was improper under the IRS rulings and procedures, and violated the University's rights under the Religion Clauses of the First Amendment. 468 F.Supp. 890, 907 (D.S.C.1978). * * *

The Court of Appeals for the Fourth Circuit, in a divided opinion, reversed. * * *

C

No. 81–1, Goldsboro Christian Schools, Inc. v. United States

Goldsboro Christian Schools is a nonprofit corporation located in Goldsboro, North Carolina. Like Bob Jones University, it was established "to conduct an institution or institutions of learning * * *, giving special emphasis to the Christian religion and the ethics revealed in the Holy scriptures." * * * The school offers classes from kindergarten through high school, and since at least 1969 has satisfied the State of North Carolina's requirements for secular education in private schools. The school requires its high school students to take Bible-related courses, and begins each class with prayer.

Since its incorporation in 1963, Goldsboro Christian Schools has maintained a racially discriminatory admissions policy based upon its interpretation of the Bible.[6] Goldsboro has for the most part accepted only Caucasians. On occasion, however, the school has accepted children from racially mixed marriages in which one of the parents is Caucasian.

Goldsboro never received a determination by the IRS that it was an organization entitled to tax exemption under § 501(c)(3). Upon audit of Goldsboro's records for the years 1969 through 1972, the IRS determined that Goldsboro was not an organization described in § 501(c)(3), and therefore was required to pay taxes under the Federal Insurance Contribution Act and the Federal Unemployment Tax Act.

* * *

The District Court for the Eastern District of North Carolina * * * assumed that Goldsboro's racially discriminatory admissions policy was based upon a sincerely held religious belief. The court nevertheless rejected Goldsboro's claim to tax-exempt status under § 501(c)(3), finding that "private schools maintaining racially discriminatory admissions policies violate clearly declared federal policy and, therefore, must be denied the federal tax benefits flowing from qualification under Section 501(c)(3)." The court also rejected Goldsboro's arguments that denial of tax-exempt status violated the Free Exercise and Establishment Clauses of the First Amendment. Accordingly, the court entered summary judgment for the Government on its counterclaim. The Court of Appeals for the Fourth Circuit affirmed, 644 F.2d 879 (CA4 1981)(per curiam). That court found an "identity for present purposes" between the Goldsboro case and the Bob Jones University case, which had been decided shortly before by another panel of that court, and affirmed for the reasons set forth in Bob Jones University. We granted certiorari in both cases,[9] and we affirm in each.

II

A

In Revenue Ruling 71–447, the IRS formalized the policy first announced in 1970, that § 170 and § 501(c)(3) embrace the common law

---

6. According to the interpretation espoused by Goldsboro, race is determined by descendance from one of Noah's three sons—Ham, Shem and Japheth. Based on this interpretation, Orientals and Negroes are Hamitic, Hebrews are Shemitic, and Caucasians are Japhethitic. Cultural or biological mixing of the races is regarded as a violation of God's command. * * *

9. After the Court granted certiorari, the Government filed a motion to dismiss, informing the Court that the Department of Treasury intended to revoke Revenue Ruling 71–447 and other pertinent rulings and to recognize § 501(c)(3) exemptions for petitioners. The Government suggested that these actions were therefore moot. Before this Court ruled on that motion, however, the United States Court of Appeals for the District of Columbia Circuit enjoined the Government from granting § 501(c)(3) tax-exempt status to any school that discriminates on the basis of race. Wright v. Regan, No. 80–1124 (CADC Feb. 18, 1982)(per curiam order). Thereafter, the Government informed the Court that it would not revoke the revenue rulings and withdrew its request that the actions be dismissed as moot. The Government continues to assert that the IRS lacked authority to promulgate Revenue Ruling 71–447, and does not defend that aspect of the rulings below. [The background and import of this rather understated version of the Government's change of position are discussed in the Notes following the case. Eds.]

"charity" concept. Under that view, to qualify for a tax exemption pursuant to § 501(c)(3), an institution must show, first, that it falls within one of the eight categories expressly set forth in that section, and second, that its activity is not contrary to settled public policy.

Section 501(c)(3) provides that "[c]orporations * * * organized and operated exclusively for religious, charitable * * * or educational purposes" are entitled to tax exemption. Petitioners argue that the plain language of the statute guarantees them tax-exempt status. They emphasize the absence of any language in the statute expressly requiring all exempt organizations to be "charitable" in the common law sense, and they contend that the disjunctive "or" separating the categories in § 501(c)(3) precludes such a reading. Instead, they argue that if an institution falls within one or more of the specified categories it is automatically entitled to exemption, without regard to whether it also qualifies as "charitable." The Court of Appeals rejected that contention and concluded that petitioners' interpretation of the statute "tears section 501(c)(3) from its roots." 639 F.2d, at 151.

It is a well-established canon of statutory construction that a court should go beyond the literal language of a statute if reliance on that language would defeat the plain purpose of the statute:

> "The general words used in the clause * * *, taken by themselves, and literally construed, without regard to the object in view, would seem to sanction the claim of the plaintiff. But this mode of expounding a statute has never been adopted by any enlightened tribunal—because it is evident that in many cases it would defeat the object which the legislature intended to accomplish. And it is well settled that, in interpreting a statute, the court will not look merely to a particular clause in which general words may be used, but will take in connection with it the whole statute * * * and the objects and policy of the law * * *." Brown v. Duchesne, 19 how. 183, 194 (1857)(emphasis added).

Section 501(c)(3) therefore must be analyzed and construed within the framework of the Internal Revenue Code and against the background of the Congressional purposes. Such an examination reveals unmistakable evidence that, underlying all relevant parts of the Code, is the intent that entitlement to tax exemption depends on meeting certain common law standards of charity—namely, that an institution seeking tax-exempt status must serve a public purpose and not be contrary to established public policy.

This "charitable" concept appears explicitly in § 170 of the Code. That section contains a list of organizations virtually identical to that contained in § 501(c)(3). It is apparent that Congress intended that list to have the same meaning in both sections.[10] In § 170, Congress used the list of

---

10. * * * There are minor differences between the lists of organizations in the two sections, see generally Liles & Blum, Development of the Federal Tax Treatment of Charities, 39 L. & Contemp. Prob. 6, 24–25 (No. 4, 1975) (hereinafter Liles & Blum). Nevertheless, the two sections are closely related; both seek to achieve the same basic goal of encouraging the development of certain organizations through the grant of tax benefits. The language of the

organizations in defining the term "charitable contributions." On its face, therefore, § 170 reveals that Congress' intention was to provide tax benefits to organizations serving charitable purposes. The form of § 170 simply makes plain what common sense and history tell us: in enacting both § 170 and § 501(c)(3), Congress sought to provide tax benefits to charitable organizations, to encourage the development of private institutions that serve a useful public purpose or supplement or take the place of public institutions of the same kind.

Tax exemptions for certain institutions thought beneficial to the social order of the country as a whole, or to a particular community, are deeply rooted in our history, as in that of England. The origins of such exemptions lie in the special privileges that have long been extended to charitable trusts.[12]

More than a century ago, this Court announced the caveat that is critical in this case:

> [I]t has now become an established principle of American law, that courts of chancery will sustain and protect * * * a gift * * * to public charitable uses, provided the same is consistent with local laws and public policy * * *.

Soon after that, in 1878, the Court commented:

> A charitable use, where neither law nor public policy forbids, may be applied to almost any thing that tends to promote the well-doing and well-being of social man.

In 1891, in a restatement of the English law of charity[13] which has long been recognized as a leading authority in this country, Lord MacNaghten stated:

> "Charity" in its legal sense comprises four principal divisions: trusts for the relief of poverty; trusts for the advancement of education; trusts for the advancement of religion; and trusts for other purposes beneficial to the community, not falling under any of the preceding heads.

These statements clearly reveal the legal background against which Congress enacted the first charitable exemption statute in 1894: charities were to be given preferential treatment because they provide a benefit to society.

---

two sections is in most respects identical, and the Commissioner and the courts consistently have applied many of the same standards in interpreting those sections. * * * To the extent that § 170 "aids in ascertaining the meaning" of § 501(c)(3), therefore, it is "entitled to great weight," * * *.

12. The form and history of the charitable exemption and deduction sections of the various income tax acts reveal that Congress was guided by the common law of charitable trusts. See Simon, The Tax–Exempt Status of Racially Discriminatory Religious Schools, 36 Tax L.Rev. 477, 485–489 (1981)(hereinafter Simon). * * *

13. The draftsmen of the 1894 income tax law, which included the first charitable exemption provision, relied heavily on English concepts of taxation; and the list of exempt organizations appears to have been patterned upon English income tax statutes. See 26 Cong.Rec. 584–588, 6612–6615 (1894).

What little floor debate occurred on the charitable exemption provision of the 1894 Act and similar sections of later statutes leaves no doubt that Congress deemed the specified organizations entitled to tax benefits because they served desirable public purposes. In floor debate on a similar provision in 1917, for example, Senator Hollis articulated the rationale:

> For every dollar that a man contributes to these public charities, educational, scientific, or otherwise, the public gets 100 percent.

In 1924, this Court restated the common understanding of the charitable exemption provision:

> Evidently the exemption is made in recognition of the benefit which the public derives from corporate activities of the class named, and is intended to aid them when not conducted for private gain. Trinidad v. Sagrada Orden, 263 U.S. 578, 581, 44 S.Ct. 204, 205, 68 L.Ed. 458 (1924).

In enacting the Revenue Act of 1938, ch. 289, 52 Stat. 447 (1938), Congress expressly reconfirmed this view with respect to the charitable deduction provision:

> The exemption from taxation of money and property devoted to charitable and other purposes is based on the theory that the Government is compensated for the loss of revenue by its relief from financial burdens which would otherwise have to be met by appropriations from other public funds, and by the benefits resulting from the promotion of the general welfare.

A corollary to the public benefit principle is the requirement, long recognized in the law of trusts, that the purpose of a charitable trust may not be illegal or violate established public policy. In 1861, this Court stated that a public charitable use must be "consistent with local laws and public policy," * * *. Modern commentators and courts have echoed that view.

When the Government grants exemptions or allows deductions all taxpayers are affected; the very fact of the exemption or deduction for the donor means that other taxpayers can be said to be indirect and vicarious "donors." Charitable exemptions are justified on the basis that the exempt entity confers a public benefit—a benefit which the society or the community may not itself choose or be able to provide, or which supplements and advances the work of public institutions already supported by tax revenues.[18] History buttresses logic to make clear that, to warrant exemption

---

18. The dissent acknowledges that "Congress intended * * * to offer a tax benefit to organizations * * * providing a public benefit," * * * but suggests that Congress itself fully defined what organizations provide a public benefit, through the list of eight categories of exempt organizations contained in § 170 and § 501(c)(3). Under that view, any nonprofit organization that falls within one of the specified categories is automatically entitled to the tax benefits, provided it does not engage in expressly prohibited lobbying or political activities. The dissent thus would have us conclude, for example, that any nonprofit organization that does not engage in prohibited lobbying activities is entitled to tax exemption as an "educational" institution if it is organized for the "instruction or training of the individual for the purpose of improving or developing his capabilities," 26 CFR § 1.501(c)(3)–1(d)(3). As Judge Leventhal noted in Green v. Connally, Fagin's school for educating English boys in the art of

under § 501(c)(3), an institution must fall within a category specified in that section and must demonstrably serve and be in harmony with the public interest.[19] The institution's purpose must not be so at odds with the common community conscience as to undermine any public benefit that might otherwise be conferred.

B

We are bound to approach these questions with full awareness that determinations of public benefit and public policy are sensitive matters with serious implications for the institutions affected; a declaration that a given institution is not "charitable" should be made only where there can be no doubt that the activity involved is contrary to a fundamental public policy. But there can no longer be any doubt that racial discrimination in education violates deeply and widely accepted views of elementary justice. Prior to 1954, public education in many places still was conducted under the pall of Plessy v. Ferguson, 163 U.S. 537, 16 S.Ct. 1138, 41 L.Ed. 256 (1896); racial segregation in primary and secondary education prevailed in many parts of the country. See, e.g., Segregation and the Fourteenth Amendment in the States (B. Reams & P. Wilson, eds. 1975).[20] This Court's decision in Brown v. Board of Education, 347 U.S. 483, 74 S.Ct. 686, 98 L.Ed. 873 (1954), signalled an end to that era. Over the past quarter of a century, every pronouncement of this Court and myriad Acts of Congress and Executive Orders attest a firm national policy to prohibit racial segregation and discrimination in public education.

An unbroken line of cases following Brown v. Board of Education establishes beyond doubt this Court's view that racial discrimination in education violates a most fundamental national public policy, as well as rights of individuals.

* * *

picking pockets would be an "educational" institution under that definition. Similarly, a band of former military personnel might well set up a school for intensive training of subversives for guerrilla warfare and terrorism in other countries; in the abstract, that "school" would qualify as an "educational" institution. Surely Congress had no thought of affording such an unthinking, wooden meaning to § 170 and § 501(c)(3) as to provide tax benefits to "educational" organizations that do not serve a public, charitable purpose.

19. The Court's reading of § 501(c)(3) does not render meaningless Congress' action in specifying the eight categories of presumptively exempt organizations, as petitioners suggest. * * * To be entitled to tax-exempt status under § 501(c)(3), an organization must first fall within one of the categories specified by Congress, and in addition must serve a valid charitable purpose.

20. In 1894, when the first charitable exemption provision was enacted, racially segregated educational institutions would not have been regarded as against public policy. Yet contemporary standards must be considered in determining whether given activities provide a public benefit and are entitled to the charitable tax exemption. In Walz v. Tax Comm'n, 397 U.S. 664, 672–673, 90 S.Ct. 1409, 1413, 25 L.Ed.2d 697 (1970), we observed: "Qualification for tax exemption is not perpetual or immutable; some tax-exempt groups lose that status when their activities take them outside the classification and new entities can come into being and qualify for the exemption." Charitable trust law also makes clear that the definition of "charity" depends upon contemporary standards. See, e.g., Restatement (Second) of Trusts, § 374, comment a (1959); Bogert § 369, at 65–67; 4 Scott § 368, at 2855–2856.

Congress, in Titles IV and VI of the Civil Rights Act of 1964, clearly expressed its agreement that racial discrimination in education violates a fundamental public policy. Other sections of that Act, and numerous enactments since then, testify to the public policy against racial discrimination.

The Executive Branch has consistently placed its support behind eradication of racial discrimination. * * *

Few social or political issues in our history have been more vigorously debated and more extensively ventilated than the issue of racial discrimination, particularly in education. Given the stress and anguish of the history of efforts to escape from the shackles of the "separate but equal" doctrine of Plessy v. Ferguson, supra, it cannot be said that educational institutions that, for whatever reasons, practice racial discrimination, are institutions exercising "beneficial and stabilizing influences in community life," Walz v. Tax Comm'n, 397 U.S. 664, 673, 90 S.Ct. 1409, 1413, 25 L.Ed.2d 697 (1970), or should be encouraged by having all taxpayers share in their support by way of special tax status.

There can thus be no question that the interpretation of § 170 and § 501(c)(3) announced by the IRS in 1970 was correct. That it may be seen as belated does not undermine its soundness. It would be wholly incompatible with the concepts underlying tax exemption to grant the benefit of tax-exempt status to racially discriminatory educational entities, which "exer[t] a pervasive influence on the entire educational process." Norwood v. Harrison, supra, 413 U.S., at 469, 93 S.Ct., at 2812. Whatever may be the rationale for such private schools' policies, and however sincere the rationale may be, racial discrimination in education is contrary to public policy. Racially discriminatory educational institutions cannot be viewed as conferring a public benefit within the "charitable" concept discussed earlier, or within the Congressional intent underlying § 170 and § 501(c)(3).[21]

C

Petitioners contend that, regardless of whether the IRS properly concluded that racially discriminatory private schools violate public policy, only Congress can alter the scope of § 170 and § 501(c)(3). Petitioners accordingly argue that the IRS overstepped its lawful bounds in issuing its 1970 and 1971 rulings.

Yet ever since the inception of the tax code, Congress has seen fit to vest in those administering the tax laws very broad authority to interpret those laws. In an area as complex as the tax system, the agency Congress vests with administrative responsibility must be able to exercise its authority to meet changing conditions and new problems. Indeed as early as 1918, Congress expressly authorized the Commissioner "to make all needful rules

---

21. In view of our conclusion that racially discriminatory private schools violate fundamental public policy and cannot be deemed to confer a benefit on the public, we need not decide whether an organization providing a public benefit and otherwise meeting the requirements of § 501(c)(3) could nevertheless be denied tax-exempt status if certain of its activities violated a law or public policy.

and regulations for the enforcement" of the tax laws. Revenue Act of 1918, ch. 18, § 1309, 40 Stat. 1057, 1143 (1919). The same provision, so essential to efficient and fair administration of the tax laws, has appeared in tax codes ever since, see 26 U.S.C.A. § 7805(a) (1976); and this Court has long recognized the primary authority of the IRS and its predecessors in construing the Internal Revenue Code, * * *.

Congress, the source of IRS authority, can modify IRS rulings it considers improper; and courts exercise review over IRS actions. In the first instance, however, the responsibility for construing the Code falls to the IRS. Since Congress cannot be expected to anticipate every conceivable problem that can arise or to carry out day-to-day oversight, it relies on the administrators and on the courts to implement the legislative will. Administrators, like judges, are under oath to do so.

In § 170 and § 501(c)(3), Congress has identified categories of traditionally exempt institutions and has specified certain additional requirements for tax exemption. Yet the need for continuing interpretation of those statutes is unavoidable. For more than 60 years, the IRS and its predecessors have constantly been called upon to interpret these and comparable provisions, and in doing so have referred consistently to principles of charitable trust law. In Treas.Reg. 45, art. 517(1)(1921), for example, the IRS denied charitable exemptions on the basis of proscribed political activity before the Congress itself added such conduct as a disqualifying element. In other instances, the IRS has denied charitable exemptions to otherwise qualified entities because they served too limited a class of people and thus did not provide a truly "public" benefit under the common law test. Some years before the issuance of the rulings challenged in these cases, the IRS also ruled that contributions to community recreational facilities would not be deductible and that the facilities themselves would not be entitled to tax-exempt status, unless those facilities were open to all on a racially nondiscriminatory basis. These rulings reflect the Commissioner's continuing duty to interpret and apply the Internal Revenue Code.

Guided, of course, by the Code, the IRS has the responsibility, in the first instance, to determine whether a particular entity is "charitable" for purposes of § 170 and § 501(c)(3).[22] This in turn may necessitate later determinations of whether given activities so violate public policy that the entities involved cannot be deemed to provide a public benefit worthy of "charitable" status. We emphasize, however, that these sensitive determinations should be made only where there is no doubt that the organization's activities violate fundamental public policy.

On the record before us, there can be no doubt as to the national policy. In 1970, when the IRS first issued the ruling challenged here, the position of all three branches of the Federal Government was unmistakably

---

22. In the present case, the IRS issued its rulings denying exemptions to racially discriminatory schools only after a three-judge District Court had issued a preliminary injunction. * * *

clear. The correctness of the Commissioner's conclusion that a racially discriminatory private school "is not 'charitable' within the common law concepts reflected in * * * the Code," Rev.Rul. 71–447, 1972–2 Cum.Bull., at 231, is wholly consistent with what Congress, the Executive and the courts had repeatedly declared before 1970. Indeed, it would be anomalous for the Executive, Legislative and Judicial Branches to reach conclusions that add up to a firm public policy on racial discrimination, and at the same time have the IRS blissfully ignore what all three branches of the Federal Government had declared.[23] Clearly an educational institution engaging in practices affirmatively at odds with this declared position of the whole government cannot be seen as exercising a "beneficial and stabilizing influenc[e] in community life," and is not "charitable," within the meaning of § 170 and § 501(c)(3). We therefore hold that the IRS did not exceed its authority when it announced its interpretation of § 170 and § 501(c)(3) in 1970 and 1971.[24]

D

The actions of Congress since 1970 leave no doubt that the IRS reached the correct conclusion in exercising its authority. It is, of course, not unknown for independent agencies or the Executive Branch to misconstrue the intent of a statute; Congress can and often does correct such misconceptions, if the courts have not done so. Yet for a dozen years Congress has been made aware—acutely aware—of the IRS rulings of 1970 and 1971. As we noted earlier, few issues have been the subject of more vigorous and widespread debate and discussion in and out of Congress than those related to racial segregation in education. Sincere adherents advocating contrary views have ventilated the subject for well over three decades. Failure of Congress to modify the IRS rulings of 1970 and 1971, of which Congress was, by its own studies and by public discourse, constantly reminded; and Congress' awareness of the denial of tax-exempt status for racially discriminatory schools when enacting other and related legislation make out an unusually strong case of legislative acquiescence in and ratification by implication of the 1970 and 1971 rulings.

* * *

---

23. Justice Powell misreads the Court's opinion when he suggests that the Court implies that "the Internal Revenue Service is invested with authority to decide which public policies are sufficiently 'fundamental' to require denial of tax exemptions." The Court's opinion does not warrant that interpretation. Justice POWELL concedes that "if any national policy is sufficiently fundamental to constitute such an overriding limitation on the availability of tax-exempt status under § 501(c)(3), it is the policy against racial discrimination in education." Since that policy is sufficiently clear to warrant Justice POWELL's concession and for him to support our finding of longstanding Congressional acquiescence, it should be apparent that his concerns about the Court's opinion are unfounded.

24. Many of the amici curiae, including Amicus William T. Coleman, Jr. (appointed by the Court), argue that denial of tax-exempt status to racially discriminatory schools is independently required by the equal protection component of the Fifth Amendment. In light of our resolution of this case, we do not reach that issue. * * *

Non-action by Congress is not often a useful guide, but the non-action here is significant. During the past 12 years there have been no fewer than 13 bills introduced to overturn the IRS interpretation of § 501(c)(3). Not one of these bills has emerged from any committee, although Congress has enacted numerous other amendments to § 501 during this same period, including an amendment to § 501(c)(3) itself. It is hardly conceivable that Congress—and in this setting, any Member of Congress—was not abundantly aware of what was going on. In view of its prolonged and acute awareness of so important an issue, Congress' failure to act on the bills proposed on this subject provides added support for concluding that Congress acquiesced in the IRS rulings of 1970 and 1971. * * *

The evidence of Congressional approval of the policy embodied in Revenue Ruling 71–447 goes well beyond the failure of Congress to act on legislative proposals. Congress affirmatively manifested its acquiescence in the IRS policy when it enacted the present 501(i) of the Code * * *. That provision denies tax-exempt status to social clubs whose charters or policy statements provide for "discrimination against any person on the basis of race, color, or religion."[25] Both the House and Senate committee reports on that bill articulated the national policy against granting tax exemptions to racially discriminatory private clubs.

Even more significant is the fact that both reports focus on this Court's affirmance of Green v. Connally, supra, as having established that "discrimination on account of race is inconsistent with an educational institution's tax exempt status." * * * These references in Congressional committee reports on an enactment denying tax exemptions to racially discriminatory private social clubs cannot be read other than as indicating approval of the standards applied to racially discriminatory private schools by the IRS subsequent to 1970, and specifically of Revenue Ruling 71–447.

III

Petitioners contend that, even if the Commissioner's policy is valid as to nonreligious private schools, that policy cannot constitutionally be applied to schools that engage in racial discrimination on the basis of sincerely held religious beliefs. As to such schools, it is argued that the IRS construction of § 170 and § 501(c)(3) violates their free exercise rights under the Religion Clauses of the First Amendment. This contention presents claims not heretofore considered by this Court in precisely this context.

This Court has long held the Free Exercise Clause of the First Amendment to be an absolute prohibition against governmental regulation of religious beliefs. As interpreted by this Court, moreover, the Free Exercise Clause provides substantial protection for lawful conduct grounded in religious belief. However, "[n]ot all burdens on religion are unconstitutional * * *. The state may justify a limitation on religious liberty by

---

25. Prior to the introduction of this legislation, a three-judge district court had held that segregated social clubs were entitled to tax exemptions. McGlotten v. Connally, 338 F.Supp. 448 (D.D.C.1972). Section 501(i) was enacted primarily in response to that decision. * * *

showing that it is essential to accomplish an overriding governmental interest." United States v. Lee, 455 U.S. 252, 257–258, 102 S.Ct. 1051 (1982)(citations omitted).

On occasion, this Court has found certain governmental interests so compelling as to allow even regulations prohibiting religiously based conduct. In Prince v. Massachusetts, 321 U.S. 158, 64 S.Ct. 438 (1944), for example, the Court held that neutrally cast child labor laws prohibiting sale of printed materials on public streets could be applied to prohibit children from dispensing religious literature. The Court found no constitutional infirmity in "excluding [Jehovah's Witness children] from doing there what no other children may do." Id., at 170, 64 S.Ct., at 444. Denial of tax benefits inevitably will have a substantial impact on the operation of private religious schools, but will not prevent those schools from observing their religious tenets.

The government interest at stake here is compelling. As discussed in Part II(B), supra, the Government has a fundamental, overriding interest in eradicating racial discrimination in education—[29]discrimination that prevailed, with official approval, for the first 165 years of this Nation's history. That governmental interest substantially outweighs whatever burden denial of tax benefits places on petitioners' exercise of their religious beliefs. The interests asserted by petitioners cannot be accommodated with that compelling governmental interest, and no "less restrictive means" are available to achieve the governmental interest.[30]

* * *

[Noting that not all burdens on religion are unconstitutional if justified by an overriding governmental interest, the Court held that the interest of eradicating racial discrimination in education substantially outweighs whatever burden denial of tax benefits may place on the exercise of their religious beliefs. The Court also summarily rejected the University's Establishment Clause challenge, observing that the Service's policy was founded on a neutral, secular basis. Eds.]

IV

The remaining issue is whether the IRS properly applied its policy to these petitioners. Petitioner Goldsboro Christian Schools admits that it "maintain[s] racially discriminatory policies," but seeks to justify those policies on grounds we have fully discussed. The IRS properly denied tax-exempt status to Goldsboro Christian Schools. Petitioner Bob Jones Uni-

---

29. We deal here only with religious *schools*—not with churches or other purely religious institutions; here, the governmental interest is in denying public support to racial discrimination in education. As noted earlier, racially discriminatory schools "exer[t] a pervasive influence on the entire educational process," outweighing any public benefit that they might otherwise provide.

30. Bob Jones University also contends that denial of tax exemption violates the Establishment Clause by preferring religions whose tenets do not require racial discrimination over those which believe racial intermixing is forbidden. [The Court summarily rejected this challenge, concluding that the IRS's policy was founded on a "neutral, secular basis." Eds.]

versity, however, contends that it is not racially discriminatory. It emphasizes that it now allows all races to enroll, subject only to its restrictions on
the conduct of all students, including its prohibitions of association between men and women of different races, and of interracial marriage.[31]
Although a ban on intermarriage or interracial dating applies to all races,
decisions of this Court firmly establish that discrimination on the basis of
racial affiliation and association is a form of racial discrimination, * * *.
We therefore find that the IRS properly applied Revenue Ruling 71–447 to
Bob Jones University.[32]

The judgments of the Court of Appeals are, accordingly,

Affirmed.

■ JUSTICE POWELL, concurring in part and concurring in the judgment.

I join the Court's judgment, along with part III of its opinion holding
that the denial of tax exemptions to petitioners does not violate the First
Amendment. I write separately because I am troubled by the broader
implications of the Court's opinion with respect to the authority of the
Internal Revenue Service (IRS) and its construction of §§ 170(c) and
501(c)(3) of the Internal Revenue Code.

I

Federal taxes are not imposed on organizations "operated exclusively
for religious, charitable, scientific, testing for public safety, literary, or
educational purposes * * *." 26 U.S.C.A. § 501(c)(3). The Code also permits a tax deduction for contributions made to these organizations.
§ 170(c). It is clear that petitioners, organizations incorporated for educational purposes, fall within the language of the statute. It also is clear
that the language itself does not mandate refusal of tax-exempt status to
any private school that maintains a racially discriminatory admissions
policy. Accordingly, there is force in Justice Rehnquist's argument that
§§ 170(c) and 501(c)(3) should be construed as setting forth the only
criteria Congress has established for qualification as a tax-exempt organization. * * * Indeed, were we writing prior to the history detailed in the
Court's opinion, this could well be the construction I would adopt. But
there has been a decade of acceptance that is persuasive in the circumstances of this case, and I conclude that there are now sufficient reasons for
accepting the IRS's construction of the Code as proscribing tax exemptions
for schools that discriminate on the basis of race as a matter of policy.

---

31. This argument would in any event apply only to the final eight months of the five
tax years at issue in this case. Prior to May 1975, Bob Jones University's admissions policy
was racially discriminatory on its face, since the University excluded unmarried Negro
students while admitting unmarried Caucasians.

32. Bob Jones University also argues that the IRS policy should not apply to it because it
is entitled to exemption under § 501(c)(3) as a "religious" organization, rather than as an
"educational" institution. The record in this case leaves no doubt, however, that Bob Jones
University is both an educational institution and a religious institution. As discussed previously, the IRS policy properly extends to all private schools, including religious schools. The IRS
policy thus was properly applied to Bob Jones University.

I cannot say that this construction of the Code, adopted by the IRS in 1970 and upheld by the Court of Appeals below, is without logical support. The statutory terms are not self-defining, and it is plausible that in some instances an organization seeking a tax exemption might act in a manner so clearly contrary to the purposes of our laws that it could not be deemed to serve the enumerated statutory purposes. And, as the Court notes, if any national policy is sufficiently fundamental to constitute such an overriding limitation on the availability of tax-exempt status under § 501(c)(3), it is the policy against racial discrimination in education. Finally, and of critical importance for me, the subsequent actions of Congress present "an unusually strong case of legislative acquiescence in and ratification by implication of the [IRS'] 1970 and 1971 rulings" with respect to racially discriminatory schools. In particular, Congress' enactment of § 501(i) in 1976 is strong evidence of agreement with these particular IRS rulings.

II

I therefore concur in the Court's judgment that tax-exempt status under § 170(c) and § 501(c)(3) is not available to private schools that concededly are racially discriminatory. I do not agree, however, with the Court's more general explanation of the justifications for the tax exemptions provided to charitable organizations. The Court states:

> Charitable exemptions are justified on the basis that the exempt entity confers a public benefit—a benefit which the society or the community may not itself choose or be able to provide, or which supplements and advances the work of public institutions already supported by tax revenues. History buttresses logic to make clear that, to warrant exemption under 501(c)(3), an institution must fall within a category specified in that section and must demonstrably serve and be in harmony with the public interest. The institution's purpose must not be so at odds with the common community conscience as to undermine any public benefit that might otherwise be conferred.

Applying this test to petitioners, the court concludes that "[c]learly an educational institution engaging in practices affirmatively at odds with [the] declared position of the whole government cannot be seen as exercising a 'beneficial and stabilizing influenc[e] in community life,' * * * and is not 'charitable,' within the meaning of § 170 and § 501(c)(3)," Quoting Walz v. Tax Comm'n, 397 U.S. 664, 673, 90 S.Ct. 1409, 1413, 25 L.Ed.2d 697 (1970).

With all respect, I am unconvinced that the critical question in determining tax-exempt status is whether an individual organization provides a clear "public benefit" as defined by the Court. Over 106,000 organizations filed § 501(c)(3) returns in 1981. Internal Revenue Service, 1982 Exempt Organization/Business Master File. I find it impossible to believe that all or even most of those organizations could prove that they "demonstrably serve and [are] in harmony with the public interest" or that they are "beneficial and stabilizing influences in community life." Nor am I prepared to say that petitioners, because of their racially discriminatory policies, necessarily contribute nothing of benefit to the community. It is clear from the substantially secular character of the curricula and degrees offered that petitioners provide educational benefits.

Even more troubling to me is the element of conformity that appears to inform the Court's analysis. The Court asserts that an exempt organization must "demonstrably serve and be in harmony with the public interest," must have a purpose that comports with "the common community conscience," and must not act in a manner "affirmatively at odds with [the] declared position of the whole government." Taken together, these passages suggest that the primary function of a tax-exempt organization is to act on behalf of the Government in carrying out governmentally approved policies. In my opinion, such a view of § 501(c)(3) ignores the important role played by tax exemptions in encouraging diverse, indeed often sharply conflicting, activities and viewpoints. As Justice Brennan has observed, private, nonprofit groups receive tax exemptions because "each group contributes to the diversity of association, viewpoint, and enterprise essential to a vigorous, pluralistic society." Far from representing an effort to reinforce any perceived "common community conscience," the provision of tax exemptions to nonprofit groups is one indispensable means of limiting the influence of governmental orthodoxy on important areas of community life.[3] Given the importance of our tradition of pluralism, "[t]he interest in preserving an area of untrammeled choice for private philanthropy is very great." Jackson v. Statler Foundation, 496 F.2d 623, 639 (C.A.2 1973)(Friendly, J., dissenting from denial of reconsideration en banc).

I do not suggest that these considerations always are or should be dispositive. Congress, of course, may find that some organizations do not warrant tax-exempt status. In this case I agree with the Court that Congress has determined that the policy against racial discrimination in education should override the countervailing interest in permitting unorthodox private behavior.

---

3. Certainly § 501(c)(3) has not been applied in the manner suggested by the Court's analysis. The 1,100–page list of exempt organizations includes—among countless examples— such organizations as American Friends Service Committee, Inc., Committee on the Present Danger, Jehovah's Witnesses in the United States, Moral Majority Foundation, Inc., Friends of the Earth Foundation, Inc., Mountain States Legal Foundation, National Right to Life Educational Foundation, Planned Parenthood Federation of America, Scientists and Engineers for Secure Energy, Inc., and Union of Concerned Scientists Fund, Inc. See Internal Revenue Service, Cumulative List of Organizations Described in Section 170(c) of the Internal Revenue Code of 1954, at 31, 221, 376, 518, 670, 677, 694, 795, 880, 1001, 1073 (Rev'd Oct. 1981). It would be difficult indeed to argue that each of these organizations reflects the views of the "common community conscience" or "demonstrably * * * [is] in harmony with the public interest." In identifying these organizations, largely taken at random from the tens of thousands on the list, I of course do not imply disapproval of their being exempt from taxation. Rather, they illustrate the commendable tolerance by our Government of even the most strongly held divergent views, including views that at least from time to time are "at odds" with the position of our Government. We have consistently recognized that such disparate groups are entitled to share the privilege of tax exemption.

I would emphasize, however, that the balancing of these substantial interests is for Congress to perform. I am unwilling to join any suggestion that the Internal Revenue Service is invested with authority to decide which public policies are sufficiently "fundamental" to require denial of tax exemptions. Its business is to administer laws designed to produce revenue for the Government, not to promote "public policy." As former IRS Commissioner Kurtz has noted, questions concerning religion and civil rights "are far afield from the more typical tasks of tax administrators—determining taxable income." Kurtz, Difficult Definitional Problems in Tax Administration: Religion and Race, 23 Catholic Lawyer 301, 301 (1978). This Court often has expressed concern that the scope of an agency's authorization be limited to those areas in which the agency fairly may be said to have expertise, and this concern applies with special force when the asserted administrative power is one to determine the scope of public policy. As Justice Blackmun has noted,

> where the philanthropic organization is concerned, there appears to be little to circumscribe the almost unfettered power of the Commissioner. This may be very well so long as one subscribes to the particular brand of social policy the Commissioner happens to be advocating at the time * * *, but application of our tax laws should not operate in so fickle a fashion. Surely, social policy in the first instance is a matter for legislative concern.

* * *

■ JUSTICE REHNQUIST, dissenting.

The Court points out that there is a strong national policy in this country against racial discrimination. To the extent that the Court states that Congress in furtherance of this policy could deny tax-exempt status to educational institutions that promote racial discrimination, I readily agree. But, unlike the Court, I am convinced that Congress simply has failed to take this action and, as this Court has said over and over again, regardless of our view on the propriety of Congress' failure to legislate we are not constitutionally empowered to act for them.

In approaching this statutory construction question the Court quite adeptly avoids the statute it is construing. This I am sure is no accident, for there is nothing in the language of § 501(c)(3) that supports the result obtained by the Court. * * * With undeniable clarity, Congress has explicitly defined the requirements for § 501(c)(3) status. An entity must be (1) a corporation, or community chest, fund, or foundation, (2) organized for one of the eight enumerated purposes, (3) operated on a nonprofit basis, and (4) free from involvement in lobbying activities and political campaigns. Nowhere is there to be found some additional, undefined public policy requirement.

The Court first seeks refuge from the obvious reading of § 501(c)(3) by turning to § 170 of the Internal Revenue Code which provides a tax deduction for contributions made to § 501(c)(3) organizations. * * * The Court seizes the words "charitable contribution" and with little discussion concludes that "[o]n its face, therefore, § 170 reveals that Congress' intention was to provide tax benefits to organizations serving charitable purposes," intimating that this implies some unspecified common law charitable trust requirement. * * *

The Court would have been well advised to look to subsection (c) where, as § 170(a)(1) indicates, Congress has defined a "charitable contribution":

> For purposes of this section, the term "charitable contribution" means a contribution or gift to or for the use of * * * [a] corporation, trust, or community chest, fund, or foundation * * * organized and operated exclusively for religious, charitable, scientific, literary, or educational purposes, or to foster national or international amateur sports competition (but only if no part of its activities involve the provision of athletic facilities or equipment), or for the prevention of cruelty to children or animals; * * * no part of the net earnings of which inures to the benefit of any private shareholder or individual; and * * * which is not disqualified for tax exemption under section 501(c)(3) by reason of attempting to influence legislation, and which does not participate in, or intervene in (including the publishing or distributing of statements), any political campaign on behalf of any candidate for public office. 26 U.S.C.A. § 170(c).

Plainly, § 170(c) simply tracks the requirements set forth in § 501(c)(3). Since § 170 is no more than a mirror of § 501(c)(3) and, as the Court points out, § 170 followed § 501(c)(3) by more than two decades, it is at best of little usefulness in finding the meaning of § 501(c)(3).

Making a more fruitful inquiry, the Court next turns to the legislative history of § 501(c)(3) and finds that Congress intended in that statute to offer a tax benefit to organizations that Congress believed were providing a public benefit. I certainly agree. But then the Court leaps to the conclusion that this history is proof Congress intended that an organization seeking § 501(c)(3) status "must fall within a category specified in that section and must demonstrably serve and be in harmony with the public interest." * * * To the contrary, I think that the legislative history of § 501(c)(3) unmistakably makes clear that Congress has decided what organizations are serving a public purpose and providing a public benefit within the meaning of § 501(c)(3) and has clearly set forth in § 501(c)(3) the characteristics of such organizations. In fact, there are few examples which better illustrate Congress' effort to define and redefine the requirements of a legislative act.

* * *

The Court suggests that unless its new requirement be added to § 501(c)(3), nonprofit organizations formed to teach pickpockets and terrorists would necessarily acquire tax exempt status. * * * Since the Court does not challenge the characterization of petitioners as "educational" institutions within the meaning of § 501(c)(3), and in fact states several times in the course of its opinion that petitioners are educational institutions, * * * it is difficult to see how this argument advances the Court's reasoning for disposing of petitioners' cases.

But simply because I reject the Court's heavy-handed creation of the requirement that an organization seeking § 501(c)(3) status must "serve and be in harmony with the public interest," does not mean that I would deny to the IRS the usual authority to adopt regulations further explaining what Congress meant by the term "educational." The IRS has fully exercised that authority in 26 CFR § 1.501(c)(3)–1(d)(3), which provides:

"(3) Educational defined—(i) In general. The term 'educational,' as used in section 501(c)(3), relates to—

"(a) The instruction or training of the individual for the purpose of improving or developing his capabilities; or

"(b) The instruction of the public on subjects useful to the individual and beneficial to the community.

"An organization may be educational even though it advocates a particular position or viewpoint so long as it presents a sufficiently full and fair exposition of the pertinent facts as to permit an individual or the public to form an independent opinion or conclusion. On the other hand, an organization is not educational if its principal function is the mere presentation of unsupported opinion.

"(ii) Examples of educational organizations. The following are examples of organizations which, if they otherwise meet the requirements of this section, are educational:

"*Example (1)*. An organization, such as a primary or secondary school, a college, or a professional or trade school, which has a regularly scheduled curriculum, a regular faculty, and a regularly enrolled body of students in attendance at a place where the educational activities are regularly carried on.

"*Example (2)*. An organization whose activities consist of presenting public discussion groups, forums, panels, lectures, or other similar programs. Such programs may be on radio or television.

"*Example (3)*. An organization which presents a course of instruction by means of correspondence or through the utilization of television or radio.

"*Example (4)*. Museums, zoos, planetariums, symphony orchestras, and other similar organizations."

I have little doubt that neither the "Fagin School for Pickpockets" nor a school training students for guerrilla warfare and terrorism in other countries would meet the definitions contained in the regulations.

Prior to 1970, when the charted course was abruptly changed, the IRS had continuously interpreted § 501(c)(3) and its predecessors in accordance with the view I have expressed above. This, of course, is of considerable significance in determining the intended meaning of the statute. [Justice Rehnquist proceeded to conclude that the position adopted by the IRS in

1970 was not entitled to any deference and that there was little or no evidence that Congress acquiesced by its failure to enact legislation to reverse the policy. Eds.]

* * *

I have no disagreement with the Court's finding that there is a strong national policy in this country opposed to racial discrimination. I agree with the Court that Congress has the power to further this policy by denying § 501(c)(3) status to organizations that practice racial discrimination. But as of yet Congress has failed to do so. Whatever the reasons for the failure, this Court should not legislate for Congress.[1]

Petitioners are each organized for the "instruction or training of the individual for the purpose of improving or developing his capabilities," 26 CFR § 1.501(c)(3)–1(d)(3), and thus are organized for "educational purposes" within the meaning of § 501(c)(3). Petitioners' nonprofit status is uncontested. There is no indication that either petitioner has been involved in lobbying activities or political campaigns. Therefore, it is my view that unless and until Congress affirmatively amends § 501(c)(3) to require more, the IRS is without authority to deny petitioners § 501(c)(3) status. For this reason, I would reverse the Court of Appeals.

NOTES AND QUESTIONS

1. *A Legislative Solution?* The opinion in *Bob Jones* does not adequately capture the political firestorm that followed the Reagan Administration's decision, on the eve of filing its brief in the Supreme Court, to abandon the Service's position denying exemptions to discriminatory schools. While the Justice Department insisted it was against race discrimination in any form, it concluded that the Service could not deny tax exemptions to discriminatory schools without specific statutory authority. Conceding defeat, it requested the Supreme Court to dismiss the cases as moot.

After the Justice Department's concession, the Court of Appeals for the District of Columbia Circuit, in related litigation, enjoined the Service from restoring exempt status to any racially discriminatory school. Wright v. Regan, Nos. 80–1124 & 82–1134 (D.C. Cir. Feb. 18, 1982) (per curiam). The Government then withdrew its request to dismiss the pending cases as moot and suggested that the court appoint counsel to support the judgments of the Fourth Circuit. The Supreme Court agreed, appointing William T. Coleman, a distinguished civil rights attorney and former Secretary of Transportation, to defend what had become the Service's former position.

---

1. Because of its holding, the Court does not have to decide whether it would violate the equal protection component of the Fifth Amendment for Congress to grant § 501(c)(3) status to organizations that practice racial discrimination. I would decide that it does not. The statute is facially neutral; absent a showing of a discriminatory purpose, no equal protection violation is established.

Several days later, in the face of a wave of protest, President Reagan proposed legislation that would have given the IRS express authority to deny tax-exempt status to schools with racially discriminatory policies. The proposal would have denied exemption to any school with a "racially discriminatory policy," which would have been defined as "[a refusal] to admit students of all races (defined to include also color and national origin) to the rights, privileges, programs, and activities usually accorded or made available to students by that organization, or if the organization refuses to administer its educational policies, admission policies, scholarship and loan programs, or other programs in a manner that does not discriminate on the basis of race." An admission policy or a program of religious training or worship that is limited to, or granted preference or priority to, members of a particular religious organization or belief would not have been considered a racially discriminatory policy as long as it was not based upon race or upon a belief that required discrimination on the basis of race. See Statement of R.T. McNamar, Deputy Secretary of the Treasury, Hearings on Legislation to Deny Tax Exemption to Racially Discriminatory Private Schools, 97th Cong., 2d Sess. 225, 229–232 (1982).

2. *Post–Decision Press Conference.* After the Supreme Court handed down its 8–1 decision in *Bob Jones University*, the Justice Department conceded that additional legislation was unnecessary to give the IRS authority to deny tax exemptions to discriminatory schools, and President Reagan told reporters, "We will obey the law." See Stephen Wermiel, U.S. Can't Grant Biased Schools Tax Exemptions, Wall St. J., May 25, 1983, at 2. The Reverend Bob Jones, Jr., whose father founded the university in 1927, was less respectful. After hearing of the decision, Rev. Jones reportedly preached a sermon in the college chapel, declaring: "We're in a bad fix when eight evil old men and one vain and foolish woman can speak a verdict on American liberties. Our nation from this day forward is no better than Russia insofar as expecting the blessings of God is concerned." See William H. Honan, Obituary of Bob Jones, Jr., N.Y. Times, Nov. 13, 1998, at C24 (national edition).

3. *IRS Enforcement Policy.* The Service's initial efforts to enforce the mandate of the courts were controversial. Guidelines issued in the 1970s and still applicable today require schools to demonstrate their racially nondiscriminatory policy in governing documents and catalogues; to make their policy known to all segments of the community through newspapers and the broadcast media; to keep detailed records evidencing compliance with the guidelines; and to file an annual statement with the IRS (now on Schedule E of Form 990 or, for schools that do not file Form 990, on Form 5578), certifying their compliance with IRS guidelines. No actual minority quotas were imposed, however, and a school practicing de facto discrimination could qualify for exemption as long as it met the publicity and recordkeeping requirements. Rev. Proc. 72–54, 1972–2 C.B. 834, as amplified in Rev. Proc. 75–50, 1975–2 C.B. 578. See also IRS Publication 557, Tax–Exempt Status for Your Organization 23–25 (rev. June 2008).

In August, 1978, in response to complaints that the IRS's enforcement of the nondiscrimination requirements was ineffective, the Carter Administration proposed a set of stricter standards, including numerical quotas, to be applied primarily to private elementary and secondary schools that had been adjudicated by a court or agency to be racially discriminatory or that were created or substantially expanded at or about the time of public school desegregation in the community and had little or no minority enrollment. The reaction to this proposal was hostile. The Service was bombarded with more than 115,000 letters of protest—"the biggest reaction anyone here can remember," according to an I.R.S. spokesman at the time. See Sanford L. Jacobs, Private Schools Pounce on IRS Proposal, Wall St.J., Nov. 6, 1978, at 13. Religious groups were particularly upset, believing the percentage test to be a quota system that was a threat to religious freedom. Jewish groups claimed that the procedure would deny an exemption to a Hebrew school because it did not have black or Spanish-speaking students.

Responding to this public outcry, the Service regrouped and issued more flexible guidelines under which a school could satisfy a "safe harbor" if minority enrollment was 20 percent of the percentage of minority age school population in the "community." But Congress blocked even these policies by freezing appropriations to implement them, and the safe harbor never went into effect.

4. *Meanwhile, Back in the Courts.* After the decision in *Bob Jones*, the Service faced inconsistent directives from Congress and the courts. Parents of black children attending public schools in several Southern states sued to compel the Service to strengthen its enforcement efforts and to deny exempt status to racially discriminatory schools throughout the United States. Reversing the D.C.Circuit, the Supreme Court held that the parents lacked standing to sue. Allen v. Wright, 468 U.S. 737, 104 S.Ct. 3315 (1984). The Court stated that the Article III doctrine of standing requires a plaintiff to allege personal injury fairly traceable to the defendant's allegedly unlawful conduct and likely to be redressed by the requested relief. It concluded that the injuries alleged by the plaintiffs were neither "judicially cognizable" nor fairly traceable to any unlawful conduct of the IRS. Id. at 753. For additional discussion of the obstacles facing third parties who seek to challenge an organization's exempt status, see Section H3 of this chapter, infra, at pp. 551–566.

Did Congressional hostility to the Carter Administration's 1978 enforcement guidelines and the Supreme Court's decision in *Wright* mean that *Bob Jones* was a hollow victory? Probably not. Revenue Procedure 75–50 (see Note 3, above) is still on the books, and subsequent developments discussed below indicate that the IRS has enforced the public policy limitation insofar as it applies to race discrimination in education but rarely beyond that.

5. *Subsequent Judicial Developments.* In Calhoun Academy v. Commissioner, 94 T.C. 284 (1990), the Tax Court upheld the Service's denial of exempt status to a private school in South Carolina because the school failed to show that it operated in good faith in accordance with a nondis-

criminatory policy toward black students. Despite a sizable local black population, Calhoun Academy never had an enrolled black student or a black applicant; it never had any employment applications from black teachers; and it did not actively recruit teachers. It did have several Asian–American students, however, and published a statement of nondiscriminatory policy in local newspapers and its own publications. In discussing the appropriate burden of proof, the court stated (94 T.C. at 297):

> Concerning what petitioner must prove, its burden in this proceeding, in broad terms, is to establish that it has a racially nondiscriminatory policy as to students. * * * More precisely, petitioner must show that it has adopted a racially nondiscriminatory policy as to students and operates in good faith in accordance with that policy. * * * If adoption of the policy is defined to mean adoption in substance rather than merely in form, then the adoption and operation elements are largely redundant. Adoption in form also does not reasonably stand as a separate element, instead serving most appropriately as a fact that contributes to an inference of good faith operation in a racially nondiscriminatory manner. Therefore, to have a separate and meaningful existence, the adoption element must be something more than adoption in form, yet something less than adoption in substance. Specifically, we define the adoption element to require more than mere adoption in form on the books of the organization, coupled with appropriate publicity and notification to the various relevant groups in the community so that adoption of the policy is known publicly.

The court went on to state that a private school may meet its burden of proof under § 501(c)(3) without establishing that it took affirmative steps on its own initiative to attract students and teachers of underrepresented races, but that "[a] conclusion that a private school generally is not required to take the specific affirmative acts suggested by [the Service] * * * does not equate with a conclusion that petitioner on the record in the instant case has satisfied its burden of proving that its operations qualify for tax-exempt status." 94 T.C. at 304. The smoking pistol, it appears, was the absence of any black students and the inability to attract them, which created an unfavorable "inference of discrimination" in view of the school's all-white history.

6. *Discriminatory Trusts.* In Private Letter Ruling 8910001 (Nov. 30, 1988), the Service ruled that a privately administered trust that otherwise qualifies for exemption under § 501(c)(3) will not be recognized as exempt if its governing instrument restricts beneficiaries to "worthy and deserving white persons." The trust had been established under a will which provided for a charitable trust " * * * for the benefit and relief of worthy and deserving white persons over the age of sixty years who were residents of a certain city and did not have sufficient income from other sources for their comfort and support." Noting that the Supreme Court's opinion in *Bob Jones* required the Service to ask whether, first, there is a public policy against a particular activity and, second, whether that public policy is so

fundamental as to require the denial or revocation of exempt status for organizations participating in that activity, the ruling concluded:

> The Court's opinion in *Bob Jones* leaves little doubt that discrimination on the basis of race, whether in an educational context or otherwise, violates a public policy so fundamental as to justify denial of charitable status to any organization otherwise described in section 501(c)(3). However, this does not mean that every racially restrictive provision justifies denial of exemption. The racial restriction must be of the type against which Federal policy is directed. It is of a type that excludes from participation in or denies the benefits of a program or activity to individuals solely on the basis of race so that it can reasonably be expected to aggravate the disparity in the educational, economic, or social levels of that group when compared with society as a whole.

> In this case, the trust's charitable program consists of making available a variety of goods and services to a charitable class consisting of needy persons over the age of sixty who are residents of the city of S. Potential beneficiaries, however, are restricted to white persons. The trust denies eligibility for benefits to members of the charitable class solely because of the race of the individual. This denial aggravates the burdens placed on those who have traditionally been the subject of discrimination and thereby fosters racial discrimination. This situation is not unlike that presented in Rev. Rul. 67–325, 1967–2 C.B. 113, wherein a racially restricted community facility was not deemed to be charitable unless all members of the community were eligible for the benefits provided. Based on the facts and circumstances of this case, the trust's activities are contrary to the clearly defined Federal public policy against racial discrimination. Therefore, the trust is [not] described in * * * section 501(c)(3) * * *.

The ruling went on to state the Service's view that *Bob Jones* "was not limited to racial discrimination in education but encompassed the eradication of racial discrimination in general." Id.

7. *Lingering Questions.* The reach of the public policy limitation remains uncertain. As Justice Powell put it in his concurring opinion, "[m]any questions remain." 461 U.S. 574, 612, 103 S.Ct. 2017 (1983). For example, would a church that discriminated on the basis of race fail to qualify for § 501(c)(3) exemption? What about a single-sex school, a private university or a § 501(c)(3) membership organization that excluded gays and lesbians, or scholarship programs targeted for racial minorities, immigrants, or white males from the suburbs? Do recent successful challenges to state-supported affirmative action programs affect the tax-exempt status of private nonprofit organizations with a significant affirmative action mission? Many of these questions are raised in the problems following this Note. The IRS has remained silent on most of them, preferring to avoid any formal pronouncements on issues that remain unsettled in the larger world beyond the tax code.

As for the sources of public policy that should inform these tax exemption questions, presumably they include the Constitution, federal and state statutes, administrative regulations and executive orders, and definitive court opinions. For some recent judicial developments that may be among these sources, see United States v. Virginia, 518 U.S. 515, 116 S.Ct. 2264 (1996) (categorical exclusion of women from educational opportunities provided by state-supported military school was denial of equal protection; proposed remedy of separate program for women did not cure constitutional violation); Faulkner v. Jones, 51 F.3d 440 (4th Cir.1995), cert. denied, 516 U.S. 910, 116 S.Ct. 331 (1995) (state's support of the Citadel, a male-only military college, violated equal protection rights of women); Podberesky v. Kirwan, 38 F.3d 147 (4th Cir.1994), cert. denied, 514 U.S. 1128, 115 S.Ct. 2001 (1995) (merit-based scholarship program limited to African-Americans at University of Maryland was unconstitutional; court rejected university's claim that program was justified by sufficient evidence of past discrimination); Grutter v. Bollinger, 539 U.S. 306, 123 S.Ct. 2325 (2003) (University of Michigan Law School's use of race as a factor in admissions decisions was not prohibited by the Equal Protection Clause because it was narrowly tailored and furthered a compelling interest in obtaining the educational benefits that flow from a diverse student body); Gratz v. Bollinger, 539 U.S. 244, 123 S.Ct. 2411 (2003) (University of Michigan's undergraduate admissions policy, which automatically awarded points to applicants who were members of underrepresented minority groups, was not narrowly tailored and thus violated the Equal Protection Clause).

The extent to which the Supreme Court's 2003 affirmative action decisions may affect § 501(c)(3) tax exemption standards is unclear. Affirmative action programs that do not use quotas or quantifiable formulas but rather look to race as a "factor" among many to promote diversity in education have now received the Supreme Court's constitutional blessing. But will the decision in Gratz v. Bollinger, where the Court declined to approve the University of Michigan's undergraduate admissions policy, jeopardize the tax exemption of a school limiting admissions to students of a particular underrepresented race or a scholarship fund limiting financial aid to minority students? Defenders of special programs, such as minority scholarships, argue that they are designed to promote equal opportunity and diversity and thus continue to pass muster under Grutter v. Bollinger. The tax exemptions of historically black colleges and universities have never been threatened with revocation. One can be fairly confident that the IRS will be slow to respond on these questions as it awaits the outcome of further litigation.

The most notable case decided since the Supreme Court's affirmative action decisions involved the Kamehameha Schools, a private school with three campuses operated by Hawaii's Bishop Estate, which has a 118-year-old history of offering admissions preference to applicants of Hawaiian ancestry. See Chapter 3C3, supra, at pp. 188–189 for discussion of other legal issues involving the Bishop Estate. In a 1999 administrative ruling, the IRS concluded that the schools' admissions policy did not violate any "established public policy" but cautioned that its ruling might need to be reexamined in light of the decision in Rice v. Cayetano, 528 U.S. 495, 120 S.Ct. 1044 (2000), where the Supreme Court held that the Fifteenth Amendment prevented racial preferences for Hawaiian natives in determining the right to vote for trustees of a state fund benefitting native Hawaiians. (The Kamehameha Schools actually did admit one non-native Hawaiian to its Maui campus in 2002, creating a furor including 7,000 petitions in opposition.) The Schools are apparently 100 percent private, having dropped ROTC and other federal government financial support. The IRS ruling thus suggests, without explicitly saying so, that if a § 501(c)(3) organization operates in a manner contrary to some constitutional principle enunciated by the Supreme Court, its tax-exempt status is in jeopardy even if receives no other federal financial assistance.

After the Supreme Court's decisions in Gratz v. Bollinger and Grutter v. Bollinger, a lawsuit was filed on behalf of John Doe, an unidentified non-Hawaiian applicant, challenging the Kamehameha Schools' admission policy as illegal race discrimination under federal civil rights laws. The Ninth Circuit, reversing the district court, held that the policies constituted unlawful race discrimination in violation of 42 U.S.C. § 1981. Doe v. Kamehameha Schools, 416 F.3d 1025 (9th Cir. 2005). The broad question before the court was whether a private school, receiving no federal funds, may legitimately restrict admission based on an express racial classification or whether such a policy was in violation of § 1981, which the Supreme Court has held to reach purely private acts of invidious discrimination. See, e.g., Runyon v. McCrary, 427 U.S. 160, 96 S.Ct. 2586 (1976). The central substantive question considered by the court was whether the Schools' affirmative action plan was based on a legitimate nondiscriminatory rationale that justified a racial preference. The Schools defended their policy as an attempt to redress hardships suffered by native Hawaiians, produce native Hawaiian leaders, and revitalize native culture. The Ninth Circuit majority found that these goals, while valid, did not justify an absolute bar to admissions for those of the non-preferred race.

In an 8–7 opinion on rehearing, however, the Ninth Circuit reversed the three-judge panel and upheld the Kamehameha Schools' Hawaiian-only admissions policy. In ruling that applicants with no Hawaiian ancestry could be denied admission without violating federal civil rights laws, the majority pointed to unique factors in the history of Hawaii and the remedial mission of the schools to counteract significant educational deficits of Native Hawaiian children. Doe v. Kamehameha Schools/Bernice Pauahi Bishop Estate, 470 F.3d 827 (9th Cir. 2006).

It was widely assumed that the Supreme Court would grant certiorari in this case because of its implications on affirmative action programs, but in May 2007 the Kamehameha Schools announced that they had settled the suit. The terms of the settlement were not disclosed.

8. *Constitutional Aspects*. Apart from the Court's brief dismissal of the First Amendment religion clause issues, *Bob Jones* was a statutory interpretation case, not a constitutional law decision. Would any constitutional problem be presented if federal tax exemptions were granted to

racially discriminatory schools? Does the answer depend on your view of the rationale for tax exemptions? Consider, for example, the conventional view that tax exemptions are government subsidies to the benefited organizations.

9. *Bob Jones University Update.* Despite losing its tax exemption, Bob Jones University grew to become a vibrant fundamentalist Christian liberal arts institution, serving 5,000 students from the United States and 43 foreign countries. The university has assembled a prominent collection of religious art that is housed in a museum and gallery. In 1992, the university "spun off" the museum, which was located on campus and was said to attract 20,000 visitors annually. The museum paid below market rent for its use of school property and displayed the art collection, which was "on loan" from the university. In Bob Jones University Museum and Gallery, Inc., 71 T.C.M. 3120 (1996), the Tax Court held that the museum qualified for exemption under § 501(c)(3) despite its close affiliation with Bob Jones University. Finding that the museum was a bona fide educational organization, the Tax Court rejected the Service's argument that the museum furthered a substantial non-exempt purpose by providing a "reputational benefit" and funneling tax-deductible contributions to the university. The court concluded that neither the rent payments nor the payment of salaries to former university employees provided an impermissible financial benefit to the nonexempt university and that any other benefits were incidental but suggested that the result might have been different if the spin-off had involved a library, cafeteria, or bookstore.

In 2000, following a controversial primary campaign appearance by then Presidential candidate George W. Bush, Bob Jones III announced on the Larry King Live television program that the university was dropping its formal ban on interracial dating. The university's web site now includes a statement that BJU does not discriminate on the basis of race, color, national or ethnic origin in admissions or any other programs. See http://www.bju.edu/admissions/nondiscrim.html. In 2008, it posted a "Statement About Race at BJU," acknowledging past failures in allowing institutional policies to be shaped by "the segregationist ethos of American culture." The University said it was "profoundly sorry" for these failures and for allowing "institutional policies to remain in place that were racially hurtful." The full statement is available at http://www.bju.edu/welcome/who-we-are/race-statement.php. According to its web site, Bob Jones University's student body now represents various ethnicities and cultures, and the university solicits financial support through separately incorporated § 501(c)(3) entities for two scholarship funds for minority applicants.

10. *For Further Reading.* David A. Brennen, The Power of the Treasury: Racial Discrimination, Public Policy, and "Charity" in Contemporary Society, 33 U.C. Davis L. Rev. 389 (2000); David A. Brennen, Charities and the Constitution: Evaluating the Role of Constitutional Principles in Determining the Scope of the Tax Law's Public Policy Limitation for Charities, 5 Fla. Tax Rev. 779 (2002); Nicholas A. Mirkay, Is It "Charitable" to Discriminate? The Necessary Transformation of Section

501(c)(3) into the Gold Standard for Charities, 2007 Wisc. L.Rev. 45 (2007); Johnny Rex Buckles, Do Law Schools Forfeit Federal Income Tax Exemption When They Deny Military Recruiters Full Access to Career Services Programs?: The Hypothetical Case of Yale University v. Commissioner, 41 Ariz. St. L. J. 1 (2009); Donald C. Alexander, Validity of Tax Exemptions & Deductible Contributions for Private Single–Sex Schools, 70 Tax Notes 225 (1996); Miriam Galston, Public Policy Constraints on Charitable Organizations, 3 Va. Tax Rev. 291 (1984); Douglas Laycock, Observation: Tax Exemptions for Racially Discriminatory Religious Schools, 60 Tex. L. Rev. 249 (1982); Karla W. Simon, The Tax–Exempt Status of Racially Discriminatory Religious Schools, 36 Tax L. Rev. 477 (1981).

PROBLEMS

Consider whether the following organizations qualify for exemption under § 501(c)(3):

(a) The Fields Aryan Church, which has never permitted African–Americans to become members or attend Sunday worship services in its 75 years as a congregation.

(b) The Role Model School, a private secondary school that restricts its faculty and student body to African–American males. A central purpose of the School is to provide a distinctive educational environment and positive role models for its students.

(c) Clara Foltz College, a private liberal arts college that only admits women as students.

(d) Blue Prep, a private high school in the New York suburbs, which has publicized its nondiscriminatory policy in accordance with IRS requirements, but only has one non-white student (the son of a United Nations delegate). Tuition is $35,000 per year, and financial aid is limited.

(e) Same as (d), above, except Blue Prep was formed in Mississippi in 1972 when public schools in its community were forced to comply with a court-imposed desegregation order.

(f) Yeshiva Brooklyn, a high school for Orthodox Jews. No person of color has ever attended the school.

(g) The Welk Scholarship Trust, which awards college scholarships to academically distinguished Caucasian graduates of high schools in North Dakota.

(h) The Johnson Scholarship Trust, which awards scholarships to deserving African–American graduates of colleges and universities in California who plan to continue their education at the graduate school level.

(i) The Boy Scouts of America ("BSA") , a private nonprofit membership organization. BSA asserts that homosexual conduct is inconsistent with its values and does not permit openly gay men to serve as scoutmasters. The Supreme Court has held that application of a state public accommodation law to require the Boy Scouts to admit gays was a violation of the organization's First Amendment right of expressive association. See Boy Scouts of America v. Dale, Chapter 10F, infra, at pp. 987–1002.

5.   Educational Organizations

Treasury Regulations: § 1.501(c)(3)–1(d)(3).

The promotion of education has long been regarded as a charitable purpose, and tax exemptions have been granted to nonprofit private schools, with little or no controversy, ever since colonial times. Although educational organizations are a sub-set of the broader "charitable" category, they raise distinct issues of interpretation under § 501(c)(3). A central question is what activities are "educational."

The regulations define "educational" purposes as (1) the instruction or training of individuals for the purpose of improving or developing their capabilities, or (2) the instruction of the public on subjects useful to individuals and beneficial to the community. Treas. Reg. § 1.501(c)(3)–1(d)(3). Examples include traditional schools and colleges; public discussion groups; and cultural institutions such as museums, zoos, planetariums, and symphony orchestras. Treas. Reg. § 1.501(c)(3)–1(d)(3)(ii). The Service has adopted a broad view of education, granting exemption to day care centers for infant children, trade schools, college bookstores, alumni associations, a jazz festival, organizations providing continuing education to doctors or lawyers, and marriage counseling services. See, e.g., San Francisco Infant School, Inc. v. Commissioner, 69 T.C. 957 (1978) (child care center); Rev. Rul. 69–538, 1969–2 C.B. 116 (bookstore); Rev. Rul. 60–143, 1960–1 C.B. 192 (alumni organization); Rev. Rul. 65–271, 1965–2 C.B. 161 (jazz festival); Rev. Rul. 65–298, 1965–2 C.B. 163 (updates for physicians). A dog obedience school was denied exemption, however, apparently on the theory that educating animals is not a valid exempt purpose. Ann Arbor Dog Training Club, Inc. v. Commissioner, 74 T.C. 207 (1980).

Organizations advocating particular viewpoints raise special problems. The regulations recognize advocacy groups as "educational" as long as they present a "sufficiently full and fair exposition of the pertinent facts" to permit a listener to form an independent opinion but not if their principal function is the mere presentation of unsupported opinion. Reg. § 1.501(c)(3)–1(d)(3). As illustrated by the materials that follow, these hazy distinctions are problematic in application and have raised constitutional questions.

Revenue Ruling 75–384

1975–2 Cum. Bull. 204.

Advice has been requested whether a nonprofit organization formed to promote world peace and disarmament by nonviolent direct action including acts of civil disobedience qualifies for exemption from Federal income tax under section 501(c)(3) or 501(c)(4) of the Internal Revenue Code of 1954.

The purposes of the organization are to educate and inform the public on the principles of pacifism and nonviolent action including civil disobedience. Its primary activity is the sponsoring of protest demonstrations and nonviolent action projects in opposition to war and preparations for war.

Protest demonstrations are conducted at military establishments, Federal agencies, and industrial companies involved with military and defense operations. Other activities consist of peace marches and protests against the use of tax monies for war purposes. The protest demonstrations constitute the primary activity of the organization. They are designed to draw public attention to the views of the organization and to exert pressure on governmental authorities. To derive the maximum publicity of an event, demonstrators are urged to commit acts of civil disobedience. Participants deliberately block vehicular or pedestrian traffic, disrupt the work of government, and prevent the movement of supplies. These activities are violations of local ordinances and breaches of public order. Incidental to demonstrations, leaflets are dispersed presenting the views of the organization.

Section 501(c)(3) of the Code provides for the exemption from Federal income tax of organizations organized and operated exclusively for charitable purposes.

Section 1.501(c)(3)–1(d)(2) of the Income Tax Regulations provides that the term "charitable" is used in section 501(c)(3) of the Code in its generally accepted legal sense. The regulation further states that the term "charity" includes lessening the burdens of government and the promotion of social welfare by organizations designed (i) to lessen neighborhood tensions; (ii) to eliminate prejudice and discrimination; (iii) to defend human and civil rights secured by law; or (iv) to combat community deterioration and juvenile delinquency.

As a matter of trust law, one of the main sources of the general law of charity, no trust can be created for a purpose which is illegal. The purpose is illegal if the trust property is to be used for an object which is in violation of the criminal law, or if the trust tends to induce the commission of crime, or if the accomplishment of the purpose is otherwise against public policy. IV Scott on Trusts Sec. 377 (3d ed. 1967). Thus, all charitable trusts (and by implication all charitable organizations, regardless of their form) are subject to the requirement that their purposes may not be illegal or contrary to public policy. See Rev. Rul. 71–447, 1971–2 C.B. 230; Restatement (Second), Trusts (1959) Sec. 377, Comment (c).

In this case the organization induces or encourages the commission of criminal acts by planning and sponsoring such events. The intentional nature of this encouragement precludes the possibility that the organization might unfairly fail to qualify for exemption due to an isolated or inadvertent violation of a regulatory statute. Its activities demonstrate an illegal purpose which is inconsistent with charitable ends. Moreover, the generation of criminal acts increases the burdens of government, thus frustrating a well recognized charitable goal, i.e., relief of the burdens of government. Accordingly, the organization is not operated exclusively for charitable purposes and does not qualify for exemption from Federal income tax under section 501(c)(3) of the Code.

Section 501(c)(4) of the Code describes civic leagues or organizations not organized for profit but operated exclusively for the promotion of social welfare.

Section 1.501(c)(4)–1(a)(2)(i) of the regulations provides that an organization is operated exclusively for the promotion of social welfare if it is primarily engaged in promoting in some way the common good and general welfare of the people of the community. An organization embraced within this section is one which is operated primarily for the purpose of bringing about civic betterments and social improvements.

Illegal activities, which violate the minimum standards of acceptable conduct necessary to the preservation of an orderly society, are contrary to the common good and the general welfare of the people in a community and thus are not permissible means of promoting the social welfare for purposes of section 501(c)(4) of the Code. Accordingly, the organization in this case is not operated exclusively for the promotion of social welfare and does not qualify for exemption from Federal income tax under section 501(c)(4).

Revenue Ruling 78–305

1978–2 Cum.Bull. 172.

Advice has been requested whether the nonprofit organization described below, which otherwise qualifies for exemption from Federal income tax under section 501(c)(3) of the Internal Revenue Code of 1954, is operated exclusively for charitable and educational purposes.

The organization was formed to educate the public about homosexuality in order to foster an understanding and tolerance of homosexuals and their problems. The organization collects factual information relating to the role of homosexual men and women in society and disseminates this information to the public.

The organization presents seminars, forums, and discussion groups, all of which are open to the public. Materials distributed to the public include copies of surveys, summaries of opinion polls, scholarly statements, publications of government agencies, and policy resolutions adopted by educational, medical, scientific, and religious organizations. The organization accumulates factual information through the use of opinion polls and independently compiled statistical data from research groups and clinical organizations. All materials disseminated by the organization contain a full documentation of the facts relied upon to support conclusions contained therein.

The organization does not participate in any political campaign, nor does it attempt to influence legislation. The organization does not advocate or seek to convince individuals that they should or should not be homosexuals.

Section 501(c)(3) of the Code provides for the exemption from federal income tax of organizations organized and operated exclusively for charitable and educational purposes.

Section 1.501(c)(3)–1(d)(3) of the Income Tax Regulations provides in relevant part that the term "educational" as used in section 501(c)(3) of the Code relates to the instruction of the public on subjects useful to the individual and beneficial to the community. The regulations further provide that an organization may be educational even though it advocates a particular position or viewpoint, so long as it presents a sufficiently full and fair exposition of pertinent facts to permit the public to form an independent opinion or conclusion.

The presentation of seminars, forums, and discussion groups is a recognized method of educating the public. See section 1.501(c)(3)–1(d)(3)(ii) of the regulations. By disseminating information relating to the role of homosexuals in society, the organization is furthering educational purposes by instructing the public on subjects useful to the individual and beneficial to the community. The method used by the organization in disseminating materials is designed to present a full and fair exposition of the facts to enable the public to form an independent opinion or conclusion. The fact that the organization's materials concern possibly controversial topics relating to homosexuality does not bar exemption under section 501(c)(3) of the Code, so long as the organization adheres to the educational methodology guidelines of section 1.501(c)(3)–(1)(d)(3).

Accordingly, the organization is operated exclusively for charitable and educational purposes and thus qualifies for exemption from federal income tax under section 501(c)(3) of the Code.

Big Mama Rag v. United States

United States Court of Appeals, District of Columbia Circuit, 1980.
631 F.2d 1030.

■ MIKVA, CIRCUIT JUDGE:

Plaintiff, Big Mama Rag, Inc. (BMR, Inc.), appeals from the order of the court below granting summary judgment to defendants and upholding the IRS's rejection of plaintiff's application for tax-exempt status. Specifically, BMR, Inc. questions the finding that it is not entitled to tax exemption as an educational or charitable organization under section 501(c)(3) of the Internal Revenue Code, 26 U.S.C. § 501(c)(3) (1976), and Treas. Reg. § 1.501(c)(3)–1(d)(2) & (3) (1959). Appellant also challenges the constitutionality of the regulatory scheme, arguing that it violates the First Amendment and the equal protection component of the Fifth Amendment and that it unconstitutionally conditions tax-exempt status on the waiver of constitutional rights.

Because we find that the definition of "educational" contained in Treas. Reg. § 1.501(c)(3)–1(d)(3) is unconstitutionally vague in violation of the First Amendment, we reverse the order of the court below.

I.   Background

BMR, Inc. is a nonprofit organization with a feminist orientation. Its purpose is "to create a channel of communication for women that would educate and inform them on general issues of concern to them." To this end, it publishes a monthly newspaper, Big Mama Rag (BMR), which prints articles, editorials, calendars of events, and other information of interest to women. BMR, Inc.'s primary activity is the production of that newspaper, but it also devotes a considerable minority of its time to promoting women's rights through workshops, seminars, lectures, a weekly radio program, and a free library.

BMR, Inc. has a predominantly volunteer staff and distributes free approximately 2100 of 2700 copies of Big Mama Rag's monthly issues. Moreover, the organization has severely limited the quantity and type of paid advertising. As the district court found, BMR, Inc. neither makes nor intends to make a profit and is dependent on contributions, grants, and funds raised by benefits for over fifty percent of its income.

Because of its heavy reliance on charitable contributions, BMR, Inc. applied in 1974 for tax-exempt status as a charitable and educational institution. That request was first denied by the IRS District Director in Austin, Texas, on the ground that the organization's newspaper was indistinguishable from an "ordinary commercial publishing practice." After BMR, Inc. filed a protest and a hearing was held in the IRS National Office, the denial of tax-exempt status was affirmed on three separate grounds:

1. the commercial nature of the newspaper; 2. the political and legislative commentary found throughout; and 3. the articles, lectures, editorials, etc., promoting lesbianism.

To enable BMR, Inc. to obtain judicial review of the IRS decision, the IRS District Director issued a final determination letter, which denied tax-exempt status on the grounds that, inter alia, the content of BMR was not educational and the manner of distribution was that of ordinary commercial publishing organizations.[4]

Appellant then brought a declaratory judgment action in the District Court for the District of Columbia. On cross-motions for summary judgment, the judge granted appellees' motion. Although the court rejected

---

4. The District Director's reasoning stated in full: The organization in publishing the newspaper is not operated exclusively for educational purposes as required by Code section 501(c)(3) as the content of the publication is not educational, the preparation of the material does not follow methods educational in nature, the distribution of the material is not valuable in achieving an educational purpose and/or the manner in which the distribution is accomplished is not distinguishable from ordinary commercial publishing practices.

appellees' argument that BMR, Inc. was not entitled to tax-exempt status because it was a commercial organization, it agreed that appellant did not satisfy the definitions of "educational" and "charitable" in Treas. Reg. § 1.501(c)(3)–1(d)(2) & (3). The court found no constitutional basis for disturbing the IRS's decision.

II.   THE REGULATORY SCHEME

Tax exemptions are granted under section 501(c) of the Internal Revenue Code to a variety of socially useful organizations, including the charitable and the educational. The Code forbids exemption of an organization if any part of its net earnings inures to the benefit of private persons or if it is an "action organization"—one that attempts to influence legislation or participates in any political campaign. Treasury regulations impose additional requirements: exempt status is accorded only to applicants whose articles of organization limit their activities to furtherance of exempt purposes (the "organizational test") or whose activities are in fact aimed at accomplishment of exempt purposes (the "operational test"). Treas.Reg. § 1.501(c)(3)–1(b) & (c) (1959).

The Treasury regulations also define some of the exempt purposes listed in section 501(c)(3) of the Code, including "charitable" and "educational." The definition of "educational" is the one at issue here: The term "educational," as used in section 501(c)(3), relates to—(a) The instruction or training of the individual for the purpose of improving or developing his capabilities; or (b) The instruction of the public on subjects useful to the individual and beneficial to the community. An organization may be educational even though it advocates a particular position or viewpoint so long as it presents a sufficiently full and fair exposition of the pertinent facts as to permit an individual or the public to form an independent opinion or conclusion. On the other hand, an organization is not educational if its principal function is the mere presentation of unsupported opinion. Treas.Reg. § 1.501(c)(3)–1(d)(3)(i) (1959).

The district court found that BMR, Inc. was not entitled to tax-exempt status because it had "adopted a stance so doctrinaire" that it could not meet the "full and fair exposition" standard articulated in the definition quoted above. Appellant's response is threefold. First, it argues, the "full and fair exposition" hurdle is not applicable at all here because BMR, Inc. is not an organization whose primary activity or principal function is advocacy of change. Second, BMR, Inc. contends that its publication does satisfy the requirements of the "full and fair exposition" standard. Finally, appellant maintains that denial of its application for tax-exempt status on the basis of the "full and fair exposition" standard is unconstitutional for a number of reasons.

Even though tax exemptions are a matter of legislative grace, the denial of which is not usually considered to implicate constitutional values, tax law and constitutional law are not completely distinct entities. In fact, the First Amendment was partly aimed at the so-called "taxes on knowledge," which were intended to limit the circulation of newspapers and therefore the public's opportunity to acquire information about governmental affairs. In light of their experience with such taxes, the framers realized, in the words of Mr. Justice Douglas, that "(t)he power to tax the exercise of a privilege is the power to control or suppress its enjoyment." Murdock v. Pennsylvania, 319 U.S. 105, 112, 63 S.Ct. 870, 874, 87 L.Ed. 1292 (1943). Thus, although First Amendment activities need not be subsidized by the state, the discriminatory denial of tax exemptions can impermissibly infringe free speech. Similarly, regulations authorizing tax exemptions may not be so unclear as to afford latitude for subjective application by IRS officials. We find that the definition of "educational," and in particular its "full and fair exposition" requirement, is so vague as to violate the First Amendment and to defy our attempts to review its application in this case.

III. VAGUENESS ANALYSIS

Vague laws are not tolerated for a number of reasons, and the Supreme Court has fashioned the constitutional standards of specificity with these policies in mind. First, the vagueness doctrine incorporates the idea of notice-informing those subject to the law of its meaning. A law must therefore be struck down if "men of common intelligence must necessarily guess at its meaning."

Second, the doctrine is concerned with providing officials with explicit guidelines in order to avoid arbitrary and discriminatory enforcement. To that end, laws are invalidated if they are "wholly lacking in 'terms susceptible of objective measurement.'"

These standards are especially stringent, and an even greater degree of specificity is required, where, as here, the exercise of First Amendment rights may be chilled by a law of uncertain meaning. Vague laws touching on First Amendment rights, noted the Supreme Court in Baggett, require (those subject to them) to "steer far wider of the unlawful zone," than if the boundaries of the forbidden areas were clearly marked, * * * by restricting their conduct to that which is unquestionably safe. Free speech may not be so inhibited. Measured by any standard, and especially by the strict standard that must be applied when First Amendment rights are involved, the definition of "educational" contained in Treas.Reg. § 1.501(c)(3)–1(d)(3) must fall because of its excessive vagueness.

We do not minimize the difficulty and delicacy of the task delegated to the Treasury by Congress under section 501(c)(3) of the Code. Words such as "religious," "charitable," "literary," and "educational" easily lend themselves to subjective definitions at odds with the constitutional limitations we describe above. Treasury bravely made a pass at defining "educational," but the more parameters it tried to set, the more problems it encountered.

The first portion of the regulation relied upon to deny BMR, Inc.'s request for tax-exempt status measures an applicant organization by whether it provides "instruction of the public on subjects useful to the individual and beneficial to the community." Treas.Reg. § 1.501(c)(3)–1(d)(3)(i)(b) (1959). The district court rejected that test with barely a murmur of disagreement from appellees. That standard, held the court below, "would be far too subjective in its application to pass constitutional muster."

We find similar problems inherent in the "full and fair exposition" test, on which the district court based affirmance of the IRS's denial of tax-exempt status to BMR, Inc. That test lacks the requisite clarity, both in explaining which applicant organizations are subject to the standard and in articulating its substantive requirements.

A.   Who Is Covered by the "Full and Fair Exposition" Test?

According to the terms of the Treasury regulation, only an organization that "advocates a particular position or viewpoint" must clear the "full and fair exposition" hurdle. Appellant maintains that the definition of an advocacy organization is to be found in the preceding subsection of the regulation, which defines the term "charitable": The fact that an organization, in carrying out its primary purpose, advocates social or civic changes or presents opinion on controversial issues with the intention of molding public opinion or creating public sentiment to an acceptance of its views does not preclude such organization from qualifying under section 501(c)(3) so long as it is not an "action" organization of any one of the types described in paragraph (c)(3) of this section. Treas.Reg. § 1.501(c)(3)–1(d)(2) (1959). The district court held that this part of the regulation was designed to cover charitable institutions and that BMR, Inc., an educational rather than a charitable organization, must meet the "full and fair exposition" standard rather than the more lenient "action organization" standard of section 1.501(c)(3)–1(d)(2). Obviously, if BMR, Inc. is an advocacy group and is not a charitable organization, it may not take cover under the "action organization" standard but must instead meet the "full and fair exposition" test.

The initial question, however, is whether or not BMR, Inc. is an advocacy group at all. What appellant turns to Treas. Reg. § 1.501(c)(3)–1(d)(2) for is the definition of "advocacy," not for the appropriate standard to be applied to advocacy organizations seeking tax-exempt status. The district court did not deal with that question, and, indeed, it is difficult to ascertain from the language of the regulation defining "educational" exactly what organizations are intended to be covered by the "full and fair exposition" standard and whether or not the definitions of advocacy groups are the same for both educational and charitable organizations.

The uncertainty of the coverage of the "full and fair exposition" standard is evidenced by its application over the years by the IRS. The Treasury Department's Exempt Organizations Handbook has defined "advocates a particular position" as synonymous with "controversial." Such a gloss clearly cannot withstand First Amendment scrutiny. It gives IRS officials no objective standard by which to judge which applicant organizations are advocacy groups-the evaluation is made solely on the basis of one's subjective notion of what is "controversial." And, in fact, only a very few organizations, whose views are not in the mainstream of political thought, have been deemed advocates and held to the "full and fair exposition" standard. The one tax-exempt homosexual organization cited by the Government as evidence that the IRS does not discriminate on the basis of sexual preference was required to meet the "full and fair exposition" standard even though it admittedly did not "advocate or seek to convince individuals that they should or should not be homosexuals." Rev.Rul. 78–305, 1978–2 C.B. 172, 173.

The Treasury regulation defining "educational" is, therefore, unconstitutionally vague in that it does not clearly indicate which organizations are advocacy groups and thereby subject to the "full and fair exposition" standard. And the latitude for subjectivity afforded by the regulation has seemingly resulted in selective application of the "full and fair exposition" standard-one of the very evils that the vagueness doctrine is designed to prevent.

B.   What Does the "Full and Fair Exposition" Test Require?

The Treasury definition of "educational" may also be challenged on the ground that it fails to articulate with sufficient specificity the requirements of the "full and fair exposition" standard. The language of the regulation gives no aid in interpreting the meaning of the test: An organization may be educational even though it advocates a particular position or viewpoint so long as it presents a sufficiently full and fair exposition of the pertinent facts as to permit an individual or the public to form an independent opinion or conclusion. On the other hand, an organization is not educational if its principal function is the mere presentation of unsupported opinion. Treas.Reg. § 1.501(c)(3)–1(d)(3) (1959). What makes an exposition "full and fair"? Can it be "fair" without being "full"? Which facts are "pertinent"? How does one tell whether an exposition of the pertinent facts is "sufficient * * * to permit an individual or the public to form an independent opinion or conclusion"? And who is to make all of these determinations?

The regulation's vagueness is especially apparent in the last clause quoted above. That portion of the test is expressly based on an individualistic—and therefore necessarily varying and unascertainable—standard: the reactions of members of the public. The Supreme Court has recognized that statutes phrased in terms of individual sensitivities are suspect and susceptible to attack on vagueness grounds. * * *

An additional source of unclarity lies in the relationship between the two sentences comprising the "full and fair exposition" test. Appellant argues that the two should be read as counter-examples—an organization fails to satisfy the test only if "its principal function is the mere presentation of unsupported opinion." The Government, on the other hand, contends that tax-exempt status must be denied BMR, Inc. if a substantial portion of its newspaper consists of unsupported opinion. Again, the language of the regulation does not resolve this issue.[13]

---

13. The IRS has adopted a list of specific guidelines to implement the Treasury definition of "educational." But those guidelines use the same conclusory terms as the

The district court's interpretation of the "full and fair exposition" test, and the one advocated by the Government, is no more precise. The district court found the Treasury regulation "capable of objective application" because "it asks only whether the facts underlying the conclusions are stated." But distinguishing facts, on the one hand, and opinion or conclusion, on the other, does not provide an objective yardstick by which to define "educational." The distinction is not so clear-cut that an organization seeking tax-exempt status—or an IRS official reviewing an application for exemption—will be able to judge when any given statement must be bolstered by another supporting statement.

One of the five examples cited by the Government as evidence of BMR's failure to meet the "full and fair exposition" test may be used to illustrate our point. Most of the article, discussing Susan Saxe's 1975 plea of guilty to charges stemming from a bank robbery in Philadelphia, is simple journalistic reporting. It discusses the terms of the plea bargain, the reaction of local feminists, the differential treatment accorded Saxe supporters and white men who went to observe the pretrial hearing, and police questioning of women in Philadelphia. In return for Saxe's plea, the Government apparently agreed, among other things, to "call off its investigation of the women's and lesbian communities" in the area and not to ask Saxe to testify against "anyone she has known or know (sic) about in the last five years." By forcing Saxe to choose between her own interests and those of other women, the article continues, "the Government has clarified for us, once again, that we, as women, are inextricably bound up with each other in the struggle."

Certainly, the author's viewpoint is not disguised in the last sentence. But is the statement one of fact or opinion? If the latter, is the author's description of the terms of the guilty plea sufficient to inform readers of the basis underlying her opinion? Or is further proof of the existence of "the struggle" necessary? If so, would the article satisfy the "full and fair exposition" test without that final statement? Neither the Treasury regulation nor the proposed fact/opinion distinction is responsive to these questions. And one's answers will likely be colored by one's attitude towards the author's point of view.

The futility of attempting to draw lines between fact and unsupported opinion is further illustrated by the district court's application of that test. The court did not analyze the contents of BMR under its proposed test but merely stated, without further explication, that the publication was not entitled to tax-exempt status because it had "adopted a stance so doctrinaire that it cannot satisfy this standard." Instead of applying the purport-

---

regulation and are not helpful in clarifying its meaning: An organization * * * may qualify * * * if (1) the content of the publication is educational, (2) the preparation of material follows methods generally accepted as "educational" in character, (3) the distribution of the materials is necessary or valuable in achieving the organization's educational and scientific purposes, and (4) the manner in which the distribution is accomplished is distinguishable from ordinary commercial publishing practices. Rev.Rul. 67–4, 1967–1 C.B. 121, 122; see Rev.Rul. 77–4, 1977–1 C.B. 141.

edly objective test the court had formulated, it was forced to resolve the case by resorting to the subjective notion of whether the publication was "doctrinaire." We can conceive of no value-free measurement of the extent to which material is doctrinaire, and the district court's reliance on that evaluative concept corroborates for us the impossibility of principled and objective application of the fact/opinion distinction.

Appellees suggest that the Treasury regulation at issue here embodies a related distinction—between appeals to the emotions and appeals to the mind.[16] Material is educational, they argue, if it appeals to the mind, that is, if it reasons to a conclusion from stated facts. Again, the required linedrawing is difficult, a problem which is compounded if the difference between the two relies on the aforementioned fact/opinion distinction.

Moreover, the Treasury regulation does not support such a narrow concept of "educational" and we cannot approve it. Nowhere does the regulation hint that the definition of "educational" is to turn on the fervor of the organization or the strength of its language. As the Supreme Court has recognized in another context, the emotional content of a word is an important component of its message.

An example raised by appellees in their brief and discussed at oral argument is illustrative. The American Cancer Society's cause may be better served by a bumper sticker picturing a skull and crossbones and saying "Smoking rots your lungs" than by one that merely states "Smoking is hazardous to your health." Both are intended to impart the same message, and they are identical in degree of specificity of the underlying facts. Although the first may be said to appeal more to the emotions, and the second to the mind, that distinction should not obscure the similarities between the two. They should be considered equal in educational content.

Even if one could in fact differentiate fact from unsupported opinion, or emotional appeals from appeals to the mind, these proposed distinctions would be inadequate definitions of "educational" because material often combines elements of each. In such cases, appellees suggested at oral argument, a quantitative test would be appropriate. But the Treasury regulation makes no mention of such a test. Even if a quantitative approach were authorized, it is unclear how much of a publication's content would have to be factual, or appeal to the mind, in order to satisfy the "full and fair exposition" standard. Also unanswered is who would apply the test and determine the requisite amount of factual material. Certainly, the Treasury regulation itself gives no clue.[18]

---

16. The court below also seemed to endorse this distinction: it read the Treasury regulation as requiring that a publication be "sufficiently dispassionate as to provide its readers with the factual basis from which they may draw independent conclusions." One can only speculate how a poetry publication would be classified under such a dichotomy.

18. In addition to advancing the two distinctions discussed above to elucidate the Treasury's definition of "educational," appellees also rely on the notion of onesidedness. They point to BMR's editorial policy of "not print(ing) any material which, by our judgment, does not affirm our struggle." We agree with the court below that the Treasury regulation may not be read to compel an educational organization to "present views inimical to its philosophy."

Thus, neither of the distinctions proposed here remedies the imprecise language of the "full and fair exposition" standard or clarifies the requirements imposed by that test.

IV.   CONCLUSION

The definition of "educational" contained in Treas.Reg. § 1.501(c)(3)–1(d)(3) lacks sufficient specificity to pass constitutional muster. Its "full and fair exposition" standard, on the basis of which the denial of BMR, Inc.'s application for tax exemption was upheld by the court below, is vague both in describing who is subject to that test and in articulating its substantive requirements.

The history of appellant's application for tax-exempt status attests to the vagueness of the "full and fair exposition" test and evidences the evils that the vagueness doctrine is designed to avoid. The district court's decision was based on the value-laden conclusion that BMR was too doctrinaire. Similarly, IRS officials earlier advised appellant's counsel that an exemption could be approved only if the organization "agree(d) to abstain from advocating that homosexuality is a mere preference, orientation, or propensity on par with heterosexuality and which should otherwise be regarded as normal." Whether or not this view represented official IRS policy is irrelevant. It simply highlights the inherent susceptibility to discriminatory enforcement of vague statutory language.

We are sympathetic with the IRS's attempt to safeguard the public fisc by closing revenue loopholes. And we by no means intend to suggest that tax-exempt status must be accorded to every organization claiming an educational mantle. Applications for tax exemption must be evaluated, however, on the basis of criteria capable of neutral application. The standards may not be so imprecise that they afford latitude to individual IRS officials to pass judgment on the content and quality of an applicant's views and goals and therefore to discriminate against those engaged in protected First Amendment activities.

We are not unmindful of the burden involved in reformulating the definition of "educational" to conform to First Amendment requirements. But the difficulty of the task neither lessens its importance nor warrants its avoidance. Objective standards are especially essential in cases such as this involving those espousing nonmajoritarian philosophies. In this area the First Amendment cannot countenance a subjective "I know it when I see it" standard. And neither can we.

This case is accordingly reversed and remanded for further proceedings consistent with this opinion.

Revenue Procedure 86–43

1986–2 Cum.Bull. 729.

SECTION 1.   PURPOSE

The purpose of this revenue procedure is to publish the criteria used by the Internal Revenue Service to determine the circumstances under which advocacy of a particular viewpoint or position by an organization is considered educational within the meaning of section 501(c)(3) of the Internal Revenue Code, and within the meaning of section 1.501(c)(3)–1(d)(3) of the Income Tax Regulations.

SECTION 2.   BACKGROUND

.01 Section 501(c)(3) of the Code provides for exemption from federal income tax for organizations that are organized and operated exclusively for purposes specified in that section, including educational purposes. Section 1.501(c)(3)–1(d)(3) of the regulations provides that the term "educational" relates to a) the instruction or training of the individual for the purpose of improving or developing his capabilities; or b) the instruction of the public on subjects useful to the individual and beneficial to the community. Under this regulation, an organization may be educational even though it advocates a particular position or viewpoint, so long as it presents a sufficiently full and fair exposition of the pertinent facts as to permit an individual or the public to form an independent opinion or conclusion. On the other hand, an organization is not educational if its principal function is the mere presentation of unsupported opinion.

.02 In applying section 1.501(c)(3)–1(d)(3) of the regulations, the Service has attempted to eliminate or minimize the potential for any public official to impose his or her preconceptions or beliefs in determining whether the particular viewpoint or position is educational. It has been, and it remains, the policy of the Service to maintain a position of disinterested neutrality with respect to the beliefs advocated by an organization. The focus of section 1.501(c)(3)–1(d)(3), and of the Service's application of this regulation, is not upon the viewpoint or position, but instead upon the method used by the organization to communicate its viewpoint or positions to others.

.03 Two recent court decisions have considered challenges to the constitutionality of section 1.501(c)(3)–1(d)(3) of the regulations. One decision held that the regulation was unconstitutionally vague. Big Mama Rag, Inc. v. United States, 631 F. 2d. 1030 (D.C.Cir.1980). However, in National Alliance v. United States, 710 F. 2d 868 (D.C.Cir.1983), the court upheld the Service's position that the organization in question was not educational. Although the latter decision did not reach the question of the constitutionality of section 1.501(c)(3)–1(d)(3), it did note that the methodology test used by the Service when applying the regulation "tend[s] toward ensuring that the educational exemption be restricted to material which substantially helps a reader or listener in a learning process." The court also noted that the application of this test reduced the vagueness found in the earlier Big Mama Rag decision.

.04 The methodology test cited by the court in National Alliance reflects the long-standing Service position that the method used by an organization in advocating its position, rather than the position itself, is the standard for determining whether an organization has educational purposes. This methodology test is set forth in Section 3 of this revenue procedure, and is used in all situations where the educational purposes of an organization that advocates a particular viewpoint or position are in question. Publication of this test represents no change either to existing procedures or to the substantive position of the Service.

SECTION 3.   CRITERIA USED TO DETERMINE WHETHER ADVOCACY BY AN ORGANIZATION IS EDUCATIONAL

.01 The Service recognizes that the advocacy of particular viewpoints or positions may serve an educational purpose even if the viewpoints or positions being advocated are unpopular or are not generally accepted.

.02 Although the Service renders no judgment as to the viewpoint or position of the organization, the Service will look to the method used by the organization to develop and present its views. The method used by the organization will not be considered educational if it fails to provide a factual foundation for the viewpoint or position being advocated, or if it fails to provide a development from the relevant facts that would materially aid a listener or reader in a learning process.

.03 The presence of any of the following factors in the presentations made by an organization is indicative that the method used by the organization to advocate its viewpoints or positions is not educational.

1.   The presentation of viewpoints or positions unsupported by facts is a significant portion of the organization's communications.

2.   The facts that purport to support the viewpoints or positions are distorted.

3.   The organization's presentations make substantial use of inflammatory and disparaging terms and express conclusions more on the basis of strong emotional feelings than of objective evaluations.

4.   The approach used in the organization's presentations is not aimed at developing an understanding on the part of the intended audience or readership because it does not consider their background or training in the subject matter.

.04 There may be exceptional circumstances, however, where an organization's advocacy may be educational even if one of more of the factors listed in section 3.03 are present. The Service will look to all the facts and circumstances to determine whether an organization may be considered educational despite the presence of one or more of such factors.

SECTION 4.   OTHER REQUIREMENTS

Even if the advocacy undertaken by an organization is determined to be educational under the above criteria, the organization must still meet all other requirements for exemption under section 501(c)(3), including the restrictions on influencing legislation and political campaigning contained therein.

NOTES

1. *Hate Groups.* Shortly after deciding *Big Mama Rag*, the D.C. Circuit considered the tax-exempt status of National Alliance, a neo-Nazi organization that sought to arouse in white Americans of European ancestry an understanding of and pride in their racial and cultural heritage. *National Alliance v. United States*, 710 F.2d 868 (1983). Central themes of National Alliance's principal publication (Attack!) were: non-whites are inferior to white Americans of European ancestry; blacks are aggressively brutal and dangerous; Jews, through their control of the media, cause U.S. policies to be harmful to the interests of whites; and communists are at fault for persuading neo-liberals that integration and equality are desirable. National Alliance called for armed confrontations between the races. Id. at 869–872.

Despite its *Big Mama Rag* precedent, the court upheld the Service's denial of exemption to National Alliance on the ground that it was not "educational." The court found that National Alliance did not rationally develop a point of view and failed to engage in "intellectual exposition." Applying what is best described as "I know it when I see it" jurisprudence, the court concluded that "the National Alliance material is far outside the range Congress could have intended to subsidize in the public interest by granting tax exemption." Id. at 873.

To help cure the constitutional infirmities of the regulations, the Service unveiled the Methodology Test, which later was promulgated as Rev. Proc. 86–43, in the *National Alliance* litigation. While noting that the Methodology Test reduced the vagueness found in *Big Mama Rag*, the court declined to rule whether the constitutional malady had been cured. It need not reach the vagueness issue, the court said, because National Alliance did not qualify as "educational" under any reasonable interpretation of the term. Id.

In The Nationalist Movement v. Commissioner, 102 T.C. 558, aff'd per curiam, 37 F.3d 216 (5th Cir.1994), cert. denied, 513 U.S. 1192, 115 S.Ct. 1256 (1995), the Tax Court upheld the constitutionality of the Methodology Test. The Nationalist Movement espoused a pro-majority philosophy. It favored white Americans and skinheads, and opposed foreigners, domestic minorities, Jews, homosexuals, immigrants, the Martin Luther King Day holiday, and Black History Month. The Tax Court found that the Methodology Test was neither aimed at the suppression of ideas nor vague or overbroad on its face, and concluded:

> Its provisions are sufficiently understandable, specific, and objective both to preclude chilling of expression protected under the First Amendment and to minimize arbitrary or discriminatory application by the IRS. The revenue procedure focuses on the method rather than the content of the presentation. In contrast, it was the potential for discriminatory denials of tax exemption based on speech content that caused the Court of Appeals for the District of Columbia Circuit to hold that the vagueness of the "full and fair exposition" standard violates

the First Amendment. Petitioner has not persuaded us that either the purpose or the effect of the revenue procedure is to suppress disfavored ideas.

Id. at 588–589.

The Tax Court went on to find that The Nationalist Movement's methodology had failed all four factors because the organization failed to support its viewpoints with facts, distorted the facts, used inflammatory and disparaging terms, and failed to educate its young followers by developing an understanding based on their background and training. Id. at 589–594.

2. *Commerciality, Inurement and Private Benefit.* Many educational organizations, such as museums, theaters and publishers, derive the bulk of their support from admission fees, subscriptions and other revenue-generating activities. Under current exemption standards, it is not inconsistent with "educational" status to raise revenue in this manner, provided that the organization's primary purpose remains educational and its net earnings neither inure to the benefit of insiders nor provide some other form of private benefit. The inurement and private benefit limitations, which are not unique to educational organizations, are considered in Section D of this chapter, infra, at pp. 445–461. Commerciality is discussed in Chapter 6.

3. *IRS and Congressional Scrutiny of Colleges and Universities.* The IRS has made colleges and universities an important audit priority, along with health care organizations. The Service's attitude is reflected in a detailed set of audit guidelines. Revenue agents are instructed to examine a wide range of activities, including financial statements, fringe benefit and retirement plans, scholarships, fundraising solicitations, investments, government-funded research contracts, political activities, college bookstore product lines, and transactions with related entities. See Internal Revenue Service, College and University Examination Guidelines, reprinted in 10 Exempt Org. Tax Rev. 618 (1994). The guidelines suggest that agents should review student newspapers and alumni publications because they may "offer a different perspective" on the operations of the institution. Id. at 343.32 (4) & (5).

In 2007, the Senate Finance Committee began to question whether more specific tax exemption standards should be applied to private colleges and universities. Areas of discussion and investigation included intercollegiate men's football and basketball programs; large university endowments and the related issue of endowment payout; and commercial activities, including technology and research alliances with for-profit companies. In October 2008, the IRS, feeling the heat, sent a detailed compliance questionnaire to 400 colleges and universities as part of a focused effort to study key areas, particularly related to endowments, executive compensation, unrelated business income, and financial aid. The questionnaire is available at http://www.irs.gov/pub/irs-tege/sample_cucp_questionnaire. pdf. The IRS eventually will issue a report on the project and, in the meantime, it has commenced selective limited-scope examinations focusing on executive compensation and unrelated business income. For discussion of congressional concerns about intercollegiate athletic programs, see Chapter 6D2b, infra, at pp. 623–624.

4. *Child Care Organizations.* Section 501(k), which was added in 1984, makes it clear that the term "educational" purposes includes providing care for children away from their homes if: (1) substantially all of the care is to enable individuals, such as the child's parents or guardian, to be gainfully employed, and (2) the services provided are available to the general public. Prior to this amendment, the Service sometimes took the position that a child care organization did not qualify for exemption if it provided only custodial care without a formal educational program.

5. *For Further Reading.* John D. Colombo, Why is Harvard Tax–Exempt? (And Other Mysteries of Tax Exemption for Private Educational Institutions), 35 Ariz.L.Rev. 841 (1993); Daniel Shaviro, From Big Mama Rag to National Geographic: The Controversy Regarding Exemptions for Educational Publications, 41 Tax L. Rev. 693 (1986); Tommy F. Thompson, The Availability of the Federal Educational Tax Exemption for Propaganda Organizations, 18 U.Cal.Davis L. Rev. 487 (1985).

PROBLEMS

Consider whether the following organizations, all of which are nonprofit corporations under state law, qualify for exemption under § 501(c)(3):

(a) Sturdley Tech University ("STU"), which has an undergraduate program and graduate programs in business, law, engineering and materials science. STU provides no financial aid to its students. Its revenue is generated from tuition (70%), government grants (10%), and sponsored research and technology licensing arrangements with for-profit companies (20%).

(b) Students Together for Individual Rights ("STIR"), an organization of law students formed to educate the public about homosexuality in order to promote understanding and tolerance of the gay and lesbian community. STIR presents seminars, forums and discussion groups, and publishes a magazine.

(c) Same as (b), above, except that a principal activity of STIR is to organize demonstrations to protest actions of businesses and government agencies that it considers to be discriminatory against gays and lesbians. Leaders of STIR often urge followers to block traffic, disrupt the activities of targeted businesses, and engage in other acts of civil disobedience.

(d) The Institute for Historical Accuracy, an organization devoted to promoting truth in history through books, journals, educational media, and conferences. Among its major projects is to "speak factually and effectively about the Jewish–Zionist grip on America's cultural and political life." It has published numerous books and essays disputing the "orthodox Holocaust extermination story" and objecting to "Jewish–Zionist" influence in the United States and much of the world.

(e) Right to Life, Inc., a nonprofit educational organization that sponsors forums, lectures and other programs dealing with abortions and pro-life alternatives. Its goals are to educate the public on the rights of the unborn. Assume that the organization does not violate the limitations on lobbying or political campaigning in § 501(c)(3) but does engage in frequent picketing and demonstrations near clinics that perform abortions.

(f) Family Planning Alternatives, an organization that provides free counseling to women on methods of avoiding unwanted pregnancies and operates an abortion clinic.

6.   RELIGIOUS ORGANIZATIONS

Since colonial times in America, and long before then in other cultures, churches and other religious organizations have enjoyed exemption from income and property taxes. Section 501(c)(3) is faithful to that tradition by granting exempt status to organizations organized and operated for "religious purposes," a category that is not limited to traditional houses of worship. Religious exemptions extend to book publishers, broadcasters, organizations conducting genealogical research, and burial societies. The exempt purposes listed in § 501(c)(3) also are not mutually exclusive. A separately incorporated parochial school may be both "religious" and "educational," and many typical "charitable" activities may be under the control or sponsorship of a particular religion or church.

Although religious tax exemptions are firmly rooted in American law and tradition, they have engendered an ongoing controversy. For a time, the debate centered on whether religious tax exemptions were constitutional. The Supreme Court settled that issue in Walz v. Tax Commission, 397 U.S. 664, 90 S.Ct. 1409 (1970), when it held that the Establishment Clause of the First Amendment was not violated by an exemption from property taxation for land and buildings owned by churches and used solely for religious worship. In upholding a New York statute that also exempted property owned by charitable, educational and other nonprofit organizations, the Court declined to justify religious tax exemptions on the social welfare services or "good works" performed by many churches. It reasoned that to emphasize so variable an aspect of the work of religious bodies would introduce an intrusive element of governmental evaluation that would undermine the constitutional policy of neutrality. The Court characterized property tax exemptions as the product of a "benevolent neutrality" that neither advanced nor inhibited religion and created only a minimal and remote "entanglement" between church and state. Although *Walz* involved a state property tax exemption, the Court suggested that the tax benefits provided by the Internal Revenue Code similarly were immune from a First Amendment challenge, but it declined to rule that religious tax exemptions were constitutionally required.

Highly sensitive questions arise when a governmental taxing authority attempts to deny exempt status to an organization that claims to be "religious" or a "church." The vast panoply of beliefs in the United States makes this definitional task inordinately delicate, which may explain why definitions of "religious purpose" or "church" are conspicuously absent from the regulations. Recognizing the constitutional difficulties that would be presented by a narrow definition, the Internal Revenue Service has advised its revenue agents to interpret "religion" broadly, encompassing even those sects that do not believe in a Supreme Being. This reluctance to define religion is necessitated by constitutional constraints. In United States v. Ballard, which involved the mail fraud prosecution of the leader of a sect who claimed to be a divine messenger with supernatural powers, the Supreme Court admonished fact finders to avoid entering the definitional quagmire:

> Man's relation to his God was made no concern of the state. He was granted the right to worship as he pleased and to answer to no man for the verity of his religious views. The religious views espoused by respondents might seem incredible, if not preposterous, to most people. But if those doctrines are subject to trial before a jury charged with finding their truth or falsity, then the same can be done with the religious beliefs of any sect. When the triers of fact undertake that task, they enter a forbidden domain.

322 U.S. 78, 87, 64 S.Ct. 882, 886 (1944). See also Chapter 10F2, infra, at pp. 1005–1010, which discusses constitutional restrictions on judicial resolution of internal church disputes.

As demonstrated by the following materials, the courts generally have avoided making value judgments on the bona fides of a religious organization except in the most egregious cases.

Holy Spirit Association v. Tax Commission

New York Court of Appeals, 1982.
55 N.Y.2d 512, 450 N.Y.S.2d 292, 435 N.E.2d 662.

■ Jones, Judge:

[This case, which involved a real property tax exemption, illustrates the difficulty of denying a governmental benefit to a "controversial" religious group. The Internal Revenue Service never litigated the question of the Unification Church's federal tax-exempt status, but it did succeed in convicting the church's leader, Reverend Sun Myung Moon, of criminal tax fraud. See United States v. Sun Myung Moon, 718 F.2d 1210 (2d Cir.1983), cert. denied, 466 U.S. 971, 104 S.Ct. 2344 (1984). Eds.]

OPINION OF THE COURT

In determining whether a particular ecclesiastical body has been organized and is conducted exclusively for religious purposes, the courts may not inquire into or classify the content of the doctrine, dogmas, and teachings held by that body to be integral to its religion but must accept that body's characterization of its own beliefs and activities and those of its adherents, so long as that characterization is made in good faith and is not sham. On this principle it must be concluded that the Unification Church has religion as its "primary" purpose inasmuch as much of its doctrine, dogmas, and teachings and a significant part of its activities are recognized as religious, and in good faith it classifies as religious the beliefs and activities which the Tax Commission (Commission) and the court below have described as political and economic.

The Holy Spirit Association for the Unification of World Christianity (the Church) is one of more than 120 national Unification Churches throughout the world propagating a common religious message under the spiritual guidance of the Reverend Sun Myung Moon, the Unification movement's founder and prophet. The Church was organized as a California nonprofit corporation in 1961, and since 1975 has maintained its headquarters in New York City.

In March, 1976 the Church applied to the Tax Commission of the City of New York under section 421 (subd. 1, par. [a])of the New York Real Property Tax Law[1] for exemption from real property taxes for the tax year beginning July 1, 1976 of three properties title to which it had acquired in 1975. * * * The majority concluded that, "although the applicant association does in certain respects bespeak of a religious association, it is in our opinion so threaded with political motives that it requires us to deny its application." Having concluded that the Church was not organized or conducted exclusively for religious purposes, the majority of the Commission had no occasion to consider whether the three properties were used exclusively for religious purposes. The dissenting members of the Tax Commission, explicitly declining to judge the validity or content of the religious beliefs of the Church or its adherents or to submit the Church's theology to analysis, concluded that the Church was organized exclusively for religious purposes and that the three properties in question were used exclusively for statutory purposes. The dissenters would therefore have granted the application.

[After reviewing a report of a Special Referee, the Appellate Division of the New York Supreme Court upheld the denial of the exemption because the Church was "inextricably interwoven with political motives and activities as to warrant denial of tax exemption." Eds.]

It is appropriate at the threshold to delineate our holding in this case— to make explicit what we are not as well as what we are called on to decide. We are not called on to determine whether the Church has any real

---

1. New York Real Property Tax Law (§ 421): "1. (a) Real property owned by a corporation or association organized or conducted exclusively for religious, charitable, hospital, educational, moral or mental improvement of men, women or children or cemetery purposes, or for two or more such purposes, and used exclusively for carrying out thereupon one or more of such purposes either by the owning corporation or association or by another such corporation or association as hereinafter provided shall be exempt from taxation as provided in this section."

religious purpose or whether any of its doctrine, dogmas, and teachings constitute a religion. In this case it is recognized that at least many of the beliefs and a significant part of the activities of the Church are religious and that the Unification movement at least in part is a religion. The determination of the Tax Commission, the report of the Special Referee, the opinion at the Appellate Division and now the arguments of the Tax Commission in our court all, at least implicitly, accept this proposition.

The issue that we confront is a narrower one—is the Church, many of whose beliefs and activities are religious, organized and conducted primarily[2] for religious purposes within the contemplation of section 421 (subd. 1, par. [a])? This, as understood by the Tax Commission and the Appellate Division, turns on whether the Church is engaged in so many or such significant nonreligious activities as to warrant the conclusion that its purpose is not primarily religious. More specifically the issue is whether the activities which have been found to be "political" and "economic" are for the purposes of that statute to be classified as secular rather than religious.

When, as here, particular purposes and activities of a religious organization are claimed to be other than religious, the civil authorities may engage in but two inquiries: Does the religious organization assert that the challenged purposes and activities are religious, and is that assertion bona fide? Neither the courts nor the administrative agencies of the State or its subdivisions may go behind the declared content of religious beliefs any more than they may examine into their validity. This principle was firmly established in Watson v. Jones, 13 Wall. [80 U.S.] 679, 728, 20 L.Ed. 666, when the Supreme Court declared that "[t]he law knows no heresy, and is committed to the support of no dogma, the establishment of no sect."

* * *

We turn then to the first avenue of inquiry allowed us, namely, whether the Church asserts that its religious doctrine and teachings embrace the challenged activities. We quote the statement with respect to the history and doctrine, dogmas and teachings of the Church from the brief of the Church in our court (without its footnote references to sources in the record).

> The Unification movement has its origins in Korea as one of the host of revivalist Christian religions that flourished there in the aftermath of the forty-year Japanese occupation (1905–1945), during which Korean religions were suppressed. Common to many of these new, patriotic religions was the theme of Korea as the modern Holy Land, birthplace of the new Messiah. This theme likewise animates the religion founded by the Reverend Moon.
>
> Unification theology is based on the teachings of the Old and New Testaments as clarified by revelations held to have been received by

---

2. The statute uses the adverb "exclusively", but we have held that it connotes "principally" or "primarily" (Matter of Association of Bar of City of N.Y. v. Lewisohn, 34 N.Y.2d 143, 153, 356 N.Y.S.2d 555, 313 N.E.2d 30).

the Reverend Moon directly from Jesus Christ beginning in 1936, and subsequently recorded by his followers in the book Divine Principle. Central to Divine Principle is the millenialist conviction that the time has come for the forces of God to reclaim the earth from the forces of Satan, and to restore "the Kingdom of God on earth."

According to Unification theology, the "great promise of Christianity" is "the return of Christ"—"not as a visiting God but as a sinless man"—to complete the work Jesus began 2,000 years ago. Unification faith holds that "when Jesus came he was the Messiah," the perfect image of God. Through the Resurrection, the Church believes, Jesus brought "spiritual salvation," but the physical institutions of this world—beginning with the family—remained unredeemed; in the Church's view, it is for the new Messiah to restore a Bride and establish the True Family serving as the foundation for ending "the existence of evil in the world," and to accomplish "not only spiritual but also physical" salvation for mankind. Adherents of the Unification faith look to the Reverend Moon to accomplish this task.

In Unification doctrine, every temporal sphere—political, cultural, and economic—is a battleground for the forces of God and the forces of Satan. God-denying Communism is deemed a singularly potent evil, threatening to overwhelm the forces of God just as Cain overwhelmed Abel; the division between North and South Korea is seen as a central providential instance of the struggle between the sons of Adam. Other temporal controversies also assume crucial spiritual significance in Unification theology.

Committed to the view that men and women need no "mediator between themselves and God," Unification faith makes no provision for a "priestly class." All members of the Church, for example, are qualified to conduct prayer services and other religious activities. Church members fall into two categories—some 7,000 members, serving the Church full-time, are engaged in some combination of evangelical, educational, pastoral, and fund-raising activities, and rely upon the Church or local Church units to meet their material needs; the remaining 30,000 members accept the tenets of the Church as their faith but devote less than full-time efforts to the Church. Representing a movement that proclaims an urgent millenialist gospel, the Church appeals primarily, but not exclusively, to the young.

There can be no doubt on the record before us that the Church has amply demonstrated that it does indeed assert that those beliefs and activities which the Tax Commission and the Appellate Division have found to be political and economic are of the essence of its religious doctrine and program. This has been the finding at every stage of this matter. The Special Referee reported that "the petitioner's theological doctrines bind petitioner to a course of political activism," that "petitioner believes that the physical world consisting of science and economics as well as the spiritual world consisting of religion have developed in accordance with 'God's providence' and that 'religion and economy relate to social life through politics'," that "it is petitioner's religious tenet that the republican form of government with separate or coequal powers held by the legislative, judicial and executive branches of government is a Satanic principle and that these three governmental branches under the present political system must be brought under a single controlling force as a condition for the second coming of the Messiah;" that "according to the Divine Principle, the forces of Satan must be subdued and Korea unified under the type of political environment where religions and science are unified in order to make the world ready for the second coming of the Messiah;" and that "it also appears that petitioner is opposed to the constitutionally mandated separation of church and State." Following a recital of illustrative examples of "political" activities, the report continues, "The petitioner's involvement in these political activities is not an escalated mobilization in behalf of a political cause. Each activity is consistent with the expression of political motives set forth in the Divine Principle and is part of an over-all plan and it is petitioner's deployment of its cadre and administrators for these activities that mark its involvement in political causes". "One of the principal tenets advanced in the Divine Principle is that there be complete integration of all economic, social and religious activities."

The Appellate Division described the referee as reporting, "that petitioner's primary purpose is religious, but that petitioner's theology, as expressed in Reverend Moon's writings binds it to a course of political activity." * * * That court itself concluded that "religious and nonreligious themes are inextricably intertwined in the doctrine", and that, "[t]herefore, despite the religious content of the doctrine, and the leitmotif of religion with which the eclectic teachings are tinged, the doctrine, to the extent that it analyzes and instructs on politics and economics has substantial secular elements." * * *

We conclude that it has been sufficiently demonstrated that what have been characterized below as political and economic beliefs and activities are in the view of the Church integral aspects of its religious doctrine and program.

We turn then to the second avenue of our restricted inquiry. No serious question can be raised on the record before us that the Church has demonstrated the sincerity and the bona fides of its assertions that in its view the political beliefs and activities of the Church and its members and the efforts which they devote to fund raising and recruitment are at the core of its religious beliefs. The Tax Commission found that the Church "does in certain aspects bespeak of a religious association"; the Special Referee reported that the Church's "primary purpose is religious" and that "it is religious in nature and nothing contained in this report should be considered as constituting a comment on the sincerity or lack of sincerity with which any members of [the Church] practices his faith." The Appellate Division concluded "that one of [the Church's] purposes is religious." We do not confront in this case an organization every aspect of whose claim to being religious is challenged, and whose bona fides might accordingly be said to be suspect.

The error of the majority of the Tax Commission, of the Special Referee and of the majority at the Appellate Division is that each asserted the right of civil authorities to examine the creed and theology of the Church and to factor out what in its or his considered judgment are the peripheral political and economic aspects, in contradistinction to what was acknowledged to be the essentially religious component. Each then took the view that beliefs and activities which could be objectively and accurately described by knowledgeable outsiders as "political" and "economic" were by that fact precluded from being classified as "religious."[6]

As stated, it is not the province of civil authorities to indulge in such distillation as to what is to be denominated religious and what political or economic. It is for religious bodies themselves, rather than the courts or administrative agencies, to define, by their teachings and activities, what their religion is. The courts are obliged to accept such characterization of the activities of such bodies, including that of the Church in the case before us, unless it is found to be insincere or sham.

Applying this principle, we conclude that on the record before us, as a matter of law, the primary purpose of the Church (much of whose doctrine, dogmas and teachings and a significant part of whose activities are recognized as religious) is religious and that the determination of the Tax Commission to the contrary is both arbitrary and capricious and affected by error of law.

Determinations with respect to the use to which each of the three individual properties is put, however, cannot be made as a matter of law. Accordingly, inasmuch as such determinations should be made in the first instance by the Tax Commission rather than by the courts, the case must be remitted to Supreme Court with directions to it to remand to the Tax Commission to make determination as to the use of each of the three properties in conformity with the views expressed in this opinion.

For the reasons stated, the judgment of the Appellate Division should be reversed, without costs, and the case remitted to Supreme Court for further remand in accordance with this opinion. * * *

General Counsel Memorandum 36993

February 3, 1977.

[A General Counsel Memorandum ("GCM") is a legal memorandum prepared by the Chief Counsel's office of the Internal Revenue Service.

---

6. If such categorization were to be undertaken we note that substantial arguments are advanced that traditional theology has always mandated religious action in social, political and economic matters. Numerous illustrations are cited of essentially religious concern and activity in areas of political and economic action in Judeo–Christian history. The point is made that virtually all of the recognized religions and denominations in America today address political and economic issues within their basic theology. (See, e.g., the briefs of the amici curiae filed in support of the position of the Church on this appeal: American Civil Liberties Union and New York Civil Liberties Union; American Jewish Congress; The Catholic League for Religion and Civil Rights; The National Association of Evangelicals, and The Center for Law and Religious Freedom of the Christian Legal Society; and National Council of Churches of Christ in the U.S.A., and New York State Council of Churches.) As reiterated, however, it is not for the courts to make judgments with reference to these substantive matters.

Although a GCM does not have the force of law and is not as authoritative as a treasury regulation or published revenue ruling, it reflects the IRS National Office's legal position on the issue under scrutiny and offers guidance in areas where there are no applicable regulations or rulings. This GCM addressed the provocative question of whether a witch's coven qualifies as a "religious organization" for purposes of § 501(c)(3) and a "church" for purposes of § 170(b)(1)(A)(i). Eds.]

* * *

FACTS

The * * * [in a GCM, the Service deletes the name of the taxpayer and certain other confidential material to maintain privacy, Eds.] was incorporated under the laws of * * * on * * * as a nonprofit religious organization. The purpose of the organization is to promote the * * * religion and the worship of deities recognized by the * * * to train priests, priestesses and other leaders of the * * * religion and to instruct members of the religious association in the history, philosophy and all other components of the stated religion. Members of the organization consider themselves to be pagans engaged in the practice of witchcraft. The organization has published a pagan manifesto, which sets forth standards of behavior for its followers. In the manifesto the members are urged to live according to the laws of nature. Judging by the available information these beliefs are sincerely held and there is no evidence in the file that the organization engages in activities that violate any laws or contravene any clearly defined public policy or policies.

The organization holds weekly services following a set ritual. There are also seasonal festivals and marriage ceremonies. The file does not show whether these ceremonies are recognized as valid marriages under applicable state laws. The organization's members worship "the horned god", but it is specifically alleged that this horned god is not the devil. Magic, healing and clairvoyance are practiced and certain animals and plants are sacred to the organization's members.

ANALYSIS

1. Code § 501(c)(3) provides that organizations organized and operated exclusively for religious, charitable and educational purposes, no part of the net earnings of which inure to the benefit of any private shareholder or individuals, are exempt under Code 501(a).

The First Amendment to the United States Constitution provides that Congress is forbidden from enacting any "law respecting an establishment of religion, or prohibiting the free exercise thereof * * *."

There are various definitions of "pagan" and "paganism" to be found in dictionaries. One definition of a "pagan" is "an irreligious person." A more frequently found definition, perhaps, is that a "pagan" is a "follower of a polytheistic religion." In the instant case the primary issue is whether the organization, whose members consider themselves to be "pagans engaged in the practice of witchcraft," may be said to be "religious" as that term is used in Code § 501(c)(3). By the preponderance of dictionary definitions, the beliefs professed by the * * * would qualify as "religious beliefs."

An analysis of the First Amendment to the Constitution of the United States indicates that it is logically impossible to define "religion". It appears that the two religious clauses of the First Amendment define "religious freedom" but do not establish a definition of "religion" within recognized parameters. An attempt to define religion, even for purposes of statutory construction, violates the "establishment" clause since it necessarily delineates and, therefore, limits what can and cannot be a religion. The judicial system has struggled with this philosophic problem throughout the years in a variety of contexts.

In Reynolds v. United States, 98 U.S. 145 (1878), the issue of the constitutionality of a law passed by Congress making the practice of polygamy by persons residing in United States Territories a criminal act was before the Supreme Court. The Court interpreted the constitutional prohibition in this way: "Congress was deprived of all legislative power over mere opinion, but was left free to reach actions which were in violation of social duties or subversive of good order." 98 U.S. at 164. Thus, finding that for some 100 years polygamy had been considered an offense against society in all the states of the union, the Court held that the statute under consideration was constitutional and valid as prescribing a rule of action for all those residing in the territories. In holding that religious belief did not except persons from operation of the statute, the Court said: " * * * while they [laws] cannot interfere with mere religious belief and opinions, they may with practices." Id. at 166. In Cantwell v. Connecticut, 310 U.S. 296 (1940), the Court endorsed Reynolds, stating " * * * the [First] Amendment embraces two concepts, freedom to believe and freedom to act. The first is absolute but, in the nature of things, the second cannot be." 310 U.S. at 303–4. See also Davis v. Beason, 133 U.S. 333, 10 S.Ct. 299, 33 L.Ed. 637 (1890) and Mormon Church v. United States, 136 U.S. 1 (1890) where the Court grappled with the same issue. While continuing to affirm the right of freedom of religious belief, the Court nevertheless held that legislation for the punishment of acts "inimical to the peace, good order and morals of society" did not violate the First Amendment.

In the last three decades the Court continued to struggle for a definition of "religion." [The GCM then discusses a line of cases, none in the tax area, in which the Supreme Court declined to define religion or determine the truth of religious beliefs and several tax exemption cases where courts held that they could not distinguish between or approve or disapprove of forms or expressions of religious faith. Eds.]

* * *

Thus, when examining an organization claiming a religious character such as the organization in the instant case, the primary rule as to religiosity is whether the organization's adherents are sincere in their beliefs. If that question is resolved affirmatively, the rule of [the cases summarized above] becomes applicable to test the use of the profits of the organization and the exclusive purposes of its existence.

In addition to the foregoing tests, an organization must conform to basic principles of charity law to qualify for recognition of exemption under Code § 501(c)(3). Thus, for example, its organizational documents cannot authorize it to engage, nor can it engage, in activities that are illegal or contrary to clearly defined public policy. See Restatement (Second), Trusts § 377 (1959); IV A. Scott, The Law of Trusts § 377 (3d ed. 1967).

Applying the above rules to this case, we have concluded on the basis of the evidence available in the administrative file that the organization's members are sincere in their beliefs, the organization is organized and operated exclusively for the claimed purposes, and there is no evidence that its organizational documents authorize it to engage in, or that it in fact engages in, activities that are illegal or contrary to any clearly defined public policy. Accordingly, and on the assumption that it otherwise qualifies, we see no reason to disagree with your proposed conclusion that the organization qualifies for recognition of exemption under Code § 501(c)(3) as a religious organization.

2.   The Service has previously considered whether a particular organization constituted a "church." In Rev. Rul. 59–129, 1959–1 C.B. 58, the * * * was held to be a church within the meaning of Code § 170(b)(1)(A). In connection with this ruling, it was observed that the * * * had (1) a distinct legal existence; (2) a recognized creed and form of worship; (3) a definite and distinct ecclesiastical government; (4) a formal code of doctrine and discipline; (5) a distinct religious history; (6) a membership not associated with any church or denomination; (7) a complete organization of ordained ministers ministering to their congregations; (8) ordained ministers selected after completing prescribed courses of study; (9) a literature of its own; (10) established places of worship; (11) regular congregations; (12) regular religious services; (13) Sunday Schools for the religious instruction of the young; and (14) schools for the preparation of its ministers. Rev. Rul. 59–129 was published in digest form and did not set forth these characteristics. These characteristics normally would be attributed to a "church" in the commonly accepted meaning of that term. In view of the fact that "church" is not defined in the Code or regulations, the above criteria are useful in determining whether, on balance, a particular religious organization, if tax-exempt, constitutes a "church." The determination is necessarily one of fact and must be made on a case by case basis.

Since it is doubtful that an organization need have all of the above characteristics in order to constitute a "church", it is helpful to examine the few court decisions relevant to this issue in order to ascertain which characteristics have been emphasized.

In Vaughn v. Chapman, 48 T.C. 358 (1967), the court was called upon to determine, inter alia, whether a religious and charitable organization was a "church" within the meaning of Code § 170(b)(1)(A)(i). The organization was interdenominational and was not affiliated with any church group or denomination. The purpose of the organization was twofold: (1) to perform dental work for missionaries, religious workers, and natives, and (2) to promote " * * * the Gospel of the Lord Jesus Christ, around the world, and the evangelization of the world on the basis of the principles of the Protestant Faith."

The organization conducted regular services in the United literature. The members of the organization were all trained in the Bible and church work. While many of its members were ordained ministers, the organization did not conduct a seminary or Bible School. All members were required to be licensed dentists.

The court, after examining the legislative history of Code § 170(b), determined that a more limited concept was intended for the term "church" than that denoted by the term "religious organization." The court stated that Congress did not intend "church" to be used in a generic or universal sense but rather in the sense of a "denomination" or "sect". The court added that a group need not necessarily have an organizational hierarchy or maintain church buildings to constitute a "church."

In holding that the organization was not a church, the court emphasized that (1) the organization's individual members maintained their affiliation with various churches; (2) the organization was interdenominational and did not seek converts to the principles of christianity generally; (3) the organization did not ordain its own ministers; and (4) the conducting of religious services by its members was not conclusive per se that the organization was a church.

In Christian Echoes National Ministry, Inc. v. United States, * * * the United States sought to revoke the Code § 501(c)(3) exempt status of a religious organization. The organization was founded and administered by an ordained minister of the Gospel of Jesus Christ. Other ordained ministers staffed the organization and were empowered to perform all sacerdotal functions on its behalf. The organization conducted numerous religious revivals in various churches throughout the United States sponsored by local congregations, and it also held regular Sunday services in Tulsa, Oklahoma. It conducted annual conventions, leadership schools, and summer sessions for the young. In upholding the organization's tax-exempt status, the [district] court concluded that [p]laintiff's organization and structure, its practices and precepts, and activities provide all the necessary elements of a "church" in the ordinary acceptance of the term and as used in the Internal Revenue Code of 1954, its amendments and applicable regulations. Plaintiff's followers together with its ordained pastors clearly constitute a congregation the same as any local church. [The court of appeals, however, upheld the revocation of Christian Echoes § 501(c)(3) exemption. Its decision was based on the organization's substantial lobbying and political campaign activities. See Section E2 of this chapter, infra, at pp. 476–488. Eds.]

In De La Salle Institute v. United States, 195 F.Supp. 891 (N.D.Cal. 1961), the court employed a "common sense" approach in determining whether a particular organization constituted a church for purposes of

Code § 511: To exempt churches, one must know what a church is. Congress must either define "church" or leave the definition to the common meaning and usage of the word; otherwise, Congress would be unable to exempt churches. The court held in that case that an incorporated religious teaching order that performs no sacerdotal functions is not a church, and the income derived by the order from the ownership and operation of a separately incorporated winery is not the income of a church, notwithstanding that both corporations were formed under church auspices.

In comparing the rationale of *Chapman*, *Christian Echoes*, and *De La Salle* to the Salvation Army characteristics underlying Rev. Rul. 59–129, it is evident that some of these characteristics have been considered more significant than others. Thus, *Chapman*, in equating "church" with denomination, stresses both the fact that the organization did not seek to attract individuals into the ranks of its membership and the fact that its members were also members of other church denominations. The court did not, on the other hand, believe that it was necessary to have a church hierarchy or church building. *Christian Echoes*, in a similar approach, emphasized that the religious organization in question had an established congregation ministered to by ordained ministers. The *De La Salle* court, rather than commenting on what a church is, analyzed the issue from the opposite point of view: what a church is not, i.e., it is not a separately incorporated teaching order that performs no sacerdotal functions, or the order's separately incorporated winery.

In the instant case the organization seeks to attract individuals into its ranks and to be accepted such individuals need not abandon their affiliation with other churches. Notwithstanding the nonabandonment factor, we have concluded that it represents a "denomination" within the *Chapman* rationale. Under the facts presented, it has trained priests and priestesses to minister to an established congregation and thus satisfies the *Christian Echoes* requirements.

Application of the other criteria underlying Rev. Rul. 59–129 to the * * * shows the following: (1) It has incorporated and has a distinct legal existence. (2) It has a recognized creed entitled "pagan manifesto" and a distinct form of worship, both unique. (3) It has a definite ecclesiastical government headed by an individual entitled "elder." (4) It has a code of doctrine and discipline. (5) It has adopted the history relating to Welsh mythology. (6) It alleges it has a complete organization with trained priests who have completed prescribed courses of study. (7) It has a vast bulk of literature relating to paganism. (8) It at the present time neither owns or leases property, however it alleges it carries on regular services. (9) It has no separate organization for the religious instruction of the young.

In addition to the above criteria it may be helpful to evaluate this organization in the light of a draft of proposed regulations defining a church for purposes of Code § 170(b)(1)(A) that was prepared, (but never issued as a notice of proposed rule-making), in 1974 * * *.

The draft provides in part: (a) Church or a convention or association of churches. A church or convention or association of churches as described in section 170(b)(1)(A)(i) if it is an organization of individuals having commonly held religious beliefs, engaged solely in religious activities in furtherance of such beliefs. The activities of the organization must include the conduct of religious worship and the celebration of life cycle events such as births, deaths and marriage. The individuals engaged in the religious activities of a church are generally not regular participants in activities of another church, except when such other church is a parent or subsidiary organization of their church. * * * Available information indicates that the * * * meets the above tests other than the "abandonment of other church" criterion, evidently adopted from *Chapman*.

Based on an overall weighing of the "normal characteristics" of churches we believe that the * * * may qualify as a church for purposes of Code § 170.

* * *

[The Los Angeles Times later publicized the Service's permissive policy toward witches with the following headline: "Out of Closet, Into Kitchen: Witches Win Nonprofit Tax Status as a Religion, Hope to Shed Evil Image." L.A. Times, Aug. 20, 1989, Part I, at 4, reprinted in Developments in the Law–Nonprofit Corporations, 105 Harv. L. Rev. 1578 (1992). Eds.]

NOTES AND QUESTIONS

1. *Religious Distinctions.* The Internal Revenue Code includes a large number of religious distinctions, some of which are significant for federal tax purposes. For example, although virtually all bona fide religious organizations qualify for exemption under § 501(c)(3), only "churches, their integrated auxiliaries and conventions or associations of churches" are relieved from filing annual informational returns with the Internal Revenue Service. I.R.C. § 6033(a)(2)(A)(i). An "integrated auxiliary" is a separate § 501(c)(3) organization, such as a seminary, mission society or youth group, that is related to a church, supported primarily from internal church sources as opposed to public or governmental sources, and meets one of the tests for avoiding private foundation status in § 509(a). Treas. Reg. § 1.6033–2(h)(1). More specifically, an organization qualifies as an integrated auxiliary if it either: (1) offers admissions, goods, services, or facilities for sale, other than on an incidental basis, to the general public and not more than 50 percent of its support comes from a combination of government sources, contributions from the general public, and receipts other than those from an unrelated business; or (2) does not offer admissions, goods, services, or facilities for sale, other than on an incidental basis, to the general public. Treas. Reg. § 1.6033–2(h)(4). See also Rev. Proc. 86–23, 1986–1 C.B. 564.

Churches and their integrated auxiliaries are conclusively presumed not to be private foundations, and they are not required to file a formal application in order to be recognized as tax-exempt. I.R.C. § 508(c)(1)(A). The IRS also is subject to special limitations on how and when it may conduct civil tax inquiries and audits of churches. I.R.C. § 7611. Even though churches are not required to apply for exempt status, many choose to do so to assure contributors that their contributions are tax-deductible.

2. *Personal Churches.* Beginning in the 1970's, the "personal church" emerged as an often comic but lamentable vehicle of tax protest. Taxpayers ranging from airline pilots and chiropractors to welders and electricians piously attempted to shelter normally taxable income by assigning their wages and property to a newly-chartered church that in turn provided lodging and a living allowance to the freshly ordained ministers. The charter often was obtained from a mail-order "parent" ministry.

Mail-order ministries received a notable blessing in 1974 when a federal district judge upheld the tax-exempt status of the Universal Life Church of Modesto, California. See Universal Life Church, Inc. v. United States, 372 F.Supp. 770 (E.D.Cal.1974). The Church had no dogma other than "to do whatever's right, to stay within the confines of the law." 372 F.Supp. at 772–773. Its founder, Kirby Hensley, proudly explained that his church was deliberately designed to exploit the tax laws in the hope that Congress and state legislatures would terminate all religious tax exemptions. In upholding the parent ULC's exemption, the district court was reluctant to impose any limits on a purported religion:

> Neither this Court, nor any branch of this Government, will consider the merits or fallacies of a religion. Nor will this Court compare the beliefs, dogmas, and practices of a newly organized religion with those of an older, more established religion. Nor will the Court praise or condemn a religion, however excellent or fanatical or preposterous it may seem. Were the court to do so, it would impinge upon the guarantees of the First Amendment.

372 F.Supp. at 776. The court's conclusion was questionable because it was not being asked to praise or condemn the "church" or pass judgment on the verity of its beliefs. The more important point was that the church had no doctrines or tenets and did not purport to offer any explanation of the ultimate meaning of life.

It took a while, but the Service ultimately was successful in revoking the exemptions of Universal Life Church "affiliates" and other personal churches whose minister and parishioners consisted of only one or two families. See, e.g., Universal Life Church, Inc. (Full Circle) v. Commissioner, 83 T.C. 292 (1984); Church of Ethereal Joy v. Commissioner, 83 T.C. 20 (1984). Rather than attempting to define religion or question religious beliefs, the courts denied exempt status on the ground that personal churches either were operated for a substantial non-exempt purpose (e.g., to run a business) or violated the inurement of private gain limitation. The cases have become far too numerous even to cite, but an instructive example is Ecclesiastical Order of the Ism of Am v. Commissioner, 80 T.C. 833 (1983), where the Tax Court denied an exemption to a promoter of religious tax benefits on the ground that the organization served a substantial non-exempt purpose. The "church" had no worship services. Rather, its theology was devoted to counseling its local chapters on the tax benefits of religious tax exemptions. The court purported not to question the sincerity of the church but nonetheless denied exempt status on the ground that it was "nothing more than a commercial tax service * * * operating under the cover of a professed religious purpose." 80 T.C. at 843.

3. *Other Grounds for Denying Exemption.* When religious organizations, including churches, are denied tax exemptions, it usually is because they have violated one or more requirements that apply to all organizations seeking § 501(c)(3) status. As developed later in this chapter and Chapter 6, exemptions have been revoked on the ground of inurement of private gain (see, e.g., Church of Scientology of California v. Commissioner, infra p. 446), excessive lobbying and political campaign activities (see, e.g., Christian Echoes National Ministry, Inc. v. United States, and Branch Ministries v. Rossotti, infra pp. 478 & 520)., and commerciality (see, e.g., Presbyterian and Reformed Publishing Co. v. Commissioner, infra p. 577).

On rare occasions, religious exemptions are denied on the ground that a claimed church is "secular" rather than "religious." A case in point is Church of the Chosen People (Demigod Socko Pantheon) v. United States, 548 F.Supp. 1247 (D.Minn.1982), where a federal district court rejected the religious claims of an organization which preached the "gay imperative" as a means of controlling overpopulation. The court held that the organization's program was "secular" because it did not address fundamental questions regarding the human condition, and because its beliefs were neither comprehensive in nature nor manifested in external forms.

Another notable case, albeit in a nontax setting, is United States v. Kuch, 288 F.Supp. 439 (D.D.C.1968), which involved the drug prosecution of a leader of the Neo–American Church, an organization of some 20,000 members who considered psychedelic drugs to be sacramental foods. The court held that the church was not a religion because the record presented "[n]o solid evidence of a belief in a supreme being, a religious discipline, a ritual, or tenets to guide one's daily existence." Id. at 444. The court was assisted in reaching these conclusions by its findings that the church had a "Catechism" ("we have a right to practice our religion, even if we are a bunch of filthy drunken bums"), official songs ("Puff, the Magic Dragon" and "Row, Row, Row Your Boat"), a church key (a bottle opener), a bulletin (known as "Divine Toad Sweat"), and a motto ("Victory Over Horseshit"). Id. at 443–44.

4. *A Test of Time?* Are tax administrators and the courts too lax in failing to define what constitutes "religion" or a "church?" Or would a governmental definition result in overly favorable treatment of mainstream religions? How should taxing authorities handle cults that may engage in brainwashing or illegal activities? Dean M. Kelley, a minister and longtime official of the National Council of Churches, has suggested a "simple, objective, external test which can be applied without entanglement to determine the bona fides of groups claiming to be churches"—the test of time. He proposes that provisional religious tax exemptions might be

granted to new organizations but that the highly preferred "church" status not be attainable until the organization shows continuing support from its adherents for a minimum period of time—such as 20, 30 or up to 50 years. During the "probationary" period, the "would-be religion" would be subject to all the information reporting, disclosure, audit and other requirements generally applicable to nonprofits. Only after the test of time is satisfied would the group be granted the preferred status of a "church." See Dean M. Kelley, Why Churches Should Not Pay Taxes 58–69 (1977).

5. *For Further Reading.* Vaughn E. James, Reaping Where They Have Not Sowed: Have American Churches Failed to Satisfy the Requirements for the Religious Tax Exemption?, 43 Cath. Law 29 (2004); Charles M. Whelan, "Church" in the Internal Revenue Code: The Definitional Problem, 45 Ford.L. Rev. 885 (1977); Stephen Schwarz, Limiting Religious Tax Exemptions: When Should the Church Render Unto Caesar, 29 U.Fla. L.Rev. 50 (1976); Boris I. Bittker, Churches, Taxes and the Constitution, 78 Yale L.J. 1285 (1969); Tax Guide for Churches and Other Religious Organizations, IRS Publication 1828 (2003), available at irs.gov/pub/irs-pdf/ p1828/pdf.

PROBLEMS

Consider whether each of the following organizations is a religious organization under § 501(c)(3) and, if so, whether the organization also is a "church":

(a) The Free Spirit Church, organized three years ago in California. The church congregation, numbering 450, reside with the church's founder and charismatic leader, David Caress, in a compound in a rural area of Southern Oregon. Its stated doctrine is to "free the spirit and enjoy life to the fullest." Local law enforcement authorities believe that illegal drug activities are being conducted inside the compound, and they are concerned that Caress and other church leaders may be sexually exploiting some young congregants.

(b) The Moral Message, a fundamentalist organization that conducts religious services, operates a network of radio stations with religious programming and publishes a weekly newsletter, and solicits funds for its operations. In the course of spreading the gospel, it often takes positions on political and social questions but does not seek to influence legislation or intervene in political campaigns.

(c) The E Street Church, which owns a townhouse in Washington, D.C. that provides below cost meals and lodging for conservative Christian members of the United States Congress. The Church also sponsors an annual National Prayer Breakfast in Washington and many state capitals and holds private Bible study meetings for its residents and their guests.

(d) The Atheist Alliance, a nonprofit organization with 5,000 members, dedicated to propagating the belief that religion is myth and superstition and that "there are no gods, no devils or angels, no heaven or hell, only the natural world." It operates bookstores and conducts meetings for its members at which the writings of prominent atheists are discussed.

7. OTHER CHARITABLE PURPOSES

Internal Revenue Code: §§ 501(e), (f), (j).

Treasury Regulations: § 1.501(c)(3)–1(d)(4) & (5).

The § 501(c)(3) family of exempt organizations has expanded over the years. In addition to the traditional exempt purposes of "religious," "charitable" and "educational," the list of permissible purposes includes "scientific," "literary," and the more specialized categories of testing for public safety, prevention of cruelty to children or animals and fostering of national or international amateur sports competition. In addition, § 501(e) deems certain "cooperative hospital service organizations"—such as an entity created by a consortium of nonprofit hospitals to perform specified services (e.g., data processing, bill collection, food preparation)—to be "charitable," while § 501(f) extends charitable status to common investment funds formed by exempt educational institutions. "Charitable risk pools," a specialized type of nonprofit entity that self-insures the insurable risks of § 501(c)(3) charities, recently has been added to the list of deemed charitable organizations. I.R.C. § 501(n).

Several of these additional exempt purposes were included in an abundance of caution. For example, "prevention of cruelty to children and animals" was added in 1918 without explanation. The Service has ruled that this category includes organizations providing funds for spaying or neutering pets (Rev. Rul. 74–194, 1974–1 C.B. 129) or ensuring humane treatment for laboratory animals (Rev. Rul. 66–359, 1966–2 C.B. 219), but does not include a club formed to promote the ownership and training of purebred dogs (Rev. Rul. 71–421, 1971–1 C.B. 229). "Literary" was added in 1921 for no discernible reason, and since that time the Service has never paused to define the term, allowing controversies over literary publications to be decided under the criteria applicable to "educational" organizations.

"Testing for public safety" was added in 1954 to overturn a case that denied exemption to the Underwriters' Laboratory, a nonprofit organization formed by fire insurance companies to test electrical appliances. See Underwriters' Laboratories v. Commissioner, 135 F.2d 371 (7th Cir.1943), cert. denied, 320 U.S. 756, 64 S.Ct. 63 (1943). The provision has been extended to organizations that test other consumer products, even if there is a benefit provided to the manufacturer (Treas. Reg. § 1.501(c)(3)–1(d)(4)), but not to drug testing organizations because of the Service's view that testing to meet Food and Drug Administration requirements serves primarily the interest of the manufacturer rather than the public (Rev. Rul. 68–373, 1968–2 C.B. 206).

Organizations operated for "scientific" purposes have raised relatively few qualification issues. The regulations provide that scientific organizations may engage in applied or fundamental research provided that they serve public rather than private interests, but exemption is denied for activities, such as testing or inspection, that are ordinarily incident to commercial operations. Treas. Reg. § 1.501(c)(3)–1(d)(5)(i), (ii).

The materials below illustrate some interpretational issues raised by the amateur sports category.

Hutchinson Baseball Enterprises, Inc. v. Commissioner

United States Court of Appeals, Tenth Circuit, 1982.
696 F.2d 757.

■ Holloway, Circuit Judge.

This is an appeal by the Commissioner of Internal Revenue from a decision by the United States Tax Court that the taxpayer Hutchinson Baseball Enterprises, Inc., is organized for the promotion, advancement, and sponsorship of recreational and amateur athletics and therefore qualifies as a charitable organization under § 501(c)(3) of the Internal Revenue Code. 26 U.S.C.A. § 501(c)(3). * * *

I

The taxpayer Hutchinson Baseball Enterprises, Inc., was incorporated on August 31, 1970, as a not-for-profit corporation under the laws of Kansas. The amended articles of incorporation provide that one of the purposes of the corporation is to "[p]romote, advance and sponsor baseball, which shall include Little League and Amateur Baseball, in the Hutchinson, Kansas area." (Certificate of Amendment to Articles of Incorporation of Hutchinson Baseball Enterprises, Inc., attached to the by-laws of Hutchinson Baseball Enterprises, Inc.). The taxpayer is involved in a variety of activities, including owning and operating the Hutchinson Broncos baseball team (the Broncos), leasing and maintaining a playing field for the use of the Broncos, American Legion teams, and a baseball camp, and furnishing instructors and coaches for the Little League and baseball camp. The taxpayer also leases the baseball field to a local junior college for a nominal fee.

The Broncos baseball team, owned by the taxpayer, plays in a semi-professional league. The Tax Court found that the Broncos is an amateur team, and that determination is not challenged on appeal. The team plays in a league consisting of seven teams based in a three-state area. The Bronco team is composed of collegiate baseball players. These players are recruited from various states around the country to play for the team during the summer. They receive no compensation for playing baseball, but they are guaranteed jobs at the minimum wage either with Hutchinson Enterprises in a non-playing capacity or with other organizations in Hutchinson, Kansas. Additionally, all team members receive free housing in a Hutchinson Junior College dormitory.

The Broncos practice and play their home games on Bud Detter Field, which is owned by the City of Hutchinson. The taxpayer Hutchinson Enterprises leases the field from the City for a monthly rental fee, with the proviso that it maintain the field and keep it in good repair. The taxpayer assumed the American Legion's lease of the field from the City of Hutchinson under an agreement with the American Legion which permits the Legion baseball team to use the field rent free and which grants Hutchinson Enterprises exclusive concession rights and profits therefrom for all events held at Detter Field. Since the taxpayer has assumed care of the field, it has improved the facility by installing new fences and screens, and by constructing new dugouts and offices, and additional bleachers to accommodate the larger crowds.

In addition to allowing the American Legion the free use of the baseball field, the taxpayer permits the Little League and the youth baseball camp run by the City of Hutchinson to have free use of the baseball field and also provides Bronco team members to serve as coaches and instructors for these activities. Moreover, the taxpayer has made Bud Detter Field available during the school year to the Hutchinson Junior College for the fee of $500. The taxpayer raises money through sales of tickets, advertising, and concessions, through contribution solicitation, and through operation of the Broncos.

On October 5, 1973, the taxpayer filed an application for exempt status under § 501(c)(3). Effective as of October 5, 1973, the Commissioner recognized the taxpayer as an exempt organization under § 501(c)(3), by a determination letter dated October 24, 1973. * * * As a result of an examination of the taxpayer's activities for the fiscal years ended July 31, 1974, and July 31, 1975, the Commissioner concluded that the taxpayer no longer qualified for exemption under § 501(c)(3) and notified the taxpayer to that effect. The Commissioner issued a final adverse determination on August 28, 1978.

The taxpayer challenged the ruling in this declaratory judgment in the Tax Court. The court's opinion stated that the term "charitable" is to be construed in its generic sense, and is not limited to classifications enumerated in the statute. The court found that the taxpayer was organized for one or more exempt purposes, that the Broncos was an amateur baseball team, and that the purpose of the taxpayer's activities with respect to the Broncos—as with those engaged in with respect to the Little League, the baseball camp, the American Legion program and the Hutchinson Community Junior College—was to advance amateur athletics, i.e., baseball, in the Hutchinson community. The court therefore held that the taxpayer satisfied the operational test and should be classified as a § 501(c)(3) organization.

II

The only issue on this appeal is whether the Tax Court erred in holding that the taxpayer qualified as a tax-exempt organization under § 501(c)(3) of the Internal Revenue Code. The facts are not in dispute and the subsidiary findings of the Tax Court are not questioned. The Commissioner challenges only the court's conclusion in favor of the taxpayer on its exempt status.

Section 501(a) provides tax exempt status for organizations described in § 501(c). [The language of § 501(c)(3) has been omitted, Eds.]

Section 501(c)(3) thus sets forth three requirements a taxpayer must meet to achieve exempt status: (1) the corporation must be organized and operated exclusively for exempt purposes; (2) no part of the corporation's net earnings may inure to the benefit of any shareholder or individual; and (3) the corporation must not engage in political campaigns or, to a substantial extent, in lobbying activities. Only the first requirement is at issue in this case. In deciding whether the taxpayer here satisfied requirement (1), we will treat in turn the Commissioner's argument that (a) the Tax Court erred in holding that the promotion of an amateur sport, without more, is a qualifying charitable activity; and (b) by reason of the fact that its predominant activity is support of the Broncos, the taxpayer is disqualified for the § 501(c)(3) exemption for organizations furthering educational or other charitable purposes.

A

The Commissioner challenges the Tax Court's conclusion that the taxpayer was entitled to the § 501(c)(3) exemption by being organized for the promotion, advancement, and sponsoring of recreational and amateur baseball.

The Commissioner argues that the sole support cited by the Tax Court for its decision is the legislative history of the amendment of § 501(c)(3) as effected by the Tax Reform Act of 1976. He says the 1976 amendment added to the organizations already enumerated in § 501(c)(3), those whose purpose is to "foster national or international amateur sports competition (but only if no part of its activities involve the provision of athletic facilities or equipment)," and stresses the more favorable treatment for fostering national and international amateur sports; that the history does not indicate that Congress was of the view that under existing law the mere promotion of amateur sports was a qualifying charitable purpose; that Congress actually recognized that promotion of amateur sports had not been viewed as a charitable purpose except where the organization engaged in sufficient instructional activities so as to qualify as an educational organization, or where the sports program was part of an overall recognized charitable activity such as the reduction of juvenile delinquency.

The Commissioner maintains that under existing law, consisting basically of revenue rulings, the fostering of amateur sports competition, without more, had not been regarded by the Commissioner as a qualifying charitable purpose; otherwise the amendment to § 501(c)(3) would have been unnecessary. He says that the Tax Court decision under the 1976 Act has the effect of imposing an added burden on such organizations generally. The anomalous result is that organizations like the taxpayer which promote local amateur sports qualify without regard to whether they provide facilities or equipment, while organizations promoting national and international sports are ineligible if they provide such facilities or equipment. Hence the Tax Court's interpretation is illogical and should be reversed.

At the outset we note that the Tax Court did not rely wholly on the legislative history of the 1976 amendment. The court persuasively reasoned that the organization's purposes in promoting numerous phases of recreational and amateur baseball for the community were of a "charitable" nature and within the broad meaning of the term "charitable" and the penumbra of § 501(c)(3). [S]ee § 1.501(c)(3)–1(d)(2), Income Tax Regulations, 26 CFR 1.501(c)(3)–1(d)(2). The regulation is pertinent in that it recognizes that the term "charitable" is to be construed in its "generally accepted legal sense and is, therefore, not to be construed as limited by the separate enumeration in section 501(c)(3) of other tax exempt purposes which may fall within the broad outlines of 'charity' as developed by judicial decisions."

The Tax Court cited Peters v. Commissioner, 21 T.C. 55. There a charitable contribution was held to have been made. The foundation benefitted was a corporation organized to furnish free public swimming facilities at a beach for residents of Cold Spring Harbor, New York, not having private facilities and not having means to acquire such facilities. A contribution was not a condition for use of the facility, which was open to contributors and noncontributors alike. The corporation was held to have been organized and operated exclusively for charitable purposes. The court found that the organization's dominant purpose was to provide convenient swimming and recreation facilities and was within the broad meaning of the term "charitable," stating (21 T.C. at 59): In its broader meaning, charity is not so limited but also embraces any benevolent or philanthropic objective not prohibited by law or public policy which tends to advance the well-doing and well-being of man.

The Commissioner cites statements from IV Scott on Trusts 2d § 374.6A (1967 ed.) and the Restatement of the Law, Trusts 2d § 374, comment n., that a trust for the mere promotion of sports is not charitable. However both authorities recognize that it has been held that a trust to promote sports among children may be upheld on the ground that it is a part of the education of children to improve their bodies as well as their minds. See also College Preparatory School for Girls of Cincinnati v. Evatt, 144 Ohio St. 408, 59 N.E.2d 142, 145. We are persuaded that in view of the various activities of the taxpayer furthering the development and sportsmanship of children and young men, Hutchinson Baseball Enterprises was properly held to qualify for the exemption as being organized and operated exclusively for charitable purposes.

Thus, on the wording of § 501(c)(3) and proper interpretation of the term "charitable," we agree with the Tax Court's ruling here. Moreover, we agree with the Tax Court's analysis of the legislative history. The Joint Committee explained the purpose of the 1976 amendment to § 501(c)(3) in statements set out in the margin.[2] In interpreting the legislative history, the Tax Court pointed to the concluding portion of the committee's "Explanation of Provision" statement, emphasized in note 2, supra, as showing that amateur athletic organizations could be exempt under 501(c)(3) prior to the 1976 amendment. We agree that the Joint Committee appeared to recognize that under prior law some amateur sports organizations did receive the favored tax-exempt status while other organizations did not. As the taxpayer points out, this recognition illustrates that Congress considered that under the existing law, the advancement of amateur athletics was a permissible charitable activity. The 1976 amendment added a further clarifying provision that organizations which foster national or international amateur sports competition are also within the exemption, subject to the restriction that they not provide athletic equipment or facilities.[3]

We thus are in agreement with the interpretation of the legislative history by the Tax Court instead of that of the Government. However, we prefer not to base our conclusion as to the state of earlier law on that subsequent legislative history. We are persuaded nevertheless that on the wording of the statute and its proper construction, the Tax Court reached the right conclusion in holding that "the furtherance of recreational and amateur sports, falls within the broad outline of 'charity' and should be so classified."

B

There remains for consideration the Commissioner's contention that the taxpayer is disqualified for the § 501(c)(3) exemption because its

---

2. The Joint Committee stated:

* * *

Reasons for Change. Prior policy on the qualification for Section 501(c)(3) status has been a source of confusion and inequity for amateur sports organizations whereby some gained favored tax-exempt status while others, apparently equally deserving, did not. The failure of some of these organizations to obtain Section 501(c)(3) status and to qualify to receive tax-deductible contributions has discouraged contributions to these organizations, and has deterred other organizations from going through the legal expense of applying to the Internal Revenue Service for recognition of Section 501(c)(3) status. Congress believes that it is, in general, appropriate to treat the fostering of national or international amateur sports competition as a charitable purpose.

Explanation of Provision. The Act permits an organization the primary purpose of which is to foster national or international amateur sports competition to qualify as an organization described in Section 501(c)(3) and to receive tax-deductible contributions, but only if no part of the organization's activities involves the provision of athletic facilities or equipment. This restriction on the provision of athletic facilities and equipment is intended to prevent the allowance of these benefits for organizations which, like social clubs, provide facilities and equipment for their members. This provision is not intended to adversely affect the qualification for charitable tax-exempt status or tax deductible contributions of any organization which would qualify under the standards of prior law.
* * *

3. As the Tax Court noted, 73 T.C. at 153, the legislative history demonstrates that this restriction was intended to prevent the providing of facilities and equipment to members of organizations such as social clubs.

predominant activity is the operation of the Hutchinson Broncos. He maintains this activity does not serve an educational or other recognized charitable purpose and was pursued to field the best team possible and win the championship of the league.

The Tax Court rejected the argument made along this line. It found that the Broncos was an amateur baseball team. The court found also that the purpose of the taxpayer's activities with respect to the Broncos—as with those it engaged in for the Little League, the baseball camp, the American Legion program and the Hutchinson Community Junior College—was to advance amateur baseball in the Hutchinson community.

The presence of a single nonexempt purpose, if substantial in nature, will destroy the exemption, regardless of the number or importance of truly exempt purposes. Nevertheless we agree with the views of the Tax Court concerning the taxpayer's support of Broncos. While the Commissioner contended in the Tax Court that the Broncos is a semi-professional team, he now expressly states in his brief that the Government is not contesting on appeal the finding that the Broncos are an amateur team. Thus we have the established fact that it is an amateur team which the taxpayer promotes.

The circumstances underlying that fact demonstrate the taxpayer's purpose of aiding development of these young athletes. The Bronco players are acquired by recruiting efforts or tryouts. They are often discovered by their high school or college coaches. The players receive free lodging in the Hutchinson Junior College dormitories during the season at the expense of Hutchinson Baseball Enterprises. The players have jobs in local industry at the minimum wage during the season. In college a large percentage of the players continue to play for college teams during their school years. Finally, an important function of the Broncos team members was that they served as instructors and coaches for Little League teams and the baseball camps.

Considering all these circumstances, we agree with the conclusion of Tax Court. The support of the Broncos and the taxpayer's other activities were for the purpose of advancing amateur baseball and served proper charitable purposes within the § 501(c)(3) exception.

AFFIRMED.

NOTES

1. *Amateur Athletics as a Charitable Purpose.* The Hutchinson Broncos qualified under § 501(c)(3) because they were "charitable" without regard to the 1976 amendment that added fostering of national and international amateur sports competition as an exempt purpose. For a contrary result, see Wayne Baseball, Inc. v. Commissioner, 78 T.C.M. 437 (1999), where the Tax Court found that more than an insubstantial part of an amateur baseball team's activities furthered the nonexempt social and recreational interests of its members. Unlike the Hutchinson Broncos, the team in *Wayne Baseball* did not promote amateur athletics by providing

instruction or facilities to the community or engaging in other charitable activities.

The Service also has granted charitable or educational exemptions to organizations that develop youth sports programs to combat juvenile delinquency and provide a "recreational outlet." See Rev. Rul. 80–215, 1980–2 C.B. 174; Rev. Rul. 65–2, 1965–1 C.B. 227. The 1976 amendment was added to extend § 501(c)(3) exempt status to other types of amateur sports organizations, such as support groups for athletes competing in the Olympics and other national and international competitions, which previously could qualify only as § 501(c)(4) social welfare organizations or § 501(c)(6) business leagues.

2. *Qualified Amateur Sports Organizations.* To qualify as an amateur sports organization under the 1976 amendment to § 501(c)(3), no part of the organization's activities may involve the provision of athletic facilities or equipment. According to the legislative history, this strange limitation was intended to preclude social clubs providing facilities and equipment for their members from sneaking into § 501(c)(3). Read literally, however, the language was broad enough to disqualify legitimate athletic support organizations that provided training facilities and equipment. This caused Congress to call a "time out" while it added yet another category—the § 501(j) "qualified amateur sports organization" ("QASO"). A QASO must be organized and operated exclusively to foster national or international amateur sports competitions by conducting the competitions or developing and supporting the competing athletes. A QASO's exemption is not adversely affected because it has a local or regional membership, and it is relieved of the restriction on providing facilities and equipment.

3. *Professional Baseball as a Charitable Purpose.* Can a professional sports team serve a charitable purpose? The estate of Ewing Kaufmann, the late former owner of the Kansas City Royals major league baseball team, received the Service's approval of a complex transaction under which the team was donated to The Greater Kansas City Community Foundation. In the late 1990s, the Foundation owned and operated the Royals in a limited partnership with local civic leaders until a local buyer was found. Additional funds were contributed to the Foundation to help cover the team's projected operating losses. The Foundation was required to use its share of any sales proceeds for charitable purposes. In approving the transaction, the Service did not rule that the team itself qualified for § 501(c)(3) exemption. The Royals were operated as a separate taxable corporation owned by the Foundation and a partnership of private investors. The IRS did find, however, that the transfer of an ownership interest in the team to the Foundation and the resulting joint venture with private investors was motivated by a charitable purpose because it "lessened the burdens of government" within the meaning of Treas. Reg. § 1.501(c)(3)–1(d)(2). See, e.g., P.L.R 9530024 (July 28, 1995). While conceding that the same could be said about retaining any large business enterprise, the ruling concluded that historically there was an "intense and unique" interest

shown by several different governmental bodies in keeping the Royals in Kansas City.

One premise of the ruling—that preserving a professional sports franchise is a quasi-governmental function—is debatable. Lost in the controversy over this questionable extension of the "reducing the burdens of government" rationale for exemption is the extraordinary generosity of the Royals' late owner, Ewing Kaufmann. Gifts of this magnitude by owners of other professional sports franchises are unlikely to become a recurring phenomenon.

For a lively critique of the Royals rulings, see Myreon Sony Hodur, Ball Four: The IRS Walks the Kansas City Royals, 19 Hastings Comm/ent L.J. 483 (1997).

PROBLEMS

Consider whether the following organizations qualify for tax exemption under either § 501(c)(3) or § 501(j):

(a) The Mixing Bowl Association, which operates an annual post-season nationally televised college football game ("The Pillsbury Mixing Bowl") in collaboration with a for-profit corporate sponsor. Net revenues from the game are distributed to the participating universities for their athletic and scholarship programs.

(b) The Butterfly Booster Club, an organization that provides moral and financial support to local swimming teams to aid in the personal development of their members, and to foster national and international swimming competition. The Club hosts meets, pays travel expenses for swimmers and coaches who attend competitions, provides training equipment, and rents time at a for-profit swim club where swimmers supported by the club train on a daily basis. The Club's board consists of ten individuals, eight of whom have children on the sponsored teams and the other two of whom own the for-profit swim club. The Club's revenues are generated from fundraising activities and contributions from parents and friends of the competitive swimmers.

(c) The Newport Harbor Foundation, which was founded by Ira Lewis, a wealthy patron of yachting, to finance the entry of his yacht, Viking Two, in the America's Cup sailing competition. Lewis personally contributed $10 million to the Foundation, and an additional $10 million will be raised from corporations, individuals, and private foundations. The Foundation will use the funds to maintain Viking Two, to compensate and house its crew, and for other expenses related to the competition. Lewis is the skipper of Viking Two but does not receive any compensation from the Foundation. Crew members are paid $35,000 per year, on average, plus living expenses.

8.   State and Local Tax Exemptions

Nonprofit organizations that derive their federal income tax exemption under § 501(c)(3) also are likely to enjoy exemption from state and local taxes. All states with a corporate income or franchise tax provide exemptions for charitable organizations and grant exemptions from state and local property taxes, at least if the organization uses the property for its exempt purposes. Public benefit organizations also may be exempt from sales and use taxes. Because of the wide variety of state and local taxing schemes, this discussion is necessarily selective, but it should be kept in mind that for many organizations, state tax benefits, especially property or sales tax exemptions, may be more important than exemption from federal income tax or even eligibility to receive tax-deductible contributions.

Income and Franchise Taxes. States vary in their approaches to granting exemption from income and corporate franchise taxes. Some, like California, import most of the requirements imposed by § 501(c)(3) but require a separate application for state income tax exemption. Others, like Delaware, provide that organizations recognized as exempt under § 501(a) and described in § 501(c) are automatically exempt from state taxes without having to file for exemption. Del. Code Ann. tit. 30, 1133. New York exempts certain nonprofit organizations from the state corporate franchise tax by regulation. 20 N.Y. Comp. Codes R. & Regs. tit. 20, § 1–3.4(b)(6). A separate application is required, but New York generally follows the Internal Revenue Service's determination. Most states have provisions comparable to the federal unrelated business income tax.

Real Property Taxes. The most dynamic area of state and local taxation affecting nonprofits is the real property tax exemption. A study by the New York University School of Law's Philanthropy and the Law program, drawing upon an earlier survey by W. Harrison Wellford and Janne Gallagher, provides a good general description of state property tax exemption schemes:

> [T]hirty-six state constitutions exempt nonprofit charities from property taxes or permit the legislature to grant such exemptions. The remaining state constitutions either generally permit granting exemptions, without restrictions on the class of eligible entities, or, if they contain no provision addressing the issue, have been interpreted as permitting exemptions for organizations carrying on activities similar to those enumerated in Code Section 501(c)(3). Generally, all states condition exemption upon prohibition of private inurement and the irrevocable dedication of assets to exempt purposes. To be exempt, most states require that the property be used either exclusively or primarily for exempt purposes. As the proportion of non-exempt use increases, so does the likelihood that all or a portion of the property will lose its exempt status. In virtually every state, property owned by an exempt entity, but dedicated to entirely non-exempt uses, will be taxed.

Bazil Facchina, Evan Showell & Jan E. Stone, Privileges & Exemptions Enjoyed by Nonprofit Organizations 45–46 (NYU Program on Philanthropy and the Law, 1993).

In reaction to their own fiscal problems and the entrepreneurial activities of many nonprofit organizations, states and municipalities have been reexamining these traditional property tax exemptions. The dollar impact of local tax exemptions on municipalities is substantial. For example, in 1993 non-governmental nonprofits in Philadelphia were exempted from nearly $45.6 million in city property taxes, $55.1 million in school district property taxes, as well as from the City's net profits tax, business privilege tax, business use and occupancy tax and parking tax. Tax exempt property constituted 25.2 percent of the city's property assessment. The assessed value of nonprofit property in Philadelphia grew from $1.2 billion in 1963 to $3.1 billion in 1993. Report of the Philadelphia Mayor's Special Committee on Nonprofits, 94 State Tax Notes 132–28, July 11, 1994. State and local officials have proceeded on several fronts: (1) tightening statutory definitions of the type of activity that qualifies as "charitable;" (2) broadening the sales tax base to include services provided by nonprofits; and (3) enacting municipal service fees or entering into agreements with nonprofits to receive payments in lieu of taxes or services in lieu of taxes to reimburse the municipality for the cost of providing essential services. See Boyd J. Black, Searching for the Revenue: Eroding State and Local Tax Exemptions, in ALI–ABA, Not-for Profit Organizations: The Challenge of Governance in an Era of Retrenchment 229 (1992). In early 1995, the District of Columbia, faced with a $600 billion budget deficit, called for a study of all tax exemptions granted to nonprofits. Prominent targets were George Washington University (holding property with an assessed value of $601 million), the World Bank ($517 million), and Georgetown University ($398.5 million). Also threatened were government instrumentalities such as the Federal National Mortgage Association and leading trade associations such as the Motion Picture Association of America. See David A. Vise, District to Go After Tax–Exempt Groups, Wash. Post, Jan. 25, 1995, A1.

While opposition to tax exemptions of nonprofit hospitals has been the primary focus of attack by state and local tax authorities, challenges have also focussed on YMCAs, nonprofit nursing facilities, residential retirement facilities, educational institutions and even churches. A common pattern is that an assessor, tax board, or lower court reflecting local pressures will revoke an exemption only to be reversed on appeal after years of litigation and substantial expense to the charity. See, e.g., Medical Center Hospital of Vt., Inc. v. City of Burlington, 152 Vt. 611, 566 A.2d 1352 (1989); City of Pittsburgh v. Board of Property Assessment Appeals, 129 Pa.Cmwlth. 69, 564 A.2d 1026 (1989); and cases discussed in Black, supra at 242–245. Several states have tightened their exemption standards. For example, New Hampshire now defines "charitable" in relation to the services performed by the organization for public good or welfare of the general public or an indefinite segment of it. It requires that an organization not provide any pecuniary profit or limit its benefits to officers or members. N.H. Rev. Stat. Ann. 72:23–1.

Other states have created statutory presumptions. In California, for example, a nonprofit hospital is presumed to be entitled to the welfare property tax exemption if it earns less than ten percent surplus revenues in a year or makes an appropriate showing of how the profit is used. Cal. Rev. & Tax'n Code § 214(a)(1); but see Rideout Hospital Foundation v. County of Yuba, 8 Cal.App.4th 214, 10 Cal.Rptr.2d 141 (1992) (hospital that earned surplus revenue in excess of ten percent can still qualify for welfare exemption from property tax if surplus is used for actual operation of exempt entity). Other states have required nonprofit hospitals to demonstrate their charitable deeds to retain exempt status. See Tex. Health & Safety Code Ann. § 311.045. The Utah State Tax Commission, in response to the Utah Supreme Court's decision in Utah County v. Intermountain Health Care, Inc., 709 P.2d 265 (Utah 1985) has issued guidelines to be applied in determining whether hospitals and nursing homes qualify for exemption from Utah real property taxes. The standards generally require a hospital to be: (1) organized as a nonprofit, (2) prohibit the inurement of net earnings and donations to the benefit of any private individuals, (3) ensure open access to medical services, regardless of race, religion, gender or ability to pay, (4) demonstrate that its policies reflect the public interest by having a broad-based governing board that meets at least annually to address community needs, and (5) enumerate and total the various ways in which it provides unreimbursed service to the community in accordance with certain measurement criteria. These standards were upheld in Howell v. County Board of Cache County, 881 P.2d 880 (Utah 1994). For further discussion of changing property tax standards for nonprofit hospitals, see Section C3b of this chapter, supra, at pp. 337–339.

Local municipalities have attempted to impose Payments-in-Lieu-of-Taxes (Pilots), Services-in-Lieu-of-Taxes (Silots) or user fees on nonprofits. Boston negotiates Pilots agreements at a uniform rate equal to the percentage of the City's operating budget devoted to essential services. In 1991, 27 nonprofits paid over $11.4 million and donated an additional $6.8 million in Silots. In 1998, Harvard University paid $1.3 million to the City of Boston as compensation for lost revenue on student housing. In 1991, it agreed to pay compensation for ten years to Cambridge for any university-owned property removed from the city's tax rolls, and in 1999 Harvard agreed to pay $40 million to Boston over 20 years as payment in lieu of property taxes on otherwise exempt property. In 1994, Philadelphia created a Pilots/Silots program which asked nonprofits to make voluntary payments to make voluntary payments of forty percent of the annual property tax they would owe if they were not tax exempt. Nonprofits would have the option of substituting up to 33% of their Pilots obligations with Silots.

No state has been more forceful in challenging nonprofit tax exemptions than Pennsylvania. The Pennsylvania Constitution allows the state legislature to exempt from taxation only "institutions of purely public charity." Pa. Constit. Art. VIII, Section 2(a)(v). In Hospital Utilization Project v. Commonwealth, 507 Pa. 1, 487 A.2d 1306 (1985), the Pennsylvania Supreme Court held that the Hospital Utilization Project (HUP), a § 501(c)(3) organization which provided statistical information to hospitals, was not a purely public charity under the Pennsylvania Constitution and therefore not entitled to a sales and use tax exemption. (A similar standard is applied for property tax exemption purposes.) The court held that for an entity to qualify as a purely public charity it must: (1) advance a charitable purpose; (2) donate or render gratuitously a substantial portion of its services; (3) benefit a substantial and indefinite class of persons who are legitimate subjects of charity; (4) relieve the government of some of its burden; and (5) operate entirely free from private profit motive. Id. at 1317. In applying these criteria to HUP, the court found that the organization did not donate its services; its beneficiaries were not an indefinite class or legitimate subjects of charity; its executives were paid too well; and its accumulation of excess revenue for capital investment suggested it did not operate entirely free from private profit motive.

Subsequent Pennsylvania cases, construing the property tax exemption statutes strictly in favor of the taxing authority, have held that all these criteria must be met. Board of Revision of Taxes of the City of Philadelphia v. American Board of Internal Medicine, 154 Pa.Cmwlth. 204, 623 A.2d 418 (1993). In School District of Erie v. Hamot Medical Center, 144 Pa.Cmwlth. 668, 602 A.2d 407 (1992), the court upheld the revocation of the tax-exempt status of a nonprofit hospital, finding that it failed to meet four of the five HUP criteria. Tax assessors have challenged other nonprofit hospitals, many of whom offered to make payments of cash or services in lieu of property taxes in order to save their exemption. In perhaps the most extraordinary case, a lower court revoked the real property exemption of Washington & Jefferson College, the nation's sixth oldest, finding the College met only one of the HUP criteria—it was operated entirely free from private profit motive. City of Washington v. Board Assessment Appeals, No. 93–7033 (Washington Co. Com. Pleas, Aug. 5, 1994).

On appeal, however, the Commonwealth Court reversed the trial court, and a divided Pennsylvania Supreme Court affirmed the Commonwealth Court, holding that the College qualified for a property tax exemption as "an institution of purely public charity." Applying the five-part *Hospital Utilization Project* test, the court found that the College: (1) advanced a charitable purpose by providing education for youths in Pennsylvania; (2) donated or rendered gratuitously a substantial portion of its services by absorbing massive tuition charges (through scholarships and the use of endowment funds for operating expenses) that otherwise would be charged to students; (3) benefitted a substantial and indefinite class of persons who are legitimate objects of charity by providing substantial aid to students who, while not poor, would not otherwise be able to afford a college education; (4) relieved the burdens of government because, like other independent colleges and universities, the College relieved the load placed on state-funded schools of higher learning; and (5) operated entirely free from private profit motive. City of Washington v. Board of Assessment, 550 Pa. 175, 704 A.2d 120 (1997).

At about the same time that the Pennsylvania Supreme Court rendered its opinion in *City of Washington*, the Commonwealth enacted a new law (Act 55) redefining the criteria for nonprofits seeking to qualify for property and sales tax exemptions in Pennsylvania. The new law incorporates the five-part *HUP* test and provides elaboration for each prong. As an example of the level of detail, nonprofits may show that they offer a substantial portion of their services for free by meeting any one of seven tests, one of which requires that an institution have a written and reasonably publicized policy that it will not turn anyone away because of inability to pay. Another provision of the new law is aimed at charities carrying on commercial business activities that are unrelated to the charity's purposes as stated in its charter or governing legal documents. The Pennsylvania legislation may be a harbinger of developments nationwide as state and local governments continue to grapple with the increased commercialism of the nonprofit sector. See Grant Williams, New Pa. Law and Court Ruling Specify Standards for Tax Exemption, Chron. Philanthropy, Dec. 11, 1997, at 41.

Other State Taxes. As this edition to went press in early 2010, many states were looking to raise new sources of revenue from nonprofit groups. Minnesota now requires charities other than churches to pay the same fees paid by residents and for-profit businesses for street lights. Hawaii is considering suspension of a range of nonprofit tax exemptions, and municipalities in Indiana and Pennsylvania are exploring whether to impose user fees on wealthier nonprofits for essential services. The mayor of Pittsburgh proposed a one percent tax on tuition charged by colleges and universities but abandoned the idea after three large Pittsburgh nonprofits agreed to increase voluntary payments to the city. These inroads on state tax exemptions are likely to continue as states face sharply declining revenues. See Stephanie Strom, States Move to Revoke Charities' Tax Exemptions, N.Y. Times, Feb. 28, 2010, at A21.

Constitutional Issues. In a case that was hailed as a major victory for charities, the Supreme Court held in a 5–to–4 opinion that a state may not deny a property tax exemption to a nonprofit organization because most of the people it serves are nonresidents. Camps Newfound/Owatonna, Inc. v. Town of Harrison, Maine, 520 U.S. 564, 117 S.Ct. 1590 (1997). The case involved a constitutional challenge by a nonprofit church-operated summer camp to a Maine law that limited or denied property tax exemptions to organizations operated principally for the benefit of nonresidents of Maine. The Court held that an otherwise generally applicable state property tax law violates the Commerce Clause if its charitable exemption excludes organizations operated primarily for the benefit of nonresidents. The Court majority reasoned that if the taxing scheme had discriminated against for-profit entities, it clearly would violate the Commerce Clause, and the same protections should extend to the nonprofit sector. In so ruling, the Court observed that it has frequently applied laws regulating commerce (e.g., labor and antitrust laws) to nonprofit organizations. See Chapter 11, infra.

The Court was not persuaded by the Town's argument that it should be able to give special benefits to charities that cater to local needs, especially those offering services the state itself otherwise would to provide.

Relying on Walz v. Tax Commission, 397 U.S. 664, 90 S.Ct. 1409 (1970), where it upheld the constitutionality of religious tax exemptions, the Court stated that there is a constitutionally significant difference between subsidies and tax exemptions.

Justice Scalia, joined by Chief Justice Rehnquist and Justices Thomas and Ginsburg, dissented, complaining that the Commerce Clause should not be invoked to prevent a state from giving tax benefits to charities that serve the state's inhabitants. Justice Thomas also wrote a separate dissent.

Camp Newfound/Owatonna attracted the attention of many large nonprofit organizations, who were concerned that a ruling in favor of Maine's property tax scheme would encourage other state and local governments to discriminate against nonprofits with a national or international presence.

For Further Reading: Property Tax Exemptions for Charities: Mapping the Battlefield (Evelyn Brody ed., 2002); Boyd J. Black, Searching for the Revenue: Eroding State & Local Tax Exemptions in Not-for-Profit Organizations: The Challenge of Governance in an Era of Retrenchment (A.L.I. ed. 1992); Margaret A. Potter & Beaufort B. Longest, Jr. The Divergence of Federal and State Policies on the Charitable Tax Exemption of Nonprofit Hospitals, 19 J. Health Pol. Pol'y & L. 393 (1994); Rebecca S. Rudnick, State and Local Taxes on Nonprofit Organizations, 22 Cap. U. L.Rev. 321 (1993); Peter Swords, Charitable Real Property Tax Exemptions in New York State–Menace or Measure of Social Progress (1981); Janne Gallagher, Sales Tax Exemptions for Charitable, Educational, and Religious Organizations, 7 Exempt Org. Tax Rev. 429 (1993).

D.   INUREMENT, PRIVATE BENEFIT AND INTERMEDIATE SANCTIONS

1.   INUREMENT OF PRIVATE GAIN

Treasury Regulations: § 1.501(c)(3)–1(c)(2).

Section 501(c)(3) organizations are prohibited from engaging in activities that result in "inurement" of the organization's net earnings to insiders, such as founders, directors, and officers. The related "private benefit" doctrine prohibits a § 501(c)(3) organization from providing a substantial economic benefit to individuals who do not exercise any substantial control over the organization. The essence of inurement is that a person in a position to influence the decisions of an organization receives disproportionate benefits, such as excessive compensation or rent, a below-market rate loan, or improper economic gain from sales or exchanges of property with the exempt organization.

Historically, the Service has invoked the inurement limitation only in the most egregious cases of insider misconduct. Since the only sanction was the ultimate death sentence—revocation of exemption—enforcement was lax. Congress gave the Service a new and more effective weapon in 1996 when it enacted the § 4958 intermediate sanctions regime. Insiders who receive excess economic benefits now are subject to monetary penalties, as are organization managers who approve of such transactions. The materials below survey the historical and contemporary aspects of inurement and private benefit and then turn to intermediate sanctions.

Church of Scientology of California v. Commissioner

United States Court of Appeals, Ninth Circuit, 1987.
823 F.2d 1310.

■ TANG, CIRCUIT JUDGE:

The Church of Scientology (Church) appeals a judgment of the Tax Court which affirmed the Commissioner's assessment of tax deficiencies and late filing penalties against the Church for the years 1970, 1971 and 1972. At issue is whether the Commissioner properly revoked the Church's tax exempt status.

I.

The Church was incorporated as a nonprofit corporation in the State of California in 1954. In 1957, the Commissioner recognized it as a tax exempt organization under § 501(c)(3) of the Internal Revenue Code of 1954. The Commissioner revoked the Church's tax exempt status in 1967. The letter of revocation stated that the Church was "engaged in a business for profit," and was "operated in a manner whereby a portion of [its] earnings inure[d] to the benefit of a private individual," and was "serving a private, rather than a public interest." * * *

On March 28, 1978, the Church filed suit in United States Tax Court challenging the Commissioner's determination of tax deficiency. In an extensive opinion, the Tax Court substantially upheld the determination of the Commissioner. 83 T.C. 381 (1984). It held that the Church did not qualify for exemption from taxation under §§ 501(a) & 501(c)(3) because: (1) the Church was operated for a substantial commercial purpose; (2) its earnings inured to the benefit of L. Ron Hubbard, his family, and OTC, a private non-charitable corporation controlled by key Scientology officials; and (3) it violated well defined standards of public policy by conspiring to prevent the IRS from assessing and collecting taxes owed by the Church. The Court also upheld the validity of the Notice of Deficiency. Finally, the Court upheld the penalties for failure to file tax returns.

II.

During the years in question, the Church of Scientology of California was the "Mother Church" of the many Scientology churches around the country. The Church propagated the Scientology faith, a religion founded by L. Ron Hubbard, through such means as the indoctrination of laity, training and ordination of ministers, creation of congregations, and provision of support to affiliated organizations.

Scientology teaches that the individual is a spiritual being having a mind and body. Part of the mind, called the "reactive mind" is unconscious and filled with mental images that are frequently the source of irrational behavior. Through the administration of a process known as "auditing" a parishioner, called a "pre-clear," is helped to erase his or her reactive mind and gain spiritual awareness. Auditing is administered individually by a trained "auditor." The auditor poses questions to the pre-clear and measures the latter's response with an electronic device called an "E–Meter" that is attached to the skin. The E–Meter assists in the identification of spiritual difficulty. Scientology teaches that spiritual awareness is achieved in stages. A disciple achieves different levels of awareness through additional auditing. The religion also offers courses to train auditors.

Scientology teaches that people should pay for whatever of value they receive. This is called the "Doctrine of Exchange." Toward the realization of this doctrine, branch churches exacted a "fixed donation" for training and auditing. Fixed donations were not based on ability to pay and with few exceptions, services were not given for free.

Scientology is an international religion with numerous churches around the world. In the 1970's, these churches were organized along hierarchical lines according to the level of services they were authorized to provide. Churches that delivered services at the lowest levels were called "franchises" and later "missions." "Class IV orgs" delivered auditing through "grade IV" and training through "level IV." "St. Hill organizations" and "advanced organizations" offered intermediate and higher level services. The branch known as "Flag" offered the highest level of training and auditing.

The California Church consisted of several divisions. The San Francisco Organization and the Los Angeles Organization were both class IV organizations. The American St. Hill Organization was located in Los Angeles and offered intermediate auditing and training. The Advanced Organization of Los Angeles provided high levels of auditing and training to persons who had completed services at a class IV organization. The Flag Operations Liaison Office, located in Los Angeles, was an administrative unit of the California Church.

In addition to auditing and training, the Church provided assistance to prisoners, ex-offenders, the elderly, the mentally ill and drug addicts. On occasion the Church assisted the poor and the sick. The Church performed christenings, funerals and wedding ceremonies free of charge, and conducted regular Sunday services. The Church's chaplain provided marriage and family counseling free of charge. The Church also provided free a specialized form of auditing geared to help people in crisis.

Flag was the highest division of the California Church. It provided spiritual leadership. It also acted as the Church's administrative center. The Flag division was headquartered aboard the ship Apollo, which cruised the Mediterranean Sea and docked in various countries along its shores. L. Ron Hubbard, his wife, Mary Sue, and their family lived aboard the Apollo with other members of the ship's crew and staff. Besides performing the highest levels of auditing and training, Flag staff members performed a variety of management functions. * * *

The Church derived income from four sources: (1) auditing and training; (2) sales of Scientology literature, recordings and E-meters; (3) franchise operations; and (4) management services. Franchise operators were required to remit ten percent of gross income to the Church. The Church offered its managerial services to branch organizations around the world for a fixed fee.

One of the policy directives of the Church was to "MAKE MONEY". The Church frequently engaged in aggressive promotion of its products and services. This promotion included market surveys and advertisements. In addition, the Church trained staff members in salesmanship techniques.

L. Ron Hubbard officially resigned his position as executive head of the California and other Scientology churches in 1966. Despite his official resignation, the Tax Court found that he continued to exert significant control over the Church by making policy statements, directives, and orders. In addition, his approval was required for all financial planning. He was the sole trustee of a major Scientology trust fund into which the Church made substantial payments. He or Mary Sue Hubbard were signatories on many Church bank accounts.

During the tax years at issue, L. Ron Hubbard and Mary Sue Hubbard received salaries from the California Church and its affiliate, the United Kingdom Church, in the following amounts * * * [the total amounts received were $20,249 in 1970, $49,648 in 1971 and $115,680 in 1972, Eds.]

During these years, L. Ron Hubbard, Mary Sue Hubbard and their four children resided for the most part aboard the Apollo. While aboard ship, the Church provided the Hubbards with free lodging, food, laundry, medical services and vitamins.

The Church made royalty payments to L. Ron Hubbard for sales of his books, tapes and E-meters. The royalties amounted to ten percent of the retail price. The Church, for example, made $104,618.27 in royalty payments to Hubbard in 1972. Additionally, Church policy required that all work pertaining to Scientology and Dianetics be copyrighted to L. Ron Hubbard. As the result of this policy, a number of publications copyrighted by L. Ron Hubbard were actually written by others. For example, Ruth Mitchell wrote the book Know Your People and Peter Gillum wrote the book How to be Successful. Additionally, a series of books called the OEC series contained policy letters, some written by L. Ron Hubbard and others written by paid employees of the Church. L. Ron Hubbard received royalty payments on the sale of all of these publications.

During the 1960's, Scientology organizations around the world were required to pay directly to L. Ron Hubbard, ten percent of their income. These payments were termed "debt repayments" because they were designed to compensate Hubbard for his work in originating the Scientology religion. The Tax Court concluded that during 1971–1972 the Church continued to make debt repayments to Hubbard.

In 1968, L. Ron Hubbard, Mary Sue Hubbard, and Leon Steinberg incorporated a Panamanian corporation called Operation Transport Corp., Ltd. (OTC). OTC was a for-profit corporation. Shortly after the corporation's formation, Hubbard, Mary Sue Hubbard and Steinberg resigned and were replaced by three Flag employees. During the years in question, the new directors performed only one function. In the summer of 1972, they approved L. Ron Hubbard's decision to transfer approximately two million dollars from an OTC bank account in Switzerland to the Apollo. The money was stored in a locked file cabinet to which Mary Sue Hubbard had the only set of keys.

Between 1971 and 1972, the Church made payments in excess of three and a half million dollars to OTC. During these years, the Church also made payments totaling nearly $175,000 to the Central Defense and Dissemination Fund. According to the Church, these payments were placed in the United States Church of Scientology Trust of which L. Ron Hubbard was the sole trustee. The trust funds were deposited in several Swiss bank accounts. L. Ron Hubbard and Mary Sue Hubbard were signatories of the accounts and L. Ron Hubbard kept the trust checkbooks.

III.

* * *

B. Inurement

Congress conferred tax exemption on churches and other organizations in recognition of the benefit society derives from the activities of these organizations. The government leaves funds in the hands of charitable organizations rather than taxing them and spending the funds on public projects. Implicit in this purpose is that charities must promote the public good to qualify for tax exemption.

Section 501(c)(3) embodies this policy. Churches are eligible for tax exempt status only if no part of their net earnings inure to the benefit of private individuals. Each phrase of the statute has significance. The term "no part" is absolute. The organization loses tax exempt status if even a small percentage of income inures to a private individual. The sole beneficiary of the church's activities must be the public at large.

Courts have construed broadly the term "net earnings". "Net earnings" includes more than gross receipts minus disbursements as shown on the books of the organization. Only those ordinary expenses necessary to the operation of the church are not included in net earnings.

The heart of § 501(c)(3) tax exempt status is the phrase "inures to the benefit." Payment of reasonable salaries to church officials does not constitute inurement. However, payment of excessive salaries will result in a finding of inurement. Inurement can also result from distributions other than the payment of excessive salaries. Unaccounted for diversions of a charitable organization's resources by one who has complete and unfettered control can constitute inurement.

Finally, the regulations define "private shareholder or individual" broadly as any person "having a personal and private interest in the activities of the organization." 26 C.F.R. § 1.501(a)–1(c).

While we remain solicitous of Congress' intent to confer tax exempt status on religious organizations, this court has previously affirmed the denial of tax exemption where church income inures to private individuals.

* * *

The finding of the Tax Court that a portion of the Church's net earnings inured to the benefit of L. Ron Hubbard, his family, and OTC, a private for-profit corporation, is a factual finding. We review this finding for clear error.

The taxpayer has the burden to demonstrate that it is entitled to tax exempt status. This is especially true in situations where there is a great potential for abuse created by one individual's control of the church. The Church must come forward with candid disclosure of the facts bearing on the exemption application. Doubts will be resolved in favor of the government.

In finding that a portion of the Church's net earnings inured to the benefit of L. Ron Hubbard, his family and OTC, the court isolated two indicia of inurement, overt and covert. The overt indicia included salaries, living expenses, and royalties. The covert indicia included "debt repayments" and L. Ron Hubbard's unfettered control over millions of dollars of Church assets. The court concluded that these indicia, when viewed in light of the self-dealing associated with them, coupled with the Church's failure to carry its burden of proof and to disclose the facts candidly, proved conclusively that the Church was operated for the benefit of L. Ron Hubbard and his family.

The Church challenges the overt indicia of inurement on the ground that the salaries, expenses and royalties, were reasonable. It notes that the court did not find them unreasonable, considered separately. The Church questions the logic of the finding that several reasonable payments add up to inurement.

The Church paid L. Ron Hubbard and Mary Sue Hubbard combined salaries of $20,249 in 1970, $49,648 in 1971 and $115,680 in 1972. We cannot say that these salaries were excessive.

In addition to Hubbard's salary, the Church paid for all of the Hubbards' living and medical expenses aboard the cruise ship Apollo. These expenses amounted to about $30,000 per year. Because it is unnecessary to our decision, we express no opinion on whether supporting a Church's founder and his family aboard a yacht cruising the Mediterranean constitutes a reasonable Church expense.

The Church also paid substantial royalties to L. Ron Hubbard for his books, recordings and E-meters. Churches, especially less established ones, rely on the distribution of church literature to propagate their beliefs. Financing church operations through the sale of religious literature does not necessarily violate the requirements for tax exemption. Furthermore, a church may pay the author reasonable compensation in the form of royalties for his literary works. However, the payments in this case, cross the line between reasonable and excessive. Here, the evidence indicates that Hubbard used the Church to generate copyrighted literature and market his products. Scientology policy mandated that any book on Dianetics and Scientology be copyrighted in the name of L. Ron Hubbard. Pursuant to this policy, a number of publications copyrighted by L. Ron Hubbard were actually written by Church employees. Furthermore, the Church encouraged its staff members to market aggressively his products. We agree with the Tax Court that the royalty payments support a finding of inurement.

The Church argues that the evidence does not support the Tax Court's finding of covert inurement. However, the record reveals that L. Ron Hubbard had unfettered control over millions of dollars in Church assets. The Church transferred several million dollars to OTC during 1970–72. These payments were designated as "charter mission expenses." L. Ron Hubbard and Mary Sue Hubbard controlled OTC funds. Sometime during 1972, OTC transferred approximately two million dollars from OTC bank accounts in Switzerland to the Apollo. The finding that OTC was a sham corporation is sustained. During the tax years in question OTC funneled millions of dollars of Church assets to L. Ron Hubbard.

The record also supports the Tax Court's conclusion that L. Ron Hubbard had unfettered control over Church of Scientology Trust Fund assets. The Church deducted payments of $28,930.34 in 1970, $67,892.40 in 1971, and $77,986.62 in 1972 to the Central Defense and Dissemination Fund. According to the Church, these payments were made to the United States Church of Scientology Trust. L. Ron Hubbard was the sole trustee of the Trust during the years in question. Trust funds were deposited in several Swiss bank accounts. L. Ron Hubbard and Mary Sue Hubbard were two of the three signatories on the Trust accounts. L. Ron Hubbard kept the Trust checkbooks. In 1972, over a million dollars was withdrawn from the Trust accounts in Switzerland and brought aboard the Apollo where it was kept in a locked file cabinet. Mary Sue Hubbard had the only keys to the cabinet.

The Church disputes that control over assets compels a finding of inurement. It argues that every Sunday morning pastors all over America collect money from parishioners and hold that money for Church uses. It asserts that OTC funds were used for expenses associated with operation of the Apollo and in providing banking services for Flag. Witnesses testified that the Church used Trust monies to defend Scientology against attack and to propagate the religion. Finally, the Church argues that the three million dollars brought aboard the Apollo from the OTC and Trust accounts remained on the Apollo during the years in question. It cites the testimony of a Trust accountant who counted the cash aboard the Apollo and testified that none of it was missing.

We find these arguments unpersuasive. Unlike the typical Saturday or Sunday when parishioners donate their money to the church, here the Church transferred millions of dollars to bank accounts controlled by a private individual who had no official responsibility for managing church assets. Although witnesses testified that the money was used for Church purposes, the Church presented little documentation to show that the majority of Trust or OTC money was actually spent on bona-fide Church activities. Finally, the self-serving testimony of a Church employee that the three million dollars remained in the Apollo safe proves nothing. The fact that there were three million dollars in the safe on the day the Church accountant checked, is not inconsistent with the Tax Court's finding that L. Ron Hubbard had unfettered control over millions of dollars in money that originated with the Church. The Church failed to come forward with testimony from key individuals such as L. Ron Hubbard and Mary Sue Hubbard and failed to present the documentation necessary to trace the source and use of OTC and Trust monies. In sum, the Church failed to carry its burden of proof in a situation where "the potential for abuse created by the [founder's] control of the Church required open and candid disclosure of facts bearing on the exemption application."

The Tax Court found that Church income inured to the benefit of L. Ron Hubbard in a "grand scale" in the form of "debt repayments." During the 1950's, Hubbard was paid a portion of the gross income of Scientology congregations, franchises and organizations. This compensation scheme was called the "proportional pay plan." During the 1960's these tithes became known as "Founding Debt Payments" (sometimes also called "LRH RR" or "LRH 10").

Although the form changed, the payments continued through the years at issue in this case. Church records indicate that between October 9, 1972 and December 28, 1972, it made debt repayments totaling $19,324.41. A policy letter dated September 7, 1972 entitled "Repayment or Due Money Collected for LRH Personally" set out a program to reimburse Hubbard for past use of Hubbard's personal income and capital; research and development of the technology of Dianetics and Scientology; and the use of Hubbard's goodwill and high credit rating. The letter establishes the post of "LRH accounts officer" to monitor collection of debt repayments.

* * *

In sum, we hold that significant sums of Church money inured to the benefit of L. Ron Hubbard and his family during the tax years 1970, 1971 and 1972. Although neither the salaries nor the living expenses necessarily constituted evidence of inurement, the cumulative effect of Hubbard's use of the Church to promote royalty income, Hubbard's unfettered control over millions of dollars of church assets, and his receipt of untold thousands of dollars worth of "debt repayments" strongly demonstrate inurement. We find no clear error.

* * *

NOTES AND QUESTIONS

1. *Scientology Update.* For almost 30 years, the Church of Scientology and the Internal Revenue Service engaged in a bitter holy war. Even while

conceding that Scientology was a bona fide religion, the Service was successful in the courts in challenging tax exemptions except for a few procedural setbacks. Its earliest substantive victory was in Founding Church of Scientology v. United States, 188 Ct.Cl. 490, 412 F.2d 1197 (1969), where the court denied exemption to what was then the parent church of the Scientology movement. On another front, the Service consistently denied income tax deductions (as either a business or medical expense, or a charitable contribution) to taxpayers who paid for "auditing" and other services provided by the Church of Scientology. See, e.g., Rev. Rul. 78–189, 1978–1 C.B. 68 (no business deduction because auditing did not maintain or improve skills in an existing trade or business); Rev. Rul. 78–188, 1978–1 C.B. 40 (no charitable deduction because taxpayer received a return benefit); Rev. Rul. 78–190, 1978–1 C.B. 74 (no medical expense deduction). In a decision with potential ramifications for other religions, the Supreme Court upheld the disallowance of charitable deductions on the ground that the taxpayers were receiving a quid pro quo. Hernandez v. Commissioner, 490 U.S. 680, 109 S.Ct. 2136 (1989).

In a surprising reversal of policy, however, the Service announced in 1993 that it had "obsoleted" its previous rulings and agreed to permit charitable deductions for auditing fees paid to the Church of Scientology. See Rev. Rul. 93–73, 1993–2 C.B. 75. At the same time, the Service granted retroactive exemptions to 25 Scientology-related organizations. These developments are discussed in Chapter 8B3, infra, at pp. 856–858.

2. *Churches and Inurement.* Applying the inurement limitation to churches is difficult because they are exempt from the usual information reporting requirements generally applicable to exempt organizations and they enjoy special protection from audits. See I.R.C. 6033; 7611. The situation is ripe for abuse. Consider, for example, the Divine Light Mission, a cult once headed by the Guru Maharaj Ji, who was reported to reside in a lavish estate and drive among the parishioners in a fleet of expensive sports cars. In the heyday of the personal church as a vehicle of tax protest, the Service had some success in revoking exemptions on inurement grounds. See, e.g., Unitary Mission Church of Long Island v. Commissioner, 74 T.C. 507 (1980) (excessive wages, loans, reimbursement of founder's travel expenses); Bubbling Well Church of Universal Love, Inc. v. Commissioner, 74 T.C. 531, aff'd 670 F.2d 104 (9th Cir.1981) (living, medical and European travel expenses).

3. *State Law Safeguards.* In addition to the general body of law regulating the fiduciary duties of officers and directors, some state nonprofit corporation laws have specific safeguards against activities that might facilitate inurement of private gain for tax purposes. For example, § 5227 of the California Corporations Code provides that no more than 49 percent of the directors of a public benefit corporation may consist of certain "interested persons," defined as persons who are being compensated by the corporation for services rendered (e.g., employees, independent contractors or otherwise) other than reasonable compensation paid to directors in that capacity, and certain family members of such directors. A public benefit

corporation in California thus must have a majority (51 percent) of directors who only serve on the board or, if they serve in any other capacity (e.g., as an employee), are not compensated for those services. Maine adopted a similar provision in 2002. Me. Rev. Stat. Ann. tit. 13–8, § 713–A. Other state law rules patrol against self-dealing transactions between the corporation and one or more directors who have a material financial interest in the transaction. See Chapter 3C3b, supra, at p. 186.

4. *Executive and Board Compensation Excess?*. In 2004, the Senate Finance Committee proposed either to limit board member compensation to a prescribed de minimis amount and impose limits on executive and other insider compensation. Executive compensation trends and the related policy issues are discussed in the Note below.

NOTE: EXECUTIVE AND TRUSTEE COMPENSATION

Model Nonprofit Corp. Act (3d ed.) § 8.11.

N.Y. Not-for-Profit Corp. Law §§ 202(a)(12), 205, 715(e), (f).

Few issues incite more outrage among the public or Congress than excessive compensation for nonprofit executives or board members. Perceived excessive salaries and benefits have served as a lightning rod of public dissatisfaction with nonprofit organizations.[1] In 1992, when former United Way President William Aramony's $463,000 salary and extraordinarily generous fringe benefits were publicized, he became the poster boy in a national debate over the appropriate level of compensation for nonprofit executives. In the course of hearings held in 1993, the press, the public and Congress discovered that other nonprofit executives received handsome compensation by any standard. Today, Aramony's salary would not be considered excessive given United Way's size and the length of his service.

Some nonprofit salaries have reached seven figures, particularly in the larger health care systems, higher education, and occasionally in the arts. The Getty Trust, the world's wealthiest arts organization, became the subject of an IRS audit and investigation by the California attorney general's office because of its compensation practices. Barry Munitz, the chief executive, received $1.2 million in compensation during a time of austerity, layoffs and program discontinuances caused by a $1 billion loss in the endowment. In addition to his compensation, Mr. Munitz also allegedly received a $72,000 Porsche Cayenne. He used Getty employees for personal errands for himself and his wife, and the museum reimbursed him for at least 30 trips involving first class travel, including a trip to Australia with his wife that cost $29,000. From mid–1998 to 2002, the Getty paid more than $60,000 on airfare for Munitz's spouse, most of it first class. Reimbursement of spousal travel is avoided at most nonprofits.

---

1. See Consuelo Lauder Kertz, Executive Compensation Dilemmas in Tax–Exempt Organizations: Reasonableness, Comparability and Disclosure, 71 Tul. L. Rev. 819 (1997); David G. Samuels & Howard Pianko, Nonprofit Compensation, Benefits & Employment Law (1998).

For many years, The Chronicle of Philanthropy has published an annual survey of compensation and benefits paid to top executives at the nation's largest § 501(c)(3) organizations. The highly selective data[2] is derived from questionnaires sent to large charities and from annual information returns (Form 990s and, for private foundations, Form 990–PFs) filed with the IRS and available for public inspection. Form 990 requires organizations to report the compensation and benefits paid to their officers, directors, trustees, and key employees who receive over $150,000 of reportable compensation, the five highest compensated employees other than officers, directors, trustees or listed key employees receiving over $100,000 in compensation from the organization or related organizations. There are also rules for listing of former employees and governing board members. "Compensation" includes salaries, bonuses and severance payments. Benefits include medical and insurance benefits, deferred compensation, future retirement benefits, housing, and other fringe benefits such as club memberships. In some situations, the reported amounts may be misleading, such as where a large severance payment is made or extraordinary relocation and housing assistance is provided in connection with the recruitment of a new chief executive.

Of the 325 nonprofit groups included in the latest Chronicle of Philanthropy survey available as this text went to press (for 2009, based on data for 2008), the median salary for chief executives (not including benefits) was $361,538. At 57 organizations, the highest paid employee was not the chief executive. The top salaries often are paid to senior administrators and top revenue-generating physicians at large urban hospital centers, with several receiving salary and benefits in excess of $1 million, and to chief investment officers and in-house money managers at universities and foundations with large endowments. In 2009, 29 percent of the 195 chief executives who responded to the question took a pay cut. The highest paid CEO was David Mongan of Partners Healthcare System in Boston, which operates nonprofit hospitals in Boston, who received $3.4 million. Glen Lowry, director of the Museum of Modern Art received $2,111,882, though he will take a 15 percent decrease for fiscal 2009. The median pay of foundation CEOs surveyed was $458,461, with the Gates Foundation's Jeff Raikes leading the pack at $990,000.

Compensation for university presidents has risen dramatically since the early 1990s. In 2007–2008 the presidents of 23 private colleges received compensation over $1 million, and the median pay for 419 colleges reviewed by the Chronicle of Higher Education was $627,750 up 6.5 percent from the previous year. The highest paid president was Shirley Ann Jackson of Rensselaer Polytechnic Institute, who received $1.6 million; close behind were David J. Sargent, president of Suffolk University, and Steadman

---

2. We say "highly selective" because this survey is based on information provided by organizations that raised the most money from private sources and the wealthiest foundations. See Noelle Barton, How the Chronicle Compiled Its Survey of Nonprofit Executive Compensation, Chron. Philanthropy, Oct. 1. 2009 at philanthropy.com. As a result, the survey is not representative of the nonprofit sector as a whole.

Upham of the University of Tulsa, both receiving $1.5 million.[3] At several major universities, employees other than the president, such as football and basketball coaches or medical school professors, are the highest paid. University of Texas football coach Mack Brown reportedly earns $5 million per year, and Nick Saban of Alabama, $4.7 million. Kentucky basketball coach John Calipari earns $4 million per year and Duke's Mike Krzyzewski received $3.6 million, not including other financial benefits earned outside the university, such as through contracts with athletic apparel companies. David Silvers, Clinical Professor of Dermatology at Columbia, was paid $3.7 million.

Defenders of the trend toward higher compensation argue that nonprofit executives should not be forced to take a vow of poverty. They point to the challenge of recruiting and retaining talented people to lead complex organizations. Moreover, nonprofit compensation is modest in relation to the private sector but, as in the for-profit world, the gap between executive compensation packages and salaries of other employees is widening.

The budget of the organization is probably the most significant factor affecting executive compensation—the larger the budget, the greater the level of compensation. Other factors include: the number of employees; national as opposed to local focus; dependence upon government funding; the particular sector of the nonprofit community; geographical location; length of executive service; and external market forces. Thus, law professors on average earn more than their colleagues in the philosophy department, presumably because the non-academic market for lawyers affects the compensation of legal educators.

NOTES AND QUESTIONS

1. *Criteria for Executive Compensation.* What criteria should determine nonprofit executive compensation? Is the appropriate analogy the remuneration received by executives of similarly sized profit-seeking corporations? On average nonprofit compensation is roughly half of what top executives of major firms with sales of $100 million earn. A 1992 study by Ernst & Young found that in comparison to chief executives of middle-market companies with revenue of less than $50 million in the New York City region, the average non-profit top executive salary was 29 percent less than the private sector chief executive's salary of $156,500. Sharon McDonnell, Many Nonprofit Leaders Don't Profit, Crain's New York Business, May 9, 1994, at 29. Is the compensation of those in politics or government the appropriate comparison? The political process keeps salaries of governmental office holders and civil service officials artificially low. What factors are similar to or differ from the nonprofit sector?

2. *Evaluating Nonprofit Compensation.* Compared to the business world, the nonprofit sector lacks empirical measures of performance such

---

3. John Hechinger, U.S. News: More College Presidents Get Million–Plus, Wall St. J., Nov. 2, 2009, at A4.

as profitability, share price, dividends, or comparative financial performance with similarly situated organizations. Criteria for compensation in the nonprofit sector are more elusive than in the business world, because it may be difficult to measure an organization's attainment of mission. See Rosabeth Moss Kanter & David Summers, Doing Well While Doing Good: Dilemmas of Performance Measurement in Nonprofit Organizations and the Need for a Multiple–Constituency Approach in The Nonprofit Sector: A Research Handbook 154 (Walter W. Powell ed., 1987).

3. *Performance–Based Compensation.* Pay for performance in the form of stock options or bonuses is the norm in the corporate world. Are such incentives appropriate in the nonprofit sector? For example, law schools and other educational institutions "profit" from their admissions operations because application fees generally exceed the costs of processing. If an aggressive admissions director can increase the number of applications by a substantial figure, why shouldn't that individual receive a bonus or reward for performance? Some nonprofit employees' tasks—fundraising and financial management come to mind—can be measured with specificity and are frequently compensated under performance criteria.

In 2003, two employees of the Harvard Management Company, the University's in-house firm that manages its endowment, each received $35 million in compensation. The top six managers collectively earned $100 million. These salaries and bonuses were based on the outstanding performance of the funds managed by the individuals rewarded. This generated alumni criticism, and a promise to review annual compensation levels of fund managers. In the fiscal year ending 2004, the top compensation to the most highly paid managers was reduced by 27 percent. The top two earned a mere $25 million each. The two managers and the president of the Harvard Management Company later resigned to form their own firms. When the Harvard endowment cratered in part because of the risky investment strategies, the managers did not have to return any compensation.

4. *Salary Caps.* Should there be absolute limits on nonprofit pay? The philosopher Michael Walzer has tried to identify some realms of life where money ought not to rule. Should the nonprofit sector be one of those spheres? Is a salary cap workable? Would a cap limit excessive compensation or will it merely lead to the creation of subsidiaries and affiliated nonprofit corporations with overlapping executives to avoid the maximum? In the business world, the $1 million limit on the deductibility of executive compensation imposed by § 162 has been ineffective because of an enormous loophole exempting performance-based pay, such as stock options. In a thorough examination of compensation of business executives and professionals, Derek Bok, former and current interim president of Harvard, urges that the nation must rethink its deepest values, motivations and priorities to harness the movement for ever higher and excessive compensation. The Cost of Talent 294–297 (1993). This may be more difficult than many consider. One of the unexpected aftermaths of the United Way salary scandal was that many nonprofit boards *increased* their executives' sala-

ries. See Jennifer Moore, 2 Years Later, a Scandal's Legacy, Chron. Philanthropy, May 17, 1994, at 28.

5. *Federal Tax Standard.* Under federal tax law the reasonableness of compensation paid by a nonprofit is judged under the same standard applied to business corporations: "only such amount as would ordinarily be paid for like services by like enterprises under like circumstances." Treas. Reg. § 1.162–7(b)(3). This presumes an arm's length transaction. In other situations the Internal Revenue Service examines the facts and circumstances and compensation for comparable positions. The intermediate sanctions legislation suggests a procedure for establishing reasonable compensation but does not reach the question of what is appropriate compensation for a particular charity.

6. *Reform Proposals.* In its June 2005 Final Report, the Panel on the Nonprofit Sector addressed the contentious issue of nonprofit compensation. The panel "discouraged" compensation to board members but opposed a flat ban and urged charities that compensated board members to disclose the amount of and reasons for the compensation and the methods used to determine its reasonableness. It also recommended a statutory ban on loans from public charities to their board members (extending the rule already in effect for private foundations), increased penalties on board members of charities who receive or approve excessive compensation, and greater transparency on Form 990 information returns, such as more detailed disclosure of the time commitment of compensated board members. Panel on the Nonprofit Sector, Final Report at 7, 61–65.

The Panel also called for more transparency on executive compensation, recommending clearer disclosure of all the elements of executive pay packages, and increased penalties on individuals who receive and managers who approve excessive compensation. It urged Congress to require nonprofit executives and other compensated insiders to demonstrate the reasonableness of their pay if the IRS alleges that it is unreasonable (query whether this is a meaningful addition to existing law?). Final Report at 7, 66–72. In opposing arbitrary compensation caps, the Panel emphasized the need for flexibility in attracting and retaining qualified leaders and it rejected a compensation standard based only or primarily on comparable positions within the charitable sector. Id. at 69–70.

7. *For Further Reading.* Jill S. Manny, Nonprofit Payments to Insiders and Outsiders: Is the Sky the Limit?, 76 Fordham L.Rev. 735 (2007).

2. PRIVATE BENEFIT

Treasury Regulations: § 1.501(c)(3)–1(d)(iii).

The inurement limitation only extends to excess economic benefits received by insiders. The related private benefit prohibition denies exemption when persons other than insiders receive more than an incidental "private benefit." The IRS and the courts view inurement and private benefit as distinct requirements. Private benefit is the broader concept because it extends beyond insiders, but the inurement proscription is unforgiving (there is no de minimis exception) while "incidental" private benefit, viewed in a qualitative and quantitative sense, is not fatal.

The private benefit limitation is a product of the regulations, which require a § 501(c)(3) organization to serve "a public rather than a private interest" and "establish that it is not organized or operated for the benefit of private interests such as designated individuals, the creator or his family, shareholders of the organization, or persons controlled, directly or indirectly, by such private interests." Treas. Reg. § 1.501(c)(3)–1(d)(1)(ii). This is just another way of saying that an organization must be operated exclusively for exempt purposes, which we already knew. The origin of the doctrine is the common law rule that a charitable trust must be formed for an unselfish purpose—i.e., its property and income must benefit a sufficiently large and indefinite charitable class rather than specific private individuals. Restatement (Third) Trusts § 28 com. a (2003). The early private benefit cases and rulings were consistent with this more limited role. See, e.g., Ginsberg v. Commissioner, 46 T.C. 47 (1966) (organization formed to dredge a navigable waterway fronting the homes of its member-donors did not qualify for exemption because the waterway was rarely used by the general public and dredging greatly benefited the property owners); Rev. Rul. 70–186, 1970–1 C.B. 129 (organization formed to preserve and improve a lake used extensively as a public recreation facility qualified for exemption even though property owners derived an incidental private benefit).

This common law private benefit concept has been gradually expanded by the IRS, primarily as a weapon in its response to changes in the health care sector. As previewed earlier (see Section C3b of this chapter, supra, at pp. 327–337), the new health care environment brought with it complex corporate structures, incentive-based compensation plans for physicians and other key personnel, and joint ventures with for-profit firms. The new economics of nonprofit health care often was driven by a desire to maximize profit while minimizing or eliminating charity care other than the obligatory open emergency room. Some arrangements involved staff physicians who did not neatly fit in the "insider" category (because they were not in any position to influence the hospital's finances) despite the IRS's attempts to elevate them. In situations where revocation of exemption based on inurement was likely to fail, the fallback argument became private benefit. See, e.g., Gen. Couns. Mem. 39862, involving an arrangement where a hospital and a group of surgeons formed a limited partnership to purchase from the hospital the right to the net revenues from a surgery clinic. The agenda was to give the surgeons a sufficient financial stake in the clinic so they would be motivated to refer patients. After first finding that the arrangement constituted inurement because the surgeons were insiders, the IRS contended in the alternative that the hospital's exemption still should be revoked because of the presence of more-than-incidental private benefit to the surgeons.

In areas other than health care, the IRS also has revoked exemptions based on private benefit in situations far removed from the doctrine's common law roots. This expanded notion of private benefit received an influential judicial endorsement in American Campaign Academy v. Commissioner, 92 T.C. 1053 (1989), where the Tax Court held that a nonprofit school operated to train individuals for careers as political campaign professionals did not qualify for § 501(c)(3) exemption because it conferred more than an incidental benefit on the Republican Party. The academy under scrutiny was created and funded by the National Republican Congressional Committee. Applicants were not required to disclose their party affiliation, but the clear implication from the record was that virtually all students were Republicans and most graduates worked for Republican candidates. The Tax Court held that even though the school provided primary benefits to a charitable class (its students, Republicans in general, the political system, or all of the above) and did not violate the inurement proscription, it nonetheless conferred more than incidental "secondary" benefits to private interests (the Republican Party) and thus did not qualify for exemption.

As illustrated by the *United Cancer Counsel* case, the IRS sought a further extension of the private benefit doctrine to charities that form a close economic alliance with a commercial fundraiser.

United Cancer Council, Inc. v. Commissioner

[supra, p. 249]

NOTES AND QUESTIONS

1. *Settlement on Remand*. As noted in Chapter 4, the Tax Court was deprived of the opportunity to reconsider *United Cancer Council* when the IRS and UCC settled their longstanding exemption dispute in February, 2000. Although the Tax Court did not provide any guidance on the private benefit issue in *UCC*, its precedential value would have been minimal in any event because the IRS's focus has begun to shift away from the inurement and private benefit doctrines with the enactment of the § 4958 intermediate sanctions regime. For a discussion of the UCC settlement, see Carolyn D. Wright, UCC, IRS Settle Decade–Long Exemption Dispute: 501(c)(3) Status Revoked for Three Years, 28 Exempt Org. Tax Rev. 189 (2000). For the text of the settlement agreement, see 28 Exempt Org. Tax Rev. 250 (2000).

How should the Tax Court have resolved the private benefit issue on remand? Did UCC violate its duty of care, resulting in a dissipation of the charity's assets, or did it simply make a bad deal that, bad as it was, still allowed UCC to make some charitable grants rather than just dissolve? Is Judge Posner suggesting that the IRS can revoke a charity's § 501(c)(3) exemption when its managers or governing board make a bad financial decision that enriches a third party "outsider?" And who should regulate the excesses of professional fundraisers—the IRS or the states?

2. *Implications*. Judge Posner's decision may influence the development of standards under § 4958. Unlike the "insiders" who can cause an

organization to lose its § 501(c)(3) exemption, § 4958 penalizes a potentially broader group of individuals and firms who wield substantial influence over the organization. Judge Posner recognized that being an insider for inurement purposes does not require having a formal title or position—a view consistent with the § 4958 regulations. The more important issue may be whether the definition of "disqualified person" extends further to firms such as Watson & Hughey, who have the economic power to overwhelm a weak charity and exploit its appealing name.

3. *Joint Ventures.* The private benefit doctrine is one of the IRS's principal weapons in evaluating joint ventures between nonprofit organizations and for-profit firms. Joint ventures are discussed in Chapter 6H2, infra, at p. 667.

4. *For Further Reading.* John D. Colombo, Private Benefit, Joint Ventures, and the Death of Healthcare as an Exempt Purpose, 34 J. Health Law 505 (2001).

3. INTERMEDIATE SANCTIONS ON EXCESS BENEFIT TRANSACTIONS

Internal Revenue Code: §§ 4958; 6033(b)(11), (12).

Treasury Regulations: §§ 1.4958–1 through–8; 1.501(c)(3)–1(f).

Background. The extreme nature of the sanctions for inurement and private benefit—revocation of exemption—and the uncertain scope of those limitations caused enforcement difficulties for the IRS. During hearings held in 1993 by the Oversight Subcommittee of the House Ways and Means Committee, then IRS Commissioner Margaret Richardson addressed the problem, observing that revocation of an exemption for minor or isolated instances of inurement can be a sanction that is greatly disproportionate to the crime. In theory, for example, a university would violate the inurement limitation by paying its president or football coach excessive compensation, but revocation of the university's exemption would be a severe penalty that would adversely affect a large and innocent community of students, faculty, staff, and alumni. And even if the organization lost its exemption, the inurement limitation would not penalize the overcompensated president or coach.

At the 1993 Hearings, IRS officials provided titillating examples of abusive transactions, including the following summaries of actual cases:

> * * * (1) a health care organization, in a clinic-type setting, controlled by a CEO and small board, all of the members of which have substantial dealings with the CEO and the organization, paid the CEO more than $1 million, including a substantial distribution from an executive compensation plan and premium payments on several hundreds of thousands of dollars in life insurance. The organization made substantial credit card payments and cash disbursements for personal expenses. The organization sold its charitable assets and began purchasing physicians' private practices at prices in excess of fair market

value, and the physicians and their staffs became employees of the organization. * * * (3) An organization which provided educational services gave its CEO a residence, including maid service and a significant compensation package, including salary, deferred compensation, expense accounts, and loans (one of which is noninterest bearing). * * * (6) A television ministry paid personal expenses for the minister, including a home mortgage, household expenses, country club membership dues, additional homes, and a house for a member of the minister's family. * * * (8) A number of organizations, nearly all of which were viable organizations with ongoing charitable programs, had virtually all of their donations absorbed by a for-profit fundraiser with very little money being made available for the organizations' charitable programs. The true fundraising costs were not discernible from looking at the annual information return, Form 990, because a substantial portion of the costs were allocated to and reported as program services rather than fundraising costs.

Report on Reforms to Improve the Tax Rules Governing Public Charities, Subcomm. on Oversight of House Comm. on Ways and Means, 103d Cong., 2d Sess. 14–15 (1994).

In response to these concerns and revelations, a consensus emerged in favor of a new regulatory scheme that would impose excise tax sanctions short of exemption revocation where a § 501(c)(3) or § 501(c)(4) organization provided excessive economic benefits to "insiders." After several false starts, Congress enacted intermediate sanctions legislation in 1996 by adding § 4958 to the Internal Revenue Code. Section 4958 is modelled on the excise taxes for self-dealing and other transgressions by private foundations (see I.R.C. §§ 4941–4945, and Chapter 7D, infra, at pp. 765–804), and the penalties for excessive lobbying by public charities (see I.R.C. §§ 501(h), 4911, and Section E4 of this chapter, infra, at pp. 497–506). In 2002, the IRS issued final regulations that have become required reading for legal advisors to exempt organizations. The highlights of these intricate regulations and some of the more important details are summarized in the text that follows.

Overview of § 4958. Section 4958 applies to an "applicable exempt organization," a category limited to organizations described in § 501(c)(3) and § 501(c)(4) other than private foundations. I.R.C. § 4958(e)(1). To prevent organizations from converting to taxable status to avoid penalties, § 4958 also applies to organizations that are not tax-exempt at the time of the excess benefit transaction under scrutiny but were described in § 501(c)(3) or § 501(c)(4) during a five-year lookback period ending on the date of the transaction. I.R.C. § 4958(e)(2); Treas. Reg. § 53.4958–2(a)(1). Governmental units or affiliates that are not subject to income tax without regard to § 501(c), including state colleges and universities, are not subject to the § 4958 regime even if they may have voluntarily applied for and received a § 501(c)(3) exemption. Treas. Reg. § 53.4958–2(a)(2)(ii).

The § 4958 sanction—"intermediate" in that it almost always is in lieu of any revocation of exemption—is an excise tax penalty on any "excess benefit transaction" between the exempt organization and a "disqualified person." I.R.C. § 4958(a), (c). The initial penalty is 25 percent of the excess benefit. It is imposed on the disqualified person, not the organization. Lesser penalties also may be imposed on one or more of the organization's "managers" who knowingly permit the organization to engage in an excess benefit transaction. I.R.C. § 4958(a)(2). The disqualified person may be liable for an additional second-tier tax of 200 percent of the excess benefit if the violation is not "corrected" within a specified period of time. I.R.C. § 4958(b). "Correction" essentially means undoing the excess benefit to the extent possible—e.g., restoring the organization to a financial position no worse than it would have been in if the disqualified person had been dealing under the highest fiduciary standards. I.R.C. § 4958(f)(6); Treas. Reg. § 53.4958–1(c)(2).

Effect on Exempt Status. According to the legislative history, the § 4958 excise taxes were intended to be the sole sanction where an excess benefit did not rise to the level where it called into question the organization's status. H.R. Rep. No. 506, 104th Cong., 2d Sess. 59, n. 15 (1996) (hereinafter "House Report"). Revocation of an organization's exemption on the ground of inurement thus will occur only in situations where the organization is no longer "charitable." The IRS has issued regulations addressing the relationship of the § 4958 intermediate sanctions regime to the proscription on inurement. Treas. Reg. § 1.501(c)(3)–1(f). They provide that even if a particular transaction is subject to intermediate sanctions, the substantive requirements for § 501(c)(3) exemption still apply—meaning that the IRS reserves the right to go beyond § 4958 and revoke an organization's exemption. In making that determination, "all relevant facts and circumstances" will be considered, taking into account these five factors:

(1) the size and scope of the organization's regular and ongoing activities that further exempt purposes before and after the excess benefit transaction or transactions occurred;

(2) the size and scope of the excess benefit transaction (collectively, if more than one) in relation to the size and scope of the organization's regular and ongoing activities that further exempt purposes;

(3) whether the organization has been involved in multiple excess benefit transactions with one or more persons;

(4) whether the organization has implemented safeguards that are reasonably calculated to prevent future violations; and

(5) whether the excess benefit transaction has been corrected, or the organization has made good faith efforts to seek correction from the disqualified persons who received excess benefits.

Treas. Reg. § 1.501(c)(3)–1(f)(2)(ii). Although the IRS will consider all these factors in combination with each other, it may assign greater or lesser weight to some than others, and it will be more favorably disposed to organizations that identify and correct excess benefit transactions before the IRS discovers them. The regulations also make it clear that correction of an excess benefit transaction after it is discovered by the IRS is never a sufficient basis for continuing to recognize exemption. Treas. Reg. § 1.501(c)(3)–1(f)(2)(iii). Six examples are provided to illustrate the operation of these rules. Treas. Reg. § 1.501(c)(3)–1(f)(2)(iv).

Disqualified Persons. Deciphering § 4958 requires a mastery of a new statutory vocabulary. The "insiders" who are potentially subject to the 25 percent tax are called "disqualified persons" ("DQPs"). A DQP is "any person who was, at any time during the five-year period [preceding the excess benefit transaction] in a position to exercise substantial influence over the affairs of the organization." I.R.C. § 4958(f)(1)(A); Treas. Reg. § 53.4958–3(a)(1). The DQP category also includes certain members of the family of the person with substantial influence and controlled entities (e.g., a corporation or partnership where more than 35 percent of the voting power is held by DQPs). I.R.C. § 4958(f); Treas. Reg. § 53.4958–3(b).

DQPs include officers, directors, trustees and their close relatives, but the lack of a formal title does not immunize an individual from DQP status if that person is in a position to exercise substantial influence. Conversely, individuals holding honorary titles are not DQPs if in reality they have no powers or ultimate responsibility. I.R.C. § 4958(f); Treas. Reg. § 53.4958–3(c). The statutory "substantial influence" standard is potentially quite broad, and soon after § 4958 was enacted, questions arose as to exactly who was or was not a DQP. For example, can a newly hired person with no prior relationship to an organization be a DQP, or are first-timers protected by a "one-free-bite" principle? What about outsiders, such as a for-profit fundraiser or partner in a joint venture, who can influence an exempt organization's activities by virtue of a contractual relationship negotiated at arm's length? Cf. United Cancer Council v. Commissioner, supra, p. 249.

The regulations provide many answers. For example, they make it clear, overturning a prior IRS legal opinion, that staff physicians at a hospital are DQPs only if they are in a position to exercise substantial influence over the affairs of the organization. Treas. Reg. § 53.4958–3(g) Examples (10) & (11). Independent contractors, such as attorneys, accountants and investment advisors, generally are not DQPs if their sole relationship to an organization is rendering professional advice and they do not have decisionmaking authority with respect to transactions from which they derive no personal economic benefit other than customary fees. Treas. Reg. § 53.4958–3(e)(3)(ii); see also Treas. Reg. § 53.4958–3(g) Example 12.

The regulations also deem three categories of "persons" as not having enough substantial influence to be DQPs: (1) other applicable § 501(c)(3) exempt organizations with respect to organizations with which, for example, they may be affiliated, (2) as to § 501(c)(4) social welfare organizations, any other § 501(c)(4) organization (leaving open the possibility that a "(c)(4)" may be a DQP with respect to transactions with a related "(c)(3)"), and (3) employees who are not statutorily-defined DQPs (such as directors, officers, or substantial contributors to the organization or related family members) and who, for the taxable year in which the benefits are provided, are not "highly compensated"—i.e., they do not receive economic benefits of more than an indexed cap ($100,000 in 2006). Treas. Reg. § 53.4958–3(d). Apart from these specifically included and excluded categories, the determination of a person's DQP status is based on all the facts and circumstances bearing on the question of substantial influence. Treas. Reg. § 53.4958–3(a), (e). The regulations provide a list of factors tending to show that a person does or does not have such influence, along with numerous examples. See Treas. Reg. § 53.4958–3(e)(2)–(3), (g).

Initial Contract Exception. The regulations address the "first timer" question with an initial contract exception crafted in response to the Seventh Circuit's *United Cancer Council* decision. Although *United Cancer Council* was not a § 4958 case, it influenced the Service to conclude that a one-free bite rule was appropriate in certain situations.

The regulations generally provide that § 4958 does not apply to any fixed payment made to a person with respect to an initial contract, regardless of whether the payment would otherwise constitute an EBT. Treas. Reg. § 53.4958–4(a)(3)(i). For this purpose, an "initial contract" is a binding written contract between an exempt organization and a person who was not a DQP immediately prior to entering into the contract. Treas. Reg. § 53.4958–4(a)(3)(iii). A "fixed payment" is an amount of cash or other property specified in the contract or determined by a specified objective "fixed formula" (e.g., a nondiscretionary bonus based on future revenue generated by the organization's activities), which is to be paid or transferred in exchange for the provision of specified services or property. Treas. Reg. § 53.4958–4(a)(3)(ii)(A). If an initial contract provides for both fixed and non-fixed (e.g., discretionary) payments, the fixed payments will not be subject to § 4958 while the non-fixed payments may be scrutinized, taking into account the DQP's entire compensation package. Treas. Reg. § 53.4958–4(a)(3)(vi).

The theory of the initial contract exception is that a person who negotiates in good faith before he is in a position to exercise substantial influence should not be subject to sanctions even if the consideration received turns out to be excessive. But immunity is not considered to be appropriate with respect to payments where future discretion must be exercised (and thus may be subject to the DQP's substantial influence) in calculating the amount or deciding whether to make a payment. For 11 examples illustrating the application of the initial contract rule, see Treas. Reg. § 53.4958–4(a)(3)(vii).

Excess Benefit Transactions: In General. An "excess benefit transaction" is any transaction in which an economic benefit is provided by an exempt organization directly or indirectly (e.g., by a taxable subsidiary) to or for the use of any DQP if the value of the benefit exceeds the value of the consideration received by the organization for providing the benefit. I.R.C. § 4958(c)(1); Treas. Reg. § 53.4958–4(a)(1), (2). Obvious examples are payment of unreasonable compensation, bargain sales, or below-market loans that benefit a DQP. In adopting a market-driven standard for compensation, Congress rejected an earlier proposal to impose a fixed dollar cap (e.g., the salary paid to the President of the United States) on compensation paid by charitable and social welfare organizations. Indeed, the legislative history states unequivocally that an individual need not accept reduced compensation because he or she renders services to a tax-exempt as opposed to a taxable organization. House Report, supra, at 56.

The regulations incorporate existing tax-law standards under § 162 in determining reasonableness of compensation. Compensation is reasonable if it is comparable to what "would ordinarily be paid for like services by like enterprises under like circumstances." Treas. Reg. § 53.4958–4(b)(1)(ii)(A). The regulations elaborate at length, providing a list of items to be considered (e.g., all forms of cash and noncash compensation, whether or not taxable, including bonuses, deferred compensation and many fringe benefits). Treas. Reg. § 53.4958–4(b)(1)(B).

Disregarded Benefits. Several types of benefits are disregarded in evaluating compensation for § 4958 purposes, including: (1) most employee fringe benefits that are excluded from gross income under § 132 (such as an employer's payments of professional dues and other employee business expenses); (2) certain expense reimbursement arrangements; (3) benefits provided to a DQP solely as a member of or volunteer for the exempt organization if the same benefit is available to the public in exchange for a membership fee of no more than $75 per year (e.g., discounts at a museum gift shop); and (4) economic benefits provided to a DQP solely as a member of a charitable class that the organization intends to benefit in connection with the accomplishment of its exempt purposes. Treas. Reg. § 53.4958–4(a)(4)(i)–(iv). An organization's payment of premiums for liability insurance covering § 4958 excise taxes or indemnification for such taxes will not constitute an EBT if the premium or indemnification is treated as compensation to the DQP when paid and the DQP's total compensation is reasonable. Treas. Reg. § 53.4958–4(a)(4).

Establishing Intent to Treat Economic Benefit as Compensation. To monitor disguised compensation, an economic benefit is not treated as consideration for services for § 4958 purposes unless the exempt organization clearly indicates its intent to treat the benefit as compensation when it is paid. To establish its intent, an organization must provide "written substantiation that is contemporaneous with the transfer of the economic benefits at issue." Treas. Reg. § 53.4958–4(c)(1). Contemporaneous substantiation can be accomplished by including the value of the benefit as wages or nonemployee compensation on an original or amended information return, such as a W–2 or 1099, unless the benefit is nontaxable, such as employer-provided medical insurance or qualified pension plan contributions. I.R.C. § 4958(c)(1)(A); Treas. Reg. § 53.4958–4(c)(1). Under a safe harbor, an organization is not required to substantiate its intent to provide an economic benefit as compensation if the benefit is excluded from the DQP's income for income tax purposes. Treas. Reg. § 53.4958–4(c)(2). As a result, although contributions to qualified retirement plans and other nontaxable benefits must be taken into account in determining if compensation is reasonable (unless specifically disregarded—e.g., de minimis and certain other fringe benefits excluded from gross income under § 132), they are not subject to the contemporaneous written substantiation requirement. All of this is supposed to make it easier for exempt organizations, but the regulations are sufficiently detailed and technical that moderately sophisticated tax advice will be required to follow the regulatory roadmap.

All these rules on establishing intent are intended to prevent an organization from claiming, after an IRS challenge, that an excess benefit was actually compensation and that the DQP's overall compensation was reasonable. That argument is essentially foreclosed unless the benefit was part of an authorized compensation package and was treated as such for tax compliance purposes. For example, assume an organization pays its executive director a $200,000 base salary plus $40,000 in various fringe benefits, and the overall compensation package is reasonable. Assume that the organization also pays $20,000 of the executive director's personal living expenses and does not include this benefit as compensation, but if it had done so the director's overall compensation still would have been reasonable. The organization's failure to establish its intent to treat the $20,000 as compensation at the time it was paid causes the payment of the living expenses to be treated as an excess benefit transaction unless the organization can show reasonable cause for the oversight. See Treas. Reg. § 53.4958–4(c)(3)(i)(B), –4(c)(4) Example 2.

If the requisite intent to treat an economic benefit as compensation is not established, the regulations permit a DQP who discovers the failure to amend his or her federal income tax return to report a benefit as income at any time prior to when the Service commences an audit of the DQP or the exempt organization. Treas. Reg. § 53.4958–4(c)(3)(i)(B).

Revenue–Sharing Transactions. A more specialized type of excess benefit transaction may result from revenue-sharing arrangements that constitute inurement to the DQP. I.R.C. § 4958(c)(2). The scope of this rule is uncertain. It potentially affects performance-based compensation arrangements and more complex deals to share revenue from intellectual property or other income-producing activities.

The proposed § 4958 regulations looked to all the facts and circumstances, including the relationship between the size of the benefit provided and the quality and quantity of services provided, as well as the service provider's ability to control the revenue-generating activities on which the compensation was based. Prop. Treas. Reg. § 53.4958–5(a). For example, incentive compensation paid to an exempt organization's in-house money manager was not an EBT when it was based on performance of the portfolio because the employee's compensation increased only when the organization received a proportional benefit. Prop. Treas. Reg. § 53.4958–5(d) Example 1. But a percentage of net revenue arrangement where the DQP controlled the revenue-generating activity and has no incentive to maximize benefits and minimize costs to the exempt organization would trigger a penalty. Prop. Treas. Reg. § 53.4958–5(d) Example 2. All this helpful guidance was removed from the final regulations while the IRS gives the issue more thought. In the meantime, revenue-sharing arrangements will be evaluated by applying the general rules governing excess benefits, leaving a lingering fog of uncertainty.

Rebuttable Presumption of Reasonableness. The regulations provide that the parties to a transaction may rely on a rebuttable presumption of reasonableness with respect to a compensation arrangement with a DQP if certain procedures are followed. See Treas. Reg. § 53.4958–6. The emphasis is on process. A transaction is presumed not to be an excess benefit transaction if:

(1) its terms are approved in advance by a governing board (or board committee) composed entirely of individuals who have no conflict of interest with respect to the transaction;

(2) prior to making a determination, these disinterested individuals obtained and relied upon appropriate comparability data (e.g., compensation levels paid by similarly situated organizations, both taxable and tax-exempt, for functionally comparable positions; independent compensation surveys by nationally recognized firms; or actual written offers from similar institutions competing for the services of the DQP); and

(3) the board adequately documented the basis for its determination (e.g., the record includes an evaluation of the individual whose compensation was being established and the basis for determining that the individual's compensation was reasonable in light of that evaluation and data).

Treas. Reg. § 53.4958–6(a)(1)–(3). A similar presumption is provided for purposes of valuing property transfers between an exempt organization and a DQP when the transaction is approved by an independent board using appropriate comparability data and adequately documenting its determination. See Id.

From a planning standpoint, the rebuttable presumption of reasonableness is an important feature of the regulatory scheme. Organizations are well advised to follow the prescribed procedures to shift the burden of proof to the Service, which then must develop sufficient contrary evidence to rebut the probative value of the evidence put forth by the parties to the transaction. Treas. Reg. § 53.4958–6(b). For example, in an unreasonable compensation controversy where the presumption applied, the Service would need to establish that the compensation data relied upon by the parties was not for a functionally comparable position or the DQP did not substantially perform the responsibilities of the position.

The rebuttable presumption was the product of lobbying by large mainstream exempt organizations with the resources and legal expertise to follow the prescribed procedures. It has the potential of providing full employment for compensation consultants who offer their services, often at great expense, to provide adequate comparability data and help nonprofit boards document the salary packages offered to their key insiders. In response to concerns about the costs of compliance, the regulations offer flexibility on the type of comparability data on which the governing body may rely. A nonprofit board will have appropriate comparability data if, given the knowledge and expertise of its members, it has information sufficient to determine whether the compensation arrangement is reasonable or a property transfer is at fair market value. Treas. Reg. § 53.4958–6(c)(2)(i). This would permit the use of less customized or internally developed data, such as an industry compensation survey or even documented phone calls, as long as the comparables were relevant to the position under scrutiny. See, e.g., Treas. Reg. § 53.4958–6(c)(iv) Examples.

For organizations with average annual gross receipts (including contributions) of less than $1 million (on average over the three years preceding the taxable year), the regulations provide additional relief by permitting these smaller nonprofits to rely on data obtained from three comparable organizations. Treas. Reg. § 53.4958–6(c)(2)(ii), (iii).

Either through ignorance or lack of resources, many affected exempt organizations will fail to satisfy the conditions for the rebuttable presumption. In those cases, the failure will not create any inference that the penalties should be imposed, but the taxpayer will bear the burden of proof, at least at the administrative level. Treas. Reg. § 53.4958–6(e).

Penalties on Organization Managers. Although exempt organizations are not penalized (except for loss of exemption in the most egregious cases) for participating in excess benefit transactions, organization managers are subject to a tax equal to 10 percent of the excess benefit (with the tax capped at $20,000 if their participation was knowing, willful, and not due to reasonable cause. I.R.C. § 4958(a)(2), (d)(2). Organization managers include officers, directors, trustees, and individuals with similar powers or responsibilities regardless of title, but not independent contractors such as attorneys, accountants, and investment advisors, and not middle managers with the power to make recommendations but not to implement decisions without approval of a superior. I.R.C. § 4958(f)(2); Treas. Reg. § 53.4958–1(d)(2)(i). If two or more managers share responsibility for the violation, they are jointly and severally liable. I.R.C. § 4958(d)(1). The best protection for an organization manager seeking to avoid an intermediate sanction is to fully disclose all the facts to a professional advisor and rely on that professional's advice, expressed in a reasoned written legal opinion, that a transaction with a DQP is not an excess benefit transaction. For that purpose, advisors include not merely lawyers but also accountants, accounting firms with expertise in valuation matters, and independent valuation experts. Treas. Reg. § 53.4958–1(d)(4)(iii). See also Treas. Reg. § 53.4958–1(d)(3)–(6) for more details and other defenses to organization manager sanctions.

Application to Supporting Organizations and Donor–Advised Funds. The Pension Protection Act of 2006 expanded the application of the intermediate sanctions rules to certain situations involving supporting organizations and donor-advised funds. These rules are discussed in Chapter 7C4, infra, at pp. 759–760 (supporting organizations) and 7B4, infra, at pp. 734–735 (donor-advised funds).

Correction and Abatement. Once it is established that an excess benefit transaction has occurred, the DQP will be subject to an additional tax equal to 200 percent of the excess benefit unless the transaction is corrected promptly. I.R.C. § 4958(b). In general, the DQP must repay an amount of money equal to the excess benefit plus any additional amount needed to compensate the organization for loss of the use of the money or other property during a period beginning on the date of the excess benefit transaction and ending on the date of correction. Treas. Reg. § 53.4958–1(c)(2)(ii). The Service also is authorized under § 4962 to abate § 4958 penalties if it is established that the violation was due to reasonable cause and not willful neglect, and the transaction at issue was corrected within the specified correction period. Treas. Reg. § 53.4958–1(c)(2)(iii).

Disclosure Requirements. Section 501(c)(3) and § 501(c)(4) organizations must disclose on their annual informational tax returns (Form 990) the names of each DQP who received an excess benefit during the taxable year and such other information as the Service may require. I.R.C. § 6033(b)(11)–(12).

Judicial Interpretation of § 4958. The first reported intermediate sanctions case involved a Mississippi family and a group of health care organizations acquired by the family in a conversion transaction. At issue was the value of the nonprofit entities when they converted to for-profit status. The IRS argued that the nonprofits were significantly undervalued, resulting in excess benefits to the insiders who orchestrated the deal.

In Caracci v. Commissioner, 118 T.C. 379 (2002), the Tax Court held that the value of the transferred assets exceeded the value of the consideration received by the § 501(c)(3) organizations and upheld $11.6 million in intermediate sanctions penalties against various disqualified persons. The decision is a lengthy and fact-bloated valuation opinion—a typical battle of the experts—with extreme positions on both sides as "opening bids." The taxpayers' appraiser determined that the nonprofit organizations had a negative fair market value, while the Service contended that, despite operating losses, the organizations had substantial values to potential purchasers. The court sided with the Service on the intermediate sanctions issues, but it declined to revoke the exempt status of the organizations, finding that intermediate sanctions were sufficient in the circumstances. The court noted that it would be preferable to preserve the exemption and permit the organizations to benefit from the "correction" provisions made available through I.R.C. §§ 4961–4963. On appeal, however, the Fifth Circuit reversed and rendered judgment for the taxpayers. Caracci v. Commissioner, 456 F.3d 444 (5th Cir. 2006). The court's opinion included a scathing critique of the IRS's valuation analysis, finding a "cascade of errors" by the government's appraiser, who had no prior experience in the home healthcare industry and spent only two days in Mississippi, one of which was devoted to retrieving lost luggage. By contrast, the court noted that the taxpayer's expert was a director of a major accounting firm with extensive industry experience who spent eight weeks preparing his appraisal. The IRS's case also was weakened when it admitted that its initial deficiency notices were excessive. The Fifth Circuit held that the Tax Court erred in failing to recognize that this concession shifted the burden of proof to the IRS.

The *Caracci* case is a testimonial to the value of an authoritative appraisal when a disqualified person is confronted with an intermediate sanctions controversy involving a conversion from nonprofit to for-profit status.

Proposed Reforms. The intermediate sanctions rules are mostly about comparables and process rather than substance. Section 4958 has not curtailed the explosive growth of compensation paid to nonprofit executives or even "outsiders," such as surgeons, investment managers, and coaches, who do not fit nearly into the definition of "disqualified person." Continued reports of excessive executive compensation and other acts of self-dealing at public charities have caused some influential members of Congress to ask whether § 4958 is too permissive. A Discussion Draft prepared by the Senate Finance Committee staff in 2004 proposed to extend the stricter § 4941 private foundation self-dealing rules to public charities, leaving only compensation to be patrolled by § 4958. If enacted, this proposal would result in a complete ban on self-dealing transactions even if the terms were fair to the charity. In its 2005 report on revenue-raising options, the Joint Committee on Taxation proposed to dilute two popular safe harbors in the § 4958 regulations—the rebuttable presumption of reasonableness and the initial contract exception—and replace them with a new (and seemingly vaguer) due diligence requirement. Under this proposal, adherence to the procedures currently required to invoke the rebuttable presumption of reasonableness would establish minimum due diligence but not result in any shift of the burden of proof. Charities would be required to disclose whether they met the minimum due diligence standard with respect to potential excess benefit transactions and, if not, they would have additional burdens to explain how they came to approve a transaction under scrutiny. Joint Committee on Taxation, Options to Improve Tax Compliance and Reform Tax Expenditures (JCS–02–05), Jan. 27, 2005, at 254–269.

In its Final Report issued in 2005, the Panel on the Nonprofit Sector took a different approach. The Panel recommended that when the IRS determines a disqualified person to have received excessive compensation, the DQP must demonstrate his or her pay package is reasonable,. Under the proposal, penalties would be imposed on board members and other organization managers who approved self-dealing or excess benefit transactions not only if they knew the transaction was improper but also if they "should have known"—by failing to exercise reasonable care, such as not adhering to minimum due diligence practices. Panel on the Nonprofit Sector, Final Report 66–72 (2005).

PROBLEMS

1. In each of the alternative situations described below, determine whether the organization risks loss of exemption under § 501(c)(3) because

of inurement of private gain or substantial private benefit, and consider whether any of the parties would be subject to intermediate sanctions penalties under § 4958:

(a) Urban Medical Center pays its chief executive officer a base annual salary of $1,000,000, and provides rent-free housing worth $80,000, free use of a car, a club membership, a standard fringe benefit package (medical and disability insurance, pension plan), and up to $100,000 in low-interest loans for personal expenses. The Medical Center also pays the physician who heads its radiology department a fixed percentage of the department's gross income. In each case, the compensation package was approved by the Medical Center's board of directors, which consists of a broad group of prominent citizens in the community.

(b) Northern Exposure Hospital ("Hospital") is the only hospital within a 100–mile radius in a rural area of Montana. Hospital has a shortage of primary care physicians. Hospital wishes to entice Dr. Joel Fishbein, who recently completed an ob/gyn residency in Seattle, to establish his practice near Hospital and become a non-employee member of its staff. Hospital's board has agreed to offer the following recruitment incentives to Dr. Fishbein: a one-time bonus of $5,000, payment of his malpractice insurance premium for one year, free office space in a building owned by Hospital for three years, a low-interest home mortgage loan, and reimbursement of moving expenses.

(c) Private University ("University") hires Coach for an initial term as head coach of its highly successful men's collegiate basketball team. The parties agree to a three-year employment contract, with the following elements: $1,200,000 base salary paid by the University; an additional $250,000 paid by University's separately incorporated alumni association; a $100,000 bonus if the basketball team advances beyond the first round of the NCAA Tournament; and free use of a car, a country club membership, and a standard fringe benefit package (including medical and disability insurance and a qualified pension plan). University expects that Coach's presence will greatly increase fundraising and so it also agrees to pay him an amount equal to five percent of the gross amount raised for the basketball program. Finally, Coach receives an additional $500,000 pursuant to a contract with a for-profit company that provides shoes and other athletic apparel for use by student-athletes at University. What if the employment contract and other benefits were in connection with a five-year contract renewal? Would the analysis be any different if Coach were employed by a state university?

(d) Church TV is a nonprofit organization that produces a weekly religious television program on various cable television networks. It was formed by Minister to carry his messages to a mass audience. The board of directors of Church TV consists of Minister, his wife and his elderly mother. Minister's brother-in-law, a recent college graduate, serves as Church TV's chief financial officer. Church TV receives $40 million in annual contributions from the public. Its annual expenses average $43 million, including a $500,000 salary and $250,000 bonus to Minister, $250,000 to Minister's wife for secretarial services, a $100,000 director's fee paid to Minister's mother, and $400,000 paid to a fashion designer to design Minister's personal and professional clothing. Church TV's assets include a broadcast studio with a cost of $2 million and a $2 million parsonage for Minister and his family. Minister's son, a contractor, built the broadcast studio under an agreement providing for cost plus 200%.

(e) World Missionaries ("World") is a nonprofit religious corporation organized to provide financial assistance, through direct grants and interest-free loans, to missionaries of Church. The organization was founded by Frank Young, a former missionary, who plans to raise funds based on mail solicitations to church and community leaders, business people and others. Missionary work is an essential component of the church's doctrine. To attract fund raisers, World proposes to offer commissions of "up to 20 percent" of any money raised on the theory that "paying a commission gets the job done better than just hiring solicitors at a set salary." Mr. Young, one of three World trustees, has already raised $200,000 and is entitled to a $20,000 (10%) commission by agreement of the board of trustees.

(f) Same as (e), above, except in addition Telemarketers, Inc., an outside for-profit fundraising firm, raised $5 million but incurred $3.5 million in fundraising expenses. Pursuant to a negotiated agreement with World's board, Telemarketers was paid a $300,000 commission, representing 20 percent of the $1.5 million raised after expenses. As a result, World netted $1.2 million from the arrangement.

(g) The Political Campaign Academy is a nonprofit school and job placement service formed and funded to train professional staff to work in political campaigns. Its purpose is "to benefit the public by fostering the training of competent professional staff in the American political process." The Academy's board is controlled by members of the Democratic National Committee. Applicants are not required to state any political affiliation, and the Academy does not engage in any actual political campaign activity, but virtually all graduates end up working for Democratic candidates.

2. Jill Woods, a resident of New York, is a member of the board of trustees of Redwoods Forever, a large public charity based in California. Jill receives no salary, but Redwoods pays all travel costs (business class air fare, lodging and meals) to attend its quarterly board meetings. In keeping with its policy to foster better camaraderie, Redwoods encourages board members to bring their spouses to meetings and pays all the spouses' travel expenses. Spouses do not attend the formal meetings but they do partici-

pate in all meals and other social events. Redwoods also pays premiums for a directors and officers liability policy that covers Jill and her fellow board members. No Form 1099's or other tax information statements are provided to board members with respect to these travel reimbursements and insurance premiums. On the advice of her tax preparer, Jill does not include these items on her income tax return.

Is Jill liable for any intermediate sanctions penalties under § 4958?

3.   Private University ("PU") is negotiating the renewal of an employment contract with Franz Arbitrage, its chief investment officer. Arbitrage is the highest paid employee of PU, earning a base salary and also an incentive fee based on the performance of the university's endowment relative to a benchmark. PU wishes to invoke the rebuttable presumption of correctness if Arbitrage's compensation package is ever challenged by the IRS. The university has requested your law firm to render a written opinion that the employment agreement with Arbitrage is not and will never be an excess benefit transaction.

(a) Who is your client? Does it matter?

(b) Is it appropriate for your firm to render a legal opinion on the reasonableness of Arbitrage's compensation? If so, what should that opinion include (and not include)?

E.   Limitations on Lobbying and Political Campaign Activities

1.   Background

A nonprofit organization qualifies for tax-exempt status under § 501(c)(3) only if: (1) "no substantial part" of its activities consists of carrying on propaganda or otherwise attempting to influence legislation, and (2) it does not participate or intervene in "any political campaign on behalf of (or in opposition to) any candidate for public office." In lieu of the vague "no substantial part" lobbying limitation, most publicly supported charities may elect to be regulated by more objective expenditure tests that permit the organization to spend certain amounts on lobbying without penalty and then imposes gradual sanctions—first an excise tax on excessive lobbying expenditures and then loss of exemption for more serious transgressions. See generally I.R.C. §§ 501(h), 4911. The Service also may impose excise tax penalties on organizations that make certain impermissible political expenditures, and on officers and trustees of the organization who are aware of these violations. See I.R.C. § 4955. These longstanding restrictions are another aspect of the border patrol function of federal tax law. They limit but do not eliminate the ability of nonprofits to influence the political process.

As a practical matter, the lobbying restrictions are relevant only to § 501(c)(3) organizations classified as public charities. A more restrictive regime applies to private foundations, which are subject to punitive excise tax penalties if they engage in *any* lobbying, regardless of its relationship to the foundation's charitable program. See I.R.C. § 4945, discussed in Chapter 7D6, infra, at pp. 795–804. By contrast, most noncharitable exempt organizations are free to lobby with respect to legislation germane to their purposes without threatening their exemption, but lobbying activities may result in partial disallowance of business deductions for dues paid to some of these organizations (e.g., trade associations and labor unions) by their for-profit members. See I.R.C. § 162(e) and Chapter 9C3, infra, at pp. 926–927.

Lobbying by charitable organizations was first limited by a 1919 Treasury regulation providing that "associations formed to disseminate controversial or partisan propaganda are not educational within the meaning of the statute." Treas. Reg. 45, art. 517 (1919 ed.). The government advanced this position with varying success in a number of cases, the most notable of which was Slee v. Commissioner, 42 F.2d 184 (2d Cir.1930). In *Slee*, the Second Circuit held that the American Birth Control League failed to qualify for exemption because it had disseminated propaganda to legislators and the public supporting the repeal of laws against birth control. In holding that the League was not operated exclusively for charitable or educational purposes, Judge Learned Hand stated that "political agitation as such" was prohibited unless the lobbying was ancillary to an organization's "end-in-chief." The court apparently would have permitted a birth control society to lobby to remove legal obstacles from its hospital work or allowed a church to lobby against a proposal to repeal Sunday blue laws because these activities were ancillary to the accomplishment of each organization's exempt purposes. But lobbying to shape public policy was viewed as a substantial noncharitable purpose. In a much quoted portion of the opinion, Judge Hand articulated a neutrality justification for this restriction:

> Political agitation as such is outside the statute, however innocent the aim, though it adds nothing to dub it "propaganda," a polemical word used to decry the publicity of the other side. Controversies of that sort must be conducted without public subvention; the Treasury stands aside from them.

42 F.2d at 185.

In 1934, Congress added the "no substantial part" lobbying limitation as a condition on § 501(c)(3) exemption, but its rationale is clouded in obscurity. Some contend that it codifies *Slee*'s distinction between permissible ancillary lobbying and impermissible independent lobbying. Others construe it as relaxing the *Slee* test by permitting insubstantial lobbying for any purpose but prohibiting "substantial" lobbying, whatever the motive. Still others point to statements in the legislative history suggesting that Congress only intended to limit lobbying that served the selfish private interests of an organization's donors and not to affect "worthy institutions." See Statement of Senator David A. Reed, 78 Cong. Rec. 5861 (1934). In 1987 Congressional hearings, a Treasury official conceded that the legislative history was "inconclusive" and that the rationale for the no substantial part limitation had "never been clearly articulated." Lobbying and Political Activities of Tax–Exempt Organizations: Hearings Before the Subcomm. on Oversight of the House Comm. on Ways and Means, 100th Cong., 1st Sess. 87 (1987) (statement of J. Roger Mentz).

In 1987, Congress concluded that these limitations were ineffective in curbing the lobbying activities of some exempt organizations and, in other circumstances, they were unduly harsh by requiring the Service to revoke exemptions for isolated political campaign activity. The Congressional response was a set of additional excise taxes in §§ 4912 and 4955 that are summarized later in this chapter.

The history of the political campaign limitation is even more obscure. The absolute ban originated as a Senate floor amendment to the Internal Revenue Code of 1954 and passed without explanatory comment apart from a statement from its sponsor, then Senator Lyndon B. Johnson, that the rule was intended to "extend" the limitation of § 501(c)(3). 100 Cong. Rec. 9604 (1954). The conventional wisdom is that Senator Johnson was out to curb the activities of a Texas foundation which had provided indirect financial support to his opponent in a senatorial primary election campaign. See Bruce R. Hopkins, The Law of Tax–Exempt Organizations § 21.1(a) (8th ed. 2003).

This section focuses principally on the federal tax law restrictions on lobbying and political campaign activities of § 501(c)(3) organizations. It then discusses the opportunities for greater political involvement through the use of § 501(c)(4) social welfare organizations and § 527 political organizations, and provides an overview of the impact of nontax rules on the politically active nonprofit.

2. The Lobbying Limitation: No Substantial Part Test

Internal Revenue Code: §§ 501(c)(3); 504; 4912.

Treasury Regulations: § 1.501(c)(3)–1(c)(3).

An organization does not qualify for exemption under § 501(c)(3) unless "no substantial part of [its] activities * * * is carrying on propaganda, or otherwise attempting, to influence legislation." Two principal issues are thus presented: (1) what constitutes "influencing legislation" (lobbying) and (2) when does lobbying become a "substantial" part of the organization's activities?

Influencing Legislation. The Service has attempted, with limited success, to give meaning to the terms "influencing legislation" and "substantial." The regulations provide that an organization will not qualify under § 501(c)(3) if it is an "action organization"—a status attained either by:

> (1) engaging in substantial attempts to influence legislation by contacting legislators or urging the public to contact them to propose, support, or oppose legislation, or advocating the adoption or rejection of legislation; or

(2) having primary objectives which may be attained only by legislation or the defeat of proposed legislation (e.g., an organization formed specifically to promote a constitutional amendment permitting prayer in the schools) and campaigning for the attainment of that objective rather than engaging in nonpartisan analysis and research and making the results available to the public.

Treas. Reg. § 1.501(c)(3)–1(c)(3).

The regulations define "legislation" to include action by Congress, state legislatures, local governing bodies or by the public in a referendum, initiative, constitutional amendment or similar procedure. Treas. Reg. § 1.501(c)(3)–1(c)(3)(ii). "Legislation" does not include action by the executive branch or independent administrative agencies. In general, attempts to influence legislation include direct contacts with legislators and their staffs to propose, support or oppose legislation ("direct lobbying") and efforts to urge the general public to contact legislators or their staffs to propose, support or oppose legislation ("grassroots lobbying").

Although generalizations are perilous in this area, cases and revenue rulings over the years provide some additional line-drawing guidance. The early cases interpreting the lobbying limitation took the position that Congress only intended to proscribe the "evil" type of lobbying that served selfish interests and was characterized by factual distortions. Lobbying for the general good would be permissible under this analysis. The Code, however, simply speaks in terms of attempts to influence legislation, whether they be good, bad or indifferent. Most courts came to the view that an organization's motives for lobbying are irrelevant. The League of Women Voters, for example, was stripped of its 501(c)(3) exemption because of excessive lobbying even though it was an integral part of its educational mission. See League of Women Voters v. United States, 148 Ct.Cl. 561, 180 F.Supp. 379 (1960), cert. denied 364 U.S. 822, 81 S.Ct. 57 (1960). In addition, if an organization's primary objective is only attainable through legislation (e.g., repeal of the federal income tax) and the organization advocates for that legislation, it will be disqualified as an action organization even if it never mentions a specific bill. See Fund for the Study of Economic Growth and Tax Reform v. IRS, 161 F.3d 755 (D.C.Cir. 1998).

An organization is not lobbying when it merely communicates with its members on issues of common interest, at least if the membership group is confined to bona fide followers. But the line is crossed if the organization exhorts its members to contact legislators or their staffs or urges the general public to do so in support of or opposition to specific pending legislation. Section 501(c)(3) organizations also are not treated as lobbying if they engage in nonpartisan analysis, study or research on legislative matters and communicate their analysis to legislators, at least if the analysis is not intended to support a particular position. Rev. Rul. 70–79, 1970–1 C.B. 127. Finally, an organization may give expert testimony or technical assistance in response to a formal request from a legislative body without jeopardizing its exemption. See, e.g., Rev. Rul. 70–449, 1970–2 C.B.

111. But an unsolicited appearance before a congressional committee to endorse or oppose a particular bill is regarded as lobbying.

When is Lobbying "Substantial?" It is not enough to define "influencing legislation." Lobbying activities lead to revocation of an organization's exemption under the general limitation only if they are a "substantial" part of the organization's activities, relative to whatever else the organization does. Nobody (including the Service) knows for sure when lobbying becomes "substantial." A few early cases attempted to devise a quantitative test, and one court held that devoting less than five percent of an organization's time and effort to lobbying was insubstantial. Seasongood v. Commissioner, 227 F.2d 907 (6th Cir.1955). In later cases, the courts opted for a subjective balancing test, under which all the facts and circumstances are sifted "in the context of the objectives and circumstances of the organization." See, e.g., Haswell v. United States, 205 Ct.Cl. 421, 500 F.2d 1133 (1974), cert. denied, 419 U.S. 1107, 95 S.Ct. 779 (1975). Relevant factors include the percentage of an organization's budget (or employee time) spent on lobbying; the continuous or intermittent nature of the organization's legislative involvement; the nature of the organization and its aims; and, realistically, the controversial nature of the organization's position and its visibility.

This balancing approach is a version of what tax lawyers refer to as the "smell test." It provides virtually no guidance to an organization wishing to influence legislation as part of its program without endangering its exempt status.

The Christian Echoes Case. Prior to the 1960's, the lobbying limitations were only sporadically enforced. The Service became more aggressive in the early days of the Kennedy administration when an "ideological organizations" project was initiated for the purpose of scrutinizing the political activities of primarily right-wing exempt organizations. The *Christian Echoes* case, below, was an outgrowth of that project.

Christian Echoes National Ministry, Inc. v. United States

United States Court of Appeals, Tenth Circuit, 1972.
470 F.2d 849, cert. denied, 414 U.S. 864, 94 S.Ct. 41 (1973).

■ Barrett, Circuit Judge.

Christian Echoes sued for refund of Federal Insurance Contribution Act (FICA) taxes for 1961 and 1963 through 1968 amounting to $103,493.08 plus statutory interest. On June 24, 1971 the District Court held that the taxpayer qualified for tax exemption under 26 U.S.C.A. Section 501(c)(3). The Government appealed to the United States Supreme Court which vacated the judgment and remanded for entry of a new decree. United States v. Christian Echoes National Ministry, Inc., 404 U.S. 561, 92 S.Ct. 663, 30 L.Ed.2d 716 (1972). The District Court entered the same decision on February 24, 1972. The Government takes this appeal therefrom.

Christian Echoes is a nonprofit religious corporation organized in 1951 under the laws of Oklahoma by Dr. Billy James Hargis, its president, chief spokesman and an ordained minister. The Articles of Incorporation state in part that the corporation is founded "to establish and maintain weekly religious, radio and television broadcasts, to establish and maintain a national religious magazine and other religious publications, to establish and maintain religious educational institutions, * * * " Article III of the Articles of Faith in the corporate by-laws reads as follows:

"We believe in God, Supreme and Eternal, and in Jesus Christ as His Son, perfect Deity, and in the Holy Comforter and Challenger of this age, The Holy Ghost, and in the Bible as the inspired Word of God.

We believe that the solution of the World's problems, economic, political and spiritual, is found by the application of Christian Teachings in the lives of men and nations rather than in political ideologies of any kind.

We believe in the Twentieth Century Reformation to combat apostate conditions with the Church. We realize atheistic world forces seek the destruction and overthrow of all the religions of the World, including particularly that founded upon the teachings of Jesus Christ. The same forces seek also the destruction of all free governments, in which the lives and property of the people are protected by civil, moral and spiritual law.

We associate ourselves together to educate and proclaim the essential truths of Christianity, and the doctrine: Jesus Christ is the Hope of the World and America is God's Greatest Nation under the Living Son. We believe in the real spiritual unity in Christ of all redeemed by His precious blood.

We believe in constitutional government, whereby religious as well as other freedoms of mankind are preserved and protected. We believe in the fundamentals of New Testament Christianity, and we propose to promulgate the eternal truths thereof at all costs."

The activities of the organization have been addressed to that theology ever since the date of incorporation.

Christian Echoes maintains religious radio and television broadcasts, authors publications, and engages in evangelistic campaigns and meetings for the promotion of the social and spiritual welfare of the community, state and nation. Dr. Hargis has stated that its mission is a battle against Communism, socialism and political liberalism, all of which are considered arch enemies of the Christian faith. Dr. Hargis testified that Christian Echoes supports "Christian conservative statesmen * * * " without regard to party political labels. The organization publishes a monthly anti-Communist magazine, Christian Crusade, a weekly "intelligence report", Weekly Crusader, and a newspaper column, "For and Against". It also distributes pamphlets, leaflets and broadcast reprints on aspects of anti-Communist activity; it distributes tapes and records of selected broad casts; and it conducts an annual anti-Communist leadership school whose goal is to answer the question, "What can my community do to stem the forces of liberalism and thus stop the growth of socialism and communism?" In 1962 it established a Summer Anti–Communist University and formed youth groups, Torchbearer Chapters, to educate the public on the threat of Communism. In 1964 Christian Echoes encouraged adults to organize local Christian Crusade chapters. Christian Echoes appealed for contributions from the public to carry on its campaign. It earned money from the sale of its publications, tapes, films and admission fees at rallies. From 1961 through 1966 its gross receipts ranged from about $677,000 to $1,000,000 per year. It spent 52% of this income on radio, television, publications and postage.

On March 12, 1953 the Internal Revenue Service ruled that Christian Echoes qualified as a tax-exempt religious and educational organization under Section 501(c)(3) of the 1954 Code, formerly Section 101(6) of the 1939 Code. * * *

In 1962 and 1963 the National Office of the Internal Revenue Service requested that the activities and financial affairs of Christian Echoes be re-examined. The IRS agents recommended no change in its exempt status. The National Office, after reviewing and analyzing the activities of Christian Echoes, recommended that the exemption be revoked. On November 13, 1964 the District Director in Oklahoma City advised Christian Echoes in a letter of the revocation of its exemption and of its protest rights. Christian Echoes filed a formal protest on June 25, 1965 after conferences with the District Director and the National Office. The District Director notified Christian Echoes on September 22, 1966 that its exempt status was being revoked for three reasons: (1) it was not operated exclusively for charitable, educational or religious purposes; (2) it had engaged in substantial activity aimed at influencing legislation; and (3) it had directly and indirectly intervened in political campaigns on behalf of candidates for public office. Christian Echoes filed further protests without avail. It paid the taxes as assessed. Christian Echoes then filed this refund suit, claiming its right to exemption.

The District Court held that the taxpayer was entitled to tax-exempt status under Section 501(c)(3). The Court ruled that Christian Echoes qualified in that no substantial part of its activities had been devoted to attempts to influence legislation or intervene in political campaigns. The Court found that the only activity of Christian Echoes relating to an attempt to influence legislation was in support of the Becker Amendment urging support of restoration of prayers in the public schools. The Trial Court accepted Dr. Hargis's interpretation of the "attempts to influence legislation" prohibition in 501(c)(3), wherein Dr. Hargis testified on cross-examination that:

"* * * it's my interpretation that as long as I don't lobby in Washington, which I never have, as long as I don't get behind a bill or post a bill which I never have, as long as I don't endorse a political candidate, which I never have * * * that by no stretch of the imagination could you say what I am doing is political * * * "

It also held that all of its activities were motivated by sincere religious convictions; that the First Amendment prohibits the Government and courts from determining whether the activities are religious or political; and that the IRS had revoked Christian Echoes' exempt status without evidence to support its action and without constitutionally justifiable cause in violation of the First Amendment. It found that the taxpayer had been denied its right to due process under the Fifth Amendment because the Government had arbitrarily selected it from organizations engaged in similar activities and had violated its published administrative procedures in the steps leading to the revocation.

The Government appealed directly to the United States Supreme Court which dismissed the appeal for lack of jurisdiction, vacated the District Court's judgment and remanded for entry of a new decree. The IRS appeals from the District Court's holding in favor of Christian Echoes following remand. The Government contends that: (1) the taxpayer failed to qualify as tax-exempt under Section 501(c)(3); (2) its interpretation and application of Section 501(c)(3) did not violate the taxpayer's rights under the First Amendment; (3) its revocation of tax-exempt status to the taxpayer under Section 501(c)(3) did not violate the taxpayer's rights of due process under the Fifth Amendment; and (4) the Commissioner did not abuse his discretion in revoking the exemption with retroactive effect.

I.

The Government contends that Christian Echoes failed to qualify as tax-exempt under Section 501(c)(3) because: (1) a substantial part of its activities consisted of carrying on propaganda, or otherwise attempting to influence legislation; and (2) it participated or intervened in political campaigns on behalf of candidates for public office. The issue raises the interpretation and application of Section 501(c)(3).

Almost since the earliest days of the federal income tax, Congress has exempted certain corporations from taxation. The exemption to corporations organized and operated exclusively for charitable, religious, educational or other purposes carried on for charity is granted because of the benefit the public obtains from their activities and is based on the theory that:

> " * * * the Government is compensated for the loss of revenue by its relief from financial burden which would otherwise have to be met by appropriations from public funds, and by the benefits resulting from the promotion of the general welfare." H.R.Rep.No.1860, 75th Cong., 3d Sess. 19 (1939).

Tax exemptions are matters of legislative grace and taxpayers have the burden of establishing their entitlement to exemptions. The limitations in Section 501(c)(3) stem from the Congressional policy that the United States Treasury should be neutral in political affairs and that substantial activities directed to attempts to influence legislation or affect a political campaign should not be subsidized.

The limitation in Section 501(c)(3) originated in the Revenue Act of 1934, allowing tax exempt status to organizations, if "no substantial part of the activities of which is carrying on propaganda, or otherwise attempting, to influence legislation." The case which led to the 1934 legislation was Slee v. Commissioner of Internal Revenue, 42 F.2d 184 (2d Cir.1930). There the Court held that the American Birth Control League was not entitled to a charitable exemption because it disseminated propaganda to legislators and the public aimed at the repeal of laws preventing birth control. The IRS denied tax exempt status because the Birth Control League's purposes were not exclusively charitable, educational or scientific. In 1954 Congress attached a further condition to exempt status by adding the bar against participation or intervention in political campaigns on behalf of candidates for public office.

A religious organization that engages in substantial activity aimed at influencing legislation is disqualified from tax exemption, whatever the motivation. The Government has at all times recognized Christian Echoes as a religious organization. Indeed, the Government acknowledges that in all of its activities, Christian Echoes has been religiously motivated.

The critical issue is whether the limitation on attempts to influence legislation should be given the narrow interpretation applied by the District Court or a broader construction. The District Court held that the only attempt to influence legislation by Christian Echoes was in its support of the Becker Amendment relating to restoration of prayers in the public schools. By this construction, there must be specific legislation before Congress in order for the "attempt to influence legislation" prohibition to come into play. We disagree. We hold that the Trial Court was clearly erroneous in this interpretation of law.

Treasury Regulation 1.501(c)(3)–1(c)(3)(ii) states that an organization will be regarded as attempting to influence legislation if the organization:

> (a) Contacts, or urges the public to contact, members of a legislative body for the purpose of proposing, supporting, or opposing legislation; or

> (b) Advocates the adoption or rejection of legislation. Legislation is defined in the regulations as: " * * * action by the Congress, by any State legislature, by any local council or similar governing body, or by the public in a referendum, initiative, constitutional amendment, or similar procedure." Treas.Reg. 1.501(c)(3)–1(c)(3)(ii)(b).

The Regulation goes well beyond the District Court's interpretation of Section 501(c)(3). It includes direct and indirect appeals to legislators and the public in general. We hold that the Regulation properly interprets the intent of Congress. A capsule review of the "substantial" activities of Christian Echoes will adequately demonstrate, we believe, that Congress intended that the limitations be given a broad or liberal interpretation.

Christian Echoes' publications, such as the Christian Crusade, contained numerous articles attempting to influence legislation by appeals to the public to react to certain issues. These articles were either authored by Dr. Hargis, members of his organization, solicited contributors, or unsolicited authors—but all such articles had the stamp of approval of Dr. Hargis before acceptance for publication. The fact that specific legislation was not mentioned does not mean that these attempts to influence public opinion were not attempts to influence legislation. For example, Christian Echoes appealed to its readers to: (1) write their Congressmen in order to influence the political decisions in Washington; (2) work in politics at the precinct level; (3) support the Becker Amendment by writing their Congressmen; (4) maintain the McCarran–Walter Immigration law; (5) contact their Congressmen in opposition to the increasing interference with freedom of speech in the United States; (6) purge the American press of its responsibility for grossly misleading its readers on vital issues; (7) inform their Congressmen that the House Committee on UnAmerican Activities must be retained; (8) oppose an Air Force Contract to disarm the United States; (9) dispel the mutual mistrust between North and South America; (10) demand a congressional investigation of the biased reporting of major television networks; (11) support the Dirksen Amendment; (12) demand that Congress limit foreign aid spending; (13) discourage support for the World Court; (14) support the Connally Reservation; (15) cut off diplomatic relations with communist countries; (16) reduce the federal payroll by discharging needless jobholders, stop waste of public funds and balance the budget; (17) stop federal aid to education, socialized medicine and public housing; (18) abolish the federal income tax; (19) end American diplomatic recognition of Russia; (20) withdraw from the United Nations; (21) outlaw the Communist Party in the United States; and (22) to restore our immigration laws.

The taxpayer also attempted to mold public opinion in civil rights legislation, medicare, the Postage Revision Act of 1967, the Honest Election Law of 1967, the Nuclear Test Ban Treaty, the Panama Canal Treaty, firearms control legislation, and the Outer Space Treaty. These appeals urging the readers to action all appeared in Christian Echoes' publications between 1961 and 1968. They were all attempts to influence legislation through an indirect campaign to mold public opinion. This was directly evidenced by Dr. Hargis' keynote address delivered at the Anti–Communist Leadership School on February 11, 1963, entitled "Counter Strategy for Counter Attack." After setting forth a 10–point program, he stated that "Your opinion isn't worth a nickel without your action to back it up."

The political activities of an organization must be balanced in the context of the objectives and circumstances of the organization to determine whether a substantial part of its activities was to influence or attempt to influence legislation. A percentage test to determine whether the activities were substantial obscures the complexity of balancing the organization's activities in relation to its objectives and circumstances. An essential part of the program of Christian Echoes was to promote desirable governmental policies consistent with its objectives through legislation. The activities of Christian Echoes in influencing or attempting to influence legislation were not incidental, but were substantial and continuous. The hundreds of exhibits demonstrate this. These are the activities which Congress intended should not be carried on by exempt organizations.

In addition to influencing legislation, Christian Echoes intervened in political campaigns. Generally it did not formally endorse specific candidates for office but used its publications and broadcasts to attack candidates and incumbents who were considered too liberal. It attacked President Kennedy in 1961 and urged its followers to elect conservatives like Senator Strom Thurmond and Congressmen Bruce Alger and Page Belcher. It urged followers to defeat Senator Fulbright and attacked President Johnson and Senator Hubert Humphrey. The annual convention endorsed Senator Barry Goldwater. These attempts to elect or defeat certain political leaders reflected Christian Echoes' objective to change the composition of the federal government.

II.

The Government contends that its application of Section 501(c)(3) does not violate the free exercise clause in the First Amendment. Christian Echoes argues strenuously that denial of its tax-exempt status is a direct infringement upon its First Amendment right of free exercise of religion, and discrimination against the religion of its followers. The District Court agreed. The District Court held that the First Amendment forbids the Government and courts from deciding whether such activities are religious or political, and if political, whether substantial. The District Court held that the Government revoked the taxpayer's exempt status without a constitutionally justifiable cause, denying the taxpayer the free exercise of religion. We disagree. We hold that the Court erred.

If we were to adopt the District Court's findings and the arguments advanced by Christian Echoes, we would be compelled to hold that Congress is constitutionally restrained from withholding the privilege of tax exemption whenever it enacts legislation relating to a nonprofit religious organization. * * * [The District Court held that courts were constitutionally prohibited from determining if a religious organization's activities were "religions" or "political," and, if political, whether substantial for the purpose of denying tax exempt status because such an inquiry would require the court to intepret the meaning of church doctrine. Eds.] We know of no legal authority supporting the [district court's] conclusion * * * . Such conclusion is tantamount to the proposition that the First Amendment right of free exercise of religion, ipso facto, assures no restraints, no limitations and, in effect, protects those exercising the right to do so unfettered. We hold that the limitations imposed by Congress in Section 501(c)(3) are constitutionally valid. The free exercise clause of the First Amendment is restrained only to the extent of denying tax exempt status and then only in keeping with an overwhelming and compelling Governmental interest: That of guarantying that the wall separating church and state remain high and firm. * * *

In light of the fact that tax exemption is a privilege, a matter of grace rather than right, we hold that the limitations contained in Section 501(c)(3) withholding exemption from nonprofit corporations do not deprive Christian Echoes of its constitutionally guaranteed right of free speech. The taxpayer may engage in all such activities without restraint, subject, however, to withholding of the exemption or, in the alternative, the taxpayer may refrain from such activities and obtain the privilege of exemption. * * * The Congressional purposes evidenced by the 1934 and 1954 amendments are clearly constitutionally justified in keeping with the separation and neutrality principles particularly applicable in this case and, more succinctly, the principle that government shall not subsidize, directly or indirectly, those organizations whose substantial activities are directed toward the accomplishment of legislative goals or the election or defeat of particular candidates. From a review of the entire record we hold that the trial court's findings of fact and conclusions of law in this area are clearly erroneous.

III.

The Government also contends that its application of Section 501(c)(3) did not arbitrarily discriminate against Christian Echoes in violation of the Fifth Amendment due process clause as found by the District Court. The Court found that the Government had arbitrarily selected Christian Echoes in violation of the due process clause. The Fifth Amendment provides that no person shall be deprived of life, liberty or property without due process of law. An organization is being discriminated against in violation of the due process clause only when there is no reasonable relationship to a proper governmental objective. In order to establish discrimination violating the due process clause, the taxpayer must show discrimination based on differences of religion, race, politics or an unacceptable classification. No discrimination is apparent in the record. The fact that the Commissioner has not proceeded against other organizations similar to Christian Echoes does not amount to a denial of due process.

The District Court also erred in its holding that the IRS's departure from its administrative procedures constituted a denial of due process. The taxpayer has not shown any prejudice by deviations from normal procedures.

* * *

Reversed.

NOTES AND QUESTIONS

1. *Policy Issues.* What is the rationale for the lobbying limitation? Consider the following asserted justifications:

   a. Excessive lobbying and other political activity is inconsistent with the concept of "charity."

b. The Treasury should be neutral in political matters and avoid subsidizing, through tax exemption and the charitable deduction, the lobbying activities of charities.

c. Charities exist to serve the public at large rather than the self-interests of their founders, members, managers or donors. They should limit their political involvement to purely nonpartisan analysis rather than taking sides in particular controversies.

d. It is "undemocratic" and "countermajoritarian" to permit charities to use public funds to influence the outcome of governmental decisions because it intensifies the disproportionate influence of their wealthy donors in the political process.

e. Excessive involvement in political controversies is divisive and polarizing, leading to a decline in the independence and strength of the charitable sector.

Are your responses to these questions influenced by the rationale for charitable tax exemptions? Does it make any difference, for example, if one justifies tax exemptions by Bittker and Rahdert's income measurement theory as opposed to one of the subsidy theories? See Section B of this chapter, supra, at pp. 297–314.

Or should there be no restraints on lobbying? Why shouldn't § 501(c)(3) organizations be permitted, as part of their charitable and educational mission, to advocate policy changes through legislation as a principal means of representing their charitable beneficiaries? Doesn't the political activity of nonprofits provide a coherent voice for otherwise underrepresented groups, enhancing the quality of public debate and leveling the playing field? Or should the restrictions be revised to permit lobbying only by those § 501(c)(3) organizations that are "charitable" in the narrower sense of representing the "public interests" of underprivileged or underrepresented groups? If so, what standards would be used to identify the "public interest" charities that would be permitted to lobby without limitation?

2. *What's Lobbying?* Did the court in *Christian Echoes* go too far in equating the phrase "attempting to influence legislation" with any expression of opinion on a public issue, including those where no specific legislation was pending? Many § 501(c)(3) organizations express views on current issues, on which legislation may or may not be pending. When is this prohibited? In fact, the regulations expressly permit an organization to advocate social change or take positions on broad public issues. Treas. Reg. § 1.501(c)(3)–1(d)(2). The lobbying limitation does not extend to attempts to influence administrative agencies? Should it?

3. *Use of the Internet for Lobbying.* Because it is a convenient and relatively inexpensive communications medium, the Internet is an effective vehicle for political advocacy, raising issues that were not contemplated when the "no substantial part" test was added to the Code. For example, assume that a § 501(c)(3) educational organization that has not made the § 501(h) election devotes over half of its web site but a relatively insignifi-

cant portion of its budget to grassroots lobbying. How should this lobbying activity evaluated in applying the "no substantial part" test? Is the location of the lobbying communication (e.g., home page or several clicks away) or number of hits relevant in making the "substantial part" determination?

4. *When is Lobbying Substantial?* How did the Tenth Circuit define "substantial?" How does an organization plan its activities to avoid violating the general lobbying limitation?

5. *Influencing Judicial Nominations.* In Notice 88–76, 1988–1 C.B. 392, the Service ruled that attempts to influence the Senate confirmation of an individual nominated by the President to serve as a federal judge constituted "carrying on propaganda or otherwise attempting to influence legislation" within the meaning of § 501(c)(3). It reasoned that "legislation" included action with respect to acts, bills, resolutions and similar items, and the Senate's action of advice and consent on judicial nominations was with respect to a "resolution or similar item." At the same time, however, the Service concluded that attempts to influence judicial confirmation proceedings did not constitute participation or intervention in a political campaign because Federal judicial nominees are not candidates for elective office. For the possibility that expenditures to influence judicial confirmations may trigger a tax under § 527, see Section E7 of this chapter, infra, at p. 537.

6. *Excise Tax on Excess Lobbying Expenditures.* In 1987, Congress concluded that revocation of exemption for excessive lobbying was an ineffective deterrent in some cases. Consider, for example, a charitable organization that uses funds raised from tax-deductible contributions for a substantial lobbying effort and then ceases operations. If the organization has little or no taxable income, it may be indifferent to revocation once its political objectives are met, and its donors' earlier charitable deductions likely would be unaffected.

To combat this problem, § 4912(a) imposes an excise tax on the organization in an amount equal to five percent of all "lobbying expenditures" for the year in which an organization loses its exemption because of substantial lobbying. The definition of "lobbying expenditures" tracks the limitation in § 501(c)(3); it includes all amounts "paid or incurred * * * in carrying on propaganda, or otherwise attempting to influence legislation." I.R.C. § 4912(d)(1). The penalty applies to all § 501(c)(3) organizations other than private foundations, churches and organizations that elect to be governed by the § 501(h) expenditure test.

An additional five percent excise tax is imposed on managers of an organization who agree to make the lobbying expenditures knowing that they were likely to cause revocation of the organization's exemption. "Managers" generally include an organization's officers, directors, trustees or employees with authority or responsibility over lobbying expenditures. A manager is not liable for the penalty, however, if his or her action was not "willful" and was due to "reasonable cause"—for example, where the manager relied on a "reasoned" opinion of counsel that the expenditures were proper. I.R.C. § 4912(b).

7. *No Conversion to § 501(c)(4) Status.* A § 501(c)(3) organization that loses its exemption because of excessive lobbying is not permitted to shift to exempt status as a social welfare organization under § 501(c)(4) even though social welfare organizations generally are permitted to lobby without limitation. I.R.C. § 504. The purpose of this lifetime ban is to prevent an organization from raising tax-deductible funds, then engaging in substantial lobbying which leads to loss of its § 501(c)(3) exemption, and then shifting to § 501(c)(4) status where it may continue to lobby, using the accumulated funds raised during its earlier charitable days. A charity that loses its exemption for excessive political activity is permitted to reapply for § 501(c)(3) status if it ceases to engage in the impermissible activities.

8. *For Further Reading.* Brian Galle, The LDS Church, Proposition 8, and the Federal Law of Charities, 103 Nw.U.L.Rev. 370 (2009); Miriam Galston, Lobbying and the Public Interest: Rethinking the Internal Revenue Code's Treatment of Legislative Activities, 71 Tex.L.Rev. 1269 (1993); Laura Brown Chisolm, Exempt Organizations Advocacy: Matching the Rules to the Rationales, 63 Ind.L.Rev. 201 (1987); Elias Clark, The Limitation on Political Activities: A Discordant Note in the Law of Charities, 46 Va.L.Rev. 439 (1960). The history of the ideological organizations project that resulted in the revocation of Christian Echoes' exempt status is chronicled in John A. Andrew III, The Other Side of the Sixties 157–164 (1997).

3. Constitutional Issues

Church groups and other free speech advocates were distressed by the Tenth Circuit's opinion in *Christian Echoes*, particularly its constitutional holding. Joining in an odd alliance with Reverend Billy James Hargis, many mainstream Protestant and Jewish organizations urged the Supreme Court to grant certiorari. Their constitutional objections can be summarized as follows:

1. As applied generally, the lobbying limitations violate the First Amendment rights of free speech and freedom to petition. More particularly, they are unconstitutional insofar as the government conditions a benefit upon the agreement of a charity and its contributors to surrender a First Amendment right without justifying such action by a compelling national policy.

2. As applied to religious organizations, the limitations violate the Establishment and Free Exercise clauses of the First Amendment in that they: (a) reflect a lack of governmental neutrality toward religion by discriminating in favor of religions that refrain from becoming involved in issues of public concern; (b) necessitate excessive surveillance by the government in the affairs of religious groups; and (c) impinge upon the free exercise rights of politically active religions by making the sacrifice of these rights a condition for tax benefits.

3. The limitations are void for vagueness and overbreadth. The principal defect is the uncertain meaning of "substantial" but similar ambiguities stem from the phrase "carrying on propaganda," "attempting to influence legislation," and "participate in . . . any political campaign." The net effect is that charitable and religious organizations are left without any guidance as to permissible conduct, chilling the exercise of their First Amendment rights.

4. The limitations violate the equal protection notions inherent in the due process clause of the Fifth Amendment insofar as they discriminate between those charities (including churches) that engage in substantial legislative activities and those that are politically inactive. The no substantial part test also discriminates on the basis of size and wealth by allowing larger organizations to devote considerable time and money to legislative involvement while jeopardizing the exemption of a smaller group that may engage in far fewer political activities in an absolute sense.

An unmoved Supreme Court denied certiorari in *Christian Echoes,* but constitutional challenges continued on more general grounds. In 1981, a panel for the D.C. Circuit held, over a strong dissent by Judge Abner Mikva, that the lobbying restrictions did not violate the First Amendment. Taxation with Representation v. Blumenthal, 81–1 USTC ¶ 9329 (D.C.Cir. 1981). On rehearing en banc, however, the Mikva position prevailed in a sweeping though short-lived 7–3 decision. Taxation With Representation v. Regan, 676 F.2d 715 (D.C.Cir.1982). The D.C. Circuit majority found that the lobbying limitations did not abridge the First Amendment rights of charitable organizations because the government was not obligated to subsidize speech. But the court held that the disparate treatment of § 501(c)(3) charities and § 501(c)(19) veterans organizations resulted in an unconstitutional classification that was not supported by any governmental interest. Veterans organizations may lobby without limitation and are eligible to receive tax-deductible contributions under § 170. Unsure of the proper remedy, the court remanded the case with instructions "to cure the constitutionally invalid operation of Section 501(c) after inviting veterans organizations to participate in framing the relief."

The Supreme Court noted probable jurisdiction in *Taxation With Representation.* Its unanimous decision upholding the constitutionality of the lobbying limitations silenced the debate.

Regan v. Taxation With Representation of Washington

Supreme Court of the United States, 1983.
461 U.S. 540, 103 S.Ct. 1997.

■ JUSTICE REHNQUIST delivered the opinion of the Court.

Appellee Taxation With Representation of Washington (TWR) is a nonprofit corporation organized to promote what it conceives to be the "public interest" in the area of federal taxation. It proposes to advocate its point of view before Congress, the Executive Branch, and the Judiciary. This case began when TWR applied for tax exempt status under § 501(c)(3) of the Internal Revenue Code, 26 U.S.C.A. § 501(c)(3). The Internal Revenue Service denied the application because it appeared that a substantial part of TWR's activities would consist of attempting to influence legislation, which is not permitted by § 501(c)(3).

TWR then brought this suit in District Court against the appellants, the Commissioner of Internal Revenue, the Secretary of the Treasury, and the United States, seeking a declaratory judgment that it qualifies for the exemption granted by § 501(c)(3). It claimed the prohibition against substantial lobbying is unconstitutional under the First Amendment and the equal protection component of the Fifth Amendment's Due Process Clause. The District Court granted summary judgment for appellants. On appeal, the en banc Court of Appeals for the District of Columbia Circuit reversed, holding that § 501(c)(3) does not violate the First Amendment but does violate the Fifth Amendment.

TWR was formed to take over the operations of two other non-profit corporations. One, Taxation With Representation Fund, was organized to promote TWR's goals by publishing a journal and engaging in litigation; it had tax exempt status under § 501(c)(3). The other, Taxation With Representation, attempted to promote the same goals by influencing legislation; it had tax exempt status under § 501(c)(4). Neither predecessor organization was required to pay federal income taxes. For purposes of our analysis, there are two principal differences between § 501(c)(3) organizations and § 501(c)(4) organizations. Taxpayers who contribute to § 501(c)(3) organizations are permitted by § 170(c)(2) to deduct the amount of their contributions on their federal income tax returns, while contributions to § 501(c)(4) organizations are not deductible. Section 501(c)(4) organizations, but not § 501(c)(3) organizations, are permitted to engage in substantial lobbying to advance their exempt purposes.

In this case, TWR is attacking the prohibition against substantial lobbying in § 501(c)(3) because it wants to use tax-deductible contributions to support substantial lobbying activities. To evaluate TWR's claims, it is necessary to understand the effect of the tax exemption system enacted by Congress.

Both tax exemptions and tax-deductibility are a form of subsidy that is administered through the tax system. A tax exemption has much the same effect as a cash grant to the organization of the amount of tax it would have to pay on its income. Deductible contributions are similar to cash grants of the amount of a portion of the individual's contributions.[4] The system Congress has enacted provides this kind of subsidy to non profit civic welfare organizations generally, and an additional subsidy to those

---

4. In stating that exemptions and deductions, on one hand, are like cash subsidies, on the other, we of course do not mean to assert that they are in all respects identical. See, e.g., Walz v. Tax Commission, 397 U.S. 664, 674–676, 90 S.Ct. 1409, 1414–1415, 25 L.Ed.2d 697 (1970); id., at 690–691, 90 S.Ct., at 1422 (Brennan, J., concurring); id., at 699, 90 S.Ct., at 1427 (opinion of Harlan, J.).

charitable organizations that do not engage in substantial lobbying. In short, Congress chose not to subsidize lobbying as extensively as it chose to subsidize other activities that non profit organizations undertake to promote the public welfare.

It appears that TWR could still qualify for a tax exemption under § 501(c)(4). It also appears that TWR can obtain tax deductible contributions for its non-lobbying activity by returning to the dual structure it used in the past, with a § 501(c)(3) organization for non-lobbying activities and a § 501(c)(4) organization for lobbying. TWR would, of course, have to ensure that the § 501(c)(3) organization did not subsidize the § 501(c)(4) organization; otherwise, public funds might be spent on an activity Congress chose not to subsidize.[5]

TWR contends that Congress' decision not to subsidize its lobbying violates the First Amendment. It claims, relying on Speiser v. Randall, 357 U.S. 513, 78 S.Ct. 1332, 2 L.Ed.2d 1460 (1958), that the prohibition against substantial lobbying by 501(c)(3) organizations imposes an "unconstitutional condition" on the receipt of tax-deductible contributions. In Speiser, California established a rule requiring anyone who sought to take advantage of a property tax exemption to sign a declaration stating that he did not advocate the forcible overthrow of the Government of the United States. This Court stated that "[t]o deny an exemption to claimants who engage in speech is in effect to penalize them for the same speech." Id., at 518, 78 S.Ct., at 1338.

TWR is certainly correct when it states that we have held that the government may not deny a benefit to a person because he exercises a constitutional right. But TWR is just as certainly incorrect when it claims that this case fits the Speiser–Perry model. The Code does not deny TWR the right to receive deductible contributions to support its non-lobbying activity, nor does it deny TWR any independent benefit on account of its intention to lobby. Congress has merely refused to pay for the lobbying out of public monies. This Court has never held that the Court must grant a benefit such as TWR claims here to a person who wishes to exercise a constitutional right.

This aspect of the case is controlled by Cammarano v. United States, 358 U.S. 498, 79 S.Ct. 524, 3 L.Ed.2d 462 (1959), in which we upheld a Treasury Regulation that denied business expense deductions for lobbying activities. We held that Congress is not required by the First Amendment to subsidize lobbying. In this case, like in Cammarano, Congress has not

---

5. TWR and some amici are concerned that the IRS may impose stringent requirements that are unrelated to the congressional purpose of ensuring that no tax-deductible contributions are used to pay for substantial lobbying, and effectively make it impossible for a § 501(c)(3) organization to establish a § 501(c)(4) lobbying affiliate. No such requirement in the code or regulations has been called to our attention, nor have we been able to discover one. The IRS apparently requires only that the two groups be separately incorporated and keep records adequate to show that tax deductible contributions are not used to pay for lobbying. This is not unduly burdensome. We also note that TWR did not bring this suit because it was unable to operate with the dual structure and seeks a less stringent set of bookkeeping requirements. Rather, TWR seeks to force Congress to subsidize its lobbying activity.

infringed any First Amendment rights or regulated any First Amendment activity. Congress has simply chosen not to pay for TWR's lobbying. We again reject the "notion that First Amendment rights are somehow not fully realized unless they are subsidized by the State." Id., at 515, 79 S.Ct., at 534 (Douglas, J., concurring).

TWR also contends that the equal protection component of the Fifth Amendment renders the prohibition against substantial lobbying invalid. TWR points out that § 170(c)(3) permits taxpayers to deduct contributions to veterans' organizations that qualify for tax exemption under § 501(c)(19). Qualifying veterans' organizations are permitted to lobby as much as they want in furtherance of their exempt purposes.[8] TWR argues that because Congress has chosen to subsidize the substantial lobbying activities of veterans' organizations, it must also subsidize the lobbying of § 501(c)(3) organizations.

Generally, statutory classifications are valid if they bear a rational relation to a legitimate governmental purpose. Statutes are subjected to a higher level of scrutiny if they interfere with the exercise of a fundamental right, such as freedom of speech, or employ a suspect classification, such as race. Legislatures have especially broad latitude in creating classifications and distinctions in tax statutes. More than forty years ago we addressed these comments to an equal protection challenge to tax legislation:

> "The broad discretion as to classification possessed by a legislature in the field of taxation has long been recognized * * *. The passage of time has only served to underscore the wisdom of that recognition of the large area of discretion which is needed by a legislature in formulating sound tax policies. Traditionally classification has been a device for fitting tax programs to local needs and usages in order to achieve an equitable distribution of the tax burden. It has, because of this, been pointed out that in taxation, even more than in other fields, legislatures possess the greatest freedom in classification. Since the members of a legislature necessarily enjoy a familiarity with local conditions which this Court cannot have, the presumption of constitutionality can be overcome only by the most explicit demonstration that a classification is a hostile and oppressive discrimination against particular persons and classes. The burden is on the one attacking the legislative arrangement to negative every conceivable basis which might support it."

We have already explained why we conclude that Congress has not violated TWR's First Amendment rights by declining to subsidize its First

---

8. The rules governing deductibility of contributions to veterans' organizations are not the same as the analogous rules for § 501(c)(3) organizations. For example, an individual may generally deduct up to 50% of his adjusted gross income in contributions to § 501(c)(3) organizations, but only 20% in contributions to veterans' organizations. Compare § 170(b)(1)(A) with § 170(b)(1)(B). Taxpayers are permitted to carry over excess contributions to § 501(c)(3) organizations, but not veterans' organizations, to the next year. § 170(d). There are other differences. If it were entitled to equal treatment with veterans' organizations, TWR would, of course, be entitled only to the benefits they receive, not to more.

Amendment activities. The case would be different if Congress were to discriminate invidiously in its subsidies in such a way as to "aim at the suppression of dangerous ideas." But the veterans' organizations that qualify under § 501(c)(19) are entitled to receive tax-deductible contributions regardless of the content of any speech they may use, including lobbying. We find no indication that the statute was intended to suppress any ideas or any demonstration that it has had that effect. The sections of the Internal Revenue Code here at issue do not employ any suspect classification. The distinction between veterans' organizations and other charitable organizations is not at all like distinctions based on race or national origin.

The Court of Appeals nonetheless held that "strict scrutiny" is required because the statute "affect[s] First Amendment rights on a discriminatory basis." Its opinion suggests that strict scrutiny applies whenever Congress subsidizes some speech, but not all speech. This is not the law. Congress could, for example, grant funds to an organization dedicated to combatting teenage drug abuse, but condition the grant by providing that none of the money received from Congress should be used to lobby state legislatures. Under Cammarano, such a statute would be valid. Congress might also enact a statute providing public money for an organization dedicated to combatting teenage alcohol abuse, and impose no condition against using funds obtained from Congress for lobbying. The existence of the second statute would not make the first statute subject to strict scrutiny.

Congressional selection of particular entities or persons for entitlement to this sort of largesse "is obviously a matter of policy and discretion not open to judicial review unless in circumstances which here we are not able to find." * * * For the purposes of this case appropriations are comparable to tax exemptions and deductions, which are also "a matter of grace [that] Congress can, of course, disallow * * * as it chooses."

These are scarcely novel principles. We have held in several contexts that a legislature's decision not to subsidize the exercise of a fundamental right does not infringe the right, and thus is not subject to strict scrutiny. Buckley v. Valeo upheld a statute that provides federal funds for candidates for public office who enter primary campaigns, but does not provide funds for candidates who do not run in party primaries. We rejected First Amendment and equal protection challenges to this provision without applying strict scrutiny. Harris v. McRae and Maher v. Roe considered legislative decisions not to subsidize abortions, even though other medical procedures were subsidized. We declined to apply strict scrutiny and rejected equal protection challenges to the statutes.

The reasoning of these decisions is simple: "although government may not place obstacles in the path of a [person's] exercise of * * * freedom of [speech], it need not remove those not of its own creation." Although TWR does not have as much money as it wants, and thus cannot exercise its freedom of speech as much as it would like, the Constitution "does not confer an entitlement to such funds as may be necessary to realize all the advantages of that freedom." As we said in Maher, "[c]onstitutional concerns are greatest when the State attempts to impose its will by force of law * * *." Where governmental provision of subsidies is not "aimed at the suppression of dangerous ideas," its "power to encourage actions deemed to be in the public interest is necessarily far broader."

We have no doubt but that this statute is within Congress' broad power in this area. TWR contends that § 501(c)(3) organizations could better advance their charitable purposes if they were permitted to engage in substantial lobbying. This may well be true. But Congress—not TWR or this Court—has the authority to determine whether the advantage the public would receive from additional lobbying by charities is worth the money the public would pay to subsidize that lobbying, and other disadvantages that might accompany that lobbying. It appears that Congress was concerned that exempt organizations might use tax-deductible contributions to lobby to promote the private interests of their members. See 78 Cong.Rec. 5861 (1934)(remarks of Senator Reed); Id., at 5959 (remarks of Senator La Follette). It is not irrational for Congress to decide that tax exempt charities such as TWR should not further benefit at the expense of taxpayers at large by obtaining a further subsidy for lobbying.

It is also not irrational for Congress to decide that, even though it will not subsidize substantial lobbying by charities generally, it will subsidize lobbying by veterans' organizations. Veterans have "been obliged to drop their own affairs and take up the burdens of the nation," "subjecting themselves to the mental and physical hazards as well as the economic and family detriments which are peculiar to military service and which do not exist in normal civil life." Our country has a long standing policy of compensating veterans for their past contributions by providing them with numerous advantages. This policy has "always been deemed to be legitimate."

The issue in this case is not whether TWR must be permitted to lobby, but whether Congress is required to provide it with public money with which to lobby. For the reasons stated above, we hold that it is not. Accordingly, the judgment of the Court of Appeals is Reversed.

■ Justice Blackmun, with whom Justice Brennan and Justice Marshall join, concurring.

I join the Court's opinion. Because 26 U.S.C. § 501's discrimination between veterans' organizations and charitable organizations is not based on the content of their speech, I agree with the Court that § 501 does not deny charitable organizations equal protection of the law. The benefit provided to veterans' organizations is rationally based on the Nation's time-honored policy of "compensating veterans for their past contributions." As the Court says, a statute designed to discourage the expression of particular views would present a very different question.

I also agree that the First Amendment does not require the Government to subsidize protected activity, and that this principle controls disposition of TWR's First Amendment claim. I write separately to make clear that in my view the result under the First Amendment depends entirely upon the Court's necessary assumption—which I share—about the manner in which the Internal Revenue Service administers § 501.

If viewed in isolation, the lobbying restriction contained in § 501(c)(3) violates the principle, reaffirmed today, "that the Government may not deny a benefit to a person because he exercises a constitutional right." Section 501(c)(3) does not merely deny a subsidy for lobbying activities; it deprives an otherwise eligible organization of its tax-exempt status and its eligibility to receive tax-deductible contributions for all its activities, whenever one of those activities is "substantial lobbying." Because lobbying is protected by the First Amendment, § 501(c)(3) therefore denies a significant benefit to organizations choosing to exercise their constitutional rights.

The constitutional defect that would inhere in § 501(c)(3) alone is avoided by § 501(c)(4). As the Court notes, TWR may use its present § 501(c)(3) organization for its nonlobbying activities and may create a § 501(c)(4) affiliate to pursue its charitable goals through lobbying. The § 501(c)(4) affiliate would not be eligible to receive tax-deductible contributions.

Given this relationship between § 501(c)(3) and § 501(c)(4), the Court finds that Congress' purpose in imposing the lobbying restriction was merely to ensure that "no tax-deductible contributions are used to pay for substantial lobbying." Consistent with that purpose, "[t]he IRS apparently requires only that the two groups be separately incorporated and keep records adequate to show that tax deductible contributions are not used to pay for lobbying." As long as the IRS goes no further than this, we perhaps can safely say that "[t]he Code does not deny TWR the right to receive deductible contributions to support its nonlobbying activity, nor does it deny TWR any independent benefit on account of its intention to lobby." A § 501(c)(3) organization's right to speak is not infringed, because it is free to make known its views on legislation through its § 501(c)(4) affiliate without losing tax benefits for its nonlobbying activities.

Any significant restriction on this channel of communication, however, would negate the saving effect of § 501(c)(4). It must be remembered that § 501(c)(3) organizations retain their constitutional right to speak and to petition the Government. Should the IRS attempt to limit the control these organizations exercise over the lobbying of their 501(c)(4) affiliates, the First Amendment problems would be insurmountable. It hardly answers one person's objection to a restriction on his speech that another person, outside his control, may speak for him. Similarly, an attempt to prevent § 501(c)(4) organizations from lobbying explicitly on behalf of their § 501(c)(3) affiliates would perpetuate § 501(c)(3) organizations' inability to make known their views on legislation without incurring the unconstitutional penalty. Such restrictions would extend far beyond Congress' mere refusal to subsidize lobbying. In my view, any such restriction would render the statutory scheme unconstitutional.

I must assume that the IRS will continue to administer §§ 501(c)(3) and 501(c)(4) in keeping with Congress' limited purpose and with the IRS' duty to respect and uphold the Constitution. I therefore agree with the Court that the First Amendment questions in this case are controlled by Cammarano v. United States, 358 U.S. 498, 513, 79 S.Ct. 524, 533, 3 L.Ed.2d 462 (1959), rather than by Speiser v. Randall, 357 U.S. 513, 518–519, 78 S.Ct. 1332, 1338, 2 L.Ed.2d 1460 (1958), and Perry v. Sindermann, 408 U.S. 593, 597, 92 S.Ct. 2694, 2697, 33 L.Ed.2d 570 (1972).

NOTES AND QUESTIONS

1. *Tax Exemption as Subsidy—Revisited*. In *Taxation With Representation*, the Court unequivocally stated that the tax exemption and charitable deduction are a "form of subsidy that is administered through the tax system" having "much the same effect as a cash grant to the organization of the amount of tax it would have to pay on its income." If tax exemptions are equivalent to cash grants from the Treasury, how could Justice Rehnquist have justified, as a constitutional matter, tax exemptions to racially discriminatory schools in the *Bob Jones University* case, supra p. 370. If the Court believes that tax exemptions are subsidies, how did religious tax exemptions pass constitutional muster in Walz v. Tax Commission?

2. *Unconstitutional Conditions*. If the right to participate in the legislative process is protected by the First Amendment, can Congress constitutionally condition that right, or any governmental benefit, on a waiver of a constitutional right? How can even a discretionary government subsidy be conditioned on a waiver of First Amendment rights? Is this the effect of the lobbying limitations in § 501(c)(3)? Or may the government constitutionally control the use of subsidized funds? In *Taxation With Representation* and the later case of *Rust v. Sullivan*, 500 U.S. 173, 111 S.Ct. 1759 (1991), where the Court rejected a First Amendment challenge to regulations banning the use of federal funds in counseling and referral programs where abortion was a method of family planning, the Supreme Court has strongly suggested that these classic "unconstitutional conditions" arguments do not apply to conditions placed on the use of public funds to subsidize an activity, at least if the conditions do not result in discrimination based on the speaker's viewpoint. This position is premised on the notion that tax exemptions and charitable contributions result in a 100 percent subsidy to the benefited organizations. Is this necessarily so? Charitable contributions only result in a subsidy, if at all, to the extent of the donor's tax savings—no more than roughly 40 percent of the gift under our current rate structure. Why shouldn't the Code at least permit § 501(c)(3) organizations to lobby with the portion of funds raised (e.g., 60 percent) from contributions that do not result in tax savings to their donors? See Chapter 4C, supra, at p. 291, for additional discussion of the unconstitutional conditions doctrine in the context of state efforts to regulate charitable solicitation.

3. *Planning.* Although the constitutional debate over the lobbying limitations ended with a resounding thud in *Taxation With Representation,* the case has not adversely affected politically active nonprofits. The Supreme Court pointed the way to a common planning strategy—the use of a § 501(c)(4) affiliate to carry out the lobbying mission of a § 501(c)(3) charity. Some organizations also have created political action committees within their § 501(c)(4) lobbying affiliates. See Section E7 of this chapter, infra, at pp. 537–539. Moreover, as we are about to discover, most § 501(c)(3) organizations may elect to be governed by objective statutory tests which permit specified expenditures for direct and grassroots lobbying.

4. *For Further Reading.* Thomas Troyer, Charities, Law–Making, and the Constitution: The Validity of the Restrictions on Influencing Legislation, 31 N.Y.U. Inst. on Fed. Tax'n 1415 (1973); Note, The Tax Code's Differential Treatment of Lobbying Under Section 501(c)(3): A Proposed First Amendment Analysis, 66 Va.L.Rev. 1513 (1980).

4. THE § 501(h) EXPENDITURE TEST ELECTION

Internal Revenue Code: §§ 501(h); 504; 4911; 6033(b)(8).

Treasury Regulations: §§ 1.501(h) –1, –2, –3; 56.4911–1, –2, –3, –4, –5, –6, –7(a) & (b).

a. INTRODUCTION

The vagueness of the "no substantial part" test prompted Congress to provide more definitive guidance for charities willing to test their lobbying under what purports to be a more precise mathematical test. Section 501(h) permits most § 501(c)(3) organizations to opt out of the "no substantial part" test and instead be governed by mechanical rules that set ceilings for different types of lobbying expenditures. Lesser violations trigger a 25 percent excise tax on excess lobbying expenditures; more flagrant excesses may trigger revocation of exemption. The election is available to most "public charities"—i.e., all organizations (except churches) not classified as "private foundations." I.R.C. §§ 501(h)(3) & (4). The exclusion of churches was the result of constitutional objections by major religious organizations to any type of limitation on their activities. Private foundations are excluded because any lobbying activity subjects them to severe excise tax penalties under § 4945. See Chapter 7D6, infra, at pp. 796–797.

The § 501(h) election is made by filing a simple one-page form (Form 5768) with the IRS. Treas. Reg. § 1.501(h)–2(a). The election is effective for all taxable years which end after the date the form is filed and begin prior to the date that the election is revoked. I.R.C. § 501(h)(6). Thus, an organization may make an effective election in the middle of the year, but a mid-year revocation will not be effective until the following year. Id.

The IRS has issued an extensive and generally helpful set of regulations interpreting the expenditure test election rules. These regulations only apply to electing charities and not to organizations subject to the no substantial part test (I.R.C. § 501(h)(7)), but they serve as nondeterminative guidelines for the many nonelecting charities that remain subject to the "no substantial part" test.

b. SPENDING LIMITS AND PENALTIES

Understanding the § 501(h) expenditure test election requires a working knowledge of many definitions, all of which are intended to establish a permissible amount of overall lobbying expenditures (direct and grassroots combined) and a separate, more restrictive, level of grassroots expenditures. To avoid the excise tax imposed by § 4911, an organization must keep its overall and grassroots lobbying expenditures below specified dollar levels. Significantly, volunteer time and other subjective factors that clouded interpretation of the no substantial part limitation are not included in this test, which looks solely to monetary expenditures. Although the rules are detailed and daunting, they are extremely permissive, and deciphering them is well worth the effort for a politically active nonprofit organization.

"Exempt purpose expenditures" are the overall measuring rod against which an organization's lobbying expenses are tested. Included are all amounts spent by the organization during the taxable year to accomplish its exempt purposes, excluding capital expenditures or the expenses of a separate fundraising unit, or investment management expenses. I.R.C. 4911(e)(1), (4); Treas. Reg. § 56.4911–4. Simply put, exempt purpose expenditures represent the organization's actual operating budget, including any lobbying expenses.

The *"lobbying nontaxable amount"* ("LNTA") is the overall amount that an organization may spend on direct and grassroots lobbying without being penalized. The LNTA is a specific percentage of the organization's exempt purpose expenditures measured by the following sliding scale:

20% of the first $500,000 of exempt purpose expenditures

15% of the next $500,000

10% of the next $500,000

5% of the excess over $1,500,000

In no event, however, may the LNTA exceed $1,000,000, a cap reached when an organization's annual budget is $17 million. I.R.C. § 4911(c)(2).

To illustrate, assume an organization has annual expenses (excluding any separate fund-raising unit) of $250,000. Its LNTA is $50,000, which is 20 percent of its budget. If the budget were $750,000, the LNTA would be $137,500—20 percent of $500,000 ($100,000) plus 15 percent of the next $250,000 ($37,500).

The *"grassroots nontaxable amount"* ("GNTA") is 25 percent of the LNTA and thus represents a separate and stricter cap on expenditures for grassroots lobbying. I.R.C. § 4911(c)(4). For example, if an organization has an LNTA of $50,000, its GNTA would be $12,500, and grassroots lobbying expenditures in excess of that cap would be subject to the 25 percent excise tax. The LNTA and GNTA are applied separately to determine an organization's exposure to the excise tax. In the example above, the organization could spend less than $50,000 on general lobbying and not exceed the LNTA, but it nonetheless would be subject to the excise tax if its grassroots expenditures exceeded $12,500.

Armed with the above definitions, the excise tax now can be explained. If overall or grassroots lobbying expenditures exceed either the LNTA or the GNTA, the organization is subject to a 25 percent excise tax on "excess lobbying expenditures"—i.e., whichever excess is greater relative to the applicable limitation. I.R.C. § 4911(a), (b).

Consider one final example. Assume an organization has an LNTA of $50,000 and a GNTA of $12,500. During the current year, its overall lobbying expenditures are $60,000, of which $35,000 are grassroots expenditures. Excess lobbying expenditures are the greater of:

(1) Lobbying Expenditures minus LNTA

($60,000 − $50,000 = $10,000); or

(2) Grassroots Expenditures minus GNTA

($35,000 − $12,500 = $22,500).

The greater of these two numbers, $22,500, is subject to the excise tax, which would be $5,625 (25 percent of $22,500). If none of the lobbying expenditures in the example had been in the grassroots category, the greater excess would have been $10,000, resulting in an excise tax of $2,500.

Expenditures exceeding the respective nontaxable amounts only trigger the excise tax, not loss of exemption. But organizations that "normally" make lobbying or grassroots expenditures in excess of 150 percent of the respective nontaxable amounts (these higher limits are referred to as "lobbying ceiling amounts") will lose their § 501(c)(3) exemption. I.R.C. § 501(h)(2); Treas. Reg. § 1.501(h)–3(b). The function of the term "normally" is to determine whether the ceiling amounts have been exceeded by aggregating expenditures over a four-year measuring period (the "base years") ending with the year under scrutiny (the "determination year"). Treas. Reg. § 1.501(h)–3(b)(1). If the sum of an electing charity's overall or grassroots lobbying expenditures exceeds the respective ceiling amounts for those four base years, the organization will lose its § 501(c)(3) exemption effective in the year following the determination year. Id. Special rules are provided for organizations with less than a four-year history. Treas. Reg. § 1.501(h)–3(b)(2). If an organization loses its exemption because of lobbying, it may not thereafter qualify for exempt status as a § 501(c)(4) social welfare organization. I.R.C. § 504(a).

Without inflicting any more detail, it should be obvious that an organization making the § 501(h) election must lobby excessively and repeatedly before it risks losing its exemption.

To prevent circumvention of the dollar limitations, § 4911(f) applies consolidation principles—aggregating expenditures of an "affiliated group" of § 501(c)(3) organizations—to determine the applicable caps on lobbying expenditures. In general, organizations are "affiliated" if they are subject to common control. For example, affiliation will exist if one organization is bound by decisions of the other on legislative issues, or the governing board of one organization includes enough representatives of the other to cause or prevent action on legislative issues. I.R.C. § 4911(f)(2). Rules also apply to aggregate lobbying expenditures of different organizations even where there is limited affiliation—e.g., where one organization controls another solely with respect to national legislation. The regulations fill in the details. See Treas. Reg. § 56.4911–7.

c. LOBBYING EXPENDITURES

Having described the spending limits and penalties for exceeding them, we turn next to the what activities are defined as lobbying and some valuable exceptions.

Lobbying Expenditures—In General. "Lobbying expenditures" are expenditures for the purpose of "influencing legislation," which is defined to include both direct lobbying (i.e., communications with legislators, their employees and other government officials who may participate in the formulation of legislation) and grassroots lobbying (attempting to influence public opinion). I.R.C. § 4911(c)(1), (e)(1). "Legislation" includes action by Congress, any state legislature, local council, or similar legislative body, and action by the public in referenda, ballot initiatives, constitutional amendments, and the like. I.R.C. § 4911(e)(2). "Action" is limited to the introduction, amendment, enactment, defeat, or repeal of legislation. I.R.C. § 4911(e)(3). Significantly, attempts to influence executive, judicial, or administrative bodies do not constitute lobbying unless the principal purpose of the communication is to influence legislation. I.R.C. § 4911(d)(2)(E); Treas. Reg. § 56.4911–2(d)(2)–(4).

Direct Lobbying. A direct lobbying communication is any attempt to influence any legislation through communication with any member or employee of a legislative body, or any other government official or employee who may participate in the formulation of the legislation but only if the principal purpose of the communication is to influence legislation. I.R.C. § 4911(d)(1)(B); Treas. Reg. § 56.4911–2(b)(1)(i). These communications are treated as direct lobbying only if they refer to specific legislation and reflect a view on the legislation. Treas. Reg. § 56.4911–2(b)(1)(ii).

Grassroots Lobbying. Grassroots lobbying is any attempt to influence legislation through communications that attempt to affect the opinion of the general public or any segment thereof. Treas. Reg. § 56.4911–2(b)(2)(i). The regulations provide that a communication will be treated as grassroots lobbying only if it: (1) refers to specific legislation (i.e., legislation that already has been introduced and specific proposed legislation that the organization either supports or opposes); (2) reflects a view on the legislation; and (3) encourages the recipient to take action with respect to the legislation. Treas. Reg. § 56.4911–2(b)(2)(ii). This definition is much more generous than a prior version of the regulations, which would have classified any communication that merely "pertained" to legislation as grass-roots lobbying.

Under the three-pronged test, a communication is not grassroots lobbying unless it includes "a call to action" with respect to specific legislation. A communication encourages its recipients to take action only if it: (1) states that the recipient should contact a legislator or employee of a legislative body or other governmental representative involved in the legislative process; (2) states the address, telephone number or similar information about a legislator or legislative staff person; (3) provides a petition, tear-off postcard or similar material for the recipient to communicate his or her views to legislators or their staffs; or (4) specifically identifies one or more legislators who will vote on the legislation as opposing the legislation, being undecided with respect to it, being the recipient's representative in the legislature or being a member of the legislative committee that will consider the legislation. Treas. Reg. § 56.4911–2(b)(2)(iii). The first three types of communications not only "encourage" but "directly encourage" the recipient to take action; communications in the fourth category only "encourage" action. The significance of this distinction is that communications in the fourth category may be within the exceptions for nonpartisan analysis, study or research or member communications (both discussed below) and thus may not be grassroots lobbying communications. Treas. Reg. § 56.4911–2(b)(2)(iv).

To illustrate the generosity of the regulations, assume an organization opposing handgun control pays for an advertisement stating:

> The State Assembly is considering a bill to make gun ownership illegal. This outrageous legislation would violate your constitutional rights and the rights of other law-abiding citizens. If this legislation is passed, you and your family will be criminals if you want to exercise your right to protect yourselves.

Under the regulations, this is not grassroots lobbying because it does not include any call to action. Treas. Reg. § 56.4911–2(b)(5)(iv) Example (4).

The regulations include one exception to the "call to action" requirement. Under the "mass media communication" rule, an organization is presumed to engage in grassroots lobbying if, within two weeks before a vote by a legislative body or committee on a "highly publicized piece of legislation", the organization makes a communication in the "mass media" (i.e., television, radio, general circulation newspapers and magazines) that "reflects a view" on the general subject of the legislation and either refers to the legislation or encourages members of the public to communicate with their legislators on the general subject of the legislation. This presumption is rebuttable if the organization can demonstrate that the communication is a type regularly made by the organization in the mass media without regard to the timing of the legislation. Treas. Reg. § 56.4911–2(b)(5)(ii).

Another helpful rule makes it clear that communications to the public with respect to referenda, initiatives, and other ballot measures are treated as direct rather than grassroots lobbying on the theory that the public itself is the legislative body on such matters. Treas. Reg. § 56.4911–2(b)(1)(iii).

The regulations elaborate on these rules with numerous examples. See Treas. Reg. § 56.4911–2(b)(4), –2(b)(5)(iv).

d. EXCEPTED COMMUNICATIONS

Another way to pose the critical definitional question is: "what isn't lobbying?" In an attempt to provide charities with more guidance and protection, § 4911(d) and the regulations provide that the following activities are not treated as "influencing legislation" for purposes of the elective regime:

(1) making available the results of nonpartisan analysis, study or research;

(2) discussion of broad social, economic, or similar problems;

(3) providing technical advice to a governmental body or committee in response to a written request;

(4) "self-defense" lobbying, such as direct communications to the legislature with respect to issues that may affect the organization's existence, tax exemption or eligibility to receive deductible contributions;

(5) communications between the organization and its bona fide "members" with respect to legislation of direct mutual interest, unless the purpose of the communication is to directly encourage the members themselves to lobby or to urge nonmembers to do so; and

(6) communications with members of the executive branch of government, unless the principal purpose is to influence specific legislation.

Nonpartisan Analysis. Nonpartisan analysis, study or research is generally defined as "an independent and objective exposition of a particular subject matter." Treas. Reg. § 56.4911–2(c)(1)(ii). Neutrality is not required. An organization may advocate a position on legislation as long as it presents sufficient facts to allow the audience to reach its own conclusion, and the results of the research may be distributed by "any suitable means" provided the communication is not targeted to those interested in only one side of the issue. Treas. Reg. § 56.4911–2(c)(1)(ii), (iv). But communications that otherwise might qualify for the exception are disqualified if they include a "call to action" by *directly* encouraging the general public to contact their legislators on the specific legislative matters. Treas. Reg. § 56.4911–2(c)(1)(vi). Moreover, even though certain analysis may be within the nonpartisan exception when it is initially prepared, subsequent use in a grassroots lobbying effort may cause the entire cost of preparing the "advocacy communication" to be treated as a grassroots expenditure. Treas. Reg. § 56.4911–2(b)(2)(v). Under a valuable safe harbor, the subsequent use rule does not apply if the organization either: (1) demonstrates a primary nonlobbying purpose (e.g., by making a substantial distribution of a study to the academic community at the same time or before it is used for lobbying), or (2) paid all the expenses for the paper at least six months before it was used for lobbying. Treas. Reg. § 53.4911–2(b)(2)(v)(D), (E). For more examples illustrating the scope of the nonpartisan analysis exception and the "subsequent use" trap, see Treas. Reg. § 56.4911–2(c)(1)(vii), –2(b)(2)(v)(H).

Discussions of Broad Social Problems. Examinations and discussions of broad social, economic and similar problems are neither direct nor grass-roots lobbying communications even if the problems are of the type with which government might ultimately deal. As long as the "discussions" do not relate to the merits of specific legislation or directly encourage recipients to take action, they are not lobbying. Treas. Reg. § 56.4911–2(c)(2).

Technical Advice. A communication is not direct lobbying if it is in response to a written request by a governmental body or committee to provide technical advice or assistance. Treas. Reg. § 56.4911–2(c)(3).

Self–Defense. The self-defense exception protects an organization's appearances before or communications with any legislative body with respect to a possible action that might affect the existence of the organization, its powers and duties, its tax-exempt status, or its eligibility to receive tax-deductible contributions. Treas. Reg. § 56.4911–2(c)(4). For example, an appearance by representatives of a § 501(c)(3) organization before the Senate Finance Committee to oppose a proposed bill to scale back the charitable deduction would not constitute direct lobbying. Id.

Member Communications. Another valuable exception permits an organization to communicate with its bona fide "members" on legislative issues of mutual interest. I.R.C. § 4911(d)(2)(D). A "member" must have more than a nominal connection with the organization; an individual whose name simply appears on a mailing list normally does not qualify. Payment of dues or donations of volunteer time (in more than a nominal amount) will help to establish an individual's "member" status. See Treas. Reg. § 56.4911–5(f).

The practical impact of this exception is that certain member communications are treated more leniently than if they had been with nonmembers. For example, a communication directed only to members that refers to and reflects a view on specific legislation of direct interest to the organization and its members is not lobbying if it does not "directly encourage" the members to engage in direct or grassroots lobbying. Treas. Reg. § 56.4911–5(b). The implication is that communications may "encourage" such lobbying (see Treas. Reg. § 56.4911–2(b)(2)(iv)) by identifying key legislators. If the same communication had been directed to nonmembers, it would have been grassroots lobbying. Similarly, assume that an organization encourages its members to contact their legislators to support a bill of direct interest to the organization. Under the more lenient member communication rules, the expenses of this communication would be treated as direct lobbying. I.R.C. § 4911(d)(3)(A); Treas. Reg. § 56.4911–5(c). If the communication had been directed to nonmembers, it would have been grassroots lobbying. But when an organization urges members to engage in grassroots lobbying on specific legislation, the costs of the communication are treated as grassroots expenditures. I.R.C. § 4911(d)(3)(B); Treas. Reg. § 56.4911–5(d).

The intellectually curious then would ask—what if a communication refers to and reflects a view on specific legislation and directly encourages the recipient to take action, and it is directed to both members and nonmembers? The regulations do not disappoint, providing that if more than half the recipients are members, the costs of the communication must be allocated between direct and grassroots lobbying under rules that vary depending on what type of lobbying is being directly encouraged! Treas. Reg. § 56.4911–5(e)(1). If the communication urges recipients to engage in direct lobbying and 15 percent or less of the distribution is to nonmember subscribers, then none of the cost of preparation or distribution is treated as a grassroots expenditure. Treas. Reg. § 56.4911–5(e)(2)(ii). For more details, see Treas. Reg. § 56.4911–5(e)(2), (3).

Allocation of Mixed–Purpose Expenditures. Charities making the § 501(h) election must allocate certain mixed-purpose expenses among nonlobbying pursuits and the two types of lobbying activities. Types of expenses requiring allocation include salaries of employees who devote part of their time to lobbying activities; costs of preparing and mailing pamphlets; costs of newspaper advertising; newsletter costs; and general overhead. Treas. Reg. § 56.4911–3(a)(1). The regulations are typically detailed on this point. If a lobbying communication is sent primarily (more than half) to bona fide members, an organization may make any reasonable allocation between lobbying and nonlobbying expenses, such as an allocation based on column inches in the publication. If the audience is primarily nonmembers, however, more stringent allocation rules apply—e.g., costs attributable to the communication that are on the same specific subject as the lobbying message must be allocated to lobbying. Treas. Reg. § 56.4911–3(a)(2).

Some readers who have read this far may wish to stop here. For those who would like an illustration, consider this example from the regulations involving a nonmembership organization ("T") that prepares a three-page document mailed to 3,000 persons on T's mailing list. The first two pages of the mailing (titled "The Need for Child Care") advocates additional child care programs and includes statistics on the number of children living in single-parent or two-worker parent homes. The third page (titled "H.R. 1") indicates T's support for a bill pending in the U.S. House, notes that the bill will provide for $10 million in additional subsidies for child care providers and ends with T's request that recipients contact their representatives to support the legislation. The entire communication is treated as grassroots lobbying (note the "call to action") on one specific subject and the expenditures of preparing and distributing all three pages are treated as "grassroots lobbying expenditures." Treas. Reg. 56.4911–3(b) Example (8). If the document has a fourth page that does not refer to the same specific subject as the lobbying message, the costs of that page would not be treated as a lobbying expenditure. Id. Example (9).

If T in the above example were a "membership" organization, and 75 percent of the recipients of the three-page document were bona fide members, T could treat half the cost of preparing and distributing the document as a nonlobbying expenditure because its purpose is to educate T's members about the need for child care. The other half would be a lobbying expenditure, of which 75 percent (attributable to the request to members to contact legislators) is "direct" lobbying and 25 percent (attributable to the request to nonmembers to contact legislators) is grassroots lobbying. Id. Example (10); Treas. Reg. § 56.4911–3(b) Example (10); see also Treas. Reg. § 56.4911–5(e)(2)(i)–(iii). If in this same example, T allocated only one percent of the costs as a lobbying expenditure because only two out of 200 printed lines in the document mentioned legislation, that allocation of expenses would be considered unreasonable. Treas. Reg. § 56.4911–3(b) Example (11); see also Treas. Reg. § 56.4911–3(a)(2)(ii).

e. REPORTING REQUIREMENTS

All § 501(c)(3) organizations required to file Form 990 must disclose on Schedule C their "attempts" to influence legislation through the use of paid staff, volunteers, media advertisements, mailings to members, legislators and the general public ,publications or broadcast statements grants to other organizations for lobbying purposes, direct lobbying, rallies and seminars, and other activities. Organizations making the § 501(h) election must report their lobbying and grassroots expenditures for the current and three preceding years and separately report any excise tax liability on IRS Form 4720.

These reporting requirements require an electing organization to allocate expenditures and general overhead to the direct and grassroots lobbying categories. This is no small chore, particularly because many expenditures may be difficult to categorize. Electing charities are well advised to require their employees to keep detailed time records so their salaries and benefits can be properly allocated. Expenses for facilities, publications, and other activities should be apportioned on some reasonable basis. Failure to keep careful records will cause difficulties in the event of an audit.

f. TO ELECT OR NOT TO ELECT

After absorbing all this detail about the § 501(h) election, it may appear that the no substantial part test is not so bad after all. Indeed, many charities prefer the vagueness of the general rules to the specificity and recordkeeping requirements of the § 501(h) election. Organizations with large budgets also may be inhibited by the regressive sliding scale and the overall $1 million ceiling on lobbying expenditures. In fact, it has been reported that relatively few eligible § 501(c)(3) organizations have made the expenditure test election.

The § 501(h) election is a prudent choice for any organization planning a highly visible lobbying program. The officers and directors will sleep more soundly knowing that the lobbying activities have not exceeded the statutory ceilings. An organization that relies primarily on volunteers also would be well advised to consider the election because time and energy are not factored into the expenditure limits. The regulations, with their permissive definitions and examples, are an additional reason why a politically active charity might prefer the "safe harbor" of the expenditure test election. An organization contemplating a one-shot lobbying effort on an issue of great importance even might choose to exceed the expenditure limits for a year or two at the price of a modest excise tax. As long as the excesses are temporary, loss of exemption should not result. A similar lobbying program evaluated under the general limitation might cause the organization to lose its exemption and be subject to the five percent excise tax under § 4912 on all of its lobbying expenditures in the year its exemption is revoked.

Some charities have feared that they will draw too much attention and risk an IRS audit by making the § 501(h) election. IRS officials have repeatedly denied that electing charities are an audit target. And if an organization were audited for excessive lobbying, it almost always would prefer the protection offered by the § 4911 regulations as opposed to the vagaries of the no substantial part test.

PROBLEM

Seniors Association for Gerontological Endeavor ("SAGE") is a non-profit § 501(c)(3) membership organization organized and operated to study the problems of the aging population and assist senior citizens. SAGE's board of trustees recently decided that the organization should become more politically active. During the current year, the board passed a resolution expressing SAGE's support for proposed legislation that would prohibit certain types of age discrimination in employment, and it developed an intense interest in legislation affecting social security benefits and medicare. From time to time, SAGE also has taken positions on local issues affecting senior citizens.

SAGE's expenditures for the current year, apart from certain additional items to be described separately below, were as follows:

Construction of New Building	$500,000
Administrative Expenses	200,000
Straight Line Depreciation	100,000
Services to Elderly	600,000
Fundraising Unit Expenses	100,000
TOTAL	$1,500,000

In addition, SAGE spent the following amounts in the current year for the purposes indicated:

(1) $150,000 for a special "Public Impact Program" designed to promote SAGE's advocacy priorities by outlining the organization's position on age discrimination and social security legislation and urging members to contact their legislators to encourage them to vote in accordance with SAGE's position on specific pending bills.

(2) $50,000 to finance a study of the problems of aged workers and to publish a report of the findings for distribution to all members of

Congress and other interested persons, including foundations, think tanks, and academic institutions.

(3) $50,000 to distribute literature to the general public in California urging support for local measures to ban age discrimination. The literature advocated SAGE's position on several pending bills and did not specifically request recipients to contact their legislators, but it identified the members of the key legislative committees that are considering the bills.

(4) $50,000 to publish a newsletter; 25% of the space in the newsletter was devoted to reporting on the prospects for passage of legislation supported by SAGE and identifying the main sponsors of the bills in the legislature; the other 75% of the newsletter reported on SAGE's many social service activities. The newsletter was mailed to SAGE's 20,000 members and to 5,000 paid subscribers (mostly libraries). Minimum SAGE membership dues are $50 per year and 80% of SAGE's members paid the minimum.

(5) $15,000 for billboards near major urban freeways with a picture of an active and healthy older American and the inscription "Don't Put Mom and Dad Out to Pasture: Eliminate Age Discrimination" and, below it, "No on 39." No other mention was made on the billboard of any pending legislation, nor was SAGE identified as the proponent of the message, but the billboards were displayed for the three weeks preceding the vote on a major statewide ballot proposition relating to age discrimination.

(6) $10,000 for full-page newspaper advertisements opposing a bill pending in Congress to reduce Medicare benefits for older Americans. The ads were strategically published during the two weeks preceding the vote but did not include any specific "call to action" or mention any legislators by name.

(7) $25,000 for mailings, radio advertisements, web site postings, e-mails, faxes, and other activities opposing a nominee for the United States Supreme Court whom SAGE regarded as an opponent of the employment rights of older Americans. These communications included a "call to action" urging recipients to contact their Senators and urge them to vote against confirmation of the nominee.

Consider the following questions:

(a) Assuming SAGE does not make the § 501(h) election, has it jeopardized its tax-exempt status as a result of its activities in the current year?

(b) If SAGE made an effective election under § 501(h), would it be liable for any excise taxes under § 4911 in the current year? If so, how might SAGE have restructured its activities to avoid excise tax exposure?

(c) If SAGE made an effective § 501(h) election and all of its expenses described above remained constant for the three years following the current year, would it jeopardize its exempt status? Will making the election serve as a "red flag" to the Internal Revenue Service, prompting a likely audit of SAGE's lobbying activity?

(d) If SAGE makes the § 501(h) election, will that complicate its ability to receive grants from private foundations?

(e) If SAGE loses its exempt status because of excessive lobbying, could it then become a § 501(c)(4) organization? Would it be subject to any other sanctions? Could SAGE promise never to lobby again and reapply for § 501(c)(3) status?

5.   POLITICAL CAMPAIGN LIMITATIONS

Internal Revenue Code: §§ 501(c)(3); 4955.

Treasury Regulations: §§ 1.501(c)(3)–1(c)(1)(iii); 53.4955–1.

Unlike the lobbying limitations, the ban on participation or intervention in political campaign activities purports to be absolute, although the Service has been known to ignore de minimis violations. In addition, § 4955 authorizes the Service to impose excise tax penalties on § 501(c)(3) charities and their managers if the organization incurs certain proscribed political expenditures discussed in more detail below.

As illustrated by the materials below, the principal interpretive questions are: (1) what constitutes participation or intervention in a political campaign, and how are these prohibited activities distinguished from permissible voter education or issue advocacy?; (2) who is a candidate for public office; (3) under what circumstances are political campaign activities of leaders or members attributed to an organization; (4) does the IRS discriminate by selectively enforcing the political campaign limitations?; and (5) does the application of the political campaign limitations to charities violate their First Amendment rights to free speech and, in the case of churches, free exercise of religion?

Revenue Ruling 2007–41

2007–1 Cum. Bull. 1421.

Organizations that are exempt from income tax under section 501(a) of the Internal Revenue Code as organizations described in section 501(c)(3) may not participate in, or intervene in (including the publishing or distributing of statements), any political campaign on behalf of (or in opposition to) any candidate for public office.

ISSUE

In each of the 21 situations described below, has the organization participated or intervened in a political campaign on behalf of (or in opposition to) any candidate for public office within the meaning of section 501(c)(3)?

LAW

Section 501(c)(3) provides for the exemption from federal income tax of organizations organized and operated exclusively for charitable or educational purposes, no substantial part of the activities of which is carrying on propaganda, or otherwise attempting to influence legislation (except as otherwise provided in section 501(h)), and which does not participate in, or intervene in (including the publishing or distributing of statements), any political campaign on behalf of (or in opposition to) any candidate for public office.

Section 1.501(c)(3)–1(c)(3)(i) of the Income Tax Regulations states that an organization is not operated exclusively for one or more exempt purposes if it is an "action" organization.

Section 1.501(c)(3)–1(c)(3)(iii) of the regulations defines an "action" organization as an organization that participates or intervenes, directly or indirectly, in any political campaign on behalf of or in opposition to any candidate for public office. The term "candidate for public office" is defined as an individual who offers himself, or is proposed by others, as a contestant for an elective public office, whether such office be national, State, or local. The regulations further provide that activities that constitute participation or intervention in a political campaign on behalf of or in opposition to a candidate include, but are not limited to, the publication or distribution of written statements or the making of oral statements on behalf of or in opposition to such a candidate.

Whether an organization is participating or intervening, directly or indirectly, in any political campaign on behalf of or in opposition to any candidate for public office depends upon all of the facts and circumstances of each case. For example, certain "voter education" activities, including preparation and distribution of certain voter guides, conducted in a non-partisan manner may not constitute prohibited political activities under section 501(c)(3) of the Code. Other so-called "voter education" activities may be proscribed by the statute. Rev. Rul. 78–248, 1978–1 C.B. 154, contrasts several situations illustrating when an organization that publishes a compilation of candidate positions or voting records has or has not engaged in prohibited political activities based on whether the questionnaire used to solicit candidate positions or the voters guide itself shows a bias or preference in content or structure with respect to the views of a particular candidate. See also Rev. Rul. 80–282, 1980–2 C.B. 178, amplifying Rev. Rul. 78–248 regarding the timing and distribution of voter education materials.

The presentation of public forums or debates is a recognized method of educating the public. See Rev. Rul. 66–256, 1966–2 C.B. 210 (nonprofit organization formed to conduct public forums at which lectures and debates on social, political, and international matters are presented qualifies for exemption from federal income tax under section 501(c)(3)). Providing a forum for candidates is not, in and of itself, prohibited political activity. See Rev. Rul. 74–574, 1974–2 C.B. 160 (organization operating a broadcast station is not participating in political campaigns on behalf of public candidates by providing reasonable amounts of air time equally available to all legally qualified candidates for election to public office in compliance with the reasonable access provisions of the Communications Act of 1934). However, a forum for candidates could be operated in a manner that would show a bias or preference for or against a particular candidate. This could be done, for example, through biased questioning procedures. On the other hand, a forum held for the purpose of educating and informing the voters, which provides fair and impartial treatment of candidates, and which does not promote or advance one candidate over another, would not constitute participation or intervention in any political campaign on behalf of or in opposition to any candidate for public office. See Rev. Rul. 86–95, 1986–2 C.B. 73 (organization that proposes to educate voters by conducting a series of public forums in congressional districts during congressional election campaigns is not participating in a political campaign on behalf of any candidate due to the neutral form and content of its proposed forums).

ANALYSIS OF FACTUAL SITUATIONS

The 21 factual situations appear below under specific subheadings relating to types of activities. In each of the factual situations, all the facts and circumstances are considered in determining whether an organization's activities result in political campaign intervention. Note that each of these situations involves only one type of activity. In the case of an organization that combines one or more types of activity, the interaction among the activities may affect the determination of whether or not the organization is engaged in political campaign intervention.

Voter Education, Voter Registration and Get Out the Vote Drives

Section 501(c)(3) organizations are permitted to conduct certain voter education activities (including the presentation of public forums and the publication of voter education guides) if they are carried out in a non-partisan manner. In addition, section 501(c)(3) organizations may encourage people to participate in the electoral process through voter registration and get-out-the-vote drives, conducted in a non-partisan manner. On the other hand, voter education or registration activities conducted in a biased manner that favors (or opposes) one or more candidates is prohibited.

Situation 1. B, a section 501(c)(3) organization that promotes community involvement, sets up a booth at the state fair where citizens can register to vote. The signs and banners in and around the booth give only the name of the organization, the date of the next upcoming statewide election, and notice of the opportunity to register. No reference to any candidate or political party is made by the volunteers staffing the booth or in the materials available at the booth, other than the official voter registration forms which allow registrants to select a party affiliation. *B* is not engaged in political campaign intervention when it operates this voter registration booth.

Situation 2. C is a section 501(c)(3) organization that educates the public on environmental issues. Candidate *G* is running for the state legislature and an important element of her platform is challenging the environmental policies of the incumbent. Shortly before the election, C sets up a telephone bank to call registered voters in the district in which Candidate G is seeking election. In the phone conversations, C's representative tells the voter about the importance of environmental issues and asks questions about the voter's views on these issues. If the voter appears to agree with the incumbent's position, C's representative thanks the voter and ends the call. If the voter appears to agree with Candidate G's position, C's representative reminds the voter about the upcoming election, stresses the importance of voting in the election and offers to provide transportation to the polls. C is engaged in political campaign intervention when it conducts this get-out-the-vote drive.

Individual Activity by Organization Leaders

The political campaign intervention prohibition is not intended to restrict free expression on political matters by leaders of organizations speaking for themselves, as individuals. Nor are leaders prohibited from speaking about important issues of public policy. However, for their organizations to remain tax exempt under section 501(c)(3), leaders cannot make partisan comments in official organization publications or at official functions of the organization.

Situation 3. President A is the Chief Executive Officer of Hospital J, a section 501(c)(3) organization, and is well known in the community. With the permission of five prominent healthcare industry leaders, including President A, who have personally endorsed Candidate T, Candidate T publishes a full page ad in the local newspaper listing the names of the five leaders. President A is identified in the ad as the CEO of Hospital J. The ad states, "Titles and affiliations of each individual are provided for identification purposes only." The ad is paid for by Candidate T's campaign committee. Because the ad was not paid for by Hospital J, the ad is not otherwise in an official publication of Hospital J, and the endorsement is made by President A in a personal capacity, the ad does not constitute campaign intervention by Hospital J.

Situation 4. President B is the president of University K, a section 501(c)(3) organization. University K publishes a monthly alumni newsletter that is distributed to all alumni of the university. In each issue, President B has a column titled "My Views." The month before the election, President B states in the "My Views" column, "It is my personal opinion that Candidate U should be reelected." For that one issue, President B pays from his personal funds the portion of the cost of the newsletter attributable to the "My Views" column. Even though he paid part of the cost of the newsletter, the newsletter is an official publication of the university. Because the endorsement appeared in an official publication of University K, it constitutes campaign intervention by University K.

Situation 5. Minister C is the minister of Church L, a section 501(c)(3) organization and Minister C is well known in the community. Three weeks before the election, he attends a press conference at Candidate V's campaign headquarters and states that Candidate V should be reelected. Minister C does not say he is speaking on behalf of Church L. His endorsement is reported on the front page of the local newspaper and he is identified in the article as the minister of Church L. Because Minister C did not make the endorsement at an official church function, in an official church publication or otherwise use the church's assets, and did not state that he was speaking as a representative of Church L, his actions do not constitute campaign intervention by Church L.

Situation 6. Chairman D is the chairman of the Board of Directors of M, a section 501(c)(3) organization that educates the public on conservation issues. During a regular meeting of M shortly before the election, Chairman D spoke on a number of issues, including the importance of voting in the upcoming election, and concluded by stating, "It is important that you all do your duty in the election and vote for Candidate W." Because Chairman D's remarks indicating support for Candidate W were made during an official organization meeting, they constitute political campaign intervention by M.

Candidate Appearances

Depending on the facts and circumstances, an organization may invite political candidates to speak at its events without jeopardizing its tax-exempt status. Political candidates may be invited in their capacity as candidates, or in their individual capacity (not as a candidate). Candidates may also appear without an invitation at organization events that are open to the public.

When a candidate is invited to speak at an organization event in his or her capacity as a political candidate, factors in determining whether the organization participated or intervened in a political campaign include the following:

- Whether the organization provides an equal opportunity to participate to political candidates seeking the same office;

- Whether the organization indicates any support for or opposition to the candidate (including candidate introductions and communications concerning the candidate's attendance); and

- Whether any political fundraising occurs.

In determining whether candidates are given an equal opportunity to participate, the nature of the event to which each candidate is invited will be considered, in addition to the manner of presentation. For example, an organization that invites one candidate to speak at its well attended annual banquet, but invites the opposing candidate to speak at a sparsely attended general meeting, will likely have violated the political campaign prohibition, even if the manner of presentation for both speakers is otherwise neutral.

When an organization invites several candidates for the same office to speak at a public forum, factors in determining whether the forum results in political campaign intervention include the following:

- Whether questions for the candidates are prepared and presented by an independent nonpartisan panel,

- Whether the topics discussed by the candidates cover a broad range of issues that the candidates would address if elected to the office sought and are of interest to the public,

- Whether each candidate is given an equal opportunity to present his or her view on each of the issues discussed,

- Whether the candidates are asked to agree or disagree with positions, agendas, platforms or statements of the organization, and

- Whether a moderator comments on the questions or otherwise implies approval or disapproval of the candidates.

Situation 7. President E is the president of Society N, a historical society that is a section 501(c)(3) organization. In the month prior to the election, President *E* invites the three Congressional candidates for the district in which Society *N* is located to address the members, one each at a regular meeting held on three successive weeks. Each candidate is given an equal opportunity to address and field questions on a wide variety of topics from the members. Society *N*'s publicity announcing the dates for each of the candidate's speeches and President *E's* introduction of each candidate include no comments on their qualifications or any indication of a preference for any candidate. Society *N*'s actions do not constitute political campaign intervention.

Situation 8. The facts are the same as in *Situation 7* except that there are four candidates in the race rather than three, and one of the candidates declines the invitation to speak. In the publicity announcing the dates for each of the candidate's speeches, Society *N* includes a statement that the order of the speakers was determined at random and the fourth candidate declined the Society's invitation to speak. President E makes the same statement in his opening remarks at each of the meetings where one of the candidates is speaking. Society *N*'s actions do not constitute political campaign intervention.

Situation 9. Minister F is the minister of Church O, a section 501(c)(3) organization. The Sunday before the November election, Minister *F* invites Senate Candidate *X* to preach to her congregation during worship services. During his remarks, Candidate *X* states, "I am asking not only for your votes, but for your enthusiasm and dedication, for your willingness to go the extra mile to get a very large turnout on Tuesday." Minister *F* invites no other candidate to address her congregation during the Senatorial campaign. Because these activities take place during official church services, they are attributed to Church *O*. By selectively providing church facilities to allow Candidate *X* to speak in support of his campaign, Church *O*'s actions constitute political campaign intervention.

Candidate Appearances Where Speaking or Participating as a Non–Candidate

Candidates may also appear or speak at organization events in a non-candidate capacity. For instance, a political candidate may be a public figure who is invited to speak because he or she: (a) currently holds, or formerly held, public office; (b) is considered an expert in a non political field; or (c) is a celebrity or has led a distinguished military, legal, or public service career. A candidate may choose to attend an event that is open to the public, such as a lecture, concert or worship service. The candidate's presence at an organization-sponsored event does not, by itself, cause the organization to be engaged in political campaign intervention. However, if the candidate is publicly recognized by the organization, or if the candidate is invited to speak, factors in determining whether the candidate's appearance results in political campaign intervention include the following:

- Whether the individual is chosen to speak solely for reasons other than candidacy for public office;

- Whether the individual speaks only in a non-candidate capacity;

- Whether either the individual or any representative of the organization makes any mention of his or her candidacy or the election;

- Whether any campaign activity occurs in connection with the candidate's attendance;

- Whether the organization maintains a nonpartisan atmosphere on the premises or at the event where the candidate is present; and

- Whether the organization clearly indicates the capacity in which the candidate is appearing and does not mention the individual's political candidacy or the upcoming election in the communications announcing the candidate's attendance at the event.

Situation 10. Historical society P is a section 501(c)(3) organization. Society P is located in the state capital. President G is the president of Society P and customarily acknowledges the presence of any public officials present during meetings. During the state gubernatorial race, Lieutenant Governor Y, a candidate, attends a meeting of the historical society. President G acknowledges the Lieutenant Governor's presence in his customary manner, saying, "We are happy to have joining us this evening Lieutenant Governor Y." President G makes no reference in his welcome to the Lieutenant Governor's candidacy or the election. Society P has not engaged in political campaign intervention as a result of President G's actions.

Situation 11. Chairman H is the chairman of the Board of Hospital Q, a section 501(c)(3) organization. Hospital Q is building a new wing. Chairman H invites Congressman Z, the representative for the district containing Hospital Q, to attend the groundbreaking ceremony for the new wing. Congressman Z is running for reelection at the time. Chairman H makes no reference in her introduction to Congressman Z's candidacy or the election. Congressman Z also makes no reference to his candidacy or the election and does not do any political campaign fundraising while at Hospital Q. Hospital Q has not intervened in a political campaign.

Situation 12. University X is a section 501(c)(3) organization. X publishes an alumni newsletter on a regular basis. Individual alumni are invited to send in updates about themselves which are printed in each edition of the newsletter. After receiving an update letter from Alumnus Q, X prints the following: "Alumnus Q, class of 'XX' is running for mayor of Metropolis." The newsletter does not contain any reference to this election or to Alumnus Q's candidacy other than this statement of fact. University X has not intervened in a political campaign.

Situation 13. Mayor G attends a concert performed by Symphony S, a section 501(c)(3) organization, in City Park. The concert is free and open to the public. Mayor G is a candidate for reelection, and the concert takes place after the primary and before the general election. During the concert, the chairman of S's board addresses the crowd and says, "I am pleased to see Mayor G here tonight. Without his support, these free concerts in City Park would not be possible. We will need his help if we want these concerts to continue next year so please support Mayor G in November as he has supported us." As a result of these remarks, Symphony S has engaged in political campaign intervention.

Issue Advocacy vs. Political Campaign Intervention

Section 501(c)(3) organizations may take positions on public policy issues, including issues that divide candidates in an election for public office. However, section 501(c)(3) organizations must avoid any issue advocacy that functions as political campaign intervention. Even if a statement does not expressly tell an audience to vote for or against a specific candidate, an organization delivering the statement is at risk of violating the political campaign intervention prohibition if there is any message favoring or opposing a candidate. A statement can identify a candidate not only by stating the candidate's name but also by other means such as showing a picture of the candidate, referring to political party affiliations, or other distinctive features of a candidate's platform or biography. All the facts and circumstances need to be considered to determine if the advocacy is political campaign intervention.

Key factors in determining whether a communication results in political campaign intervention include the following:

- Whether the statement identifies one or more candidates for a given public office;

- Whether the statement expresses approval or disapproval for one or more candidates' positions and/or actions;

- Whether the statement is delivered close in time to the election;

- Whether the statement makes reference to voting or an election;

- Whether the issue addressed in the communication has been raised as an issue distinguishing candidates for a given office;

- Whether the communication is part of an ongoing series of communications by the organization on the same issue that are made independent of the timing of any election; and

● Whether the timing of the communication and identification of the candidate are related to a non-electoral event such as a scheduled vote on specific legislation by an officeholder who also happens to be a candidate for public office.

A communication is particularly at risk of political campaign intervention when it makes reference to candidates or voting in a specific upcoming election. Nevertheless, the communication must still be considered in context before arriving at any conclusions.

Situation 14. University *O*, a section 501(c)(3) organization, prepares and finances a full page newspaper advertisement that is published in several large circulation newspapers in State *V* shortly before an election in which Senator *C* is a candidate for nomination in a party primary. Senator *C* represents State *V* in the United States Senate. The advertisement states that S. 24, a pending bill in the United States Senate, would provide additional opportunities for State *V* residents to attend college, but Senator *C* has opposed similar measures in the past. The advertisement ends with the statement "Call or write Senator *C* to tell him to vote for S. 24." Educational issues have not been raised as an issue distinguishing Senator *C* from any opponent. S. 24 is scheduled for a vote in the United States Senate before the election, soon after the date that the advertisement is published in the newspapers. Even though the advertisement appears shortly before the election and identifies Senator *C*'s position on the issue as contrary to *O*'s position, University *O* has not violated the political campaign intervention prohibition because the advertisement does not mention the election or the candidacy of Senator *C*, education issues have not been raised as distinguishing Senator *C* from any opponent, and the timing of the advertisement and the identification of Senator *C* are directly related to the specifically identified legislation University *O* is supporting and appears immediately before the United States Senate is scheduled to vote on that particular legislation. The candidate identified, Senator C, is an officeholder who is in a position to vote on the legislation.

Situation 15. Organization R, a section 501(c)(3) organization that educates the public about the need for improved public education, prepares and finances a radio advertisement urging an increase in state funding for public education in State *X*, which requires a legislative appropriation. Governor *E* is the governor of State *X*. The radio advertisement is first broadcast on several radio stations in State *X* beginning shortly before an election in which Governor *E* is a candidate for re-election. The advertisement is not part of an ongoing series of substantially similar advocacy communications by Organization *R* on the same issue. The advertisement cites numerous statistics indicating that public education in State *X* is under funded. While the advertisement does not say anything about Governor *E*'s position on funding for public education, it ends with "Tell Governor *E* what you think about our under-funded schools." In public appearances and campaign literature, Governor *E*'s opponent has made funding of public education an issue in the campaign by focusing on Governor *E*'s veto of an income tax increase the previous year to increase funding of public education. At the time the advertisement is broadcast, no legislative vote or other major legislative activity is scheduled in the State X legislature on state funding of public education. Organization R has violated the political campaign prohibition because the advertisement identifies Governor E, appears shortly before an election in which Governor E is a candidate, is not part of an ongoing series of substantially similar advocacy communications by Organization R on the same issue, is not timed to coincide with a non election event such as a legislative vote or other major legislative action on that issue, and takes a position on an issue that the opponent has used to distinguish himself from Governor E.

Situation 16. Candidate A and Candidate B are candidates for the state senate in District W of State X. The issue of State X funding for a new mass transit project in District W is a prominent issue in the campaign. Both candidates have spoken out on the issue. Candidate A supports funding the new mass transit project. Candidate B opposes the project and supports State X funding for highway improvements instead. P is the executive director of C, a section 501(c)(3) organization that promotes community development in District W. At C' s annual fundraising dinner in District W, which takes place in the month before the election in State X, P gives a lengthy speech about community development issues including the transportation issues. P does not mention the name of any candidate or any political party. However, at the conclusion of the speech, P makes the following statement, "For those of you who care about quality of life in District W and the growing traffic congestion, there is a very important choice coming up next month. We need new mass transit. More highway funding will not make a difference. You have the power to relieve the congestion and improve your quality of life in District W. Use that power when you go to the polls and cast your vote in the election for your state senator." C has violated the political campaign intervention as a result of P's remarks at C's official function shortly before the election, in which P referred to the upcoming election after stating a position on an issue that is a prominent issue in a campaign that distinguishes the candidates.

Business Activity

The question of whether an activity constitutes participation or intervention in a political campaign may also arise in the context of a business activity of the organization, such as selling or renting of mailing lists, the leasing of office space, or the acceptance of paid political advertising. In this context, some of the factors to be considered in determining whether the organization has engaged in political campaign intervention include the following:

- Whether the good, service or facility is available to candidates in the same election on an equal basis,

- Whether the good, service, or facility is available only to candidates and not to the general public,

- Whether the fees charged to candidates are at the organization's customary and usual rates, and

● Whether the activity is an ongoing activity of the organization or whether it is conducted only for a particular candidate.

Situation 17. Museum K is a section 501(c)(3) organization. It owns an historic building that has a large hall suitable for hosting dinners and receptions. For several years, Museum K has made the hall available for rent to members of the public. Standard fees are set for renting the hall based on the number of people in attendance, and a number of different organizations have rented the hall. Museum K rents the hall on a first come, first served basis. Candidate P rents Museum K's social hall for a fundraising dinner. Candidate P's campaign pays the standard fee for the dinner. Museum K is not involved in political campaign intervention as a result of renting the hall to Candidate P for use as the site of a campaign fundraising dinner.

Situation 18. Theater L is a section 501(c)(3) organization. It maintains a mailing list of all of its subscribers and contributors. Theater L has never rented its mailing list to a third party. Theater L is approached by the campaign committee of Candidate Q, who supports increased funding for the arts. Candidate Q's campaign committee offers to rent Theater L's mailing list for a fee that is comparable to fees charged by other similar organizations. Theater L rents its mailing list to Candidate Q's campaign committee. Theater L declines similar requests from campaign committees of other candidates. Theater L has intervened in a political campaign.

Web Sites

The Internet has become a widely used communications tool. Section 501(c)(3) organizations use their own web sites to disseminate statements and information. They also routinely link their web sites to web sites maintained by other organizations as a way of providing additional information that the organizations believe is useful or relevant to the public.

A web site is a form of communication. If an organization posts something on its web site that favors or opposes a candidate for public office, the organization will be treated the same as if it distributed printed material, oral statements or broadcasts that favored or opposed a candidate.

An organization has control over whether it establishes a link to another site. When an organization establishes a link to another web site, the organization is responsible for the consequences of establishing and maintaining that link, even if the organization does not have control over the content of the linked site. Because the linked content may change over time, an organization may reduce the risk of political campaign intervention by monitoring the linked content and adjusting the links accordingly.

Links to candidate-related material, by themselves, do not necessarily constitute political campaign intervention. All the facts and circumstances must be taken into account when assessing whether a link produces that result. The facts and circumstances to be considered include, but are not limited to, the context for the link on the organization's web site, whether all candidates are represented, any exempt purpose served by offering the link, and the directness of the links between the organization's web site and the web page that contains material favoring or opposing a candidate for public office.

Situation 19. M, a section 501(c)(3) organization, maintains a web site and posts an unbiased, nonpartisan voter guide that is prepared consistent with the principles discussed in Rev. Rul. 78–248. For each candidate covered in the voter guide, M includes a link to that candidate's official campaign web site. The links to the candidate web sites are presented on a consistent neutral basis for each candidate, with text saying "For more information on Candidate X, you may consult [URL]." M has not intervened in a political campaign because the links are provided for the exempt purpose of educating voters and are presented in a neutral, unbiased manner that includes all candidates for a particular office.

Situation 20. Hospital N, a section 501(c)(3) organization, maintains a web site that includes such information as medical staff listings, directions to Hospital N, and descriptions of its specialty health programs, major research projects, and other community outreach programs. On one page of the web site, Hospital N describes its treatment program for a particular disease. At the end of the page, it includes a section of links to other web sites titled "More Information." These links include links to other hospitals that have treatment programs for this disease, research organizations seeking cures for that disease, and articles about treatment programs. This section includes a link to an article on the web site of O, a major national newspaper, praising Hospital N's treatment program for the disease. The page containing the article on O's web site contains no reference to any candidate or election and has no direct links to candidate or election information. Elsewhere on O's web site, there is a page displaying editorials that O has published. Several of the editorials endorse candidates in an election that has not yet occurred. Hospital N has not intervened in a political campaign by maintaining the link to the article on O's web site because the link is provided for the exempt purpose of educating the public about Hospital N's programs and neither the context for the link, nor the relationship between Hospital N and O nor the arrangement of the links going from Hospital N's web site to the endorsement on O's web site indicate that Hospital N was favoring or opposing any candidate.

Situation 21. Church P, a section 501(c)(3) organization, maintains a web site that includes such information as biographies of its ministers, times of services, details of community outreach programs, and activities of members of its congregation. B, a member of the congregation of Church P, is running for a seat on the town council. Shortly before the election, Church P posts the following message on its web site, "Lend your support to B, your fellow parishioner, in Tuesday's election for town council." Church P has intervened in a political campaign on behalf of B.

HOLDINGS

In situations 2, 4, 6, 9, 13, 15, 16, 18 and 21, the organization intervened in a political campaign within the meaning of section 501(c)(3).

In situations 1, 3, 5, 7, 8, 10, 11, 12, 14, 17, 19 and 20, the organization did not intervene in a political campaign within the meaning of section 501(c)(3).

Branch Ministries v. Rossotti

United States Court of Appeals, District of Columbia Circuit, 2000.
211 F.3d 137.

■ Buckley, Senior Judge:

Four days before the 1992 presidential election, Branch Ministries, a tax-exempt church, placed full-page advertisements in two newspapers in which it urged Christians not to vote for then-presidential candidate Bill Clinton because of his positions on certain moral issues. The Internal Revenue Service concluded that the placement of the advertisements violated the statutory restrictions on organizations exempt from taxation and, for the first time in its history, it revoked a bona fide church's tax-exempt status because of its involvement in politics. Branch Ministries and its pastor, Dan Little, challenge the revocation on the grounds that (1) the Service acted beyond its statutory authority, (2) the revocation violated its right to the free exercise of religion guaranteed by the First Amendment and the Religious Freedom Restoration Act, and (3) it was the victim of selective prosecution in violation of the Fifth Amendment. Because these objections are without merit, we affirm the district court's grant of summary judgment to the Service.

I. BACKGROUND

A.   Taxation of Churches

The Internal Revenue Code ("Code") exempts certain organizations from taxation, including those organized and operated for religious purposes, provided that they do not engage in certain activities, including involvement in "any political campaign on behalf of (or in opposition to) any candidate for public office." 26 U.S.C. § 501(a), (c)(3) (1994). Contributions to such organizations are also deductible from the donating taxpayer's taxable income. Id. § 170(a). Although most organizations seeking tax-exempt status are required to apply to the Internal Revenue Service ("IRS" or "Service") for an advance determination that they meet the requirements of section 501(c)(3), id. § 508(a), a church may simply hold itself out as tax exempt and receive the benefits of that status without applying for advance recognition from the IRS. Id. § 508(c)(1)(A).

* * *

The unique treatment churches receive in the Internal Revenue Code is further reflected in special restrictions on the IRS's ability to investigate the tax status of a church. The Church Audit Procedures Act ("CAPA") sets out the circumstances under which the IRS may initiate an investigation of a church and the procedures it is required to follow in such an investigation. 26 U.S.C. § 7611. Upon a "reasonable belief" by a high-level

Treasury official that a church may not be exempt from taxation under section 501, the IRS may begin a "church tax inquiry." Id. § 7611(a). A church tax inquiry is defined, rather circularly, as any inquiry to a church (other than an examination) to serve as a basis for determining whether a church—(A) is exempt from tax under section 501(a) by reason of its status as a church, or (B) is ... engaged in activities which may be subject to taxation.... Id. § 7611(h)(2). If the IRS is not able to resolve its concerns through a church tax inquiry, it may proceed to the second level of investigation: a "church tax examination." In such an examination, the IRS may obtain and review the church's records or examine its activities "to determine whether [the] organization claiming to be a church is a church for any period." Id. § 7611(b)(1)(A), (B).

B.   Factual and Procedural History

Branch Ministries, Inc. operates the Church at Pierce Creek ("Church"), a Christian church located in Binghamton, New York. In 1983, the Church requested and received a letter from the IRS recognizing its tax-exempt status. On October 30, 1992, four days before the presidential election, the Church placed full-page advertisements in USA Today and the Washington Times. Each bore the headline "Christians Beware" and asserted that then-Governor Clinton's positions concerning abortion, homosexuality, and the distribution of condoms to teenagers in schools violated Biblical precepts. The following appeared at the bottom of each advertisement: This advertisement was co-sponsored by the Church at Pierce Creek, Daniel J. Little, Senior Pastor, and by churches and concerned Christians nationwide. Tax deductible donations for this advertisement gladly accepted. Make donations to: The Church at Pierce Creek. [mailing address]. * * *

The advertisements did not go unnoticed. They produced hundreds of contributions to the Church from across the country and were mentioned in a New York Times article and an Anthony Lewis column which stated that the sponsors of the advertisement had almost certainly violated the Internal Revenue Code. Peter Applebome, Religious Right Intensifies Campaign for Bush, N.Y. Times, Oct. 31, 1992, at A1; Anthony Lewis, Tax Exempt Politics?, N.Y. Times, Dec. 1, 1992, at A15.

The advertisements also came to the attention of the Regional Commissioner of the IRS, who notified the Church on November 20, 1992 that he had authorized a church tax inquiry based on "a reasonable belief ... that you may not be tax-exempt or that you may be liable for tax" due to political activities and expenditures. Letter from Cornelius J. Coleman, IRS Regional Commissioner, to The Church at Pierce Creek (Nov. 20, 1992), reprinted in App. at Tab 5, Ex. F. The Church denied that it had engaged in any prohibited political activity and declined to provide the IRS with certain information the Service had requested. On February 11, 1993, the IRS informed the Church that it was beginning a church tax examination. Following two unproductive meetings between the parties, the IRS revoked the Church's section 501(c)(3) tax-exempt status on January 19, 1995, citing the newspaper advertisements as prohibited intervention in a political campaign.

The Church and Pastor Little (collectively, "Church") commenced this lawsuit soon thereafter. This had the effect of suspending the revocation of the Church's tax exemption until the district court entered its judgment in this case. See 26 U.S.C. § 7428(c). The Church challenged the revocation of its tax-exempt status, alleging that the IRS had no authority to revoke its tax exemption, that the revocation violated its right to free speech and to freely exercise its religion under the First Amendment and the Religious Freedom Restoration Act of 1993, 42 U.S.C. § 2000bb (1994) ("RFRA"), and that the IRS engaged in selective prosecution in violation of the Equal Protection Clause of the Fifth Amendment. After allowing discovery on the Church's selective prosecution claim, Branch Ministries, Inc. v. Richardson, 970 F.Supp. 11 (D.D.C.1997), the district court granted summary judgment in favor of the IRS. Branch Ministries, Inc. v. Rossotti, 40 F.Supp.2d 15 (D.D.C.1999).

The Church filed a timely appeal, and we have jurisdiction pursuant to 28 U.S.C. § 1291. We review summary judgment decisions de novo, * * *.

II. ANALYSIS

The Church advances a number of arguments in support of its challenges to the revocation. We examine only those that warrant analysis.

A.   The Statutory Authority of the IRS

The Church argues that, under the Internal Revenue Code, the IRS does not have the statutory authority to revoke the tax-exempt status of a bona fide church. It reasons as follows: section 501(c)(3) refers to tax-exempt status for religious organizations, not churches; section 508, on the other hand, specifically exempts "churches" from the requirement of applying for advance recognition of tax-exempt status, id. § 508(c)(1)(A); therefore, according to the Church, its tax-exempt status is derived not from section 501(c)(3), but from the lack of any provision in the Code for the taxation of churches. The Church concludes from this that it is not subject to taxation and that the IRS is therefore powerless to place conditions upon or to remove its tax-exempt status as a church.

We find this argument more creative than persuasive. The simple answer, of course, is that whereas not every religious organization is a church, every church is a religious organization. More to the point, irrespective of whether it was required to do so, the Church applied to the IRS for an advance determination of its tax-exempt status. The IRS granted that recognition and now seeks to withdraw it. CAPA gives the IRS this power. * * *

[The court found that the IRS had statutory authority under I.R.C. § 7611 to revoke the tax exemption of a church that violated the limitations on political campaign activity in § 501(c)(3) and then turned to the church's free exercise challenges. Eds.]

B. First Amendment Claims and the RFRA

The Church claims that the revocation of its exemption violated its right to freely exercise its religion under both the First Amendment and the RFRA. To sustain its claim under either the Constitution or the statute, the Church must first establish that its free exercise right has been substantially burdened. * * * We conclude that the Church has failed to meet this test.

The Church asserts, first, that a revocation would threaten its existence. See Affidavit of Dan Little dated July 31, 1995. ("The Church at Pierce Creek will have to close due to the revocation of its tax exempt status, and the inability of congregants to deduct their contributions from their taxes."). The Church maintains that a loss of its tax-exempt status will not only make its members reluctant to contribute the funds essential to its survival, but may obligate the Church itself to pay taxes.

The Church appears to assume that the withdrawal of a conditional privilege for failure to meet the condition is in itself an unconstitutional burden on its free exercise right. This is true, however, only if the receipt of the privilege (in this case the tax exemption) is conditioned upon conduct proscribed by a religious faith, or ... denie[d] ... because of conduct mandated by religious belief, thereby putting substantial pressure on an adherent to modify his behavior and to violate his beliefs. Jimmy Swaggart Ministries, 493 U.S. at 391–92 (internal quotation marks and citation omitted). Although its advertisements reflected its religious convictions on certain questions of morality, the Church does not maintain that a withdrawal from electoral politics would violate its beliefs. The sole effect of the loss of the tax exemption will be to decrease the amount of money available to the Church for its religious practices. The Supreme Court has declared, however, that such a burden "is not constitutionally significant." Id. at 391; see also Hernandez v. Commissioner, 490 U.S. 680, 700, 109 S.Ct. 2136, 104 L.Ed.2d 766 (1989) (the "contention that an incrementally larger tax burden interferes with [ ] religious activities ... knows no limitation").

In actual fact, even this burden is overstated. Because of the unique treatment churches receive under the Internal Revenue Code, the impact of the revocation is likely to be more symbolic than substantial. As the IRS confirmed at oral argument, if the Church does not intervene in future political campaigns, it may hold itself out as a 501(c)(3) organization and receive all the benefits of that status. All that will have been lost, in that event, is the advance assurance of deductibility in the event a donor should be audited. See 26 U.S.C. § 508(c)(1)(A); Rev. Proc. 82–39 § 2.03. Contributions will remain tax deductible as long as donors are able to establish that the Church meets the requirements of section 501(c)(3).

Nor does the revocation necessarily make the Church liable for the payment of taxes. As the IRS explicitly represented in its brief and reiterated at oral argument, the revocation of the exemption does not convert bona fide donations into income taxable to the Church. See 26 U.S.C. § 102 ("Gross income does not include the value of property acquired by gift...."). Furthermore, we know of no authority, and counsel provided none, to prevent the Church from reapplying for a prospective determination of its tax-exempt status and regaining the advance assurance of deductibility—provided, of course, that it renounces future involvement in political campaigns.

We also reject the Church's argument that it is substantially burdened because it has no alternate means by which to communicate its sentiments about candidates for public office. In Regan v. Taxation With Representation, 461 U.S. 540, 552–53, 103 S.Ct. 1997, 76 L.Ed.2d 129 (1983) (Blackmun, J., concurring), three members of the Supreme Court stated that the availability of such an alternate means of communication is essential to the constitutionality of section 501(c)(3)'s restrictions on lobbying. The Court subsequently confirmed that this was an accurate description of its holding. See FCC v. League of Women Voters, 468 U.S. 364, 400, 104 S.Ct. 3106, 82 L.Ed.2d 278 (1984). In Regan, the concurring justices noted that "TWR may use its present § 501(c)(3) organization for its nonlobbying activities and may create a § 501(c)(4) affiliate to pursue its charitable goals through lobbying." 461 U.S. at 552.

The Church has such an avenue available to it. As was the case with TWR, the Church may form a related organization under section 501(c)(4) of the Code. See 26 U.S.C. § 501(c)(4) (tax exemption for "[c]ivic leagues or organizations not organized for profit but operated exclusively for the promotion of social welfare"). Such organizations are exempt from taxation; but unlike their section 501(c)(3) counterparts, contributions to them are not deductible. See 26 U.S.C. § 170(c); see also Regan, 461 U.S. at 543, 552–53. Although a section 501(c)(4) organization is also subject to the ban on intervening in political campaigns, see 26 C.F.R. § 1.501(c)(4)–1(a)(2)(ii) (1999), it may form a political action committee ("PAC") that would be free to participate in political campaigns. Id. § 1.527–6(f), (g) ("[A]n organization described in section 501(c) that is exempt from taxation under section 501(a) may, [if it is not a section 501(c)(3) organization], establish and maintain such a separate segregated fund to receive contributions and make expenditures in a political campaign.").

At oral argument, counsel for the Church doggedly maintained that there can be no "Church at Pierce Creek PAC." True, it may not itself create a PAC; but as we have pointed out, the Church can initiate a series of steps that will provide an alternate means of political communication that will satisfy the standards set by the concurring justices in *Regan*. Should the Church proceed to do so, however, it must understand that the related 501(c)(4) organization must be separately incorporated; and it must maintain records that will demonstrate that tax-deductible contributions to the Church have not been used to support the political activities conducted by the 501(c)(4) organization's political action arm. See 26 U.S.C. § 527(f)(3); 26 C.F.R. § 1.527–6(e), (f).

That the Church cannot use its tax-free dollars to fund such a PAC unquestionably passes constitutional muster. The Supreme Court has consistently held that, absent invidious discrimination, "Congress has not violated [an organization's] First Amendment rights by declining to subsidize its First Amendment activities." Regan, 461 U.S. at 548; see also Cammarano v. United States, 358 U.S. 498, 513, 79 S.Ct. 524, 3 L.Ed.2d 462 (1959) ("Petitioners are not being denied a tax deduction because they engage in constitutionally protected activities, but are simply being required to pay for those activities entirely out of their own pockets, as everyone else engaging in similar activities is required to do under the provisions of the Internal Revenue Code.").

Because the Church has failed to demonstrate that its free exercise rights have been substantially burdened, we do not reach its arguments that section 501(c)(3) does not serve a compelling government interest or, if it is indeed compelling, that revocation of its tax exemption was not the least restrictive means of furthering that interest.

Nor does the Church succeed in its claim that the IRS has violated its First Amendment free speech rights by engaging in viewpoint discrimination. The restrictions imposed by section 501(c)(3) are viewpoint neutral; they prohibit intervention in favor of all candidates for public office by all tax-exempt organizations, regardless of candidate, party, or viewpoint. Cf. Regan, 461 U.S. at 550–51 (upholding denial of tax deduction for lobbying activities, in spite of allowance of such deduction for veteran's groups).

C.   Selective Prosecution (Fifth Amendment)

The Church alleges that the IRS violated the Equal Protection Clause of the Fifth Amendment by engaging in selective prosecution. In support of its claim, the Church has submitted several hundred pages of newspaper excerpts reporting political campaign activities in, or by the pastors of, other churches that have retained their tax-exempt status. These include reports of explicit endorsements of Democratic candidates by clergymen as well as many instances in which favored candidates have been invited to address congregations from the pulpit. The Church complains that despite this widespread and widely reported involvement by other churches in political campaigns, it is the only one to have ever had its tax-exempt status revoked for engaging in political activity. It attributes this alleged discrimination to the Service's political bias.

To establish selective prosecution, the Church must "prove that (1) [it] was singled out for prosecution from among others similarly situated and (2) that [the] prosecution was improperly motivated, i.e., based on race, religion or another arbitrary classification." United States v. Washington, 705 F.2d 489, 494 (D.C.Cir.1983). This burden is a demanding one because "in the absence of clear evidence to the contrary, courts presume that [government prosecutors] have properly discharged their official duties." United States v. Armstrong, 517 U.S. 456, 464, 116 S.Ct. 1480, 134 L.Ed.2d 687 (1996) (internal quotation marks and citation omitted).

At oral argument, counsel for the IRS conceded that if some of the church-sponsored political activities cited by the Church were accurately reported, they were in violation of section 501(c)(3) and could have resulted in the revocation of those churches' tax-exempt status. But even if the Service could have revoked their tax exemptions, the Church has failed to establish selective prosecution because it has failed to demonstrate that it was similarly situated to any of those other churches. None of the reported activities involved the placement of advertisements in newspapers with nationwide circulations opposing a candidate and soliciting tax deductible contributions to defray their cost. As we have stated, [i]f . . . there was no one to whom defendant could be compared in order to resolve the question of [prosecutorial] selection, then it follows that defendant has failed to make out one of the elements of its case. Discrimination cannot exist in a vacuum; it can be found only in the unequal treatment of people in similar circumstances. * * *

Because the Church has failed to establish that it was singled out for prosecution from among others who were similarly situated, we need not examine whether the IRS was improperly motivated in undertaking this prosecution.

III.   CONCLUSION

For the foregoing reasons, we find that the revocation of the Church's tax-exempt status neither violated the Constitution nor exceeded the IRS's statutory authority. The judgment of the district court is therefore

Affirmed.

NOTE: CHURCHES AND POLITICAL CAMPAIGN ACTIVITY: RECENT SKIRMISHES AND PROPOSED REFORMS

A Strategically Timed Sermon. On October 31, 2004, the Sunday preceding the 2004 Presidential election, the Reverend Dr. George F. Regas, Rector Emeritus of All Saints Church in Pasadena, California, preached a sermon entitled "If Jesus Debated Senator Kerry and President Bush." All Saints is an Episcopal congregation of 3,500 members with a longstanding liberal anti-war tradition. Reverend Regas began by telling congregants that "Jesus does win. And I don't intend to tell you how to vote," and "[g]ood people of profound faith will be for either George Bush or John Kerry for reasons deeply rooted in their faith." He then joked that when he was rector, some parishioners described his modus operandi as: "We can just agree to disagree. You go your way and I'll go God's way."

Reverend Regas's sermon imagined what would be said if Jesus were debating the 2004 Presidential candidates. He speculated that Jesus would view the war in Iraq as "the most extreme form of terrorism," and would ask the candidates "[w]hy is so little mentioned about the poor" because "poverty is a religious issue and it is central to the presidential election." He surmised that Jesus's heart would break at tax cuts for the wealthiest Americans while the poor were getting poorer and the health care crisis was getting worse. On the issue of abortion, Reverend Regas imagined that Jesus would say: "Shame on all those conservative politicians in the nation's Congress and in state legislatures who have for years 'so proudly proclaimed their love for children when they were only fetuses—but ignored their needs after they were born.' "

The sermon concluded: "When you go into the voting booth on Tuesday, take with you all that you know about Jesus, the peacemaker. Take all that Jesus means to you. Then vote your deepest values. Amen."

The full text of the sermon is available on the All Saints Church web site at http://www.allsaints-pas.org/sermons-and-transcripts.

On the next day, the Los Angeles Times reported Reverend Regas's sermon along with these other political messages from houses of worship throughout the country:

- An evangelical church in Ohio distributed Christian Coalition voters guides, which stated they were "educational" and not to be construed as an endorsement of any candidate or party.

- A Catholic church bulletin in Wisconsin urged parishioners to vote and distributed voters guides not naming either candidate but delivering a message that clearly opposed controversial positions taken by Senator Kerry.

- The pastor of an African–American congregation in New Mexico told congregants to let their voice be heard and suggested President Bush's faith did not outweigh the many problems of his presidency.

- The pastor of a large evangelical church in Colorado exhorted congregants to vote and reportedly said: "If evangelicals vote, then Bush will win. If they don't, then Kerry could win."

Josh Getlin, The Race for the White House: Pulpits Ring With Election Messages, L.A. Times, Nov. 1, 2004, at A1.

Six months after the election, the IRS notified All Saints Church that it was conducting a tax inquiry, expressed concerns about Reverend Regas's sermon, and requested answers to specific questions about the church's operations. The examination was part of a broader IRS investigation of political campaign activities of charities during the 2004 election cycle. The church hired able tax counsel, who disagreed that the "guest sermon" of a former pastor could jeopardize the church's exemption. He added that, in any event, the sermon did not endorse or oppose any candidates, did not officially represent the church's position, but rather represented the speaker's personal opinion while reflecting the church's longstanding core moral values during a period of worship.

The revelation that All Saints Church was being threatened with loss of exemption led to charges that conservative churches also had engaged in improper campaign activity. Particular targets were two evangelical churches in Ohio which were accused of using their facilities to promote President Bush and the Republican candidate for governor through voter registration drives, invitation of conservative candidates to church functions, and participation in partisan political events. See Stephanie Strom, Group Seeks I.R.S. Inquiry of 2 Ohio Churches Accused of Improper Campaigning, N.Y. Times, Jan. 16, 2006, at A9.

The All Saints Church examination ended in September 2007. The IRS announced that although it found the church to have violated the political campaign limitations, it decided not to revoke the church's exemption or impose any excise tax penalty. In other words, never mind—but don't do it again. The church demanded an explanation and apology but neither was extended. See Press Release, All Saints Church, Pasadena Demands Correction and Apology from IRS (Sept. 23, 2007), available at http://www.all saints-pas.org/site/PageServer?pagename=IRS_Exam_splash.

Assume you were a lawyer and board member of All Saints Church and were asked to review Reverend Regas's sermon before it was delivered and advise the church whether the sermon constituted prohibited political campaign activity. What's your advice? Has the IRS gone too far in investigating the campaign activities of churches, or is it obligated to do so? Has the IRS not gone far enough?

The 2008 Presidential Campaign. The 2008 Presidential campaign brought with it the inevitable allegations and occasional IRS investigations of impermissible political activity by churches. A widely reported probe involved the United Church of Christ's 50th anniversary General Synod, which was held in June 2007 at the Hartford (Ct.) Civic Center. The conclave was attended by an estimated 10,000 church members and included an address by Presidential candidate Barack Obama, who reportedly discussed his "personal spiritual journey" along with his positions on various issues such as health care. Several news articles reported that at least forty Obama volunteers staffed campaign tables promoting his campaign outside the convention center. In February 2008, the IRS requested the church to respond to a list of specific questions about the event. Several months later, it concluded that the church had not violated the political campaign limitations in § 501(c)(3), noting that Senator Obama attended the event as a church member, not a candidate, and the church was careful to tell those in attendance not to engage in any political activities. The campaign volunteers were found to be outside the church's control. For press reports, see Suzanne Sataline, IRS Probes Church Over Obama Speech, Wall St. J., Feb. 27, 2008, at A10; Suzanne Sataline, IRS Clears Obama's Church, Wall St. J., May 22, 2008, at A6.

On another front, the Alliance Defense Fund, a conservative advocacy group, enlisted ministers to defy the political campaign limitation during the 2008 Presidential campaign by preaching from the pulpit on the moral qualifications of candidates for public office. The Fund's goal was to create a test case to challenge the constitutionality of the limitation insofar as it applied to churches. For press coverage of complaints urging the IRS to revoke exemptions of participating churches, see Simon Brown, IRS Must Act on Pulpit Freedom Sunday, Former Official Says, 62 Exempt Org. Tax. Rev. 146 (2009).

Brushfire at Liberty University. In May 2009, Liberty University in Lynchburg, Virginia, which was founded by the Reverend Jerry Falwell and his son, reportedly told the student Democratic club that it was no longer eligible for university recognition and would cease to receive funding from student activity fees. The basis for this decision was that the goals of the Democratic party were contrary to Liberty's evangelical Christian outlook.

Americans United for the Separation of Church and State reacted promptly, asking the IRS to revoke Liberty's tax-exempt status because of impermissible political campaign activity. Liberty then instituted a new policy classifying all political clubs as "unofficial" and thus ineligible for funding but able to use the university's name and facilities as long as any campus events were "appropriate and compatible" with Liberty's Christian mission. This compromise was accepted by the Liberty University College Democrats, and no IRS action is expected.

Proposed Legislation. Almost annually, members of Congress have introduced legislation to allow churches to engage in limited political campaign activity without jeopardizing their tax exemptions. H.R. 235, proposed in 2003 by Rep. Walter B. Jones (R–N.C.), would permit political campaign activity by churches in the form of homilies, sermons, teaching dialectics, or other representations made during religious services or gatherings. Earlier proposals would have allowed churches to participate in political campaigns in any manner provided the participation was not a substantial part of their activities. An alternative bill would have permitted religious organizations to spend up to 20 percent of their budget on lobbying and 5% on political campaign activity. See Fred Stokeld, Bill Allowing Limited Church Political Activity Stirs Debate, 41 Exempt Org. Tax Rev. 14 (2003).

In 2004, an amendment to a House tax bill (H.R. 4520) would have given clergy and churches more leeway than other § 501(c)(3) organizations to endorse candidates and otherwise engage in political campaign activity. The Safe Harbor for Churches provision generally would have permitted members of the clergy to endorse candidates if they made it clear they were acting as private citizens and did not use church funds or facilities, and would have allowed clergy to make up to two deliberate and three unintentional political endorsements within the house of worship in a calendar year without any penalty. At about the same time, it was reported that President Bush's reelection campaign was seeking to enlist members of friendly conservative congregations to distribute campaign information at their places of worship. The predictable outcry followed (the proposal and its timing "simply reeks to high heaven, literally," said Rev. Barry Lynn, executive director of Americans for the Separation of Church and State). See David B. Kirkpatrick, Bush Appeal to Churches Seeking Help Raises Doubt, N.Y. Times, July 2, 2004, at A15. The safe harbor provision ultimately was dropped from the final bill approved by the House. Subsequent efforts to create a statutory exception for churches have been unsuccessful. Should Congress enact a law precluding the IRS from enforcing the political activity ban with respect to sermons inside a house of worship or internal communications from church leaders to members?

NOTES

1. *Who's a Candidate?* "Candidates" for public office generally include individuals offering themselves or proposed by others for national,

state, or local elective public office. Treas. Reg. § 1.501(c)(3)–1(c)(3)(iii). The election need not be contested nor must it involve the participation of political parties. Rev. Rul. 67–71, 1967–1 C.B. 125. An individual who declares his or her intention to run for public office is clearly a candidate, and the term also was construed in the *Christian Echoes* case to include incumbents who had not formally announced their candidacy but were likely to do so. But a person's status as a prominent public figure does not automatically equate to "candidate" status despite public speculation about a future run for office. See Tech. Adv. Mem. 9130008. Individuals nominated for appointment to a judgeship are not candidates. Notice 89–76, 1988–2 C.B. 392.

2. *What's Nonpartisan?* The IRS permits § 501(c)(3) organizations to engage in nonpartisan activities such as voter education and get-out-the-vote drives. "Nonpartisan" has never been clearly defined, and attempts at a bright line test are probably futile. At the very least, an organization may not expressly advocate for or against particular candidates or parties. Voter registration efforts, however, are considered nonpartisan even if they are targeted at groups (e.g., minorities, low-income, the homeless) that are likely to favor a particular political party. But registration drives apparently are partisan if they target people with a viewpoint on a particular issue (e.g., pro-life or fiscal conservative). Much of the law here is anecdotal.

3. *Rating Candidates.* The political campaign limits extend to the rating of candidates for elective judgeships, even if the election is nonpartisan and the rating activity is conducted by a politically neutral local bar association to educate the public. See Association of the Bar of the City of New York v. Commissioner, 858 F.2d 876 (2d Cir.1988), where the court held that the term "candidate for public office" includes anyone who is running in an election even if no political parties are involved.

4. *Excise Taxes on Political Expenditures.* Section 4955 authorizes the Service to impose excise tax penalties on certain political expenditures of § 501(c)(3) organizations. These taxes may be imposed in addition to or, perhaps in the case of isolated violations, in lieu of revocation. The § 4955 tax and two additional penalties (§ 6852 and § 7409) discussed below were enacted in response to publicized examples of § 501(c)(3) organizations operated under the guise of "think tanks" and used by candidates to support their political ambitions. See Subcomm. on Oversight, House Comm. on Ways and Means, Hearings on Lobbying and Political Activities of Tax–Exempt Organizations (1987). In addition, concerns had been raised about a § 501(c)(3) organization that used tax-deductible contributions to oppose the reelection of members of Congress who had not supported aid to the Nicaraguan Contras.

Section 4955 provides for a two-tiered excise tax on specified political expenditures of a § 501(c)(3) organization and on the agreement of its managers to make the expenditure. Two types of expenditures are targeted: (1) amounts paid or incurred to participate or intervene in a political campaign on behalf of any candidate for public office (sound familiar?), and (2) certain expenditures of organizations formed primarily for the purpose of promoting a person's candidacy, or used primarily for that purpose and effectively controlled by the candidate. I.R.C. § 4955(d). The first category tracks the § 501(c)(3) limitation. The second is more specific and includes amounts paid for a candidate's speeches and travel, expenses of conducting polls and surveys, advertising expenses, and any other expense that has the primary effect of promoting public recognition of the candidate. I.R.C. § 4955(d)(2). One wonders how an organization incurring any of the second type of taxable expenditure could have qualified for exemption under § 501(c)(3) in the first place!

The § 4955 initial excise tax on the organization is 10 percent of each forbidden political expenditure is imposed on the organization. A separate tax of 2½ percent of the expenditure (up to a ceiling of $5,000 per expenditure) is imposed on any organization "manager" who agrees to the expenditure knowing that it is impermissible—unless the manager's agreement is "not willful and is due to reasonable cause." Second-tier taxes (100 percent of the expenditure for the organization, 50 percent, with a $10,000 cap, on the knowing manager) are imposed if the political expenditure is not "corrected" within a specified period of time. "Correction" is accomplished by recovering part or all of the expenditure to the extent possible and by establishing safeguards to prevent future political expenditures. If all these steps are taken, even the first-tier taxes may be waived if the expenditure was not "willful and flagrant." I.R.C. § 4962(c). See Treas. Reg. § 53.4955–1(d), (e).

If the Service determines that an organization's violation of the limitation on political campaign expenditures is flagrant, it may immediately assess the excise taxes described above as well as any income taxes due and also may file an action in federal district court to enjoin or halt any future political expenditures by the organization if certain procedural requirements are met. I.R.C. § 6852; § 7409.

Although these new rules are designed to broaden the enforcement powers of the Service against wrongdoers, the excise taxes also might be applied as an alternative to revocation of exemption in the case of an organization that, perhaps inadvertently, makes political expenditures but is willing to undo the damage by recovering the funds (e.g., from the benefited candidate) and promising never to do it again. The Service, however, believes that § 4955 should not be used as an intermediate sanction except in very limited circumstances. See FY 1993 EO CPE, supra, at 417.

5. *For Further Reading.* Lloyd H. Mayer, Politics at the Pulpit: Tax Benefits, Substantial Burdens, and Institutional Free Exercise, 89 B.U.L.Rev. 1137 (2009); Laura Brown Chisolm, Sinking the Think Tanks Upstream: The Use and Misuse of Tax Exemption Law to Address the Use and Misuse of Tax–Exempt Organizations by Politicians, 51 U.Pitt.L.Rev. 577 (1990); Laura Brown Chisolm, Politics and Charity: A Proposal for Peaceful Coexistence, 58 Geo.Wash.L.Rev. 308 (1990); Deirdre Dessingue, Politics and the Pulpit 2008: A Guide to the Internal Revenue Code

Restrictions on the Political Activity of Religious Organizations (The Pew Forum on Religion & Public Life, 2008).

6.   THE § 501(c)(4) ALTERNATIVE

Internal Revenue Code: §§ 501(c)(4); 527.

A § 501(c)(3) organization may conclude that it is unable to meet its political objectives within the strictures of either the no substantial part test or § 501(h) expenditure test election. It also may wish to influence political campaigns or engage in more targeted issue advocacy. In those cases, the § 501(c)(3) charity often will form an affiliated § 501(c)(4) organization to conduct lobbying and other political activities. This type of dual structure was specifically noted by the Supreme Court in the *Taxation With Representation* case, supra p. 489, when it upheld the constitutionality of the lobbying limitations on § 501(c)(3) organizations.

Section 501(c)(4) confers tax-exempt status on "[c]ivic leagues and organizations not organized for profit but operated exclusively for the promotion of social welfare." See Chapter 9B, infra, at p. 910. As illustrated by Revenue Ruling 71–530, below, "social welfare" has been defined liberally to include virtually any charitable or educational cause that does not violate the law. More importantly, social welfare organizations qualify for exemption even if a substantial part of their activities consists of lobbying or political activities provided those activities are germane to the organization's social welfare purposes. The principal disadvantage of § 501(c)(4) status is that contributions to the organization are not tax-deductible.

Revenue Ruling 71–530

1971–2 Cum. Bull. 237.

Advice has been requested whether the nonprofit organization described below qualifies for exemption from Federal income tax under section 501(c)(4) of the Internal Revenue Code of 1954.

The organization was formed to promote the common good and welfare of the general public through the presentation, at legislative and administrative hearings on tax matters, of views directed at the improvement of the tax system. It selects individuals who the organization believes qualified to represent the interests of the general public in matters of tax policy. Such individuals include members of the tax bar, public finance economists, teachers of accounting and tax law, and other tax specialists. The organization alerts them as soon as tax issues arise in their fields of expertise, and aids them in preparing and publicizing their testimony. It receives contributions from the general public which are used to cover the cost of transporting witnesses, reproducing witness statements, publicizing recommendations on proposed tax changes, and the payment of salaries and other office expense.

Section 501(c)(4) of the Code provides for the exemption from Federal income tax of civic leagues or organizations not organized for profit but operated exclusively for the promotion of social welfare.

Section 1.501(c)(4)–1(a)(2) of the Income Tax Regulations provides that an organization is operated exclusively for the promotion of social welfare if it is primarily engaged in promoting in some way the common good and general welfare of the people of the community.

Section 1.501(c)(4)–1(a)(2)(ii) of the regulations states that a social welfare organization may qualify under section 501(c)(4) even though it is an "action" organization described in 1.501(c)(3)–1(c)(3)(iv) if it otherwise qualifies under the section.

Section 1.501(c)(3)–1(c)(3)(iv) of the regulations provides that an organization is an "action" organization if it has the following two characteristics: (a) its main or primary objective or objectives (as distinguished from its incidental or secondary objective) may be attained only by legislation or a defeat of proposed legislation; and (b) it advocates, or campaigns for, the attainment of such main or primary objective or objectives as distinguished from engaging in nonpartisan analysis, study, or research and making the results thereof available to the public.

Through presentations by qualified witnesses on pending or proposed tax legislation, the organization is promoting the common good and general welfare of the community by assisting legislators and administrators concerned with tax policy. Such activity helps the legislators and administrators form better judgments about the legislation.

The fact that the organization's only activities may involve advocating changes in law does not preclude the organization from qualifying under section 501(c)(4) of the Code. See regulations cited above.

Accordingly, it is held that the organization qualifies for exemption from Federal income tax as a social welfare organization under section 501(c)(4) of the Code. Contributions to it are not deductible by donors under the provisions of section 170(c)(2) of the Code.

* * *

NOTES

1. *Relationship Between a § 501(c)(3) Organization and its § 501(c)(4) Affiliate.* A § 501(c)(3) organization can control its § 501(c)(4) affiliate provided that the "(c)(4)" is a separate legal entity whose activities are not supported by tax-deductible contributions. "Control" is often ensured by a governance structure that gives the § 501(c)(3) parent the authority to appoint all or a majority of the § 501(c)(4) subsidiary's board of directors. The two organizations may operate side-by-side if they keep separate books, avoid commingling funds, and provide that, upon any dissolution, the assets of the § 501(c)(3) organization may not be distributed to the lobbying affiliate. The board of directors of the two organizations may overlap, and

the "(c)(3)" can effectively control the "(c)(4)'s" policies as long as the finances of each organization are kept separate. Sharing of space and personnel is permitted, provided that the "(c)(4)" reimburses the "(c)(3)" for its share of direct costs and general overhead.

2. *Political Campaign Activities.* The IRS permits a § 501(c)(4) social welfare organization to engage in political campaign activities, including endorsement of candidates, targeted voter registration drives, and distribution of voter guides, as long as the organization is "primarily" engaged in activities that further its social welfare purposes. Rev. Rul. 81–95, 1981–1 C.B. 332. Whether a § 501(c)(4) organization is "primarily engaged in promoting social welfare" is determined based on "facts and circumstances," such as expenditures, other resources (e.g., buildings and equipment) and volunteer time devoted to the activity; the manner in which the organization's activities are conducted; and the purposes furthered by its various activities. Raymond Chick & Amy Henchey, Political Organizations and I.R.C. 501(c)(4), Exempt Organizations Continuing Prof. Educ. Technical Instruction Program 191 (1995). There is no official bright line test, but some practitioners take the position that a § 501(c)(4) organization will not risk its tax exemption if it confines political expenditures to less than 50 percent of total expenditures.

Social welfare organizations also may create political action committees ("PACs"), which usually are structured as separate segregated funds (rather than separate legal entities), to raise money from members for campaign activities. In an affiliated organization structure, the § 501(c)(3) parent must not involve itself in these electoral activities. For example, a charity's tax-deductible contributions should not be diverted to a PAC, and a PAC should not be controlled directly by a charity.

3. *Other Tax Consequences of Political Activities.* Although a properly structured § 501(c)(3)/§ 501(c)(4)/PAC combination will not threaten the tax-exempt status of the § 501 entities, certain types of expenditures may trigger a tax liability under rules designed to ensure that politically active exempt organizations are taxed comparably to political organizations under the special limited tax-exempt regime of § 527.

Under § 527, a political organization is any organization, including parties, committees, associations, or funds, that is organized and operated primarily to directly or indirectly accept contributions and make expenditures for certain "exempt" functions. Political organizations are not taxed on the dues and contributions they receive for their electioneering and other political activities, but they generally are taxed at the highest corporate income tax rate on any business or investment income. I.R.C. § 527(b), (c). Contributions by individual donors to political organizations are not tax-deductible nor are they subject to federal gift tax. I.R.C. § 2501(a)(5). Gifts to § 501(c)(4) advocacy organizations also are not tax-deductible, but they may be taxable gifts for federal gift tax purposes if they exceed the annual exclusion (currently $13,000 per donor).

Section 501(c) exempt organizations become subject to the § 527 tax regime if they make expenditures for an "exempt function"—defined as "influencing or attempting to influence the selection, nomination, election, or appointment of any individual to any Federal, State, or local public office, or office in a political organization, or the election of Presidential or Vice–Presidential electors, whether [the] individual or electors are selected, nominated, elected, or appointed." I.R.C. 527(e)(2). As used for this purpose, the term "exempt" has nothing to do with "exempt purposes" under § 501(c)(3) but rather is a reference to the exempt functions of a typical political organization. For more details on the scope of "exempt function" activities, see Treas. Reg. § 1.527–2(c). The amount taxed is the lesser of the organization's net investment income or the aggregate amount spent for exempt functions. I.R.C. § 527(f)(1). "Net investment income" consists of dividends, interest, rent, royalties, and capital gains, less directly related expenses. I.R.C. § 527(f)(2).

To illustrate, assume a § 501(c)(4) advocacy organization has $400,000 of net income, of which $100,000 is net investment income, and it spends $150,000 during the year on political campaign activities that constitute "exempt functions" as defined in § 527(e)(2). The organization will be subject to tax at the highest applicable corporate rate (currently 35%) on the lesser of: (1) its exempt function expenditures, or (2) the organization's net investment income. In the example, the § 501(c)(4) organization would be subject to an income tax of $35,000 (35% x $100,000 net investment income). If its political expenditures had been only $80,000, the tax would be 35 percent of that lesser amount, or $28,000.

An organization with no investment income does not need to be concerned with this tax. An organization with a large endowment can avoid the tax by establishing a separate segregated fund and allocating to it a share of the organization's dues. I.R.C. § 527(f)(3). For tax purposes, the fund will be treated as a separate organization and, if it has no investment income, it will not be taxable with respect to its political expenditures. Care must be taken not to commingle funds or "loan" money to the segregated fund to preserve its separate tax status.

In some situations, expenditures for public advocacy communications by § 501(c)(4) organizations (as well as § 501(c)(5) labor unions and § 501(c)(6) trade associations) may subject those organizations to tax under § 527. The IRS has issued a published ruling that provides extensive analysis (with lists of positive and negative factors) of when advocacy expenditures relating to a public policy issue are or are not for an exempt function. Rev. Rul. 2004–6, 2004–1 C.B. 328. The ruling includes six detailed examples of the "all facts and circumstances" test mandated by the regulations. Two of these examples are particularly instructive. In Situation 1, a full-page advertisement prepared and financed by a labor union supported increased spending on law enforcement. The ads were published on a regular basis throughout the year, including one shortly before a U.S. Senatorial election, and urged readers to contact their Senators and representatives in Congress and ask them to support the increased funding. The IRS ruled that the advertisement was not an "exempt function." Despite the timing, the ad did not mention any candidate's position on the issue, no votes were scheduled, the ad was part of a year-long campaign, and there was nothing to suggest support or opposition of any candidate based on the issue being advocated.

In Situation 3, a § 501(c)(4) health care advocacy group ran a full-page ad in major newspapers shortly before an election urging federal assistance for a public hospital and noting that a U.S. Senator up for reelection supported the group's position. The timing of the ad, the targeting of voters, and identification of a candidate's position was enough to classify the expense as an exempt function expenditure even though federal funding of hospitals was not an issue raised in the campaign.

PROBLEM

Incorporate by reference the facts describing Seniors Association for Gerontological Endeavor ("SAGE") in the problem at p. 506, supra. Consider whether the proposed activities described below would jeopardize SAGE's tax-exempt status under § 501(c)(3) or subject SAGE to excise tax liability under § 4955. If you are concerned about any of the activities, please advise SAGE how it might make changes to minimize any tax risks.

(a) SAGE formally endorses a candidate for Governor who is sympathetic to the organization's positions.

(b) The chair of SAGE's board of directors signs a statement formally opposing the reelection of an incumbent Senator who is not sympathetic to SAGE's positions.

(c) SAGE publishes a voter's guide, listing state legislators and informing SAGE's members how each legislator voted on subjects of interest to SAGE. Is the timing of this publication relevant?

(d) SAGE allows some of its members and employees to use the organization's telephones and copying machine to encourage people to attend a rally on behalf of a candidate who is widely known to share SAGE's position on issues affecting older Americans.

(e) SAGE conducts a voter registration project urging senior citizens to register to vote and assisting them to obtain absentee ballots.

(f) SAGE sponsors candidates' forums in legislative districts with large senior citizen populations. All major party candidates are invited to participate (minor party candidates are excluded). SAGE selects the moderator and controls the format.

(g) SAGE rents its mailing lists to political candidates who favor SAGE's position on public issues.

(h) SAGE establishes and supports a political action committee to raise funds from its members to support candidates for public office.

(i) SAGE forms a § 501(c)(4) affiliate, known as SAGE Advocates, which engages in lobbying, and it also establishes the SAGE Political Action Committee to support candidates for public office. SAGE makes grants to its § 501(c)(4) affiliate for lobbying purposes, but the affiliate otherwise raises its own funds. SAGE makes its mailing list available to the PAC without charge.

7.   SECTION 527 POLITICAL ORGANIZATIONS: REPORTING AND DISCLOSURE REQUIREMENTS

As discussed above, § 527 provides a form of limited tax-exempt status for "political organizations," a broad category embracing political parties, political action committees, and funds created to support candidates and causes at the federal, state and local levels. Section 527 organizations are exempt from federal income tax on contributions they receive, and donors are exempt from federal gift tax on their contributions. Net investment income of political organizations is taxable at the highest corporate income tax rate (currently 35 percent).

Unlike § 501(c) tax-exempt organizations, § 527 organizations are not required to apply for their special exempt status or file annual Form 990 information returns. Those "527s" with taxable investment income must file an annual return (Form 1120–POL), which reports taxable income and deductible expenses but does not include information on the specific activities of the organization or other sources of its revenue. Tax returns filed by political organizations historically were not subject to the public disclosure and inspection requirements applicable to § 501(c) organizations, but § 527 organizations that seek to influence federal campaigns by engaging in "express advocacy" must disclose their activities and contributors to the Federal Election Commission. "Express advocacy" generally means advocating the election or defeat of specific candidates for federal elective office by using magic words such as "vote for" and "vote against."

Beginning in the mid–1990s, political activists, exploiting arcane inconsistencies in the tax and election laws, began to form § 527 organizations to funnel vast sums of unregulated "soft money" to benefit political causes and candidates through activities such as voter education and issue advocacy. The principal goals of these new stealth vehicles were to: (1) avoid public disclosure of their activities and sources of income under both tax and election laws, (2) avoid federal election law limits on contributions, and (3) allow donors to contribute unlimited amounts without the potential gift taxes they would incur if the contributions were made to a § 501(c)(4) advocacy organization.

The emergence of § 527 organizations was the subject of some scholarly discourse during the 1998 election campaign. See, e.g., Frances R. Hill, Probing the Limits of Section 527 to Design a New Campaign Finance Vehicle, 22 Exempt Org. Tax Rev. 205 (1998). But it was not until the 2000 primary season that campaign finance reformers and the media began to expose these secretive groups as the loophole of choice for raising and spending unlimited amounts on political activity without any tax liability or disclosure obligation. See John M. Broder & Raymond Bonner, A Political Voice, Without Strings, N.Y. Times, March 29, 2000, at A1. Examples of § 527 groups outed by journalists and reform advocates were Republicans for Clean Air, which broadcast advertisements critical of Senator John McCain before the March 2000 Super Tuesday primaries and reportedly was financed by a major supporter of George W. Bush, and Business Leaders for Sensible Priorities, created by the founders of Ben and Jerry's Ice Cream to argue for less spending on weapons and more on education.

Congress responded by passing narrowly tailored legislation to require § 527 organizations to disclose their activities and donors. Among other things, § 527 groups must: (1) notify the IRS within 24 hours of their creation; (2) file periodic reports (more frequently in election years) of their activities and expenses; and (3) disclose their contributors unless they are already required to do so with the Federal Election Commission. Sanctions, including monetary penalties and possible loss of exempt status, will be imposed for noncompliance. Congress also directed the IRS to make all this information available to the public on the Internet.

Although the § 527 reporting and disclosure legislation brought the most secretive § 527 groups into the sunshine, it does not reach other tax-exempt organizations often used for political advocacy, such as § 501(c)(4) social welfare organizations, § 501(c)(5) labor unions, and § 501(c)(6) trade associations. As a result, some stealth soft money migrated back to § 501(c)(4) organizations and, possibly, even to § 501(c)(3) charities (under the guise of "education") and for-profit entities.

Soon after the legislation was enacted, lawsuits challenged the constitutionality of the § 527 disclosure and reporting rules. In National Federation of Republican Assemblies v. United States, 218 F.Supp.2d 1300 (S.D. Ala. 2002), a federal district court held that the disclosure rules imposed by § 527(j) violated free speech rights under the First Amendment insofar as they require disclosure of expenditures for federal electoral advocacy and of expenditures and contributions in connection with state and local advocacy. The court also held that § 527(j) violated the equal protection component of the Due Process Clause to the extent it requires political organizations to disclose expenditures. The court upheld the constitutionality of the rules requiring disclosure of contributions in connection with federal electoral advocacy. On appeal, however, the Eleventh Circuit reversed and dismissed the case for lack of jurisdiction. The court reasoned that the monetary penalties imposed on political organizations for failing to disclose their electoral advocacy expenditures and contributions imposed conditions on the receipt of a tax subsidy and thus must be treated as part of an overall taxing scheme for which injunctive and declaratory relief was procedurally barred (e.g., under I.R.C. § 7421(a), the "Anti–Injunction Act"). Mobile Republican Assembly v. United States, 353 F.3d 1357 (11th Cir. 2003).

For Further Reading. Miriam Galston, Emerging Constitutional Paradigms and Jutifications for Campaign Finance Regulation: The Case of 527 Groups, 95 Geo.L.J. 1181 (2007); Lloyd H. Mayer, The Much Maligned 527 and Institutional Choice, 87 B.U.L.Rev. 625 (2007); Donald B. Tobin, Anonymous Speech and Section 527 of the Internal Revenue Code, 37 Ga.L.Rev. 611 (2003); Frances R. Hill, Softer Money: Exempt Organizations and Campaign Finance, 32 Exempt Org. Tax Rev. 27 (2001); Martin A.

Sullivan, More Disclosure From 501(c)'s: Poison Pill or Good Policy, 29 Exempt Org. Tax Rev. 10 (2000).

8.   OTHER REGULATION OF POLITICAL ACTIVITIES OF NONPROFIT ORGANIZATIONS

Federal laws impose various other restrictions on lobbying and campaign activity by nonprofit organizations. Some of these restrictions were enacted in response to real and perceived abuses and reflect the persistent theme that lobbying, despite its prevalence throughout American history, is undesirable or at least must be closely regulated. This discussion is limited to an overview of the major nontax statutes and regulations applicable to the nonprofit sector.

Federal Lobbying Disclosure Act. The Lobbying Disclosure Act of 1995 ("the Act") establishes a comprehensive regime for registration and reporting of lobbying activities at the federal level. Among other things, the Act requires exempt and non-exempt organizations to register and file semi-annual reports on their lobbying activities if: (1) the organization has at least one employee who is a "lobbyist" (as defined), and (2) the organization incurs or expects to incur expenditures on "lobbying activities" of $20,000 or more in a six-month period. A "lobbyist" is an employee who makes at least two "legislative contacts" and devotes at least 20 percent of his or her time to "lobbying activities."

The question remains—what is lobbying for purposes of the Act? Charities that have made the § 501(h) election for federal tax purposes may elect to use the federal tax definition of "influencing legislation" and the tax rules for computing lobbying expenditures for purposes of determining their obligations under the Lobbying Disclosure Act. The definition of lobbying under the Act, however, differs significantly from the tax definitions in §§ 4911 and 162(e). For example, the Act does not cover efforts to influence state and local legislative bodies or grassroots lobbying at any level, but it does include most "self-defense" lobbying and efforts to influence executive branch decisions through contacts with members of Congress or with executive branch officials. Politically active charities thus are faced with a strategical choice as to which definition to use in determining their obligations under the Act.

Churches and their integrated auxiliaries are exempt from the registration and reporting requirements of the Lobbying Disclosure Act, but outside lobbyists retained by a church are subject to it. Although private foundations are not permitted to lobby, as that term is defined for federal tax purposes, they are still subject to the Act if they engage in activities that are treated as lobbying under the Act but not under federal tax law. In addition to the registration and reporting requirements, the Act includes monetary sanctions for violations and a prohibition on receipt of federal funds by § 501(c)(4) organizations that lobby, but they may establish a separate § 501(c)(4) affiliate to engage in privately-funded lobbying. Many state and local governments also have reporting and registration requirements for lobbying activity.

Restrictions on Use of Federal Funds for Lobbying. Rules promulgated by the Office of Management and Budget prohibit some nonprofits from using federal funds for lobbying at the federal and state levels. See OMB Circular A–122, Cost Principles for Nonprofit Organizations, 49 Fed.Reg. 18,260 (April 27, 1984). The definitions of lobbying are similar but not identical to those employed under the federal tax laws. The OMB regulations do not restrict a nonprofit's overall lobbying expenses if none of those expenses are paid with funds obtained through federal grants or contracts. Legislation enacted in 1989 under the sponsorship of Senator Robert Byrd of West Virginia also forbids the use of federally appropriated funds for lobbying purposes and requires disclosure of lobbying activities and expenses by organizations that are seeking federal grants, contracts, loans, and the like. This legislation covers attempts to influence executive agencies as well as the legislature. Nonprofit organizations are specifically subject to the Byrd Amendment. See generally 31 U.S.C.A. § 1352 (1988).

Federal Election and Campaign Finance Law Restrictions. Federal election and campaign finance laws and the election laws of some states restrict for-profit and nonprofit corporations from making certain types of direct campaign contributions and other political expenditures and limit the amount that individuals may contribute directly to political candidates. They also regulate political action committees and require disclosure of political contributions in federal elections. See generally Federal Election Campaign Act, 2 U.S.C.A. §§ 431–455 (1988).

The federal election laws rival the tax law for their technical complexity. This discussion is limited to an overview of their impact on the nonprofit sector. In general, a distinction is drawn between "express advocacy," such as advocating the election or defeat of a specific candidate by using certain magic words like "vote for" or "vote against," and other partisan activities. Federal election law also distinguishes between direct contributions to candidates or campaigns and expenditures for communications that may be supportive but are "independent" and not coordinated with a specific campaign or political party.

The impact of federal election law on § 501(c) organizations depends on which type of nonprofit is engaging in the activity. Section 501(c)(3) organizations are less affected because the tax law already bars them from engaging in express advocacy on behalf of candidates. But the tax law does not prohibit social welfare organizations, labor unions and trade associations from political activity as long as it is not their primary purpose. Prior to 2010, federal election law prohibited these noncharitable nonprofit corporations from spending money from their general treasury for express advocacy on behalf of candidates. This direct advocacy ban was extended in 2002 by the Bipartisan Campaign Reform Act—popularly known as "McCain/Feingold"—to independent expenditures for "electioneering communications," which generally are broadcast, cable or satellite communications that refer to a clearly identified federal candidate and are distributed to the relevant electorate within 30 days of a primary or political convention or 60 days of a general election.[1] McCain/Feingold also requires any person, including § 501(c)(4) advocacy groups, who make disbursements to produce and air an electioneering communication totaling more than $10,000 during a calendar year to disclose their expenditures and the sources of the funds in a public filing.

A narrow sub-category of § 501(c)(4) organization may spend money directly for express advocacy, including "electioneering communications." This exception for "qualified nonprofit corporations" ("QNCs") was first carved out by the Supreme Court in Federal Election Commission v. Massachusetts Citizens for Life, 479 U.S. 238, 107 S.Ct. 616 (1986), where the Court held that it was unconstitutional to restrict the electioneering activities of a nonprofit "pro-life" § 501(c)(4) advocacy organization. The Court distinguished this advocacy group from a business corporation, finding that it was "formed to disseminate political ideas, not to amass capital." Id. at 259. In response, the Federal Election Commission issued regulations allowing a QNC to make independent expenditures for express advocacy or electioneering communications if the organization was formed for the express purpose of promoting identified political ideas, but only if the group does not take corporate or labor donations and refrains from any related or unrelated business activities. See 11 C.F.R. § 114.10.[2]

In Austin v. Michigan Chamber of Commerce, 494 U.S. 652, 110 S.Ct. 1391 (1990), however, the Court held that state-imposed restrictions on political expenditures were constitutionally applied to a § 501(c)(6) business league. Rejecting the First Amendment free speech arguments of the Michigan Chamber of Commerce, the Court found that a nonprofit corporation must be organized "to promot[e] political ideas" rather than engage in business activities in order to be constitutionally exempt from political expenditure limitations. Id. at 662. Or so we thought until the Supreme Court's 5–4 opinion in Citizens United v. Federal Election Commission, 130 S.Ct. 876 (2010), where the Court held that the ban on corporate independent expenditures from general treasury funds for express advocacy or electioneering communications was an unconstitutional abridgement of free speech.[3]

---

1. Even after McCain/Feingold, however, corporations still could make expenditures through their separate political action committees, which are strictly regulated by federal election law and are subject to contribution limits, burdensome recordkeeping, and disclosure requirements. Political action committees formed by corporations must rely on voluntary donations from members or employees rather than general treasury funds.

2. To retain their tax exemptions, however, political campaign activities may not be a QNC's primary purpose. QNCs also may not make direct contributions to federal candidates or political committees. See 11 CFR § 114.10(c)(4)(ii). In Federal Election Commission v. Beaumont, 539 U.S. 146, 123 S.Ct. 2200 (2003), the Supreme Court declined to create a constitutionally grounded exception to permit unlimited direct *contributions* by nonprofit organizations engaged in ideological advocacy.

3. *Citizens United* does not overturn the ban on direct corporate contributions to candidates or expenditures for communications that are coordinated with campaigns.

Citizens United was a § 501(c)(4) nonprofit corporation that released a documentary highly critical of then Presidential candidate Hillary Clinton shortly before the 2008 primary elections. After finding that the documentary was an electioneering communication, the Court overruled *Austin*. The majority opinion forcefully articulates the view that the First Amendment applies to corporations and rejects arguments that the ban on electioneering communications is necessary to prevent the "distorting" effects of large aggregations of corporate wealth or prevent corruption. The Court concluded that no sufficient governmental interest justified limits on political speech of for-profit or nonprofit corporations. By an 8–1 vote, however, it upheld the disclosure requirements and the mandate to include "disclaimers" (that tell the electorate who is speaking) in any electioneering communication. The Court viewed disclosure as a less restrictive alternative to more comprehensive speech regulation that was justified by a governmental interest in providing the electorate with information.

The effect of the *Citizens United* decision is that all corporations, not just the ideological groups that qualified for the QNC exception, are now free to spend unlimited amounts on broadcast advertisements advocating a particular candidate's election or defeat, and for-profit corporations may donate general treasury funds to nonprofit groups that engage in express advocacy. The implications of *Citizens United* on the nonprofit sector have yet to unfold, but a consensus is emerging on some possibilities. First, the decision does not open the door for § 501(c)(3) charities to spend money on political campaigns because they remain muzzled by the tax law prohibitions discussed earlier in this chapter. But query whether *Citizens United* may inspire a new constitutional challenge to the § 501(c)(3) limitations on lobbying and political activity on free speech grounds despite the repeated rejection of those arguments by the courts? Second, *Citizens United* allows § 501(c)(4) social welfare organizations, as well as labor unions and trade associations, to make unlimited independent expenditures in federal and most likely state elections. These groups no longer must rely on their heavily regulated PACs to engage in electoral advocacy. Finally, much of this nonprofit electioneering can be funded by wealthy individuals and for-profit corporations—a strategy that, without further changes in the law, may preserve anonymity. Tax law does not require public disclosure of donors to social welfare organizations, labor unions and trade associations, and federal election law disclosure rules have been interpreted to apply only to contributions earmarked for campaign activity.

As this text went to press, efforts were underway to enact further legislation to curtail the permissive impact of *Citizens United* without running afoul of the First Amendment.

For Further Reading. Miriam Galston, When Statutory Regimes Collide: Will Wisconsin Right to Life and Citizens United Invalidate Federal Regulation of Campaign Activity?, available at SSRN: http://ssrn.com/abstract=1572511 (March 2010); Lloyd H. Mayer, The Effect of the Bipartisan Campaign Reform Act on Exempt Organizations, 41 Exempt Org. Tax Rev. 23 (2003); Frances R. Hill, *McConnell* and the Code: Exempt Organizations and Campaign Finance, 45 Exempt Org. Tax Rev. 71 (2004).

9.   POLICY ISSUES: USE AND ABUSE OF NONPROFIT ORGANIZATIONS FOR PARTISAN POLITICAL ACTIVITIES

The use of nonprofit organizations as fronts for political causes and candidates has been widely reported for decades. Both § 501(c)(3) and § 501(c)(4) organizations have been used to circumvent federal and state election law contribution limits and disclosure requirements. For example, in the early 1990s, a Republican Party political action committee (GOPAC) developed a voter outreach project to disseminate the Republican Party's agenda. The project included a course (Renewing American Civilization) taught at two small colleges by then House Speaker Newt Gingrich. The thrust of Gingrich's message was that the United States should replace its current welfare state with an "opportunity society." With funding provided first by the Abraham Lincoln Opportunity Fund and later by the Progress and Freedom Foundation, both § 501(c)(3) organizations with close ties to GOPAC, the course was broadcast nationwide by satellite television. The House Ethics Committee charged Rep. Gingrich with violating House rules by failing to seek the advice of tax counsel regarding the use of tax-deductible funds for political purposes and for providing inaccurate information to the committee when he said the course was completely nonpartisan. See In the Matter of Representative Newt Gingrich, H.Rep. No. 105–1, 105th Cong., 1st Sess. (1997). After a lengthy investigation, Rep. Gingrich accepted a reprimand and fine without conceding any violation of tax law. Three years later, the IRS ruled that the Progress and Freedom Foundation had not engaged in any impermissible political activity by sponsoring Gingrich's course. Calling it a "close case," the Service concluded that the course was nonpartisan and that the private interests of Mr. Gingrich and the Republican Party were served only incidentally by the use of tax-exempt funds. It noted that the content of the course "was educational and never favored or opposed a candidate for public office." Tech. Adv. Mem. (unreleased) (Dec. 1, 1998), reprinted in 23 Exempt Org. Tax Rev. 512 (1999).

At the same time, the IRS revoked the tax-exempt status of the Abraham Lincoln Opportunity Fund but later reversed itself and also retroactively restored the tax exemption of another organization (the Howard H. Callaway Foundation) with ties to former House Speaker Newt Gingrich. The IRS concluded that the previous revocations were not warranted. See Fred Stokeld, Tax–Exempt Status Restored to Groups With Gingrich Ties, 40 Exempt Org. Tax Rev. 139 (2003). Lawyers for the two organizations stated that the reversals were made after the IRS reviewed transcripts and videotapes of the controversial television programs and concluded that they were nonpartisan. As one lawyer put it, "If you didn't know Newt Gingrich's political affiliation, you wouldn't be able to tell if the program were produced by Republicans or Democrats or Libertarians or the Girl Scouts—it's simply that nonpartisan." J. Christine Harris, Attorney for "Gingrich Groups" Says News Reports Are Inaccurate, 40 Exempt Org. Tax Rev. 254, 256 (2003). Media reports and some Democratic members of Congress took a more skeptical view, suggesting that political pressure caused the IRS to reverse itself. These charges were strongly denied by the senior IRS officials with oversight responsibility over the review process. J. Christine Harris, IRS Reps Offer More Insight Into Review of Gingrich Groups, 99 Tax Notes 1761 (June 23, 2003).

Some commentators expressed concern that the IRS reversal in the Gingrich case opens up a huge loophole by permitting § 501(c)(3) organizations to solicit tax-deductible contributions for improper political campaign activity, effectively circumventing contribution limits and disclosure requirements. See, e.g., David Johnston, Ruling May Open Financial Loophole: IRS Reversal Over Gingrich Lectures Seen as Highly Unusual, N.Y. Times, June 8, 2003, § 1, at 37.

Another celebrated controversy involved the Christian Coalition, which was founded by Rev. Pat Robertson and sought tax-exempt status under § 501(c)(4). One of the Coalition's principal activities was the the distribution of millions of voter guides in churches on the Sunday before major elections. The guides evidenced a bias for or against particular political candidates and legislative proposals. After a lengthy examination, the IRS ruled in 1999 that the Coalition did not qualify under § 501(c)(4). The Coalition promptly reorganized, forming both a § 527 political organization for election-related activities and an affiliated § 501(c)(4) organization to engage in education and advocacy. See Carolyn D. Wright, Christian Coalition Fails to Obtain Tax–Exempt Status, 25 Exempt Org. Tax Rev. 9 (1999).

In 2005, the Christian Coalition settled its dispute with the IRS, which restored the Coalition's § 501(c)(4) status after reaching agreement on detailed criteria for the preparation and distribution of "nonpartisan" voter guides. Among other things, the voter guides must survey a broad range of issues, ask questions of candidates in a clear and unbiased manner, give all candidates an opportunity to respond, and display at least six questions (and answers) directed to each candidate. See Gregory L. Colvin, IRS Gives Christian Coalition a Green Light for New Voter Guides, 50 Exempt Org. Tax Rev. 353 (2005).

NOTES AND QUESTIONS

1. *Political Agendas.* The use of § 501(c)(3) organizations to disguise political activity is generally motivated by several overlapping goals: (1) to give donors a charitable deduction for what otherwise would be a nondeductible political contribution; (2) to avoid federal election law limitations on "hard money" contributions and other regulation by the Federal Election Commission; and (3) to avoid the public disclosure of political contributions mandated by federal and state election laws. In other scenarios, a § 501(c)(4) organization is used; although no tax deduction is allowed, contributions and expenditures are not subject to the federal election law disclosure requirements.

2. *Experts Disagree.* It should be apparent by now that the law in this area is hopelessly murky and thus ripe for exploitation. Newt Gingrich's

satellite seminar is a good example of how experts disagree on the scope of the political campaign limitations in § 501(c)(3). The special counsel to the House Ethics Committee, after consultation with experienced tax counsel, concluded that Gingrich's course conferred more than insubstantial benefits to GOPAC and Republican candidates. Although conceding that the content of the course was more ideological than politically partisan, the report pointed to Gingrich's political motivation and the role of Republican Party officials and financial support of GOPAC. Other tax specialists argued, however, that the course was no different than the strategically timed issue advocacy conducted by a broad range of § 501(c)(3) organizations. See, e.g., Leslie Lenkowsky, Newt Tax Violation Hard to Find, and Terrence Scanlon & William J. Lehrfeld, And Don't Believe the Partisan Spin, Wall St. J., Jan. 3, 1997, at A8. Should resolution of the Gingrich matter have turned on subjective factors, such as partisan intent? It appears that the IRS's decision to clear the Progress and Freedom Foundation of any tax law violations was based on its evaluation of the content of the course rather than the underlying political motives.

3. *For Further Reading.* Adriana Riviere, Comment: 527s: The New Frontier for Election Law and Associational Rights, 60 U.Miami L. Rev. 261 (2006); Gregg D. Polsky & Guy–Uriel E. Charles, Regulating Section 527 Organizations, 73 Geo. Wash L.Rev. 1000 (2005); Robert Paul Meier, The Darker Side of Nonprofits: When Charities and Social Welfare Groups Become Political Slush Funds, 147 U.Pa.L.Rev. 971 (1999); Brent Coverdale, A New Look at Campaign Finance Reform: Regulation of Nonprofit Organizations Through the Tax Code, 46 U.Kans.L.Rev. 155 (1997).

PROBLEM

The Institute for Public Policy is a "think tank" founded by Lute Stormy, a prominent member of the U.S. House of Representatives, to conduct research on economics and public policy. The Institute relies on gifts and grants from individuals, corporations, and foundations, most of whom also have directly and indirectly supported Rep. Stormy's political agenda. Funds are used to publish reports, conduct symposia, and sponsor a weekly closed-circuit television seminar taught by Rep. Stormy. The Institute is not directly involved in any partisan political activity, but its activities and emphasis are consistent with the legislative initiatives of interest to Rep. Stormy and supported by his political party. Does the Institute qualify for tax-exempt status under § 501(c)(3)? Should it?

F.   Procedural Issues

1.   Judicial Determinations of Exempt Status

Internal Revenue Code: § 7428.

Prior to 1976, organizations that failed to obtain a favorable exemption ruling from the Internal Revenue Service or were threatened with revocation of their exemption had great difficulty obtaining judicial review of the IRS's adverse determination. As a practical matter, the organization's only legal recourse was to await a monetary controversy involving an income or employment tax deficiency or a disallowed charitable contributions deduction for one of its donors. This could take years and, in the meantime, the organization would be unable to assure its contributors that their gifts were tax-deductible. Attempts by organizations to obtain more immediate relief were rebuffed by the courts on procedural grounds. See, e.g., Bob Jones University v. Simon, 416 U.S. 725, 94 S.Ct. 2038 (1974) and Alexander v. "Americans United" Inc., 416 U.S. 752, 94 S.Ct. 2053 (1974), where the Supreme Court held that declaratory judgment actions were precluded by the Anti–Injunction Act (I.R.C. § 7421(a)) and other procedural barriers.

In *Bob Jones University v. Simon*, the Supreme Court invited Congress to remove these obstacles to dispute resolution:

> Congress has imposed an especially harsh regime on 501(c)(3) organizations threatened with loss of tax-exempt status and with withdrawal of advance assurance of deductibility of contributions. * * * The degree of bureaucratic control that, practically speaking, has been placed in the Service over those in [the position of Bob Jones University] is susceptible to abuse, regardless of how conscientiously the Service may attempt to carry out its responsibilities. Specific treatment of not-for-profit organizations to allow them to seek preenforcement review may well merit consideration.

416 U.S. at 749–750. In a dissenting opinion in the companion *Americans United* case, Justice Blackmun lamented the "unfettered power of the Commissioner [of Internal Revenue]" to issue exemption rulings in a system that did not provide a meaningful avenue for judicial review. 416 U.S. at 774.

Prompted by these Supreme Court decisions and the lobbying efforts of the exempt organizations community, Congress enacted § 7428 as part of the Tax Reform Act of 1976. Under that section, organizations may bring declaratory judgment actions in the Tax Court, the U.S. Court of Federal Claims and the Federal District Court for the District of Columbia in actual controversies relating to qualification for exemption under § 501(c)(3), classification as a private foundation or private operating foundation, and eligibility to receive tax-deductible charitable contributions under § 170(c)(2). This remedy enables aggrieved organizations to proceed directly to court from an administrative controversy without having to await a specific monetary dispute with the IRS.

Section 7428 confers jurisdiction only in cases where there is an "actual controversy," such as when the organization has obtained an adverse notice of final determination, or the IRS has failed to make a timely determination on the organization's initial or continuing exemption qualification or private foundation classification. There is no jurisdiction to review rulings regarding the effect of a proposed transaction, at least where no formal steps have been taken by the IRS to revoke the organization's exemption. The Tax Court has liberally interpreted the "actual controversy" requirement. It has accepted jurisdiction, for example, in cases where the IRS granted a favorable advance nonprivate foundation ruling to an organization based on its public support while simultaneously declining to issue a definitive ruling that the organization qualified as a church. See, e.g., Foundation of Human Understanding v. Commissioner, 88 T.C. 1341 (1987). An actual controversy existed in these cases because church classification is more favorable.

Congress did not intend that § 7428 would supplant the normal administrative process. Section 7428(b)(2) thus requires that a declaratory judgment is not available unless an organization demonstrates to the court that it has exhausted all administrative remedies available to it within the IRS. Specifically, it must show that it filed a substantially completed Form 1023, timely submitted all additional information requested to complete the application, and exhausted all administrative appeals within the Service, including appeals to the National Office. If the Service fails to take action on an application, the organization is not deemed to have satisfied the exhaustion requirement until the expiration of 270 days from the date on which a substantially completed application or request for determination has been filed. I.R.C. § 7428(b)(2). If the organization hears nothing from the IRS after the 270–day period expires, it ordinarily may bring an action under § 7428, unless it has been uncooperative at the administrative level—for example, by failing to supply requested information.

Most § 7428 declaratory judgment actions are brought in the Tax Court, which has promulgated a detailed set of rules to govern this procedure. See Tax Court Rule 210 et seq. The Tax Court has expressed a strong preference for disposing of declaratory judgment actions on the basis of the administrative record. Tax Court Rule 217. Additional evidence will be admitted only for good cause shown, and the court rarely finds good cause. See, e.g., Houston Lawyer Referral Service v. Commissioner, 69 T.C. 570 (1978). The administrative record includes the organization's request for a determination (the Form 1023 on an original application), all documents submitted in connection with the request, all protests and related papers submitted during the appeals process, any relevant tax and informational returns, the adverse IRS notice, and the organization's charter and other enabling documents.

Contributions Made During Judicial Proceedings. If a previously exempt organization loses its status as an eligible charitable donee under § 170(c)(2) and challenges the IRS's action in a § 7428 proceeding, contributions made to the organization while the litigation is pending will continue to be deductible up to the date of the final judicial determination even though the court ultimately upholds the IRS's position. I.R.C. § 7428(c)(1). This relief is only available where the IRS has revoked an organization's exempt status and not where an initial application is denied. The notice of revocation must have been formally published by the IRS, and the organization must have initiated a timely declaratory judgment proceeding.

To obtain relief under § 7428(c), a contributor must have clean hands. Thus, a deduction will not be allowed if the contribution was made by an individual who was responsible for the activities that were the basis for the revocation of exemption. I.R.C. § 7428(c)(3). In addition, the maximum amount of contributions to an organization made by any one individual (husbands and wives are treated as one contributor for this purpose) that are allowed during the entire pendency of the litigation may not exceed $1,000. I.R.C. § 7428(c)(2).

2. Information Return and Disclosure Requirements

Internal Revenue Code: §§ 6033(a), (b); 6104(a)(1)(A) & (C), (b), (d); 6652(c).

Treasury Regulations: § 301.6104(d)–3, –4, –5.

Information Returns. Section 6033(a) generally requires exempt organizations to file an annual informational return that reports all receipts and disbursements and any other information that the Service may require by forms or regulations. Most exempt organizations must file Form 990. For 2010 and later years, organizations with gross receipts of less than $200,000 and total assets of less than $500,000 may file the short-form equivalent, Form 990–EZ. Private foundations must file Form 990–PF. Any exempt organization that is liable for the unrelated business income tax (see Chapter 6, infra) also must file Form 990–T and, if it expects its tax for the year to exceed $500, the organization must make quarterly payments of estimated tax on unrelated business income. Recent versions of Form 990, Form 990–PF and their instructions are reproduced in the Statutes, Regulations and Forms Supplement.

Mandatory exemptions from the filing requirement are granted to churches, their integrated auxiliaries, and conventions or associations of churches; certain organizations that are not private foundations and have annual gross receipts that normally do not exceed $5,000; and religious orders, with respect to their exclusively religious activities. I.R.C. § 6033(a)(2)(A). Exercising its discretionary authority under under § 6033(a)(2)(B), the IRS has raised the annual gross receipts threshold from $5,000 of gross receipts to $25,000 ($50,000 for 2010 and later years) for all exempt organizations that are not private foundations and for most state and U.S. governmental organizations, and for certain organizations affiliated with governmental units, such as state colleges and universities, and public libraries and museums. I.R.S. Ann. 82–88, 1982–25 I.R.B 23; I.R.S. Ann. 94–117, 1994–39 I.R.B. 19.

Effective for taxable years beginning after 2006, a "notice" requirement has been imposed on small exempt organizations that are not required to file Form 990. Beginning in 2009 tax years, small charities must stay on the IRS's radar screen by filing an annual report providing their legal name, mailing and web site address, tax identification number, name and address of a principal officer, and evidence of their continuing basis for exemption from Form 990 filing requirements. Failure to provide this notice for three consecutive years will result in revocation of the organization's exemption unless it shows reasonable cause or is otherwise able to beg for mercy. I.R.C. § 6033(i)(1). Small organizations also must furnish notice to the IRS when their existence is terminated. I.R.C. § 6033(i)(2). The IRS has developed an "E-postcard" (Form 990–N) for small organizations to use in fulfilling their annual reporting obligation. The E–Postcard is not really a postcard—it is a mandatory electronic filing procedure unless a small organization elects to file a paper copy of the regular Form 990. The notice is due by the fifteenth day of the fifth month after the close of the organization's tax period. Churches and certain church-related affiliates and most government entities are exempt from this requirement. See T.D. 9366, 72 Fed. Reg. 64147.

The Revised Form 990. In 2007, the IRS unveiled a draft of a redesigned Form 990 information return. The final Form 990 that emerged from over a year of discussion, including 3,000 pages of comments on the IRS web site, has an 11–page core form along with 16 schedules many of which will not apply to most organizations. The new form is based on three guiding principles: (1) enhancing transparency to provide the IRS and the public with a realistic picture of the organization, (2) promoting compliance by accurately reflecting the organization's operations so the IRS may efficiently assess the risk of noncompliance, and (3) minimizing the filing burden. Highlights include a summary page providing a snapshot of the organization's key financial, compensation, governance, and operational information; a section dedicated to information about the organization's governance and its compliance with best practices; and schedules focusing on areas of interest to the public, such as political activity, compensation, and noncash contributions, activities outside the United States, gaming activities, and specific sub-sectors such as schools and hospitals.

Part VI of the redesigned Form 990 asks numerous questions about governance and management. Some examples are: (1) did the organization become aware during the year of a material diversion of its assets?; (2) did the organization contemporaneously document meetings or written actions taken by its governing body?; (3) was a copy of the Form 990 provided to the organization's governing board before it was filed?; (4) does the organization have a written conflict of interest policy, whistleblower policy, and document retention and destruction policy; and (5) did the process for determining compensation of the CEO and other top officers and key employees include a review and approval by independent persons, comparability data, and contemporaneous substantiation of the deliberation and decision? Critics have argued that the questions imply that these "best practices" are legal requirements for tax exemption when they are not, causing negative answers to mislead the public when taken out of context. And many of the questions poach on what historically has been the jurisdiction of state law. The IRS has remained resolute, however, justifying the questions on the relationship between good governance and fiscal oversight.

For the impact of the redesigned Form 990 on hospitals, see Section C3b of this chapter, supra, at p. 323, and for the expanded requirements on reporting compensation, see Section D1, supra, at p. 445.

Disclosure and Inspection. In a continuing effort to make exempt organizations more accountable, Congress has enacted and expanded a variety of public disclosure and inspection requirements that apply to both the Internal Revenue Service and the organization.

The IRS must make available for public inspection at the National Office and the appropriate field offices all Forms 990 and approved applications for exemption. I.R.C. § 6104(a)(1)(A), (b). Trade secrets and information that would adversely affect national defense are exempt from disclosure, as is the schedule of major contributors that is required as an attachment to the Form 990. I.R.C. § 6104(a)(1)(D), (b).

All organizations exempt from tax under § 501(c) or § 501(d) must make available for inspection their application for exemption, along with all supporting documents, and their annual informational returns for the most recent three years. The documents must be made available at the organization's principal office during regular business hours and at regional or district offices with three or more employees. I.R.C. 6104(d)(1)(A). Tax-exempt organizations also must provide copies of their exemption applications and Form 990's for the three most recent tax years to anyone who requests them. The copies ordinarily must be provided immediately if the request is made in person or within 30 days if in writing. I.R.C. § 6104(d)(1)(B). Under prior law, requestors only could inspect these documents at the organization's office and had no right to demand copies. If a copy is requested, the organization may charge only for reasonable copying and mailing costs. For the many details on the obligation to make copies, see Treas. Reg. § 301.6104(d)–3(d).

Organizations that make their documents widely available, such as by posting an exact and downloadable reproduction on the Internet, are not required to provide photocopies, but they still must make returns available for inspection at their offices. I.R.C. § 6104(d)(4); Treas. Reg. § 301.6104(d)–4. In response to this opportunity, more organizations use the Internet to meet the "widely available" standard.

In expanding the disclosure requirements, Congress was mindful that some highly visible charities would be the target of harassment campaigns, and it authorized the IRS to issue regulations providing relief in appropriate cases. I.R.C. § 6104(d)(4). The regulations define a harassment campaign as "a single coordinated effort to disrupt the operations of a tax-exempt organization, rather than to collect information about the organization." Treas. Reg. § 301.6104(d)–5(b). Examples of harassment include a sudden increase in the number of request for copies, an extraordinary number of requests made through form letters, or numerous requests containing language "hostile" to the organization. Id. If a sudden increase in requests for copies is the result of national media attention and there is no evidence that the requests are part of an organized campaign to disrupt the organization's operations, no relief will be available even if the requests place a burden on the organization. Treas. Reg. § 301.6104(d)–5(f) Example 1. The regulations elaborate on the procedures an organization must follow to establish that it is the victim of a harassment campaign. Treas. Reg. § 301.6104(d)–5(d).

Form 990s and 990–PFs of public charities and private foundations are now widely available on the Internet. The best source is Guide Star, which posts information on most U.S. charities at www.guidestar.org. The greater accessibility of financial data has provided a wealth of information to journalists and scholars and has resulted in a heightened level of scrutiny of the nonprofit sector.

Penalties. An exempt organization that fails to file a required information return is subject to a penalty of $20 per day, with a maximum penalty of the lesser of $10,000 or 5 percent of gross receipts. I.R.C. § 6652(c)(1)(A). The penalties are increased for organizations with gross receipts exceeding $1 million. Id. Penalties also may be imposed on the managers of the organization who knowingly fail to file a return or provide information after a request from the Service. I.R.C. § 6652(c)(1)(B). Responsible officials of an exempt organization who refuse to provide copies of documents or allow public inspection are subject to penalties of $10 for each day the failure continues up to a maximum of $5,000 per return. I.R.C. § 6652(c)(1)(C), (D). Additional penalties may be imposed for willful noncompliance or fraud. I.R.C. §§ 6685; 7207.

3.   STANDING BY THIRD PARTIES TO CHALLENGE EXEMPT STATUS

Some of the most provocative substantive tax exemption controversies have never been decided on the merits because of insurmountable procedural obstacles. The courts generally are only willing to entertain controversies involving adverse determinations by the Internal Revenue Service with respect to particular organizations. Interested third parties whose taxes are not directly affected by the Service's actions or administrative policy have met with little success in their attempts to challenge tax benefits granted to others.

But it is not for lack of trying. As discussed earlier in this chapter, low-income individuals and their representatives were held to lack standing to challenge the Service's shift from a "relief of the poor" to a "community benefit" exemption standard for hospitals. Simon v. Eastern Kentucky Welfare Rights Organization, 426 U.S. 26, 96 S.Ct. 1917 (1976). The Supreme Court held in Allen v. Wright, 468 U.S. 737, 104 S.Ct. 3315 (1984) that parents of black children attending public schools lacked standing to challenge the Service's procedures for denying exemption to racially discriminatory private schools. A group of for-profit travel agents failed in their attempt to enjoin the Service from granting exempt status on nonprofit organizations that offered travel tour packages to their members at below-market prices. American Society of Travel Agents v. Blumenthal, 566 F.2d 145 (D.C.Cir.1977), cert. denied, 435 U.S. 947, 98 S.Ct. 1533 (1978). Dr. Lenora Fulani, a minor party candidate for President in 1988, met with mixed success in challenging the tax-exempt status of organizations that failed to include her in nationally televised candidates' debates. The Second Circuit held that Dr. Fulani did have standing to challenge the exempt status of the League of Women Voters Education Fund for failing to include her in Presidential primary debate, but dismissed her case on the merits. Fulani v. League of Women Voters Educ. Fund, 882 F.2d 621 (2d Cir.1989). But Dr. Fulani was denied standing in a related case brought to challenge the exempt status of the Commission on Presidential Debates, which sponsored later debates after the League of Women Voters temporarily receded from the process. Fulani v. Brady, 935 F.2d 1324 (D.C.Cir.1991). And she failed again in a challenge to her exclusion from a 1992 Democratic party debate co-sponsored by the League of Women Voters Education Fund and Cable News Network. Fulani v. Bentsen, 35 F.3d 49 (2d Cir.1994)(Dr. Fulani suffered no injury traceable to League's conduct because CNN still would have prevented her from participating; prior Second Circuit decision distinguished on ground that League was sole sponsor of 1988 debates and its action caused actual harm to Dr. Fulani's campaign).

The obstacles faced by third parties are well summarized in the *Abortion Rights Mobilization* case, which follows. The suit was brought by a consortium of abortion rights groups, civil liberties organizations, clergy, and individual taxpayers acting in various capacities, all seeking to challenge the tax exemption of the Roman Catholic Church, which the plaintiffs alleged was engaging in political activities on abortion issues that were inconsistent with the Church's tax-exempt status. The litigation took a circuitous route, but it ended predictably when the Second Circuit denied standing, and the Supreme Court later denied certiorari.

In re United States Catholic Conference

United States Court of Appeals, Second Circuit, 1989.
885 F.2d 1020, cert. denied 495 U.S. 918, 110 S.Ct. 1946.

■ CARDAMONE, CIRCUIT JUDGE:

This appeal is before us for a second time. The Supreme Court has remanded the matter for a determination of whether the United States District Court for the Southern District of New York (Carter, J.) had subject matter jurisdiction over the instant lawsuit that challenged the tax-exempt status of the Roman Catholic Church in the United States. The specific issue is whether the plaintiffs, who initiated this litigation to force the government to revoke the Catholic Church's tax-exempt status, satisfy the standing requirements of Article III. For the reasons discussed below, we hold that they do not.

I.   Background

A.   The Plaintiffs

Plaintiffs in this appeal are united in their commitment to a woman's right to obtain a legal abortion. This suit was instituted originally by 20 individuals and nine organizations. We assume familiarity with their specific identities as set forth in the district court's opinion. See Abortion Rights

Mobilization, Inc. v. Regan, 544 F.Supp. 471, 474 (S.D.N.Y.1982). Some are no longer parties. Of the nine original organizational plaintiffs, for example, the district court held that five abortion clinics lacked standing and dismissed their complaints. The district court did grant standing to an organization called the Women's Center for Reproductive Health, because it is run by a Presbyterian minister who is also a plaintiff. We discuss the Women's Center with the clergy plaintiffs. The three remaining organizations are Abortions Rights Mobilization Inc. (ARM), the National Women's Health Network Inc. (NWHN) and the Long Island National Organization For Women–Nassau, Inc. (Nassau–NOW). The former two are pro-choice organizations that are non-profit, tax-exempt organizations as defined in § 501(c)(3) of the Internal Revenue Code (Code). 26 U.S.C.A. § 501(c)(3). Nassau–NOW shares ARM's and NWHN's objectives, but is exempt from taxes under § 501(c)(4), rather than (c)(3).

Twenty individual plaintiffs also bring this suit. They include Protestant ministers and Jewish rabbis. In contrast to the views of the Catholic Church, they believe that abortion is morally permissible under some circumstances. Many of the individual plaintiffs donate money to or serve as directors of the organizational plaintiffs. The individual plaintiffs vote and pay taxes.

B. Pertinent Statutory Framework

Before reciting the history of the prior legal proceedings, an understanding of two pertinent sections of the Code is necessary, as a preliminary matter, to appreciate what is at stake in this litigation. As noted, the Catholic Church and organizational plaintiffs ARM and NWHN are tax-exempt under § 501(c)(3). That section states that qualifying religious or civic public interest organizations need not pay federal taxes. The trade-off for the benefit of this exemption is that no substantial part of the organization's activities may include "carrying on * * * propaganda, or otherwise attempting, to influence legislation * * * [nor may it] participate in, or intervene in (including the publishing or distributing of statements), any political campaign on behalf of any candidate for public office." Thus, the quid pro quo for § 501(c)(3) tax-exemption is a restraint on an organization's right to try to influence the political process. This limitation has been held constitutional. Section 501(c)(3) status is advantageous to the supporters of an organization as well as the organization itself because § 170 of the Code permits donors to § 501(c)(3) entities to claim a deduction for their contributions. This deduction gives the donor an economic incentive to contribute. For example, a donor in a 28 percent tax bracket actually pays only 72 cents for every dollar contributed to the Catholic Church because of the deduction. Consequently, organizations like the Church and plaintiffs ARM and NWHN have enhanced fundraising abilities because they are able to offer donors the lure of the § 170 deduction.

C. The Dispute

The plaintiffs object to the Internal Revenue Service's (IRS) enforcement—or, as they describe it, nonenforcement—of § 501(c)(3)'s prohibition on lobbying and campaigning. Because this appeal arises from a motion to dismiss for want of standing, we must accept all of the plaintiffs' allegations as true and draw all inferences in their favor.

Plaintiffs first allege that the Catholic Church is repeatedly violating § 501(c)(3)'s prohibition on campaigning in order to promote the tenet that abortion is immoral and should therefore be made unlawful. For instance, plaintiffs point to the Church's "Pastoral Plan for Pro–Life Activities," which they claim is an organized effort to mobilize the entire Church in a "three-fold educational, pastoral and political effort to outlaw abortions in the United States." The complaint also alleges that through its priests and officials, the Catholic Church has endorsed or supported pro-life political candidates and opposed pro-choice candidates by publishing articles in its bulletins, attacking or endorsing candidates from the pulpit, distributing partisan letters to parishioners, and urging its members to donate to and sign petitions of "right to life" committees and candidates. Similarly, plaintiffs contend that the Church has contributed substantial sums of money to "right to life" and other political groups which have, directly or indirectly, supported the political candidacies for public office of persons favoring anti-abortion legislation.

Plaintiffs' other major contention is that the IRS knows about the Catholic Church's alleged political activities and has ignored these activities rather than either revoking the Church's tax-exempt status under § 501(c)(3), or not renewing the Church's annual exemption. They therefore assert that the government has "exempted the Roman Catholic Church from the strictures of the law and from the government's enforcement efforts," and that the IRS treats the Catholic Church more favorably than those organizations that are pro-choice. Yet plaintiffs do not allege that the IRS has penalized them for violating the Code; in fact, they assert that they have not violated § 501(c)(3) by electioneering, and do not intend to. Rather, they want the government to enforce the strictures of § 501(c)(3) against the Catholic Church. Thus, plaintiffs do not complain about their own tax status—their challenge is directed solely against the Catholic Church's exemption.

The complaint and affidavits also spell out the asserted harms plaintiffs suffer as a result of the Church's and the IRS' acts. Because the nature of the claimed harm is an integral component in standing analysis, it will be fully analyzed in the later discussion of standing.

D.   Prior Proceedings

[The court then reviewed the early procedural history of the case, during which the district court granted the Catholic Church's motion to dismiss it as a defendant but also held the Church in contempt for its resistance to discovery as a non-party witness. Eds.]

On appeal, the Church argued that it was improperly held in contempt in the action because the district court lacked subject matter jurisdiction over the case before it due to plaintiffs' lack of standing. We held that, as a non-party contemnor, the Church itself lacked standing to challenge plaintiffs' standing in the main suit, and that as a non-party witness it could only challenge a contempt finding when the district court was without even colorable jurisdiction. Hence, we had no occasion to reach the underlying question now before us of plaintiffs' standing. See In re United States Catholic Conference, 824 F.2d 156 (2d Cir.1987). The Supreme Court reversed, holding that a non-party witness held in contempt had standing to challenge the district court's subject matter jurisdiction. United States Catholic Conference v. Abortion Rights Mobilization, Inc., 487 U.S. 72, 108 S.Ct. 2268, 101 L.Ed.2d 69 (1988). Upon remand from the Supreme Court, we now must analyze whether plaintiffs have standing to sue the government for conferring tax-exempt status to the Catholic Church.

II. DISCUSSION

A. Standing Analysis

In Allen v. Wright, 468 U.S. 737, 104 S.Ct. 3315, 82 L.Ed.2d 556 (1984), the Supreme Court made clear that standing is not merely a prudential inquiry into whether a court should exercise jurisdiction, but is rooted in Article III's "case" or "controversy" requirement and reflects separation of powers principles. Thus, when a plaintiff lacks standing to bring suit, a court has no subject matter jurisdiction over the case. Deceptively simple to state, standing entails a complex three-pronged inquiry. First, plaintiffs must show that they have suffered an injury in fact that is both concrete in nature and particularized to them. Second, the injury must be fairly traceable to defendants' conduct. Third, the injury must be redressable by removal of defendants' conduct. The second and third prongs-traceability and redressability—often dovetail; essentially, both seek a causal nexus between the plaintiff's injury and the defendant's assertedly unlawful act. To establish standing, a plaintiff must plead all three elements.

B. Application to This Case

Standing in the case at hand is alleged under a number of theories that require a general overview in order to match the category of plaintiff to the asserted basis for standing. The prior proceedings have distilled standing theories that view plaintiffs as clergy, voters, and taxpayers. We first address those theories relied upon by the district court in finding that plaintiffs had standing, and then consider a fourth theory—competitive advocate standing—not explicitly addressed below.

1. Clergy Standing

Clergy plaintiffs claim standing under the Establishment Clause of the First Amendment. That clause provides: "Congress shall make no law respecting an establishment of religion * * *." The amended complaint alleges that "The failure of the government defendants to apply the Code equally to the * * * Church is in effect a subsidy of the Church's efforts to further its religious aims in the political sphere, a subsidy not granted to law-abiding * * * plaintiffs, who hold contrary religious beliefs." This constitutes an unconstitutional establishment of religion. Without reaching the merits, the district court held that the clergy plaintiffs and the religiously affiliated Women's Center for Reproductive Health (collectively clergy plaintiffs) had standing under the Establishment Clause because they were "denigrated by government favoritism to a different theology." Thus, it concluded that the IRS "hampers and frustrates these plaintiffs' ministries." The appropriateness of this holding turns on whether the stigma plaintiffs allege is a cognizable injury in fact. We think the district court erred by translating plaintiffs' genuine motivation to sue into a personalized injury in fact.

It is true that an injury claimed to derive from a violation of the Establishment Clause can be spiritual in nature. Nonetheless, the injury must be particularized to the individuals who sue. * * * The Establishment Clause does not exempt clergy or lay persons from Article III's standing requirements. Here, the clergy plaintiffs have not been injured in a sufficiently personal way to distinguish themselves from other citizens who are generally aggrieved by a claimed constitutional violation. For that reason, they lack standing.

Both Valley Forge and Allen v. Wright support this conclusion. In Valley Forge, an organization dedicated to ensuring separation of church and state sued the Secretary of Health, Education and Welfare for conveying, without consideration, surplus government property to a religiously affiliated college. The Valley Forge plaintiffs made the same argument as the instant clergy plaintiffs—that by conferring a benefit to a third party that was a religious entity, the government had violated the Establishment Clause. The Supreme Court considered whether plaintiffs had been injured as taxpayers—a subject we address below—and as "separationists" bent on policing the Establishment Clause. Accepting the sincerity of plaintiffs' ire at the alleged violation of the Establishment Clause, it held that such distress was not cognizable unless plaintiffs could "identify any personal injury suffered by them as a consequence of the alleged constitutional error * * *." It was not enough to point to an assertedly illegal benefit flowing to a third party that happened to be a religious entity. Absent a particularized injury, plaintiffs could not maintain suit.

In Allen v. Wright, the plaintiffs were parents of black children who attended public schools. They sued the IRS, asserting that it was duty-bound to deny tax-exempt status to racially discriminatory private schools, and its failure to do so impaired desegregation of the public school system. In Allen v. Wright, as here, plaintiffs' complaint centered on the tax-exempt status of a third party. The parents asserted two injuries, only one of which is pertinent to this case—harm from the fact that the government was giving financial assistance to private discriminatory schools. The Supreme Court held that the parents did not have standing and made several points on the injury in fact requirement.[4] Relying on Schlesinger v.

---

4. The Supreme Court held that although diminished opportunity for plaintiffs' children to obtain desegregated public education stated a cognizable injury in fact, the complaint failed to satisfy the standing requirement of traceability and redressability.

Reservists Committee to Stop the War, 418 U.S. 208, 94 S.Ct. 2925, 41 L.Ed.2d 706 (1974)(Reservists), the Court stated that "an asserted right to have the Government act in accordance with law is not sufficient, standing alone, to confer jurisdiction on a federal court." Parents did not derive standing by claiming "stigmatizing injury" caused by racial discrimination because "such injury accords a basis for standing only to 'those persons who are personally denied equal treatment' by the challenged discriminatory conduct." The Supreme Court then emphasized that when the injury asserted is an "abstract stigmatic injury," the requirement that a plaintiff be personally injured takes on heightened importance.

The clergy plaintiffs' complaint in the instant case suffers from the same defects as the parents' complaint in Allen v. Wright and the separationists' complaint in *Valley Forge*: The primary injury of which they complain is their discomfiture at watching the government allegedly fail to enforce the law with respect to a third party. As in *Valley Forge*, the instant plaintiffs state that defendants have violated their "sincere and deeply held belief in the separation of church and state." This injury can hardly be called personalized to the clergy plaintiffs. They can point to no illegal government conduct directly affecting their own ministries. Thus, the injury the clergy complain of could be asserted by any member of the public who disagrees with the views of the Catholic Church and the IRS in granting it a tax exemption.

Similarly, because the clergy have neither been personally denied equal treatment under the law nor in any way prosecuted by the IRS, their self-perceived "stigma" does not amount to a particularized injury in fact. To hold the clergy plaintiffs' injury cognizable would turn the federal court into "a forum in which to air * * * generalized grievances about the conduct of government." Hence, the clergy's complaint collapses into that of an offended bystander, insufficient to meet Article III's standing requirements. A mere "claim that the Government has violated the Establishment Clause does not provide [plaintiffs] a special license to roam the country in search of governmental wrongdoing and to reveal their discoveries in federal court."

This analysis is unchanged by the fact that the plaintiffs in this case are clergy. To rebut the argument that they have not suffered a particularized injury, these plaintiffs contend that what distinguishes them from the ordinary member of the public who takes issue with the Church and IRS is that they are members of the clergy. In our view, the holding in *Valley Forge* and its progeny would have been the same even had those plaintiffs been members of the clergy rather than Americans United For Separation of Church and State because "standing is not measured by the intensity of the litigant's interest or the fervor of his advocacy."

Moreover, granting standing to clergy qua clergy raises several troubling issues. Granting standing to the instant ministers and rabbis on the basis that they were directly and personally injured by the IRS' actions solely on account of their stature within their churches and synagogues would require us to give greater credence to the clergy's beliefs than the beliefs of their parishioners. Thus, to hold that a religious leader is more qualified to bring an Article III "case" or "controversy" than a member of his congregation seemingly entails an impermissible invasion into a church's or a synagogue's internal hierarchy and its autonomy. And, as the district court correctly noted, the Establishment Clause protects religions from secular interference.

Second, granting standing to enforce the Establishment Clause to clergy qua clergy might itself violate the same clause by constituting governmental favoritism of religion over non-religion. The Supreme Court has made clear that the Establishment Clause prohibits not only government endorsement of a given sect, but also forbids the government from generally favoring religion over secularism. Thus, the strength, intensity, or knowledge of one's religious beliefs obviously is not a criterion upon which to confer standing because such a rule would deny to non-believers the same benefits of maintaining suit. As Thomas Jefferson stated in his much quoted metaphor, the Establishment Clause was designed to build "a wall of separation between church and State." Plaintiffs point to no authority for a standing doctrine exception to this principle of separation between church and state. To read plaintiffs' complaint as stating a particularized injury simply because it is dressed in clerical garb would only weaken the foundation of Jefferson's metaphorical wall. As a consequence, stripped of the assertedly unique status of clergy, plaintiffs' injury is as generalized as that asserted in *Valley Forge* and Allen v. Wright, and their complaint must be similarly dismissed.

2. Taxpayer Standing

The taxpayer plaintiffs allege that they are "harmed because the government's subsidy of the * * * Church's illegal political activities is the equivalent of a government expenditure to establish a religion in violation of the First Amendment to the Constitution." In essence, they complain that not only is the government making illegal use of tax revenue, but also that they, as taxpayers, are forced to contribute to the government's asserted subsidy of the Catholic Church.

We set forth briefly the requirements for taxpayer standing, which are somewhat more specific than those for standing generally. The basic rule is that taxpayers do not have standing to challenge how the federal government spends tax revenue. See Frothingham v. Mellon, 262 U.S. 447, 488, 43 S.Ct. 597, 601, 67 L.Ed. 1078 (1923). In Flast v. Cohen, the Supreme Court created an exception to the *Frothingham* rule, holding that taxpayer standing is available to challenge Establishment Clause violations when the allegedly unconstitutional action was authorized by Congress under the taxing and spending clause of Art. I, § 8. Subsequent cases made clear the narrowness of *Flast's* exception to *Frothingham's* rule against taxpayer standing.

Then *Valley Forge*—handed down in the interim between the filing of the instant complaint and the motion to dismiss—caused some commentators to conclude that the taxpayer standing theory was virtually a dead letter. Hence, plaintiffs abandoned this theory in the district court. Following the Supreme Court's more recent decision in Bowen v. Kendrick, 108 S.Ct. 2562, 101 L.Ed.2d 520 (1988)(holding that taxpayers had standing to challenge the application of the Adolescent Family Life Act (AFLA)), plaintiffs renew before us their taxpayer standing arguments. In light of the protracted history of this litigation, it is appropriate to consider this issue now, if for no other reason than to prevent a third appeal.

The Supreme Court in *Kendrick* distinguished *Valley Forge* by emphasizing that in the latter case the decision by the executive agency to dispose of the surplus federal property—though made pursuant to a federal statute—was not a challenge to Congress' taxing and spending power because the statute's mandate derived from the property clause of Art. IV, § 3. In so doing, the Supreme Court clarified that taxpayer standing exists to challenge the executive branch's administration of a taxing and spending statute; the challenge need not be directed exclusively at Congress. But *Kendrick's* discussion of *Valley Forge* does not breathe new life into plaintiff's moribund taxpayer standing theory, as shall become evident.

In *Kendrick*, it was Congress that decided how the AFLA funds were to be spent, and the executive branch, in administering the statute, was merely carrying out Congress' scheme. See id. at 2580 ("[A]ppellees' claims call into question how the funds authorized by Congress are being disbursed pursuant to the AFLA's statutory mandate."). Thus, the Supreme Court held that taxpayers had standing to challenge whether Congress' decision under the taxing and spending clause had violated the limits imposed by the Establishment Clause.

Plaintiffs in the instant case do not challenge Congress' exercise of its taxing and spending power as embodied in § 501(c)(3) of the Code; they do not contend that the Code favors the Church. The Supreme Court, as noted, has already upheld the constitutionality of that section. Instead, they argue that the IRS, in allegedly closing its eyes to violations by the Church, is disregarding the Code's mandate and the Constitution. The complaint centers on an alleged decision made solely by the executive branch that in plaintiffs' view directly contravenes Congress' aim. The instant case is therefore distinguishable from *Kendrick*. In that case, there was "a sufficient nexus between the taxpayer's standing as a taxpayer and the congressional exercise of taxing and spending power, notwithstanding the role the Secretary plays in administering the statute." Here, there is no nexus between plaintiffs' allegations and Congress' exercise of its taxing and spending power. Hence, *Kendrick* does not alter the requirements of taxpayer standing to allow the instant plaintiffs to challenge how the IRS administers the Code. Consequently, plaintiffs fall within *Frothingham's* general rule denying taxpayer standing.

3. Voter Standing

The voter plaintiffs allege that they are injured because the IRS' refusal to revoke the Catholic Church's tax-exempt status "impairs and diminishes plaintiffs' right to vote." When it granted plaintiffs' "voter standing," the district court relied on Baker v. Carr, 369 U.S. 186, 82 S.Ct. 691, 7 L.Ed.2d 663 (1962). The district court's appellation of this theory as "voter standing" as applied to this case is a misnomer; plaintiffs' asserted basis for standing has nothing to do with voting. In Baker v. Carr, the Supreme Court held that disadvantaged voters had standing to challenge Tennessee's apportionment plan. The wrong that plaintiffs sought to vindicate in Baker v. Carr and in those cases that construed it was the dilution of their vote relative to the vote of other citizens of the same state—a direct, cognizable injury.

The Supreme Court has also held that disadvantaged voters may challenge an apportionment plan that is gerrymandered, that is, a plan whose voting district lines are drawn to reduce or eliminate the voting leverage of a given group of voters. It is undisputed that the instant plaintiffs do not allege that their vote has been diluted or that voting district lines have been gerrymandered to favor the Church or that anyone has "stuffed the ballot box" with votes for Church-backed candidates or that anyone has been prevented from voting. In short, plaintiffs here do not allege the particularized and objectively ascertainable injury in fact that sustained standing in the malapportionment cases. We therefore hold that Baker v. Carr and its progeny are inapposite and provide no basis for granting voter standing to these plaintiffs.

4.   Competitive Advocate Standing

We consider finally whether the plaintiffs may have standing under a theory that the district court did not explicitly consider, yet which derives from its discussion of "voter standing." This theory may be labeled as "Competitive Advocate Standing." It is addressed separately from voter standing for analytical clarity and because it presents a closer question.

Plaintiffs allege that they are injured "by the unequal enforcement of the Code by [the government] * * * which constitutes an illegal, unfair and unconstitutional distortion of the political process by the government * * *." They argue that their chance of electoral success is diminished because they do not receive the advantage that the Church receives from the government's asserted non-enforcement of the Code: The ability to campaign without losing tax-exemption under § 501(c)(3), and the ability nonetheless to offer their contributors a tax deduction for donating. "In the inherently competitive political arena an advantage granted to one competitor automatically constitutes a hardship to the others." The essence of this charge is that the IRS' non-enforcement of the Code creates an uneven playing field, tilted to favor the Catholic Church. The fatal flaw in the argument is that plaintiffs are not players in that arena or on that field.

The Supreme Court has found cognizable injuries to economic competitors. Implicit in the reasoning of those opinions is a requirement that in order to establish an injury as a competitor a plaintiff must show that he personally competes in the same arena with the party to whom the government has bestowed the assertedly illegal benefit. Only then does the plaintiff satisfy the rule that he was personally disadvantaged.

The economic competitor cases arose as banks diversified their functions, moved into new business areas, and became competitors of firms that had traditionally provided those services into which the banks sought to expand. The Supreme Court held that the organizations from which the banks sought to take away business—that is, with whom they sought to compete—had standing to challenge the banks' expansion into non-banking functions.

In each of these cases the banks obtained governmental rulings allowing them to compete on the same "playing field" as the plaintiffs. The results would have been different had the travel agents, for example, sought to complain about the bank's incursion into the data processing business. It is equally inappropriate to allow the present plaintiffs to challenge the IRS' treatment of the Church, since by their own admission they choose not to match the Church's alleged electioneering with their own. Therefore, they are not competitors.

* * * Plaintiffs' allegations of a political system biased against them by illegal government conduct are troubling. But, just as the Supreme Court has refused to recognize an Establishment Clause exception to standing doctrine, so must the requirements of Article III be applied with equal rigor to cases concerning participation in the political process. There is "no principled basis on which to create a hierarchy of constitutional values or a complementary 'sliding scale' of standing which might permit respondents to invoke the judicial power of the United States."

Like the claims of the clergy plaintiffs, the instant competitor claims lack particularized injury in fact. By asserting that an advantage to one competitor adversely handicaps the others, plaintiffs have not pleaded that they were personally denied equal treatment. They concede their tax status was correctly assessed by the IRS. Moreover, the complaint indicates that no plaintiff is currently a political candidate for public office. Plainly, the whole point of this lawsuit is plaintiffs' contention that it is illegal for the Catholic Church as a § 501(c)(3) recipient to participate actively in the political process. And, recognizing that potential illegality and the value of their own exemptions under §§ 501(c)(3) and (c)(4), plaintiffs state that they have refused to engage in electioneering to counter the Church's pro-life stance. Partly as a result of this self-imposed restraint, plaintiffs chose not to compete.

It may be argued that to qualify as competitor advocates plaintiffs need not go so far as to run for office or lobby; rather, they may simply advocate the pro-choice cause and stop short of supporting candidates. But that argument fails to answer the nagging question of why these individuals and organizations are then the appropriate parties to call a halt to the alleged wrongdoing. It is obvious that plaintiffs express their pro-choice views strongly and articulately. Yet such strongly held beliefs are not a substitute for injury in fact.

A further problem with recognizing a competitor advocate theory of standing in the present case is that it would be difficult to deny standing to any person who simply expressed an opinion contrary to that of the

Catholic Church. Affording standing on that basis would lack a limiting principle, and would effectively give standing to any spectator who supported a given side in public political debate. Cf. J.H. Ely, Democracy and Distrust 103 (1980)(courts should intervene when the playing field is tilted, not when they think the wrong side has scored). This is precisely the problem the Supreme Court addressed in *Valley Forge* when it denied standing to plaintiffs who sued as taxpayers and citizens. We think that result would have been the same even had they called themselves "competitor advocates"—as proponents of a theory of the Establishment Clause different than that held by the government or the college that received the government benefit.

* * *

We do not foreclose the possibility that political competitors may state a cognizable injury; instead, we simply hold that the theory cannot be sustained here. Putting out into the stormy sea of this litigation, it is prudent to closely hug the shores of the pleaded facts and established law, and not venture out any further than we must. As a consequence, because we hold that plaintiffs have not pleaded a direct injury in fact, we need not decide whether the two other standing requirements of traceability and redressability have been met.

III. CONCLUSION

It could be argued that if no one among this diverse group of plaintiffs has standing to challenge the IRS' application of 501(c)(3) to the Church, then perhaps no one could ever have standing to raise this issue. But such is irrelevant for determining whether the "case" or "controversy" requirement has been satisfied. As the Supreme Court noted, that "view would convert standing into a requirement that must be observed only when satisfied." Moreover, the lack of a plaintiff to litigate an issue may suggest that the matter is more appropriately dealt with by Congress and the political process.

Without reaching or deciding whether there are prudential reasons not to exercise jurisdiction, we conclude that plaintiffs have not met the Article III minimum requirements for standing. In sum, we hold that none of the plaintiffs has standing, that the district court therefore did not have subject matter jurisdiction, that the contempt adjudication must be vacated, and that the order denying the motion to dismiss the case must be reversed and the plaintiffs' complaint dismissed.

Reversed and complaint dismissed.

■ JON O. NEWMAN, CIRCUIT JUDGE, dissenting:

The Court today rules that tax-exempt organizations advocating the right to an abortion have no standing to challenge the actions of the Internal Revenue Service in failing to enforce against the Catholic Church the statutory requirement that prohibits tax-exempt organizations from "participat[ing] in, or interven[ing] in * * * any political campaign * * *." 26 U.S.C.A. § 501(c)(3)(1982). The Court reaches this result by concluding that the "pro-choice" organizations are not competitors of the Catholic Church in the political arena on the subject of abortion. Because I believe that conclusion is incorrect—indeed, that it is contrary to the undisputed facts of the abortion controversy in Twentieth Century America, I respectfully dissent.

The majority begins its analysis by labeling the issue that divides us as "Competitive Advocate Standing." I think that is an admirable designation. The majority then recognizes that standing is frequently recognized for those who seek to challenge the lawfulness of governmental actions that inure to the benefit of their competitors. The majority then concludes that the competitor standing rule of these cases does not apply to the tax-exempt "pro-choice" organizations that are plaintiffs in this suit because they do not intervene in political campaigns.

That conclusion rests on a needlessly narrow view of both the realities of American political life and the contours of the doctrine of competitive advocate standing. To be an advocate in the political arena in this country, organizations and their members need not intervene in the campaign of any particular candidate for public office. Political advocacy takes many forms. To promote their views, a few people run for office. Others support candidates. But most Americans advocate their side of public issues by standing up for what they believe through a wide range of activities beyond the formal processes of electoral politics. They speak to their friends and neighbors; they participate in community activities; they devote their time, their energy, and sometimes their money to their causes. All who engage in these activities are competing in the arena of public advocacy with those who choose to support differing points of view by various forms of advocacy, including backing like-minded political candidates.

The competition necessary to confer competitor standing need not be in the identical activity of one's economic or philosophical opponent. When the Texas Monthly challenged the tax exemption of religious magazines, it did not wish to compete in the precise activity of publishing religious magazines. It wished to compete in the broader field of magazine publishing, and it was accorded standing to challenge the economic benefit of a tax exemption conferred upon the competitive publisher of a religious magazine. So here, plaintiffs Abortion Rights Mobilization, Inc. and the National Women's Health Network, Inc. do not wish to compete in the political arena with the Catholic Church on the issue of abortion by the precise technique of supporting candidates for public office. Instead, they have chosen to compete in advocating their side of the abortion issue by distributing information on the availability of abortions, by speaking, writing, and marching, and by championing in countless other ways the cause of abortion rights.

If the words are to have any meaning at all, these plaintiffs are indisputably "competitive advocates" of the Catholic Church on the issue of abortion.

The majority reckons with the argument that the plaintiff 501(c)(3) organizations might qualify as competitive advocates if they "simply advocate the pro-choice cause and stop short of supporting candidates." The argument is dismissed by the assertion that the strongly held beliefs of the plaintiffs "are not a substitute for injury in fact." Of course, they are not. But no one claims they are. The injury in fact is the competitive disadvantage the plaintiff organizations are obliged to endure when, accepting at this stage the allegations of the complaint, the Catholic Church is permitted to violate the tax laws by using tax-exempt donations to support the "anti-abortion" side of the national debate through contributions to like-minded political candidates, while the plaintiff organizations must confine their advocacy of the "pro-choice" side to those insubstantial lobbying activities that the tax laws permit. If the allegations of the complaint are true, and plaintiffs seek only the opportunity to prove them, the plaintiff organizations are seriously injured both in the eyes of the law and in the real world of political advocacy by the significant advantage currently enjoyed by the Catholic Church as a result of governmental action that violates the tax laws. According to the complaint, the Catholic Church is using its tax-free funds to support political candidates who oppose the right to an abortion; the plaintiff 501(c)(3) organizations, abiding by the terms of the tax law, are limited to other forms of advocacy. Both sides are competing in the arena of public advocacy, but governmental action is tolerating a law violation that enables one side to promote its cause with a significant technique denied to the other side. That should be sufficient to permit the claim of law violation to be litigated.

In the majority's view, the plaintiff 501(c)(3) organizations and the Catholic Church are not competitors in the arena of public advocacy on the issue of abortion because the plaintiffs "choose not to match the Church's alleged electioneering with their own." That makes it sound as if the plaintiff 501(c)(3) organizations have simply decided as a matter of personal preference that they do not wish to match the Church's alleged electioneering. But the decision to forgo electioneering is not a matter of personal preference, it is obedience to a requirement of an act of Congress. I fail to understand why any person or organization, seeking to challenge a violation of federal law, should be denied access to a federal court for the reason that it is obeying the law.

The majority further supports its rejection of competitive advocate standing by expressing concern that such standing would be too extensive, that "it would be difficult to deny standing to any person who simply expressed an opinion contrary to that of the Catholic Church." I think this fear is groundless. The competition that most clearly creates standing in this case is not between the Catholic Church and every citizen who holds a contrary view on the issue of abortion. Such citizens are not limited by a statute that they are prepared to prove the Catholic Church is violating to their disadvantage. The competition is between those tax-exempt organizations that are abiding by the limitations of section 501(c)(3) in their advocacy on the abortion issue and the Catholic Church, which is violating these limitations in the advocacy of its point of view on the issue. Whether an individual citizen could challenge the Church's tax exemption on the theory that its unlawful support of political candidates is aided by tax-free donations unavailable to the ordinary citizen is a question far beyond the narrow issue we are required to decide in this case. A standing doctrine is entirely within manageable bounds when it recognizes the competition among organizations all of which are subject to the same statutory restraint and permits the law-abiding competitors to challenge the governmental action that enables one organization to violate that restraint to the detriment of the others.

A variant of the competitive advocate doctrine should also confer standing on the one plaintiff that is a 501(c)(4) organization, Long Island National Organization for Women–Nassau ("Nassau NOW"). This plaintiff, by qualifying as a tax-exempt organization under section 501(c)(4), is not subject to the restraints on political activity imposed by section 501(c)(3), but is obliged to solicit donations that are not tax deductible to the donors. Like the 501(c)(3) plaintiffs, Nassau–NOW competes with the Catholic Church in the arena of public advocacy on the issue of abortion, but does so under a competitive disadvantage that is different from the one existing between the Church and the 501(c)(3) plaintiffs. The latter may not support political candidates at all, while the Church, though barred from doing so, provides such support (according to the complaint). Nassau–NOW may engage in political activity but only with donations that cost its donors 100 cents on the dollar, while the Church supports political candidates with tax deductible donations that cost its donors only 67, 72, or 85 cents for every dollar contributed, depending on whether they are in the 33%, 28% or 15% bracket. That competitive disadvantage, arising from what plaintiffs are prepared to prove is a violation of law, is also sufficient to confer standing on the entity that is disadvantaged.

Whether any of the other plaintiffs have standing presents issues that I need not decide. We are asked to adjudicate the lawfulness of a contempt citation for refusing lawful discovery requests that has been challenged solely on the ground that the District Court lacks jurisdiction over the subject matter of the complaint. If any one plaintiff has standing to bring this lawsuit, the jurisdiction of the District Court to require compliance with the discovery requests is established, and the contempt judgment against the recalcitrant witnesses should be affirmed. For these reasons, I respectfully dissent.

ON REHEARING

■ Per Curiam:

Appellants have sought rehearing, alleging inconsistency between the opinion in this case and an opinion issued by another panel in Fulani v. League of Women Voters Education Fund, 882 F.2d 621 (2d Cir.1989). In *Fulani*, competitor standing was accorded to a political candidate to challenge her exclusion from a televised debate in which her political rivals were invited to participate. A majority of the panel concluded that she suffered sufficient injury to establish standing. In the present case, though this panel is divided as to whether the plaintiffs are sufficiently in competition with the Catholic Church to have suffered injury that confers standing, we are in agreement that the competition in *Fulani* is more direct and immediate than that shown here.

The petition for rehearing is denied.

NOTES AND QUESTIONS

1. *Postscript.* The day after the Supreme Court denied certiorari in *Abortion Rights Mobilization*, the organization's president, Lawrence Lader, was quoted as saying, "I just don't know how you'd come up with a plaintiff to fit the Court's definition of standing." Linda Greenhouse, Supreme Court Roundup; Suit on Church Tax Status and Abortion Fails, N.Y. Times, May 1, 1990, at A18. Was Mr. Lader correct? Could the plaintiffs have positioned themselves more effectively to obtain standing? What if they had sought tax exemption under § 501(c)(3) for an organization that stated unequivocally that it intended to engage in political activities on abortion issues? Once the application was denied, could the organization survive a standing challenge in its suit to enjoin the Catholic Church's exemption?

2. *For Further Reading.* Note, Standing to Challenge Tax–Exempt Status: The Second Circuit's Competitive Political Advocate Theory, 58 Fordham L. Rev. 723 (1990); Note, Voter Standing: A New Means for Third Parties to Challenge the Tax–Exempt Status of Nonprofit Organizations?, 16 Hastings Const. L.Q. 453 (1989).

CHAPTER 6

COMMERCIAL ACTIVITIES AND UNRELATED BUSINESS INCOME

A. INTRODUCTION

As previewed in Chapter 1, a nonprofit organization is not prohibited from making an economic profit. Many nonprofits engage in activities that are "commercial" in the sense that they resemble businesses conducted by for-profit firms. A revenue generating activity may be the exempt organization's very reason for existence (e.g., a health care provider or religious publisher), a support function that may or may not make a profit (e.g., a museum cafeteria or gift shop), a business activity unrelated to the organization's exempt purposes that is conducted to raise funds to support its core mission, or (worst case) an unrelated business that dedicates its profits to expand or buy other companies.

The "commercialization" of the nonprofit sector has been widely publicized and hotly debated for years. Over 50 years ago, the popular press warned of the perceived abuses of tax exemption. A December, 1948 front-page story in The New York Times described how universities were being used as tax shelters for business profits.[1] Two years later, an article in Fortune magazine was titled with the exhortation: "The Abuse of Tax Exemption: It Has Got to the Point Where Something Has to Be Done About It."[2] As this chapter will reveal, something *was* done in 1950. But since then, commercial activities have increased, attracting the attention of the small business community, Congressional taxwriting committees, the Internal Revenue Service, muckraking journalists, *New Yorker* cartoons[3] and last, but not least, economists and legal scholars.

As the debate has raged, for-profit firms complain that they are victims of unfair competition, while nonprofit organizations counter that income-producing activities are vital to support their missions and reduce dependence on government and private philanthropy. Some major charities, principally in health care, higher education and the arts, have raised the stakes by conducting commercial activities through complex structures, such as corporate subsidiaries and joint ventures with for-profit entities

---

1. Benjamin Fine, University Dollars Yielding Tax–Free Business Profits, N.Y. Times, Dec. 13, 1948, at A1, A29.

2. Fortune, May 1950, at 74.

3. A December 15, 1976 cartoon depicted Santa Claus saying to his elves, "I've been thinking. This year, instead of *giving* everything away, why don't we charge a little something." The authors thank Professor John Simon for this discovery.

and private investors. The IRS has responded by devoting more of its resources to patrolling the charity/business border and uncovering transactions where nonprofits are used as facilitators for tax avoidance by for-profit taxpayers. Congress has barked but rarely bitten, confining itself to occasional inquiries and threats, usually followed by inaction or special interest relief legislation.

The contemporary conventional wisdom is that the nonprofit sector is undergoing a commercial transformation. More nonprofits are said to be straying from their stated mission as they increasingly mimic for-profit firms. At the same time, for-profit firms are encroaching on traditional nonprofit turf in areas such as education and health care. There is not uniform agreement as to whether these sector-blurring trends are desirable. The excerpt that follows, from a study by economists and social scientists, describes the phenomenon.

Burton A. Weisbrod, The Nonprofit Mission and Its Financing: Growing Links Between Nonprofits and the Rest of the Economy

To Profit or Not to Profit: The Commercial Transformation of the Nonprofit Sector 1–4 (Burton A. Weisbrod, ed. 1998).

Massive change is occurring in the nonprofit sector. Seemingly isolated events touching the lives of virtually everyone are, in fact, parts of a pattern that is little recognized but has enormous impact; it is a pattern of growing commercialization of nonprofit organizations:

Nonprofit *hospitals* are launching health clubs open to the public, with the latest exercise equipment and Olympic-size swimming pools, generating substantial profits and threatening the for-profit fitness center industry.

Nonprofit *museums* are opening glitzy retail shops, generating revenue that is now a larger percentage of operating income than that from federal funding or admissions and memberships.

Nonprofit *universities* are engaging in research alliances with private firms and suppressing research findings that are unfavorable to those firms' profit prospects.

Nonprofits in various industries are forming for-profit subsidiaries, engaging in joint ventures with private firms, and paying executives compensation at "Fortune 500" levels.

Commercialism in the nonprofit sector sounds like a paradox: Nonprofits are supposed to be different from private firms, for whom commercialism is their very lifeblood. To some people, though, the uniqueness of nonprofit organizations is by no means self-evident; perhaps they are really not different from private firms, but are just as influenced by business motives and opportunities for self-aggrandizement.

Late in 1997 two apparently unrelated events brought front-page headlines. One involved a contract between the American Medical Association and the Sunbeam Corporation, a manufacturer of consumer electronic products, with the AMA promising to endorse Sunbeam products, such as heating pads and vaporizers, in return for payments expected to yield millions of dollars. The other involved the purchase by Chicago's Field Museum of Natural History of "Sue," the largest complete *Tyrannosaurus rex* fossil in existence—the $8.3 million cost being financed largely by McDonald's and the Walt Disney Company. McDonald's will get several "life-size replicas of the ferocious dinosaur, one of the most widely recognized dinosaurs and a powerful promotional tool," and one of the replicas will be displayed at McDonald's DinoLand USA attraction at Disney's new Animal Kingdom theme park. In addition, the museum will display the original in its new McDonald's Fossil Preparatory Laboratory, and there is talk of miniatures, with the Field Museum name, being included in hamburger Happy Meals.

Both the AMA and Field Museum cases involved nonprofit, tax-exempt organizations contracting to receive multimillion-dollar payments from private firms. Both arrangements generated money but also criticism. The criticism of the AMA was so intense that its top leadership resigned and the AMA broke the agreement with Sunbeam, resulting in a $20 million breach-of-contract lawsuit.

The nonprofit sector has been both criticized and acclaimed. The rationale for its special tax treatment and subsidies rests on the belief that it provides services that are materially different from, and preferred to, the services that private enterprise provides. * * * [Prof. Weisbrod then describes the growth of the nonprofit sector and suggests that it reflects an increase in the gap between perceived social needs and the capacity of government to provide these public-type services. Eds.]

As the nonprofit sector grows, the debate over its proper role in a modern economy continues, periodically grabbing public attention: private firms claim they are victims of "unfair competition" from subsidized, tax-exempt, nonprofits, pressuring lawmakers to restrict nonprofits' commercial activities; the federal government considers revising the personal income tax in ways that will affect incentives to donate to charitable nonprofits; local governments introduce the latest device for extracting money from supposedly tax-exempt nonprofits.

In short, what brings the activities into the limelight is their links with the rest of the economy. Contrary to the common view, nonprofits are far from independent of private enterprise and government. They compete with and collaborate with these other organizations in countless ways in their efforts to finance themselves, to find workers, managers, and other resources to produce their outputs, and to develop markets for those outputs.

Professor Weisbrod's study went on to examine the extent to which increasing commercialization affects the behavior of nonprofit organizations, both generally and in specific sectors such as health, education and the arts. This chapter has a narrower focus, limiting its coverage to the tax system's response to the pursuit of profit by nonprofits. The conduct of a business by an otherwise tax-exempt organization raises two distinct issues under current federal income tax law: first, does the activity adversely affect the organization's exempt status and second, if not, should the net income of certain business activities nonetheless be taxed and how far should this tax extend. Part B of this chapter considers the tax exemption question, focusing primarily on § 501(c)(3) charities. Parts C through E survey the history, policy and basic structure of IRS's principal border patrol sentry, the unrelated business income tax, or "UBIT," as we shall come to know it. For those with the time and fortitude for more advanced study, the next three parts of the chapter address computation issues, including strategic allocation of expenses, and the special problems raised by complex structures such as taxable subsidiaries and joint ventures. The chapter concludes with a brief look at reform proposals.

For Further Reading. Joseph J. Cordes & C. Eugene Steurle (eds.), Nonprofits & Business (Urban Institute Press, 2009).

B. IMPACT OF COMMERCIAL ACTIVITIES ON EXEMPT STATUS

1. INTRODUCTION

Internal Revenue Code: § 502

Treasury Regulations: § 1.501(c)(3)–1(b)(1)(i), –1(c)(1), –1(e).

The impact of commercial activity on tax exemption is an untidy area of the law. No intelligent discussion can begin without at least a sneak preview of the unrelated business income tax, familiarly known as the UBIT, which is covered in depth later in this chapter. Since the UBIT's enactment in 1950, charitable and most other exempt organizations have been taxable on any net income from an "unrelated" trade or business. Very generally, and ignoring many specialized exceptions, an unrelated trade or business is an income-producing activity (other than passive investing) that is regularly carried on and not "substantially related" to an organization's exempt purposes apart from the need for income to support its charitable or other exempt mission. See I.R.C. §§ 511–514. The UBIT was enacted in response to real and perceived abuses by tax-exempt organizations, charges of unfair competition from the business community, and—like any tax bill—to raise revenue. At the same time, Congress added § 502, which provides that an organization operated for the primary purpose of carrying on a trade or business for profit shall not be exempt from tax under § 501 on the ground that all of its profits are payable to one or more tax-exempt organizations. This provision denies exemption to so called "feeder corporations," which are entities that operate a business as their sole activity and typically are obligated to pay over their profits to an affiliated § 501(c)(3) organization.

Under pre-UBIT case law, a charity conducting an unrelated business, even as its sole activity, qualified for exemption if its net profits were used to support an exempt purpose or were paid over to a bona fide charity. Even feeder corporations qualified—e.g., a shoe store obligated by its charter to distribute its profits to support a school. The theory, as articulated by the Supreme Court in dictum and then with greater clarity in later circuit court decisions, was that the destination of income, not its source, was the ultimate test of exemption. See Trinidad v. Sagrada Orden, 263 U.S. 578, 44 S.Ct. 204 (1924); Roche's Beach, Inc. v. Commissioner, 96 F.2d 776 (2d Cir. 1938); C.F. Mueller Co. v. Commissioner, 190 F.2d 120 (3d Cir.1951). When it enacted the UBIT and decided to tax "unrelated" business income, Congress discarded the destination of income test for UBIT purposes. But the standards for § 501(c)(3) exemption were not altered except in the narrow case of feeder corporations described in § 502.

There is no bright line test to answer the question of whether and to what extent the conduct of commercial activity jeopardizes qualification for exemption under § 501(c)(3). The statute merely requires an organization to be organized and operated "exclusively" for one or more of the enumerated exempt purposes. Looking next at the regulations, an organization's articles of incorporation (or trust agreement) may not "expressly empower" it to "engage, other than as an insubstantial part of its activities, in activities which in themselves are not in furtherance of one or more exempt purposes." Treas. Reg. § 1.501(c)(3)–1(b)(1)(i). Notably, the focus here is on substantial nonexempt *activities*, not on whether or not an organization's primary purpose is charitable. The regulations later warn that an organization will fail the organizational test if its articles empower it to "engage in a manufacturing business." Treas. Reg. § 1.501(c)(3)–1(b)(1)(iii). Read literally, these regulations seem to say that there is little leeway for "substantial" unrelated business activities.

Similarly, the operational test regulations, after interpreting "exclusively" as used in § 501(c)(3) to mean "primarily," go on to provide that an organization will not qualify for exemption "if more than an insubstantial part of its activities is not in furtherance of an exempt purpose." Treas. Reg. § 1.501(c)(3)–1(c)(1). Although the regulations offer no guidance on what types of activities do or do not further an exempt purpose, they seem to leave some room for insubstantial commercial activity, whatever its motivation. They later elaborate by providing that an organization will qualify for § 501(c)(3) exemption "although it operates a trade or business as a substantial part of its activities, if the operation of such trade or business is in furtherance of the organization's exempt purpose or purposes and if the organization is not organized or operated for the primary purpose of carrying on an unrelated trade or business, as defined in Section 513." Treas. Reg. § 1.501(c)(3)–1(e). An organization's primary purpose is to be determined by all the facts and circumstances, "including the size and extent of the trade or business and the size or extent of the activities which are in furtherance of one or more exempt purposes." Id.

The regulations are susceptible to varying interpretations. Many courts and commentators see them as importing a "commerciality" doctrine into § 501(c)(3). Under this theory, an otherwise qualified § 501(c)(3) organization does not lose its exemption by engaging in insubstantial business activities, even if they are unrelated to its exempt purposes. Substantial business activities also are permissible if they are "in furtherance of" (does that mean "related to"?) exempt purposes. But exemption is denied if unrelated trade or business activities are "substantial" in relation to charitable activities because at that point the organization's "primary purpose" is a trade or business. See, e.g., Joint Committee on Taxation, Historical Development and Present Law of the Federal Tax Exemption for Charities and Other Tax–Exempt Organizations (JCX–29–05), 51–52 (April 19, 2005), which assumes that this articulation of the commerciality doctrine is an accurate statement of current law.

It follows under this view that if an organization's unrelated business activities are "insubstantial," its exemption is secure and the only sanction is the UBIT. But if unrelated business income (net or gross?) exceeds some blurry substantiality benchmark (some cautious advisors assume it is 20 percent of total revenue for planning purposes, others say it is higher, and the most adventuresome think there is no limit), the organization no longer qualifies for exemption, whether or not the revenue is used to subsidize a charitable activity. This theory loosely links the exemption qualification question with the UBIT relatedness standard. It has caused risk-averse exempt organizations to establish subsidiary corporations to conduct any major unrelated business. In many of the cases and IRS rulings, however, the inquiry begins and ends with an amorphous "all the facts and circumstances" smell test that never even mentions the UBIT.

A contrary and more permissive view is that current law does not impose any per se limit on the amount of unrelated business income or activity for § 501(c)(3) qualification purposes. Proponents point to an IRS ruling holding that an organization relying on commercial revenue for its sole source of support qualifies for § 501(c)(3) exemption if it conducts a charitable grantmaking program "commensurate in scope with its financial resources." Rev. Rul. 64–182, infra p. 586. This theory assumes that, in enacting the UBIT, Congress did not intend to overturn the destination of income test for exemption qualification purposes except in the narrow case of § 502 feeder corporations. It follows that any amount of unrelated business income is permissible provided that the organization's "primary purpose" is charitable, as measured (somehow) by the exceedingly vague commensurate-in-scope standard.

As we said, this area is untidy. The materials below elaborate on this introductory snapshot, illustrating the tension between charity and commerce as it relates to § 501(c)(3) exemption in a few typical settings.

2.   THE COMMERCIALITY DOCTRINE

Goldsboro Art League v. Commissioner

Tax Court of the United States, 1980.
75 T.C. 337.

OPINION

■ TIETJENS, JUDGE: Respondent determined that petitioner is not exempt from Federal income tax under section 501(c)(3). The prerequisites for declaratory judgment having been satisfied, petitioner has, pursuant to section 7428, invoked the jurisdiction of this Court. The issue for our determination is whether petitioner is operated exclusively for one or more exempt purposes delineated in section 501(c)(3).

Petitioner, a nonprofit North Carolina corporation incorporated on May 24, 1971, has its principal office in Goldsboro, N.C. On November 20, 1978, the District Director of Internal Revenue, Atlanta, EP/EO Service Unit, received petitioner's application for recognition of exemption. On October 26, 1979, respondent issued to petitioner a final adverse ruling letter which denied petitioner tax-exempt status for the following reasons: "You are not operated exclusively for any exempt purpose within the meaning of section 501(c)(3) of the Code. You are operated in furtherance of a substantial commercial purpose. Further, you serve private rather than public interests."

Petitioner's charter states that it is organized for the following purposes: to promote the appreciation of and participation in the visual arts; to promote and encourage the expression of creativity through the creative arts; to promote education in the fine arts; to sponsor a creative arts center to provide a facility for instruction, creation and display of paintings, statuary and objects of creative arts; but the corporation shall not pursue any purpose or carry on any activity inconsistent with Sections 501(c)(3) and 170(c)(2) of the Internal Revenue Code.

Petitioner has 12 board members whose professional backgrounds include careers in business, law, education, art, and religion. The president of petitioner, for 1978–79, has a master of divinity degree from Duke University and is Director of Continuing Education at Wayne Community College. Petitioner's vice president is an attorney; its secretary, an interior designer; and its treasurer, an accountant.

Petitioner is the hub of many art activities in Wayne County and is known throughout the State for the quality of its programs. There are no other art museums, galleries, or similar facilities of significant note available within Wayne, or any contiguous, county.

Petitioner operates the Goldsboro Art Center (hereinafter center) which furnishes various educational and charitable services to the community. Specifically, the Center sponsors art classes in conjunction with Wayne Community College (hereinafter college), in such areas as watercolor, oil, and acrylic painting; pottery; interior design; macrame and weaving. The center offers an average of 20 to 25 classes quarterly for approximately 250 students. In addition, on its own, petitioner offers courses for children in pottery, drawing, discovering art, puppetry, creative stitchery, and painting.

The center sponsors art demonstrations, including one at the Wayne County Agricultural Fair each year, and workshops in, for example, Japanese watercolor techniques and Ink Resist (wash techniques). In conjunction with the college and the North Carolina Art Society, the center sponsors film series, including the 13–part "Civilization" series narrated by Sir Kenneth Clark.

Petitioner owns 52 pieces of art as a permanent collection[5] which it displays in various public buildings throughout Wayne County, including the college, Wayne Memorial Hospital, the Wayne County administration building, the Goldsboro City Hall Annex, the Goldsboro fire and police complex, the Wayne County revenue building, city parks and recreation, and the Wayne County Public Library. The artwork is hung and maintained by members of petitioner. Local Scout troops, school groups, clubs, and other interested persons are given tours of the center, and an estimate of over 400 people are involved in the center's activities each week.

The director of the center gives a series of lectures on art at the Goldsboro High School humanities classes and speaks to both elementary and secondary Goldsboro and Wayne County public school classes. The director of the center also participates in Wayne County and Goldsboro school system's "career day" each year. Likewise, petitioner conducts art oriented workshops for teachers in Goldsboro and Wayne County and public exhibits of the artwork of Goldsboro and Wayne County public school children. Petitioner offers the Goldsboro Camera Club space for a darkroom. Petitioner organizes bus tours to the North Carolina Museum of Art in Raleigh. Petitioner also sponsors tours to the two local State-supported mental institutions.

Petitioner has some paid employees, but it relies heavily on volunteer help. It also hires some of its staff through the Youth Improvement Program, CETA, the Retired Senior Volunteer Program, and the Community College Work Study Program.

Besides these activities, petitioner operates two public galleries, the Art Market and the Art Gallery. All artworks in these galleries are selected by jury procedures to insure artistic quality and integrity. The Art Market and the Art Gallery are similar in that they both exhibit and sell artwork except that the former invites displays from numerous artists, while the latter only features one artist each month. The Art Market has paintings, drawings, sculpture, etchings, serigraphs, lithographs, weavings, pottery, and mobiles. These galleries often exhibit an artist's more daring work.

---

5. On petitioner's books, these works are valued at $614.70, but most were donated by the artists themselves and are, therefore, valued at cost and at significantly less than their fair market value. Petitioner estimates their market value to be more than $30,000.

Petitioner's sales are made pursuant to a mutual understanding between petitioner and the artist without a written contract specifying the
terms of sales. Petitioner collects any sales proceeds and turns over that
money, less approximately 20–percent commission for estimated expenses,
to the artist. [The court then discussed the gallery's relatively minor
receipts and expenses for the years in question. Gross receipts never
exceeded $6,500 per year and, after deducting amounts paid to the artists
and other expenses, net profits were negligible, never exceeding $750. The
organization's total revenues from all sources in 1976–1978 were, respectively, approximately $47,109, $47,440, and $57,289. Eds.]

* * *

Petitioner contends that it is operated exclusively for exempt purposes,
that the sale of artwork in its galleries is an incidental activity but one
which helps it pursue its exempt purposes, that petitioner is not operated
in furtherance of a substantial commercial purpose, and that the primary
purpose of the sales, as well as petitioner's other activities, is to further the
public's appreciation of art and not to serve private interests.

Respondent, by contrast, argues that since petitioner's activities are
indistinguishable from activities required in operating a commercial art
gallery for profit, petitioner is operated for a substantial commercial
purpose; therefore, respondent asserts, under Better Business Bureau v.
United States, 326 U.S. 279 (1945), petitioner may not qualify for exemption under section 501(c)(3) despite the presence of any number of truly
exempt purposes.

Moreover, respondent maintains that providing individual artists with
direct monetary benefits derived from the sale of created artworks serves
more than incidentally the private interests of designated individuals.

Respondent's final ruling letter denied petitioner exempt status on the
grounds that it is not operated exclusively for any exempt purpose, that it
is operated in furtherance of a substantial commercial purpose, and that it
serves private rather than public interests. Petitioner has the burden of
proof to show that respondent's determination is wrong.

We find that petitioner has sustained its burden and is exempt from
Federal taxation under section 501(c)(3).

In order to be exempt under section 501(c)(3), an organization must
qualify under both the organizational and the operational tests. Sec.
1.501(c)(3)–1(a)(1), Income Tax Regs. Respondent does not question that
petitioner qualifies for exemption under the organizational test; rather,
respondent's denial of exemption is based on his conclusion that petitioner
does not satisfy the operational test.

The operational test requires an organization's activities to be primarily those which accomplish one or more exempt purposes as specified in
section 501(c)(3) and not, except to an insubstantial part, those which do
not further an exempt purpose. Sec. 1.501(c)(3)–1(c)(1), Income Tax Regs.
A substantial nonexempt purpose will disqualify an organization from tax

exemption despite the number or the importance of its exempt purposes. Better Business Bureau v. United States, supra. The operational test focuses on the purpose and not on the nature of the activity. An organization may engage in a trade or business as long as its operation furthers an exempt purpose and its primary objective is not the production of profits. An organization is not operated exclusively for one or more exempt purposes, however, unless it serves a public rather than a private interest. Sec. 1.501(c)(3)–1(d)(1)(ii), Income Tax Regs. * * * Whether an organization satisfies the operational test is a question of fact.

Included among the exempt purposes are "educational" and "charitable" purposes. Sec. 1.501(c)(3)–1(d)(1)(i)(b) and (f), Income Tax Regs. "Educational" is defined as:

(a) The instruction or training of the individual for the purpose of improving or developing his capabilities; or

(b) The instruction of the public on subjects useful to the individual and beneficial to the community.

Sec. 1.501(c)(3)–1(d)(3), Income Tax Regs. The promotion of the arts has consistently been recognized as both charitable and educational. Indeed, respondent does not question that the overwhelming purpose of petitioner's art classes, films, museum tours, and display of its permanent collection is charitable or educational. Respondent, however, contends that two of petitioner's activities, the operations of its Art Market and Art Gallery, further a substantial commercial purpose and serve the private interests of individual professional artists. He argues that the evidence indicates that the sales activity is an end in itself rather than a means of accomplishing an exempt purpose.

We disagree with respondent's conclusions and find that the evidence presented here confirms, as petitioner suggests, that the purpose of the Art Gallery and Art Market is primarily to foster community awareness and appreciation of contemporary artists and to provide a constant flow of art for students to study art and painting techniques.

Among the factors we consider in determining whether an organization is operated to further a substantial commercial purpose are the particular manner in which an organization's activities are conducted, the commercial hue of these activities, and the existence and amount of profit from these activities.

In the instant case, since there are no other art museums or galleries in the area, petitioner has found difficulty attracting artists to exhibit their work without the incentive of the Art Gallery and Art Market.[6] Petitioner has a jury to select which works will be displayed, and we find it significant that the works are chosen not for their salability but for their representation of modern trends. Exhibiting an artist's more daring works in a part of

---

6. That there may be other possible means of attracting artists to exhibit their work is not, as respondent suggests, determinative. It is sufficient that we find that petitioner's purpose in these activities is an exempt one.

the country where there are no nearby art museums or galleries illustrates that petitioner's purpose is primarily to educate rather than to sell.

Moreover, petitioner's activities with respect to the Art Market and Art Gallery must be viewed in connection with petitioner's other activities. The clear impression that we get from the record is one of petitioner's dedication to teach the public, through a variety of means, to appreciate art. We find that petitioner's sales activities are incidental to its other activities and serve the same overall objective of art education. This is not a case where the other activities are adjunct to petitioner's sales, but, rather, where petitioner's sales activities are secondary and incidental to furthering its exempt purpose. * * *

We are convinced, moreover, that petitioner is not operating these galleries for a profit. Petitioner retains only approximately 20 percent of the gross receipts from the sales and uses this amount to defray its expenses. A review of petitioner's books for 3 years shows that petitioner has either made no profit or, at most, a negligible one, for these years.

[The court also rejected the IRS's private benefit and inurement arguments. Eds.]

Because petitioner is organized and operated exclusively for an exempt purpose, is not operated in furtherance of a substantial commercial purpose, and serves public rather than private interests, petitioner is entitled to exemption from Federal taxation under sections 501(a) and 501(c)(3).

Decision will be entered for the petitioner.

Presbyterian and Reformed Publishing Co. v. Commissioner

United States Court of Appeals, Third Circuit, 1984.
743 F.2d 148.

■ ADAMS, CIRCUIT JUDGE.

This is an appeal from a decision of the United States Tax Court affirming the Internal Revenue Service's (IRS) revocation of tax-exempt status for a religiously-oriented publishing house. The Tax Court's decision affirming the termination of the publisher's 52–year–old tax-exemption under 26 U.S.C.A. § 501(c)(3)(1982), was based on its conclusion that the publisher had become a profitable venture with only an attenuated relationship to the church with which it claims an affiliation. For the reasons set forth below, the decision of the Tax Court will be reversed.

I.

In 1931, the Presbyterian and Reformed Publishing Company (P & R) was incorporated to

> * * * state, defend and disseminate (through every proper means connected with or incidental to the printing and publishing business) the system of belief and practice taught in the Bible, as that system is

now set forth in the Confession of Faith and Catechisms of the Presbyterian Church in the United States of America.

P & R's charter requires that any income otherwise available as a dividend be used to improve its publications, extend their influence, or assist institutions "engaged in the teaching or inculcating" of the "system of belief and practice" of the Orthodox Presbyterian Church (OPC).

The IRS granted P & R tax-exempt status in 1939, stating,

> Your actual activities consist of publishing a religious paper known as "Christianity Today," a Presbyterian journal devoted to stating, defending, and furthering the gospel. Your income is derived from subscriptions, contributions and gifts and is used to defray maintenance and general operating expenses.

From the beginning, P & R has been closely linked—although not formally affiliated—with the OPC, a Presbyterian group dedicated to its view of reformed Presbyterian theology and, in particular, to the doctrine of Biblical Christianity set forth in the Westminster Confession of Faith. P & R's central editorial criterion is whether a book chosen for publication would make a "worthy contribution * * * to the reformed [Presbyterian] community." One independent publisher characterized P & R's books as lacking in "common ground" with the "nonreformed mind" and "offensive" to all but the "truly reformed."

One of P & R's three incorporators and original directors founded the OPC in 1932, one year after P & R's incorporation. Seven of P & R's nine directors are either officials at Westminster Theological Seminary of Philadelphia or pastors of OPC or OPC-affiliated denominations. On January 1, 1976, P & R changed its charter to specify OPC's seminary, the Westminster Theological Seminary of Philadelphia, as the recipient of all P & R assets in case of dissolution, citing Westminster's common dedication to Biblical Christianity and the Westminster Confession.

The organizational structure of P & R further underscores its close ties to the OPC. Since 1931, the publishing house has been run by three successive generations of the Craig family. Samuel, Charles, and Bryce Craig each worked without compensation at what amounted to a family concern whose business was conducted at the Craigs' kitchen table; all three Craigs were ministers. The record is devoid of evidence indicating any lessening of ties between P & R and the OPC.

From its inception until 1969, the company could claim no income over and above expenses. Indeed, the Craigs themselves often contributed personal funds in order to keep the corporation afloat (Samuel donated $500 in 1939 and $3,000 in 1954; Charles donated a total of $19,600 from 1955 to 1963). Until 1973, P & R relied exclusively on volunteers to help the Craigs with editing, packing, shipping, and clerical work.

Beginning in 1969, however, P & R experienced a considerable increase in economic activity as a result of the sudden and unexpected popularity of books written by Jay Adams, a Westminster Theological faculty member. P & R reported gross profits of over $20,000 for 1969, almost twice as much in 1970, and subsequent escalations culminating in over $300,000 in gross profits in 1979. By 1979, P & R had seven paid employees assisting Bryce Craig, one with a salary of $12,500, and five with salaries under $6,250 (all five full-time employees were OPC officials or members). Bryce Craig himself began receiving a salary of $12,000 in 1976, which increased, to $15,350 by 1979.

As early as March 2, 1974, P & R notified the Internal Revenue Service that it was accumulating surplus cash as a "building fund." In 1976, P & R used this fund to purchase 5–1/2 acres of land in Harmony, New Jersey, close to both an OPC community and Harmony Press, the printer for both P & R and OPC. In 1978, construction of a combined warehouse and office building in Harmony was completed at a cost of $263,000; an additional $27,000 was spent in 1979 for equipment.

After an audit, the IRS issued a revocation of P & R's tax-exempt status in 1980 on the grounds that P & R was not "operating exclusively for purposes set forth in 501(c)(3)" and was "engaged in a business activity which is carried on similar to a commercial enterprise." The IRS made this revocation retroactive, to apply from January 1, 1969 onward.

The Tax Court affirmed the revocation in a December 23, 1982 opinion, but held that the IRS abused its discretion in making the revocation retroactive to 1969. Instead, it set the effective revocation date at 1975, based upon its declaration that as of that year P & R "had acquired a truly commercial hue" and the company "was aware * * * that IRS agents had been raising serious questions [about its exemption]." To support its determination that P & R came to be "animated" by a "substantial commercial [and thus nonexempt] purpose" in 1975, the Tax Court relied primarily on three lines of evidence: first, P & R's "soar[ing] net and gross profits" between 1969 and 1979; second, the fact that P & R set prices which generated "consistent and comfortable net profit margins," rather than lowering prices to encourage a broader readership; and, third, P & R's purchase and sale of books to and from Baker Book Stores (a commercial publishing house), which "must have * * * overlapp[ed] in subject matter" with commercial publishers. * * * The Tax Court deemed this sufficient to support the proposition that P & R was in "competition with commercial publishers." * * *[2]

---

2. The Tax Court appended a list of additional "profit motivated" decisions: Other activities as well indicate that petitioner was animated by a substantial commercial purpose. It consciously attempted to transform itself into a more mainline commercial enterprise: It searched out more readers; it employed paid workers; it dropped money-losing plans; it paid substantial royalties; it made formal contracts with some authors; and, of course, it expanded into a new facility from which it could continue to reap profits. Further, petitioner was not affiliated or controlled by any particular church organization and this nondenominational character "contributes to the resemblance between its publishing activities and those of commercial, non-exempt publishers of Christian literature with whom * * * [it] competes." Inc. Trustees of Gospel Wkr. Soc. v. United States, [510 F.Supp. 374,] 379, n. 16 [D.D.C. (1981)]. Petitioner argues that it accumulated profits to expand so that it could publish more books and thus reach more readers. We recognize that petitioner used a large amount of its accumulated profits for the new Harmony facility; this new facility probably aided petitioner

On P & R's motion for reconsideration, the Tax Court issued a second opinion on April 8, 1983, leaving its prior judgment intact and rejecting P & R's argument that its "profit" figures should have been adjusted to reflect accumulations for the building fund. The Tax Court suggested that the new building furthered commercial purposes as much as religious purposes, and noted that "gross profit margins" did not fall after the building was completed. Finally, the Tax Court emphasized that P & R's accumulations exceeded its expenditures for the new building. P & R's motion to reconsider also sought to distinguish its OPC-affiliated activity from that of generic Christian publishers. The Tax Court rejected this point, stating that "the denominational or nondenominational character of an organization has never been a controlling criterion." * * *.

II.

The principal issue we must address is at what point the successful operation of a tax-exempt organization should be deemed to have transformed that organization into a commercial enterprise and thereby to have forfeited its tax exemption. The Tax Court answered this question by looking at the composite effects of the broad-scale increase in commercial activity, the accumulation of capital, the company's "profitability," and the development of a professional staff. Although these indicia of non-exempt business activity are all relevant, we are troubled by the inflexibility of the Tax Court's approach. It is doubtful that any small-scale exempt operation could ever increase its economic activity without forfeiting tax-exempt status under such a definition of non-exempt commercial character. Thus, we believe that the statutory inclusion or exclusion of P & R should be considered under a two-prong test: first, what is the purpose of an organization claiming tax-exempt status; and, second, to whose benefit does its activity inure?

This two-prong inquiry is drawn directly from the wording of 501(c)(3) and the legislative history of its enactment. The statute explicitly cites as qualifying for tax exemption those entities "organized exclusively for religious, charitable * * * or educational purposes." Indeed, the statute's original sponsor cited the religious publishing house as the archetypal example of the contemplated tax-exempt organization. In the words of the sponsor, Senator Bacon:

> [T]he corporation which I had particularly in mind as an illustration at the time I drew this amendment is the Methodist Book Concern, which has its headquarters in Nashville, which is a very large printing establishment, and in which there must necessarily be profit made, and there is a profit made exclusively for religious, benevolent, charitable, and educational purposes, in which no man receives a scintilla of individual profit. Of course if that were the only one, it might not be a matter that you would say we would be justified in changing these

---

in increasing its productivity and distribution. Such increase, however, may also be indicative of a commercial enterprise. We are not convinced that one of the significant reasons for expansion was not the commercial one of wishing to expand production for profit.

provisions of law to meet a particular case, but there are in greater or less degree such institutions scattered all over this country. If Senators will mark the words, the amendment is very carefully guarded, so as not to include any institution where there is any individual profit, and further than that, where any of the funds are devoted to any purpose other than those which are religious, benevolent, charitable, and educational.

44 Cong.Rec., pt. 4, at 4151 (1909).

This passage directly supports the two-part test set forth today. The legislative history refers to a "very large printing establishment * * * in which there must necessarily be profit made" as within the scope of the exemption. Significantly, Senator Bacon's remarks point to the purpose of the publishing house and the absence of personal profit, rather than the volume of business, as the hallmarks of non-taxable activity. Assuming that large religious or educational publishers may qualify for an exemption, and assuming that not all such publishers are created as large entities, the question becomes one of defining the standards by which the growth in volume of a publisher will not in itself jeopardize the tax exemption.

In the case at hand, the "purpose" prong of the two-part test is the more difficult to administer. Therefore, we will turn first to the question of inurement, and then return to the question of purpose.

A.

[The court held that there was no basis for concluding that P & R's increased commercial activity inured to the personal benefit of any individual. Eds.]

Therefore, if P & R is to be denied tax-exempt status, it must be as a result of the first prong of the test set forward today: the purpose of P & R would have to be incompatible with 501(c)(3).

B.

In order to come within the terms of § 501(c)(3), an organization seeking tax-exempt status must establish that it is organized "exclusively" for an exempt purpose. In the leading case elucidating the purposes considered exempt under § 501(c)(3), the Supreme Court in Better Business Bureau v. U.S., 326 U.S. 279, 283, 66 S.Ct. 112, 114, 90 L.Ed. 67 (1945), stated, "[t]he presence of a single [non-exempt] purpose, * * * substantial in nature, will destroy the exemption." The Court found that the Better Business Bureau of the District of Columbia was not exempt because a substantial purpose was "the mutual welfare, protection and improvement of business methods among merchants." Id. at 281, 66 S.Ct. at 113. Nevertheless, Better Business Bureau is a relatively straightforward case because of the presence of an explicit non-exempt commercial purpose by the organization claiming the exemption. P & R, to the contrary, claims that it is animated by no commercial motive and therefore falls squarely within the statutory exemption. Thus, the Tax Court's decision in the present case rests on the evaluation of what it deemed to be the true but unspoken motive of P & R.

Any exploration of unarticulated or illicit purpose necessarily involves courts in difficult and murky problems. When the legality of an action depends not upon its surface manifestation but upon the undisclosed motivation of the actor, similar acts can lead to diametrically opposite legal consequences. In the field of equal protection law, for instance, similar state actions having disproportionate impacts upon minorities may be upheld or struck down depending upon the weighing of various indicia of "discriminatory intent." * * *

The difficulties inherent in any legal standard predicated upon the subjective intent of an actor are further compounded when that actor is a corporate entity. In such circumstances, courts forced to pass upon a potentially illicit purpose have looked for objective indicia from which the intent of the actor may be discerned. In reviewing the decision of the Tax Court in the present case, therefore, the question is whether the proper indicia were relied upon in concluding that P & R was animated by a purpose alien to the statutory exemption of § 501(c)(3).

The Tax Court properly framed the inquiry as to whether P & R's purpose was within § 501(c)(3) as follows: Where a nonexempt purpose is not an expressed goal, courts have focused on the manner in which activities themselves are carried on, implicitly reasoning that an end can be inferred from the chosen means. If, for example, an organization's management decisions replicate those of commercial enterprises, it is a fair inference that at least one purpose is commercial, and hence nonexempt. And if this nonexempt goal is substantial, tax exempt status must be denied. Clearly, petitioner's conduct of a growing and very profitable publishing business must imbue it with some commercial hue. How deep a tint these activities impart can best be evaluated by looking at certain factors deemed significant in cases involving religious publishing companies, as well as in other pertinent cases.

There are two aspects of the Tax Court's opinion regarding P & R's purpose that require careful examination. First is the Tax Court's conclusion that "petitioner was not affiliated or controlled by any particular church and [that] this nondenominational character 'contributes to the resemblance between its publishing activities and those of commercial, nonexempt publishers of Christian literature with whom * * * [it] competes.'" * * * Given the close connection between P & R and the OPC, the absence of formal control of P & R by any particular church is not dispositive of the question of the fundamental ties between its goals as a publishing house and the dogma espoused by the OPC. In Inc. Trustees [v. United States, 510 F.Supp. 374 (D.D.C.1981), Eds.], the court's decision that a gospel-oriented press failed to qualify for § 501(c)(3) status did not turn on the extent of the press' formal affiliation with a church. Rather, the court focused on the virtually complete cessation of religious activity by the church, the church's unexplained accumulation of millions of dollars, and the fact that some officers of the affiliated publishing concern were drawing salaries ranging from $42,000 to over $100,000. The Tax Court itself seems to have recognized the non-dispositive nature of formal affiliation in its decision on the motion for reconsideration, where it stated, "the denominational or nondenominational character of an organization has never been a controlling criterion."

The second point, P & R's accumulation of "profits," causes greater difficulty. Although the profits of P & R constituted only one of the factors enumerated and discussed by the Tax Court in its opinion, the memorandum filed upon P & R's motion for reconsideration makes clear that the Tax Court's principal concern was the "presence of substantial profits." The Tax Court computed P & R's profits by subtracting the cost of goods sold from the gross sales of books to arrive at the gross profits. The sum of other expenses was in turn subtracted from the gross profits to derive the net profit schedule used by the Tax Court in determining P & R's profitability. These net profits peaked at $106,180 in 1975, the year the Tax Court decided that P & R had acquired a truly commercial character. On reconsideration, the Tax Court added that the gross profits margin of P & R did not fall even after the new building was constructed.

We do not read § 501(c)(3) or its legislative history to define the purpose of an organization claiming tax-exempt status as a direct derivative of the volume of business of that organization. Rather, the inquiry must remain that of determining the purpose to which the increased business activity is directed. As the Tax Court itself observed, "the presence of profitmaking activities is not per se a bar to qualification of an organization as exempt if the activities further or accomplish an exempt purpose." Aid to Artisans, Inc. v. Commissioner, 71 T.C. 202, 211 (1978). Despite the long history of § 501(c)(3) and the numerous organizations that have claimed its coverage, no regulation or body of case law has defined the concept of "purpose" under this provision of the Tax Code with sufficient clarity to protect against arbitrary, ad hoc decision-making.

The Tax Court's analysis of P & R's accumulation of profits in the present context could, absent a clearer articulation of the legal standard for tax-exempt status, lead to such arbitrary or ad hoc treatment. We are particularly concerned that although the Tax Court acknowledged that P & R informed the IRS as early as March 2, 1974 of its accumulation of funds to purchase or build an office and warehouse, the opinion tabulates the company's cash-on-hand, and cites this as an important factor in concluding that P & R was motivated by a non-exempt purpose.

There is no doubt that unexplained accumulations of cash may properly be considered as evidence of commercial purpose. Although no regulations govern cash accumulations in the 501(c)(3) context, we are guided by the accumulated earnings tax, 26 U.S.C.A. § 531 et seq. (1982). [The court's discussion of the accumulated earnings tax is omitted. Eds.]

Although we recognize that the Tax Court is entitled to deference in determining the existence of a substantial, non-exempt purpose, that court must focus on facts which indicate a purpose falling outside the ambit of section 501(c)(3). In this case, the Tax Court focused primarily on two factors—the lack of affiliation with a particular church and the accumulation of profits. As we have shown, neither factor indicates the presence of a non-exempt purpose here. Therefore, we must consider the balance of the record to determine whether all the evidence taken together supports a finding of non-exemption. Such an examination reveals no additional evidence of improper motives.

III.

Two competing policy considerations are present in situations where tax-exempt organizations begin to expand the scope of their profit-generating activities. On the one hand, the simple act of accumulating revenues may properly call into question the ultimate purpose of an organization ostensibly dedicated to one of the enumerated pursuits under § 501(c)(3). On the other hand, success in terms of audience reached and influence exerted, in and of itself, should not jeopardize the tax-exempt status of organizations which remain true to their stated goals.

Our concern is that organizations seeking § 501(c)(3) status may be forced to choose between expanding their audience and influence on the one hand, and maintaining their tax-exempt status on the other. If this were a stagnant society in which various ideas and creeds preserve a hold on a fixed proportion of the population, this concern would evaporate. A large religious institution with a broad base of support, such as one of the more established churches, could be the springboard for large-scale publishing houses dedicated to advancing its doctrines and be assured of qualifying for § 501(c)(3) coverage. A small denomination, such as the OPC, could then have within its penumbra only a small-scale operation run off a kitchen table. In such circumstances, any attempt by a publisher adhering to the views of the small denomination to expand its scope of activities would properly raise questions relating to its continued eligibility for tax-exempt status.

This view does not reflect either the dynamic quality of our society or the goals that generated the grant of tax-exempt status to religious publishers. The sudden popularity of an erstwhile obscure writer, such as Jay Adams, cannot, by itself, be the basis for stating that P & R has departed from its professed purpose any more than an increase in congregations would call into question the OPC's continued designation as a church. Such a standard would lead to an inequitable disparity in treatment for publishers affiliated with mainstream churches as opposed to small offshoots.

Accordingly, the decision of the Tax Court will be reversed.

Revenue Ruling 67–4

1967–1 Cum. Bull. 121.

Advice has been requested whether a nonprofit organization formed and operated as described below qualifies for exemption from Federal income tax under section 501(c)(3) of the Internal Revenue Code of 1954.

The organization was formed to encourage scientific research in, and to disseminate educational information about, specific types of physical and mental disorders. This is accomplished by publishing a journal which contains abstracts of current information from the world's medical and scientific publications. The journal is sold, below cost, to the public.

The organization's staff consists of leading pathologists, other medical specialists, and teachers, most of whom donate their services. The organization receives income from the sale of subscriptions, contributions, and government grants. Its operating deficits are defrayed by contributions.

Section 501(c)(3) of the Code provides for the exemption from Federal income tax of organizations organized and operated exclusively for charitable, educational, and scientific purposes.

Section 1.501(c)(3)–1(d)(2) of the Income Tax Regulations defines the term "charitable" as used in section 501(c)(3) of the Code as including the advancement of education or science.

Revenue Ruling 66–147, C.B. 1966–1, 137, holds that the publication of abstracts of scientific and medical articles by an organization contributes to the advancement of education and science by providing an effective means for the increased dissemination and application of such knowledge.

An organization engaged in publishing scientific and medical literature may qualify for exemption from Federal income tax under section 501(c)(3) of the Code if (1) the content of the publication is educational, (2) the preparation of material follows methods generally accepted as "educational" in character, (3) the distribution of the materials is necessary or valuable in achieving the organization's educational and scientific purposes, and (4) the manner in which the distribution is accomplished is distinguishable from ordinary commercial publishing practices.

The methods used in preparing and presenting the abstracts conform to methods traditionally accepted as "educational" in character. The organization provides a reference to literature on the research undertaken in the area, and enables the afflicted to receive improved instruction and treatment. The distribution of the abstracts is carried out essentially in a "charitable" manner, in the sense that there is a public benefit derived from the distribution. The charges for the publication recover only a portion of the costs.

Accordingly, the organization qualifies for exemption from Federal income tax under section 501(c)(3) of the Code.

* * *

This case is distinguishable from that in Revenue Ruling 60–351, C.B. 1960–2, 169, involving an organization which is publishing a magazine and selling it to the general public in accordance with ordinary commercial publishing practices.

NOTE AND QUESTIONS

As the commerciality cases and rulings demonstrate, the IRS and the courts are often preoccupied with whether an activity under scrutiny has a "commercial hue." Efficiently managed businesses that make money, retain earnings for expansion, and compete with for-profit firms are especially vulnerable, whether or not the activity also might be characterized as "charitable," "educational," "religious," or "scientific." Is this analysis consistent with the operational test regulations? They seek to determine, first, whether a "trade or business" is a substantial part of the organization's activities (if not, then no problem, whether or not the business is related or unrelated) and, if so, whether it is "in furtherance of" the organization's exempt purpose. Does "in furtherance of" mean "substantially related to" an exempt purpose (importing standards used for the UBIT), or is it enough that business profits are used to subsidize a charitable activity? Can an unrelated business ever be in furtherance of an organization's exempt purposes? In what circumstances does a business become an organization's "primary purpose?" And what if the business is, in and of itself, the organization's exempt purpose?

3.   The Commensurate–in–Scope Doctrine

Revenue Ruling 64–182

1964–1 Cum Bull. 186.

A corporation organized exclusively for charitable purposes derives its income principally from the rental of space in a large commercial office building which it owns, maintains and operates. The charitable purposes of the corporation are carried out by aiding other charitable organizations, selected in the discretion of its governing body, through contributions and grants to such organizations for charitable purposes. Held, the corporation is deemed to meet the primary purpose test of section 1.501(c)(3)–1(e)(1) of the Income Tax Regulations, and to be entitled to exemption from Federal income tax as a corporation organized and operated exclusively for charitable purposes within the meaning of section 501(c)(3) of the Internal Revenue Code of 1954, where it is shown to be carrying on through such contributions and grants a charitable program commensurate in scope with its financial resources.

* * *

NOTES AND QUESTIONS

1. *Commensurate-in-Scope: A Confused History.* Revenue Ruling 64–182 has been interpreted as clearly demonstrating that the destination of income test is alive and well. But was the rental activity in that ruling even a "trade or business?" As developed later in this chapter, most rental income is excluded from the UBIT tax base, as are dividends, interest and royalties, presumably on the theory that passive investing does not present any border patrol problem.

Revenue Ruling 64–182 is brief and relatively uninformative. It evolved from an internal IRS debate culminating in a detailed legal memorandum concluding that the operational test regulations permit an organization to qualify for exemption despite substantial unrelated business activities if its primary purpose is charitable. See Gen. Couns. Mem. 32869 (Oct. 9, 1963). Under this analysis, "in furtherance of" does not mean "related." An organization's "primary purpose" is to be determined based on whether it has a "real, bona fide, or genuine charitable purpose, as manifested by the charitable accomplishments of the organization, and not a mathematical measuring of business purpose as opposed to charitable purpose." Id.

In a 1971 General Counsel Memorandum, the IRS effectively "gave away the store" in considering this hypothetical fact pattern that goes well beyond the 1964 published ruling:

> A large department store creates a nonprofit corporation to take over and operate its business assets. The articles of incorporation and bylaws of the nonprofit corporation contain a statement that the purpose of the organization is to engage in charitable works by contributing to those exempt organizations exempt under section 501(c)(3) which are selected by the officers of the nonprofit corporation in their role as trustees. The articles and bylaws further provide that all proceeds derived from the business operation commensurate with its financial resources will be expended annually in its program of charitable giving. Is the corporation deemed a feeder organization? Is it, on the other hand, considered to be primarily engaged in charitable activities within the meaning of the regulations?

> * * *

> Assuming that all the assets of the organization referred to in your first series of questions have been effectively dedicated to some charitable objective, we believe that, aside from section 502, such organization could engage in an indeterminate amount of business and still be exempt under section 501(c)(3) so long as it can be said that there is a reasonable operation of the property for the beneficial use of charity. In such case, we would regard it as being operated exclusively for charitable purposes, and not for the primary purpose of carrying on unrelated trade or business within the meaning of regulations section 1.501(c)(3)–1(e). Thus, we would hold that, in accord with Rev. Rul. 64–182, the organization would be entitled to exemption under Code section 501(c)(3).

Gen. Couns. Mem. 34682 (Nov. 17, 1971). For some other older authorities applying the commensurate-in-scope doctrine, see Help the Children, Inc. v. Commissioner, 28 T.C. 1128 (1957) (organization contributing less than one percent of bingo revenues to charity did not qualify for exemption because its principal activity was the profitable operation of a commercial bingo business); Tech. Adv. Mem. 200021056 (organization formed to give financial assistance to needy women qualifies for § 501(c)(3) exemption even though 66 percent of its revenue was from operation of an unrelated business; IRS reasons that an unrelated business used to raise funds for a charitable purpose is "in furtherance of" a charitable purpose and does not constitute a substantial non-exempt purpose). For a contrary view, see Orange County Agricultural Society v. Commissioner, 893 F.2d 529 (2d Cir. 1990) (organization that received one-third of its income from an automobile racetrack was operated for a substantial non-exempt purpose, but revocation of exemption also was based on inurement of private gain).

Are GCM 34682 and the other cited authorities correct statements of the law? Do they properly interpret the § 501(c)(3) operational test regulations? If the answer is no, how much unrelated business is (or should be) permissible? Assuming that the commensurate-in-scope doctrine is good law, its scope is unclear because the IRS does not consistently or coherently apply the doctrine. Would it be possible to quantify the doctrine, or at least establish a safe harbor? Or is it best to muddle through with the "facts and circumstances" smell test used in many of the decided cases and rulings?

2. *Revival of the Doctrine.* After many years of near dormancy, the IRS resurrected the commensurate-in-scope doctrine for the purposes of denying tax exemption to organizations without any meaningful charitable program. In Private Letter Ruling 200818023 (May 2, 2008), the organization under scrutiny described itself as a worldwide humanitarian evangelistic Christian missionary, but its principal activity was sponsoring "asset exchange programs" through the sale of annuities. Less than half of one percent of the funds received by the organization was devoted to charitable activities. The IRS ruled that the organization was not "charitable" because it was organized and operated for the "primary purpose of carrying on an unrelated trade or business" and, unlike the grantmaking department store in Revenue Ruling 64–182, it did "not carry on a charitable program that is commensurate in scope with [its] financial resources." The Service also has indicated its intention to apply the commensurate-in-scope doctrine as a tool to determine whether charities are spending money efficiently and effectively. See Grant Williams, IRS Denies Tax–Exempt Status to Group That Spends Too Little Money on Charitable Programs, Chron. Philanthropy, May 15, 2008, at 29. A useful follow-up would be to issue further guidance in the form of a published ruling with more challenging and informative fact patterns.

3. *What's a Feeder?* A "feeder corporation" generally is a controlled subsidiary of an exempt organization that carries on a trade or business for profit. Section 502(a) makes it clear that a feeder corporation will not be entitled to tax-exempt status on the ground that all of its profits are payable to one or more exempt organizations. Feeders are thus fully taxable entities even if *part* of their income might have been exempt if it had been earned directly by the exempt parent. Section 502 has been extended to deny exemption to certain shared-service organizations formed by several unrelated entities to serve special needs—e.g., a laundry serving a group of hospitals. See HCSC–Laundry v. United States, 450 U.S. 1, 101 S.Ct. 836 (1981). As discussed later in this chapter (see Section H1, infra, at pp. 663–664), feeders are not necessarily bad. Indeed, if an exempt organi-

zation is clearly engaged in an unrelated business, spinning the business off into a taxable subsidiary may be desirable from a planning standpoint.

Not all subsidiaries of exempt organizations are *taxable* "feeders." If a subsidiary is operated exclusively (i.e., primarily) for exempt purposes, it may obtain exempt status—e.g., where it carries on a trade or business that is substantially related to an exempt mission. In addition, the regulations provide that a separate corporation can avoid taxable feeder status if its activities are an "integral part" of its exempt parent's activities, such as an organization operated for the sole purpose of furnishing electric power to a tax-exempt university. Treas. Reg. § 1.502–1(b). The integral part doctrine was discussed in the context of nonprofit hospitals and HMOs in Chapter 5C3b, supra, at p. 337.

The quoted portion of the 1971 GCM discussed in Note 1, above, seems to finesse (avoid?) the question of whether the organization under scrutiny was a § 502 feeder corporation. A thorough reading of the GCM reveals that it narrowly construed § 502, concluding that it only applies to organizations that are legally obligated (e.g., by their charter or contract) to pay over their profits to a specific charity. On the other hand, an organization would not be a feeder if the distribution of its income was discretionary in the sense that the trustees or directors were under no legal or equitable duty to distribute income to a specific (affiliated?) charity. GCM 34682 (Nov. 17, 1971). As a practical matter, these "non-feeder" grantmaking organizations would have to qualify as a public charity because of the limits in § 4943 on excess business holdings of private foundations. See Chapter 7C4, infra. A strategy to avoid private foundation status would be to establish a support relationship with one or more public charities. See I.R.C. § 509(a)(3) and Chapter 7B4, infra.

In CRSO v. Commissioner, 128 T.C. 153 (2007), the Tax Court held that a nonprofit corporation that rented out two parcels of debt-financed commercial real estate as its sole activity and distributed the net proceeds to a public charity named in its articles of incorporation was operated for the primary purpose of carrying on a "trade or business" and thus was a taxable feeder corporation under § 502. The taxpayer argued that its leasing activity did not rise to the level of a "trade or business" and also pointed to a special rule in § 512(b)(1) providing that the term "trade or business" shall not include the deriving of rents that are excluded from unrelated business taxable income under § 512(b)(3). Relying on Treas. Reg. § 1.502–1(d)(2), the court found that not all the rent would be excluded from UBTI because the property was debt-financed and thus the activity was a "trade or business" under the statutory scheme.

4. *Other Approaches.* Are the IRS and the courts too lenient in their treatment of commercial activity? Charities have become very imaginative in broadening their tax-exempt purposes to encompass activities that are virtually indistinguishable from for-profit businesses. Is this a problem? If so, how might the tax exemption border be more effectively patrolled—by narrowing the definition of charity, or refining what is meant by "commercial?" Would it be sufficient to rely on the UBIT to tax "insubstantial"

unrelated business income and revoke exemption only when such income becomes substantial, as measured by an agreed upon mathematical benchmark? Discussion of these difficult questions is best deferred until the UBIT is studied and mastered.

5. *For Further Reading.* Travis L.L. Blais & Christopher T. Bird, Should the Commensurate Test Force Greater Spending by Public Charities, 63 Exempt Org. Tax Rev. 31 (April 2009); John D. Colombo, Regulating Commercial Activity by Exempt Charities: Resurrecting the Commensurate-in-Scope Doctrine, 39 Exempt Org. Tax Rev. 341 (2003); John D. Colombo, Commercial Activity and Charitable Tax Exemption, 44 Wm. & Mary L. Rev. 487 (2002); Jessica Pena & Alexander L.T. Reid, Note: A Call for Reform of the Operational Test for Unrelated Commercial Activity in Charities, 76 N.Y.U. L. Rev. 1855 (2001); Thomas C. Troyer, Quantity of Unrelated Business Consistent with Charitable Exemption—Some Clarification, 56 Tax Notes 1075 (1992); Kenneth C. Eliasberg, Charity and Commerce: Section 501(c)(3)—How Much Unrelated Business Activity?, 21 Tax L. Rev. 53 (1965).

PROBLEMS

Consider whether the following nonprofit organizations, all of which receive little or no financial support from charitable donations, qualify for tax exemption under § 501(c)(3). Assume that none of the organizations is a private foundation.

(a) Alcoholic Artifacts is engaged in the purchase and sale of products made by recovering alcoholics, drug addicts, and ex-offenders. The purpose of the organization is to provide employment opportunities for individuals handicapped by alcoholism, drug dependence and other problems of urban poverty.

(b) The Downtown YMCA is located near the financial district of a major city and offers memberships to the general public for an initiation fee of $250 plus dues of $100 per month. Its facilities include a gymnasium, fitness center, racquetball courts, swimming pool and sun deck, and carpeted locker room facilities with showers, spas and saunas. Located nearby are several for-profit health clubs offering comparable facilities.

(c) Charitable Consultants of Topeka provides managerial and consulting services on a cost basis to an unrelated group of § 501(c)(3) charities in Eastern Kansas. The services of the organization include writing job descriptions and training materials, recruiting personnel, advising on fund raising and endowment management and other administrative and accounting matters.

(d) The Bay Area Chronicle publishes a daily newspaper (print and online) that includes national, state and local news, sports, investigative reporting, and editorial opinion. The Chronicle is the successor to a for-profit company that published a daily newspaper in the region for over 100 years but was forced to go out of business due to mounting losses. The Chronicle's revenue comes from subscription income (20%), advertising (40%), and grants from private foundations and individuals (40%). It takes positions on state and local issues but does not endorse candidates for public office.

(e) The Christian Charter School, a religious educational institution not affiliated with any particular denomination, has 2,500 students from pre-school through 12th grade, and a profitable publishing division that produces and markets religious textbooks throughout the world. Gross receipts from the publishing division represent 60% of the organization's total gross receipts, while publishing division expenditures are less than half of overall expenditures. Assume that the publishing activity is an unrelated trade or business.

(f) The Rubber Soul Conservancy, a § 509(a)(3) supporting organization, is organized and operated to provide financial support to five arts and cultural organizations in New York City. It derives 75% of its gross revenue from investment income and 25% from the operation of a fashionable shoe store in Manhattan. Annual grants average 4% of the value of the Conservancy's net assets, including the shoe store business.

(g) Same as (f), above, except all the Conservancy's revenue is from operation of the shoe store.

(h) Same as (g), above, except average annual grants ($10,000 per year) are less than 1% of the value of the Conservancy's net assets.

(i) Same as (g), above, except the Conservancy is controlled by the Manny Planetarium, a § 501(c)(3) public charity, and it is obligated by its charter to distribute all its net profits annually to the Planetarium.

C. THE UNRELATED BUSINESS INCOME TAX: HISTORY AND POLICY

As we have seen, a nonprofit organization does not necessarily lose its tax-exempt status by engaging in commercial activities. But what if it engages in a business with no discernible relationship to its exempt purposes and directly competes with for-profit businesses? Consider, for example, a university-owned pizza parlor that solicits business from the general public, underpricing an off-campus establishment that must pay taxes on its income. Should the university's exemption extend to its pizza profits on the theory that, like tuition and endowment income, the profits are used for educational purposes? Or should those earnings be taxed to eliminate the potential for unfair competition? And if unfair competition is the problem, why not tax profits from any competitive business, such as a prosperous university bookstore, even if it is closely related to the school's educational mission?

These questions set the stage for a study of one of the most contentious topics in the law of tax-exempt organizations—the unrelated business income tax. Subject to a host of exceptions, the "UBIT," as it is familiarly known, is generally imposed on the net income of any trade or business that is regularly carried on by an exempt organization and which is not substantially related to the organization's exempt purposes. I.R.C. § 511 et seq. This chapter continues with a brief history of the UBIT and a survey of the current tax policy debate. It then considers the application and scope of the UBIT, with an emphasis on contemporary controversies and emerging complex structures, and concludes by evaluating some proposals for reform.

1. HISTORICAL BACKGROUND

When the unrelated business income tax was added to the Internal Revenue Code in 1950, it represented a legislative retreat from unbridled tax exemption for nonprofit organizations. The prevailing view had been that an organization conducting a business nonetheless qualified for exemption if its profits were dedicated to charitable or other exempt purposes. The origins of this destination of income test can be traced back to a dispute between the Insular Collector of the Philippine Islands, then under U.S. jurisdiction, and Sagrada Orden de Predicadores, an ancient Philippine religious order with missions throughout the Far East. The order derived the bulk of its income from large real estate and securities holdings and more modest revenue from the sale of wine, chocolates and other articles for use within its religious missions. The Insular Collector, even while conceding that the religious charity was organized and operated for exempt purposes, argued that it was not operated "exclusively" for such purposes because it derived significant revenue from commercial sources. In Trinidad v. Sagrada Orden,[1] the Supreme Court ruled that the charity qualified for tax exemption, holding that the earliest predecessor of § 501(c)(3) permitted exempt organizations to have net income and "said nothing about the source of the income, but makes the destination the ultimate test of exemption."[2] In discussing the organization's income from the sale of wines and chocolates, the court observed that all goods sold by Sagrada Orden were either for religious use or "incidental" to the charity's missionary activities.[3]

An important principle from *Sagrada Orden*—that an organization may be "exclusively" operated for exempt purposes even if it engages in some insubstantial income-producing activities—was discussed earlier in this chapter.[4] A close reading of *Sagrada Orden* does not reveal that the

---

1. 263 U.S. 578, 44 S.Ct. 204 (1924).

2. Id. at 581, 44 S.Ct. at 205.

3. Id. at 582, 44 S.Ct. at 206.

4. See Section B of this chapter, supra, at pp. 570–572.

religious charity was engaged in any business that was unrelated to its exempt purposes. The bulk of its revenue was from passive investments, and its sales of wine and chocolates apparently were related to its religious mission. Yet dictum from this landmark case gave birth to another principle: a tax-exempt organization does not lose its exemption by virtue of the conduct of an "unrelated" business as long as its profits are dedicated to charitable or other exempt purposes.

The "destination of income" test had its heyday in the 1930s and 1940s as a handful of exempt organizations began engaging in commercial activities, either directly or through separate "feeder" entities that operated a business and distributed the profits to their tax-exempt owners. In one of the earliest cases, the Second Circuit upheld the exempt status of a corporation operating a large bathing beach business near Far Rockaway in New York City. The organization's revenues, which came from the rental of bath houses, bathing suits, towels and beach-related concessions, all were paid over to a charitable foundation created by the late owner of the beach. The court held that a corporation engaged exclusively in commercial activities qualified for tax-exempt status so long as all of its net profits were turned over to a legitimate charitable organization.[5] In a later and more notorious case, the Third Circuit held that C.F. Mueller Co., then the nation's largest manufacturer of noodles and macaroni, qualified for exemption under § 501(c)(3) because its pasta profits were distributed to its sole shareholder, New York University, for the exclusive benefit of its School of Law.[6] This case was working its way through the courts as Congress debated the first UBIT bill. It prompted Representative John Dingell to warn that unless action was taken "the macaroni monopoly will be in the hands of the university * * * and eventually all the noodles produced in this country will be produced by corporations held or created by universities," depriving the Treasury of any tax revenue from an entire industry.[7]

Relying on the destination of income test, more nonprofits began engaging in commercial activities having no relationship to their exempt purposes. Although New York University was best known for its School of Law's macaroni business, the university also owned Howes Leather Company, American Limoges China, and Ramsey Corporation, a manufacturer of piston rings.[8] Other nonprofits acquired real estate from for-profit taxpayers, usually borrowing to finance the purchase, and then leased the property back to the seller for a lengthy term, servicing the loan with tax-free

---

5. Roche's Beach, Inc. v. Commissioner, 96 F.2d 776 (2d Cir.1938). Judge Learned Hand dissented, noting correctly that Trinidad v. Sagrada Orden was distinguishable because the business income in that case was "very trifling." 96 F.2d at 779. Judge Hand believed that a "business subsidiary" should not be exempt, without regard to where its income was destined.

6. C.F. Mueller Co. v. Commissioner, 190 F.2d 120 (3d Cir. 1951).

7. Hearings Before the House Comm. on Ways and Means, 81st Cong., 2d Sess. 579–80 (1950).

8. For more on this early history, see Donald L. Sharpe, Unfair Business Competition and the Tax on Income Destined for Charity: Forty–Six Years Later, 3 Fla. Tax Rev. 367, 380–383 (1996).

rental income from the lease. In 1942, the Treasury Department prodded Congress to hold hearings on the subject, and two perceived abuses were identified: loss of revenue and unfair competition. But it was not until the Revenue Act of 1950 that Congress finally responded. First, it imposed a tax on the "unrelated business income" of most (but not all)[9] tax-exempt organizations. Second, it withdrew exempt status from feeder corporations by providing, in the predecessor to current § 502, that an organization primarily engaged in a trade or business for profit does not qualify for exemption merely because its profits are destined for charitable ends. The legislative history indicates that Congress's primary concern was the perceived problem of unfair competition. Both the House and Senate Reports stated that:[10]

> The problem at which the tax on unrelated business income is directed is primarily that of unfair competition. The tax-free status of [section 501(c)(3)] organizations enables them to use their profits tax-free to expand operations, while their competitors can expand only with the profits remaining after taxes. Also, a number of examples have arisen where these organizations have, in effect, used their tax exemptions to buy an ordinary business. That is, they have acquired the business with little or no investment on their own part and paid for it in installments out of subsequent earnings—a procedure which usually could not be followed if the business were taxable.

The statutory regime that we are about to study, however, says little or nothing about competition, and it is apparent that the need for revenue to finance the Korean War and more generalized concerns over fairness and public perceptions greatly influenced enactment of the UBIT.[11]

The 1950 legislation forever altered the economic stakes of unrelated business activity by most nonprofits, but it did not completely address the problem. Churches had successfully lobbied for a complete exemption from the UBIT, as did social clubs and fraternal beneficiary societies. When churches began exploiting their favored status, even the sensibilities of religious leaders were offended, a condition that was exacerbated by unfavorable publicity and constitutional challenges.[12] After much deliberation, the mainstream religious community shifted its position and, in 1969, the National Council of Churches and the United States Catholic Conference urged Congress to eliminate the UBIT church exemption. Congress willingly obliged in the Tax Reform Act of 1969 by extending the tax to churches as well as social clubs and fraternal beneficiary societies. At the same time,

---

9. Churches, social clubs, and fraternal beneficiary societies were exempt from the earliest version of the UBIT.

10. H.R.Rep. No. 2319, 81st Cong., 2d Sess. 38 (1950); S.Rep. No. 2375, 81st Cong., 2d Sess. 28–29 (1950).

11. See particularly President Truman's admonitions "to improve the fairness of the tax system, to bring in some additional revenue, and to strengthen [the] economy." 96 Cong. Rec. 769, 771 (1950) (President's Message to Congress).

12. For much of this history, see Stephen Schwarz, Limiting Religious Tax Exemptions: When Should the Church Render Unto Caesar?, 29 U.Fla.L.Rev. 50, 94–96 (1976).

it expanded the scope of the tax to patrol against a new form of abusive debt-financed acquisition by tax exempt organizations that had been endorsed by the Supreme Court.[13] The 1969 legislation significantly tightened the UBIT in several other respects but any business activities that were substantially related to the exempt purposes of an organization were left untouched, even if they were in direct competition with a for-profit taxpayer.

The subsequent history of the UBIT is a series of piecemeal changes, most of which are specialized exemptions added at the behest of lobbyists representing a particular nonprofit sub-sector. Every so often, complaints about unfair competition from segments of the small business community are sufficiently loud to prompt Congress to engage in a comprehensive review. The last major episode was in 1987, when Representative J.J. Pickle of Texas presided over extensive hearings by the House Ways and Means Committee's Oversight Subcommittee. The Hearings resulted in three volumes of fascinating testimony and a discussion draft (excerpted at the end of this chapter) proposing significant reforms but resulting in no immediate legislation.

The commercial activities of exempt organizations raise profoundly complex and perhaps insoluble policy issues about the role of the nonprofit sector and the rationale for tax exemption. The policy debate inevitably will continue as long there is a public perception that nonprofits are unfairly competing with private firms while straying from their stated mission.

NOTES AND QUESTIONS

1. *Destination of Income Test.* What was so bad about the destination of income test? If the rationale for exempt status under § 501(c)(3) is to subsidize organizations that provide a public benefit, relieve the burdens of government and foster pluralism, why shouldn't the tax exemption extend to all the organization's sources of revenue? Some of the academic theories discussed in Chapter 5 explain tax exemption as a subsidy to correct the undersupply of goods and services that suffer from the twin failures of the private market and government? Do those theories justify subsidizing an unrelated business? For example, under Hall and Colombo's donative theory, is taxing unrelated business income irrelevant as long as the organization has the requisite level of donative support? See John D. Colombo & Mark A. Hall, The Charitable Tax Exemption 175–179 (1995).

2. *Unfair Competition or Profit Motive?* Is income from an unrelated business taxable only if the exempt organization is competing with a for-profit firm? Most courts considering this question have concluded that the presence or absence of competition with for-profits, while an important objective of the tax, is not determinative. In their view, the more critical question is whether the organization has a profit motive and operates the business in a commercial manner. Noting that the statutory language has

---

13. Commissioner v. Brown, 380 U.S. 563, 85 S.Ct. 1162 (1965). For further discussion of these "bootstrap acquisition" transactions, see Section E2 of this chapter.

never required a showing of unfair competition, these decisions emphasize that the UBIT was enacted not only to eliminate a form of unfair competition but also to raise revenue by closing a loophole. See, e.g, Clarence LaBelle Post No. 217, Veterans of Foreign Wars of the United States v. United States, 580 F.2d 270 (8th Cir.1978) (income from bingo games subject to UBIT even though organization did not compete because only nonprofit entities may operate bingo games under local law); Louisiana Credit Union League v. United States, 693 F.2d 525 (5th Cir.1982). For a contrary view that requires a showing of unfair competition, see Hope School v. United States, 612 F.2d 298 (7th Cir.1980).

3. *For Further Reading.* Ethan Stone, Adhering to the Old Line: Uncovering the History and Political Function of the Unrelated Business Income Tax, 54 Emory L.J. 1475 (2005); Harvey P. Dale, About the UBIT, N.Y.U. 18th Conf. on Tax Planning for 501(c)(3) Organizations § 9 (1990); Donald L. Sharpe, Unfair Business Competition and the Tax on Income Destined for Charity: Forty–Six Years Later, 3 Fla. Tax Rev. 367 (1996); Kenneth C. Eliasberg, Charity and Commerce: Section 501(c)(3)—How Much Unrelated Business Activity?, 21 Tax L.Rev. 53 (1965); Note, The Macaroni Monopoly: The Developing Concept of Unrelated Business Income of Exempt Organizations, 81 Harv.L.Rev. 1280 (1968).

2. POLICY CONSIDERATIONS: FAIRNESS, EFFICIENCY AND PUBLIC RELATIONS

Echoing the theme that pervades the legislative history of the UBIT, the regulations state that "the primary objective of [the tax] was to eliminate a source of unfair competition by placing the unrelated business activities of certain exempt organizations upon the same tax basis as the non-exempt business endeavors with which they compete." Treas. Reg. § 1.513–1(b). The small business community, led by the Office of Advocacy of the U.S. Small Business Administration and a consortium of other trade groups, has emphasized competitive imbalance in urging Congress to expand the reach of the UBIT and improve its enforcement. These concerns gained prominence during hearings held in 1987 by the Oversight Subcommittee of the House Ways and Means Committee.

Some tax law scholars and economists, however, have questioned the underlying economic assumptions that appear to have influenced the enactment and expansion of the UBIT. The following materials survey the debate.

Statement of Joseph O'Neil, Chairman, Business Coalition for Fair Competition, at Hearings Before the Subcommittee on Oversight, House Ways and Means Committee

100th Cong. 1st Sess. 217–220 (Ser. 100–26, 1987).

[The Business Coalition for Fair Competition is an alliance of trade and professional associations and businesses formed in 1983 to articulate the concerns of the business community on the subject of unfair competition. This excerpt is from testimony of BCFC's chairman at the 1987 House UBIT hearings. Many years later, it remains a concise articulation of one side of the policy debate. Eds.]

The Importance of Nonprofits in Our Society

At the outset, let me make clear what this testimony is *not* about, and why BCFC believes legislative solutions are needed.

Our purpose is not to denigrate the vital role of nonprofits. The spirit of voluntarism, our ability to balance a system which emphasizes self-reliance with the common welfare of all, is what makes this nation unique. We acknowledge the importance of the independent nonprofit sector and its essential contributions in education, basic research, and charitable endeavors. We are particularly proud of the participation of our small businesses in charitable endeavors. Small business owners serve on the boards of many local nonprofit institutions such as the YMCA, the university, the hospital, or the United Way. At the annual pancake festival you will most likely find that the local restaurant owner has contributed the maple syrup. Many nonprofits play a critical role in society. For example, universities educate the highly trained engineers, scientists and other professionals needed for the jobs of the future. Nonprofit trade and professional associations promote professional and ethical conduct as well as improvements in the quality of goods and services.

* * *

What Are the Unfair Advantages?

Unfair competition itself is easy to define, yet difficult to quantify. The unfair advantage is derived from the granting of special status by an external source, almost always the government, which either permits the entity to avoid governmental "burdens" (e.g., taxes) or to obtain direct support (e.g., grants). The exemption from federal taxation is the most significant of these advantages. Others include exemption from state and local taxes, lower subsidized postal rates, and antitrust exemptions, to name a few. Congress only recently granted another privilege to nonprofits, the ability to obtain contracts from the government on a sole source basis.

Tax-exemption is the most recognized unfair advantage, but it is difficult to measure the extent of that advantage. The Internal Revenue Code includes a provision that requires the nonprofit to pay an unrelated business income tax on activities deemed to be unrelated. * * * Although a lower postal rate or an antitrust exemption is important, there is no doubt that tax-exemption drives the nonprofit issue. It is the linchpin of the nonprofit system.

A significant "benefit" of nonprofit status is the aura of the government imprimatur. While the "aura" has been described as a rationale for the existence of nonprofits, it, in fact, has emerged as a major business advantage. The "contract failure" theory suggests nonprofits assure the public of quality and performance in services for which the consumer is not able to make such judgments. The evidence now suggests that, increasingly, the aura serves as a marketing tool as much as a method of quality control and protection.

The Impact of Unfair Competition

How do these exemptions or privileges provide advantage within the marketplace? The obvious answer is that the exemptions allow the nonprofit to lower the price of the goods or services. A less obvious advantage is the ability to sustain the costs of market entry. The chance to devote more resources to advertising, to produce a better product and to underwrite new products is a tremendous advantage. The National Geographic Society, for example, through nonprofit donations is able to commit vast sums to the production of the magazine, which in turn creates new donors.

The damage of unfair competition is difficult to assess because the problem is national in scope, but local in impact. This explains, in part, why the phenomenon hits the small business sector particularly hard. The competition takes place on an institution-by-institution basis. A small business competes against one university or one hospital. The central activity is the provision of service. Service, except for a limited number of franchise operations, does not lend itself to a national marketing strategy. A key index, if one were able to compile the data, is "opportunity lost." How many sales were not made by the for-profit, how many jobs were not created as the result of the sales not made, or the taxes not paid on those sales? In a growing market, if a firm's sales increase 50% but a nonprofit has siphoned off another 50% of the potential growth, how is one to know?

What is clear is that nonprofits have become increasingly reliant on income-producing activities. Contributions as a percentage of income have decreased from 17 to 13 percent, and dues have decreased from 26 to 12 percent between 1946 and 1978. Other income has increased from 57 to 75 percent. The nonprofit sector has gained marketshare, and it is easier to document their gain rather than small business' loss. The correlation is clear, and not surprisingly, the concept of the for-profit business community regarding unfair competition has risen in direct proportion to the increase in the sale of goods and services by nonprofits.

How Nonprofits Compete

Areas in which businesses go head to head with nonprofits include food service, testing laboratories, retail sales of books and computers, travel, recreation, nurseries, day care, hearing aids, veterinarians, blood banks, consulting engineers, medical equipment suppliers, pencil makers, specialty advertisers, hotels, bus operators, printing, construction, laundries, janitorial services, waste hauling, electrical, plumbing and heating contracting to name a few. * * *

Why Nonprofits Compete

There are two types of competitors. In a number of fields, such as health care, the nonprofit has been dominant provider of the service and it is the for-profit that has sought a foothold in the market. In the second case, the nonprofit has expanded, entering a thriving for-profit market. The reasons for this latter expansion are clear. "Escalating expenses, declining revenue and a rising demand for highly technical services have forced many exempt organizations into the commercial arena." More accurately it is escalating expenses, declining revenue, and *excess* capacity that have forced the exempts to look to the commercial arena. Nonprofits are professionally operated, and sophisticated management will adapt to maximize resources. At the same time, self interest dictates that managers and employees will seek to protect their efforts. The laundry industry provides a classic example. Nonprofit hospital laundries have learned to capitalize on their resources. Consider the statements of these nonprofit managers: "We intend to turn St. Elizabeth's into a profit making operation." "This guarantees employment for our staff of 32 and allows us to think about hiring more." Meanwhile for-profit laundries have been able to document a corresponding loss of marketshare. One such business owner reports a drop of marketshare from approximately 28–30 percent to 20 percent shortly after the nonprofit laundry expanded its marketing efforts.

The trend towards for-profit performance of activities which have been the province of nonprofits presents an entirely different set of questions. Changes in our society, particularly the growth of health insurance, have created a situation where ability to pay is no longer the dominant factor in determining who receives health care. Either way, there is no organized body of law or economics to explain adequately why nonprofits exist or why governments grant such status to particular enterprises. As early as 1601, the British had conferred preferred status on charitable institutions through the Statute of Uses. In the U.S., the first tax-exemptions surfaced in the Tariff of 1894. Since that time Congress has added over twenty-five specific statutory categories but "not [as] the result of any planned legislative scheme, and [exemptions] have never been set forth as part of any unified concept of exemption."

Academicians have advanced a number of theories to explain the existence of nonprofits. The predominant explanation is the contract failure theory, which states that a consumer "needs an organization that he can trust", and the nonprofit, because of the legal constraints under which it must operate, is likely to serve that function better than its for-profit counterpart. The second theory is the "public goods" theory, which suggests that nonprofits provide services the government would otherwise have to provide to the citizenry. Both the Congress and the courts have provided added credibility to this theory. Small business counters with the assertion that the public good rationale actually begs the question. The existence of for-profits should be prima facie evidence that the government would not have to provide the service. Further, one can ask why the Government does not subsidize all providers, whether for-profit or nonprofit.

One rationale for tax-exemption is that it fosters volunteerism and the principle of volunteerism is part and parcel of our society and culture. What makes the U.S. economy truly unique is the balance between self reliance and the common good. However, tax-exemption does not have an inherent bearing on the relationship. Nonprofit status without the tax-exemption should foster volunteerism under this theory. The motivation of the volunteer, in addition to the desire to contribute to the common good, is the knowledge that no individual will benefit or profit from the work of volunteers. Two commentators have succinctly summed up the common justifications for a tax-exemption and the counter arguments thereto:

> *"Nonprofits are better suited than for-profits to produce public good because everyone should have access to public goods at the lowest possible price.* The classic example of a public good is a lighthouse; society is served when all boats use its light. It is very difficult to charge a price for the service because you cannot deny the light to those who do not pay. Some observers think of health care services as this kind of public good. A nonprofit organization, theoretically freed from worrying too much about costs and from raising money, can better deliver such services at the lowest possible price.

> This argument confuses funding with production. Government funding underwrites public goods and services that the private marketplace would otherwise not produce in sufficient quantity. The organizational form whose output is most cost effective-whether for-profit, nonprofit, or public-should receive such government funding to produce the needed services.

> *Nonprofit organizations have the same motives and rationales—and are subject to the same controls—as public organizations.* But nonprofits are not the same as public organizations because they have few outside controls on their activities. The free market sector is watchdogged by everything from the stock market to government regulatory agencies and consumer advocate organizations. Government institutions have somewhat fewer controls on their performance, like the voting process and bureaucratic budgetary control. Nonprofits have even fewer; boards of trustees appoint their members who are then subjected to little outside scrutiny. Although some observers believe donors act as a control, in reality they are hardly involved with the impact or results of their donations.

> *Nonprofit managers operate from a moral base that makes them more trustworthy than for-profit managers because the mission of their organization is not to make money but to serve society.* Nonprofits are supposedly more worthy to receive private donations than for-profits because their managers will not divert them into the organization's bottom line. Given the weaker controls on nonprofits, however, it is unclear why nonprofit managers should not be equally likely to direct such funds into larger salaries, organizational perquisites, and excessively large staffs.

> *Nonprofits are better suited than for-profits to provide services their customers cannot evaluate, such as education or health care, in part because they sacrifice growth to quality.* This argument assumes a naive

consumer whose existence we doubt. Given a choice between two organizations that offer the same service, the American customer is more likely than ever to pick the one with the better performance no matter what its form. More consumers are well-educated today than ever before. Recent sharp declines in deaths from heart disease in the United States, for example, are caused primarily by self-induced changes in life-styles, not from counsel by the medical profession. Further, no one has proven that nonprofits are reluctant to grow; they have tripled since World War II, and their income now represents more than 9% of GNP."

[Mr. O'Neil went on to propose "solutions" to the unfair competition problem, some of which are discussed in Section I of this chapter, infra, at pp. 696–702. Eds.]

NOTES AND QUESTIONS

1. *Why and How is the Competition Unfair?* How, specifically, are for-profit businesses harmed by their tax-exempt competitors? Is it because nonprofits charge lower prices for comparable services? For-profit firms also could lower their prices. Is it because nonprofits can accumulate earnings and expand faster if they are exempt from income tax while for-profits only can expand with after-tax profits? Economically, who is adversely affected by unfair competition? And if unfair competition is the problem, why is most investment income, such as interest and rent, not taxed? Would repeal of the UBIT result in widespread displacement of for-profit firms?

2. *Economic Perspectives: Fairness.* In tax policy parlance, "horizontal equity" is the principle that taxpayers with equal income should pay the same amounts of tax. In questioning the underlying economic assumptions in the UBIT policy debate, Professor Susan Rose–Ackerman has identified two different claims based on the notion of horizontal equity. The first compares firms within the same industry and asserts that it is unfair for the tax system to favor one competitor over another. The second approach compares for-profit firms across different industries—those with and those without tax-exempt competitors—and asserts that for-profits that compete with both taxable and tax-exempt firms are disadvantaged. Susan Rose–Ackerman, Unfair Competition and Corporate Income Taxation, 34 Stan. L.Rev. 1017, 1019–1021 (1982).

Professor Rose–Ackerman argues that unfairness does not result from competition between firms in the same industry. In her view, the impact of tax exemption is less upon the for-profit firms than upon their investors, and the unfair competition is with investors in industries that do not face competition from tax favored firms. As a result, similarly situated investors earn different returns. Investors in an industry with competition from nonprofits are asked to bear a greater share of the social costs of tax favoritism to nonprofits than investors in firms without nonprofit competition. Rose–Ackerman suggests that the only way nonprofits can affect profits is through excessive entry into a particular industry so that the industry has more firms earning lower gross returns than the for-profit investors anticipated. In other words, nonprofits will enter a field, causing marginally profitable for-profit firms to leave because they will be earning subcompetitive returns. She concludes that if the nonprofit sector's productive business investments were spread across the economy, they would be unlikely to have any competitive impact. But since the UBIT prevents such dispersion, nonprofits must concentrate their profitable endeavors on those few lines of business that are substantially related to their exempt purposes. It thus is more likely that the permissible business activities of nonprofits will impose losses on competitive for-profit firms.

And so what does one conclude from all of this? Professor Rose–Ackerman's thesis is that the UBIT creates more unfairness than it can possibly prevent and should be repealed. Id. at 1038. Other commentators also have questioned the effectiveness of the UBIT in preventing unfair competition by nonprofits. But this debate has proceeded on a wholly theoretical level. As the commentators concede, empirical work is virtually non-existent. See also Boris I. Bittker & George K. Rahdert, The Exemption of Nonprofit Organizations from Federal Income Taxation, 85 Yale L.J. 299, 316–326 (1976); William A. Klein, Income Taxation and Legal Entities, 20 UCLA L.Rev. 13, 61–68 (1972).

3. *Economic Perspectives: Efficiency.* Professor Henry Hansmann believes that the UBIT policy debate has been muddled by casting the issue in terms of fairness. In his view, the more fundamental concern is economic efficiency. From that perspective, he concludes that the argument for retaining the UBIT in roughly its present form is overwhelming. Henry B. Hansmann, Unfair Competition and the Unrelated Business Income Tax, 75 Va.L.Rev. 605, 607 (1989).

Professor Hansmann agrees with Rose–Ackerman that repeal of the UBIT would not result in widespread displacement of for-profit firms. Id. at 610. But he argues that failure to apply the corporate income tax to unrelated businesses operated by nonprofits could result in a number of inefficiencies. For example, if the UBIT were repealed, universities, foundations and pension funds that now invest a substantial portion of their endowments in a diversified portfolio of common stocks would have a strong incentive to invest in wholly owned businesses. The result would be an incentive for nonprofits to increase their investment risk through decreased diversification. Id. at 615.

Hansmann also argues that repeal of the UBIT would lead to managerial inefficiency because nonprofits have no stockholders and thus less incentive to minimize costs or maximize revenues. Moreover, repeal would give nonprofits too great an incentive to accumulate assets rather than spend for their exempt purposes. Finally, Hansmann maintains that repeal of the UBIT would shrink the corporate tax base because nonprofits would purchase wholly owned exempt businesses through debt-financed acquisitions. Id. at 622. Although Hansmann concludes that the case for repealing or considerably broadening the UBIT is weak, he urges that serious reform is needed in defining (and contracting) the scope of the basic underlying exemption. Id. at 634–635.

4. *Historical Perspective: The Political Function of the UBIT*. Professor Ethan Stone has made a compelling case that the UBIT was the result of a reaction by Congress to problems of perception created when charities began to engage in politically embarrassing commercial activities. These public relations problems coincided with the expansion of the progressive income tax rates in the 1940s. Some for-profit firms began to use charities (among others) as tax shelter facilitators. These developments, along with some widely publicized "uncharitable-like" commercial activities by high profile organizations, threatened the traditional "good works" rationale of tax exemption. Professor Stone's research also reveals that in the years preceding enactment of the UBIT, there is almost no evidence of taxpaying businesses complaining about unfair competition.

Professor Stone concludes that Congress enacted the UBIT to discourage charities from engaging in nontraditional activities that make them look uncomfortably uncharitable while preserving tax exemption for "related" businesses and passive investment income. So viewed, the primary function of the UBIT is political symbolism: the UBIT deters charities from engaging in activities that look bad. See Ethan Stone, Adhering to the Old Line: Uncovering the History and Political Function of the Unrelated Business Income Tax, 54 Emory L.J. 1475 (2005).

5. *For Further Reading*. Office of Advocacy, U.S. Small Business Administration, Unfair Competition by Nonprofit Organizations with Small Business: An Issue for the 1980s (1984); General Accounting Office, Tax Policy: Competition Between Taxable Business and Tax–Exempt Organizations (1987); W. Harrison Wellford and Janne G. Gallagher, Unfair Competition? The Challenge to Tax Exemption (1988).

D.   THE NATURE OF AN UNRELATED TRADE OR BUSINESS

1.   IMPOSITION AND RATES OF TAX

Internal Revenue Code: § 511(a), (b).

The unrelated business income tax applies to virtually all organizations otherwise exempt from tax under § 501(a), including qualified pension and profit-sharing plans, and state colleges, universities, and their subsidiaries. I.R.C. § 511(a)(2). The tax does not apply to certain United States instrumentalities, such as the Federal Deposit Insurance Corporation and the Federal National Mortgage Association. I.R.C. §§ 511(a)(2); 501(c)(1). See Gen. Couns. Mem. 38737 (June 1, 1981). Except in the case of trusts, unrelated business taxable income is taxable at corporate income tax rates, which range from 15 percent on the first $25,000 of taxable income to 34 percent for taxable income over $75,000 and peak at 35 percent for taxable income over $10 million. I.R.C. §§ 511(a)(1); 11(b). Trusts are taxable at the compressed trust rates in § 1(e), which in 2010 reached the top 35 percent bracket at a mere $11,050 of taxable income. I.R.C. § 511(b)(1). In view of the differential in tax rates, an exempt organization with substantial net income from an unrelated business will save taxes by conducting the business in a corporation.

2. TAXABLE AND EXCEPTED ACTIVITIES

Internal Revenue Code: § 513(a), (c), (f), (h), (i).

Treasury Regulations: § 1.513–1, –4, –7.

The principal target of the UBIT is income derived from profit-seeking activities not related to an organization's exempt purposes. Congress did not intend to tax income from "related" activities, such as admission fees to theaters and museums, college tuition, fees paid by hospital patients, or dues paid by members of labor unions, trade associations, and social clubs. And since the tax was aimed at the problem of unfair competition, most forms of investment income, such as dividends, interest, rents and royalties, are exempt from the UBIT, except in the case of social clubs and a few more specialized types of exempt organizations.

Three conditions must be met for an activity to be classified as an unrelated trade or business: (1) the activity must be a "trade or business"; (2) it must be "regularly carried on"; and (3) it must not be substantially related to an organization's exempt purposes, aside from the need for funds derived from the activity. I.R.C. § 513(a); Treas. Reg. § 1.513–1(a).

The threshold question is whether the organization is engaged in a trade or business. In general, a "trade or business" includes "any activity carried on for the production of income from the sale of goods or performance of services." Treas. Reg. § 1.513–1(b). An activity will not lose its identity as a trade or business merely because it is carried on within a larger aggregate of similar activities which may or may not be related to the exempt purposes of the organization. I.R.C. § 513(c); Treas. Reg. § 1.513–1(b). Under this fragmentation approach, an "unrelated" business need not be wholly separate from the exempt activities of the organization. Thus, the sale of medications and supplies to the general public by a hospital pharmacy does not escape characterization as an unrelated business merely because the pharmacy also furnishes these products to the hospital and its patients. Similarly, even though the publication of a magazine is related to the exempt purposes of an organization, its advertising revenue likely will be taxable.

The "regularly carried on" test relates to the frequency and continuity of the activity as compared with similar activities of nonexempt organizations. Congress believed that intermittent activities would not pose any threat of unfair competition. Treas. Reg. § 1.513–1(c). An organization thus will not be subject to the UBIT if it briefly conducts an income-producing activity of a kind that a taxable business would conduct on a year-round basis (e.g., a fundraising auction). But if income-producing activities are of a kind normally undertaken by for-profit firms only on a "seasonal" basis, the conduct of comparable activities by an exempt organization during a significant portion of the season ordinarily will constitute the regular conduct of a trade or business. Id. Some of the special problems raised by the "regularly carried on" test are illustrated later in this chapter.

The "substantially related" test is more difficult to apply. The regulations offer little more than abstract generalizations, requiring an examination of the relationship between the business and the organization's exempt purposes. To be "related" to an exempt purpose, there must be a substantial causal relationship—i.e., the activity must "contribute importantly" to the accomplishment of the exempt purpose. Treas. Reg. § 1.513–1(d). All the facts and circumstances control, but particular emphasis is placed on the size and extent of the activity. Thus, if a business is conducted on a scale larger than necessary to carry out an exempt purpose, it is more likely to be treated as unrelated. The potential for competition with a commercial counterpart is another important factor. Id.

These general rules are subject to numerous qualifications, conditions, and exceptions. Three types of activities are specifically excluded from the definition of an unrelated trade or business: (1) a trade or business where substantially all of the labor is performed by unpaid volunteers, (2) a business carried on by a § 501(c)(3) organization or a state college or university primarily for the convenience of members, students, patients, officers or employees (e.g., a university cafeteria), and (3) the sale of donated merchandise (e.g., a thrift shop). See I.R.C. § 513(a)(1)–(3). More specialized exceptions are provided for activities such as bingo (I.R.C. § 513(f)), certain corporate sponsorship payments that do not constitute advertising (I.R.C. § 513(i)), convention and trade shows (I.R.C. § 513(d)(3)(A)), distribution of low-cost items as part of fundraising solicitations (I.R.C. § 513(h)(1)), public entertainment at events such as state fairs (I.R.C. § 513(d)(2)(A)), services for small hospitals (I.R.C. § 513(e)), and rental of telephone poles (I.R.C. § 513(g)). The Code also contains numerous "modifications" which have the effect of exempting virtually all forms of passive income from the UBIT provided the income is not derived from debt-financed property. I.R.C. §§ 512(b); 514.

The materials that follow illustrate the range of current issues on the evolving concept of an unrelated trade or business.

a. ADVERTISING

United States v. American College of Physicians

Supreme Court of the United States, 1986.
475 U.S. 834, 106 S.Ct. 1591.

■ JUSTICE MARSHALL delivered the opinion of the Court.

A tax-exempt organization must pay tax on income that it earns by carrying on a business not "substantially related" to the purposes for which the organization has received its exemption from federal taxation.

The question before this Court is whether respondent, a tax-exempt organization, must pay tax on the profits it earns by selling commercial advertising space in its professional journal, The Annals of Internal Medicine.

I

Respondent, the American College of Physicians, is an organization exempt from taxation under § 501(c)(3) of the Internal Revenue Code. The purposes of the College, as stated in its articles of incorporation, are to maintain high standards in medical education and medical practice; to encourage research, especially in clinical medicine; and to foster measures for the prevention of disease and for the improvement of public health. The principal facts were stipulated at trial. In furtherance of its exempt purposes, respondent publishes The Annals of Internal Medicine (Annals), a highly regarded monthly medical journal containing scholarly articles relevant to the practice of internal medicine. Each issue of Annals contains advertisements for pharmaceuticals, medical supplies, and equipment useful in the practice of internal medicine, as well as notices of positions available in that field. Respondent has a longstanding policy of accepting only advertisements containing information about the use of medical products, and screens proffered advertisements for accuracy and relevance to internal medicine. The advertisements are clustered in two groups, one at the front and one at the back of each issue.

In 1975, Annals produced gross advertising income of $1,376,322. After expenses and deductible losses were subtracted, there remained a net income of $153,388. Respondent reported this figure as taxable income and paid taxes on it in the amount of $55,965. Respondent then filed a timely claim with the Internal Revenue Service for refund of these taxes, and when the Government demurred, filed suit in the United States Claims Court.

The Claims Court held a trial and concluded that the advertisements in Annals were not substantially related to respondent's tax-exempt purposes. Rather, after finding various facts regarding the nature of the College's advertising business, it concluded that any correlation between the advertisements and respondent's educational purpose was incidental because "the comprehensiveness and content of the advertising package is entirely dependent on each manufacturer's willingness to pay for space and the imagination of its advertising agency." Accordingly, the court determined that the advertising proceeds were taxable.

The Court of Appeals for the Federal Circuit reversed. It held clearly erroneous the trial court's finding that the advertising was not substantially related to respondent's tax-exempt purpose. The Court of Appeals believed that the trial court had focused too much on the commercial character of the advertising business and not enough on the actual contribution of the advertisements to the education of the journal's readers. It held that respondent had established the requisite substantial relation and its entitlement to exemption from taxation. We granted the Government's petition for certiorari, and now reverse.

II

The taxation of business income not "substantially related" to the objectives of exempt organizations dates from the Revenue Act of 1950. The statute was enacted in response to perceived abuses of the tax laws by tax-exempt organizations that engaged in profit-making activities. Prior law had required only that the profits garnered by exempt organizations be used in furtherance of tax-exempt purposes, without regard to the source of those profits. * * * As a result, tax-exempt organizations were able to carry on full-fledged commercial enterprises in competition with corporations whose profits were fully taxable. * * * See Revenue Revision of 1950 * * * (describing universities' production of "automobile parts, chinaware, and food products, and the operation of theatres, oil wells, and cotton gins"). Congress perceived a need to restrain the unfair competition fostered by the tax laws.

Nevertheless, Congress did not force exempt organizations to abandon all commercial ventures, nor did it levy a tax only upon businesses that bore no relation at all to the tax-exempt purposes of an organization, as some of the 1950 Act's proponents had suggested. Rather, in the 1950 Act it struck a balance between its two objectives of encouraging benevolent enterprise and restraining unfair competition by imposing a tax on the "unrelated business taxable income" of tax-exempt organizations. 26 U.S.C. § 511(a)(1).

"Unrelated business taxable income" was defined as "the gross income derived by any organization from any unrelated trade or business * * * regularly carried on by it * * *." § 512(a)(1). Congress defined an "unrelated trade or business" as "any trade or business the conduct of which is not substantially related * * * to the exercise or performance by such organization of its charitable, educational, or other purpose or function constituting the basis for its exemption * * *." § 513(a). Whether respondent's advertising income is taxable, therefore, depends upon (1) whether the publication of paid advertising is a "trade or business," (2) whether it is regularly carried on, and (3) whether it is substantially related to respondent's tax-exempt purposes.

III

A

Satisfaction of the first condition is conceded in this case, as it must be, because Congress has declared unambiguously that the publication of paid advertising is a trade or business activity distinct from the publication of accompanying educational articles and editorial comment.

In 1967, the Treasury promulgated a regulation interpreting the unrelated business income provision of the 1950 Act. The regulation defined "trade or business" to include not only a complete business enterprise, but also any component activity of a business. Treas.Reg. § 1.513–1(b), 26 CFR § 1.513–1(b)(1985). This revolutionary approach to the identification of a "trade or business" had a significant effect on advertising, which theretofore had been considered simply a part of a unified publishing business. The new regulation segregated the "trade or business" of selling advertising space from the "trade or business" of publishing a journal, an approach commonly referred to as "fragmenting" the enterprise of publishing into its component parts:

> "[A]ctivities of soliciting, selling, and publishing commercial advertising do not lose identity as a trade or business even though the advertising is published in an exempt organization periodical which contains editorial matter related to the exempt purposes of the organization." 26 CFR § 1.513–1(b)(1985).

In 1969, Congress responded to widespread criticism of those Treasury regulations by passing the Tax Reform Act of 1969, Pub.L. 91–172, 83 Stat. 487 (1969 Act). That legislation specifically endorsed the Treasury's concept of "fragmenting" the publishing enterprise into its component activities, and adopted, in a new § 513(c), much of the language of the regulation that defined advertising as a separate trade or business:

> "Advertising, etc., activities * * * an activity does not lose identity as a trade or business merely because it is carried on * * * within a larger complex of other endeavors which may, or may not, be related to the exempt purposes of the organization." 26 U.S.C. § 513(c).

The statute clearly established advertising as a trade or business, the first prong of the inquiry into the taxation of unrelated business income.

The presence of the second condition, that the business be regularly carried on, is also undisputed here. The satisfaction of the third condition, however, that of "substantial relation," is vigorously contested, and that issue forms the crux of the controversy before us.

B

According to the Government, Congress and the Treasury established a blanket rule that advertising published by tax-exempt professional journals can never be substantially related to the purposes of those journals and is, therefore, always a taxable business. Respondent, however, contends that each case must be determined on the basis of the characteristics of the advertisements and journal in question. Each party finds support for its position in the governing statute and regulations issued by the Department of the Treasury.

In its 1967 regulations, the Treasury not only addressed the "fragmentation" issue discussed above, but also attempted to clarify the statutory "substantially related" standard found in § 513(a). It provided that the conduct of a tax-exempt business must have a causal relation to the organization's exempt purpose (other than through the generation of income), and that "the production or distribution of the goods or the performance of the services from which the gross income is derived must *contribute importantly* to the accomplishment of [the exempt] purposes." Treas.Reg. § 1.513–1(d)(2)(emphasis added). In illustration of its new test for substantial relation, the Treasury provided an example whose interpretation is central to the resolution of the issue before us. Example 7 of Treas.Reg. § 1.513–1(d)(4)(iv) involves "Z," an exempt association formed to advance the interests of a particular profession and drawing its membership from that profession. Z publishes a monthly journal containing articles and other editorial material that contribute importantly to the tax-exempt purpose. Z derives income from advertising products within the field of professional interest of the members:

> "Following a practice common among taxable magazines which publish advertising, Z requires its advertising to comply with certain general standards of taste, fairness, and accuracy; but within those limits the form, content, and manner of presentation of the advertising messages are governed by the basic objective of the advertisers to promote the sale of the advertised products. While the advertisements contain certain information, the informational function of the advertising is incidental to the controlling aim of stimulating demand for the advertised products and differs in no essential respect from the informational function of any commercial advertising. Like taxable publishers of advertising, Z accepts advertising only from those who are willing to pay its published rates. Although continuing education of its members in matters pertaining to their profession is one of the purposes for which Z is granted exemption, the publication of advertising designed and selected in the manner of ordinary commercial advertising is not an educational activity of the kind contemplated by the exemption statute; it differs fundamentally from such an activity both in its governing objective and in its method. Accordingly, Z's publication of advertising does not contribute importantly to the accomplishment of its exempt purposes; and the income which it derives from advertising constitutes gross income from unrelated trade or business." § 1.513–1(d)(4)(iv), Example 7.

The Government contends both that Example 7 creates a per se rule of taxation for journal advertising income and that Congress intended to adopt that rule, together with the remainder of the 1967 regulations, into law in the 1969 Act. We find both of these contentions unpersuasive.

Read as a whole, the regulations do not appear to create the type of blanket rule of taxability that the Government urges upon us. On the contrary, the regulations specifically condition tax exemption of business income upon the importance of the business activity's contribution to the particular exempt purpose at issue, and direct that "[w]hether activities productive of gross income contribute importantly to the accomplishment of any purpose for which an organization is granted an exemption depends *in each case* upon the facts and circumstances involved," § 1.513–1(d)(2) (emphasis added). Example 7 need not be interpreted as being inconsistent with that general rule. Attributing to the term "example" its ordinary meaning, we believe that Example 7 is best construed as an illustration of one possible application, under given circumstances, of the regulatory standard for determining substantial relation.

The interpretative difficulty of Example 7 arises primarily from its failure to distinguish clearly between the statements intended to provide hypothetical facts and those designed to posit the necessary legal consequences of those facts. Just at the point in the lengthy Example at which the facts would appear to end and the analysis to begin, a pivotal statement appears: "the informational function of the advertising is incidental to the controlling aim of stimulating demand for the advertised products." The Government's position depends upon reading this statement as a general proposition of law, while respondent would read it as a statement of fact that may be true by hypothesis of "Z" and its journal, but is not true of Annals.

We recognize that the language of the Example is amenable to either interpretation. Nevertheless, several considerations lead us to believe that the Treasury did not intend to set out a per se statement of law. First, when the regulations were proposed in early 1967, the Treasury expressed a clear intention to treat all commercial advertising as an unrelated business. When the regulations were issued in final form, however, following much criticism and the addition of Example 7, they included no such statement of intention. Second, a blanket rule of taxation for advertising in professional journals would contradict the explicit case-by-case requirement articulated in Treas.Reg. § 1.513–1(d)(2), and we are reluctant to attribute to the Treasury an intention to depart from its own general principle in the absence of clear support for doing so. Finally, at the time the regulations were issued, the 1950 Act had been interpreted to mean that business activities customarily engaged in by tax-exempt organizations would continue to be considered "substantially related" and untaxed. A per se rule of taxation for the activity, traditional among tax-exempt journals, of carrying commercial advertising would have been a significant departure from that prevailing view. Thus, in 1967 the idea of a per se rule of taxation for all journal advertising revenue was sufficiently controversial, its effect so substantial, and its statutory authorization so tenuous, that we simply cannot attribute to the Treasury the intent to take that step in the form of an ambiguous example, appended to a subpart of a subsection of a subparagraph of a regulation.

It is still possible, of course, that, regardless of what the Treasury actually meant by its 1967 regulations, Congress read those regulations as creating a blanket rule of taxation, and intended to adopt that rule into law in the 1969 Act. The Government appears to embrace this view, which it supports with certain statements in the legislative history of the 1969 Act. For example, the Government cites to a statement in the House Report, discussing the taxation of advertising income of journals published by tax-exempt organizations:

> "Your committee believes that a business competing with taxpaying organizations should not be granted an unfair competitive advantage by operating tax free unless the business contributes importantly to the exempt function. It has concluded that by that standard, advertising in a journal published by an exempt organization is not related to the organization's exempt functions, and therefore it believes that this

income should be taxed." H.R.Rep. No. 91–413, pt. 1, p. 50 (1969), U.S.Code Cong. & Admin.News 1969, pp. 1645, 1695.

Similar views appear in the Senate Report:

* * *

Based on this [legislative history], the Government argues that the 1969 Act created a per se rule of taxation for advertising income. The weakness of this otherwise persuasive argument, however, is that the quoted discussion appears in the Reports solely in support of the legislators' decision to enact § 513(c), the provision approving the fragmentation of "trade or business." Although § 513(c) was a significant change in the tax law that removed one barrier to the taxation of advertising proceeds, it cannot be construed as a comment upon the two other distinct conditions— "regularly carried on" and "not substantially related"—whose satisfaction is prerequisite to taxation of business income under the 1950 Act. Congress did not incorporate into the 1969 Act the language of the regulation defining "substantial relation," nor did the statute refer in any other way to the issue of the relation between advertising and exempt functions, even though that issue had been hotly debated at the hearings. Thus, we have no reason to conclude from the Committee Reports that Congress resolved the dispute whether, in a specific case, a journal's carriage of advertising could so advance its educational objectives as to be "substantially related" to those objectives within the meaning of the 1950 Act.

It is possible that the Committees' discussion of advertising reflects merely an erroneous assumption that the "fragmentation" provision of § 513(c), without more, would establish the automatic taxation of journal advertising revenue. Alternatively, the quoted passages could be read to indicate the Committees' intention affirmatively to endorse what they believed to be existing practice, or even to change the law substantially. The truth is that, other than a general reluctance to consider commercial advertisements generally as substantially related to the purposes of tax-exempt journals, no congressional view of the issue emerges from the quoted excerpts of the Reports. Thus, despite the Reports' seeming endorsement of a per se rule, we are hesitant to rely on that inconclusive legislative history either to supply a provision not enacted by Congress, or to define a statutory term enacted by a prior Congress. * * * We agree, therefore, with both the Claims Court and the Court of Appeals in their tacit rejection of the Government's argument that the Treasury and Congress intended to establish a per se rule requiring the taxation of income from all commercial advertisements of all tax-exempt journals without a specific analysis of the circumstances.

IV

It remains to be determined whether, in this case, the business of selling advertising space is "substantially related"—or, in the words of the regulation, "contributes importantly"—to the purposes for which respondent enjoys an exemption from federal taxation. Respondent has maintained throughout this litigation that the advertising in Annals performs an educational function supplemental to that of the journal's editorial content.

Testimony of respondent's witnesses at trial tended to show that drug advertising performs a valuable function for doctors by disseminating information on recent developments in drug manufacture and use. In addition, respondent has contended that the role played by the Food and Drug Administration, in regulating much of the form and content of prescription-drug advertisements, enhances the contribution that such advertisements make to the readers' education. All of these factors, respondent argues, distinguish the advertising in Annals from standard commercial advertising. Respondent approaches the question of substantial relation from the perspective of the journal's subscribers; it points to the benefit that they may glean from reading the advertisements and concludes that benefit is substantial enough to satisfy the statutory test for tax exemption. The Court of Appeals took the same approach. It concluded that the advertisements performed various "essential" functions for physicians, and found a substantial relation based entirely upon the medically related content of the advertisements as a group.

The Government, on the other hand, looks to the conduct of the tax-exempt organization itself, inquiring whether the publishers of Annals have performed the advertising services in a manner that evinces an intention to use the advertisements for the purpose of contributing to the educational value of the journal. Also approaching the question from the vantage point of the College, the Claims Court emphasized the lack of a comprehensive presentation of the material contained in the advertisements. It commented upon the "hit-or-miss nature of the advertising," and observed that the "differences between ads plainly reflected the advertiser's marketing strategy rather than their probable importance to the reader." "[A]ny educational function [the advertising] may have served was incidental to its purpose of raising revenue." Id., at 535.

We believe that the Claims Court was correct to concentrate its scrutiny upon the conduct of the College rather than upon the educational quality of the advertisements. For all advertisements contain some information, and if a modicum of informative content were enough to supply the important contribution necessary to achieve tax exemption for commercial advertising, it would be the rare advertisement indeed that would fail to meet the test. Yet the statutory and regulatory scheme, even if not creating a per se rule against tax exemption, is clearly antagonistic to the concept of a per se rule for exemption for advertising revenue. Moreover, the statute provides that a tax will be imposed on "any trade or business the conduct of which is not substantially related," 26 U.S.C. § 513(a)(emphasis added), directing our focus to the manner in which the tax-exempt organization operates its business. The implication of the statute is confirmed by the regulations, which emphasize the "manner" of designing and selecting the advertisements. See Treas.Reg. § 1.513–1(d)(4)(iv), Example 7, 26 CFR § 1.513–1(d)(4)(iv), Example 7 (1985). Thus, the Claims Court properly directed its attention to the College's conduct of its advertising business, and it found the following pertinent facts:

> "The evidence is clear that plaintiff did not use the advertising to provide its readers a comprehensive or systematic presentation of any aspect of the goods or services publicized. Those companies willing to

pay for advertising space got it; others did not. Moreover, some of the advertising was for established drugs or devices and was repeated from one month to another, undermining the suggestion that the advertising was principally designed to alert readers of recent developments [citing, as examples, ads for Valium, Insulin and Maalox]. Some ads even concerned matters that had no conceivable relationship to the College's tax-exempt purposes." 3 Cl.Ct., at 534 (footnotes omitted).

These facts find adequate support in the record. * * * Considering them in light of the applicable legal standard, we are bound to conclude that the advertising in Annals does not contribute importantly to the journal's educational purposes. This is not to say that the College could not control its publication of advertisements in such a way as to reflect an intention to contribute importantly to its educational functions. By coordinating the content of the advertisements with the editorial content of the issue, or by publishing only advertisements reflecting new developments in the pharmaceutical market, for example, perhaps the College could satisfy the stringent standards erected by Congress and the Treasury. In this case, however, we have concluded that the Court of Appeals erroneously focused exclusively upon the information that is invariably conveyed by commercial advertising, and consequently failed to give effect to the governing statute and regulations. Its judgment, accordingly, is

Reversed.

■ CHIEF JUSTICE BURGER, with whom JUSTICE POWELL joins, concurring.

Most medical journals are not comparable to magazines and newspapers published for profit. Their purpose is to assemble and disseminate to the profession relevant information bearing on patient care. The enormous expansion of medical knowledge makes it difficult for a general practitioner—or even a specialist—to keep fully current with the latest developments without such aids. In a sense these journals provide continuing education for physicians—a "correspondence course" not sponsored for profit but public health.

There is a public value in the widest possible circulation of such data, and advertising surely tends to reduce the cost of publication and hence the cost to each subscriber, thereby enhancing the prospect of wider circulation. Plainly a regulation recognizing these realities would be appropriate. Such regulations, of course, are for the Executive Branch and the Congress, not the courts. I join the opinion because it reflects a permissible reading of the present Treasury regulations.

b.   INTERCOLLEGIATE ATHLETICS

Revenue Ruling 80–296

1980–2 Cum. Bull. 195.

ISSUE

Is the sale of broadcasting rights to an annual intercollegiate athletic event by an organization exempt from federal income tax under section

501(c)(3) of the Internal Revenue Code unrelated trade or business within the meaning of section 513?

FACTS

The organization was created by a regional collegiate athletic conference, made up of universities exempt under section 501(c)(3) of the Code, for the purpose of conducting an annual competitive athletic game between the champion of the conference and another collegiate team. The annual game generates income from various sources including admission charges and the sale of exclusive broadcasting rights to a national radio and television network.

LAW AND ANALYSIS

Section 513(a) of the Code defines the term "unrelated trade or business" as any trade or business the conduct of which is not substantially related (aside from the need of an organization for income or funds or the use it makes of the profits derived) to the exercise or performance by an organization of its exempt function.

Section 1.513–1(d)(2) of the Income Tax Regulations provides that a trade or business is "substantially related" only if the production or distribution of the goods or the performance of the service from which the gross income is derived contributes importantly to the accomplishment of the purposes for which exemption is granted. Whether activities productive of gross income contribute importantly to the accomplishment of any purpose for which an organization is granted exemption depends in each case upon the facts and circumstances involved.

College and university athletic organizations that promote certain aspects of athletic competition have generally been held to be educational and thus exempt from federal income tax. An athletic program is considered to be an integral part of the educational process of a university, and activities providing necessary services to student athletes and coaches further the educational purposes of the university. See Rev. Rul. 67–291, 1967–2 C.B. 184. See also Rev. Rul. 64–275, 1964–2 C.B. 142.

The Service has traditionally taken the position that income from paid admissions to college and university athletic events, regardless of the number of persons in attendance or the amount of paid admissions, is not taxable as income from unrelated trade or business because the events themselves are related to the educational purposes of the colleges and universities. This position is consistent with the following language contained in the Committee Reports on the Revenue Act of 1950, in which the predecessor to section 513 of the Code was enacted.

> Athletic activities of schools are substantially related to their educational functions. For example, a university would not be taxable on income derived from a basketball tournament sponsored by it, even where the teams were composed of students from other schools. (H.R. Rep. No. 2319, 81st Cong., 2d Sess. 37, 109 (1950), 1950–2 C.B. 380, 458.)

Of course, income of an educational organization from charges for admissions to football games would not be deemed to be income from an unrelated business, since its athletic activities are substantially related to its athletic program. (S. Rep. No. 2375, 81st Cong., 2d Sess. 29, 107 (1950), 1950–2 C.B. 483, 505.)

On the basis of the facts and circumstances presented in this case the educational purposes served by intercollegiate athletic activities are identical whether conducted directly by individual universities or by their regional athletic conference. Also, the educational purposes served by exhibiting a game before an audience that is physically present and exhibiting the game on television or radio before a much larger audience are substantially similar. Therefore, the sale of the broadcasting rights and the resultant broadcasting of the game contributes importantly to the accomplishment of the organization's exempt purposes.

HOLDING

The sale of broadcasting rights, under the circumstances described, is substantially related to the purpose constituting the basis for the organization's exemption and is not unrelated trade or business within the meaning of section 513 of the Code.

National Collegiate Athletic Ass'n v. Commissioner

United States Court of Appeals, Tenth Circuit, 1990.
914 F.2d 1417.

■ SEYMOUR, CIRCUIT JUDGE.

The National Collegiate Athletic Association (NCAA), the petitioner in this case, appeals from the decision of the tax court, which determined a deficiency of $10,395.14 in unrelated business income tax due for the 1981–1982 fiscal year. On appeal, the NCAA challenges the court's conclusion that revenue received from program advertising constituted unrelated business taxable income under I.R.C. § 512, not excludable from tax as a royalty under section 512(b)(2), I.R.C. § 512(b)(2). We reverse.[2]

I.

The NCAA is an unincorporated association of more than 880 colleges, universities, athletic conferences and associations, and other educational organizations and groups related to intercollegiate athletics, for which it has been the major governing organization since 1906. The NCAA is also an "exempt organization" under section 501(c)(3) of the Code, I.R.C. § 501(c)(3), and hence is exempt from federal income taxes. One of the purposes of the NCAA, as described in the organization's constitution, is "to supervise the conduct of * * * regional and national athletic events

---

2. Our determination that the advertising revenue is not unrelated business taxable income obviates the need to consider whether the income should nonetheless be excluded from taxation as a royalty under I.R.C. § 512(b)(2).

under the auspices of this Association." Pursuant to this purpose, the NCAA sponsors some seventy-six collegiate championship events in twenty-one different sports for women and men on an annual basis. The most prominent of these tournaments, and the NCAA's biggest revenue generator, is the Men's Division I Basketball Championship. The tournament is held at different sites each year. In 1982, regional rounds took place at a variety of sites, and the Louisiana Superdome in New Orleans was the host for the "Final Four," the tournament's semifinal and final rounds. In that year, the Championship consisted of forty-eight teams playing forty-seven games on eight days over a period of almost three weeks. The teams played in a single-game elimination format, with each of the four regional winners moving into the Final Four.

The NCAA contracted with Lexington Productions, a division of Jim Host and Associates, Inc. ("Host" or "Publisher"), in 1981 to print and publish the program for the 1982 Final Four games.[3] The purpose of such programs, according to the NCAA's then-director of public relations, is

> "to enhance the experience primarily for the fans attending the game * * *. [It also] gives the NCAA an opportunity to develop information about some of its other purposes that revolve around promoting sports [as a] part of higher education and demonstrating that athletes can be good students as well as good participants."

Prior to the middle of the 1970s, the host institution produced the Final Four program. The NCAA took over production until the late 1970s, when it began contracting with Host for the Final Four program. In 1982, Host began producing the programs for all rounds of the Championship. The motive for contracting the program production to Host was, according to the NCAA, to achieve consistency and quality at each round's game sites; making a profit was not the primary incentive.

The "Official Souvenir Program" for the 1982 Final Four round of the tournament was some 129 pages long, and it featured pictures of NCAA athletes such as Michael Jordan and articles on the NCAA itself, on New Orleans, on individual athletes, on championships from prior years, and on the Final Four teams: Georgetown, Houston, Louisville, and North Carolina. Advertisements made up a substantial portion of the program, some of which were placed by national companies. Among the products and services so displayed were Buick automobiles, Miller beer, Texaco motor oil, Fuji film, Maxwell House coffee, Nike sneakers, McDonald's fast food, Coca–Cola soda, Xerox photocopiers, ESPN cable network, and Popeye's Famous Fried Chicken. Other advertisers were local New Orleans merchants. A number of the New Orleans advertisements, including those for

---

3. The agreement read in part: [Under the agreement, the NCAA granted Host the exclusive right to publish the Final Four program and to act as the NCAA's exclusive agent for the sale of advertising. Advertising in the program was not to exceed 35% of the total pages, and the NCAA reserved the right of final approval for all advertising. Host agreed to pay to the NCAA the sum of $50,000 or 51% of net revenues, whichever was greater]. The parties also entered into an oral agreement under which Host produced a uniform program for the regional tournament games.

restaurants, hotels, and rental cars, apparently were directed at out-of-town tournament attendees. But these advertisements were exceeded in number by those placed by New Orleans/Louisiana companies not specifically related to the tourist industry. Among the local advertisers were the Canal Barge Company, the National Bank of Commerce in Jefferson Parish, Breit Marine Surveying, Inc., Pontchartrain Materials Corp., McDermott Marine Construction, and Tri–Parish Construction & Materials, Inc.[4]

The NCAA's total revenue from the 1982 Men's Division I Basketball Championship was $18,671,874. The NCAA reported none of this amount as unrelated business taxable income on its federal income tax return for the fiscal year ending August 31, 1982. The Commissioner mailed the NCAA a notice of deficiency in which he determined that the NCAA was liable for $10,395.14 in taxes on $55,926.71 of unrelated business taxable income from the program advertising revenue. The NCAA petitioned the tax court for a redetermination of the deficiency set forth by the Commissioner. The tax court determined that this revenue was unrelated business taxable income, and that it was not excludable from the tax as a royalty.

* * *

III.

Section 511 of the Code imposes a tax on the unrelated business taxable income of exempt organizations. Section 512(a)(1) of the Code defines the term "unrelated business taxable income" as "the gross income derived by any organization from any unrelated trade or business * * * regularly carried on by it * * *." The term "unrelated trade or business" means "any trade or business the conduct of which is not substantially related * * * to the exercise or performance by such organization" of its exempt function. I.R.C. § 513(a). Under the heading "Advertising, etc., activities," section 513(c) provides that "the term 'trade or business' includes any activity which is carried on for the production of income from the sale of goods or the performance of services * * *. An activity does not lose identity as a trade or business merely because it is carried on * * * within a larger complex of other endeavors which may, or may not, be related to the exempt purposes of the organization." I.R.C. § 513(c).

The NCAA's advertising revenue therefore must be considered unrelated business taxable income if: "(1) It is income from trade or business; (2) such trade or business is regularly carried on by the organization; and (3) the conduct of such trade or business is not substantially related (other than through the production of funds) to the organization's performance of its exempt functions." Treas. Reg. § 1.513–1(a). If a taxpayer shows that it does not meet any one of these three requirements, the taxpayer is not liable for the unrelated business income tax.

---

4. Only the Final Four program was included in the record, and so we use it as an example. The NCAA's director of public relations testified that the program for the earlier rounds differed very little from the Final Four program. See rec., vol. II, at 33.

The NCAA concedes that its program advertising was a "trade or business" not "substantially related" to its exempt purpose. The only question remaining, therefore, is whether the trade or business was "regularly carried on" by the organization. The meaning of the term "regularly carried on" is not defined by the language of the statute. Accordingly, we turn to the Treasury Regulations for assistance.[5]

Section 1.513–1(c) of the Treasury Regulations provides a discussion of the phrase "regularly carried on." The general principles set out there direct us to consider "the frequency and continuity with which the activities productive of the income are conducted and the manner in which they are pursued." Treas. Reg. § 1.513–1(c)(1)(emphasis added). As a cautionary note, the regulations emphasize that whether a trade or business is regularly carried on must be assessed "in light of the purpose of the unrelated business income tax to place exempt organization business activities upon the same tax basis as the nonexempt business endeavors with which they compete." Id.

The regulations then move beyond the general principles and set out a process for applying the principles to specific cases. The first step is to consider the normal time span of the particular activity, and then determine whether the length of time alone suggests that the activity is regularly carried on, or only intermittently carried on. See id. § 1.513–1(c)(2)(i). If the activity is "of a kind normally conducted by nonexempt commercial organizations on a *year-round* basis, the conduct of such [activity] by an exempt organization over a period of only a few weeks does not constitute the regular carrying on of trade or business." Id. (emphasis added). As an example of a business not regularly carried on, the regulations describe a hospital auxiliary's operation of a sandwich stand for only two weeks at a state fair. In contrast, the regulations deem the operation of a commercial parking lot every Saturday as a regularly-carried-on activity. Id.

If the activity is "of a kind normally undertaken by nonexempt commercial organizations only on a seasonal basis, the conduct of such activities by an exempt organization during a significant portion of the season ordinarily constitutes the regular conduct of trade or business." Id. (emphasis added). The operation of a horse racing track several weeks a year is an example of a regularly-conducted seasonal business, because such tracks generally are open only during a particular season. Id.

A primary point of contention in this case is whether the NCAA's advertising business is normally a seasonal or year-round one, and whether it is intermittent or not. The tax court noted that the Commissioner looked at the short time span of the tournament, concluded that it was as much a "seasonal" event as the operation of a horse racing track, and then argued that the time involved in the tournament program advertising made it a

---

5. We of course accord the Treasury Regulations deference unless they are unreasonable or plainly inconsistent with the Code. See Commissioner v. Portland Cement Co., 450 U.S. 156, 169, 101 S.Ct. 1037, 67 L.Ed.2d 140 (1981). Neither party challenges the validity of the regulations, and both argue that they provide the analytical framework for our inquiry here.

regularly carried on business. The court observed that the NCAA, which did not agree with the Commissioner's "season" conclusion, also focused on the tournament itself in contending that the event's short time span made the activity in question intermittent. The tax court rejected these arguments as "plac[ing] undue emphasis on the tournament itself as the measure for determining whether petitioner regularly carried on the business at issue * * *. Although sponsorship of a college basketball tournament and attendant circulation of tournament programs are seasonal events, the 'trade or business' of selling advertisements is not."

We agree that to determine the normal time span of the activity in this case, we should consider the business of *selling advertising space*, since that is the business the Commissioner contends is generating unrelated business taxable income. There is no dispute that the tournament itself is substantially related to the NCAA's exempt purpose and so, unlike the horse racing track, it should not be the business activity in question. See American College of Physicians, 475 U.S. at 839 ("Congress has declared unambiguously that the *publication of paid advertising* is a trade or business activity *distinct* from the publication of accompanying * * * articles")(emphasis added). Since the publication of advertising is generally conducted on a year-round basis, we conclude that if the NCAA's sale of program advertising was conducted for only a few weeks, that time period could not, standing alone, convert the NCAA's business into one regularly.

In regard to the question of how long the NCAA conducted its advertising business, the tax court stated that "it is inappropriate to decide whether the trade or business at issue is regularly carried on solely by reference to the time span of the tournament itself." The tax court, observing that the agency relationship between the NCAA and Host allowed the court to attribute Host's activities to the NCAA, noted that the NCAA had "not produced any evidence * * * regarding the extent or manner of Host's conduct in connection with the solicitation, sale, and publication of advertising for the tournament programs." The court went on to conclude that "without such evidence [the NCAA] has not proven that neither it nor Host carried on the activity of selling program advertising regularly. [The tax court] will not assume Host's conduct in this regard was infrequent or conducted without the competitive and promotional efforts typical of other commercial endeavors." We believe the tax court focused its analysis in the wrong direction.

The tax court held, and the Commissioner argues, that the amount of preliminary time spent to solicit advertisements and prepare them for publication is relevant to the regularly-carried-on determination, and that the length of the tournament is not relevant. This position is contrary to the regulations and to existing case law. The language of the regulations alone suggests that preparatory time should not be considered. The sandwich stand example in the regulations, for instance, included a reference only to the two weeks it was operated at the state fair. See Treas. Reg. § 1.513–1(c)(a)(i). The regulations do not mention time spent in planning the activity, building the stand, or purchasing the alfalfa sprouts for the sandwiches.

The case closest to the one here also does not evaluate preparatory time. In that case, Suffolk County Patrolmen's Benevolent Ass'n v. Commissioner, 77 T.C. 1314 (1981), an exempt organization staged a professional vaudeville show every year as a fundraising event, using a company with which it had contracted. The organization derived the vast majority of its receipts from the sale of advertising in a program guide distributed to show patrons and to anyone who requested it. The shows generally consisted of three or four performances stretching over two weekends. The tax court found that preparation for the shows and the program, including the solicitation of advertisements, lasted eight to sixteen weeks, but it then emphasized that "nowhere in the regulations or the legislative history of the tax on unrelated business income is there any mention of time apart from the duration of the event itself * * *. The fact that an organization seeks to insure the success of its fundraising venture by beginning to plan and prepare for it earlier should not adversely affect the tax treatment of the income derived from the venture."

As in *Suffolk County*, the advertising here was solicited for publication in a program for an event lasting a few weeks. The NCAA did put on evidence as to the duration of that event. While the length of the tournament is irrelevant for purposes of assessing the normal time span of the business of selling advertising space, we hold that, contrary to the tax court's conclusion, the tournament must be considered the actual time span of the business activity sought to be taxed here. The length of the tournament is the relevant time period because what the NCAA was selling, and the activity from which it derived the relevant income, was the publication of advertisements in programs distributed over a period of less than three weeks, and largely to spectators.[7] Obviously, the tournament is the relevant time frame for those who chose to pay for advertisements in the program. This case is unlike American College of Physicians, 475 U.S. at 836, where advertisements were sold for each issue of a monthly medical journal. Accordingly, we conclude that the NCAA's involvement in the sale of advertising space was not sufficiently long-lasting to make it a regularly-carried-on business solely by reason of its duration.

The next step of the regulation's analysis is to determine whether activities which are intermittently conducted are nevertheless regularly carried on by virtue of the manner in which they are pursued. In general, according to the regulations, "exempt organization business activities which are engaged in only discontinuously or periodically will not be considered regularly carried on if they are conducted without the competitive and promotional efforts typical of commercial endeavors." Treas. Reg. § 1.513–1(c)(2)(ii). As an example of an activity not characteristic of

---

7. There was testimony that some programs also were sold to members of the public not attending the tournament, but who wanted the program as a souvenir of the tournament. See Suffolk County Patrolmen's Benevolent Ass'n v. Commissioner, 77 T.C. 1314, 1317 (1981) (vaudeville show program made available to any nonpatron who requested it).

commercial endeavors, the regulations refer to "the publication of advertising in programs for sports events or music or drama performances." Id. (emphasis added). The NCAA places considerable emphasis on this latter sentence and criticizes the tax court, which stated only that there was insufficient evidence from which the court could draw conclusions on the manner of Host's conduct of its advertising activities. As the NCAA stresses, the tax court did not distinguish the 1982 Basketball Championship from the "sports events" referred to in the regulation above.

On appeal, the Commissioner initially agreed with the tax court that the record was devoid of evidence with which the NCAA could show that Host's efforts were not of a sufficiently competitive and promotional nature. But the Commissioner then went on to focus on the Final Four program, a part of the record. He characterized the program's advertisements as "typical print media advertisements," and distinguished them from the advertisements in the vaudeville show programs, which " 'more closely resembled complimentary contributions than commercial selling agents.' " The sentence referring to sports events in the regulations was, according to the Commissioner, directed more at advertising in high school sports programs than at the type of advertising in the program here.

Addressing first the tax court's conclusion, we fail to see what evidence in addition to the advertisements themselves the tax court could require. The regulations discuss the business of advertising but refer only to advertisements published in programs, and not to any efforts to secure the advertisements. In *Suffolk County*, the tax court disregarded all but the advertisements themselves and stated that it is "entirely reasonable for an exempt organization to hire professionals in an effort to insure the success of a fundraiser, and there are no indications [in the applicable statutes and regulations] * * * that the use of such professionals would cause an otherwise infrequent intermittent activity to be considered regularly carried on." 77 T.C. at 1323.

The Commissioner's assertion that the advertisements themselves are of a commercial nature deserves more discussion. It is true that a number of the advertisements are virtually indistinguishable from those that might appear in magazines like Sports Illustrated. A substantial number of other advertisements, however, particularly those placed by Louisiana companies not engaged in the tourist industry, seem to us to resemble more closely the "complimentary contributions" of Suffolk County.

The difficult question of whether the NCAA's advertising is of the type envisioned as commercial in nature, or instead as consistent with that connected to the "sports events" referred to in the regulations, is not one which we must answer now, however. For the final step in the process spelled out by the regulations requires us to consider whether, promotional efforts notwithstanding, an intermittent activity occurs "so infrequently that neither [its] recurrence nor the manner of [its] conduct will cause [it] to be regarded as trade or business regularly carried on." Treas. Reg. § 1.513–1(c)(2)(iii). We conclude that the advertising here is such an infrequent activity. The programs containing the advertisements were distributed over less than a three-week span at an event that occurs only once a year. We consider this to be sufficiently infrequent to preclude a determination that the NCAA's advertising business was regularly carried on.

Our conclusion is buttressed by the regulation's admonition that we apply the regularly-carried-on test in light of the purpose of the tax to place exempt organizations doing business on the same tax basis as the comparable nonexempt business endeavors with which they compete. See Treas. Reg. § 1.513–1(c)(1). The legislative history of the unrelated business income tax also convinces us that we must consider the impact an exempt organization's trade or business might have on its competition. The tax was a response to the situation prevailing before 1950, when an exempt organization could engage in any commercial business venture, secure in the knowledge that the profits generated would not be taxed as long as the destination of the funds was the exempt organization. The source of those funds did not affect their tax status. * * * As more and more exempt organizations began acquiring and operating commercial enterprises, there were rumblings in Congress to do away with the perceived advantage enjoyed by these organizations. The case which most forcefully brought this point home was that involving the C.F. Mueller Co. That company, a leading manufacturer of macaroni products, was in 1947 acquired and organized for the purpose of benefitting the New York University's School of Law, a tax-exempt educational institution.[8] See C.F. Mueller, 190 F.2d at 121. This acquisition prompted an outcry from a number of sources.

In President Truman's 1950 message to Congress, for example, he stated that " 'an exemption intended to protect educational activities has been misused in a few instances to gain competitive advantage over private enterprise through the conduct of business * * * entirely unrelated to educational activities.' " Primarily to "restrain the unfair competition fostered by the tax laws," Congress imposed a tax on the business income of exempt organizations, but only on that income substantially unrelated to the organization's exempt purposes.[9] See Revenue Act of 1950, Pub. L. No. 814, § 301, 64 Stat. 906, 947.

Although we have observed that the purpose of the unrelated business income tax was to prevent unfair competition[10] between companies whose

---

8. New York University also owned a leather company and chinaware manufacturing operations. Other educational institutions operated a number of enterprises: automobile parts, cotton gins, oil wells, theaters, an airport, a radio station, a hydroelectric plant, haberdasheries, citrus groves, and cattle ranches. See Kaplan, Intercollegiate Athletics and the Unrelated Business Income Tax, 80 Colum. L. Rev. 1430, 1432 & n.8 (1980).

9. Although prevention of unfair competition was the main purpose behind the unrelated business income tax, revenue raising concerns also played a role in Congress' actions, for Congress feared that exempt organizations, with a tax-induced competitive advantage, would drive other enterprises out of business. Congress believed this would mean that " 'eventually all the noodles produced in this country will be produced by corporations held or created by universities * * * and there will be no revenue to the Federal Treasury from this industry. That is our concern.' "

10. The term "unfair competition" is the hallmark of the unrelated business income tax, but the content of that term has been called into question. As one commentator has noted,

earnings are taxed and those whose are not, it is not necessary to prove or disprove the existence of actual competition. But analyzing the business in question in terms of its possible effect on prospective competitors helps to explain why an activity can occur "so infrequently" as to preclude a designation as a business regularly carried on. While the operation of a parking lot on a weekly basis occurs sufficiently frequently to threaten rival parking lot owners, the hospital auxiliary's annual sandwich stand is too infrequent a business to constitute a threat to sandwich shop owners. The competition in this case is between the NCAA's program and all publications that solicit the same advertisers. The competition thus includes weekly magazines such as Sports Illustrated and other publications which solicit automobile, beverage, photocopier, and fried chicken advertisements, to name a few. Viewed in this context, we conclude that the NCAA program, which is published only once a year, should not be considered an unfair competitor for the publishers of advertising. Application of the unrelated business tax here therefore would not further the statutory purpose. We hold that the NCAA's advertising business was not regularly carried on within the meaning of the Code.

The decision of the tax court is REVERSED.

NOTES

1. *The IRS Disagrees.* The Service did not acquiesce to the Tenth Circuit's decision in *NCAA.* See A.O.D. 1991–015. Although it strongly disagreed with the decision, the Service announced that it would not seek Supreme Court review because there was no conflict between the circuits but it would continue litigating the issue "in appropriate cases." Id.

2. *Taxing Intercollegiate Athletics Revenue.* College football and basketball programs are big business. According to a report prepared in 2009 by the Congressional Budget Office, the NCAA men's basketball tournament generated about $143 million in revenue in 2008, and college football bowl games earned a similar amount. The CBO report found that in the case of NCAA Division IA schools (the largest programs that meet certain minimum standards for football) 60 to 80 percent of the athletic department revenue comes from "commercial" activities, such as ticket sales, advertising, distributions from conferences, and media rights. This commercial share of revenue is seven to eight times more than for the rest of the schools' activities and programs. See Congressional Budget Office, Tax Preferences for College Sports (May 2009), available at http://www.cbo.gov/ftpdocs/100xx/doc10055/05–19–CollegiateSports.pdf.

According to the latest publicly available Form 990, the NCAA had about $636 million in program service revenue (and $610.3 million in

---

"different tax treatment * * * implies only that N.Y.U. would keep a larger share of Mueller's profits than would Ronzoni's owners * * *. Why must a fair tax code treat students and scholars who are the beneficiaries of Mueller's profits as if they were 'equal to' Ronzoni's investors?" Rose–Ackerman, Unfair Competition and Corporate Income Taxation, 34 Stan. L. Rev. 1017, 1020 (1982).

expenses) in 2007 but only $191,811 in donations. Of the total gross program service revenue, $548.2 million was from television rights fees, and another $46 million from bowl games and other tournaments. Only $17.6 million came from ticket sales. Notwithstanding this "commercial hue," the NCAA has long been recognized as tax-exempt under § 501(c)(3) on the ground that intercollegiate athletics are part of a college's educational program. As the preceding materials demonstrate, this link between the athletic program and education has helped the NCAA shelter its substantial revenue from football and basketball programs from the UBIT. In the section of the NCAA's 2007 Form 990 categorizing its income-producing activities, only $56,735 of gross income was from unrelated trade or business activities.

Should Congress attempt to subject the "commercial" revenue of the NCAA and intercollegiate athletic programs to the UBIT? If it did so, would the affected universities owe much tax? The likely answer to the second question is no. The Congressional Budget Office report concluded that removing tax preferences currently available to university athletic departments would not significantly alter the nature of the programs or raise much tax revenue. The report assumed that as long as athletic departments remain a part of the overall university, schools would be able to allocate expenses strategically to shift revenue, costs, or both between the taxed and untaxed sectors and reduce the bottom line of the taxable sector to zero. A more promising approach would be to target certain revenue sources, such as royalties from the sale of branded merchandise or corporate sponsorship, but Congress has shown no inclination to do so although there have been rumblings. In 2006, then House Ways and Means Committee chair Bill Thomas sent a detailed questionnaire asking the NCAA, among other things, what benefits the organization provided to taxpayers in exchange for its tax exemption and why should the federal government subsidize the athletic activities of educational institutions when that subsidy was being used to help pay for escalating coaches' salaries, costly chartered travel, and state-of-the-art athletic facilities? Chairman Thomas's letter and a detailed response from then NCAA president Miles Brand are available on the NCAA's web site at http://www.ncaa.org.

3. *For Further Reading*. John D. Colombo, The NCAA, Tax Exemption, and College Athletics, 2010 U.Ill.L.Rev. 109; Richard L. Kaplan, Intercollegiate Athletics and the Unrelated Business Tax, 80 Colum.L.Rev. 1430 (1980).

c.   MUSEUM GIFT SHOPS

Revenue Ruling 73–104
1973–1 Cum.Bull. 263.

Advice has been requested whether, under the circumstances described below, the sales activities of an educational organization that is exempt from Federal income tax under section 501(c)(3) of the Internal Revenue

Code of 1954 constitutes unrelated trade or business within the meaning of section 513 of the Code.

The organization maintains and operates an art museum devoted to the exhibition of modern art. The museum offers for sale to the general public greeting cards that display printed reproductions of selected works from the museum's collection and from other art collections. The proportions of the reproductions are determined by the form of the original work and care is taken with respect to other technical aspects of the reproduction process. Each card is imprinted with the name of the artist, the title or subject matter of the work, the date or period of its creation, if known, and the museum's name. The cards contain appropriate greetings and are personalized on request.

The organization sells the cards in the shop it operates in the museum. It also publishes a catalogue in which it solicits mail orders for the greeting cards. The catalogue is available at a small charge and is advertised in magazines and other publications throughout the year. In addition, the shop sells the cards at quantity discounts to retail stores. As a result, a large volume of cards are sold at a significant profit.

Section 511(a) of the Code imposes a tax upon the unrelated business taxable income (as defined in section 512) of organizations exempt from Federal income tax under section 501(c)(3). Section 512(a) of the Code defines "unrelated business taxable income" as income from any "unrelated trade or business" regularly carried on by the organization as computed in the manner provided in section 512.

The term "unrelated trade or business" is defined in section 513 of the Code as any trade or business the conduct of which is not substantially related (aside from the need of such organization for income or funds or the use it makes of the profits derived) to the exercise or performance by such organization of its exempt functions.

Section 513(c) of the Code and section 1.513–1(b) of the Income Tax Regulations provide that trade or business includes any activity which is carried on for the production of income from the sale of goods.

Section 1.513–1(d)(2) of the regulations provides that a trade or business is "substantially related" to purposes for which exemption is granted only if the production or distribution of the goods from which the gross income is derived "contributes importantly" to the accomplishment of those purposes.

The museum is exempt as an educational organization on the basis of its ownership, maintenance, and exhibition for public viewing of works of art. The sale of greeting cards displaying printed reproductions of art works contributes importantly to the achievement of the museum's exempt educational purposes by stimulating and enhancing public awareness, interest, and appreciation of art. Moreover, a broader segment of the public may be encouraged to visit the museum itself to share in its educational functions and programs as a result of seeing the cards. The fact that the cards are promoted and sold in a clearly commercial manner at a profit and in competition with commercial greeting card publishers does not alter the fact of the activity's relatedness to the museum's exempt purpose.

Accordingly, it is held that these sales activities do not constitute unrelated trade or business under section 513 of the Code.

Revenue Ruling 73–105

1973–1 Cum.Bull. 264.

Advice has been requested whether, under the circumstances described below, the sales activities of an art museum exempt from Federal income tax as an educational organization under section 501(c)(3) of the Internal Revenue Code of 1954 constitute unrelated trade or business within the meaning of section 513 of the Code.

The organization maintains and operates an art museum devoted to the exhibition of American folk art. It operates a shop in the museum that offers for sale of the general public: (1) reproductions of works in the museum's own collection and reproductions of artistic works from the collections of other art museums (these reproductions take the form of prints suitable for framing, postcards, greeting cards, and slides); (2) metal, wood, and ceramic copies of American folk art objects from its own collection and similar copies of art objects from other collections of art works; and (3) instructional literature concerning the history and development of art and, in particular, of American folk art. The shop also rents originals or reproductions of paintings contained in its collection. All of its reproductions are imprinted with the name of the artist, the title or subject matter of the work from which it is reproduced, and the museum's name.

Also sold in the shop are scientific books and various souvenir items relating to the city in which the museum is located.

Section 511(a) of the Code imposes a tax upon the unrelated business taxable income (as defined in section 512) of organizations exempt from Federal income tax under section 501(c)(3). Section 512(a) of the Code defines "unrelated business taxable income" as the gross income from any "unrelated trade or business" regularly carried on by the organization as computed in the manner provided in section 512.

The term "unrelated trade or business" is defined in section 513 of the Code as any trade or business the conduct of which is not substantially related (aside from the need of such organization for income or funds or the use it makes of the profits derived) to the exercise or performance by such organization of its exempt functions.

Section 1.513–1(d)(2) of the Income Tax Regulations provides that trade or business is "substantially related" to purposes for which exemption is granted only if the production or distribution of the goods from which the gross income is derived "contributes importantly" to the accomplishment of those purposes.

Section 513(c) of the Code and section 1.513–(b) of the regulations provide that trade or business includes any activity which is carried on for the production of income from the sale of goods. An activity does not lose its identity as trade or business merely because it is carried on within a larger aggregate of similar activities or within a larger complex of other endeavors which may not be related to the exempt purposes of the organization.

Thus, sales of a particular line of merchandise any be considered separately to determine their relatedness to the exempt purpose. Section 1.513–1(d)(2) of the regulations emphasizes that it is the particular facts and circumstances involved in each case which determines whether the activities in question contribute importantly to the accomplishment of any purpose for which the organization is exempt.

An art museum is exempt as an educational organization on the basis of its ownership, maintenance, and exhibition for public viewing of an art collection. The sale and rental of reproductions of works from the museum's own collection and reproductions of artistic works not owned by the museum contribute importantly to the achievement of the museum's exempt educational purpose by making works of art familiar to a broader segment of the public, thereby enhancing the public's understanding and appreciation of art. The same is true with respect to literature relating to art.

Accordingly, it is held that these sales activities do not constitute unrelated trade or business under section 513 of the Code.

On the other hand, scientific books and souvenir items relating to the city where the museum is located have no causal relationship to art or to artistic endeavor and, therefore, the sale of these items does not contribute importantly to the accomplishments of the subject organization's exempt educational purpose which, as an art museum, is to enhance the public's understanding and appreciation of art. The fact that some of these items could, in a different context, be held related to the exempt educational purpose of some other exempt educational organization does not change the conclusion that in this context they do not contribute to the accomplishment of this organization's exempt educational purpose.

Additionally, under the provisions of section 513(c) of the Code, the activity with respect to sales of such items does not lose identity as trade or business merely because the museum also sells articles which do contribute importantly to the accomplishment of its exempt function.

Accordingly, it is held that the sale of those articles having no relationship to American folk art or to art generally, constitutes unrelated trade or business under section 513 of the Code.

d. CORPORATE SPONSORSHIP ACTIVITIES

Background. In the early 1990s, the IRS provoked a major controversy by threatening to tax the income received by exempt organizations from corporate sponsorship arrangements. In a celebrated technical advice memorandum, the Service ruled that the corporate sponsorship revenue received by two § 501(c)(3) organizations that conducted college football bowl games was taxable. Tech. Adv. Memo 9147007. Although the ruling deleted the names of the affected organizations, it was well known that they were the Mobil Cotton Bowl and the John Hancock Bowl. See, e.g., Bowl Ruling May Affect Others, Chron. of Philanthropy, Dec. 17, 1991. The Mobil Oil Corporation reportedly paid over $1 million to sponsor the "Mobil Cotton Bowl," in return for which Mobil's name and logo were prominently displayed on the playing field, scoreboards, uniforms, paper cups, and all related print material connected with the New Year's Day event. Id.

In its "Cotton Bowl ruling" the Service concluded that the corporate sponsor's payment was made with an expectation of receiving a substantial return benefit for the "well-positioned visual images" displayed at the bowl game. Tech. Adv. Memo 9147007. The ruling's premise was that the activity went beyond mere "donor acknowledgment" and was more akin to advertising—thus, it was a trade or business, regularly carried on and not substantially related to the organization's exempt purposes.

College football fans and other nonprofit sector advocates reacted with alarm, fearing that the UBIT might be extended to a wide range of donor acknowledgement activities such as corporate sponsored art exhibits, Little League teams, walkathons, public broadcasting programs, and even named professorships at universities. After reading piles of mail, the Service first issued somewhat threatening audit guidelines and then retreated considerably in proposed regulations issued in 1993. Congress finally entered the fray in 1997 by enacting a specific statutory exclusion that is largely based on the generous proposed regulations. Final regulations interpreting § 513(i) were issued in 2002. Treas. Reg. § 1.513–4.

Qualified Sponsorship Payments. Section 513(i) excludes from the term "unrelated trade or business" the activity of soliciting and receiving "qualified sponsorship payments" (QSPs). A QSP is any payment (including cash payments, transfers of property and performance of services) made by a person engaged in a trade or business ("the sponsor") with respect to which there is no arrangement or expectation that the sponsor will receive any substantial return benefit other than the use or acknowledgement of the sponsor's name, logo, or product lines in connection with the activities of the exempt organization that receives the payment. I.R.C. § 513(i)(2)(A); Treas. Reg. § 1.513–4(c)(1) & 2(iv). A "substantial return benefit" does not include any goods or service that have an insubstantial value, such as complimentary tickets, pro-am playing slots in a golf tournament, or donor receptions. Return benefits also are deemed to be "insubstantial" and thus are disregarded if their aggregate fair market value is not more than 2 percent of the payment. Treas. Reg. § 1.513–4(c)(2)(ii).

Activities covered by the QSP exclusion may include a single event (such as a bowl game, walkathon or television program); a series of related events (such as a concert series or sports tournament); an activity of extended or indefinite duration (such as an art exhibit); or continuing support of an exempt organization's operation. See Preamble to Regulations on Corporate Sponsorship, T.D. 8991, F.R. 20433, reprinted in 36 Exempt Org. Tax Rev. 419 (2002). A payment may be a QSP even if the sponsored activity is not substantially related to the recipient organization's exempt purposes. Treas. Reg. § 1.513–4(c)(1).

Section 501(i) acts as a safe harbor, insulating payments that come within its reach from the UBIT. If the QSP safe harbor does not apply, a sponsorship payment is not necessarily taxable but must be evaluated under general UBIT principles apart from § 513(i). For example, a payment may not be taxable because the activity generating it is not regularly carried on. Treas. Reg. § 1.513–4(d)(1)(i).

Advertising. The QSP exclusion does not extend to payments received for advertising the sponsor's products or services. For this purpose, "advertising" means messages that include qualitative or comparative language, price information, etc., or other indications of savings or value, endorsements, and the like. I.R.C. § 513(i)(2)(A). Treas. Reg. § 1.513–4(c)(2)(v). Payments contingent upon the level of attendance at one or more events, broadcast ratings, or other factors indicating the degree of public exposure, also do not qualify for the QSP exclusion. I.R.C. § 513(i)(2)(B)(i); Treas. Reg. § 1.513–4(e)(2). But the fact that a sponsorship payment is contingent on an event taking place or being broadcast is not, in and of itself, fatal, nor is the distribution or display of a sponsor's products to the general public at a sponsored event. See id. and Joint Committee on Taxation, General Explanation of Tax Legislation Enacted in 1997 ("1997 General Explanation"), 105th Cong., 1st Sess. (1997).

A payment does not qualify as a QSP if it entitles the sponsor to the use or acknowledgement of its name, logo, or product lines in a regularly published periodical of the exempt organization that is not related to and primarily distributed in connection with a specific sponsored event. I.R.C. § 513(i)(2)(B)(ii)(I); Treas. Reg. § 1.513–4(b). Whether or not such a payment is taxable depends upon an application of general UBIT principles relating to periodical advertising, as developed in the regulations (see Treas. Reg. § 1.513–1(d)(4)(iv) Example 7) and the case law (see, e.g., United States v. American College of Physicians, supra p. 605). In addition, the QSP safe harbor does not apply to payments made in connection with any qualified convention or trade activity, as defined in § 512(d)(3). I.R.C. § 513(i)(2)(B)(ii)(II); Treas. Reg. § 1.513–4(b).

Dual Purpose Payments. To the extent that a portion of a payment (if made as a separate payment) would be a qualified sponsorship payment, that portion and the other portion will be treated separately for purposes of the QSP exclusion. I.R.C. § 513(i)(3); Treas. Reg. § 1.513–4(d)(1), –4(f) Examples 2 and 3. Thus, if a payment entitles the sponsor to both product advertising and the use or acknowledgement of the sponsor's name or logo by an exempt organization, the amount of the payment that exceeds the fair market value of the product advertising would not be taxable. The regulations place the burden of establishing the fair market value of any substantial return benefit on the exempt organization. Id. To illustrate, assume a corporate sponsor pays $100,000 to a museum to sponsor an art exhibit and receives in return $5,000 of "pure" advertising. Under a tainting rule in an earlier version of the regulations, the entire $100,000 would have been taxable, but § 501(i) only taxes the $5,000 in advertising revenue and not the $95,000 sponsorship income.

Exclusive Sponsorship and Provider Arrangements. The right to be an exclusive sponsor of an activity (without any advertising or other substantial return benefit to the payor)—such as for a museum exhibit or bowl game with a single corporate sponsor—is generally not considered to be a substantial return benefit. Treas. Reg. § 1.513–4(c)(2)(vi)(A), –4(f) Example 4. But an exclusive *provider* agreement—such as where, in return for a payment, an exempt organization agrees that products or services that compete with the payor's products or services will not be sold in connection with one or more of the exempt organization's activities—generally results in a substantial return benefit, causing the arrangement to fall outside the QSP safe harbor. Treas. Reg. § 1.513–4(c)(2)(vi)(B). If a payor receives both exclusive sponsorship and exclusive provider rights in exchange for making a payment, the fair market value of the exclusive provider arrangement and any other substantial return benefit is determined first in making the required allocation between taxable and excluded payments. Treas. Reg. § 1.513–4(f) Example 6. To illustrate, assume the increasingly common situation where a university receives a substantial payment from a soft drink company or athletic gear manufacturer and agrees in return that only that company's products may be sold on campus. Under the regulations, the payment would not come within the QSP safe harbor, but that does not necessarily resolve the ultimate question of whether the payment is taxable under general UBIT principles.

Web Sites and Hyperlinks. Another important question is whether links between Internet sites of an exempt organization and a sponsor constitute potentially taxable advertising. The regulations respond with two helpful examples. In the first, the mere posting of a list of sponsors along with hyperlinks to their web sites on an exempt organization's web site is treated as an acknowledgement if there is no promotion of products or advertising. But if the exempt organization provides a hyperlink to a sponsor's web site where the organization then endorses the sponsor's product, the endorsement is advertising and falls outside the QSP safe harbor. See Treas. Reg. § 1.513–4(f) Examples 11 and 12.

Impact on Public Charity Status. QSPs in the form of money or property (but not services) qualify as public support in determining whether an organization qualifies as a public charity and thus avoids private foundation status under §§ 170(b)(1)(A)(vi) or 509(a)(2). Treas. Reg. § 1.509(a)–3(f)(1), (3) Examples 2 and 3. See Chapter 7B, supra.

For Further Reading. Frances R. Hill, Corporate Sponsorship in Transactional Perspective: General Principles and Special Cases in the Law of Tax–Exempt Organizations, 13 U. Miami Ent. & Sports L. Rev. 5 (1995); David A. Brennen, The Proposed Corporate Sponsorship Regulations: Is the Treasury Department "Sleeping with the Enemy?" 6 Kan. J.L. & Pub.

Pol'y (1996); Nathan Wirtschafter, Note, Fourth Quarter Choke: How the IRS Blew the Corporate Sponsorship Game, 27 Loy.L.A.L.Rev. 1465 (1994).

NOTES AND QUESTIONS

1. *The Substantially Related Test.* Is substantial "relatedness" the appropriate standard for determining whether an exempt organization's business activity should be taxed? Does the test offer adequate guidance to exempt organizations and the Service? Have the courts and the Service applied the test too leniently, causing exempt organizations to exploit it? For example, is it reasonable to conclude that a symphony gift shop's sale of T-shirts with the likeness of a composer, an art museum's sale of Rodin pasta, Monet olive oil, or Cezanne baseballs, or an environmental organization's mail order sale of panda bears "contribute importantly" to the exempt purposes of these organizations?

At the 1987 Hearings of the House Ways and Means Oversight Subcommittee, Treasury Department officials testified that the relatedness test had "conceptual merit," but they expressed concern that its "inherent generality is a source of administrative difficulty." Although the Treasury made no substantive legislative recommendations, it proposed more detailed reporting rules to serve as a source of data for a more informed study of the adequacy of the relatedness test. See Statement of O. Donaldson Chapoton, 1 Hearings Before the Subcomm. on Oversight of the House Committee on Ways and Means, Unrelated Business Income Tax, 100th Cong., 1st Sess. 37–39 (Ser. 100–26, 1987) (hereinafter "1987 House Hearings"). For additional proposed reforms, which remain on the legislative back burner, see Section I of this chapter, infra, at pp. 696–702.

2. *The Convenience Exception.* The legislative history indicates that the exception for businesses carried on primarily for the convenience of members, students, patients, officers or employees was enacted to exempt university dining halls and dormitories, hospital cafeterias, and laundries serving students and patients. Why is this exception necessary? Why don't these activities escape the UBIT because they are substantially related to the organization's exempt purposes?

3. *Low–Cost Articles Exception.* Under another special exception, the distribution by charitable and veterans organizations of certain low-cost items incident to the solicitation of charitable contributions is not a taxable activity. I.R.C. § 513(h)(1); Treas. Reg. § 1.513–1(b). Congress enacted this safe harbor rule to protect organizations that distribute small items (such as greeting cards) as part of a fundraising campaign. In general, a low-cost article is one costing the organization not more than $5 (this amount is indexed); in 2010 it was $9.60. I.R.C. § 513(h)(2). The charitable solicitation requirement is met if the distribution is made without the recipient's request or consent, the distributed items are accompanied by a request for a donation, and the solicitation includes a statement that the recipient may keep the article, whether or not a contribution is made. I.R.C. § 513(h)(3).

4. *Bingo Exception.* Income from bingo games, but not from other games of chance, is exempt from the UBIT if the bingo game is "not an activity ordinarily carried out on a commercial basis," and conduct of the game does not violate any state or local law. I.R.C. § 513(f). If these tests are not met, a regularly conducted bingo or other gambling activity is an unrelated business. Not all bingo qualifies for the § 513(f) exception. The courts have held that "instant" or pull tab bingo, a game of chance in which individuals place wagers by purchasing a card and pulling off sealed tabs to determine if the revealed numbers match a preprinted winning combination, does not qualify for the UBIT exception. See, e.g., Julius M. Israel Lodge of B'nai B'rith No. 2113 v. Commissioner, 98 F.3d 190 (5th Cir. 1996).

5. *Tip Jars and Pickle Cards.* In addition to bingo, many small nonprofit organizations raise funds from more esoteric (at least to the uninitiated, which includes the authors) gambling activities. For example, tip jars are gambling devices in which players purchase sealed pieces of paper containing numbers or symbols entitling the player to a prize. In Vigilant Hose Co. of Emmitsburg v. United States, 87 A.F.T.R.2d 2001–2398 (D. Md. 2001), the court found that proceeds from tip jars placed in taverns for the benefit of a volunteer fire department did not constitute UBTI. The for-profit taverns administered the activity, with the nonprofit's role being limited to obtaining a county permit and taking a share of the profits. On these facts, the court concluded that the organization's activities did not rise to the level of a trade or business and, in so doing, it declined to impute the taverns' activities to the nonprofit organization under an agency theory.

Pickle cards are another form of legal gambling activity for nonprofit organizations in Nebraska. In Education Athletic Ass'n v. Commissioner, 77 T.C.M. (CCH) 1525 (1999), the Tax Court held that a § 501(c)(3) educational organization that received all of its financial support from the sale of pickle cards to Nebraska liquor establishments was engaged in an unrelated trade or business even though state law prohibited for-profit firms from the activity. Despite the lack of any unfair competition, the court concluded that the organization's sale of the pickle cards was not substantially related to its exempt purposes and thus the profits were taxable. As a result, the organization failed to qualify as a public charity under § 509(a)(2) but, notably, its § 501(c)(3) exemption was not challenged.

6. *Associate Member Dues.* Trade associations, labor unions, and some agricultural organizations have attempted to avoid the UBIT by disguising revenue for certain services or benefits as dues paid by "associate members." Several federal postal unions pushed the envelope by charging dues to associate members who were not even required to be postal workers but joined the unions primarily to obtain access to low-cost group insurance. In most cases, associate members have no voting rights, but occasionally they may have limited legal rights that on closer scrutiny are devoid of substance. The courts have been unreceptive to these arrangements. See, e.g.,

National League of Postmasters of the United States v. Commissioner, 86 F.3d 59 (4th Cir.1996); National Ass'n of Postal Supervisors v. United States, 944 F.2d 859 (Fed.Cir.1991); American Postal Workers Union v. United States, 925 F.2d 480 (D.C.Cir.1991). After a period of further controversy (and lobbying), Congress enacted § 512(d), which provides that § 501(c)(5) agricultural and horticultural organizations will not be taxable on any portion of membership dues not exceeding $100 by reason of any benefits or privileges to which the members are entitled. In Rev. Proc. 97–12, 1997–1 Cum. Bull. 631, the Service extended this statutory safe harbor by indicating that it would not treat income from associate member dues paid to § 501(c)(5) or § 501(c)(6) organizations as UBTI unless the associate member category was formed or availed of for the principal purpose of avoiding the UBIT.

7. *UBIT Compliance.* Exempt organizations with $1,000 or more of gross income from an unrelated trade or business are required to file a Form 990–T (Exempt Organization Business Income Tax Return) on which they compute and pay their tax. I.R.C. § 6012(a)(2); Treas. Reg. § 1.6012–2(e). Quarterly payments of estimated tax also are required for organizations that anticipate $500 or more of UBIT liability for a taxable year. I.R.C. § 6154(h). Very few exempt organizations owe any unrelated business income tax. In 2006, the most recent year for which reliable data is available, collected UBIT revenue was $555.7 million and returns were filed by 43,520 organizations (of which 32.5 percent were § 501(c)(3) charities). Only 40 percent of the 14,157 § 501(c)(3) organizations filing UBIT returns in 2006 reported any unrelated business income, and only about 50 percent of all exempt organizations filing UBIT returns reported any tax liability. Jael Jackson, Unrelated Business Income Tax Returns 2006, IRS Statistics of Income Bulletin (Winter 2010), at 148, 152. It is likely that there is some underreporting of unrelated business income by exempt organizations and, significantly, these statistics do not reflect any businesses conducted through for-profit, taxable subsidiaries.

Legislation enacted in 2006 eventually will shed more light on the commercial activities of charities, which now must make their UBIT returns (Form 990–T) publicly available with only limited exceptions for redaction of items, such as trade secrets, that might adversely affect the organization. I.R.C. § 6104(d)(1)(A)(ii). For guidance on the public inspection rules for Form 990–T's, see I.R.S. Notice 2008–49, 2008–49 I.R.B. 979.

PROBLEMS

1. Sturdley University is a prominent private university, with an undergraduate college and graduate colleges of law, medicine and agriculture. Sturdley controls several separately incorporated entities, some of which are described below. Evaluate the unrelated business tax consequences of the following activities:

(a) The Sturdley University Alumni Association, a separately incorporated § 501(c)(3) organization, operates a travel tour program open to all members of the Association and their immediate families. Last year, the Association made four mailings to its approximately 30,000 members announcing nine tours to various destinations around the world. The brochures described a special discount fare arrangement and stated that the tours included sightseeing and visits to historic sites. No formal educational program was conducted in connection with any trip. The Association works with various commercial travel agencies in planning the tours under arrangements whereby each participating travel agent pays the Association a per person fee.

(b) The University athletic department operates a campus golf course, used by the college golf team (3%), other students (27%), faculty and staff (20%) and the general public (50%). Public users are required to pay fees comparable to those charged by nearby commercial golf courses.

(c) The Sturdley College of Agriculture operates a commercial dairy adjacent to the campus. The primary purpose of the dairy is to teach the art of farming. The dairy has a store on campus where it sells products such as milk, butter, cheese and ice cream.

(d) The University has a large auditorium on campus that is used for class registrations, intercollegiate athletic events and commencement exercises. On average, the auditorium is used 75 days a year for events for which tickets are sold, including rock concerts, closed-circuit television presentations of boxing matches, and professional basketball games. All these events are open to the public and generate substantial revenues for the University.

(e) The University operates a summer sports camp for high school students, charging fees comparable to those charged by for-profit summer camps.

(f) The University's intercollegiate football and basketball programs generate substantial revenues, including admission fees, radio and television receipts, and the sale of advertising in programs and advertising space at the football stadium and basketball arena. The advertisements are for fast food restaurants, insurance companies, soft drinks, automobiles, and banks.

(g) The Sturdley Medical Center, a large teaching hospital, operates a 500–car parking garage adjacent to the hospital for the use of patients, staff, visitors and the general public. On many weekends, the garage also is used by spectators attending various concerts and sporting events at the auditorium and Sturdley Stadium.

(h) The Medical Center operates a pharmacy, primarily to sell prescription drugs to patients and persons visiting private physicians in an adjacent medical office building owned by the hospital.

(i) The Sturdley Daily News, the student daily newspaper, derives revenue from advertising for local businesses serving the university community.

2.   The Museum of Provocative Art is a large urban museum with a wide variety of modern and traditional exhibits. Will it be subject to the unrelated business income tax if it realizes income from the operation of:

(a) A cafeteria and snack bar on museum premises for use by its staff, employees, visiting members of the public and employees of nearby businesses.

(b) A gift shop and bookstore, where it sells greeting cards, expensive books for coffee table display, art reproductions, jewelry, ceramics, stuffed animals and t-shirts with the museum logo.

(c) Same as (b), above, except that the museum also sells all the items available in the gift shop through a mail order catalog that is distributed nationwide.

(d) Same as (b), above, except the shop is a "satellite" facility located 25 miles from the museum in a suburban shopping mall.

(e) A theater on museum premises used for the showing of educational films during museum hours and as an ordinary motion picture theater for public entertainment during the evening.

(f) Sponsorship of a major new exhibit by a leading soft drink manufacturer. In exchange for a $500,000 payment, the corporate sponsor's name is included in the title of the event and is prominently displayed in all promotional literature and publicity. Special VIP showings and receptions are provided for the corporation's executives and their friends, and the corporate sponsor has the exclusive right to sell its soft drinks at the museum's cafeteria and vending machines.

E.   EXCLUSIONS FROM UNRELATED BUSINESS TAXABLE INCOME

Internal Revenue Code: §§ 512(a)(1), (b)(1)–(5), (7)–(9), (13), (15).

Treasury Regulations: §§ 1.512(b)–1(a)(1), (b), (c)(2)–(5), (d)(1).

The computation of unrelated business taxable income ("UBTI") is governed by § 512(a)(1), which defines UBTI as the gross income derived from the unrelated business less expenses directly connected with the carrying on of the trade or business, both computed with certain modifications in § 512(b). Most of these "modifications" are actually exclusions from the unrelated business tax base. As such, they are appropriately examined first, before turning to the more mechanical computation and expense allocation issues.

1.   PASSIVE INVESTMENT INCOME

When it first enacted the UBIT in 1950, Congress stated that passive investment income was long recognized as a proper source of revenue for charitable and educational organizations and was not likely to cause competitive problems for taxable businesses. S.Rep. No. 2375, 81st Cong., 2d Sess. (1950). In keeping with this policy, the most significant exclusions from UBTI are for traditional forms of passive investment income, such as dividends, interest, annuities, rents and royalties. I.R.C. § 512(b)(1)–(4). The exclusion extends to all gains from the sale, exchange or other disposition of property other than inventory and property primarily held for sale to customers in the ordinary course of a trade or business. I.R.C. § 512(b)(5). In effect, all capital gains are excluded unless the property is debt-financed. Gain on the sale of depreciable property used in an unrelated trade or business is taxable to the extent it is treated as ordinary income under the depreciation recapture provisions. Treas. Reg. § 1.1245–6(b).

In recognition of the growing investment sophistication of the nonprofit sector, this traditional list has been expanded to exclude income from modern investment and risk management strategies such as options, securities lending transactions, notional principal contracts and short sales. Treas. Reg. § 1.512(b)–1(a)(1); see also I.R.C. §§ 512(a)(5); 512(b)(5). As to short sales, see Rev. Rul. 95–8, 1995–1 C.B. 107.

As developed later in this chapter (see infra pp. 651–663), the passive investment income exclusions generally are unavailable if the income is derived from debt-financed property (e.g., dividends from securities purchased with borrowed funds). I.R.C. § 512(b)(4). In addition, some forms of investment income received from a 50 percent or more controlled subsidiary may be taxable. See I.R.C. § 512(b)(13).

2. Rents

The rules for the rent exclusion vary, depending on whether the rent is derived from real or personal property, or from a mixed lease. Real property rents are excludable in full, even if they are derived from an actively managed real estate rental business. I.R.C. § 512(b)(3)(A)(i). Personal property rents (e.g., from a lease of computer or medical equipment) are excludable only if derived from a mixed lease and the rents attributable to the personal property are an "incidental" (not more than 10 percent) part of the total rents received under the lease. I.R.C. § 512(b)(3)(A)(ii); Reg. § 1.512(b)–1(c)(2)(ii). If the amount attributable to personal property is more than incidental but not more than 50 percent of the total, the real property rent is excludable but the personal property rent is not. But if the personal property rent exceeds 50 percent of the total, then none of the rent is excludable. I.R.C. § 512(b)(3)(B)(i); Treas. Reg. § 1.512(b)–1(c)(2)(iii)(a). In making these determinations, the terms of the lease are not necessarily conclusive if the amounts allocated are unrealistic. See Treas. Reg. § 1.512(b)–1(c)(2)(iv), Example.

Rents dependent on profits or income derived by any person from the real property do not qualify for the exclusion unless they are based on a fixed percentage of gross receipts or sales. I.R.C. § 512(b)(3)(B)(ii). To prevent an obvious end-run around these requirements, multiple leases (i.e., separate leases with respect to real and personal property) are considered as one lease if the real and personal property covered by the lease have an "integrated use." Treas. Reg. § 1.512(b)–1(c)(3)(iii).

Amounts paid for the occupancy of space do not qualify for the rent exclusion if the property owner renders services for the convenience of the occupant, as in a hotel, boarding house, parking lot, or warehouse. Services are considered rendered to the occupant if they are "primarily for his convenience and are other than those usually or customarily rendered in connection with the rental of rooms or other space for occupancy only." Treas. Reg. § 1.512(b)–1(c)(5).

3.   ROYALTIES

Charities with valuable intellectual property frequently enter into contractual arrangements to license a wide range of intangible assets, such as a charity's name, reputation, logo, mailing lists, and technology. These arrangements rarely create tax problems under current law. First, they usually are insubstantial relative to the totality of the nonprofit's activities. Second, § 512 excludes from unrelated business taxable income "all royalties ... whether measured by production or by gross or taxable income from the property," less directly connected deductions. The Code does not define "royalty" for UBIT purposes, and the legislative history is silent as to why royalties were included in what otherwise is a list of more traditional passive investment income items. It is reasonable to assume Congress thought mineral royalties and revenue from licensing various forms of intellectual property were among the properly excludable passive sources of support. As it has been interpreted, the royalty exclusion is exceedingly broad, extending to virtually all payments for the right to use intangible property, including income received for the use of valuable intellectual property rights, such as patents, trademarks, and copyrights, but not to compensation for services rendered by the owner of the licensed property. See Treas. Reg. § 1.512(b)–1(b). Even when significant services are required in connection with a licensing arrangement, UBIT exposure can be minimized by using a taxable subsidiary or unrelated third party to perform the services. This bifurcation strategy separates the royalty and services income and preserves the § 512(b) exclusion for the bulk of the revenue generated from the arrangement.

There are valid business reasons for a charity to license intellectual property. Licensing permits the organization to obtain outside marketing expertise and relieves it of the risks and burdens of manufacturing and distributing the licensed product. Similar factors influence the decision to license valuable patents. Although the upside is more limited, so is the downside risk. The vast majority of licensing arrangements do not require a charity to devote much of its time to the enterprise. Manufacturing, marketing, distribution, and all the "active" elements of a trade or business are handled by the for-profit licensee. A major concern is to prevent the licensee from misusing the nonprofit's reputation, The IRS permits tax-exempt licensors to retain quality control, and royalty payments may be based on a percentage of gross sales, but the line is crossed if a charity becomes actively involved in the development and marketing of the product. See, e.g., Rev. Rul. 81–178, 1981–2 C.B. 135.

Because the royalty concept is so elastic, nonprofit organizations have been encouraged to enter into licensing arrangements to exploit their valuable forms of intangible property rather than developing them directly. The IRS has attempted with limited success to recharacterize some of these licensing arrangements as joint ventures, product endorsements, or the rendering of services for compensation. Some of the most contentious disputes have involved whether revenues from the rental of an exempt organization's mailing list and participation in affinity credit card programs were excludable royalties. In a typical mailing list rental deal, an organization seeks to exploit its valuable donor base by permitting other organizations to "rent" the names and addresses of members in exchange for a fee. A list broker and computer service bureau are engaged to handle the promotion and administration of the arrangement, limiting the nonprofit organization's role to reviewing rental requests and approving the proposed mailings. Affinity credit card programs are arrangements where a well known organization—often a university or "brand name" charity—agrees to permit a bank to issue credit cards with the organization's name and logo in exchange for a small percentage of the amounts charged on the card. Solicitation and marketing are handled by the issuer of the card or one of its affiliates, with the nonprofit organization's cooperation.

The legal issue in the mailing list and affinity card cases is whether the payments received are excludable royalties. In a series of cases, the IRS argued that the royalty exclusion was limited to payments for the use of intangible property where the subject of the payment was "passive" in nature. Under this narrow construction, mailing list and affinity card arrangements were "active," not "passive" and thus not within the exclusion. Most courts rejected the IRS's active/passive distinction and interpreted "royalty" to mean payments made to an owner of property for the right to use the property in exchange for the payment of a fee. See, e.g., Sierra Club v. Commissioner, 86 F.3d 1526 (9th Cir. 1996); but see Disabled American Veterans v. United States, 227 Ct.Cl. 474, 650 F.2d 1178 (1981). These courts distinguished royalties from compensation for services rendered by the owner of property. Most mailing list arrangements escaped the UBIT under this reasoning because the organizations outsourced marketing and administrative tasks. Affinity card arrangements were similar but raised more issues of fact—for example, did a nonprofit organization perform services when it cooperated in a marketing effort and performed some administrative and endorsement services? The courts uniformly sided with the taxpayers on these issues, finding that the fees received were for the use of valuable intangible property rights, not services rendered. See, e.g., Oregon State University Alumni Ass'n v. Commissioner, 71 T.C.M. (CCH) 1935 (1996); Alumni Ass'n of the University of Oregon v. Commissioner, 71 T.C.M. (CCH) 2093 (1996); and Mississippi State University Alumni, Inc. v. Commissioner, 74 T.C.M. (CCH) 458 (1997). Faced with this string of defeats, the IRS finally surrendered.

NOTES AND QUESTIONS

1. *Statutory Mailing List Exception.* Section 513(h)(1)(B), enacted in 1986, exempts amounts derived by most § 501(c)(3) and veterans organizations from the rental or exchange of donor lists to or with other such exempt organizations. The exception does not extend to § 501(c)(4) organizations, such as the Sierra Club, and it does not exempt income from mailing list rentals to for-profit organizations. In enacting this amendment, Congress included a typical reminder in the legislative history that no inference was intended as to whether or not revenue from mailing list activities other than those expressly described in § 513(h)(1)(B) were taxable. Staff of the Joint Committee on Taxation, General Explanation of the Tax Reform Act of 1986, 100th Cong., 1st Sess. 1325 (Jt. Comm. Print 1987). The issue thus lives on.

2. *Policy Issues.* Should exempt organizations be allowed to use licensing or endorsement arrangements to convert the earnings of an unrelated trade or business into an excludable royalty that likely is tax-deductible by the for-profit payor? Is the exempt organization receiving passive investment income in these royalty arrangements or is it acting more like a joint venturer? Should it make any difference if the royalty is based on net or gross income, or whether the exempt organization has the right to control the manufacture and marketing of the licensed product? Why isn't licensing a trademark or logo a commercial exploitation of the organization's goodwill? For more on these policy issues and possible reforms, see Section I of this chapter, infra, at pp. 700–701.

4.   RESEARCH INCOME

Income from technology transfer and sponsored research is another rich source of nondonative revenue for universities and other leading nonprofit research centers. The dramatic surge of technology transfer opportunities for research institutions was spurred by the enactment in 1980 of the Bayh–Dole Act, which permits universities to patent and license for profit technologies developed by its research team. Prior to Bayh–Dole, title to inventions developed wholly or partially with federal funding reverted to the government. The technology transfer boom also was driven by factors such as the privatization trend, which reduced government support and forced research institutions to seek other funding sources; the technology explosion and the opportunities for universities to profit from its growth; and the desire of faculty to share the profits from their discoveries, as Bayh–Dole permits.

Under current law, typical technology transfer alliances can be structured so that the tax-exempt licensors are not subject to the UBIT. Patent royalties qualify for the § 512(b) exclusion, even when a university accepts equity in partial consideration for a license to develop the intellectual property. Even without the royalty exclusion, educational and scientific organizations have a good case that their patent licensing and corporate supported research income is not taxable because these activities are substantially related to their exempt purposes. To remove most lingering doubt, Congress also has provided three statutory exclusions from UBTI for research income if the research is:

(1) Performed for the United States, any agency or instrumentality of the federal government, or a state or local government. I.R.C. § 512(b)(7).

(2) Performed by a college, university or hospital "for any person." I.R.C. § 512(b)(8).

(3) "Fundamental" (as distinguished from "applied") and the results are freely made available to the general public. I.R.C. § 512(b)(9).

The regulations limit the reach of these exclusions by distinguishing "research" activities from other activities "of a type ordinarily carried on as an incident to commercial or industrial operations, for example, the ordinary testing or inspection of materials or products or the designing or construction of equipment, buildings, etc." Treas. Reg. § 1.512(b)–1(f)(4). In addition, the term "fundamental research" does not include research carried on for the primary purpose of commercial or industrial applications. Id.

In a 1976 ruling, the Service set forth factors to be considered in determining whether income from commercially sponsored research conducted by a scientific organization would be subject to the UBIT. See Rev. Rul. 76–296, 1976–2 C.B. 141. If the results of commercially sponsored research projects are published in a form available to the public within a reasonably short time after completion, the organization is treated as engaging in scientific research in the public interest even if the sponsor retains ownership rights in the research results. But if the scientific organization agrees to withhold publication beyond the time reasonably necessary to obtain patents or agrees to forego publication entirely, its income from conducting the commercially sponsored research is subject to the UBIT.

5.   A MONOGRAMMED EXCLUSION

Section 512(b)(15) contains a curious "modification" excluding from UBTI the income and deductions of any trade or business of providing certain "federally licensed services" by a religious order that carried on the business prior to May 27, 1959, provided that less than 10 percent of the net income is used for other than the order's exempt purposes and the Service is satisfied that competitive rates are being charged. It is widely believed that this exclusion was enacted (embroidered?) for a radio station in New Orleans that is owned and operated by Jesuit-affiliated Loyola University. The call letters of the station are monogrammed into three separate sub-sections of Section 512(b)(15) ("which . . .; which . . .; less . . ."). See Philip M. Stern, The Rape of the Taxpayer 40–41 (1973), which attributes this provision to the cultivated sense of humor of the late Senator Russell Long of Louisiana.

PROBLEMS

1.   Sturdley University has a vast complex of athletic facilities, including a superb football stadium, 20 lighted tennis courts with dressing room facilities, an art museum, a variety of eating facilities, and a large on-campus bookstore. What are the tax consequences to Sturdley of the following activities:

(a) Leasing the football stadium as a practice facility to a professional football team during July and August. Under the lease agreement, the University will maintain the playing surface and provide dressing room, linen and security services.

(b) Renting space in the art museum for special events such as corporate receptions, cocktail parties, weddings and dinners. In a normal year, the museum is used for 25 to 30 outside events. University personnel handle the furniture set-up and, as required by its liquor license, they are required to purchase and serve any alcoholic beverages. Volunteer docents are available at most events to lead tours and discuss exhibits at the museum.

(c) An exclusive marketing agreement with a soft drink company under which the University, in exchange for a fee, agrees to grant the company exclusive rights to sell its products and display its logo and familiar slogan, at all University eating facilities, vending machines and concession stands.

(d) Leasing the tennis complex to a local country club, which will operate a satellite facility and pay the University rent based on a fixed percentage of the gross receipts derived by the club from the use of the complex.

(e) Licensing the University's name and logo for use on Sturdley University athletic apparel (T-shirts, shorts, sweatshirts) and a University-label wine ("Sturdley Cabernet") that is sold in the on-campus bookstore and through mail-orders to alumni, parents and others on the alumni association's mailing list. The University retains the right to approve all the merchandise and is paid a royalty based on a percentage of the net income from sales.

(f) Providing the University's mailing list, logo, and a photograph of the campus to Bancorp, which offers a no-fee Sturdley VISA credit card to all alumni of the University. The alumni association, through an unrelated list manager, provides mailing labels for all "Sturdley card" marketing materials. Bancorp provides all other services related to the credit cards and pays the University a fee based on a small percentage of total cardholder sales volume.

2.   Golden Gate Hospital leases space in its adjacent medical building to a group of doctors who provide medical services to private patients. It also leases medical equipment to various doctors and for-profit medical partnerships. Is the income derived by the Hospital taxable as unrelated business income?

F. COMPUTATION OF UNRELATED BUSINESS TAXABLE INCOME

Internal Revenue Code: § 512(a).

Treasury Regulations: § 1.512(a)–1(a), (b), (c), (d), (e), (f)(1).

1. ALLOCATION OF EXPENSES

As previewed above, UBTI, the base on which the UBIT is computed, is defined in § 512(a)(1) as the gross income derived from any unrelated trade or business less allocable deductions for business expenses, losses, depreciation and other items "directly connected" with the unrelated business. I.R.C. § 512(a)(1). The computation is not as simple as the statute suggests. Reaching the bottom line is complicated by the necessity of allocating deductions between the unrelated trade or business and the exempt activities of the organization. If an organization is unable to avoid the UBIT under the myriad exclusions already discussed, it often can utilize the expense allocation rules to reduce or eliminate the bottom line figure.

Directly Connected. To be "directly connected" with the carrying on of an unrelated trade or business, an expense generally must have a "proximate and primary relationship" to that business. Treas. Reg. § 1.512(a)–1(a). This relationship exists in two situations: (1) the expenses are attributable solely to an unrelated business, in which case they are fully deductible (Treas. Reg. § 1.512(a)–1(b)), or (2) the expenses are attributable to the dual use of facilities or personnel, requiring an allocation between exempt and business functions on a "reasonable basis" (Treas. Reg. § 1.512(a)–1(c)). Thus, if employees are used for both exempt and business activities, their compensation must be allocated on a reasonable basis, and the amount allocated to the business is considered to be "directly connected." Treas. Reg. § 1.512(a)–1(c). The regulations suggest an allocation based on time devoted to the various activities. Depreciation and other expenses on a building can be allocated by reference to the space used for the various activities unless there is a more reasonable basis for the allocation. Id.

Exploitation of Exempt Functions. Organizations engaging in an unrelated business that "exploits" an exempt function may be able to minimize their UBIT exposure by allocating expenses of the exempt activity to the taxable business. The regulations permit this type of allocation in certain limited situations.

In general, expenses attributable to the exploitation of an exempt function are not deductible in computing UBTI on the theory that the items are incident to the conduct of an exempt purpose and thus do not possess a sufficient relationship to the unrelated trade or business. Treas. Reg. § 1.512(a)–1(d). Under a special and very generous rule, if an unrelated trade or business is of a kind carried on for profit by a taxable organization and if the exempt activity exploited by the business also is comparable to activities normally conducted by taxable organizations in pursuance of such a business, the expenses attributable to the exempt activity are deductible to the extent that: (1) they exceed the income (if any) attributable to the exempt activity, and (2) the allocation of the excess expenses to the unrelated activities does not result in a loss from the unrelated trade or business. Treas. Reg. § 1.512(a)–1(d)(2).

To illustrate, assume that Friends of the Sea, an exempt environmental organization with 20,000 members, mails advertising literature for consumer products to its members under a contract with an advertising agency. The mailing activity is an unrelated business that exploits the membership list developed in the conduct of the organization's exempt functions. The expenses solely attributable to the advertising business are deductible. But since development of the membership lists is not an activity usually conducted by for-profit organizations, no part of the cost of developing the membership list is deductible in computing UBTI. Treas.Reg. § 1.512(a)–1(e), Example.

Advertising in an exempt organization's journal is a typical example of exploitation of an exempt function. May the expenses attributable to the production and distribution of the journal be deducted against the taxable advertising income? Within limits, the answer is yes since the exempt activity (publication of the journal) is of "a type normally conducted by taxable organizations in pursuance of such [a] business." Treas. Reg. § 1.512(a)–1(d)(2). The regulations provide elaborate rules for allocating expenses in the advertising area. Treas. Reg. § 1.512(a)–1(f)(2)–(7).

If expenses of an exempt activity are deductible in computing UBTI, the regulations provide an allocation procedure that may limit the deductible amount. Exempt function expenses first must be allocated to the income derived from or attributable to that function—e.g., expenses of publishing a journal first must be allocated to subscription income, if any. Any excess then may be allocated to the unrelated business income. But no allocation of the excess is permitted to the extent that such an allocation would result in a net operating loss from the unrelated business. Finally, the excess may not be allocated to any other unrelated trade or business that does not exploit the same exempt function—e.g., excess expenses attributable to a periodical may not be applied against income from a manufacturing activity. Treas. Reg. § 1.512(a)–1(d)(2). But several businesses exploiting the same exempt function may be consolidated. Treas. Reg. § 1.512(a)–1(f)(7).

As illustrated by the *Rensselaer Polytechnic Institute* case, which follows, the allocation of expenses between related and unrelated activities of dual use facilities has proven to be one of the more difficult aspects of computing unrelated business taxable income.

Rensselaer Polytechnic Institute v. Commissioner

United States Court of Appeals, Second Circuit, 1984.
732 F.2d 1058.

■ PRATT, CIRCUIT JUDGE:

The issue before us is not only one of first impression; it is also of considerable financial significance to many of our colleges and universities.

When a tax-exempt organization uses one of its facilities, as in this case a fieldhouse, for both tax-exempt purposes and for the production of unrelated business income, what portion of its indirect expenses such as depreciation may it deduct from its unrelated business income pursuant to I.R.C. § 512 (1982)? May it allocate those expenses, as prescribed by Treas. Reg. § 1.512(a)–1(c), on any "reasonable" basis? Or must it first establish, as the commissioner here argues, that the expense would not have been incurred in the absence of the business activity? Finding no conflict between the regulation and the statute and finding no error in the determination of the tax court that RPI's method of allocation was reasonable, we reject the commissioner's position and affirm the tax court's judgment, which approved apportioning the fieldhouse's idle time in proportion to the hours devoted to exempt and not exempt uses.

The facts are undisputed. Rensselaer Polytechnic Institute (RPI) is a non-profit educational organization entitled to tax-exempt status under I.R.C. § 501(c)(3). It owns and operates a fieldhouse which it devotes to two broad categories of uses: (1) student uses, which include physical education, college ice hockey, student ice skating, and other activities related to RPI's tax-exempt educational responsibilities; and (2) commercial uses, which include activities and events such as commercial ice shows and public ice skating, that do not fall within its tax-exempt function. For the fiscal year 1974, the net income from commercial use of the fieldhouse constituted "unrelated business taxable income" which was subject to taxation under I.R.C. § 511(a)(1).

The dispute is over the amount of unrelated business tax due from RPI for 1974 and, since there is no disagreement over the gross income, $476,613, we must focus on the deductible expenses. The parties have classified RPI's applicable deductible expenses in three groups. The first group, "direct expenses," are those that can be specifically identified with particular commercial uses. For the year in question direct expenses amounted to $371,407, and the parties have always agreed to their deductibility.

The second group, "variable expenses", are those which vary in proportion to actual use of the fieldhouse, but which cannot be identified with particular events. They were originally in dispute before the tax court, but neither side has appealed that part of the decision below which (a) found the total variable expenses to be $197,210; and (b) allocated them on the basis of actual use, as claimed by RPI, rather than total availability, as claimed by the commissioner.

This appeal involves the third group, "fixed expenses", which do not vary in proportion to actual use of the facility. The amounts of fixed expenses incurred with respect to the fieldhouse were stipulated to be:

Salaries and fringe benefits	$ 59,415
Depreciation	29,397
Repairs and Replacements	14,031
Operating Expenditures	1,356
	$104,199

Narrowly stated, the issue is how these fixed expenses should be allocated between RPI's dual uses: the exempt student use and the taxable commercial use. RPI contends it is entitled to allocate the fixed expenses on the basis of relative times of actual use. Thus, in computing that portion of its deductible expenses, RPI multiplies the total amount of fixed expenses by a fraction, whose numerator is the total number of hours the fieldhouse was used for commercial events, and whose denominator is the total number of hours the fieldhouse was used for all activities and events-student and commercial combined.

The commissioner argues that the allocation of fixed expenses must be made not on the basis of times of actual use, but on the basis of total time available for use. Thus, he contends the denominator of the fraction should be the total number of hours in the taxable year. In practical terms, the difference between the two methods of allocation amounts to $9,259 in taxes.

Below, the tax court agreed with RPI's method of allocating on the basis of actual use, finding it to be "reasonable" within the meaning of Treas. Reg. § 1.512(a)–1(c). The commissioner appeals, contending (a) that the tax court's otherwise reasonable allocation based on actual use does not satisfy the statutory requirement that in order to be deductible an expense must be "directly connected with" the unrelated business activity; (b) that the cases the tax court relied on below, dealing with allocation of home office expenses between business and personal use, are inapposite; and (c) that strict application of the "directly connected with" language of the statute is "necessary to prevent serious abuse of the tax exemption privilege."

It has been the consistent policy of this nation to exempt from income taxes a corporation, like RPI, that is "organized and operated exclusively for * * * educational purposes * * *". I.R.C. § 501(c)(3). This preferred treatment to educational, as well as religious, charitable, and scientific institutions, was established simultaneously with the first income tax enacted by congress in 1913, and has been continued in identical language through a series of revenue acts down to and including the current provision contained in I.R.C. § 501. * * * So firm was the policy shielding educational institutions from taxation that, despite repeated challenges by the commissioner, the statute was consistently interpreted to exempt from taxation all income earned by an exempt corporation, even that obtained from activities unrelated to its tax-exempt educational purposes.

Recognizing, however, the unfair competitive advantage that freedom from income taxation could accord tax-exempt institutions that entered the world of commerce, congress, in 1950, extended the income tax to the "unrelated business income" of certain tax-exempt institutions, including educational corporations. Pub. L. No. 81–814, § 301, 64 Stat. 906, 947 (1950)(codified at I.R.C. § 511–513). Its objective in changing the law was to eliminate the competitive advantage educational and charitable corporations enjoyed over private enterprise, without jeopardizing the basic purpose of the tax-exemption. * * *

With this historical background in mind, we turn to the applicable statute and regulations. Section 512 of the code defines as "unrelated business taxable income" gross income derived from unrelated business activities less deductions "directly connected with" such activities. Treas. Reg. § 1.512(a)–1(a) further defines the term "directly connected with", and provides that "to be 'directly connected with' the conduct of unrelated business for purposes of section 512, an item of deduction must have proximate and primary relationship" to that business. Two subsequent subsections of that regulation define "proximate and primary relationship" in the context of (a) items that are attributable solely to the unrelated business, Treas. Reg. § 1.512(a)–1(b); and (b) as in this case, items that are attributable to facilities or personnel used for both exempt and unrelated purposes, Treas. Reg. § 1.512(a)–1(c). The latter regulation provides:

> (c) Dual use of facilities or personnel. Where facilities are used both to carry on exempt activities and to conduct unrelated trade or business activities, expenses, depreciation and similar items attributable to such facilities (as, for example, items of overhead), shall be allocated between the two uses on a reasonable basis. Similarly, where personnel are used both to carry on exempt activities and to conduct unrelated trade or business activities, expenses and similar items attributable to such personnel (as, for example, items of salary) shall be allocated between the two uses on a reasonable basis. The portion of any such items so allocated to the unrelated trade or business activity is proximately and primarily related to that business activity, and shall be allowable as a deduction in computing unrelated business taxable income in the manner and to the extent permitted by section 162, section 167 or other relevant provisions of the Code.

Treas. Reg. § 1.512(a)–1(c)(emphasis added).

Thus, when allocated "on a reasonable basis," expenses attributable to such facilities or personnel-which expressly include such "indirect expenses" as depreciation and overhead—are by definition "proximately and primarily related" to the business. They are therefore "directly connected with" the unrelated business activity and expressly made deductible by the regulation.

Under this regulation, therefore, the critical question is whether the method of allocation adopted by RPI was "reasonable". The tax court found that it was, and, giving due regard to its expertise in this area, ABKCO Industries, Inc. v. Commissioner, 482 F.2d 150, 155 (3d Cir.1973), we see no error in that conclusion. Apportioning indirect expenses such as depreciation on the basis of the actual hours the facility was used for both exempt and taxable purposes sensibly distributes the cost of the facility among the activities that benefit from its use. In addition, the method is consistent with that followed by the tax court in the most common dual-use situation, home office deduction cases. * * *

Indeed, the commissioner does not claim that RPI's allocation method is factually unreasonable, but instead contends solely that the method is not "reasonable", because by permitting depreciation during "idle time", when the fieldhouse is not being used at all, it contravenes the statutory requirement that deductible expenses be "directly connected with" RPI's unrelated business activities. By advancing this argument, however, the commissioner ignores his own definition of the concept "directly connected with" included in Treas. Reg. § 1.512(a)–1(a) discussed above. In addition, the commissioner would have us adopt a more stringent interpretation of "directly connected with" in § 512 than has been applied for over sixty years to the same concept in the commissioner's regulations governing the deductibility of ordinary and necessary business expenses. See Treas. Reg. § 1.162–1(a). Moreover, the logical extension of his position would require the commissioner to deny depreciation deductions to all businesses for those periods when their assets are idle. Such a view, however, would contravene the basic concepts underlying the commissioner's elaborate regulations governing depreciation generally. See Treas. Reg. § 1.167(a)–1 et seq.

For an expense to be "directly connected with" an activity, the commissioner argues that it must be one that would not have been incurred in the absence of the activity. But whether or not the fieldhouse is actually put to any business use, depreciation of the facility continues. We cannot accept the commissioner's argument, therefore, because it would in effect eliminate entirely all deductions for indirect expenses such as depreciation, a result that is not required by statute and that is directly contrary to the regulation.

* * *

Some concern has been expressed that RPI's allocation method would provide an incentive for educational institutions to abuse their tax-exempt status. The argument is a red herring. Use of educational facilities for producing unrelated business income is not tax abuse; on the contrary, as we have pointed out above, such non-exempt activities have been consistently permitted and, since 1950, expressly approved by congress. Moreover, should the trustees of a particular tax-exempt educational institution so pervert its operations that the institution no longer "engages primarily in activities which accomplish * * * [its exempt purposes]", Treas. Reg. § 1.501(c)(3)–1(c)(1), the commissioner has adequate remedies available to correct any abuse or even terminate the exemption.

The judgment appealed from is affirmed.

■ MANSFIELD, CIRCUIT JUDGE (Dissenting):

I respectfully dissent.

Rensselaer Polytechnic Institute ("RPI") is a tax-exempt institution only because it has dedicated itself and its property in perpetuity to "charitable" and "educational purposes." 26 U.S.C. § 501(c). Its unrelated business income less "deductions * * * which are directly connected with the carrying on of such trade or business" is taxable. 26 U.S.C. § 501(b), 512(a). We are here asked to permit the college to deduct from its commercial business income fixed expenses that would normally be allocated on a time basis to periods when the college's property is not being used for trade or business but for its educational purposes.

In my view such expenses are not "directly connected" with the institution's commercial business activities within the meaning of § 512(a) and are therefore not deductible form its business income. On the contrary, they are attributable to time when the facilities exist for educational purposes. Indeed, it could reasonably be argued that since RPI would, absent part-time use of its fixed assets for commercial purposes, be required to absorb all depreciation of such assets, no such depreciation is "directly connected" with its commercial business operations. RPI represented in its petition to the Tax Court that "[t]he main function of the fieldhouse is to provide a suitable facility necessary to allow petitioner to carry out *its total educational responsibilities*." (Emphasis added). Although some allocation may be permissible, I do not believe RPI should be allowed to give its commercial use any credit for time when its facilities exist for educational use. To do so would give a tax exempt institution an unfair tax advantage over commercial institutions. The majority reaches this result only by what appears to be a misinterpretation of the governing statute and regulations.

In my view the fundamental error underlying the majority's decision is its assumption that tax-exempt institutions are governed for tax deduction purposes by the same standards as those governing taxable businesses. That assumption conflicts with legislative intent, economic reality, and the express wording of the pertinent statute and regulations. When Congress in 1950 passed legislation subjecting tax-exempt organizations to income tax on unrelated business income, it was concerned both with removing the unfair competitive advantage enjoyed by tax-exempt institutions and with assuring that the unrelated business income would produce a fair amount of revenue for the public fisc. However, it was confronted with inherent differences between regular taxable business and a non-profit university engaged mainly in educational activity and only partially in income-producing commercial activities. These differences precluded a wholesale transfer and application to a university of the same deduction principles as those governing regular commercial businesses.

In the case of a commercial business devoted solely to making a profit, its entire operation is subject to a tax on its income. Regardless how it chooses to allocate its business expenses between divisions, the net income from all divisions is taxable. The IRS therefore has no quarrel with an "reasonable" allocation of deductible expenses between branches of the operation. The tax-exempt university, on the other hand, is fundamentally different in that one of its "divisions"—the educational function—is not subject to taxation. The university will therefore always have an incentive to minimize the allocation of expenses attributed to the educational function, and correspondingly to maximize the deduction for unrelated business activity. This incentive, which is not present in the ordinary business setting, requires a stricter standard of deductibility for tax-exempt organizations than for purely profit-seeking firms. The government cannot, in the case of an educational institution engaged in unrelated commercial business activity, afford to take the same relaxed approach as with wholly-taxable businesses and to accept any allocation the taxpayer may deem "reasonable."

Thus, the majority achieves parity only in the most superficial sense. The identical rule of deductibility is imposed, but it is imposed on organizations that have different characteristics and are therefore affected differently by the same rule. To whatever extent Congress sought to place wholly taxable and exempt organizations on the same footing, it was concerned not with such technical legal tests but with the real after-tax situations of the two different types of organization. Yet the majority's approach, which claims to provide equal treatment, actually leaves the tax-exempt organizations with the very advantage that the majority claims Congress was trying to eliminate.

That Congress adopted a narrower test of deductibility for the tax-exempt organization is clearly reflected in the statute. 26 U.S.C. § 512 allows such an organization to take those "deductions allowed by this chapter which are directly connected with" its unrelated business income (emphasis added). The underlined language is imposed as an additional requirement for tax-exempt institutions not faced by purely profit-oriented businesses.

* * *

For these reasons, I would reverse the Tax Court's decision.

2.   OTHER COMPUTATION ISSUES

Several of the modifications in § 512(b) affect the computation of unrelated business taxable income. Net operating losses ("NOLs") are allowable as a deduction in computing UBTI and may be carried back and forward as in a normal business activity. I.R.C. § 512(b)(6). Only income and deduction items not excluded from the UBIT are taken into account for NOL purposes, and any preceding years in which the organization was not an exempt organization are ignored in computing NOLs, including carrybacks and carryforwards. For the details, see Treas. Reg. § 1.512(b)–1(e).

Nonprofit corporations subject to the UBIT generally may deduct charitable contributions in an amount up to 10 percent of UBTI computed without regard to the contributions. I.R.C. § 512(b)(10). Contributions in excess of the 10 percent limit may be carried over for five years, but no carryover is allowed to the extent it increases a net operating loss carryover. The contributions need not be connected to the unrelated business but they must be paid to another qualified organization. I.R.C. § 512(b)(10); Treas. Reg. § 1.512(b)–1(g). Trusts may deduct contributions in the same amounts as allowed for individuals, but the percentage limitations in § 170(b) are determined in relation to UBTI rather than adjusted gross income. I.R.C. § 512(b)(11); Treas. Reg. § 1.512(b)–1(g)(2).

A "specific deduction" of $1,000 is allowed in computing UBTI, but this deduction may not create or increase a net operating loss. I.R.C. § 512(b)(12). The deduction is limited to $1,000 irrespective of the number of unrelated businesses in which the organization engages. Church units may be eligible for separate $1,000 deductions (per parish, diocese, province, etc.) provided that the local units are not separate entities and the parent organization files a consolidated return. I.R.C. § 512(b)(12); Treas. Reg. § 1.512(b)–1(h)(2).

PROBLEMS

1. State College uses its multi-purpose indoor athletic center for intercollegiate basketball and hockey games, student intramural activities, professional athletic events and commercial entertainment. During the current year the College earned $500,000 in gross revenue from commercial use of the facility. Assume that this revenue is subject to the unrelated business tax.

Expenses for the facility for the current year were as follows: $300,000 of direct expenses for commercial events (setting up the facility, paying extra security guards, etc.), $100,000 of variable expenses (e.g., expenses that vary with the use of the facility), and $100,000 of fixed expenses (e.g., expenses, such as depreciation, repairs, and salaries) that do not vary with the use of the facility.

Assume for convenience that there are 9,000 hours during the year, and the use of the athletic facility is as follows: 600 hours for commercial events, 4,200 hours for activities substantially related to the College's exempt purposes, and 4,200 hours of idle time.

Compute the College's unrelated business taxable income from this facility for the current year.

2. Save the Porpoise ("STP") is a § 501(c)(3) environmental organization. One of its activities is the publication of a quarterly journal, The Porpoise, that is distributed to its 10,000 members who pay annual dues of $40 per year. STP also distributes 5,000 additional copies of The Porpoise to nonmembers (such as libraries), who pay $20 per year. During the current year, STP derived $600,000 in gross revenue from the sale of commercial advertising in the Porpoise. Its direct costs of selling and publishing the advertising were $400,000. STP's other costs in producing and distributing The Porpoise were $350,000.

   (a) What is STP's unrelated business taxable income from its advertising activity?

(b) Same as (a), above, except assume STP sold only 500 copies of The Porpoise to nonmembers at $20 per year and STP's members could elect not to receive the journal, in which case their dues would be reduced from $40 per year to $24 per year. During the current year, 3,000 members elected to receive the journal and pay the full $40 annual dues.

(c) Same as (a), above, except that STP had a net loss from the advertising activity of $30,000 and also earned $50,000 of unrelated business taxable income from another business activity (not advertising). What is STP's aggregate UBTI from the two activities?

G.   UNRELATED DEBT-FINANCED INCOME

Internal Revenue Code: §§ 514(a); (b); (c)(1)–(4), (7), (9)(A)–(D), (E).

Treasury Regulations: § 1.514(b)–1(a), (b), (d).

If an exempt organization borrows in order to acquire income-producing property, all or part of that income, less allocable deductions, may be included in UBTI under § 514 even if it otherwise would have been excluded under § 512(b). This expansion of the unrelated business tax to embrace income from debt-financed investments was in response to a variety of transactions aimed at circumventing the UBIT and exploiting an organization's tax-exempt status. A few words of background may be helpful to introduce this technical topic.

When the UBIT was first enacted, charities were viewed as being in a unique position to trade on their tax exemptions by acquiring property such as real estate on credit and then leasing the property back to the seller without payment of taxes by either party. A typical transaction might have been structured as follows:

Charity buys rental property from Taxpayer, paying little or nothing down and financing the balance of the purchase price with a 20–year purchase money mortgage. Charity then enters into a net lease arrangement with Taxpayer, who agrees to pay all expenses on the property and remit a net rental to Charity. The tax-free rent received by Charity enables it to amortize the mortgage and still realize a profit. Taxpayer, in turn, enjoys capital gains treatment on the sale (often spreading his gain via the installment method of reporting) and is able to shelter its income from operating the property to a nominal amount through the deductions for rent and other expenses.

In 1950, Congress responded by imposing the UBIT on rentals from leases of real property and certain personal property if the lease term exceeded five years and the property was acquired with borrowed funds. The amount taxed generally was the gross rent multiplied by a percentage computed by dividing the total outstanding debt by the adjusted basis of the property, less a similar percentage of expenses attributable to the property. See Revenue Act of 1950, ch. 994, § 301(a). Creative tax advisors devised other transactions to circumvent this early legislation. For example, some exempt organizations made debt-financed acquisitions of going businesses that were liquidated tax-free by the charity, which then leased the assets back to a new entity created by the former owners of the for-profit business. Attempts by the Service to curb these transactions by requiring sellers to report their gains as ordinary income or revoking the charity's tax exemption were generally unsuccessful. See, e.g., Commissioner v. Brown, 380 U.S. 563, 85 S.Ct. 1162, 14 L.Ed.2d 75 (1965).

Fearing an erosion of the tax base and an unchecked growth of charitable organizations without any commensurate increase in their level of donative support, Congress expanded § 514 in 1969 to include in UBTI any passive investment income of an exempt organization to the extent that the property generating the income was acquired, directly or indirectly, with borrowed funds. But § 514 goes far beyond the transactions at which it was originally aimed. For example, stocks and bonds purchased on margin may constitute debt-financed property and, as a result, their dividend and interest income will be partially taxable.

Section 514 provides that an exempt organization must include in its UBTI a certain percentage—known as the "debt/basis fraction"—of gross income from debt-financed property, less a similar percentage of allocable deductions. I.R.C. § 514(a)(1)–(3). The types of income items potentially covered are rent, royalties, interest, dividends, and capital gains. "Debt-financed property" is defined as any tangible or intangible property held for the production of income with respect to which there exists an "acquisition indebtedness" at any time during the taxable year. I.R.C. § 514(b)(1); Treas. Reg. § 1.514(b)–1(a). Property is considered held for the production of income if it is held for operating profit or gain on a disposition of the property. Treas. Reg. § 1.514(b)–1(a). Familiar examples of debt-financed property are rental real estate subject to a mortgage and corporate stock purchased in part with borrowed funds. The statutory definition is qualified by numerous exceptions, most of which are intended to exempt property related to the organization's exempt purposes. I.R.C. § 514(b)(1); Treas. Reg. § 1.514(b)–1(b).

"Acquisition indebtedness" is generally defined as any unpaid debt incurred to acquire or improve property, including in some cases debt incurred before or after the acquisition or improvement. The most obvious example of acquisition indebtedness occurs when an organization acquires or improves income-producing property with borrowed funds, but the definition is broader in order to cover other borrowing that is closely connected with the acquisition or improvement of the property. The regulations provide that the "facts and circumstances" of each situation will determine whether the incurrence of a debt is reasonably foreseeable. The fact that the need to incur a debt may not have been foreseen before the acquisition does not necessarily mean that a later incurrence of the debt was not reasonably foreseeable. Treas. Reg. § 1.514(c)–1(a)(1).

The debt-basis fraction is used to determine the percentage of debt-financed income that must be included in UBTI. The fraction is generally determined by comparing the "average acquisition indebtedness" with respect to the debt-financed property to its adjusted basis. The fraction varies with the passage of time, as the debt is amortized and the basis is adjusted through depreciation, improvements, etc. I.R.C. § 514(a)(1).

Although § 514 was aimed at real estate, it has a much broader reach, as illustrated by the *Bartels Trust* case, which follows.

Bartels Trust v. United States

United States Court of Appeals, Second Circuit, 2000.
209 F.3d 147, cert. denied, 531 U.S. 978, 121 S.Ct. 426 (2000).

■ WEXLER, DISTRICT JUDGE:

Plaintiff-appellant, The Henry E. & Nancy Horton Bartels Trust for the Benefit of the University of New Haven ("Taxpayer"), appeals from a judgment of the United States District Court for the District of Connecticut (Eginton, J.), upon an order granting Taxpayer's motion for reconsideration and, on reconsideration, affirming an order granting the government's motion for summary judgment and denying Taxpayer's cross-motion for summary judgment in Taxpayer's refund action. Because we agree with the district court that Taxpayer's securities purchased on margin constitute debt-financed property and that income derived therefrom is subject to the unrelated business income tax ("UBIT") under §§ 511–14 of the Internal Revenue Code ("Code"), 26 U.S.C. §§ 511–14, we affirm.

I. BACKGROUND

[The taxpayer was a § 501(c)(3) organization formed to provide support for the University of New Haven. It qualified as a "supporting organization" under § 509(a)(3) of the Code. During the taxable years in question, taxpayer purchased securities on margin, borrowing from its broker. It filed Form 990–T, reporting the income from its margin-financed securities and later filed a claim for refund, which the IRS denied. This tax refund suit followed. The district court granted the IRS's motion for summary judgment, and the taxpayer appealed to the Second Circuit. Eds.]

II. DISCUSSION

* * *

B. Unrelated Business Income Tax

An organization exempt from tax under § 501 of the Code may be subject to the UBIT on income it derives from a trade or business unrelated to its exempt purpose. See 26 U.S.C. § 501(b). Section 511(b) imposes the UBIT on tax-exempt trusts for "unrelated business taxable income," as defined in § 512. Id. § 511(b). Under § 512(a), "unrelated business taxable income" is defined, in general, as the "gross income derived by any organization from any unrelated trade or business (as defined in section 513) regularly carried on by it, less the deductions ... directly connected with the carrying on of such trade or business." Id. § 512(a)(1). Section 513, in turn, defines "unrelated trade or business" to include any trade or business "the conduct of which is not substantially related (aside from the need of such organization for income or funds or the use it makes of the profits derived) to the exercise or performance by such organization of its charitable, educational, or other purpose or function constituting the basis for its exemption under section 501"—subject to certain exceptions not applicable here. Id. § 513(a).

As a general rule, § 512 excludes from tax passive investment income, such as interest, dividends, and royalties, received by exempt organizations. Nevertheless, such investment income is taxable if derived from "debt-financed property," as defined in § 514. Thus, while § 512(b) generally excludes certain items of income from "unrelated business taxable income," it nullifies these exclusions for income derived from "debt-financed property," providing: "Notwithstanding paragraph (1), (2), (3), or (5), in the case of debt-financed property (as defined in section 514) there shall be included, as an item of gross income derived from an unrelated trade or business, the amount ascertained under section 514(a)(1)...." Id. § 512(b)(4). Section 514(a)(1) requires that income earned from "debt-financed property" be treated as income derived from an unrelated trade or business (in the proportion that the basis of the property bears to the amount financed) for purposes of determining unrelated business taxable income. Id. § 514(a)(1). The taxability of income from debt-financed property has no effect on the tax-exempt organization's tax-exempt status, but the income the organization derives from debt-financed property is subject to the UBIT as income from an unrelated trade or business. See id. § 501(b).

"Debt-financed property" is defined as "any property which is held to produce income and with respect to which there is an acquisition indebtedness (as defined in subsection (c)) at any time during the taxable year." Id. § 514(b)(1). Expressly excluded from debt-financed property is "any property substantially all the use of which is substantially related (aside from the need of the organization for income or funds) to the exercise or performance by such organization of its charitable, educational, or other purpose or function constituting the basis for its exemption under section 501." Id. § 514(b)(1)(A)(i).

Section 514(c)(1), in turn, defines "acquisition indebtedness" generally as "the indebtedness incurred by the organization in acquiring or improving [debt-financed property]." Id. § 514(c)(1)(A). Expressly excluded from acquisition indebtedness is "indebtedness the incurrence of which is inherent in the performance or exercise of the purpose or function constituting the basis of the organization's exemption, such as the indebtedness incurred by a credit union described in section 501(c)(14) in accepting deposits from its members." Id. § 514(c)(4).

C. Imposition of UBIT on Taxpayer's Income Derived from Securities Purchased on Margin

Taxpayer argues that the income it derived from securities purchased on margin is not subject to the UBIT because: (1) Taxpayer's securities investment activities, including margin trading, do not constitute conduct of a "trade or business" under the Code; (2) neither Taxpayer nor any third-party (i.e., UNH or Gilder, Gagnon) derived a direct or indirect "unfair competitive advantage" over taxable entities from Taxpayer's margin trading and the income derived therefrom; (3) Taxpayer's securities purchased on margin are not "debt-financed property" under § 514(b)(1); and (4) the exceptions to "debt-financed property" and "acquisition indebtedness" under § 514(b)(1)(A)(i) and § 514(c)(4), respectively, apply to exclude Taxpayer's income derived from securities purchased on margin from the UBIT. We disagree with Taxpayer's arguments, each of which we address below, and hold, as did the district court, that Taxpayer's income derived from margin-financed securities is subject to the UBIT under §§ 511–14 of the Code.

1.   Unrelated Trade or Business

Taxpayer initially argues that its securities investment activities, particularly its margin trading, do not constitute a "trade or business" under the Code, and, therefore, the income it derived from margin-financed securities is not subject to the UBIT. In this respect, Taxpayer argues that in determining whether an exempt organization's income is subject to the UBIT as "unrelated business taxable income" the following three requirements must be met: "(1) [i]t is income from trade or business; (2) such trade or business is regularly carried on by the organization; and (3) the conduct of such trade or business is not substantially related (other than through the production of funds) to the organization's performance of its exempt functions." Treas.Reg. § 1.513–1(a); see United States v. American College of Physicians, 475 U.S. 834, 838–39, 106 S.Ct. 1591, 89 L.Ed.2d 841 (1986). Taxpayer maintains that the first prong of this test is not met because Supreme Court decisions, such as Higgins v. Commissioner, 312 U.S. 212, 61 S.Ct. 475, 85 L.Ed. 783 (1941), and Whipple v. Commissioner, 373 U.S. 193, 83 S.Ct. 1168, 10 L.Ed.2d 288 (1963), hold that securities investing is not the conduct of a "trade or business." As further set out below, we find no merit to Taxpayer's argument.

Under the plain language of the UBIT, the purchase of securities on margin is a purchase using borrowed funds; therefore, under § 514(c), the securities are subject to an "acquisition indebtedness." See Elliot Knitwear Profit Sharing Plan v. Commissioner, 614 F.2d 347, 348–51 (3d Cir.1980). Thus, the margin-financed securities constitute "debt-financed property" under § 514(b)(1). As "debt-financed property," § 512(b)(4) and § 514(a)(1) require that the income derived from these securities be treated "as an item of gross income derived from an unrelated trade or business" (in the proportion that the basis of the property bears to the amount financed), and, therefore, this income is included in the § 512 computation of unrelated business taxable income. See, e.g., id. (holding securities purchased on margin are subject to UBIT, as margin-financed securities are debt-financed property, and § 514(a) requires treating income derived therefrom as income from unrelated trade or business). Thus, Taxpayer's reliance on Supreme Court decisions construing "trade or business" in other contexts and under the general test for determining unrelated business taxable income is misplaced because § 512(b)(4) and § 514(a)(1) require that Taxpayer's income derived from margin-financed securities be treated as income derived from an unrelated trade or business.

2. Unfair Competition

Despite the plain language of the UBIT, and its straightforward applicability to the income Taxpayer derived from margin-financed securities, Taxpayer argues that the UBIT does not apply here because neither Taxpayer nor any third-party derived, directly or indirectly, an "unfair competitive advantage" over taxable entities. Taxpayer asserts that because there has been no showing of "unfair competition," the income it derived from margin-financed securities is not subject to the UBIT. We find no merit to this argument.

[In rejecting the taxpayer's unfair competition argument, the court noted that nothing in the plain language of the statute required a showing of unfair competition and the legislative history, while referring to unfair competition, indicated it was not the sole purpose of the UBIT. The court concluded that even though Congress enacted the UBIT primarily to eliminate unfair competition, it chose language going beyond the evil it sought to correct in order to close the loophole at which § 514 was aimed. Eds.]

Accordingly, we reject Taxpayer's argument that unfair competition must be shown for the imposition of the UBIT on income it derived from margin-financed securities.

3. "Held to Produce Income"

Next, Taxpayer argues that its margin-financed securities are not "debt-financed property" because § 514(b)(1) defines "debt-financed property" as property that is "held to produce income," and this phrase should be interpreted to include only "periodic" income. We find no merit to this argument for at least two reasons. First, Taxpayer cites no authority for this construction of § 514(b)(1), and there is nothing in the statutory language or legislative history of the UBIT supporting this restrictive interpretation. Second, the applicable regulation specifically construes "income" under § 514(b)(1) as including both capital gains and recurring or "periodic" income (e.g., dividends). In this respect, Treasury Regulation § 1.514(b)–1(a) defines "debt-financed property" as

> any property which is held to produce income (e.g., rental real estate, tangible personal property, and corporate stock), and with respect to which there is an acquisition indebtedness (determined without regard to whether the property is debt-financed property) at any time during the taxable year. The term "income" is not limited to recurring income but applies as well to gains from the disposition of the property.

Treas. Reg. § 1.514(b)–1(a) (emphasis added). Although Taxpayer urges us to reject the Commissioner's interpretation of the UBIT, we must sustain the regulation unless it is "unreasonable and plainly inconsistent" with the statute.

Section 61(a) of the Code broadly defines income to include "all income from whatever source derived," and lists, as examples, both periodic income (e.g., dividends and interest) and nonperiodic income (e.g., compensation for services; gross income derived from business; and gains derived from dealings in property). 26 U.S.C. § 61(a)(1), (2), (3), (4), (7). There is nothing in the statutory language to suggest that this general definition of "income" is inapplicable to § 514(b)(1) or to justify limiting § 514(b)(1) to "periodic" income. Moreover, the legislative history of the UBIT does not indicate that Congress intended to tax only "periodic" income under those provisions. Accordingly, we reject Taxpayer's argument that § 514(b)(1)'s reference to "debt-financed property" includes only "periodic" income.

4.   Exceptions to Acquisition Indebtedness and Debt–Financed Property

Finally, Taxpayer argues that even if the income it derived from margin-financed securities would otherwise constitute unrelated business income under §§ 511 and 512, the exceptions to "debt-financed property" and "acquisition indebtedness" under § 514(b)(1)(A)(i) and § 514(c)(4), respectively, apply to exclude this income. In this respect, Taxpayer argues that its income is not taxable because (1) the securities it purchased on margin are "substantially related" to its exempt purpose under the § 514(b)(1)(A)(i) exception to "debt-financed property"; and (2) its purchase of securities on margin is "inherent" to its exempt purpose under the § 514(c)(4) exception to "acquisition indebtedness." We find no merit to Taxpayer's argument, as both exceptions are inapplicable here.

The leading case addressing these exceptions is *Elliot Knitwear*, which involved a tax-exempt employee profit-sharing plan which derived income from margin-financed securities. See Elliot Knitwear, 614 F.2d at 348. In holding the income subject to the UBIT, the Third Circuit rejected the plan's argument that its margin account fell within the § 514(c)(4) exception to acquisition indebtedness because the margin account was "inherent" in the plan's exempt purpose, and the plan's further argument that the margin account fell within the § 514(b)(1)(A)(i) exception to debt-financed property because the margin account was "substantially related" to the plan's exempt purpose, namely, accumulation of income for employees for their retirement. *See id.* at 349–51. The court held that "inherent," as used in § 514(c)(4), is synonymous with "essential," and concluded that, while investing on margin may have been desirable for the plan, it was not essential to its tax-exempt purpose of providing employee participation in the employer's profits. Id. at 349–50. The court reasoned that "while investment of the fund probably is inherent to its tax-exempt purpose, debt-financed investment is not." Id. at 350. Thus, the court held that the "purchase of securities on margin is not inherent to the purpose of a tax-exempt profit-sharing plan within the meaning of section 514(c)(4)" and, therefore, not within the exception to "acquisition indebtedness." Id.

As for the plan's argument that the § 514(b)(1)(A)(i) exception to debt-financed property applied, the court first observed that "[i]t is the property itself, and not the income generated by the property, that must be substantially related to the exempt purpose of the organization." Id. In rejecting the plan's argument, the court reasoned:

> It is expected that the buying and selling of income-producing property will be a method utilized to increase and accumulate income and gains, but such investment activity is a means to accomplish the purpose of deferred compensation it is not the purpose itself of the Plan. Even assuming, arguendo, that investment of contributions for accumulation of income is a function of the Plan, indebtedness or acquisition of securities on margin is not necessary for such accumulation or that purpose.

Id. Moreover, the court recognized that the "statute does not exclude property that is substantially related by virtue of 'the need of the organization for income or funds.'" Id. (quoting 26 U.S.C. § 514(b)(1)(A)(i)).

We find the *Elliot Knitwear* court's reasoning persuasive, and accordingly conclude that Taxpayer's purchase of securities on margin does not fall within the "inherent" purpose exception or the "substantially related" exception to § 514.

Taxpayer's exempt purpose is to provide funds to support UNH's educational programs. Taxpayer's purchase of securities on margin is not "inherent" or essential to that purpose. Indeed, many alternative investments, whether involving borrowed funds or not, are available to Taxpayer for generating income. Taxpayer's indebtedness incurred from its margin borrowing is readily distinguishable from the statute's example of indebtedness that is "inherent" to an organization's exempt purpose, namely, "the indebtedness incurred by a credit union * * * in accepting deposits from its members." 26 U.S.C. § 514(c)(4). Taxpayer need not purchase securities on margin to generate income from trading in securities.

For similar reasons, Taxpayer's securities purchased on margin are not "substantially related" to Taxpayer's exempt purpose of supporting UNH's educational programs. As the Third Circuit noted in Elliot Knitwear, the use of the property itself, not the income generated by the property, must be substantially related to the exempt purpose. Elliot Knitwear, 614 F.2d at 350. Taxpayer's argument ignores that the exception does not apply to property "substantially related" merely by virtue of "the need of the organization for income or funds." While margin-financed securities may be useful to accomplish that exempt purpose by their ability to generate income, their purchase and use is not substantially related to Taxpayer's tax-exempt purpose within the meaning of § 514(b)(1)(A)(i). See id.

Thus, Taxpayer's borrowing to purchase securities is not "inherent" to its exempt purpose; and its margin-financed securities are not "substantially related" to its exempt purpose. Accordingly, the district court correctly held that the exceptions in § 514(b)(1)(A)(1) and § 514(c)(4) do not apply.

III. CONCLUSION

We have reviewed Taxpayer's remaining arguments raised on appeal and find them to be without merit. For the above reasons, we affirm the judgment of the district court.

NOTES AND QUESTIONS

1. *Strike Two.* Another trust established by Henry and Nancy Bartels made essentially the same argument in the Court of Federal Claims, which reached the same result as the Second Circuit. Henry E. & Nancy Horton Bartels Trust ex rel. Cornell University v. United States, 88 Fed. Cl. 105 (2009). In explaining the debt-financed income rules, the court quoted Albert Einstein's famous lament, "The hardest thing in the world to understand is the income tax." 88 Fed. Cl. at 118.

2. *Avoiding § 514.* In many typical situations, § 514 is avoidable because of the numerous exceptions summarized in this Note.

Substantially Related Use. If "substantially all" of the use of the property is "substantially related" to the exercise or performance of the organization's exempt purposes, no part of the property is treated as debt-financed. I.R.C. § 514(b)(1)(A)(i). "Substantially all" is defined by the regulations to be 85 percent or more. The extent to which property is used for a particular purpose is determined on the basis of all the facts, particularly time and space. Treas. Reg. § 1.514(b)–1(b)(1)(ii). "Related use" does not include the need of the organization for income or the use it makes of the profits derived from the property. Treas. Reg. § 1.514(b)–1(b)(1)(i). For example, assume that University owns an office building that is debt-financed. If at least 85 percent of the building is used for university activities, the fact that 15 percent may be rented to outsiders will not cause the property to be debt-financed.

Dual Use. If property is used for both exempt activities and to produce income (but less than 85 percent of the property is substantially related to exempt activities), the property will be considered debt-financed only in proportion to the non-exempt use. I.R.C. § 514(b)(1)(A)(ii). For example, assume that University owns an office building subject to a large mortgage. Two floors are used for university administration; the other two floors are rented to the public. Only the rented portion of the building is debt-financed. Treas. Reg. § 1.514(b)–1(b)(1)(iii) Example (2).

Unrelated Business Income. If the income from the property is subject to the UBIT under the general rules in §§ 511 to 513, it is not debt-financed unless the income results from the sale or exchange of non-inventory property. I.R.C. § 514(b)(1)(B). For example, an exempt organization that provided substantial services in connection with a rental real estate activity, as in the case of an apartment hotel, would be taxable on its rental income even if the property were not debt-financed.

Research Income. In keeping with prior themes, property used in certain research activities is not debt-financed if the income is excludable from UBTI under §§ 512(b)(7), (8) or (9). I.R.C. § 514(b)(1)(C).

Volunteers, Convenience Activities and Thrift Shops. Mirroring the general UBIT exceptions for these activities, property used in a trade or business described in § 513(a)(1) (relating to services performed by volunteers), § 513(a)(2) (activities conducted for the convenience of students, patients, customers, etc.) and § 513(a)(3) (sale of donated merchandise) is not debt-financed. I.R.C. § 514(b)(1)(D).

Neighborhood Land Property. A rather elaborate exception to the definition of debt-financed property applies in cases where an organization acquires income-producing real estate for future use for exempt purposes. Known as the "neighborhood land rule," this exception is available if the following requirements are met:

(1) The real property must be acquired for the principal purpose of using the land but not the improvements in the exempt activities of the organization within ten years after it is acquired. The intent to use the property in an exempt manner may not be abandoned within the 10–year period. I.R.C. § 514(b)(3)(A).

(2) The property must be in the "neighborhood" of other property owned and used by the organization for its exempt purposes. Id. Property is considered in the "neighborhood" if it is contiguous to the other property or would be but for the intervention of a road, street, railroad, stream, etc. Treas. Reg. § 1.514(b)–1(d)(1)(ii).

(3) If the acquired property is not contiguous with the exempt purpose property, it is still treated as "in the neighborhood" if it is within one mile of the property and the facts and circumstances indicate that the acquisition of contiguous property was not feasible. Id.

(4) If structures exist on the property when it is purchased, the organization's intended use requires the structures to be demolished. I.R.C. § 514(b)(3)(C)(i).

The neighborhood land exception applies for no more than ten years after the property is acquired. It applies for years 6–10 only if the organization can establish to the satisfaction of the Service that conversion for use in an exempt activity within ten years after the purchase is "reasonably certain." (Churches have 15 years.) I.R.C. § 514(b)(3)(A), (E). This special burden of proof must be met by a ruling request filed at least 90 days before the end of the fifth year after acquisition. Treas. Reg. § 1.514(b)–1(d)(1)(iii).

If the organization fails the above tests, either because the property is not in the neighborhood or the organization is unable to prove in years 6–10 that it is "reasonably certain" that the land will be converted, the exception nonetheless applies (and is given retroactive effect) if the organization in fact converts the land to exempt use within ten years of its purchase. I.R.C. § 514(b)(3)(B).

Exception for Certain Leveraged Real Property. Section 514(c)(9) contains an important exception for indebtedness incurred with respect to real estate held by qualified pension and profit sharing trusts, certain educational organizations described in § 170(b)(1)(A)(ii) and their affiliated support organizations described in § 509(a)(3), and certain § 501(c)(25) holding companies.[1] Stripped of detail, debt incurred by these "qualified organizations" to acquire or improve any real property is not "acquisition indebtedness" provided that:

(1) The acquisition price is a fixed amount determined as of the date of acquisition or completion of the improvement;

(2) The amount of the debt, or the time for making payment, is not dependent on profits derived from the property;

(3) The property is not leased back to the seller or to any person related to the seller within the § 267(b) attribution rules, except under a "small lease" exception in § 514(c)(9)(G)(i) a qualified organization may lease back to the seller up to 25 percent of the leasable floor space in a building (or complex of buildings) if the lease is on commercially reasonable terms;

(4) In the case of a qualified pension or profit sharing trust, the property is not acquired from or leased back to certain "disqualified persons," as defined in § 4975(e)(2), subject to the "small lease" exception described in (3), above;

(5) Neither the seller, a party related to the seller, nor a disqualified person provides financing in connection with the acquisition or improvement unless the financing is on commercially reasonable terms;

(6) If the real property is held by a partnership, the partnership must meet all the foregoing requirements and, in addition, all the partners must be qualified organizations as defined in § 514(c)(9)(C), and certain other mind boggling requirements must be met. Since those requirements require a mastery of partnership tax, this explanation will go no further.

I.R.C. § 514(c)(9)(B) & (c)(9)(G).

3. *Policy for the Leveraged Real Estate Exception.* It has been suggested that the only reason why the generous exemption in § 514(c)(9) was enacted is that "some people wanted it" in order to achieve greater investment diversification for the nonprofit organizations that they represented! 4A Bittker & Lokken, Federal Taxation of Income, Estates and Gifts ¶ 103.4.3 (3d ed. 2003). When first enacted in 1980, the exception only applied to qualified pension trusts. Their lobbyists argued that they were at a competitive disadvantage relative to banks and insurance companies.

---

1. Section 501(c)(25) title holding companies pass through their income to their shareholders or beneficiaries. These beneficial owners may utilize the § 514(c)(9) exception with respect to amounts passed through to them only if they are qualified pension trusts, or the types of educational organizations described in § 170(b)(1)(A)(ii). I.R.C. § 514(c)(9)(F).

Over the Treasury's objection, the exception was extended to schools (as narrowly defined in § 170(b)(1)(A)(ii)) in 1984, and in 1986 to certain real estate title holding companies. Employee retirement plans at least can make the argument that their income eventually will be taxed to the employees and the beneficiaries. That same rationale does not extend to educational organizations and title holding companies.

The § 514(c)(9) exception includes anti-abuse rules. For example, the purchase price may not be contingent on earnings, leasebacks to the seller are not permitted, and the seller may not finance the acquisition unless the financing is on "commercially reasonable terms." Why should the exception be limited to pension plans, schools, and their title holding companies? Why shouldn't it extend to all § 501(c)(3) organizations and to debt-financed property other than real estate?

4. *For Further Reading.* Suzanne Ross McDowell, Taxation of Unrelated Debt–Financed Income, 34 Exempt Org. Tax Rev. 197 (2001); William H. Weigel, Unrelated Debt–Financed Income: A Retrospective and a Modest Proposal, 50 Tax Law. 625 (1997); Suzanne Ross McDowell, Taxing Leveraged Investments of Charitable Organizations: What is the Rationale? 39 Case West.L.Rev. 705, 712–723 (1988).

PROBLEM

Hospital owns a 20–story building one block from its urban headquarters. Hospital's cost basis in the building is $800,000, and the property is encumbered by a $600,000 mortgage. Consider whether the rentals from the building are subject to the unrelated business income tax in the following alternative situations:

(a) Hospital rents 90 percent of the building to research physicians for purposes related to its cancer treatment facility and 10 percent to commercial tenants for unrelated purposes.

(b) Same as (a), above, except 60 percent of the use is by research physicians and 40 percent by commercial tenants.

(c) Same as (b), above, except Hospital received the building as a contribution from Benefactor, who had owned it for ten years before making the lifetime gift.

(d) Hospital operates the building as a hotel and restaurant.

(e) Hospital operates the building as an apartment house for the general public.

(f) Assume Hospital acquired the building, which previously had been operated as a residential hotel, with the intent of demolishing the structure and using the property for a new medical research facility. It continues to rent space to the general public for seven years while seeking city approval for the project.

(g) Same as (e), above, except that the building is never demolished and Hospital eventually renovates it for exempt purpose use.

(h) Would the result be different in any of the above alternatives if Hospital were a university?

H.   COMPLEX STRUCTURES AND OTHER SPECIAL PROBLEMS

1.   THE USE OF CONTROLLED SUBSIDIARIES

a.   PLANNING CONSIDERATIONS

Some nonprofit organizations choose to conduct commercial activities through a wholly owned for-profit subsidiary. This structure is not motivated solely by tax considerations. The tax-exempt parent may wish to insulate itself from the liabilities of the business activity; use compensation arrangements, fringe benefit plans or accounting methods that are more suitable for a for-profit entity; employ different management structures for its various activities; expand access to investment capital; avoid public disclosure of certain sensitive financial information; and circumvent regulatory obstacles. Tax considerations also may play a role in the decision because dropping the taxable activity into a subsidiary may protect an exempt organization against a challenge to its exempt status. Under current exemption qualification standards, the activities and income of separate controlled entities generally are not taken into account in determining whether an organization's "primary purpose" is a tax-exempt purpose—at least if the parent does not exercise day-to-day operational control over the subsidiary's activities. Exempt organizations thus may conduct substantial unrelated business activities through subsidiaries without risking their exemption even though their favored tax status might be threatened if they conducted the same activities directly. Moreover, taxable subsidiaries are sometimes used to serve as the general partner when an exempt organization engages in a joint business venture with for-profit entrepreneurs and investors. The organization might jeopardize its exemption if it served directly as a general partner in ventures where the partnership activity does not otherwise further the organization's exempt purposes.

Another planning strategy is to use a controlled subsidiary to reduce the overall tax burden resulting from an unrelated business activity. For example, an exempt organization could use a for-profit subsidiary to conduct both an unprofitable exempt activity and a taxable business, enabling losses from the related business to offset profits of the unrelated activity. This helpful allocation of expenses could not be accomplished if all the activities were conducted directly by the exempt organization.

Under current law, the separate identity of a controlled subsidiary is almost always respected by the Service. In this area, the venerable tax doctrine of substance over form gives way to an equally hoary line of cases that respect a corporation's separate existence.[1] The business activities of

---

1. See, e.g., Moline Properties, Inc. v. Commissioner, 319 U.S. 436, 63 S.Ct. 1132, 87 L.Ed. 1499 (1943); National Carbide Corp. v. Commissioner, 336 U.S. 422, 69 S.Ct. 726, 93

the subsidiary ordinarily are not attributed to the parent if (1) the purposes for which the subsidiary is formed are the equivalent of business activities, or (2) the subsidiary subsequently carries on business activities.[2] But if the parent so controls the affairs of the subsidiary that it is merely an instrumentality of the parent, the separate corporate status of the subsidiary can be disregarded. Id. Against this permissive background, the use of complex structures has proliferated, particularly in the health care sector, where a medical center often consists of a tax-exempt parent acting essentially as a holding company for a multitude of taxable and tax-exempt subsidiaries.

During its scrutiny of the UBIT in the late 1980s, the Oversight Subcommittee of the House Ways and Means Committee made several specific proposals to limit the use of controlled subsidiary tax avoidance strategies. A particularly controversial recommendation would have required the activities of an exempt parent and its controlled subsidiaries to be treated as an integrated enterprise in determining whether an organization's primary purpose was a tax-exempt purpose. This and other proposals never were enacted, but the controversy over complex structures lingers as a major policy issue in the law of tax-exempt organizations. The policy issues are discussed further in Section I of this chapter, infra, at pp. 701–702, infra.

For Further Reading. Eugene Steuerle, When Nonprofits Conduct Exempt Activities as Taxable Enterprises, in Urban Institute–Hauser Center Emerging Issues in Philanthropy Brief (Nov. 2000); James J. Mc-Govern, The Use of Taxable Subsidiary Corporations by Public Charities—A Tax Policy Issue for 1988, 41 Tax Notes 1125 (1988); Ellen P. Aprill, Lessons from the UBIT Debate, 45 Tax Notes 1105 (1989), reprinted in 2 Exempt Org. Tax Rev. 687 (1990).

b. PAYMENTS FROM CONTROLLED ORGANIZATIONS

An exempt organization operating an unrelated trade or business might be tempted to segregate its business activities in a wholly owned subsidiary and then convert otherwise taxable business income into excluded income through the payment of interest, rent, royalties or other items that are deductible by the taxable subsidiary and excludable by the exempt parent. For many years, § 512(b)(13) has blocked this opportunity by tracing the passive income back to the subsidiary's business operations and treating it as UBTI to the parent to the extent it was not taxed to the

---

L.Ed. 779 (1949). For a rare case where the Service successfully denied a § 501(c)(3) exemption because of the activities of a for profit subsidiary, see Orange County Agric. Soc'y v. Commissioner, 893 F.2d 529 (2d Cir.1990).

2. See Gen. Couns. Mem. 39326 (Jan. 17, 1985), where an exempt organization was formed to provide hospital management and support activities to nonprofit hospitals. The business became successful and the organization wished to expand its operation to include governmental and educational agencies and for-profit entities. Since the expanded activities likely would be viewed as inconsistent with the organization's charitable purposes, it dropped down the management business to a for-profit subsidiary.

subsidiary. This result is accomplished by including all or part of certain investment income items received from controlled entities in the parent's UBTI.

These special rules apply to interest, annuities, royalties and rent (but not dividends) received by a "controlling organization" from a "controlled entity." I.R.C. § 512(b)(13)(C). In the case of a stock corporation, "control" is defined as ownership (by vote or value) of more than 50 percent of the stock of the corporation. I.R.C. § 512(b)(13)(D)(i)(I). In the case of a partnership, "control" requires ownership of more than 50 percent of the profits or capital interests. I.R.C. § 512(b)(13)(D)(i)(II). In all cases, "control" means ownership of more than 50 percent of the beneficial interests in the entity. I.R.C. § 513(b)(13)(D)(i)(III). These control tests were tightened in 1997 to prevent several avoidance opportunities that were available under prior law.

Constructive ownership rules, borrowed from the corporate tax world (see I.R.C. § 318), apply in determining control. I.R.C. § 512(b)(13)(D)(ii). To illustrate with one simple example, assume Charity owns 100 percent of the stock of Holding Company, which in turns owns 100 percent of the stock of one or more second-tier subsidiaries that conduct unrelated businesses. Charity is treated under § 318 as owning 100 percent of the second-tier subsidiary. Under prior law, which did not provide any indirect ownership rules, Charity would not have been in control of a second-tier subsidiary and thus could have received tax-free payments of rent, interest, royalties, or annuities. This "double drop down" strategy was utilized successfully by several well-known exempt organizations. In a widely publicized case, the National Geographic Society, a § 501(c)(3) organization best known for its National Geographic magazine, created a for-profit holding company that in turn controlled second-tier subsidiaries engaged in various television, film, on-line and map-making businesses. See Marlis L. Carson, Exploring the UBIT's Frontier: A National Geographic Production, 69 Tax Notes 1432 (1995); Constance L. Hays, Seeing Green in a Yellow Border: Quest for Profits Is Shaking a Quiet Realm, N.Y. Times, Aug. 3, 1997, § 3, at 1, 12, 13.

If § 512(b)(13) applies, the taxable portion of the otherwise excluded payments received by the controlling exempt organization is determined under "look-through" rules that seek to preserve one level of tax within the affiliated structure. The rules apply to a "specified payment" (interest, annuity, royalty, or rent) from a controlled entity to the controlling organization. I.R.C. § 512(b)(13)(A), (C). If the controlled entity is itself an exempt organization, the parent must include a specified payment in its gross income to the extent that the payment reduced the net UBTI or increased any net unrelated loss of the exempt subsidiary. I.R.C. § 512(b)(13)(A), (B)(i)(II). If the controlled entity is not tax-exempt, a similar "matching" principle requires the subsidiary first to determine the portion of its taxable income that would have been UBTI if it were an exempt organization with the same exempt purposes as the parent. The parent then includes in its gross income that portion of the payment that reduced the hypothetical UBTI (or increased net unrelated loss) of the controlled entity. I.R.C. § 512(b)(13)(A), (B)(i)(I). In either case, the parent is allowed all deductions directly connected with amounts treated as derived from an unrelated trade or business. I.R.C. § 512(b)(13)(A).

Ever since § 512(b)(13) was tightened, a group of adversely affected nonprofit organizations have been lobbying for a "fair market value" exception that would allow payments of interest, rent, royalties and annuities from controlled subsidiaries to their tax-exempt parents to be excluded from UBTI as long as they were made at "fair market value." Supporters of this proposal argue that § 512(b)(13) tries "to kill an ant with a sledgehammer" and violates rather than enforces basic tax principles. Under this theory, the only problem is when the subsidiary pays an inflated price to the parent for property or services. So viewed, the cure goes beyond the abuse, and the proper remedy is to replace § 512(b)(13) with an arm's length standard similar to § 482, which polices abusive income-shifting transactions between commonly controlled taxpayers in the for-profit sector.

A simple and superficially appealing example illustrates the opposition's point. Assume an exempt organization ("P") has a wholly owned subsidiary ("S") that engages in an unrelated business. P owns a building that is available for rental as office space. If P leases the space to S at market rates, S can deduct the rent which is then taxable to P under § 512(b)(13). If P leases the space to an unrelated third party ("U"), U can deduct the rent, and it will not be taxable to P. The after-tax return from the building is lower, so the argument goes, when P leases space to S as compared to a lease to U, causing exempt organizations to be driven away from contractual relationships with subsidiaries and toward third parties. If P used its control position to cause S to pay above-market rent, *that* would shift UBTI from S to P, but only to the extent of the excess—thus the argument for a fair market value standard.

In the Pension Protection Act of 2006, Congress finally enacted a temporary "fair market value" exception with limited application. Section 512(b)(13)(E) provides that the general rule in § 512(b)(13) shall apply only to the portion of interest, rent, annuity, or royalty payments received or accrued in a taxable year that exceeds the amount of the specified payment that would have been paid or accrued if the payment had been determined under the arms length standard principles used under § 482 to patrol transactions between commonly controlled taxpayers. As a result, if a payment by a controlled subsidiary to its tax-exempt parent exceeds "fair market value," this excess amount generally is included in the parent's unrelated business taxable income. A 20 percent valuation misstatement penalty is imposed on excess payments received by a controlling parent. I.R.C. §§ 512(b)(13)(E)(ii); 6033(h).

As first enacted, the fair market value exception applied to payments made pursuant to a binding written contract in effect on August 17, 2006 (or renewal of such a contract on substantially similar terms) and received or accrued before January 1, 2008. It later was extended to apply to payments received or accrued before January 1, 2010. A further one-year extension was included in a pending "extenders" bill that had not yet been enacted as this book went to press.

NOTES AND QUESTIONS

1. *Policy Concerns.* Is § 512(b)(13) based on a flawed premise? Assume that an exempt organization leases space or licenses its logo to an unrelated third party in exchange for rent or a royalty. These payments may be deducted by the payor and will not be taxable to the exempt organization. Why should the same type of payment, assuming it is not excessive, be included in UBTI if it is received from a controlled entity? Congress historically has rejected these arguments, most recently when it tightened the control test in § 512(b)(13). As explained by the Joint Committee on Taxation staff, one purpose of § 512(b)(13) is to prevent taxable subsidiaries from reducing their otherwise taxable income by borrowing, leasing, or licensing assets from a tax-exempt parent at inflated levels. But even if the payments are not inflated, the provision "is intended to prevent a tax-exempt parent from obtaining what is, in effect, a tax-free return on capital invested in the subsidiary" if the subsidiary is conducting an active business. Staff of Joint Committee on Taxation, General Explanation of Tax Legislation Enacted in 1997, 105th Cong., 1st Sess. 239–240 (1997). Does this explanation make sense?

2. *Fair Market Value Exception?* In evaluating the proposed fair market value exception, consider an exempt organization that is engaged in a profitable unrelated business. If that business is operated directly by the organization, the profits are taxable. Why should the organization be able to eliminate all or part of the taxable income from this same business simply by conducting it through a taxable subsidiary that arranges to make payments of interest, rent and royalties to its tax-exempt parent? Would the fair market value standard be easier or more difficult to administer than the current rule in § 512(b)(13)?

3. *For Further Reading.* Daniel Halperin, The Unrelated Business Income Tax and Payments from Controlled Entities, 109 Tax Notes 1443 (Dec. 12, 2005); Harry L. Gutman, Taxing Transactions Between Exempt Parents and Their Affiliates, 26 Exempt Org. Tax Rev. 45 (1999); Michael Schler, Letter to the Editor: The Implicit Rationale for Section 512(b)(13), 84 Tax Notes 1329 (Aug. 30, 1999); Fred Stokeld, EO Specialists Have Doubts About Section 512(b)(13) Modification, 17 Exempt Org. Tax Rev. 246 (1997).

2.   JOINT VENTURES

a.   INTRODUCTION

Background. In the search for new sources of revenue, some nonprofit organizations have entered into joint ventures with for-profit firms. Proponents of joint ventures contend that they provide a healthy alternative for nonprofits to advance their mission while eliminating total reliance on more traditional sources of funding. They also are said to create economic efficiencies and permit nonprofits to benefit from the managerial expertise of their for-profit partners. See generally Michael I. Sanders, Joint Ventures Involving Tax–Exempt Organizations (3d ed. 2007).

The principal areas in which joint ventures have been employed are health care, low-income housing, education, and the arts. Legal structures vary, as do the roles played by the nonprofit partner, which may be an active manager, passive investor, or some combination. The early joint ventures were structured as general or more often limited partnerships. More recently, limited liability companies have become the vehicle of choice. Some joint ventures are conducted through less formal contractual arrangements such as joint operating and licensing agreements. Joint ventures raise a variety of legal and tax issues, including: (1) the appropriate legal structure for the venture, (2) whether the nonprofit partner is adhering to its fiduciary duty, (3) the impact of the venture on the nonprofit partner's tax-exempt status, and (4) to what extent the net income from a joint venture is subject to the unrelated business income tax. Structures attracting the most attention to date are "whole charity" (almost always hospital) joint ventures and the far more prevalent ancillary joint ventures. In a "whole charity" joint venture, all or virtually all of a charity's assets are transferred to an LLC or limited partnership which usually is managed by an affiliate of the for-profit partner. The charity typically becomes a grantmaking entity, but for tax purposes it is deemed to be engaged as well in the activities of the partnership or LLC. The joint venture is said to be "whole" because it is the substantial or sole activity of the exempt organization, apart from grantmaking.

In an ancillary joint venture, the exempt organization's participation is not its sole activity. For example, in a hospital ancillary joint venture, the activity could be a core function (e.g., the anesthesiology department), or relatively insubstantial (e.g., a dialysis unit), or a support function (e.g., a laundry). In a university setting, an ancillary joint venture might be a technology alliance, an on-campus hotel, an agreement between the education department with a video conferencing facility, or a link between the law or business school and a for-profit publisher or continuing education provider.

A successful joint venture can be an effective means for a nonprofit organization to raise private capital and earn valuable unrestricted revenue. Many joint ventures are justified as directly advancing the nonprofit partner's core mission, or at least "contributing importantly" to exempt purposes. It is reasonable to assume that the motives of the for-profit partners are market oriented. Most for-profit joint venturers in health care, education, and housing seek to profit from the nonprofit partner's reputation, name recognition, intellectual capital, and "fuzzy good" image, or to take advantage of targeted tax benefits such as low-income housing credits. Some examples, gathered from press releases, news reports, private rulings, and shop talk, offer a glimpse at the variety of contemporary joint ventures.

In the interest of brevity, some important details and nuances have been omitted.

In June 2006, Baptist Health System of East Tennessee announced that it had signed a letter of intent to form a joint venture with for-profit Triad Hospitals to operate Baptist's four hospitals. Triad will have 80 percent ownership and Baptist will retain 20 percent; governance will be shared 50:50; physicians will have at least 50 percent board representation and "be given the immediate opportunity to invest in the new joint venture." The infusion of capital will permit Baptist to immediately pay off $210 million in debt. According to the chair of Baptist's board, the hospitals will "maintain the Baptist faith-based mission and commitment to charity care at the current level."[1] This is what we will come to know as a whole hospital joint venture.

Community Neighborhood Housing, Inc. ("CNH") is a § 501(c)(3) charity dedicated to providing low-income housing in compliance with IRS safe harbor guidelines. To obtain the necessary capital and efficiently utilize federal low-income housing tax credits allocated to it by its home state, CNH enters into a limited partnership with For–Profit Syndicators ("FPS"), a pool of for-profit investors, to own and operate a low-income housing complex.[2] CNH will serve as the sole general partner, and FPS will be a limited partner, providing 99 percent of the equity capital for the project. FPS's participation is motivated by the ability to obtain low-income housing tax credits. The partnership agreement provides that CNH will have operational control of the project, which must be operated in a manner that is consistent with CNH's charitable purposes. In keeping with standard industry practice, the agreement obligates CNH to provide various indemnifications and guarantees to FPS, such as an indemnification for any loss or damage attributable to environmental hazards and guarantees to advance funds if necessary for completion of construction or to cover operating deficits.

In 2004, the University of Delaware and for-profit Shaner Hotel Group formed Blue Hen Hotel, LLC, to develop and operate a 126–room hotel on university land near the central campus. The university owns a 75 percent interest and Shaner, which will manage the hotel as a Court-yard by Marriott, owns 25 percent. Students in the university's hotel, restaurant and institutional management school work at the hotel, which is adjacent to the university's 40,000 square foot and highly profitable conference center.[3] This is an ancillary joint venture.

---

1. Press Release, June 14, 2006, available at http://www.baptistoneword.org/whatsnew/ newsreleases/newsDetail.asp?id=284.

2. This is a generic example of a typical low-income housing joint venture, adapted from a letter to the IRS from two leading practitioners.

3. Maureen Milford, A University Tries Its Hand at a For–Profit Hotel, N.Y. Times, Aug. 18, 2005, at 5. The university's web site reports that students are involved in all aspects of the hotel, from the front office to accounts and engineering, sales and marketing—"students will have total immersion in the hotel industry" in "a working laboratory." See http://www.udel.

In 2006, Showtime Networks and the Smithsonian Institution announced an agreement to develop Smithsonian Networks, a cable television channel to produce and broadcast a cable television channel, Smithsonian on Demand, with programming to be drawn from the Smithsonian's collections and curators. Under the agreement, commercial filmmakers who wish to make "more than incidental" use of Smithsonian archives or curators must receive approval from this venture. According to news reports, Showtime agreed to pay the Smithsonian a flat fee for the rights plus additional fees based on the number of subscribers to the service and will pay the cost of producing roughly 100 hours of programming a year.[4] In response to queries from Congress and others, the Smithsonian stated that the agreement will not restrict public access to Smithsonian resources, only commercial *use* of those resources.[5] The Smithsonian also entered to an agreement with HarperCollins to publish "Smithsonian Books" in areas such as science, American history, and design.[6]

In 1998, the University of California at Berkeley and Novartis, a multinational pharmaceutical company, entered into a five-year agreement under which Novartis gave UC Berkeley $25 million to fund basic research at a department in the College of National Resources. Berkeley granted Novartis first refusal rights on approximately one-third of the department's discoveries and two of five seats on the departmental research committee, which determines how the money will be spent. The agreement gave the faculty access to Novartis's proprietary genomic data base if they agreed to sign a confidentiality provision requiring them to keep the information secret.[7] The UC–Novartis joint venture was contractual and did not involve the creation of a separate entity.

In 2003, the National Wildlife Federation and Home Depot entered into a multifaceted agreement under which Home Depot stores offered selected products (e.g., jugs of Pro's Choice Wild Bird Mix and bird feeders designed to keep out bird-eating snakes) bearing the Federation's logo. The Federation reportedly will earn a portion of the

edu/hotel. Since the University of Delaware, as a public university, is not obligated to file a Form 990 information return, it is impossible to determine if the hotel partnership gives rise to any unrelated business income. It is fair to assume, however, that the business is treated as a "related" activity because of the student involvement.

4. Edward Wyatt, Smithsonian–Showtime Deal Raises Concerns, N.Y. Times, March 31, 2006, at A11.

5. Oversight Hearing on the Smithsonian Business Ventures: Hearing Before House Comm. on House Administration, 109th Cong. (2006) (testimony of Lawrence M. Small), available at http://cha.house.gov/hearings/Testimony.aspx?TID=765.

6. See Harper Collins press release, Feb. 10, 2005, available at http://www.harpercollins.com/press/display.asp?ACT=showid&ID=321.

7. The Berkeley–Novartis deal was widely reported. See, e.g., Eyal Press & Jennifer Washburn, The Kept University, Atlantic Monthly (March 1, 2000). In July 2005, UC Berkeley entered into an alliance with Yahoo to operate a research lab near the Berkeley campus. Verne Kopytoff, Yahoo Cements UC Partnership, S.F. Chronicle, July 15, 2005, at C1.

proceeds from the sale of products and an annual fee for its part in other joint promotions that Home Depot uses to persuade customers of its commitment to the environment. The Federation also received a grant from Home Depot's corporate foundation.[8] Home Depot has entered into a similar marketing alliance with the American Association of Retired Persons, a § 501(c)(4) organization, to sell products specifically aimed at older adults.[9] These are examples of licensing, marketing, and corporate sponsorship agreements.

The IRS's Early Hostility: The Per Se Prohibition. The IRS initial position was that a charity could not qualify for § 501(c)(3) exemption if it served as a general partner in a joint venture with for-profit limited partners. The rationale was that this type of alliance was a vehicle to share profits with private individuals and, under partnership law, a charity's service as a general partner created an inherent conflict between its fiduciary duty to maximize profit for the for-profit partners and adherence to its tax-exempt mission. The IRS also was concerned that the unlimited liability of the nonprofit general partner exposed its charitable assets while protecting the private investors from liability. See, e.g., Gen. Couns. Mem. 36293 (May 30, 1975).

In Plumstead Theatre Society, Inc. v. Commissioner,[10] the Tax Court rejected the Service's per se prohibition. The court held that a nonprofit theater company did not lose its exemption because, as one of a variety of planned activities to promote the arts, it served as a general partner in a limited partnership to co-produce the play, "First Monday in October," at the (nonprofit) John F. Kennedy Center in Washington, D.C. Plumstead contributed a portion of its intellectual property rights in the play in exchange for a 36.5 percent profit and loss interest in the partnership. The limited partners, including several individuals and a for-profit motion picture company, contributed $100,000 cash for the remaining 63.5 percent. Without extensively discussing the joint venture aspect, the Tax Court held that the partnership did not cause Plumstead to be operated for a private rather than a public purpose. Critical findings were that the purpose of the joint venture was to raise capital to further Plumstead's exempt purposes and the dealings between the parties were at arm's length. Other favorable factors were: (1) Plumstead, as general partner, controlled the venture; (2) the joint venture was only one of many different activities in which Plumstead planned to engage (and thus was what we now would call an "ancillary" joint venture); (3) Plumstead was not obligated to return any

---

8. See Elizabeth Schwinn, Constructing a Marketing Deal: Home Depot Venture Could be a Sign of the Future, Chron. Philanthropy, Aug. 7, 2003, at 24.

9. See, e.g., Eric Dash, AARP Agrees to Endorse Home Depot Products, N.Y. Times, Dec. 2, 2004, at C10. AARP, a § 501(c)(4) organization, has numerous other marketing deals for products ranging from elder-friendly cell phones and luggage to health insurance and even motorcycle insurance. See Claudia H. Deutsch, AARP Wants You (to Buy Its Line of Products), N.Y. Times, Oct. 28, 2005, at C1.

10. 74 T.C. 1324 (1980), aff'd per curiam, 675 F.2d 244 (9th Cir. 1982).

capital contribution made by the limited partners from its own funds; and (4) none of the limited partners was an officer or director of Plumstead.[11]

The Two–Part Test: Charitability and Private Benefit. After *Plumstead*, the IRS reconsidered its position, concluding that a charity's participation as a general partner in a joint venture with for-profit limited partners would not automatically result in loss of exemption. Rather, joint ventures would be evaluated by asking two questions: (1) does the charity's participation in the joint venture further its exempt purposes (the "charitable purpose" test), and (2) does the legal structure of the joint venture permit the charity to operate exclusively for exempt purposes and not for an impermissible private benefit (the "private benefit" test). See, e.g., Gen. Couns. Mem. 39005 (June 28, 1983). If the answer to either question was "no," exemption would be denied.

Applying this two-part test, the IRS began to scrutinize a variety of transactions, most of which were low-income housing partnerships or ancillary joint ventures in which a health care provider joined with a for-profit firm or private investors to carry out a particular function, such as magnetic resonance imaging, surgery, physical therapy or dialysis. In most of these cases, the charitable purpose test was met without great difficulty. The greater hurdle was the private benefit limitation, which was grounded in the IRS's concern that joint ventures created a potential conflict of interest between maximizing investment return for the private investors and the organization's exempt mission. The early private rulings required partnership agreements to include sufficient safeguards and protections. Several later rulings appeared to more permissive, looking not so much to structural safeguards as to the presence or absence of direct or indirect economic benefits to the limited partners, as evidenced by disproportionate allocations of profits and losses, nominal capital contributions by the limited partners, and the charity's assumption of all the risk or liability for partnership losses. See, e.g., Gen. Couns. Mem. 39732 (May 19, 1988).

The two-part test was criticized as more rigid than it needed to be to protect the integrity of § 501(c)(3). One complaint was that partnerships are separate legal entities and, like corporate subsidiaries, they should not in themselves jeopardize an organization's exemption absent other negative factors, such as inurement of private gain. A second was that the commercial nature of a partnership should not adversely affect qualification for exemption if that same business, if conducted directly by the organization without taxable partners, would not have been a problem because, for example, it was consistent with or substantially related to the organization's exempt purposes. And even if the business was unrelated, that only should expose the charity to the unrelated business income tax, not loss of exemption.

The Control Test. The emergence of the whole hospital joint venture caused the IRS to refine its position. Whole hospital joint ventures were a response to rapid market forces in the health care sector, the decline of the

---

11. 74 T.C. at 1333–1334.

traditional community hospital, and a shift from "fee-for-service" to "managed care" financing mechanisms. These pressures forced many nonprofit hospitals to form alliances, first with private physicians and clinics and later with larger for-profit hospital systems. The most extreme step was the conversion transaction, in which a nonprofit hospital was acquired by a for-profit firm. See Chapter 2E, supra, at p. 113. Whole hospital joint ventures were viewed as a more palatable alternative for nonprofit hospitals who needed to affiliate with a larger system in order to survive but balked at an outright sale or conversion. The stated goal in most cases was to preserve, albeit in altered form, the cherished community benefit and the accompanying tax exemption under § 501(c)(3). See Chapter 5C3b, supra, at pp. 323–327. Whole hospital joint ventures were promoted as a win/win transaction that would stem the tide of conversions. Proponents argued that the economies of scale and greater access to more cost-efficient managed care contracts was critical to survival of the nonprofit hospital and its charitable mission. Charitability would be preserved by a shared governance structure and provisions in the joint venture agreement requiring adherence to the § 501(c)(3) community benefit standard through such factors as an open emergency room, open medical staff, community board, nondiscriminatory treatment of Medicare and Medicaid patients, and (possibly) some charity care, research and teaching activities.

The for-profit firm also expected to come out a winner—why else would it enter into such a transaction if it did not expect to make a profit? Significantly, the prototype transaction enabled the for-profit firm to obtain day-to-day control over an entire hospital for a capital contribution equal to not more than half (and usually less) than its true fair market value. The desired result was increased market share and all the accompanying economic advantages and growth opportunities.

The response of the IRS and the courts to these developments and the IRS's position on ancillary joint ventures are surveyed in the materials that follow.

b.   WHOLE HOSPITAL JOINT VENTURES: THE CONTROL TEST

Revenue Ruling 98–15

1998–1 Cum. Bull. 718.

ISSUE

Whether, under the facts described below, an organization that operates an acute care hospital continues to qualify for exemption from federal income tax as an organization described in § 501(c)(3) of the Internal Revenue Code when it forms a limited liability company (LLC) with a for-profit corporation and then contributes its hospital and all of its other operating assets to the LLC, which then operates the hospital.

FACTS

Situation 1

A is a nonprofit corporation that owns and operates an acute care hospital. A has been recognized as exempt from federal income tax under § 501(a) as an organization described in § 501(c)(3) and as other than a private foundation as defined in § 509(a) because it is described in § 170(b)(1)(A)(iii). B is a for-profit corporation that owns and operates a number of hospitals.

A concludes that it could better serve its community if it obtained additional funding. B is interested in providing financing for A's hospital, provided it earns a reasonable rate of return. A and B form a limited liability company, C. A contributes all of its operating assets, including its hospital to C. B also contributes assets to C. In return, A and B receive ownership interests in C proportional and equal in value to their respective contributions.

C's Articles of Organization and Operating Agreement ("governing documents") provide that C is to be managed by a governing board consisting of three individuals chosen by A and two individuals chosen by B. A intends to appoint community leaders who have experience with hospital matters, but who are not on the hospital staff and do not otherwise engage in business transactions with the hospital.

The governing documents further provide that they may only be amended with the approval of both owners and that a majority of three board members must approve certain major decisions relating to C's operation, including decisions relating to any of the following topics: A. C's annual capital and operating budgets; B. Distributions of C's earnings; C. Selection of key executives; D. Acquisition or disposition of health care facilities; E. Contracts in excess of $x per year; F. Changes to the types of services offered by the hospital; and G. Renewal or termination of management agreements.

The governing documents require that C operate any hospital it owns in a manner that furthers charitable purposes by promoting health for a broad cross section of its community. The governing documents explicitly provide that the duty of the members of the governing board to operate C in a manner that furthers charitable purposes by promoting health for a broad cross section of the community overrides any duty they may have to operate C for the financial benefit of its owners. Accordingly, in the event of a conflict between operation in accordance with the community benefit standard and any duty to maximize profits, the members of the governing board are to satisfy the community benefit standard without regard to the consequences for maximizing profitability.

The governing documents further provide that all returns of capital and distributions of earnings made to owners of C shall be proportional to their ownership interests in C. The terms of the governing documents are legal, binding, and enforceable under applicable state law.

C enters into a management agreement with a management company that is unrelated to A or B to provide day-to-day management services to C. The management agreement is for a five-year period, and the agreement is renewable for additional five-year periods by mutual consent. The management company will be paid a management fee for its services based on C's gross revenues. The terms and conditions of the management agreement, including the fee structure and the contract term, are reasonable and comparable to what other management firms receive for similar services at similarly situated hospitals. C may terminate the agreement for cause.

None of the officers, directors, or key employees of A who were involved in making the decision to form C were promised employment or any other inducement by C or B and their related entities if the transaction were approved. None of A's officers, directors, or key employees have any interest, including any interest through attribution determined in accordance with the principles of § 318, in B or any of its related entities.

Pursuant to § 301.7701–3(b) of the Procedure and Administrative Regulations, C will be treated as a partnership for federal income tax purposes.

A intends to use any distributions it receives from C to fund grants to support activities that promote the health of A's community and to help the indigent obtain health care. Substantially all of A's grantmaking will be funded by distributions from C. A's projected grantmaking program and its participation as an owner of C will constitute A's only activities.

Situation 2

D is a nonprofit corporation that owns and operates an acute care hospital. D has been recognized as exempt from federal income tax under § 501(a) as an organization described in § 501(c)(3) and as other than a private foundation as defined in § 509(a) because it is described in § 170(b)(1)(iii). E is a for-profit hospital corporation that owns and operates a number of hospitals and provides management services to several hospitals that it does not own.

D concludes that it could better serve its community if it obtained additional funding. E is interested in providing financing for D's hospital, provided it earns a reasonable rate of return. D and E form a limited liability company, F. D contributes all of its operating assets, including its hospital to F. E also contributes assets to F. In return, D and E receive ownership interests proportional and equal in value to their respective contributions.

F's Articles of Organization and Operating Agreement ("governing documents") provide that F is to be managed by a governing board consisting of three individuals chosen by D and three individuals chosen by E. D intends to appoint community leaders who have experience with hospital matters, but who are not on the hospital staff and do not otherwise engage in business transactions with the hospital.

The governing documents further provide that they may only be amended with the approval of both owners and that a majority of board members must approve certain major decisions relating to F's operation, including decisions relating to any of the following topics: A. F's annual capital and operating budgets; B. Distributions of F's earnings over a required minimum level of distributions set forth in the Operating Agreement; C. Unusually large contracts; and D. Selection of key executives.

F's governing documents provide that F's purpose is to construct, develop, own, manage, operate, and take other action in connection with operating the health care facilities it owns and engage in other health care-related activities. The governing documents further provide that all returns of capital and distributions of earnings made to owners of F shall be proportional to their ownership interests in F.

F enters into a management agreement with a wholly-owned subsidiary of E to provide day-to-day management services to F. The management agreement is for a five-year period, and the agreement is renewable for additional five-year periods at the discretion of E's subsidiary. F may terminate the agreement only for cause. E's subsidiary will be paid a management fee for its services based on gross revenues. The terms and conditions of the management agreement, including the fee structure and the contract term other than the renewal terms, are reasonable and comparable to what other management firms receive for similar services at similarly situated hospitals.

As part of the agreement to form F, D agrees to approve the selection of two individuals to serve as F's chief executive officer and chief financial officer. These individuals have previously worked for E in hospital management and have business expertise. They will work with the management company to oversee F's day-to-day management. Their compensation is comparable to what comparable executives are paid at similarly situated hospitals.

Pursuant to § 301.7701–3(b). F will be treated as a partnership for federal tax income purposes.

D intends to use any distributions it receives from F to fund grants to support activities that promote the health of D's community and to help the indigent obtain health care. Substantially all of D's grantmaking will be funded by distributions from F. D's projected grantmaking program and its participation as an owner of F will constitute D's only activities.

LAW

Section 501(c)(3) provides, in part, for the exemption from federal income tax of corporations organized and operated exclusively for charitable, scientific, or educational purposes, provided no part of the organization's net earnings inures to the benefit of any private shareholder or individual.

Section 1.501(c)(3)–1(c)(1) of the Income Tax Regulations provides that an organization will be regarded as operated exclusively for one or more exempt purposes only if it engages primarily in activities which accomplish one or more of such exempt purposes specified in § 501(c)(3). An organization will not be so regarded if more than an insubstantial part of its activities is not in furtherance of an exempt purpose. In Better Business Bureau of Washington, D.C. v. United States, 326 U.S. 279, 283 (1945), the Court stated that "the presence of a single . . . [non-exempt] purpose, if substantial in nature, will destroy the exemption regardless of the number or importance of truly . . . [exempt] purposes."

Section 1.501(c)(3)–1(d)(1)(ii) provides that an organization is not organized or operated exclusively for exempt purposes unless it serves a public rather than a private interest. It further states that "to meet the requirement of this subdivision, it is necessary for an organization to establish that it is not organized and operated for the benefit of private interests. . . ."

Section 1.501(c)(3)–1(d)(2) provides that the term "charitable" is used in § 501(c)(3) in its generally accepted legal sense. The promotion of health has long been recognized as a charitable purpose. See Restatement (Second) of Trusts, §§ 368, 372 (1959); 4A Austin W. Scott and William F. Fratcher, The Law of Trusts 368, 372 (4th ed. 1989). However, not every activity that promotes health supports tax exemption under § 501(c)(3). For example, selling prescription pharmaceuticals certainly promotes health, but pharmacies cannot qualify for recognition of exemption under § 501(c)(3) on that basis alone. Federation Pharmacy Services, Inc. v. Commissioner, 72 T.C. 687 (1979), aff'd, 625 F.2d 804 (8th Cir.1980) ("Federation Pharmacy"). Furthermore, "an institution for the promotion of health is not a charitable institution if it is privately owned and is run for the profit of the owners." 4A Austin W. Scott and William F. Fratcher, The Law of Trusts § 372.1 (4th ed. 1989). See also Restatement (Second) of Trusts, § 376 (1959). This principle applies to hospitals and other health care organizations. As the Tax Court stated, "[w]hile the diagnosis and cure of disease are indeed purposes that may furnish the foundation for characterizing the activity as 'charitable,' something more is required." * * *

In evaluating whether a nonprofit hospital qualifies as an organization described in § 501(c)(3), Rev. Rul. 69–545, 1969–2 C.B. 117, compares two hospitals. The first hospital discussed is controlled by a board of trustees composed of independent civic leaders. In addition, the hospital maintains an open medical staff, with privileges available to all qualified physicians; it operates a full-time emergency room open to all regardless of ability to pay; and it otherwise admits all patients able to pay (either themselves, or through third party payers such as private health insurance or government programs such as Medicare). In contrast, the second hospital is controlled by physicians who have a substantial economic interest in the hospital. This hospital restricts the number of physicians admitted to the medical staff, enters into favorable rental agreements with the individuals who control the hospital, and limits emergency room and hospital admission substantially to the patients of the physicians who control the hospital. Rev. Rul. 69–545 notes that in considering whether a nonprofit hospital is operated to serve a private benefit, the Service will weigh all the relevant facts and circumstances in each case, including the use and control of the hospital. The revenue ruling concludes that the first hospital continues to qualify as an organization described in § 501(c)(3) and the second hospital does not because it is operated for the private benefit of the physicians who control the hospital.

Section 509(a) provides that the term "private foundation" means a domestic or foreign organization described in § 501(c)(3) other than an organization described in § 509(a)(1), (2), (3), or (4). The organizations described in § 509(a)(1) include those described in § 170(b)(1)(A)(iii). An organization is described in § 170(b)(1)(A)(iii) if its principal purpose is to provide medical or hospital care.

Section 512(c) provides that an exempt organization that is a member of a partnership conducting an unrelated trade or business with respect to the exempt organization must include its share of the partnership income and deductions attributable to that business (subject to the exceptions, additions, and limitations in § 512(b)) in computing its unrelated business income. * * *

* * *

In Plumstead Theatre Society, Inc. v. Commissioner, 74 T.C. 1324 (1980), aff'd, 675 F.2d 244 (9th Cir.1982) ("Plumstead"), the Tax Court held that a charitable organization's participation as a general partner in a limited partnership did not jeopardize its exempt status. The organization co-produced a play as one of its charitable activities. Prior to the opening of the play, the organization encountered financial difficulties in raising its share of costs. In order to meet its funding obligations, the organization formed a limited partnership in which it served as general partner, and two individuals and a for-profit corporation were the limited partners. One of the significant factors supporting the Tax Court's holding was its finding that the limited partners had no control over the organization's operations.

In Broadway Theatre League of Lynchburg, Virginia, Inc. v. U.S., 293 F.Supp. 346 (W.D.Va.1968) ("Broadway Theatre League"), the court held that an organization that promoted an interest in theatrical arts did not jeopardize its exempt status when it hired a booking organization to arrange for a series of theatrical performances, promote the series and sell season tickets to the series because the contract was for a reasonable term and provided for reasonable compensation and the organization retained ultimate authority over the activities being managed.

In Housing Pioneers v. Commissioner, 65 T.C.M. (CCH) 2191 (1993), aff'd, 49 F.3d 1395 (9th Cir.1995), amended 58 F.3d 401 (9th Cir.1995) ("Housing Pioneers"), the Tax Court concluded that an organization did not qualify as a § 501(c)(3) organization because its activities performed as co-general partner in for-profit limited partnerships substantially furthered a non-exempt purpose, and serving that purpose caused the organization to serve private interests. The organization entered into partnerships as a one percent co-general partner of existing limited partnerships for the purpose of splitting the tax benefits with the for-profit partners. Under the management agreement, the organization's authority as co-general partner was narrowly circumscribed. It had no management responsibilities and could describe only a vague charitable function of surveying tenant needs.

In est of Hawaii v. Commissioner, 71 T.C. 1067 (1979), aff'd in unpublished opinion 647 F.2d 170 (9th Cir.1981) ("est of Hawaii"), several for-profit est organizations exerted significant indirect control over est of Hawaii, a non-profit entity, through contractual arrangements. The Tax Court concluded that the for-profits were able to use the non-profit as an "instrument" to further their for-profit purposes. Neither the fact that the for-profits lacked structural control over the organization nor the fact that amounts paid to the for-profit organizations under the contracts were reasonable affected the court's conclusion. Consequently, est of Hawaii did not qualify as an organization described in § 501(c)(3).

In Harding Hospital, Inc. v. United States, 505 F.2d 1068 (6th Cir. 1974) ("Harding"), a non-profit hospital with an independent board of directors executed a contract with a medical partnership composed of seven physicians. The contract gave the physicians control over care of the hospital's patients and the stream of income generated by the patients while also guaranteeing the physicians thousands of dollars in payment for various supervisory activities. The court held that the benefits derived from the contract constituted sufficient private benefit to preclude exemption.

ANALYSIS

For federal income tax purposes, the activities of a partnership are often considered to be the activities of the partners. Aggregate treatment is also consistent with the treatment of partnerships for purpose of the unrelated business income tax under § 512(c). * * * In light of the aggregate principle * * * reflected in § 512(c), the aggregate approach also applies for purposes of the operational test set forth in § 1.501(c)(3)–1(c). Thus, the activities of an LLC treated as a partnership for federal income tax purposes are considered to be the activities of a nonprofit organization that is an owner of the LLC when evaluating whether the nonprofit organization is operated exclusively for exempt purposes within the meaning of § 501(c)(3).

A § 501(c)(3) organization may form and participate in a partnership, including an LLC treated as a partnership for federal income tax purposes, and meet the operational test if participation in the partnership furthers a charitable purpose, and the partnership arrangement permits the exempt organization to act exclusively in furtherance of its exempt purpose and only incidentally for the benefit of the for-profit partners. See Plumstead and Housing Pioneers. Similarly, a § 501(c)(3) organization may enter into a management contract with a private party giving that party authority to conduct activities on behalf of the organization and direct the use of the organization's assets provided that the organization retains ultimate authority over the assets and activities being managed and the terms and conditions of the contract are reasonable, including reasonable compensation and a reasonable term. See Broadway Theatre League. However, if a private party is allowed to control or use the non-profit organization's activities or assets for the benefit of the private party, and the benefit is not incidental to the accomplishment of exempt purposes, the organization will fail to be organized and operated exclusively for exempt purposes. See est of Hawaii; Harding; § 1.501(c)(3)–1(c)(1); and § 1.501(c)(3)–1(d)(1)(ii).

Situation 1

After A and B form C, and A contributes all of its operating assets to C, A's activities will consist of the health care services it provides through C and any grantmaking activities it can conduct using income distributed to C. A will receive an interest in C equal in value to the assets it contributes to C, and A's and B's returns from C will be proportional to their respective investments in C. The governing documents of C commit C to providing health care services for the benefit of the community as a whole and to give charitable purposes priority over maximizing profits for C's owners. Furthermore, through A's appointment of members of the community familiar with the hospital to C's board, the board's structure, which gives A's appointees voting control, and the specifically enumerated powers of the board over changes in activities, disposition of assets, and renewal of the management agreement. A can ensure that the assets it owns through C and the activities it conducts through C are used primarily to further exempt purposes. Thus, A can ensure that the benefit to B and other private parties, like the management company, will be incidental to the accomplishment of charitable purposes. Additionally, the terms and conditions of the management contract, including the terms for renewal and termination are reasonable. Finally, A's grants are intended to support education and research and give resources to help provide health care to the indigent. All of these facts and circumstances establish that, which A participates in forming C and contributes all of its operating assets to C, and C operates in accordance with its governing documents. A will be furthering charitable purposes and continue to be operated exclusively for exempt purposes.

Because A's grantmaking activity will be contingent upon receiving distributions from C, A's principal activity will continue to be the provision of hospital care. As long as A's principal activity remains the provision of hospital care. A will not be classified as a private foundation in accordance with § 509(a)(1) as an organization described in § 170(b)(1)(A)(iii).

Situation 2

When D and E form F, and D contributes its assets to F, D will be engaged in activities that consist of the health care services it provides through F and any grantmaking activities it can conduct using income distributed by F. However, unlike A, D will not be engaging primarily in activities that further an exempt purpose. "While the diagnosis and cure of disease are indeed purposes that may furnish the foundation for characterizing the activity as 'charitable,' something more is required." Sonora, 46 T.C. at 525–526. See also Federation Pharmacy; Sound Health; and Geisinger. In the absence of a binding obligation in F's governing documents for F to serve charitable purposes or otherwise provide its services to the community as a whole. F will be able to deny care to segments of the community, such as the indigent. Because D will share control of F with E, D will not be able to initiate programs within F to serve new health needs within the community without the agreement of at least one governing board member appointed by E. As a business enterprise, E will not necessarily give priority to the health needs of the community over the consequences for F's profits. The primary source of information for board members appointed by D will be the chief executives, who have a prior relationship with E and the management company, which is a subsidiary of E. The management company itself will have broad discretion over F's activities and assets that may not always be under the board's supervision. For example, the management company is permitted to enter into all but "unusually large" contracts without board approval. The management company may also unilaterally renew the management agreement. Based on all these facts and circumstances, D cannot establish that the activities it conducts through F further exempt purposes. "[I]n order for an organization to qualify for exemption under § 501(c)(3) the organization must 'establish' that it is neither organized nor operated for the 'benefit of private interests.' " Federation Pharmacy, 625 F.2d at 809. Consequently, the benefit to E resulting from the activities D conducts through F will not be incidental to the furtherance of an exempt purpose. Thus, D will fail the operational test when it forms F, contributes its operating assets to F, and then serves as an owner to F.

HOLDING

A will continue to qualify as an organization described in § 501(c)(3) when it forms C and contributes all of its operating assets to C because A has established that A will be operating exclusively for a charitable purpose and only incidentally for the purpose of benefiting the private interests of B. Furthermore, A's principal activity will continue to be the provision of hospital care when C begins operations. Thus, A will be an organization described in § 170(b)(1)(A)(iii) and thus, will not be classified as a private foundation in accordance with § 509(a)(1), as long as hospital care remains its principal activity.

D will violate the requirements to be an organization described in § 501(c)(3) when it forms F and contributes all of its operating assets to F because D has failed to establish that it will be operated exclusively for exempt purposes.

NOTES

1. *Judicial Endorsement of the Control Test.* Revenue Ruling 98–15 was the IRS's first published ruling on the tax consequences of whole hospital joint ventures. The ruling focuses primarily on the level of control retained by the tax-exempt partner and provides examples at the good and

bad ends of the spectrum. It has been criticized for offering little guidance on the more prevalent middle ground situations.

The control test has been endorsed by the few courts to consider it. See St. David's Health Care System, Inc. v. United States, 349 F.3d 232 (5th Cir. 2003); Redlands Surgical Services v. Commissioner, 113 T.C. 47 (1999), aff'd per curiam, 242 F.3d 904 (9th Cir. 2001). The leading precedent involved the IRS's revocation of the tax exemption of St. David's Health Care System, which for many years owned and operated a hospital and related health care facilities in Austin, Texas. In the mid–1990s, St. David's encountered financial difficulties and concluded that it should consolidate with another health care organization. After failed attempts to join forces with a city hospital and another tax-exempt health care system, it entered into a limited partnership with an affiliate of Columbia/HCA Healthcare ("HCA"), a nationwide for-profit corporation. HCA already had a presence in the Austin suburbs and was interested in expanding into the urban market. St. David's contributed all of its assets to the newly formed partnership in exchange for a 45.9 percent interest, and HCA contributed its Austin-area facilities in exchange for 54.1 percent. The partnership hired an HCA subsidiary to provide day-to-day management, and an HCA affiliate served as the managing general partner. Each partner had the power to appoint six members of the partnership's 12–person governing board. The partnership agreement contained certain safeguards to preserve the charitable nature of the facility (e.g., the manager was required to abide by the community benefit standard), and St. David's had the unilateral legal right to dissolve the venture if the partnership did not act in accordance with the recognized community benefit standard for tax exemption.

When its exemption was revoked, St. David's paid the disputed tax and sued for a refund in federal district court—a wise choice of forum. After pausing to characterize the operational test as "a horrible amalgamation of negatives arranged like an inside joke prompting laughter only from seasoned and sadistic bureaucrats,"[3] the district judge granted St. Davids' motion for summary judgment, finding that the hospital had "substantially more control than the for-profit partner" despite its lack of formal voting control. In response to the Service's argument that St. David's failed to provide sufficient charity care, the court found that the hospital met the community benefit standard by providing *emergency* care regardless of ability to pay.[4]

On appeal, the IRS emphasized that St. David's had ceded control over the partnership and failed to meet the community benefit standard by lacking the requisite "community board." St. David's viewed the critical question as one of function, not control, and emphasized that its partnership provided free emergency room care and was open to all persons, regardless of ability to pay (the IRS disputed this contention), and used its

---

3. St. David's Health Care System, Inc. v. United States, 2002–1 USTC ¶ 50,452 (W.D.Tex., June 7, 2002).

4. Id.

share of profits to fund research grants and other health-related initiatives. The Fifth Circuit, purporting to apply the IRS's control test, scrutinized the partnership documents to determine if St. David's had ceded control. Because it was "uncertain," it held that genuine issues of material fact required it to vacate the summary judgment in favor of St. David's and remand the case to the district court for further proceedings.

The Fifth Circuit's opinion included a long list of observations and conclusions, which offer some guidance in structuring a successful whole activity joint venture. Favorable factors included: (1) the for-profit manager was required to operate the facilities in compliance with the community benefit standard; (2) the parties had equal representation on the governing board, giving St. David's veto power; (3) St. David's had the power to appoint the initial CEO, subject to approval of HCA's board members, and either party unilaterally could remove the CEO; and (4) St. David's had the power to dissolve the partnership if it received legal advice from a mutually acceptable attorney that its participation in the partnership would hinder its tax-exempt status. Unfavorable factors were: (1) because St. David's did not control a majority of the governing board, it had veto power but no power to initiate action without HCA's consent; and its authority to appoint the board chair was insufficient because the chair was unable to initiate actions without a majority of the full board; (2) because the hospital manager was a for-profit subsidiary of HCA, it was "not apparent" that the manager would be inclined to serve charitable interests and more likely that it would prioritize the noncharitable interests of its for-profit parent; (3) St. David's primary means to enforce adherence to the community benefit standard was to take legal action, which would be time-consuming and expensive; it was unrealistic to expect St. David's to resort to litigation every time a decision was made that conflicted with that standard; and (4) although St. David's had 50 percent board representation, the board's power was limited in scope and did not extend to day-to-day operational decisions; as a practical matter, St. David's could not overrule a management decision that fell outside the range of the Board's authority.

And then there were the "uncertainties" that dictated the Fifth Circuit's decision to send the case back to the trial court. The court was unsure whether St. David's ever would be willing to exercise its option to cancel the for-profit manager's contract without HCA's consent or, if it did terminate the current manager, whether a new manager would prioritize charitable purposes. Moreover, although St. David's had the power to appoint and terminate the CEO, there were instances cited by the IRS where the CEO failed to comply with the partnership agreement (e.g., no reports of charity care were furnished until IRS audit commenced), suggesting that St. David's was unable to enforce a provision of the partnership agreement specifically dealing with charity care. Finally, the court surmised that it was unlikely St. David's would exercise its dissolution power even if the partnership strayed from its charitable mission because the partnership agreement included a non-compete clause providing that, in the event of dissolution, neither partner can "compete" in the Austin area for two years. Since St. David's only served Austin, its facilities would in effect cease to exist if the partnership were dissolved.

On remand, the case was tried by a jury, and St. David's emerged victorious. The judge's instructions were based on the IRS's control test and requested the jury to find whether or not St. David's retained sufficient control over the operations of the partnership to ensure they were conducted primarily for charitable purposes and only incidentally for the private benefit of HCA/Columbia. St. David's introduced evidence on the control issue that reportedly was not effectively challenged by the government, and it also is said to have presented undisputed testimony that the partnership's hospitals provided significant charity care in their emergency rooms. The jury rendered a verdict in favor of St. David's. Shortly thereafter, the government and St. David's reached an out-of-court settlement under which St. David's retained its tax exemption. See Fred Stokeld, St. David's Settles With IRS, Retains Tax Exempt Status, 45 Exempt Org. Tax Rev. 13 (July 2004).

2. *For Further Reading.* John D. Colombo, Private Benefit, Joint Ventures, and the Death of Healthcare as an Exempt Purpose, 34 J.Health Law 505 (2001).

c. ANCILLARY JOINT VENTURES

The typical structure of an ancillary joint venture was described by the IRS in its 1998 training manual for exempt organization specialists:

> A hospital ancillary joint venture refers to those joint venture arrangements where an exempt organization that operates a hospital or other health care facility owns an interest in a joint venture with a for-profit entity to operate a particular service. The exempt organization, usually part of a health care system, owns and operates a hospital as well as other health care facilities or services, such as ambulatory surgery center, MRI, or home health care services. It transfers the assets of the health care facility or service to the joint venture; or contributes funds to establish the ancillary service. The for-profit partner contributes cash equal to the fair market value of the exempt organization facility transferred to the joint venture. The joint venture owns and operates the health care facility or service. The exempt organization still owns and operates the hospital facility.

> Thus, unlike the whole hospital joint venture structure, or the hospital subsidiary joint venture arrangement, the exempt organization does not contribute all of its operating assets nor is the participation by the exempt organization in the joint venture its sole activity. In the hospital ancillary joint venture, the activity conducted by the exempt organization through the joint venture arrangement is generally not the sole activity of the exempt organization, and it may not be a substantial part of the organization's activities. Instead, the exempt partner will continue to operate its hospital and other health care facilities and services.

Mary Jo Salins, Judy Kindell & Marvin Friedlander, Whole Hospital Joint Ventures, FY 1999 IRS Exempt Organizations Professional Education Technical Instruction Program 1 (1998).

Revenue Ruling 98–15 and the whole hospital joint ventures cases did not shed much light on the tax treatment of ancillary joint ventures and left tax advisors uncertain as to the relevance of a nonprofit partner's control in determining if such joint ventures jeopardized an organization's exemption. The IRS studied these issues for several years and, in 2004, it issued the published ruling which follows.

Revenue Ruling 2004–51

2004–1 Cum.Bull. 974.

ISSUES

1.   Whether, under the facts described below, an organization continues to qualify for exemption from federal income tax as an organization described in § 501(c)(3) of the Internal Revenue Code when it contributes a portion of its assets to and conducts a portion of its activities through a limited liability company (LLC) formed with a for-profit corporation.

2.   Whether, under the same facts, the organization is subject to unrelated business income tax under § 511 on its distributive share of the LLC's income.

FACTS

M is a university that has been recognized as exempt from federal income tax under § 501(a) as an organization described in § 501(c)(3). As a part of its educational programs, M offers summer seminars to enhance the skill level of elementary and secondary school teachers.

To expand the reach of its teacher training seminars, M forms a domestic LLC, L, with O, a company that specializes in conducting interactive video training programs. L's Articles of Organization and Operating Agreement ("governing documents") provide that the sole purpose of L is to offer teacher training seminars at off-campus locations using interactive video technology. M and O each hold a 50 percent ownership interest in L, which is proportionate to the value of their respective capital contributions to L. The governing documents provide that all returns of capital, allocations and distributions shall be made in proportion to the members' respective ownership interests.

The governing documents provide that L will be managed by a governing board comprised of three directors chosen by M and three directors chosen by O. Under the governing documents, L will arrange and conduct all aspects of the video teacher training seminars, including advertising, enrolling participants, arranging for the necessary facilities, distributing the course materials and broadcasting the seminars to various locations. L's teacher training seminars will cover the same content covered in the

seminars M conducts on M's campus. However, school teachers will participate through an interactive video link at various locations rather than in
person. The governing documents grant M the exclusive right to approve
the curriculum, training materials, and instructors, and to determine the
standards for successful completion of the seminars. The governing documents grant O the exclusive right to select the locations where participants
can receive a video link to the seminars and to approve other personnel
(such as camera operators) necessary to conduct the video teacher training
seminars. All other actions require the mutual consent of M and O.

The governing documents require that the terms of all contracts and
transactions entered into by L with M, O and any other parties be at arm's
length and that all contract and transaction prices be at fair market value
determined by reference to the prices for comparable goods or services. The
governing documents limit L's activities to conducting the teacher training
seminars and also require that L not engage in any activities that would
jeopardize M's exemption under § 501(c)(3). L does in fact operate in
accordance with the governing documents in all respects.

M's participation in L will be an insubstantial part of M's activities
within the meaning of § 501(c)(3) and § 1.501(c)(3)–1(c)(1) of the Income
Tax Regulations.

Because L does not elect under § 301.7701–3(c) of the Procedure and
Administration Regulations to be classified as an association, L is classified
as a partnership for federal tax purposes pursuant to § 301.7701–3(b).

LAW

Exemption under § 501(c)(3)

Section 501(c)(3) provides, in part, for the exemption from federal
income tax of corporations organized and operated exclusively for charitable, scientific, or educational purposes, provided no part of the organization's net earnings inures to the benefit of any private shareholder or
individual.

Section 1.501(c)(3)–1(c)(1) provides that an organization will be regarded as operated exclusively for one or more exempt purposes only if it
engages primarily in activities that accomplish one or more of the exempt
purposes specified in § 501(c)(3). Activities that do not further exempt
purposes must be an insubstantial part of the organization's activities. In
Better Business Bureau of Washington, D.C. v. United States, 326 U.S. 279,
283 (1945), the Supreme Court held that "the presence of a single . . . [non-
exempt] purpose, if substantial in nature, will destroy the exemption
regardless of the number or importance of truly . . . [exempt] purposes."

Section 1.501(c)(3)–1(d)(1)(ii) provides that an organization is not
organized or operated exclusively for exempt purposes unless it serves a
public rather than a private interest. To meet this requirement, an organization must "establish that it is not organized or operated for the benefit of
private interests. . . ."

Section 1.501(c)(3)–1(d)(2) defines the term "charitable" as used in § 501(c)(3) as including the advancement of education.

Section 1.501(c)(3)–1(d)(3)(i) provides, in part, that the term "educational" as used in § 501(c)(3) relates to the instruction or training of the individual for the purpose of improving or developing his capabilities.

Section 1.501(c)(3)–1(d)(3)(ii) provides examples of educational organizations including a college that has a regularly scheduled curriculum, a regular faculty, and a regularly enrolled body of students in attendance at a place where the educational activities are regularly carried on and an organization that presents a course of instruction by means of correspondence or through the utilization of television or radio.

Joint Ventures

Rev. Rul. 98–15, 1998–1 C.B. 718, provides that for purposes of determining exemption under § 501(c)(3), the activities of a partnership, including an LLC treated as a partnership for federal tax purposes, are considered to be the activities of the partners. A § 501(c)(3) organization may form and participate in a partnership and meet the operational test if 1) participation in the partnership furthers a charitable purpose, and 2) the partnership arrangement permits the exempt organization to act exclusively in furtherance of its exempt purpose and only incidentally for the benefit of the for-profit partners.

Redlands Surgical Services, 113 T.C. 47, 92–93 (1999), aff'd 242 F.3d 904 (9th Cir. 2001), provides that a nonprofit organization may form partnerships, or enter into contracts, with private parties to further its charitable purposes on mutually beneficial terms, "so long as the nonprofit organization does not thereby impermissibly serve private interests." The Tax Court held that the operational standard is not satisfied merely by establishing "whatever charitable benefits [the partnership] may produce," finding that the nonprofit partner lacked "formal or informal control sufficient to ensure furtherance of charitable purposes." Affirming the Tax Court, the Ninth Circuit held that ceding "effective control" of partnership activities impermissibly serves private interests. 242 F.3d at 904.

St. David's Health Care System v. United States, 349 F.3d 232, 236–237 (5th Cir. 2003), held that the determination of whether a nonprofit organization that enters into a partnership operates exclusively for exempt purposes is not limited to "whether the partnership provides some (or even an extensive amount of) charitable services." The nonprofit partner also must have the "capacity to ensure that the partnership's operations further charitable purposes." Id. at 243. "[T]he non-profit should lose its tax-exempt status if it cedes control to the for-profit entity." Id. at 239.

Tax on Unrelated Business Income

Section 511(a), in part, provides for the imposition of tax on the unrelated business taxable income (as defined in § 512) of organizations described in § 501(c)(3).

Section 512(a)(1) defines "unrelated business taxable income" as the gross income derived by any organization from any unrelated trade or business (as defined in § 513) regularly carried on by it less the deductions allowed, both computed with the modifications provided in § 512(b).

Section 512(c) provides that, if a trade or business regularly carried on by a partnership of which an organization is a member is an unrelated trade or business with respect to the organization, in computing its unrelated business taxable income, the organization shall, subject to the exceptions, additions, and limitations contained in § 512(b), include its share (whether or not distributed) of the gross income of the partnership from the unrelated trade or business and its share of the partnership deductions directly connected with the gross income.

Section 513(a) defines the term "unrelated trade or business" as any trade or business the conduct of which is not substantially related (aside from the need of the organization for income or funds or the use it makes of the profits derived) to the exercise or performance by the organization of its charitable, educational, or other purpose or function constituting the basis for its exemption under § 501.

Section 1.513–1(d)(2) provides that a trade or business is "related" to an organization's exempt purposes only if the conduct of the business activities has a causal relationship to the achievement of exempt purposes (other than through the production of income). A trade or business is "substantially related" for purposes of § 513, only if the causal relationship is a substantial one. Thus, to be substantially related, the activity "must contribute importantly to the accomplishment of [exempt] purposes." Section 1.513–1(d)(2). Section 513, therefore, focuses on "the manner in which the exempt organization operates its business" to determine whether it contributes importantly to the organization's charitable or educational function. United States v. American College of Physicians, 475 U.S. 834, 849 (1986).

ANALYSIS

L is a partnership for federal tax purposes. Therefore, L's activities are attributed to M for purposes of determining both whether M operates exclusively for educational purposes and therefore continues to qualify for exemption under § 501(c)(3) and whether M has engaged in an unrelated trade or business and therefore may be subject to the unrelated business income tax on its distributive share of L's income.

The activities M is treated as conducting through L are not a substantial part of M's activities within the meaning of § 501(c)(3) and § 1.501(c)(3)–1(c)(1). Therefore, based on all the facts and circumstances, M' s participation in L, taken alone, will not affect M's continued qualification for exemption as an organization described in § 501(c)(3).

Although M continues to qualify as an exempt organization described in § 501(c)(3), M may be subject to unrelated business income tax under

§ 511 if L conducts a trade or business that is not substantially related to the exercise or performance of M's exempt purposes or functions.

The facts establish that M's activities conducted through L constitute a trade or business that is substantially related to the exercise and performance of M's exempt purposes and functions. Even though L arranges and conducts all aspects of the teacher training seminars, M alone approves the curriculum, training materials and instructors, and determines the standards for successfully completing the seminars. All contracts and transactions entered into by L are at arm's length and for fair market value, M's and O's ownership interests in L are proportional to their respective capital contributions, and all returns of capital, allocations and distributions by L are proportional to M's and O's ownership interests. The fact that O selects the locations and approves the other personnel necessary to conduct the seminars does not affect whether the seminars are substantially related to M's educational purposes. Moreover, the teacher training seminars L conducts using interactive video technology cover the same content as the seminars M conducts on M's campus. Finally, L's activities have expanded the reach of M's teacher training seminars, for example, to individuals who otherwise could not be accommodated at, or conveniently travel to, M's campus. Therefore, the manner in which L conducts the teacher training seminars contributes importantly to the accomplishment of M's educational purposes, and the activities of L are substantially related to M's educational purposes. Section 1.513–1(d)(2). Accordingly, based on all the facts and circumstances, M is not subject to unrelated business income tax under § 511 on its distributive share of L's income.

HOLDINGS

1.   M continues to qualify for exemption under § 501(c)(3) when it contributes a portion of its assets to and conducts a portion of its activities through L.

2.   M is not subject to unrelated business income tax under § 511 on its distributive share of L's income.

PROBLEM

Sturdley University, long recognized as tax-exempt under § 501(c)(3), is a private, nonprofit university with an undergraduate college and professional schools in law, business and medicine. To further its educational mission and raise revenue, Sturdley's business school is exploring whether to enter into a joint venture with ExecutiveEd.com ("Dot Com"), a for-profit provider of on line education to business executives. Under the proposal, the Sturdley School of Business will develop the courses and contribute its name, logo and the services of selected faculty. Dot Com will contribute cash, and a Dot Com subsidiary will manage the venture for a fee under a five-year renewable contract. All operational decisions, including marketing and fee structure, will be made by Dot Com. The venture will be structured as a limited liability company ("LLC") under state law.

In exchange for their respective contributions, Sturdley and Dot Com each will take back a 50 percent LLC interest and have equal representation on the LLC's governing board. Disputes will be resolved through binding arbitration. Income, expenses and distributions will be allocated equally.

Will this joint venture have an adverse effect on Sturdley's tax-exempt status? What factors are relevant in making this determination? Accepting the IRS's current position on joint ventures, what safeguards or other steps would you suggest to protect Sturdley's tax exemption?

3. PARTNERSHIPS AND S CORPORATIONS

Internal Revenue Code: § 512(c)(1), (e).

Treasury Regulations: § 1.512(b)–1(h)(2).

Service Bolt & Nut Co. v. Commissioner

United States Tax Court, 1982.
78 T.C. 812.

OPINION

■ NIMS, JUDGE: * * *.

[The primary issue in this case was whether a tax-exempt profit-sharing trust realized "unrelated business taxable income" in its capacity as a limited partner in various partnerships that were engaged in a wholesale fastener distribution business. The same issue is raised with respect to other § 501(c) organizations which realize income from limited partnership investments. Eds.]

Notwithstanding their general income tax exemption under section 501(a), section 511 imposes a tax on profit-sharing trusts qualified under section 401(a) to the extent such trusts receive "unrelated business taxable income." The primary dispute in this case is whether petitioners received any unrelated business taxable income within the meaning of section 511 as a result of holding limited partnership interests in various wholesale fastener distributing partnerships.

Petitioners argue that a limited partnership interest is a passive investment that cannot, unlike a general partnership interest, produce unrelated business taxable income.

Respondent, on the other hand, contends that a limited partnership interest is no different from a general partnership interest for purposes of the section 511 tax: Both can produce unrelated business taxable income.

The concept of and tax imposed upon unrelated business income of exempt organizations derives essentially from Supplement U of the 1939 Code. In its latter codification, this concept appears at sections 511 through 515. Section 511 imposes a tax on the unrelated business taxable income (as defined in section 512) of certain tax-exempt organizations. As regards the treatment of income from partnership interests held by exempt organizations, the relevant provisions of the 1954 Code are sections 512(c) and 513(b). Section 512(c) provides:

(c) SPECIAL RULES APPLICABLE TO PARTNERSHIPS.—If a trade or business regularly carried on by a partnership of which an organization is a member is an unrelated trade or business with respect to such organization, such organization in computing its unrelated business taxable income shall, subject to the exceptions, additions, and limitations contained in subsection (b), include its share (whether or not distributed) of the gross income of the partnership from such unrelated trade or business and its share of the partnership deductions directly connected with such gross income. If the taxable year of the organization is different from that of the partnership, the amounts to be so included or deducted in computing the unrelated business taxable income shall be based upon the income and deductions of the partnership for any taxable year of the partnership ending within or with the taxable year of the organization.

Section 513(b) provides in relevant part:

(b) SPECIAL RULE FOR TRUSTS.—The term "unrelated trade or business" means, in the case of—

* * *

(2) a trust described in section 401(a), or section 501(c)(17), which is exempt from tax under section 501(a); any trade or business regularly carried on by such trust or by a partnership of which it is a member.

Petitioners contend that these references to partnerships in sections 512(c) and 513(b) apply only in the case of general partnership interests held by exempt organizations and not to limited partnership interests. They argue that limited partnership income is analogous to such passive-income items as dividends, interest, royalties, and some rents. Congress, petitioners argue, could not have meant to make taxable the income from a passive investment such as a limited partnership interest, where the exempt organization could not actively manage the business in a fashion to result in unfair competition. We disagree.

In examining the application of a particular statute, our first reference must be to the words of that statute. Here, the provisions in question (secs. 512(c) and 513 (b)) impose a tax on an exempt organization's distributive share of partnership gross income (less allocable deductions) attributable to a partnership's regularly carrying on a trade or business unrelated to the exempt organization's purpose. The only statutory requirement for the imposition of this tax is that the organization be a "member" of such a partnership. Petitioners would limit the meaning of the word "member" to "general partner." There is nothing in the language or structure of these sections to demand or even justify reading into them petitioners' narrower requirement. * * *

Additionally, the legislative history of these sections does not support petitioners' narrow reading. In discussing the application of the Supplement U tax in the case of partnership interests, both the House and Senate reports from 1950 contain the following example: For example, if an exempt educational institution is a silent partner in a partnership which runs a barrel factory and such partnership also holds stock in a pottery manufacturing corporation, the exempt organization would include in its unrelated business income its share of the barrel factory income, but not its proportionate share of any dividends received by the partnership from the pottery corporation. * * * While, as petitioners point out, a "silent partner" is not necessarily the same thing as a "limited partner," we think the above example clearly demonstrates Congress' intent to include exempt organizations' distributive shares of partnership income within the Supplement U tax, regardless of whether, as partners, they behaved in an active or passive manner with regard to the management of the partnership's unrelated trades or businesses.

Indeed, it would have been unlikely for Congress to have thought otherwise. One problem which Congress was addressing in the Supplement U tax was the availability of pools of tax-exempt income which gave previously nontaxable trades or businesses unfair competitive advantages over their taxable counterparts. In the case of a partnership, these pools of income can be created when a partner who otherwise would have to withdraw some of his partnership income each year to pay the tax on his distributive share of partnership income does not have to withdraw any cash from the partnership because he has no income tax to pay. Whether the tax-exempt partner actively manages the underlying unrelated partnership business or not is thus irrelevant to the issue of whether the partnership as a whole has an unfair competitive advantage from the accumulation of an unwithdrawn pool of tax-exempt income.

* * *

In short, we decline to strain the construction of the word "member" in sections 512(c) and 513(b) and defeat the intent of Congress. Therefore, we hold that an exempt trust which is a limited partner may receive unrelated business taxable income (within the meaning of section 512) through a limited partnership upon which the trust is taxable under section 511. Since it is undisputed that the wholesale fastener partnerships in which petitioners were members engaged in the type of activity which falls within the section 513(a) definition of unrelated trade or business, respondent's determinations of petitioners' liabilities for the tax imposed by section 511 must be sustained.

* * *

NOTES AND QUESTIONS

1. *Policy Considerations.* What is the policy of § 512(c)? Exempt organizations generally are not taxed on income derived from passive investments. If an exempt organization chooses to invest in an active business as a limited partner, why is it subject to the UBIT when it would

not be taxed on dividends and interest from other types of investments? The answer lies in the need to ensure that income from an unrelated business is subject to at least one level of tax. If the business is conducted by a "C corporation," its net income will be subject to the corporate income tax, and thus earnings distributed as dividends to tax-exempt investors need not be taxed again as they would be if they were received by taxable shareholders. Partnerships and limited liability companies (which are taxed as partnerships), by contrast, are not subject to tax but rather pass through their income and deductions to their partners or members. Section 512(c) treats any unrelated business income of a partnership as if it were realized directly by its tax-exempt partners, even if they do not actively participate in management of the enterprise. This rule is faithful to the pass-through principles of partnership taxation and precludes an easy end run around the policy of the UBIT.

2. *Investment Partnerships*. Many wealthy exempt organizations, such as private foundations or universities with large endowments, engage in a variety of sophisticated investment strategies, often through investment pools known generically as "hedge funds." For the nontax aspects of nontraditional investments, see Chapter 3C5c, supra, at pp. 213–216. These investment pools are unregulated in the sense that, unlike mutual funds, they are exempt from most regulation under federal and state securities and investment company laws. To qualify for this special status, access to private investment partnerships is limited to wealthy individuals and large institutional investors who meet certain tests qualifying them as "sophisticated" under federal securities laws.

Virtually all domestic investment pools are structured as limited partnerships or limited liability companies in order to avoid the corporate income tax. The specific investment strategies of these funds vary widely, ranging from the classic hedge fund that seeks to minimize risk by holding both long and short market positions, to real estate and venture capital funds, and to more exotic investments in risk and event arbitrage transactions, debt of financially distressed companies, foreign currency, and harvestable timber.

If an exempt organization is a limited partner in an investment partnership, its share of dividends, interest, rent, capital gains and other forms of passive investment income is not included in UBTI because the reach of § 512(c) is limited to active business income. If a hedge fund uses leverage, however, a tax-exempt partner likely will be taxable on at least part of its otherwise excluded investment income because of the unrelated debt-financed property rules in § 514. To avoid these tax problems, large investment pools catering to tax-exempt investors typically incorporate offshore "blocker" funds, often in the Cayman Islands. For example, a Cayman Islands Exempted Company can be structured to avoid corporate income tax either in the United States or its offshore domicile. Since the fund is a corporation, its net income does not pass-through to the tax-exempt investors, and problems with unrelated debt-financed income are avoided. Distributions by offshore funds to their investors are ordinarily treated as dividends excluded from UBTI by § 512(b).

If debt-financed real estate is held by a partnership, any tax-exempt partners that are "qualified organizations" (e.g., pension trusts and schools) may qualify for the § 514(c)(9)(A) exception from acquisition indebtedness (see Section G of this chapter, supra, at pp. 661–662), but only if certain additional requirements are met. I.R.C. § 514(c)(9)(B)(vi), (E); 168(h)(6). Very generally, the Congressional agenda is to prevent partnerships consisting of both taxable and tax-exempt partners from making strategic allocations to realize tax benefits that could not be achieved using a more direct route. Understanding the details requires a mastery of the arcane world of partnership allocations, a topic mercifully beyond the scope of this Note.

3. *Limited Liability Companies.* Limited liability companies are generally taxed like partnerships for federal tax purposes unless they elect to be taxed as corporations. As a result, they have limited utility for tax-exempt organizations conducting a substantial unrelated trade or business because, like partnerships but unlike C corporations, the business activities of an LLC are attributed to its tax-exempt owner. It follows that LLCs are not effective vehicles to protect against loss of tax exemption or avoid the UBIT. In some situations, however, the attribution of activities is a good thing—for example, it may permit a nonprofit hospital that contributes its operating assets to a joint venture with a for-profit partner to retain its public charity status, assuming the co-owned facility conforms to the community benefit standard and the nonprofit partner does not cede control.

Single-member LLCs have become more widely used by nonprofit organizations for non-tax reasons—primarily to insulate their tax-exempt parent from liability by holding real property (an alternative to using a § 501(c)(2) title holding company) or to conduct high-risk "substantially related" activities, such as clinical trials of pharmaceuticals, that could expose the tax-exempt parent to liability. For tax purposes, single-member LLCs are treated as "disregarded entities" unless they elect to be taxed as C corporations and thus they have no need to apply for separate tax-exempt status.

4. *S Corporations.* Like partnerships and limited liability companies, S corporations are generally not subject to federal income tax at the entity level. The income, deductions, and other tax items of an S corporation pass through to its shareholders in proportion to their ownership interests. Unlike partnerships and LLCs, S corporations are subject to strict eligibility limitations. For example, an S corporation may have no more than 100 shareholders; its shareholders are limited to individuals, estates, certain types of trusts, and a few specialized categories; and it may only have one class of stock. See I.R.C. §§ 1361 et seq. Over the years, however, Congress has been relaxing these limitations, and since 1998 S corporations may have exempt organizations as shareholders. I.R.C. § 1361(c)(6).

In liberalizing the S corporation eligibility requirements, Congress took steps to preclude tax-exempt shareholders from circumventing the UBIT. To preserve at least one level of tax, § 512(e)(1) provides that an exempt organization's interest in an S corporation "shall be treated as an interest in an unrelated trade or business." As a result, the organization's share of the corporation's income, loss, deduction, and other tax items, as well as any gain or loss on a disposition of S corporation stock, is taken into account in computing the exempt organization's UBTI. The items passing through to a tax-exempt shareholder's UBTI include its pro rata share of the corporation's dividends, interest, rents, and capital gains. These passive investment income items would be excluded from UBTI if they were realized through a partnership or LLC. S corporations raise a host of other unique UBIT issues that must be considered by an organization in evaluating whether it should purchase or accept a gift of S corporation stock. For a good discussion of this largely uncharted area, see Christopher R. Hoyt, Subchapter S Stock Owned by Tax–Exempt Organizations: Solutions to Legal Issues, 22 Exempt Org. Tax Rev. 25 (1998).

4.   SOCIAL CLUBS

Internal Revenue Code: § 512(a)(3).

The UBIT has a much broader reach in the case of § 501(c)(7) social clubs and a handful of other exempt organizations. A social club's UBTI includes all of its gross income other than "exempt function income," less directly related deductions. I.R.C. § 512(a)(3)(A). This rule has the effect of taxing social clubs on their investment income. The theory is that the club's members would be individually taxable on their dividends and interest and must pay for social and recreational activities with after-tax income. They should not be able to obtain a more favorable result by pooling their investments in an exempt entity that uses the resulting income to support the members' recreational pursuits.

"Exempt function income" includes dues, fees and charges paid by the club's members for goods, facilities and services that are related to the club's exempt functions. It also includes amounts set aside for charitable purposes, such as where a college fraternity or sorority sets aside funds for scholarships. I.R.C. § 512(a)(3)(B). Finally, gain from the sale of assets used in the performance of a social club's exempt functions (e.g., the sale of a club house) are not taxable to the extent that the proceeds are reinvested in assets used for a comparable function within a specified period of time. I.R.C. § 512(a)(3)(D).

Computation of the unrelated business taxable income of a social club requires an allocation of business expenses and depreciation between exempt function income and taxable receipts. One common strategy used by social clubs to reduce their bottom line UBTI is to deduct net losses from nonmember activities, such as the sale of food and beverages, against taxable investment income. Some clubs claimed these deductions even when the nonmember business was not carried out with a profit motive.

This issue worked its way up to the Supreme Court, which held in a 6–3 opinion that social clubs may offset losses incurred from nonmember activities against investment income only if the nonmember sales were motivated by an intent to make a profit. Portland Golf Club v. Commissioner, 497 U.S. 154, 110 S.Ct. 2780 (1990). Profit motive, for this purpose, was interpreted by the Court to mean an intent to generate receipts in excess of costs.

I. Proposals for Reform

As previewed earlier in this chapter, the scope and application of the unrelated business income tax attracted increasing scrutiny in the 1980's, culminating in extensive hearings by the Subcommittee on Oversight of the House Ways and Means Committee in 1987 and 1988. In mid–1988, the Subcommittee circulated a draft report and recommendations, which were quickly leaked to the press. See Subcommittee on Oversight of the House Committee on Ways and Means, 100th Cong., 2d Sess., Draft Report Describing Recommendations on the Unrelated Business Income Tax (Comm. Print 1988) (hereinafter "Draft Report"). By 1989, the momentum had shifted, and UBIT reform began moving to the back burner, where it remained during the budget-driven tax legislative gridlock that typified much of the 1990's. The Draft Report nonetheless remains "on the shelf" and is poised to serve as the focal point for discussion if and when the UBIT debate is resurrected.

After flirting with some alternative formulations (e.g., a "directly related" test), the Oversight Subcommittee recommended the retention of the conceptual framework of the UBIT, including the "substantially related" test. It observed, however, that the test had proven to be vague, difficult to administer and unevenly enforced. Draft Report at 29–34. The Subcommittee concluded that further clarification was needed to identify particular income-producing activities that were fundamentally not "related" in nature. The excerpt below sets forth some of the Subcommittee's specific recommendations to supplant the substantially related test with respect to the certain categories of revenue-producing activities.

Subcommittee on Oversight of House Ways and Means Committee, Draft Report Describing Recommendations on the Unrelated Business Income Tax

100th Cong., 2d Sess. (Comm. Print 1988).

* * *

b. Gift shop, bookstore, catalog and mail order activities.

Recommendation: Income derived from the sale of goods through gift shop, bookstore, catalog, and mail order activities (whether the sale takes place on or off the premises of the exempt organization) should be treated as income derived from an unrelated trade or business, subject to the exceptions described below. For this purpose, the term sale of goods includes rental of goods (e.g., the rental of video cassettes by a bookstore or gift shop). However, the sale or rental of medical equipment and devices, or pharmaceutical drugs and goods, is governed by the rule described at c., below.

[The Report then carved out several limited exceptions. For all exempt organizations other than schools and hospitals, the UBIT would not apply to: (1) sales of "mementos" (e.g., T-shirts, tote bags, etc., with the organization's logo) costing not more than $15, (2) sales of reproductions by museums, libraries, historical societies, or other organizations maintaining collections if the reproductions cost no more than $50 and the object reproduced was part of the organization's own collection or exhibits, and (3) items, whatever their cost, that are "primarily educational" and whose content relates to the exempt purposes of the organization (e.g., income derived by a museum of modern sculpture from a bookstore sale of a general art history textbook, but items of a "primarily decorative or functional" nature would be taxable). In the case of hospital gift shops, the UBIT would not apply to income from the sale of goods used primarily by or for patients, such as flowers, candy, toiletries, reading materials and pajamas, whether or not the items were purchased for a patient. In the case of educational institutions, the UBIT would not apply to income from the sale to students of goods with a retail price of $15 or less or to income from the sale of higher priced goods to students that furthered the institution's educational programs and "are not common consumer goods." Books and computer software would be exempted, but not appliances, cameras, televisions, VCRs and recreational sports equipment. Special rules were provided for the sale of computers by an educational institution. Sales to students would be exempted if the student submitted a statement signed by a faculty member that the computer was required for the student's course work, but income from the sale of computers to students would be taxable "to the extent that the number of otherwise exempt sales made by the institution during a year exceeds half the total number of full-time students attending the institution during that year." Eds.]

c. Activities related to medical equipment and devices, pharmaceutical drugs and goods, and laboratory testing

Recommendation: Income derived from the sale or rental of medical equipment and devices (including hearing aids, portable X-ray units, and oxygen tanks), the sale of pharmaceutical drugs and goods, and the performance of laboratory testing should be treated as income derived from an unrelated trade or business, subject to the following two exceptions.

First, the UBIT should not apply to income from the sale or rental of such items to patients of the organization deriving the income (e.g., to patients of the hospital), or from the performance of laboratory testing for such patients. For this purpose, the term patient has the same meaning as used for UBIT purposes under present law. * * *

Second, the UBIT should not apply to income from the sale or rental of such an item to, or the providing of laboratory testing for, persons who are not patients of the organization if such item or service is not otherwise available in the immediate geographic area.

d.   Fitness, exercise, and similar health-promotion activities

Recommendation: Income derived by a charitable organization from fitness, exercise, and similar health-promotion activities (such as classes or programs in aerobics, weightlifting, racquetball, or swimming) should be treated as income derived from an unrelated trade or business unless the facility at which the activity is conducted independently serves a primarily charitable purpose. The required charitable purpose could be demonstrated by various factors, such as service to low-income, elderly, or handicapped individuals, youth, or by providing service to the community as a whole.

The present-law treatment of "special-fee" activities should be retained. For example, if members of a section 501(c)(3) community recreational organization could use the organization's weightlifting or exercise room only by paying an additional charge that precludes participation by the general community, income from the special-fee activity would be unrelated business income.

e.   Travel and tour service activities

Recommendation: Income derived from travel and tour activities should be treated as income derived from an unrelated trade or business, subject to the exception described below. For purposes of this rule, the term travel and tour activities would not include local transportation activities of a charitable nature, such as the transportation of needy individuals to medical facilities for treatment of the transportation of elderly individuals to senior citizen centers for meals or to pharmacies to purchase medicine, but would include such activities as the transportation of individuals to tourist attractions or vacation spots.

Under the exception, the UBIT should not apply (1) to income derived by an educational institution from travel or tour activities conducted for the benefit of its students or faculty members ("students") if the travel or tour is part of the degree program curriculum of the institution, or (2) to a de minimis amount of income attributable to participation in such travel or tours by individuals who are neither its students nor faculty members ("nonstudents"). For this purpose, de minimis should be defined as income attributable to five percent or less of the available participation in the qualified travel or tour. For example, if a university arranges a bus trip with seating for 40 persons to an art museum in connection with its art history degree program, sells 38 tickets to students, and makes the two seats not purchased by students available to other individuals, then income from the two nonstudents would not be subject to UBIT. If students purchased only 35 tickets and the remaining five seats were sold to nonstudents, the income attributable to three of the five nonstudent tickets would be treated as unrelated business income.

f.   Ancillary food sale or service activities

Recommendation: Income derived from food sale or service activities that are ancillary to an organization's exempt purpose should be treated as income derived from an unrelated trade or business, subject to the exception described below. For example, if a museum operates a sidewalk cafe or other food facility that can be patronized by the general public without entering the museum building, or provides catering services for a private reception held in a museum when it is not open to the general public (or in a part of the museum closed to the general public), income from such activities would be subject to the UBIT. Similarly, income derived by a hospital from a catering-type service whereby the hospital prepares and delivers meals to members of the general public would be treated as unrelated business income. Under this rule, the UBIT would not apply where food services are provided as part of the organization's primary exempt function, such as where a charitable organization delivers meals to elderly individuals at their residences (or serves meals to the elderly at a senior citizen's center) as a charitable activity, or provides food at shelters for the homeless.

Under the exception, the UBIT should not apply to income derived from food sale or service activities of a section 501(c)(3) organization (or State college or university) that both (1) are provided on the organization's premises, and (2) are provided primarily for students, faculty, patients, employees, or members of the organization, or visitors to the organization. For example, food sales at a cafeteria within a museum while the museum is open to the public, or at on-premises hospital or school cafeterias, would qualify for the exception, as would on-premise food vending machine sales and concession sales at sports or cultural events.

g.   Veterinary activities

Recommendation: Income derived from veterinary activities should be treated as income derived from an unrelated trade or business, subject to three exceptions. The UBIT should not apply to income from (1) spaying and neutering, (2) measures to protect the public health (such as rabies shots), and (3) emergency surgery (or other emergency services) if determined by a veterinarian to be necessary for the health of the animal.

h.   Hotel facility activities

Recommendation: Income derived from operation of a hotel facility that is patronized by the general public should be treated as income derived from an unrelated trade or business. The term hotel facility does not include hospitals, nursing homes, hospices, youth homes and hostels, away-from-home lodging (based on need) for parents of hospitalized children, or dormitories, fraternities, or sororities of educational institutions (to the extent such educational institution facilities are used by students, faculty, or staff).

i. Retail sales of condominiums and time-sharing units

Recommendation: Income derived from retail sales of condominiums or time-sharing units should be treated as income derived from an unrelated trade or business. The term retail sale does not include a sale of a condominium or time-sharing unit that has been donated as a charitable contribution to the organization if such income otherwise would be excludable from the UBIT pursuant to sections 512(b)(5) and 514.

j. Affinity credit card and other affinity merchandising activities

Recommendation: Income derived from affinity credit card or other affinity merchandising activities (whether or not such income is labeled as "royalties") should be treated as income derived from an unrelated trade or business.

For this purpose, the term affinity credit card refers to a credit card that carries the name or identifying logo of an exempt organization; the term other affinity merchandising refers to a catalog or similar sales literature that carries the name or identifying logo of an exempt organization and that offers ordinary commercial merchandise (such as household or gardening items) or services (such as long-distance telephone service). Under these so-called affinity arrangements, the exempt organization typically furnishes its membership or contributor mailing list to the credit card or merchandising business, enters into a contractual arrangement for exclusive use of the exempt organization's name or logo, and in effect endorses or promotes obtaining and using the particular company's credit card, ordering catalog items from the merchandising company, or using services of the commercial business.

These affinity arrangements are distinguishable from, and this recommendation does not apply with respect to, a practice sometimes referred to as "cause-related fund raising." Under this practice, charitable contributions (qualifying for deduction under section 170) are made by a business which merely has informed the public that an amount will be donated to the charity based on the sales of its products or use of its services, and has not entered into a contractual arrangement with the charity under which the business receives any consideration from the charity (such as the exclusive right to use the charity's name or logo on a particular type of product). For example, if a retail fast-food chain advertises that for each soft drink purchased at its restaurants it will donate one cent to a named charity, and subsequently makes a charitable contribution to the charity measured by the number of such sales, and the charity does not endorse the product except by allowing use of its name or logo, the donation received by the charity would not constitute unrelated business income.

k. Theme or amusement park activities

Recommendation: Income from theme or amusement park activities should be treated as income derived from an unrelated trade or business.

* * *

NOTES

1. *Other Recommendations.* The Draft Report also recommended repeal of the "convenience" exception in § 513(a)(2), concluding that its unduly broad interpretation had the effect of freeing exempt organizations from the responsibility for deciding whether particular activities were substantially related to the organization's exempt functions. Draft Report at 49–50. The Subcommittee concluded that activities traditionally covered by this exception, such as college dining halls and dormitories and hospital parking lots, would remain exempt under the substantially related test, but that more tangential revenue-producing activities, such as the operation of gas stations and the sale of common consumer goods, would no longer be protected. Id.

One of the more controversial recommendations was to tax any royalty income measured by net or taxable income derived from the licensed property, except for research income. Even royalty income not measured by net or taxable income (e.g., a flat fee royalty arrangement) would have been taxed if the organization either created the property right being licensed or was active in marketing the property right, with exceptions for licensing arrangements furthering the organization's exempt purpose and for research. Draft Report at 51–52. The Report specifically stated that licensing a trademark or logo in an attempt to foster name recognition would not, in itself, be treated as furthering an organization's exempt function. Id. But a children's educational organization that licensed its name or self-created intangible property for use on books or video cassettes would continue to be exempt on the theory that the arrangement furthered the organization's educational purposes. Id. at 52.

The Report also recommended several reforms that would more closely regulate the use of taxable subsidiaries. Under one proposal, the taxable income of a nonexempt controlled subsidiary could be no less than the amount of unrelated business taxable income if the income-producing activity had been carried on directly by the tax-exempt parent. Draft Report at 54–55. This rule was designed to preclude a taxable subsidiary from carrying on a profitable unrelated business along with a money-losing business activity that would be "related" if carried on directly by the exempt parent. Another proposal—to modify the "control" test in § 512(b)(13)—was adopted by Congress in the Taxpayer Relief Act of 1997. See Section H1 of this chapter, supra, at p. 664.

The Report recommended far more specific rules for allocation of expenses. In the case of dual use facilities, only the marginal costs attributable to the taxable activity would be deductible if the facility were used 25 percent or less of the time (measured by actual, not total available, use) for a taxable activity. If the facility were used 26 to 75 percent of the time for a taxable activity, then a portion of all costs attributable to the facility (including depreciation and general administrative costs) would be allocable to the taxable activity based on that activity's percentage of actual use. If the facility were used more than 75 percent of the time for a taxable activity, then all costs attributable to the facility would be deductible except for marginal costs related to tax-exempt use. In that case, however, any losses generated by the unrelated taxable activity could not be used to offset taxable income from other sources. Id. at 56–57. In the case of advertising, the Report recommended that publication and circulation expenses of an exempt organization periodical should not be deductible against advertising revenue.

The Oversight Subcommittee's final recommendation was an "aggregation rule" under which the Service, in determining whether an organization's "primary purpose" was a tax-exempt purpose under § 501(c), could take into account the activities of any of the organization's 80 percent or more subsidiaries. This determination, which could lead to revocation of exemption, was to be made based on a variety of factors, including the time and attention given by the parent's governing board and staff to taxable and unrelated business activities, the organization's mix of income and expenditures, and its expectation of earning a profit. Id. at 63–65.

2. *For Further Reading.* Thomas A. Troyer, Changing UBIT: Congress in the Workshop, 41 Tax Notes 1221 (1988).

CHAPTER 7

PRIVATE FOUNDATIONS

A. THE UNIVERSE OF PRIVATE FOUNDATIONS

1. INTRODUCTION

Within the extended family of § 501(c)(3) organizations, the Internal Revenue Code makes a critical distinction between private foundations and public charities. Defined generically, a foundation is a fund of private wealth established for charitable purposes, often in perpetuity. Most private foundations receive their support from a single individual or corporate source or from a close-knit family group. The principal function of most private foundations is to make grants to other nonprofit organizations, qualified individuals and government entities, but some "operating foundations" directly engage in one or more active programs, such as research or the operation of a museum. Public charities, by contrast, derive most of their support from government or the general public, or the nature of their activities makes them accountable to a broader constituency.

Although the warning signs came earlier, it was not until 1969 that Congress singled out private foundations for special regulation through the federal tax system. The intricate regime examined in this chapter was the result of a growing impression, supported more by anecdotal evidence than thoughtful empirical analysis, that private foundations were more susceptible to abuse than public charities. Congress has since relaxed some of the punishment inflicted on foundations and shifted much of its recent scrutiny to public charities. But the Code continues to police private foundations more strictly. The details will follow, but it is useful at the outset to summarize the principal badges of tax inferiority.

First, the income tax treatment of gifts to private foundations is less favorable than for contributions to public charities. For purposes of determining an individual donor's income tax charitable deduction, stricter percentage limitations are imposed on charitable gifts to private grantmaking foundations. Gifts of cash and ordinary income property to public charities are subject to an annual limitation of 50 percent of adjusted gross income with a five-year carryover of any excess. I.R.C. § 170(b)(1)(A). This limitation is reduced to 30 percent for gifts to private foundations. I.R.C. § 170(b)(1)(B). Gifts of long-term capital gain property (such as stock and most real estate) to private foundations are subject to a 20 percent limitation, as compared to the 30 percent cap applicable to public charities. I.R.C. § 170(b)(1)(B), (D). Income tax deductions for gifts of appreciated capital gain property (other than certain publicly traded stock) to private foundations are limited to the donor's basis in the contributed property, while taxpayers generally may deduct the full fair market value if capital gain property is donated to a public charity. I.R.C. § 170(e)(1)(B)(ii). These distinctions, however, are limited to the income tax charitable deduction. Gifts and bequests to both public charities and private foundations are fully deductible for federal gift and estate tax purposes. I.R.C. §§ 2055; 2522.

Second, private foundations are subject to a two percent excise tax on their net investment income, including capital gains. I.R.C. § 4940. The rate can be reduced to one percent for foundations that increase their charitable distributions by a specified amount. I.R.C. § 4940(e).

Third, private foundations are subject to federal excise tax sanctions if they engage in various proscribed activities such as self-dealing, excessive ownership of business interests, and investments that jeopardize the organization's charitable purposes, or if they make certain forbidden "taxable expenditures." Penalties also may be imposed if a private foundation fails to meet income distribution requirements designed to ensure that the foundation's charitable payout is reasonably related to its endowment. I.R.C. §§ 4941–4945.

This chapter has been designed to accommodate coverage of the tax rules classifying and regulating private foundations in varying degrees of depth. For those seeking a user-friendly overview, the first two sections should suffice. They describe the universe of private foundations in the United States, summarize the history and policy of the current regulatory scheme, survey the distinction between public charities and private foundations and the scope of the private foundation excise taxes, and explore the positive role that family foundations play in the world of philanthropy. Subsequent sections flesh out the details and consider planning strategies that enable an organization to avoid private foundation status or, if that is not feasible, to navigate successfully around the tax landmines.

The excerpt below, from a handbook published by The Council on Foundations,[1] sets the stage.

David F. Freeman, The Handbook on Private Foundations

The Council on Foundations 1–9 (Rev. Ed. 1991).

The roots of philanthropy go back many centuries, and philanthropic organizations exist in many cultures. In the United States, many individuals, families, and corporations have chosen a unique institution—the private foundation—to carry out their charitable purposes. Private foundations have played an important role in U.S. history during the last century, supporting cultural, social, and scientific efforts. Today private foundations continue to offer donors special opportunities to contribute to society.

---

1. The Council on Foundations, based in Washington, D.C., is a membership organization of foundations established in 1949 to promote and strengthen organized philanthropy. It includes most major U.S. foundations among its members.

Foundations in the United States date from the end of the nineteenth century, when Andrew Carnegie, John D. Rockefeller, and other industrial pioneers first chose to apply parts of their accumulating wealth to public purposes. Unlike European philanthropists, they faced no governmental restrictions or royal monopoly on good works. The corporate form or organization had served them well in the pursuit of profits, and with no public agency to direct them otherwise, they found it only natural to adapt this same device for the achievement of charitable objectives.

These early foundations were created years before income or estate taxes became a serious factor. Moreover, when federal progressive taxes on income, gifts, and estates were enacted in the second decade of the twentieth century, our government not only exempted charities, including foundations, from income tax but also encouraged gifts to them by permitting donors' deductions from income, gift, and estate taxes. Such deductions, intended as incentives, had their desired effect. By the late 1980s, nearly 30,000 foundations were in existence, many of them created by persons of relatively modest wealth. [See infra p. 711 for the most recently available data on grantmaking foundations. Eds.]

A prime reason for this remarkable growth has been the foundation's flexibility. It can respond to a need as it becomes manifest, it can strike out quickly in new directions, and it can give in a single community or throughout the world.

WHAT'S IN A NAME?

In 1957, two foundation watchers offered very different answers to the question, "What is a foundation?" To author Dwight MacDonald, the Ford Foundation was "a large body of money completely surrounded by people who want some."

F. Emerson Andrews developed the second definition in his pioneering work, *Philanthropic Foundations*. It was adopted by the Foundation Center in the first edition of *The Foundation Directory* and remains substantially unchanged today:

> A foundation [is] a nongovernmental, nonprofit organization with its own funds (usually from a single source, either an individual, family, or corporation) and program managed by its own trustees and directors, which was established to maintain or aid educational, social, charitable, religious, or other activities serving the common welfare primarily by making grants to other nonprofit organizations.

This definition readily fits most of the organizations described in this handbook. But the grantmaking field has no copyright on the name *foundation*—it is a term freely used by noncharitable organizations, by other kinds of charities, and increasingly by governmental agencies. Ordinarily this confusion is a minor irritant, making problems for statisticians of the field, but not a matter of general concern. On occasion, however, the public image of grantmaking foundations is damaged by the publicized misdeeds or excesses of other types of "foundations" not subject to the same close regulation.

Just as the presence of the word foundation in an organization's name is no guarantee that it is a grantmaking foundation, the reverse is also true. The titles of many foundations contain synonyms such as *fund, endowment,* and *trust,* but others use no such identifier at all—for example, Carnegie Corporation of New York; DeRance, Inc.; and Research Corporation.

* * *

TYPES OF FOUNDATIONS

The *independent foundation* is a term coined by the Council on Foundations to distinguish private foundations established and funded by individuals or families from those funded by corporations. Also adopted for statistical use by the Foundation Center, the independent foundation category is by far the largest and most varied. It includes the large, long-established foundations as well as the smallest foundations.

Most independent foundations are established by contributions from an individual donor or family. In many instances, the donor and other family members participate actively in the foundation's direction. Large foundations usually have professional staff, but the smaller ones typically do not and are run entirely by their directors or trustees on a volunteer basis. Over time, a foundation launched with close ties to a donor and family often tends to develop a character and style of its own, becoming less personalized and more of an institution in its own right.

Most independent foundations are endowed, that is, they have a principal fund and make their grants essentially from investment income. Some, particularly smaller foundations, make grants from funds that are contributed periodically by living donors. Foundations that operate initially on this pass-through basis often receive an endowment at a later stage.

Corporate foundations are those established by business corporations as a means of carrying out systematic programs of charitable giving. They are classified as private foundations and are legally separate from the corporation. Corporations, whether giving through a foundation or direct giving program, frequently focus on the educational, cultural, and social welfare needs of communities where the company facilities and employees are located. They often sponsor programs to match employee gifts to charity. The corporate foundation board of directors is usually composed of senior executives and directors of the company, and staff is often recruited from within the company—although in recent years some corporations have hired staff from outside the corporation who are experienced in community work. Few corporate foundations have large endowments. Most receive and distribute funds each year from current profits of the parent company and have endowments equivalent to only one or two years of annual giving. * * *

Community foundations differ significantly in structure and in other respects from independent and corporate foundations. Community foundations have multiple sources of funding and a local or regional focus in their giving. Commonly they administer investments and charitable distributions separately; investments are managed professionally, often by trustee banks. The grantmaking and other charitable activities are directed by a governing body or distribution committee representative of community interests. The assets of a community foundation consist of a number of component funds with varying charitable purposes.

Community foundations are classified as public charities under the 1969 Tax Reform Act and accordingly are subject to fewer and different regulations than private foundations. Gifts to them qualify for maximum income tax deductibility. The number and size of community foundations have grown tremendously in the last 20 years. This is in part because of the requirement that they raise funds to meet a public support test. It may also have partly resulted from the help provided to newly forming or revitalizing community foundations by special programs sponsored by the Council on Foundations, the Ford Foundation, and the C.S. Mott Foundation. However, a major reason for their popularity among donors is the ease with which funds can be established and the variety of giving options available to donors. * * *

An *operating foundation* is a private foundation that primarily conducts programs of its own, expending its funds directly for the conduct of its own charitable activities rather than making grants to others. Examples include the J. Paul Getty Trust, which operates museum activities, and the Russell Sage Foundation, which conducts and publishes research. The distinction between operating foundations and those that are primarily grantmaking has long been recognized in the foundation field. The 1969 Tax Reform Act recognized this distinction by establishing a separate category, with more favorable tax status, for operating foundations. Approximately 3,000 organizations are classified by the Internal Revenue Service (IRS) as private operating foundations. The vast majority of private foundations are classified as private "nonoperating" * * *.

GENERAL AND SPECIAL PURPOSE FOUNDATIONS

Most donors charter their foundations with general purposes to support a wide range of charitable activities that change from time to time, as the directors or trustees determine. Others, either by choice of the managers or by virtue of the charter, may have one or more special purposes. A special purpose may be extremely broad, such as the advancement of science or health, or quite limited and specific, such as research into the causes and cure of alcoholism. Frequently, foundation managers select trustees and staff for a special-purpose foundation because of their interest or expertise in the field of emphasis.

Whether or not they incorporate geographic limitations into their charters, most small general-purpose foundations and a few large ones restrict their giving to a region, state, or city. Many special-purpose foundations and the largest of the general-purpose foundations, however, give regionally, nationally, and internationally.

FOUNDATIONS IN SOCIETY

The Andrews/Foundation Center definition of a private foundation * * * is helpful in describing the range of organizations in which we are primarily interested. However, it fails to position foundations in the voluntary sector of our society. The voluntary, independent nonprofit, or third sector, as it is variously called, is an important partner with government and business in the myriad activities that collectively make up our way of life. Within the voluntary sector, foundations play both a supportive and an innovative role, serving as important channels through which profits earned by individuals and businesses are distributed to the public in goods and services. Their influence within the voluntary sector is not dependent on the dollar volume of their grants, which is small in comparison to government spending. Rather, it lies in their flexibility in responding to needs, their willingness to take risks, and in the pluralistic nature of foundation decision making.

No other country has so many alternatives to government funding for a good idea or a new approach to an old problem. The value of foundations as alternative funding sources lies in the likelihood that at least one grantmaker will be willing to take a chance on a particular organization or individual, making possible an experiment that may gain public acceptance and broad support.

This is not to suggest that it is easy to get a grant from a foundation. Some of the staffed foundations that keep track of the number of qualified requests they decline each year report the percentage of turndowns is about 85 percent and rising. This trend is partly due to increased demand for private contributions in the wake of government cutbacks during the 1980s. But the adage, "if at first you don't succeed, try, try again," is still sound advice to the grantseeker.

The range of activities recognized by the IRS as within a charitable organization's exempt purposes constantly widens. Even contributions to businesses that operate for profit can qualify as charitable if made, for example, to help racial minorities establish themselves in the free enterprise system. Foundation grants have triggered other extensions of the definition of what is charitable, such as special guidelines including public interest work in law and voter education activities.

There is much discussion among scholars and practitioners about foundation grantmaking philosophy. Some say foundations are more concerned with research on the underlying causes of social or health problems, while others contend that they are more involved in funding the delivery of needed services. It is probably more accurate to say that they are concerned with both. Thus, while some foundations working on the problems of the inner city may fund studies of economic or demographic trends, others seek to help new community organizations wrestling with immediate problems such as homelessness, drug abuse, or unemployed young people.

We can learn valuable lessons from the relatively short experience of organized grantmaking. For example, a few foundations have traditionally shown considerable willingness to stay with a particular problem or project over a period of years—a capability that distinguishes them from most government funding sources. The Rockefeller Foundation's long and successful battle against yellow fever is a favorite example. That same foundation and others have shown equal persistence in the funding of agricultural research leading to the miracle rice and grain strains that have increased crop yields so markedly as part of the "green revolution" in Asia, Africa, and Latin America. And, in future years we may find that long-term commitments from private foundations such as the Robert Wood Johnson Foundation and others will be instrumental in finding a cure and developing prevention strategies for AIDS.

Although grantmaking may be their primary function, many foundations offer more than money. Staffed foundations and actively involved trustees of unstaffed ones frequently develop expertise in a special area of interest and become informal clearinghouses of information about new approaches to problems and funding sources other than their own. Often foundations bring together people working in the same or related fields for mutually helpful discussion and planning.

Although most foundations are blessed with broad charters, in practice many narrow their areas of current interest. This sharpening of focus serves several useful purposes. If these interests are clearly defined and publicized, it helps grantseeking agencies to target their appeals for support. And the grantmaker, having become familiar with both the problems and the imaginative people who are working toward solutions in a special field, is able to make better-informed grant decisions.

Examples of both the "staying power" of foundations and the advantages of selecting areas of special interest (taken from a long list of past accomplishments) include reform of medical education, early work on population problems, and development of policy-oriented research institutes such as the Brookings Institution and the Institute of Medicine of the National Academy of Sciences.

Nonprofit organizations look to grantmaking foundations to provide funding for experimental and high-risk projects. But with many research, educational, and service agencies heavily dependent on government project funding, general support grants from smaller foundations are also vitally important. In these and many other ways, foundations are demonstrating their continuing usefulness.

FOUNDATIONS AND GOVERNMENT

Much has been written about the degree to which government has "taken over" the funding of the voluntary sector. It is true that government support of nonprofit institutions equals that of private contributions, and government spending on charitable activities such as health care and job training dwarfs private spending. But since foundations are able to change the direction and emphasis of their programs with little or no lead time, many new opportunities have opened up *because* of heavy government funding in fields traditionally thought of as the concern of the private sector. For example, government funding of health services through Medicare and Medicaid has created demand for new types of health practitioners; Robert Wood Johnson, Commonwealth, Kaiser, and other foundations have conducted studies, made grants to educational institutions, funded demonstration projects, and otherwise moved to help identify ways to meet the demand.

In the environmental field, foundations have long played an important role by preserving wilderness areas, barrier islands, and historic buildings. This function continues to be an important one, especially because of the speed with which foundations and grantees such as the Nature Conservancy and Trust for Public Land can move. In addition, foundations monitor government conservation programs and allow environmental disputes between government agencies to be ventilated. And on occasion, powerful coalitions of public interest law firms and voluntary membership organizations (many of whom were launched by or are funded by foundations) generate lawsuits to force corporations or government agencies to comply with environmental protection laws and regulations. Foundations have been willing to take risks in this area and in others through support of pilot projects, studies, and investigative reporting. These and similar activities have often influenced or changed public policies.

Trends in the 1980s indicated that government funding in certain areas may have reached its limit, resulting in a larger demand for foundation dollars for basic services, especially for the disadvantaged. Foundation boards and staffs find themselves in new roles, sometimes working in tandem with government agencies to fund programs. Foundations are also contributing more dollars to issues such as public education—areas that have traditionally been considered to be the concern of the public sector.

LEGAL STATUS OF FOUNDATIONS

Foundations in the United States typically are created and organized under state law either as corporations or trusts and enjoy federal tax exemption under the Internal Revenue Code. Neither these laws nor others give the term *foundation* a precise or fixed legal meaning. Indeed, many of the state statutes under which foundations are created and operate do not use the word at all.

The Internal Revenue Code refers to foundations in various contexts related to not-for-profit organizations, but it leaves the term undefined. However, the relatively new phrase *private foundation*, introduced by the 1969 Tax Reform Act, does have a technical meaning. Unfortunately, the code defines private foundations not by what they are, but by what they are not. Moreover, the phrase private foundation creates confusion because the word *private* tends to blur an essential fact: Foundations are committed to public purposes, even though their assets are derived from private sources.

The code's definition by exclusion of private foundation operates in this fashion. Starting with the universe of voluntary organizations described in Section 501(c)(3), the code excludes broad groups such as churches, schools, hospitals, government, and publicly supported charities and their affiliates. (Publicly supported charities derive much of their support from the general public and reach out in other ways to a public constituency.) The code refers to all of the above kinds of excluded organizations as *public charities*. Section 501(c)(3) organizations remaining after these exclusions are considered private foundations.

Thus, organizations are included in the remainder as private foundations that are not really grantmaking foundations at all. These may include museums, homes for the aged, and libraries, among others. The IRS considers these organizations private foundations if they have been endowed by an individual or a single family or if they were established as public charities and lose that status by failing to prove that they have received ongoing financial support from the general public.

NOTE: DIMENSIONS OF THE FOUNDATION COMMUNITY

According to the latest authoritative count as this edition of the text went to press, there were an estimated 75,187 private grantmaking foundations in the United States at the end of 2007. These foundations had approximately $687 billion in total assets (the total is down significantly as a result of the financial crisis that began in 2008) and made aggregate annual grants of $44.4 billion in 2007. Most foundations have less than $1 million in assets and make annual grants of less than $100,000. The largest foundations (with assets of $50 million or more), although representing less than two percent of all foundations, control roughly two-thirds of the assets and award half of all grants.

Based on the most recent available public information, the ten wealthiest U.S. grantmaking foundations measured by total assets, were:

Rank	Foundation	Total Assets
1	Bill and Melinda Gates Foundation	$38,921,022,000
2	The Ford Foundation	11,184,655,197
3	W. K. Kellogg Foundation	8,058,127,639
4	Robert Wood Johnson Foundation	7,200,000,000
5	William and Flora Hewlett Foundation	6,208,980,453
6	Lilly Endowment	5,718,809,917
7	John D. and Catherine T. MacArthur Foundation	5,014,059,260
8	David and Lucile Packard Foundation	4,650,858,492
9	Gordon and Betty Moore Foundation	4,509,705,996
10	Andrew W. Mellon Foundation	4,363,563,000

Sources: Foundation Center, Foundation Growth and Giving Estimates (2009); foundation annual reports.

2.   The Distinction Between Private Foundations and Public Charities: Historical Origins*

The first harbingers of Congress's desire to treat private foundations as second class citizens came in the Revenue Act of 1950, which added to the Internal Revenue Code a set of rules withdrawing tax-exempt status from organizations that engaged in certain "prohibited transactions," such as loans without adequate security, payment of unreasonable compensation, bargain sales, and preferential rendering of services to related parties. Rules also were enacted to patrol against unreasonable accumulations of income, substantial expenditures for nonexempt purposes, or investments that jeopardized the ability of a charity to carry out its exempt purposes. The legislative history reveals Congress's concern that some charities—specifically, certain charitable trusts and private foundations—were abusing the privileges of their exempt status by benefiting donors, their families and other insiders. Congress exempted churches, schools, hospitals and certain publicly supported organizations from the potential sanctions, apparently because they were viewed as less susceptible to the perceived abuses.

By the mid–1950s, these distinctions between charitable organizations were incorporated in the rules governing the income tax charitable deduction. Historically, an individual donor's annual charitable deduction has been limited to a certain percentage of the donor's adjusted gross income. In 1954, the overall percentage limitation was raised from 20 to 30 percent, but only for gifts to religious orders, schools and colleges, hospitals, and churches. The change was justified as a way to help the favored institutions obtain "the additional funds they need, in view of their rising costs and the relatively low rate of return they are receiving on endowment funds." S.Rep.No. 1622, 83d Cong., 2d Sess. 29 (1954); H.Rep.No. 1337, 83d Cong., 2d Sess. 25 (1954). In 1956, the higher limitation was extended to a narrow type of medical research organization and, in 1962, to organizations that supported state universities. The extra 10–percent deduction (along with several other benefits, such as eligibility for a five-year carryover of contributions that exceeded the annual ceiling) was extended again in 1964 to other organizations that derived a substantial part of their total support from governmental sources or from direct or indirect contributions from the general public. These incremental changes had the effect of narrowing the *disfavored* category to private foundations and a miscellany of other § 501(c)(3) organizations that could not demonstrate the requisite public support.

---

* Much of this history is derived from Laurens Williams and Donald V. Moorehead, An Analysis of the Federal Tax Distinctions Between Public and Private Charitable Organizations, in IV U.S. Dept. of the Treasury, Research Papers Sponsored by the [Filer] Commission on Private Philanthropy and Public Needs 2099 (1977), and Peter Dobkin Hall, A Historical Overview of the Private Nonprofit Sector, in The Nonprofit Sector: A Research Handbook 3, 19–20 (Walter W. Powell ed., 1987).

Professor Boris Bittker explained this caste system as embodying two distinctions, resting on different rationales suggested but not clearly articulated in the legislative history. First, Congress may have intended to benefit operating over nonoperating charities on the theory that the operating charities needed special assistance to maintain or expand their activities at accustomed levels in the face of increased costs and declining endowment yields. Grantmaking charities, it seemed, could more easily retrench or postpone their activities. Second, the distinction between public and private charities may have been based on the view that public charities satisfied more pressing social needs, or had been endorsed by a form of public referendum. Churches, schools and hospitals fell into the "charmed circle" irrespective of their public support—presumably because they were the most venerable (and influential) members of the charitable sector. See Boris I. Bittker, Should Foundations Be Third–Class Charities?, in The Future of Foundations 132, 142–143 (Fritz F. Heimann ed., 1973).

The increasing regulation of private foundations was not entirely unexpected. Throughout the first half of the 20th century, large pools of philanthropic wealth were periodically subjected to critical scrutiny by a diverse ideological coalition. In 1916, the Walsh Commission, which was investigating industrial relations, concluded that the small group of wealthy families controlling American industry were extending their reach to education and "social service" by creating "enormous privately managed funds for indefinite purposes." Among other things, the Commission recommended that these institutions be required to obtain a federal charter that limited their size, prohibited accumulations of unexpended income, and opened their books to government inspection. Two Congressional investigations in the 1950s were somewhat more balanced, but concerns remained about public accountability, the unhealthy influence of foundations over social science research and education, and the leftist and collectivist leanings of some foundations. In 1952, the Cox Commission concluded its report by asking whether foundations had supported persons and projects that "tended to weaken or discredit the capitalistic system as it exists in the United States and to favor Marxist socialism." The 1954 Reece Commission recommended a limit on the life of a foundation, and it would have required mandatory distribution of income, restrictions on corporate control, and a complete prohibition on all political activity.

The movement against private foundations picked up considerable steam in the 1960s, primarily because of the efforts of populist Congressman Wright Patman of Texas. The barrage began in 1962 with extensive hearings culminating in a lengthy report that identified abuses ranging from misuse of funds to operation of businesses at a competitive advantage. A 1965 Treasury Department report concluded that private foundations played an important and valuable role in American philanthropy but identified three broad areas for legislative attention. First, the Treasury concluded that the use of foundations produced an undue lag between the charitable gift generating the tax benefit (the transfer of wealth to the foundation) and the use of the funds for charitable purposes. Second, the Treasury was concerned that foundations were becoming a disproportionate segment of the national economy. Third, foundations were said to represent dangerous concentrations of social and economic power. Among the recommended legislative solutions were a ban on self-dealing, an annual charitable payout requirement, a limit on foundation holdings in business enterprises, less beneficial tax treatment for gifts of appreciated property to private foundations, prohibitions on borrowing by foundations, and a rule requiring the family of the founding donor to reduce its representation on the governing board to no more than 25 percent after the first 25 years of a foundation's existence.

It was against this background that Congress turned its attention to comprehensive tax reform in the late 1960s. In so doing, it mounted an attack on private foundations that culminated in the Tax Reform Act of 1969. The 1969 legislation was shaped by the political dynamics of that period. An appreciation of the setting in which the regulatory regime emerged can only enhance understanding of the technical material to follow.[1] In early 1969, with a large segment of the public in open revolt against the unfairness of the tax laws, the House Ways and Means Committee commenced hearings on proposed legislation targeted at private foundations.

Some of the provisions of the House bill were the product of anecdotal testimony, such as when Representative John Rooney, a Brooklyn, New York Democrat, told the committee that a private foundation funded by a wealthy political opponent tried to unseat him by using its money and influence. Another influential witness was McGeorge Bundy, then president of The Ford Foundation and a former Harvard College dean and key player in the Kennedy and Johnson administrations. Under Bundy's leadership, the Ford Foundation made controversial grants to encourage voter registration in African–American and Hispanic communities and assisted senior members of the staff of Senator Robert Kennedy after his assassination with travel fellowships to "ease the transition from public to private life." Bundy defended the Ford Foundation grants in testimony that most observers accurately described as defensive and condescending, prompting this response from one House committee member; "I went into that hearing this morning basically friendly to the foundations; I came out feeling that if Bundy represents the prevailing attitude among them, they are going to have to be brought down a peg. For all their Ph.D's, they are not above the law."[2] Bundy was followed by John D. Rockefeller 3d, who while supporting continued tax benefits for philanthropy, casually admitted that thanks to the then unlimited charitable deduction for certain donors he had not paid any federal income tax since 1961. Other revelations and incidents, such as modest financial payments from private foundations to two U.S. Supreme Court justices, raised the temperature even higher.

With momentum established, the anti-foundation bandwagon moved to the Senate, where the Finance Committee heard pleas for restraint from

---

1. For a lively chronicle of the political climate during the gestation period of the 1969 legislation, see Waldemar A. Nielsen, The Big Foundations 7–17 (1972).

2. Id. at 12.

mainstream nonprofit sector lobbyists and support for stricter regulation from an odd coalition of populist liberals and conservatives. The anti-foundation forces prevailed and the basic structure of the regulatory regime crafted by the House survived virtually intact. As we will see, most of the private foundation excise tax rules—such as the strict prohibition on self dealing, the absolute ban on lobbying and political campaign expenditures, and the limitations on study and travel grants to individuals, were an outgrowth of the 1969 House and Senate deliberations and the earlier work of Representative Patman and the Treasury Department.

NOTES AND QUESTIONS

1. *The Role of Private Foundations.* Do private foundations represent a "shadow government" that acts as a political force partially financed by public funds, without accountability to the electorate? Should they steer clear of public controversy and limit their activities to support of traditional charitable activities such as scientific and medical research? Is it fundamentally undemocratic for foundations to exert their influence in a democratic society? Or do foundations inform democracy by offering different and innovative solutions to social problems?

Most private foundations exist in perpetuity. Would it be preferable if the law required them to have a limited life span, such as 50 to 100 years? Would term limits protect against departure from the original donor's grantmaking intent? During the Senate's consideration of the Tax Reform Act of 1969, Senator Albert Gore, Sr. (father of the 2000 Presidential candidate), a populist from the left, joined with some conservatives to press for a mandatory limit on the life of any private foundation. The Senate Finance Committee bill approved a 40–year limit, but it was removed during the Senate floor debate.

2. *For Further Reading.* Joel Fleishman, The Foundation: A Great American Secret (2007); Thomas A. Troyer, The 1969 Private Foundations Law: Historical Perspectives on Its Origins and Underpinnings, 27 Exempt Org. Tax Rev. 52 (2000); John A. Edie, Congress and Foundations, in Teresa Odendahl (ed.), America's Wealthy and the Future of Foundations (1987); John G. Simon, Charity and Dynasty Under the Federal Tax System, 5 The Probate Lawyer 1 (Summer 1978); Fritz F. Heimann (ed.), The Future of Foundations (1973); Marion R. Fremont–Smith, Foundations and Government (1965).

3.   COMMUNITY FOUNDATIONS

Not all "foundations" are private. A community foundation is a § 501(c)(3) organization created to receive and administer funds contributed by members of a particular community and to disburse those funds for charitable purposes within that community. The typical community foundation has a broadly representative governing board and its funds are administered professionally. Because they receive their support from a broad constituency, community foundations are public charities and, as explained in the excerpt below, donors often find them to be a desirable alternative to a private foundation.

John A. Edie, First Steps in Starting a Foundation

Council on Foundations 35–38 (4th ed.1997).

THE COMMUNITY FOUNDATION OPTION

As one type of traditional charity, the community foundation has the tax advantages of being publicly supported and does not have the disadvantages of being a private foundation. This section explains how the community foundation differs from other public charities and why it is an attractive option in a variety of circumstances.

Community foundations do not have a separate, legal classification in the tax code. In almost every circumstance community foundations are classified as traditional charities under Section 509(a)(1). However, their history goes back to 1914 and thus predates the tax code itself. The Council on Foundations defines a community foundation as a tax exempt, nor-for-profit, autonomous, publicly supported philanthropic institution comprised primarily of permanent funds endowed by many separate donors for the long-term benefit of the residents of a defined geographic area. Even though community foundations do not have a separate legal classification, the Treasury regulations defining publicly supported organizations of the Traditional charity variety provide great detail about the rules governing community trusts or community foundations. In contemplating the formation of a new foundation focusing on local needs, one would be well advised to learn the advantages of utilizing an existing community foundation or creating a new one to service the local community.

Community foundations develop, receive and administer endowment funds from private sources and manage them under community control for charitable purposes primarily focused on local needs. Their grants are normally limited to charitable organizations within a specific identified region or local community, and their charitable giving and other charitable activities are overseen by a board of directors representing the diversity of community interests. Originally conceived as a vehicle primarily for those desiring to leave property by will in perpetuity, community foundations have broadened their range over the years to accept more lifetime and short-term gifts.

Community foundations have two major purposes: to seek funds from private sources to build a pool of capital for local philanthropic purposes, and to allocate and distribute such funds for public needs.

Developers of a Capital Pool for Philanthropy

A community foundation attracts capital in ways not intended to impede the efforts of local service organizations to raise annual operating support. It is a supplement to federated funds and other agencies, not a competitor. It seeks its resources from testators, living donors, business corporations, other nonprofit organizations, trade associations, clubs and occasionally from units of government.

In bringing resources into a pool, the community foundation enhances the utility of each fund by developing an endowment of size sufficient to tackle community problems. By pooling resources, a community foundation can support one joint staff (as opposed to different staffs for each fund), and can take advantage of the obvious economies of scale.

Distributors of Funds for Philanthropy

Having drawn capital resources together, a community foundation distributes funds as its governing body determines or to charitable agencies and fields of interest designated by donors at the time of making their gifts. Its staff, supported by pooled resources, is able to become well acquainted with the emerging and changing needs of the local community, and thus provides professional expertise rarely available otherwise to private donors, corporations, unstaffed private foundations and other grantmakers. The permanence of a community foundation ensures the ongoing presence of such expertise; and the public structure of both its governing body and its procedures ensures that its grantmaking choices are responsive to community needs.

Since the formation of the first community foundation in Cleveland in 1914, this institution has grown in popularity around the nation. In 1997, there were more than 400 community foundations with assets ranging from a few thousand dollars to over $1 billion. Together, community foundations hold assets in excess of $13 billion and distribute annually more than $900 million. In addition to the main purpose just outlined, each community foundation has certain basic characteristics in common, as summarized here.

Form

Community foundations are created as trusts or nonprofit corporations whose charitable distributions are made by a distribution committee in the trust form, or by a board of directors in the corporate form. In the trust form, banks or other investment firms serve as trustees under a common governing instrument that may be executed using similar language by each local institution that agrees to accept funds constituting a part of that community's foundation. In some communities, one bank serves as sole trustee; but in most areas, a number of institutions with trust powers accept funds under the declaration of trust of their community's foundation. In the trust form, banks or other institutions, as trustees, manage the investment function; a distribution committee or board of directors manages the distribution function. In the nonprofit corporation form, the board of directors often performs both functions.

Geography and Size

A community foundation operates primarily to serve a chosen area, but on occasion it may accept funds for distribution outside that area. Generally, each community foundation serves an area of natural cohesion whether it be a city, greater metropolitan area, county or state. While there is no specific minimum geographic size required, the smaller the population, the fewer the number of potential donors and corporations likely to be available to provide the basic support.

Governing Body

The Treasury regulations governing most community foundations require that all the combined or pooled funds (component parts) be subject to a common governing body or distribution committee which directs or, in the case of a fund designated for specific beneficiaries, monitors the distribution of all of the funds exclusively for charitable purposes. The governing body must represent the broad interests of the public rather than the personal or private interests of a limited number of donors. Community foundations frequently satisfy this public representation requirement by filling positions on the governing body with: 1) public officials, 2) members appointed by public officials, 3) persons with special knowledge in a particular field or discipline in which the community foundation operates, and/or 4) community leaders such as members of the clergy, educators or civic leaders.

Range of Service to Donors

Community foundations provide a wide variety of ways to respond to the needs of donors whether the gifts are permanent or short-term. Unrestricted funds are most sought after by community foundations because they provide the governing body with the maximum amount of flexibility to respond to the most pressing needs of the community. Designated funds are created by the donor *at the time of transferring the assets* and specifically name the agency or agencies to receive the benefit of the fund. Donor-advised funds are created by the donor, reserving at the time of making the gift the privilege (from time to time thereafter) to recommend agencies to receive grants. However, the ultimate power to make all grant decisions must lie with the governing body and such recommendations can be redirected. Field-of-interest funds are established by a donor by specifying at the time of asset transfer some broadly identified field of charitable concern. Examples would be health, education or cultural arts. In any of the various funds noted above, a donor can name the fund thereby providing an opportunity to give his or her family name a place in the philanthropic history of the community. Community foundations normally charge a fee for these donor services, often based on a percentage of the value of the corpus of the fund.

Variance Power

Treasury regulations for most community foundations require that the governing body have a variance power. Specifically, the rules state that the governing body must have the power (alone or with court approval) "to modify any restriction or condition on the distribution of funds for any specified charitable purposes or to specified organization if in the sole judgment of the governing body * * * such restriction or condition becomes, in effect, unnecessary, incapable of fulfillment, or inconsistent with the charitable needs of the community or area served." The concept of including a variance power in the design of a community foundation has been present since the first one was formed in Cleveland. In fact, providing a variance power was a major reason for starting a community foundation since it provided a reasonable mechanism to avoid having the donor's restriction become obsolete or impossible to fulfill (sometimes called the rule of the dead hand).

* * *

NOTES

1. *Growth of Community Foundations.* Virtually every major city in the United States is served by a community foundation. Community foundations have enjoyed tremendous growth. According to the latest available data, the assets of community foundations reached $56.7 billion in 2007, a 13.5 percent increase from 2006, and grants paid in 2007 reached an all-time high of $4.6 billion, more than triple the number of grants made in 1996. Foundation Center, Key Facts on Community Foundations (May 2009). As this text went to press in early 2010, the top ten community foundations, ranked by market value of assets, were:

Rank	Foundation	Total Assets
1.	Tulsa Community Foundation	$3,740,241,151
2.	Cleveland Foundation	2,183,913,190
3.	New York Community Trust	2,135,691,023
4.	Silicon Valley Community Foundation	1,943,885,894
5.	Chicago Community Trust	1,841,684,803
6.	California Community Foundation	1,257,906,849
7.	The Oregon Community Foundation	1,214,146,698
8.	Greater Kansas City Community Foundation	1,183,724,020
9.	Marin Community Foundation (California)	1,180,106,202
10.	The Columbus Foundation (and affiliates)	1,045,016,666

Source: The Foundation Center Statistical Information Service.

2. *For Further Reading.* Christopher R. Hoyt, Legal Compendium for Community Foundations (1996).

4. OTHER PRIVATE FOUNDATION ALTERNATIVES

The major advantages of a private foundation are flexibility and control. For donors who are willing to relinquish a measure of control, several other alternative vehicles, such as donor-advised funds and supporting organizations, offer many of the advantages of a private grantmaking foundation without the added expense, reduced tax benefits, or additional regulation. Donor-advised funds are discussed in Section B4 of this chapter, infra at pp. 730–736. Supporting organizations are separate legal entities established to support one or more existing public charities. They are an attractive alternative when a donor who is willing to forego absolute control desires the tax benefits of a lifetime gift to a public charity and prefers the structure offered by an independent charitable entity without all the regulatory limitations imposed on private foundations. Supporting organizations are previewed in Section B1 of this chapter, infra, at pp. 726–727, and discussed in more detail in Section C4, infra, at pp. 751–763.

5. The Present (and Future) of Private Foundations

The birth rate of private foundations declined sharply after the Tax Reform Act of 1969. An early study by the Council on Foundations and the Yale Program on Nonprofit Organizations revealed that wealthy donors were deterred by the increased regulation, the tax disincentives for lifetime gifts, the administrative burdens, and the availability of alternative philanthropic vehicles such as community foundations, donor-advised funds, and supporting foundations. According to the study, attorneys played a major role in discouraging the formation of foundations during the 1970's and early 1980's. Overreacting to the 1969 legislation, they conveyed the message that foundations were expensive, time consuming, inefficient and complicated—"a mine field for somebody who doesn't know what they are doing." Francie Ostrower, The Role of Advisors to the Wealthy in The Future of Foundations 247 et seq. (Teresa Odendahl ed., 1987). This negative environment caused many existing private foundations to dissolve or transfer their assets to community foundations.

More recently, however, private foundations have enjoyed a resurgence as Congress relaxed some of the disincentives and philanthropists and their advisors adapted to the regulatory regime. The enormous wealth accumulated by entrepreneurs and investors in the late 1990s bull market and beyond was a major stimulus to the foundation birth and growth rates, causing the total number of foundations to increase nearly 70 percent by the end of that decade. The Foundation Center, Foundation Yearbook (2002). Financial service companies, consultants, and sophisticated estate planners also have played a role by including foundations in their list of attractive "products." Publicity surrounding several enormous gifts to new and existing foundations has contributed to a bandwagon effect among the actual and aspiring affluent. All these developments have confirmed the emergence of the family foundation as a growth industry and a powerful force within the world of philanthropy.

Why did philanthropists rediscover private foundations despite the legal "mine field" that almost caused their extinction? The nontax motivations for creating a foundation are many, including: (1) providing a formal structure to administer family charitable giving and a strategic buffer between an affluent family and the many charities who seek contributions; (2) building a charitable endowment that will last well beyond the founder's life and serve as a permanent memorial to the family's values; (3) giving a donor greater influence and control over donated funds; (4) providing a vehicle for family unity; (5) offering younger family members a meaningful role in their communities (and sometimes a job); (6) personal fulfillment; and (7) status.

Wealth transfer tax savings also are influential. With the prospect of a 45 percent (or higher?) federal estate tax rate on wealth transfers over $3.5 million, a substantial bequest to a private foundation often becomes the culminating event in a wealthy individual's estate plan. This type of "philanthropic inheritance" avoids turning family assets over to the government through taxes and permits enormous pools of wealth to remain under family control for generations.[1] Many private foundations are initially funded during the wealth creator's life at a relatively modest level and receive the bulk of their endowment at the founder's death, when they qualify for a 100 percent estate tax charitable deduction.

Foundations still have their detractors, even from within the world of philanthropy. Some critics argue that private foundations are self-indulgent status symbols that support "pet projects" of the donor and are motivated largely by tax avoidance. They view public charities as more deserving of favorable tax treatment because they are more broadly representative of and thus accountable to the community at large. As the debate continues, the tax treatment of private foundations and public charities is slowly converging as Congress has shifts its scrutiny to the real and perceived abuses of public charities, including some of the popular private foundation alternatives discussed in this chapter.

For Further Reading. Kathryn W. Miree & Jerry J. McCoy, Family Foundation Handbook (2001); Bruce R. Hopkins & Jody Blazek, Private Foundations: Tax Law and Compliance (3d ed. 2009).

B.   PRIVATE FOUNDATIONS VS. PUBLIC CHARITIES: AN OVERVIEW

1.   THE TAX DEFINITION OF A PRIVATE FOUNDATION

Considering the vast regulatory scheme aimed at private foundations, one might have assumed that Congress would have told us what a private foundation "is." Curiously, it did just the opposite. The Code defines private foundations by exclusion, providing in § 509(a) that all § 501(c)(3) domestic or foreign organizations are private foundations unless they come within any of the following four categories of "nonprivate" foundations:

    (1) § 509(a)(1) "traditional public charities"—more specifically, those organizations described in 170(b)(1)(A)(i)–(vi). Very generally, this group includes churches, schools, hospitals, medical research insti-

---

1. To the surprise of just about everyone, the long scheduled temporary repeal of the estate tax went into effect on January 1, 2010, but the estate tax is set to be resurrected in 2011 with higher rates and lower exemptions. Permanent estate tax repeal, if it ever happens, would alter the planning agenda and reduce a major tax incentive for forming a private foundation. For the potential impact of estate tax repeal on charitable giving, see Chapter 8A, infra, at pp. 826–827.

tutions, support arms of state universities, governmental units, and broad publicly supported organizations that enjoy favored treatment for purposes of the charitable income tax deduction.

(2) § 509(a)(2) "broad publicly supported organizations"—another breed of public charity, sometimes referred to as "gross receipts" or "membership" organizations, that receive more than one-third of their support from gifts, grants, fees and "gross receipts" from admissions, sales of goods or services, where the fee-generating activity is related to the performance of the organization's exempt purposes.

(3) § 509(a)(3) "supporting organizations," which are not publicly supported but have a closely defined control or programmatic relationship with one or more public charities.

(4) § 509(a)(4) "testing for public safety" organizations, a specialized category of no great consequence that will not be discussed further.

All of these organizations share the characteristic of "publicness" in that they rely on public support or are accountable to a broad constituency. As such, they are seen as less susceptible to the abuses that motivated Congress to regulate private foundations more stringently. The excerpt below, from a guidebook published by The Council on Foundations, elaborates on the three major types of "nonprivate" foundations.

John A. Edie, First Steps in Starting a Foundation

Council on Foundations 8–13 (4th ed. 1997).

Exception 1: Traditional Charities and Publicly Supported Organization #1

The traditional charity exception contains the largest number of organizations. The term traditional is not used in the tax code, but is offered here to distinguish the various categories in shorthand form.

The first exception is really a list of many different legal exceptions that include many traditional institutions: churches, colleges, universities, schools, nonprofit hospitals, medical research institutes, support organizations to schools and governmental units. If the organization qualifies under the legal definition of any one of these traditional institutions, it is sufficiently public and will not be classified as a private foundation.

Congress felt that churches were sufficiently public because by definition they were composed of a broad segment of the community that actively participated in the day-to-day operations of the organization and contributed funds to it regularly. Similarly, educational institutions by definition include faculty and student bodies and parents paying tuition. Medical institutions (such as nonprofit hospitals) also could fall under the definition of public based on the involvement of the medical profession, and the fact that patients constantly use the institution for medical care. In short, each institution could not survive without continually convincing a reasonably large segment of the public that its operation and services are worthwhile. By similar reasoning, governmental units were sufficiently public, because their continued existence depended upon the oversight and approval of publicly elected officials. Note that all governmental units escape private foundation status through Exception 1. Governmental units are treated as public charities even though they are not classified under Section 501(c)(3).

A newly formed organization also can fall under this first exception as a traditional charity in another way. Even though it may not satisfy the legal definition of the various institutions just noted, it may qualify by being publicly supported. The test of publicness here is different. It is not the inherent nature (or definition) of the church, school or hospital that is important here. The question is whether the organization can meet certain public support tests. Can the organization demonstrate that a certain portion of its total support comes directly or indirectly from public contributions?

If one is contemplating the formation of an organization whose primary source of funding will be public donations and/or government support, the traditional charity format is the preferred type of organization to form. The organization will not be classified as a private foundation (through Exception 1—Traditional) because it will meet one of two public support tests. Traditional charities such as the Red Cross, the YMCA, the United Way and the Audubon Society meet this definition. However, certain organizations whose purpose primarily is grantmaking (such as community foundations) also can satisfy the rules for this classification.

For publicly supported charities under this first exception, there are two tests. If the charity fails to meet the first test, it may fall back to the second test. The first test is called the **mechanical test** because it relies on a mathematical formula. If over the most recent five-year period, public support equals or exceeds one-third of total eligible support, the charity has met the test and will qualify as a public charity.

Public support divided by total support equals the support fraction. The rules for what counts as public support and what does not are complex; this is one of many areas where legal counsel is especially important. Generally, the types of support that count as *public* support and are included in both the top and the bottom half of the support fraction are:

1. Contributions from individuals, foundations, trusts or corporations.

2. Support from governmental units.

3. Membership dues, if the basic purpose of such payment is to support the organization rather than to purchase admissions, merchandise, services or the use of facilities.

All public support counts as part of total support. The types of support that *cannot* count as public support but are included in *total* support making up the bottom half of the fraction are:

1. Gross investment income.

2. Contributions and dues from individuals, foundations, trusts or corporations that exceed two percent of total support for the applicable period.

3. Net income from unrelated business activities.

In constructing the support fraction to see if the one-third test has been met, the organization must exclude from both the top and bottom half any income received from the exercise of the exempt function of the foundation (admission fees, fees for services, etc.). * * *

If the organization fails to meet the mechanical test, it has a second chance and may resort to the **facts and circumstances test.** Under this test, the organization may fall below the one-third test, but—as the name suggests—it may still qualify depending on all the facts and circumstances. To qualify under this test, the organization must demonstrate adequate evidence of three different elements:

1. The total amount of government and public support must equal or exceed an absolute minimum ten percent of total support for the applicable period.

2. It must be organized and operated to attract new and additional public and governmental support on a continuous basis; and

3. It must demonstrate by other facts and circumstances that it is entitled to be recognized as public rather than private. Two of several factors considered here are: to what degree the board of directors represents the general public (rather than merely the donors), and to what extent services or facilities of the organization are available to the general public.

In summary, the first exception (Traditional Charities and Publicly Supported Organization #1) is quite flexible, and meeting the public support requirements is not onerous. Consequently, it is the most frequently used form of public charity.

* * *

Exception 2: Gross Receipts Charities or Publicly Supported Organization #2

The second type of public charity also must meet a public support test. Part of the legacy of the 1969 tax legislation was recognizing that certain organizations that relied in large part on gross receipts from tax-exempt activities also should qualify for the more favored tax advantages of the traditional charities. As noted above, the traditional charity may not include as public support any receipts obtained from carrying out its exempt function. A Gross Receipts charity—as the name suggests—can count such support as public. Again, the term gross receipts is not actually used in this section of the tax code, but it is offered here to avoid the use of more technical language.

To qualify as a Gross Receipts charity, two tests must be met. The first is a different **public support test.** To satisfy this test, the organization normally must receive more than one-third of its total support from any combination of (1) qualifying gifts, grants, contributions or membership fees, *and* (2) gross receipts from admissions, sales of merchandise, performance of services or furnishing of facilities in activities related to its exempt functions. Examples of public charities that commonly fall under this classification are symphonies, opera companies and a wide variety of organizations that provide charitable services for a fee.

As with traditional charities, the support fraction is calculated over [a five-year period]. However, you have *no* facts and circumstances test to fall back on. The one-third public support percentage is an absolute minimum.

The second test that must be met is the **investment income test.** Under this test, the organization must show that the total of its investment income and net unrelated business income does not exceed one-third of its total support.

It bears repeating that what constitutes total support versus public support for both Traditional charities and Gross Receipts charities is highly technical and complex and, therefore, skilled counsel is essential. Two examples of this complexity for Publicly Supported Charity #2 are worth noting:

Limits on Substantial Contributors: In adding up public support to qualify as a Publicly Supported Charity #2, the contribution of *any* amount from a disqualified person (including substantial contributors) cannot count as public support (in the top half) but nonetheless counts as total support (in the bottom half). A substantial contributor to a Publicly Supported Charity #2 is one who contributes more than $5,000; and that amount must exceed two percent of the total support ever received by the organization by the close of that tax year. Contributions from substantial contributors can count as public support for a traditional charity (subject to the two percent limit described above).

$5,000 or One Percent Limit on Gross Receipts: A Gross Receipts charity cannot count as *public* support gross receipts from any person or governmental unit that exceeds the greater of $5,000 or one percent of total support for that year. However, any gross receipts that exceed this limit must be counted as part of *total* support in meeting the one-third test. As noted above, gross receipts received by a traditional charity may not count as public support.

If this discussion of public support leaves you hopelessly confused, do not feel alone. The U.S. Tax Court stated that these rules are "almost frighteningly complex and technical." * * * However, you should be left with the understanding that: (1) two different types of publicly supported organization classifications are available, each with different advantages and disadvantages, and (2) sound legal advice on which option best fits the reader's needs is indispensable.

Exception 3: Supporting Organization

The supporting organization is a third type of public charity category. Because of the complexity of the rules, an attempt to provide details on how to qualify as a supporting organization would be foolish in the context of this book. Instead, the intent here is to provide a rough understanding of what a supporting organization is and how it can be used.

Four important points should be stressed. First, this option is becoming a popular choice among those starting foundations. Second, its requirements are flexible, enabling it to be used in a variety of different circumstances. Third, its great advantage is that it does not require meeting any public support test and, *at the same time*, it enables the organization to obtain the advantages of being a public charity. Finally, establishing a supporting organization without expert legal counsel is virtually impossible.

How does a supporting organization acquire sufficient publicness to qualify as a public charity? A supporting organization is like a barnacle; it attaches itself to (or supports) another public charity (or charities), and—in effect—acquires the public charity status of the organization or organizations it supports. The biggest problem is to make sure the barnacle sticks. In other words, the supporting organization must be carefully constructed to meet the complex tests required by the law and regulations. The two essential tests are a **purpose test** and a **control test.** The purpose test requires the supporting organization to benefit or carry out a purpose of the supported organization, ordinarily a public charity. The control test requires that the supported organization control the supporting organization. However, the definition of control is fairly broad and can be satisfied easily in most cases. Perhaps two examples of typical supporting organizations will aid the reader's understanding.

> **Trust example:** Mr. and Mrs. X endow a trust with $1 million to provide scholarships to public high school students in a particular city. The sole trustee is the local community foundation. No public support or fundraising is provided. The scholarships are paid from the investment income. The trust can qualify as a public charity because it is a supporting organization of a community foundation (one example of a traditional charity).

> **Corporate example:** Mr. and Mrs. Y establish a nonprofit corporation with an endowment of $1 million to help a local church in eliminating poverty in a particular city. In the articles of incorporation, they name a local church as the supported organization, and the church appoints three of five members to the foundation's board. Mr. and Mrs. Y are the other two board members. This foundation can qualify as a public charity since it is a supporting organization of another public charity.

Two other general limitations are worth mentioning:

Specified public charities: Normally it is expected that the charity or charities that will be supported will be specifically identified in the governing instruments by name. However, under some circumstances, specific identification can be avoided by identifying beneficiary organizations by class or purpose so long as other more technical tests are also met.

Limitation on control: A supporting organization may not be controlled directly or indirectly by one or more disqualified persons (meaning substantial contributors to the foundation and their families). Control in this context means having 50 percent or more of the voting power of the organization or the right to exercise veto power over the activities of the foundation.

* * *

[Additional requirements to qualify as a supporting organization and other limitations on their structure and operation were added by the Pension Protection Act of 2006 and are discussed in Section C4 of this chapter, infra, at pp. 751–763. Eds.]

2.   PRIVATE OPERATING FOUNDATIONS

The Internal Revenue Code distinguishes between traditional grant-making foundations and private operating foundations. Operating foundations do more than just make grants for charitable purposes; they also conduct their own charitable programs. The typical operating foundation receives its funding from a large gift or bequest from the founding donor. The income from the resulting endowment is used to support an active charitable enterprise, such as the operation of a museum, library, research institute, or public park. An example of a large private operating foundation is the J. Paul Getty Museum in Los Angeles.

Private operating foundations are subject to the entire regulatory regime applicable to private foundations, but they enjoy several notable advantages. The principal benefit is that donors to operating foundations may take advantage of the more favorable income tax charitable deduction rules applicable to public charities. Contributions to operating foundations qualify for the higher 50 percent limitation on contributions of cash and ordinary income property and the 30 percent limitation on contributions of capital gain property, and they are not subject to the reduction for unrealized built-in gain on certain gifts of appreciated capital gain property. I.R.C. § 170(b)(1)(A)(vii). Operating foundations also are exempt from the income distribution requirement applicable to nonoperating foundations under 4942.

Qualification as a private operating foundation requires satisfying an "income test," which generally requires the foundation to use "substantially all" (85 percent or more) of its income directly for the active conduct of charitable activities rather than for grantmaking. In addition, a private operating foundation must meet one of the following three tests, each of which is described only generally:

1.   The **assets test**, under which a foundation must show that at least 65 percent of all its assets are devoted directly to the active conduct of

the foundation's exempt function activities (e.g., operation of a museum) or to functionally-related businesses (e.g., low-income housing), or both, or consist of stock of a foundation-controlled corporation, 65 percent or more of the assets of which are so devoted. I.R.C. § 4942(j)(3)(B)(i). Investment assets are included in the denominator of the testing fraction but may not be counted in satisfying the 65 percent test.

2. The **endowment test**, under which the foundation normally must expend funds directly for the active conduct of its exempt purposes in an amount equal to 3–1/3 percent of the fair market value of its net investment assets. I.R.C. § 4942(j)(3)(B)(ii).

3. The **support test**, under which the foundation must receive at least 85 percent of its support from the general public and five or more unrelated exempt organizations, provided that not more than 25 percent of the foundation's support is received from any one exempt organization and not more than half of the support is normally received from gross investment income. I.R.C. § 4942(j)(3)(B)(iii).

The regulations elaborate considerably on these requirements, covering such matters as the relevant testing periods and the treatment of various receipts and expenses for purposes of the numerous tests. See Treas. Reg. § 53.4942(b).

3. PRIVATE FOUNDATION EXCISE TAXES

The centerpiece of the private foundation regulatory regime is a set of excise taxes imposed on private foundations and their managers (e.g., trustees, officers and other insiders) for the types of infractions that Congress concluded were susceptible to the greatest abuse. These taxes impose gradual punishment, beginning with a slap on the wrist (an "initial tax") and the opportunity to seek absolution by a process known as "correction." Those who do not correct are subject to a far more confiscatory second-level tax. Only the most flagrant violators risk loss of tax-exempt status and, in the very worst cases, confiscation of all their assets. An abatement procedure provides relief from the first-tier taxes in some cases, but ignorance of the law ordinarily does not justify exoneration. Congress also enacted a modest excise tax on a private foundation's net investment income, ostensibly to pay for all the bureaucracy needed to audit and monitor the new regime.

The excise taxes are extremely intricate and go beyond whatever abuses had been prevalent in the foundation community. The following description briefly summarizes the regulatory system, stripped of details. To ease comprehension, the text avoids the use of limiting language such as "in general" and "ordinarily," but it should be understood that exceptions and refinements abound in this area, and a legal advisor to a private foundation should never rely on a mere overview.

Excise Tax on Investment Income (§ 4940). Section 4940 imposes a tax of two percent on a private foundation's net investment income, a tax base that includes items such as dividends, interest, royalties, and net capital gains, less directly related expenses. At one time the rate was four percent, but Congress reduced it after discovering that the tax raised far more than what was needed to administer the system. Foundations may reduce their excise tax rate to one percent by making additional distributions for charitable purposes.

Self–Dealing (§ 4941). The self-dealing provisions penalize virtually any transaction between a private foundation and its "disqualified persons," even if the deal is at arm's length. Section 4946 defines "disqualified person" broadly to include major donors (known technically as "substantial contributors"), trustees and officers of the foundation, members of their families, some of their business associates and related business entities such as corporations and partnerships. In theory, the penalty can apply even if the act of self-dealing benefits the foundation. Among the prohibited transactions are sales, exchanges and leases of property; lending of money; and furnishing of goods, services or facilities. A foundation may pay reasonable compensation to a disqualified person, however, for services necessary to carry out the foundation's exempt purposes.

The initial penalty is 10 percent of the amount involved in the transaction on the self-dealer and 5 percent (with a $20,000 per act cap) on foundation managers who participate and know what they are doing. Second-tier taxes of 200 percent and 50 percent (with a $20,000 cap), respectively, of the amount involved are imposed if the self-dealing act is not corrected within a specified period.

Minimum Distribution Requirements (§ 4942). Private foundations must make annual "qualifying distributions" in an amount equal to 5 percent of the fair market value of their net investment assets. The penalty for failure to meet this charitable payout requirement is an excise tax of 30 percent of the undistributed income, with a second-tier penalty of 100 percent if the shortfall is not distributed within a specified correction period. Qualifying distributions include grants for charitable purposes, reasonable administrative costs related to the grantmaking process (e.g., staff salaries), payments to acquire assets used in the conduct of the foundation's exempt activities, and expenses of conducting direct charitable activities (e.g., a research project). Certain amounts set-aside for future projects and "program-related investments" (e.g., scholarship loans or an equity investment in a community development project) also satisfy the payout requirement. A foundation generally has two years (the current taxable year and the following year) to make the required distributions.

Excess Business Holdings (§ 4943). Congress concluded that it was inappropriate for a private foundation to hold a substantial stake in the principal donor's family business. To implement this policy, § 4943 imposes a tax on a foundation's "excess business holdings," which are defined for most purposes as any holdings that exceed a 20 percent ownership interest in the enterprise, reduced by the percentage owned by disqualified persons. For example, if disqualified persons own 11 percent, the foundation's interest must be limited to 9 percent. If disqualified persons own more than

20 percent, the foundation must completely divest, except under a de minimis rule a foundation can always own less than 2 percent of any business irrespective of the percentage held by disqualified persons. Grace periods of from 5 to 10 years are provided to divest holdings received by gift or bequest. If effective control of the business is held by owners who are not disqualified persons, the limit may be raised to 35 percent. The initial tax is 5 percent of the value of the excess holdings. An additional tax of 200 percent is imposed if the foundation fails to make the required divestiture within a correction period. Section 4943 also applies to donor-advised funds and some types of supporting organizations.

Jeopardy Investments (§ 4944). Private foundations are subject to a 10 percent penalty on amounts invested in a manner that jeopardizes the carrying out of their exempt purposes. Foundation managers who knowingly participate in the jeopardy investment also are subject to a 5 percent penalty (with a $10,000 cap). Failure to correct will result in a second-tier tax of 25 percent against the foundation and 5 percent (with a $20,000 cap) against any sinning foundation managers. Determining whether an investment crosses the jeopardy line is a factual question, with the emphasis placed on the care and prudence of the board of directors. An exception is granted for program-related investments made to achieve a charitable objective rather than to produce income (e.g., a low-interest loan to a minority business).

Taxable Expenditures (§ 4945). Section 4945 contains a list of expenditures that Congress believed were inconsistent with a private foundation's proper mission. Taxable expenditures include any expenditures for lobbying; electioneering and voter registration; grants to individuals; grants to any organization that is not classified as a public charity; and (lest anything be forgotten) any other expenditure for noncharitable purposes. An initial tax of 20 percent of the prohibited expenditure is imposed on the foundation and 5 percent on foundation managers (with a $10,000 cap) who agree to the expenditure and know it is subject to a penalty. Additional taxes of 100 percent on the foundation and 50 percent on the foundation manager (with a $20,000 cap) are imposed if the action is not corrected. This only begins to tell the story. Section 4945 contains numerous exceptions—for example, grants to individuals are permitted if certain grantmaking procedures are pre-approved by the IRS. Grants to organizations that are not public charities are allowed if the foundation exercises "expenditure responsibility"—a bureaucratic but ultimately surmountable legal requirement designed to ensure that the funds are used solely for charitable purposes.

4. Donor–Advised Funds

Internal Revenue Code: §§ 170(f)(18); 4943(e)(1)–(3); 4958(c)(2), (f)(1)(E), (f)(7)–(8); 4966; 4967.

a. INTRODUCTION

Donor-advised funds have become widely recognized as flexible, low cost and tax-efficient alternatives to private foundations. In a typical donor-advised fund, an individual or family contributes cash or appreciated property to a public charity, which enters into an agreement with the donor to establish a philanthropic "fund." The fund usually bears the name of the donor or another individual that the donor selects.[1] The public charity assumes legal control over how the assets are invested and distributed, but the donor-advisor may recommend grants under guidelines established by the organization sponsoring the fund. Although nonbinding, virtually all these grant recommendations are accepted if the grantee is a qualified U.S. public charity. Some donor-advised funds permit donors to recommend investments, usually from a menu of mutual funds. A donor-advised fund typically terminates at the death of the donor (or the donor's spouse), and any remaining assets are distributed for charitable purposes. A more recent trend, however, is to permit donors to appoint successor advisors for at least one generation or to create a named endowment for a particular charitable purpose if the amount remaining in the fund at the donor's death is over a certain dollar threshold. Lifetime gifts to donor-advised funds qualify for current income tax deductions,[2] but the donor may defer selecting the ultimate recipients until later years. This feature enables a donor to make a large gift (e.g., of highly appreciated stock) in high-income years and use the fund to make grants over time. In the meantime, earnings within the fund are not taxable.

Donor-advised funds have existed for over 75 years, but they remained mostly in the shadows until the 1980s. They were pioneered by community foundations and religions federations and have enjoyed enormous growth since being discovered and adapted by several large financial services firms and a few independent organizations formed solely to administer donor-advised funds. According to the latest survey by the Chronicle of Philanthropy, the 90 or so largest donor-advised fund "sponsors" had $22.3 billion in combined assets at the end of 2008 (down from $23.7 billion in 2007 but way up from approximately $13 billion in 2003) and made combined grants of $5.4 billion. Some of the largest donor-advised fund programs are charitable entities formed by financial services firms. The prototype for this relatively new breed of charity was the Fidelity Charitable Gift Fund, founded in 1991, which by the end of 2008 had amassed over $3.8 billion, making it one of the wealthiest public charities in the United States. For a minimum initial tax-deductible gift of $10,000, donors may "bank" their charitable dollars in a named or anonymous fund and recommend grants to virtually any charity on the IRS approved list. All the Fund's investments are managed by Fidelity Investments for a fee that varies based on the balance in the fund and the number of annual

---

1. Related vehicles are the donor-designated fund, where a donor makes an irrevocable gift, usually to a community foundation, and designates specific charitable organizations to which grants will be made, and a field-of-interest fund established to support a particular charitable purpose, such as the arts or education.

2. Income tax deductions are disallowed, however, if the donor-advised fund sponsor is a veterans organization, fraternal society, cemetery company or what we will come to know as a Type III supporting organization that is not functionally integrated with its supported organization. I.R.C. § 170(f)(18)(A).

transactions. Several other financial services firms, such as Vanguard and Charles Schwab, offer similar philanthropic "products" that are said to provide all the advantages of a private foundation.

Commercially sponsored funds contributed to the growth of charitable giving in the 1990s, but they were not warmly received within the world of philanthropy. Concerns were expressed about the close relationship between these funds and their commercial sponsors. The funds also have been criticized for their marketing emphasis and failure to carry out any charitable program or to monitor the grantmaking of their donor-advisers. Initially, the Fidelity Charitable Gift Fund gave almost unbridled discretion to donors, allowing them to make grants to their own private foundations or to foreign charities. Some fund sponsors permitted donors to pay off legally binding pledges or receive personal benefits in return for their grants without reducing their charitable deduction. When these practices were publicized, Fidelity adopted new rules prohibiting donors from funneling money to private foundations and mandating the annual distribution of at least five percent of the Fund's assets for charitable purposes. Most of the funds sponsored by financial services firms now have clear guidelines that conform to all legal requirements, but some critics remain dissatisfied, asserting that the sole purpose of creating the "commercial" funds was to generate investment management fees for the sponsor. Virtually all donor-advised fund sponsors charge an administrative fee, ranging from .60 to 1.5 percent of the value of the fund, and separate investment management fees.

Donor-advised funds were not regulated by statute until passage of the Pension Protection Act of 2006. The Act provided the first definitions and added a new layer of regulation requiring more transparency and penalizing donors and related parties who receive personal economic benefits and fund sponsors that make inappropriate distributions.

b. DEFINITION OF DONOR–ADVISED FUND

The Internal Revenue Code defines a donor-advised fund ("DAF") as any fund or account that is separately identified by reference to the contributions of a donor or donors; is owned and controlled by a "sponsoring organization" ("SPORG"), such as a community foundation or other public charity that maintains one or more DAFs where the donor or any person appointed by the donor has or reasonably expects to have advisory privileges over either distributions or investments of amounts held in the fund by reason of the donor's status as a donor. I.R.C. § 4966(d)(2)(A). The presence of an "advisory privilege" may be evident from a written document, such as a fund agreement, or by a pattern of reciprocal conduct between the donor and the SPORG. The privilege need not have existed at the time of the original contribution—e.g., it could arise later when the donor gives advice that is regularly followed by the SPORG.

Two types of funds are excluded from the DAF definition. The first exception is for funds that benefit a single designated organization or governmental entity. I.R.C. § 4966(d)(2)(B)(I). This exception excludes from DAF status an endowment fund owned and controlled by a SPORG even if it is named after its principal donor and the donor has advisory privileges with respect to the distribution of amounts held in the fund to that organization.

The second exception is for funds where the donor or his designee offers advice on grants to individuals for travel, study or similar purposes provided that:

(1) the advisory privileges are performed exclusively by the donor-advisor in that person's capacity as a member of a committee all of the members of which are appointed by the SPORG;

(2) the committee is not controlled by the donor or donor-advisor or any person related to them; and

(3) all grants from the fund are awarded on an objective and nondiscriminatory basis pursuant to a procedure approved in advance by the SPORG's board, and such procedure meets the requirements of § 4945(g) (relating to grants to individuals by private foundations).

I.R.C. § 4966(d)(2)(B).

The Treasury is granted authority to grant additional exemptions for funds advised by a committee not controlled by the donor or any person appointed by the donor to advise on distributions from the fund, or if the fund benefits a single identified charitable purpose, such as a fund formed to aid individuals affected by a particular natural or civic disaster. I.R.C. § 4966(d)(2)(C).

c. TAXABLE DISTRIBUTIONS AND PROHIBITED BENEFITS

Taxable Distributions. Section 4966 imposes excise taxes of 20 percent (on the SPORG) and five percent with a $10,000 cap (on any "fund manager" who knowingly agrees to the distribution) on the amount of each "taxable distribution" made from a donor-advised fund. The "fund managers" who may be subject to the taxable distributions penalty are officers, directors, trustees or persons having similar responsibilities who agree to the making of a taxable distribution. I.R.C. § 4966(a)(2). This new tax effectively prohibits certain DAF grants altogether and requires "expenditure responsibility" (a more rigorous standard of due diligence that is borrowed for this purpose from the private foundation excise tax regime) for certain other types of distributions.

Taxable distributions do not include distributions to most U.S. public charities, their sponsoring organizations, other DAFs, government entities, and supporting organizations that are not "disqualified" SOs. A "taxable distribution" is any grant from a DAF to:

(1) an individual;

(2) any entity other than a public charity or governmental entity described in § 170(b)(1)(A) if the distribution is not for a charitable purpose; or

(3) unless the SPORG exercises expenditure responsibility, to "disqualified SOs," most private grantmaking foundations, and foreign charities.

I.R.C. § 4966(c)(1). A "disqualified" SO is any Type III SO that is not functionally integrated or any Type I, II or functionally integrated SO if the DAF's donor or designated donor-advisor and persons related to them directly or indirectly control the organization that the SO supports. I.R.C. § 4966(d)(4). It seems appropriate at this point to wish readers good luck in deriving these rules from the convoluted statutory language and to remind them not to blame the messenger.

Prohibited Benefits. Section 4967 imposes an excise tax on the advice of any donor, donor-advisor, family member, or 35–percent controlled entity of a donor or donor-advisor that results in a more than incidental benefit from the grantee as a result of recommended distributions from a DAF. The tax is 125 percent of the amount of the prohibited benefit. Any fund manager of a SPORG who approves a distribution from a DAF knowing that it would result in more than an incidental benefit to the persons listed above will be subject to an excise tax equal to 10 percent of the amount of the benefit, not to exceed $10,000 for any one distribution. I.R.C. § 4967(a)(2), (b)(2). To prevent double penalties for the same offense, the excise tax on prohibited benefits will not apply if an intermediate sanctions excise tax has been imposed under § 4958 with respect to the distribution. I.R.C. § 4967(b). There is no requirement to "correct" by repaying the amount of prohibit benefits penalties to the charity.

Examples of prohibited benefits are distributions from a donor-advised fund to pay college tuition for a donor's children (an egregious abuse that few reputable fund sponsors have permitted) or receiving in return for a grant an economic benefit that would have reduced a charitable deduction if the grant had been a direct contribution from the donor. Most fund sponsors interpret this rule as precluding them from making grants for events such as dinners and auctions even if the donor separately pays for the value of the return benefits (e.g., the cost of the dinner) with personal funds.

d. OTHER SANCTIONS AND PENALTIES

Intermediate Sanctions. In another response to concerns that some donor-advised funds were providing personal benefits to their donor-advisors and others, Congress extended the § 4958 intermediate sanctions rules to various types of potentially abusive transactions. The effect is to preclude any grant, loan, payment of compensation, or "other similar payment" by a DAF to a donor, donor-advisor, or persons related to them, by treating those entire payments (and not just the excess benefit portion) as excess benefit transactions under § 4958 and thus subject to a 25 percent excise tax. I.R.C. §§ 4958(c)(2), (f)(7). Bona fide sales or leases of property are not subject to this automatic excess benefit transaction rule, nor are payments of compensation by a SPORG to a person who is both a donor with respect to a DAF and a service provider with respect to the SPORG unless the payment (e.g., a grant, loan or compensation) is viewed as a payment from the DAF and not from the SPORG. Amounts repaid as a result of correcting an excess benefit transaction under this rule may not be held in any DAF but most go into the SPORG's general funds.

In situations not already covered by the automatic excess benefit transaction rule, the generally applicable intermediate sanctions rules are extended to transactions between a DAF and its disqualified persons, with the DQP category under § 4958 expanded for this purpose to include donors and donor-advisors with respect to a DAF. I.R.C. § 4958(f)(1)(E). In addition, an "investment advisor" and persons related to investment advisors are treated as DQPs with respect to a SPORG for which the advice is provided. I.R.C. § 4958(f)(1)(F). "Investment advisors" means any person (other than an employee of a SPORG) compensated by the SPORG for managing the investments of, or providing investment advice with respect to, assets maintained in DAFs owned by the SPORG. I.R.C. § 4958(f)(8). The effect of this rule is to subject investment advisors who receive excess benefits (query how to determine "excess" in this well-compensated industry) to § 4958 intermediate sanctions penalties even if they otherwise are not DQPs because they are not in a position to exercise influence with respect to the SPORG.

Excess Business Holdings. Donor-advised funds are subject to the excise tax imposed by § 4943 on excess business holdings. As a result, donors no longer can "park" an interest in a family controlled business indefinitely in a DAF. Like private foundations, DAFs have five years after receipt of a gift or bequest to divest any excess business holdings and another five years if the DAF can demonstrate hardship. Business holdings of the SPORG outside of its donor-advised funds are not affected. For more details, see Section D4 of this chapter, infra, at pp. 791–792.

e. REPORTING AND DISCLOSURE

Contributions to DAFs are subject to additional substantiation requirements that are the donor's responsibility but, as a practical matter, require the SPORG to state in its contemporaneous written gift acknowledgment that it has exclusive legal control over the contributed assets. I.R.C. § 170(f)(18)(B). SPORGs must disclose on their Form 990 information return the number of DAFs they administer, and the aggregate contributions to and grants from the funds during the year. Charities applying for exemption after August 17, 2006 must disclose whether they intend to maintain DAFs and, if so provide information on how the program will be operated—e.g., how they plan to notify donors that the funds are owned by the charity and that distributions may not confer private benefits on donors. I.R.C. § 6033(k).

f. LINGERING POLICY QUESTIONS

The Pension Protection Act of 2006 directed the Treasury to conduct a study to consider whether charitable contribution deductions are appropriate for gifts to DAFs; whether DAFs should be subject to a payout requirement; whether retention of advisory rights is consistent with the treatment of transfers as completed gifts; and whether the preceding issues are relevant with respect to other forms of charitable gifts. See I.R.S. Notice 2007–21, inviting public comments on this study by April 7, 2007. Many comments were received, but the eagerly awaited study had not yet been released as of early 2010.

5. Pass–Through Foundations and Pooled Common Funds

Internal Revenue Code: § 170(b)(1)(A)(vii), (b)(1)(F)(ii), (iii).

Two types of private grantmaking foundations—the pass-through (or conduit) foundation and the pooled common fund—are subject to the entire private foundation regulatory regime except for the limitations on the charitable deduction in § 170. More specifically, they are entitled to the more liberal percentage limitations and their donors are not required to reduce their deductions for gifts of appreciated capital gain property by the amount of the built-in gain.

Pass–Through Foundations. A pass-through foundation must pass through all contributions made to it during the taxable year within two and one-half months after the end of the tax year in which the gifts are made. The definition is actually a bit more technical in that the requirement is to make "qualifying distributions," as defined in § 4942(g), equal to 100 percent of the value of its contributions received. For this purpose, qualifying distributions include grants to other charities and certain costs of administering the grantmaking program. See I.R.C. § 170(b)(1)(F)(ii).

Pass-through foundations are used by philanthropists who wish to launch a charitable entity during their lives, enjoying the favorable income tax benefits, and then more fully endow the foundation at death. The trade-off for the more liberal income tax treatment is the pass-through requirement, but this vehicle presents a few advantages over direct gifts from the donor. First, reasonable administrative costs, such as salaries to foundation staff, count as qualifying distributions but might not be tax-deductible if paid directly by an individual donor. Second, donors achieve a current income tax deduction but have a grace period of several months to decide the ultimate recipients of their charitable largesse. Third, a foundation may elect in and out of pass-through status from year to year. Thus, in years where the liberal deduction rules in § 170 are desirable, it can make the election; in other years, the foundation may elect out and only be required to meet the minimum distribution requirements (generally, five percent of its endowment) of § 4942. See Section D3 of this chapter, infra, at pp. 781–789.

Pooled Common Funds. The pooled common fund is a little-known charitable vehicle with the following characteristics:

1. One or more donors may make contributions that are pooled into a common fund.

2. The donor (or his or her spouse) may retain the right to designate annually the organizations to which the income attributable to his or her contribution shall be given.

3. The donee organizations must be public charities described in § 509(a)(1).

4. The fund's governing instrument must require it to distribute, and it in fact must pay out (including administrative costs):

   a. All of its adjusted net income (as defined) to one or more eligible charities not later than two and one-half months after the end of the taxable year in which the income was earned or realized.

   b. All the corpus attributable to any donor's contribution to the fund to one or more eligible charities not later than one year after the death of the donor (or the donor's surviving spouse if that spouse has the right to designate the recipients of corpus).

I.R.C. § 170(b)(1)(F)(iii).

The pooled common fund offers donors the advantage of the more liberal charitable income tax deduction rules without the requirement to pass through all gifts on a relatively current basis. It allows donors to retain full control over the ultimate recipients of their gifts and, if desired, to pool funds with close family members and other donors. Like donor-advised funds, the pooled common fund also permits donors with fluctuating income to coordinate their annual giving levels, giving more in high income years while retaining a steady level of giving overall. They also can "bank" charitable funds for a major gift in the future while achieving current charitable deductions. But a pooled common fund is not a suitable vehicle for establishing an endowed grantmaking foundation in perpetuity because the corpus must be paid out to qualifying public charities within a year of the donor's death.

PROBLEM

1. Consider generally whether the following § 501(c)(3) organizations are public charities or private foundations:

(a) The Bay Cities Free Clinic is an outpatient facility providing medical services to low-income residents of a major urban community. The Clinic receives all its funding from Dr. Trish Largess, its founder, and her immediate family.

(b) The Progressive Advocacy Institute is a public policy think tank that makes fellowship and research grants in the area of social justice. The Institute was formed with a $30 million bequest from a single donor and supports its operations through investment income and gifts from the founding donor's children.

(c) The Green Foundation seeks to educate the general public on issues related to sustainability. For the current taxable year and the four years preceding the current year, the Foundation received the following support:

Interest income	$240,000
Government grant	100,000
Income from sale of books	160,000
Individual contributions (none more than $1,000)	120,000
Bequest from founder (not an "unusual grant")	200,000

(d) Same as (c), above, except $40,000 of the $120,000 in individual contributions were from donors who gave $1,000 or less and $80,000 was from Julie Green, the surviving spouse of the organization's founder.

(e) The Cyberspace Cultural Center is a technology museum created six years ago with a $30 million gift from Cy Space and his wife, Sissy. For the current year and the four preceding years, it received the following support:

Dividend income	$1,000,000
Admission fees	300,000
Grant from public charity	200,000
Gift from Cy Space	200,000
Individual contributions (none more than $1,000)	100,000

(f) The Global Law School Foundation was founded with a $20 million gift from George Porous, a hedge fund manager. It derives all of its $600,000 in annual support from investment income. The Foundation provides general support in equal shares to international law programs at three law schools, all of which are public charities. Its seven-person board consists of George Porous, his two children, his lawyer, and the deans of the three supported law schools.

2. Nate Brown and Kwan Lee are a married couple in their 40's with a net worth of $30 million, most of which consists of low-basis common stock in Froogle, Inc., a publicly traded company where Nate and Kwan are employed as executives. During the current year, Nate and Kwan anticipate unusually high taxable income ($4 million) because of a large capital gain realized on the sale of some of their Froogle stock. They are both active in the community and wish to make a gift of $5 million of Froogle stock this year to a philanthropic vehicle from which they may make future gifts to a wide variety of charitable organizations. They prefer to give anonymously. Keeping in mind their goals, consider generally the pros and cons of the following alternative giving vehicles for Nate and Kwan's contribution:

(a) A private foundation.

(b) A donor-advised fund at their local community foundation.

(c) A donor-advised fund at a § 501(c)(3) organization founded and administered by a major financial services firm.

(d) A § 509(a)(3) supporting organization.

C. AVOIDING PRIVATE FOUNDATION STATUS: THE DETAILS

The preceding sections provided an overview of the federal tax treatment of private foundations, including the rules distinguishing private foundations from public charities. For those with the intellectual curiosity or professional obligation to explore further, we turn here to a more technical examination of the tax definition of a private foundation and some strategies for avoiding private foundation status. Because this chapter has been designed to provide both a self-standing overview along with this more detailed coverage, some repetition is unavoidable for those who choose to read on. Any overlap is likely to be pedagogically beneficial, however, because the private foundation classification rules are seldom mastered on a first reading.

1. THE DISQUALIFIED PERSON RULES

Internal Revenue Code: §§ 4946; 507(d)(2).

Treasury Regulations: §§ 53.4946–1(a); 1.507–6(b)(1).

Like any complex statute, the private foundation rules are littered with terms of art. The term "disqualified person" is particularly important. For example, in testing the level of an organization's public support, contributions from disqualified persons count less than gifts from outsiders, and in some cases they do not count at all. The self-dealing penalty in 4941 applies to transactions between a private foundation and disqualified persons, and the holdings of disqualified persons in a business enterprise may affect a foundation's permissible business holdings.

A "disqualified person" with respect to a private foundation includes the following: a "substantial contributor" (defined below), a "foundation manager" (also defined below), a more than 20 percent owner of a business entity that is a substantial contributor, a member of the family (yet another definition) of any of the foregoing, and corporations, partnerships, trusts or estates in which any of the foregoing (as a group) have greater than 35 percent ownership interests. I.R.C. § 4946(a).

A few specialized categories of "disqualified person" apply for purposes of the self-dealing and excess business holdings rules. They will be discussed in the context of the penalties to which they relate. See I.R.C. § 4946(a)(1)(H), (I).

Substantial Contributor. The major category of disqualified person consists of substantial contributors to the foundation and members of the family of substantial contributors. A substantial contributor is any person (including natural persons as well as entities, such as corporations or other private foundations) who has contributed or bequeathed an aggregate amount of more than $5,000 to the foundation, if that amount is more than

2 percent of the total contributions and bequests received by the foundation from its inception through the end of its taxable year in which the contribution or bequest is received. The creator of a charitable trust is always a substantial contributor. I.R.C. § 507(d)(2). The determination of a donor's substantial contributor status is made annually on the last day of a foundation's taxable year, but a donor "joins the club" as of the first date that the foundation received from the donor an amount sufficient to make him a substantial contributor. Id.; Treas. Reg. § 1.507–6(b)(1). With one exception described below, the donor remains a substantial contributor for time immemorial (including after one's death!), even if the person's aggregate gifts fall short of the 2 percent threshold in the future. Id.

In identifying substantial contributors, contributions and bequests are taken into account at their fair market value on the date the foundation receives the gift, except (historians take note) any gifts received before October 9, 1969 are treated for valuation purposes as having been received on that date. I.R.C. § 507(d)(2)(B)(i) & (ii). Individuals are treated as making all contributions and bequests made by their spouse, but not by other members of their family. I.R.C. § 507(d)(2)(B)(iii).

The principal donors to a private foundation almost always are substantial contributors. For example, assume Mr. and Mrs. Donor each give $1 million in appreciated stock to fund the Donor Foundation. Each is treated as giving $2 million—an amount well in excess of $5,000 and constituting 100 percent of the foundation's total gifts. The inquiry is more challenging for smaller donors. To illustrate, assume that Giver makes a mid-year gift of $6,000 cash to Foundation, which has received a total of $100,000 of gifts and bequests as of the end of that year. Since Giver's gift exceeds $5,000 and is more than 2 percent of the year-end total (2% of $100,000 = $2,000), he is a substantial contributor. But if Giver made the same $6,000 mid-year gift at a time when the foundation's total gifts were $100,000, but subsequent gifts raised the foundation's total to $1,000,000 by year-end, Giver would not be a substantial contributor because his gift does not exceed $20,000 (2% of $1,000,000) as of the end of the year.

At one time, the rule was "once a substantial contributor, always a substantial contributor." As will become clearer below, this status could taint related family members and their spouses even though they had nothing to do with the foundation. In the meantime the foundation may have received large gifts from other donors, diluting any historic influence a substantial contributor may have once derived from his or her contribution. Section 507(d)(2)(C) addresses this problem by providing that a person ceases to be treated as a substantial contributor as of the close of a foundation's taxable year if, for a ten-year period ending at the close of that year, the contributor or any related person neither makes any contribution to the foundation nor serves as its foundation manager. In addition, the Service must determine that the aggregate contributions made by the contributor and related persons (including appreciation of contributed property while held by the foundation) are "insignificant" when compared with the aggregate amount of contributions made by "one other person."

I.R.C. § 507(d)(2)(C)(i)(III). To illustrate, assume Donor makes a $10,000 cash gift to Foundation, which has received total contributions of $100,000 as of the end of Year 1. Donor makes no further gifts and, as of the end of Year 11, Foundation's aggregate gifts are $1,000,000, of which $500,000 was received from a person unrelated to Donor. Donor would lose substantial contributor status at the end of Year 11 because no gifts had been made for 10 years and Donor's $10,000 gift is "insignificant" when compared with the $500,000 received from the unrelated person.

Foundation Manager. A "foundation manager" is another type of disqualified person. Foundation managers include officers, directors, trustees, or individuals having similar powers or responsibilities. I.R.C. § 4946(a)(1)(B), (b)(1). Other foundation employees with authority or responsibility regarding particular matters also are treated as managers with respect to any act, or failure to act, within their scope of authority or responsibility, but the regulations make it clear that a person who is a foundation manager solely under this "responsible employee" rule is not a disqualified person for any other purpose. Treas. Reg. § 53.4946-1(f)(4).

Owners of Substantial Contributors. As noted above, corporations, partnerships, trusts and other entities may become substantial contributors. In addition, persons owning more than 20 percent of these entities are also treated as disqualified persons. Specifically, the ownership threshold is crossed by owning more than 20 percent of the voting stock of a corporation, of the profits interests of a partnership, or of the beneficial interests of other entities. I.R.C. § 4946(a)(1)(C). Nothing is simple. Stock ownership is determined by applying the § 267(c) attribution rules, with the definition of "family" modified slightly to include only an individual's spouse, ancestors, children, grandchildren, great grandchildren, and the spouses of these lineal descendants (siblings and more distant lineal descendants are dropped). I.R.C. § 4946(a)(3). Additional technical rules are provided to determine constructive ownership of interests in partnerships, trusts and other entities. See I.R.C. § 4946(a)(4).

Family Members. "Members of the family" of a substantial contributor, a foundation manager, or a more than 20 percent owner of a substantial contributor also are disqualified persons. I.R.C. § 4946(a)(1)(D). An individual's "family" includes his or her spouse, ancestors, children, grandchildren, great grandchildren, and the spouses of children, grandchildren and great grandchildren. I.R.C. § 4946(d). At one time, the disqualified person taint meandered forever through the family tree, but Congress—perhaps fearful that all of civilization ultimately would become disqualified people—revised the rule to halt the spreading virus at the great grandchildren's generation.

Related Entities. To ensure that Congressional intent could not be circumvented through the use of related entities, the term "disqualified person" includes any corporation, partnership, trust, or estate if more than 35 percent of the corporation's voting stock, the partnership's profits interests, or the trust or estate's beneficial interests is owned by the four types of disqualified persons discussed above—i.e., substantial contributors, more than 20 percent owners of substantial contributors, foundation managers, and members of the family of any of the foregoing. I.R.C. § 4946(a)(1)(E), (F), (G). The § 267 attribution rules once again apply in determining ownership interests.

2.   Traditional Public Charities: § 509(a)(1)

Internal Revenue Code: §§ 509(a)(1), (d); 170(b)(1)(A)(i)–(vi).

Treasury Regulations: §§ 1.170A–9(a), (b), (d)(1), (e); –9T(f)(1)–(4)(v), (6), (7).

Most organizations that avoid private foundation status come within the exception provided by § 509(a)(1) for traditional and publicly supported charities described in § 170(b)(1)(A)(i) through (vi). These organizations historically have been favored for charitable income tax deduction purposes. They sometimes are referred to as "50 percent charities" because cash contributions to them may be deducted by individual donors up to an annual limit of 50 percent of adjusted gross income. Traditional public charities fall into six sub-categories, five of which are exempted because of the nature of their activities and the sixth because of the level of public financial support that they receive.

a.   ORGANIZATIONS ENGAGING IN INHERENTLY PUBLIC ACTIVITIES

Churches or Conventions or Associations of Churches. The first exclusion from private foundation status is for churches and conventions and associations of churches. I.R.C. 170(b)(1)(A)(i). As discussed in Chapter 5, not every religious organization is a "church." The regulations do not define "church," but the courts occasionally have been forced to do so, usually applying 14 church characteristics employed by the Internal Revenue Service. According to the Tax Court, a minimum requirement for "church" status is a body of believers or communicants that assemble regularly in order to worship. See, e.g., Foundation of Human Understanding v. Commissioner, 88 T.C. 1341 (1987) (acq.); Chapter 5C6, supra, at pp. 415–431. A "convention or association of churches" is a regional or national umbrella organization that consists of member churches, usually of the same denomination, such as the National Council of Churches, the Union of American Hebrew Congregations, and the National Catholic Conference. See Rev. Rul. 74–224, 1974–1 C.B. 61.

Educational Organizations. Traditional public charities also include educational organizations that maintain a "regular faculty and curriculum" and normally have a "regularly enrolled body of pupils or students in attendance * * *." I.R.C. § 170(b)(1)(A)(ii). This category includes primary and secondary schools, colleges, universities and nonprofit vocational schools. Treas. Reg. § 1.170A–9(c).[1] Advocacy organizations that qualify as

---

1.   In September 2008, the IRS made significant changes to the regulations under § 170(b)(1)(A)(vi) and § 509(a)(2). Some nonsubstantive changes resulted in new section

"educational" under 501(c)(3) would not fall into this narrower classification. The primary function of an educational organization must be "the presentation of formal instruction." Id. The Service has construed this requirement liberally in several published rulings. See, e.g., Rev. Rul. 73–434, 1973–2 C.B. 71 (26–day survival course for young people); Rev. Rul. 78–309, 1978–2 C.B. 123 (martial arts school).

Hospitals and Medical Research Organizations. The hospitals that avoid private foundation status include any organization for which the "principal purpose or function is the providing of medical or hospital care." I.R.C. § 170(b)(1)(A)(iii). Inpatient care need not be provided, but the term "hospital" is not broad enough to include convalescent homes, homes for children or the aged, or facilities for training the handicapped. Treas. Reg. § 1.170A–9(d)(1).

"Medical research organizations" qualify if they are directly engaged in the continuous active conduct of medical research in conjunction with a hospital and if they commit contributions received to such research for use within five years of the time of the gift. I.R.C. § 170(b)(1)(A)(iii). Formal affiliation with a hospital is not required—only an "understanding" that the research organization and the hospital will cooperate and engage in a "joint effort." Treas. Reg. § 1.170A–9(d)(2)(vii). For more guidance on the nature of "medical research" and the extent of pursuits necessary to qualify under this provision, see Treas. Reg. § 1.170A–9(d)(2). This specialized exemption reportedly was created to cover organizations founded by Howard Hughes and the DuPont family, but it has a wider net.

Support Organizations for State Colleges and Universities. Organizations formed to support state colleges and universities are not private foundations if they normally receive a substantial part of their support from governmental sources or from direct or indirect contributions from the general public, or from a combination of those sources. I.R.C. 170(b)(1)(A)(iv). This category includes separately incorporated entities formed to conduct building fund drives, maintain scholarship funds, support athletic programs and the like. The determination of public support generally follows the guidelines applicable to § 170(b)(1)(A)(vi) organizations (see discussion below), although permitted sources of support from governmental entities are somewhat narrower. See Treas. Reg. § 1.170A–9(c)(2).

Governmental Units. This category of nonprivate foundation includes the United States, its political subdivisions, the District of Columbia, and all other governmental bodies listed in § 170(c)(1). I.R.C. § 170(b)(1)(A)(v). Singling out governmental units in § 170 is significant for purposes of the charitable income tax deduction, but excluding them from private foundation status may be unnecessary because most governmental units do not

designations (e.g., former § 1.170A–9(b) is now § 1.170A–9(c)). Substantive changes are reflected in "temporary" regulations that, unlike proposed regulations, become effective when they are issued. The temporary regulations apply to taxable years beginning on or after January 1, 2008.

derive their federal tax exemption from § 501(c)(3), and only § 501(c)(3) organizations can be private foundations.

b. PUBLICLY SUPPORTED ORGANIZATIONS

Section 170(b)(1)(A)(vi) describes the first of two types of publicly supported organizations excluded from private foundation status because of the breadth of their financial support. The exclusion is based on the notion that an organization dependent upon the general public or government for its support will be publicly accountable. This category of public charity must:

> [n]ormally receive a substantial part of its support (exclusive of income received in the exercise or performance by such organization of its charitable, educational, or other purpose or function constituting the basis for its exemption under § 501(a)) from a governmental unit * * * or from direct or indirect contributions from the general public.

I.R.C. § 170(b)(1)(A)(vi).

The regulations elaborate considerably, providing two alternative sub-tests to measure the requisite public support and defining the critical statutory terms. See generally Treas. Reg. § 1.170A–9T(f). We shall first outline the two sub-tests and then flesh out the remaining details.

Mathematical Test. An organization will be treated as a public charity for its current year and the next taxable year if public and governmental contributions equal at least one-third of the total support received by the charity over a testing period that generally consists of the current year and the four taxable years immediately preceding that year. Treas. Reg. 1.170A–9T(f)(2).

Facts and Circumstances Test. An organization that fails to meet the mathematical test still can qualify as a public charity if it generates at least 10 percent public support during the testing period and is "so organized and operated as to attract new and additional public or governmental support on a continuous basis." Treas. Reg. § 1.170A–9T(f)(3). An active fund raising program, including a membership structure, is helpful in meeting the "attraction of public support" requirement.

In addition to the 10 percent and attraction of public support requirements, the organization must establish, based on "all pertinent facts and circumstances," that it is publicly supported. Treas. Reg. § 1.170A–9T(f)(3)(ii). The regulations list five factors, stating that the weight accorded to any one of them may differ depending upon the nature and purpose of the organization and the length of time it has been in existence:

(1) *Percentage of Financial Support.* The higher the percentage of public support above 10 percent, the lesser is the organization's burden of establishing its publicly supported nature through other factors. The burden increases, conversely, as public support falls toward 10 percent. Treas. Reg. § 1.170A–9T(f)(3)(iii).

(2) *Sources of Support.* Public support is best demonstrated by a representative number of supporters rather than members of a single family group. In considering breadth of support, the regulations consider "the type of organization involved, the length of time it has been in existence, and whether it limits its activities to a particular community or region or to a special field which can be expected to appeal to a limited number of persons." Treas. Reg. § 1.170A–9T(f)(3)(iv).

(3) *Representative Governing Body.* A governing board that is representative of broad public or community interests is preferable to a narrow group. The regulations suggest a board comprised of public officials acting in that capacity; of individuals selected by public officials; of persons having special knowledge or expertise in the foundation's field of interests; of community leaders and others representing a broad cross-section of community views; and, in the case of membership organizations, of individuals elected by a broadly based membership. Treas. Reg. § 1.170A–9T(f)(3)(v).

(4) *Availability of Public Facilities or Services and Public Participation.* Organizations that generally provide facilities or services directly for the benefit of the general public on a continuing basis—e.g., museums, libraries, symphonies—are more easily able to demonstrate that they are publicly supported. In addition, the fact that educational or research organizations regularly publish and disseminate scholarly studies is considered evidence that they are publicly supported. The regulations list a number of other factors that are considered evidence of public support. Treas. Reg. § 1.170A–9T(f)(3)(vi).

(5) *Additional Factors Pertinent to Membership Organizations.* Membership organizations can demonstrate their public support by soliciting a broad cross-section of the public and having activities that are likely to appeal to persons having some broad common interest, such as educational activities in the case of alumni associations, or musical activities in the case of symphonies. Treas. Reg. § 1.170A–9T(f)(3)(vii).

Both the mechanical and the facts and circumstances tests require the organization to calculate its public support over a testing period by using a fraction that compares public support (the numerator) with total support (the denominator). The regulations provide the definitions needed to make this calculation.

Total Support. Total support includes gifts and grants from individuals, corporate donors, public charities, private foundations, and other nonprofit organizations; bequests; government grants made to enable the organization to provide a service to or maintain a facility for the direct benefit of the public; membership fees paid for general support of the organization; net income from unrelated business activities; gross investment income (excluding capital gains); tax revenues levied by a governmental unit for the benefit of the organization; and the value of services or facilities furnished without charge to the organization by a government unit (exclusive of what is generally provided free to the public). All income derived by the organization from the performance of its exempt functions—such as tuition, admission fees to a museum or theater, proceeds from the sale of merchandise—is excluded from total support for purposes of § 170(b)(1)(A)(vi). I.R.C. § 509(d); Treas. Reg. § 1.170A–9T(f)(6) & (7). Also excluded are the value of donated services (e.g., a volunteer's time) and certain "unusual grants," which are discussed below.

Public Support. Public support includes gifts, bequests and grants from the general public, government grants, membership fees, tax revenues levied specifically to benefit the organization, and the value of government provided services or facilities. Donations from any private source (e.g., a corporation, individual, trust or private foundation) are included in public support only to the extent they do not exceed two percent of the total support received by the organization over the measuring period. In applying the two percent limitation, an individual's contributions are aggregated with gifts made during the measuring period by certain members of the donor's family. Significantly, contributions from government entities and other public charities are not subject to the two percent limitation. Treas. Reg. § 1.170A–9T(f)(6), (7) & (8).

Unusual Grants. An "unusual grant" may be excluded from both the top and bottom of the public support fraction if including the grant would cause the organization to fail the public support test. An unusual grant is a substantial gift or bequest to an organization that: (1) is attracted by reason of the organization's publicly supported nature, (2) is unusual or unexpected with respect to its amount, and (3) by reason of its size, adversely affects the organization's public charity status. Treas. Reg. § 1.170A–9T(f)(6)(ii). Because gifts and grants are fully included in total support but are not included in public support to the extent they exceed the two percent cap, the ability to exclude unusual grants can be very helpful in preserving the public charity status of an organization receiving an unexpected windfall from a generous donor.

In evaluating whether a contribution qualifies as an unusual grant, the Service considers a long list of factors, no one of which is determinative. For example, a grant is more likely to be unusual if: (1) it is made by a person with no prior connection to the organization rather than by a member of the founding family or a member of the board of directors, (2) it is a bequest rather than a lifetime gift, (3) the gift is of cash or marketable securities rather than an illiquid asset that is unrelated to the organization's exempt purposes, (4) the organization regularly solicits funds, (5) if the organization has a broad based governing board, and (6) no material restrictions are imposed on the grant. Treas. Reg. § 1.170A–9T(f)(6)(iii); Rev. Proc. 81–7, 1981–1 C.B. 621.

Testing Period. The statute cryptically requires that a public charity "normally" must receive substantial public support. The term "normally" is construed by the regulations, which were revised in September 2008.

Under the old rules, public support for a current tax year was tested by looking to the four years immediately preceding that year or, alternatively, to the four years immediately preceding the year before the current year— e.g., 2008 public support was tested by looking to 2005 through 2008 or 2004 through 2007. Under the new rules, the public support computation testing period is now a full five years: the current year and the four preceding years. An organization that meets a public support test for any current taxable year is treated as publicly supported for that year and the immediately succeeding taxable year. For example, an organization using a calendar year that meets a public support test for 2011 based on its support for the 2007–2011 computation period will be classified as a public charity for 2011 and also 2012 even if it does not meet a public support test for 2008–2012. If it then is unable to meet a public support test for 2013 (based on the 2009–2013 computation period), it will be classified as a private foundation as of the beginning of 2013. Treas. Reg. § 1.170A–9T(f)(4)(i).

To coordinate the public support tests with the redesigned Form 990, support must be reported using the organization's overall method of accounting (e.g., cash or accrual). The previous regulations required the cash method for support computation purposes even if the organization used a different method. Under the old rules, organizations that experienced "substantial and material changes" in the sources of support for the current year—i.e., the year being tested—were permitted to use a five-year testing period, including the current year, to measure public support. The new regulations eliminate this exception because it is obsolete now that the general testing period is five years, including the year being tested.

Obtaining and Maintaining Public Charity Classification. Historically, a new § 501(c)(3) organization seeking to qualify as a publicly supported charity was required to obtain an advance ruling from the IRS. If the organization demonstrated to the IRS's satisfaction that it could "reasonably be expected" to meet one of the public support tests in § 170(b)(1)(A)(vi) or § 509(a)(2) during its first five years, it would receive a ruling recognizing its public charity classification. The 2008 regulations eliminate the advance ruling process. As discussed above, an organization that demonstrates in its exemption application that it can "reasonably be expected" to meet either the one-third public support test or the facts and circumstances test during its first five years will be classified as a public charity for that entire period and will not be subject to any private foundation excise taxes regardless of the level of public support it actually receives during those five years. In determining whether an organization can reasonably be expected to meet either the mathematical or "facts and circumstances" public support test of § 170(b)(1)(A)(vi), the regulations provide that the "basic consideration" is whether its organizational structure, current or proposed programs or activities, and actual or intended method of operation are such as can reasonably be expected to attract the type and level of support that is necessary to meet these those tests. The various factors applied under the ten percent plus facts and circumstances test are considered in making this determination. Treas. Reg. § 1.170A–9T(f)(4)(v)(B).

Beginning with its sixth year, an organization must demonstrate to the IRS (on Schedule A of Form 990, as revised beginning for 2008 tax years) that it actually does meet one of the public support tests, looking to the current tax year and the four immediately preceding years. If it fails to do so, it will be reclassified as a private foundation and be liable for the § 4940 excise tax on investment income and be subject to the other private foundation excise taxes. Treas. Reg. §§ 1.170A–9T(f)(4) & (5).

3. "Gross Receipts" and Membership Organizations: § 509(a)(2)

Internal Revenue Code: § 509(a)(2). Review §§ 507(d)(2); 509(d); 4946.

Treasury Regulations: § 1.509(a)–3(a)(1), (b)(1); –3T(a)(2), (c)(1), (d), (e)(1) & (2).

A different type of publicly supported organization is described in § 509(a)(2). To come within this escape hatch, an organization must enjoy broad public support measured by a positive support test and a negative investment income test. Specifically, a § 509(a)(2) organization first must demonstrate that it "normally" receives more than one-third of its total support from any combination of gifts, grants, contributions, membership fees, admission charges, and fees from the performance of exempt functions. I.R.C. § 509(a)(2)(A). Second, it must establish that it normally does not receive more than one-third of its support from the sum of gross investment income and unrelated business income less federal taxes imposed on that income. I.R.C. § 509(a)(2)(B). Congress included the additional category of public charity at the behest of certain organizations that derive substantial public support through their exempt function activities but are not heavily dependent on investment income. Because § 170(b)(1)(A)(vi) excludes exempt function income in testing for public support, another test was necessary to protect organizations that traditionally derived much of their revenue from tax-exempt activities. The legislative history indicates that § 509(a)(2) was intended to cover "symphony societies, garden clubs, alumni associations, Boy Scouts, Parent–Teacher Associations and many other membership organizations." S.Rep. No. 552, 91st Cong., 2d Sess. 461 (1969).

Total Support. The "total support" denominator of both the positive and negative fractions in § 509(a)(2) includes gifts, grants, contributions, and membership fees; "gross receipts" from admissions, sales of merchandise, performance of services or furnishing of facilities in an activity which is not an unrelated trade or business; net income from unrelated business activities; gross investment income, excluding capital gains; tax revenues levied for the organization's benefit and either paid to or expended on behalf of the organization; and the value of services or facilities furnished by the government specifically to the organization without charge. I.R.C. § 509(d).

Good Support. The numerator of the positive support fraction includes gifts, grants, contributions and fees received from governmental sources, public charities, or any other person who is not a disqualified person with respect to the organization as well as gross receipts from the conduct of exempt functions. I.R.C. § 509(a)(2)(A). Thus, gifts from substantial contributors or other insiders do not count as good support. Gross receipts from the conduct of exempt functions also are excluded from the numerator in any taxable year to the extent that they exceed the greater of $5,000 or one percent of the organization's support for that year. This limitation is intended to ensure that organizations relying on § 509(a)(2) maintain a broad-based program of income-generating sales or services.

The regulations go on at some length to distinguish grants (which are not subject to this limitation) and gross receipts. "Gross receipts" are amounts received from an activity where the organization provides a specific service, facility or product to serve the direct and immediate needs of the payor rather than to confer a direct benefit upon the general public. See Treas. Reg. § 1.509(a)–3(g).

Gross Investment Income. The negative support test set forth in § 509(a)(2)(B) provides that no more than one-third of the organization's total support may consist of: (1) gross investment income (consisting of interest, dividends, payments with respect to securities loans, rents, and royalties) and (2) the net of unrelated business taxable income over the unrelated business tax imposed by Section 511. The regulations also provide that an organization's gross investment income includes amounts distributed from the gross investment income of another organization. See Treas. Reg. § 1.509(a)–5(a)(1) for the details.

Unusual Grants. In measuring support for both the positive public support and negative investment income tests, an organization may exclude any unusual grants if they would have an adverse effect. The criteria for determining whether a particular contribution is an unusual grant are the same as those already discussed under § 170(b)(1)(A)(vi). See p. 746, supra, and Treas. Reg. § 1.509(a)–3T(c)(3).

Testing Period. The positive and negative support fractions are calculated by aggregating the organization's sources of support over the same rolling five-year testing period discussed earlier in connection with the § 170(b)(1)(A)(vi) public support test. Treas. Reg. § 1.509(a)–3T(c), (e). If the tests are met for the current year, the organization avoids private foundation status under § 509(a)(2) for that year and the following year. Rules similar to those applicable under § 170(b)(1)(A)(vi) also apply to newly created organizations. Treas. Reg. § 1.509(a)–3T(c)(1)(iv).

PROBLEM

This problem offers an opportunity to apply the tests for public charity status under §§ 170(b)(1)(A)(vi) and 509(a)(2).

The Burbank Foundation, a § 501(c)(3) organization, was organized many years ago by Amanda Burbank and her husband, Earl, each of whom became "substantial contributors" as a result of their founding gifts. The purposes of the Foundation are to support a broad range of charitable activities, concentrating specifically on the problems of the environment. The Foundation has six directors, including three members of the Burbank family and three local community leaders. The Foundation's President is Walter Russell, the husband of Aretha Burbank Russell, who is the daughter of Amanda and Earl Burbank.

For the years 2006–2010, the Foundation's gross revenues were as follows (figures are in thousands of dollars):

	2006	**2007**	**2008**	**2009**	**2010**
Dividends	125	125	125	125	150
Government grants	25	25	25	25	25
Sierra Club grant	—	25	—	25	—
Individual donations	50	25	150	25	40
Fundraising dance	25	25	20	30	20
Sale of environmental posters	25	25	30	20	40
Total	$250	$250	$350	$250	$275

No one person purchased more than $100 in tickets to the fundraising dance, an annual event. Half the price of each ticket to the dance was treated as a deductible charitable contribution, and the other half was for the food and entertainment provided at the event. The posters were sold to a diverse group of people except for the Sierra Club, a § 501(c)(4) organization, which made an annual bulk purchase of $10,000 worth of posters (included in the above totals). The Foundation has received a letter ruling that the poster sales were an activity substantially related to its exempt purposes and thus did not constitute an unrelated trade or business.

Individual donations to the Foundation came from a diverse group of supporters and were in amounts of $500 or less. No person gave more than $500 except that in both 2006 and 2008, Walter Russell made $20,000 in cash gifts, and in 2008 the Foundation received a $100,000 bequest (included in "individual donations" in the table above) from Willard Ginsburg, a Vermont philanthropist, who had never made any previous gifts to the Foundation. The Sierra Club's grants to date have not exceeded two percent of the total contributions and bequests received by the Foundation.

(a) Who are the disqualified persons with respect to the Burbank Foundation?

(b) Is the Burbank Foundation a "private foundation" for year 2010? Consider §§ 170(b)(1)(A)(vi) and 509(a)(2).

4.   SUPPORTING ORGANIZATIONS: § 509(a)(3)

Internal Revenue Code: § 509(a)(3), (f).

Treasury Regulations: § 1.509(a)–4(a)(1)–(4), (f)(1)–(4).

a.   INTRODUCTION

Section 509(a)(3) provides a final refuge from private foundation status to organizations that maintain a support relationship with one or more publicly supported charities or governmental entities that are known as the "supported organizations." I.R.C. § 509(f)(3). An organization avoids private foundation status as a "supporting organization" if it is:

1. Organized and at all times thereafter operated exclusively for the benefit of, to perform the functions of, or to carry out the purposes of one or more public charities described in either § 509(a)(1) or § 509(a)(2).

2. Operated, supervised, or controlled by, supervised or controlled in connection with, operated in connection with, one or more of these public charities; and

3. Not controlled, directly or indirectly, by one or more "disqualified persons" other than foundation managers and the public charities that it supports.

A translation will follow shortly. For now, to provide context for the challenging struggle to come, it may be helpful to revisit some of the more common uses of supporting organizations, or "SOs" as they have become known. An SO can be an attractive vehicle for involving a family with a public charity through an independent entity that bears the family's name while avoiding some of the disadvantages of private foundation status. For example, a philanthropist may wish to fund a charitable foundation with lifetime gifts of stock in a closely held corporation.[1] Unlike a private foundation, most (but not all) supporting organizations are not required to dispose of "excess business holdings," such as stock in a family company. SOs are not subject to the two percent tax on net investment income, and contributions of appreciated long-term capital gain property, including closely-held stock, are generally deductible to the extent of 30 percent of the donor's adjusted gross income, without reduction by the amount of the built-in gain. The trade-off is that donors who establish SOs give up the level of control they would have with a private foundation, and since 2006 certain types of grantmaking SOs with the loosest relationship to their supported organizations are subject to greater regulation that brings them closer to private foundations.

---

1. Supporting organizations also are employed in several prosaic but practical contexts. For example, some public charities (e.g., universities and hospitals) use SOs to hold real estate, pool and manage investments, hold and manage technology assets, or as a part of a complex structure where separate nonprofit entities are desirable to avoid regulatory obstacles or provide managerial flexibility.

For many years, supporting organizations were relatively unknown except to well informed insiders. The dense regulations were enough to discourage generalist advisers from recommending them to their clients. The handful of attorneys who mastered the rules quietly counseled donors on the "win win" upside of supporting organizations, and more aggressive advisers and "product marketers" devised structures to allow donors and their families to maintain the same degree of practical control they would have with a private foundation, but without all the regulatory hassle. Congress paid scant attention to the potential for abuse until a 1998 front page article in the Wall Street Journal "outed" supporting organizations, providing colorful examples of wealthy billionaires who donated illiquid assets such as ranch land, antique cars and closely held stock to grantmaking charities that rarely made grants and were loosely governed by the donor and his supposedly independent friends and retainers.[2] The relationship between these supporting organizations and the charities they supported was often remote, precluding the sort of accountability check that Congress contemplated when it excluded SOs from private foundation status.

The Wall Street Journal article and other anecdotal reports caused Congress to begin considering corrective legislation. Critics argued that SOs should be required to adhere to all or most of the stringent rules on self-dealing and charitable payout applicable to private foundations and that the looser Type III SOs should be eliminated or more closely regulated. Nonprofit sector advocates pointed to the important role played by some Type III SOs, such as those that support public colleges and universities, government entities, hospital systems, and foreign charities. See, e.g., Panel on the Nonprofit Sector, Strengthening Transparency, Governance, Accountability of Charitable Organizations: A Final Report to Congress and the Nonprofit Sector 46–47 (June 2005). The debate raged for several years, but a determined Congress finally acted in the Pension Protection Act of 2006 by adding an intricate new overlay on what already was a complex regulatory regime.

b. PERMISSIBLE RELATIONSHIPS

The first step in deciphering § 509(a)(3) and its accompanying regulations is to understand the three types of sanctioned relationships between the supporting and supported organizations. Without one of these relationships, an organization will not qualify as a public charity under § 509(a)(3). The type of relationship also has an impact on the other statutory tests that must be met and the level of regulation.

A supporting organization may be: (1) operated, supervised or controlled by, (2) supervised or controlled in connection with, or (3) operated in connection with, one or more publicly supported charities. Treas. Reg. § 1.509(a)–4(f)(2). Thus, it is possible to satisfy the statute by establishing

---

2. Monica Langley, The SO Trend: How to Succeed in Charity Without Really Giving: A "Supporting Organization" Lets the Wealthy Donate Assets, Still Keep Control, Wall St. J., May 29, 1998, at A1.

a relationship of tight control (analogous to a parent owning a subsidiary), or to provide more autonomy to the supporting organization ("operated in connection with"). Any relationship must ensure, however, that the supporting organization is "responsive to the needs or demands of one or more publicly supported organizations" and that the supporting organization "will constitute an integral part of, or maintain a significant involvement in, the operations of one or more publicly supported organizations." Treas. Reg. § 1.509(a)–4(f)(3). Type I and Type III SOs will lose their status if they accept gifts from a person who, together with certain related persons, controls the governing body of a supported organization. I.R.C. § 509(f)(2). Type III SOs may not support any charity not organized in the United States. I.R.C. § 509(f)(1)(A).

Type I: Operated, Supervised, or Controlled By. The first and most restrictive type of relationship is established when a majority of the officers, directors or trustees of the supporting organization must be appointed or elected by the governing body or officers of the supported organization. The regulations give the example of a separately incorporated university press whose board of governors is selected by the university's trustees on recommendation of the university president. Treas. Reg. § 1.509(a)–4(g)(2) Example (1). The organization or organizations that control the supporting organization need not be those directly benefited by it, provided that the purposes of the controlling organizations are carried out by means of the benefits afforded the latter organizations. See Treas. Reg. § 1.509(a)–(4)(g)(1)(ii). An example is a trust that pays its net income to three hospitals in a particular community for research, and its trustees are appointed by the president of a local university, some of whose faculty members do research in the hospitals. Treas. Reg. § 1.509(a)–4(g)(2) Example (3).

Type II: Supervised or Controlled in Connection With. This relationship is analogous to that of brother-sister corporations—i.e., there must be common supervision or control over both the supporting and supported organizations. Merely making payments (mandatory or discretionary) to one or more named public charities will not suffice to establish this type of relationship. Rather, the control or management of the supporting organization must be vested in the same persons that control or manage the supported public charity. Treas. Reg. § 1.509(a)–4(h).

Type III: Operated in Connection With. This is the most flexible of the permissible statutory relationships but also the most strictly regulated. Under proposed regulations issued in 2009,[3] a Type III SO must comply with a notification requirement and meet both a responsiveness test and an integral part test. The notification requirement and responsiveness test are the same for all Type III SOs, but the integral part test differs depending on whether the Type III SO is "functionally integrated" or "non-function-

---

3. As of early 2010, these regulations were still "proposed." They will become effective when published as final or temporary and then will apply to tax years beginning after the date of such publication. Prop. Treas. Reg. I.R.C. § 1.509(a)–4(i)(11)–(12).

ally integrated" (stay tuned for an explanation of this distinction, which was added to the law in 2006).

Starting with the notice requirement, the proposed regulations require a Type III SO to provide to each of its supported organizations: (1) a written notice addressed to a principal officer of the supported organization identifying the SO and describing the amount and type of support provided in the past year; (2) a copy of the SO's most recently filed Form 990; and (3) a copy of the SO's governing documents (just once, not annually, unless there are amendments). I.R.C. § 509(f)(1)(A); Prop. Treas. Reg. § 1.509(a)–4(i)(2).

A Type III supporting organization meets the responsiveness test if it is responsive to the needs and demands of a supported organization. "Responsiveness" is established through interlocking boards or officer structures, or by a "close and continuous working relationship" between the officers, directors or trustees of both organizations. By reason of this symbiosis, the supported organization must have a "significant voice" in the investment policies, the timing of grants, the manner of making grants, and the selection of recipients, "and in otherwise directing the use of the income or assets" of the supporting organization. Prop. Treas. Reg. § 1.509(a)–4(i)(2), (3).[4]

The "integral part" test operates differently depending on whether or not the Type III SO is "functionally integrated" to its supported organizations. Described generically, functionally integrated SOs do something other than just making grants, and in that respect they are similar to private operating foundations. Of course, the definition in the proposed regulations is more technical. A Type III SO is functionally integrated with its supported organization and thus satisfies the integral part test if it engages in activities "substantially all" of which directly further the exempt purposes of the supported organization (or organizations) to which it is responsive by performing the functions of, or carrying out the purposes of, such organizations and that, but for the involvement of the SO, would normally be engaged in by the supported organization.[5] An example would be a nonprofit religious publishing house that publishes works for a discrete number of churches in a particular geographic region and has a

---

4. Prior to 2006, Type III SOs formed as charitable trusts could satisfy the responsiveness test if the supported organizations named in the trust instrument had the power to enforce the trust and compel an accounting under state law. This permissive rule was repealed in 2006. Charitable trusts now must meet the general responsiveness test, presumably by showing a close and continuing working relationship with their supported organizations since their trustees will not have been appointed by or be an officer, director or trustee of those supported organizations. See Prop. Treas. Reg. § 1.509(a)–4(i)(3)(iv).

5. A narrow alternative test permits an SO that serves as the parent of its supported organization or organizations to qualify as functionally integrated. Parent status is achieved by exercising a substantial degree of control over the supported organizations' policies, programs and activities and by the ability to appoint or elect a majority of the officers, directors or trustees of the supported organizations. An example is an integrated hospital system, consisting of a parent—the functionally integrated SO—and supported organizations that perform various functions. Prop. Reg. § 1.509(a)–4(i)(4)(i)(B).

governing board that includes an official from one of the churches and other board members drawn from the church congregations. Prop. Reg. § 1.509(a)–4(i)(4)(iv) Example 3. An SO does not "directly further" the purposes of its supported organizations by fundraising, grantmaking, or investing and managing non-exempt use assets (e.g., investments).[6] Prop. Treas. Reg. § 1.509(a)–4(i)(4)(i)(A).

Nonfunctionally integrated Type III SOs are essentially grantmaking entities. To satisfy the integral part test, they must make qualified charitable distributions (i.e., grants) in an amount equal to five percent of the fair market value of their non-exempt use (i.e., investment) assets[7] and pass an "attentiveness" sub-test. Prop. Reg. § 1.509(a)–4(i)(5). The attentiveness sub-test requires the SO to distribute at least one-third of its required payout (called the "distributable amount") to one or more supported organizations that are attentive to the SO and with respect to which the SO meets the responsiveness test. Attentiveness is demonstrated when the SO either: (1) provides 10 percent or more of a supported organization's total support; (2) provides a level of support that is necessary to avoid the interruption of the carrying on of a particular function or activity of the supported organization; or (3) provides an amount of support that based on all the facts and circumstances is a sufficient part of a supported organization's total support to ensure attentiveness. Prop. Reg. § 1.509(a)–4(i)(5)(iii). An SO cannot meet the attentiveness test by distributions to a donor-advised fund at the supported organization. Prop. Treas. Reg. § 1.509(a)–4(i)(5)(iii)(C). See Lapham Foundation v. Commissioner, 389 F.3d 606 (6th Cir. 2004), which reached a similar result prior to the 2006 statutory changes.

c.   ORGANIZATIONAL AND OPERATIONAL TESTS

A supporting organization must be organized and operated exclusively for the benefit of one or more public charities. Treas. Reg. § 1.509(a)–4(b). The regulations enforce this statutory requirement with an "organizational" and an "operational" test.

Organizational Test. Like the general organizational test for § 501(c)(3) tax exemption, the § 509(a)(3) organizational test is concerned solely with the language used in the supporting organization's articles of incorporation or other governing instrument. The articles must limit the organization's purposes to exclusively benefitting, performing the functions of, or carrying out the purposes of the supported organization or organiza-

---

6. Under an exception, an SO that supports a single governmental entity, such as alumni association supporting a public university, may treat investing and managing non-exempt use assets as activities that directly further an exempt purpose if a "substantial part" of the SO's total activities directly further the exempt purposes of the governmental entity. Prop. Treas. Reg. § 1.509(a)–4(i)(4)(iii), –4(i)(4)(iv) Example 7.

7. For purposes of this distribution requirement, the proposed regulations incorporate many of the calculation, valuation and carryover rules that are used in determining the private foundation payout under § 4942, except amounts set aside for future charitable distributions do not count. See Prop. Treas. Reg. § 1.509(a)–4(i)(6)–(8) and Section D3 of this chapter, infra, at pp. 782–785.

tions, all of which must be public charities described in §§ 509(a)(1) and (a)(2). The articles may not empower the organization to engage in any activities that do not further those purposes. Treas. Reg. § 1.509(a)–4(c)(1)–(3).

A critical element of the organizational test is the general requirement that the supported organizations be designated specifically by name. Treas. Reg. § 1.509(a)–4(d)(2). A specific designation is not required, however, if there has been a historic and continuing relationship between the supporting and supported organizations so that a substantial identity of interest has developed between them. Treas. Reg. § 1.509(a)–4(d)(2)(iv). In addition, the beneficiary charities can be identified by "class or purpose" (e.g., "all the institutions of higher learning" in a particular state) rather than by name if the organizations' relationship satisfies either the "operated, supervised or controlled by" or "supervised or controlled in connection with" test. Treas. Reg. § 1.509(a)–4(d)(2)(i). The regulations also elaborate on the circumstances when a substitution of specified beneficiaries will be permitted. Treas. Reg. § 1.509(a)–4(d)(3) & (4).

The IRS has been known to interpret the organizational test rather strictly, with unfortunate ramifications for otherwise worthy organizations that commit a technical foot fault in drafting their articles of incorporation. For example, in Revenue Ruling 75–387, 1975–2 C.B. 216, the IRS ruled that a charitable trust formed to provide college scholarships to graduates of a high school in a particular county failed the organizational test. The trustee was a bank, but the scholarship recipients were selected by a committee of school superintendents who had no authority over the administration of the trust. The trust instrument lacked the requisite statement of purpose, and the trustee was completely independent of the benefitted schools, which were not named beneficiaries. For similar reasons, the trust lacked one of the three prescribed relationships. It didn't matter that the educational purposes of the trust were consistent with those of the schools and governmental units.

The courts have been more lenient than the IRS in interpreting the organizational test for scholarship-granting organizations. For example, the Tax Court has held that no particular magic language is required in a foundation's organizational documents to state that a § 509(a)(3) organization is organized to benefit a specified public charity. See Warren M. Goodspeed Scholarship Fund v. Commissioner, 70 T.C. 515 (1978), nonacq. 1981–2 C.B. 3, where a charitable trust (established by a will) whose net income was to be used to pay for the education at Yale College of graduates of a Massachusetts public high school qualified under § 509(a)(3) even though the will did not specifically state that the trust was organized exclusively for Yale's benefit. In Cockerline Memorial Fund v. Commissioner, 86 T.C. 53 (1986), the court held that the historic relationship between a scholarship granting trust and colleges and universities in Oregon was sufficient to qualify the trust under 509(a)(3) even though the Will creating the trust did not specify the benefited organizations.

Operational Test. The operational test requires that the supporting organization must engage "solely in activities which support or benefit the specified publicly supported organizations." Treas. Reg. § 1.509(a)–4(e)(1). The supporting organization need not pay its income to the supported organization to meet this requirement. Instead, it may carry on an independent activity or program benefiting the supported organization. Treas. Reg. § 1.509(a)–4(e)(2). The example in the regulations is of a separately incorporated alumni association of a university that uses its dues and other income "to support its own program of educational activities for alumni, faculty, and students * * * and to encourage alumni to maintain a close relationship with the university and to make contributions to it." Treas. Reg. § 1.509(a)–4(e)(3) Example (1).

d. CONTROL TEST

Although a supporting organization may achieve substantial autonomy by operating "in connection with" more than one public charity, it may not be controlled "directly or indirectly" by one or more disqualified persons (other than foundation managers and/or the charities it is required to support). I.R.C. § 509(a)(3)(C). Control is determined with reference to the aggregate power of disqualified persons to require the organization to perform any significant act or prevent such an act. See Treas. Reg. § 1.509(a)–4(j). The revenue ruling that follows is a good example of the concept of "indirect" control.

Revenue Ruling 80–207

1980–2 Cum. Bull 193.

ISSUE

Is an organization which makes distributions to a university, under the circumstances described below, a supporting organization within the meaning of section 509(a)(3) of the Internal Revenue Code if it is controlled by a disqualified person and the employees of a disqualified person?

FACTS

The organization is exempt from federal income tax under section 501(c)(3) of the Code. Its purpose is to make distributions to a university described in section 509(a)(1) and section 170(b)(1)(A)(ii).

The organization is controlled by a four member board of directors. One of these directors is a substantial contributor to the organization. Two other directors are employees of a business corporation of which more than 35 percent of the voting power is owned by the substantial contributor. The remaining director is chosen by the university. None of the directors has a veto power over the organization's actions.

LAW AND ANALYSIS

Section 509(a)(3)(C) of the Code provides that in order to qualify as other than a private foundation under section 509(a)(3), an organization may not be controlled directly or indirectly by one or more disqualified persons (as defined in section 4946) other than foundation managers and other than one or more organizations described in section 509(a)(1) or (2).

Section 4946 provides that the term "disqualified person" includes a substantial contributor to an organization, and a corporation of which a substantial contributor owns more than 35 percent of the total combined voting power.

Section 1.509(a)–4(j) of the Income Tax Regulations provides that a supporting organization will be considered to be controlled directly or indirectly by one or more disqualified persons if the voting power of such persons is 50 percent or more of the total voting power of the organization's governing body or if one or more of such persons has the right to exercise veto power over the actions of the organization. However, all pertinent facts and circumstances will be taken into consideration in determining whether a disqualified person does in fact indirectly control an organization.

Because only one of the organization's directors is a disqualified person and neither the disqualified person nor any other director has a veto power over the organization's actions, the organization is not directly controlled by a disqualified person under section 1.509(a)–4(j) of the regulations. However, in determining whether an organization is indirectly controlled by one or more disqualified persons, one circumstance to be considered is whether a disqualified person is in a position to influence the decisions of members of the organization's governing body who are not themselves disqualified persons. Thus, employees of a disqualified person will be considered in determining whether one or more disqualified persons controls 50 percent or more of the voting power of an organization's governing body.

Two of the organization's four directors are also employees of a corporation that is itself a disqualified person because more than 35 percent of its voting power is owned by a disqualified person. Because a majority of its board of directors consists of a disqualified person and employees of a disqualified person, the organization is indirectly controlled by disqualified persons within the meaning of section 509(a)(3)(C) of the Code.

HOLDING

Since the organization is controlled by a disqualified person and the employees of a disqualified person, under the circumstances described above, it is not a supporting organization within the meaning of section 509(a)(3) of the Code.

e. OTHER OPERATIONAL RULES AND SANCTIONS

The Pension Protection Act of 2006 added several other operational limitations on supporting organizations. In some cases, only Type III SOs were singled out. These rules narrow the regulatory divide between supporting organizations and private foundations.

Automatic Excess Benefit Rule. Congress concluded that some supporting organizations were being used to provide economic benefits to the families of their founding donors, such as paying salaries to the founder's child for minimal services rendered. The response was overkill—a punitive expansion of the § 4958 intermediate sanctions rules. For transactions occurring after July 25, 2006, all three types of SOs are effectively prohibited from making grants, loans, paying compensation, or making "similar payments"[1] to a "substantial contributor,"[2] a member of the family of a substantial contributor and to certain business entities they control (using a 35 percent test for control). These payments are automatically treated as excess benefit transactions, and the substantial contributor who receives them is subject to an excise tax penalty of 25 percent of the full amount of the payment, not merely the excess benefit. In addition, an organization manager who participates in the making of the payment, knowing that it was in one of the forbidden categories, is subject to a tax of 10 percent of the amount paid. The second-tier taxes and other rules of § 4958 also apply to such payments. I.R.C. § 4958(c)(3).

The automatic excess benefit rule also applies to loans by SOs to a § 4958 disqualified person,[3] a category that in some situations may be broader than substantial contributor—e.g., DQPs include officers, directors and other employees with substantial influence whether or not they are substantial contributors to the SO. I.R.C. § 4958(c)(3)(A)(i)(II). The impact is severe because the entire amount of the loan is treated as an excess benefit subject to the 25 percent excise tax imposed by § 4958.

The odd upshot of the automatic excess benefit rule is that SOs are treated more harshly than private foundations in that SOs may not even pay reasonable compensation to substantial contributors and their family members while private foundations are still permitted to do so. Charitable sector advocates have proposed legislation to overturn this odd disconnect and permit SOs to pay reasonable compensation to substantial contributors

---

1. According to the legislative history, "similar payments" include expense reimbursements but not payments made pursuant to a bona fide sale or lease of property with a substantial contributor. Sales and leases may be subject to the general intermediate sanctions rules, however, if the substantial contributor is a disqualified person. Joint Committee on Taxation, General Explanation of Tax Legislation Enacted in the 109th Congress 650–651 (2007).

2. For purposes of this provision, a "substantial contributor" ("SC") is any person (other than a public charity that is not an SO) who contributed or bequeathed an aggregate amount of more than $5,000 to the So if such amount is more than two percent of the total contributions and bequests received before the close of the organization's taxable year in which the contribution or bequest is received from the donor whose status is being tested or, in the case of a trust, its creator. I.R.C. § 4958(c)(3)(C)(i)(I).

3. DQPs of all three types of SOs are now also treated as DQPs with respect to organizations supported by the SO for purposes of § 4958 even if they have no other relationship with or influence over the supported charity. I.R.C. § 4958(f)(1)(D).

and reimburse their reasonable and necessary expenses but, as of early 2010, no action had been taken on this proposal.

No Support for Foreign Charities. Type III SOs are prohibited from supporting organizations not organized in the United States, with transitional relief delaying the application of this prohibition for three years for existing organizations. I.R.C. § 509(f)(1)(B). The effect is that U.S. charities established principally to provide financial or other assistance to a foreign charity, sometimes referred to as "friends of" organizations) will not qualify as SOs if they do not have broad public support, but they still may be able to qualify as public charities under §§ 170(b)(1)(A)(vi) or 509(a)(2) if either of those public support tests is met.

Excess Business Holdings. The private foundation excess business holdings rules have been extended to non-functionally integrated Type III SOs and Type II SOs that accept gifts from persons (other than a public charities that are not SOs) who effectively control the governing body of a supported organization of the SO. See Section D4 of this chapter, infra, at pp. 789–793, for elaboration on the excess business holdings rules.

Grants by Private Foundations to SOs. Another form of punishment adversely affects private foundations that make grants to SOs. Grants from private nonoperating foundations to non-functionally integrated Type III SOs, or to Type I and II SOs if a disqualified person with respect to the foundation directly or indirectly controls either the SO or any supported organization of that SO, will not count as a "qualifying distribution" for purposes of the § 4942 private foundation payout requirement. I.R.C. § 4942(g)(4)(A). The IRS is also authorized to define other conditions under which payments by a private foundation to an SO would not be appropriate and thus not count as a qualifying distribution. I.R.C. § 4942(g)(4)(A)(ii)(II). Any amount that does not count as a qualifying distribution under this rule is treated as a taxable expenditure under § 4945. I.R.C. § 4945(d)(4)(A)(ii). See Section D5 of this chapter, infra, at pp. 795–803 for elaboration on taxable expenditures penalties.

Disclosure. All SOs are required to file an annual Form 990, regardless of their gross receipts, and indicate whether they are Type I, II or III and identify their supported organizations. They also must demonstrate annually that they are not controlled by one or more disqualified persons and certify that the majority of their governing body is comprised of individuals selected on the basis of their special knowledge or expertise in the SO's particular field or because they represent the community served by the supported public charities. I.R.C. § 6033(*l*).

Other Procedural Rules. Several provisions added by the Pension Protection Act of 2006, such as the restriction on grants by private foundations and donor-advised funds to certain types of SOs, require a grantmaker to be aware of the grantee's specific public charity status. Historically, this information was often unclear or difficult to determine—it was enough just to know the grantee was some type of public charity. Indeed, some public charities were not sure of their own status. All this uncertainty caused many private foundations to suspend making grants to any type of SO for fear that the grants would not count toward their payout requirement and trigger a taxable expenditure penalty. And some SOs that historically avoided private foundation status under § 509(a)(3) discovered they had sufficient public support to qualify as public charities under the tests in § 170(b)(1)(A)(vi) or § 509(a)(2), motivating them to seek reclassification to what are now more favorable categories. In response to this problem, the IRS has provided simplified procedures to permit eligible organizations to submit a written request for reclassification from an SO to a public charity under § 509(a)(1) or § 509(a)(2) and for private foundations seeking clarification of a grantee's SO status. I.R.S Ann. 2009–62, 2009–33 I.R.B. 247; Rev. Proc. 2009–32, 2009–28 I.R.B. 142.

PROBLEM

Paul and Frances Ross are a wealthy couple in their early 60's. They have three children, all in their 30's. Mr. and Mrs. Ross have been discussing estate planning options with their attorney and are interested in establishing a family charitable foundation. Their major asset is $30 million of common stock in Ross Cosmetics, Inc., a closely-held family corporation. Members of the Ross family own 85 percent of the stock; the remaining 15 percent is owned by employees of the company.

Mr. and Mrs. Ross have been advised that serious problems would be presented if they were to donate their Ross Cosmetics stock to a family foundation. Because the stock is their major asset, they are exploring techniques to avoid private foundation status but still establish a philanthropic vehicle over which their family would have substantial influence and control. The Rosses are anxious to involve their descendants in the activities of the foundation, which they hope will serve as a continuing memorial to the Ross Cosmetics dynasty, and they would like their daughter, Rhoda, to serve as part-time executive director for an annual salary of $40,000 per year.

Paul and Frances are major donors to their local Jewish Community Federation, which is classified as a public charity under § 170(b)(1)(A)(vi). The Federation, in turn, makes grants to a wide variety of Jewish and some secular charities in the community. The Ross children are more interested in supporting environmental organizations and in establishing scholarship funds for disadvantaged students.

The Rosses recently attended a seminar where they learned about the advantages in establishing a "supporting foundation" for the benefit of a public charity. It is their understanding that such a foundation would not be a "private foundation" if it were carefully structured. Based on this information, they decided to create The Ross Family Supporting Foundation, to be operated exclusively for charitable, educational or religious purposes by supporting activities for the benefit of or to carry out the purposes of the Jewish Community Federation. The new entity gradually will be funded with a $10 million gift of Ross Cosmetics stock. All the income from the stock will be distributed in the discretion of the board of directors. The board will consist of Paul, Frances, their daughter Rhoda, and two unrelated family friends, one of whom is vice-president of Ross Cosmetics, Inc. None of the proposed directors is currently an employee, officer or director of the Jewish Community Federation.

    (a) Why are Mr. and Mrs. Ross so anxious to avoid private foundation status?

    (b) If the Rosses are willing to limit their financial support to the Jewish Community Federation, why don't they simply donate the funds directly? Why should they go to the trouble of creating a separate entity?

    (c) Will the Ross Foundation, as currently proposed, qualify for exemption under § 501(c)(3)?

    (d) Will the Ross Foundation qualify as a supporting organization under § 509(a)(3)? If not, is it possible to restructure the proposal to achieve § 509(a)(3) status? Consider the three types of permissible relationships, the impact of your choice on the composition of the governing board and the operation of the foundation, and any other operational issues that would conflict with the family's goals.

    (e) Suppose the Ross children express concern about the emphasis of the Foundation and propose to broaden the purposes as follows: "to further the dual causes of Jewish philanthropy and arresting the problems of urban poverty." Is this feasible? If not, how might the same objectives be achieved and how should the Foundation's organizational documents reflect those objectives?

    (f) Suppose the Rosses want their foundation to have as its sole purpose the creation and maintenance of a public interest law program at the Vanguard College of the Law, a well-established independent nonprofit law school. Officials of the law school have been reluctant to expand public interest programs in the past but, tempted by the Rosses' generosity, they have informally agreed to undertake such a program. What considerations should be taken into account in structuring this type of supporting organization? Could the foundation, once formed, later amend its articles and shift its support to another law school if it becomes dissatisfied with Vanguard's program?

    (g) What if the Rosses wish to create a charitable trust, the sole purpose of which is to provide college scholarships to graduates of public high schools in Los Angeles County, California. Recipients will be selected by a committee composed of the Superintendent of the Unified School District, the principal of the largest public high school in the county and a third member selected by the other two. The trust will be administered by a bank. Would the trust qualify as a § 509(a)(3) supporting organization?

    (h) What if the Ross children wish to create a separate foundation whose sole purpose was to support the purely educational activities of a § 501(c)(5) labor organization? Would this type of supporting organization qualify under §§ 501(c)(3) and 509(a)(3)?

5.   PRIVATE OPERATING FOUNDATIONS

Internal Revenue Code: § 4942(j)(3).

Treasury Regulations: §§ 53.4942(b)–1(a)(1), (b), (c); –2, –3(a), (b)(1).

Within the private foundation family, the Code distinguishes between private operating foundations, which directly engage in charitable or educational activities, and nonoperating or grantmaking foundations. Very generally, a private operating foundation ("POF") is a § 501(c)(3) organization that has not escaped private foundation status, often because of an abundance of investment income, but which meets certain statutory tests that entitle it to avoid some of the strictures that burden grantmaking foundations. The distinctive characteristics of private operating foundations include:

(1) Contributions to POFs are deductible by individual donors to the same extent as contributions to public charities—i.e., they are not subject to the special 30 percent limitation on contributions of cash and ordinary income property, the 20 percent limitation on contributions of capital gain property, and the reduction of unrealized built-in gain on gifts of appreciated capital gain property.

(2) Certain POFs, known as "exempt operating foundations," are exempt from the excise tax on investment income.

(3) POFs are not subject to the § 4942 payout requirement.

(4) Grants to POFs ordinarily may be counted by the donor foundation as "qualifying distributions" in satisfaction of the § 4942 payout requirement.

(5) Other private foundations that make grants to "exempt operating foundations" are relieved from exercising "expenditure responsibility" with respect to the grants.

A POF is defined in § 4942(j)(3) as a foundation that makes "qualifying distributions directly for the active conduct" of its exempt-function activities that are equal in value to substantially all of the lesser of its "adjusted net income" or its "minimum investment return" (five percent of the value of its investment assets). For this purpose, "substantially all" means 85 percent. Treas. Reg. § 53.4942(b)–1(c). Where "qualifying distributions" exceed the foundation's minimum investment return, substantially all of those distributions must be made directly for the conduct of exempt function activities. Treas. Reg. § 53.4942(b)–1(a)(1)(ii).

This initial test for POF status, known as the "income test," requires an understanding of several statutory terms of art that are amplified in the regulations. For example, are capital expenditures to acquire assets to be used directly in the conduct of the foundation's exempt activities considered as qualifying distributions? The answer is yes; the conduct of such activities also qualify. But payments to individuals (e.g., scholarships or grants) ordinarily fail to qualify unless the foundation maintains a "significant involvement" in a charitable, educational or other activity within the context of which those grants are made. Thus, where an exempt purpose of the foundation is the relief of poverty or human distress, and its exempt activities are designed to "ameliorate conditions among a poor or distressed class of persons or in an area subject to poverty or natural disaster," and the foundation maintains a salaried or volunteer staff to supervise its activities on a continuing basis, the grants will qualify for purposes of the substantially all test. For elaboration and other examples, see Treas. Reg. § 53.4942(b)–1(b)(2).

In addition to meeting the "income" test, a POF must satisfy one of three alternative tests relating to its use of assets, operating expenditures or support.

Assets Test. Under the assets test, substantially more than half (i.e., 65 percent or more) of the assets of the foundation must be devoted directly to the foundation's exempt function activities or to functionally-related businesses, or both, or consist of stock of a corporation controlled by the foundation, substantially all of the assets of which are so devoted. I.R.C. § 4942(j)(3)(B)(i).

Expenditures Test. The organization normally must spend an amount that is not less than two-thirds of its minimum investment return directly for the active conduct of its exempt activities. I.R.C. § 4942(j)(3)(B)(iii).

Support Test. The organization must receive substantially all of its support (other than gross investment income) from the general public and from five or more exempt organizations that are not related to one another, and not more than 25 percent of the foundation's support may be received from any one such exempt organization, and not more than half the foundation's support may normally be received from gross investment income. I.R.C. § 4942(j)(3)(B)(iii).

The above tests may be applied on a year-by-year basis. A foundation qualifies as a POF by satisfying the activity test, and either the assets, expenditures or support test, for any three taxable years during a four-year period consisting of the taxable year in question and the three immediately preceding taxable years. Alternatively, the foundation may aggregate all pertinent items for the four-year period and qualify on the basis of those aggregate amounts. It may not, however, use one method (for example, the three-out-of-four-year test) to satisfy the income test and the other to satisfy the assets, expenditures or support test. Reg. § 53.4942(b)–3(a).

6.   INFORMATION REPORTING AND DISCLOSURE REQUIREMENTS

Internal Revenue Code: §§ 6033(c); 6104(d).

As discussed in Chapter 5, most exempt organizations must file an annual information return with the Internal Revenue Service. I.R.C.

§ 6033. These returns (Form 990 for public charities, Form 990–PF for private foundations) are public documents that are available for inspection at various designated IRS offices and on the Internet. Unlike public charities, private foundations must include an itemized statement of all grants made or approved for future payment, with the name and address of grantees and the purpose and amount of each grant, and they must complete a detailed schedule showing that they have complied with the five percent payout requirement. Like most public charities, private foundations must make their annual Form 990–PF (as well as their application for exemption) available for public inspection at their principal office during regular business hours or upon written request, as discussed below. I.R.C. § 6104(a). They also must provide to any individual who makes a request a "take home" copy of Form 990 and Form 990–PF (in the case of a private foundation) for the three most recent taxable years, and a copy of the organization's exemption application (Form 1023). Monetary penalties are imposed on the foundation and its managers for failure to comply with these requirements. I.R.C. § 6685.

Because of the unusual amount of detail required, the annual information return filed by a large foundation is likely to be quite bulky (some exceed 500 pages), making duplication and mailing of the returns expensive and administratively burdensome. When it expanded the disclosure requirements, Congress directed the Treasury to consider the unique issues that private foundations might face. The IRS issued final regulations governing the public disclosure of private foundation annual information returns and exemption applications. These regulations are very similar to the generally applicable disclosure rules governing other exempt organizations except that private foundations, unlike public charities, must disclose the names and addresses of their contributors. Under the regulations, a private foundation must provide copies of its three most recent annual information returns and its exemption application in response to an in-person request or within 30 days of receipt of a written request. Private foundations no longer are required to publish a notice in a local newspaper announcing that their information return is available for inspection. See generally Treas. Reg. § 301.6104(d)–1.

A significant development on the disclosure front has been the posting on the Internet of the most recent tax information returns for virtually every U.S. private foundation and the Form 990s for most public charities. The full collection of Form 990–PFs is available to scholars, grantseekers, journalists and voyeurs thanks to GuideStar, a joint project of Philanthropic Research, Inc. and the Urban Institute's National Center for Charitable Statistics. See http://www.guidestar.org.

D. PRIVATE FOUNDATION EXCISE TAXES

Sections 4940 through 4945 impose excise taxes on private foundations, foundation managers, and in some cases principal donors and government officials. With one exception (the § 4940 tax on net investment income), these excise taxes impose monetary sanctions for specific abuses enumerated in the statute. The initial sanctions serve as a warning and an invitation to "correction" of the abuse. If correction does not occur within a designated time period, much larger second-tier penalties are imposed. Repeated transgressions that go uncorrected may lead to termination of the foundation and confiscation of all its assets by the government. Exceptions, monetary caps, opportunities for abatement, and other relief provisions abound throughout the complex scheme.

Mastery of the excise tax rules—a highly technical but obligatory exercise for legal advisors to private foundations—requires familiarity with the statutory provisions and a daunting set of regulations.

1. TAX ON NET INVESTMENT INCOME: § 4940

Internal Revenue Code: § 4940.

Treasury Regulations: § 53.4940(a)–1(a), (c), (d), (e), (f).

In General. Section 4940 imposes a two percent excise tax on a private foundation's net investment income.[1] The tax was justified as a special fee to finance the expenses of auditing private foundations and enforcing the regulatory scheme. It thus has become known as the "audit tax" even though the revenue raised is not earmarked for the IRS's budget. The § 4940 tax rate initially was four percent, but Congress reduced it to two percent in 1978 after discovering that the higher rate produced more than twice the revenue needed to administer all of the exempt organizations provisions. When subsequent studies revealed that audit tax receipts continued to far exceed the costs of administration, Congress reduced the rate to one percent for foundations making additional distributions for charitable purposes. The § 4940 tax is a persistent source of controversy. The foundation community sees it as a punitive measure that reduces funds available for charitable purposes and unfairly singles out foundations. Supporters of the tax argue that foundations, especially those with large endowments, should pay for some of the costs of government.

Net Investment Income. The tax is imposed on "net investment income," which is the sum of "gross investment income" and "capital gain net income," less related expenses of producing and collecting the income. I.R.C. § 4940(c)(1). Gross investment income includes dividends, interest, rents, royalties, payments with respect to loans of securities, and income from notional principal contracts, annuities, and other substantially similar income from ordinary and routine investments, but not tax-exempt bond interest and any income subject to the unrelated business tax. I.R.C. § 4940(c)(2), (5).

---

1. Exempt operating foundations are wholly exempt from the tax on net investment income. I.R.C. § 4940(d)(1). This is an exceedingly narrow category confined to organizations that had private operating foundation status in 1983 and meet certain other conditions. Newly created foundations do not qualify.

"Capital gain net income" is the excess of capital gains over capital losses from dispositions of property used for the production of gross investment income, such as interest, dividends, rents and royalties and dispositions of income-producing property used in an unrelated business unless that gain is already subject to the unrelated business income tax, and even currently unproductive property held for capital gain through appreciation. I.R.C. § 4940(c)(4)(A). Capital losses may be netted against capital gains for the taxable year, but excess capital losses are not deductible against gross investment income, and no capital loss carryovers are allowed. I.R.C § 4940(c)(4)(C). Capital gain net income includes gains from the sale of property "used" for the production of the various types of investment income if the property "is of a type that generally produces" such income, even if the foundation sells the income-producing property immediately after receiving it as a gift or bequest. Treas. Reg. § 53.4940–1(f)(1). See Greenacre Foundation v. United States, 762 F.2d 965 (Fed.Cir. 1985).

The tax base was expanded in 2006 to overrule case law that strictly interpreted § 4940 by excluding any form of income that was not specifically enumerated in the statute, such as certain currently unproductive investment property held for appreciation. See, e.g., Zemurray Foundation v. United States, 687 F.2d 97 (5th Cir. 1982). The legislative history explains that this expanded definition is even intended to include gains or losses from the disposition of property used to further an exempt purpose but, once implementing regulations are adopted, such gains need not be recognized if the property was held for exempt use at least one year and it is exchanged for like kind property to be used for exempt purposes under applicable principles for like kind exchanges under § 1031. I.R.C. § 4940(c)(4)(D). See Joint Committee on Taxation, General Explanation of Tax Legislation Enacted in the 109th Congress 618 (2007).

In computing net investment income, a foundation may deduct ordinary and necessary expenses (including straight line depreciation and cost depletion) paid or incurred for the production or collection of gross investment income or for the management, conservation or maintenance of property held for the production of such income. I.R.C. § 4940(c)(3). Typical deductible expenses are investment advisory fees, salaries paid to foundation employees who manage the endowment, depreciation on property used to manage investments, and investment interest. See Treas. Reg. § 53.4940–1(e).

Rate Reduction. Section 4940(e) reduces the tax rate from two to one percent for foundations that make equivalent increases in their qualifying distributions for charitable purposes. The term "qualifying distributions" has the same meaning as in § 4942(g)—very generally, it refers to amounts distributed or set aside for charitable purposes and expenses of administering the foundation's charitable program. Specifically, to qualify for the rate reduction a foundation's qualifying distributions for the year must equal or exceed the sum of: (1) the value of the foundation's assets for that year multiplied by the foundation's average percentage charitable payout for a "base period" consisting of the five taxable years preceding the current year (or the foundation's existence, if it has less than a five-year history), and (2) one percent of net investment income. I.R.C. § 4940(e)(2)(A). Foundations in their first year of existence do not qualify for any rate reduction. To illustrate, assume that a foundation has investment assets with a value of $10 million at all times during the current year and the preceding five years. Assume further that, on average, the foundation has made $500,000 of qualifying distributions for the five-year base period, and that its net investment income for the current year is $600,000. The foundation will qualify for the one percent rate reduction (a savings of $6,000) if its qualifying distributions for the current year equal or exceed the sum of: $500,000 (net investment assets multiplied by average payout) plus $6,000 (one percent of net investment income), or $506,000. In effect, a foundation that is able to maintain its historical distribution level may substitute additional qualifying distributions for the extra one percent of audit tax.

Two other operating rules complete the picture. First, to prevent the general formula described above from requiring continually higher payout rates to qualify for the rate reduction (a "distributions escalator"), § 4940(e)(3)(C) provides that, for any year in the base period that the audit tax rate was reduced, the amount of qualifying distributions made by the foundation during that year also is reduced by the amount of the rate reduction. In practice, this rule provides at best only partial relief, and foundations that have made grants in excess of their payout requirement may find it increasingly difficult to achieve a rate reduction. Second, the reduction is not available for a given year if, at any time during the base period, the foundation has incurred a penalty under § 4942 for failing to meet the minimum payout requirement. I.R.C. § 4940(e)(2)(B).

PROBLEM

The Lifton Foundation, a § 501(c)(3) organization classified as a private nonoperating foundation, had the following assets on January 1 of the current year:

	Basis	**Value**
Lifton Pea Co. stock	$10,000	$4,500,000
Real Estate	80,000	200,000
Cash	50,000	50,000
Undeveloped parcel	200,000	300,000
Works of art (on loan to museum)	25,000	75,000
Office furniture	10,000	8,000
State of Connecticut bonds	300,000	250,000

During the current year, the Foundation had the following income, expenses and losses:

Income
Dividends on Lifton Pea stock $225,000

Capital gain from sale of parcel	100,000
Rentals from real estate	20,000
Interest on Connecticut bonds	12,000

Expenses and Loss

General administrative expenses	$ 40,000
Scholarship grants	120,000
Maintenance of real estate (including straight line depreciation)	10,000
Purchase of various works of art	25,000
Loss on sale of Connecticut bonds	50,000

Assume that no expenses are directly related to producing either the dividend or the interest income.

(a) What is the Lifton Foundation's § 4940 excise tax liability for the current year?

(b) In general, what steps can be taken by the Foundation to reduce its tax rate from 2 to 1 percent?

2. SELF-DEALING: § 4941

Internal Revenue Code: § 4941(a), (b), (c), (d)(1), (2)(A)–(G), (e).

Treasury Regulations: §§ 53.4941(a)–1(a), (b), (c); 53.4941(d)–1(a), (b)(1), (2), (4)–(8); 53.4941(d)–2(a), (b)(1) & (2), (c), (d), (e), (f), (g); 53.4941(d)–3.

Much of the criticism of private foundations that influenced the 1969 legislation was directed at the ability of foundation insiders and related persons to use the foundation's resources for private gain. Prior law had penalized self-dealing transactions by certain § 501(c)(3) organizations if they favored substantial contributors and other insiders. The only federal sanction, however, was revocation of the organization's exempt status, and regulation of self-dealing under state nonprofit law was uneven and largely ineffective. The arm's length standard of prior law was subjective, and enforcement efforts proved ineffective, inhibited by the draconian sanction. Congress also believed that even arm's-length transactions permitted insiders to benefit improperly, such as when an insider sells property to a foundation at a fair price but the sale is made to provide liquidity to the insider at a time when other buyers can't be found. In response to these concerns, Congress decided to penalize a broad range of self-dealing transactions, whether or not they disadvantaged the foundation.

a. ACTS OF SELF–DEALING

Section 4941(d)(1) identifies five categories of self-dealing transactions between a private foundation and its disqualified persons, and one additional category limited to certain dealings with government officials. The "special rules" in § 4941(d)(2) offer several helpful exceptions for innocent transactions that otherwise would fall within the broad sweep of the self-dealing concept. As is the norm in the private foundations area, the regulations elaborate considerably.

Sales and Exchanges. A sale or exchange of property between a private foundation and a disqualified person is an act of self-dealing even if the transaction is at fair market value or, remarkably, even if the foundation receives a bargain. I.R.C. § 4941(d)(1)(A). Transfers of encumbered real or personal property by a disqualified person to the foundation are treated as sales or exchanges if the foundation expressly assumes the debt or takes subject to a mortgage or lien placed on the property within the 10–year period preceding the transfer. I.R.C. § 4941(d)(2)(A).

An important exception is provided for certain transactions between a private foundation in its capacity as a shareholder of a corporation that is a disqualified person. Liquidations, mergers, redemptions, recapitalizations and similar corporate transactions are not treated as acts of self-dealing if all the securities of the same class as that held by the foundation are subject to the same terms and those terms provide for receipt by the foundation of not less than fair market value. I.R.C. § 4941(d)(2)(F).

Leases. A lease of property between a private foundation and a disqualified person is an act of self-dealing. The regulations carve out an exception for rent-free leases by a disqualified person to a foundation if payments by the foundation for janitorial services, utilities and other maintenance costs are not made to the disqualified person. Treas. Reg. § 53.4941(d)–2(b)(2).

Loans. The "lending of money or other extension of credit" between a private foundation and a disqualified person is an act of self-dealing. Interest-free loans by a disqualified person to a foundation are excepted where the loan proceeds are used exclusively by the foundation in pursuit of its exempt purposes. I.R.C. § 4941(d)(1)(B) & (d)(2)(B).

Furnishing of Goods, Services or Facilities. The furnishing of goods, services or facilities between a private foundation and a disqualified person is an act of self-dealing, except where the goods, services or facilities are furnished by the disqualified person without charge and used by the foundation in pursuit of its exempt purposes. I.R.C. § 4941(d)(1)(C) & (d)(2)(C). A second exception applies where the goods, services or facilities are furnished by the private foundation to the disqualified person on terms not more favorable than those made available to the general public. I.R.C. § 4941(d)(2)(D).

Payment of Compensation. The payment of compensation or reimbursement of expenses by a foundation to a disqualified person is an act of self-dealing unless the payment is not excessive and is for personal services which are "reasonable and necessary to carrying out the exempt purpose" of the foundation. In no event may the foundation pay any compensation to a "government official." I.R.C. § 4941(d)(1)(D) & (d)(2)(E).

Use or Transfer of Assets or Income. Congress did not want to leave any stone unturned. Its final catch-all category provides that any transfer by a private foundation of its income or assets to or for the use or benefit of a disqualified person is an act of self-dealing. I.R.C. § 4941(d)(1)(E). For example, the Service has ruled that the placing of paintings owned by a private foundation in the residence of a substantial contributor comes within this category. Rev. Rul. 74–600, 1974–2 C.B. 385.

Payments to Government Officials. Any agreement by a private foundation to make a payment of money to a government official, even if the payment is reasonable in amount, is an act of self-dealing. I.R.C. § 4941(d)(1)(F). An individual is a "government official" if, at the time of any particular act of self-dealing, he or she holds various elective or appointive offices specified in § 4946(c). This long list includes the President and Vice President of the United States, all members of Congress, federal judges and cabinet members, high-level employees of all three branches of the federal government, staff members in the U.S. Senate or House who earn at least $15,000 a year in compensation, elected or appointed state and local governmental officials who earn at least $20,000 a year, and any "personal or executive assistant or secretary" to any of the foregoing. For more details, see Treas. Reg. § 53.4946–1.

The government official self-dealing rule is subject to several exceptions. For example, a foundation may agree to employ or make a grant to a government official for any period after termination of government service if the agreement is made no more than 90 days before that service terminates. See Treas. Reg. § 53.4941(d)–3(e)(8). Other exceptions cover certain narrowly defined types of scholarships, prizes, awards, pension benefits, de minimis gifts, and travel expense reimbursements. See I.R.C. § 4941(d)(2)(G) and Treas. Reg. § 53.4941(d)–3(e).

Disaster Relief Payments. Prior to September 11, 2001, it was unclear whether disaster-relief payments by company-sponsored private foundations to employees were acts of self-dealing. The concern was that such assistance was tantamount to an employee benefit program that provided an impermissible private benefit. For example, the IRS had ruled that a private foundation established, funded and controlled by a particular employer for the purpose of providing disaster relief for its employees did not qualify as a charitable organization under § 501(c)(3) because the foundation was not operated solely for charitable purposes and was providing a benefit on behalf of the employer in violation of the prohibition on private inurement. See, e.g., P.L.R. 199914040.

The Victims of Terrorism Tax Relief Act of 2001 (§ 111) eased the path for employer-sponsored foundations that make relief payments in connection with disasters resulting from certain terrorist or military actions, Presidentially declared disasters, disasters resulting from an accident involving a common carrier, or any other event determined by the Secretary of the Treasury to be catastrophic (collectively "qualified disasters"). The IRS now must presume that such qualified disaster payments made by company foundations to employees or their families are consistent with the foundation's charitable purposes if: (1) eligible beneficiaries are a sufficiently large or indefinite group to constitute a "charitable class;" (2) the recipients are selected based on an objective determination of need; and (3) the selection is made by an independent selection committee or adequate substitute procedure to ensure that any benefit to the employer is incidental or tenuous. If the presumption applies, a foundation's payments will be treated as made for charitable purposes and will not constitute acts of self-dealing.

b. THE TAX COST OF SELF–DEALING

Initial Tax. In keeping with the general scheme of the foundation excise taxes, penalties for self-dealing are imposed at two levels. An initial tax is imposed on any disqualified person (other than a foundation manager only acting as such) who participates in an act of self-dealing. Notably, a penalty is not imposed on the foundation itself. Failure to correct the evil act within an appropriate period of time triggers the second-level tax. The initial tax on the self-dealer is ten percent of the "amount involved" with respect to the act of self-dealing for each year or part of a year in the taxable period. I.R.C. § 4941(a)(1). The "amount involved" is the greater of the amount of money and the fair market value of the other property given, or the amount of money and the fair market value of the other property received, valued as of the date of the act of self-dealing. I.R.C. § 4941(e)(2). The "taxable period" begins with the act of self-dealing and ends on the earliest of: (1) the date of mailing of an IRS deficiency notice, (2) the date on which the first-level tax is assessed, or (3) the date on which the act of self-dealing is fully corrected. I.R.C. § 4941(e)(1).

A tax of five percent of the amount involved (up to $20,000 per act) also is imposed on a foundation manager who participates in an act of self-dealing knowing it was such an act if the participation was not willful and due to reasonable cause for each year (or part thereof) in the taxable period. I.R.C. § 4941(a)(2).

Correction and Second Level Tax. "Correction" requires undoing the transaction to the extent possible, provided the foundation's financial position is not worse than it would be if the disqualified person were dealing under the "highest fiduciary standards." I.R.C. § 4941(e)(3). The regulations provide amplification, essentially imposing a restitution plus profits (if any) requirement. Treas. Reg. § 53.4941(e)–1(c). Failure to correct triggers the second-level tax of 200 percent of the amount involved on the self-dealer and 50 percent on the obstinate or ignorant foundation manager who refuses to agree to all or part of the correction. I.R.C. § 4941(b)(1), (b)(2). For this purpose, the "amount involved" means the greater of the amount of money paid or the highest fair market value during the taxable period. I.R.C. § 4941(e)(2)(B).

Abatement of First–Tier Excise Taxes. In connection with its 1984 reexamination of the private foundation sanctions, Congress concluded that the first-level excise tax should be abated in certain cases if the "taxable event was due to reasonable cause and not to willful neglect" and correction is accomplished within the appropriate correction period. I.R.C. § 4962(a). Congress found no justification for extending abatement relief to acts of self-dealing, however, because the penalty tax is payable by the self-dealer and not the foundation, and since "commercial transactions between disqualified persons and foundations are generally prohibited." H.R. Rep. No. 98–432 (Part 2), 98th Cong., 2d Sess. 1472 (1984). See I.R.C. § 4962(b). The conferral of abatement authority reflects an awareness that innocent transgressions of the private foundation rules commonly occur, and that a rigid penalty is often inappropriate. Query whether the most appealing case for equitable consideration can be made on behalf of the "innocent" self-dealer, to whom abatement relief is not available?

* * *

The *Madden* case, which follows, is a real-world example of the reach of the § 4941 self-dealing penalty regime. It demonstrates the importance of carefully interpreting the statute and regulations before advising a private foundation and its managers about their potential exposure to self-dealing penalties.

Madden v. Commissioner

United States Tax Court, 1997.
74 T.C.M. (CCH) 440.

■ FAY, JUDGE:

MEMORANDUM FINDINGS OF FACT AND OPINION

[The taxpayers in this case were John Madden, his wife, Marjorie, their daughter, Cynthia, and several business entities controlled by the Madden family. Mr. Madden was the founder of John Madden Co., which developed and managed commercial properties including Greenwood Plaza, a major office complex in Denver, Colorado. The taxpayers formed a private foundation to operate an outdoor museum (hereinafter "Museum") located in Greenwood Plaza. Mr. and Mrs. Madden and their daughter all served as directors or officers of Museum and thus were "foundation managers" within the meaning of § 4946(b). John Madden also owned a 75 percent stake in GMC, a maintenance and janitorial company that performed services for many of the buildings in the complex, including Museum. Because it was controlled by Mr. Madden, GMC was a "disqualified person" with respect to Museum.

Museum's collection consisted primarily of sculptures and other exhibits designed to withstand the outdoor elements. Most of the pieces were located along public thoroughfares running through the complex or in atriums on the ground floor of some of the buildings. In addition to displaying its works, Museum conducted tours and offered art courses to the community.

John Madden Co. furnished rent-free office space to Museum and allowed Museum to use the company's accounting system free of charge. Museum also relied on building owners, including John Madden Co., to provide space free of charge for displays of its collection. Museum often held special events, such as wedding receptions and bar mitzvahs, in the complex and charged a fee for the use of space furnished by building owners. In connection with these events, it paid GMC fees for maintenance and janitorial services. The fee arrangement was entered into after John Madden Co.'s chief executive officer, Sherry Manning, told Cynthia Madden that GMC could charge Museum for its services as long as the fee was no higher than the fair market rate for comparable services rendered.

Museum also mistakenly made small payments for repairs to artwork owned by John Madden personally, but Mr. Madden promptly reimbursed Museum, and it made a $3,000 payment to an unrelated company (Form, Inc.) in connection with an art exhibit, fulfilling a contractual obligation of John Madden Co.

The IRS asserted that GMC was liable for § 4941(a)(1) self-dealing penalties and that John, Marjorie and Cynthia Madden were liable for § 4941(a)(2) foundation manager self-dealing penalties in connection with payments made by Museum to GMC. The IRS also claimed that Museum owed unrelated business income tax on its revenue from the special events and the leasing of space; the excerpts from the opinion below are limited to the self-dealing issues. Eds.]

OPINION

* * *

Issue 3. Payments to GMC

Section 4941 imposes an excise tax for acts of "self-dealing" that occur between a private foundation and a "disqualified person". Sec. 4941(a)(1). The parties agree that GMC is a "disqualified person" with respect to the Museum, a private foundation. For the purposes of this section, "self-dealing" includes the "furnishing of goods, services, or facilities between a private foundation and a disqualified person". Sec. 4941(d)(1)(C). However, section 4941(d)(2) provides several exceptions for certain arrangements that would otherwise constitute self-dealing transactions. Specifically, section 4941(d)(2)(E) provides:

> the payment of compensation (and the payment or reimbursement of expenses) by a private foundation to a disqualified person for personal services which are reasonable and necessary to carrying out the exempt purpose of the private foundation shall not be an act of self-dealing if the compensation (or payment or reimbursement) is not excessive
> * * *

Throughout the years at issue, the Museum contracted with GMC to perform general maintenance, janitorial, and custodial functions. Respondent maintains that payments to GMC for services performed are self-dealing transactions within the ambit of section 4941(d)(1)(C). Petitioner replies that these transactions fit within the exception in section 4941(d)(2)(E) as "personal services" which are reasonable and necessary to carry out the Museum's exempt functions. As might be expected, respondent disagrees.

The resolution of this issue depends solely on whether or not the functions that GMC performed fall within the definition of "personal services" of section 4941(d)(2)(E). Before making this determination, a review of the legislative history of section 4941 is helpful.

Prior to 1969, sections 501(a) and 503(a), (b), and (d) had imposed severe sanctions for transactions that resulted in the diversion of funds to a creator or substantial contributor of a tax-exempt organization. Further, in order to prevent tax-exempt foundations from being used to benefit their creators or substantial contributors, Congress had established a set of arm's-length standards for dealings between the foundations and these disqualified individuals. H. Rept. 91–413 (Part 1), at 21 (1969), 1969–3 C.B. 200, 214.

Nevertheless, Congress noted that abuses involving tax-exempt organizations continued. Congress believed the abuses resulted from the significant enforcement problems posed by the arm's-length standards. Id. Therefore, section 4941 was enacted as part of subchapter A of a new chapter 42 added to the Internal Revenue Code by the Tax Reform Act of 1969 (the 1969 Act), Pub.L. 91–172, sec. 101(b), 83 Star. 487, 499.

One of the stated goals of the 1969 Act was to minimize the need for an arm's-length standard by generally prohibiting self-dealing transactions. Specifically, the 1969 Act prohibited the following transactions between a foundation and a disqualified person: (1) The sale, exchange or lease of property; (2) the lending of money; (3) the furnishing of goods, services or facilities; (4) the payment of compensation to a disqualified person; (5) the transfer or use of foundation property by a disqualified person; and (6) payments to Government officials. S. Rept. 91–552, at 29 (1969), 1969–3 C.B. 423, 443. If the foundation and a disqualified person entered into a prohibited transaction, then the 1969 Act imposed various levels of sanctions.

The question before us is whether the functions performed by GMC qualify as "personal services" under section 4941(d)(2)(E). Thus, we must construe what activities Congress intended would qualify as personal services. At the outset, we can look to the regulations interpreting the statute. While those regulations do not define the term "personal services", they offer several examples of activities that constitute "personal services". See sec. 53.4941(d)–3(c)(2), Foundation Excise Tax Regs. The activities set out in the examples include legal services, investment management services, and general banking services. Id.

Respondent argues that the character of the services performed by GMC, namely maintenance, janitorial, and security, are different than those outlined in the regulations. We agree. The services in the regulations are essentially professional and managerial in nature. These types of services contrast with the nature of the services rendered by GMC.

GMC contends any activity is a service where capital is not a major factor in the production of income. Under this interpretation, as set out in the brief, "the sale of goods is not the rendering of personal services, but certainly all other services which assist the private foundation in carrying on its legitimate business are personal services." We cannot agree with GMC's interpretation of the statute. First, this position would nullify the prohibition against furnishing services contained in section 4941(d)(1)(C), because almost any service would be a "personal service" and fall within the exception. The statute draws an explicit distinction between a "charge" for "furnishing of goods, services, or facilities", see sec. 4941(d)(1)(C) and (2)(C), and the payment of "compensation" "for personal services", see sec. 4941(d)(1)(D) and (2)(E). GMC's argument equating a charge for services with compensation for personal services significantly erodes this distinction.

Second, GMC's interpretation of the term "personal services" contravenes congressional intent, as expressed in the above legislative history. We think it is clear that Congress intended to prohibit self-dealing. Consequently, any exceptions to the self-dealing transactions rules should be construed narrowly. We therefore reject GMC's broad interpretation of the term "personal services" and conclude that the janitorial services provided by GMC do not meet the definition of "personal services". Accordingly, we find that the payments made by the Museum to GMC constitute "self-dealing" within the meaning of section 4941(d)(1)(C), and, as a consequence, GMC is liable for the self-dealing excise tax under section 4941(a)(1).

Issue 4. Excise Tax on Payments Made by the Museum to GMC

We shall next turn our attention to whether petitioner, petitioner's wife, and petitioner's daughter (the foundation managers) are liable under section 4941(a)(2) for payments made to GMC by the Museum. In general, section 4941(a)(1) imposes an excise tax on the self-dealer for each self-dealing transaction. When an excise tax is imposed under section 4941(a)(1), then section 4941(a)(2) may impose excise taxes on the management of the foundation as well. Section 4941(a)(2) provides:

> In any case in which a tax is imposed by [section 4941(a)] paragraph (1), there is hereby imposed on the participation of any foundation manager in an act of self-dealing between a disqualified person and a private foundation, knowing that it is such an act, a tax equal to [now 5 percent, Eds.] of the amount involved with respect to the act of self-dealing for each year (or part thereof) in the taxable period, unless such participation is not willful and is due to reasonable cause. * * *

Thus, this tax is imposed only when (1) a tax is imposed under section 4941(a)(1), (2) the participating foundation manager knows that the act is an act of self-dealing, and (3) the participation by the foundation manager is willful and is not due to reasonable cause. Sec. 53.4941(a)–1(b)(1), Foundation Excise Tax Regs. Respondent must prove, by clear and convincing evidence, that the foundation managers participated knowingly in the self-dealing transaction. Sec. 7454(b); Rule 142(c).

We first turn to the regulations to provide the initial guidance in applying section 4941(a)(2). The regulations interpret what the statute requires for knowing participation. Section 53.4941(a)–l(b)(3), Foundation Excise Tax Regs., states:

a person shall be considered to have participated in a transaction "knowing" that it is an act of self-dealing only if—

(i) He has actual knowledge of sufficient facts so that, based solely upon such facts, such transaction would be an act of self-dealing,

(ii) He is aware that such an act under these circumstances may violate the provisions of federal tax law governing self-dealing, and

(iii) He negligently fails to make reasonable attempts to ascertain whether the transaction is an act of self-dealing, or he is in fact aware that it is such an act.

The regulations specify that the term "knowing" does not mean "having reason to know", but evidence that shows a person has a reason to know a fact is relevant in determining whether that person has actual knowledge. of that fact. Id. These regulations were adopted in 1972, 3 years after the passage of the statute, and have not been substantially modified since that time. Therefore, we must give appropriate weight to the regulations in interpreting the statute. Commissioner v. South Texas Lumber Co., 333 U.S. 496, 68 S.Ct. 695, 92 L.Ed. 831 (1948).

We have found no other cases that have analyzed the foundation manager excise tax under section 4941(a)(2). However, the Tax Court analyzed the foundation manager excise tax under section 4945(a)(2) in Thorne v. Commissioner, 99 T.C. 67, 1992 WL 166157 (1992). These statutes were both enacted as part of the chapter 42 reforms of the 1969 Act, and the statutes, as well as the respective regulations promulgated thereunder, contain nearly identical language. Thus, the analysis contained in Thorne v. Commissioner, supra, is highly probative in interpreting the excise tax of section 4941(a)(2). We concluded in Thorne v. Commissioner that the threshold determination under the knowledge requirement is ascertaining the extent of the taxpayer's factual knowledge concerning the expenditures and not whether the taxpayer actually knew the expenditures were prohibited under the statute.

The parties have stipulated that the foundation managers were aware both that GMC was a disqualified person vis-a-vis the Museum, and that some transactions between a private foundation and a disqualified person are considered "self-dealing" under section 4941(d). Further, the parties have agreed that the foundation managers were aware self-dealing is defined as, inter alia, a direct furnishing of goods, services, or facilities between a private foundation and a disqualified person. In addition, the parties have agreed that the foundation managers were aware the Museum was making payments to GMC, and the managers did not oppose the making of these payments. On the basis of these facts, we conclude respondent has proven, by clear and convincing evidence, that the foundation managers possessed actual knowledge of sufficient facts concerning the transactions to establish the arrangements with GMC were self-dealing transactions.

Respondent has satisfied both the first and second requirements of section 4941(a)(2). First, we have concluded that, under section 4941(a)(1), an excise tax should be imposed on the payments from the Museum to GMC. Second, respondent has established that the foundation managers possessed sufficient "knowledge" concerning the self-dealing payments to GMC. Next, we shall evaluate whether the foundation managers made the payments willfully and without reasonable cause, the third requirement under section 4941(a)(2).

The regulations define "willful" participation by the foundation manager as conduct that is "voluntary, conscious, and intentional." Sec. 53.4941(a)–1(b)(4), Foundation Excise Tax Regs. On the basis of the facts, we conclude the foundation managers voluntarily and intentionally caused the Museum to enter into the transactions with GMC. Accordingly, we sustain respondent's determination that the participation of the foundation managers was willful.

Additionally, the foundation managers' participation in these transactions must not be due to reasonable cause. The regulations explain that "A foundation manager's participation is due to reasonable cause if he has exercised his responsibility on behalf of the foundation with ordinary business care and prudence." Sec. 53.4941(a)–1(b)(5), Foundation Excise Tax Regs. The foundation managers were aware that GMC was a disqualified person with respect to the Museum, and they were aware that tax laws prohibited self-dealing transactions. Nevertheless, they proceeded to contract with GMC to provide services to the Museum without first attempting to get advice from their counsel concerning the implications of these arrangements. This demonstrates a failure to exercise their responsibilities with ordinary business care and prudence.

The foundation managers argue that they acted on the advice of Dr. Sherry Manning. Dr. Manning, a former president of a women's college, has experience with nonprofit organizations. Thus, the foundation managers claim that they exercised ordinary prudence in relying on Dr. Manning's advice. We cannot agree. Dr. Manning is not a lawyer, and she does not otherwise have any special expertise in foundation tax law. Further, although she had been the president of a college, there is no indication in the record that Dr. Manning gained any experience in running foundations. Clearly, the foundation managers were aware of the potential problems with paying fees to GMC, as prior to the hiring of Dr. Manning, GMC had simply rendered the services for free. We conclude the foundation managers did not exercise ordinary prudence by relying on the advice of Dr. Manning and not seeking the advice of counsel regarding these payments. Accordingly, we hold that the foundation managers are liable for the foundation manager excise tax under section 4941(a)(2) for payments made by the Museum to GMC.

Issue 5. Excise Tax on Other Payments Made by the Museum

Respondent determined that the foundation managers are liable for the foundation manager excise tax under section 4941(a)(2) for two payments made by the Museum that benefited petitioner and a third payment by the Museum that benefited the Company. Specifically, the two payments which benefited petitioner, in the amounts of $2,304 and $1,343, were made by the Museum for work done to petitioner's artwork. A third payment, in the amount of $3,000, related to a financial obligation of the Company which was actually paid by the Museum. As discussed supra, a foundation manager excise tax under section 4941(a)(2) may be imposed where (1) a tax should be imposed under section 4941(a)(1), (2) the participating foundation manager knows that the act is an act of self-dealing, and (3) the participation by the foundation manager is willful and is not due to reasonable cause. Sec. 53.4941(a)–l(b)(1), Foundation Excise Tax Regs. Respondent must carry the burden of proving by clear and convincing evidence that the foundation managers participated knowingly in the transaction. Sec. 7454(b); Rule 142(c).

The foundation managers have conceded that each of these payments constitutes self-dealing under section 4941(a)(1). However, respondent must still prove that the foundation managers knew the act was an act of self-dealing. Also, the participation by the foundation managers must be willful and not due to reasonable cause.

As noted supra, the Company provided accounting services to the Museum. Two invoices relating to artwork repairs were received by the accounting department of the Company. The accounting personnel, assuming that the work had been performed on artwork owned by the Museum, made payments of $2,304 and $1,343 by checks drawn upon the Museum's bank account. In fact, the artwork belonged to petitioner, and the payments should have been made from petitioner's personal account.

Far from having actual knowledge of sufficient facts about the two transactions, the evidence indicates that the foundation managers lacked any knowledge concerning these transactions. Immediately upon learning of the payments a few days after they were made, petitioner's daughter corrected both of the transactions, and petitioner reimbursed the Museum for the expense. Under these circumstances, we conclude respondent erred in imposing the foundation manager excise tax on these two transactions.

The record is less than complete regarding the $3,000 payment made for the benefit of the Company. The payment was made by the Museum on behalf of the Company, a disqualified person. The Company has not reimbursed the Museum. Respondent, again, must prove by clear and convincing evidence that the foundation managers participated knowingly in this transaction. Sec. 7454(b); Rule 142(c). Respondent has failed to carry this burden. First, respondent has not shown that petitioner or petitioner's wife had any knowledge of this transaction. We refuse to presume that, because the transaction occurred, petitioner or petitioner's wife must have known about it. Consequently, we do not sustain respondent's determination with respect to petitioner or petitioner's wife as it relates to this transaction.

As for petitioner's daughter, the facts must be examined more closely. The $3,000 payment related to a contract with Form, Inc., for the creation of an outdoor art exhibit. The subject matter of the contract comports directly with the Museum's exempt purpose, and the contract was signed by petitioner's daughter as a director of the Museum. However, the John Madden Co. is the named party in the contract, not the Museum. The payment by the Museum for setting up the outdoor exhibit satisfied a financial obligation of the Company under the contract with Form, Inc., and the parties agree that it is a self-dealing payment to the Company.

Petitioner's daughter testified that she was aware of the payment made by the Museum. As evidenced by this testimony, she was knowledgeable about the subject matter of the contract. However, based on the testimony and surrounding facts, we conclude that her actions do not constitute knowing participation in a self-dealing transaction. Petitioner's daughter testified that the foundation managers intended to have the Museum shoulder the responsibility for the exhibit, not the Company. She believed, at the time of the payment, that responsibility for the financial obligation rested with the Museum. As a consequence, petitioner's daughter did not view this payment as benefiting the Company. Given these circumstances, we conclude respondent has failed to prove by clear and convincing evidence that petitioner's daughter knowingly entered into a self-dealing transaction. Accordingly, we do not sustain respondent's determination with respect to petitioner's daughter as it relates to this $3,000 transaction.

PROBLEMS

1.   The Lifton Foundation ("the Foundation") is a § 501(c)(3) organization classified as a private nonoperating foundation. The Foundation's President is Olga Lifton Rothschild, granddaughter of Archibold Lifton, who created the Foundation in 1970 with a substantial gift of Lifton Pea Corporation stock. Other substantial gifts have been made by Archibold's wife, Claribel, and by Roger Ogleby, a distant cousin of Olga Rothschild. Assume that Archibold and Claribel Lifton and Roger Ogleby are "substantial contributors." The Foundation's net assets are $25 million.

Which of the following transactions during the current year are likely to create excise tax liability for self-dealing under § 4941? In each case in which you conclude that there is such liability, determine: (a) against whom the tax will be imposed; (b) the probable amount of the tax; and (c) the procedure and time period in which to correct the act and the ramifications of failing to do so within the prescribed period.

(a)   Payment of $75,000 per year compensation to Olga for her services as President, and $5,000 in reimbursement of travel expenses for other family members and their spouses to attend the annual meeting of the board of directors at the family's summer retreat.

(b)   Leasing of office space by the Foundation on a rent-free basis in a townhouse owned by Olga Rothschild.

(c) Sharing of office space with Lifton family members in a commercial building owned by an unrelated party; the Foundation reimburses the family members for its share of rent and related expenses.

(d) Payment by the Foundation of a legally binding charitable pledge made by Olga to her alma mater to commemorate her 25th college reunion.

(e) Hanging of paintings from the Foundation's collection at the home of Peggy Rothschild, Olga's daughter.

(f) Receipt by Olga and other Lifton family members of preferred seating at opera and symphony performances, and member benefits at museums, resulting from the Foundation's substantial grants to these cultural institutions.

(g) Sale by the Foundation of an undeveloped parcel on March 15 to Olga's husband, Dick, for $300,000, its fair market value. As foundation manager, Olga was aware of the sale but did not know that a sale at fair market value would constitute an act of self-dealing. For this purpose, assume that the IRS issues a statutory notice of deficiency three years after March 15 of the current year, asserting that the sale is an act of self-dealing and assume, alternatively, that:

(1) Dick continues to own the land, which is now worth $500,000.

(2) Dick develops the land, now a shopping center worth $1,500,000.

(3) Dick's plan to develop the land fails and he sells the land for $250,000 seven months after its acquisition.

(h) Payment by the Foundation of $5,000 in directors and officers liability insurance premiums to cover the potential liability of its trustees for wrongful acts committed in their official capacity.

(i) Scholarship grant of $1,000 to Olga's granddaughter, Henrietta.

(j) Payment of an honorarium of $1,000 plus travel expenses to Hiram Goldsmith, legislative assistant to a United States Senator, for a speech sponsored by the Foundation and delivered for the Senator by Mr. Goldsmith.

2. If the transactions described in Problem 1, above, all occur in the current year, is it likely that the Foundation or any other person will be liable for taxes or penalties in addition to those imposed by § 4941? See, e.g., I.R.C. §§ 507(c); 6684.

3. CHARITABLE DISTRIBUTION REQUIREMENTS: § 4942

Internal Revenue Code: § 4942(a), (b), (c), (d), (e), (g)(1)–(3), (h), (j)(1), (2) & (4).

a. INTRODUCTION

It always has been assumed that a § 501(c)(3) organization will regularly disburse its funds for charitable purposes. Prior to 1969, however, some charities held unproductive assets or accumulated income, neglecting their charitable commitment. Although the Code provided that some foundations would lose their exemption if its accumulations of income were "unreasonable" in amount and duration, the standards were vague and sanctions were difficult to enforce.

To encourage more consistent generosity, § 4942 requires all private nonoperating foundations to make certain minimum annual distributions for charitable purposes. The required payout is measured with reference to a percentage of the foundation's investment assets. A foundation that fails to meet the minimum payout requirement is subject to an excise tax on its "undistributed income." If any of the required payout remains undistributed as of the beginning of the second (or any succeeding) taxable year following the current taxable year, a first-level tax equal to 30 percent of that undistributed amount is imposed; continuing failure to satisfy the statute gives rise to a more severe second-level penalty equal to 100 percent of the undistributed income. I.R.C. § 4942(a), (b).

To illustrate, assume that a private foundation formed on January 1, 2008, is required by § 4942 to distribute $100,000 for that year. The foundation would be subject to the initial excise tax under § 4942 if all or part of the 2008 distributable amount were not distributed as of January 1, 2010. If, however, the foundation had a $50,000 shortfall as of the beginning of 2010, it would be subject to a tax of $15,000 (30% x $50,000 of undistributed income) and the liability would continue for each succeeding taxable year in which the remaining payout requirement were not met. Continuing transgressions would also trigger the more severe second-level penalty equal to 100 percent of the undistributed income.

b. OPERATION OF § 4942

Distributable Amount. To avoid the § 4942 tax, a foundation must not have "undistributed income," which is defined by § 4942(c) as the foundation's "distributable amount" for the taxable year less "qualifying distributions" attributable to that year. The "distributable amount" is equal to the foundation's "minimum investment return" reduced by the § 4940 audit tax and any unrelated business income tax imposed on the foundation. I.R.C. § 4942(d).

Minimum investment return ("MIR") is equal to five percent of the excess of the fair market value of all assets of the foundation (other than those used directly in carrying out its exempt purposes) over any acquisition indebtedness to which those assets are subject. I.R.C. § 4942(e)(1). The "MIR" concept guarantees that a foundation's charitable activity, as measured by its grant-making or more direct expenditures for charitable purposes, bears some reasonable relationship to its size. The specific determination of MIR presents inevitable questions of valuation. For example, readily marketable securities are valued on a monthly basis, and the annual valuation must be an average of the monthly values determined. I.R.C. § 4942(e)(2)(A). Other assets may be valued less frequently—e.g., real property may be valued by independent appraisals at five-year intervals.

Treas. Reg. § 53.4942(a)–2(c)(4)(iv). For securities, reductions in value for blockage or similar factors are appropriate where the foundation establishes that a reduction in value would accompany any liquidation, but blockage discounts are limited to 10 percent of market prices. I.R.C. § 4942(e)(2)(B).

Assets used directly to carry out a foundation's exempt purposes are excluded in determining MIR on the theory that they do not produce any income that is available for distribution. Examples of excluded assets are the buildings, equipment and supplies used in managing a foundation's exempt activities—but not the facilities used in administering a foundation's investments. Treas. Reg. § 53.4942(a)–2(c)(3). Also excluded are assets "held for use" in an exempt activity (e.g., an office building purchased for use as a national headquarters but temporarily rented to commercial tenants) and "program-related investments" (e.g., low-interest student loans). Id. Other examples of excluded related-function assets include: paintings loaned to museums and schools (Rev. Rul. 74–498, 1974–2 C.B. 387); an island preserved for ecological and historical purposes (Rev. Rul. 75–207, 1975–1 C.B. 361); and assets of a business for which substantially all of the work is performed by volunteers (Rev. Rul. 76–85, 1976–1 C.B. 357).

Qualifying Distributions. A foundation satisfies its payout requirement by making "qualifying distributions." In general, a "qualifying distribution" is any amount paid to accomplish a proper charitable purpose, or any amount paid to acquire an asset to be used in carrying out such a purpose. I.R.C. § 4942(g)(1). Most qualifying distributions are grants, but direct expenditures to advance the foundation's proper purposes also qualify. Excluded, however, are (1) distributions to an organization controlled by the foundation or one or more disqualified persons, and (2) distributions to other nonoperating foundations, unless the distributee commits to passing such amount through by the end of the succeeding year. I.R.C. § 4942(g)(1), (3).

Qualifying distributions include reasonable and necessary administrative expenses paid to accomplish the foundation's exempt purposes, but not investment expenses and other costs of managing the foundation's endowment. Treas. Reg. § 53.4942(a)–3(a)(2). "Grant administrative expenses" include expenses allocable to the making of grants, such as costs of evaluating grant applications, expenses incurred to administer and evaluate grants, and expenses for post-grant review.

Effective for payments made after August 17, 2006, private foundations may not count as qualifying distributions payments to Type III supporting organizations that are not functionally integrated with the organizations they support, or to all other types of SOs if they or the organizations they support are directly or indirectly controlled by a disqualified person of the private foundation. The Treasury also has the authority to define other conditions under which a payment by a private foundation to a supporting organization would not be appropriate and thus not counted as a qualifying distribution. I.R.C. § 4942(g)(4).

Set–Asides. From time to time a foundation may find it advisable to establish an internal fund for future expenditures in a charitable activity. For example, it may choose to fund a scientific research program of such magnitude that it requires an accumulation of funds before the project commences. Or it may wish to accumulate funds in connection with a matching-grants program in which the distributee is expected to raise an amount to match the foundation's future contribution. Section 4942(g)(2) permits such "set-aside" amounts to qualify as current distributions provided that the amount will be paid for a specific project within five years (and the foundation satisfies the Service as to that prospect), and either the foundation establishes that the project is one which can better be accomplished by such set-aside than by immediate payment or meets certain other complex requirements in § 4942(g)(2)(B).

The amount set aside need not be an accumulation of income. It is sufficient if the foundation sets aside, by means of a bookkeeping entry, the amount of its minimum investment return for the preceding year and earmarks it for a specific project. Rev. Rul. 78–148, 1978–1 C.B. 380. But the set-aside must advance the project. In Rev. Rul. 79–319, 1979–2 C.B. 388, a set-aside made so that the foundation could control the funds during a three-year museum construction period and receive income thereon, was held not to be a qualifying distribution. Compare Rev. Rul. 74–450, 1974–2 C.B. 388 (conversion of land into park under four-year construction contract justified set-asides against future payments).

Incorrect valuation. Where a foundation fails to make adequate qualifying distributions solely because it incorrectly valued assets for purposes of determining minimum investment return, the statute affords relief from tax provided that:

a. the failure to value the asset properly was not willful and was due to reasonable cause, and

b. "make-up" distributions are made within the "allowable distribution period" (as defined by 4942(j)(2)); the foundation notifies the Service that the necessary amount has been distributed; and the make-up distribution is treated, under the tracing rules of the statute, as made out of income for the year as to which the incorrect valuation occurred.

I.R.C. § 4942(a)(2).

Source of Qualifying Distributions. The initial § 4942 tax is imposed only if the "distributable amount" for the taxable year is not expended by qualifying distributions made by the end of the following year. I.R.C. § 4942(a). The statute provides that qualifying distributions are treated as first made out of the undistributed income for the immediately preceding year, then out of the undistributed income for the present year, and finally out of corpus. To enable a foundation to correct a distributions deficiency for a year prior to the immediately preceding year, however, the foundation may elect to treat any distribution that otherwise would be treated as out of the current year's distributable amount, or out of corpus, as a distribution for the year in which correction is necessary. I.R.C. § 4942(h).

If by chance the foundation's distributions during the preceding five years (the "adjustment period") exceed its distributable amount for those years, then the excess distributions may be used to reduce the foundation's distributable amount for the taxable year. I.R.C. § 4942(i).

c. POLICY ISSUES: ADJUSTING THE PAYOUT RATE

A longstanding debate over the appropriate payout rate for private foundations escalated in response to controversial legislation introduced in May 2003 by Rep. Roy Blunt, a Missouri Republican, and Rep. Harold Ford, Jr., a Tennessee Democrat. Section 105 of the Charitable Giving Act of 2003 (H.R. 7) would have amended § 4942(g)(1) by removing reasonable and necessary administrative expenses from the calculation of "qualifying distributions" for purposes of the 5 percent payout requirement. The effect would be to increase the amount that private foundations must pay in grants and direct charitable programs. Proponents argued that they were trying to help cash-strapped charities by forcing foundations to distribute more of their endowment for charitable purposes, and to curb what they saw as a trend of excessive administrative expenses, especially compensation.

The payout rate amendment attracted wide attention, and the response was predictably mixed. Most officials of large private foundations were strongly opposed, as was Independent Sector, an umbrella group that represents over 700 nonprofit and philanthropic institutions. They argued that reasonable operating expenses, such as the staff time devoted to evaluation and monitoring grantees, technical assistance to improve the effectiveness of grantees, research, and public education programs are essential components of a well-managed foundation's core mission. Some mainstream insiders reacted with ominous predictions that the proposal would ensure the ultimate demise of foundations by forcing them to distribute more than the investment return on their endowments. Critics of the proposal also argued that if excessive administrative expenses are the problem, the appropriate solution is more IRS enforcement of the abusers or targeted legislation to limit administrative costs (e.g., caps on compensation paid to foundation executives). See Harvy Lipman & Ian Wilhelm, Pressing Foundations to Give More, Chron. Philanthropy, May 29, 2003, at 7.

Others from both ends of the political spectrum applaud the goal of putting more money into the hands of charities in light of the weak economy and declines in government and private support. The National Committee for Responsive Philanthropy projects that eliminating administration expenses from "qualifying distributions" would generate more than $4 billion in additional grants annually without endangering the long-term survival of foundations. The NCRP study found that in 2001, the 100 largest U.S. private foundations counted $883 million of administrative expenses toward their annual 5 percent payout requirement, and nearly

$350 million of that amount was for staff salaries and trustee compensation. Helping Charities, Sustaining Foundations: Reasonable Tax Reform Would Aid America's Charities, Preserve Foundation Perpetuity and Enhance Foundation Effectiveness and Efficiency, available at www.ncrp.org/HelpingCharities.pdf.

The Blunt/Ford proposal was another chapter in an ongoing dialogue over the appropriate foundation payout rate. A 1999 report prepared for the National Network of Grantmakers by Perry Mehrling, an economics professor at Barnard College, argued that higher payout means higher grants, and higher grants mean more nonprofit activity. Professor Mehrling's study concluded that historical asset returns have generally exceeded the minimum payout level but foundations remained wedded to the 5 percent minimum payout as a spending benchmark, suppressing charitable distributions at a time of growing need in society. He took issue with the conclusions in reports commissioned in 1991 and 1995 by the Council on Foundations that five percent was the optimal payout to protect foundation assets from being eroded by inflation. According to Professor Mehrling, a typical foundation could have afforded a payout rate as high as eight percent during the period from 1974 to 1995 without reducing its corpus. Spending Policies for Foundations: The Case for Foundations (National Network of Grantmakers, 1999). Notably, perhaps, the Mehrling study was released at the peak of the 1990s stock market boom, when equity investment returns were averaging 20 percent or more per year. But reports commissioned in 1999 by the Council on Foundations and Goldman Sachs warned against increasing the payout rate to prevent erosion of the real value of foundation assets. They argue that lower initial spending results in higher aggregate spending over time. See DeMarche Associates, Spending Policies and Investment Planning for Foundations: A Structure for Determining a Foundation's Asset Mix (3d ed. 1999); Goldman Sachs Asset Management, Sustainable Spending, Policies for Foundations and Endowments (1999).

Economists, former members of Congress, academics and a handful of prominent philanthropists have joined the discussion, ratcheting up the level of discourse without reaching any consensus. In collaboration with former Senator Bill Bradley, the consulting firm of McKinsey & Co. has argued that "time value of money" principles support a higher payout rate because a dollar of charity given today is worth more to society than a dollar given in the future. Paul J. Jansen & David M. Katz, For Nonprofits, Time is Money, The McKinsey Quarterly, no. 1 (2002); Bill Bradley & Paul Jansen, Faster Charity, N.Y. Times, May 15, 2002, at 23. Some philanthropists contend that foundations must increase their payout today to solve social problems (e.g., global warming) that will cause untold harm to future generations if they are not addressed promptly. A few large foundations (most with first generation donors still alive) have gone so far as to plan their own demise by spending themselves out of existence rather than maintaining endowments. The motivations for increased spending range from philosophical opposition to endowments to a personal desire of some founding donors to give their money away while they are still living rather than entrust grantmaking to their descendants or professional foundation managers. They assume future causes and needs can be funded by the next generation of philanthropists and beyond. See David Bank, Giving While Living: Some Foundations Have a New Idea: Spend It All Now, Wall St. J., Sept. 10, 2002, at A1.

Are foundation grants made in the future of lesser social value than those made currently? Should § 4942 reflect a preference for present generations of charitable beneficiaries, or should the payout rate be set to maintain the real economic value of foundation endowments in perpetuity and, if so, what is the appropriate rate? Or should there be a limited life for foundations (e.g., 50 years, as was once proposed but rejected) after which all remaining funds must be released for immediate use for charitable purposes? For a thoughtful and balanced review of these questions that rejects McKinsey's "time value of money" methodology and explains how a higher payout rate can lead to less money actually paid out and, conversely, a lower payout rate results in more distributed over time, see Michael Klausner, When Time Isn't Money: Foundation Payout Rates and the Time Value of Money, Stan. Soc. Innovation Rev., Spring 2001, at 50.

The payout debate has been an effective consciousness raiser for the foundation community. In the last analysis, the current approach is a good compromise. Whatever the trade-offs between present and future generations may be, foundations should be required to devote some of their resources annually for charitable purposes, and the 5 percent benchmark is workable and familiar. Foundations wishing to spend more are free to do so. Many smaller foundations choose to exceed the 5 percent benchmark, and some very large foundations, usually influenced by the founding donor, have made a conscious decision to accelerate spending as part of a plan to distribute all their assets by a future date. If excessive administrative expenses are seen as an abuse, Congress would be better advised to address that problem more directly, such as by giving the IRS more resources to enforce the self-dealing rules in § 4941 or by considering, as rough justice, a cap on the administrative expenses that can be included in calculating qualifying distributions.

PROBLEM

The Wang Foundation ("Wang"), a private operating foundation, commenced operations on January 1, 2009, when it was funded with the following gifts:

Asset	Donor	Adj. Basis	F.M.V.
10,000 shs. Wang Inc. stock (10% of total shs. outstanding)	Tom Wang	$370,000	$3,970,000
Cash	Mary Wang	30,000	30,000
Office Building	Lemon, Inc.	80,000	150,000
Furniture/Fixtures	Lemon, Inc.	20,000	20,000

Unless otherwise indicated, assume for convenience that the assets and values remain unchanged throughout the years covered by the problem, and that no blockage discount is allowed for the Foundation's stock in Wang, Inc.

Wang was organized to encourage the education of underprivileged youth in Northern California by seeking to identify urban high schools with a high percentage of disadvantaged students, to make grants to these schools to establish special educational programs, to award college scholarships, and to make student loans. Wang administers its programs in a building donated by a for-profit corporation, and employs a full-time director, a secretary, and one staff member who spends virtually all of her time visiting schools and counseling students. The building also is frequently used for meetings between high school students and representatives of various colleges.

In 2009, Wang's income consisted of $250,000 of dividends and a $360,000 long-term capital gain from the sale of 1,000 shares of Wang, Inc. stock on December 31, 2009. The foundation's expenses were as follows:

Administrative expenses	$7,000
Salaries	50,000
Maintenance of building	10,000
Depreciation	6,000
Grants to schools	18,000
Scholarship awards	40,000
Student loans	20,000
Investment advisory fee	5,000

On January 1, 2010, Wang used the $380,000 gross proceeds from the sale of Wang, Inc. stock to purchase all the outstanding common stock of a small company engaged in preparing students for standardized college entrance examinations. Wang hoped that it could use the resources of this company to increase the test scores of disadvantaged students, but it had no immediate plans to change the nature of the business. At the same time, the remaining Wang, Inc. stock was sold and the proceeds were reinvested in a diversified portfolio of securities. Assume that the average value of the portfolio during 2010 was $3,420,000.

Receipts during 2010 were as follows:

Dividends	$ 160,000
Interest	80,000
Long-term Capital Gain	3,240,000
Short-term Capital Gain	20,000
Repayment of Student Loans	6,000

Expenditures in 2010 were exactly the same as in 2009 in each category except that scholarships were $50,000 and student loans were $30,000.

Consider the following questions:

(a) Should Wang have made additional distributions in 2009 or 2010 to avoid the § 4942(a) tax?

(b) To avoid any tax under § 4942, what amount must Wang distribute in 2011?

(c) May Wang satisfy its distribution requirements by creating an account on its books of $500,000 and earmarking the amount for an accelerated summer school tutoring program on the condition that the City of San Jose, before January 1, 2017, appropriates an equal amount for the same purpose?

4.   EXCESS BUSINESS HOLDINGS: § 4943

Internal Revenue Code: § 4943(a), (b), (c)(1)–(3), (5)–(7), (d); skim § 4943(c)(4).

Treasury Regulations: § 53.4943–1, –3(a), (b), –6(a).

a.   INTRODUCTION

One of the principal abuses that Congress sought to curb in 1969 was the perpetuation of control of a closely-held family business through substantial private foundation ownership of equity or proprietary interests. Foundation managers, often wearing shareholder and officer hats as well, were said to place the interests of the business ahead of the charitable responsibilities of the foundation. The legislative history of the 1969 Act cited several egregious examples, including one where a foundation controlled 45 separate businesses: fifteen were clothing manufacturers, seven engaged in the real estate business, six operated retail stores, one owned and managed a hotel, and others carried on printing, hardware and jewelry businesses. See S.Rep. No. 552, 91st Cong., 1st Sess. (1969).

The income-distribution mandate of § 4942 represents one solution to this problem. Congress went further, however, by limiting the extent to which a business may be controlled by a private foundation and its major donors. Section 4943 generally provides that a foundation and its disqualified persons together may not own more than 20 percent of the voting stock of a corporation or equivalent interests in a partnership. The value of holdings in excess of those permitted are subject to an initial tax of 10 percent, and a second-level tax of 200 percent for failure to dispose of the excess holdings during a statutorily prescribed correction period. I.R.C. § 4943(a), (b).

b.   OPERATION OF § 4943

Permitted and Excess Holdings. Section 4943(c)(1) defines "excess business holdings" as the amount of stock that a private foundation must dispose of to a person other than a disqualified person in order for its remaining holdings to be "permitted holdings." "Permitted holdings" in a corporation are 20 percent of the corporation's voting stock less the percentage of such stock held by all disqualified persons. I.R.C. § 4943(c)(2)(A). A private foundation is thus permitted to own 20 percent of the voting stock of a corporation, reduced by the percentage of voting stock owned by all disqualified persons. Where all disqualified persons together do not own more than 20 percent of voting stock, the private foundation may own nonvoting stock in any amount. Id.

To illustrate, assume that the Stewart Foundation owns 11 percent of the voting stock of Rainbow Fabrics, Inc.; the chair of the Stewart board owns 3 percent; and other disqualified persons (descendants of a substantial contributor) own 9 percent. Since the aggregate holdings of the foundation and its disqualified persons are 23 percent, the foundation has excess business holdings. But since all disqualified persons together do not own more than 20 percent, any nonvoting shares held by the foundation are treated as permitted holdings.

Congress apparently selected 20 percent as the critical benchmark on the theory that more than 20 percent ownership may represent control of a corporation when shares are otherwise widely dispersed. The same policy prompted Congress to relax the rules when effective control can be shown to reside elsewhere. If the private foundation and all disqualified persons together do not own more than 35 percent of the voting stock, and it can be established that effective control of the corporation is in other nondisqualified persons, then the overall limitation is 35 percent rather than 20 percent. I.R.C. § 4943(c)(2)(B). See Rev. Rul. 81–111, 1981–1 C.B. 509 (may qualify for 35 percent limit by proving unrelated party or "cohesive group" exercises control, but not by showing that foundation and disqualified persons cannot exercise control).

Both the 20 percent and 35 percent rules are modified by a de minimis rule, which provides that if the foundation, together with any other private foundations to which it is considered related under § 4946(a)(1)(H), does not own more than two percent of the voting stock and not more than two percent in value of all outstanding shares of the corporation, it will not be treated as having any excess business holdings without regard to the holdings of disqualified persons. I.R.C. § 4943(c)(2)(C).

Similar albeit less precise rules are provided for unincorporated business enterprises. To determine permitted holdings in a partnership, the foundation's "profits interest" is aggregated with the profits interests of all disqualified persons and substituted for the voting stock measure applicable to corporations, and "capital interest" is used in lieu of nonvoting stock. I.R.C. § 4943(c)(3)(A); Treas. Reg. § 53.4943–3(c). No business whatsoever may be conducted as a proprietorship. I.R.C. § 4943(c)(3)(B). In the highly unusual event that a business in which the foundation has an interest is conducted in the form of a trust, the foundation's beneficial interest in such trust, together with those of its disqualified persons, is substituted for the voting stock measure applicable to corporate stock ownership. I.R.C. § 4943(c)(3)(C).

Excluded from the definition of "business enterprise" and thus not subject to the excess business holdings penalties are businesses that are functionally related (e.g., a business that is related to the foundation's exempt purposes) or a business where at least 95 percent of the gross income is derived from passive sources (e.g., dividends, interest, rent and the like). I.R.C. § 4943(d)(3).

Attribution Rules. In computing the holdings of any business enterprise, stock or other interests owned directly or indirectly by a corporation, partnership, estate, or trust are considered as owned proportionately by the beneficial owners. I.R.C. § 4943(d)(1). In order to establish the extent of a foundation's permitted holdings, therefore, it often is necessary to undertake a rather extensive fact-finding mission, and to inquire, particularly of trustees and estate administrators, as to the extent of their holdings in the business in question. The responsibility of the foundation managers is considerable—and so, too, are the enforcement problems. The regulations suggest that the foundation send an annual questionnaire to each foundation manager, substantial contributor, etc., requesting a listing of all actual and beneficial holdings of interests in enterprises in which the foundation has interests in excess of the 2 percent de minimis rule. Treas. Reg. § 53.4943–2(a)(1)(v)(B).

Gifts and Bequests. Business interests received by gift or bequest after May 26, 1969 that cause a foundation to have excess business holdings are treated, along with prior holdings of the foundation if it was not then in an excess business holdings position, as held by a disqualified person (rather than by the foundation) during the five-year period beginning on the date such holdings are received. The foundation thus has a five-year period to correct the problem created by the gift or bequest. I.R.C. § 4943(c)(6). Where a foundation receives "an unusually large gift or bequest of diverse business holdings or holdings with complex corporate structures," the Service may extend the five-year disposition period to ten years. I.R.C. § 4943(c)(7). An extension will be granted, however, only if the foundation establishes that it has made diligent attempts to dispose of the excess holdings within the initial five-year period and that disposition was not possible other than at a distress sale price. Id.

Disposal of Excess Business Holdings. The Code and regulations offer several avenues of avoidance from the excess business holdings tax. The simplest method allows a foundation a 90–day correction period from the time it discovers an excess business holdings problem. The 90–day period begins to run on the date "on which [the foundation] knows, or has reason to know, of the event which caused it to have such excess business holdings." Treas. Reg. § 53.4943–2(a)(1)(ii). Even a purchase by the foundation will not subject it to liability, where the excess can be shown to be attributable to prior acquisitions by disqualified persons of which the foundation managers were unaware. The foundation's innocence, which is crucial to the 90–day escape, is established on the basis of all relevant "facts and circumstances." Treas. Reg. § 53.4943–2(a)(1)(v).

c. APPLICATION OF EXCESS BUSINESS HOLDINGS RULES TO DONOR–ADVISED FUNDS AND CERTAIN SUPPORTING ORGANIZATIONS

During its investigation of donor-advised funds and supporting organizations, Congress concluded that these private foundation alternatives were being used by some donors to maximize tax benefits on gifts of interests in closely held businesses and circumvent the excess business holdings rules. If these same gifts had been made to a private foundation, the income tax deduction would have been limited to the donor's basis rather than fair market value, and the foundation would have been required to divest its holdings to avoid a § 4943 penalty, possibly diluting the family's control. These end runs were curtailed when Congress extended the excess business holdings rules to donor-advised funds and some supporting organizations.

In the case of donor-advised funds, the term "disqualified person" is redefined to include donors, other donor-advisors, members of their families, and 35–percent controlled entities of any of the foregoing. Transitional rules similar to those applicable to private foundations are provided to ease the pain. For example, a donor-advised fund would have five years to divest any new excess business holdings acquired by gift or bequest. See I.R.C. §§ 4943(e); 4943(c)(4)–(6).

The excess business holdings rules also apply to Type III supporting organizations (other than functionally integrated Type IIIs) and Type II SOs that accept any gift from a person (other than a public charity not including an SO) who controls, alone or with family members and 35–percent controlled entities, the governing body of a supported organization of the SO. I.R.C. §§ 4943(f)(3); 509(f)(2)(B).[1] The legislative history explains that "control" for this purpose includes "the ability to exercise effective control," such as where the SO's supported organization has a five-member board composed of the SO's donor, a family member, the donor's personal attorney, and two independent directors. Joint Committee on Taxation, General Explanation of Tax Legislation Enacted in the 109th Congress 653, n. 996 (2007). Oddly (or so it seems to the authors), § 4943 was not extended to Type I SOs or functionally integrated Type III SOs.

In applying § 4943 to SOs, the term "disqualified person" is more expansive than the § 4946 definition applicable to private foundations. Borrowing from the intermediate sanctions rules, Congress broadly defined DQP to include persons who can exercise substantial influence over the SO's affairs during the five-year period preceding the transaction, substantial contributors (as defined in § 4958(c)(3)(c)) and persons related to the foregoing, and (accept our apologies in advance) any organization that is effectively controlled by the same person or persons who control the supporting organization or any organization substantially all of the contributions to which were made by the same person or persons who made substantially all of the contributions to the supporting organization, or members of that person's family. I.R.C. § 4943(f)(4). Congress apparently did not want to leave out any possible suspect!

d. TRANSITIONAL RULES

Private foundations with excess business holdings as of May 26, 1969 may rely on transitional rules that provide ample time to dispose of the

---

1. The IRS may exempt the excess business holdings of any organization from the application of § 4943 if the organization establishes to the IRS's satisfaction that the excess holdings are consistent with the organization's exempt purposes. I.R.C. § 4943(f)(2). A custom tailored exemption provides that excess business holdings do not include the holdings of any Type III SO if, as of November 18, 2005 and at all times thereafter, the holdings are held for the benefit of the community pursuant to a directive by a state attorney general or other appropriate state official with jurisdiction over the organization. I.R.C. § 4943(f)(6).

holdings without the economic loss that might result from an immediate forced divestiture. Fortunately, the importance of the transitional rules has waned considerably, and inflicting further torture by reviewing them risks violating the Geneva Convention. Suffice it to note that business interests held by a foundation on May 26, 1969, or acquired subsequently under a will executed before that date or pursuant to a trust that was irrevocable on that date, qualify for more liberal divestiture schedules. In general, the more extensive the holdings of the foundation and its disqualified persons, the longer the period allowed. See I.R.C. § 4943(c)(4)(B). Similarly, affected supporting organizations with excess business holdings as of the effective date of the Pension Protection Act of 2006 qualify for transitional relief.

PROBLEM

The James Irving Foundation, a private foundation, was organized in 1994 by James Irving and his wife, Esther, each of whom contributed 9,000 shares of Irving Co. common stock. On that date and at the present time, the outstanding Irving Co. common stock (totalling 100,000 shares) was held as follows:

Irving Foundation	18,000 shares
James Irving	3,000 shares
Esther Irving	3,000 shares
Leola Irving Smythe	3,000 shares
Craft Industries	22,000 shares
Unrelated shareholders	51,000 shares

Leola Irving Smythe is the daughter of James and Esther Irving. Craft Industries is not related to the Irving family; it acquired all of its shares last year in a tender offer. None of the "unrelated shareholders" owns as much as one percent of the stock.

(a) Do the Foundation's present holdings create any excess business holdings problem? If so, how could the problem be avoided? Consider, among other things, the possibility of the Foundation selling all or part of its stock to other shareholders, or the corporation redeeming stock held by the Foundation in order to achieve any necessary divestiture.

(b) Same as (a), above, except that the Foundation owns only 2,000 shares, and James and Esther and Leola Irving Smythe own 25,000 shares in the aggregate.

(c) Same as (a), above, except that the Foundation received its 18,000 shares two years ago as a bequest from the late Rosalie Irving, the mother of James Irving.

(d) Same as (a), above, except the Foundation is a non-functionally integrated Type III supporting organization that was formed in 2007.

5.   JEOPARDY INVESTMENTS: § 4944

Internal Revenue Code: § 4944.

Treasury Regulations: § 53.4944–1, –3(a).

In theory, the income distribution requirements, sanctions against excess business holdings, and state law standards of fiduciary duty should guarantee a diversified and reasonably productive investment portfolio. But Congress also was concerned that a private foundation's governing board might make investments that would jeopardize the foundation's endowment. To ensure that the foundation's portfolio strategy creates no more than a tolerable level of risk, § 4944 imposes an excise tax of ten percent on any amount invested by a private foundation "in such a manner as to jeopardize the carrying out of any of its exempt purposes * * *." I.R.C. § 4944(a). As defined by the regulations, a jeopardy investment occurs:

> if it is determined that the foundation managers, in making such investment, have failed to exercise ordinary business care and prudence, under the facts and circumstances prevailing at the time of making the investment, in providing for the long-and short-term financial needs of the foundation to carry out its exempt purposes.
>
> Treas. Reg. § 53.4944–1(a)(2)(i).

Jeopardy can be a quantitative matter. Thus, a foundation with $10 million in assets which allocates ten percent of its portfolio to speculative growth stocks in various industries should not have any excise exposure under § 4944. On the other hand, a foundation that risks nearly all of its endowment in speculative ventures or loses the bulk of its investments in a Ponzi scheme without conducting adequate due diligence is unlikely to survive close audit scrutiny by the IRS. The standards to be applied on audit are not precise. Despite extensive regulations, the determination of jeopardy turns on all the facts and circumstances, including "the need for diversification." Treas. Reg. § 53.4944–1(a)(2)(i). The following investments are considered worthy of "close scrutiny:" margin trading; commodity futures; working interests in oil and gas wells; options and straddles; warrants; and short sales.

Notably excepted from the prohibitions of § 4944 are program-related investments, which are defined as investments "the primary purpose of which is to accomplish one or more of the [charitable, religious, etc.] purposes described in section 170(c)(2)(B) and no significant purpose of which is the production of income or the appreciation of property." I.R.C. § 4944(c). The regulations suggest a "but for" test—i.e., would the investment have been made but for the relationship between the investment and the accomplishment of the foundation's exempt activities. Treas. Reg. § 53.4944–3(a)(2)(i). For example, assume a foundation invests in an urban renewal project in a deteriorating inner-city neighborhood. Assistance in the financing of such a project involves significant risks, to be sure, and probably an unfavorable interest rate, but the project is intended to advance a charitable purpose of the foundation. See Treas. Reg. § 53.4944–3(b).

A private foundation that makes a jeopardy investment is subject to an initial tax of ten percent of the amount invested for each taxable year or part thereof. Additional taxes may be imposed if the investment is "not removed from jeopardy." I.R.C. § 4944(a)(1), (b)(1). In addition, participating foundation managers are subject to a ten percent first-level tax (up to a maximum of $10,000) and a ten percent second-level tax (up to $10,000), unless such participation is not willful and is due to reasonable cause. I.R.C. § 4944(a)(2), (d)(2). Under the regulations, however, managers are protected if they act on the advice of legal counsel "expressed in a reasoned written legal opinion" that the particular investment will not jeopardize the foundation's exempt purposes. Similarly, reliance upon the advice of investment counsel, expressed in writing, that a particular investment will provide for the "long-and short-term financial needs of the foundation" will provide a defense to the penalty even though the investment turns out badly. Reg. § 53.4944–1(b)(2)(v).

PROBLEMS

1. The Prudence Foundation has net assets worth $10 million, of which $2 million is cash recently received as a gift from Maude Prudence, the president of its board. The remaining $8 million is invested in a diversified portfolio of stocks and bonds.

Evaluate whether the following investments being considered by the Foundation's board for the $2 million cash would be treated as jeopardy investments:

(a) High-yield (and high-risk) subordinated corporate debentures.

(b) Commodity futures, stock index futures, options, and other derivative instruments.

(c) Undeveloped real estate.

(d) Below-market loans to low-income farmers in a depressed rural area.

2. Assume in Problem 1, above, that the Prudence Foundation invested 80% of its portfolio with a hedge fund managed by Bernard Madoff. Five years later, its entire investment was lost when it was discovered that Madoff's firm had engaged in a Ponzi scheme. Does the Foundation or any of its board have any excise tax exposure under § 4944? What additional facts would you need to know to make that determination?

6.   TAXABLE EXPENDITURES: § 4945

Internal Revenue Code: §§ 4945; 4946(c).

Treasury Regulations: §§ 53.4945–1(a), (d), –4, –5, –6; skim § 53.4945–3.

a.   INTRODUCTION

Section 4945 penalizes a private foundation for making certain expenditures that Congress considered to be inappropriate even when the expenditures may be consistent with the foundation's charitable purposes. The obligations created by § 4945 are constant, necessitating evaluation of each foundation grant or expenditure against the requirements of the statute. Some expenditures are forbidden entirely, while others are permitted if the foundation satisfies additional guidelines. Section 4945 thus may influence some private foundations to limit their grants to public charities to escape the burdens of oversight responsibility and the possibility of penalty.

If a private foundation makes a taxable expenditure, it is subject to an initial tax of 20 percent of the amount expended. I.R.C. § 4945(a)(1). Foundation managers who "knowingly" agree to the making of a taxable expenditure are subject to a 5 percent tax, up to a $10,000 ceiling. I.R.C. § 4945(a)(2), (c). Additional sanctions (100 percent on the foundation, 50 percent of the amount on the manager up to $20,000) are imposed for failures to correct the initial transgression. I.R.C. § 4945(b), (c).

b. TYPES OF TAXABLE EXPENDITURES

Section 4945(d) lists the following five categories of proscribed expenditures, each of which is discussed in more detail below: (1) propaganda and lobbying, (2) influencing legislation and financing voter registration drives, (3) grants to individuals, (4) grants to organizations other than public charities, and (5) expenditures for noncharitable purposes.

Propaganda and Lobbying. Any amount paid (i) for grassroots lobbying, or (ii) to "influence legislation through communication with any member or employee of a legislative body, or with any other government official or employee who may participate in the formulation of the legislation" (except technical advice provided pursuant to written request) will be a taxable expenditure. I.R.C. § 4945(e). The statute and regulations, however, carve out several qualifications and exceptions.

"Legislation" includes action by legislatures but not by executive, judicial or administrative bodies. Treas. Reg. § 53.4945–2(a), referring to Treas. Reg. § 56.4911–2(d). Quasi-legislative entities, such as school boards, housing authorities, etc., whether elective or appointive, are considered administrative bodies. Id.

Expenditures by a private foundation for nonpartisan analysis, study, or research, are not considered to be "lobbying communications" and thus are not taxable expenditures. Treas. Reg. § 53.4945–2(d)(1). As long as the foundation presents a "sufficiently full and fair exposition of the pertinent facts" that enables the public to form an independent opinion, no penalty will attach, whether the communication is to the public at large or is directed to legislators. Treas. Reg. § 53.4945–2(d)(1)(ii). Expenditures in connection with examinations and discussions of broad social, economic, and similar problems also are not considered to be lobbying. Treas. Reg. § 53.4945–2(d)(4).

Another valuable exception is provided for amounts expended in connection with providing technical assistance to a governmental body or committee in response to a written request. Treas. Reg. § 53.4945–2(d)(2).

Thus, whenever possible, a foundation seeking to communicate with a legislature should do so by invitation. Yet another exception applies when the amounts expended to influence proposed legislation may affect the foundation's existence, its powers and duties, its tax-exempt status, or the deductibility of contributions to it. Treas. Reg. § 53.4945–2(d)(3).

Where a foundation makes a program-related investment (see I.R.C. § 4944(c)), and the recipient engages in lobbying, the investing foundation will not be liable for any penalty, provided that funds were not earmarked for lobbying, and the recipient obtains a § 162 (ordinary and necessary business) deduction for the lobbying expenditure. Treas. Reg. § 53.4945–2(a)(4). Grants to public charities also create no liability, provided that there is no earmarking for a use which would violate any § 4945(d) provision and no agreement whereby the granting foundation may cause the grantee to engage in any such prohibited activity. Treas. Reg. § 53.4945–2(a)(5).

Elections and Voter Registration Drives. Section 4945(d)(2) somewhat redundantly proscribes expenditures to "influence the outcome of any specific public election or to carry on * * * any voter registration drive." As discussed earlier in connection with qualification for tax-exempt status, electioneering expenses should cause an organization to lose its exempt status under § 501(c)(3). Congress nonetheless included them in § 4945's forbidden list in response to reports that foundations were using their funds to finance voter registration drives in limited geographical areas or publicizing the views of certain political candidates. See S. Rep. No. 552, 91st Cong., 1st Sess. 454 (1969).

Under a narrow exception, amounts paid in connection with certain nonpartisan and broadly supported voter registration activities, if carried on in five or more states, are not taxable expenditures. I.R.C. § 4945(f); Treas. Reg. § 53.4945–3(b). Although it has been suggested that this exception furnishes the only means by which a private foundation may support voter registration, a non-earmarked general purpose grant to a public charity (e.g, a community development organization) which conducts voter registration as an educational (and nonpartisan) aspect of its general programs seems likely to create a problem for the foundation only if its grantee is deemed to have engaged in prohibited political campaign activities. See Treas. Reg. § 53.4945–2(a)(5).

Grants to Individuals. Historically, private foundations have made grants to individuals, typically in the form of scholarships. This traditional activity is impeded somewhat by § 4945(d)(3), which treats grants to an individual "for travel, study, or other similar purposes" as a taxable expenditure unless the grant is made pursuant to a procedure approved "in advance" by the Service, which must be satisfied that the grant either: (1) constitutes a scholarship or fellowship excludable from gross income by the grantee under § 117(a) and is used for study at a § 170(b)(1)(A)(ii) institution (i.e., a regular college, university, etc.); (2) constitutes a prize or award (as defined in § 74(b)); or (3) is made to "achieve a specific objective, produce a report or other similar product, or improve or enhance a * * * capacity, skill or talent of the grantee." I.R.C. § 4945(g).

As explained by the drafters of the 1969 legislation, the rule was designed to preclude foundations from making ostensibly educational grants which are made "to enable people to take vacations abroad, to have paid interludes between jobs, and to subsidize the preparation of materials furthering specific political viewpoints." S.Rep. No. 91–552, 91st Cong., 1st Sess. 47 (1969).

A principal exception to the prohibition on grants to individuals relates to scholarships. To secure approval of a scholarship-granting procedure, the foundation must demonstrate not only a sensible and objective selection procedure but also must show that its scholarship program is genuinely charitable—e.g., does not constitute a disguised fringe benefit to the children of the employees of a corporate contributor. Service guidelines indicate that the number of scholarships awarded should not exceed 25 percent of eligible applicants, or in the case of a company foundation scholarship plan, 10 percent of the number of employees' children who can be shown to be eligible for grants. Rev. Proc. 76–47, 1976–2 C.B. 670. See also Rev. Proc. 80–39, 1980–2 C.B. 772, as to employer-related foundation loan programs. Note that approval of "scholarship" grant procedures carries no guarantee that grants will be excluded from grantees' gross income as "scholarships" under 117. See, e.g., Rev. Rul. 77–44, 1977–1 C.B. 355. The foundation also must monitor the academic performance of its scholarship grantees by making arrangements to receive reports of grades at least once a year or, as to advanced studies, to receive a brief progress report. Treas. Reg. § 53.4945–4(c)(2).

The regulations require the Service to respond to a request for approval of grant-making procedures within 45 days. Treas. Reg. § 53.4945–4(d)(3). If no response is received, the procedures are deemed approved until notice is received. See Rev. Rul. 81–46, 1981–1 C.B. 514. Conversely, even though a grant-making procedure is ultimately approved, grants made prior to submission to the Service will constitute taxable expenditures. German Society of Maryland, Inc. v. Commissioner, 80 T.C. 741 (1983).

Given the relative ease with which grants may be made to public charities, it might be tempting for a private foundation simply to select such an organization as the recipient of a grant ultimately destined to support the study or research of a particular individual. The regulations provide a surprising latitude to do so, provided that the grantee organization exercises ultimate discretion over the selection of the individual recipients and the terms of the award. See Examples at Treas. Reg. § 53.4945–4(a)(4)(iv).

Payments for services of consultants are not considered grants. Treas. Reg. § 53.4945–4(a)(2); Rev. Rul. 74–125, 1974–1 C.B. 327. Nor are payments to research assistants of the foundation's individual grantee, if not selected by the foundation. Rev. Rul. 81–293, 1981–2 C.B. 218.

Grants to Certain Supporting Organizations. The Pension Protection Act of 2006 added grants to certain supporting organizations to the list of taxable expenditures. See I.R.C. § 4945(d)(4) and Section C4e of this chapter, supra, at p. 760.

Grants to Other Organizations. If a private foundation makes a grant to an organization that is not a public charity, it must exercise "expenditure responsibility" in order to avoid taxable expenditure treatment. I.R.C. § 4945(d)(4). Under § 4945(h) and the accompanying regulations, that responsibility involves pre-grant investigations and adequate follow-up procedures to determine that the grant is appropriately spent, and that the grantee has adequately reported upon its progress. The granting foundation is obligated to report to the Service in some detail as to the use of all grants subject to expenditure responsibility.

Public charities have benefited from the burden of the expenditure responsibility requirement. Indeed, many private foundations, as a matter of policy, decline to make grants to organizations other than public charities to avoid the expenditure responsibility requirement. But as explained below, the burden may not be so great for the well-advised foundation.

Expenditures for Noncharitable Purposes. To make certain that nothing was forgotten, Congress added a final category of taxable expenditures—amounts paid "for any purpose other than one specified in section 170(c)(2)(B)." I.R.C. § 4945(d)(5). In effect, this covers all foundation outlays that are not made for a charitable purpose. The regulations provide considerable elaboration. Thus, expenditures to acquire and manage investments, payment of taxes, and any payment which constitutes a qualifying distribution are excepted. Treas. Reg. § 53.4945–6(b). But unreasonable administrative expenses or fees (unless incurred in the good faith belief of reasonableness and necessity), and certain payments to noncharitable organizations are listed as examples of forbidden outlays. Id.

c.   EXPENDITURE RESPONSIBILITY

John A. Edie, Expenditure Responsibility: "It's Easier Than You Think"

in The Handbook on Private Foundations 248–253 (1991).

Expenditure responsibility "can't get no respect." It's the Rodney Dangerfield of grantmaking. Maids don't do windows, and private foundations don't do expenditure responsibility. Yet, a growing number of private foundations are finding the exercise of expenditure responsibility to be a regular and surprisingly routine part of their grantmaking.

Last spring in the middle of a speech in New York City, I was asked to explain what steps were required to do expenditure responsibility. When I finished a brief explanation, several members of the audience expressed amazement at how simple it sounded. One questioner said, "We do most of that already with every grant." Despite this common reaction, once the procedure is explained, I am continually confronted with grantmakers who avoid expenditure responsibility like the plague.

* * *

This potential penalty [under § 4945] for giving to a nonpublic charity has created the misconception among many in the foundation field that a private foundation can give only to a Section 501(c)(3) organization. This simply is not true. There are many organizations to which a private foundation may make a grant even though the grantee is not a public charity. Examples include chambers of commerce, labor unions, trade associations, fraternal orders (such as Rotary), other private foundations, or even for-profit companies. However, to avoid the penalty when giving to nonpublic charity grantees, the private foundation must, in Congress's words, "exercise expenditure responsibility."

In other words, the private foundation must exercise the oversight job normally done by IRS for public charities. Since such a grant is going to a private foundation or to an organization that is *not* organized and operated exclusively for charitable purposes, the grantor foundation must take the steps necessary to see that the funds are appropriately spent. Before spelling out the basic steps required to exercise expenditure responsibility correctly, it is important to make clear that this process is not as easy nor as safe as simple grants to universities or to the United Way. The required procedures and documents must be designed with care and should definitely be approved by your legal counsel. But once established, procedures are very similar to what many foundations already undertake for many, if not all, of their grants. While it is certainly true that staffed foundations are more likely to make expenditure responsibility grants, more and more smaller foundations are finding this procedure to be much easier than they had first thought.

There are four basic requirements for expenditure responsibility: (1) a pregrant inquiry, (2) a written agreement, (3) regular reports from the grantee, and (4) a report to IRS by the grantor. A brief summary of each of these requirements is set out below, and the reader can obtain sample procedures and documents from the Council on Foundations. However, it bears repeating that any system for exercising expenditure responsibility should be approved by legal counsel.

As a first step, a private foundation must conduct an inquiry of the potential grantee that is complete enough to give a reasonable person assurance that the grantee will use the grant for proper, charitable purposes. As Treasury regulations state, such a pregrant inquiry "should concern itself with matters such as (a) the identity, prior history and experience (if any) of the grantee organization and its managers; and (b) any knowledge which the private foundation has (based on prior experience or otherwise) of, or other information which is readily available concerning the management, activities, and practices of the grantee organization." Some foundations design a simple pregrant inquiry check sheet that is completed by a foundation official and kept on file. The regulations also make clear that the "scope" of the inquiry will vary from case to case depending on "the size and purpose of the grant, the period over which it is to be paid, and the prior experience which the grantor has had with the capacity of the grantee to use the grant for the proper purposes."

WRITTEN AGREEMENT

In making an expenditure responsibility grant, the foundation may not simply write a check. Rather, a written agreement (or contract) must be signed by "an appropriate officer, director or trustee of the grantee organization." This requirement for a written agreement is where legal counsel is most vital because the regulations are quite specific about what must be included.

However, once a "form" contract (or "boilerplate" as lawyers call it) has been developed and approved, completing the rest of the blank spaces in the "form" contract is fairly easy. The blanks to fill in can be as simple as name of grantee, name and title of grantee official signing the agreement, the date of the agreement, the length of the grant period, the date (or dates) by which a written report (or reports) on the status of the grant must be submitted, and the grant's specific charitable purpose (or purposes). The regulations are clear in indicating that the purpose of the grant must be spelled out in writing.

The rest of the private foundation's standard expenditure responsibility agreement will never change (unless amended by counsel). However, the regulations require that the grantee sign an agreement that includes each of the following four commitments:

1. To repay any portion of the amount granted that is not used for the purposes of the grant.

2. To submit full and complete annual reports on the manner in which the funds are spent and the progress made in accomplishing the purposes of the grant.

3. To maintain records of receipts and expenditures and to make its books and records available to the grantor at reasonable times.

4. Not to use any of the funds:

   To undertake any activity that is not charitable;

   To carry on propaganda, or otherwise attempt to influence legislation;

   To influence the outcome of any specific public election, or to carry on, directly or indirectly, any voter registration drive;

   To make any grants to individuals for travel, study or similar purposes unless such grants comply with the requirements to which private foundations are subject; or

   To make any grants that would require expenditure responsibility unless such grants comply with the requirements to which private foundations are subject.

There may be other provisions of agreement that your legal counsel may wish to include. For example, a foundation may wish to state that the grantee understands that the grantor intends to monitor and evaluate the activities funded by the grant, and that the grantor may discontinue, modify, or withhold part or all of the grant funds when, in its judgment, such action is necessary to comply with the law or regulations.

REPORTS FROM THE GRANTEE

Since Treasury regulations do not spell out the details of what must be included in the grantee's report, it is probably wise for your legal counsel to include them in the "form" contract.

The regulations state, "The grantee shall make such reports as of the end of its annual accounting period within which the grant or any portion thereof is received and all such subsequent periods until the grant funds are expended in full or the grant is otherwise terminated." For example, if grantee X receives a two-year expenditure responsibility grant on May 1, 1990 and grantee X has an accounting period ending on June 30, reports would be due "within a reasonable period of time" after June 30, 1990; after June 30, 1991; and after June 30, 1992. The grantee must make a final report (the June 30, 1992, report in the example above) with respect to "all expenditures made from such funds (including salaries, travel, and supplies) and indicating the progress made toward the goals of the grant." The grantor is not required to conduct "any independent verification" of such reports "unless it has reason to doubt their accuracy or reliability," and may rely on adequate records or other sufficient evidence (such as a statement by an appropriate officer, director, or trustee of the grantee organization).

Finally, if the grantee receiving the expenditure responsibility grant is other than a private foundation, the grantee must agree to maintain continuously the grant funds "in a separate fund dedicated to one or more charitable purposes." In other words, the noncharitable grantee may not simply commingle funds that are dedicated exclusively for charitable purposes with those that are not.

Failure by the grantee to provide the required reports could subject the grantor to a penalty unless the grantor makes a reasonable effort to obtain the reports and withholds any future payments until they are received.

REPORTING TO THE IRS

Every private foundation is required to file a tax return within four and one-half months after the end of its tax year. For each year in which it has made an expenditure responsibility grant, it must answer "yes" to the appropriate question * * *. In addition, it must add a schedule to the tax return, providing a brief summary paragraph on each expenditure responsibility grant's status. An example, as suggested by the IRS, is Form 990–PF for the hypothetical Oak Foundation:

Grantee: Allen Reid Museum of Fine Arts, 31 Meyers St., Atlanta, Ga. 30301.
Date paid: April 7, 1985. Amount $15,000.
Purpose: For the partial support of a major renovation and expansion of the museum facilities.

Amount of grant spent by grantee: $15,000.
Diversion: To the knowledge of the foundation, and based on the report furnished by the grantee, no part of the grant has been used for other than its intended purpose.

Date of report for grantee: Final report January 8, 1986.

* * *

For some, the requirements of expenditure responsibility will seem more complicated than their normal grantmaking procedures. But many will note, for any grant, that a pregrant inquiry is regularly performed, their foundation requires use of a standard grant agreement form, and some kind of written report is required from the grantee. For these foundations, the added steps of satisfying the requirements of expenditure responsibility will be relatively easy to accomplish.

PROBLEMS

In each part of this problem, determine whether the described private foundation may properly make the proposed grant or other expenditure and, if so, whether any conditions should attach to the grant for the protection of the foundation:

(a) The Eli Stern Foundation, formed in 1937 "to advance the welfare and education of the employees of Eli Stern & Co.," a shoe manufacturer which employs 7,000 persons, intends to announce its annual grant of 200 scholarships in the amount of $1,000 each to children of employees.

(b) Exploring for Peace, Inc., intends to make a $100,000 grant to support an expedition to map several of the uncharted Amazon River tributaries. It wants the project to be led by Dr. Ferris Murple, a prominent geographer and cartographer of the University of New Hampshire.

(c) The Blue Dolphin Foundation, which has long supported marine research, has been approached by a private operating foundation, Friends Under the Sea, Inc., which seeks a grant of $50,000 to study the sounds of whales.

(d) The Wilderness Fund proposes to place a full-page advertisement in the Sunday Los Angeles Times criticizing the Governor of California for proposing cutbacks in the public recreation budget and urging the legislature to pass a scenic rivers bill which would create 40,000 acres of state parks.

(e) The Public Conscience Trust, which has in the past supported research in American history, is considering a grant of $500,000 to a recently organized § 501(c)(3) organization, The Citizens' Crusade, which will conduct as its sole activity voter registration drives. Such drives will soon begin in New York, Florida, California and Pennsylvania, and will concentrate on registration of voters who will be eligible to cast their ballots for the first time in the next Presidential election.

(f) The Public Conscience Trust also is considering a grant of $250,000 to finance an empirical study by Simon Catchpole, an authority on the mass media, as to the effect of digital satellite dishes on (a) the gross national product, (b) the national divorce rate, (c) the national birth rate, and (d) the incidence of violent crimes. If the study tends to prove that the new dishes are inimical to the well-being of the nation, may the Trust:

(1) publish it?

(2) send copies to each member of Congress?

(3) send Mr. Catchpole, study in hand, to the Federal Communications Commission?

(g) The Bakst Foundation, created in 1966 by M. Charles Bakst for the purpose of encouraging investigative journalism, wishes to make grants to the person whose work represents the best example of investigative reporting on matters concerning the Federal government. All U.S. journalists will be eligible for the award, and the winner would be chosen by majority vote of an independent selection committee appointed by the Foundation's trustees.

(h) What if the grants in (g), above, were to outstanding journalists to be used for financing a three-month trip throughout Europe for the purpose of broadening the recipient's understanding of the common market?

(i) The Human Rights Foundation wishes to make a $50,000 grant to the Southeast Asia Refugee Coalition, an organization formed in Indonesia, to investigate and remedy human rights violations. See Treas. Reg. § 53.4945–5(a)(4).

E.   TERMINATION OF PRIVATE FOUNDATION STATUS

Internal Revenue Code: § 507.

Section 507 governs the tax consequences of a termination of a § 501(c)(3) organization's status as a private foundation. Foundations may give up the status voluntarily, or they may be terminated involuntarily for "willful repeated acts" or a "willful and flagrant act (or failure to act)" giving rise to liability for a Chapter 42 tax. See I.R.C. § 507(a)(2).

1.   INVOLUNTARY TERMINATION

Involuntary termination is not a joyous event. The Code imposes a confiscatory "termination tax" equal to the lower of: (1) the aggregate historical tax benefits of exemption to the foundation and its substantial contributors (dating back to its organization or February 28, 1913, whichever is later), plus interest, or (2) the value of the net assets of the foundation. So much for the foundation! I.R.C. § 507(c), (d).

The Service has the authority to abate any portion of the termination tax if the private foundation distributes all of its net assets to one or more public charities, each of which has been in existence as such for at least 60 months, or upon assurance that appropriate corrective action has been initiated under state law. I.R.C. § 507(g). The regulations provide no indication as to how liberally the Service may exercise its authority. See Treas. Reg. § 1.507–1(b)(9).

2.   VOLUNTARY TERMINATION

A private foundation may avoid the dreaded termination tax by transferring its assets to one or more public charities or by operating itself as an organization described in §§ 509(a)(1), (2) or (3). Many smaller private foundations chose voluntary termination after becoming frightened by the 1969 legislation. By far the simplest route to relief from the burdens of private foundation status is simply to distribute all the foundation's assets to one or more public charities each of which has been in existence and so described for at least 60 months. I.R.C. § 507(b)(1)(A). In order to do so, however, notice must be given to the Service.

If the foundation wishes to convert to public charity or supporting organization status, it must give notice to the Service and embark upon a five-year qualification measuring period. I.R.C. § 507(b)(1)(B). An advance ruling based on the expectancy of operating as a public charity may be obtained under Treas. Reg. § 1.507–2(e). If the organization fails to qualify for the entire 60–month period, it nonetheless will escape the private foundation regime for any year within that period for which it does meet the public charity requirements.

A final alternative is abdication. A foundation may accomplish a voluntary termination simply by notifying the Service of its intent to do so, without proposing to transfer its assets to other public charities, or to operate itself as such an organization. In that case, the foundation becomes liable for the § 507(c) termination tax. The regulatory burdens persist until rigor mortis fully sets in. The regulations provide that the foundation's notice must "set forth in detail the computation and amount" of tax owing, and, unless a request for abatement is made, full payment of the tax must be made when the statement is filed. Treas. Reg. § 1.507–1(b)(1).

Common situations where a private foundation may wish to terminate include: (1) disagreements within the founding family, or a desire for branches of the family to go their separate ways, (2) a desire to change the legal form (e.g., from trust to corporation), (3) simplicity, such as eliminating the expense and responsibility of administering a separate entity, or (4) a preference, possibly to achieve greater tax benefits, to make grants through a donor-advised fund or supporting organization.

For many years, foundations wishing to terminate incurred the expense of obtaining a private ruling as an insurance policy against the § 507 termination tax. The IRS finally responded by issuing the two published rulings that, while beyond the scope of our coverage, are valuable roadmaps for terminating foundations. The rulings provide several different toll-free exit ramps from private foundation status. See Rev. Rul. 2002–28, 2002–1 C.B. 941 (a private foundation transfers all of its assets to one or more private foundations); Rev. Rul. 2003–13, 2003–1 C.B. 305 (a private foundation distributes all of its net assets to one or more public charities).

CHAPTER 8

CHARITABLE CONTRIBUTIONS

A. INTRODUCTION

1. HISTORICAL ORIGINS[1]

The first charitable income tax deduction was enacted in 1917 as part of a tax bill that raised federal tax rates to help finance the costs of entering World War I. Ever since, the charitable deduction has been a prominent feature of our income tax system. The legislative history is typically sparse, but excerpts from the floor debate reveal Congress's belief that the steeper tax rates would reduce funds donated to needy schools, hospitals, churches, and other charitable organizations. Proponents of the charitable deduction argued that private donations came from the "surplus" of an individual's income. As Senator Hollis of New Hampshire put it:

> * * * After they have done everything else they want to do, after they have educated their children and traveled and spent their money on everything they really want or think they want, then, if they have something left over, they will contribute it to a college or to the Red Cross or for some scientific purposes. Now, when war comes and we impose these very heavy taxes on incomes, that will be the first place where the wealthy men will be tempted to economize, namely, in donations to charity. They will say, "Charity begins at home."[2]

The estate and gift tax charitable deductions have an equally venerable history. The unlimited deduction for charitable bequests now found in § 2055 was added in 1918, two years after enactment of the first federal estate tax. The deduction was justified on the familiar ground that wealth transferred for charitable, educational and religious uses should not be burdened by a tax because the funds would be used for a public purpose.[3] The gift tax charitable deduction in § 2522 is similarly entrenched in our wealth transfer tax system.

---

1. Much of this early history of the charitable deduction is derived from John A. Wallace & Robert W. Fisher, The Charitable Deduction Under Section 170 of the Internal Revenue Code, in IV Research Papers Sponsored by the [Filer] Commission on Private Philanthropy and Public Needs 2131 (1977).

2. Remarks of Senator Hollis, 55 Cong. Rec. 6728 (1917).

3. See John Holt Myers, Estate Tax Deduction for Charitable Benefits: Proposed Limitations, in IV Research Papers Sponsored by the [Filer] Commission on Private Philanthropy and Public Needs 2299 (1977).

In succeeding tax bills, Congress has justified the charitable deduction, like tax exemptions generally, as an efficient alternative to government support for those nonprofit organizations providing a public benefit. Early Congressional advocates also believed that individuals should not be taxed on the portion of their income devoted to charity. The underlying premise of this argument was that the income tax should be imposed only upon consumable income—i.e., the taxpayer's gross income, less the costs of earning it *and* the taxpayer's charitable contributions. As developed later in this chapter, these theories continue to be advanced whenever critics seek to curtail or eliminate the charitable deduction.

The 1917 predecessor of current § 170 allowed an income tax deduction for:

> Contributions or gifts made within the year to corporations or associations organized and operated exclusively for religious, charitable, scientific, or educational purposes, or to societies for the prevention of cruelty to children or animals, no part of the net income of which inures to the benefit of any private stockholder or individual, to an amount not in excess of 15 per centum of the taxpayer's taxable net income as computed without the benefit of this paragraph.

The current version of § 170 expands this once elegant concept to more than 34 pages in the most recent Commerce Clearing House edition of the Internal Revenue Code, and the regulations exceed 100 pages, small print, double column! This once inspired a prominent law professor to suggest that an entire four-unit basic income tax course could be taught solely by studying § 170. Our goals here are somewhat more modest. After a survey of the policy issues, this chapter provides an overview of the tax aspects of charitable giving, emphasizing those issues of greatest interest to donors, charitable fundraisers, trustees of nonprofit organizations, and their legal and financial advisors.

2. Policy Issues

The policy debate over the charitable deduction is reminiscent of the controversy surrounding the rationale for tax exemptions. A central question is whether the charitable deduction is a subsidy—a "tax expenditure" in modern tax policy parlance—and, if so, whether it is a proper mechanism for providing government support to the charitable sector. Some critics of the deduction ask why the government should provide undifferentiated support to all public charities without evaluating their relative needs, or why it should provide any support to religious organizations. And even if a subsidy is appropriate, the question remains whether it should come from the tax system and, if so, whether the structure of the current tax regime is defensible as a policy matter. Other critics claim that the system violates principles of equity and fairness in a democratic society because organizations benefiting the most from the charitable deduction cater to the tastes of the upper class "cultural elite." The charitable deduction also has been challenged as an inefficient incentive because it principally benefits higher income taxpayers and does not significantly influence the giving patterns of low and middle-income donors who are taxed at lower rates and do not itemize deductions.

Defenders of the charitable deduction reject the notion of an inefficient subsidy and argue that contributions do not constitute personal consumption and thus are not appropriately included in a normative income tax base. They answer the claims of upper class privilege by emphasizing the contributions of private philanthropy to a dynamic pluralistic society and the range of innovative options offered beyond those provided by the government and business sectors.

The first excerpt below, from the 1975 report of the Commission on Private Philanthropy and Public Needs (known as the Filer Commission), frames the debate. It is followed by excerpts by Professor William Andrews, who argues that charitable contributions are not properly included in a normative income tax base, and Teresa Odendahl, who offers an anthropologist's perspective on the role of philanthropy in American culture.

Giving in America: Toward a Stronger Voluntary Sector

Report of the [Filer] Commission on Private Philanthropy and Public Needs 107–111 (1975).

Philosophical Challenge

A major challenge to the philosophical basis of the charitable deduction lies in the contention that charitable giving is not that different from other kinds of personal outlays and therefore should not be treated differently under the income tax. This viewpoint is summarized in a study for the Commission by Paul R. McDaniel of Boston College Law School. " * * * Most economists and social psychologists," he writes, "take the 'scientific' view that charitable contributions are not simply individual sacrifices for the public good, but are actually consumption spending * * * In making a charitable gift, the individual is seen as purchasing status, the perpetuation of his social values, or on a less mercenary level, the satisfaction resulting from doing a 'good deed.' * * * And one can inquire as to whether the deduction operates equitably as an incentive system to induce this form of consumption."

Overlapping this argument in recent years has been the more vigorous and somewhat less abstract contention of tax reformers that the charitable deduction is not distinct from a number of other deductions that have been built into the income tax, and that all of them are wanting by the yardstick of equity.

According to this viewpoint, all tax immunities are forms of government subsidy to whatever activity benefits from nontaxation. This is not a new idea. A president of Harvard University, Charles William Eliot, acknowledged and attacked this way of looking at tax immunity a century ago. "It has been often asserted," he said, "that to exempt an institution from taxation is the same thing as to grant it money directly from the public treasury. This statement is sophistical and fallacious." But the tax-immunity-as-subsidy viewpoint has gained considerable influence among tax analysts in recent years. It was adopted by the federal government in 1968 when the Treasury Secretary's annual report included a "tax expenditure" section. This section lists the amounts by which the government is seen to be subsidizing various areas through forms of nontaxation or reduced taxes. * * *

Nor is the tax expenditure viewpoint limited to tax analysts or government ledgers. A ghetto activist in Hartford who challenges the pattern of corporation and foundation philanthropy in that city was quick to evoke the viewpoint during an interview for a Commission report. His position: "These corporations and foundations are tax exempt. Therefore, part of the money they spend is my money. Therefore, they should have regulatory restrictions placed upon them that will force them to meet specific social criteria * * *." The result of one foundation's practices, he charged later, was "to use charitable giving—a form of federal subsidy-to perpetuate the effects of past discrimination."

When seen as a form of government subsidy or expenditure, the charitable deduction, like other personal income tax deductions, is open to charges of inequity because of a pattern that is, in effect, the inverse of the progressive structure of the income tax. The higher a person's income the higher the rate of taxation under the income tax and therefore the more the government forgoes—or "spends" in the tax-expenditure view—for any portion of such income not taxed. In other words, the government adds proportionately more of the subsidy to a high-income taxpayer's giving and proportionately less to the low-income taxpayer's contribution.

Stanley S. Surrey of Harvard Law School, formerly Assistant Secretary of the Treasury for Tax Policy, is the foremost proponent of this way of looking at tax deductions, starting with his advocacy of a tax-expenditure budget while he was in the Treasury Department. Talking of the charitable deduction in a Commission discussion, Surrey illustrated the tax-expenditure viewpoint in this way:

> "Let us look at this subsidy to charities which is given by the charitable deduction. Well, it was a very peculiar subsidy. It's sort of an upside-down affair. As you know, if a person in the 70 per cent bracket [the highest marginal bracket at the time] gives a sum of money, he is able to deduct that sum of money from his tax base, and in effect he is only giving 30 per cent, whereas when a person in the 14 per cent bracket gives a sum of money, he is giving 86 per cent. Or to put it differently, if a $200,000 person gives 10 per cent of his income to charity, it really costs the government $14,000 to get $6,000 out of that person * * * If a $12,000 person gives 10 per cent of his income to charity, it costs the government $324 to get $876 from this person. The charitable deduction works just upside down." * * *

The tax-expenditure viewpoint and its implications are by no means universally accepted. A major argument that has been raised against the whole notion of tax "expenditures" is that it implies that all income covered by tax laws is government money. It is only in this light, it is contended, that non-taxation can be seen as a subsidy or expenditure.

The equity implications of the tax-expenditure viewpoint are also challenged by those who argue that the alleged disparity of tax expenditures in favor of high-income taxpayers is merely the mirrored reflection of the progressive income tax, which is structured against them. In other words, nontaxation of portions of higher incomes because of tax exemptions or deductions is only higher, can only be viewed as a greater government expenditure, because the tax rates are set higher for upper-income levels to begin with.

Perhaps the principal counter-argument to the tax-expenditure viewpoint as far as its application to the charitable deduction goes rests with the "income definition" rationale for the deduction. According to this reasoning, tax allowances for philanthropic giving cannot be looked at or measured in the same way as tax privileges for other purposes because money given to charity is not an element of income that should be subject to government's taxing power to begin with. Boris I. Bittker of Yale Law School posed the "income definition" argument against the "tax-expenditure" viewpoint this way in the same Commission discussion in which Stanley Surrey took part:

" * * * The concept of income is not settled, cannot be settled the way one can define water as H_2O or lay down the laws of gravity * * * Income is a political, economic, social concept which takes its meaning from the society in which the term is used, in my view. And there are many definitions of income * * * But at the very core of the only definition that has the benefit of a consensus, there is a concept of consumption * * * I would assert that consumption certainly consists of what one spends on food, shelter and clothing for himself, his family, friends, what one saves to pass on to heirs and so on * * * But 2,000 years of religious, philosophical and ethical views suggest that what one gives to charity can properly be viewed differently * * * If, as I think, we have a powerful sense of difference between giving to charity and spending in other respects, I see no reason at all why in defining income one shouldn't exclude those items like charitable contributions that our whole history tells us represent a special kind of use of one's funds."

Yet another view that the Commission heard expressed by tax experts was that those who support the charitable deduction should have no argument with the tax-expenditure viewpoint, but should be willing to view tax savings from the charitable deduction as a form of tax expenditure and simply assert that, for special reasons associated with philanthropic giving, it was a desirable form of tax expenditure, whereas other forms were not necessarily desirable. This view in turn has been challenged on the grounds that to regard charitable tax savings as a form of government expenditure is to undermine the "income definition" case for the deduction, because it means conceding that the charitable deduction is not fundamentally different from other deductions and allowances.

The pros and cons of the tax-expenditure viewpoint continue to be argued, often heatedly, as do its implications for the charitable and other deductions. Meanwhile, however, the viewpoint seems to be taking an even firmer hold within government. The tax-expenditure part of the Treasury Secretary's report was instituted in 1968 by administrative decision. In 1974, Congress wrote the tax-expenditure viewpoint into law: it passed legislation requiring that as of 1975 a tax-expenditure section be included in the federal budget. In all likelihood, tax exemptions, deductions, credits—including those benefiting nonprofit organizations—will be increasingly scrutinized by Congress as if they were forms of government spending, whatever the implications.

William D. Andrews, Personal Deductions in an Ideal Income Tax

86 Harv.L. Rev. 309, 344–348, 356–358, 371–372, 374–375 (1972).

The charitable contribution deduction is generally described as a subsidy to charitable giving and thus to the activities of qualified charitable organizations. The effect of the deduction has been likened to a matching gift program under which an employer makes matching gifts to charities supported by its employees. There is something peculiar, of course, about the Government spending funds with so little control over their allocation or use. Furthermore, this is an unusual matching gift program because the rate at which gifts are matched varies directly with the taxpayer's marginal tax rate bracket: wealthy taxpayers find their gifts much more generously matched than do lower bracket taxpayers. * * *

But I do not believe, nor do I think most serious practical students of the subject believe, that the charitable contribution deduction is as irrational as this explanation makes it sound. To be sure, there are anomalies arising out of the allowance of a deduction for the fair market value of appreciated property without any offsetting recognition of gain. But as to simple cash contributions, the charitable deduction makes more sense than tax expenditure analysis would indicate. If we want our theories to express our judgments, therefore, we should seek to give the deduction a better explanation.

* * * [T]here are substantial grounds for excluding from our definition of taxable personal consumption whatever satisfactions a taxpayer may get from making a charitable contribution. * * * [T]here are * * * good reasons why a charitable contribution may rationally be excluded from the concept of taxable personal consumption. In the case of alms for the poor, for instance, the charitable contribution results in the distribution of real goods and services to persons presumably poorer and in lower marginal tax brackets than the donor. These goods and services, therefore, should not be taxed at the higher rates intended to apply to personal consumption by the donor. In the case of philanthropy more broadly defined—the support of religion, education, and the arts-benefits often do not flow exclusively or even principally to very low bracket taxpayers. But the goods and services produced do have something of the character of common goods whose enjoyment is not confined to contributors nor apportioned among contributors according to the amounts of their contributions. There are a number of

reasons for defining taxable personal consumption not to include the benefit of such common goods and services. The personal consumption at which progressive personal taxation with high graduated rates should aim may well be thought to encompass only the private consumption of divisible goods and services whose consumption by one household precludes their direct enjoyment by others.

Various objections can be made to this analysis. It can be argued that the exercise of power over the distribution of goods and services is what constitutes taxable personal consumption even if that power is exercised in favor of somebody else. Or it can be argued that the pleasure or satisfaction one presumably gets from supporting philanthropic enterprises is a component of consumption. But at least this analysis and the objections to it focus on the problem of how to treat philanthropy as an intrinsic issue of personal tax policy, instead of just assuming that the purpose underlying the deduction must be something outside the realm of tax policy.

It is convenient to take up first the case of alms for the poor, then philanthropy more broadly defined, and finally the special problems that arise when charitable contributions are made out of accumulated wealth rather than current earnings.

A.   Alms for the Poor

Consider a taxpayer who simply contributes some of his earnings to an organization which redistributes them to or for the needy. In such a case the consumption or accumulation of real goods and services represented by the funds in question has been shifted to the recipients rather than the donor and should not be subjected to taxation at rates designed to apply to the donor's standard of living and saving. If the redistributed funds are used for ordinary consumption by the recipients, then in principle the funds should be taxed to the recipients at their rates—although in practice the recipients' total income may often fall below a taxable level. The matter is essentially one of rates. Under a graduated rate schedule the personal consumption and accumulation of well-to-do taxpayers is intended to be curtailed much more than that of the poor. Yet if a wealthy taxpayer were to be taxed at his high rate even on the income that he donated to the poor, the probable effect would be a reduction in the amount received by the donees. For all practical purposes, such a scheme would tax the consumption of the poor at the rate intended for the wealthy taxpayer. The effect of the charitable contribution is to avoid this result.

Moreover, the charitable contribution deduction operates to treat a taxpayer who redistributes his income by giving alms like other taxpayers who effect a redistribution of income directly. A businessman, for example, may pay generous wages, higher than he would have to pay in order to secure the services he needs. If he does so, within reason, we would not tax him on the additional income he could have earned by paying less. He has arranged his business in a way that diverts more income to employees and less to himself; the tax law generally will deal with the income as so redistributed.

More to the point, perhaps, a doctor might choose to spend one day a week in a clinic without charging for his services. More generally he might simply treat impecunious patients for less than the going rate. In either case he has foregone in favor of the patients whom he treats some of the personal consumption and accumulation he could have had. We do not tax the doctor on the value of his services or the excess of the value of his services over the fee he charges. We tax the doctor only on the personal consumption and accumulation he achieves by the exercise of his profession, not on what he could have achieved if he chose to maximize his personal financial gain.

Another professional man, a tax lawyer for example, may have skills that are not so directly useful to the poor as those of the doctor. If he wishes to devote part of his professional energies to the welfare of the poor, the efficient way to do it may well be to continue practicing his profession for paying clients but to turn over part of his fees for distribution among the poor or for the purchase of other services to meet their needs. The charitable contribution deduction operates to treat the tax lawyer like the doctor, by taxing him only on the amount of personal consumption and accumulation he realizes from the practice of his profession, not on what he could have realized if he had not given part of his fees away.

* * *

B.   Philanthropy More Broadly Defined

For many kinds of charitable contributions the foregoing analysis will not quite do because the benefits of the contributions do not go entirely to the poor. More than half of all charitable deductions are for contributions to churches, whose activities are conducted for rich and poor alike and often on a more comfortable and expensive scale in wealthy neighborhoods than in poor ones. Many contributions are to private schools, whose student bodies are probably still disproportionately representative of the affluent part of the population. Some contributions go to support artistic enterprises, ordinary and esoteric, in which most of the poor are likely to have little interest. Moreover, the activities of such organizations are frequently ones in which contributors participate more or less directly for their own edification or pleasure.

Such contributions also differ from alms for the poor because they represent an affirmative allocation of resources by the contributor to a particular activity whose benefits are not taxed to the recipients. In theory, though not in practice (and it is typically not important in practice), alms should be counted as income to the recipient, so that deduction by the donor is only a matter of reassigning taxability to the person whose consumption is supported, as in the case of alimony. But when a group of wealthy people support a church, a school, a research institute, or a symphony orchestra, the effect of the charitable contribution deduction is to eliminate the enjoyment of the output of that activity from the tax base altogether. A community of people that supports a church will pay less in taxes than a community of people with the same total income, similarly distributed, that spends less on its church and more on its private homes.

Nevertheless, the benefits produced by charitable contributions have certain shared characteristics which provide the basis for principled arguments in favor of deduction. Almost all charitable organizations other than those that distribute alms to the poor produce something in the nature of common or social goods or services. The benefit produced by a contribution to a private school, for example, may not inure primarily to the poor, but neither does it inure solely to the contributor. Even when contributors are almost all members who share in the product of the organization, as in the case of a church, the product is essentially a common good to be enjoyed by the members without regard to relative contributions and usually is at least open to enjoyment by others.

Common goods have several characteristics relevant for our purposes. Principally, their enjoyment is not limited exclusively or even primarily to those who pay for them. That might be stated merely as a matter of external benefits: a wealthy man cannot purchase and enjoy the sound of a new church organ without conferring a benefit on his fellow parishioners. Unlike the typical external effect of private consumption, however, the benefit conferred on others is of the same kind as that enjoyed by the contributor himself.

Moreover, it is typically the case that the benefits produced by a charitable organization are free goods in the sense that one person's enjoyment of them will not directly impair another's enjoyment. Attendance at church on a particular Sunday, use of the town library, or listening to a symphony orchestra broadcast will not immediately prevent someone else from doing the same thing. Of course, pure public goods are relatively rare. Use of the library does not immediately prevent others from using it; but if too many use it too much, then its utility will be impaired. The conditions under which a town common can serve effectively for common use are very limited. And students' places in schools are sometimes quite scarce. But as among the students, once admitted to a school or to a particular class, many of the educational opportunities offered have this quality of common goods.

The underlying problem with respect to contributions to churches, schools, museums, and similar charities is whether the common goods they produce should be reflected in the consumption component of personal income of any of the individuals associated with them.

* * *

C.   Charity by the Idle Rich

The discussion thus far has dealt with a taxpayer who contributes part of his earnings to a charitable organization, and it has been pointed out that the effect of the deduction is to treat such a taxpayer as if he had devoted part of his energies directly toward the promotion of charitable enterprises, instead of earning money. Many charitable contributions, however, are made by wealthy people from accumulated wealth or unearned income. Thus, the question arises whether a deduction for them can be justified on grounds such as those we have been exploring.

1. *Contributions Out of Investment Income.* Consider first a taxpayer with an income solely from dividends who contributes one third to charity and lives on the rest. It cannot be argued very directly that a charitable deduction will operate to treat him as if he were performing services for the charity instead of earning money and turning it over, since he is not earning any money in any event. Nor can it be argued in this situation that the incentive effect of the charitable contribution deduction serves to offset the disincentive effect of the tax on remunerative employment. There may seem to be more reason, therefore, to take the taxpayer's income as fixed and to tax it without regard to use in order to make the tax neutral with respect to expenditure choices.

But I think the deduction is still justified along the lines indicated in this paper for two reasons. First, most taxpayers in the long run do face earnings or investment decisions with respect to which the tax is not neutral and which may have some relation to their level of charitable giving. The deduction will therefore operate to offset the bias of the tax itself insofar as income is devoted to charitable uses. Second, even if that is not so for a particular taxpayer, considerations of equity require that he be allowed a charitable contribution deduction if other taxpayers are. For reasons that include a consideration of incentive effects on most taxpayers, we have decided that taxable consumption should embrace only private, preclusive, household consumption. To make income a measure of consumption thus defined, plus accumulation, a deduction must be allowed for expenditures for other things, whatever the source of the income. The deduction should be allowed, therefore, whenever charitable contributions are made out of taxable ordinary income, whether earned or unearned.

2. *Unrealized Capital Appreciation.* In the case of a donation of appreciated capital assets to a charitable organization, present law generally allows a deduction for fair market value without taking into account that there is unrealized gain represented by the excess of fair market value over the taxpayer's basis. The argument in this paper will not support that rule. The argument here is concerned only with adjusting gross income to make it a more accurate measure of private consumption plus accumulation by allowing a deduction to offset the inclusion in gross income of receipts that have been turned over to philanthropic use. Since the effect of the fair market value rule is to allow a tax deduction for an amount, the unrealized gain, that will never be included in gross income, it clearly goes beyond that rationale.

Whatever its origin, the fair market value rule must now be viewed as a subsidy or artificial inducement, above and beyond mere tax exemption, for philanthropic giving. The magnitude of the subsidy is a function of the amount of unrealized appreciation in relation to the basis of the property and the taxpayer's rates of tax, being greatest for taxpayers in highest brackets and with most appreciation. For a taxpayer in the top rate brackets whose property has a nominal basis, the rule operates in a sense to make the Government take over the whole cost of a charitable donation. * * *

                                  * * *

    5. *Conclusion.* In general, then, the argument of this paper, that the purpose of the deduction is to help create an income tax that imposes a uniform graduated burden on aggregate personal private consumption and accumulation, supports a deduction for contributions only to the extent that funds out of which each contribution is made have otherwise been included in computing taxable income. That limitation is clearly exceeded in the case of the deduction of fair market value of appreciated capital assets without recognition of the unrealized gain. It raises difficulties in other cases where some current receipts or prior accumulations may have been taxed at less than current ordinary rates. But the difficulties are not solely, or even primarily, a product of the charitable contributions deduction, since they already exist with respect to capital gains or prior accumulations that may be devoted to current private consumption without ever bearing tax at current ordinary income rates. The capital gain rules in particular are inconsistent with the underlying thesis that the tax should be evenly laid on total consumption plus accumulation without distinctions according to differences in source, and the charitable contribution deduction only puts that inconsistency into sharper focus.

Teresa Odendahl, Charity Begins at Home: Generosity and Self Interest Among the Philanthropic Elite

3–5, 232–240 (1990).

CULTURE, GENEROSITY, AND POWER

    Elite American philanthropy serves the interests of the rich to a greater extent than it does the interests of the poor, disadvantaged, or disabled. * * * Voluntary organizations supported and directed by wealthy philanthropists divert decision making in the arts, culture, education, health, and welfare from public representatives to a private power elite.

    Paradoxically, although people of all classes participate in nonprofit groups, most of these organizations are controlled by a few, and many charities benefit the rich more than they do the poor. The vast majority of nonprofit agencies and programs do not primarily serve the needy. Many elite philanthropists are civic-minded and sincere, but the system they help to maintain may actually reduce the extent to which basic human services are provided on a democratic basis.

    By studying rich people and their charitable endeavors, I have identified a nationwide "culture of philanthropy." Those who inherited "old money" and the richest Americans, usually with "new money," tend to be the most involved in voluntary activities. But they contribute disproportionately to private universities, the arts, and culture, rather than to community health clinics, legal aid programs, or other projects for the poor. There are thousands of good causes in which millionaires have little interest. Those are not the subject of this book, although they are certainly affected by the neglect of the wealthy.

Not all millionaires in the United States are serious philanthropists. My guess is that fewer than half of the wealthy are charitably minded. Those who regularly contribute large sums of money to nonprofit organizations, serve on several volunteer boards of directors, and spend much of their time raising additional resources for charity from colleagues, friends, and relatives belong to a select social group.

* * *

In addition, and of great importance, is the fact that through their charitable activities, wealthy philanthropists and their advisers sponsor what we think of as "high culture"—ballet, opera, symphony, theater, and the visual arts. Rich children learn to value these "serious" cultural forms that on the whole are produced by nonprofit organizations. But there is more to philanthropic culture than breeding and taste.

Through their donations and work for voluntary organizations, the charitable rich exert enormous influence in society. As philanthropists, they acquire status within and outside of their class. Although private wealth is the basis of the hegemony of this group, philanthropy is essential to the maintenance and perpetuation of the upper class in the United States. In this sense, nonprofit activities are the nexus of a modern power elite.

The culture of philanthropy is manifest in the common behavior and manners, economic status, and sociocultural institutions, as well as in the shared attitudes, ideas, perceptions, tastes, and values of this group whose members frequently interact with one another. The "established" wealthy are socialized in the family and by exclusive preparatory schools and private colleges. Their interaction continues throughout adulthood as business associates, friends, leaders of local and national voluntary organizations, and relatives by birth and marriage. Elite culture is passed from generation to generation, and from those with old money to the newly rich.

Class and culture are related but not identical. Although the elite who participate in the culture of philanthropy are usually members of the upper class, not everyone in this class endorses a particular way of life. And some middle-class individuals—notably certain "professionals," who serve the wealthy as, for example, personal advisors and private foundation staff—often have perspectives and values similar to their employers and exist within the same charitable system.

My use of the term culture in connection with philanthropy is intentional: the word carries so many subtle applicable meanings. The rich are integral members of the wider society. In certain respects the charitable elite are so aware of prevalent middle-class cultural norms that they deny their affluence and privilege and do not present or even think of themselves as being upper-class. This book is primarily about wealthy people who belong to a distinctive culture that is, in the anthropological sense, a subculture.

* * *

THE RESTRUCTURING OF ELITE PHILANTHROPY

The philanthropy of the wealthy serves many purposes, but primarily it assists in the social reproduction of the upper class. Private contributions by the elite support institutions that sustain their culture, their education, their policy formulation, their status—in short, their interests. This is not to say that the charitable giving of the rich is unworthy, or wholly detrimental to the larger society. Funding of the arts may provide the general population with greater access to high culture. Elite schools do not serve the wealthy alone but also enroll a sizable proportion of scholarship students. A new wing at a children's hospital or money for medical research may ultimately save many lives. Corporate and foundation grants for economic development or housing can be worthwhile, especially since the government has moved away from funding in these areas. Small amounts of money to grassroots, poverty, and social-change projects are absolutely basic to their survival.

The vast majority of these nonprofit agencies, groups, organizations, programs, and institutions do good work that is essential in our society. I have not been criticizing them or their performance. The evidence, however, indicates that they have been stretched thin because of federal cutbacks. Social services have suffered more than any others, and philanthropy—elite or otherwise—has not made up the difference. At least half of all private contributions come from the upper class. As I have stressed in the preceding chapters, most of this money does not go to aid the poor, and we must ask whether the funding of the wealthy serves the public good. Is this the type of human service deployment we want in a "pluralistic" society?

Even one of the leading proponents of pluralism, the political scientist Robert A. Dahl, has argued for the necessity of redistributing wealth and income. He acknowledges that in the United States the full achievement of pluralist democracy has been curtailed; all citizens do not have the opportunity to participate effectively in organizations that have an impact on the political process. Because certain groups have greater access than others to resources, "the preferences of their members count for more than the preferences of citizens who belong to weaker organizations." The "final control over the agenda" is not shared equally. "The unequal resources that allow organizations to stabilize injustice also enable them to exercise unequal influence in determining what alternatives are seriously considered." A central ingredient in a solution to the dilemmas posed by Dahl is progressive taxation and redistribution.

The difficulty, of course, is that a majority of elite philanthropists already object to what they consider excessive taxation. They view their charitable giving as an alternative to even higher taxes. In addition they derive immense personal satisfaction from their philanthropic activities.

The rich continue to view any money that was once theirs as still theirs. They think of their contributions as private money going for the public good. It thus follows, the elite earnestly professed during interviews, that they should make decisions about "their" money. In this way the upper class, rather than the majority of the population, through a political process, defines the public good. The wealthy, however, feel entitled to this prerogative. After all, are they not better qualified as leaders, especially given their superior culture and knowledge?

I have argued that the elite control, influence, or want to control the organizations they fund in significant ways. Thus an already powerful group has disproportionate authority in many nonprofit endeavors. Once again, this does not mean that rich people run all the private cultural, educational, health, and welfare organizations in the country. But they do have the strongest voices in many of the biggest, most prestigious enterprises and institutions. When the elite or the foundations they have funded deem projects to be unworthy of their time and money, these causes suffer because they must increase their efforts in order to secure smaller sums from more contributors.

Furthermore, wealthy board members make decisions about the disposition of more than their "own" funds. Many nonprofit groups still take in sizable government revenue as well as smaller contributions from thousands of middle- and working-class donors. The charitable tax break for itemizers has also resulted in lost income to the State. In effect, these are not private efforts but public endeavors.

At its best, the philanthropy system provides a check against corporate or government domination or indifference. It is also inextricably linked with business and political affairs. Individual nonprofit groups can be important players in a kind of balance of power, as "independent centers of thought, action, involvement, and pressure." This is the type of pluralism that we should promote. I would not do away with the system, but I strongly believe that it needs to be restructured.

Given the widespread support for charity, how might the system be reformed to serve the public interest? A variety of policy options and recommendations about elite philanthropy are outlined in the remainder of this chapter. An equitable tax system would lay the foundation for such reforms. Each alternative offered is built upon the need for accountability from donors, the government, intermediaries, and nonprofit service providers as well as the desirability of a representative process. Public awareness, educational, and organizing programs could foster the participation of more citizens in philanthropy and work against elite control. Clear guidelines and standards for foundations, other grant-makers, and nonprofit governance in general would encourage fairness. There is a way for us to continue to be partners with our own government in providing for the common good. And there are several strategies for building individual choice, without elite control, into the process.

EQUITABLE TAXATION

Taxation has been the mechanism that provides revenues for the funding of national defense, public works, and public goods. Almost all Americans these days feel that they suffer from taxation. Curiously, even the wealthy are perturbed, although it is undeniable that the real tax burden is carried disproportionately by the middle class. Within the framework of a modern capitalist system, and leaving aside for the moment the particular responsibilities of a democracy to its citizens, there appears to be no alternative to taxation short of the nationalization of industry. There has to be some source of income. A reformed system could be devised along the following lines.

No Nonprofit Public Policy

Charitable policy is currently enacted through a tax code premised on the notion that individual philanthropy is altruistic and should be rewarded. Yet some contributions are clearly more altruistic than others and some organizations more highly geared than others toward serving the public good. Americans need to rethink the system by which nonprofit groups are categorized as tax-exempt under the rulings of the Internal Revenue Service. The code could, for example, require a more representative decision and governance process within individual charities, and base their exemption status partially on these criteria. Except for due care and fiduciary responsibility, the legal requirements of most voluntary groups are extremely limited; there is little regulation of the field and almost no distinction between the services that the various tax-exempt organizations actually perform.

The main exception is the private foundation, which has been treated differently since the Tax Reform Act of 1969. This act was a specific and fairly successful attempt to limit the power exercised by the wealthy through the grant-making institutions they endow. It did not, however, apply to the individual contributions of the upper class, to the elite organizations they tend to support, or to other charitable trusts and vehicles.

Certain endeavors more clearly fill a public role than others, and they should receive a larger tax break. We do have a precedent in this regard. Those who donate to public charities, for example, receive the largest deduction, 50 percent, whereas those who create or contribute to private foundations are given only a 30 percent deduction. (This disparity represents a recognition of the basic differences in the functions and roles of these types of organizations.) In addition, an individual or family cannot have a controlling business interest in the assets that comprise the endowment of a private foundation, whereas closely held assets may be contributed to other kinds of charitable vehicles, such as support organizations.

We might want to insure that people who donate money to the organizations serving the neediest members of our society will receive the greatest tax benefits. Or, a full tax exemption might be given only if the general population is free to use the services of the agency. A related option would be to require that certain nonprofit groups meet a "public interest" or "public support" test. In order to be accorded public charity status, even grant-making organizations would have to demonstrate that they have widespread support and boards of trustees that are representative of the communities to be served. Gifts to nonprofit institutions that are exclusionary or offer services for high fees would get reduced tax breaks. In the case of private schools, for example, the number of scholarships offered might be required to equal or even exceed the number of tuition-paying students in order for the institution to be accorded a particular tax standing. People of all classes could still have the option to give to whatever nonprofit group they might choose, but the tax benefits would be based on the nature of the work done by that group.

Income Tax

Whether or not philanthropy is to be viewed as an alternative form of taxation, when people are given choice about where "their" money goes, more democratic safeguards need to be instituted. If the income tax system were equitable across classes, there would be a charitable deduction for all citizens or for none. The present system is untenable. A fair income tax system would also be effectively progressive, and corporations would pay their share. * * *

Another consequence of the inequality in the tax system is that it encourages the wealthy to give large contributions which allow them to control nonprofit organizations. An obvious way to limit individual power over specific groups in particular and public policy in general would be to place an annual ceiling on gifts to any one charitable agency, as we do for contributions to national political campaigns. This option would undoubtedly be unpopular with many nonprofit groups that depend heavily on large gifts, especially elite preparatory schools and universities. And the increased work of fundraising could take away from the basic goals or services of the organization. But many groups that are not supported by the wealthy already face this dilemma. Perhaps a compromise would be to allow a fully deductible contribution up to a certain amount, and to limit tax breaks over that sum. It might also be stipulated that there be no limits on contributions to public charities and foundations that meet a public-support test.

In contrast to major donations, smaller gifts do become public because they are immediately absorbed into a common fund, or in the case of single works of art, into a larger collection. It is difficult to be precise about the exact figure that would constitute a major donation, but perhaps $10,000 is a good "dividing line." Or the breakoff point might change depending on the size of the budget of the recipient group. In any event, the specifics of these recommendations would require much discussion among all who would be concerned, and resolution within the political arena.

Estate Taxes

As we have seen, our inheritance system perpetuates inequality and the concentration of wealth. We have a myth in this country that all people are equal at birth. But almost by definition the majority of the poor are unable to accumulate possessions that they can pass on to their children or others when they die. Middle-class individuals, if they do not end up in a nursing home, may have something, perhaps a house, for their offspring to inherit. Only the rich bequeath charitable trust funds, seats on foundation boards, non-charitable trust funds, and vast fortunes to their children. As we have seen, their children grow up in a different world-of culture, good education, and privilege. If we in the United States were to drastically alter or even disallow the inheritance system, then our people might start off more equal at birth.

Another alternative to the present system would be to eliminate loopholes like annuities, special gifts, and split-interest trusts that enable the wealthy to avoid inheritance taxation. For example, charitable lead and remainder trusts enable the wealthy to sidestep taxation by receiving assets tax-free simply because for some period of time their interest income went to charity.

We might, however, want to continue to provide incentives for direct bequests to truly charitable nonprofit organizations or public foundations. The same basic guidelines that are adopted for income tax deductions might be applied to estate plans. Wealthy individuals and others with considerable assets would pay lower or even minimum estate taxes if a bequest were made to a group that clearly met and maintained full tax-exempt status.

NOTE: POLICY ASPECTS OF THE ESTATE TAX CHARITABLE DEDUCTION

Proponents of the tax expenditure concept have extended their analysis to the federal wealth transfer taxes. Viewing the charitable estate and gift tax charitable deduction as a spending measure that departs from a normative transfer tax structure, they contend that the deduction must be justified in terms of need, efficiency, or equity. See, e.g., Paul R. McDaniel, James R. Repetti & Paul L. Caron, Federal Wealth Transfer Taxation: Cases and Materials 561, 565–569 (6th ed. 2009). Professor McDaniel and others have argued that the deduction mechanism concentrates in very wealthy estates the foregone revenue that results from allowing the deduction. This "upside-down effect," they contend, undercuts the fundamental argument in favor of the charitable deduction based on the need for a pluralistic approach to the solution of social problems. See id. Tax expenditures theorists propose to replace the estate and gift tax charitable deductions with a more carefully tailored federal direct matching grant program.

In response, Professor John Simon has attempted to extend the tax-base defining rationales for tax exemptions and the charitable income tax deduction to the wealth transfer taxes. He argues:

Just as income is based on consumption and accumulation and the [income-defining] rationale asserts that this consumption is the private consumption of non-"public" * * * goods and services, we can perhaps say that the definition of personal wealth for estate tax purposes should refer to those assets available for the private accumulation or consumption of non-"public" * * * goods and services. A testamentary charitable contribution reduces the amount of assets available for such private consumption and accumulation; hence, under this analysis, it is logical to exclude these contributions from the definition of wealth for purposes of the estate tax. Here, as in the case of the income tax, it would be concluded that the government is subsidizing no one when it affords a charitable deduction.

John G. Simon, Charity and Dynasty Under the Federal Tax System, 5 The Probate Lawyer 22–23 (Summer 1978). Professor Simon also concludes that while the charitable deduction may be a "non-egalitarian law," it still serves to benefit all classes of citizens including those who do not receive direct tax benefits. Id. at 56 et seq.

Unlike the income tax charitable deduction, which is subject to annual percentage limitations, the estate and gift tax deductions are unlimited. As a result, the wealthiest Americans can and often do avoid paying any significant estate tax when they die because they leave virtually all their wealth to charity—usually a private foundation controlled by their family. This has prompted proposals to limit the estate tax charitable deduction to 50 percent of a decedent's gross estate and to restrict or deny a deduction for gifts and bequests to private foundations. Not surprisingly, nonprofit sector advocates and some tax theorists vigorously oppose these suggestions. They argue that limiting the charitable estate tax deduction would reduce charitable bequests, particularly to private colleges and universities, without much offsetting gain in equity or tax revenues. See, e.g., Michael J. Boskin, Estate Taxation and Charitable Bequests, in III Research Papers Sponsored by the Commission on Private Philanthropy and Public Needs 1453 (1977); Boris I. Bittker, Charitable Bequests and the Federal Estate Tax: Proposed Restrictions on Deductibility, 31 Rec. Ass'n B. City N.Y. 159 (1976).

NOTES AND QUESTIONS

1. *The Charitable Deduction as a Tax Expenditure.* Since 1974, Congress has required a listing of tax expenditures in the federal budget. For this purpose, tax expenditures are defined as revenue losses due to preferential provisions of the federal tax laws. Estimates of tax expenditures are released periodically by the Office of Tax Analysis of the Treasury Department and the Joint Committee on Taxation. The Joint Committee has estimated that the total revenue loss attributable to the charitable deduction will be $237.6 billion for the 2009–2013 fiscal years. The charitable deduction ranks as one of the top ten expenditures. The deduction for home mortgage interest ranked first, costing $ 572.9 billion for the 2009–2013 period. The exclusion of employers' contributions for employee medical insurance premiums and medical care ranked second, with tax expenditures of $568.3 billion for the same period. See Joint Committee on Taxation,

Estimates of Federal Tax Expenditures for Fiscal Years 2009–2013 (JCS–1–10), January 11, 2010.

2. *Philanthropy and the Cultural Elite.* Teresa Odendahl's thesis is that elite philanthropy, instead of relieving social and economic inequality, actually exacerbates it. She argues that private schools and other nonprofit institutions of "high culture" have a disproportionate influence and limited public accountability and that federal tax policy reinforces this syndrome. Odendahl's goal of rethinking the qualification criteria for tax-exempt status presents a challenge similar to that raised by the legal theorists. But her agenda suffers from considerable imprecision. Would private foundations still be eligible charitable donees under her proposed reforms? Should favored tax-exempt status be conditioned on the representative composition of an organization's governing board or a "public interest" test? Would it be appropriate to place a cap on a taxpayer's annual charitable deduction for gifts to a single institution—for example, limit the deduction to $10,000 per year per charitable donee? What would be the impact on charitable giving if the estate tax charitable deduction were subject to a dollar or percentage limitation, or if the federal wealth transfer taxes were repealed?

3. *Charitable Deduction for Non–Itemizers.* Only taxpayers who itemize deductions obtain any tax benefit from the charitable deduction. Should the deduction also be available to taxpayers who claim the standard deduction? Would this provide a greater inducement for donations from low-income taxpayers? In 1975, the Filer Commission recommended extending the charitable deduction to non-itemizers and went so far as to propose a "double charitable deduction" for families with incomes of less than $15,000 a year. These low-income taxpayers would have been allowed to deduct 200 percent of their gifts to charity! Giving in America: Toward a Stronger Voluntary Sector, Report of the Commission on Private Philanthropy and Public Needs 135 (1975). In 1981, Congress amended the Code to permit non-itemizers to deduct a portion of their charitable contributions, but the provision expired at the end of 1986.

The introduction of bills to resurrect some type of charitable deduction for non-itemizers has become an annual ritual in Congress. Proponents cite the encouragement of philanthropy and benefits to low and middle-income taxpayers. Opponents point to additional complexity and undermining the policy of the standard deduction. The most recent legislative proposal would have allowed non-itemizers to deduct their cash contributions in excess of $210 ($420 in the case of a joint return) in addition to taking the standard deduction, but taxpayers who itemized deductions would not have been permitted to deduct the first $210 (or $420 for joint filers) of their gifts to charity. The proposal was seriously considered but never enacted.

4. *Itemized Deductions Floor.* For many years, most itemized deductions, including the charitable deduction, were subject to a reduction rule enacted by Congress in 1990 as a phantom tax rate increase for high-income taxpayers. Single individuals and married couples filing joint returns were required to reduce their total itemized deductions (except for a few exempted items) by three percent of the excess of those deductions over

an indexed threshold ($166,800 in 2009), but not by more than 80 percent of the itemized deductions subject to this limit. I.R.C. § 68. Beginning in 2006, the § 68 limitation was gradually phased out until it was eliminated in 2010 but, unless Congress takes further action, the phase-out will reappear in 2011. The Obama administration favors restoring the phase-out.

Whether or not the itemized deduction phase-out rule reduces the tax benefits of charitable giving is a matter of some debate. What is not debatable is that phase-outs have significant complexity costs and contribute to taxpayer (and student?) confusion. Tax rate increases, by contrast, are easy to understand.

5. *Limiting the Tax Benefit of Charitable Deduction for Wealthy Donors.* Early in his first 100 days, President Obama proposed another approach to limit the tax benefit derived from most itemized deductions, including the charitable deduction, for high-income taxpayers. Under current law, the tax savings from a charitable deduction vary depending on the donor's marginal income tax bracket. For example, assume a taxpayer donates $100,000 cash to a public charity. If that $100,000 otherwise would be taxed at the highest marginal regular tax rate (35 percent in 2010), the deduction saves the donor $35,000 in federal taxes, as compared to $28,000 in tax savings for a taxpayer with a top marginal bracket of 28 percent.

Under the proposal, the tax benefit of a charitable deduction for purposes of the regular income tax would be limited to no more than 28 percent whenever the deduction otherwise would reduce taxable income in the higher brackets (which the Obama administration proposes to increase to 36 percent and 39.6 percent). Taxpayers subject to the alternative minimum tax, which has a broader base but a lower top rate of 28 percent, also would be adversely affected. The tax benefit cap was intended to make the tax system more progressive (and fair?) and raise revenue to help finance health care reform. See Joint Committee on Taxation, Description of Revenue Provisions Contained in the President's Fiscal Year 2010 Budget Proposal; Part One: Individual Income Tax and Estate and Gift Tax Provisions (JCS–2–09), at 123–130 (2009).

The proposal received a chilly response from legislators and howls of protest from the charitable sector, especially charities that rely on large gifts from wealthy donors. It remains on the shelf and could be revived as Congress continues to search for ways to raise revenue without explicitly raising tax rates.

6. *Impact of Estate Tax Repeal on Philanthropy.* The federal estate tax was repealed, effective January 1, 2010, but it is set to be reinstated in 2011, reverting back to the higher rates (up to 55 percent) and lower lifetime exemption ($1 million) that were in effect prior to 2002 unless Congress takes further action, which it is likely to do before the end of 2010.

While Congress has been shuffling its feet, a policy debate on the merits and implications of permanent estate tax repeal has been ongoing. A major talking point for opponents of complete repeal is the negative impact on charitable giving. A study conducted in 2003 by the Brookings Institution and the Urban Institute estimated that charities will lose approximately $10 billion a year through reduced bequests and lifetime gifts if there were no estate tax. Jon M. Bakija & William G. Gale, Effects of Estate Tax Reform on Charitable Giving, Tax Policy Issues and Options, Urban–Brookings Tax Policy Center (No. 6, July 2003). A 2004 Congressional Budget Office report agreed that the estate tax provides a powerful incentive for charitable bequests and also influences wealthy individuals to donate more when they are alive. Robert McClelland & Pamela Greene, The Estate Tax and Charitable Giving, Congressional Budget Office (CBO), July 2004. The CBO report concluded that for the year 2000 alone estate tax repeal would have resulted in a 16 to 28 percent decrease of charitable bequests and an overall loss of charitable donations of $13 to $25 billion.

Proponents of estate tax repeal argue that charities will not suffer much of a loss because taxpayers would have more disposable wealth, stimulating increased giving. One study, noting that very wealthy taxpayers give less to charity during their lives and considerably more at death, suggested that elimination of the estate tax would encourage the wealthy to give more while they were alive and less at death, without necessarily reducing total giving. David Jouthian, Charitable Giving in Life and at Death, in Rethinking Estate and Gift Taxation 350–374 (William G. Gale, James R. Hines & Joel Slemrod, eds., Brookings Institution 2001).

Despite the conventional wisdom that charities would suffer from estate tax repeal, the nonprofit sector was strangely silent in the early debate, perhaps fearing that opposition to repeal would alienate wealthy donors. See Stephanie Strom, Charities Silent on Costly Estate Tax Repeal, N.Y. Times, April 24, 2005, at § 1, 28. Eventually, however, a few mainstream groups, such as Independent Sector and the Council for Advancement of Education, took public positions against full permanent repeal, citing the devastating impact on charitable giving. See, e.g., Independent Sector, The Estate Tax and Charitable Giving (2005), available at www.independentsector.org/programs/gr/estatetax.

7. *For Further Reading.* Stanley S. Surrey, Pathways to Tax Reform 223–232 (1973); Boris I. Bittker, Charitable Contributions: Tax Deductions or Matching Grants, 28 Tax L.Rev. 37 (1972); Paul R. McDaniel, Federal Matching Grants for Charitable Contributions: A Substitute for the Income Tax Deduction, 27 Tax L. Rev. 377 (1972); John K. McNulty, Public Policy and Private Charity: A Tax Policy Perspective, 3 Va. Tax Rev. 229 (1984); John G. Simon, Charity and Dynasty Under the Federal Tax System, 5 The Probate Lawyer 22 (Summer 1978); Mark P. Gergen, The Case for a Charitable Contributions Deduction, 74 Va.L.Rev. 1393 (1988); Lawrence M. Stone, Federal Tax Support of Charities and Other Exempt Organizations: The Need for a National Policy, 1968 U.S.C. Tax Inst. 27; Mark G. Kelman, Personal Deductions Revisited: Why They Fit Poorly in an "Ideal" Income Tax and Why They Fit Worse in a Far from Ideal World, 31 Stan.L.Rev. 831, 838–851 (1979); Charles T. Clotfelter, Tax–Induced Dis-

tortions in the Voluntary Sector, 39 Case West.L.Rev. 663 (1988); Francie Ostrower, Why the Wealthy Give: The Culture of Elite Philanthropy (1996); Symposium: Corporate Philanthropy: Law, Culture, Education and Politics, 41 N.Y.L.Sch.L.Rev. 753 (1997); Miranda Perry Fleischer, Theorizing the Charitable Tax Subsidies: The Role of Distributive Justice, 87 Wash U.L. Rev. 505 (2009).

B.   Charitable Contributions: Basic Principles

Internal Revenue Code: § 170(c).

1.   Qualified Donees

a.   IN GENERAL

The definition of a charitable contribution in § 170(c) consists of a list of the following five categories of organizations that qualify to receive tax-deductible gifts:

1. Governmental entities, including the United States, the District of Columbia, states, possessions and political subdivisions, provided the gift is made for exclusively public purposes. I.R.C. § 170(c)(1).

2. Domestic corporations, community chests, funds, or foundations that are organized and operated exclusively for religious, charitable, scientific, literary or educational purposes, to prevent cruelty to children or animals, or to foster national or international amateur sports competition, provided that no part of the organization's net earnings inure to the benefit of any private shareholder or individual and the organization does not violate the lobbying and political campaign limitations in § 501(c)(3). I.R.C. § 170(c)(2). This is the same group of organizations eligible for tax-exempt status under § 501(c)(3), except that "testing for public safety" is not a qualifying purpose under § 170. In the case of gifts by corporate donors to a charitable trust or other noncorporate donee, a charitable deduction is allowed only if the gift is to be used within the United States or any of its possessions. I.R.C. § 170(c)(2), flush language. Gifts by corporations to domestic corporate donees, however, are not subject to any place-of-use restriction and thus may be expended outside the United States. Rev. Rul. 69–80, 1969–1 C.B. 65.

3. Veterans organizations (including certain ancillary entities), subject to a no inurement of private gain limitation. I.R.C. § 170(c)(3).

4. Domestic fraternal lodges, if the gift is from an individual and is to be used exclusively for religious, charitable, scientific, literary, or educational purposes, or for the prevention of cruelty to children or animals. I.R.C. § 170(c)(4).

5. Nonprofit cemetery companies owned and operated exclusively for the benefit of their members, which also are subject to a no inurement of private gain limitation. I.R.C. § 170(c)(5).

With a few minor differences, the first four categories of organizations in the above list also are eligible to receive tax-deductible gifts for federal estate and gift tax purposes. I.R.C. §§ 2055(a); 2522(a).

Most qualified donees are included in the IRS's Publication 78, also known as "The Cumulative List," a bulky multi-volume book that lists all organizations that have obtained a favorable determination under § 170(c) from the Service. The list also is available on the IRS's web site at www.irs. gov. In general, a contributor may rely upon the Cumulative List until the Service publishes a formal notice of revocation or change of classification (e.g., from public charity to private foundation). A donor who knows that the organization's exempt status was revoked, was aware that revocation was imminent, or was responsible for or aware of the circumstances leading to the revocation, may not rely on the Cumulative List. See Rev. Proc. 82–39, 1982–2 C.B. 759.

b. INTERNATIONAL GIVING

The growth of global philanthropy has stimulated greater interest in tax planning for contributions by U.S. donors for use beyond the borders of the United States. The arcane and often formalistic tax regime that regulates international giving places a high premium on knowing the "right way" to structure a gift for use abroad. Section 170 appears to place a geographical water's edge limitation on the income tax deduction for individual contributions by requiring qualified donees to be created or organized within the United States, including any state, the District of Columbia, and U.S. possessions. I.R.C. § 170(c)(2)(A). But the Code does not restrict the area in which deductible contributions may be used for charitable purposes. Reg. § 1.170A–8(a)(1). As illustrated by Revenue Ruling 63–152, which follows, U.S. noncorporate taxpayers may deduct contributions made for use abroad provided the gifts are made to a domestic charity that is not legally obligated to pay over the donated funds to a foreign recipient. Donations by corporations to charitable trusts, however, are only deductible if the donated funds are used within the United States and its possessions. I.R.C. § 170(c), flush language.

Revenue Ruling 63–252

1963–2 Cum.Bull. 101.

Advice has been requested as to the deductibility, under section 170 of the Internal Revenue Code of 1954, of contributions by individuals to a charity organized in the United States which thereafter transmits some or all of its funds to a foreign charitable organization.

* * *

In determining whether contributions to or for the use of a particular corporation, trust, community chest, fund, or foundation are deductible, it must first be determined that the recipient organization was validly created or organized in the United States, a state or territory, the District of

Columbia or a possession of the United States, as required by section 170(c)(2)(A) of the Code. If the organization does not qualify under section 170(c)(2)(A) of the Code—that is, it was not created or organized in the United States, etc.—a contribution thereto is not deductible under section 170 of the Code. It must further be found that the recipient was organized and operated exclusively for one of the purposes stated in section 170(c)(2)(B) of the Code, namely, religious, charitable, scientific, literary, or educational purposes or for the prevention of cruelty to children or animals, and that it meets the remaining requirements of section 170(c)(2) of the Code.

Assuming that an organization otherwise meets the requirements set forth in section 170(c)(2) of the Code, a further problem arises where that organization is required to turn all or part of its funds over to a foreign charitable organization. As noted above, contributions directly to the foreign organization would not be deductible. The question presented here is whether the result should differ when funds are contributed to a domestic charity which then transmits those funds to a foreign charitable organization.

Prior to the passage of the Revenue Act of 1938 there were no restrictions as to the place of creation of charitable organizations to which individuals might make deductible contributions. * * * The rule as to individual contributions was changed with the passage of the Revenue Act of 1938. Section 23(o) of that Act provided that contributions by individuals were deductible only if the recipient was a "domestic" organization. Section 224 of the Revenue Act of 1939 substituted for the requirement that a qualifying organization be "domestic," the requirement that it have been "created or organized in the United States or in any possession thereof," etc. In substantially the same form, this requirement was re-enacted as section 170(c)(2)(A) of the 1954 Code.

At the outset, it should be noted that section 170(c)(2)(A) of the Code relates only to the place of creation of the charitable organization to which deductible contributions may be made and does not restrict the area in which deductible contributions may be used. Compare the last sentence in section 170(c)(2) of the Code, which requires that certain corporate contributions be used within the United States. Accordingly, the following discussion should not be construed as limiting in any way the geographical areas in which deductible contributions by individuals may be used.

The deductibility of the contributions here at issue will be discussed in connection with five illustrative examples set out below. The "foreign organization" referred to in each of the examples is an organization which is chartered in a foreign country and is so organized and operated that it meets all the requirements of section 170(c)(2) of the Code excepting the requirement set forth in section 170(c)(2)(A) of the Code. The "domestic organization" in each example is assumed to meet all the requirements in section 170(c)(2) of the Code. In each case, the question to be decided is whether the amounts paid to the domestic organization are deductible under section 170(a) of the Code.

(1) In pursuance of a plan to solicit funds in this country, a foreign organization caused a domestic organization to be formed. At the time of formation, it was proposed that the domestic organization would conduct a fund-raising campaign, pay the administrative expenses from the collected fund and remit any balance to the foreign organization.

(2) Certain persons in this country, desirous of furthering a foreign organization's work, formed a charitable organization within the United States. The charter of the domestic organization provides that it will receive contributions and send them, at convenient intervals, to the foreign organization.

(3) A foreign organization entered into an agreement with a domestic organization which provides that the domestic organization will conduct a fund-raising campaign on behalf of the foreign organization. The domestic organization has previously received a ruling that contributions to it are deductible under section 170 of the Code. In conducting the campaign, the domestic organization represents to prospective contributors that the raised funds will go to the foreign organization.

(4) A domestic organization conducts a variety of charitable activities in a foreign country. Where its purposes can be furthered by granting funds to charitable groups organized in the foreign country, the domestic organization makes such grants for purposes which it has reviewed and approved. The grants are paid from its general funds and although the organization solicits from the public, no special fund is raised by a solicitation on behalf of particular foreign organizations.

(5) A domestic organization, which does charitable work in a foreign country, formed a subsidiary in that country to facilitate its operations there. The foreign organization was formed for purposes of administrative convenience and the domestic organization controls every facet of its operations. In the past the domestic organization solicited contributions for the specific purpose of carrying out its charitable activities in the foreign country and it will continue to do so in the future. However, following the formation of the foreign subsidiary, the domestic organization will transmit funds it receives for its foreign charitable activities directly to that organization.

It is recognized that special earmarking of the use or destination of funds paid to a qualifying charitable organization may deprive the donor of a deduction. In S.E. Thomason v. Commissioner, 2 T.C. 441 (1943), the court held that amounts paid to a charitable organization were not deductible where the contributions were earmarked for the benefit of a particular ward of the organization. Similarly, see Revenue Ruling 54–580, C.B. 1954–2, 97. These cases indicate that an inquiry as to the deductibility of a contribution need not stop once it is determined that an amount has been paid to a qualifying organization; if the amount is earmarked, then it is appropriate to look beyond the fact that the immediate recipient is a qualifying organization to determine whether the payment constitutes a deductible contribution.

Similarly, if an organization is required for other reasons, such as a specific provision in its charter, to turn contributions, or any particular contribution it receives, over to another organization, then in determining whether such contributions are deductible it is appropriate to determine whether the ultimate recipient of the contribution is a qualifying organization. * * * Moreover, it seems clear that the requirements of section 170(c)(2)(A) of the Code would be nullified if contributions inevitably committed to go to a foreign organization were held to be deductible solely because, in the course of transmittal to the foreign organization, they came to rest momentarily in a qualifying domestic organization. In such cases the domestic organization is only nominally the donee; the real donee is the ultimate foreign recipient.

Accordingly, the Service holds that contributions to the domestic organizations described in the first and second examples set forth above are not deductible. Similarly, those contributions to the domestic organization described in the third example which are given for the specific purpose of being turned over to the foreign organization are held to be nondeductible.

On the other hand, contributions received by the domestic organization described in the fourth example will not be earmarked in any manner, and use of such contributions will be subject to control by the domestic organization. Consequently, the domestic organization is considered to be the recipient of such contributions for purposes of applying section 170(c) of the Code. Similarly, the domestic organization described in the fifth example is considered to be the real beneficiary of contributions it receives for transmission to the foreign organization. Since the foreign organization is merely an administrative arm of the domestic organization, the fact that contributions are ultimately paid over to the foreign organization does not require a conclusion that the domestic organization is not the real recipient of those contributions. Accordingly, contributions by individuals to the domestic organizations described in the fourth and fifth examples are considered to be deductible.

* * *

NOTES

1. *Treaties.* In limited cases, United States taxpayers may deduct contributions to foreign charities under a treaty. For example, gifts to certain Canadian, Israeli, and Mexican charities may be deductible under the terms of tax treaties provided that the donor has income from sources within those countries.

2. *Grants to Foreign Charities by Private Foundations, Donor-Advised Funds and Supporting Organizations.* Private foundations in the United States have become increasingly involved in international philanthropy. In Rev. Proc. 92–94, 1992–2 C.B. 507, the Internal Revenue Service

provided a simplified procedure to assure that foundation grants to foreign grantees will be treated as "qualifying distributions" for purposes of the § 4942 foundation payout requirements and will not be treated as "taxable expenditures" under § 4945. The problem arises because most foreign grantees do not have exemption classification rulings from the Internal Revenue Service. Under the revenue procedure, grants to foreign charities will comply with the private foundation rules if the foundation obtains an affidavit of the grantee or an opinion of counsel of either the grantor or grantee that the grantee's operations and sources of support make it likely that the grantee would have qualified as a public charity or private operating foundation if it had been a domestic organization.

The Pension Protection Act of 2006 included several provisions restricting international grantmaking through donor-advised funds and supporting organizations. In the case of donor-advised funds, a grant to a foreign charity will trigger a taxable distributions penalty under § 4966 unless the organization sponsoring the fund exercises expenditure responsibility in accordance with the rules in § 4945(h). According to the legislative history, an alternative approach would be for the sponsoring organization to make a good faith determination, known in private foundation parlance as an "equivalency determination," that the foreign grantee would qualify as a public charity if it were organized in the United States. Joint Committee on Taxation, General Explanation of Tax Legislation Enacted in the 109th Congress, 642, n. 948 (2007). The Pension Protection Act of 2006 also effectively precludes any § 509(a)(3) support relationship with a foreign charity by requiring that to qualify as a supporting organization, the supported organization must be organized in the United States. I.R.C. § 509(f)(1)(B)(i).

3. *Financing Terrorism.* As discussed in Chapter 1, the September 11, 2001 terrorist attacks forced the IRS to focus attention on the use of charitable organizations as a significant source of funding for terrorist activities throughout the world. In a few cases, the government determined that funds had been funneled overseas through U.S. public charities and private foundations, often without the donors' knowledge. See Chapter 1A, supra, at p. 17. In 2002, the Treasury Department issued anti-terrorist financing "best practices" guidelines for U.S. charities and requested comments from the nonprofit community. A spirited dialogue ensued, as several influential organizations complained that the guidelines were impractical and would chill international grantmaking. These critics urged the Treasury to rely instead on existing law to address any problems. See, e.g., Section of Taxation, American Bar Association, Comments on International Charitable Activities, reprinted in 41 Exempt Org. Tax Rev. 278 (Aug. 2003). In November, 2005, the Treasury issued revised guidelines that were somewhat less onerous than the earlier version but still require an extensive vetting process for international grantmakers. See U.S. Department of the Treasury Anti–Terrorist Financing Guidelines: Voluntary Best Practices for U.S.–Based Charities (Nov. 2005), available at www. treas.gov/press/releases/js3035.htm.

4. *For Further Reading.* Harvey P. Dale, Foreign Charities, 48 Tax Lawyer 657 (1995); Victoria B. Bjorklund, International Philanthropy Exploring New Ways to Accomplish International Goals, Including Activities of U.S. Charities Abroad, 21 NYU Conf. on Tax Planning for 501(c)(3) Organizations § 8 (1993); Kimberly S. Blanchard, U.S. Taxation of Foreign Charities, 8 Exempt Org. Tax Rev. 719 (1993).

c. FISCAL SPONSORS

Assume that an individual or group engaging in a short-term or embryonic project is seeking to raise tax-deductible contributions from individual or corporate donors, or grants from private foundations or government agencies. The project may be an educational film, a theater production, or an international human rights program—all activities that comfortably would qualify as "charitable" if carried out directly by a § 501(c)(3) organization. Because they will be short-lived or are still in the formative stages, these projects might not justify the expense of creating a separate tax-exempt entity. Yet without formal recognition from the Internal Revenue Service, the prospect of raising substantial funds is slim to none.

The nonprofit sector has developed and refined the "fiscal sponsorship" concept to respond to these concerns. As described in a leading guidebook on the subject:

> Fiscal sponsorship arrangements typically arise when a person or group (we will call this a project) wants to get support from a private foundation, a government agency, or tax-deductible donations from individual or corporate donors. By law or preference, the funding source will make payments only to organizations with 501(c)(3) tax status. So the project looks for a 501(c)(3) sponsor to receive the funds and pass them on to the project.

Gregory L. Colvin, Fiscal Sponsorship: 6 Ways to Do it Right (2005).

Fiscal sponsorships are contractual arrangements that are memorialized in a written agreement. Sponsors typically provide accounting, gift processing, and other administrative services, and an institutional relationship in exchange for a fee. The sponsored project retains practical control over its mission and programs and is responsible for fundraising, but the sponsor has legal control over the project's finances.

Fiscal sponsors are sometimes called "fiscal agents," but the term "agent" is a misnomer and should be avoided. To comply with IRS guidelines, the sponsoring exempt organization should not act as a mere agent of the nonexempt project. Rather, the charity must retain legal control and ensure that the project furthers the charity's exempt purposes and does not result in any inurement of private gain to the project leaders. Id. Contributions to a charity that are simply earmarked by the donor for a particular individual or nonexempt organization are deductible where the charitable donee lacks discretion and control over the donated funds.

2. FORM AND TIMING

Treasury Regulations: § 1.170A–1(a), (b), (g).

A contribution is tax-deductible if it is made either "to" or "for the use of "a qualified donee. Gifts made directly to individuals, however worthy or needy they may be, are not deductible. The term "for the use of "permits a charitable deduction for gifts that benefit a charity even though not made directly "to" the organization. The term has been interpreted to include gifts made in trust for an organization's benefit.

Gifts to support individuals who perform services for a particular charity are not deductible where the charity does not have control over the donated funds. This principle is illustrated by Davis v. United States, 495 U.S. 472, 110 S.Ct. 2014 (1990), where the Supreme Court held that funds transferred by parents to their two sons while the sons served as full-time unpaid missionaries for the Church of Jesus Christ of Latter-day Saints were not deductible as contributions "to or for the use of" the Church. In *Davis*, the taxpayers argued that their payments were contributions "for the use of" the Church or, alternatively, were deductible as unreimbursed expenditures incident to the rendering of services to a charitable organization. The Supreme Court strictly interpreted the phrase "for the use of" as meaning "in trust for" and went on to conclude that a defining characteristic of a trust arrangement is that the beneficiary has the legal power to enforce the trustee's duty to comply with the trust terms. Since the taxpayers in *Davis* did not donate the funds in trust or a similarly enforceable legal arrangement for the benefit of the Church, the Court held that the funds were not donated "for the use of" the Church within the meaning of § 170. The Court also rejected the taxpayers' alternative argument, finding that taxpayers may claim charitable deductions only for unreimbursed expenditures made in connection with their own services, not those of third parties.

NOTES

1. *Out-of-Pocket Expenses*. Payments that further an organization's charitable activities, such as unreimbursed expenses of volunteers and board members, are deductible even if the payment is not made directly to the charity. The out-of-pocket expense deduction extends to travel expenses, subject to a "no smile" rule that disallows a deduction for transportation, meals and lodging "unless there is no significant element of personal pleasure, recreation, or vacation in such travel." I.R.C. § 170(j). In determining the deduction for unreimbursed expenses for using a passenger automobile, § 170(i) prescribes a special rate of 14 cents per mile. Unreimbursed expenditures are treated as contributions "to" a charity (rather than "for the use of") and thus are subject to the higher 50 percent limitation on cash contributions in § 170(b)(1)(A). See Rockefeller v. Commissioner, 676 F.2d 35 (2d Cir.1982); Rev. Rul. 84–61, 1984–1 C.B. 39.

2. *Students in the Taxpayer's Household.* Section 170(g) provides a limited charitable deduction (generally $50 per month) for amounts paid to maintain individuals as members of the taxpayer's household. This provision applies to certain arrangements between taxpayers and qualified charitable organizations which provide educational opportunities in the United States for full-time students in the 12th or lower grades.

3. *Payment Requirement.* Whatever their method of accounting, individual taxpayers may deduct charitable contributions only in the year in which they are unconditionally paid. Treas. Reg. § 1.170A–1(a). Payment is accomplished by placing the contributed property beyond the dominion and control of the donor. Thus, a cash contribution made by a check that clears in due course will be effective as of the date of mailing, even if it is not received and deposited by the charity until the following year. Treas. Reg. § 1.170A–1(b). Contributions made by a credit card are deductible when the charge is made to the donor's account, regardless of when the cardholder pays the bank. Rev. Rul. 78–38, 1978–1 C.B. 67. Gifts of stock registered in certificate form in the taxpayer's name are not considered complete until stock is transferred on the corporation's books. Treas. Reg. § 1.170A–1(b). But if a donor mails a properly endorsed stock certificate to a charity or to a broker who is acting as an agent for the charity, the gift will be effective as of the date of mailing if the certificate reaches the charity in the normal course of the mails. Id. If securities held by the donor in "street name" in a brokerage or custody account are transferred to an account in the charity's name, the gift is effective as of the date of the transfer.

4. *Pledges.* Even if a pledge is enforceable under state law, neither the act of making the pledge nor the delivery of the donor's own promissory note will constitute "payment" for purposes of the charitable deduction. Rev. Rul. 68–174, 1968–1 C.B. 81. A deduction is allowable only when the pledge is satisfied or the note is paid. Treas. Reg. § 1.170A–1(a). As to the enforceability of pledges to nonprofit organizations, see Mary Frances Budig, Gordon T. Butler & Lynne M. Murphy, Pledges to Non–Profit Organizations: Are They Enforceable and Must They Be Enforced? (New York University School of Law Program on Philanthropy and the Law, 1993).

5. *Corporate Donors.* A corporation using the accrual method of accounting may elect to deduct contributions authorized by its board of directors before the end of its taxable year and paid on or before the fifteenth day of the third month of the following year. I.R.C. § 170(a)(2); Reg. § 1.170A–11(b).

6. *Options.* An option granted to a charitable donee to purchase property at a bargain price does not produce a charitable deduction at the time of the grant. A deduction is allowed at the time the option is exercised. The amount of the charitable deduction is the excess of the fair market value of the property at that time over the exercise price. Rev. Rul. 82–197, 1982–2 C.B. 72.

3.   WHAT IS A CHARITABLE GIFT?

a.   RETURN BENEFITS: IN GENERAL

Treasury Regulations: § 1.170A–1(h).

To be tax-deductible, a charitable contribution must be made with donative intent. A transfer does not qualify as a gift if the transferor receives a return benefit, such as goods or services with a measurable fair market value. The burden is on the taxpayer to show that she intended to make a gift and in fact donated an amount with a value exceeding the fair market value of any goods or services received from the donee. Treas. Reg. § 1.170A–1(h). In the celebrated *Duberstein* case, the Supreme Court loosely defined a gift as a transfer of money or property without adequate consideration and with no expectation of a return benefit.[1] Under *Duberstein*, the requisite donative intent is present if the transfer is made out of "detached and disinterested generosity," an elusive and highly factual standard. In the more recent *American Bar Endowment* case, the Court stated that "[a] payment of money generally cannot constitute a charitable contribution if the contributor expects a substantial benefit in return. * * * The *sine qua non* of a charitable contribution is a transfer of money or property without adequate consideration."[2]

As illustrated by the materials that follow, whether a donor has made a gift or is receiving a quid pro quo has become an increasingly important question as the Internal Revenue Service has heightened its scrutiny of the vast array of return benefits provided to donors by charitable organizations.

Revenue Ruling 67–246

1967–2 Cum. Bull. 104.

Advice has been requested concerning certain fund-raising practices which are frequently employed by or on behalf of charitable organizations and which involve the deductibility, as charitable contributions under section 170 of the Internal Revenue Code of 1954, of payments in connection with admission to or other participation in fund-raising activities for charity such as charity balls, bazaars, banquets, shows, and athletic events.

Affairs of the type in question are commonly employed to raise funds for charity in two ways. One is from profit derived from sale of admissions or other privileges or benefits connected with the event at such prices as their value warrants. Another is through the use of the affair as an occasion for solicitation of gifts in combination with the sale of the

---

1. Commissioner v. Duberstein, 363 U.S. 278, 285, 80 S.Ct. 1190, 1196 (1960). In *Duberstein*, the Court was interpreting the appropriate standard for determining whether a transfer qualified as a gift for purposes of § 102, which excludes gifts from gross income.

2. United States v. American Bar Endowment, 477 U.S. 105, 116, 118, 106 S.Ct. 2426, 2433 (1986).

admissions or other privileges or benefits involved. In cases of the latter type the sale of the privilege or benefit is combined with solicitation of a gift or donation of some amount in addition to the sale value of the admission or privilege.

The need for guidelines on the subject is indicated by the frequency of misunderstanding of the requirements for deductibility of such payments and increasing incidence of their erroneous treatment for income tax purposes.

In particular, an increasing number of instances are being reported in which the public has been erroneously advised in advertisements or solicitations by sponsors that the entire amounts paid for tickets or other privileges in connection with fund-raising affairs for charity are deductible. Audits of returns are revealing other instances of erroneous advice and misunderstanding as to what, if any, portion of such payments is deductible in various circumstances. There is evidence also of instances in which taxpayers are being misled by questionable solicitation practices which make it appear from the wording of the solicitation that taxpayer's payment is a "contribution," whereas the payment solicited is simply the purchase price of an item offered for sale by the organization.

Section 170 of the Code provides for allowance of deductions for charitable contributions, subject to certain requirements and limitations. To the extent here relevant a charitable contribution is defined by that section as 'a contribution or gift to or for the use of' certain specified types of organizations.

To be deductible as a charitable contribution for Federal income tax purposes under section 170 of the Code, a payment to or for the use of a qualified charitable organization must be a gift. To be a gift for such purposes in the present context there must be, among other requirements, a payment of money or transfer of property without adequate consideration.

As a general rule, where a transaction involving a payment is in the form of a purchase of an item of value, the presumption arises that no gift has been made for charitable contribution purposes, the presumption being that the payment in such case is the purchase price.

Thus, where consideration in the form of admissions or other privileges or benefits is received in connection with payments by patrons of fund-raising affairs of the type in question, the presumption is that the payments are not gifts. In such case, therefore, if a charitable contribution deduction is claimed with respect to the payment, the burden is on the taxpayer to establish that the amount paid is not the purchase of the privileges or benefits and that part of the payment, in fact, does qualify as a gift.

In showing that a gift has been made, an essential element is proof that the portion of the payment claimed as a gift represents the excess of the total amount paid over the value of the consideration received therefor. This may be established by evidence that the payment exceeds the fair market value of the privileges or other benefits received by the amount claimed to have been paid as a gift.

Another element which is important in establishing that a gift was made in such circumstances, is evidence that the payment in excess of the value received was made with the intention of making a gift. While proof of such intention may not be an essential requirement under all circumstances and may sometimes be inferred from surrounding circumstances, the intention to make a gift is, nevertheless, highly relevant in overcoming doubt in those cases in which there is a question whether an amount was in fact paid as a purchase price or as a gift.

Regardless of the intention of the parties, however, a payment of the type in question can in any event qualify as a deductible gift only to the extent that it is shown to exceed the fair market value of any consideration received in the form of privileges or other benefits.

In those cases in which a fund-raising activity is designed to solicit payments which are intended to be in part a gift and in part the purchase price of admission to or other participation in an event of the type in question, the organization conducting the activity should employ procedures which make clear not only that a gift is being solicited in connection with the sale of the admissions or other privileges related to the fund-raising event, but also, the amount of the gift being solicited. To do this, the amount properly attributable to the purchase of admissions or other privileges and the amount solicited as a gift should be determined in advance of solicitation. The respective amounts should be stated in making the solicitation and clearly indicated on any ticket, receipt, or other evidence issued in connection with the payment.

In making such a determination, the full fair market value of the admission and other benefits or privileges must be taken into account. Where the affair is reasonably comparable to events for which there are established charges for admission, such as theatrical or athletic performances, the established charges should be treated as fixing the fair market value of the admission or privilege. Where the amount paid is the same as the standard admission charge there is, of course, no deductible contribution, regardless of the intention of the parties. Where the event has no such counterpart, only that portion of the payment which exceeds a reasonable estimate of the fair market value of the admission or other privileges may be designated as a charitable contribution.

The fact that the full amount or a portion of the payment made by the taxpayer is used by the organization exclusively for charitable purposes has no bearing upon the determination to be made as to the value of the admission or other privileges and the amount qualifying as a contribution.

Also, the mere fact that tickets or other privileges are not utilized does not entitle the patron to any greater charitable contribution deduction than would otherwise be allowable. The test of deductibility is not whether the right to admission or privileges is exercised but whether the right was accepted or rejected by the taxpayer. If a patron desires to support an affair, but does not intend to use the tickets or exercise the other privileges being offered with the event, he can make an outright gift of the amount he wishes to contribute, in which event he would not accept or keep any ticket or other evidence of any of the privileges related to the event connected with the solicitation.

The foregoing summary is not intended to be all inclusive of the legal requirements relating to deductibility of payments as charitable contributions for Federal income tax purposes. Neither does it attempt to deal with many of the refinements and distinctions which sometimes arise in connection with questions of whether a gift for such purposes has been made in particular circumstances.

The principles stated are intended instead to summarize with as little complexity as possible, those basic rules which govern deductibility of payments in the majority of the circumstances involved. They have their basis in section 170 of the Code, the regulations thereunder, and in court decisions. The observance of these provisions will provide greater assurance to taxpayer contributors that their claimed deductions in such cases are allowable.

Where it is disclosed that the public or the patrons of a fund-raising affair for charity have been erroneously informed concerning the extent of the deductibility of their payments in connection with the affair, it necessarily follows that all charitable contribution deductions claimed with respect to payments made in connection with the particular event or affair will be subject to special scrutiny and may be questioned in audit of returns.

In the following examples application of the principles discussed above is illustrated in connection with various types of fund-raising activities for charity. Again, the examples are drawn to illustrate the general rules involved without attempting to deal with distinctions that sometimes arise in special situations. In each instance, the charitable organization involved is assumed to be an organization previously determined to be qualified to receive deductible charitable contributions under section 170 of the Code, and the references to deductibility are to deductibility as charitable contributions for Federal income tax purposes.

Example 1:

The M Charity sponsors a symphony concert for the purpose of raising funds for M's charitable programs. M agrees to pay a fee which is calculated to reimburse the symphony for hall rental, musicians' salaries, advertising costs, and printing of tickets. Under the agreement, M is entitled to all receipts from ticket sales. M sells tickets to the concert charging $5 for balcony seats and $10 for orchestra circle seats. These prices approximate the established admission charges for concert performances by the symphony orchestra. The tickets to the concert and the advertising material promoting ticket sales emphasize that the concert is sponsored by, and is for the benefit of M Charity.

Notwithstanding the fact that taxpayers who acquire tickets to the concert may think they are making a charitable contribution to or for the benefit of M Charity, no part of the payments made is deductible as a charitable contribution for Federal income tax purposes. Since the payments approximate the established admission charge for similar events, there is no gift. The result would be the same even if the advertising materials promoting ticket sales stated that amounts paid for tickets are "tax deductible" and tickets to the concert were purchased in reliance upon such statements. Acquisition of tickets or other privileges by a taxpayer in reliance upon statements made by a charitable organization that the amounts paid are deductible does not convert an otherwise nondeductible payment into a deductible charitable contribution.

Example 2:

The facts are the same as in Example 1, except that the M Charity desires to use the concert as an occasion for the solicitation of gifts. It indicates that fact in its advertising material promoting the event, and fixes the payments solicited in connection with each class of admission at $30 for orchestra circle seats and $15 for balcony seats. The advertising and the tickets clearly reflect the fact that the established admission charges for comparable performances by the symphony orchestra are $10 for orchestra circle seats and $5 for balcony seats, and that only the excess of the solicited amounts paid in connection with admission to the concert over the established prices is a contribution to M.

Under these circumstances a taxpayer who makes a payment of $60 and receives two orchestra circle seat tickets can show that his payment exceeds the established admission charge for similar tickets to comparable performances of the symphony orchestra by $40. The circumstances also confirm that amount of the payment was solicited as, and intended to be, a gift to M Charity. The $40, therefore, is deductible as a charitable contribution.

Example 3:

A taxpayer pays $5 for a balcony ticket to the concert described in Example 1. This taxpayer had no intention of using the ticket when he acquired it and he did not, in fact, attend the concert.

No part of the taxpayer's $5 payment to the M Charity is deductible as a charitable contribution. The mere fact that the ticket to the concert was not used does not entitle the taxpayer to any greater right to a deduction than if he did use it. The same result would follow if the taxpayer had made a gift of the ticket to another individual. If the taxpayer desired to support M, but did not intend to use the ticket to the concert, he could have made a qualifying charitable contribution by making a $5 payment to M and refusing to accept the ticket to the concert.

Example 4:

A receives a brochure soliciting contributions for the support of the M Charity. The brochure states: "As a grateful token of appreciation for your help, the M Charity will send to you your choice of one of the several articles listed below, depending upon the amount of your donation." The remainder of the brochure is devoted to a catalog-type listing of articles of merchandise with the suggested amount of donation necessary to receive each particular article. There is no evidence of any significant difference between the suggested donation and the fair market value of any such article. The brochure contains the further notation that all donations to M Charity are tax deductible.

Payments of the suggested amounts solicited by M Charity are not deductible as a charitable contribution. Under the circumstances, the amounts solicited as "donations" are simply the purchases prices of the articles listed in the brochure.

Example 5:

A taxpayer paid $5 for a ticket which entitled him to a chance to win a new automobile. The raffle was conducted to raise funds for the X Charity. Although the payment for the ticket was solicited as a "contribution" to the X Charity and designated as such of the face of the ticket, no part of the payment is deductible as a charitable contribution. Amounts paid for chances to participate in raffles, lotteries, or similar drawings or to participate in puzzle or other contests for valuable prizes are not gifts in such circumstances, and therefore, do not qualify as deductible charitable contributions.

* * *

Example 8:

In order to raise funds, W Charity plans a theater party consisting of admission to a premiere showing of a motion picture and an after-theater buffet. The advertising material and tickets to the theater party designate $5 as an admission charge and $10 as a gift to W Charity. The established admission charge for premiere showings of motion pictures in the locality is $5.

Notwithstanding W's representations respecting the amount designated as a gift, the specified $10 does not qualify as a deductible charitable contribution because W's allocation fails to take into account the value of admission to the buffet dinner.

Example 9:

The X Charity sponsors a fund-raising bazaar, the articles offered for sale at the bazaar having been contributed to X by persons desiring to support X's charitable programs. The prices for the articles sold at the bazaar are set by a committee of X with a view to charging the full fair market value of the articles.

A taxpayer who purchases articles at the bazaar is not entitled to a charitable contribution deduction for any portion of the amount paid to X for such articles. This is true even though the articles sold at the bazaar are acquired and sold without cost to X and the total proceeds of the sale of the articles are used by X exclusively for charitable purposes.

* * *

Example 12:

To assist the Y Charity in the promotion of a Halloween Ball to raise funds for Y's activities, several individuals in the community agree to pay the entire costs of the event, including the costs of the orchestra, publicity, rental of the ballroom, refreshments, and any other necessary expenses. Various civic organizations and clubs agree to undertake the sale of tickets for the dance. The publicity and solicitations for the sale of the tickets emphasize the fact that the entire cost of the ball is being borne by anonymous patrons of Y and by the other community groups, and that the entire gross receipts from the sale of the tickets, therefore, will go to Y Charity. The price of the tickets, however, is set at the fair market value of admission of the event.

No part of the amount paid for admission to the dance is a gift. Therefore, no part is deductible as a charitable contribution. The fact that the event is conducted entirely without cost to Y Charity and that the full amount of the admission charge goes directly to Y for its uses has no bearing on the deductibility of the amounts paid for admission, but does have a bearing on the deductibility of the amounts paid by the anonymous patrons of the event. The test is not the cost of the event to Y, but the fair market value of the consideration received by the purchaser of the ticket or other privileges for his payment.

NOTES

1. *Donee Estimates of Return Benefits.* Charities should provide their donors with a good faith estimate of the value of any return benefits. In so doing, they may use any reasonable method to determine value. If the service or product is available commercially, using a valuation within the range of retail prices normally is acceptable. If it is not available commercially, the estimate should be made by comparing the return benefit to comparable goods or services. The regulations provide an example of a museum that allows donors to hold private events in exchange for a sufficiently large donation. In this type of case, they authorize a valuation based on the cost of leasing ballrooms in two hotels in the same community with similar amenities and capacity. Treas. Reg. § 1.6115–1(a)(3). The unique qualities of the museum (e.g., its collection) can be disregarded, as may "celebrity presence" at a fundraiser or other special event. Id.

2. *Administrative Guidelines: Benefits with Insubstantial Value.* The IRS has provided charities with administrative guidelines and safe harbors to help them advise donors about benefits received in return for contributions. See Rev. Proc. 90–12, 1990–1 C.B. 471. In response to concerns that some small items would be difficult or burdensome to value, the guidelines

provide that a benefit may be so inconsequential or insubstantial that the full amount of a contribution may be deducted.

Benefits received in connection with a payment to a charity will be considered to have insubstantial fair market value if the payment occurs in the context of a fundraising campaign[1] in which the charity informs patrons how much of their payment is a deductible contribution, and either:

(1) The fair market value of all of the benefits received in connection with the payment is not more than 2 percent of the payment, or $50, whichever is less [the $50 limitation is indexed for inflation; in 2010, it was $96, Eds.], or

(2) The payment is $25 [adjusted for inflation; in 2010, the amount was $48, Eds.] or more and the only benefits received in connection with the payment are token items (bookmarks, calendars, key chains, mugs, posters, tee shirts, etc.) bearing the organization's name or logo. For this purpose, the cost (as opposed to fair market value) of all of the benefits received by a donor must, in the aggregate, be within the limits established for "low cost articles" under § 513(h)(2).[2]

Rev. Proc. 90–12, supra, § 3.01.

In determining whether a return benefit has "insubstantial value," newsletters or program guides (other than "commercial quality" publications) are treated as if they do not have a measurable fair market value or cost if their primary purpose is to inform members about the activities of an organization and if they are not available to nonmembers by paid subscription or through newsstand sales. Whether a publication is considered a commercial quality publication depends upon all of the facts and circumstances. Generally, publications that contain articles written for compensation and that accept advertising will be treated as commercial quality publications having measurable fair market value or cost. Professional journals (whether or not articles are written for compensation and

---

1. A fundraising campaign must be designed to raise tax-deductible contributions, and employ procedures requiring the charity to determine the fair market value of the benefits offered in return for contributions (using a reasonable estimate if an exact determination is not possible), and to state in all its solicitations in any medium, as well as in tickets, receipts, or other documents issued in connection with contributions, how much is and is not deductible. If a charity is providing only insubstantial benefits in return for a payment, fundraising materials should include a statement to the effect that: "Under Internal Revenue Service guidelines the estimated value of the benefits received is not substantial; therefore the full amount of your payment is a deductible contribution." Rev. Proc. 90–12, supra, § 3.01.

2. The general rule under § 170 is that the deductible amount of a contribution is determined by taking into account the fair market value, not the cost to the charity, of any benefits received in return. For purposes of this safe harbor, however, the cost to the charity may be used in determining whether the benefits are insubstantial. An item is a "low cost article" if its cost does not exceed $5, increased for years after 1987 by a cost-of-living adjustment under section 1(f)(3). For 2010, the amount was $9.60. For donated goods or services, the organization's cost can be a reasonable estimate of the amount it would have to pay for the items or services in question. Rev. Proc. 90–12, supra, §§ 3.06–3.07.

advertising is accepted) are normally treated as commercial quality publications. Id. at §§ 3.02–3.04.[3]

3. *Membership Dues*. Membership fees and dues paid to qualified donees (e.g., museums) are deductible only to the extent the amount paid exceeds any return benefits. The regulations provide that some de minimis benefits may be disregarded if they are received in return for annual payments of $75 or less. Examples of disregarded membership benefits include free or discounted admission or parking and preferred access to and discounts on the purchase of goods and services. See Treas. Reg. § 1.170A–13(f)(8)(i)(B).

4. *Information Disclosure of Return Benefits*. A charity that receives a payment of more than $75 that is in part a contribution and in part consideration for goods and services provided to the payor (a "quid pro quo" contribution) must provide the donor with a written statement that includes a good faith estimate of the value of those goods and services and informs the donor that only the excess of the contribution over the value of the return benefits is deductible. I.R.C. § 6115(a). For this purpose, a "quid pro quo" contribution does not include any payment made to a religious organization in return for which the taxpayer receives "solely an intangible religious benefit that generally is not sold in a commercial transaction outside the donative context." I.R.C. § 6115(b). For further discussion of the substantiation and disclosure regulations, see Section B5 of this chapter, *infra*.

b. INTANGIBLE RELIGIOUS BENEFITS

Sklar v. Commissioner

United States Court of Appeals, Ninth Circuit, 2008.
549 F.3d 1252.

■ WARDLAW, CIRCUIT JUDGE:

Michael and Marla Sklar ("the Sklars") appeal from a decision of the Tax Court affirming the disallowance of deductions they claimed for tuition and fees paid to their children's Orthodox Jewish day schools. We have jurisdiction pursuant to 26 U.S.C. § 7482(a)(1), and we affirm.

I. FACTUAL AND PROCEDURAL BACKGROUND

A. Taxpayers

The Sklars are Orthodox Jews who in 1995 had five school-aged children. Rather than send their children to public school to meet California State educational requirements, the Sklars enrolled each of their children in one of two Orthodox Jewish day schools, Emek Hebrew Acade-

---

3. The "cost" of a commercial quality publication includes the costs of production and distribution and must be computed without regard to income from advertising or newsstand or subscription sales. Id.

my ("Emek") and Yeshiva Rav Isacsohn Torath Emeth Academy ("Yeshiva Rav"). They did so "because of their sincerely and deeply held religious belief that as Jews they have a religious obligation to provide their children with an Orthodox Jewish education in an Orthodox Jewish environment." In 1995, the Sklars paid a total of $27,283 to Emek and Yeshiva Rav which included $24,093 for tuition, $1300 for registration fees, $1715 for other mandatory fees, and $175 for an after school Mishna program at Emek.[3] During 1995, Emek and Yeshiva Rav each were exempt from federal income tax under I.R.C. § 501(c)(3), which provides tax exempt status for certain institutions "organized and operated exclusively for religious, charitable, . . . or educational purposes," among others. Both schools also qualified as organizations described in I.R.C. § 170(b)(1)(A), which allows donors to deduct charitable donations to qualifying institutions.

Both schools provided daily exposure to Jewish heritage and values. Their goals included educating their students in Jewish heritage and values, as well as the tenets of the Jewish faith. To this end, time was allocated in the school day for prayers and religious studies, students were required to adhere to Orthodox Jewish dress codes, and boys and girls attended classes separately.

A child's day at each school included specified hours devoted to courses in religious studies and specified hours devoted to secular studies. The length of time that each student participated in secular classes, as opposed to religious studies, and the length of the total school day varied with the gender and grade level of the particular student.

Quality secular education that fulfilled the mandatory education requirements of the State of California also was a goal of both schools. Emek sought to provide a thorough and well-balanced curriculum in both religious and secular studies so that every student could succeed "in the most rigorous yeshiva [(Jewish)] high schools and other institutions of higher learning." Yeshiva Rav sought to prepare its students for matriculation to yeshiva high schools and to attend a college or seminary.

During the school years in issue, the Sklars paid tuition and mandatory fees to Emek and Yeshiva Rav for their children's education. To ensure payment, the Sklars, like other parents, were required to contract with each school to pay, and to give to each school postdated checks covering, the tuition for the upcoming school year. Both schools provided tuition discounts to families based on financial need, if documented by detailed financial information submitted to the schools' scholarship committees, but the Sklars did not seek or receive such assistance. Although an Orthodox Rabbinic ruling precluded either school from expelling students from the Jewish studies program during the school year, nonpayment of tuition could result in expulsion from secular studies and the schools' refusal to allow the children to register for classes in the subsequent school year.

---

3. Mishna is the study of Jewish oral law.

B.   The Prior Litigation

In 1993, the Sklars learned of a confidential closing agreement[4] the Internal Revenue Service ("IRS") had executed with the Church of Scientology that purportedly allowed deductions for certain religious educational services such as auditing and training. The Sklars subsequently amended their tax returns for 1991 and 1992, and filed a return for 1993, including new deductions for a portion of the tuition they had paid to their children's schools. See Sklar, 125 T.C. at 288. The IRS allowed these deductions, apparently under the impression that the Sklars were Scientologists. See id. The Sklars claimed similar deductions in 1994, but these were disallowed. Id. at 288–89. The IRS Notice of Deficiency explained that because the costs were for personal tuition expenses, they were not deductible. The Sklars pursued an unsuccessful petition for redetermination before the Tax Court regarding their 1994 deductions, which subsequently came before us. Judge Reinhardt, writing for our Court in an opinion joined by Judge Pregerson, upheld the Tax Court's denial of the deduction. See Sklar v. Comm'r (Sklar I) 282 F.3d 610 (9th Cir.2002), amending and superseding Sklar v. Comm'r, 279 F.3d 697 (9th Cir.2002).

In *Sklar I*, the Sklars made virtually identical arguments to those they assert here, based predominantly on their theories that a portion of their tuition payments are tax deductible because they received in exchange only intangible religious benefits and the Scientology Closing Agreement is an unconstitutional establishment of religion from which they should also benefit.

The *Sklar I* panel soundly rejected the Sklars' argument that certain 1993 amendments to the Tax Code rendered their tuition payments deductible as payments to exclusively religious organizations for which the Sklars received only intangible religious benefits. 282 F.3d at 612–14. Specifically, the panel noted that the amendments addressed "clearly procedural provisions" and that the deduction the Sklars alleged would be "of doubtful constitutional validity." Id. at 613.

Next, the *Sklar I* panel held that the IRS was compelled to disclose the contents of its Closing Agreement with the Church of Scientology, at least to the extent it fell under I.R.C. § 6104(a)(1)(A), see 282 F.3d at 614–18, and that such disclosure was necessary as a practical matter because the agreement affects "not just one taxpayer or a discrete group of taxpayers, but a broad and indeterminate class of taxpayers with a large and constantly changing membership." Id. at 617. Further, the panel held "where a closing agreement sets out a new policy and contains rules of general applicability to a class of taxpayers, disclosure of at least the relevant part

---

4.   Under § 7121 of the Internal Revenue Code, the IRS is authorized to execute "closing agreements." A closing agreement is "an agreement in writing with any person relating to the liability of such person (or of the person or estate for whom he acts) in respect of any internal revenue tax for any taxable period." I.R.C. § 7121(a), see also 26 C.F.R. § 301.7121–1. Such closing agreements are intended to be "final and conclusive, and, except upon a showing of fraud or malfeasance, or misrepresentation of a material fact," shall not be reopened or annulled. I.R.C. § 7121(b).

of that agreement is required in the interest of public policy." Id. In *Sklar I*, the panel therefore rejected the argument that the closing agreement made with the Church of Scientology, or at least the portion establishing rules or policies that are applicable to Scientology members generally, is not subject to public disclosure. The IRS is simply not free to enter into closing agreements with religious or other tax-exempt organizations governing the deductions that will be available to their members and to keep such provisions secret from the courts, the Congress, and the public. Id. at 618. The *Sklar* I panel nevertheless opined, without resolving the issue, that the Tax Court's ruling that the Closing Agreement was irrelevant to the deductibility of the Sklars' tuition payments was "in all likelihood correct." Id. It continued:

> The Tax Court concluded that the Sklars were not similarly situated to the members of the Church of Scientology who benefitted from the closing agreement. While we have no doubt that certain taxpayers who belong to religions other than the Church of Scientology would be similarly situated to such members, we think it unlikely that the Sklars are. Religious education for elementary or secondary school children does not appear to be similar to the "auditing" and "training" conducted by the Church of Scientology. Id. at 618 n. 13; see also Hernandez v. Comm'r, 490 U.S. 680, 684–85, 109 S.Ct. 2136, 104 L.Ed.2d 766 (1989) (describing "auditing" and "training").

The *Sklar I* panel then turned to the Sklars' Establishment Clause and administrative consistency arguments. Although it was not required to decide those issues because the Sklars had "failed to show that their tuition payments constitute a partially deductible 'dual payment' under the Tax Code," Sklar I, 282 F.3d at 620, the panel noted that had it been required to do so, it would have first concluded that the IRS policy constitutes an unconstitutional denominational preference under Larson v. Valente, 456 U.S. 228, 102 S.Ct. 1673, 72 L.Ed.2d 33 (1982). See Sklar I, 282 F.3d at 618–19. The panel reasoned that the denominational preference embodied in the Closing Agreement was unconstitutional because it "cannot be justified by a compelling governmental interest." Id. However, the panel indicated it would not be willing to extend that preference to other religious organizations for three reasons: First, an extension of the preference would amount to state sponsorship of all religions, which the panel doubted "Congress or any agency of the government would intend." Id. at 619–20. Second, an extension of the preference would be "of questionable constitutional validity under Lemon," because administering the policy "could require excessive government entanglement with religion."[5] Id. at

---

5. In Hernandez v. Commissioner, 490 U.S. 680, 109 S.Ct. 2136, 104 L.Ed.2d 766 (1989), the Supreme Court rejected the claim that payments made to the Church of Scientology for purely religious education and training were deductible as gifts or contributions under I.R.C. § 170. Id. at 692–94, 109 S.Ct. 2136. Among other reasons it gave for its decision, the Court explained that "the deduction petitioners seek might raise problems of entanglement between church and state." Id. at 694, 109 S.Ct. 2136; see also infra Part II.B (discussing § 170 and Hernandez).

620, 91 S.Ct. 2105. Third, the requested policy appeared to violate I.R.C. § 170. Id.

The panel also indicated it would reject the Sklars' administrative consistency claim because it "seriously doubted" that the Sklars were similarly situated to the Scientologists.[6] The panel further stated that even if the Sklars were similarly situated, "because the treatment they seek is of questionable statutory and constitutional validity under § 170 of the IRC, under *Lemon,* and under *Hernandez,* we would not hold that the unlawful policy set forth in the closing agreement must be extended to all religious organizations." Id. at 620, 91 S.Ct. 2105.

Finally, relying on United States v. American Bar Endowment, 477 U.S. 105, 106 S.Ct. 2426, 91 L.Ed.2d 89 (1986), the *Sklar I* panel rejected the argument that the Sklars' tuition payments were deductible as a "dual payment" or "quid pro quo payment," a payment made in part as consideration for goods and services and in part for charitable purposes. In *American Bar Endowment,* the Supreme Court held that the taxpayer must satisfy a two-part test to be entitled to the § 170 deduction for a quid pro quo payment:

> First, the payment is deductible only if and to the extent it exceeds the market value of the benefit received. Second, the excess payment must be made with the intention of making a gift.

477 U.S. at 117, 106 S.Ct. 2426 (internal citation and quotation marks omitted). The *Sklar I* panel held that the Sklars failed to introduce evidence demonstrating both "that any dual tuition payments they may have made exceeded the market value of the secular education their children received," 282 F.3d at 621, or "that they intended to make a *gift* by contributing such 'excess payment.' " Id. The panel also suggested that for the purpose of demonstrating the first part of the *American Bar Endowment* test, the "market value" for the tuition payments would be the cost of a comparable secular education offered by private schools, evidence the Sklars had failed to introduce, perhaps, because of the "practical realities of the high cost of education." Id.

C.   The Current Litigation

On their 1995 tax return, the Sklars claimed $15,000 in deductions for purported charitable contributions that comprised a portion of their five children's tuition at Emek and Yeshiva Rav. The deduction was based on their estimate that 55% of the tuition payments were for purely religious education, an estimate supported by letters submitted two years later (in 1997) that were drafted by each of the schools at the Sklars' request. Sklar, 125 T.C. at 288–89.

---

6. Judge Silverman, concurring, concluded that the question of whether the Sklars were "similarly situated" to the Scientologists had "no bearing on whether the tax code permits the Sklars to deduct the costs of their children's religious education as a charitable contribution." Sklar I, 282 F.3d at 622. Rather, he concluded that the Sklars were absolutely barred from taking the deduction by the Internal Revenue Code and Supreme Court precedent. See id. at 622–23.

The IRS disallowed the $15,000 deduction. The IRS also determined the Sklars had "failed to meet the substantiation requirements of Internal Revenue Code Section 170(f)(8) with respect to the disallowed $15,000.00 of claimed charitable contributions." The Sklars petitioned the Tax Court for a redetermination of deficiency, asserting that (1) the tuition and fee payments to exclusively religious schools are deductible under a dual payment analysis to the extent the payments exceeded the value of the secular education their children received (a question left somewhat open in *Sklar I*); (2) Sections 170(f)(8) and 6115 of the Internal Revenue Code, as enacted in 1993, authorized the deduction of tuition payments for religious education made to exclusively religious schools (an issue all but foreclosed by *Sklar I*); and (3) that the 1993 Closing Agreement between the Commissioner and the Church of Scientology constitutionally and administratively requires the IRS to allow other taxpayers to take the same charitable deductions for tuition payments to their religious schools (a question the panel discussed at length but declined to decide in *Sklar I*). Before the Tax Court, the Sklars and the IRS stipulated that in 1993 the IRS had executed a confidential closing agreement with the Church of Scientology, settling several outstanding issues between the IRS and the Church of Scientology. See id. at 298. Under this agreement, members of the Church of Scientology were authorized to deduct as charitable contributions at least 80% of the fees for qualified religious services provided by the Church of Scientology. See id. at 298–99.

The Tax Court again rejected the Sklars' arguments, holding that the tuition and fee payments to the Jewish Day Schools were not deductible under any of the Sklars' theories.[7] [The court then summarized the Tax Court's holdings. Ed.]

II. DISCUSSION

* * *

B. The Sklars' 1995 Tuition Payments Are Not Deductible as Charitable Contributions Under the Internal Revenue Code

Section 170 of the Internal Revenue Code allows taxpayers to deduct "any charitable contribution," defined as "a contribution or gift to or for the use of" certain eligible entities enumerated in § 170(c), including those exclusively organized for religious purposes and educational purposes. I.R.C. § 170(a)(1), (c). "[T]o ensure that the payor's primary purpose is to assist the charity and not to secure some benefit," we require such contributions to be "made for detached and disinterested motives." Graham v. Comm'r, 822 F.2d 844, 848 (9th Cir.1987). Therefore, "quid pro quo" payments, where the taxpayer receives a benefit in exchange for the payment, are generally not deductible as charitable contributions. See Hernandez v. Comm'r, 490 U.S. 680, 689–91, 109 S.Ct. 2136, 104 L.Ed.2d 766 (1989). In keeping with this framework, tuition payments to parochial

---

7. The Tax Court also ruled that the Sklars were not liable for an accuracy-related penalty the IRS had imposed under I.R.C. § 6662, an issue not before us on this appeal.

schools, which are made with the expectation of a substantial benefit, or quid pro quo, "have long been held not to be charitable contributions under § 170." Id. at 693, 109 S.Ct. 2136; see also DeJong v. Comm'r, 309 F.2d 373, 376 (9th Cir.1962) ("The law is well settled that tuition paid for the education of the children of a taxpayer is a family expense, not a charitable contribution to the educating institution.").

In *Hernandez*, the Supreme Court considered "whether taxpayers may deduct as charitable contributions payments made to branch churches of the Church of Scientology"[8] in return for services known as "auditing" and "training." 490 U.S. at 684, 109 S.Ct. 2136. Both are considered forms of religious education. "Auditing" involves a form of spiritual counseling whereby a person gains spiritual awareness in one-on-one sessions with an auditor. By participating in "training," a person studies the tenets of Scientology, gains spiritually, and may seek to become an auditor. Members of the Church of Scientology sought to deduct payments for auditing and training as charitable contributions for religious services. The Court held that such payments for religious educational services "do not qualify as 'contribution[s] or gift[s].'" Id. at 691, 109 S.Ct. 2136. Rather, "[t]hese payments were part of a quintessential quid pro quo exchange: in return for their money, petitioners received an identifiable benefit, namely, auditing and training sessions." Id. The Court reasoned "'[t]he sine qua non of a charitable contribution is a transfer of money or property without adequate consideration." Id. (quoting American Bar Endowment, 477 U.S. at 118, 106 S.Ct. 2426).

The Court further rejected the taxpayers' argument that a quid pro quo analysis was not even appropriate, because the payments for auditing and training services resulted in receipt of a purely religious benefit. Id. at 692–93, 109 S.Ct. 2136. The Court first found no support in the language of § 170, which makes "no special preference for payments made in the expectation of gaining religious benefits or access to a religious service." Id. at 693, 109 S.Ct. 2136. Second, the Court reasoned that accepting the taxpayers' "deductibility proposal would expand the charitable contribution deduction far beyond what Congress has provided." Id. at 693, 109 S.Ct. 2136. For example, "some taxpayers might regard their tuition payments to parochial schools as generating a religious benefit or as securing access to a religious service," which would be incorrect because "such payments ... have long been held not to be charitable contributions under § 170." Id. Finally, the Court noted that "the deduction petitioners seek might raise problems of entanglement between church and state" because it would "inexorably force the IRS and reviewing courts to differentiate 'religious'

---

8. In Hernandez, the Commissioner had stipulated before the Tax Court that "the branch churches of Scientology are religious organizations entitled to receive tax-deductible charitable contributions under the relevant sections of the Code." 490 U.S. at 686, 109 S.Ct. 2136. This stipulation isolated the statutory issue of "whether payments for auditing or training sessions constitute 'contribution[s] or gift[s]' under § 170." Id. Similarly, the parties to the current litigation stipulated before the Tax Court "that an agreement dated October 1, 1993, between the Commissioner and the Church of Scientology settled several longstanding issues." 125 T.C. at 298.

benefits from 'secular' ones." Id. at 694, 109 S.Ct. 2136. While declining to pass on the constitutionality of such hypothetical inquiries, the Court noted that " 'pervasive monitoring' for the 'subtle or overt presence of religious matter' is a central danger against which we have held the Establishment Clause guards." Id. (quoting Aguilar v. Felton, 473 U.S. 402, 413, 105 S.Ct. 3232, 87 L.Ed.2d 290 (1985)). Thus, the *Hernandez* decision clearly forecloses the Sklars' argument that there is an exception in the Code for payments for which one receives purely religious benefits.

1. The 1993 Amendments to the Tax Code Did Not Overrule Hernandez

To circumvent *Hernandez's* clear holding, the Sklars resurrect their *Sklar I* argument that the 1993 amendments to IRS §§ 170(f)(8) and 6115 overruled the Court's holding in *Hernandez* that only gifts or contributions may be deducted under § 170. According to the Sklars, the 1993 amendments provide for the deduction of tuition payments for which they receive only intangible religious benefits. We agree with the Tax Court that the Sklar's interpretation of the 1993 amendments is misguided.

Amended § 170(f)(8) requires the taxpayer to "substantiate * * * the contribution by a contemporaneous written acknowledgment of the contribution by the donee organization." I.R.C. § 170(f)(8)(A). This acknowledgment must include an estimate of the value of any goods or services the donor received in exchange, "or, if such goods or services consist solely of intangible religious benefits, a statement to that effect." I.R.C. § 170(f)(8)(B)(iii). The amendment also defines an "intangible religious benefit" as one "which is provided by an organization organized exclusively for religious purposes and which generally is not sold in a commercial transaction outside the donative context." Id. As the Tax Court correctly held, *Sklar,* 125 T.C. at 296–97, and as we have previously suggested, Sklar I, 282 F.3d at 613, this amendment creates an exception only to the new substantiation requirement created by § 170(f)(8)(A). Nothing in the amendment's language suggests that Congress intended to expand the types of payments that are deductible contributions. As the *Sklar I* panel explained:

> Given the clear holding of *Hernandez* and the absence of any direct evidence of Congressional intent to overrule the Supreme Court on this issue, we would be extremely reluctant to read an additional and significant substantive deduction into the statute based on what are clearly procedural provisions regarding the documentation of tax return information, particularly where the deduction would be of doubtful constitutional validity.

The second pertinent 1993 amendment requires donee organizations to disclose limitations on the deductibility of certain quid pro quo payments to the donors of such payments. See I.R.C. § 6115. Amended § 6115(a) requires any organization that "receives a quid pro quo contribution in excess of $75" to provide the donor with a written statement declaring that the deductible portion of the contribution cannot include "the value of the goods or services provided by the organization," along with "a good faith estimate of the value of such goods or services." However, § 6115(b) explains:

> *For purposes of this section,* the term "quid pro quo contribution" means a payment made partly as a contribution and partly in consideration for goods or services provided to the payor by the donee organization. A quid pro quo contribution does not include any payment made to an organization, organized exclusively for religious purposes, in return for which the taxpayer receives solely an intangible religious benefit that generally is not sold in a commercial transaction outside the donative context.

I.R.C. § 6115(b) (emphasis added). The Sklars read the exemption from the disclosure requirement for organizations organized exclusively for religious purposes which provide solely an intangible religious benefit completely out of context. The *Sklar I* panel explained why the Sklars' reading of the exemption is unsupportable:

> [Section] 6115 requires that tax-exempt organizations inform taxpayer-donors that they will receive a tax deduction only for the amount of their donation above the value of any goods or services received in return for the donation and requires donee organizations to give donors an estimate of this value, exempting *from this estimate requirement* contributions for which solely intangible religious benefits are received.

282 F.3d at 613.

Nor does the legislative history of these amendments even mention *Hernandez,* and the House Report specifically states that, although the new requirements apply only to quid pro quo contributions for *commercial* benefits, "[n]o inference is intended ... [regarding] whether or not any contribution outside the scope of the bill's substantiation or reporting requirements is deductible (in full or in part) under the present-law requirements of section 170." H.R.Rep. No. 103–111, at 786 n. 170 (1993), reprinted in 1993 U.S.C.C.A.N. 378, 1017 n. 170. Thus, the House Report confirms that Congress intended to preserve the status quo ante, and hardly serves as support for the Sklars' argument.[10]

To put to rest the Sklars' statutory claim, we now hold that neither the plain language of the 1993 amendments nor the accompanying legislative history indicates any substantive change to Hernandez's holding that payment for religious education to religious organizations is not deductible. We agree with the observation of both the Tax Court and the *Sklar I* panel that had Congress intended to overrule judicial precedent and to provide charitable contributions for tuition and fee payments to religious organiza-

---

10. In light of certain well-established deductible payments to religious organizations in exchange for intangible religious benefits, such as pew rents and church dues, see Hernandez, 490 U.S. at 701–02, 109 S.Ct. 2136, it seems plausible that Congress contemplated these sorts of contributions in amending §§ 170(f)(8) and 6115 in a manner that did not impose the arduous task of valuing the intangible religious benefits, such as the ability to participate in religious celebrations, that donors receive in exchange for these contributions.

tions that provide religious education, it would have expressed its intention more clearly. See 282 F.3d at 613, 125 T.C. at 296–97.

2.   The Tuition Payments Were Not Dual Payment Contributions

The Tax Court correctly concluded that no part of the Sklar's tuition payments is deductible under a "dual payment analysis." See Sklar, 125 T.C. at 290–94, 299–300. In *American Bar Endowment,* the Supreme Court considered the question of the extent to which payments to organizations that bear the "dual character" of a purchase and a contribution are deductible under § 170. 477 U.S. at 116–18, 106 S.Ct. 2426. IRS Revenue Ruling 67–246 had set forth a two-part test for determining the extent to which such payments are deductible:

> First, the payment is deductible only if and to the extent it exceeds the market value of the benefit received. Second, the excess payment must be "made with the intention of making a gift."

Id. at 117, 106 S.Ct. 2426 (quoting Rev. Rul. 67–246, 1967–2 Cum. Bull. 104, 105 (1967)). The Court held that Revenue Ruling 67–246 embodied the proper standard, reasoning: "The *sine qua non* of a charitable contribution is a transfer of money or property without adequate consideration. The taxpayer, therefore, must at a minimum demonstrate that he purposely contributed money or property in excess of the value of any benefit he received in return." Id. at 118, 106 S.Ct. 2426.

* * *

The Sklars again have failed to meet their burden of satisfying either prong of the two-part test for a dual payment, and we seriously doubt that they could ever make the showing that would support a "dual payment" deduction for tuition for combined religious and secular education.[11] In *Sklar I,* the panel concluded that the Sklars failed to satisfy the requirements for partial deductibility of their tuition payments. Our analysis has not changed, despite the Sklars' effort to introduce evidence as to market value.

First, the *Sklar I* panel reasoned that the Sklars "failed to show that they intended to make a *gift* by contributing any such 'excess payment.' " 282 F.3d at 621. In fact, the Sklars have never even *argued*—not in *Sklar I,* not before the Tax Court and not before us—that they intended to make a gift as a portion of their tuition payment. Indeed, the record is to the contrary. In their brief, the Sklars explain at length that they pay the tuition and fees to send their children to Orthodox Jewish schools because it is a religious imperative of Orthodox Judaism. They "sent their children to Yeshiva Rav Isacsohn and Emek in 1995 because of their sincerely and deeply held religious belief that as Jews they have a religious obligation to provide their children with an Orthodox Jewish education in an Orthodox Jewish environment." Because they paid for religious education out of their

---

11. Indeed, the Tax Court expressed skepticism as to whether a dual payment analysis would ever be appropriate in this context. See 125 T.C. at 293 ("[M]ore fundamentally, the record speaks to whether a dual payments analysis applies in this case at all.").

own deeply held religious views, and because the record demonstrates that throughout the school day-during recess, lunch and secular, as well as religious, classes-the schools inculcate their children with their religion's lifestyle, heritage, and values, the Sklars have actually demonstrated the absence of the requisite charitable intent.

Second, the *Sklar I* panel reasoned that "the Sklars have not shown that any dual tuition payments they may have made exceeded the market value of the secular education their children received." Id. The panel stated that the Sklars needed to present evidence that their total payments exceeded "[t]he market value [of] the cost of a comparable secular education offered by private schools." Id. Before the Tax Court, the Sklars introduced expert testimony asserting that "Catholic schools are the most reasonable comparison benchmarks for the schools attended by the Sklar children." Based on his estimation of tuition paid for Archdiocesan Catholic schools[12] in Los Angeles County in 1995, the Sklars' expert concluded that the market value of the secular education the Sklars' children received was between $1483 and $1724, such that in 1995 the Sklars made "excess payments" of almost $5000 per child. The Sklars' expert also included tuition data for other Los Angeles schools in his report. The Tax Court correctly concluded that the evidence in the record indicated: "(1) Some schools charge more tuition than Emek and Yeshiva Rav Isacsohn, and some charge less; and (2) the amount of tuition petitioners paid is unremarkable and is not excessive for the substantial benefit they received in exchange; i.e., an education for their children." 125 T.C. at 293–94. Before us, the Sklars have failed to demonstrate—or even argue on appeal—that the Tax Court's factual findings as to the data set forth in their expert's report are clearly erroneous.

Thus, the Tax Court did not err by concluding that the Sklars failed to show that any part of their tuition fees was a charitable deduction, subject to a dual payment analysis. We conclude that under *Hernandez* and the Internal Revenue Code, their tuition and fee payments must be treated like any other quid pro quo transaction, even if some part of the benefit received was religious in nature. *See* 490 U.S. at 691–94, 109 S.Ct. 2136. We therefore agree with the Tax Court that the Sklars' tuition is not deductible, in whole or in part, under § 170.

C. The 1993 Closing Agreement Does Not Constitutionally and Administratively Require the IRS To Allow Charitable Deductions for the Sklars' Tuition Payments to Religious Schools

[In this part of the opinion, the court rejected the Sklars' arguments that, since the IRS allowed similar deductions for members of the Church

---

12. The flaws in the expert report itself are too numerous to mention, but we point out only one: the archdiocesan schools are subsidized in large measure by the parishes in the Archdiocese in order to force down the costs of education and to afford all Catholic children the opportunity to attend Catholic schools. Thus, by choosing archdiocesan schools as the basis for his comparative market value, the Sklars' expert guaranteed that the tuition and fees paid to the Sklars' schools would greatly exceed the tuition at the archdiocesan Catholic schools.

of Scientology as part of a comprehensive settlement, the disallowance of deductions for Orthodox Jewish religious education violates the Establishment Clause and principles of administrative consistency. They also argued that the agreement with Scientology constitutionally and administratively precluded the IRS from disallowing their deductions for school tuition and fees, which are "jurisprudentially indistinguishable" from the auditing and training provided by the Church of Scientology.

Like the Tax Court and Ninth Circuit panel in *Sklar I*, the court found that the Sklars were not similarly situated to the Scientologists because "tuition and fee payments to schools that provide secular and religious education as part of one curriculum are quite different from payments to organizations that provide exclusively religious services." It also rejected the claims of unconstitutional denominational preference and administrative inconsistency because "[t]o conclude otherwise would be tantamount to rewriting the Tax Code, disregarding Supreme Court precedent, only to reach a conclusion directly at odds with the Establishment Clause—all in the name of the Establishment Clause." The court was concerned that if it allowed the deductions claimed by the Sklars, the "logic" of such a holding "would extend to all members of religious organizations who benefit from educational services that are in whole or part religious in nature." Eds.]

CONCLUSION

The Tax Court correctly affirmed the IRS's disallowance of deductions the Sklars claimed for tuition and fees paid to their children's Orthodox Jewish day schools. The decision of the Tax Court is AFFIRMED.

NOTES AND QUESTIONS

1. *Confusion About Scientology.* In Hernandez v. Commissioner, 490 U.S. 680, 109 S.Ct. 2136 (1989), the Supreme Court held that payments made by members of the Church of Scientology to branch chapters for "auditing" and "training" services were not deductible as charitable contributions. The Court provided this description of the theology underlying the payments:

> Scientologists believe that an immortal spiritual being exists in every person. A person becomes aware of this spiritual dimension through a process known as "auditing." Auditing involves a one-to-one encounter between a participant (known as a "preclear") and a Church official (known as an "auditor"). An electronic device, the E-meter, helps the auditor identify the preclear's areas of spiritual difficulty by measuring skin responses during a question and answer session. Although auditing sessions are conducted one on one, the content of each session is not individually tailored. The preclear gains spiritual awareness by progressing through sequential levels of auditing, provided in short blocks of time known as "intensives."
>
> The Church also offers members doctrinal courses known as "training." Participants in these sessions study the tenets of Scientolo-

gy and seek to attain the qualifications necessary to serve as auditors. Training courses, like auditing sessions, are provided in sequential levels. Scientologists are taught that spiritual gains result from participation in such courses.

The Church charges a "fixed donation," also known as a "price" or a "fixed contribution," for participants to gain access to auditing and training sessions. These charges are set forth in schedules, and prices vary with a session's length and level of sophistication. In 1972, for example, the general rates for auditing ranged from $625 for a 12 1/2–hour auditing intensive, the shortest available, to $4,250 for a 100–hour intensive, the longest available. Specialized types of auditing required higher fixed donations: a 12 1/2–hour "Integrity Processing" auditing intensive cost $750; a 12 1/2–hour "Expanded Dianetics" auditing intensive cost $950. This system of mandatory fixed charges is based on a central tenet of Scientology known as the "doctrine of exchange," according to which any time a person receives something he must pay something back. In so doing, a Scientologist maintains "inflow" and "outflow" and avoids spiritual decline.

490 U.S. at 684–685.

The Court concluded that the auditing and training payments were not gifts because they were part of a "quintessential quid pro quo exchange." Influential factors were the taxpayer's receipt of an "identifiable benefit;" the Church had fixed price schedules, calibrating fees to the length and level of services; no free services were provided; and the proceeds from auditing and training were the Church's primary source of income.

The Church also argued that the IRS had violated its First Amendment rights to freedom of religion and engaged in administrative inconsistency by allowing a charitable deduction for dues and other payments to churches and synagogues for their religious services while denying deduction to Scientologists for comparable intangible religious benefits. The Court rejected the First Amendment claims and ducked the selective prosecution argument, finding an insufficient factual record at the trial level as to the types and structure of these religiously-motivated payments to other faiths. In their dissent, Justices O'Connor and Scalia characterized the IRS's position as "a singular exception to its 70–year practice of allowing fixed payments indistinguishable from those made by[the Scientologists] to be deducted as charitable contributions." 490 U.S. at 704. The dissenters found these "irrational distinctions" to be unprincipled and constitutionally discriminatory.

As discussed by the Ninth Circuit in *Sklar*, the IRS—despite the victory in *Hernandez*—settled its long battle against the Church of Scientology in 1993, granted tax-exempt status to numerous Scientology entities, and "obsoleted" the 1978 revenue ruling in which it had disallowed charitable deductions for "fixed donations" to the church. Rev. Rul. 93–73, 1993–2 C.B. 75. The settlement agreement was not released to the public, and the Service did not explain why it had abandoned a legal position on the charitable deduction issue that had been sustained by the Supreme Court.

The terms of the 1993 settlement eventually were leaked to the public, first by the Wall Street Journal in an Internet posting and then more broadly in the mainstream press. See, e.g., Douglas Frantz, $12.5 Million Deal with IRS Lifted Cloud Over Scientologists, N.Y. Times, Dec. 31, 1997, at A1 and A13. In exchange for a payment of $12.5 million, the Service agreed to discontinue audits of thirteen Scientology entities, abate tax penalties, and grant exempt status to 114 domestic Scientology branches. The church agreed to drop its lawsuits against the Service and to create a special oversight committee to monitor the church's tax compliance and report annually to the Service for three years. This is an unusually high level of government oversight of a religious organization. The entire closing agreement is reprinted in 19 Exempt Org. Tax Rev. 227 (1998).

Some former IRS officials praised the Service for its innovative approach to resolving a long and bitter dispute, while other commentators criticized the Service for "caving" in response to continued harassment by the Church of Scientology. See Fred Stokeld, Purported Closing Agreement Reveals Scientology Paid Government $12.5 Million, 19 Exempt Org. Tax Rev. 152 (1998).

Is *Hernandez* still good law? How could it not be? If it is, how could the IRS legally enter into the closing agreement with the Church of Scientology? Are you sympathetic to the arguments of the Sklars, or are they overreaching by attempting to deduct expenses for personal consumption? Would the result in *Sklar* been different if the Sklars could have proven that their children were only receiving "religious" education?

2. *For Further Reading.* Allan J. Samansky, Deductibility of Contributions to Religious Institutions, 24 Va. Tax Rev. 65 (2004).

4.   Percentage Limitations and Carryovers

Internal Revenue Code: § 170(b), (d)(1).

When it first enacted the charitable income tax deduction in 1917, Congress did not intend the deduction to be unlimited. The earliest predecessor of § 170 limited an individual taxpayer's charitable deduction to 15 percent of the donor's "net income." Since then, Congress has become so enamored of the percentage limitation concept that it has constructed a mind numbing web of often overlapping rules that contributes to the corpulence of § 170. The limitations reflect a judgment that no taxpayer should completely avoid federal income tax by making charitable contributions. As a practical matter, they affect only the most generous philanthropists.

Several different types of percentage limitations apply for purposes of determining an individual taxpayer's income tax charitable deduction. The "basic percentage limitation" varies based on the type of organization receiving the gift. Other limitations apply to gifts of long-term capital gain property. Finally, the percentage limitation applicable to a particular gift also is affected by whether the gift is "to" or merely "for the use of" the charity. The percentage limitations for individual taxpayers are applied with reference to the taxpayer's "contribution base," which is defined as "adjusted gross income * * * computed without regard to any net operating loss carryback to the taxable year * * *." I.R.C. § 170(b)(1)(F).

The Basic 50% and 30% Limitations. Qualified recipients of charitable contributions are divided into two general categories for purposes of the basic percentage limitation. The preferred group—known as "50 percent charities"—includes schools, hospitals, churches, medical research organizations, government entities, publicly supported charities and certain operating and supporting foundations. I.R.C. § 170(b)(1)(A). The second and less favored category—the "30 percent charities"—consists primarily of private foundations. For the background of these distinctions, see Chapter 7A2, infra, at pp. 712–715.

Gifts of cash and ordinary income property to 50 percent charities qualify for the maximum allowable annual charitable deduction—50 percent of a donor's contribution base. Contributions in excess of the 50 percent limit may be carried forward and deducted, subject to the same 50 percent limit, over the five taxable years following the gift. I.R.C. § 170(d)(1). Gifts to private foundations generally may be deducted up to a 30 percent limit, with a five-year carryover of any excess. I.R.C. § 170(b)(1)(C). In addition, gifts "for the use of" even the most favored group of charities (e.g., gifts in trust) are subject to the 30 percent limit.

In applying these limitations, gifts to 50 percent charities are considered first. Gifts to 30 percent charities are currently deductible only to the extent that, when added to gifts to 50 percent charities, they do not result in total gifts exceeding the overall 50 percent limit. Stated more technically, the 30 percent limit is the lesser of: (1) 30 percent of a donor's contribution base for the year, or (2) 50 percent of the contribution base less gifts that qualify for the 50 percent limit. I.R.C. § 170(b)(1)(B).

To illustrate the relationship between the basic limitations, assume Donor ("D") has adjusted gross income (D's "contribution base") of $100,000 and contributes $40,000 cash to Public Charity and $25,000 to Private Foundation. D's gift to Public Charity, which is counted first, is fully deductible because it does not exceed the 50 percent limit, but only $10,000 of D's gift to Private Foundation is currently deductible. Although the private foundation gift did not exceed 30 percent of D's contribution base, it is deductible only to the extent of the difference between 50 percent of D's contribution base ($50,000) and the amount of D's gifts to 50 percent charities ($40,000). The $15,000 excess may be carried over for the five succeeding years.

Gifts of Capital Gain Property. The basic percentage limitations described above apply to gifts of cash and ordinary income property. Additional limitations are imposed on gifts of long-term capital gain property, a category consisting of capital and § 1231 assets (e.g., securities, art and other collectibles, and most investment real estate) which, if sold, would result in long-term capital gain. I.R.C. § 170(b)(1)(C)(iv). A capital asset is "long-term" when it has been held for more than one year. I.R.C. § 1222(3).

A donor may deduct the fair market value of gifts of capital gain property to "50 percent" public charities to the extent that the total amount for the year does not exceed 30 percent of the donor's contribution base. Any excess may be carried forward for five years, subject in each succeeding year to the same percentage limitation. I.R.C. § 170(b)(1)(C). Special rules discussed later in this chapter may reduce the amount of the charitable deduction for gifts of certain tangible personal property that is not used by the donee for its exempt purposes. See I.R.C. § 170(e)(1)(B)(i). See Section C3 of this chapter, infra, at pp. 876–877.

Some gifts of capital gain property to private foundations may be subject to double punishment. In general, the amount of the gift first must be reduced by the long-term capital gain that would have been recognized if the donor had sold rather than contributed the property. I.R.C. § 170(e)(1)(B)(ii).[1] This reduced amount (or the fair market value, if property with a basis in excess of its value is contributed) then may be deducted only to the extent of 20 percent of the donor's contribution base. I.R.C. § 170(b)(1)(D).

Special Stepdown Election. A special elective provision permits a donor to avoid the 30 percent limitation on gifts of capital gain property to the favored group of charities and instead be subject to the 50 percent limitation. The trade-off is that the donor must reduce the value of all gifts of appreciated capital gain property to those organizations by the entire gain that would have been recognized if the property had been sold for its fair market value rather than contributed. I.R.C. § 170(b)(1)(C)(iii). If this election is made, it applies to all gifts of capital gain property made during the year and to any carryovers from and to the year in which the election is made.

The effect of the stepdown election is that the charitable deduction is limited to the donor's basis in the donated capital gain property. The election may be useful when the amount of appreciation inherent in the property is small or where the gift is so large that the donor would not have been able to deduct its full value, even over the five-year carryover period, if the gift were subject to the 30 percent limitation.

Relationship Between the Percentage Limitations. The relationship between the various percentage limitations is very technical, especially in years when a donor has both current gifts and contribution carryovers from prior years and has made gifts of both cash and capital gain property to the different categories of donees. Fortunately, excellent computer software is available to sort out these relationships, either at the planning stage or

---

1. The reduction to basis rule does not apply, however, to gifts of "qualified appreciated stock," a category that generally includes publicly traded securities provided that the donor and certain related persons have not contributed more than 10 percent of the corporation's outstanding stock to private foundations. I.R.C. § 170(e)(5).

when preparing the donor's tax return. For purposes of this overview, it will suffice to summarize the ordering rules that emerge from the many examples in the § 170 regulations. In any given year, a donor's charitable deduction is determined by taking into account contributions in the following order: (1) gifts qualifying under the 50 percent limitation actually made during the year, (2) carryovers of 50 percent contributions made during the preceding five years, (3) contributions of cash and ordinary income property made to 30 percent charities during the current year, (4) carryovers of excess 30 percent cash and ordinary income property contributions made during the preceding five years, (5) contributions of 30 percent capital gain property made during the year, (6) carryovers of excess 30 percent capital gain property from the preceding five years, (7) contributions of 20 percent capital gain property made during the year, and (8) carryovers of excess 20 percent capital gain property from the preceding five years. But as we said, software is available, so never mind—and we'll skip the examples!

Corporate Contributions. The percentage limitation on charitable contributions by corporations is 10 percent of the corporation's taxable income, after certain technical adjustments. I.R.C. § 170(b)(2). Amounts in excess of this limit may be carried forward and deducted in the five years following the gift. I.R.C. § 170(d)(2). Gifts authorized during the year by accrual method corporations may be deducted even if not actually paid up to two months and fifteen days after the close of the year, provided an election to that effect is made. See I.R.C. § 170(a)(2). Contributions by Subchapter S corporations, which generally are not taxable entities, pass through to the shareholders, who may deduct their respective portion subject to the appropriate percentage limitations applicable to individuals. Similar pass-through rules apply to contributions by partnerships and limited liability companies.

For Further Reading. For scholarly discussion of the policy for the percentage limitations, see Miranda Perry Fleischer, Generous to a Fault? Fair Shares and Charitable Giving, 93 Minn. L. Rev. 165 (2008).

5.   SUBSTANTIATION AND COMPLIANCE RULES

Internal Revenue Code: §§ 170(f)(8); 6113; 6115; 6710; 6714.

Treasury Regulations: § 1.170A–13(a), (f); 1.6115–1.

Individual taxpayers deduct charitable contributions on Schedule A of Form 1040, listing on separate lines their cash and property contributions. It is sufficient to list the aggregate amount of cash contributions, without providing a list of donees and specific amounts. In the event of an audit, however, taxpayers must substantiate their gifts. Historically, this could be accomplished by providing a cancelled check, a receipt from the donee showing the name of the charity and the amount and date of the gift, or "other reliable written records" showing the information required on a receipt. Treas. Reg. § 1.170A–13(a).

Despite attempts by the Internal Revenue Service to educate charities and their donors, Congress ultimately concluded that more rigorous substantiation and disclosure requirements were necessary to patrol against inflated charitable deductions and misleading solicitations. The Senate Finance Committee explained why these changes were necessary:[1]

> Difficult problems of tax administration arise with respect to fundraising techniques in which an organization that is eligible to receive tax deductible contributions provides goods or services in consideration for payments from donors. Organizations that engage in such fundraising practices often do not inform their donors that all or a portion of the amount paid by the donor may not be deductible as a charitable contribution. Consequently, the committee believes that there will be increased compliance with present-law rules governing charitable contribution deductions if a taxpayer who claims a separate charitable contribution of $250 or more is required to obtain substantiation from the donee indicating the amount of the contribution and whether any goods, service, or privilege was received by the donor in exchange for making the contribution. In addition, the committee believes it is appropriate that when a charity receives a *quid pro quo* contribution in excess of $75 (i.e., a payment exceeding $75 made partly as a gift and partly in consideration for a benefit furnished to the payor), the charity should inform the donor that the deduction under section 170 is limited to the amount by which the payment exceeds the value of the goods or service furnished by the charity, and should provide a good faith estimate of the value of such goods or service.

Substantiation of Gifts of $250 or More. To implement this policy, Congress enacted § 170(f)(8), which provides that no charitable deduction shall be allowed for a separate contribution of $250 or more unless the taxpayer substantiates the contribution with a contemporaneous written acknowledgement from the donee organization. The responsibility for obtaining this substantiation lies with the donor. The acknowledgment must include the following information: (1) the amount of cash and a description (but not the value) of any property other than cash contributed, (2) whether the donee provided any return benefits in the form of goods or services, and (3) a description and good faith estimate of the value of any goods or services provided to the donor in exchange for making the gift, or if such goods or services consist solely of "intangible religious benefits," a statement to that effect. I.R.C. § 170(f)(8)(B); Treas. Reg. § 1.170A–13(f)(2). The term "intangible religious benefit" is defined as any intangible religious benefit provided by an organization organized exclusively for religious purposes and where the benefit is not sold in a commercial transaction outside the donative context. I.R.C. § 170(f)(8)(B). No particular form is prescribed for the charity's acknowledgment, but it is clear that a cancelled check is not sufficient. The contemporaneous requirement is

---

1. Explanation of Senate Finance Committee Revenue Provisions, Revenue Reconciliation Act of 1993, 103d Cong., 1st Sess. 221 (1993).

met if the acknowledgement is obtained on or before the earlier of the date that the taxpayer files a return for the year of the contribution, or the due date (including extensions) for filing the return. I.R.C. § 170(f)(8)(C); Treas. Reg. § 1.170A–13(f)(3). These special substantiation rules are waived for the donor if the donee organization files an annual information return reporting all the required information on gifts of $250 or more made during the year. I.R.C. § 170(f)(8)(D).

The substantiation rules raise numerous technical questions that seem trivial when viewed in isolation but can be important to charitable organizations engaged in substantial fundraising. Guidance can be found in the regulations, which make it clear that separate payments are treated as separate contributions and thus are not aggregated for purposes of the $250 threshold, and that contributions made by payroll deductions will be treated as separate payments. Treas. Reg. § 1.170A–13(f)(1), (11).

Substantiation of Gifts of Less than $250. Beginning in 2007, donors are subject to stricter substantiation rules for cash gifts of less than $250. They must have reliable written proof, such as a bank or credit card record (e.g., a cancelled check will suffice) or a written communication from the charity (e-mails are permitted), providing the date and amount of the contribution. A diary or other informal record of small gifts no longer will suffice. I.R.C. § 170(f)(17). The regulations exempt unreimbursed expenses under $250 for services rendered to charity. For guidance on how to handle these new recordkeeping requirements for gifts made by payroll deduction, see I.R.S. Notice 2006–110, I.R.B. 2006–51 I.R.B. 1127.

Information Disclosure for Quid Pro Quo Contributions. A charitable organization that receives a *quid pro quo* contribution in excess of $75 must provide, in connection with the solicitation or receipt of the contribution, a good faith estimate of the value of the goods or services and inform the donor in writing that only the excess of the contribution is deductible. I.R.C. § 6115(a); Treas. Reg. § 1.6115–1(a)(1). A "quid pro quo" contribution is a payment that is "made partly as a contribution and partly in consideration [for return benefits in the form of] goods or services." I.R.C. § 6115(b). For example, if a donor pays $100 to attend a fund raising event and receives in exchange a $40 dinner, the charity must inform the donor that only $60 is tax-deductible. The legislative history states that the disclosure must be made in a manner that is reasonably likely to come to the donor's attention; small print is thus discouraged. The disclosure requirement does not apply if the goods or services provided have "insubstantial value" (see Rev. Proc. 90–12, discussed supra, at pp. 843–845), or if the contributor receives solely an intangible religious benefit that is provided by an organization organized exclusively for religious purposes and the benefit generally is not sold in a commercial transaction outside the donative context. I.R.C. § 170(f)(8)(B); Treas. Reg. § 1.6115–1(a)(2), –1(b).

If a charity fails to make the required disclosure, it is subject to a penalty of $10 per contribution, capped at $5,000 for any particular fundraising event or mailing. I.R.C. § 6714. The penalty is waived if the charity can show that its failure was due to reasonable cause. Id. The penalties are triggered if an organization either fails to make any disclosure in connection with a *quid pro quo* contribution or makes an incomplete or inaccurate disclosure, such as a determination of the value of the return benefits that is not in good faith. Id.

Information Disclosure of Nondeductibility of Contributions. During its closer scrutiny of fundraising practices of nonprofit organizations in the late 1980s, Congress discovered many nonprofits ineligible to receive tax-deductible contributions were not disclosing their proper status to potential contributors and, in some cases, were actually implying in solicitations that contributions were deductible when in fact they were not. Particular targets of this scrutiny were § 501(c)(4) lobbying organizations. To patrol against these abuses, § 6113 generally requires fundraising solicitations by or on behalf of tax-exempt donees that do not qualify to receive deductible contributions, or by any political organization defined in § 527(e), to include an express statement in a conspicuous and easily recognizable format that contributions to the organization are not tax-deductible. I.R.C. § 6113(a), (b)(1). Exceptions are provided for small organizations (with average annual gross receipts not exceeding $100,000), fraternal organizations with respect to solicitations for exclusively charitable purposes, and any solicitation made by letter or telephone call if the letter or call is not part of a coordinated fundraising campaign soliciting more than 10 persons during the calendar year. I.R.C. § 6113(b)(2), (3) & (c)(2). Monetary penalties are imposed for noncompliance with these rules unless the failure was due to reasonable cause. I.R.C. § 6710.

Internet Fundraising: Some Special Problems. Fundraising over the Internet raises additional questions in addition to the state law charitable solicitation issues discussed in Chapter 4.

Some solicitations are made by for-profit firms on behalf of specified charitable organizations. Contributions are collected through secure connections using credit cards and the solicitor remits the gift to the charity after keeping a fee. If the solicitor is acting as the charity's agent, the full amount of the gift should be deductible, with the fee being treated as an expense of the charity. In other cases (and how is the donor to know?), the fee would not be a deductible contribution because the intermediary is the donor's agent. The legal relationship of the solicitor to the charity also may affect the timing of a deduction. If the solicitor is the donor's agent, the gift is not complete until remitted to the charity, but a deduction should be available upon a click of the mouse if the solicitor is the charity's agent.

In Announcement 2000–84, 2000–42 I.R.B. 385, the Service asked for comments on whether e-mail acknowledgements and disclosures of "quid pro quo" return benefits satisfied the substantiation and disclosure rules in §§ 170(f)(8) and 6115. The answer in both cases is yes, at least if the electronic acknowledgements can be printed out and contain the required information. A related question is whether Internet solicitations (either on a web site or by e-mail) are in "written or printed form" within the meaning of I.R.C. § 6113(c)(1)(A), in which case organizations (such as § 501(c)(4) advocacy groups) that are not eligible to receive deductible gifts must include an express statement to that effect in "a conspicuous and easily recognizable format."

What about a web surfer who visits an on line "charity mall" where "commissions" paid by on-line merchants on all purchases made through the site are remitted to charities selected by the purchasers from a list. For example, assume that a charitable mall, in response to a "frequently asked question," advises donors that they may not take any tax deduction because they are buying goods and services at regular prices and not making a donation directly to the charity. May the merchants (who don't select the donee) take the deduction? Or what if a web-based solicitor allows members to purchase products from vendors who then send back rebates which the buyer either may keep or designate to selected charities? In this situation, should members be told that rebates designated to charities are tax-deductible because the member may keep the rebate or donate it?

Noncash Contributions. Additional valuation and substantiation rules apply to gifts of property other than cash. These rules are discussed in Section C7 of this chapter, infra at pp. 884–887.

For Further Reading. Bruce R. Hopkins, The Tax Law of Charitable Giving (3d ed. 2005); Christina L. Nooney, Tax–Exempt Organizations and the Internet, 27 Exempt Org. Tax Rev. 33 (2000); Catherine E. Livingston, Tax–Exempt Organizations and the Internet: Tax and Other Legal Issues, 31 Exempt Org. Tax Rev. 419 (2001).

PROBLEMS

Determine whether the following contributions are tax-deductible under § 170 and, if not, suggest how the transfer might be restructured to achieve an income tax deduction:

(a) Concerned Citizen makes a $1,000 payment to the United States government to help reduce the national debt.

(b) Ira Weisel donates $10,000 to Community Foundation, a § 170(c) charity, on the understanding that the funds will be transferred to a foreign charitable organization that provides food and shelter to needy residents of Third World countries.

(c) Dan Kaye, a prominent geologist, donates $50,000 to the Sturdley University Department of Geology and earmarks the gift to support the research of two graduate students who work in his laboratory under his supervision.

(d) Edith Calderon volunteers five hours a week at St. Anthony's Soup Kitchen, a charitable organization that provides meals for the homeless. She also incurs travel expenses for two cross-country trips per year in connection with her service as an alumni trustee of her undergraduate alma mater.

(e) Barnabas Collins, who has a rare blood type, donates blood with a fair market value of $5,000 to the American Red Cross.

(f) Gordon Haines, a wealthy personal injury lawyer, donates $5 million to State Law School. In recognition of the gift, the Law School renames its library as The Haines Legal Information Center.

(g) Tyrone Johnson, a third-year law student, buys 10 tickets to a raffle sponsored by his school's Public Interest Law Foundation (at $1 per ticket), fully aware that he has only a small chance at winning the first prize: a free bar review course worth $1,200. Each of the raffle tickets states that the "donation" is "tax-deductible as provided by law."

(h) After several glasses of chablis, Celine Kane makes the winning bid ($5,000) on a baseball autographed by the 1955 New York Yankees at the annual Country Day School Auction. A reliable collector's guide values similar autographed balls at $2,400.

(i) Donna Davies pays $250 for a "patron" ticket to a benefit concert to benefit The Metropolitan Symphony. A comparable ticket for a regular concert would cost $75. As a "patron," Donna is recognized as such in the printed program and entitled to a Fritos-champagne-and-caviar reception honoring Placido Domingo following the performance.

(j) Same as (i), above, except Donna has no intention of attending the event.

(k) Dan Stein contributes $5,000 annually to the Sturdley University athletic program booster fund, for which he receives a biweekly newsletter about the college athletic program and the right to purchase preferential seating at football and basketball games. The seats sold to those who donate $5,000 or more are not available to other alumni or the general public.

(l) Rhoda Powell is a member of Temple Sinai, a large Reform Jewish synagogue. Her annual dues are $1,600, which are based on her income according to a dues policy approved by the synagogue's board. As a member, she is entitled to attend weekly services and other events (which usually are also open to non-members on a space-available basis) and receives reserved seat tickets to the Jewish High Holy Day services (which non-members may not attend). She also paid $2,500 during the current year for after-school religious and Hebrew classes for her son, Ben, who is preparing for his Bar Mitzvah.

(m) Emil Perini makes a $350 cash contribution to Charity by mailing a check on December 31 of Year One. Charity receives and deposits the check on January 5 of Year Two, but it does not mail Emil any acknowledgement. Charity's original solicitation form stated: "Your cancelled check shall serve as your receipt."

(n) Same as (m), above, except that Emil gave $250 on April 1 and another $100 on December 1.

(o) Same as (m), above, except Emil makes his contribution on the Internet by charging $350 to his credit card. He pays his credit card bill on January 15 of Year Two. Charity sends him an e-mail acknowledgment of the gift.

C.   NONCASH CONTRIBUTIONS

Internal Revenue Code: §§ 170(a)(3), (b)(1)(C) & (D), (e)(1), (5) & (7); (f)(12) & (16); (o); 1011(b).

Treasury Regulations: §§ 1.170A–1(c)(1) & (2).

1.   CAPITAL GAIN PROPERTY

Subject to the percentage limitations discussed earlier, noncash contributions generally are deductible in an amount equal to the fair market value of the donated property on the date of the gift. Gifts of "capital gain property," such as appreciated securities or real estate held by the taxpayer for more than one year, offer attractive tax benefits. The donor avoids tax on the gain that would have been recognized if the donated property had been sold, and she may deduct the full fair market value of the property subject to the applicable percentage limitations. I.R.C. § 170(b)(1)(C). A full fair market value deduction, however, is not available for gifts of appreciated capital gain property (other than certain publicly traded stock) to a private foundation. In determining the charitable deduction, the donor's gift must be reduced by the amount of long-term capital gain that would have been recognized if the property had been sold for its fair market value rather than contributed. I.R.C. § 170(e)(1)(A) & (B)(ii). As previewed earlier, this "stepdown" rule is one of the most significant disadvantages of making lifetime gifts of property such as closely held stock or real estate to a private foundation. In addition, the deductible amount is subject to a 20 percent limitation with a five-year carryover. I.R.C. § 170(b)(1)(D).

It is not advisable to contribute capital gain property that is worth less than its basis because the donor will be unable to deduct the loss. If a sale of property would result in a deductible loss, the donor should sell the property, deduct the loss, and donate the proceeds to charity.

Philanthropic taxpayers who are about to sell appreciated property occasionally find it attractive to contribute the property and let the charity complete the sale. For example, a donor may own publicly traded stock for which a tender offer is outstanding or may be negotiating the sale of real estate. In these situations, the donor will avoid recognizing the gain inherent in the contributed property only if the contribution is made prior to an unconditional sale. The charity must not be obligated to sell the property as a condition of the gift. Similarly, a contribution of closely held stock followed by a redemption will not be treated as a constructive dividend to the donor-shareholder if the charity is not legally obligated to tender the stock to the company. See, e.g., Rev. Rul. 78–197, 1978–1 C.B. 83. As illustrated by the *Blake* case, which follows, an implied understanding between the donor and the charity may cause the donor's delicate tax plan to self destruct if the Service is able to successfully invoke the step transaction doctrine.

Blake v. Commissioner

United States Court of Appeals, Second Circuit, 1982.
697 F.2d 473.

■ OAKES, CIRCUIT JUDGE:

This appeal presents a familiar problem in the tax law involving step-transaction analysis. The context is one in which a taxpayer "contributes" a substantially appreciated asset to a charitable organization which then liquidates the contribution and purchases another asset from the taxpayer. The question in this case is whether the taxpayer is entitled to treat the transfer of the first asset—corporate stock—as a contribution and treat the transfer of the second asset—a yacht—as a sale, or whether, as the Tax Court held, the transactions here must be recharacterized for tax purposes as a sale of the stock by the taxpayer followed by a contribution to the charity of the vessel. The vessel, it might be noted, was sold by the charity shortly after it had been purchased from the taxpayer for a little less than half of what the charity paid the taxpayer out of the proceeds of the stock. The taxpayer contends that the charity had no legally binding obligation to purchase the yacht and that absent such an obligation the transactions here must be treated according to the form they took: a contribution followed by a sale of an asset. We disagree. We hold that in this case the charity would have been legally obligated to purchase the yacht and that, even if it were not legally obligated, the Tax Court's finding that the transactions were undertaken pursuant to an understanding arrived at in advance is sufficient to sustain the Commissioner's position. We therefore affirm the Tax Court, Arnold Raum, Judge, in its decision that the gain realized on the sale of the stock was attributable to the taxpayer. It follows that only the market value of the yacht, not challenged on this appeal, was deductible as a contribution.

I. Facts

The taxpayer in this case, S. Prestley Blake, was a co-founder and major stockholder in the Friendly Ice Cream Corporation. In 1972, Blake purchased the yacht "America" for $500,000. The America is a replica of the original yacht America, built in 1851, after which the America's Cup race is named. Although not particularly well suited to racing or chartering, the yacht does have a certain mystique owing to its historical associations. Subsequent to the transactions recounted below, the America became familiar nationally because it was featured in the Tall Ships' Sail to New York City during the Bicentennial celebration of 1976. Blake, however, had nothing but trouble with the yacht. The vessel required frequent repair, and Blake found various captains and crews unsatisfactory. With one exception, Blake's ambition to defray expenses associated with owning the boat through chartering was never realized. He ultimately decided to dispose of the yacht; in his own words, he "had to get rid of [the America] at all costs," because it "was taking too much * * * time and concern."

Blake had made a number of charitable gifts throughout his career, particularly in western New England, his home and the place where he started business. He attempted to donate the America to Mystic Seaport in Mystic, Connecticut, but that institution declined the gift. More unhappy cruises followed. Some time later, Blake approached the Kings Point Fund, Inc. (the Fund), a qualified charitable organization associated with the United States Merchant Marine Academy at Kings Point, New York. In January and February of 1975, Blake and the superintendent of the Academy discussed the possibility of the Academy's use of the America as a training vessel, and the Superintendent wrote Blake a letter in late February of 1975 confirming the Academy's interest in the proposition. The letter expressed gratitude for Blake's "extremely generous offer to donate" the America and to "provide an additional annual grant of $10,000 towards its maintenance." The record indicates that the Fund's directors had discussed the possibility of acquiring the America at an earlier meeting where it was suggested that the boat be kept for at least two years and that Blake donate $10,000 annually and that twelve other major donors be solicited to raise an additional $125,000 for upkeep. On March 13, 1975, some two weeks after the Superintendent wrote Blake, the Fund's directors met again. It was reported at the meeting that Blake was "very receptive to donating his YACHT AMERICA to the Kings Point Fund" and the minutes of the meeting indicate that "[f]urther negotiation packages to this acquisition [were] to be discussed." A motion to acquire the America, subject to the consent of the Superintendent and approval of legal counsel, carried the Board unanimously.

In the meanwhile, Blake was apparently consulting with his tax lawyers. Four days after the March 13 meeting, he wrote the Fund that he had transferred 35,000 shares of Friendly stock "to advance your training program for young cadets in a way that you see fit." The stock had an adjusted basis in Blake's hands of $98, but a market value of $686,875 at the time of transfer. The Fund immediately sold the stock in a series of transactions netting $701,688.89. At an April 8, 1975, meeting of the Fund's directors, it was reported that "Mr. Blake had donated * * * $714,000 * * * worth of Friendly Ice Cream stock" to the Fund, that the Fund "then sold same," and that $675,000 "is to be used to purchase the yacht AMERICA and the remainder is to be used toward the maintenance of the vessel." The Board unanimously accepted "the generous donation of Mr. P. Blake to be used for the purchase of the yacht America and her maintenance." Almost immediately, however, the Board set out to sell the yacht; at a June 17, 1975, meeting a possible sale was discussed which would allow the Academy to use the vessel for the Bicentennial "Tall Ships Parade." This sale was approved, the minutes noting that it would "net the

Fund over $200,000." Presumably this sale was carried out over the summer; the minutes of a meeting of September 18, 1975, show that, in addition to selling half a dozen other smaller craft, the Fund sold the America for $250,000, netting it some $200,000. The taxpayer does not dispute that, but for his expectation that the Fund would purchase the vessel, he might not have contributed the stock. But he argues that he had, at most, an expectation in this regard because there was no binding, enforceable commitment on the Fund's part to purchase the vessel. He points out that the directors of the Fund were free not to purchase the yacht if they determined that it would not be in the Fund's best interests to do so and that he alone bore the risk that events occurring between the transfer of the stock and either its sale or the purchase of the yacht would reduce the value of the stock or the yacht respectively. Thus, the taxpayer argues, there was a mere "coincidence" of two transactions and the principles underlying the tax treatment of charitable contributions require separate treatment of these transactions in the absence of an obligation binding the charity to purchase an asset of the contribution.

Under Grove v. Commissioner, 490 F.2d 241 (2d Cir.1973), the taxpayer argues reversal is required. *Grove* is presented to us as in a line of cases including, e.g., Palmer v. Commissioner, 62 T.C. 684 (1974), aff'd on other grounds, 523 F.2d 1308 (8th Cir.1975), acq'd in Rev.Rul. 78–197, 1978–1 C.B. 83; * * *. We will first examine whether there was a legally binding agreement in this case, although this point was neither relied upon by the Tax Court nor particularly argued by the Commissioner, because the premise of the taxpayer's argument is that there was no legal obligation whatsoever. We will then address the Tax Court's holding that the understanding between the parties was alone sufficient to justify recharacterization of these transactions, irrespective whether the understanding was legally enforceable.

II.   The Fund's Obligation to Blake

If there was a legally binding agreement on the Fund's part to purchase the vessel with the entirety of the proceeds derived from the sale of the transferred stock, the taxpayer seems to concede that there would be no contribution here in excess of the fair market value of the yacht at the time of its transfer. The existence of such an obligation is determined, of course, with reference to state law. [The court then surveyed the various state laws that might govern the transaction. Eds.]

* * *

We need not decide which of the three states' law would govern, however, because we are certain that each state would consider the Fund legally obligated to purchase the America under a theory of promissory estoppel on the facts of this case. Under this theory, a mere gratuitous promise by the Fund that it would purchase the America became legally binding when Blake acted in reliance on such an assurance. * * *

The taxpayer argues that no legal obligation arose on the charity's part to purchase the vessel because he "gave the shares * * * absolutely, parting with all control over them." But, far from negating the existence of an obligation, the transfer itself gave rise to an obligation, under the decisions cited above, if the taxpayer made the transfer in reliance upon an assurance that the charity would use the proceeds of the asset for a specific purpose. Although the taxpayer maintains that the charity made no commitment upon which the reliance in the form of the transfer could be premised, the Tax Court's findings are to the contrary. The Tax Court concluded, upon the record in its entirety, that the transfer of stock was made "with the understanding that the stock would be sold, that the yacht would be turned over to the fund, and that virtually all of the proceeds of the sale of the stock would end up in [the taxpayer's] hands." The individual who served as the Fund's negotiator in dealing with Blake was unable to testify at trial as to any express oral agreement between the Fund and Blake, but a Fund director testified that it was the Board's understanding that the negotiator had agreed that the stock proceeds would be used to "purchase" the vessel. That the Board's "understanding" accurately reflected an understanding between Blake and the Fund's negotiator is supported by the fact that, as of the March 13, 1975, meeting, the directors agreed to take "such steps as necessary to acquire the YACHT AMERICA" and were aware that "further negotiation packages to acquisition [were] to be discussed." Further support is provided by the minutes of the Fund's April 8, 1975, meeting, which note the approval of a motion "to accept the generous donation of Mr. P. Blake to be used for the purchase of the yacht America and her maintenance." Finally, Blake himself testified on direct examination that he would not have made a donation as substantial as the amount of the market value of the stock he transferred "except for the boat thing."

On the basis of the Tax Court's factual findings as to the understanding between the taxpayer and the charity, we have little difficulty concluding that Blake would have had an enforceable cause of action under a promissory estoppel theory. * * * The same public policy considerations that support the enforcement of promises made by individuals to charitable organizations also support the enforcement of promises made by a charity in connection with a contribution. As the former Assistant Superintendent of the Merchant Marine Academy and twenty-five-year director of the Fund testified at trial, if the Fund had not purchased the America with the proceeds of the stock, if it "had simply taken Mr. Blake's money and run," the "gifting of future yachts would have been severely jeopardized." We therefore reject the taxpayer's contention that the Fund was not legally obligated to "purchase" the yacht, and this is enough to satisfy the case law referred to us. Grove v. Commissioner, supra, and the other cases cited by the taxpayer for the proposition that there must be a legally binding obligation on a charity's part before a transfer that is ostensibly a contribution can be recharacterized are therefore simply inapposite because there was a legal obligation here.

III.   The "Understanding" Between Blake and the Fund

The Tax Court found as a factual matter that there existed an "understanding" between Blake and the Fund with respect to the disposition of the proceeds the Fund realized from sale of the stock. Even if this understanding fell short of a legal obligation, it amounted to more than mere wishful thinking on the taxpayer's part and thus refutes the contention that these transactions were merely coincidental. It also serves to distinguish this case from Grove v. Commissioner, supra, if not from all the other cases the taxpayer cites here. In *Grove*, this court relied on the Tax Court's finding there was not even an informal agreement that the charity would deal with the contributed asset in a manner providing a tax benefit to the taxpayer. The majority opinion in *Grove* declined to infer an understanding from a pattern of activity benefiting the taxpayer in the "absence of any supporting facts in the record," an approach with which the author of this opinion took issue. But this case does not present us with the same difficulty. Here, the Tax Court found an understanding and we are quite firmly convinced that this finding was not clearly erroneous. Our review of the record satisfies us that "[t]here was evidence to support the findings of the Tax Court, and its findings must therefore be accepted."

[The court then proceeded to distinguish several cases relied upon by the taxpayers. Eds.]

* * *

More troublesome is the case of Palmer v. Commissioner, 62 T.C. 684 (1974), aff'd on other grounds, 523 F.2d 1308 (8th Cir.1975), which held that even an expectation of a stock redemption would not warrant denying charitable contribution status. The Service, in Revenue Ruling 78–197, 1978–1 C.B. 83, acquiesced in *Palmer*, stating that it would treat redemption proceeds under facts similar to Palmer as income to the donor "only if the donee is legally bound, or can be compelled by the corporation, to surrender the shares for redemption." The Service cited both *Grove* and *Carrington* as support for its position; what we have said above indicates our belief that this Ruling reads too much into those decisions. Where there is, as here, an expectation on the part of the donor that is reasonable, with an advance understanding that the donee charity will purchase the asset with the proceeds of the donated stock, the transaction will be looked at as a unitary one. A wooden view that would require legal enforceability of an understanding or obligation to purchase the asset contemplated to be donated ab initio is not what the tax law contemplates. At least, this circuit will not take it to do so.

Judgment affirmed.

2.   Ordinary Income Property

Section 170(e)(1) significantly reduces the tax benefits for gifts of ordinary income property. Ordinary income property is property that, if sold by the taxpayer for its fair market value, would result in ordinary income or short-term capital gain. Examples include inventory, other property held primarily for sale to customers in the ordinary course of the taxpayer's trade or business ("dealer property"), depreciable property to the extent that gain on a sale would be "recaptured" and taxed as ordinary income, stock and other capital assets held for one year or less, certain preferred corporate stock (§ 306 stock), and works of art or other intellectual property created by the donor.

Charitable gifts of ordinary income property are not subject to the special 30 percent limitation that applies to most gifts of capital gain property, but the donor is required to reduce the gift by the amount of gain that would not have been long-term capital gain if the property had been sold for its fair market value rather than contributed to charity. I.R.C. § 170(e)(1)(A). Put less technically, taxpayers who donate ordinary income property may only deduct their basis (usually cost) of that property. The purpose of this rule is to place these donors in roughly the same position that they would occupy if the ordinary income property had been sold and the proceeds were contributed to a charity.

To illustrate, assume that Donor contributes to Charity $10,000 of stock that she acquired seven months ago for $4,000. Because the stock has not been held for more than one year and thus would generate short-term capital gain if it were sold, it is ordinary income property. Donor thus must reduce her charitable deduction to $4,000. If she had held the same stock for more than one year at the time of her donation, her deduction (before application of any percentage limitation) would have been $10,000.

The ordinary income property "stepdown" rule is subject to a significant exception for corporate contributions of inventory to a public charity for a use that is related to the donee's exempt purposes and if the inventory is used "solely for the care of the ill, the needy, or infants." I.R.C. § 170(e)(3). Examples include gifts of food or drugs. If this exception applies, the usual reduction for gifts of ordinary income property is limited under a complex formula that has the effect of allowing a deduction for the lesser of (1) twice the basis of the property, or (2) the basis of the property plus 50 percent of the unrealized appreciation.

The ordinary income property rules significantly reduce the tax benefits for contributions of inventory and other "dealer" property. As illustrated by Revenue Ruling 79–256, which follows, the Service has expanded the definition of "dealer" to prevent efforts by taxpayers (and facilitating tax shelter promoters) to circumvent these rules.

Revenue Ruling 79–256

1979–2 Cum.Bull. 256.

ISSUE

In the situations described below, does section 170(e) of the Internal Revenue Code apply and thus require that the amount of the taxpayers' charitable contributions be reduced by any gain that would not have been long-term capital gain if the donated property had been sold by the taxpayer at its fair market value?

FACTS

Situation 1. For a number of years the taxpayer was engaged in the activity of raising ornamental plants, as a hobby. In 1978, as in prior years, the taxpayer donated a large number of plants to various charities, after having held the donated plants for the long-term holding period for a capital asset under section 1222(3) of the Code. The cost of the plants contributed in 1978 was 25x dollars, and they had a total fair market value of 200x dollars when they were contributed. Approximately the same ratio of cost to fair market value existed in the prior years.

Situation 2. The taxpayer is not a dealer in objects of art. In 1977, the taxpayer purchased a substantial part of the total limited edition of a particular lithograph print by an established artist for a total price of 25x dollars. In 1978, after having held the prints for more than a year, the taxpayer donated the prints to various art museums. The total fair market value of the prints was 100x dollars when they were contributed.

LAW AND ANALYSIS

Section 170(a) of the Code allows as a deduction any charitable contribution payment of which is made within the taxable year.

Section 1.170A–1(c)(1) of the Income Tax Regulations provides that, if a charitable contribution is made in property other than money, the amount of the contribution is the fair market value of the property at the time of the contribution.

Section 170(e)(1)(A) of the Code provides that the amount of any charitable contribution of property shall be reduced by the amount of gain that would not have been long-term capital gain if the property had been sold by the taxpayer at its fair market value.

Section 1.170A–4(a)(1) of the regulations provides that section 170(e)(1)(A) requires that the amount of a charitable contribution of "ordinary income property" be reduced by the amount of gain that would not have been recognized as long-term capital gain if the property had been sold by the donor at fair market value at the time such property was contributed.

Section 1.170A–(4)(b)(1) of the regulations provides that the term "ordinary income property" means property on which any of the gain would not have been long-term capital gain if the property had been sold by the donor at its fair market value at the time of its contribution. The term "ordinary income property" includes, for example, property held by a donor primarily for sale to customers in the ordinary course of the donor's trade or business.

Thus, under section 170(e)(1)(A) of the Code and the corresponding regulations, the determination whether property contributed to charity is ordinary income property requires that the donor be placed in the position of a seller of such property. Even though a donor is not engaged in a trade or business, the frequency and continuity of the contributions may be such as to be substantially equivalent to the activities of a dealer selling property in the ordinary course of a trade or business. Under such circumstances, the items contributed would be treated as ordinary income property.

In both Situation 1 and Situation 2, the contributions were not made after a period of accumulation and enjoyment by the taxpayers of the property contributed. On the contrary, the contributed property was produced (Situation 1) or purchased (Situation 2) in bulk and distributed to various donees. In Situation 1, the taxpayer's continuous production and disposition of plants are the equivalent of the activities of a commercial nursery business. In Situation 2, the taxpayer's bulk acquisition and subsequent disposal of a substantial part of the total limited edition of prints are substantially equivalent to the activities of a commercial art dealer. Therefore, under the presumed sale requirement of section 170(e)(1)(A) of the Code, the items contributed in both situations will be treated as ordinary income property.

HOLDING

In both Situation 1 and Situation 2, the amount of each taxpayer's contribution must be reduced, under section 170(e) of the Code, by the excess of the fair market value of the contributed property as of the dates of contribution over each taxpayer's cost. Therefore, the amount of each taxpayer's contribution is limited, for purposes of section 170 of the Code, to its cost to the donor. However, the treatment provided under section 170(e) does not imply that a taxpayer is engaged in a trade or business for the purposes of any other section of the Code. Furthermore, the holding of this revenue ruling is equally applicable to taxpayers who, under comparable circumstances, produce or acquire types of property other than those involved in the two situations.

NOTES

IRA Rollovers. An owner of a traditional IRA who has reached the age of 59–½ may withdraw funds from the IRA without incurring a penalty but the distribution is taxable as ordinary income except to the extent it is attributable to after-tax contributions (i.e., contributions to the IRA for which the taxpayer did not receive a tax deduction). The IRA owner then may contribute the withdrawn funds to charity, claiming a charitable deduction subject to the applicable percentage limitation in § 170(b) (generally, 50 percent of adjusted gross income for gifts to public charities).

From 2006 to 2009, individuals age 70–½ or older could exclude from gross income IRA distributions of up to $100,000 per year to "50–percent" (primarily public) charities described in § 170(b)(1)(A). I.R.C. § 408(d)(8). Distributions to supporting organizations and donor-advised funds did not qualify for the exclusion. To prevent double dipping, charitable IRA rollovers that qualified for the exclusion were not tax-deductible under § 170.

Distributions had to be made directly from the IRA plan administrator to the charity, and they counted toward the IRA minimum distribution requirement. IRA distributions to split-interest vehicles such as charitable remainder trusts did not qualify for the exclusion.

The IRA rollover exclusion expired at the end of 2009 but, as this edition went to press in early 2010, efforts were underway to extend it another year or, better still, to make the exclusion permanent and expand its benefits.

What type of taxpayer would be in a position to take advantage of this provision?

Gifts of Food and Book Inventory. Temporary legislation that expired at the end of 2009 provided an enhanced deduction to business taxpayers (C corporations and individuals) for gifts of food and book inventory. In general, instead of being limited to the donor's basis, the allowable charitable deduction was the lesser of the fair market value of the inventory or twice the taxpayer's basis in the contributed property, subject to a few technical limitations. See I.R.C. §§ 170(e)(3)(C) (food); 170(e)(3)(D) (books to schools). These provisions were extended twice before they expired. As this edition went to press in early 2010, Congress was considering yet another one-year extension.

3. Tangible Personal Property

In General. A donor generally may take a full fair market value deduction for gifts of tangible personal property such as art objects, jewelry, antiques, books, automobiles, or yachts. A reduction rule applies, however, if the property is not used by the donee in the conduct of its exempt purposes or functions. In that event, the amount of the gift must be reduced by the long-term capital gain that the donor would have recognized if the property had been sold for its fair market value rather than contributed. I.R.C. § 170(e)(1)(B). In other words, as with gifts of ordinary income property, the charitable deduction generally is limited to the donor's basis in the contributed property. If this reduction rule applies, the gift is not subject to the 30 percent limitation on gifts of capital gain property (thus, the basic 50 percent limitation applies), but this often is of little solace in light of the tax benefits lost from reducing the charitable deduction to the donor's basis.

In evaluating whether contributed property is used in the conduct of a charity's exempt functions, the regulations provide that it must be "reasonable to anticipate" that the organization will use the property for some exempt purpose. Treas. Reg. § 1.170A–4(b)(3)(ii). Examples include a gift of art to a museum for its collection, or rare books to a library. But the reduction rule applies if the donor can reasonably anticipate that the charity will sell the property—e.g., at a fundraising auction.

The Pension Protection Act of 2006 added another anti-abuse rule aimed at gifts of tangible personal property not used by the donee for its exempt purposes. For contributions made after September 1, 2006, a donor who takes a full fair market value deduction for a gift of exempt use property with a claimed value of more than $5,000 that is sold, exchanged, or otherwise disposed of by the donee within three years after the donor contributed the property must recapture the tax benefits by including in gross income in the year of the disposition the difference between the deduction allowed and the donor's basis in the donated property. For dispositions in the year the gift was made, the punishment is to limit the charitable deduction to the donor's basis. I.R.C. §§ 170(e)(1)(B)(i)(II); 170(e)(7). See also I.R.C. § 6050L(a)(2)(A).

The recapture rule does not apply if an officer of the donee provides a written statement to the donor certifying that the charity's use of the property was a "substantial exempt use," describing how that use furthered its purposes or function, and further certifying that the intended use at the time of the contribution later had become impossible or infeasible to implement. IRC § 170(e)(7)(B)(ii), (D). Civil penalties are imposed on any person who fraudulently identified property as "exempt use" when it was not intended for such use.

As discussed in more detail below, additional anti-abuse legislation applies to particular types of donated property.

Cars, Boats and Airplanes. As donations of used cars emerged as a popular form of charitable giving, Congress and the IRS became justifiably concerned that taxpayers were inflating tax deductions by claiming excessive valuations. This practice was encouraged by advertisements suggesting that donors could base their deduction on "Blue Book" value even for used cars destined to be towed to the junkyard. A 2003 General Accounting Office study validated these concerns. Based on an examination of 733,000 charitable deductions claimed for vehicle donations in 2000, the GAO report found that the majority of charities received cash proceeds of less than 5 percent of the value claimed on the donor's tax return. Apart from overvaluation, a charity's share also was reduced by large fees charged by fundraisers and for-profit intermediaries. See Vehicle Donations: Benefits to Charities and Donors but Limited Program Oversight (GAO–04–73, Nov. 2003), available at http://www.gao.gov.

To curb these abuses, Congress enacted strict new rules on vehicle donations. In general, for contributions made after December 31, 2004, the charitable income tax deduction for gifts of a "qualified vehicle" (motor vehicle, boat or airplane) with a claimed value of more than $500 is limited to the lesser of the fair market value of the vehicle on the date of the contribution or the gross proceeds from the sale of the vehicle by the charity. I.R.C. § 170(f)(12)(A)(i), (E). Donors must obtain and attach to their tax return a contemporaneous written acknowledgment (within 30 days of the sale of the vehicle) that includes detailed information, such as the identification number of the vehicle, a certification that the sale was an arm's length transaction between unrelated parties, and the gross proceeds from the sale. I.R.C. § 170(f)(12)(A)(i), (B), (C). Stiff monetary penalties will be imposed on charities for knowingly furnishing a false or fraudulent receipt or knowingly failing to furnish a timely and complete acknowledgement. I.R.C. § 6720.

The deduction is not limited to the gross proceeds received from sale when the charity: (1) makes a "significant intervening use" of the vehicle— e.g., regular use on a daily basis for a year or more to deliver food to the elderly or disabled; (2) materially improves the vehicle—e.g., major repairs that significantly increase its value, not mere painting or cleaning; or (3) gives or sells the vehicle at a significantly below-market price to a needy individual in furtherance of charitable purposes—e.g., helping poor people who need a means of transportation. I.R.C. § 170(f)(12)(B)(ii); I.R.S. Notice 2005–44, § 3.02. If one of these exceptions applies, the charity's written acknowledgment must contain a certification of such intervening use, material improvement, or transfer to the needy. I.R.C. § 170(f)(12)(B); I.R.S. Notice 2005–44, 2005–1 C.B. 1287, § 3.03.

Donors who claim a deduction of $500 or less are not subject the new rules and may take a fair market value deduction (up to $500) if they comply with the generally applicable substantiation rules in § 170(f)(8). The IRS has announced that "dealer retail value" listed in a "used vehicle pricing guide" (e.g. Blue Book) is not an acceptable measure of value for this purpose. Rather, for contributions of vehicles made after June 3, 2005, "fair market value" may not exceed the "private party sale price" (usually less than "dealer retail") listed in a pricing guide for a comparable vehicle. I.R.S. Notice 2005–44, supra, § 5. See also I.R.S. Publication 526, at 10–11 (2009).

In the unlikely event that the fair market value of the vehicle exceeds the taxpayer's basis and the vehicle is not used by the charity to further its exempt purposes, the charitable deduction is limited to the donor's basis under the general reduction rule in § 170(e)(1) discussed above.

Intellectual Property. The American Jobs Creation Act of 2004 also placed new restrictions on gifts of patents or other intellectual property that are capital assets. (There was no need to cover copyrights and other types of "ordinary income" property that already are subject to the deduction limits in § 170(e)(1)(A).) Section 170(e)(1)(B)(iii), which applies to contributions made after June 3, 2004, limits an initial charitable contribution to the lesser of the donor's basis in the contributed property or its fair market value.

Under a novel "open gift" approach, additional deductions in the year of the contribution or the twelve subsequent years may be allowed (provided the gift is not made to a private nonoperating foundation) based on a specified percentage of the "qualified donee income" (i.e., income allocable to the intellectual property itself, not the activity in which the property is used) received or accrued by the charitable donee with respect to the contributed property. The percentage is 100 percent for the first two years and then gradually declines to 10 percent after ten years. I.R.C. § 170(m). The additional charitable deduction is allowed only to the extent that the aggregate of the amounts calculated under the sliding scale exceed the amount of the deduction claimed upon initial contribution of the property.

I.R.C. § 170(m)(2). Additional deductions are subject to special reporting and substantiation requirements (e.g., the taxpayer must obtain written proof from the charitable donee of the amount of the qualified donee income, and the donee must file annual information returns with the IRS). I.R.C. § 6050L(b).

Used Clothing and Household Goods. In a 2005 report on revenue-raising options, the staff of the Joint Committee on Taxation proposed strict limits on the charitable deduction for gifts of clothing and household items to curb valuation abuses. The Joint Committee was concerned about the lack of uniform standards for establishing the value of these types of gifts and the tendency of many taxpayers to claim excessive deductions based on the "sentimental value" they may place on them. Joint Committee on Taxation, Options to Improve Tax Compliance and Reform Tax Expenditures (JCS–02–05) 288–292 (Jan. 27, 2005).

In another 2005 report, the Panel on the Nonprofit Sector opposed any maximum ceiling on gifts of clothing and household items, arguing that it was arbitrary and would be a "significant disincentive for taxpayers to make generous contributions of a number of items or high-end items rather than re-sell those items and retain the cash for their own use." Final Report 58–60. The Panel noted that many types of donated items, such as appliances, high-quality furniture and some clothing, may have a substantial re-sale value and were vital to the successful operation of thrift shops, programs that assist homeless families, charity auctions, and the like. Id. at 59. In lieu of a cap, the Panel suggested clearer standards for establishing value, such as IRS-approved "value guides" for commonly donated items. Id. at 60.

When Congress addressed this issue in the Pension Protection Act of 2006, it acknowledged the problems identified by the Joint Committee but took a different approach. Section 170(f)(16) permits a deduction for contributions of clothing and household items only if the donated item is in "good used condition or better." The IRS may deny by regulation a deduction for any clothing or household item which has "minimal monetary value" (used undergarments are an example cited in the legislative history). I.R.C. § 170(f)(16)(B). These limitations do not apply, however, to any contribution of a single item of clothing or a household item for which a deduction of more than $500 is claimed if the taxpayer includes with his return a qualified appraisal with respect to the donated property. I.R.C. § 170(f)(16)(C). For purposes of these new limits, "household items" are defined to include furniture, furnishings, electronics, appliances, linens, and other similar items, but not food, paintings, antiques, other art objects, jewelry and gems, and collectibles. I.R.C. § 170(f)(16)(D).

Taxidermy Property. Among the more exotic charitable giving abuses recently uncovered by Congress involved donations of big-game trophies— mounted parts and skins of dead animals captured on African safaris and other expeditions and donated by the philanthropic hunters to "wildlife museums." Congress's interest was piqued by a Washington Post article reporting that the hunter/philanthropists were claiming excessive deductions based on inflated appraisals. According to the report, many gifts were made to a rarely visited museum in rural Nebraska that stored most of the dead animal mounts in a railroad car for a little over two years and then sold them for much less than their claimed charitable deduction value. See Marc Kaufman, Big-game Hunting Brings Big Tax Breaks, Washington Post, April 5, 2005, at A01.

In response to this "phoniness," as it was described by then Senate Finance Committee chair Charles Grassley, Congress enacted new rules on contributions of "taxidermy property," which is defined as "[a] mounted work of art which contains any part of a dead animal." I.R.C. § 170(f)(15)(B). For contributions after July 25, 2006 by the person "who prepared, stuffed or mounted" the taxidermy property or paid for the preparation, stuffing, or mounting, the charitable deduction is limited to the lesser of the donor's basis or the fair market value of the property. In determining basis, only the cost of preparing, stuffing, or mounting (and not indirect costs, such as expenses of the safari or hunting trip) are taken into account. I.R.C. §§ 170(e)(1)(B)(iv); 170(f)(15)(A).

4. BARGAIN SALES

A "bargain sale" is a sale of property for less than its fair market value. Bargain sales to charitable organizations offer two major benefits: (1) a charitable deduction for the bargain element (the fair market value of the property less the sale price), and (2) reduction of the tax that the donor would pay if the property had been sold for its full fair market value. Bargain sales have proven particularly useful where a donor wishes to donate part of a substantial piece of property that is not easily divided (such as real estate) and to receive cash for the remaining portion.

A bargain sale to a charitable organization is bifurcated for tax purposes into a sale and a charitable gift. Under a special rule only applicable to bargain sales to charity, the donor's basis in the property must be allocated between the sale and gift transactions in proportion to the respective fair market values of each portion. I.R.C. § 1011(b). As a result, the donor is taxed on the difference between the sale price and the portion of the basis allocated to the sale part of the transaction.

To illustrate, assume that Donor ("D") owns a parcel of unimproved investment real estate with a fair market value of $100,000 and an adjusted basis of $50,000. D sells the property to Charity for $40,000 cash. D's charitable contribution is the $60,000 "bargain element"—i.e., the $100,000 fair market value of the property less the $40,000 sales proceeds received by D. Because this is a contribution of capital gain property, the $60,000 gift will be subject to the 30 percent limitation in § 170(b)(1)(C). D then must proceed to determine her gain on the sale portion of the transaction. D's amount realized is $40,000. Under § 1011(b), her basis in the sale portion is 40 percent (the ratio of the $40,000 sale price to the $100,000 value of the property) of her $50,000 total basis, or $20,000, and her taxable gain is thus $20,000 ($40,000 amount realized, minus $20,000 adjusted basis). See Treas. Reg. § 1.1011–2(a); 1.170A–4(c)(2).

A charitable gift of encumbered property is treated as a bargain sale to the extent that the outstanding liability exceeds the portion of the donor's adjusted basis allocated to the sale portion of the transaction. See, e.g., Guest v. Commissioner, 77 T.C. 9 (1981). Gifts of limited partnership interests also may constitute bargain sales when the partnership property is subject to indebtedness.

5.   PARTIAL INTERESTS (NOT IN TRUST)

Donors historically have favored giving techniques that allow them to take a current income tax deduction for the value of a future interest in property while they retain a right to current income or enjoyment of the donated property. The Code contains intricate rules, summarized later in this chapter, for charitable gifts of income or remainder interests in trust. Section 170(f)(3) imposes comparable restrictions on gifts of partial interests not in trust by providing that the retained present interest either must be a guaranteed annuity or unitrust interest. In addition, § 170(a)(3) provides that a contribution of a remainder interest in tangible personal property is deductible only when all intervening noncharitable interests have expired. This seemingly superfluous rule postpones a charitable deduction for a gift of a remainder interest in tangible personal property, such as a work of art or other collectible, when the donor or a related party retains the right to possess and enjoy the property.

The limitations on deductions for partial interests not in trust are subject to three major exceptions. Two of these exceptions—for contributions of qualified conservation easements and gifts of remainder interests in a personal residence or farm-are discussed later in this chapter. See Section C6, infra, at pp. 882–884, and Section D4, infra, at p. 895. A third exception applies to gifts of an undivided portion of a donor's entire interest in property. I.R.C. § 170(f)(3)(B)(ii); Treas.Reg. § 1.170A–7(b)(1). This exception permits donors to obtain a current deduction for a donation of a work of art or real estate by contributing a fractional interest in the property. After the gift, the donor and the charity are co-owners, typically sharing the property on a seasonal basis. Some art donors, however, pushed the envelope by taking a current deduction for a fractional interest gift without giving up possession of the donated property even for part of the year. These donors took the position, supported by case law, that the charitable donee only must have a legal right to possession for the fractional portion of the year equal to its ownership interest and that actual physical possession was unnecessary. See, e.g., Winokur v. Commissioner, 90 T.C. 733 (1988). Museums were willing to forego possession during a donor's lifetime if they were assured of obtaining complete ownership after the donor's death.

In the Pension Protection Act of 2006, Congress responded to this problem by enacting strict new rules that have virtually eliminated fractional gifts of art. For gifts made after August 17, 2006, no income or gift tax charitable deduction is allowed for contributions of fractional interests in tangible personal property unless, immediately before the gift, the entire interest in the property is held by the taxpayer or the taxpayer and the donee. The IRS is authorized to issue regulations providing an exception where all persons owning an interest in the property make proportional contributions of an undivided portion of their respective amounts. I.R.C. § 170(o)(1).

When a donor makes subsequent gifts of a fractional interest, which is common with gifts of art, the fair market value of that gift for charitable deduction purposes must be the lesser of: (1) the value used at the time of the initial contribution, or (2) the fair market value at the time the subsequent gift is made. I.R.C. § 170(o)(2). As initially enacted, this valuation rule for subsequent gifts was problematic when the final fraction was transferred by bequest. For example, assume Donor contributes to Museum a 10 percent interest in a work of art worth $5 million and claims a $500,000 charitable income tax deduction. Seven years later, when the art is worth $20 million, Donor dies, bequeathing the remaining 90 percent interest to Museum. Donor's estate would include the $18 million value of his 90 percent interest, but the estate tax charitable deduction would be limited to $4.5 million (90 percent of the original $5 million value). In the Tax Technical Corrections Act of 2007, Congress removed the subsequent gifts valuation rule for estate and gift tax purposes, permitting a charitable deduction for the fair market value as of the decedent's estate tax valuation date.

Two other rules have diminished the allure of fractional interest gifts. First, a charity receiving a fractional interest gift must take "substantial physical possession" of the property and use it in a manner related to its exempt purposes. Second, the donor must contribute his entire interest within ten years of the date of the initial fractional interest gift (or by the date of death, if sooner). Violations of these requirements will cause the donor's previous charitable deductions to be recaptured and a penalty equal to 10 percent of the amount recaptured also will be imposed. I.R.C. § 170(o)(3).

Art lovers and museums, contending that lifetime art gifts are threatened with extinction, strongly objected to this legislation, and efforts are ongoing to have it modified or repealed.

6.   QUALIFIED CONSERVATION CONTRIBUTIONS

To encourage the preservation and protection of land and certain unique buildings, § 170(f)(3)(B)(iii) allows a charitable deduction for gifts of "qualified conservation contributions" that meet certain highly technical rules set forth in § 170(h). The term "qualified conservation contribution" entails these three requirements:

(1) The gift must be of a "qualified property interest," which is defined as the donor's entire interest in the property (except for certain mineral interests), a remainder interest, or a perpetual restriction on the use that may be made of the property. I.R.C. § 170(h)(2).

(2) The contribution must be made to a "qualified organization," a category that includes certain governmental units, public charities, or organizations controlled by and supporting a public charity or governmental unit. I.R.C. § 170(h)(3).

(3) The contribution must be exclusively for one or more specified "conservation purposes," including: preservation of land areas for outdoor recreation by, or education of, the general public; protection of a relatively natural habitat of fish, wildlife, plants, or similar ecosystems; preservation of open space, including farms and forest land, where the preservation is for the scenic enjoyment of the general public or pursuant to a clearly delineated governmental policy and will yield a significant public benefit; and preservation of an historically important land area or a certified historic structure. I.R.C. § 170(h)(4)(A).

Valuation of a conservation easement typically is based on a "before and after" approach under which the value of the contributed easement is the difference between the fair market value of the property without the restriction and the fair market value after it is encumbered by the easement, based on the objective uses of the property. Reg. § 1.170A–14(h)(3)(i).

Conservation easements have become very popular with wealthy landowners. They require a customized legal agreement between the owner and a qualified donee, which is often a local nature conservancy or land trust. The donee typically allows the owner to continue using and enjoying the property, which may include a residence, but the easement restricts future use, often by limiting further development in perpetuity. The donee of the easement is responsible for monitoring and enforcing the restrictions.

In its 2005 report on revenue-raising options, the Joint Committee on Taxation identified conservation easements as a major trouble spot for tax administrators. The report summarized the problem as follows:

> Charitable deductions of qualified conservation contributions, including conservation and facade easements, present serious policy and compliance issues. Valuation is especially problematic because the measure of the deduction (i.e., generally the difference in fair market value before and after placing the restriction on the property) is highly speculative, considering that, in general, there is no market and thus no comparable sales data for such easements. In many instances, present law does not require that the preservation or protection of conservation be pursuant to a clearly delineated governmental conservation policy, only requiring such a policy in cases of open space preservation if the preservation is not for the scenic enjoyment of the general public. As a result, taxpayers and donee organization have considerable flexibility to determine the conservation purpose served by an easement or other restriction, enabling taxpayers to claim substantial charitable deductions for conservation easements that arguably do not serve a significant conservation purpose.

The Joint Committee staff proposed several reforms, including eliminating the charitable deduction altogether for easements related to personal residences, substantially reducing the deduction for other qualified conservation contributions, and patrolling valuation abuses more carefully by imposing new appraisal standards. In the Pension Protection Act of 2006, however, Congress moved in the opposite direction by temporarily (through 2009) increasing the applicable percentage limitation from 30 to 50 percent for qualified conservation contributions, providing for a 15–year (rather than 5–year) carryover for contributions that exceed the 50 percent limitation (with some technical ordering rules for taxpayers who make other gifts during the same year), and raising the limit to 100 percent of the taxpayer's contribution base for certain eligible farmers and ranchers. I.R.C. § 170(b)(1)(E).

The 2006 legislation also tightened the rules for gifts of facade easements, where an owner gives up rights to make modifications to a historic building while retaining ownership of the property. A contribution relating to the exterior of a building now must preserve the entire exterior, not just its facade, and must provide that no portion of that exterior may be changed or altered in a manner inconsistent with its historical character. In certain cases, filing fees and additional appraisal and reporting requirements are imposed. I.R.C. §§ 170(h)(4)(B), (f)(13).

7. VALUATION AND APPRAISAL REQUIREMENTS

For most noncash contributions, the donor's charitable deduction is the fair market value of the donated property. For this purpose, the regulations adopt the usual definition of fair market value—the price at which property would change hands in an arm's-length transaction between a willing buyer and a willing seller. Reg. § 1.170A–1(c)(2). In the case of publicly traded securities, valuation is easily determined by reference to published quotations. The charitable deduction for a listed security is the mean (i.e., average) of the highest and lowest quoted selling prices on the date of the gift, without regard to the net proceeds realized by the charitable donee on a subsequent sale of the security. Reg. § 20.2031–2(b)(1). Gifts of closely held stock, real estate, art and other hard to value property raise far more difficult valuation questions and have been susceptible to abuse by donors who are seeking inflated charitable contribution deductions. Congress has responded with its usual arsenal of penalties for overvaluations and detailed reporting and appraisal requirements for substantial gifts of property.

Form 8283: Gifts of $5,000 or Less. Noncash charitable contributions in excess of $500 must be reported to the Internal Revenue Service on Form 8283, which is an attachment to the donor's income tax return.[1] The information required on the form varies depending on the type and amount of the gift. Charitable gifts with a claimed value of $5,000 or less per item

---

1. A copy of Form 8283, including instructions, is reproduced in the Statutes, Regulations and Forms Supplement.

(or group of similar items) and gifts of publicly traded securities (even if the deduction exceeds $5,000) are reported on Schedule A of Form 8283. The information requested includes a description of the donated property, the date of the contribution, the date the property was acquired by the donor, how the donor acquired the property, the donor's cost or other tax basis, the fair market value of the property and the method used to determine fair market value. Additional information is required for gifts of less than entire interest in property or gifts subject to restrictions. See Form 8283, Section A, Part II.

Appraisal Requirements: Gifts Over $5,000. No charitable deduction is allowed for contributions of property by individuals, partnerships and corporate donors with a claimed value of more than $5,000 unless the donor obtains a "qualified appraisal" and provides an "appraisal summary" on Part B of Form 8283. I.R.C. § 170(f)(11)(A)(i), (C). A "qualified appraisal" is one which: (1) is made not earlier than 60 days prior to the date of the contribution (this does not restrict the number of days after the contribution but merely limits appraisals made in advance of the gift); (2) is prepared, signed and dated by a "qualified appraiser," who generally must be someone who holds himself out to the public as an appraiser, is familiar with the type of property being appraised, and is unrelated to the donor or donee; (3) includes certain specific information, such as a detailed description of the property and its condition, the valuation method used, the specific basis for the valuation, etc.; and (4) is not based on a percentage of the appraised value of the property or the amount allowed as a deduction. See I.R.C. § 170(f)(11)(E) and Treas.Reg. § 1.170A–13(c) for more detail.

Although a qualified appraisal is necessary to substantiate a charitable deduction, the donor is not required to attach a complete copy to his tax return except in the case of art contributions with a claimed value of $20,000 or more or any property contribution for which a deduction of more than $500,000 is claimed. I.R.C. § 170(f)(11)(D); IRS Form 8283 (rev. Dec. 2006), Sec. B. In all other cases, only an "appraisal summary" is required. The summary consists of certain general information on the donated property. It requires the appraiser to certify that he is qualified under the rules, and the donee must acknowledge that it is a qualified recipient of charitable contributions and received the donated property on the date indicated.

Donee Information Return. The appraisal requirement is buttressed by a donee information return rule. A donee that sells property donated to it with a value in excess of $5,000 within three years of the date of the gift must file an information return (Form 8282) with the Internal Revenue Service. I.R.C. § 6050L. Donees also must provide a description of how they used the asset, whether the use was related to the organization's exempt purpose or function and, if so, the donee must include the written certification required by § 170(e)(7)(D). The reporting requirement is waived for items valued at less than $500 where the donor has signed a declaration to that effect on Form 8283, and for items consumed or distributed without consideration in furtherance of the donee's charitable purpose.

Penalties. If an amount claimed as a charitable deduction is 150 percent or more than the correct value as finally determined, the donor is subject to a substantial valuation misstatement penalty of 20 percent of the amount by which the donor's tax is understated as a result of the inflated valuation. I.R.C. § 6662(e). If the value claimed is 200 percent or more of the correct amount, the penalty is increased to 40 percent of the tax understatement. I.R.C. § 6662(h). For estate and gift tax purposes, a valuation misstatement is "substantial" if the claimed value is 65 percent or less of the correct value and is "gross" if the claimed value is 40 percent or less of the correct amount. I.R.C. § 6662(g). The penalty may be waived only if the donor can show that he or she relied on a qualified appraisal and the donor made a good faith investigation of the value of the contributed property. I.R.C. § 6664(c)(2). An appraiser who is found to have provided an appraisal knowing that it will result in an underpayment of tax also is subject to penalties. See I.R.C. § 6701.

NOTES AND QUESTIONS

1. *Policy Issues.* Why does § 170 permit a charitable deduction for the full fair market value of appreciated capital gain property without requiring the donor to recognize the gain inherent in the property? Without giving the matter much thought, the Internal Revenue Service ruled in 1923 that allowing a full fair market value deduction was an appropriate interpretation of the statute. This rule acts as a powerful inducement for large gifts of stock, real estate and art, particularly by wealthy supporters of private universities and museums. Critics of the appreciated property charitable deduction contend that it sharply departs from normative tax principles and is inequitable. In recommending that the deduction be limited to the lesser of the fair market value of donated property or the donor's basis, indexed for inflation, a 1984 Treasury Department report stated:

> The current treatment of certain charitable gifts of appreciated property is unduly generous and in conflict with basic principles governing the measurement of income for tax purposes. In other circumstances where appreciated property is used to pay a deductible expense, or where such property is the subject of a deductible loss, the deduction allowed may not exceed the taxpayer's adjusted basis plus any gain recognized. Thus, a taxpayer generally may not receive a tax deduction with respect to untaxed appreciation in property. The current tax treatment of certain charitable gifts departs from this principle by permitting the donor a deduction for the full value of the property, including the element of appreciation with respect to which the donor does not realized gain.

U.S. Treasury Department, Report to the President, 2 Tax Reform for Fairness, Simplicity, and Economic Growth 72–74 (1984).

Congress rejected the Treasury's 1984 recommendation but in 1986 it included the unrealized appreciation inherent in contributed capital gain property as a tax preference item for purposes of the alternative minimum tax. For many wealthy donors, this had the effect of significantly reducing the tax benefits of gifts of appreciated property. After a concerted lobbying effort by the nonprofit sector, Congress gradually repealed this provision, initially with respect to gifts of tangible personal property and in 1993 for all gifts of appreciated capital gain property to public charities.

This issue moved back to the front burner during the heightened Congressional scrutiny of the nonprofit sector in 2005 and 2006. In its 2005 report on revenue-raising options, the Joint Committee on Taxation staff observed that "[t]he determination of fair market value creates a significant opportunity for error or abuse by taxpayers making charitable contributions of property" and complained that valuation is a "difficult and resource intensive issue for the IRS to identify, audit, and litigate." Joint Committee on Taxation, Options to Improve Tax Compliance and Reform Tax Expenditures (JCS–02–05) 296 (Jan. 27, 2005). It went on to note that charitable donees had no incentive to challenge inflated valuations and may even directly support them in their zeal to secure a desired gift. The Joint Committee also suggested that noncash contributions often entail significant diversions of resources from a charity's mission or require a charity to incur substantial transaction costs and thus should not be as favored as gifts of cash or marketable securities. Id.

One option proposed by the Joint Committee would limit the income tax deduction for noncash contributions (other than marketable securities) to the lesser of the donor's basis or the fair market value on the date of the gift. This would extend the rule currently applicable to gifts of ordinary income property and non-exempt use tangible personal property to gifts of real estate, art, and other capital gain property. Under an alternative option, an exception to this strict "lesser of basis or value" rule would be carved out for contributions of property used by the donee to substantially further its exempt purposes (e.g., art to an art museum) but with a reduction of the donor's tax benefits if the donee disposed of such exempt use property within three years of the contribution date. Id. at 297–299.

The Joint Committee report explored other possible approaches, including strengthening present law appraisal rules, initially limiting the donor's deduction to the lesser of basis or value but increasing the deduction if the charity were to sell the property for a greater amount within a short time after the contribution (so much for simplicity), or (quite radically) simply eliminating any deduction for gifts of property other than cash or marketable securities on the grounds of simplicity (no valuation disputes) and efficiency (cash is of the most use to charity and does not involve transaction costs). Id. at 304–307.

Not surprisingly, the Panel on the Nonprofit Sector opposed all these recommendations except for strengthening the appraisal requirements, expanding penalties on taxpayers who claim inflated valuations, and imposing new penalties on appraisers who knowingly inflate valuations. Panel on the Nonprofit Sector, Final Report at 53–55.

2. *Art Valuations*. The Internal Revenue Service has an Art Advisory Panel that meets several times a year to determine a value for all donated

works of art with a claimed value of $20,000 or more. The Panel includes museum curators and directors, art scholars, art dealers, and representatives from major auction houses, all of whom serve without compensation. The recommendations made by the Panel are used by the Service in its audit, administrative appeals, and litigation functions. A taxpayer may obtain an advance "statement of value" for donated works of art after the contribution is made but before the taxpayer files a federal income tax return claiming a charitable deduction. Rev. Proc. 96–15, 1996–1 C.B. 627. The procedure is limited to items for which the taxpayer has obtained an appraisal of $50,000 or more, and requires the taxpayer to pay a $2,500 "user fee" to the Service. Taxpayers must submit their qualified appraisals to the Service, which then issues a statement either approving the appraisal or disagreeing and indicating the basis of its disagreement and its own determination of value. In cases where the Service disagrees, the taxpayer may accept the Service's valuation or submit additional support with the tax return on which the deduction is claimed.

PROBLEMS

1. Donor is a single taxpayer who is considering whether to make a charitable gift of appreciated property with a fair market value of $100,000 and an adjusted basis to Donor of $20,000. Potential donees are Public Charity, which is described in § 170(b)(1)(A)(vi), and Private Foundation. Consider generally the tax consequences of the charitable gift in the following alternative situations:

   (a) Donor contributes publicly traded stock acquired more than a year ago to Public Charity.

   (b) Same as (a), above, except the contribution is made to Private Foundation.

   (c) Public Charity is a library. The donated property is a collection of rare books and Donor is a rare book dealer.

   (d) Same as (c), above, except Donor is not a rare book dealer and acquired the books for investment more than one year ago.

   (e) Public Charity is a law school. The donated property is an antique automobile that Public Charity intends to sell at a fund-raising auction, using the proceeds for a student scholarship fund.

   (f) Public Charity is an art museum, and Donor is an artist. The donated property is a work of art painted by Donor and is being donated for the museum's collection.

   (g) Same as (f), above, except that Donor is a collector who acquired the work of art more than a year ago. The museum intends to keep the painting in storage for a year and then sell it and use the proceeds to acquire works of art that are more compatible with its collection.

(h) Same as (g), above, except Donor contributes a 25% fractional interest in the work of art but retains custody of it for the entire year on the understanding that he will make a specific bequest of the remaining fractional interest to the museum at his death.

(i) Donor loans the work of art to the museum for an entire year for an exhibit and then takes it back.

(j) For which of the gifts in the alternatives above must Donor complete and attach a Form 8283 to her income tax return?

(k) For which of the gifts in the alternatives above must Donor obtain a qualified appraisal?

(l) Assume that the donated art in (g), above, is fully deductible, but on audit it is determined to have a fair market value of only $50,000 rather than the $100,000 claimed by Donor on her income tax return. To what extent, if any, will Donor be subject to a valuation overstatement penalty?

2.   Consider the tax consequences of the following charitable gifts:

(a) Environmentalist ("E") owns a parcel of undeveloped land in which he has an adjusted basis of $100,000 and which is subject to an outstanding nonrecourse mortgage of $300,000. The fair market value of the land, as determined by a qualified appraisal, is $400,000. E's adjusted gross income for the current year (apart from this transaction) is $150,000. E wishes to contribute the parcel to The Land Trust, a public charity, which will take the property subject to the outstanding mortgage.

(b) Generous Giver ("GG") owns a 300–acre ranch in Montana where she spends the months of July and August. She wishes to grant the Girl Scouts the exclusive use of the ranch, on a year-to-year basis, during the remaining 10 months.

(c) Todd Hugo owns a 200 acre property in Western Massachusetts that the Hugo family has used as a summer retreat for many decades. Directly adjacent to the Hugo property is a 500–acre parcel owned by the estate of a recently deceased neighbor. The Berkshire Land Trust ("the Trust") is a § 501(c)(3) organization dedicated to land conservation. Hugo proposes to donate appreciated stock to the Trust in an amount sufficient to allow the Trust to acquire the 500–acre parcel. The Trust then will convey 250 of those acres to Hugo subject to a conservation easement permitting the construction of only two residences in return for Hugo's grant of a conservation easement restricting development of his 200 acre property. An appraiser is prepared to write a report stating that the exchange is for equal value.

(d) In (c), above, suggest an alternative plan that would involve less tax risk to the parties.

D. Planned Giving Techniques

1. Introduction

The terms "planned giving" and "deferred giving" do not appear in the Internal Revenue Code or the Treasury Regulations. These terms were created by charitable fundraisers to describe a variety of sophisticated "plans" by which donors make a substantial gift to a charitable organization. The "plan" can be as simple as a pledge during the donor's lifetime to make an outright bequest to endow a chair or scholarship fund at a university. The more typical planned gift involves a more complex arrangement, such as a gift in trust where the donor or his family retains some present or future rights in the property. Planned gifts may be made during the donor's lifetime or at death; in either case, significant tax savings may be achieved if the gift is properly structured.

The topic of planned giving is much too technical for detailed coverage in a survey course on nonprofit organizations. The goal here is to become familiar with the planned giving universe by outlining the principal techniques and providing some typical illustrative cases. Bibliographic references are provided at the end of this section for those who might wish to study this area in the considerable depth that is required for charitable fundraisers, philanthropists, and their legal advisors.

The principal vehicles for planned giving are:

(1) *Charitable Remainder Trusts.* A charitable remainder trust is one of several types of planned giving techniques where a donor makes a gift of property in trust and retains an interest for himself and/or other noncharitable beneficiaries for life or a term of years. In general, there are two types of charitable remainder trusts: annuity trusts and unitrusts. An annuity trust pays out a fixed annual dollar amount to the income beneficiary; the amount is a specific percentage (but not less than 5 percent) of the initial fair market value of the property contributed to the trust. Payments may be made annually or at more frequent intervals. A unitrust is similar except that the income beneficiary, who usually is the donor, receives annual payments based on a fixed percentage of the trust assets as valued each year, or in some cases the annual net income of the trust if it is less than the fixed percentage. In either format, the remainder goes to the charity after the death of the income beneficiary or beneficiaries.

(2) *Pooled Income Funds.* A pooled income fund is a common trust to which a donor transfers cash or securities that are commingled for investment purposes with property transferred to the fund by other donors. The donor or any person designated by the donor is paid an annual amount of income based on the rate of return of the fund.

After the death of the income beneficiary or beneficiaries, the remainder passes to the charity.

(3) *Remainder Interest in a Personal Residence or Farm.* As discussed earlier, charitable gifts of future interests in property that are not made to one of the trust vehicles described above do not offer any tax benefits. In the case of a personal residence or farm, however, a donor may contribute a remainder interest while retaining lifetime use for himself or others and take a charitable deduction for the actuarial value of the remainder interest.

(4) *Charitable Gift Annuity.* A charitable gift annuity is a contract under which a charitable organization, in exchange for an irrevocable gift of cash or property, promises to pay a fixed amount each year to a designated beneficiary for life. The amount of the annuity is determined by actuarial tables. At the time the gift is made, the donor may take a charitable deduction for the difference between the value of the gift and the value of the annuity.

(5) *Charitable Lead Trusts.* A charitable lead trust is the mirror image of a charitable remainder trust. It is a gift in trust with a specified annuity or unitrust amount payable to a charity or group of charities for a term of years. At the end of the charitable income term, the remainder either reverts to the donor or, more commonly, it passes to younger family members, such as children or grandchildren.

2.   CHARITABLE REMAINDER TRUSTS

Apart from simple bequests, charitable remainder trusts are the most widely used planned giving vehicles. In 1969, Congress significantly tightened the requirements to qualify gifts to split-interest trusts for income, gift and estate tax benefits. Prior law permitted donors to claim charitable deductions that did not correlate with the amount that ultimately would be received by the charitable remainder beneficiary. The purpose of the intricate new ground rules was to eliminate these potentially large discrepancies. As a condition to obtaining tax benefits, gifts of partial interests in trust must be made to a "charitable remainder annuity trust" or a "charitable remainder unitrust," as defined in § 664(d). I.R.C. § 170(f)(2)(A). Charitable remainder trusts are most frequently created during a donor's lifetime, but they also may be established at death, in a decedent's will or revocable living trust. In all cases, the charitable deduction—be it for income, gift or estate tax purposes—is determined actuarially and is the present value of the charity's right to receive the corpus of the trust when the noncharitable interests expire. A trust created after July 28, 1997 generally will not qualify as a charitable remainder trust unless the actuarial value of the remainder interest is at least 10 percent of the net fair market value of the property transferred to the trust. I.R.C. §§ 664(d)(1)(D), (d)(2)(D).

Charitable Remainder Annuity Trusts (§ 664(d)(1)). A charitable remainder annuity trust ("CRAT") is a trust from which a specified amount (not less than five percent and not more than 50 percent of the initial fair market value of the assets transferred to the trust) must be paid to the donor and/or other named income beneficiaries, either for the life of the named noncharitable beneficiaries or a specific period of time that may not exceed 20 years. The payments must be made at least annually, but the trust may provide for payments at more frequent intervals, such as quarterly or monthly. The frequency of the payments affects the valuation of the charitable remainder interests.

Since the annuity is fixed, it is unaffected by the accounting income actually earned by the trust. If this income is insufficient, the trustee is required to meet the payout requirement from previously accumulated income (including capital gains) or corpus. If the income exceeds the required payout, it accumulates in the trust. If the trust holds real estate, closely held stock or other illiquid assets that may not generate sufficient income to meet the payout requirement, the trustee is required either to liquidate the assets or transfer fractional portions to the beneficiary. Particularly careful advance planning is thus required for any CRAT that may face a liquidity problem.

No additional gifts may be made to a CRAT after its initial funding, and the trust may not authorize the trustee to invade corpus for the benefit of the noncharitable income beneficiaries. I.R.C. § 664(d)(1)(B).

Charitable Remainder Unitrusts § 664(d)(2). A unitrust is similar to an annuity trust with the important exception that it pays the donor or other noncharitable beneficiaries a variable annuity computed as a fixed percentage (not less than five percent) of the net fair market value of the trust assets valued at least annually. A unitrust is a better inflation hedge than an annuity trust because the payout fluctuates with the value of the trust assets. On the other hand, the guaranteed payout of an annuity trust provides more security if the value of the trust assets should decline.

Section 664(d)(3) also authorizes an alternative "income only" unitrust format that permits the payment of the lesser of: (1) a fixed percentage of the trust's annual value (not less than five percent and not more than 50 percent), or (2) the net income of the trust. The trust also may (but is not required to) include a "makeup" provision which is triggered if the actual income is lower than the percentage amount for one or more years and is higher in a later year. In that case, the excess income can be paid to the beneficiaries up to the amount necessary to "make up" past shortfalls.

The "net income with make-up" (NIMCRUT) format is a particularly flexible device when the property transferred to the trust does not currently produce income (e.g., raw land or closely held stock) and may not be sold for some time after the gift is made. If a trust is a NIMCRUT, the trustee is not required to distribute corpus while the low-yielding property is retained and may make larger distributions after the property is sold. An even more attractive variation is the "flip" unitrust, which begins as an income-only CRUT and converts to a standard fixed payout when the illiquid or unproductive asset is sold or on certain other events. The Service will approve a flip if it is triggered by the sale of an unmarketable asset or other events such as marriage, divorce, death, or birth of a child. See Reg. § 1.644–3(a)(1)(i)(c)–(e).

Another feature unique to unitrusts is that additional deductible gifts may be made by the grantor after the trust is initially funded. When the trust is funded with hard-to-value assets such as closely held stock or real estate, a disadvantage of a unitrust is the requirement to value the assets at least annually.

Determining the Donor's Charitable Deduction. The charitable income and gift tax deduction for a donor who makes a lifetime gift to a charitable remainder trust is the present value of the charitable remainder interest, determined from the Service's actuarial and mortality tables. These valuations are based on tables that incorporate the applicable discount rate for the month in which the valuation date falls or, if the taxpayer elects, either of the two preceding months. I.R.C. § 7520(a). The applicable rate varies monthly and is set at 120 percent of an index known as the "Federal Mid–Term Rate." The amount of the charitable deduction is thus a function of the annuity or unitrust payment; the length of the noncharitable income payout period; the frequency of payment of the annuity or unitrust amount; and, for annuity trusts, the § 7520 rate. A similar approach is used for determining the charitable estate tax deduction for bequests to a charitable remainder trust. See I.R.C. § 2055(e)(2).

To illustrate, assume 70–year old Donor contributes $300,000 of appreciated stock to a charitable remainder annuity trust, retaining a $15,000 (5 percent) annuity for her life, payable annually, with the remainder passing to a designated public charity. At the time of the gift, the applicable discount rate under § 7520 is 4 percent. Using the appropriate actuarial valuation tables, Donor's charitable income tax deduction is determined as follows:

Amount of Annuity	$15,000
Annuity Factor for Age 70	10.0589
Present Value of Annuity	150,884
Present Value of Remainder	149,116

Donor's charitable deduction is thus $149,116, subject to the 30 percent limitation for gifts of capital gain property to public charities. If Donor had contributed cash, the 50 percent limitation would have applied. If the charitable remainder beneficiary were a private foundation, the percentage limitations would be reduced to 30 percent (for cash gifts) and 20 percent (gifts of capital gain property).

Income Taxation of the Trust and its Beneficiaries. A charitable remainder trust generally is exempt from all federal income taxes except in the rare case where it has unrelated business taxable income. In that event, it is subject to an excise tax equal to 100 percent of its UBTI. I.R.C. § 664(c). As a result, when a charitable remainder trust sells appreciated property contributed by a donor, the gain is not taxable to the trust although, under rules described below, it may be taxable to the life income beneficiaries when it is distributed.

The beneficiaries of a charitable remainder trust are taxable on the amounts distributed to them, but the character of that income is determined based on a unique "tier system" that looks to the historic income of the trust since its creation. Distributions are first taxed as ordinary income to the extent of the trust's ordinary income for the current year and undistributed ordinary income from prior years. Within the ordinary income category, distributions are first deemed made from ordinary income subject to tax at the highest marginal rates (e.g., interest, rents) and then from "qualified dividends," which through 2010 are subject to a maximum tax rate of 15 percent when received by individual taxpayers. Any remaining portion of the distribution is taxed as capital gain to the extent of current and past undistributed capital gains, with short-term gains deemed distributed first; then as "other" (i.e., tax-exempt) income to the extent of current and past exempt income of the trust; and finally as a nontaxable distribution of corpus. I.R.C. § 664(b); Treas. Reg. § 1.664–1(d).

To illustrate, assume Donor contributes $500,000 of nondividend paying publicly traded growth stock with a basis of $100,000 to a charitable remainder annuity trust that pays a 7 percent annuity ($35,000) per year. The CRAT immediately sells the stock, realizing a $400,000 long-term capital gain, and invests the proceeds in a corporate bond yielding 8 percent ($40,000 interest income) annually. The annual $35,000 payout to Donor is deemed to come entirely from the current ordinary income of the trust. If the proceeds had been invested entirely in an 8 percent tax-exempt bond, the trust would have no ordinary income and thus the $35,000 payout would be taxed as "second-tier" long-term capital gain to Donor until the $400,000 long-term capital gain from the sale of the stock is exhausted through distributions.

Application of Private Foundation Restrictions. Section 4947(a)(2) provides that split-interest charitable trusts are subject to some of the restrictions applicable to private foundations. Specifically, a qualifying charitable remainder trust is subject to the prohibitions on self-dealing in § 4941 and the taxable expenditure rules in § 4945. See Chapter 7D, supra, at pp. 769–781, 795–804.

3. Pooled Income Funds

A pooled income fund is a trust, created and administered by a public charity, which consists of commingled property contributed by many donors who retain life income interests in their pro rata shares of the net income earned by the fund. See I.R.C. § 642(c)(5). Pooled income funds are particularly attractive to smaller donors. They provide a means for diversifying investments without incurring the tax that otherwise would result if the donor sold appreciated property and reinvested the proceeds. See I.R.C. § 642(c)(5).

Pooled income funds are like mutual funds. A donor who contributes cash or property to the fund acquires "units" of participation that entitle the donor to periodic distributions of income that usually continue for the life of the donor or one or more other living persons. The annual income received by a beneficiary is dependent on the fund's rate of return. Some larger charities maintain different types of pooled income funds to accommodate their donors' goals—e.g., a relatively stable fixed-income fund along with a lower-yielding balanced fund that seeks moderate growth and thus the potential of higher income in later years.

A donor to a pooled income fund receives a current income tax deduction for the actuarial value of the charitable remainder interest. I.R.C. § 170(f)(2)(A). Valuation is dependent on several variables, including the value of the donated property, the age of the income beneficiary or beneficiaries, the historical rate of return of the fund, or an assumed rate of return for new funds. The fund itself is generally exempt from tax, but income received by the beneficiary is taxable at ordinary income rates.

4. REMAINDER INTEREST IN PERSONAL RESIDENCE OR FARM

One of the few partial interests in property that qualifies for charitable income, gift and estate tax deductions is a remainder interest in a personal residence or farm. If the interest is contributed during the donor's lifetime, the donor may take an income tax deduction for the actuarial value of the remainder interest, discounted to reflect straight line depreciation on the improvements. See I.R.C. §§ 170(f)(3)(B)(i), (f)(4); Treas.Reg. § 1.170A–12. In a typical arrangement, the donor continues living in the residence or on the farm during his or her life, and at death the property passes to charity.

To qualify as a personal residence, the property need not be the donor's *principal* residence. Vacation homes also may qualify. A "farm" includes the land and buildings used by the donor for the production of crop, fruits, agricultural products, or sustenance of livestock.

5. CHARITABLE GIFT ANNUITIES

A charitable gift annuity involves the transfer of property to a charitable organization in return for the charity's commitment to pay an annual sum certain to the donor for the donor's life, or for the joint lives of the donor and the donor's spouse. A charitable deduction is allowed for the amount transferred to charity that exceeds the actuarially determined present value of the annuity. In general, the annual amounts received by the donor is taxed according to the normal rules for the taxation of annuities. Thus, a portion of each annuity payment is a tax-free return of capital, and a portion is taxable as ordinary income. See I.R.C. § 72.

When a donor transfers appreciated property to acquire the annuity, the transaction is treated as a bargain sale for tax purposes. A portion of the donor's basis in the transferred asset is allocated to the gift portion of the transaction, and the balance is allocated to the purchase of the annuity. The gain from the "sale part" may be spread over the period during which payments are received if the annuitant is the donor or the donor's spouse. If the annuitant is a third party, the entire gain is taxable in the year of the gift. See Treas. Reg. § 1.170A–1(d); 1.1011–2(b).

6.   Charitable Lead Trusts

Charitable lead trusts provide for a gift of income to charity for a period of time with the remainder either returning to the grantor or passing to noncharitable beneficiaries, usually children or grandchildren of the grantor. One type of lead trust—the "grantor lead trust"—is used principally to obtain a current income tax deduction equal to the actuarial value of the charitable income interest. The more widely used format—the "nongrantor lead trust"—is an estate planning technique designed to provide income to charity for a specified term and then to pass the property to family members at little or no wealth transfer tax cost. In either case, the trust must provide for payments to a specified charity or charities not less than annually, and the payments must be in the form of a fixed annuity or a unitrust interest.

Grantor Lead Trusts. A grantor lead trust is useful when the donor is seeking a current income tax charitable deduction in a year when his or her marginal income tax rate is unusually high relative to later years. Grantor lead trusts have little or no appeal when tax rates are relatively flat or are gradually increasing over time because the trade-off for a current income tax deduction for the actuarial value of the charitable income interest is that the donor is taxable on the trust income at a higher rate during the term of the trust even though she does not receive the income. If a donor expects to be in a lower marginal tax bracket in the future, however, the present value of the current deduction may outweigh the present value of the future tax liability on the trust income.

Nongrantor Lead Trusts. The nongrantor lead trust does not provide a current income tax deduction but it may be a useful technique for shifting wealth to younger generations. If properly structured, a nongrantor lead trust allows a donor to benefit a favored charity for a period of time and then pass the property either outright or in a continuing trust to family members at relatively little transfer tax cost. If a nongrantor lead trust is established during the donor's life, a current gift tax deduction is available for the actuarial value of the charitable lead interest. If a lead trust is created upon the donor's death, the donor's estate is entitled to an estate tax charitable deduction for the value of the charitable lead interest. In either case, the remainder passing to family members is a taxable gift or bequest at the time the trust is created. The amount of the taxable gift may be minimized by synchronizing the required charitable payout with the term of the trust—a result more easily accomplished when the applicable discount rate under § 7520 is lower rather than higher.

The problems that follow illustrate some prototype cases where charitable split-interest trusts may be utilized effectively.

PROBLEMS

1. Julius Sims is a 65 year old bachelor with a net worth of approximately $1.6 million and adjusted gross income of $200,000 per year. His assets include 10,000 shares of publicly traded Pacific Wiper Co. stock, which he acquired many years ago for $50,000. The stock is now worth $500,000, but it pays a meager dividend of 50 cents per share. Julius is interested in diversifying his portfolio, but he does not relish the prospect of the large capital gains tax that he would incur if he were to sell or all or part of his Pacific Wiper stock. Julius has no close relatives and plans to leave the bulk of his estate to the Sturdley College of Business Administration to establish the Julius Sims Professorship.

Consider the following proposal that has been suggested by a financial planner. Julius will transfer his entire 10,000 shares of Pacific Wiper stock to a charitable remainder annuity trust. Julius will retain an annual annuity of $35,000, and the remainder will be distributed on Julius's death to Sturdley College, a public charity which will serve as Trustee. During discussions with representatives of Sturdley's development office, an understanding has been reached that Sturdley will sell the Pacific Wiper stock and reinvest the proceeds in a diversified portfolio of stocks and bonds. Assume that at the time the stock is transferred to the trust, the applicable rate under § 7520 for the month of the gift and the two prior months is 6% (and thus the annuity valuation factor is 9.9301).

(a) In general, what are the income tax consequences to Julius when he creates the trust? Would the result be the same if Julius simply retained a life income interest in the trust, with the remainder to go to Sturdley College.

(b) What is the income tax treatment of the trust during Julius's life?

(c) What are the income tax consequences to Julius when he receives his $35,000 annual annuity? Is your answer affected by the Trustee's investment strategy?

(d) Would Julius have jeopardized the tax benefits for himself and the trust if he had reserved the right to change the charitable remainder beneficiary at any time during his life?

(e) Is it appropriate for Sturdley College to serve as Trustee of a charitable remainder trust created for its benefit? Could Julius have served as Trustee?

(f) When Julius dies, will the trust property be included in his gross estate for federal estate tax purposes?

(g) In general, how would the income tax consequences change if the applicable § 7520 rate was lower than 6%?

(h) Assume that Julius's lawyer is not competent to draft a charitable remainder trust and would prefer the planning, drafting, and other details to be handled by the development office of Sturdley College. Is it appropriate for the charity to assist the donor in this manner?

May the charity pay the expenses for a competent lawyer to plan and draft the trust?

2. Garth Coleman is a wealthy 65–year old widower. He has $2 million of his own funds and recently inherited a $10 million estate from his wife, Marian. Garth is a loyal alumnus of Private Law School ("PLS") and was recently named as chair of its Board of Visitors. He regularly makes charitable gifts to PLS averaging about $20,000 per year but will be expected to give more in his role as chair of the Board of Visitors. Garth ultimately would like to leave his wealth to his children and grandchildren. Would it make sense for Garth to consider establishing a nongrantor charitable lead trust that would pay a specific amount to PLS for a period of time and then distribute the assets remaining in trust to his children? Consider generally the design of the trust and the tax consequences of such an arrangement.

PART FOUR

MUTUAL BENEFIT AND PRIVATE MEMBERSHIP ORGANIZATIONS

CHAPTER 9

TAX EXEMPTION: MUTUAL BENEFIT AND OTHER NONCHARITABLE ORGANIZATIONS

A. THE RATIONALE FOR TAX EXEMPTION

This chapter considers the diverse family of "noncharitable" nonprofits that exist primarily to further the common goals of their members rather than the public at large. The major categories are social welfare organizations, a type of hybrid charity created by the law; mutual benefit organizations such as labor unions, trade and professional associations, social clubs, fraternal lodges, cooperatives; and a myriad of other more specialized entities ranging from cemetery companies to black lung trusts. Mutual benefit and other noncharitable organizations generally are not eligible to receive tax-deductible contributions,[1] and they do not share most of the other tax benefits enjoyed by § 501(c)(3) charities such as preferred postal rates, property tax exemptions, exemption from unemployment taxes, and the ability to issue tax-exempt bonds.

Since mutual benefit organizations are viewed as providing only an incidental (or no) public benefit and may not be subject to the nondistribution constraint, one might ask why this chapter is even necessary. Is there a normative principle that explains why organizations serving the narrow economic or social interests of their members have long been exempt from federal income tax? Can tax exemptions for mutual benefit nonprofits be explained by the traditional subsidy theories that justify the charitable exemption? Perhaps because their tax benefits are not as generous or extensive as those enjoyed by their charitable counterparts, mutual benefit organizations have not been as closely scrutinized by the taxing authorities or legal scholars. The excerpt below is one of the few attempts in the tax literature to articulate a coherent rationale for exemption.

---

1. The few exceptions are veterans organizations, fraternal societies (if the gift is used for charitable purposes), and cemetery companies. I.R.C. § 170(c)(3)–(5).

Boris I. Bittker and George K. Rahdert, The Exemption of Nonprofit Organizations From Federal Income Taxation

85 Yale L.J. 299, 348–357 (1977).

In general terms, mutual benefit organizations are operated to provide goods and services to their members at cost. Any excess of gross revenues over costs may appear to violate this purpose, but since they do not endeavor to generate profits from membership patronage, a year-end surplus could be viewed as an overcharge which, if promptly refunded to the members, should not be classified as "income." This is in fact how patronage refunds by consumers' cooperative societies are treated, reflecting the fact that the society would have had nothing resembling "income" if it had reduced its prices in order to avoid a year-end surplus. And since actual price reductions would have prevented the society from having any income, one might favor the same tax-free result if the "overcharges" are retained by the mutual society to benefit the members in future years by permitting charges to be reduced or facilities to be expanded without additional cost. Alternatively—but with the same nontaxable result—a mutual society's "profit" from membership patronage might be regarded as a deposit or capital contribution by the members to finance future activities or facilities. If the members of a commune estimate their expenses for food at $500 per person and pay this amount in advance to their purchasing agent, one would not expect the group, as an entity, to realize income if the cost turned out to be only $450 per person, even if the excess was retained for the commune's future needs rather than refunded to the members. To classify the excess as income would be tantamount to taxing the members because they were astute shoppers or because they performed unpaid services for the society.

Much could be said for a comprehensive statutory rule embodying the foregoing rationale, but—as is often true of the Internal Revenue Code—Congress has preferred piecemeal legislation to broad generalizations. Similarly, Congress did not prescribe a set of across-the-board rules governing the investment income, profit-oriented activities and transactions with nonmembers, of mutual benefit organizations, but instead established many divergent taxing systems, which turn on such variables as the organization's size, function, history, and occupational or geographic characteristics. The most important categories of mutual benefit organizations are discussed hereafter.

A.   Social Clubs

Clubs organized and operated exclusively "for pleasure, recreation, and other nonprofitable purposes" have been exempt since 1916. As originally enacted, the exemption was denied if any part of the club's net earnings inured to the benefit of any "private shareholder or member." In 1924, the word "member" was excised from this restriction, and the door was opened to two substantial tax advantages: the building up of a tax-free endowment, and the exemption from tax of profits derived from dealings with nonmembers.

First, the members of a social club could build up its capital with their initiation fees and dues, immunizing the income generated by these contributions from tax, even though it served to reduce the club's charges to its members in later years. Of course, if the dues and fees were invested in such assets as a golf course or a clubhouse, the use of the exempt organization to acquire these properties would not result in a tax savings for the members, because if the members invested in recreational or social property individually or as joint tenants rather than through a "conduit" organization, their ownership and use of these facilities would not itself create taxable income. But if the club converted the contributions into income-producing endowment, it got an exemption that was not available to the members as individuals. In effect, therefore, they could earmark part of their own income-producing capital to be used, free of income taxes, to pay for their pleasure or recreation.[136] Second, social clubs enjoyed an even more dramatic advantage in that profits generated by their transactions with nonmembers were also exempt from tax, despite use of these profits to reduce the fees paid by members or to provide better facilities without cost to them.

Before 1969, when this state of affairs was drastically altered by legislation, the courts intervened from time to time to limit the scope of these tax advantages. Although the adjective "social" is a label rather than an operative statutory phrase, the statutory term "club," in conjunction with the Code's references to "pleasure" and "recreation," was held to require "some sort of commingling of members," with the result that groups like automobile clubs serving a mutual interest without social contact among the members were held not to qualify. The courts found another restraint in the statutory requirement that a club be operated exclusively for "nonprofitable purposes," which was interpreted to disqualify clubs with excessive amounts of income from nonmembership patronage or separate business activities. Even if a social club avoided these pitfalls, however, the Tax Reform Act of 1969 substantially reduced its tax advantages by expanding the reach of the tax on "unrelated business taxable income." With minor exceptions, a social club's income from investments and from non-member patronage is now taxable.

As a consequence of the 1969 changes, the major significance of a social club's exemption at present is that it is not taxed on "profits" arising from goods, facilities, and services furnished to members and their dependents and guests. This residual tax advantage is minimal if the club is regarded as a true association of its members, since any profit from one year's operations will at most be used to reduce membership charges in another

---

136. A nonexempt club might attempt to achieve the same result, by using endowment or business income to reduce its charges to members for their use of its social facilities, and deducting the maintenance expenses under § 162 in a manner reminiscent of the incorporated country estates and yachts that gave rise to § 543(a)(6) of the personal holding company provisions. * * *

year. A relentless search for income in this context, of course, would disclose that some members derive an economic advantage from expenditures by their fellow members. Thus, if the club's sole charge is an annual membership fee, those who use the club's facilities frequently are subsidized by the other members, just as a trencherman benefits from splitting a restaurant bill equally after dining with a group of abstemious friends. But if the friends' overpayment is subjected to analysis, it qualifies as a tax-free gift to the person paying less than his true share of the bill. Perhaps the benefits accruing to a member of a social club who pays less than his share of its costs, at the expense of members paying more than their share, can also be characterized as a gift, even though the bonds of affection among the members are more attenuated than is customary in the case of most gifts.

B. Consumers' Cooperatives and Similar Organizations

The Internal Revenue Code contains a single set of rules to govern the tax treatment of two quite different types of cooperative societies-consumers' cooperatives, organized primarily to supply food and other household goods to their members; and marketing cooperatives, organized by farmers, dairymen, and other producers to market their agricultural products. The far greater economic importance of marketing cooperatives, coupled with a risk that agricultural profits may slip untaxed through a statutory crevice between the cooperative and its members, has given rise to elaborate provisions to ensure that all income will be reported by one or the other of these potential taxpayers. The tax status of consumers' cooperatives emerges almost as an afterthought from the same network of rules.

Under the basic statutory scheme, as applied to consumers' cooperatives, the organization enjoys no explicit tax exemption, but it is allowed to exclude patronage dividends from its taxable income. These distributions are not taxed to the members, on the theory that they represent belated reductions in the cost of household goods. The net effect is that the organization is taxed in full on income from business with nonmembers; it is taxed on transactions with its members only to the extent that overcharges are not refunded, and it can reduce its taxable income from membership transactions by either charging less or refunding more. Earnings from membership patronage retained by the organization to provide working capital or expand its facilities, however, are subject to tax, even though, as suggested earlier, they might be appropriately exempted on the ground that they represent savings by the members to reduce their future living expenses.

Although they perform substantially the same functions as consumers' cooperatives, various other organizations are granted blanket tax exemption (save for their unrelated business income) by the Internal Revenue Code. This miscellaneous group of exempt organizations includes:

1. Fraternal lodges and employee associations providing life, sickness, accident, or other benefits to members and dependents.

2. Local life insurance associations, and mutual irrigation, telephone, and similar companies, if at least 85 percent of their income is paid by members to defray expenses and losses.

3. Cemetery companies operated for the benefit of their members, or not for profit.

4. Credit unions.

5. Insurance companies (primarily fire and casualty companies) whose premiums and investment income do not exceed $150,000.

Profits accruing to these organizations from membership patronage, which is probably the sole or dominant source of their income in most cases, qualify for exemption under the rationale outlined above for exclusion of the patronage dividends of cooperatives. Income from investment or nonmembership patronage, however, would not be immune from tax under this conduit rationale, and the statutory exemption of income from these sources probably reflects benign neglect more than thoughtful attention.[148]

C. Labor Unions

Section 501(c)(5) exempts "labor organizations" in unqualified language, carrying forward a provision of the Revenue Act of 1913. The Regulations state that the organization's net earnings must not inure to the benefit of any member, a restriction of doubtful validity unless loosely construed, since the statutory provision must have been intended, and has been consistently interpreted, to exempt labor unions engaged in collective bargaining on behalf of their members. The prohibition is also virtually retracted by another part of the Regulations themselves, conditioning the exemption on the organization's dedication to "the betterment of the conditions" of its membership. Moreover, the Internal Revenue Service has ruled that unions do not lose their exemption by paying sickness, death, accident, or other benefits to members. In revoking an earlier ruling to the contrary, the Service said that "labor organizations were exempted for the very reason that they operated, in part, as mutual benefit organizations providing [such] benefits to their members."

---

148. In addition to consumer cooperatives, agricultural and horticultural organizations have been consistently included in the statutory list of exempt organizations since 1913. Although the statute does not describe these organizations further, the Regulations state that their objectives must be "the betterment of the conditions of those engaged in such pursuits, the improvement of the grade of their products, and the development of a higher degree of efficiency in their respective occupations" and that they must not allow their net earnings to inure to the benefit of their members. Treas. Reg. § 1.501(c)(5)–1(a)(1958).

Given these limitations, organizations qualifying under § 501(c)(5) have much in common with business leagues, exempt under § 501(c)(6), and with social welfare organizations exempt under § 501(c)(4). * * *

Farmers' cooperatives, whether engaged in purchasing supplies and equipment for their members or in marketing their produce, are subject to special rules. * * * Hence the organizations qualifying under § 501(c)(5) are probably of minor importance. The few published rulings refer to the sponsorship of county fairs, improvement of livestock, and soil testing as appropriate objectives of these organizations. * * *

Approached *ab initio*, the exemption of labor unions is best examined in the context of the principles governing business expenses. Dues paid by a union member are deductible as ordinary and necessary business expenses under § 162 because the organization serves as his collective bargaining agent in a profit-seeking endeavor and in otherwise seeking to improve his conditions of employment. If the dues are not immediately spent by the union, but are invested and retained for future contingencies (in a strike fund, for example), the member's share of the union's investment income might be imputed back to him. But then the member should be allowed an offsetting deduction when the income so imputed is later spent by the organization on his behalf, because he could deduct similar expenditures from his own private (and taxable) investment income.

As in the case of business leagues, exempting the organization's accumulated income is the equivalent of currently imputing its income to its members but allowing them to deduct these amounts when they are ultimately used by the union, except that the time value of the money slips past the tax collector. Alternatively, if the union's accumulated income permits dues to be reduced in future years (or activities to be expanded without additional cost to the membership), the fact that the members will deduct a smaller amount for dues in these years than if they paid in full for the union's activities will compensate the Treasury, albeit belatedly, for the revenue lost by exempting the union's income when realized-again, except for the time value of the money.[155]

D. Business Leagues

Since 1913, business leagues, chambers of commerce, and boards of trade have been exempt from income taxation if not organized for profit and if their net earnings do not inure to the benefit of any private shareholder or individual. Real estate boards were added to the statutory list in 1928 and professional football leagues in 1966.[156] Trade associations are the most common instances of exempt "business leagues," along with professional groups like the American Bar Association and the American Medical Association.

For most qualifying organizations, the statutory prohibitions of § 501(c)(6) against a profit orientation and the inurement of net earnings to private benefit must be loosely interpreted, as was no doubt intended by Congress from the outset. Strictly construed, these limits would close the door to organizations serving the business interests of an industry, since these activities inure to the benefit of their profit-motivated members. Such a construction would confine § 501(c)(6) to organizations not in need of its protection-those devoted to the general welfare of society, which qualify for

---

155. * * * Since the membership's composition changes over time, the group to whom the union's investment income would be imputed is not identical with the group that will benefit from future lower dues. As pointed out earlier * * *, there is a similar disparity in the case of social clubs.

156. § 501(c)(6). The 1966 committee reports do not disclose why baseball was not given the same treatment as football. If the House Committee on Un–American Activities were still on the warpath, surely it would want to investigate this disparagement of our national sport.

exemption as charitable or social welfare organizations under § 501(c)(3) or (4). The statutory prohibitions of § 501(c)(6), therefore, have not been interpreted to preclude the commonly understood objectives of chambers of commerce and similar organizations.

As summarized by the Regulations, the activities of a business league

should be directed to the improvement of business conditions of one or more lines of business as distinguished from the performance of particular services for individual persons. An organization whose purpose is to engage in a regular business of a kind ordinarily carried on for profit, even though the business is conducted on a cooperative basis or produces only sufficient income to be self-sustaining, is not a business league.

In administration, the interpretative problems under § 501(c)(6) have primarily concerned the boundary between business leagues and taxable joint business ventures. Although § 501(c)(6) does not by any means impose a high standard of altruism, it has been held to exclude organizations created by business competitors to coordinate or centralize their advertising or purchasing activities, engage in research for their exclusive benefit, furnish credit reports and collect delinquent accounts, or otherwise advance their special business interests; § 501(c)(6) does require some showing of benefit to the public. Less frequently, it is necessary to decide whether a business league's devotion to the public interest so outweighs its service to its membership as to justify classification as a charitable or educational organization. Charitable status is ordinarily of minor importance, however, since tax exemption as a business league is usually as satisfactory as exemption under § 501(c)(3). To be sure, the latter status permits gifts to be deducted by the donors as charitable contributions, but this is no more (and, occasionally, less) advantageous than deducting them as business expenses under § 162. While charitable status would be preferred to a § 501(c)(6) exemption if gifts are sought from exempt foundations or other nonmember donors, a business league could obtain deductible contributions by organizing an affiliated entity devoted solely to its charitable objectives. An example is the American Bar Association's American Bar Endowment.

Once it is recognized that § 501(c)(6) organizations ordinarily serve the business objectives of their members, the justification for their statutory exemption is exposed as rickety. There would be no great difficulty in applying familiar principles of income computation to their activities, nor in fixing an appropriate level of taxation for an organization whose membership is composed of corporations whose income is taxed predominantly at a fixed rate. On the other hand, the exercise would, to a large degree, be self-defeating. First, their charges to members would no doubt be increased to offset the tax, and the additional amounts would be deductible by the members as business expenses; their own taxes would thus be reduced by about one-half of the taxes paid by the organization. Second, as a more drastic response, the organization could operate at or near its breakeven point, generating little or no income to be taxed, and increasing its charges to its members when necessary.

Viewed as an alternative to the hypothetical charges that could be deducted by its members, a business league's tax exemption, which covers its investment income, is not without a plausible rationale. The principal residual objection to the § 501(c)(6) exemption is that if large reserves are currently being accumulated by the organization against nebulous and distant future needs, its members are able to delay income tax liability—and thus save the time value of the deferred taxes—by taking immediate deductions for the league's future business expenditures and by excluding from income the organization's endowment income.

NOTES AND QUESTIONS

1. *Subsidy and Capital Formation Theories*. To what extent does the traditional subsidy theory explain the exemption for mutual benefit organizations? Is Congress trying to encourage mutual benefit nonprofits to perform their various roles? Or is the income tax exemption the product of historical factors, inattention, or the political power of the benefited groups? Some academic theorists justify the exemption by arguing that mutual benefit organizations arise in response to the failure of the private markets. Because mutual benefits are the most efficient suppliers of their goods and services, these theorists assert, they should be granted exemption from tax in order to increase their retained earnings available for growth. See, e.g., Henry Hansmann, The Rationale for Exempting Nonprofit Organizations from Corporate Income Taxation, 91 Yale L.J. 54, 95–96 (1981).

2. *Investment Income*. Why should the passive investment income of mutual benefit organizations be exempt from tax? Do Bittker and Rahdert adequately explain why the exemption reaches this far? In 1987, the staff of the Joint Committee on Taxation floated a proposal to tax the investment income of trade associations and labor unions, but it was never seriously considered. The idea remained largely dormant outside of academic circles until the Clinton Administration, in its fiscal year 2000 budget submission, proposed to raise revenue by taxing investment income of trade associations in excess of $10,000. The arguments for and against this proposal are summarized by the staff of the Joint Committee on Taxation in the excerpt that follows.

Excerpt From Joint Committee on Taxation, Description of Revenue Provisions Contained in the President's Fiscal Year 2000 Budget Proposal

106th Cong., 1st Sess. 279–281 (JCS 1–99, Feb. 22, 1999).

1. Subject investment income of trade associations to tax

In general

Under present law, dues payments by members of an organization described in section 501(c)(6) generally are deductible. In addition, the organization generally is not subject to tax on its investment income. Thus, members of such an organization are able to fund future operations of the organization through deductible dues payments, even though the members would have been subject to tax on the earnings attributable to such dues payments if they had been retained and invested by the members and paid at the time the organization had expenses. Supporters of the Administration proposal argue that the tax-exempt treatment accorded to organizations described in section 501(c)(6) should not extend to the accumulation of assets on a tax-free basis. Thus, it can be argued that such organizations should be subject to tax on earnings attributable to amounts collected in excess of the amounts needed to fund current operations of the organization.

Opponents of the proposal will argue that the proposal does not permit organizations described in section 501(c)(6) to plan for anticipated expenditures, such as the purchase of a headquarters building. Thus, it could be argued that the proposal has the effect of forcing such an organization to collect substantial dues from members in the year in which an extraordinary expense arises and that this will have the effect of penalizing those individuals who are members at the time of an extraordinary expense. On the other hand, the Administration proposal does not subject the first $10,000 of investment earnings to tax, and thus allows an organization described in section 501(c)(6) to accumulate some assets to meet future expenses.

Opponents of the proposal also may contend that it is not appropriate to extend the tax treatment of social clubs (and other mutual benefit organizations) to other organizations described in section 501(c)(6), because the purposes and activities of these types of entities are not analogous. The purpose of a social club is to provide to its members benefits of a recreational or social nature, which generally would not be deductible if directly paid for by the members. Accordingly, it is considered appropriate to prevent such benefits from being provided through tax-free investment income. In contrast, expenditures for many of the activities of a trade association (e.g., although not expenditures for lobbying or political activities * * *) would be deductible by the association's members if carried on by the members directly, because the expenditures would constitute ordinary and necessary business expenses under section 162(a).

Alternatively, opponents might argue the proposal is too narrow because it would not impose tax on the investment income of organizations exempt under other provisions of section 501 (for example, labor, agricultural or horticultural organizations under sec. 501(c)(5)). On the other hand, it could be argued that such organizations are not analogous to the ones taxed under the proposal, or to organizations subject to [the unrelated business income tax] under present law on all gross income other than exempt function income.

* * *

Economic analysis of proposal

In general, the dues collected by a trade association are established at levels that are intended to provide sufficient funds to carry out the exempt purposes of the trade association. That is, the trade association ultimately spends all dues collected on the exempt purposes of the trade association. The effect of the present-law exclusion from UBIT for certain investment income of trade associations is that if the trade association collects $1.00 of dues today, but does not incur expenses until some point in the future, the association will have an amount with a present value of $1.00 available to meet those expenses. For example, if interest rates are 10 percent and the trade association collects $1.00 in January 1999, but incurs no expenses until January 2000, at that time it will have $1.10 available to meet expenses.

The deductibility of dues paid by the trade association member to the trade association effectively reduces the cost of paying such dues. Depending upon whether investment earnings of trade associations predominantly are earned and used to fund current year operations or whether substantial balances of assets are carried forward for a number of years, the present-law exclusion from UBIT for investment income of trade associations may permit the trade association and its members to effectively lower the cost of the trade associations's dues below the cost reduction created solely by deductibility of dues.

* * *

NOTES AND QUESTIONS

1. *Lobbying Against Taxing the Lobbyists.* The Clinton Administration's proposal would have taxed the wealthiest special interest trade associations—namely, lobbyists. Not surprisingly, the intended targets responded by lobbying against the proposal. A spokesman for the Chamber of Commerce described the plan as "a stake driven at the very heart of nonprofit organizations." Jacob M. Schlesinger, Clinton Plan to Tax Lobbyists' Investment Gains Hits Home in a Fury of Faxes, Letters, Web Sites, Wall St. J., Feb. 17, 1999, at A24. Trade groups argued that their investment income is derived from funds accumulated as a result of "prudent fiscal planning" and used for public services. Id. Despite its theoretical appeal, the proposal was not well received and is unlikely to be revived in the near term. For a thoughtful discussion of the issue, see Analysis of Administration's Year 2000 Budget Proposal to Tax the Investment Income of Trade Associations, ABA Tax Section, in 25 Exempt Org. Tax Rev. 138 (1999).

2. *Why Not Labor Unions?* Why was the Clinton Administration's proposal limited to § 501(c)(6) trade associations? Shouldn't the investment income of labor unions also be taxed? Do individual members of labor unions receive the same tax benefits from their dues payments as corporate members of trade associations?

B.   SOCIAL WELFARE ORGANIZATIONS

Internal Revenue Code: § 501(c)(4).

Treasury Regulations: § 1.501(c)(4)–1.

Section 501(c)(4) confers exempt status on "civic leagues or organizations not organized for profit but operated exclusively for the promotion of social welfare." Social welfare organizations are a breed of public benefit organization and are regulated like charities under the laws of many states, but they differ markedly from § 501(c)(3) charities because of their inability to receive tax-deductible contributions as well as their ability to engage in substantial lobbying activities.

To qualify for exemption under § 501(c)(4), an organization must be primarily engaged in promoting in some way the common good and general welfare of the community, such as "by bringing about civic betterments and social improvements." Treas. Reg. § 1.501(c)(4)–1(a)(2). "Social welfare" is thus quite similar to "charitable," the major difference being that attempts to influence legislation are not considered "charitable" purposes but are nonetheless regarded as compatible with the promotion of social welfare. This distinction is rather odd in view of the fact that promotion of social welfare is an example of a charitable purpose. See Treas. Reg. § 1.501(c)(3)–1(d)(2).

As discussed earlier in the text (see Chapter 5E6, supra, at pp. 532–536, "social welfare" does not include direct or indirect participation in political campaigns on behalf of candidates for public office; social activities for the benefit, pleasure or recreation of members; or the conduct of a business with the general public in a manner similar to commercial operations. Treas. Reg. § 1.501(c)(4)–1(a)(2)(ii). Lobbying is permissible, of course, but illegal activities such as civil disobedience are regarded as an impermissible means of promoting social welfare.

As a practical matter, apart from its role as the Code section of choice for politically active advocacy groups, § 501(c)(4) has become the default choice ("dumping ground"?) for organizations that fail to make the grade as a § 501(c)(3) charity but nonetheless may provide some public benefit. For example, the IRS historically has granted § 501(c)(4) status to nonprofit health maintenance organizations that fail to provide the requisite "community benefit" required by § 501(c)(3). Certain neighborhood groups and homeowners associations that enforce restrictive covenants and preserve open space for a limited geographical area have been held to qualify under § 501(c)(4) even though they would not benefit a sufficiently broad charitable class to fit within § 501(c)(3). See, e.g., Rev. Rul. 75–286, 1975–2 C.B. 210 (organization engaged in preserving and beautifying a city block); Rancho Santa Fe Association v. United States, 589 F.Supp. 54 (S.D.Cal. 1984) (homeowner's association).

C.   LABOR, AGRICULTURAL AND HORTICULTURAL ORGANIZATIONS

Internal Revenue Code: § 501(c)(5).

Treasury Regulations: § 1.501(c)(5)–1.

Section 501(c)(5) provides a tax exemption for labor, agricultural and horticultural organizations. In general, these groups must "have as their objects the betterment of the conditions of those engaged in such pursuits, the improvement of the grade of their products, and the development of a higher degree of efficiency in their respective occupations." Treas. Reg. § 1.501(c)(5)–1(a)(2). Section 501(c)(5) embraces not only the typical collective bargaining unit but also includes associations formed to educate union members, process grievances, and engage in litigation and lobbying activities. See, e.g., Rev. Rul. 76–31, 1976–1 C.B. 157. Inurement of net earnings to any member is prohibited, but the payment of death, sickness, accident or similar benefits to members is permitted if provided under a plan aimed at bettering the conditions of the members. See, e.g., Rev. Rul. 62–17, 1962–1 C.B. 87.

The case that follows, involving a foreign pension fund's efforts to achieve tax-exempt status under § 501(c)(5), is one of the few contemporary controversies over the definition of a labor organization.

Stichting Pensioenfonds Voor de Gezondheid v. United States

United States Court of Appeals, District of Columbia Circuit, 1997.
129 F.3d 195, cert. denied, 525 U.S. 811, 119 S.Ct. 43 (1998).

■ TATEL, CIRCUIT JUDGE:

A Dutch pension fund jointly controlled by employers and unions and claiming to be a "labor organization" as described in section 501(c)(5) of the Internal Revenue Code challenges the Internal Revenue Service's denial of its application for exemption from federal income taxation. Because tax exemptions require unambiguous proof and because we can find no authority directly entitling the pension fund to an exemption, we affirm the district court's grant of summary judgment to the United States.

I

Appellant Stichting Pensioenfonds Voor de Gezondheid, Geestelijke en Maatschappelijke Belangen (the "Fund") is a Dutch pension plan formed in 1969 following negotiations between labor unions representing hospital workers and the Dutch national hospital employers' association. Soon after the Fund's formation, the Dutch government granted it "compulsory treatment," thus requiring all private hospitals and their employees to participate. The Fund has since expanded to include fourteen health and social welfare sectors in the Netherlands. The Fund has no principal place of business in the United States, nor does it engage in any trade or business here.

A board of directors controls the Fund's management and assets. Pursuant to Dutch law, employers and unions each appoint half of the board's twelve directors. The six employer directors and the six union directors enjoy equal voting power. If all directors are not present at a meeting, each side may only cast as many votes as the side with the fewer directors. On all policy issues, employer and union directors must agree, or the board may not act. Unions and employers also designate equal numbers of directors to all committees formed by the board.

As the second largest private pension fund in the Netherlands, the Fund covered approximately one million people as of December 31, 1993, some of whom were union members and some of whom were not. About 600,000 were active contributing members. Some 330,000 of the remaining members were "sleepers," a Dutch idiom referring to employees no longer working in industry sectors covered by the Fund but entitled to receive pension benefits upon retirement by virtue of previous employment. The remaining members were retirees already receiving pension benefits.

Both employers and employees contribute to the Fund. The board of directors establishes required contribution rates, as well as the respective portions of the total contribution paid by employers and employees.

The Fund invests in U.S. stocks and mutual funds. In 1993, its U.S. security custodians withheld and paid to the U.S. Treasury over eight million dollars in income tax. Claiming tax-exempt status as a labor organization under section 501(c)(5) of the Internal Revenue Code, the Fund filed a claim for this amount. Receiving no response from the Service, the Fund filed suit in the U.S. District Court for the District of Columbia.

Noting that taxpayers must prove exemptions "unambiguously," and finding that the Fund lacked "a sufficient nexus with a more traditional labor organization to qualify as a tax-exempt labor organization itself," the district court granted summary judgment for the United States. In doing so, the district court rejected the Fund's alternative argument that, even if not entitled to tax-exempt status, it should have received a refund pursuant to section 7805(b) of the Code. We review the district court's grant of summary judgment de novo.

II

Because the Constitution confers upon Congress exclusive authority to collect taxes to provide for the general welfare of the United States, U.S. Const. art. I, § 8, cl. 1, only Congress itself may create exemptions from federal tax laws. Given the importance of taxation and the general presumption in favor of taxing all sources of income, courts may not infer exemptions when Congress has not clearly provided for them. See 1 Jacob Mertens, Jr., The Law of Federal Income Taxation § 3.49 (Nov. 1991). For this reason, the Supreme Court has consistently held for over a century that a taxpayer must "unambiguously" prove entitlement to an exemption: * * * "As taxation is the rule, and exemption the exception, the intention to create an exemption must be expressed in clear and unambiguous terms * * *. Legislation which relieves any species of property from its due proportion of the burdens of the government must be so clear that there can be neither reasonable doubt nor controversy in regard to its meaning," Yazoo & Miss. Valley R.R. Co. v. Thomas, 132 U.S. 174, 183, 10 S.Ct. 68, 72, 33 L.Ed. 302 (1889). As Justice Cardozo said for a unanimous court over sixty years ago, "Exemptions from taxation are not to be enlarged by implication if doubts are nicely balanced." Trotter v. Tennessee, 290 U.S. 354, 356, 54 S.Ct. 138, 139, 78 L.Ed. 358 (1933). With this extremely high standard in mind, we search for some direct authority that unquestionably and conclusively entitles the Fund to the exemption it seeks.

We begin, of course, with the Internal Revenue Code. Section 501(c)(5) exempts labor, agricultural, and horticultural organizations from taxation. The Code neither defines the term "labor organization" nor elaborates on its meaning. The legislative history, moreover, provides no unambiguous guidance. The early twentieth-century congressional debates on whether to include the term "labor organization" in section 501(c)'s precursor had nothing to do with whether jointly controlled entities providing pension benefits should be exempt from federal taxation. Instead, the debates focused on whether the Code's exemption for "fraternal beneficiary societies * * * providing for the payment of life, sick, accident, or other benefits to members" would be understood as covering all labor organizations, a question that Congress answered negatively when it explicitly exempted labor organizations. See 44 Cong. Rec. 4154–55 (1909). We agree with the district court that this legislative history provides "little help" in understanding the scope of the term "labor organization."

We next turn to the Treasury Regulation that defines the term "labor organization," but which is ultimately unhelpful. It says: The organizations contemplated by section 501(c)(5) as entitled to exemption from income taxation are those which: (1) Have no net earnings inuring to the benefit of any member, and (2) Have as their objects the betterment of the conditions of those engaged in such pursuits, the improvement of the grade of their products, and the development of a higher degree of efficiency in their respective occupations. 26 C.F.R. § 1.501(c)(5)–1(a) (1997). A nonprofit entity, the Fund clearly satisfies sub-paragraph (1). While the Fund may also satisfy the first of sub-paragraph (2)'s requirements—it has as its object the betterment of employee financial conditions—it cannot meet the other two requirements: it works neither to improve products nor to develop higher degrees of efficiency. The Fund urges us to read subparagraph (2) disjunctively, but given the plain meaning of the word "and" we cannot do so. See C.K. Ogden, Basic English International Second Language 132 (1968) ("And is used for joining words together: The man and the woman are married. Or is used for the idea of one of two: The man or the woman is married."). Although this conclusion would otherwise end this case—the regulation does not unambiguously entitle the Fund to an exemption—the Service did not rely on the regulation in its brief or at oral argument. Because the Service itself does not argue that the regulation excludes the Fund from labor organization status, we decline to decide the case on that basis.

Finding help in neither the Code nor the regulation, we look next to the IRS's Revenue Rulings, the second most important agency pronouncements that interpret the Code. Applying the Code to specific situations, Revenue Rulings bind both the Service and the taxpayer. Although Revenue Rulings "do not have the force and effect of Treasury Department Regulations," they are "published to provide precedents to be used in the disposition of other cases, and may be cited and relied upon for that purpose." 26 C.F.R. § 601.601(d)(2)(v)(d) (1997). But because "each Revenue Ruling represents the conclusion of the Service as to the application of the law to the entire state of facts involved, taxpayers, Service personnel, and others concerned are cautioned against reaching the same conclusion in other cases unless the facts and circumstances are substantially the same." 26 C.F.R. § 601.601(d)(2)(v)(e). The Fund can thus prevail only by identifying a Revenue Ruling awarding an exemption in a case having facts and circumstances "substantially the same" as this case. Examining the relevant Revenue Rulings carefully, we find no such controlling authority.

The Service has issued fifteen Revenue Rulings under section 501(c)(5). Eleven deal with organizations completely controlled by unions and thus do not involve facts and circumstances substantially similar to those in this case. Of the four that concern jointly controlled organizations, three award tax exemptions, but none of the organizations covered by those rulings is substantially similar to the Fund. See Rev. Rul. 78–42, 1978–1 C.B. 158; Rev. Rul. 75–473, 1975–2 C.B. 213; Rev. Rul. 59–6, 1959–1 C.B. 121. To begin with, the organizations do not provide pension benefits. Rulings 78–42 and 59–6 deal with apprenticeship committees that provide training and education to employees, while Ruling 75–473 involves a jointly controlled dispatch hall that allocates work assignments to union members and adjudicates grievances over working conditions. Moreover, the labor organizations that the Service found exempt in these three rulings focus primarily on improving employee conditions on the job, while the Fund has as its purpose improving employee benefits after the job, i.e. pension benefits. The three Rulings also differ from this case because none involves organizations governed by foreign law. Simply because the Service has awarded tax exemptions to labor organizations dually controlled under American law does not mean that it would necessarily have to reach the same conclusion for organizations dually controlled under foreign law, particularly since exempting foreign pension plans means that their earnings will escape all U.S. taxation. Earnings of exempt domestic funds, by comparison, are taxed when benefits are paid to recipients.

The Fund argues that it should receive an exemption because it conducts appropriate labor organization activities. That an organization performs activities "appropriate" to labor organizations, however, does not make it a labor organization under these Revenue Rulings. The Service has said only that a labor organization not itself a labor union that engages in appropriate labor union activities "may" qualify for an exemption. Rev. Rul. 75–473. The Service does not end its inquiry upon finding that the organization carries out an "appropriate" union activity. Instead, the Service examines the specific facts of each case, looking to other factors such as the organization's purpose, see Rev. Rul. 78–42; Rev. Rul. 59–6, and the nexus between the organization's activities and the parent labor union's objectives, see Rev. Rul. 75–473. Although providing and administering pension plans for workers is certainly an appropriate and traditional union function, we find no basis for an exemption in this case because the Revenue Rulings do not unambiguously stand for the proposition that any organization bearing some connection to a traditional labor union and performing appropriate or traditional union functions is necessarily an exempt labor organization.

* * *

The Fund has failed to meet its heavy burden of demonstrating unambiguous entitlement to tax-exempt status. We find nothing in the Code, the regulation, or the Revenue Rulings that even comes close to stating that a jointly controlled pension plan governed by foreign law is a labor organization exempt from federal taxation. Our doubts about the Fund's entitlement to tax-exempt status are not even "nicely balanced."

We recognize that in Morganbesser v. United States, 984 F.2d 560 (2d Cir.1993), the Second Circuit, with one judge dissenting, held that a jointly controlled pension fund is entitled to tax-exempt status under section 501(c)(5). Unlike this case, however, *Morganbesser* involved a pension fund organized under U.S. law. The Second Circuit, moreover, relied on the precedentially dubious GCMs, never mentioning or applying the "unambiguous" standard that we find controlling. In any event, the Treasury Department has now promulgated a regulation providing that "[a]n organization is not an organization described in section 501(c)(5) if the principal activity of the organization is to receive, hold, invest, disburse, or otherwise manage funds associated with * * * pension or other retirement savings plans or programs." 62 Fed.Reg. 40,447, 40,449 (1997) (adding proposed 26 C.F.R. § 1.501(c)(5)–1(b)(1)). Although both parties agree that this purely prospective regulation has no relevance to the case before us, we mention it to point out that Morganbesser had a brief life.

III

[The court then rejected the Fund's alternative argument that the Service had engaged in unfair discrimination by denying the Fund an exemption while granting favorable private rulings to two comparable British multiemployer pension funds.]

NOTES

1. *Pension Funds.* Qualified pension trusts are exempt from tax under § 501, but they must satisfy a long list of technical requirements in I.R.C. § 401 et seq. The *Stichting* case was an attempted end run around

these rules by a foreign multiemployer pension fund seeking to avoid tax on its U.S. investment income. As noted in the opinion, the Second Circuit's opinion in Morganbesser v. United States reached a contrary result, suggesting the possibility of a conflict in the circuits. The Supreme Court resisted the temptation to address this fascinating issue, however, by denying certiorari in *Stichting*. The issue may well be resolved prospectively by the regulation discussed at the end of the *Stichting* opinion.

2. *Agricultural and Horticultural Organizations*. Agricultural organizations are exempt if they engage in the art or science of cultivating land, harvesting crops or aquatic resources, or raising livestock. See I.R.C. § 501(g). To be exempt under § 501(c)(5), an agricultural organization must be devoted to encouraging the development of better agricultural and horticultural products and to the betterment of the conditions of persons engaged in agriculture. If the organization's activities are directed toward the improvement of marketing or other business conditions, it must pass muster under the qualification standards for a business league under § 501(c)(6).

3. *Political Activities*. Section 501(c)(5) organizations do not jeopardize their exempt status by lobbying and seeking to influence political campaigns as long as these pursuits do not become the organization's primary purpose. This longstanding policy withstood a constitutional challenge by aerospace workers who sought to strip their union's tax exemption because part of their dues were being used for partisan political purposes. In denying standing, the D.C. Circuit concluded that tax exemptions to labor unions did not amount to a government subsidy and that consequently there was an insufficient nexus between the exemption and any government involvement in the union's political activities. See Marker v. Shultz, 485 F.2d 1003 (D.C.Cir.1973). Certain political expenditures of § 501(c)(5) organizations are subject to federal and state election regulation law restrictions, however, and direct political expenditures may trigger a tax on a union's investment income under § 527(f). See Chapter 5E6, supra, at pp. 534–535.

D. Trade Associations and Other Business Leagues

Internal Revenue Code: §§ 501(c)(6); 162(e); 6033(e).

Treasury Regulations: § 1.501(c)(6)–1; 1.162–29.

Section 501(c)(6) exempts nonprofit business leagues, chambers of commerce, real estate boards, boards of trade and professional football leagues. This important category includes many influential trade associations, such as the American Medical Association, the American Bar Association, the National Association of Manufacturers, and The National Football League. The primary advantages of § 501(c)(6) status are that dues and investment income received by the organization are exempt from tax, and similar income tax exemptions frequently are available from state and local taxes. Exempt status also may provide an intangible advantage for a trade association in the eyes of the general public and governmental officials.

A business league is defined as an association of persons organized to promote a common business interest provided the organization does not engage in a regular business of a kind ordinarily carried on for profit. Its activities must be directed to the improvement of business conditions of "one or more lines of business" as distinguished from the performance of particular services for individuals. Treas. Reg. § 1.506(c)(6)–1. No part of the net earnings of the organization may inure to the benefit of any private individual. Section 501(c)(6) organizations must provide benefits to an entire industry (e.g., plastics manufacturers) or a component geographical branch (e.g., California hot tub contractors). But they may limit their membership provided there is a common business interest (e.g., business and professional women or candidates for a professional degree in a particular field). See Rev. Rul. 76–400, 1976–2 C.B. 153; Rev. Rul. 77–112, 1977–1 C.B. 149.

1. The Line of Business Requirement

Guide International Corporation v. United States

United States Court of Appeals, Seventh Circuit, 1991.
948 F.2d 360.

■ Kanne, Circuit Judge.

Guide International Corporation is a nonprofit organization whose purpose is to develop data processing products and services, and to provide a forum for the exchange and dissemination of information concerning data processing equipment and systems. In 1971, the Internal Revenue Service determined that Guide was exempt from tax as a nonprofit business league under § 501(c)(6) of the Internal Revenue Code. However, Revenue Ruling 83–164, 1983–2 C.B. 95 put Guide's tax-exempt status into question.[2] To obtain a binding determination of its tax-exempt status, Guide filed income tax returns for the years 1984, 1985, and 1986, and, thereafter, filed for refund of taxes paid with those returns. No action was taken on Guide's claim and Guide brought suit. On cross-motions for summary judgment, the district court found that Guide failed to qualify as a business league and granted summary judgment in favor of the government. Guide appeals and we affirm.

* * *

The facts are undisputed. Guide was formed in 1956 and incorporated in Missouri in 1969 as a nonprofit association. Guide's purposes, as set forth in its Articles of Incorporation, are the following: (a) The promotion

---

2. The ruling held that an organization whose members represent diversified businesses that own, rent, or lease computers produced by a single computer manufacturer does not qualify for exemption from federal income tax as a business league under § 501(c)(6).

of sound professional practices with respect to the uses of data processing equipment and systems. (b) The exchange and dissemination of information concerning data processing equipment and systems. (c) The participation with manufacturers of data processing equipment (including hardware, software and peripheral equipment) in the improvement and development of products, standards, and education. Guide's By-laws state that its primary purposes include "communicat[ing] to the IBM Corporation user needs in all technical areas of interest" and "review[ing], comment[ing] and exchang[ing] information on products and services related to the equipment needed to qualify for GUIDE membership." The By-laws restrict membership to organizations who own large-scale computer equipment manufactured by International Business Machines (IBM mainframes).

Guide's membership includes major corporations from diverse fields, as well as educational and governmental organizations. Many of the members compete against each other, and some compete against IBM. Guide is managed by a board of directors, who are members of the organization. Guide's principal activity is the sponsorship of week-long conferences that are held three times a year and focus on data processing matters. Representatives of IBM and other persons are invited to speak at the conferences on topics chosen by Guide's management. Although IBM and manufacturers of compatible peripheral equipment present data processing products at the conferences, all sales and recruitment activities are prohibited. IBM provides administrative personnel, a personal computer, copiers and refreshments at the meetings. The information presented and discussed at the conferences is communicated to IBM.

Guide also conducts research involving data processing equipment manufactured by IBM and other companies. Project papers and other resource materials prepared by Guide are maintained in a library and are generally available to all interested parties, including non-members.

Guide argues that the district court erred in determining it was not a business league under § 501(c)(6). The principal issue before the district court was whether Guide satisfies the requirement of Treasury Regulation § 1.501(c)(6)–1 (26 C.F.R. § 1.501(c)(6)–1) that its activities "be directed to the improvement of business conditions of one or more lines of business as distinguished from the performance of particular services for individual persons."

Relying on National Muffler Dealers Ass'n, Inc. v. United States, 440 U.S. 472, 99 S.Ct. 1304, 59 L.Ed.2d 519 (1979), the district court found that Guide fails to meet the line of business test because it primarily serves the interests of IBM and the users of IBM computers rather than the data processing industry as a whole.

In *National Muffler*, the United States Supreme Court adopted the Internal Revenue Commissioner's interpretation of the line of business test that an association which is not industrywide should not be exempt. 440 U.S. at 484, 99 S.Ct. at 1310. But see Pepsi–Cola Bottlers' Ass'n v. United States, 369 F.2d 250 (7th Cir.1966) (not followed by Rev.Rul. 68–182, 1968–

1 C.B. 263 (1968), and disapproved by *National Muffler*, 440 U.S. at 476, 99 S.Ct. at 1306). Accordingly, the Court denied a tax exemption to an association of franchisees of one brand of muffler because the association did not improve conditions of an industrial line, but, instead, promoted a particular product at the expense of others in the industry.

Here, the district court acknowledged that although Guide's stated purpose is to facilitate the use and exchange of information regarding data processing equipment in general, the primary benefit inures to IBM which is only a segment (70 to 75%) of the mainframe computer business, not a line of business.

Guide argues that this case is distinguishable from *National Muffler* because its activities improve several lines of business by enabling its members to perform data processing more efficiently. This argument is in direct conflict with Revenue Ruling 83–164 and was rejected in National Prime Users Group, Inc. v. United States, 667 F.Supp. 250 (D.Md.1987). Revenue Ruling 83–164 held that an organization that directs its activities to the users of one brand of computers improves the business conditions in only segments of the various lines of business to which its members belong. Similarly, in *National Prime Users Group*, the court denied a tax exemption to an association whose members consisted of users of computers of a single manufacturer because the association only improved conditions for members in those lines of businesses that used the particular computers. The court found an inherent competitive advantage for the computer manufacturer. We believe that the Revenue Ruling and the decision of the district court in Maryland were correct.

Therefore, while Guide's members reflect a wide variety of businesses, no single business is enhanced and Guide only benefits IBM and those individuals within various lines of business who use IBM mainframes. Moreover, the district court found that Guide primarily advances IBM's interests and that any benefit to its members and other data processing companies who use information prepared by Guide is incidental.

We agree with the district court's characterization of Guide as a powerful marketing tool for IBM. Guide's conferences provide IBM customers with the opportunity to learn about IBM products and services and IBM receives feedback about those products and services which influences product development. The district court properly found that Guide fails to qualify as an exempt business league under § 501(c)(6).

The judgment of the district court is Affirmed.

NOTE

Bluetooth Sig is an organization with over 4,000 members, including major technology companies such as Apple, Microsoft, IBM, Hewlett Packard and Sony. It was formed as a nonprofit organization to advance the common business interests in the development and regulation of technical standards for "Bluetooth" wireless products and it applied to the IRS for tax-exempt status under § 501(c)(6). In Bluetooth SIG, Inc. v. United States, 2008–1 USTC ¶ 50,177 (D. Wash. 2008), the court upheld the IRS's denial of exemption, finding that: (1) the organization's activities in developing and marketing Bluetooth technology were of a kind ordinarily carried on for profit, and (2) the activities were not directed to the improvement of business conditions for "one or more lines of business" but rather offered particular services for association members.

2.   No Conduct of Business for Profit Requirement

Associated Master Barbers & Beauticians of America v. Commissioner

United States Tax Court, 1977.
69 T.C. 53.

■ Dawson, Judge:

[Associated Master Barbers & Beauticians of America was organized in 1924 for the purpose of "promoting such unity of sentiment and action among the Master Barbers throughout America, joining them closer together for united protection." Among its activities were the administration of certain insurance programs for its members and the publication of a magazine, first known as Master Barber and Beautician Magazine and later as The Professional Men's Hairstylist and Barber's Journal. The magazine included news and information of the trade, such as shampooing methods and shaving techniques, and articles dealing with the various benefits, goods, services and insurance programs offered to members. The association also sent representatives to "The World Hairstyling Olympics," an international conclave held for the purpose of exchanging hairstyling techniques with professionals in foreign countries. The Service revoked the organization's exempt status under § 501(c)(6) on the ground that it had engaged in a regular business for profit. Eds.]

OPINION

Issue 1. Tax–Exempt Status Under Section 501(c)(6)

* * *

Section 1.501(c)(6)–1, Income Tax Regs., provides:

A business league is an association of persons having some common business interest, the purpose of which is to promote such common interest and not to engage in a regular business of a kind ordinarily carried on for profit. It is an organization of the same general class as a chamber of commerce or board of trade. Thus, its activities should be directed to the improvement of business conditions of one or more lines of business as distinguished from the performance of particular services for individual persons. An organization whose purpose is to engage in a regular business of a kind ordinarily carried on for profit, even though the business is conducted on a cooperative basis or produces only sufficient income to be self-sustaining, is not a business league. * * *

These regulations have remained basically unchanged for many years and have been held valid by various courts. They may be deemed to have been approved in effect by reenactment of the statutory exemption provision in the same terms since their adoption and permitting the administrative interpretation to become settled. American Automobile Association v. Commissioner, 19 T.C. 1146, 1158 (1953).

Petitioner has the burden of proving that it meets the requirements of the statute. A statute creating an exemption must be strictly construed, and any doubt must be resolved in favor of the taxing power. The essential requirements of an organization exempt under section 501(c)(6) were spelled out in American Automobile Association v. Commissioner, as follows:

> (1) It must be an association of persons having a common business interest.

> (2) Its purpose must be to promote that common business interest.

> (3) It must not be organized for profit.

> (4) It should not be engaged in a regular business of a kind ordinarily conducted for a profit.

> (5) Its activities should be directed toward the improvement of business conditions of one or more lines of business as opposed to the performance of particular services for individual persons.

> (6) Its net earnings, if any, must not inure to the benefit of any private shareholder or individual.

Petitioner must meet each of these requirements in order to qualify as a tax-exempt business league.

* * *

Petitioner is clearly an association of persons having a common business interest. Members of the Associated Master Barbers & Beauticians of America, Inc., associate themselves in order to professionalize their services and ensure the establishment of an adequate income for services provided. The purpose for which petitioner was formed was to promote the common business interests of its members. That purpose was set forth in its constitution and rule book. In addition, petitioner was not organized for profit. It was incorporated in 1924 as a nonprofit organization. Its intention to operate as a nonprofit organization was stated in its articles of incorporation. Thus, the petitioner meets the first three requirements set out above.

The crux of respondent's position, however, is that the petitioner fails to meet the last three requirements. He contends that the services provided by the petitioner to both members and nonmembers were activities which are of a kind ordinarily carried on for profit. In particular, respondent points to petitioner's self-insurance programs and its involvement with the various insurance programs underwritten by independent insurance companies as evidence that it is engaged in a regular business of a kind ordinarily conducted for profit.

To the contrary, the petitioner maintains that the income from its insurance programs is related to the exempt function of its organization. Central to its position is that an association promotes the good of a profession as a whole when it provides proper protection and fringe benefits for the members of a profession who would otherwise not have any security, protection, or benefits. Thus the operation of an insurance program, argues petitioner, is related to the exempt purpose of the organization.

We agree with the respondent. Petitioner established a basic death benefit plan in 1928 and a basic sick benefit plan in 1932. In addition, a voluntary supplemental benefit plan was initiated in 1955. From October 1, 1966, to September 30, 1971, petitioner administered and self-insured the basic sick and death benefit plans and the supplemental benefit plan. Its national officers and employees kept records on what insurance program each member participated in, processed claims for benefits, and paid benefits with respect to the numerous insurance programs provided by the petitioner.

A new basic benefit program, approved on August 15, 1972, was underwritten by Globe Life Insurance Co. Those members age 66 and above were not eligible for the new program. They continued to receive benefits under the old basic benefit program. Petitioner continued to operate and administer its self-insurance programs including the basic sick and death benefit plans for those members age 66 and above. In addition, Globe Life Insurance Co. required petitioner to collect premiums from its members, keep records of payments made, determine whether the insured was still a member, and process claims for benefits.

A large majority of petitioner's members participated in the self-insurance plans offered by petitioner. During the taxable year ended September 30, 1967, 6,971 of petitioner's 9,041 members participated in the sick and death benefit plans, while 2,220 participated in the voluntary supplemental benefit plan. During the taxable year ended September 30, 1970, 5,010 of petitioner's 6,832 members participated in the sick and death benefit plans, while 941 participated in the voluntary supplemental benefit plan. During the taxable year ended September 30, 1971, 4,366 of petitioner's 5,964 members participated in the sick and death benefit plans, while 960 participated in the voluntary supplemental benefit plan.

In addition, the number of claims processed by petitioner was substantial. During the taxable year ended September 30, 1967, it processed and paid 596 claims under the basic plan (sick and death) and 124 claims under the voluntary supplemental plan. During the taxable year ended September 30, 1970, it processed 497 claims under the basic plan and 104 claims under the voluntary supplemental plan. During the taxable year ended September

30, 1971, it processed 453 claims under the basic plan and 91 claims under the voluntary supplemental plan.

We think the evidence clearly demonstrates that petitioner was engaged in a regular business of a kind ordinarily carried on for profit during all the taxable years in question. Its officers and employees were involved on a daily basis with recordkeeping, processing claims for benefits, paying claims, and performing other administrative duties in connection with such insurance activities. As we see it, the petitioner was engaging in an insurance business—a business of the type which is ordinarily carried on for profit.

* * *

In our judgment the petitioner herein is engaged in a regular business of a kind ordinarily carried on for profit, namely, the insurance business. However, it is true that an organization whose principal purpose and activity is such as to qualify for "business league" exemption does not lose its exempt status by engaging in incidental activities which standing alone would be subject to taxation. It is therefore necessary for us to examine the extent of petitioner's insurance activities to see if they constitute only incidental, as opposed to substantial, activities.

Petitioner argues that the time which the employees of an association devote to its various functions is a proper measure of "activity." It further argues that the evidence here shows that the time petitioner's employees devoted to its insurance activities was only 15 percent for the taxable years ended September 30, 1967, September 30, 1970, and September 30, 1971, and only 10 percent for the taxable year ended September 30, 1973. Thus, it is asserted that the insurance activities were only "incidental."

Respondent, on the other hand, contends that we should look to petitioner's financial data, such as its statement of receipts and disbursements for the taxable years at issue, to determine the extent of petitioner's insurance activities. See Evanston–North Shore Board of Realtors v. United States, supra.

During the taxable year ended September 30, 1967, receipts from the basic sick and death benefit funds and the voluntary supplemental benefit fund amounted to $115,876.32; and disbursements totaled $96,720.95. These amounts constituted 43 percent and 35 percent, respectively, of total receipts and total disbursements during that year. During the taxable year ended September 30, 1970, receipts and disbursements from the basic sick and death benefit funds and the voluntary supplemental benefit fund amounted to $94,547 and $95,584, respectively. These amounts constituted 31 percent and 30 percent, respectively, of total receipts and disbursements for that year. During the taxable year ended September 30, 1971, receipts and disbursements from the basic sick and death benefit funds and the voluntary supplemental benefit fund amounted to $87,400 and $85,931, respectively. These amounts constituted 31 percent and 32 percent, respectively, of total receipts and disbursements for that year. During the taxable year ended September 30, 1973, receipts and disbursements from the basic sick and death benefits funds and the voluntary supplemental benefit fund amounted to $22,549 and $47,363, respectively. These amounts constituted 11 percent and 21 percent, respectively, of total receipts and disbursements for that year.

While we think that both time and financial data should be considered in determining the extent of an organization's nonexempt activities, we view the petitioner's evidence, consisting of the testimony of Chris Hood, an employee, J. Nelson Snyder, a former employee, and Gerald St. Onge, petitioner's national president at the time he testified, as having little probative value with regard to the percentage of time spent on the insurance programs. What is clear from the record is that numerous clerical duties had to be performed and voluminous records were kept on the petitioner's various insurance programs. Evidence as to the numerous records that had to be kept, the entries that had to be made on each record, and the processing of claims for benefits establishes to our satisfaction that a substantial amount of time was devoted to the insurance programs. The time spent, combined with the persuasive financial data available, convinces us that the petitioner's insurance activities were not merely incidental. They were substantial.

For these reasons we conclude that the petitioner failed to meet the fourth requirement necessary to qualify for exemption under section 501(c)(6). In our opinion it was engaging in a regular business of a kind ordinarily carried on for profit.

With respect to the fifth requirement for exemption, the record contains substantial evidence of the performance of "particular services" for individual persons and comparatively little evidence of activities designed to promote the hairstyling profession. In all of the years at issue the petitioner provided and offered numerous benefits to individual members in the form of various types of insurance, goods, and services. In addition to the self-insurance programs it administered and financed, the petitioner initiated a new basic benefit program in 1972 which was underwritten by Globe Life Insurance Co. In July 1967, the major benefit insurance program was initiated and underwritten by Zurich Insurance Co. This program provided, on a voluntary basis to the members, monthly disability income protection and death benefits. During the years at issue, the petitioner also offered a cancer insurance policy underwritten by an insurance company to its members; a malpractice and personal liability insurance policy underwritten by an insurance company; and a hospitalization insurance plan underwritten by Craftsman Life Insurance Co., and later, by Hanover Insurance Co. The petitioner also offered to its members a voluntary retirement insurance program which was in effect only during its taxable years ended September 30, 1970, and September 30, 1971.

Besides the numerous insurance programs, the petitioner offered its members an eyeglass and prescription lens replacement service. It sold its local chapters certain supplies. It sold its members hair and beard styling charts, a "carlow book," style of the month binders, appointment books, and white nylon hair cloths. It sold its members shop emblems and association jewelry. It also sold a standard textbook and an examination for the textbook, as well as a special hairstyling book.

These insurance and other activities, which formed the bulk of the activities performed by petitioner during the years of issue, did not contribute to the improvement of business conditions in one or more lines of business as opposed to the performance of particular services for individuals. Consequently, we conclude that the petitioner has failed to satisfy the fifth requirement for exempt status under section 501(c)(6). The record contains substantial evidence of activities of a type termed "particular services" by the regulations, but little evidence of activities designed to improve business conditions in the barbering and beautician professions. Because these activities serve as a convenience or economy to petitioner's members in the operation of their businesses, we think they constitute "particular services" as proscribed by the regulation. By providing insurance or textbooks for its members, the petitioner relieves its members of obtaining insurance or textbooks on an individual basis from a nonexempt commercial business. If the petitioner did not provide these goods and services, its individual members would have to obtain them from nonexempt businesses at a substantially increased cost. Thus, the organization is rendering "particular services" for the individual members as distinguished from an improvement of business conditions in the barbering and beautician professions generally.

Accordingly, we sustain respondent's determination revoking the exempt status of petitioner under section 501(c)(6) for the years at issue herein. The petitioner is taxable as a corporation under section 11 of the Code.

NOTES

1. *Monopoly Businesses*. What if a nonprofit organization seeking § 501(c)(6) status engages in a business but does not compete with other commercial enterprises because it constitutes a monopoly? The Service contends that *potential* competition with for-profit businesses is fatal. See, e.g., Jockey Club v. United States, 133 Ct.Cl. 787, 137 F.Supp. 419 (1956), denying § 501(c)(6) status to a thoroughbred racing organization which published "The American Stud Book," a popular volume listing bloodlines of purebreds, and "Racing Calendar," an almanac for the horsey set. Although Jockey Club had a monopoly, the court found that commercial competition was foreseeable.

In MIB, Inc. v. Commissioner, 80 T.C. 438 (1983), the Tax Court upheld the § 501(c)(6) exemption of an organization that collected and exchanged confidential underwriting information about applicants for life insurance among its members in order to deter fraud and misrepresentation. The membership consisted of virtually the entire U.S. life insurance industry, and there were no competing organizations providing the same service. Revenues, including "assessments" to members and service charges, were substantial ($11,400,000 in 1978), but there was no foreseeable competition. On appeal, however, the First Circuit reversed, holding that the modus operandi of M.I.B. was to perform direct services for its individual members rather than improving business conditions as a whole. MIB, Inc. v. Commissioner, 734 F.2d 71 (1st Cir.1984). The court reasoned that the ultimate inquiry is "whether the association's activities advance the members' interests generally, by virtue of their membership in the industry, or whether they assist members in the pursuit of the individual businesses." 734 F.2d at 78. A negative factor was that members' assessments were not uniform but varied in approximate proportion to the specific services received.

2. *Unrelated Business Income Tax.* Even if an organization qualifies for exemption under § 501(c)(6), it remains taxable on the net income from any business activities unrelated to its exempt purposes. Treas. Reg. § 1.506(c)(6)–1. Since enactment of the unrelated business income tax, there have been fewer reported controversies involving qualification for § 501(c)(6) status and far more disputes over whether particular income-generating activities are taxable.

3.   LOBBYING AND OTHER POLITICAL ACTIVITIES

The Internal Revenue Code does not impose any express limitation on the lobbying or other political activities of § 501(c)(6) organizations. Indeed, the Service has ruled that a trade association may qualify for exemption under § 501(c)(6) even though its sole or principal activity is the advocacy of legislation beneficial to the common business interests of its members. Rev. Rul. 61–177, 1961–2 C.B. 117. But the nature and extent of a trade association's lobbying and other political activities may adversely affect the ability of its for-profit members to deduct their dues as business expenses.

Impact of Lobbying on Deduction of Membership Dues. In general, trade association membership dues are tax-deductible under § 162. For many years, § 162(e) disallowed a business deduction for expenses incurred in connection with either attempts to influence the general public on legislation ("grassroots" lobbying) or participation or intervention in political campaigns on behalf of or in opposition to candidates for public office. Consistent with that policy, the portion of trade association membership dues attributable to grassroots lobbying or political campaign activities also was not deductible. In 1993, Congress extended the deduction disallowance to all amounts paid in connection with "influencing legislation" and direct communications with high-level executive branch officials to influence their official actions or positions. I.R.C. § 162(e)(1). In so doing, it further limited the membership dues deduction.

As amended, § 162(e) has become a minefield of rules that only will be summarized here to provide a sense of their impact on tax-exempt trade associations. "Influencing legislation" is defined as "any attempt to influence any legislation through communicating with any member or employee of a legislative body or with any government official or employee who may participate in the formulation of legislation." I.R.C. § 162(e)(4)(A). This definition is expanded to include research, preparation, planning or coordination of an attempt to influence legislation. I.R.C. § 162(e)(5)(C). A "lobbying communication" must refer to and reflect a view on specific legislation, or it must clarify, modify, or provide support for views reflected in a prior lobbying communication. Treas. Reg. § 1.162–29(b)(3). "Legislation" includes the usual actions with respect to Acts, bills, and resolutions, as well as proposed treaties submitted by the President to the Senate for its advice and consent. I.R.C. §§ 162(e)(4)(B); 4911(e)(2); Treas. Reg. § 1.162–29(b)(4).

An exception excludes from the definition of "influencing legislation" any attempts to influence local bodies, such as county or city councils. I.R.C. § 162(e)(2). A de minimis rule excludes from disallowance "in-house expenditures" provided that they do not exceed $2,000 (without regard to overhead). I.R.C. § 162(e)(5)(B)(i). In-house expenditures are lobbying expenditures other than payments to a professional lobbyist or association dues that are allocable to lobbying. I.R.C. § 162(e)(5)(B)(ii).

These rules affect trade associations in several different ways. First, § 162(e)(3) disallows a business deduction for the portion of membership dues paid to any noncharitable exempt organization that is allocable to the kinds of lobbying and political campaign expenses ("§ 162(e) expenses") that are not deductible under § 162(e). To illustrate, assume that Corporation pays $1,000 in annual dues to exempt Trade Association, which spends 30 percent of its annual budget on direct lobbying. Corporation would not be able to deduct $300 (30 percent) of its dues. See Treas. Reg. § 1.162–28 for permissible methods of allocating costs to lobbying activities. Second, noncharitable exempt organizations must include on their annual Form 990 informational return their total § 162(e) expenses and the total amount of membership dues allocable to those expenses. I.R.C. § 6033(e)(1)(A)(i). Third, unless they are protected by the de minimis rule described above, these organizations must make a reasonable estimate of the portion of dues attributable to § 162(e) expenses and notify dues paying members at least annually of the amount that is not deductible. I.R.C. § 6033(e)(1)(A)(ii). Alternatively, an exempt organization may avoid the notification requirement by electing to pay a "proxy tax," at the highest corporate tax rate applicable for the taxable year, on the total amount of its § 162(e) expenditures (up to the amount of dues received during the year). The proxy tax is imposed automatically if an organization fails to notify its members of the nondeductible portion of their dues. § 6033(e)(2)(A).

In a final burst of complexity, § 6033(e)(3) waives the reporting requirement for organizations that establish to the Service's satisfaction that substantially all (90 percent or more, according to the legislative history) of the dues paid to the organization are "not deductible without regard to section 162(e)." This apparently means that an organization receiving the bulk of its dues from individuals who cannot deduct them is exempt from any reporting requirement.

Constitutional Issues. Prior to the enactment of § 162(e), the Treasury had promulgated regulations disallowing any business deduction for lobbying expenditures, be they direct or grassroots. In Cammarano v. United States, 358 U.S. 498, 79 S.Ct. 524 (1959), the Supreme Court upheld the constitutionality of these regulations, which the Service had applied to disallow a deduction claimed by beer and liquor dealers for expenses incurred in attempts to urge voters to defeat state initiative measures that would have put them out of business. In rejecting the taxpayer's First Amendment challenge, the Court said:

> Petitioners are not being denied a tax deduction because they engage in constitutionally protected activities, but are simply being required to pay for those activities entirely out of their own pockets, as everyone else engaging in similar activities is required to do under the provisions of the Internal Revenue Code. Nondiscriminatory denial of deduction from gross income to sums expended to promote or defeat legislation is plainly not "aimed at the suppression of dangerous ideas." * * * Rather, it appears to us to express a determination by Congress that since purchased publicity can influence the fate of legislation which will affect, directly or indirectly, all in the community, everyone in the community should stand on the same footing as regards its purchase so far as the Treasury of the United States is concerned.

After *Cammarano* was decided, Congress enacted the pre–1994 version of § 162(e), which expressly permitted the deduction of direct lobbying expenses but continued to disallow a deduction for grassroots expenses. In the 1993 legislation, Congress reverted to the Treasury's earlier policy by disallowing business deductions for both direct and grassroots lobbying. Is this constitutional? Is it sound tax policy? Does it unfairly limit the expression of views on legislative matters by the corporate community? Are the tax rules that apply to business taxpayers consistent with the treatment of nonprofit organizations and their donors or members?

Some of these constitutional questions were revisited when a coalition of trade associations challenged the provisions in §§ 162(e) and 6033(e) that forbid members of tax-exempt organizations from deducting the portion of their dues allocable to lobbying expenses and require organizations either to notify members of the nondeductible portion of their dues or pay a 35 percent proxy tax on lobbying expenses. Applying "rational basis" scrutiny, the D.C. Circuit, affirming the federal district court, held that the challenged provisions did not violate First Amendment free speech rights or discriminate against organizations that lobby because the statutory scheme bore a rational relationship to the legislative goal of eliminating any tax subsidy for lobbying and preventing taxpayers from circumventing that goal. In finding no free speech burden, the court emphasized that a § 501(c)(6) organization could avoid any obligation to allocate dues or pay a proxy tax by dividing itself into two separate tax-exempt entities, one of which engages exclusively in lobbying and one that completely refrains from lobbying. American Society of Association Executives v. United States,

195 F.3d 47 (D.C.Cir.1999). Is § 501(c)(6) tantamount to a subsidy? Would it be a subsidy if the Clinton Administration's proposal to tax investment income of § 501(c)(6) organizations had been enacted?

Other Political Activities. Nothing in the Code or regulations specifically prohibits § 501(c)(6) organizations from engaging in political campaign activities. The conventional wisdom is that a business league will not jeopardize its exempt status by engaging in political activities that promote the common business interests of its members provided that campaign activity is not the organization's primary purpose. Section 501(c)(6) organizations are subject to regulation under federal and state election laws, however, and their investment income may be taxable under § 527 to the extent the organization incurs certain types of political expenditures. See Chapter 5E6, supra, at pp. 534–536, for the tax treatment of political activities of § 501(c) organizations and for an overview of federal election law regulations, including the impact of the Supreme Court's decision in Citizens United v. Federal Election Commission, 130 S.Ct. 876 (2010).

Enhanced Disclosure of Compensation. The new and improved Form 990 information return expands compensation reporting requirements for all § 501(c) organizations, not just charities. It requires public disclosure of the names, positions and earnings for all "key employees" with "reportable compensation" (generally, W–2 wages) greater than $150,000 if those employees have significant responsibilities within the organization and are one of the 20 employees at the top of the pay scale. Form 990 previously required this information for officers, directors, and the five other most highly compensated employees. Some large trade associations, including the National Football League, complained that the new requirements invaded the privacy of key employees who have become subject to the public disclosure requirements. They sought to have the information redacted by the IRS, but no exception was included in the final version of Form 990 released in early 2009. It remains to be seen whether the NFL and other trade associations would be willing to forego tax-exempt status to keep this information private.

The NFL's member teams are not tax exempt, nor are its various taxable subsidiaries. Even if the NFL were taxable, it apparently would not owe any tax. According to its most recently available Form 990 (for the 2008 fiscal year), the NFL had $169.7 million in total revenue and $204.9 million in expenses, resulting in a $35.2 million deficit. A significant portion of the expenses was attributable to compensation, including commissioner Roger Goodell's base pay of $5,219,694, and $704,104 in contributions to employee benefit and deferred compensation plans on his behalf. The privacy concern, however, was for lower echelon employees, such as its executive vice president for communications, who reportedly said: "I finally get to the point where I'm making 150 grand and they want to put my name and address on the form so the lawyer next door who makes a million dollars can laugh at me." See Amy Elliott & Fred Stokeld, NFL Wants to Withhold Salaries of Highly Paid Employees from Public, 61 Exempt Org. Tax Rev. 279 (2008). The Office of the Commissioner of Baseball, known as

Major League Baseball, also is tax-exempt under § 501(c)(6). Its fiscal year 2008 information return reported $141.2 million of revenue, offset by exactly the same amount of expenses. Commissioner Bud Selig's base compensation was $17,470,491, not including pension contributions and expense allowances.

For Further Reading. Jasper L. Cummings, Jr., Tax Policy, Social Policy, and Politics: Amending Section 162(e), 9 Exempt Org. Tax Rev. 137 (1994); Miriam Galston, Lobbying and the Public Interest: Rethinking the Internal Revenue Code's Treatment of Legislative Activities, 71 Tex.L.Rev. 1269 (1993); George Cooper, The Tax Treatment of Business Grassroots Lobbying: Defining and Attaining Public Policy Objectives, 68 Colum.L.Rev. 801 (1968).

PROBLEMS

1. Determine whether the following organizations are exempt from tax under § 501(c)(6):

(a) Dialogue, a nonprofit membership organization of business and professional women formed to promote the acceptance of women in business and the professions. The group sponsors luncheons and dinner meetings devoted to discussion of career opportunities for women; awards scholarships to promising women in local professional schools; and presents a "young-woman-of-the-month" award.

(b) Merchants of the Mall, Inc., an association composed of all the business tenants and the corporate owner of a suburban shopping center. Membership in the organization is mandatory under the terms of the tenants' leases, and no businesses other than tenants of the center are permitted to join. The purpose of the organization is to serve as a means of communication and exchange of views between the developer and the tenants and to serve as the governing body for enforcing rules respecting the common areas of the center. Income is from membership dues assessed according to the amount of business space rented.

2. The National Association of Industrialists ("NAI") is a nationwide trade association exempt from tax under § 501(c)(6). It has taken a strong position that recent proposals in the state legislature to impose a timetable for implementation of new occupational safety standards will have a drastic economic impact, forcing layoffs and causing some businesses to cease operations. The Association has contacted its members to urge them to ask their employees and customers to oppose enactment of the legislation because of its detrimental effect on their businesses. It also has paid a professional lobbyist to monitor the legislation and to help draft position papers that will be sent to all members of the legislature. Do these activities constitute "lobbying communications" and, if so, what in general are the tax consequences to NAI and its members?

E. Social Clubs and Fraternal Organizations

Internal Revenue Code: §§ 501(c)(7), (8) & (10); 501(i).

Treasury Regulations: § 1.501(c)(7)–1.

1. Introduction

Section 501(c)(7) grants exempt status to "clubs organized for pleasure, recreation, and other nonprofitable purposes" provided that substantially all of the club's activities serve these exempt purposes and no part of its net earnings inures to the benefit of any private shareholder. As previewed earlier and developed at greater length later in this text, the exemption under § 501(c)(7) does not extend to a club's investment income (e.g., dividends, interest and most capital gains) or to its net revenue from dealings with non-members. See I.R.C. § 512(a)(3), which in effect limits a club's exemption to "exempt function income," such as dues and charges for goods and services to members and their guests, and Chapter 6H4, supra, at pp. 695–696.

To qualify as a "club," the Service requires personal contacts and fellowship. "Commingling" of the members must play a material part in the life of the organization. See Rev. Rul. 69–635, 1969–2 C.B. 126. The membership must evidence an "identity of purpose"—for example, a flying club consisting of members who enjoy flying for recreation. Rev. Rul. 74–30, 1974–1 C.B. 137. An organization will not qualify if it is operated primarily as a service to its members—for example, a flying club operated to save money for pilots by sharing facilities. Rev. Rul. 70–32, 1970–1 C.B. 132.

Two types of fraternal organizations qualify for exemption. The first category—organizations providing life, sickness, accident or other benefits to their members or dependents and which operate under the lodge system or for the exclusive benefit of members of a fraternal society under the lodge system—are exempt as "fraternal beneficiary societies" under § 501(c)(8). Organizations that operate under the lodge system and devote all their net earnings exclusively to religious, charitable, scientific, literary, educational and fraternal purposes and which do not provide for the payment of life, sickness, accident or other benefits are exempt as "domestic fraternal societies" under § 501(c)(10). This second category reportedly was added to cover the Masons, who engage in many charitable pursuits but do not offer insurance programs for their members.

The exemption for fraternal organizations is not limited to their exempt function income; investment income also is exempt from tax. Moreover, contributions by an individual to a fraternal society operating under the lodge system are tax-deductible if the donation is "used exclusively for religious, charitable, scientific, literary or educational purposes, or for the prevention of cruelty to children or animals." I.R.C. § 170(c)(4).

As demonstrated by the *Zeta Beta Tau* case, which follows, the more generous tax treatment of fraternal organizations can motivate a college fraternity or sorority to contend that it is more fraternal than social.

Zeta Beta Tau Fraternity, Inc. v. Commissioner

United States Tax Court, 1986.
87 T.C. 421.

■ SWIFT, JUDGE:

In a timely statutory notice of deficiency respondent determined a deficiency in the unrelated business income tax of petitioner for its taxable year ending June 30, 1971, in the amount of $1,936. The only issue for decision is whether petitioner, a tax-exempt social club described in section 501(c)(7), also qualifies as a tax-exempt domestic fraternal society described in section 501(c)(10). If so, petitioner's income from investments is not taxable as unrelated business income and petitioner is not liable for an underpayment of tax.

FINDINGS OF FACT

* * *

Petitioner was organized as a New York corporation in 1907. Petitioner is the central organization of the Zeta Beta Tau national college fraternity (hereinafter referred to as "Zeta Beta"). Associated with Zeta Beta are approximately 80 local chapters. Also associated with Zeta Beta are approximately 80 corporations (hereinafter referred to as the "house corporations") that individually own each building in which the local fraternity houses are located. Zeta Beta also operates the Zeta Beta Tau Foundation, Inc., and the NFEF Foundation, Inc. Zeta Beta, its associated local chapters, and the house corporations were granted tax-exempt status by respondent in 1940 under the provisions of section 101(a), Internal Revenue Code of 1939, the predecessor to section 501(c)(7).

Under the provisions of its national constitution and code of rules, the officers and directors of Zeta Beta's governing body, the supreme council, are selected by representatives of the local chapters who meet annually at a national convention. The supreme council meets periodically and acts as the legislative, executive, and judicial authority of Zeta Beta. Zeta Beta also employs an administrative staff. The principal purpose of Zeta Beta's central staff is to serve as the coordinating and governing organization of the local chapters, house corporations, and private foundations that comprise the Zeta Beta national college fraternity.

Zeta Beta also provides various programs, services, and publications to the local chapters, their members, and the house corporations. The services and publications provided by Zeta Beta include a philanthropic and social service programming guide, a dance marathon guide, a fraternity magazine, awards to local chapters and members for scholastic and public service achievements, information concerning scholarship and emergency student loan programs, a leadership school for undergraduate members, and a monthly newsletter containing articles on professional schools, study tips, financial aid information, and social news from local chapters throughout the United States. Zeta Beta itself does not engage in any significant social activities.

Each local chapter of Zeta Beta adopts its own constitution and bylaws and generally exercises substantial autonomy in the governance of its affairs. The local chapter may not, however, adopt any rule that contravenes Zeta Beta's constitution or code of rules. Generally, each local chapter does not incorporate as a separate entity. Each chapter, however, files its own annual Federal tax returns (Forms 990, Return of Organization Exempt from Tax). The assets, liabilities, receipts, and expenses of local chapters are not included on Zeta Beta's Federal tax returns. Zeta Beta also does not file a separate group information return with respondent on behalf of local chapters.

Each house corporation associated with Zeta Beta is separately incorporated and serves as the owner and manager of the local fraternity house. The house corporations individually file annual Federal tax returns (Forms 990), and Zeta Beta does not include the assets, liabilities, receipts, or expenses of the individual house corporations in its Federal tax returns. Each house corporation is, however, subordinate to Zeta Beta and subject to its general supervision.

The Zeta Beta Tau Foundation, Inc. (hereinafter referred to as the "ZBT Foundation") provides scholarship and loan assistance to undergraduate students who belong to the fraternity. The ZBT Foundation also issues fellowship grants to graduate students in return for their management advice to local chapters of Zeta Beta. The NPEF Foundation, Inc., supports Zeta Beta research and publication programs, chapter house libraries, and leadership development workshops. Both the ZBT Foundation and the NPEF Foundation are recognized by respondent as exempt from Federal income taxes under section 501(c)(3).

As of 1985, Zeta Beta had approximately 104,500 members, of which 4,500 were undergraduate college students and 100,000 were alumni members. Zeta Beta's local chapters provide the undergraduate student members of Zeta Beta housing and meals, social activities, and opportunities for charitable service within their communities. Usually, only a portion of the members of a local chapter reside at the fraternity house. Local chapters generally provide daily meals to its members.

Social activities of each chapter typically include homecoming weekend for alumni and parents, a fall "football weekend," a winter carnival, and a formal dance in the spring. Depending on budgetary considerations and the calendar of social events sponsored by the college, local chapters sponsor additional social events at the fraternity house. The costs of the social events typically are borne by individual members of the chapter.

Local chapters of Zeta Beta also participate in public service activities, such as blood drives, Easter Seal drives, and the transportation of elderly citizens to the polls on election day. Some local chapters regularly sponsor an annual dance marathon to raise funds for charity.

Local chapters of Zeta Beta compete with other college fraternities in scholastic achievement. Chapter members help each other adjust to college life and generally aid in each other's personal development. At times, upperclassmen and graduate student members of Zeta Beta assist and supervise other members of Zeta Beta in their studies. Most Zeta Beta fraternity houses contain a library for use by members. Of the approximately 100,000 alumni, approximately 5,100 contributed money in 1984 to Zeta Beta. An additional 600 alumni participated in Zeta Beta activities in 1984.

The parties agree that Zeta Beta and its subordinate local chapters operate under the lodge system and do not pay insurance benefits to members within the meaning of section 501(c)(10). Zeta Beta concedes that (together with its subordinate local chapters and house corporations) it is a national college fraternity within the meaning of section 1.501(c)(10)–1, Income Tax Regs.

On August 18, 1972, Zeta Beta filed a Return of Organization Exempt from Tax (Form 990) for its taxable year ended June 30, 1971. On June 15, 1973, Zeta Beta filed its Exempt Organization Business Income Tax Return (Form 990–T) for its taxable year ended June 30, 1971. In November of 1975, Zeta Beta filed with respondent an application for a determination that it was tax exempt as a domestic fraternal society under section 501(c)(10). Zeta Beta's application was denied on June 26, 1976. In his letter denying the application, respondent noted that Zeta Beta had "always operated * * * exclusively for educational, charitable, or fraternal purposes," but that as a national college fraternity, it was precluded from tax exemption under section 501(c)(10) by section 1.501(c)(10)–1, Income Tax Regs.

On July 8, 1976, Zeta Beta protested respondent's denial of its application for tax-exempt classification as a domestic fraternal society under section 501(c)(10), and requested reconsideration thereof. On September 30, 1977, respondent reaffirmed its denial of Zeta Beta's application. Respondent's notice of deficiency at issue herein followed.

Respondent's computation of the deficiency herein is based on his inclusion in Zeta Beta's unrelated business income the investment income Zeta Beta received in its taxable year ending June 30, 1971.

OPINION

Generally, tax-exempt organizations described in section 501(c) are taxed at regular corporate rates on unrelated business income. Sec. 511(a). The term "unrelated business taxable income" is defined as the gross income derived from any unrelated trade or business regularly carried on by an organization, less allowable deductions that are directly connected with the conduct of the trade or business. Sec. 512(a). In general, investment income such as dividends, interest, annuities, royalties, rents derived from real property, and capital gains, are excluded from the exempt organization's unrelated business income. Sec. 512(b)(1).

Unrelated business income is described differently, however, for, among other organizations, tax-exempt social clubs described in section 501(c)(7). In the case of a section 501(c)(7) social club, unrelated business taxable income includes all income generated by the organization other than "exempt function income" less expenses related to exempt function income. Sec. 512(a)(3)(A). Exempt function income is defined as the gross income derived from dues, fees, charges, or similar amounts received from organization members or their guests for goods, facilities, or services in furtherance of the tax-exempt purposes of the organization. Sec. 512(a)(3)(B). The result of this difference in the computation of unrelated business taxable income is that investment income of section 501(c)(7) social clubs is taxed as unrelated business income, whereas investment income of section 501(c)(10) fraternal organizations generally is not taxed as unrelated business income.

Zeta Beta, as the central organization of a national college fraternity, received its long-standing tax exemption under the predecessor of section 501(c)(7). Zeta Beta argues, however, that it also properly may be classified as a domestic fraternal society under section 501(c)(10), and that its investment income, therefore, should not be subject to the unrelated business income tax.

Section 501(c)(10), a new category of tax-exempt organizations that was added to the Internal Revenue Code by the Tax Reform Act of 1969, provides a tax exemption for—

(10) Domestic fraternal societies, orders, or associations, operating under the lodge system—

(A) the net earnings of which are devoted exclusively to religious, charitable, scientific, literary, educational, and fraternal purposes, and

(B) which do not provide for the payment of life, sick, accident, or other benefits.

Treasury regulations relating to section 501(c)(10) expressly state that national college fraternities do not qualify under section 501(c)(10). Section 1.501(c)(10)–1, Income Tax Regs., provides as follows:

* * *

Any organization described in section 501(c)(7), such as, for example, a national college fraternity, is not described in section 501(c)(10) and this section. [Emphasis added.]

Zeta Beta argues that it is an organization that is precisely described by the language of section 501(c)(10) because it is a fraternal society that operates under the lodge system, it does not provide insurance benefits to members, and because its net earnings are devoted exclusively to religious, charitable, scientific, literary, educational, and fraternal purposes. Zeta Beta further argues that it cannot be distinguished factually from organizations such as the Masons, Moose, or Elks clubs which usually are classified by respondent as tax exempt under section 501(c)(10). Zeta Beta, therefore, contends that section 1.501(c)(10)–1, Income Tax Regs., in its exclusion of national college fraternities from tax exemption under section 501(c)(10), establishes an arbitrary distinction that discriminates between two similarly situated taxpayers (namely, national college fraternities and organizations such as the Masons) and is, therefore, to that extent invalid.

Zeta Beta also contends that its classification as a tax-exempt organization described in section 501(c)(7) does not preclude its additional classification under section 501(c)(10). Zeta Beta concludes that if it meets the precise description of a section 501(c)(10) organization, there is no express or implied legislative policy that would deny it an exemption thereunder just because it also may be classified as a section 501(c)(7) social club.

Respondent argues that Zeta Beta is not an organization described in section 501(c)(10) because of the clear congressional intent that national college fraternities be exempt from tax as social clubs under section 501(c)(7). Respondent contends that national college fraternities such as Zeta Beta are fundamentally different from those fraternal organizations, such as the Masons, that Congress intended to qualify for tax exemption under section 501(c)(10). Finally, respondent argues that even if a national college fraternity could qualify for tax exemption under section 501(c)(10), the net earnings of Zeta Beta herein are not exclusively devoted to the exempt purposes listed in section 501(c)(10)(A). For the above reasons, respondent argues that Zeta Beta properly may be classified only as a section 501(c)(7) tax-exempt social club.

After careful review of the relevant statutory provisions, the legislative history thereof, and the facts of this case, we agree with respondent that a national college fraternity such as Zeta Beta may not properly be classified as a domestic fraternal society described in section 501(c)(10).

Contrary to Zeta Beta's contention, the relevant statutory language is not clear and unambiguous. As we recently stated—

> Trying to understand the various exempt organization provisions of the Internal Revenue Code is as difficult as capturing a drop of mercury under your thumb. There are currently 23 categories of exempt organizations under section 501(c) and five categories of organizations recognized as qualified donees of tax deductible contributions under section 170(c). Rarely is it clear that an organization would qualify only under one of the categories of section 501(c), and often it is clear that an organization would qualify under a number of the categories, even though a particular organization may have applied for and actually received its exemption letter under a single provision of section 501(c).

There is an extensive body of legislative history explaining the changes in 1969 to the unrelated business income tax provisions of the Code and of the addition of paragraph 10 to section 501(c). A decision herein based solely on the statutory language would be based on a mere "toss of the coin." Reference to the relevant legislative history, on the other hand, provides significant insight into the relevant statutory language. Under such circumstances, we would be remiss if we were to ignore such assistance.

As explained, the tax exemption for domestic fraternal organizations in section 501(c)(10) had its genesis in the Tax Reform Act of 1969 and arose specifically out of the imposition of the unrelated business income tax on investment income of membership organizations described in sections 501(c)(7) and (c)(9). Congress recognized that a tax-exempt social club or similar group organized for recreational or social purposes merely was an extension of the individual members and that it would be inappropriate to impose a tax on the social club as a separate entity. S. Rept. No. 91–552 (1969), 1969–3 C.B. 423, 429. One court summarized the rationale as follows:

> Congress has determined that in a situation where individuals have banded together to provide recreational facilities on a mutual basis, it would be conceptually erroneous to impose a tax on the organization as a separate entity. The funds exempted are received only from the members and any "profit" which results from overcharging for the use of the facilities still belongs to the same members. No income of the sort usually taxed has been generated; the money has simply been sifted from one pocket to another, both within the same pair of pants. * * * McGlotten v. Connally, 338 F.Supp. 448, 458 (D.D.C.1972).

Where, however, the tax-exempt membership organization receives investment income and uses the tax free income to pay for recreational services offered to its members, the members receive an unintended benefit. As explained in the Senate committee report—

> where the organization receives income from sources outside the membership, such as income from investments (or in the case of employee benefit associations, from the employer), upon which no tax is paid, the membership receives a benefit not contemplated by the exemption in that untaxed dollars can be used by the organization to provide pleasure or recreation (or other benefits) to its membership. For example, if a social club were to receive $10,000 of untaxed income from investment in securities, it could use that $10,000 to reduce the cost or increase the services it provides to its members. In such a case, the exemption is no longer simply allowing individuals to join together for recreation or pleasure without tax consequences. Rather, it is bestowing a substantial additional advantage to the members of the club by allowing tax-free dollars to be used for their personal recreational or pleasure purposes. The extension of the exemption to such investment income is, therefore, a distortion of its purpose. (S. Rept. No. 91–552, supra at 470.)

The House report accompanying the Tax Reform Act of 1969 notes similar concern with respect to fraternal societies, as follows:

The receipt of untaxed income by fraternal beneficiary societies for use in providing recreational or social facilities in furtherance of the organization's fraternal purpose creates a similar problem to that of social clubs. * * * (H. Rept. No. 91–413 (1969), 1969–3 C.B. 199, 231.)

Congress recognized, however, that investment income also could be used by tax exempt membership organizations to further the exempt purposes of the organizations and that in such cases the tax on investment income would be inappropriate. Accordingly, the statutory exception found in section 512(a)(3)(B)(i) and (ii) for such income was enacted. As originally proposed by the House, only investment income of fraternal beneficiary associations and employees' beneficiary associations would have been eligible to qualify for this exception. In the Senate Finance Committee, however, the House version was changed to include investment income of social clubs where the investment income of social clubs was set aside for educational or charitable purposes. The Senate committee report explains the change as follows:

> In extending the exemption, the committee intends in the case of *national organizations of college fraternities and sororities* that amounts set aside for scholarships, student loans, loans on local chapter housing, leadership and citizenship schools and services, and similar activities, be classified as amounts used for educational or charitable purposes under this provision. [Emphasis added].

The express reference in the above legislative history to investment income of "national organizations of college fraternities and sororities," makes it very clear that Congress considered the investment income of such organizations to be generally subject to the new unrelated business income tax provisions.

* * *

Zeta Beta's emphasis on its similarity to section 501(c)(10) organizations such as the Masons also is not persuasive. Clearly, like the Masons, Zeta Beta operates under the lodge system and its local chapters engage in some activities that concededly further the charitable and educational goals of the fraternity. We agree with respondent, however, that the predominant purpose of Zeta Beta and its local chapters is to provide housing, board, and social activities for its undergraduate student members. In that respect, Zeta Beta is fundamentally different from fraternal organizations such as the Masons.

Even if we could find no relevant distinction between the purposes and activities of Zeta Beta and the Masons, it is not for this Court to counteract by judicial decision what we conclude is the congressional intent to treat national college fraternities in a manner different from fraternal organizations such as the Masons. Congress has "broad latitude in creating classifications and distinctions in tax statutes." Regan v. Taxation with Representation of Washington, 461 U.S. 540, 547–548 (1983).

Zeta Beta argues that its existing tax exemption under section 501(c)(7) does not preclude it from receiving an additional tax-exempt classification under section 501(c)(10), if it meets the qualifications thereof. As we stated earlier, in some situations an organization may qualify for tax exemption under a number of paragraphs of section 501(c). We have concluded, however, that national college fraternities are intended by Congress to be treated as exempt under section 501(c)(7) and not under section 501(c)(10).

Zeta Beta concedes that college fraternities historically have been granted tax-exempt classification under section 501(c)(7). If Congress had intended in 1969 to change that policy and to allow national college fraternities to be exempt under section 501(c)(10), it is reasonable to conclude that some mention of such a policy change would have been made in the extensive legislative history that accompanied the passage of the Tax Reform Act of 1969. To the contrary, that history (as well as the legislative history accompanying the 1976 amendments to section 501(c)(7)) reiterates the long-standing treatment of national college fraternities as tax-exempt organizations under section 501(c)(7) and the predecessors thereof.

We also note the agreement among commentators that national college fraternities and sororities are tax-exempt social clubs described in section 501(c)(7) and are subject to the unrelated business income tax on investment income. See, e.g., P. Treusch & N. Sugarman, Tax–Exempt Charitable Organizations, ch. 3, sec. E2.03 at 128 (1983); B. Hopkins, The Law of Tax–Exempt Organizations, sec. 18.1 at 303 (1983).

The prohibition in section 1.501(c)(10)–1, Income Tax Regs., on national college fraternities obtaining their tax exemption under section 501(c)(10) is a valid and reasonable interpretation of the statutory provisions as explained above. Treasury regulations must be sustained unless unreasonable and plainly inconsistent with the language, history, and purpose of a statute.

In light of the congressional intent that national college fraternities qualify for their tax-exempt status under section 501(c)(7), and not section 501(c)(10), we agree with respondent that Zeta Beta is not an organization described in section 501(c)(10), and that Zeta Beta is taxable on its investment income under section 512(a)(3)(A).

Accordingly,

Decision will be entered for the respondent.

2.   DISCRIMINATION

McGlotten v. Connally

United States District Court, District of Columbia, 1972.
338 F.Supp. 448.

■ BAZELON, CHIEF JUDGE.

[Plaintiff, an African American allegedly denied membership in a local lodge of the Benevolent and Protective Order of Elks solely because of his race, brought this class action to enjoin the granting of federal tax benefits to fraternal and non-profit organizations that excluded non-whites from membership. After rejecting various jurisdictional arguments raised by the Service, the court turned to the merits. Eds.]

* * *

II. *Failure to State a Claim Upon Which Relief Can Be Granted*

As noted above, plaintiff advances three separate theories in support of his right to relief. He challenges the constitutionality of the statute if, and to the extent that, it authorizes the grant of tax exempt status to nonprofit clubs and fraternal orders, and makes deductible contributions to such fraternal orders. He alternatively claims that the Internal Revenue Code does not authorize the deductibility of contributions to fraternal orders. Finally, plaintiff claims that both exemption from taxation and deductibility of contributions are federal financial assistance in violation of Title VI of the Civil Rights Act of 1964. Since a motion to dismiss for failure to state a claim tests the legal sufficiency of each count of the complaint, we must consider the counts separately.

A. *Constitutionality of Federal Tax Benefits to Segregated Organizations*

Better than one hundred years ago, this country sought to eliminate race as an operative fact in determining the quality of one's life. The decision has yet to be fully implemented. As Mr. Justice Douglas has pointedly stated: "Some badges of slavery remain today. While the institution has been outlawed, it has remained in the minds and hearts of many white men." The minds and hearts of men may be beyond the purview of this or any other court; perhaps those who cling to infantile and ultimately self-destructive notions of their racial superiority cannot be forced to maturity. But the Fifth and Fourteenth Amendments do require that such individuals not be given solace in their delusions by the Government. Nor is this emphasis on the conduct of the Government misplaced. "Government is the social organ to which all in our society look for the promotion of liberty, justice, fair and equal treatment, and the setting of worthy norms and goals for social conduct. Therefore something is uniquely amiss in a society where the government, the authoritative oracle of community values, involves itself in racial discrimination." Where that involvement is alleged, the courts have exercised the most careful scrutiny to ensure that the State lives up to its own promise.

Here plaintiff challenges the constitutionality of various provisions of the Internal Revenue Code to the extent that they authorize the grant of Federal tax benefits to organizations which exclude nonwhites from membership. These provisions exempt from income taxation nonprofit clubs (§ 501(c)(7)) and fraternal orders (§ 501(c)(8)) and make individual contributions to such fraternal orders deductible for income, estate, and gift taxes if the contributions are used "exclusively for religious, charitable, scientific, literary or educational purposes, or for the prevention of cruelty to children or animals." §§ 170(c)(4), 642(c), 2055, 2106(a), 2522. Plaintiff's claim thus leads us into the murky waters of the "state action" doctrine, for we must determine whether by granting tax benefits to private organizations which discriminate on the basis of race in membership, the Federal Government has supported or encouraged private discrimination so as to have itself violated plaintiff's right to the equal protection of the laws.

While a century ago, the phrase "state action"[31] may have sufficiently demarcated the extent of lawful state participation in private discrimination, that clarity has long since vanished in the wake of the greatly expanded role of government in a modern, industrial society. Whether by licensing, contract, or tax, few activities are left wholly untouched by the arm of Government. The responsibilities of the Government under the Fifth and Fourteenth Amendments, however, are not diluted by the expanded scope of Government, and our inquiry has become necessarily more detailed. "[O]nly by sifting facts and weighing circumstances can the nonobvious involvement of the State in private conduct be attributed its true significance." Burton v. Wilmington Parking Authority, 365 U.S. 715, 722, 81 S.Ct. 856, 860, 6 L.Ed.2d 45 (1961).

1. The Deductibility of Contributions to Fraternal Orders.

To demonstrate the unconstitutionality of the challenged deductions plaintiff must, of course, show that they in fact aid, perpetuate, or encourage racial discrimination. He alleges, subject to proof at trial, both the substantiality of the benefits provided[37] and a causal relation to the discrimination practiced by the segregated organizations.[38] But more is required to find a violation of the Constitution. Every deduction in the tax laws provides a benefit to the class who may take advantage of it. And the withdrawal of that benefit would often act as a substantial incentive to eliminate the behavior which caused the change in status. Yet the provision of an income tax deduction for mortgage interest paid has not been held sufficient to make the Federal Government a "joint participant" in the bigotry practiced by a homeowner. An additional line of inquiry is essential, one considering the nature of the Government activity in providing the

31. Since the grant of tax benefits is certainly an act of the state, it might be more accurate to state the question as whether the act of exemption violates the Fifth Amendment. Cf. Reitman v. Mulkey, 387 U.S. 369, 392, 87 S.Ct. 1627, 18 L.Ed.2d 830 (Harlan, J. dissenting). Nonetheless, the determination of when state involvement is sufficient either to bring otherwise private discrimination within the aegis of the Fifth or Fourteenth Amendment, or to evoke a duty on the part of the government to prevent that discrimination, has traditionally been styled one of "state action." Little clarity is gained at this stage by attaching a different label to the same inquiry depending on who is the defendant.

37. There is no question that allowing the deduction of charitable contributions in fact confers a benefit on the organization receiving the contribution. The court in Green v. Kennedy, supra note 11, described "the impact of Federal tax * * * deduction" as a "matching grant," and we agree.

38. We do not find it significant that plaintiff does not allege, as was the case in Green v. Kennedy, that the charitable purposes to which the federal funds are put are in themselves discriminatory. Plaintiff alleges that he and others in his position are denied the opportunity to help determine the purposes to which the funds are devoted. Paternalism should not be confused with equality.

challenged benefit and necessarily involving the sifting and weighing prescribed in Burton.

The rationale for allowing the deduction of charitable contributions has historically been that by doing so, the Government relieves itself of the burden of meeting public needs which in the absence of charitable activity would fall on the shoulders of the Government. "The Government is compensated for its loss of revenue by its relief from financial burdens which would otherwise have to be met by appropriations from public funds." H.Rep. No. 1860, 75th Cong., 3rd Sess. 19 (1938). And here the Government does more than simply authorize deduction of contributions to any cause which the individual taxpayer deems charitable. The statute, regulations, and administrative rulings thereunder, define in extensive detail not only the purposes which will satisfy the statute, but the vehicles through which those purposes may be achieved as well. A contribution, even for an approved purpose, is deductible only if made to an organization of the type specified in § 170 and which has obtained a ruling or letter of determination from the Internal Revenue Service. Thus the government has marked certain organizations as "Government Approved" with the result that such organizations may solicit funds from the general public on the basis of that approval.

In our view, the Government has become sufficiently entwined with private parties to call forth a duty to ensure compliance with the Fifth Amendment by the parties through whom it chooses to act. We see no difference in the degree to which the Government has "place[d] its power, property and prestige behind the admitted discrimination," Burton v. Wilmington Parking Authority, supra, at 725, 81 S.Ct. at 862, where a private restaurant in a government owned parking facility refuses service to black patrons, and where a tax supported organization by its constitution admits only "white male citizens."[43]

The public nature of the activity delegated to the organization in question, the degree of control the Government has retained as to the purposes and organizations which may benefit, and the aura of Government approval inherent in an exempt ruling by the Internal Revenue Service, all serve to distinguish the benefits at issue from the general run of deductions available under the Internal Revenue Code. Certain deductions provided by the Code do not act as matching grants, but are merely attempts to provide for an equitable measure of net income. Others are simply part of the structure of an income tax based on ability to pay. We recognize that an additional class of deductions—such as accelerated depreciation for rehabilitated low income rental property, or deductions for mortgage interest-do act as "incentives" favoring certain types of activities.

---

43. See Pitts v. Department of Revenue, * * *. The court there held that the grant of exemption from property taxation to organizations which discriminate on the basis of race in their membership violates the Fourteenth Amendment. The statute in question, Wis.Stat. § 70.11(4), made exemption available only to particular organizations, and the parties agreed "that the exemptions are granted on the reasoning that the organizations benefitted serve a public purpose."

But unlike the charitable deductions before us, these provisions go no further than simply indicating the activities hoped to be encouraged; they do not expressly choose fraternal organizations as a vehicle for that activity and do not allow such organizations to represent themselves as having the imprimatur of the Government. This seems to us a significant difference of degree in an area where no bright-line rule is possible.

2. *The Exemption From Income Tax for Nonprofit Clubs and Fraternal Orders.*

The exemptions from income taxation for nonprofit clubs (§ 501(c)(7)) and fraternal orders (§ 501(c)(8)) present more difficult problems. Because their tax treatment is not identical, we consider the exemptions for the two types of groups separately.

Nonprofit Clubs

Plaintiff's claim of unconstitutional aid to private discrimination rests on the following syllogism: Since the Government imposes a tax on all income, § 61(a), and then exempts from taxation the income of nonprofit clubs, an affirmative benefit or subsidy has been provided the exempted groups. After the Tax Reform Act of 1969, the treatment of exempt nonprofit clubs is that all their income, including passive investment income, is taxed at regular corporate rates. They are, however, allowed the equivalent of a deduction for "exempt function income," defined essentially as income derived from members. It is therefore this deduction which provides the allegedly unconstitutional aid.

Unlike the deduction for charitable contributions, the deduction for "exempt function income" does not operate to provide a grant of federal funds through the tax system. Rather, it is part and parcel of defining appropriate subjects of taxation. Congress has determined that in a situation where individuals have banded together to provide recreational facilities on a mutual basis, it would be conceptually erroneous to impose a tax on the organization as a separate entity. The funds exempted are received only from the members and any "profit" which results from overcharging for the use of the facilities still belongs to the same members. No income of the sort usually taxed has been generated; the money has simply been shifted from one pocket to another, both within the same pair of pants. Thus the exclusion of member generated revenue reflects a determination that as to these funds the organization does not operate as a separate entity.

That the Government provides no monetary benefit does not, however, insulate its involvement from constitutional scrutiny. The lease in Burton was, as far as the record shows, entirely arm's length with no provision of federal property at less than market value. Encouragement of discrimination through the appearance of governmental approval may also be sufficient involvement to violate the Constitution. But here the necessary involvement is not readily apparent. Section 501(c)(7) does not limit its coverage to particular activities; exemption is given to "[c]lubs organized and operated exclusively for pleasure, recreation and other nonprofitable purposes * * * " (emphasis added.) Thus there is no mark of Government approval inherent in the designation of a group as exempt. Congress has simply chosen not to tax a particular type of revenue because it is not within the scope sought to be taxed by the statute. And however dysfunctional the "state action" limitation is at a time when the nation has sufficiently matured that the elimination of racial discrimination is a cornerstone of national policy, it still means that Congress does not violate the Constitution by failing to tax private discrimination where there is no other act of Government involvement. To find a violation solely from the State's failure to act would, however laudably, eliminate the "state action" doctrine and that must come from the Supreme Court. The motion to dismiss is granted as to the claim that the exemption for § 501(c)(7) nonprofit clubs violates the Constitution.

Fraternal Orders

The exemption given to fraternal organizations under § 501(c)(8) stands on different footing. Unlike nonprofit clubs, fraternal organizations are taxed only on "unrelated business taxable income" defined as "any trade or business the conduct of which is not substantially related (aside from the need of such organization for income or funds or the use it makes of the profits derived) to the exercise or performance by such organization of its charitable, educational, or other purpose or function constituting the basis for the exemption under section 501 ..." The crucial impact of this differential treatment is that the passive investment income of fraternal orders is not taxed. This exemption cannot be explained simply by the inappropriateness of taxing the organization as a separate entity in this situation. Here individuals are providing funds which are then invested for the purposes of benefiting the contributing members, and the exemption of this income is a "benefit" provided by the Government.

We think this exclusion, provided only to particular organizations with particular purposes, rather than across the board, is sufficient government involvement to invoke the Fifth Amendment. By providing differential treatment to only selected organizations, the Government has indicated approval of the organizations and hence their discriminatory practice, and aided that discrimination by the provision of federal tax benefits.

B.   Claim That the Internal Revenue Code Does Not Authorize the Deductibility of Contributions to Segregated Fraternal Organizations.

Plaintiff also alleges that the deductibility of contributions to fraternal organizations which exclude nonwhites from membership is not authorized by the Internal Revenue Code.[59] Contributions to fraternal organizations exempt under § 501(c)(8) are deductible under §§ 170(c)(4), 642(c), 2055, 2106(a), and 2522, if used exclusively for the purposes there listed. Plaintiff argues that because such contributions also perpetuate the existence of an

---

59. Under Count 3 of the complaint, unlike the other counts, Plaintiff attacks only the deductibility of contributions and not the tax exempt status of the organizations themselves.

organization which discriminates on the basis of race, the exclusivity requirement is not satisfied.

Only recently a three-judge court of this District considered the application of the statutes in question to the benefits granted to segregated private schools. Green v. Connally, 330 F.Supp. 1150 (D.D.C.1971), aff'd sub nom. Coit v. Green, 404 U.S. 997, 92 S.Ct. 564, 30 L.Ed.2d 550 (1971) (mem.). The Court there held that since "the Congressional intent in providing tax deductions and exemptions is not construed to be applicable to activities that are either illegal or against public policy," the overwhelming federal policy against segregated education required that the Internal Revenue Code "no longer be construed so as to provide private schools operating on a racially discriminatory premise the support of the exemptions and deductions which Federal tax law affords to charitable organizations and their sponsors."

In *Green*, the Court felt its construction of the Code was "underscored by the fact that it obviates the need to determine * * * serious constitutional claims." Since the constitutional claim here, unlike in *Green*, was challenged by a motion to dismiss, and since we therefore cannot avoid plaintiff's serious constitutional claim, we have already determined that the tax deductions in question, if authorized, would violate the Fifth Amendment. As such, we would be bound to interpret the Code as not allowing the deduction of contributions to segregated fraternal orders. We do not think, however, that the correctness of that construction depends on the finding of state action which underlies our constitutional determination. [The court supported this conclusion by referring to the Thirteenth Amendment's delegation of authority to Congress to pass laws necessary to abolish slavery and the Congressional policy, articulated in the 1964 Civil Rights Act, that race discrimination cannot be practiced by those receiving federal financial assistance. As a result, the Internal Revenue Code could not be construed to allow the deduction of contributions to organizations which exclude nonwhites from membership. The court then considered the plaintiff's allegations that the granting of federal tax benefits to organizations excluding non-whites from membership was a form of federal financial assistance in violation of Title VI of the 1964 Civil Rights Act. It concluded that while the tax deduction for charitable contributions and the tax exemption for fraternal orders did constitute "federal financial assistance," the exemption of social clubs did not. Eds.]

III. *Conclusion*

We have no illusion that our holding today will put an end to racial discrimination or significantly dismantle the social and economic barriers that may be more subtle, but are surely no less destructive. Individuals may retain their own beliefs, however odious or offensive. But the Supreme Court has declared that the Constitution forbids the Government from supporting and encouraging such beliefs. By eliminating one more of the "nonobvious involvement[s] of the State in private conduct," we obey the Court's command to quarantine racism.

NOTES

1. *Section 501(i).* After *McGlotten* was decided, Congress enacted § 501(i), which disqualifies a social club from exemption if at any time during its taxable year the charter, bylaws, or other governing instruments of the organization, or any written policy statement, contain a provision which provides for discrimination against any person on the basis of race, color or religion. The prohibition is intended to extend to discrimination against guests and other persons, such as employees. In 1980, at the behest of the Knights of Columbus, Congress added an exception to § 501(i) permitting clubs and certain auxiliaries of fraternal societies to discriminate on the basis of religion, if they in good faith limit their membership to members of a particular religion in order to further their principles, rather than to exclude individuals of a particular race or color.

2. *Other Legal Issues.* Other legal problems of private membership associations are considered in Chapter 10, infra.

3. *For Further Reading.* Boris I. Bittker & Kenneth M. Kaufman, Constitutionalizing the Internal Revenue Code, 82 Yale L.J. 51 (1972).

3. Nonmember Activities

At one time, a social club qualified for exemption under § 501(c)(7) only if it was "organized and operated exclusively for pleasure, recreation * * * and similar exempt purposes." In 1976, Congress relaxed the "exclusively" requirement. A club now qualifies if "substantially all" of its activities are for the recreational and other exempt purposes listed in the Code. This amendment was intended to make it clear that a social club may receive outside income, including investment income, without losing its exempt status and to permit clubs to derive a somewhat higher level of income from the use of their facilities or services by non-members. The trade-off is that this type of income may be taxable as unrelated business income.

The legislative history provides the following guidelines to measure the permissible extent of nonmember income:

(1) A club may receive up to 35 percent of its gross receipts, including investment income, from nonmember sources.

(2) In applying the 35 percent test above, not more than 15 percent of total gross receipts may be derived from the use of the club's facilities or services by the general public.

(3) If a club has outside income that exceeds either the 35 or 15 percent limits, a facts and circumstances test will be applied to determine qualification for exemption under § 501(c)(7).

(4) For purposes of these tests, "gross receipts" means receipts from normal and usual activities of the club, including charges, admissions, membership fees, dues, assessments, investment income and normal recurring capital gains on investments but excluding initiation fees and capital contributions. Where a club receives unusual

amounts of bunched income—e.g., gain from the sale of its club-house—that income will not be included in the gross receipts formula.

See S. Rep. No. 94–1318, 94th Cong., 2d Sess. (1976).

It is important to remember that satisfying the safe harbor tests for nonmember income does not automatically protect a club from loss of exemption. A club still may be disqualified if its members do not "commingle" sufficiently or if the club engages in excessive activities, even of a non-income producing nature, that do not serve its exempt purposes. Private inurement is also prohibited. For example, the Service takes the position that where a club has different membership classes which enjoy the same rights and privileges but are treated differently for purposes of dues and initiation fees, inurement of private gain may result because the classes paying the lower dues are being subsidized by the members of the classes paying more. See Rev. Rul. 70–48, 1970–1 C.B. 133.

PROBLEMS

1. Consider whether the following organizations are exempt as social clubs under § 501(c)(7):

   (a) The Suburban Golf and Country Club has 450 members, none of whom are African–American or Jewish. Neither the club's charter nor any written policy statements authorize discrimination on the basis of race or religion, but new members must obtain five "sponsors" who already belong to the club. This policy has been in effect during the club's 92 years of operation.

   (b) The Oyster Cracker Club, a dining club in a major U.S. city, has 1,100 male members of all races, creeds and colors but no women members. Women are not permitted in the main dining room or bar, but they may be guests at functions held in the club's private rooms.

   (c) Same as (b), above, except the club has only women members.

2. The Argonaut Club, which has both men and women members, provides traditional services that include a dining room, lounges and private rooms for meetings and parties. The club is known for its wonderful food. In an effort to provide more services for members (and raise revenue), the club is considering the activities described below. Which, if any, of these activities will jeopardize the club's tax-exempt status?

   (a) Sale of food products, such as turkey and ham platters and baked goods, to members to be consumed off the club's premises. The products could be packaged as gift items or for the convenience of members seeking "take out" service.

   (b) Sale of flower arrangements to be taken off club property.

   (c) Renting club parking spaces to members to be used while they are at work.

(d) Renting rooms to members who live in the suburbs but wish to stay overnight in the city while attending the theater, symphony or club functions.

(e) Engaging in any of the foregoing transactions with nonmembers.

F.   OTHER MUTUAL BENEFIT ORGANIZATIONS

1.   VETERANS ORGANIZATIONS

Until 1972, veterans organizations were exempt as social welfare organizations under § 501(c)(4) or as social clubs under § 501(c)(7). To protect veterans organizations from exposure to the unrelated business tax on income derived from insuring their members, Congress created a new exemption category in § 501(c)(19) and added a specific unrelated business tax exemption for veterans groups in § 512(a)(4). In addition, contributions to veterans organizations are tax-deductible under § 170(c)(3).

A veterans organization qualifies for exemption under § 501(c)(19) if:

(1) It is organized in the United States or its possessions;

(2) At least 75 percent of its members are past or present "members of the Armed Forces" (whether or not "war veterans") and substantially all the other members are cadets or spouses, widows or widowers of members of the Armed Forces or cadets;

(3) At least 97.5 percent of its members are veterans, students in college or university ROTC programs, students at armed services academies, and spouses and surviving spouses of these veterans or students; and

(4) No part of the net earnings of the organization inures to the benefit of any private shareholder or individual.

See also Treas. Reg. § 1.501(c)(19)–1(b).

The regulations elaborate on the permissible exempt purposes of a veterans organization. They include assisting disabled veterans and current members of the armed forces and their dependents, entertaining and caring for hospitalized veterans, perpetuating the memory of deceased veterans and comforting their survivors, carrying on traditional charitable and educational programs, sponsoring patriotic activities, providing insurance benefits, and providing social and recreational activities for members. Treas. Reg. § 1.501(c)(19)–1(c). Significantly, veterans organizations historically have been permitted to lobby in furtherance of these exempt purposes without limitation. The Supreme Court has upheld the constitutionality of this favorable treatment of veterans organizations as compared to § 501(c)(3) public charities. See Regan v. Taxation With Representation of Washington, 461 U.S. 540, 103 S.Ct. 1997 (1983), Chapter 5E3, supra, at p. 489.

Section 501(c)(23) confers exempt status on a separate (and narrow) category of organization that was founded before 1880 and whose principal purpose is to provide insurance and other benefits to veterans or their dependents provided that more than 75 percent of the organization's members are present or past members of the armed forces.

2.   POLITICAL ORGANIZATIONS

Political organizations are a hybrid form of tax-exempt organization. For tax purposes, a political organization is a group or fund organized and operated primarily to accept contributions or make expenditures for an "exempt function." I.R.C. § 527(e)(1). Exempt functions include influencing or attempting to influence the selection, nomination, election, or appointment of individuals to any Federal, state, or local public office or office in a political organization, or the election of Presidential or Vice Presidential electors, whether or not these individuals are selected, nominated, elected, or appointed. I.R.C. § 527(e)(2).

Political organizations are taxable on their "political organization taxable income," which is defined as the organization's gross income other than "exempt function income" less directly related expenses of the nonexempt income. I.R.C. § 527(b), (c)(1). Exempt function income includes: (1) contributions, (2) membership dues, fees, and assessments, (3) proceeds from political fundraising events and sales of campaign materials, and (4) proceeds of bingo games, to the extent all these amounts are segregated for use for the organization's exempt functions. I.R.C. § 527(c)(3).

All of this means that political organizations are not taxed on contributions and other income generated by their political activities, but in theory they are taxable, at the highest corporate rate (currently 35 percent), on their net investment income. I.R.C. § 527(b)(1). As a practical matter, even if a political organization has investment income, it may be able to avoid tax under § 527 by establishing a "separate segregated fund" (a simple checking or savings account would suffice) to receive contributions and make political expenditures. I.R.C. § 527(f)(3); Treas. Reg. § 1.527–2(b)(1). Segregated funds are treated as separate entities for tax purposes.

Section 527(f) links the taxing scheme outlined above to those § 501(c) organizations—primarily § 501(c)(4) social welfare organizations, § 501(c)(5) labor unions, and § 501(c)(6) business leagues—that make expenditures for an exempt function, such as participating in a political campaign or seeking to influence a nomination of a Supreme Court appointee. These organizations generally are taxed on the lesser of their net investment income, or the aggregate amount spent for exempt functions. I.R.C. § 527(f)(1). The application of § 527 to an exempt organization that controls an affiliated political action committee and issues related to § 527 organizations are discussed in Chapters 5E6 and 5E7, supra, at pp. 532–539.

3.   TITLE HOLDING COMPANIES

Exempt organizations occasionally form separate nonprofit entities to hold title to their property, collect the income, pay expenses, and distribute the net earnings to the exempt parent-beneficiary. Nonprofits first formed title holding companies to overcome state law obstacles to direct holding of title to real property. More recently, title holding companies have served to insulate exempt organizations from liability, enhance the owner's ability to borrow against the property, simplify accounting and management, and facilitate compliance with state property law requirements.

Section 501(c)(2) grants exempt status to a title holding company that may hold any type of property (not just real estate), usually for the benefit of one exempt organization. Section 501(c)(25) confers exemption to corporations or trusts organized for the exclusive purpose of holding title to real property, and collecting and remitting the income to one or more qualified exempt organizations (including pension trusts and § 501(c)(3) organizations) provided that the entity has no more than 35 shareholders or beneficiaries. The purpose of § 501(c)(25), which was added to the Code in 1986, was described as follows by the Joint Committee on Taxation staff:

> The Congress concluded that smaller, unrelated tax-exempt organizations should be able to pool investment funds for purposes of investing in real property through a title-holding company * * * with generally the same tax treatment as is available to a larger tax-exempt organization having a title-holding subsidiary that is tax-exempt as an organization described in section 501(c)(2).

Staff of Joint Comm. on Taxation, 99th Cong., 2d Sess., General Explanation of the Tax Reform Act of 1986 at 1328 (Comm. Print 1987).

Prior to 1993, title holding companies lost their exempt status if they generated any unrelated business income from activities other than collecting income from their property and remitting it to their exempt parent-beneficiary. Treas. Reg. § 1.501(c)(2)–1. In 1993, however, Congress enacted an obscure but important amendment that permits all § 501(c)(2) and § 501(c)(25) title holding companies to receive up to 10 percent of gross income from incidental unrelated business activities without affecting their exempt status. I.R.C. § 501(c)(25)(G). The change was intended to provide relief to title holding companies holding large properties, such as apartment houses or shopping centers, that derived income from parking garages and vending machines. H.R.Rep. No. 103–111, 103d Cong., 1st Sess. 618–619 (1993).

4.   Other Exempt Organizations

The remaining categories of mutual benefit organizations may be vitally important to their founders and members, but they are highly specialized and thus beyond the scope of our coverage. They include: nonprofit cemetery companies (I.R.C. § 501(c)(13)); employee benefit organizations, such as voluntary employee beneficiary associations (I.R.C. § 501(c)(9)); trusts to provide group legal services (I.R.C. § 501(c)(20)); trusts to provide supplemental unemployment compensation benefits (I.R.C. § 501(c)(17)); local teachers' retirement funds (I.R.C. § 501(c)(11)); trusts to compensate coal miners for disability or death due to certain diseases covered by the Black Lung laws (I.R.C. § 501(c)(21)); and various types of mutual insurance, ditch and irrigation, cooperative electric, and telephone companies (I.R.C. § 501(c)(12), (14)–(16)). In addition, home-owners associations may elect to be treated as exempt organizations, limiting their tax liability to 30 percent of their investment income and amounts received from nonmembers for the use of association property. I.R.C. § 528.

CHAPTER 10

SPECIAL PROBLEMS OF PRIVATE MEMBERSHIP ASSOCIATIONS

A. INTRODUCTION

Note, State Power and Discrimination by Private Clubs: First Amendment Protection for Nonexpressive Associations

104 Harv. L. Rev. 1835, 1838–1839 (1991).

Americans have traditionally cherished and vigorously exercised their freedom to form clubs and voluntary associations. In 1820 Alexis de Tocqueville commented that "[b]etter use has been made of association and this powerful instrument of action has been applied to more varied aims in America than anywhere else in the world." For de Tocqueville, the right to form an association was a natural right of man, "by nature almost as inalienable as individual liberty," and Americans exercised it actively. "Americans of all ages, all stations in life, and all types of disposition are forever forming associations. * * * There are not only commercial and industrial associations * * * but others of a thousand different types— religious, moral, serious, futile, very general and very limited, immensely large and very minute." De Tocqueville's observation remains valid today.

Although it may often be difficult to discern the social value of a single association, in the aggregate, private voluntary associations serve a number of important values. Associations play a critical role in individual self-definition and provide an important context in which individuals pursue personal happiness. Many private clubs, for example, provide fellowship and a comfortable environment for social interaction. On a broader, socio-political level, private associations foster democratic values and aid in the process of free self-government. Not only do private associations serve civic republican values of participation, but they are also an important counter-weight to the power of the state. In addition, private associations are the principal building blocks of societal diversity and pluralism. Given the multiculturalism, mobility, and impersonality of the modern world, many commentators argue that the values of private association are more important now than they were in the early years of the republic.

INTRODUCTORY NOTE

What are the rights of members of private clubs and other voluntary associations? When can members utilize the courts for either specific relief, to obtain an injunction, a declaratory judgment, a writ of mandamus or procure an award of monetary damages for a perceived wrong? What theories can members allege to trigger judicial intervention in the affairs of private organizations? In what situations can the government on its own initiative intervene in the affairs of private organizations? At what point or under what circumstances do the strictures of the Constitution intrude upon associations? Are there limits to the power of an organization to expel a member?

Courts have utilized several theories to justify intrusion into the affairs of private associations. The expulsion of a member might deprive her of a property or contractual right. A procedurally improper expulsion could be a tort because the member's relationship to the organization may be the true basis for protection. See Zechariah Chafee, The Internal Affairs of Associations Not for Profit, 43 Harv. L. Rev. 993, 1007 (1930).

The essence of freedom to form voluntary associations is the freedom to determine which individuals one will select as members. Or, as the United States Supreme Court said in Roberts v. United States Jaycees, 468 U.S. 609, 623, 104 S.Ct. 3244, 3252 (1984), freedom of association "plainly presupposes a freedom not to associate." In controlling admission to private associations, is there a right to discriminate because of members' rights of freedom of association, privacy, or the First Amendment? What are the state interests in providing equal access to private organizations? Where should the balance be drawn? In this chapter, we examine members' rights in associations, when courts will intervene in matters of expulsion or admission, the limits to an organization's freedom of association, and the special issues raised when religious organizations seek to regulate their internal affairs.

B.   JUDICIAL INTERVENTION INTO PRIVATE ASSOCIATION AFFAIRS

Zechariah Chafee, The Internal Affairs of Associations Not for Profit

43 Harv.L.Rev. 993, 993–995 (1930).

The bitterness of a dispute is apt to be inversely proportionate to the area of conflict. Family rows are proverbial for their violence. A similar acerbity pervades quarrels in clubs, trade unions, professional associations, secret societies, churches, and educational institutions. Even a decisive defeat within the organization does not always discourage the losers. Their blood is up, and they are almost sure to carry the fight into the courts, hoping for better fortune on a fresh field of battle. What welcome should such suits receive? Corporations, partnerships, joint adventures, joint stock companies, and business trusts are frequently the objects of judicial control, but their business activities naturally cause public concern, and the bodies which we are considering exist for other purposes than making money. How far should the state consent to settle through its courts the internal affairs of these non-profit-making associations?

A typical example of such internal disputes was presented by the expulsion of Colonel Dawkins in 1878 from the Travellers' Club, of which he had been for more than twenty years a member. That case, which led to the judicial statement of several widely accepted principles of law, may serve as the focus of our problems. The colonel had not confined his militancy to the field, and this was by no means his first controversy. His career in the Coldstream Guards had been enlivened and then abruptly terminated by a succession of altercations, beginning in 1859 with an undeserved reprimand from his superior officer, and ending with two courts martial in which he was the central figure. The second of these retired him in 1865 on half pay, condemning him as an officer but not as a gentleman. But the colonel had just begun to fight. After failing to get his commanding officer, Lord Rokeby, court-martialed, he sued him unsuccessfully for false imprisonment and conspiracy to reduce Dawkins' rank. A year or two later he tried an action of libel against his previous commanding officer, Lord Paulet, for sending a damaging report about Dawkins to the adjutant general. Losing again, he brought an action of libel against Lord Rokeby for his testimony against the colonel at one of the courts martial. After a third series of defeats in every court up to the House of Lords, the colonel sued three members of the final court martial, including Prince Edward of Saxe Weimar, for conspiracy in reporting to the commander in chief that Dawkins was unfit for his military duties. For the fourth time, judgment for the defendants.

Thus was our law of torts enriched through the colonel's pertinacity. Although the public would regard Dawkins as a quarrelsome nuisance, and the psychiatrists would classify him as afflicted by the litigious variety of mental disease, we lawyers should think of him as one of those all too rare benefactors of the law praised by Von Ihering in his *Struggle for Law*, who at the cost of great inconvenience and expense to themselves establish fundamental legal principles by big lawsuits over small claims. Yet so little recognition has been given him that he is absent from the Dictionary of National Biography, and even his first name is unknown.

The colonel's greatest achievement in law-making was still to come. Two years after his final failure to bring most of the leaders of the British army to strict accountability in the courts, he turned author and produced a pamphlet entitled, *A Farce and a Villainy—Heads I Win, Tails You Lose*, which reflected on the conduct of Lieutenant General Stephenson, a member of the disastrous court martial. Dawkins enclosed this pamphlet in a wrapper marked, "Dishonourable Conduct of lieutenant General Stephenson," and sent it by mail to the general at the Horse Guards. Now the general was also a member of the Travellers' Club, and the matter was soon brought to the attention of the club committee, which under the rules had power to find "the conduct of any member, either in or out of the clubhouse, * * * injurious to the character and interests of the club." After Dawkins had first refused to explain and then refused to resign, the committee made such a finding of injurious conduct, and thereupon called a general meeting of the club, which expelled the colonel by a vote of 108 to 36. Dawkins then sued the club trustees and the committee for a declaration that his expulsion was improper, and for an injunction restraining them from interfering with his use of the club's buildings and property. For the last time he lost his case, but he obtained from the Court of Appeal a lucid statement of the law of clubs. And so Colonel Dawkins passed out of legal history.

NOTES AND QUESTIONS

1. *Court Intervention.* In Dawkins v. Antrobus, 17 Ch.D. 615 (C.A. 1881), the case discussed by Professor Chafee, the court said that its role was to determine whether the expulsion of Colonel Dawkins was according to the rules of the club and whether the procedures were bona fide and the honest exercise of the club's powers. The court would not examine the merits of the decision.

Under what circumstances will a court intervene in the affairs of a private association? What would a court do if there was no reason for the expulsion?

2. *The Social and Economic Costs of Expulsion from a Private Association.* One should not downplay the severity of the consequences of expulsion from a private association. Even if a legal claim can be filed, damages may provide inadequate relief. Excommunication of a believer from a church can be the spiritual equivalent of capital punishment or even worse—eternal damnation. A wrongfully ejected member of a social club may find her reputation amongst peers permanently tarnished. Members of a labor union may lose their opportunity to pursue a livelihood if expelled. A student expelled from a school is branded for years and his life's chances forever may be affected. When punishment is sufficiently severe or unfair, courts will intercede.

3. *The Scope of Judicial Inquiry.* When a claimant seeks judicial relief, the court must determine whether the alleged conduct is wrong in a legal sense, whether it is appropriate for judicial relief, and if so, what should be the scope of judicial intervention and whether an appropriate legal remedy can be fashioned. If the answers to these questions are affirmative, the court must then weigh the validity of the claim and fashion the appropriate relief. Developments in the Law—Judicial Control of Private Associations, 76 Harv. L. Rev. 983, 990 (1963). Damages may not suffice, and courts have fashioned equitable relief.

NOTE: EXERCISE OF GOVERNMENT–LIKE POWERS BY PRIVATE ASSOCIATIONS

Constitutional limitations on associations have been applied where the private organization exercises state-like powers or authority delegated by the state. Marsh v. Alabama, 326 U.S. 501, 66 S.Ct. 276 (1946) (individual could not be prosecuted for criminal trespass for proselytizing her religion in company town after being ordered to leave by Company); Shelley v. Kraemer, 334 U.S. 1, 68 S.Ct. 836 (1948) (Fourteenth Amendment prohibited judgment enforcement of restrictive covenants based on race or color). More recently, the issue has arisen with the expansion of community associations, private residential enclaves that range from cooperative apartment buildings to walled neighborhoods of free-standing houses. See Evan McKenzie, Privatopia: Homeowner Associations and the Rise of Residential Private Government (1994); Lisa J. Chadderdon, No Political Speech Allowed: Common Interest Developments, Homeowners Associations, and Restrictions on Free Speech, 21 J. Land Use & Envtl.L. 233 (2006); Steven Siegel, The Constitution and Private Government: Toward the Recognition of Constitutional Rights in Private Residential Communities Fifty Years After Marsh v. Alabama, 6 Wm & Mary Bill Rts. J. 461 (1998). Condominium and homeowners associations are frequently described as "residential private governments" that exercise legislative, judicial and executive powers over those living within their territorial boundaries. Stewart E. Sterk, Minority Protection in Residential Private Governments, 77 B.U.L.Rev. 273 (1997); Note, The Rule of Law in Residential Associations, 99 Harv. L. Rev. 472 (1985); Uriel Reichman, Residential Private Governments: An Introductory Survey, 43 U. Chi. L. Rev. 253 (1976). They exert extraordinary governmental-like powers over their residents' conduct, property rights, and lifestyle.

These private developments often have rules that are far more restrictive than municipal government, from one vote per family instead of one person one vote to restrictions on the posting of signs or flags. States generally have deferred to the rule making power of community associations. Note, Judicial Review of Condominium Rulemaking, 94 Harv. L. Rev. 647, 652 (1981). Except in cases of racial discrimination and restriction of non-commercial speech, courts have not been particularly solicitous of requests for constitutional review on grounds of state action. Robert G. Natelson, Law of Property Owners Associations § 4.6.5 (1989 & 1997 Supp.).

In City of Ladue v. Gilleo, 512 U.S. 43, 114 S.Ct. 2038 (1994), the Supreme Court unanimously struck down an ordinance which banned all residential signs except those falling within one of ten exemptions. The principal purpose of the ordinance was to minimize the usual clutter associated with such signs. The Court found that the regulation restricted too little speech because the exemptions discriminated on the basis of the sign's messages, and that it prohibited too much protected speech. The Court said that displaying a sign from ones' own residence provided information about the speaker's identity, an important component of many attempts to persuade. Residential signs were also an unusually cheap and convenient form of communication. If Ladue had occurred in a private property owners association, would such a bylaw as the ordinance been upheld? See Committee for a Better Twin Rivers v. Twin Rivers Homeowner's Ass'n, 192 N.J. 344, 929 A.2d 1060 (2007).

C.   MEMBERSHIP AS A PROPERTY RIGHT

It is common to mutual benefit organizations for members to purchase interests in the organization when they join. The following case examines the extent to which membership becomes a property right.

Lambert v. Fishermen's Dock Cooperative, Inc.

Supreme Court of New Jersey, 1972.
61 N.J. 596, 297 A.2d 566.

■ MOUNTAIN, J.

[Plaintiff joined the Fisherman's Dock Association, a cooperative, by purchasing two shares of stock for $125. Several years later his membership was terminated by the cooperative's board of directors because he was no longer engaged in the fishing industry, did no business with the cooperative and was ineligible for membership. Plaintiff objected that he did not receive the amount to which he was entitled upon redemption of his shares. Eds.]

In 1957, the time plaintiff became a stockholder, a by-law of the association stated that upon termination of membership a stockholder was entitled to receive the "fair book value" of his shares. In 1962 this by-law was amended to provide that henceforth, instead of "fair book value," a retiring member would be entitled to a return only of the price he had originally paid for his stock. Plaintiff strongly objected to this amendment at the time of its adoption. Both the certificate of association and the by-laws at all times contained provisions authorizing the amendment of the by-laws by majority vote of the membership.

The trial court agreed with plaintiff that the amended by-law, altering the consideration to be received upon the redemption of shares from fair book value to original purchase price, was invalid as violating a contract, infringing upon a vested right, and exceeding such authority as was bestowed upon the majority by its reserved power to amend by-laws. The Appellate Division disagreed, holding that the power reserved to the majority to amend the by-laws of the association was ample to support the questioned amendment and therefore the amendment became binding upon the plaintiff upon its adoption. Upon this crucial point we find ourselves in agreement with the trial judge.

It is the law generally that a reserved right to amend the by-laws of an association, whether to be exercised by the majority or, in some cases, a larger proportion of stockholders, members or directors, is a limited rather than an absolute right, even though the reservation is expressed in broad and general terms. It is often said that such a right to amend may not be extended so as to impair or destroy a contract or vested right, that it does not authorize the adoption of an amendment which will have such an effect, and that in general the exercise of such a right should be confined to matters touching the administrative policies and affairs of the corporation, the relations of members and officers with the corporation and among themselves, and like matters of internal concern.

In New Jersey this rule, that a reserved power to amend by-laws may not affect basic rights, has found expression in a number of cases; interestingly, most of these deal with societies and associations which are similar to the defendant cooperative in that they were created to foster some kind of mutual benefit. * * *

Elsewhere the general rule limiting the exercise of the reserved right to amend by-laws to such matters as will not substantially affect basic rights of stockholders or members has been applied to cooperatives like the defendant. In Whitney v. Farmers Co-op. Grain Co., 110 Neb. 157, 193 N.W. 103 (1923), at the time plaintiff became a stockholder-member, a by-law of the defendant provided that it would repurchase his stock at a designated price in the event that he should later move out of the marketing area. This by-law was later rescinded. Plaintiff thereafter moved from the area so that he was no longer able to avail himself of defendant's services, whereupon he requested the defendant to repurchase his stock in accordance with the original by-law. This the defendant refused to do, pointing out that the by-law had been rescinded and that plaintiff had originally agreed to be bound by all defendant's by-laws, both those then in existence and those thereafter adopted. The court found for the plaintiff, holding that the reserved right to amend, even though coupled with plaintiff's original agreement to be bound by any subsequent exercise thereof, did not justify defendant's abrogation of its contract to repurchase. * * *

Accordingly we hold that the amended by-law adopted in 1962 by Fishermen's Dock Cooperative was ineffective to divest the plaintiff of the right given him under the by-law in effect when he purchased his stock, namely, to receive upon the termination of his membership, the fair book value of his shares.

* * *

NOTE

Property Rights of Withdrawing Members. In an omitted part of Lambert v. Fishermen's Dock Cooperative, the court asked but did not answer the question whether a former member of a cooperative or mutual benefit association is entitled to the assets upon dissolution. The general rule is that in the absence of contrary provisions in the bylaws or certificate of incorporation, members of an association who withdraw acquire no severable right to any of the property or funds of the organization. Title to property rests in the remaining members whether membership is terminated by the member's own act, by the organization or where a majority of members leave, or the organization subsequently dissolves. Thus, withdrawal of membership has the effect of resignation of all rights in the property. See Raulston v. Everett, 561 S.W.2d 635 (Tex.Civ.App.1978); DeBruyn v. Golden Age Club of Cheyenne, 399 P.2d 390 (Wyo.1965). Elimination of voting rights of members is limited by notions of fairness. See Ferry v. San Diego Museum, 180 Cal.App.3d 35, 225 Cal.Rptr. 258 (1986), supra p. 133.

D.   EXPULSION OF MEMBERS

Revised Model Nonprofit Corp. Act § 6.21.

Cal. Corp. Code § 7341.

Owen v. Rosicrucian Fellowship

District Court of Appeal, California, 1959.
173 Cal.App.2d 112, 342 P.2d 424.

■ MUSSELL, JUSTICE.

Juanita Owen and Grace Sawyer, as members of the Rosicrucian Fellowship, a church corporation, seek a writ of mandamus to compel the defendant members of the board of directors of the corporation to reinstate petitioners as members thereof and to permit them to examine the mailing list of membership of the corporation. The trial court rendered judgment denying plaintiffs' petition and discharging the alternative writ of mandamus theretofore entered. Plaintiffs appeal from the judgment.

As stated in the pretrial order herein, petitioners contend that they were unlawfully expelled from membership in the Rosicrucian Fellowship corporation and were illegally denied the right to inspect the membership list. The respondents contend that the petitioners were first suspended and then expelled in accordance with the by-laws and rules and regulations of the church corporation and that by reason of the suspension and expulsion, any right of petitioners to examine the corporate records expired, and that, in any event, the demand of petitioners was not reasonably related to their interests as members of said corporation.

There is no serious dispute as to the material facts involved. They are set forth in a written stipulation attached to the pretrial order and in the findings of the trial court. Summarized, they are as follows:

The Rosicrucian Fellowship is a church corporation and at all times here involved its by-laws provided for the suspension and expulsion of members in rules and regulations duly and regularly adopted for such suspension and expulsion. These rules and regulations provide, in substance, that upon receipt of a written complaint signed by a member in good standing of the church corporation, against another member, the board of directors shall have the power by majority vote to suspend the accused member pending a hearing of the charges at a subsequent meeting; that notice of said hearing and charges be given by mail to the accused member; that at the subsequent meeting, the board of directors, after hearing evidence for and against the accused, has the power by majority vote to reprimand, exonerate or expel said member.

Prior to January 26, 1958, petitioners Juanita Owen and Grace Sawyer were members of the church corporation. On January 25, 1958, they delivered to defendants a written demand for inspection of the membership records of the Rosicrucian Fellowship, and on February 22 the said board of directors adopted a resolution denying petitioners the right to inspect the membership register. On January 25 the board of directors received from a member of the corporation letters complaining of certain acts of Juanita Owen and Grace Sawyer and on January 26, 1958, the board of directors adopted resolutions expelling petitioners. At a special duly and regularly called meeting on February 22, 1958, the board passed resolutions revoking the resolutions of January 26 and reinstating petitioners. Resolutions were then adopted suspending each of said petitioners pending hearing of said letters of complaint at the next regular meeting of the board to be held on April 19, 1958. Written notice of this hearing was mailed to petitioners and, on April 19, 1958, the board heard evidence as to whether or not the petitioners should be exonerated, reprimanded, expelled or suspended as probationers and as members of the corporation. The board thereupon adopted separate resolutions expelling petitioners Owen and Sawyer as members of the church corporation.

The trial court found that the defendant board of directors had complied with each and every procedural requirement of the by-laws, rules and regulations of said church corporation; that the defendant board had exclusive jurisdiction to expel the petitioners by said resolutions adopted on April 19, 1958; that any right of petitioners to inspect the mailing list of membership or the corporate records of the church corporation existed only so long as petitioners were members thereof; that any such right expired and terminated with the adoption of the resolutions on April 19, 1958, expelling petitioners. The court then concluded that since petitioners had been suspended and expelled by the board in accordance with the by-laws, rules and regulations of the corporation, the court had no jurisdiction to compel their reinstatement, and that petitioners, having been so suspended and expelled, had no right to inspect the mailing list or other corporate records of the church corporation. Judgment was then entered denying the petition and discharging the writ theretofore issued.

Petitioners appeal from the judgment, contending that they had a property right in the membership of the church corporation; that this property right was established by the decision in Rosicrucian Fellowship v. Rosicrucian Fellowship Non–Sectarian Church, 39 Cal.2d 121, 245 P.2d 481, and that the trial court therefore had jurisdiction to try the issue of the propriety of their ouster and the good faith of respondents in expelling appellants.

The evidence shows that the board of directors of the church corporation suspended and expelled the petitioners in accordance with the by-laws and rules and regulations of the church and the trial court properly held that it had no jurisdiction to order their reinstatement.

As is said in Rosicrucian Fellowship v. Rosicrucian, etc., Ch., 39 Cal.2d 121, 132, 245 P.2d 481, 488: " * * * A person who joins a church covenants expressly or impliedly that in consideration of the benefits which result from such a union he will submit to its control and be governed by its laws, usages and customs whether they are of an ecclesiastical or temporal character to which laws, usages, and customs he assents as to so many stipulations of a contract. The formal evidence of such contract is contained in the canons of the church, the constitution, articles, and by-laws of the society, and the customs and usages which have grown up in connection with these instruments."

The right to membership in the corporation here involved is subject to the by-laws, rules and regulations of the church corporation. There is no evidence in the record before us that the suspension and expulsion of petitioners was not in accord with the by-laws, rules and regulations of the corporation. In Rosicrucian Fellowship v. Rosicrucian, etc., Ch., supra, 39 Cal.2d 121, 131, 245 P.2d 481, 487, the following rule is stated: "The general rule that courts will not interfere in religious societies with reference to their ecclesiastical practices stems from the separation of the church and state, but has always been qualified by the rule that civil and property rights would be adjudicated." The case does not hold that membership in a church corporation is not subject to the by-laws, rules and regulations of the corporation.

In Dyer v. Superior Court, 94 Cal.App. 260, 269, 271 P. 113, it is held that civil authorities cannot disregard the decisions of the church tribunals; that whenever the question of discipline, or of faith, or ecclesiastical rule, custom, or law has been decided by the highest of the church judicatories to which the matter has been carried, the legal tribunals must accept such decisions as final, and as binding on them, in their application to the case before them.

In Church of Christ of Long Beach v. Harper, 83 Cal.App. 41, 46–47, 256 P. 476, 478, the court said: "Civil courts in this country have no ecclesiastical jurisdiction. They cannot revise or question ordinary acts of church discipline, or properly interfere with that part of church management which concerns the spiritual welfare and discipline of the members, but only when rights of property are involved."

In Erickson v. Gospel Foundation of California, 43 Cal.2d 581, 585, 275 P.2d 474, 477, the court said: "The courts have recognized different rules of law relating to review of the action to an organization in expelling a member, depending on the nature of the particular group involved and the character and extent of the member's interest. For example, it has been held that one may not be expelled from an organization such as a labor union or a mutual benefit society, where property rights are attached to membership, without notice and a reasonable opportunity to defend against the charges made. The courts have always been reluctant to interfere with actions taken by religious organizations with respect to their internal affairs, and it has been commonly held that the expulsion of a member by a proper tribunal of such an association will not be reviewed where no property right is involved.''

In the instant case a hearing was had on notice and petitioners had a reasonable opportunity to defend against the charges made.

Petitioners no doubt had a right to inspect the membership list involved so long as they were members of the church corporation. However, counsel for petitioners and respondents admitted that this property right was coextensive with membership in the corporation.

The trial court was correct in ruling that it did not have jurisdiction to order the reinstatement of petitioners under the facts shown by the record herein.

The judgment is affirmed.

■ GRIFFIN, P. J., and SHEPARD, J., concur.

■ Hearing denied; PETERS, J., dissenting.

Bernstein v. Alameda–Contra Costa Medical Association

California District Court of Appeal, 1956.
139 Cal.App.2d 241, 293 P.2d 862.

■ WOOD, JUSTICE.

[Dr. Samuel Bernstein was expelled from the Alameda–Contra Costa Medical Association when the Association's council found that he was guilty of seven charges of violation of the Principles of Medical Ethics of the American Medical Association. Section 14 of Chapter I of the local association's by-laws declared that a ''member who * * * violates * * * any of the provisions of the Principles of Medical Ethics of the American Medical Association, shall be liable to censure, suspension or expulsion.'' Section 4 of Article IV of Chapter III of the Principles stated: ''When a physician does succeed another physician in charge of a case, he should not disparage by comment or insinuation, the one who preceded him. Such comment or insinuation tends to lower the confidence of the patient in the medical profession and so reacts against the patient, the profession and the critic.'' In the course of internal association and trial court proceedings four of the charges were dropped. The trial court found the evidence sufficient as to three of the remaining charges and concluded that Dr. Bernstein was entitled to no relief.

In the first of the remaining charges, Dr. Bernstein, in the course of preparing a pathological report on one George Hill, who was deceased, criticized an earlier pathological report on Hill prepared by another doctor. Bernstein gave a copy of his report to the deceased's widow for use as evidence in an administrative hearing in support of her claim for benefits under the workers' compensation law. Eds.]

* * *

It seems abundantly clear that Dr. Bernstein's report was requested by a litigant for use as evidence in a judicial proceeding; was prepared and delivered by the doctor, in response to that request, solely for that purpose; and was put to that very use by the litigant.

That makes it a "privileged publication," a publication (written or oral) " * * * made * * * [i]n any * * * judicial proceeding * * *." In such a case, the privilege is absolute. The use of this report as evidence before the Industrial Accident Commission characterizes the author of it as a witness. The testimony of a witness in a judicial proceeding is uniformly accorded the same degree of privilege as is accorded the pleadings therein. Thus, it is established in this state that statements made in an affidavit (testimony in written form) filed in a judicial proceeding enjoy this privilege.

The policy of making such statements privileged i[s] obvious. If parties and witnesses were subject to slander and libel actions for utterances made or filed in a judicial proceeding the administration of justice would be hampered and the judicial process throttled. The same policy should ban a medical association by-law which holds over each of the members the threat of expulsion if in his testimony (oral or written) before a court or other judicial body he "disparages, by comment or insinuation," another physician. With such a threat ever facing him, he must weigh carefully and well his every utterance lest through some slip of the tongue he "insinuate" something about another physician which his county medical council may, perchance, deem "disparaging" and, as such just cause for censure, suspension, or expulsion. It is inconceivable that the law could tolerate the holding of such a sword of Damocles over any medical witness in any judicial proceeding.[5]

We are loath to read into the Principles of Medical Ethics an intent upon the part of the American Medical Association to interfere with the judicial process. We find it unnecessary to do so. The canon here involved contains not a single word about the duty of one physician toward another when testifying as a witness in a judicial proceeding. It is a fair inference from such silence that the American Medical Association when it formulated its Principles of Medical Ethics harbored no intent to arrogate to itself the state's prerogative of defining the duties of witnesses in judicial proceedings and the prescribing of penalties for the violation of such duties.

---

5. It has been held that an association's by-laws are not enforceable if against public policy. Bennett v. Modern Woodmen of America, 52 Cal.App. 581, 584–585, 199 P. 343, hearing by Supreme Court denied; * * *. A by-law which provided for expulsion of a member upon his exercising his right to petition the legislature was held invalid in Spayd v. Ringing Rock Lodge No. 665, 270 Pa. 67, 113 A. 70, 14 A.L.R. 1443. * * * It has been held incompetent for an association to expel a member for testifying in a legal proceeding to the disadvantage of the association. * * *

Moreover, section 4 speaks of a physician who "succeeds" another physician "in charge of a case." He is not to disparage the physician who "preceded" him in charge of the case, for such conduct tends to lower the confidence of the "patient" in the medical profession and reacts against the "patient," the profession and the critic. This suggests a doctor-patient relationship and one doctor succeeding another in that relationship. It is difficult to fit the actors in the present drama into such a picture. It is hard to visualize the coroner or the widow or the body of the decedent as a patient in charge, first, of Dr. Ellis and, later, of Dr. Bernstein.

There is no escape from the conclusion that the evidence does not show a violation of section 4 in the Hill case.

The Muir Case.

The charge was that Dr. Bernstein violated section 1 of Article IV of Chapter III of the Principles of Medical Ethics [the principle essentially said that a physician should not second guess another physician, Eds.] in that "on March 10, 1951, Mrs. Leo F. Muir was a patient of Dr. M. L. Lipton, and was in Pittsburg Community Hospital for delivery of her second child. It was decided that a Caesarean section was necessary and the patient was moved from the labor room to surgery. Just prior to this removal, Dr. Bernstein was scrubbing for a delivery and he engaged a nurse in conversation within hearing distance of Mr. and Mrs. Muir. Dr. Bernstein commented to the nurse, and the comment was heard by Mr. and Mrs. Muir, that this was the poorest excuse for a section that he had ever seen and that 'if she (Mrs. Muir) pushed one through, she can push another through.'"

The trial court found the evidence sufficient to sustain a finding that this charge constituted an intentional violation of said section 1. Our examination of the record convinces us that the court's finding is correct and cannot be disturbed.

[In the third incident the court found that there was no basis for disturbing the trial court's finding that Dr. Bernstein's conduct in stating to patient's brother that she should not be operated on, though patient had been so scheduled by her own physician, constituted an intentional violation of the medical association's canon proscribing a physician from doing anything to diminish the trust reposed by a patient in her own doctor. Eds.]

* * *

Is This a Justiciable Controversy?

The respondent association advances the argument that "membership in a professional nonprofit association such as respondent in which the members have no severable interest in the property of the association, is not the subject of judicial intervention as there is no property right involved." That is an inadequate and inaccurate statement of the applicable principles which have been succinctly expressed by the Supreme Court in these words: "In any proper case involving the expulsion of a member from a voluntary unincorporated association, the only function which the courts may perform is to determine whether the association has acted within its powers in good faith, in accordance with its laws and the law of the land." Smith v. Kern County Medical Ass'n, 19 Cal.2d 263, 265, 120 P.2d 874, 875. * * * "Any matter of policy involved in the adoption of the by-laws, the code of ethics, and the resolution in conformity therewith, is a question for the membership itself and is not debatable here so long as it is not shown that such policy is in violation of law."

We entertain no doubt that the issues discussed herein are justiciable and that mandamus affords an appropriate proceeding for their judicial consideration. * * *

[The court ordered the trial council to set aside its order of expulsion and to determine the penalty to be imposed in the light of the revised findings. Eds.]

NOTES

1. *Expulsions from Professional Organizations.* Even where expulsion or censure from a professional organization does not lead to an interference with an ability to earn a living, associations, particularly those with a quasi-public status, are held to reasonable standards of due process. Sanctions by a professional association have an impact that transcends the organization because they convey to the community that the individual was found lacking by her peers. McCune v. Wilson, 237 So.2d 169 (Fla.1970) (professional ethics committee of appraisers association required to adhere to fair standards); Salkin v. California Dental Ass'n, 176 Cal.App.3d 1118, 224 Cal.Rptr. 352 (4th Dist. 1986).

2. *Process of Inquiry.* When a member is expelled from a group and brings suit, what is the course of judicial inquiry? The starting point would be the organization's own procedures. The organization will respond that it followed its rules. When a court evaluates a group's rules or past practices, difficulties can arise when it enters what Professor Chafee called the "dismal swamp" where only the organization can speak with confidence. Zechariah Chafee, The Internal Affairs of Associations Not for Profit, 43 Harv. L. Rev. 993, 1023–1026 (1930); Developments in the Law–Judicial Control of Private Associations, 76 Harv. L. Rev. 983, 991 (1963). Courts will shy away from determining particularly difficult or arcane issues such as whether "goats are sheep in disobedience" as one Primitive Baptist congregation sought guidance, Canterbury v. Canterbury, 143 W.Va. 165, 100 S.E.2d 565 (1957); or disputes involving the proper interpretation of the doctrine of "plenary inspiration," Mertz v. Schaeffer, 271 S.W.2d 238 (Mo.Ct.App.1954). Thus, unless there are significant property, constitutional or contractual interests involved, or actions in patent bad faith, courts give substantial deference to the rules of the private association.

3. *Substantive Limits on Association Activity.* Even if an association follows its own procedures in good faith, there are limits to the actions the

organization can take against a member. Clearly an association cannot justify expulsion or sanction on the ground that a member refused to violate the law. Developments in the Law–Private Associations, supra, at 1006–1111. Beyond actions that harm society's rules are there limits to disciplinary actions organizations may take against members? Does the nature of the organization relate to the extent of discipline or punishment of members? Under what principles should a court determine the validity of the group's actions?

4. *Post Expulsion Punishment.* How far can an organization go in punishing its members? Can discipline extend beyond membership? In Guinn v. Church of Christ of Collinsville, 775 P.2d 766 (Okla.1989) the plaintiff, a member of the fundamentalist Collinsville Church of Christ, was accused by church elders of having a sexual relationship with a non-member of the congregation in violation of church precepts, which subjected her to a disciplinary procedure that was to last more than one year. The parishioner attended several meetings before the congregation but was warned by the elders that if she did not repent they would commence a withdrawal of fellowship, a disciplinary procedure in which members of the congregation shun the offending member. The elders threatened to divulge to the congregation her sexual involvement with her companion. Despite the plaintiff's pleas, and her decision to withdraw from membership, which was not doctrinally possible, the elders publicly branded her a fornicator and distributed the information to four other area Church of Christ congregations to be read aloud during services.

The plaintiff sued on the basis of the torts of outrage and invasion of privacy. A jury trial resulted in a verdict in favor of the plaintiff and against the elders and the Church in the amount of $205,000 in actual and $185,000 in punitive damages plus $44,737 in prejudgment interest. The appellate court rejected the argument that the suit involved governmental interference with First Amendment rights and required judicial abstention because the controversy concerned the allegedly tortious nature of religiously motivated acts rather than their orthodoxy *vis-a-vis* established church doctrine. The court held that the disciplinary actions taken by the elders against plaintiff before she withdrew her membership from the church did not justify judicial interference because of First Amendment considerations. It found that the parishioner's right of withdrawal of consent to submit to the disciplinary decisions of the church was constitutionally unqualified. Her waiver of such right to withdraw required knowing consent. By continuing to discipline plaintiff after her withdrawal, the elders invaded her privacy and caused emotional distress outside of First Amendment protection. The court dismissed the plaintiff's tort claims and damages awarded for pre-withdrawal conduct.

What if the penalty for violating church doctrines was placing the offender in public stocks for two days or in a closet for three? Would the First Amendment protections apply? Cf. Madsen v. Erwin, 395 Mass. 715, 481 N.E.2d 1160, 1167 (1985); Bear v. Reformed Mennonite Church, 462 Pa. 330, 341 A.2d 105, 107–108 (1975). If the Elders had instructed the other church members to continue to shun the plaintiff after she withdrew from the congregation, could she sue for emotional distress? See Paul v. Watchtower Bible & Tract Soc., 819 F.2d 875, 883 (9th Cir.1987), cert. denied, 484 U.S. 926, 108 S.Ct. 289 (1987).

5. *Procedural Limitations on Association Action.* Courts are more reluctant to investigate on a *de novo* basis the merits of and the action taken in an association's dispute with a member than whether the association has followed its own procedures. Developments in the Law–Private Associations, supra, at 1020. If the breach of association procedures is minimal, courts may waive it if there is substantial compliance with the rules. Association procedures do not require the full formalities of due process that one expects in the court room. Procedural fairness requires some notice of the charges and meeting date as well as the right to defend oneself. The degree of process demanded depends upon the size and purpose of the organization and the nature of the charges.

NOTE: EXPULSION FROM SOCIAL ORGANIZATIONS

Conduct which might not warrant expulsion from an organization where membership is a condition to earning one's livelihood (such as exclusion of a doctor from a medical association or a worker from a labor union) or essential to the enjoyment of a contractual or property right may allow exclusion from a private, purely social, organization.

1. *Offensive Views and Associates.* Todd Blodgett was a member of the University Club, a private association in Washington, D.C. He worked for groups that promoted "right-wing" political causes and was hired as an independent contractor for Liberty Lobby, an organization run by Willis Carto. Blodgett sold advertising in *The Spotlight,* a newspaper in which Liberty Lobby took anti-Israeli and anti-Zionist stands. Blodgett's association with Carto and Liberty Lobby was unpopular with many of the University Club's members. No Club by-law or rule limited the type of guest who could be invited to the premises, but in an effort to placate his fellow members, Blodgett voluntarily stopped bringing Carto to the Club. In March 1999 William Pierce, a nationally known white supremacist and chairman of the National Alliance, see Chapter 5C5, supra, at p. 412, contacted Blodgett, seeking to purchase his shares of stock in Resistance Records, which Blodgett himself characterized as "a purveyor of hate music." The two men dined at the Club in April 1999 and discussed a sale of the stock. Eventually, Blodgett sold his interest in the record label to Pierce for $15,000. Pierce's appearance at the Club did not cause a disturbance or engender controversy at the time. A few months later, the Washington Post published an article about Pierce entitled "The Pied Piper of Racism." It reported that Pierce and Blodgett had dined at the Club and had "haggled over" control of Resistance Records. The next day Blodgett sent the Club's Board of Governors a letter apologizing for the publicity caused by Pierce's visit.

The Club's Board of Governors conducted an investigation reviewing Blodgett's behavior in the Club, including previous allegations of anti-Semitism, the factual basis of the Post article, and his professional involvement with hate group organizations. Blodgett was encouraged to resign but refused. He was suspended pending the outcome of the investigation. Blodgett was sent copies of all e-mail and correspondence from Club members to the Board related to the investigation, as well as a copy of the investigative report, which contained typed summaries of the interviews conducted. (The summaries did not disclose the identities of the individuals who had been interviewed). After hearing from Blodgett and his counsel, the Board voted 8–2 to afford Blodgett an opportunity to resign and, if he refused, to expel him. He was expelled.

Blodgett sued, alleging the expulsion unconstitutionally infringed his First Amendment freedom of expressive association, a breach of due process and the obligation of good faith and fair dealing and a violation of the District of Columbia Human Rights Act, which prohibits *inter alia* discrimination against political affiliation and source of income in places of public accommodation. In Blodgett v. University Club, 930 A.2d 210 (2007), the District of Columbia Court of Appeals affirmed the expulsion. It held that a member of a voluntary association facing discipline is not entitled to the same type of process afforded under civil and criminal justice systems. When courts do interfere with the management and internal affairs of a voluntary association, they look to common law concepts of fundamental fairness, rather than Fifth Amendment due process concepts. The club had complied with that standard. Common law fundamental fairness did not require disclosure to Blodgett of the identities of Club members and staff who spoke with the investigative committee. Nor did Blodgett's expulsion, based on his use of the Club's facilities to conduct business with persons who publicly expounded racist and anti-Semitic views, constitute discrimination based on source of income for purposes of provision of the Human Rights Act. Did Blodgett's behavior warrant expulsion, or was this an example of the power of the press?

2. *Disputes With the Association.* In Waugaman v. Skyline Country Club, 277 Ala. 495, 172 So.2d 381 (1965) the plaintiff sued for damages for allegedly wrongful expulsion from the Skyline Country Club. The plaintiff had been a member in good standing when his wife was seriously injured on the club's golf course. After unsuccessful negotiations were conducted with the club's insurance carrier, the plaintiff and his wife filed suit against the club. Eight days later, the plaintiffs were expelled from Skyline. They alleged that the ejection was wrongful and malicious and caused by their lawsuit, and that the expulsion occurred without notice, hearing or the opportunity to be heard.

The court upheld the ouster, stating:

> We think there is a marked distinction between associations such as trade unions, societies providing credit loans, sick, death and other benefits, professional associations, trading exchanges and like organizations, affecting a person's right to earn a living on one hand, and

private social clubs on the other. Certain conduct, which might not justify expulsion from some other type of association, where membership is a condition to earning a livelihood, or essential to the enjoyment of a contract or property right, may justify expulsion from a private social club, which usually has the primary purpose of affording pleasant, friendly and congenial social relationship and association between the members. * * *

We have no statute governing expulsion procedure in social clubs in Alabama. Therefore, the Constitution and the By-laws of a social club constitute a contract between it and its members, and as one of the incidents of membership, a member consents to accept liability to expulsion, if ordered in accordance with the club's regulations, provided that those regulations are valid and do not violate public policy. In Board of School Commissioners of Mobile County v. Hudgens, 274 Ala. 647, 151 So.2d 247, we said: "One who becomes a member of an association is deemed to have known and assented to its by-laws, rules and regulations and cannot be heard to object to their enforcement thereafter, and such person may validly agree to be bound by the constitution, by-laws, rules and regulations of an association existing at the time the membership begins or those that may be thereafter adopted in accordance with the constitution of such association. * * *" There is no averment that appellant's expulsion was not effected in the exact procedure outlined in the by-laws, and construing the allegations of the pleader more strongly against him on demurrer, we conclude compliance with the section.

277 Ala. at 497–498, 172 So.2d at 382–383.

In Bernstein v. The Players, 120 Misc.2d 998, 466 N.Y.S.2d 897 (1983), Nahum Bernstein, an attorney and member of The Players Club, questioned certain financial transactions involving a club member and an employee; implied that some of the matters involved criminal conduct; and stated that if the information sought was not forthcoming, legal action would be commenced to obtain it. Following an extensive investigation by a select committee of the club, a report was issued that concluded there was no substance or validity to the charges, and they had been recklessly made. Bernstein then wrote to the chair of the club expressing shock at the comments in the report and suggesting that the Committee members resign. The club's managing committee then suspended Bernstein on the grounds that the charges had been recklessly made against the club's management and were prejudicial to the club. He was later served with a formal statement of charges and notice of a hearing which was resulted in Bernstein's expulsion and subsequent suit for reinstatement. The court upheld the expulsion, stating that it only would review an internal dispute if there were a showing that the hearing was in bad faith, fraudulent, or utterly unsupported by evidence.

3. *Conduct Unbecoming.* Courts have upheld expulsions for unbecoming conduct on the premises of a tennis club, even when there were procedural errors in the initial proceedings. See Garvey v. Seattle Tennis

Club, 60 Wash.App. 930, 808 P.2d 1155 (Wash.App.1991). However, in Kendrick v. Watermill Beach Club, 8 Misc.2d 798, 165 N.Y.S.2d 1009 (1957), the suspension of a member's spouse, who constantly complained, was annulled because of the vague notice in the charges. In Johnson v. Green Meadow Country Club, 222 Mont. 405, 721 P.2d 1287 (1986), the plaintiff complained about the club pro arbitrarily reducing his golf handicap and then received a letter of reprimand from the club. The Supreme Court of Montana held that the fact that the golfer received no notice before the letter of reprimand did not violate his due process rights.

4. *Statutorily Mandated Fairness.* Several states have provisions that provide that a member of an organization cannot be expelled except pursuant to a fair and reasonable procedure that is carried out in good faith. See, Cal. Corp. Code 7341; Minn. Stat. Ann. 317A.411; Miss. Code Ann. 79–11–189.

Section 7341 of the California Corporations Code was construed in Aluisi v. Fort Washington Golf and Country Club, 42 Cal.Rptr.2d 761 (Ct.App.1995), which involved expulsion from a golf club for using "vulgar, filthy, and demeaning remarks made in the presence of women members * * * in the area between the Pro Shop and Grille Room." * * * The board had concealed the identities of two witnesses and considered matters undocumented in his membership file without notice or a chance to respond. The trial court ruled this deprived him of a fair hearing. The appellate court affirmed. Calif. Corp. Code § 7341(b) provides that any expulsion, suspension, or termination must be done in good faith and in a fair and reasonable manner. A procedure is fair and reasonable when its provisions are set forth in the bylaws or copies of such provisions are sent to members. Fifteen days prior notice must be given of expulsion, suspension or termination, and the accused is provided an opportunity to be heard, orally or in writing, not less than five days before the effective date of the expulsion, suspension or termination by a body or person authorized to make such a decision. Id. § 7341(c). The lack of confrontation of the witnesses and of notice of the additional allegations established the plaintiff did not receive a fair trial. (In declining to review *Aluisi*, the California Supreme Court ordered the opinion below to be "depublished." As a result, it may not be cited as authority.)

PROBLEMS

Consider in the following problems whether the actions of the association would be upheld:

(a) Kilroy Military Academy is a secular secondary school preparing young men and women for careers in the military. A student, Edward Bailey, is expelled for failure to attend chapel.

(b) The Bullmoose Party, one of three major political parties in Delaware County Nevada, requires a loyalty oath of all members that they will support all candidates nominated for office. John Gruen, a party member, refuses to support one of the Bullmoose endorsed candidates because he believes him to be dishonest, and he is expelled from the party.

(c) The Roustabout Union, which represents workers at carnivals and circuses, requires all members to wear coats and ties in public so as to improve the union's image. Ted Williams, a member, refuses and is expelled.

(d) During a strike the Roustabout Union orders workers to wear a coat and green tie as a symbol of unity and to improve the public image of union members. Williams refuses and is expelled.

E. ADMISSION OF MEMBERS

For most physicians, hospital privileges are absolutely essential to a medical practice. The denial or revocation of staff privileges has severe economic consequences. The right of physicians to practice their profession, however, must be balanced by the need for peer review to preserve the quality of medical care administered to patients. Historically, doctors have exercised almost complete control over the admission of other doctors. The justification is that the credentialing system ensures the quality of health care provided by the hospital.

Falcone v. Middlesex County Medical Society

Superior Court of New Jersey, 1960.
62 N.J.Super. 184, 162 A.2d 324, aff'd 34 N.J. 582, 170 A.2d 791 (1961).

■ VOGEL, J.S.C.

This is an action in lieu of Mandamus by the plaintiff, Dr. Italo J. Falcone, to compel the defendant, Middlesex County Medical Society, to admit the plaintiff to full membership in the defendant association. The complaint also prays an adjudication of the plaintiff's rights, and such other relief as may be just.

The defendant society contends that the court may not compel the defendant society to accept plaintiff as a member for the reason that the defendant is a voluntary association and, as such, may freely exercise independent judgment in the selection of its membership.

In the alternative, the defendant society contends that even though a court may compel admission of a qualified person to membership, the plaintiff herein is not qualified because he does not have an M.D. degree based upon four years of study in a medical school approved by the American Medical Association (hereinafter referred to as the A.M.A.).

* * *

A factual projection indicates that the plaintiff, Dr. Italo J. Falcone, a citizen of the United States, was born in Newark, New Jersey, on March 6, 1923, ever since which time he has been a resident of this State; and more particularly, since January 1, 1952 he has resided at 247 Livingston Avenue, New Brunswick, in this county. The facts further indicate that the plaintiff pursued undergraduate work at Rutgers University and Villanova College from September 1941 until September 1943, in an accelerated program equivalent to three years of undergraduate work. From September 1943 until September 1946 plaintiff was enrolled in an accelerated program at the Philadelphia College of Osteopathy in Philadelphia, Pennsylvania; and in 1946 the plaintiff received the degree of Doctor of Osteopathy (D.O.) from the Philadelphia College of Osteopathy. The Philadelphia College of Osteopathy was not at that time, nor is it today, a medical college approved by the A.M.A.

After receiving his D.O. degree, the plaintiff served a one-year internship and a three-year residency at the Detroit Osteopathic Hospital, which internship and residency likewise were not recognized by the A.M.A.

In 1950 the plaintiff presented his credentials from the Philadelphia College of Osteopathy and the Detroit Osteopathic Hospital to the New Jersey State Board of Medical Examiners, on the basis of which he was permitted to take the State Board medical examination, which examination, administered by the State Board of Medical Examiners, he was successful in passing. On November 8, 1950 this plaintiff received a license to practice medicine and surgery in the State of New Jersey. The State Board of Medical Examiners recognizes the degree of D.O. granted by the Philadelphia College of Osteopathy, as well as other osteopathic schools, as a prerequisite for admission to the physicians' examination. The license granted to this plaintiff is the same as that granted to doctors holding the degree of Doctor of Medicine (M.D.), and entitles plaintiff to the very same rights and privileges. See N.J.S.A. 45:9–1 et seq.

Thereafter, and more particularly in 1951, the plaintiff attended the Medical School of the University of Milan, Italy, for a period of approximately seven months. The University of Milan gave the plaintiff academic credit for three years of medical school based on his courses of study at the Philadelphia College of Osteopathy, and awarded him the degree of Doctor of Medicine (M.D.) on or about November 12, 1951. The University of Milan, College of Medicine, is recognized as an approved medical school by the A.M.A.

After receiving his degree from the University of Milan, the plaintiff served a 16–month internship at St. Peter's Hospital in New Brunswick, New Jersey. The internship program at St. Peter's Hospital is approved by the A.M.A Plaintiff also served a three- or four-month residency in surgery at the Jersey City Medical Center. The aforesaid residency was not one accredited by the American College of Surgeons or the A.M.A.

Since the latter part of 1951 or early 1952 plaintiff has maintained an office with his father, a licensed physician, for the practice of medicine and general surgery, at 247 Livingston Avenue, in New Brunswick, New Jersey. He is registered, according to law, with the County Clerk of Middlesex County.

In the latter part of 1953 the plaintiff was admitted to the defendant Middlesex County Medical Society as an associate member. The by-laws of the defendant society provide that a physician may not be an associate member for more than two consecutive years. At the time of his admission into associate membership by the defendant society plaintiff's application, admitted into evidence, did not indicate plaintiff's osteopathic education, nor his internship and residency at an osteopathic hospital. The application informed the society that plaintiff had an M.D. degree from the University of Milan, and had completed an internship at St. Peter's Hospital in New Brunswick, New Jersey.

During the period of his associate membership in defendant society the plaintiff was a member of the medical staffs of the Middlesex General Hospital and St. Peter's Hospital, both in New Brunswick, and was permitted to admit his patients and to treat them therein. Both of the latter institutions require that a staff physician be a member of the Middlesex County Medical Society.

While the plaintiff was an associate member the defendant society learned that plaintiff's M.D. degree was based upon one academic year of study at the University of Milan and credit for three years of study at the Philadelphia College of Osteopathy, the latter not being a medical school approved by the defendant society.

By reason of the aforesaid facts the judicial medical ethics committee of the defendant society refused to recommend Dr. Falcone for active membership, and the general membership of the defendant society, at a regular meeting, also declined to admit the plaintiff to active membership. * * *

After the defendant society deleted the plaintiff's name from its membership list, the Middlesex General Hospital and St. Peter's Hospital terminated the plaintiff's staff membership, and precluded him from admitting and treating his patients in these respective institutions.

The plaintiff appealed from the decision of the defendant county society to the judicial council of the State Medical Society, and received a hearing from that body on January 27, 1957. The State Society's judicial council refused to interfere with the defendant county society's action. Thereupon the plaintiff appealed to the judicial council of the A.M.A., which body opined that it did not have jurisdiction to hear the plaintiff's appeal.

The testimony by various physicians, some of whom, hostile to this plaintiff, nevertheless had the opportunity to observe the professional work of Dr. Falcone, indicates that the plaintiff is an ethical and capable physician. There is no evidence in the record that the plaintiff actually practiced osteopathy, but, on the contrary the testimony reveals that the plaintiff practiced the same system of medicine as that practiced by the members of the defendant county society.

* * *

The record indicates that the judicial medical ethics committee applies a rule for membership requiring four years of study at a medical college approved by the A.M.A.

The Middlesex County Medical Society is a component part of the Medical Society of New Jersey, and is governed by the latter's laws. The State Society was founded July 23, 1766, and the Legislature of the State of New Jersey granted a charter to the State Medical Society in 1864. Every person who becomes a member of the county medical society automatically becomes a member of the State Society. Each component society is the judge of the qualifications of its own members, subject to the right of approval of the State Society.

The State Society may revoke the charter of a component society where the component society has acted in conflict with the letter or spirit of the constitution and by-laws of the State Society.

* * *

The State Medical Society of New Jersey is a part of a federation of medical societies called the American Medical Association. As a constituent member of the A.M.A. the State Medical Society is bound to observe the Principles of Medical Ethics of the A.M.A.

Section 3 of the Principles of Medical Ethics of the A.M.A. provides: "A physician should practice a method of healing founded on a scientific basis, and he should not voluntarily associate professionally with anyone who violates this principle."

It is noteworthy that the second affirmative defense asserted by the defendant society embraces the contention that the plaintiff is ineligible for membership for the reason that section 3 of the Principles of Medical Ethics has been construed to mean that any voluntary association by physicians with osteopaths is unethical, and since the license authorizing him to practice medicine and surgery in the State of New Jersey indicates that he received a D.O. degree, under their construction, he is unfit for association with his confreres who also practice medicine and surgery in the State of New Jersey.

It will likewise be noted at this point that considerable testimony was taken with particular reference to the plaintiff's failure to have supplied all of the required information on the original application for associate membership, as well as his failure to have detailed information on the supplemental application for active membership. The court makes this comment for the reason that notwithstanding any right that the defendant society may have had by reason of this alleged failure on the part of the plaintiff, if any right existed, nevertheless, it elected to defend its position on the ground "that the Plaintiff has failed to comply with a Rule that requires four years of study in a Medical College approved by the A.M.A."

The immediate problem is a determination as to what extent the court may intervene with respect to the action taken by the defendant society barring this plaintiff from active membership.

Legal precedent indicates that the courts have been reluctant to interfere in the internal affairs of voluntary organizations. * * *

However, in cases involving exclusion from those medical societies which controlled the right to practice medicine, even the earlier cases granted writs of Mandamus to compel admission in appropriate cases.

Despite the rigid rule imposed by some courts precluding judicial relief in exclusion cases, the courts have found various theories upon which to grant relief in an increasingly greater number of cases involving expulsions or suspensions from medical societies. One theory developed by the courts is the contract theory.

The contract theory projects the view that the laws of an organization constitute a contract between a member and the organization. Therefore, the contract is enforceable in equity when the organization acts contrary to its own laws.

Other courts have demanded that an applicant for judicial relief have a civil or property right in an organization as a condition precedent to judicial intervention.

In other cases regarding expulsions from medical societies the courts have held that there is a judicial remedy without indulging in theoretical polemic. Bernstein v. Alameda–Contra Costa Medical Association, * * *

Legal writers have criticized the property and contract theories. Professor Chafee recognized that there may be serious injuries without loss of any property right. The real interests of membership cannot be measured in terms of rights of property. As early as 1930, in his landmark article in the Harvard Law Review, Professor Chafee saw the trend toward protection of interests of personality. He criticized the contract theory as artificial, and noted that both the contract and property theories frequently give rise to legal fictions. Neither theory looks to the substance of the injuries resulting from expulsion or loss of membership in an organization. * * *

Recognizing that the real interests in an exclusion or an expulsion case are personal, rather than proprietary or contractual, the distinction which has arisen between expulsions and exclusions from voluntary organizations appears to be one of fiction, rather than of substance. A loss to one excluded from an organization may be as great, or greater, than a loss to one expelled or suspended therefrom. Chafee, "The Internal Affairs of Associations Not for Profit," 43 Harv. L. Rev. 93, 1022 (1930).

A proper rule herein must be based on what the courts have actually done, rather than upon the theories upon which they have purported to base their decisions.

When the injury to the party expelled or excluded has been real enough, or has conflicted with some public policy, the courts have granted relief. Contrary to their theoretical discussions, the courts have, in fact, looked to the nature of the particular organization involved and to the degree of harm arising out of the particular act of the organization. Though the courts have tended to designate all private organizations as "voluntary" they have proceeded to distinguish among them in granting or denying judicial intervention. * * *

This court is of the opinion that where an organization is in fact involuntary and/or is of such a nature that the court should intervene to protect the public, and where an exclusion results in a substantial injury to a plaintiff, the court will grant relief, providing that such exclusion was contrary to the organization's own laws, was without procedural safeguards, or the application of a particular law or laws of an organization was contrary to public policy. It follows that each case must stand upon its own facts.

Applying the above rule to the case at bar, the court must determine (1) the nature of the defendant society; (2) whether or not the injury complained of herein is substantial; and if the findings in (1) and (2) justify judicial scrutiny of the defendant's action, the court must proceed to determine (3) whether the defendant society applied proper procedural safeguards, (4) whether the defendant society acted in accordance with its own laws; and, if so, (5) whether the defendant's laws, as applied here, were reasonable and consistent with public policy.

(1) A review of the entire record indicates to this court that the defendant Middlesex County Medical Society combined with the other component parts of the State Medical Society of New Jersey and the American Medical Association, has virtual monopolistic control of the practice of medicine. The practical effect of such a monopoly is to prevent nonmembers of the society from practicing medicine in the overwhelming majority of hospitals in this State. Society members control the staffs of all approved hospitals, and society members serve on the accrediting bodies for hospitals and medical schools. Eligibility for membership in the county medical society is a requirement for hospital staff membership promulgated by the joint commission on the accreditation of hospitals, which commission is composed of society members. Failure to observe that rule on the part of a hospital results in loss of accreditation. Withdrawal of accreditation from a hospital means that the hospital may not thereafter have an approved internship and residency program with which to attract young doctors. It also means that the hospital will be able to attract few, if any, society members, for the medical staff.

Although the A.M.A. and its constituent and component parts have been designated by many courts as voluntary organizations, other courts and legal writers have recognized the involuntary nature of these associations. * * *

Many authorities cited by the defendant society deal with fraternal and social organizations, emphasizing with great particularity that in organizations of such character the right of election and selection of membership has been reserved to them as a matter of law. It is well settled that in this latter class of organizations membership may be increased or decreased at will, without regard to standards, arbitrariness or otherwise, and without judicial interference.

The status of the defendant society, however, must be distinguished, for the reason that the Middlesex County Medical Society is not a fraternal or social organization. As a practical matter, it is virtually an institution that controls the practice of medicine in the hospitals located within this county. Membership in the defendant society is essential for any doctor wishing to freely and fully pursue his profession in Middlesex County.

The defendant society is far more than a private organization; a fact that will readily be developed from its own genesis. The State of New Jersey has clothed the parent State Medical Society with the authority to grant the degree of Doctor of Medicine. The State of New Jersey has also imposed the duty and privilege upon the parent State Medical Society to submit the names of three of its members, for the consideration of the Governor, one of whom is to be selected for appointment to the State Board of Medical Examiners, when a vacancy exists.

The monopolistic control by the defendant society of the practice of medicine in the county necessarily carries with it certain public responsibilities. It may not escape these responsibilities by designating itself as a private, voluntary association.

The court finds that the defendant society is an involuntary organization, clothed with such public responsibilities that its actions are subject to judicial scrutiny.

(2) The plaintiff, here, Dr. Falcone, has, in the opinion of the court, suffered substantial injury by virtue of his exclusion from the defendant society. * * *

The testimony indicates that a physician bereft of county society membership is barred from admitting a patient to an accredited hospital, and is also prevented from a professional visitation of any patient in the institution.

* * *

(5) The remaining question is whether the defendant society contravenes the public policy of the State by the imposition of a rule requiring four years of study at a medical college approved by the A.M.A.

The State Board of Medical Examiners has inspected and approved the Philadelphia College of Osteopathy, in which institution this plaintiff successfully completed his training. By virtue hereof, this plaintiff was eligible to take the examination given to all candidates for the privilege of the practice of medicine in this State, and successfully passed such examination; on the basis of which he was issued a license to practice medicine and surgery in New Jersey. The license issued this plaintiff bestowed upon him the same rights and privileges as those granted to Doctors of Medicine licensed by the State. Notwithstanding his certification by the State Board of Medical Examiners as an individual authorized to practice medicine and surgery in New Jersey, he is being precluded from the practice of his profession in hospitals approved by the A.M.A.

The defendant society, through its monopolistic organization, thus prevents the graduates of the Philadelphia College of Osteopathy from practicing medicine to the fullest extent, even though the State of New Jersey has granted that privilege. The defendant society, by virtue of its action, has thwarted the public policy of the State which grants licenses to practice medicine and surgery to graduates of the Philadelphia College of Osteopathy, who successfully complete the required examination.

The rule of the defendant society requiring four years of study in a medical college approved by the A.M.A., as applied to Dr. Falcone, contravenes the public policy of the State. It is in the interest of the State that all physicians and surgeons be given the opportunity to prove their qualifications to a hospital without the necessity of first establishing membership in the defendant society as a basic qualification for an opportunity to display their talents as physicians. Here is a blatant illustration of the defendant society's creating itself as an intermediary between the licensed physician and a hospital; an effort we hold to be offensive to the public policy of this State.

* * *

In our enlightened age, could anyone doubt that if the limitation here imposed, namely, that a duly licensed physician and surgeon would be denied the right to practice medicine in a hospital unless he was a member of the defendant county society, were to be incorporated as part of our statute law, that the same would not be stricken as being unconstitutional and a denial of equal protection under the law?

Again it will be noted, the defendant society contends that, in the interest of public health and welfare, the standard it has adopted for membership in the defendant society, translated in the rule being applied to this plaintiff, requiring four years of study in a medical school approved by the A.M.A., is a necessary prerequisite in the public interest. However, the defendant society has lost sight of the fact that the plaintiff, here, has been admitted to the practice of medicine and surgery in the State of New Jersey, and by virtue of such licensure is entitled to practice medicine and surgery to the same extent as every other licensed physician in this State.

Notwithstanding the aforesaid, this plaintiff is, nevertheless, being denied admission in the defendant society, with consequences to him more fully set forth in the complaint under review.

* * *

For the reasons herein assigned, the court declares the action taken by the defendant Middlesex County Medical Society in excluding the plaintiff, Dr. Italo J. Falcone, from active membership, void and of no effect.

The court will order the defendant society to admit the plaintiff to full membership.

An appropriate order conforming with this opinion may be presented.

NOTES AND QUESTIONS

1. *Fiduciary Responsibility to the Public. Falcone* was affirmed on appeal, 34 N.J. 582, 170 A.2d 791, on somewhat different grounds. The

Supreme Court viewed the County Medical Society as possessing monopoly control over the use of hospital facilities. It was not a typical voluntary membership association but one with which the public is concerned and engaged in activities vitally affecting the health and welfare of the people. The Society's power was viewed as a fiduciary responsibility to be exercised in a reasonable and lawful manner for the advancement of the interests of the medical profession and the public. The unwritten requirement of four years' attendance at A.M.A. approved medical colleges affected Falcone's fundamental right to work and was viewed as arbitrary and unreasonable, having no relation to the advancement of medical science or elevating professional standards and ran counter to public policy and justice.

2. *Federal Antitrust Violations.* Another avenue of protest for physicians excluded from staff privileges is the use of federal antitrust law which in recent years has expanded into health care settings. Antitrust claims arise out of staff privileges because of the way hospitals are organized. Usually, the hospital board delegates the right to make decisions about clinical privileges to the physicians serving on the hospital's medical staff. For antitrust purposes medical staff physicians are not only professional colleagues but independent practitioners with their own economic interests to protect in competition with the applicant. When excluded the physician will raise the charge of anticompetitive activity. William S. Brewbaker III, Antitrust Conspiracy Doctrine and the Hospital Enterprise, 74 B.U. L. Rev. 67, 68 (1994).

3. Would the court have ordered Dr. Falcone's admission if he had not met the state licensing standards? If an association is compelled to admit all practitioners, will this result in lower standards for the profession in general and damage the reputation of the particular association?

4. What may have been the real reason the Medical Society denied Dr. Falcone admission?

F. PRIVATE ASSOCIATIONS AND THE CONSTITUTION

1. FREEDOM OF ASSOCIATION

The Supreme Court has on several occasions discussed the conflicting interests between protecting an organization's freedom of association and society's compelling interest in eradicating discrimination. The following case offers a useful discussion of the parameters of this constitutional right and its limitation in the face of other compelling interests.

Roberts v. United States Jaycees

Supreme Court of the United States, 1984.
468 U.S. 609, 104 S.Ct. 3244.

■ JUSTICE BRENNAN delivered the opinion of the Court.

[The United States Jaycees, a national young men's civic and service organization, limited membership to young men between the ages of 18 and

35. Associate membership was available to women and older men, but they could not vote or hold local or national office. Two local Jaycee chapters in Minnesota admitted women as regular members and, as a result, the national Jaycee organization imposed a number of sanctions. When these chapters were notified by United States Jaycees that revocation of their charters was to be considered, members of both chapters filed discrimination charges with the Minnesota Department of Human Rights, alleging that the exclusion of women from full membership violated the Minnesota Human Rights Act (Act), which makes it "an unfair discriminatory practice * * * [t]o deny any person the full and equal enjoyment of goods, services, facilities, privileges, advantages, and accommodations of a place of public accommodation because of race, color, creed, religion, disability, national origin, or sex."

Before a hearing on the state charges, United States Jaycees sued the state officials in federal court to prevent enforcement of the Act, alleging that, by requiring the Jaycees to accept women as regular members, application of the Act would violate the male members' constitutional rights of free speech and association. Eventually, the Minnesota Supreme Court held that the United States Jaycees was "a place of public accommodation" within the meaning of the Act. The Jaycees then amended their federal complaint to claim that the Minnesota Supreme Court's interpretation of the Act rendered it unconstitutionally vague and overbroad. After trial, the district court entered judgment in favor of the state officials. The court of appeals reversed, holding that application of the Act to United States Jaycees' membership policies would produce a "direct and substantial" interference with its freedom of association guaranteed by the First Amendment, and, in the alternative, that the Act was vague as construed and applied and hence unconstitutional under the Due Process Clause of the Fourteenth Amendment. Eds.]

* * *

II

Our decisions have referred to constitutionally protected "freedom of association" in two distinct senses. In one line of decisions, the Court has concluded that choices to enter into and maintain certain intimate human relations must be secured against undue intrusion by the State because of the role of such relationships in safeguarding the individual freedom that is central to our constitutional scheme. In this respect, freedom of association receives protection as a fundamental element of personal liberty. In another set of decisions, the Court has recognized a right to associate for the purpose of engaging in those activities protected by the First Amendment-speech, assembly, petition for the redress of grievances, and the exercise of religion. The Constitution guarantees freedom of association of this kind as an indispensable means of preserving other individual liberties.

* * *

A

The Court has long recognized that, because the Bill of Rights is designed to secure individual liberty, it must afford the formation and preservation of certain kinds of highly personal relationships a substantial measure of sanctuary from unjustified interference by the State. Without precisely identifying every consideration that may underlie this type of constitutional protection, we have noted that certain kinds of personal bonds have played a critical role in the culture and traditions of the Nation by cultivating and transmitting share ideals and beliefs; they thereby foster diversity and act as critical buffers between the individual and the power of the State. Moreover, the constitutional shelter afforded such relationships reflects the realization that individuals draw much of their emotional enrichment from close ties with others. Protecting these relationships from unwarranted state interference therefore safeguards the ability independently to define one's identity that is central to any concept of liberty.

The personal affiliations that exemplify these considerations, and that therefore suggest some relevant limitations on the relationships that might be entitled to this sort of constitutional protection, are those that attend the creation and sustenance of a family—marriage; childbirth; the raising and education of children; and cohabitation with one's relatives. Family relationships, by their nature, involve deep attachments and commitments to the necessarily few other individuals with whom one shares not only a special community of thoughts, experiences, and beliefs but also distinctively personal aspects of one's life. Among other things, therefore, they are distinguished by such attributes as relative smallness, a high degree of selectivity in decisions to begin and maintain the affiliation, and seclusion from others in critical aspects of the relationship. As a general matter, only relationships with these sorts of qualities are likely to reflect the considerations that have led to an understanding of freedom of association as an intrinsic element of personal liberty. Conversely, an association lacking these qualities—such as a large business enterprise-seems remote from the concerns giving rise to this constitutional protection. Accordingly, the Constitution undoubtedly imposes constraints on the State's power to control the selection of one's spouse that would not apply to regulations affecting the choice of one's fellow employees.

Between these poles, of course, lies a broad range of human relationships that may make greater or lesser claims to constitutional protection from particular incursions by the State. Determining the limits of state authority over an individual's freedom to enter into a particular association therefore unavoidably entails a careful assessment of where that relationship's objective characteristics locate it on a spectrum from the most intimate to the most attenuated of personal attachments. We need not mark the potentially significant points on this terrain with any precision. We note only that factors that may be relevant include size, purpose, policies, selectivity, congeniality, and other characteristics that in a particular case may be pertinent. In this case, however, several features of the

Jaycees clearly place the organization outside of the category of relationships worthy of this kind of constitutional protection.

The undisputed facts reveal that the local chapters of the Jaycees are large and basically unselective groups. * * * Apart from age and sex, neither the national organization nor the local chapters employs any criteria for judging applicants for membership, and new members are routinely recruited and admitted with no inquiry into their backgrounds. In fact, a local officer testified that he could recall no instance in which an applicant had been denied membership on any basis other than age or sex.

In short, the local chapters of the Jaycees are neither small nor selective. Moreover, much of the activity central to the formation and maintenance of the association involves the participation of strangers to that relationship. Accordingly, we conclude that the Jaycees chapters lack the distinctive characteristics that might afford constitutional protection to the decision of its members to exclude women. We turn therefore to consider the extent to which application of the Minnesota statute to compel the Jaycees to accept women infringes the group's freedom of expressive association.

* * *

B

An individual's freedom to speak, to worship, and to petition the Government for the redress of grievances could not be vigorously protected from interference by the State unless a correlative freedom to engage in group effort toward those ends were not also guaranteed. According protection to collective effort on behalf of shared goals is especially important in preserving political and cultural diversity and in shielding dissident expression from suppression by the majority. * * * Consequently, we have long understood as implicit in the right to engage in activities protected by the First Amendment a corresponding right to associate with others in pursuit of a wide variety of political, social, economic, educational, religious, and cultural ends. In view of the various protected activities in which the Jaycees engage, that right is plainly implicated in this case.

* * *

The right to associate for expressive purposes is not, however, absolute. Infringements on that right may be justified by regulations adopted to serve compelling state interests, unrelated to the suppression of ideas, that cannot be achieved through means significantly less restrictive of associational freedoms. We are persuaded that Minnesota's compelling interest in eradicating discrimination against its female citizens justifies the impact that application of the statute to the Jaycees may have on the male members' associational freedoms.

* * *

[I]n explaining its conclusion that the Jaycees local chapters are "place[s] of public accommodations" within the meaning of the Act, the

Minnesota court noted the various commercial programs and benefits offered to members and stated that, "[l]eadership skills are 'goods,' [and] business contacts and employment promotions are 'privileges' and 'advantages' ". * * * Assuring women equal access to such goods, privileges, and advantages clearly furthers compelling state interests.

In applying the Act to the Jaycees, the State has advanced those interests through the least restrictive means of achieving its ends. Indeed, the Jaycees have failed to demonstrate that the Act imposes any serious burdens on the male members' freedom of expressive association. * * * Over the years, the national and local levels of the organization have taken public positions on a number of diverse issues, and members of the Jaycees regularly engage in a variety of civic, charitable, lobbying, fundraising and other activities worthy of constitutional protection under the First Amendment. There is, however, no basis in the record for concluding that admission of women as full voting members will impede the organization's ability to engage in these protected activities or to disseminate its preferred views. The Act requires no change in the Jaycees' creed of promoting the interests of young men, and it imposes no restrictions on the organization's ability to exclude individuals with ideologies or philosophies different from those of its existing members. * * * Moreover, the Jaycees already invite women to share the group's views and philosophy and to participate in much of its training and community activities. Accordingly, any claim that admission of women as full voting members will impair a symbolic message conveyed by the very fact that women are not permitted to vote is attenuated at best.

* * *

In any event, even if enforcement of the Act causes some incidental abridgement of the Jaycees' protected speech, that effect is no greater than is necessary to accomplish the State's legitimate purposes. As we have explained, acts of invidious discrimination in the distribution of publicly available goods, services, and other advantages cause unique evils that government has a compelling interest to prevent-wholly apart from the point of view such conduct may transmit. Accordingly, like violence or other types of potentially expressive activities that produce special harms distinct from their communicative impact, such practices are entitled to no constitutional protection. In prohibiting such practices, the Minnesota Act therefore "responds precisely to the substantive problem which legitimately concerns" the State and abridges no more speech or associational freedom than is necessary to accomplish that purpose.

III

[The Court held that the Minnesota statute was not unconstitutionally vague under the void for vagueness doctrine nor overbroad. Eds.]

IV

The judgment of the Court of Appeals is Reversed.

■ Justice Rehnquist concurs in the judgment.

■ The Chief Justice and Justice Blackmun took no part in the decision of this case.

■ Justice O'Connor, concurring in part and concurring in the judgment.

[Justice O'Connor would have applied a different standard than the majority—a commercial-noncommercial test. Associations engaged predominantly in protected expression would be classified as expressive, and all others as commercial, with the latter receiving only minimal constitutional protection. The Jaycees were a "commercial" organization. The strict scrutiny standard, available to expressive associations, was unwarranted for organizations whose activities were not predominantly of the type protected by the First Amendment. For Justice O'Connor, the critical factor in assessing a claim of a right to discriminate was the state's goal of ensuring nondiscriminatory access to commercial opportunities in our society. If an association is more commercial than expressive, Justice O'Connor would uphold any rational regulation of its activities or membership. Eds.]

NOTE: BOARD OF DIRECTORS OF ROTARY INTERNATIONAL v. ROTARY CLUB OF DUARTE AND NEW YORK STATE CLUB ASSOCIATION v. CITY OF NEW YORK

In Board of Directors of Rotary International v. Rotary Club of Duarte, 481 U.S. 537, 107 S.Ct. 1940 (1987), the United States Supreme Court found that the application to Rotary International of California's Unruh Act, Cal. Civ. Code 51, which entitles all persons, regardless of sex, to full and equal accommodations, advantages, facilities, privileges, and services in all business establishments in the state, did not interfere unduly with Rotary Club members' freedom of private association nor violate the First Amendment right of expressive association. Rotary International allowed women to attend meetings, give speeches, receive awards, and form auxiliary organizations, but its constitution excluded women from membership. Because it had admitted women to active membership, the Duarte California Rotary Club's membership in the international organization was terminated.

In determining whether a particular association was sufficiently intimate or private to warrant constitutional protection, a court should consider factors such as size, purpose, selectivity, and whether others are excluded from critical aspects of the relationship. The Rotary Club was found not deserving of protection because of the particularly large size of local clubs, the high turnover rate among club members, the inclusive nature of the membership, and the fact that the clubs welcomed the inclusive nature of the membership, the public purposes behind Rotary's service activities and the club's encouragement of strangers and the media coverage of many activities. The Unruh Act's slight impingement of members' rights was justified by the State's compelling interest in eliminating discrimination against women and assuring them equal access to public accommodations.

The Unruh Act sometimes has been interpreted expansively by California courts. For example, in Isbister v. Boys' Club of Santa Cruz, Inc., 40 Cal.3d 72, 707 P.2d 212, 219 Cal.Rptr. 150 (1985), the California Supreme Court held that the Unruh Act's language "business establishments of every kind whatsoever" included nonprofit places of accommodation such as the Boys Club of Santa Cruz which owned a gymnasium and swimming pool. Membership was open to all Santa Cruz boys between the ages of eight and eighteen but excluded females.

However, in Curran v. Mount Diablo Council of the Boy Scouts of America, 17 Cal.4th 670, 952 P.2d 218, 72 Cal.Rptr.2d 410 (1998), the California Supreme Court held that a local Boy Scout council that excluded a former eagle scout and recipient of numerous scout honors for an adult leader position because of his homosexuality was not a "business establishment" subject to the anti-discrimination provisions of the Unruh Act, California's public accommodation statute. The Court distinguished *Isbister* on the grounds that the boys club in that case demonstrated that it was a place of public amusement because of the prominence of its recreational facilities, its availability to the entire youthful population with the sole condition that its users be male, and a line of federal cases finding recreational activities of YMCAs to be places of public accommodation. In contrast, the Boy Scouts' functions and activities were unrelated to the promotion or advancement of the economic or business interests of its members. Its primary function was the inculcation of a specific set of values in its members. Scouts met regularly in small groups to foster close friendship, trust and loyalties, and the members had to participate in a variety of activities, ceremonies, and rituals that were designed to teach the moral principles to which the organization subscribed. Four judges wrote concurring opinions; two would have overruled *Isbister*. As a private organization under California law, could the Boy Scouts discriminate against African–Americans or women?

New York State Club Association v. City of New York, 487 U.S. 1, 108 S.Ct. 2225 (1988) involved an amendment to New York City's Human Rights Law, which prohibited discrimination by any place of public accommodation, resort or amusement. The amendment expanded the law's reach to include private clubs of more than 400 members that provided "regular meal service" and received regular payments "directly or indirectly from or on behalf of nonmembers for the furtherance of trade or business." The city found these two characteristics to be significant in pinpointing organizations which were "commercial" in nature, and "where business deals are often made and personal contacts valuable for business purposes, employment and professional advancement are formed." The amendment was directed at several exclusive men's clubs where important business was conducted in the absence of women.

A consortium of private clubs filed suit against the city seeking a declaration that the law was invalid on various state grounds and unconstitutional on its face under the First and Fourteenth Amendments and requested that defendants be enjoined from enforcing it. The clubs were unsuccessful in the state and lower federal courts and appealed to the Supreme Court, which affirmed.

The Court found that the law did not infringe on the associational rights of members of private clubs because on its face it did not affect in any significant way the ability of individuals to form associations that advocated public or private viewpoints. The Court identified the characteristics targeted by the Human Rights Law amendment—venues where business transactions were conducted and networking occurred that was valuable for business, employment and professional advancement. It concluded that these characteristics were at least as significant in defining the nonprivate nature of these associations because of the kind of role nonmembers played, as was the regular participation of strangers at meetings, which it emphasized in *Roberts* and *Rotary*. The Court concluded that on its face the amendment would not affect "in any significant way" the ability of individuals to form associations to advocate public or private viewpoints. It did not require the clubs "to abandon or alter" any activities that were protected by the First Amendment. If a club sought to exclude individuals who did not share the views that the club's members wished to promote, the amendment erected no obstacle to this end. Instead, it merely prevented an association from using race, sex, and the other specified characteristics as shorthand measures in place of what the city considered to be more legitimate criteria for determining membership.

NOTES AND QUESTIONS

1. What is the justification for state prohibitions of discrimination by private clubs? What was the harm of the restrictive policy in all three clubs? What are the advantages of access to civic, eating, or athletic clubs? Under the Court's analysis, would there have been a difference in result if the clubs were all female and discriminated against men?

2. Do the holdings in *Roberts*, *Rotary* and *New York Club Association* mean that private organizations cannot discriminate against women? Is the Court's distinction between intimate and non-intimate affiliations valid? The ultimate question becomes whether an association appears to be an extension of more of the home or of the marketplace. Most affiliations are in between. Is there a direct correlation between size, selectivity, and intimacy?

3. The association was not organized for expressive purposes in any of the cases. Isn't merely joining an organization an act of expression? See Lathrop v. Donohue, 367 U.S. 820, 882, 81 S.Ct. 1826, 1858 (1961) (Douglas, J., dissenting).

4. *Withdrawing Favorable Tax Treatment*. Section 501(i) of the Internal Revenue Code denies exemption to certain social clubs if the charter, bylaws or governing documents contain a provision which provides for discrimination against any person on the basis of race, color, or religion. See Chapter 9E2, supra, at p. 946. This is a trap only for the unwary and would not apply to clubs that discriminate on the basis of practice rather

than through formal written documents. Other suggested approaches have been to deny any business expense deduction for dues paid to discriminatory clubs or by defining "public accommodations" as organizations that derive more than 20 percent of their income from expenditures in furtherance of business. See Michael Burns, The Exclusion of Women from Influential Men's Clubs: The Inner Sanctum and the Myth of Full Equality, 18 Harv. C.R.—C.L.L. Rev. 321, 387 (1983). Since 1993, however, club dues are no longer tax-deductible, whether or not the club discriminates. I.R.C. § 274(a)(3). Professor Deborah L. Rhode has suggested an approach that ties public sanctions to public entanglements. Clubs willing to forgo tax advantages, employer contributions or state licenses could retain their separated status. Association and Assimilation, 81 N.W.U.L. Rev. 106, 129 (1986). Isn't this what Local Law 63 presumed in the N.Y. Club Association case?

5. *Exemptions for Truly Private Associations.* All three of the preceding Supreme Court decisions dealt with statutorily defined discrimination. All public accommodations legislation carves out exemptions in favor of truly private associations by specific language or interpretive gloss. William Buss, Discrimination by Private Clubs, 67 Wash. U.L. Rev. 815, 838 (1989). Title II of the Civil Rights Act exempts discrimination by "a private club or other establishment not in fact open to the public." Title II, Civil Rights Act of 1964, 42 U.S.C.A. 201(e). Even New York City's legislation exempted from coverage "any institution, club, or place of accommodation that was distinctly private." The Minnesota statute in *Jaycees* applied only to "public" business and the California statute in *Rotary* covered "business establishments". Will courts encroach upon "truly private" associations by expansive interpretations of statutes?

Boy Scouts of America v. Dale

Supreme Court of the United States, 2000.
530 U.S. 640, 120 S.Ct. 2446.

■ Chief Justice Rehnquist delivered the opinion of the Court.

Petitioners are the Boy Scouts of America and the Monmouth Council, a division of the Boy Scouts of America (collectively, Boy Scouts). The Boy Scouts is a private, not-for-profit organization engaged in instilling its system of values in young people. The Boy Scouts asserts that homosexual conduct is inconsistent with the values it seeks to instill. Respondent is James Dale, a former Eagle Scout whose adult membership in the Boy Scouts was revoked when the Boy Scouts learned that he is an avowed homosexual and gay rights activist. The New Jersey Supreme Court held that New Jersey's public accommodations law requires that the Boy Scouts admit Dale. This case presents the question whether applying New Jersey's public accommodations law in this way violates the Boy Scouts' First Amendment right of expressive association. We hold that it does.

I

James Dale entered scouting in 1978 at the age of eight by joining Monmouth Council's Cub Scout Pack 142. Dale became a Boy Scout in 1981 and remained a Scout until he turned 18. By all accounts, Dale was an exemplary Scout. In 1988, he achieved the rank of Eagle Scout, one of Scouting's highest honors.

Dale applied for adult membership in the Boy Scouts in 1989. The Boy Scouts approved his application for the position of assistant scoutmaster of Troop 73. Around the same time, Dale left home to attend Rutgers University. After arriving at Rutgers, Dale first acknowledged to himself and others that he is gay. He quickly became involved with, and eventually became the copresident of, the Rutgers University Lesbian/Gay Alliance. In 1990, Dale attended a seminar addressing the psychological and health needs of lesbian and gay teenagers. A newspaper covering the event interviewed Dale about his advocacy of homosexual teenagers' need for gay role models. In early July 1990, the newspaper published the interview and Dale's photograph over a caption identifying him as the copresident of the Lesbian/Gay Alliance.

Later that month, Dale received a letter from Monmouth Council Executive James Kay revoking his adult membership. Dale wrote to Kay requesting the reason for Monmouth Council's decision. Kay responded by letter that the Boy Scouts "specifically forbid membership to homosexuals."

* * *

[The Court then traced the path of the case through the lower New Jersey courts. Eds.]

The New Jersey Supreme Court * * * held that the Boy Scouts was a place of public accommodation subject to the public accommodations law, that the organization was not exempt from the law under any of its express exceptions, and that the Boy Scouts violated the law by revoking Dale's membership based on his avowed homosexuality. * * * [T]he court concluded that the Boy Scouts' "large size, nonselectivity, inclusive rather than exclusive purpose, and practice of inviting or allowing nonmembers to attend meetings, establish that the organization is not 'sufficiently personal or private to warrant constitutional protection' under the freedom of intimate association." With respect to the right of expressive association, the court "agree[d] that Boy Scouts expresses a belief in moral values and uses its activities to encourage the moral development of its members." But the court concluded that it was "not persuaded . . . that a shared goal of Boy Scout members is to associate in order to preserve the view that homosexuality is immoral." Accordingly, the court held "that Dale's membership does not violate the Boy Scouts' right of expressive association because his inclusion would not 'affect in any significant way [the Boy Scouts'] existing members' ability to carry out their various purposes.'" The court also determined that New Jersey has a compelling interest in eliminating "the destructive consequences of discrimination from our society," and that its public accommodations law abridges no more speech than is necessary to accomplish its purpose. * * *

We granted the Boy Scouts' petition for certiorari to determine whether the application of New Jersey's public accommodations law violated the First Amendment.

II

In Roberts v. United States Jaycees, 468 U.S. 609, 622, 104 S.Ct. 3244 (1984), we observed that "implicit in the right to engage in activities protected by the First Amendment" is "a corresponding right to associate with others in pursuit of a wide variety of political, social, economic, educational, religious, and cultural ends." This right is crucial in preventing the majority from imposing its views on groups that would rather express other, perhaps unpopular, ideas. See ibid. stating that protection of the right to expressive association is "especially important in preserving political and cultural diversity and in shielding dissident expression from suppression by the majority"). Government actions that may unconstitutionally burden this freedom may take many forms, one of which is "intrusion into the internal structure or affairs of an association" like a "regulation that forces the group to accept members it does not desire." Forcing a group to accept certain members may impair the ability of the group to express those views, and only those views, that it intends to express. Thus, "[f]reedom of association * * * plainly presupposes a freedom not to associate."

The forced inclusion of an unwanted person in a group infringes the group's freedom of expressive association if the presence of that person affects in a significant way the group's ability to advocate public or private viewpoints. New York State Club Assn., Inc. v. City of New York, 487 U.S. 1, 13, 108 S.Ct. 2225 (1988). But the freedom of expressive association, like many freedoms, is not absolute. We have held that the freedom could be overridden "by regulations adopted to serve compelling state interests, unrelated to the suppression of ideas, that cannot be achieved through means significantly less restrictive of associational freedoms." Roberts, supra, at 623.

To determine whether a group is protected by the First Amendment's expressive associational right, we must determine whether the group engages in "expressive association." The First Amendment's protection of expressive association is not reserved for advocacy groups. But to come within its ambit, a group must engage in some form of expression, whether it be public or private.

Because this is a First Amendment case where the ultimate conclusions of law are virtually inseparable from findings of fact, we are obligated to independently review the factual record to ensure that the state court's judgment does not unlawfully intrude on free expression. The record reveals the following. The Boy Scouts is a private, nonprofit organization. According to its mission statement:

"It is the mission of the Boy Scouts of America to serve others by helping to instill values in young people and, in other ways, to prepare them to make ethical choices over their lifetime in achieving their full potential.

"The values we strive to instill are based on those found in the Scout Oath and Law:

Scout Oath

On my honor I will do my best
To do my duty to God and my country
and to obey the Scout Law;
To help other people at all times;
To keep myself physically strong,
mentally awake, and morally straight

Scout Law

A Scout is:

Trustworthy	Obedient
Loyal	Cheerful
Helpful	Thrifty
Friendly	Brave
Courteous	Clean
Kind	Reverent"

Thus, the general mission of the Boy Scouts is clear: "[T]o instill values in young people." The Boy Scouts seeks to instill these values by having its adult leaders spend time with the youth members, instructing and engaging them in activities like camping, archery, and fishing. During the time spent with the youth members, the scoutmasters and assistant scoutmasters inculcate them with the Boy Scouts' values—both expressly and by example. It seems indisputable that an association that seeks to transmit such a system of values engages in expressive activity. See Roberts, supra, at 636 (O'CONNOR, J., concurring) ("Even the training of outdoor survival skills or participation in community service might become expressive when the activity is intended to develop good morals, reverence, patriotism, and a desire for self-improvement").

Given that the Boy Scouts engages in expressive activity, we must determine whether the forced inclusion of Dale as an assistant scoutmaster would significantly affect the Boy Scouts' ability to advocate public or private viewpoints. This inquiry necessarily requires us first to explore, to a limited extent, the nature of the Boy Scouts' view of homosexuality.

The values the Boy Scouts seeks to instill are "based on" those listed in the Scout Oath and Law. The Boy Scouts explains that the Scout Oath and Law provide "a positive moral code for living; they are a list of 'do's' rather than 'don'ts.'" The Boy Scouts asserts that homosexual conduct is inconsistent with the values embodied in the Scout Oath and Law, particularly with the values represented by the terms "morally straight" and "clean."

Obviously, the Scout Oath and Law do not expressly mention sexuality or sexual orientation. And the terms "morally straight" and "clean" are by no means self-defining. Different people would attribute to those terms very different meanings. For example, some people may believe that engaging in homosexual conduct is not at odds with being "morally straight" and "clean." And others may believe that engaging in homosexual conduct is contrary to being "morally straight" and "clean." The Boy Scouts says it falls within the latter category.

The New Jersey Supreme Court analyzed the Boy Scouts' beliefs and found that the "exclusion of members solely on the basis of their sexual orientation is inconsistent with Boy Scouts' commitment to a diverse and 'representative' membership * * * [and] contradicts Boy Scouts' overarching objective to reach 'all eligible youth.'" The court concluded that the exclusion of members like Dale "appears antithetical to the organization's goals and philosophy." But our cases reject this sort of inquiry; it is not the role of the courts to reject a group's expressed values because they disagree with those values or find them internally inconsistent.

The Boy Scouts asserts that it "teach[es] that homosexual conduct is not morally straight," and that it does "not want to promote homosexual conduct as a legitimate form of behavior." We accept the Boy Scouts' assertion. We need not inquire further to determine the nature of the Boy Scouts' expression with respect to homosexuality. But because the record before us contains written evidence of the Boy Scouts' viewpoint, we look to it as instructive, if only on the question of the sincerity of the professed beliefs.

A 1978 position statement to the Boy Scouts' Executive Committee, signed by Downing B. Jenks, the President of the Boy Scouts, and Harvey L. Price, the Chief Scout Executive, expresses the Boy Scouts' "official position" with regard to "homosexuality and Scouting":

"Q. May an individual who openly declares himself to be a homosexual be a volunteer Scout leader?

"A. No. The Boy Scouts of America is a private, membership organization and leadership therein is a privilege and not a right. We do not believe that homosexuality and leadership in Scouting are appropriate. We will continue to select only those who in our judgment meet our standards and qualifications for leadership."

Thus, at least as of 1978—the year James Dale entered Scouting—the official position of the Boy Scouts was that avowed homosexuals were not to be Scout leaders.

A position statement promulgated by the Boy Scouts in 1991 (after Dale's membership was revoked but before this litigation was filed) also supports its current view:

"We believe that homosexual conduct is inconsistent with the requirement in the Scout Oath that a Scout be morally straight and in the Scout Law that a Scout be clean in word and deed, and that homosexuals do not provide a desirable role model for Scouts."

This position statement was redrafted numerous times but its core message remained consistent. * * *

The Boy Scouts publicly expressed its views with respect to homosexual conduct by its assertions in prior litigation. * * * We cannot doubt that the Boy Scouts sincerely holds this view.

We must then determine whether Dale's presence as an assistant scoutmaster would significantly burden the Boy Scouts' desire to not "promote homosexual conduct as a legitimate form of behavior." As we give deference to an association's assertions regarding the nature of its expression, we must also give deference to an association's view of what would impair its expression. That is not to say that an expressive association can erect a shield against antidiscrimination laws simply by asserting that mere acceptance of a member from a particular group would impair its message. But here Dale, by his own admission, is one of a group of gay Scouts who have "become leaders in their community and are open and honest about their sexual orientation." Dale was the copresident of a gay and lesbian organization at college and remains a gay rights activist. Dale's presence in the Boy Scouts would, at the very least, force the organization to send a message, both to the youth members and the world, that the Boy Scouts accepts homosexual conduct as a legitimate form of behavior.

Hurley is illustrative on this point. There we considered whether the application of Massachusetts' public accommodations law to require the organizers of a private St. Patrick's Day parade to include among the marchers an Irish–American gay, lesbian, and bisexual group, GLIB, violated the parade organizers' First Amendment rights. We noted that the parade organizers did not wish to exclude the GLIB members because of their sexual orientations, but because they wanted to march behind a GLIB banner.

* * *

Here, we have found that the Boy Scouts believes that homosexual conduct is inconsistent with the values it seeks to instill in its youth members; it will not "promote homosexual conduct as a legitimate form of behavior." As the presence of GLIB in Boston's St. Patrick's Day parade would have interfered with the parade organizers' choice not to propound a particular point of view, the presence of Dale as an assistant scoutmaster would just as surely interfere with the Boy Scout's choice not to propound a point of view contrary to its beliefs.

The New Jersey Supreme Court determined that the Boy Scouts' ability to disseminate its message was not significantly affected by the forced inclusion of Dale as an assistant scoutmaster because of the following findings:

> "Boy Scout members do not associate for the purpose of disseminating the belief that homosexuality is immoral; Boy Scouts discourages its leaders from disseminating any views on sexual issues; and Boy Scouts includes sponsors and members who subscribe to different views in respect of homosexuality."

We disagree with the New Jersey Supreme Court's conclusion drawn from these findings.

First, associations do not have to associate for the "purpose" of disseminating a certain message in order to be entitled to the protections of the First Amendment. An association must merely engage in expressive activity that could be impaired in order to be entitled to protection. For example, the purpose of the St. Patrick's Day parade in Hurley was not to espouse any views about sexual orientation, but we held that the parade organizers had a right to exclude certain participants nonetheless.

Second, even if the Boy Scouts discourages Scout leaders from disseminating views on sexual issues—a fact that the Boy Scouts disputes with contrary evidence—the First Amendment protects the Boy Scouts' method of expression. If the Boy Scouts wishes Scout leaders to avoid questions of sexuality and teach only by example, this fact does not negate the sincerity of its belief discussed above.

Third, the First Amendment simply does not require that every member of a group agree on every issue in order for the group's policy to be "expressive association." The Boy Scouts takes an official position with respect to homosexual conduct, and that is sufficient for First Amendment purposes. In this same vein, Dale makes much of the claim that the Boy Scouts does not revoke the membership of heterosexual Scout leaders that openly disagree with the Boy Scouts' policy on sexual orientation. But if this is true, it is irrelevant. The presence of an avowed homosexual and gay rights activist in an assistant scoutmaster's uniform sends a distinctly different message from the presence of a heterosexual assistant scoutmaster who is on record as disagreeing with Boy Scouts policy. The Boy Scouts has a First Amendment right to choose to send one message but not the other. The fact that the organization does not trumpet its views from the housetops, or that it tolerates dissent within its ranks, does not mean that its views receive no First Amendment protection.

Having determined that the Boy Scouts is an expressive association and that the forced inclusion of Dale would significantly affect its expression, we inquire whether the application of New Jersey's public accommodations law to require that the Boy Scouts accept Dale as an assistant scoutmaster runs afoul of the Scouts' freedom of expressive association. We conclude that it does.

State public accommodations laws were originally enacted to prevent discrimination in traditional places of public accommodation—like inns and trains. Over time, the public accommodations laws have expanded to cover more places. New Jersey's statutory definition of " '[a] place of public accommodation' " is extremely broad. The term is said to "include, but not be limited to," a list of over 50 types of places. Many on the list are what one would expect to be places where the public is invited. For example, the statute includes as places of public accommodation taverns, restaurants, retail shops, and public libraries. But the statute also includes places that often may not carry with them open invitations to the public, like summer camps and roof gardens. In this case, the New Jersey Supreme Court went a step further and applied its public accommodations law to a private entity without even attempting to tie the term "place" to a physical location. As the definition of "public accommodation" has expanded from clearly commercial entities, such as restaurants, bars, and hotels, to membership organizations such as the Boy Scouts, the potential for conflict between state public accommodations laws and the First Amendment rights of organizations has increased.

We recognized in cases such as *Roberts* and *Duarte* that States have a compelling interest in eliminating discrimination against women in public accommodations. But in each of these cases we went on to conclude that the enforcement of these statutes would not materially interfere with the ideas that the organization sought to express. * * * We thereupon concluded in each of these cases that the organizations' First Amendment rights were not violated by the application of the States' public accommodations laws.

In *Hurley*, we said that public accommodations laws "are well within the State's usual power to enact when a legislature has reason to believe that a given group is the target of discrimination, and they do not, as a general matter, violate the First or Fourteenth Amendments." But we went on to note that in that case "the Massachusetts [public accommodations] law has been applied in a peculiar way" because "any contingent of protected individuals with a message would have the right to participate in petitioners' speech, so that the communication produced by the private organizers would be shaped by all those protected by the law who wish to join in with some expressive demonstration of their own." And in the associational freedom cases such as *Roberts*, *Duarte*, and *New York State Club Assn.*, after finding a compelling state interest, the Court went on to examine whether or not the application of the state law would impose any "serious burden" on the organization's rights of expressive association. So in these cases, the associational interest in freedom of expression has been set on one side of the scale, and the State's interest on the other.

* * *

The state interests embodied in New Jersey's public accommodations law do not justify such a severe intrusion on the Boy Scouts' rights to freedom of expressive association. That being the case, we hold that the First Amendment prohibits the State from imposing such a requirement through the application of its public accommodations law.

JUSTICE STEVENS' dissent makes much of its observation that the public perception of homosexuality in this country has changed. Indeed, it appears that homosexuality has gained greater societal acceptance. But this is scarcely an argument for denying First Amendment protection to those who refuse to accept these views. The First Amendment protects expression, be it of the popular variety or not. And the fact that an idea may be embraced and advocated by increasing numbers of people is all the more reason to protect the First Amendment rights of those who wish to voice a different view.

* * *

We are not, as we must not be, guided by our views of whether the Boy Scouts' teachings with respect to homosexual conduct are right or wrong; public or judicial disapproval of a tenet of an organization's expression does not justify the State's effort to compel the organization to accept members where such acceptance would derogate from the organization's expressive message. "While the law is free to promote all sorts of conduct in place of harmful behavior, it is not free to interfere with speech for no better reason than promoting an approved message or discouraging a disfavored one, however enlightened either purpose may strike the government."

The judgment of the New Jersey Supreme Court is reversed, and the cause remanded for further proceedings not inconsistent with this opinion.

It is so ordered.

[The Appendix to the opinion of the Court is omitted. Eds.]

■ JUSTICE STEVENS, with whom JUSTICE SOUTER, JUSTICE GINSBURG and JUSTICE BREYER join, dissenting.

* * *

The majority holds that New Jersey's [public accommodations] law violates BSA's right to associate and its right to free speech. But that law does not "impos[e] any serious burdens" on BSA's "collective effort on behalf of [its] shared goals," nor does it force BSA to communicate any message that it does not wish to endorse. New Jersey's law, therefore, abridges no constitutional right of the Boy Scouts.

I

* * *

In this case, Boy Scouts of America contends that it teaches the young boys who are Scouts that homosexuality is immoral. Consequently, it argues, it would violate its right to associate to force it to admit homosexuals as members, as doing so would be at odds with its own shared goals and values. This contention, quite plainly, requires us to look at what, exactly, are the values that BSA actually teaches.

* * *

[Justice Stevens then examined the Boy Scouts' Statement of Mission as expressed through its publications. Eds.]

It is plain as the light of day that neither one of these principles— "morally straight" and "clean"—says the slightest thing about homosexuality. Indeed, neither term in the Boy Scouts' Law and Oath expresses any position whatsoever on sexual matters.

BSA's published guidance on that topic underscores this point. Scouts, for example, are directed to receive their sex education at home or in school, but not from the organization: "Your parents or guardian or a sex education teacher should give you the facts about sex that you must know." Boy Scout Handbook (1992) To be sure, Scouts are not forbidden from asking their Scoutmaster about issues of a sexual nature, but Scoutmasters are, literally, the last person Scouts are encouraged to ask: "If you have questions about growing up, about relationships, sex, or making good decisions, ask. Talk with your parents, religious leaders, teachers, or Scoutmaster." Ibid. Moreover, Scoutmasters are specifically directed to steer curious adolescents to other sources of information[.] "If Scouts ask for information regarding * * * sexual activity, answer honestly and factually, but stay within your realm of expertise and comfort. If a Scout has serious concerns that you cannot answer, refer him to his family, religious leader, doctor, or other professional." Scoutmaster Handbook (1990). More specifically, BSA has set forth a number of rules for Scoutmasters when these types of issues come up: "You may have boys asking you for information or advice about sexual matters. * * * " How should you handle such matters? "Rule number 1: You do not undertake to instruct Scouts, in any formalized manner, in the subject of sex and family life. The reasons are that it is not construed to be Scouting's proper area, and that you are probably not well qualified to do this." Rule number 2: If Scouts come to you to ask questions or to seek advice, you would give it within your competence. A boy who appears to be asking about sexual intercourse, however, may really only be worried about his pimples, so it is well to find out just what information is needed. "Rule number 3: You should refer boys with sexual problems to persons better qualified than you [are] to handle them. If the boy has a spiritual leader or a doctor who can deal with them, he should go there. If such persons are not available, you may just have to do the best you can. But don't try to play a highly professional role. And at the other extreme, avoid passing the buck."

In light of BSA's self-proclaimed ecumenism, furthermore, it is even more difficult to discern any shared goals or common moral stance on homosexuality. Insofar as religious matters are concerned, BSA's bylaws state that it is "absolutely nonsectarian in its attitude toward * * * religious training."

II

The Court seeks to fill the void by pointing to a statement of "policies and procedures relating to homosexuality and Scouting" signed by BSA's President and Chief Scout Executive in 1978 and addressed to the members of the Executive Committee of the national organization. The letter says that the BSA does "not believe that homosexuality and leadership in Scouting are appropriate." * * *

Four aspects of the 1978 policy statement are relevant to the proper disposition of this case. First, at most this letter simply adopts an exclusionary membership policy. But simply adopting such a policy has never been considered sufficient, by itself, to prevail on a right to associate claim.

Second, the 1978 policy was never publicly expressed—unlike, for example, the Scout's duty to be "obedient." It was an internal memorandum, never circulated beyond the few members of BSA's Executive Committee. It remained, in effect, a secret Boy Scouts policy. Far from claiming any intent to express an idea that would be burdened by the presence of homosexuals, BSA's public posture—to the world and to the Scouts themselves—remained what it had always been: one of tolerance, welcoming all classes of boys and young men. In this respect, BSA's claim is even weaker than those we have rejected in the past.

Third, it is apparent that the draftsmen of the policy statement foresaw the possibility that laws against discrimination might one day be amended to protect homosexuals from employment discrimination. Their statement clearly provided that, in the event such a law conflicted with their policy, a Scout's duty to be "obedient" and "obe[y] the laws," even if "he thinks [the laws] are unfair" would prevail in such a contingency. * * * At the very least, then, the statement reflects no unequivocal view on homosexuality. Indeed, the statement suggests that an appropriate way for BSA to preserve its unpublished exclusionary policy would include an open and forthright attempt to seek an amendment of New Jersey's statute. ("If he thinks these rules and laws are unfair, he tries to have them changed in an orderly manner rather than disobey them.")

Fourth, the 1978 statement simply says that homosexuality is not "appropriate." It makes no effort to connect that statement to a shared goal or expressive activity of the Boy Scouts. Whatever values BSA seeks to instill in Scouts, the idea that homosexuality is not "appropriate" appears entirely unconnected to, and is mentioned nowhere in, the myriad of publicly declared values and creeds of the BSA. That idea does not appear to be among any of the principles actually taught to Scouts. Rather, the 1978 policy appears to be no more than a private statement of a few BSA executives that the organization wishes to exclude gays—and that wish has nothing to do with any expression BSA actually engages in.

* * *

It is clear, then, that nothing in these policy statements supports BSA's claim. The only policy written before the revocation of Dale's membership was an equivocal, undisclosed statement that evidences no connection between the group's discriminatory intentions and its expressive interests. * * *

BSA's inability to make its position clear and its failure to connect its alleged policy to its expressive activities is highly significant. By the time Dale was expelled from the Boy Scouts in 1990, BSA had already been engaged in several suits under a variety of state antidiscrimination public accommodation laws challenging various aspects of its membership policy. * * * [I]t was clearly on notice by 1990 that it might well be subjected to state public accommodation antidiscrimination laws, and that a court might one day reject its claimed right to associate. Yet it took no steps prior to

Dale's expulsion to clarify how its exclusivity was connected to its expression. It speaks volumes about the credibility of BSA's claim to a shared goal that homosexuality is incompatible with Scouting that since at least 1984 it had been aware of this issue—indeed, concerned enough to twice file amicus briefs before this Court—yet it did nothing in the intervening six years (or even in the years after Dale's expulsion) to explain clearly and openly why the presence of homosexuals would affect its expressive activities, or to make the view of "morally straight" and "clean" taken in its 1991 and 1992 policies a part of the values actually instilled in Scouts through the Handbook, lessons, or otherwise.

III

BSA's claim finds no support in our cases. We have recognized "a right to associate for the purpose of engaging in those activities protected by the First Amendment—speech, assembly, petition for the redress of grievances, and the exercise of religion." Roberts, 468 U.S., at 618. And we have acknowledged that "when the State interferes with individuals' selection of those with whom they wish to join in a common endeavor, freedom of association * * * may be implicated." Ibid. But "[t]he right to associate for expressive purposes is not * * * absolute"; rather, "the nature and degree of constitutional protection afforded freedom of association may vary depending on the extent to which * * * the constitutionally protected liberty is at stake in a given case." Indeed, the right to associate does not mean "that in every setting in which individuals exercise some discrimination in choosing associates, their selective process of inclusion and exclusion is protected by the Constitution." New York State Club Assn., Inc. v. City of New York, 487 U.S. 1, 13, 108 S.Ct. 2225 (1988). For example, we have routinely and easily rejected assertions of this right by expressive organizations with discriminatory membership policies, such as private schools, law firms, and labor organizations. In fact, until today, we have never once found a claimed right to associate in the selection of members to prevail in the face of a State's antidiscrimination law. To the contrary, we have squarely held that a State's antidiscrimination law does not violate a group's right to associate simply because the law conflicts with that group's exclusionary membership policy.

* * *

Several principles are made perfectly clear by *Jaycees* and *Rotary Club*. First, to prevail on a claim of expressive association in the face of a State's antidiscrimination law, it is not enough simply to engage in some kind of expressive activity. Both the Jaycees and the Rotary Club engaged in expressive activity protected by the First Amendment, yet that fact was not dispositive. Second, it is not enough to adopt an openly avowed exclusionary membership policy. Both the Jaycees and the Rotary Club did that as well. Third, it is not sufficient merely to articulate some connection between the group's expressive activities and its exclusionary policy.

* * *

The relevant question is whether the mere inclusion of the person at issue would "impose any serious burden," "affect in any significant way," or be "a substantial restraint upon" the organization's "shared goals," "basic goals," or "collective effort to foster beliefs." Accordingly, it is necessary to examine what, exactly, are BSA's shared goals and the degree to which its expressive activities would be burdened, affected, or restrained by including homosexuals.

The evidence before this Court makes it exceptionally clear that BSA has, at most, simply adopted an exclusionary membership policy and has no shared goal of disapproving of homosexuality. BSA's mission statement and federal charter say nothing on the matter; its official membership policy is silent; its Scout Oath and Law—and accompanying definitions—are devoid of any view on the topic; its guidance for Scouts and Scoutmasters on sexuality declare that such matters are "not construed to be Scouting's proper area," but are the province of a Scout's parents and pastor; and BSA's posture respecting religion tolerates a wide variety of views on the issue of homosexuality. Moreover, there is simply no evidence that BSA otherwise teaches anything in this area, or that it instructs Scouts on matters involving homosexuality in ways not conveyed in the Boy Scout or Scoutmaster Handbooks. In short, Boy Scouts of America is simply silent on homosexuality. There is no shared goal or collective effort to foster a belief about homosexuality at all—let alone one that is significantly burdened by admitting homosexuals.

As in Jaycees, there is "no basis in the record for concluding that admission of [homosexuals] will impede the [Boy Scouts'] ability to engage in [its] protected activities or to disseminate its preferred views" and New Jersey's law "requires no change in [BSA's] creed." And like Rotary Club, New Jersey's law "does not require [BSA] to abandon or alter any of" its activities. The evidence relied on by the Court is not to the contrary. The undisclosed 1978 policy certainly adds nothing to the actual views disseminated to the Scouts. It simply says that homosexuality is not "appropriate." There is no reason to give that policy statement more weight than Rotary International's assertion that all-male membership fosters the group's "fellowship" and was the only way it could "operate effectively." As for BSA's post-revocation statements, at most they simply adopt a policy of discrimination, which is no more dispositive than the openly discriminatory policies held insufficient in Jaycees and Rotary Club; there is no evidence here that BSA's policy was necessary to—or even a part of—BSA's expressive activities or was every taught to Scouts.

Equally important is BSA's failure to adopt any clear position on homosexuality. * * * A State's antidiscrimination law does not impose a "serious burden" or a "substantial restraint" upon the group's "shared goals" if the group itself is unable to identify its own stance with any clarity.

IV

The majority pretermits this entire analysis. It finds that BSA in fact " 'teach[es] that homosexual conduct is not morally straight.' " This conclusion, remarkably, rests entirely on statements in BSA's briefs.

* * *

This is an astounding view of the law. I am unaware of any previous instance in which our analysis of the scope of a constitutional right was determined by looking at what a litigant asserts in his or her brief and inquiring no further. It is even more astonishing in the First Amendment area, because, as the majority itself acknowledges, "we are obligated to independently review the factual record." It is an odd form of independent review that consists of deferring entirely to whatever a litigant claims. But the majority insists that our inquiry must be "limited," because "it is not the role of the courts to reject a group's expressed values because they disagree with those values or find them internally inconsistent."

* * *

To prevail in asserting a right of expressive association as a defense to a charge of violating an antidiscrimination law, the organization must at least show it has adopted and advocated an unequivocal position inconsistent with a position advocated or epitomized by the person whom the organization seeks to exclude. If this Court were to defer to whatever position an organization is prepared to assert in its briefs, there would be no way to mark the proper boundary between genuine exercises of the right to associate, on the one hand, and sham claims that are simply attempts to insulate nonexpressive private discrimination, on the other hand. Shielding a litigant's claim from judicial scrutiny would, in turn, render civil rights legislation a nullity, and turn this important constitutional right into a farce. Accordingly, the Court's prescription of total deference will not do.
* * *

V

* * *

The majority, though, does not rest its conclusion on the claim that Dale will use his position as a bully pulpit. Rather, it contends that Dale's mere presence among the Boy Scouts will itself force the group to convey a message about homosexuality—even if Dale has no intention of doing so. The majority holds that "[t]he presence of an avowed homosexual and gay rights activist in an assistant scoutmaster's uniform sends a distinc[t] * * * message," and, accordingly, BSA is entitled to exclude that message. In particular, "Dale's presence in the Boy Scouts would, at the very least, force the organization to send a message, both to the youth members and the world, that the Boy Scouts accepts homosexual conduct as a legitimate form of behavior."

* * *

It is true, of course, that some acts are so imbued with symbolic meaning that they qualify as "speech" under the First Amendment. At the same time, however, "[w]e cannot accept the view that an apparently limitless variety of conduct can be labeled 'speech' whenever the person engaging in the conduct intends thereby to express an idea." Though participating in the Scouts could itself conceivably send a message on some level, it is not the kind of act that we have recognized as speech. Indeed, if merely joining a group did constitute symbolic speech; and such speech were attributable to the group being joined; and that group has the right to exclude that speech (and hence, the right to exclude that person from joining), then the right of free speech effectively becomes a limitless right to exclude for every organization, whether or not it engages in any expressive activities. That cannot be, and never has been, the law.

The only apparent explanation for the majority's holding, then, is that homosexuals are simply so different from the rest of society that their presence alone—unlike any other individual's—should be singled out for special First Amendment treatment. Under the majority's reasoning, an openly gay male is irreversibly affixed with the label "homosexual." That label, even though unseen, communicates a message that permits his exclusion wherever he goes. His openness is the sole and sufficient justification for his ostracism. Though unintended, reliance on such a justification is tantamount to a constitutionally prescribed symbol of inferiority. * * *

[It] is not likely that BSA would be understood to send any message, either to Scouts or to the world, simply by admitting someone as a member. Over the years, BSA has generously welcomed over 87 million young Americans into its ranks. In 1992 over one million adults were active BSA members. The notion that an organization of that size and enormous prestige implicitly endorses the views that each of those adults may express in a non-Scouting context is simply mind boggling. Indeed, in this case there is no evidence that the young Scouts in Dale's troop, or members of their families, were even aware of his sexual orientation, either before or after his public statements at Rutgers University. * * *

VI

Unfavorable opinions about homosexuals "have ancient roots." Over the years, however, interaction with real people, rather than mere adherence to traditional ways of thinking about members of unfamiliar classes, have modified those opinions. A few examples: The American Psychiatric Association's and the American Psychological Association's removal of "homosexuality" from their lists of mental disorders; a move toward greater understanding within some religious communities; Justice Blackmun's classic opinion in Bowers; Georgia's invalidation of the statute upheld in Bowers; and New Jersey's enactment of the provision at issue in this case. * * *

That such prejudices are still prevalent and that they have caused serious and tangible harm to countless members of the class New Jersey seeks to protect are established matters of fact that neither the Boy Scouts nor the Court disputes. That harm can only be aggravated by the creation of a constitutional shield for a policy that is itself the product of a habitual way of thinking about strangers. As Justice Brandeis so wisely advised, "we must be ever on our guard, lest we erect our prejudices into legal principles."

If we would guide by the light of reason, we must let our minds be bold. I respectfully dissent.

■ [The decision of Mr. Justice Souter with whom Justices Ginsburg and Breyer join, dissenting, is omitted. Eds.]

PROBLEMS

1. The County of Rebok, Illinois passes an ordinance prohibiting discrimination on the basis of racial, religious, ethnic, national origin, or gender criteria. Could the county apply the statute to the following organizations?

   (a) A 15 member current events discussion club that excludes African–Americans.

   (b) The Protestant Lawyers Bar Association, which admits only those of Protestant faith and provides professional training and networking opportunities for its members. Seventy-five percent of the lawyers in Rebok County belong.

   (c) The Gaelic Club, which promotes Irish heritage, is only open to Irish–Americans.

   (d) The Black and Tan Society, an organization of North Ireland Protestants that admits all except those of Irish heritage who are Roman Catholic.

   (e) The Ku Klux Klan, which refuses to admit persons of color, Catholics, or Jews.

2. The Harlem African American Chamber of Commerce is an organization of 350 African American business people that meets monthly and addresses the concerns of Black-owned businesses in the Harlem section of New York City. Caucasian and Asian business-people are excluded from membership. Under Jaycees, Rotary, and N.Y. Club, would the exclusions be permissible?

NOTE: UNIVERSITY NONDISCRIMINATION POLICIES AND STUDENT RELIGIOUS ORGANIZATIONS

The tension between freedom of association and a university nondiscrimination policy has arisen in several recent cases involving official recognition of student groups by public law schools. Pending before the Supreme Court as this edition went to press is Christian Legal Society Chapter of University of California, Hastings College of the Law v. Martinez, cert. granted, 130 S.Ct. 795 (2009). The Christian Legal Society of Hastings College of the Law was a local chapter of the Christian Legal Society, a national organization. Like many educational institutions, Hastings, which is a self-standing public law school affiliated with the University of California, has a broad nondiscrimination policy that covers all aspects of college life including student activities. Student organizations at Hastings must be registered to obtain various benefits provided by the law school, including the use of the school's name and logo, the use of certain means of communicating with Hastings students, access to particular law school facilities, and eligibility to apply for limited funds. Hastings' interpretation of its nondiscrimination policy requires registered groups to allow any interested student to participate and serve as voting members and officers even if they disagree with the mission of the group. CLS was denied registration as a student organization on the ground that its members were required to affirm a Statement of Faith that obligated officers and members to adhere to orthodox Christian beliefs, which CLS interpreted as including a prohibition on sexual conduct between persons of the same sex.

The law school would not allow CLS to register as a student organization unless it opened its membership to all students irrespective of their religious beliefs or sexual orientation. CLS sued in federal court, alleging that its rights to freedom of expressive association, free speech and freedom of religion were violated. The district court, in a decision affirmed by the Ninth Circuit in a two-sentence unsigned disposition,[1] held that CLS's speech rights were not violated because the nondiscrimination policy affected conduct not speech—i.e., it regulated what CLS must do if it wanted to become registered. The court reasoned that Hastings through its registration policy had created a limited public forum, which was viewpoint-neutral and reasonable. CLS's rights of expressive association were not infringed as the college was not directly ordering the organization to admit students but merely placing conditions on the use of its campus as a forum and CLS's eligibility to receive a small subsidy available to registered student organizations. Does this decision mean a Muslim students association must admit Buddhists, or an atheist group offer membership and even leadership positions to believers in God?

A similar issue was raised In Christian Legal Society v. Walker, 453 F.3d 853 (7th Cir. 2006), where a chapter of the Christian Legal Society sued Southern Illinois University. SIU's law school dean had declined to recognize CLS on the ground that it violated the university's nondiscrimination policy by denying membership to students who engaged in or affirmed homosexual conduct. A divided Seventh Circuit, reversing the district court, granted a request for a preliminary injunction to compel the university to restore CLS's official status after finding that CLS had shown a likelihood of success on the merits. The court concluded that application of the university's nondiscrimination policy would have significantly affected CLS's ability to sincerely and effectively convey a message of disapproval of certain types of conduct if at the same time it had to accept members who engaged in that conduct. It also held that the university's interest in preventing discrimination did not outweigh the organization's interest in expressing its views, and found that it was unclear whether CLS had even violated any university policy because no students were denied membership

---

1. Neither the district court nor Ninth Circuit decisions were officially reported, but they are available on Westlaw. The district court decision is Christian Legal Society Chapter of University of California v. Kane, 2005 WL 850864 (N.D.Cal. April 12, 2005), aff'd, 319 Fed.Appx. 645 (9th Cir. 2009).

based on sexual orientation, and CLS had not discriminated in employment because it had no employees.

1. *For Further Reading.* Joan W. Howarth, Teaching Freedom: Exclusionary Rights of Student Groups, 42 U.C. Davis L. Rev. 889 (2009); Note, Leaving Religious Students Speechless: Public University Antidiscrimination Policies and Religious Student Organizations, 118 Harv. L. Rev. 2882 (2005); Charles J. Russo & William Thro, The Constitutional Rights Of Politically Incorrect Groups: Christian Legal Society v. Walker As An Illustration, 33 J.C. & U.L. 361 (2006); Mark Andrew Snider, Viewpoint Discrimination by Public Universities: Student Religious Organizations and Violations of University Nondiscrimination Policies, 61 Wash. & Lee L. Rev. 841 (2004); Eugene Volokh, Freedom of Expressive Association and Government Subsidies, 58 Stan. L. Rev. 1919 (2006).

2. *Male Only Fraternities.* Can a male fraternity discriminate on the basis of sex? The College of Staten Island ("CSI"), a unit of the City University of New York, required student groups to comply with CSI's nondiscrimination policy in order to obtain recognition, which would offer a variety of benefits including the use of CSI's facilities, insurance, and rights to use of the CSI name. Chi Iota was a social fraternity that did not admit women. Although the fraternity identified itself as a Jewish organization devoted to "the inculcation of the traditional values of men's college social fraternities, community service and the expression of Jewish culture," most of its members were non-practicing Jews. It welcomed non-Jewish members, and several current members were not Jewish. Many of the fraternity's activities involved nonmembers.

Chi Iota was denied college recognition, because it failed to comply with CSI's nondiscrimination policy by discriminating against women. The fraternity filed suit alleging it was an intimate association and being forced to admit women would be an unconstitutional burden on its associational rights. The district court, applying a strict scrutiny standard, granted a preliminary injunction because CSI's policy affected a constitutionally protected interest. The Court of Appeals for the Second Circuit reversed. Chi Iota v. City University of New York, 502 F.3d 136 (2d Cir. 2007). Rather than apply a categorical strict scrutiny approach in dealing with association-rights cases, the court asked whether a balancing of all pertinent facts justified the state intrusion on the particular associational freedom. It measured the degree of the fraternity's associational interest by examining its size, purpose, selectivity and whether others were excluded from critical aspects of the relationship. The court found the size limitation was the product of circumstances and not a desire to maintain intimacy. The fraternity did employ care in selecting members, but upon a graduation it lost contact with its members and had to replace them. Most of those who attended the first recruitment rush were invited back. Chi Iota's purposes were inclusive, broad public minded goals that did not depend for their promotion on close-knit bonds. The fraternity involved nonmembers in several crucial aspects of its existence and gave parties to which nonmembers were encouraged to attend. The court held that the college's denial of recognition was not a substantial imposition on the fraternity's rights of association because the state had a substantial interest in prohibiting sex discrimination, which was no less compelling because federal antidiscrimination statutes exempted fraternities.

2.   JUDICIAL INTERVENTION INTO CHURCH DISPUTES

Owen v. Rosicrucian Fellowship

[p. 959, supra]

The Constitutional guarantee of free exercise of religion affords religious organizations substantial autonomy in conducting their internal affairs. Courts ordinarily will dismiss church doctrinal disputes as beyond their competence and will abstain from adjudicating the merits unless the determination of rights to the use of church property is necessary. Note, Developments in the Law–Judicial Control of Private Associations, 76 Harv. L. Rev. 983, 1055 (1963). In this latter situation, courts will defer to the ecclesiastical autonomy on all doctrinal questions.

As discussed in the excerpt below, church disputes arise in a number of contexts: disagreements over the ownership of church property, the retention of ministers, whether church buildings should be replaced, the expulsion of members and the process involved, or allegations of breach of fiduciary duties by church officials in the handling of property.

Ira Mark Ellman, Driven from the Tribunal: Judicial Resolution of Internal Church Disputes

69 Calif. L. Rev. 1378, 1382–1389, 1397–1400 (1981).

A court drawn into an internal religious dispute will surely become "entangled" in church affairs. Judicial authority will be brought to bear on a religious matter in which the state has no apparent secular interest. Almost any church dispute can be characterized as doctrinal, and it seems self-evident that the religion clauses forbid secular authorities from making pronouncements identifying the true doctrine. There could hardly be more certain markers of the "forbidden domain." The independence of churches and the religious freedom of their members are apparently endangered by intervention.

Internal religious disputes, however, unlike other religion cases, do not involve a meddlesome government gratuitously inserting itself into church affairs. They are requests by one faction of the church—sometimes by both factions—that the court act as referee. The stakes may be distinctly secular, as where property is concerned. Moreover, almost all cases involve the kind of dispute that the court would normally decide in the context of a secular nonprofit association and involve rights ordinarily recognized under corporation, contract, or trust law. * * *

Since its 1871 decision in Watson v. Jones, the Supreme Court, as well as most state courts, has assumed that the judiciary could intervene more freely to settle disputes in "congregational" churches than in "hierarchial" churches.[19] Under this traditional analysis, courts have often held that there is a rule of deference to the decisions of the central hierarchies that effectively bars any review of their decisions. The Supreme Court cases do not, however, support any rule of deference to hierarchical church authorities. Rather, the Court has employed a number of different rationales from case to case, in a groping and not entirely consistent fashion that has continued through its most recent decision, Jones v. Wolf. * * *

The literature of church disputes contains repeated references to the 1871 Supreme Court decision in Watson v. Jones. *Watson* involved a local congregation in Louisville, called the Walnut Street Presbyterian Church. The congregation had divided into two factions during the Civil War. A majority of the congregation's ruling "elders" were of the proslavery faction, while a majority of the church members were of the antislavery faction. The antislavery faction, with the support of the central Presbyterian Church, chose new elders, but the incumbents refused to recognize them. An action was brought to oust the proslavery elders from their control over the church property. The proslavery faction had meanwhile joined forces with sympathizers in other congregations to form the Presbyterian Church of the Confederate States, the hierarchy to which this faction now claimed allegiance. They rejected the original hierarchy, claiming that it had abandoned the "true" Presbyterian faith.

The issue in *Watson* was control over the property of the Walnut Street Church, but its facts raised almost every question that arises in court adjudication of church disputes: In this fight between competing sets of "elders," what weight should the court give to the hierarchy's endorsement? Which hierarchy? Should a court consider that claim that the original hierarchy's departure from the faith robbed it of its authority? Were the new, antislavery elders properly chosen under church rules?

---

19. While the distinction between the two categories may not always be clear, the essential difference in the Court's view is that the hierarchical church has a central authority to which local congregations are subject, while in the congregational church there is no authority over the local congregation. * * * The extent of central church authority may vary, of course; it might include final power over doctrinal matters, and a role in the selection of clergymen for the local congregation. On the other hand, while congregational churches may have national denominational associations, those are merely voluntary vehicles for such joint action as the member churches may wish to participate in, and have no ecclesiastical or secular authority over the local congregations. The Baptists are probably the most numerous denomination with a congregational polity, and courts have repeatedly treated Baptist churches as congregational for the purpose of this constitutional doctrine. * * * [T]he line between hierarchical and congregational churches is anything but clear, and in at least one case, an association of Baptist churches has been found to be hierarchical. * * *

Most other large Protestant denominations as well as the Roman Catholic Church are hierarchical in structure. At various times the Presbyterian Church, the Methodist Church, and the Lutheran Church have all been held to be hierarchical for the purpose of this doctrine. * * * In the case of the Lutheran Church, however, the courts have gone both ways. * * *

Should a court examine those rules to decide whether the new elders were in fact entitled to office?

The Court avoided most of these questions with a narrow ruling. It held that by setting up the competing hierarchy, the proslavery elders withdrew from the church and therefore abandoned any property rights in it which they might have had. This conclusion led to a decision for the antislavery faction of the local church, and implied as well that the original hierarchy had not been supplanted. Although logic required no further elaboration, the Court took the opportunity presented by the case to treat the entire question of church disputes in a comprehensive fashion. * * *

Four basic propositions in *Watson* have had such a continuing life. The first proposition is rather straightforward: Disputes between factions of congregational churches "must be determined by the ordinary principles which govern voluntary associations." *Watson* clearly contemplated courts performing the contract function in such cases, and performing it by application of ordinary contract rules. It assumes, for example, that the court might examine church documents to decide whether a particular decision may be made by the officers of the church, or whether it requires a vote of the congregation. * * *

Watson's three remaining principles are intended to apply to hierarchical churches, and it is these three which have caused the difficulties. All three require civil courts to accept as binding the decisions of church authorities in questions of "discipline, faith, ecclesiastical rule, custom, or law." But *Watson* offers three different rationales for this conclusion. These three rationales have generated three principles for handling church disputes.

[The contract] principle requires a court to sustain hierarchical decisions because "all who unite themselves to such a body do so with an implied consent to this government, and are bound to submit to it." *Watson* adds that appeals from decisions of church tribunals should be allowed when "the organism itself provides." When church members, by joining the church, have implicitly agreed to be bound by a hierarchy's decisions, the court will not review those decisions. But the court defers to the hierarchy only because the parties' agreement makes deference appropriate. This approach is consistent with that employed for congregational churches, as well as secular organizations, because it applies the parties' agreement.

Watson says that a civil court should never decide ecclesiastical questions because "the law knows no heresy, and is committed to the support of no dogma, the establishment of no sect." This is the "ban on doctrinal decisions." * * *

This final principle [strict deference] from *Watson* assumes that there is some overriding concern for religious autonomy that cannot be successfully satisfied if doctrine and contract form the only limits on judicial intervention. * * * It requires the court to defer to the hierarchy even when challengers make such jurisdictional or procedural objections to its decisions.

The strict deference principle is thus significantly different from the other principles enunciated in *Watson*. It conflicts with the contract principle, which is founded on the parties' "consent to be bound." * * * For example, under the ban on doctrinal decisions, courts could not review the substance of a hierarchical determination of the morality of abortion, yet it could consider a claim that church law preserves to local congregations the right to choose their minister. * * *

Its most recent decision, Jones v. Wolf, decided in 1979, indicates that five members of the Court may have second thoughts about strict deference [to a hierarchy's decision.]; * * * *Jones* approved a limited application of contract principles in judicial decisions involving church disputes. No clear rule has emerged from *Jones*, however, because the Court was closely divided and the majority opinion left many questions unanswered.

In *Jones*, the Court again dealt with a Presbyterian congregation in Georgia that had decided to declare its independence from the central church. The local congregation was split over the withdrawal, however, and a commission appointed by the hierarchy concluded that the loyal minority faction was the "true congregation." Representatives of that faction brought an action in Georgia state court to oust the disloyal majority from their control over the property.

* * *

[T]he Georgia courts found no language of trust in favor of the hierarchy in the deeds or in the Book of Church Order, the "constitution" setting forth the governing rules for Presbyterian churches. The Georgia court therefore concluded that the congregation's majority had absolute title to the church property, and could take it with them when they seceded from the national organization.

The Supreme Court vacated the Georgia court's decision in a five to four vote. The opinion, written by Justice Blackmun, approved the Georgia court's use of "neutral principles": to decide that the local congregation, and not the mother church, controlled church property. It remanded the case, however, because the state court did not adequately explain the grounds for its determination that the local congregation should be controlled by the majority faction.

Jones was the first time a Court majority explicitly recognized the advantages of allowing religious organizations to adopt their own organizational structures through deeds, constitutions, or agreements and, of enforcing these arrangements on the same basis as any other private agreements. The majority's neutral principles doctrine is not the simple application of ordinary contract and trust law principles, however. The *Jones* Court, * * * limited the use of contract principles by barring judicial construction of religious terms that might be found in the relevant documents. It said a court encountering religious terms must follow the interpretation given by the "authoritative ecclesiastical body." The Court approved of the Georgia court's application of "neutral principles" because no forbidden interpretation was involved.

The Court was troubled, however, by the Georgia court's assumption that the majority of the congregation controlled the local church. Justice Blackmun said that a state court may employ an initial presumption of majority rule, but must afford some method for rebutting it. He approved "any method," so long as it did not "impair free exercise rights" or lead to court entanglement in "matters of religious controversy." For example, he suggested that a corporate charter that provided for an alternate way of deciding a local church's governance would be adequate to overcome the presumption. He added, however, that "if" Georgia law provided that the will of the local congregation is to be determined according to church rules, the courts must defer to the central hierarchy's decision.

The implication of the "if" in the Court's discussion is that Georgia has the freedom, if it chooses, to declare church rules irrelevant to its determination, and to make the presumption of majority rule rebuttable only by some explicit provision in the property deed or corporate charter. On remand, the Georgia court chose to ignore the implication that it need not consider church rules. The court said that the presumption of majority rule could be overcome "by reliance upon neutral status, corporate charters, relevant deeds, *and the organizational constitutions of the denomination*." It announced that its review "of those sources," presumably including the church rules contained in the "organizational constitutions," disclosed no provision rebutting the presumption of majority rule.

Justice Powell's opinion for the four dissenters * * * rejected "neutral principles" as a feasible alternative. Having determined that the Presbyterian Church has a hierarchical form of government, and that the local congregation was a member of it, Justice Powell would have deferred to the decision of the hierarchy's tribunal, vesting control, and thus ownership of the property, in the loyal minority faction. That analysis intentionally ignores any organizational documents or deed language that might have placed some independent rights in the local congregation, for under strict deference such an inquiry would be irrelevant. Since the mother church had identified the loyal minority as the true congregation, there was no dispute between the congregation and the central church. And the hierarchy's exclusion of the disloyal majority was of course unreviewable. It is apparent that under strict deference a court would always enforce the hierarchy's view.

The decision in *Jones* makes it difficult to know just what latitude civil courts are now permitted in resolving church disputes. While the *Jones* majority clearly appreciated the appeal of decision rules based on ordinary contract and trust law principles—"neutral principles"—it was unwilling to embrace that approach without limitation. The difficulty lies in understanding the nature of this limitation. First, in what circumstances are documents too ecclesiastical in tone to permit judicial determination of their meaning? * * * Did the Court intend to make the hierarchy's right to control a local church turn on local law rather than on the church's own rules? What local laws would be unconstitutional because they violated free exercise rights or led to entanglement of civil courts in religious affairs? These questions remain unanswered.

* * *

The Supreme Court decisions from *Watson* to *Jones* suggest a troubled court unable to find an acceptable framework for analysis of the basic issue: what is the proper rule for civil courts to apply when asked to adjudicate internal church disputes?

NOTES

1. *The Limits of Religiously Motivated Acts*. Are there some religiously motivated acts that are undeserving of First Amendment protection? What if a wife religiously believed church doctrine held that it was her duty to burn herself on the funeral pyre of her dead husband? Would it be beyond the power of civil government to prevent such practices? See Reynolds v. United States, 98 U.S. (8 Otto) 145, 166–167, 25 L.Ed. 244 (1879).

2. *For Further Reading*. Michael William Galligan, Note, Judicial Resolution of Intrachurch Disputes, 83 Colum. L.Rev 2007 (1983); Patty Gerstenblith, Civil Court Resolution of Property Disputes Among Religious Organizations, 39 Am. U.L.Rev. 513 (1990); Kent Greenawalt, Hands Off! Civil Court Involvement in Conflicts Over Religious Property, 98 Colum.L.Rev. 1843 (1998); Developments in the Law–Religion and the State, Pt. VI Government Regulation of Religious Organizations, 100 Harv. L.Rev. 1606, 1740 (1987); William G. Ross, The Need for An Exclusive and Uniform Application of "Neutral Principles" in the Adjudication of Church Property Disputes, 32 St. Louis U.L.J. 263 (1987); Giovan Harbour Venable, Note: Courts Examine Congregationalism, 41 Stan. L.Rev. 719 (1989); Michael Weisberg, Balancing Cultural Integrity Against Individual Liberty: Civil Court Review of Ecclesiastical Judgments, 25 U. Mich. J.L.Ref. 955 (1992); David Young & Steven W. Tigges, Into the Religious Thicket— Constitutional Limits on Civil Court Jurisdiction Over Ecclesiastical Disputes, 47 Ohio St. L.J. 475 (1986).

PART FIVE

OTHER LEGAL ISSUES AFFECTING NONPROFIT ORGANIZATIONS

CHAPTER **11**   Antitrust and Nonprofits

CHAPTER 11

ANTITRUST AND NONPROFITS

A. INTRODUCTION

Sherman Act §§ 1, 2.

Clayton Act §§ 1, 7, 11.

The central thrust of antitrust law is to preserve and promote competition. The Sherman Act (15 U.S.C.A. §§ 1–7) and other antitrust statutes attempt to prevent concentrations of economic power that limit competition. In the words of the Supreme Court, the Sherman Act: " * * * was designed to be a comprehensive charter of economic liberty aimed at preserving free and unfettered competition as the rule of trade. * * * [U]nrestrained interaction of competitive forces will yield the best allocation of our economic resources, the lowest prices, the highest quality and the greatest material progress * * * [T]he policy unequivocally laid down by the act is competition." Northern Pac. R.R. v. United States, 356 U.S. 1, 4, 78 S.Ct. 514, 517 (1958). The primary beneficiary of the antitrust laws is the consumer. Jefferson Parish Hosp. Dist. No. 2 v. Hyde, 466 U.S. 2, 13, 104 S.Ct. 1551, 1558 (1984).

The Sherman Act's two main provisions provide that every contract, combination or conspiracy that unreasonably restrains trade or commerce is illegal (§ 1), and that every person who monopolizes trade, or attempts to monopolize or conspires to do so, shall have committed a felony (§ 2). The Clayton Act (15 U.S.C.A. §§ 12–14, 19–22, 27) declares illegal price discrimination—i.e., sales of a product at different prices to similarly situated buyers, exclusive dealing contracts requiring buyers to deal only with the seller, certain corporate mergers, and interlocking directorates. In evaluating a merger under § 1 of the Sherman Act or § 7 of the Clayton Act, courts consider the percentage of business the new merged entity would control, the strength of remaining competition, whether the action sprung from business requirements or purpose to monopolize, the possible development of the industry, consumer demands, and other characteristics of the market. United States v. General Dynamics Corp., 415 U.S. 486, 94 S.Ct. 1186 (1974); United States v. Columbia Steel Co., 334 U.S. 495, 527, 68 S.Ct. 1107, 1124 (1948).

In determining whether a business combination unreasonably restrains trade under the Sherman Act, courts have used two basic approaches: the *per se* rule and the rule of reason. The *per se* doctrine labels as illegal any practice to which it applies regardless of the reasons for the practice and without extended inquiry as to its effects. The rule of reason calls for a broad inquiry with respect to the purpose and the effects of the challenged business practice. Courts have sometimes used an abbreviated or "quick look" rule of reason, an intermediate standard, where *per se* condemnation is inappropriate, but no elaborate industry analysis is required to demonstrate the anticompetitive character of a suspected restraint. The *per se* rule has been applied to horizontal restraints—attempts to fix prices, to allocate territories, or to boycott various persons, as well as to certain vertical restraints—relationships that deal with buyers and sellers and the chain of distribution. In most cases involving nonprofit organizations, a rule of reason analysis has been utilized, permitting a broader inquiry into the special nature of the particular nonprofit.

Does "trade or commerce" include any activity in which an organization realizes financial gain even though the pursuit of profit is not its principal purpose, or does it include only those the activities of organizations whose primary purpose is to realize financial gain? The answer is the former. In the words of a leading treatise "All of the possible objectives of antitrust law—from efficient resource allocation, minimum production costs, and maximum innovation to equal access to the market and 'fair' distribution according to competitive standards—can implicate the activities of non-profit organizations. If the behavior is anticompetitive, the consequences are equally detrimental whether or not the actor pays dividends to its owners." Phillip Areeda & Herbert Hovenkamp, Antitrust Law § 261a (3d. ed. 2006 & 2009 Supp.). The courts have applied the antitrust laws to several kinds of mutual benefit nonprofits: labor unions, trade associations, amateur athletic associations, and medical regulatory associations. See generally Note, Antitrust and Nonprofit Entities, 94 Harv. L. Rev. 802 (1981). These organizations have been accused of collusive or exclusionary conduct. Although the organizations are organized in the nonprofit form, they are agents of for profit firms and individuals, so courts have ignored the nonprofit status and treat them functionally as if they were for profit organizations. Tomas J. Philipson & Richard A. Posner, Antitrust in the Not–For–Profit Sector, 52 J.L. & Econ. 1 (2009). Fewer cases have involved public benefit organizations. The extent to which the antitrust laws apply to nonprofits ultimately depends upon the purpose of those statutes. In Apex Hosiery Co. v. Leader, 310 U.S. 469, 60 S.Ct. 982 (1940) where the Supreme Court held union monopolization did not violate the antitrust laws, the court stated: "The end sought [by the Sherman Act] was the prevention of restraints to free competition in business and commercial transactions * * *." Id. at 493.

Subsequent Supreme Court decisions clearly have demonstrated that nonprofit status by itself does not provide sanctuary from the Sherman Act.[1] In Goldfarb v. Virginia State Bar, 421 U.S. 773, 95 S.Ct. 2004 (1975), which involved a challenge to minimum fees established by a county bar

---

1. The Robinson–Patman Act, 15 U.S.C.A. §§ 13–13c, 21a, which prohibits price discrimination that lessens competition, contains an exemption, § 13c, for supplies purchased for their own use by schools, colleges, universities, public libraries, churches, hospitals and charitable institutions not operated for profit.

association, the Bar maintained that competition was "inconsistent with the practice of a profession because enhancing profit is not the goal of professional activities," 421 U.S. at 786. The Supreme Court stated that Congress intended to strike as broadly as it could in § 1 of the Sherman Act, and to read so wide an exemption as urged by the Bar would be contrary to that purpose. Other nonprofit professional associations have come within the Sherman Act or the Federal Trade Commission Act.[2] See California Dental Ass'n v. F.T.C., 526 U.S. 756, 119 S.Ct. 1604 (1999); National Society of Professional Engineers v. United States, 435 U.S. 679, 98 S.Ct. 1355 (1978); Arizona v. Maricopa County Medical Society, 457 U.S. 332, 102 S.Ct. 2466 (1982); FTC v. Indiana Fed'n Dentists, 476 U.S. 447, 106 S.Ct. 2009 (1986). Judge Richard Posner in Hospital Corp. of America v. FTC, 807 F.2d 1381, 1390 (7th Cir.1986), cert. denied, 481 U.S. 1038, 107 S.Ct. 1975 (1987) observed: "Non-profit status affects the method of financing the enterprise * * * and the form in which profits * * * are distributed, and it may make management somewhat less beady-eyed in trying to control costs. * * * But no one has shown that it makes the enterprise unwilling to cooperate in reducing competition."

This chapter examines the application of the antitrust statutes to nonprofits by focusing on two important illustrations—first, mergers of nonprofit hospitals and second, group standardization of financial aid awards in higher education. In both the health care and education sectors, the usual commercial relationships are skewed by the type of services provided. The health care industry has certain characteristics which affect the normal laws of supply and demand including: third party payment which makes consumers of services less sensitive to the true costs of care; the absence of information and ability to monitor quality, which forces patients to follow the recommendations of their doctors, reducing the consumer incentive to "shop" for medical care; barriers to entry for new health care providers, such as certificates of need and licensing requirements; and ethical considerations in favor of creating available health care services to the largest number of people regardless of their ability to pay, causing demand to flow from need rather than from price or supply. Health Care Committee, Section of Antitrust Law, The Antitrust Health Care Handbook II 5–6 (3d ed. 2004).

In their application to higher education the antitrust laws clash against noncommercial virtues that restrain competition such as maximizing the number of scholarships to expand the pool of poorer students attending elite institutions or creating eligibility rules to preserve the special nature of college athletics. The Supreme Court, however, has not looked favorably or with complete clarity on noncommercial justifications for restraints on competition. Compare National Society of Professional Engineers v. United States, supra at 691 (1978) (noncommercial explanations can never justify

---

2. 15 U.S.C. § 45. The FTC Act gives the Federal Trade Commission authority to enforce the antitrust statutes and prohibits unfair competition and deceptive acts or practices. It overlaps with § 1 of the Sherman Act. FTC v. Indiana Federation of Dentists, 476 U.S. 447, 454–455, 106 S.Ct. 2009 (1986).

restraints on price competition) with NCAA v. Board of Regents, 468 U.S. 85, 102, 104 S.Ct. 2948, 2961 (1984) (regulations that prohibit pay for athletes or require class attendance preserve integrity of "product" and can only be accomplished by mutual agreement.)

B. HEALTH CARE

Clayton Act §§ 7, 11.

Federal Trade Commission Act § 4.

Barry R. Furrow, Sandra H. Johnson, Timothy S. Jost & Robert L. Schwartz, The Law of Health Care Organization and Finance

448–452 (1991).

The purpose of the antitrust laws is to prohibit private conduct that restrains trade, i.e., that impedes competition in markets for goods and services. * * * [M]any impediments exist in health care markets and some of these obstacles are attributable to intentional conduct on the part of health care professionals and institutions. Recent years have seen vigorous enforcement activity to remove these barriers, thus a competent health care attorney must have some familiarity with the antitrust laws. * * *

For most of this century, however, medical professionals and organizations engaged in health care escaped serious scrutiny. Beginning only in 1975, when the Supreme Court rejected the conventional wisdom that health care providers were exempt from antitrust enforcement as "learned professions," has antitrust law begun to play an important role in regulating the health care industry.

The application of the federal antitrust statutes to health care, however, continues to present problems related to the peculiarity of health care enterprises as compared to other businesses: What place is there for defenses related to concerns over the quality of health care in a statutory regime designed to enhance competition and to leave such issues to the market? Do not-for-profit health care providers conform to traditional economic assumptions about competitors? If they do not, should they somehow be treated differently under the statutes? What impact do regulatory controls such as certificate of need and professional licensure have on the application of federal antitrust law? Do market failures in health care, particularly imperfect information, suggest special approaches to applying antitrust law?

Section 1 of the Sherman Act provides: "Every contract, combination * * * or conspiracy, in restraint of trade or commerce among the several States * * * is hereby declared to be illegal." 15 U.S.C.A. § 1. This short statement raises three major issues requiring explanation. First, the activities prohibited by Section 1—contracts, combinations and conspiracies—require joint or collusive action. They require that two or more persons have acted together. A claim based on Section 1, then, must include proof of a concerted activity. One of the questions this presents in health care is whether a hospital and its medical staff are capable of conspiring or whether they should be treated, in effect, as one person. Second, the federal antitrust laws only proscribe restraints of "interstate commerce." Though the Supreme Court has shown a willingness to interpret this provision quite liberally, whether it reaches to the denial of staff privileges by a single hospital of a single doctor, for example, remains to be finally decided. Third, what kind of agreements restraining trade are prohibited by the Act? *All* contracts restrain trade, as they represent a commitment to provide particular services or goods to one party and set the price to the contracting buyer such that price thereafter is no longer allowed to change in response to competitive bids from other potential buyers or sellers. It was necessary, therefore, early in the history of Section 1, for the courts to interpret the statute to prohibit only "unreasonable" restraints of trade.

In recent years the Supreme Court and others have moved away from a rigid dichotomy between *per se* and rule of reason analysis, and now view the two forms as complementary modes of analysis. Thus, * * * the courts will now consider, however briefly, procompetitive justifications for suspect practices before attaching the *per se* label. Similarly, courts will truncate the inquiry under the rule of reason when they find convincing proof (such as a reduction in output or an absence of plausible justifications) that the conduct unreasonably restrains trade. During the past few years, the Supreme Court and others have at times indicated dissatisfaction with the *per se* rule. As the courts have begun to consider the application of the *per se* rule to activities in the health care setting, some have shied away from the presumptive illegality required by a *per se* violation, perhaps as a remnant of the deference that historically had been granted the "learned professions." As the courts have modified the *per se* rule at least in health care cases, some have used a "shorthand" form of the rule of reason in which the court examines the apparent effects of the activity but does not engage in the rather intensive examination required for full treatment under the rule of reason. This approach is still evolving but has been used in a number of health care cases.

Courts generally view horizontal restraints, as compared to vertical restraints, as more likely to violate the statute. Horizontal restraints are those among competitors at the same level of production or distribution. Examples include an agreement among area hospitals to charge the same *per diem* room prices (possibly, price-fixing); an agreement among physicians to refuse to admit patients to hospitals that employ non-physician health care professionals (possibly, a group boycott); or agreements between two hospitals in adjacent towns to market their services only in their own town or between two hospitals not to develop ancillary services already offered by the other (possibly, division of markets). Vertical restraints involve concerted action between competitors at different levels of production or distribution; for example, between buyers and sellers or manufacturers and retailers. Economic analysis of vertical restraints suggests that these restraints are likely to have significant pro-competitive effects and so may be inappropriate for the *per se* rule. A possible exception, still appropriate for *per se* treatment, is the tying arrangement, where a seller refuses to sell a product as to which it has power to control the market unless the buyer also purchases another "tied" product. Where do staff privileges decisions fit in this analysis? Are they horizontal restraints among competing physicians? Or are they vertical restraints between the "buyer" of physician services (the hospital) and the "seller" (the physicians)?

The concept of market power is critical to most Section 1 and all Section 2 claims. Under the rule of reason, Section 1 claims require that the plaintiff prove that the defendant has "market power." Section 2 of the Sherman Act prohibits monopolization and attempts to monopolize. A claim of illegal monopolization requires proof that the defendant enjoys sufficient market power to allow it to exclude competitors or control price. A second requirement to establish monopolization is the willful acquisition or maintenance of power as distinguished from growth or development resulting from a superior product, business skill or accident. To satisfy this requirement, courts tend to require plaintiff to show that the power was achieved or is maintained through illegitimate business practices.

Definition of a market for discerning market power requires two determinations. What is the relevant product market? And, what is the relevant geographic market? For example, for a hospital, is the relevant product in-patient services only, or does the hospital's product also include out-patient services? What range of products compete with the hospital's products? May consumers, for example, substitute non-hospital-based out-patient surgery for in-patient surgery? Is the relevant geographic market for a hospital the political subdivision (i.e., the city or the county) in which it is located; or its standard metropolitan statistical area; or all zip code areas from which the hospital draws any, or a significant number, of patients? Once the market is defined, the defendant's share of that market must be determined as a proxy for the defendant's market power. Other factors in addition to market share, such as ease of entry, may bear importantly on whether the market share data actually reflects market power.

Market definition is also critical to a major prohibition of the Clayton Act relevant to the health care industry. Section 7 of the Clayton Act prohibits mergers and acquisitions where the effect may be to "substantially lessen competition" or to "tend to create a monopoly." 15 U.S.C.A. § 18. (The Clayton Act also prohibits tying or exclusive dealing contracts and price discrimination.) In order to test the legality of a proposed merger or acquisition, a court must define the market share of the entities prior to the transaction and of the resulting organization after the transaction. As hospitals consolidate in response to cost containment and more intense competition, merger cases will become much more frequent.

Finally, Section 5 of the Federal Trade Commission Act prohibits unfair methods of competition (which include all Sherman Act and Clayton

Act violations) and unfair deceptive acts or practices (including deceptive advertising). Section 5 has been interpreted to grant the FTC the authority to enforce in civil suits the provisions of the Sherman Act and the Clayton Act. * * * The Department of Justice has authority to enforce the Sherman Act through both civil and criminal proceedings and the Clayton Act through civil actions. Finally, any person "injured" by a violation of the antitrust laws may bring a civil suit to enjoin the illegal act or practice or to recover treble damages. A prevailing plaintiff is also entitled to attorney's fees and costs. Not surprisingly, private parties have brought the vast majority of antitrust suits in health care. Individual physicians have sued hospitals over the denial of staff privileges. Nurse practitioners have sued doctors and hospitals over lack of access to facilities. Everyone has sued the private professional associations, such as the American Medical Association, that dominate health care.

There are several statutory and judicially-crafted defenses to antitrust liability, some of which are of importance to health care antitrust litigation. The antitrust state action doctrine exempts from antitrust liability actions taken pursuant to a clearly expressed state policy to restrict free competition, where the challenged conduct is under the active control and supervision of the state. The high degree of state regulation of health care has spawned state action defenses, in, for example, staff privileges cases, ultimately with little success. The McCarran–Ferguson Act generally exempts the "business of insurance" from antitrust enforcement to the extent that the particular insurance activities are regulated by state law. (This should not be taken to mean, however, that "insurance companies" are exempt from antitrust scrutiny). The Noerr–Pennington doctrine, developed in two Supreme Court cases in the 1960s, protects the exercise of the First Amendment right to petition the government, so long as the "petitioning" is not merely a "sham" to cover anti-competitive behavior. This defense is relevant in lobbying efforts on health care issues and to participation in administrative proceedings, such as certificate of need, each of which may lead to an outcome that lessens competition. The most recent statutory defense relevant to health care is the Health Care Quality Improvement Act, enacted by Congress in 1986, which grants limited immunity for peer review activities.

QUESTIONS

1. In an inquiry over anti-competitive practices, would a defense of preserving the quality of health care be justified when the antitrust laws seek to promote competition and allow the marketplace to determine quality?

2. Do nonprofit health care providers such as hospitals conform to the economic assumptions about for-profit competitors? If not, how should they be treated under the antitrust statutes?

NOTE: HOSPITAL MERGERS

Hospital mergers, once rare in the United States, became common in the 1980s as part of a broader structural transformation of the hospital industry and the development of new technologies and health care practices. Jonathan Baker, The Antitrust Analysis of Hospital Mergers and the Transformation of the Hospital Industry, 51 L. & Contemp. Probs. 93 (1988). During this period the application of the antitrust laws to health care institutions, even though nonprofit, became clearer than in the past.

The escalation of health care costs resulting from the passage of Medicare and Medicaid legislation in the 1960s forced Congress, commencing in 1974, to place limitations upon the amount of health care consumers might receive in hospitals. In the late 1970's, large hospital capital expenditures became subject to supervision of state regulatory boards through the requirement of a Certificate of Need (CON). Id. 96–97. Congress introduced the Prospective Pricing System (PPS) for Medicare reimbursement in 1983. Social Security Amendments of 1983, Pub. L. No. 98–21, Sections 601–697, 97 Stat. 85, 149–72 (codified as amended in scattered sections of 42 U.S.C.A.). PPS replaced the cost-based Medicare reimbursement system which allowed hospitals to bill Medicare for all reasonable charges for services provided to a patient no matter how extended the stay. Barry Furrow, et al., Health Law § 13–10 (1991). It provided for standardized predetermined payments to hospitals, reimbursing a hospital a fixed amount based upon patient diagnosis regardless of how much of the treatment of the diagnosed illness cost the hospital. PPS also capped physician reimbursement.

By rewarding cost-efficient hospital practices, PPS encouraged hospitals to reduce costs. PPS led to a decline in hospital admissions, stays and occupancy rates. Baker, supra, at 98–99. However, it impacted upon certain types of hospitals disproportionately. Institutions with significant commitments to uncompensated care and to individuals covered by Medicaid, such as many nonprofit hospitals, were affected by PPS more than hospitals whose patients were commercially insured or paid their own medical bills. William G. Kopit & Robert W. McCann, Toward a Definitive Antitrust Standard for Nonprofit Hospital Mergers, 13 J. Health Pol'y & Law 635, 638 (1988). This new market environment increased competition between hospitals and created additional pressures to reduce costs.

Accompanying PPS's introduction was the emergence of health maintenance organizations and preferred provider organizations, which lower health care costs through the conservative use of medical services and an emphasis on preventative care. These alternative health care providers increased price and non-price competition for hospitals. Furrow et al., supra, at § 13–12. Technological change also affected the demand for hospital services. Many treatments previously performed only in hospitals came to be performed on an outpatient basis at free standing medical, surgical and diagnostic centers. David L. Glazer, Comment: Clayton Act Scrutiny of Nonprofit Hospital Mergers: The Wrong Rx for Ailing Institutions, 66 Wash. L. Rev. 1041 (1991). The result of these changes, which transformed the American health care system, has been a rash of hospital mergers.

In 2009 there were 52 hospital mergers with a value of $1.676 billion, down from 60 mergers in 2008 worth $2.5796 billion. Irving Levin Report, Healthcare M & A for 2009 Reaches Second Highest Level in Decade, Jan. 19, 2010, available at http://www.levinassociates.com/pr2010/pr1001mamq4. When challenging hospital mergers the government has used Section 7 of the Clayton Act, which prohibits mergers or acquisitions that "tend to create a monopoly". 15 U.S.C.A. § 18. As United States v. Rockford, below, indicates, there is some question whether § 7 applies to nonprofit organizations. Mergers among health care providers are scrutinized by the Department of Justice or the Federal Trade Commission. In examining hospital mergers for antitrust concerns, the Department of Justice has attempted to determine whether a reduction in the number of firms in a particular market substantially increases the likelihood of collusion or other anti-competitive consequences. Baker, supra, at 114.

Since 1968 the Department of Justice has issued merger guidelines. The most recent edition, published in 1992 jointly with the Federal Trade Commission, uses a five-step analysis to evaluate whether horizontal merg-ers, acquisitions, tender offers or joint ventures between or among competi-tors will impermissibly lessen competition. Department of Justice & Feder-al Trade Commission Horizontal Merger Guidelines, 57 Fed. Reg. 41552 (1992), 4 Trade Reg. Rep. (CCH) ¶ 13,104 (Apr. 2, 1992), amended May 5, 1992 and April 8, 1997. The Guidelines' five-step analysis aids in determin-ing whether the combination leads to adverse competitive effects: (1) The definition, measurement and concentration of the relevant market in which the merging firms operate; (2) The potential adverse competitive effects flowing from the merger; (3) Whether entry into the relevant market by new firms would be "timely, likely, and sufficient" to counteract any adverse effects of the merger on competition; (4) Whether the merger would result in "significant net efficiencies"; and (5) whether either merging party qualifies as a "failing firm." Health Care Committee, Sec-tion of Antitrust Law, The Antitrust Health Care Handbook II 56–57 (1993).

In September 2009, the Department of Justice and the Federal Trade Commission announced that they would solicit public comments and hold a series of five workshops to consider potential revisions to the Guidelines, which had remained unchanged for seventeen years. The review process is intended to ensure that the Guidelines accurately reflect current agency practice and incorporate developments in the fields of economics and antitrust analysis. At the final workshop in January 2010, an assistant attorney general in the antitrust division stated that the review process has identified "gaps between the Guidelines and actual agency practice" as well as developments in merger analysis. In particular, the sequential nature of the Guidelines' five-step analytical process should be deemphasized in favor of a more integrated fact-driven analysis directed at competitive effects. See Christine A. Varney, An Update on the Review of the Horizontal Merger

Guidelines, Remarks as Prepared for the Horizontal Merger Guidelines Review Project's Final Workshop, January 26, 2010, available at http:// www.justice.gov/atr/public/speeches/254577.htm. There was no indication when new guidelines would be issued.

In a leading case, In re Hospital Corp. of America, 106 F.T.C. 361 (1985), aff'd Hospital Corp. of Am. v. FTC, 807 F.2d 1381 (7th Cir.1986), cert. denied, 481 U.S. 1038, 107 S.Ct. 1975 (1987), the Hospital Corp. of America (HCA), a proprietary hospital chain, acquired Hospital Affiliates International in a $650 million stock transaction. As a result, HCA obtained ownership or management of five acute area hospitals in the Chattanooga, Tennessee area. Several months later HCA obtained control of a sixth Chattanooga hospital through its acquisition of the Health Care corporation. HCA thereby became owner or manager of seven of the fourteen hospitals in the six-county Chattanooga metropolitan area. Ultimately, HCA was ordered to divest itself of two of the facilities acquired in its purchase of HIA and HCC and enjoined from further acquisitions in the Chattanooga area without prior FTC approval.

One of the arguments used by HCA to deflect the possible lack of competition resulting from the merger was that several of the hospitals in the Chattanooga area were nonprofit institutions. HCA claimed the nonprofit hospitals had no incentive to maximize profits but would seek to maximize output of the number of patients treated, and nonprofit hospitals had other objectives such as providing the most sophisticated and highest quality care available or pursuing religious or governmental goals. Thus, collusion would not occur because the for-profit and nonprofit competitors had no common interests. The Federal Trade Commission disagreed, commenting that the nonprofit status of market participants was no guarantee of competitive behavior. It noted that nonprofit hospital administrators might seek to maximize their personal benefits and comfort through profit-seeking activities and concluded that the specific characteristics of the nonprofit hospitals in the Chattanooga area market made anti-competitive behavior a reasonable probability. HCA, manager of two of six nonprofit hospitals in the Chattanooga area and two other major nonprofit hospitals, had incentives to participate in price collusion, because it had to subsidize unreimbursed care for indigents out of the rates charged to paying customers. Therefore, the hospitals could not compete through price cutting.

In 1988 the Department of Justice focused on nonprofit hospital mergers and attempted to enjoin the combinations of nonprofit hospitals in Roanoke, Virginia and Rockford, Illinois.

United States v. Rockford Memorial Corp.

United States Court of Appeals, Seventh Circuit, 1990.
898 F.2d 1278, cert. denied, 498 U.S. 920, 111 S.Ct. 295.

■ POSNER, CIRCUIT JUDGE.

The United States brought suit under section 7 of the Clayton Act and section 1 of the Sherman Act (15 U.S.C. §§ 18, 1) to enjoin a merger of the two largest hospitals—both nonprofits—in Rockford, Illinois, a city of 140,000 people. The district judge held that the merger violated section 7, and issued the injunction; he did not reach the section 1 charge.

The defendants appeal, arguing first that section 7 does not apply to a merger between nonprofit enterprises. Surprisingly, this is an issue of first impression at the appellate level, with the exception of an unpublished opinion by the Fourth Circuit, of which more later. Section 7 provides that "[1] no person * * * shall acquire * * * the whole or any part of the *stock or other share capital* and [2] no person *subject to the jurisdiction of the Federal Trade Commission* shall acquire the whole or any part of the assets of another person," where the effect may be substantially to lessen competition, or to tend to create a monopoly. (Emphasis added.) Illinois law forbids a nonprofit corporation to have, and these hospitals do not have, stock or share capital. So the clause we have labeled [1] would seem not to apply. And, the defendants argue, the FTC has no jurisdiction over a nonprofit corporation—so that the merger is not covered by the clause referring to asset acquisitions, clause [2], either—because section 4 of the Federal Trade Commission Act confines the Commission's jurisdiction under the Act to a "company * * * or association, incorporated or unincorporated, which is organized to carry on business for its own profit or that of its members." 15 U.S.C. § 44 [in 1999 the Supreme Court held that the F.T.C. Act applies to nonprofits, California Dental Ass'n v. F.T.C., 526 U.S. 756, 119 S.Ct. 1604 (1999), Eds.]

The first argument, knocking out clause [1], is strong. The second argument, however, in assuming that the reference in section 7 to "person[s] subject to the jurisdiction of the Federal Trade Commission" is to the Federal Trade Commission Act, overlooks the possibility that the reference is actually to the provision in the Clayton Act itself concerning the jurisdiction of the FTC—namely section 11, 15 U.S.C. § 21. Section 11 vests authority to enforce the prohibitions of the Clayton Act in five agencies. These are the Interstate Commerce Commission, with respect to the common carriers regulated by that Commission; the Federal Communications Commission, with respect to the common carriers regulated by it; ditto for the Civil Aeronautics Board (now defunct); the Federal Reserve Board, for banks; and, for everyone else, the FTC: "Authority to enforce compliance with sections 2, 3, 7, and 8 of this Act by the persons respectively subject thereto is hereby vested in * * * the Federal Trade Commission where applicable to all other character of commerce." Section 11 goes on to prescribe the procedure to be followed by these commissions and boards that have been given jurisdiction to enforce the Act. The procedure is self-contained and does not depend on particular provisions in the agencies' organic statutes, so that when in 1950 Congress amended section 7 to broaden its reach, it amended section 11 as well. We believe that the force of the assets-acquisition provision in section 7 is, therefore, merely to exempt mergers in the regulated industries enumerated in section 11. Areeda & Turner, Antitrust Law ¶ 906, at p. 797 n. 2 (1989 Supp.). Those industries do not include the hospital industry. The Clayton Act evinces a purpose of limiting the Federal Trade Commission's jurisdiction vis-a-vis that of other federal agencies charged with enforcing the Act in the industries that they regulate, but it evinces no purpose of exempting nonprofit firms in industries within the domain that the Act bestows on the Commission ("all other character of commerce").

The government amazingly has failed to make this argument (thus waiving it), substituting an unnecessarily venturesome argument that the acquisition of control of a nonprofit corporation is the acquisition of that corporation's stock or share capital within the meaning of section 7 (and hence comes within clause [1]), even though a nonprofit corporation does not have any stock or share capital and could not under relevant state law. The government points out that in United States v. Philadelphia National Bank, 374 U.S. 321, 335–49, 83 S.Ct. 1715, 1726–33, 10 L.Ed.2d 915 (1963), the Supreme Court held that a bank merger was a stock acquisition for purposes of section 7, though in corporate law it is an asset acquisition. There was no indication, the Court pointed out, that Congress had by its references to the FTC in sections 7 and 11 intended to exempt mergers by regulated firms; and while the acquiring firm in a merger does not actually acquire the stock of the acquired firm—it acquires the assets, in exchange either for stock of the acquiring firm or, in the case of a consolidation (the actual transaction in that case), for new stock—the effect is the same. Id. at 336–38, 83 S.Ct. at 1726–27.

The approach to statutory interpretation that informs Philadelphia National Bank is controversial, but it is neither indefensible nor irrelevant to the interpretive question in the present case. The approach, premised on recognition that legislative draftsmanship is often a rushed and clumsy process, deficient in foresight, tries to carry out the purposes of the statute insofar as these can be inferred, even if the result is a wide departure from literal meaning. But whatever its merits, it is not an approach in vogue in the Supreme Court at the moment and we hesitate to push it further than it was pushed in Philadelphia National Bank. We would be pushing it further if we read the words "stock" and "share capital" in section 7 as if they were synonyms for "control" (which is what would be acquired by this merger), although there are passages in the Philadelphia Bank opinion that can be quoted in support of the extension.

We are especially reluctant to test the elasticity of our interpretive powers without good reason, the only reason here being that the government overlooked a solid argument, based on section 11 of the Clayton Act, which would eliminate the loophole that the government rather desperately asks us to fill by a far-out interpretation of section 7. We decline the invitation, and conclude that as the parties have framed the issues the merger is not subject to section 7. The qualification is important, for we believe (contrary to United States v. Carilion Health System, 707 F.Supp. 840, 841 n. 1 (W.D.Va.), aff'd without opinion, 892 F.2d 1042 (4th Cir. 1989)) that the merger is subject to section 7, once the reference in that section to the jurisdiction of the FTC is understood, as we think it should be understood, to refer to section 11 of the Clayton Act rather than to section 4 of the FTC Act.

The government has a fallback position, however: the merger violates section 1 of the Sherman Act, as charged alternatively in the complaint. Although the district judge did not find it necessary to reach the issue, we can do so, without impropriety, since the subordinate findings that the judge made demonstrate a section 1 violation. We can affirm a decision by a district court on an alternative ground that has not been waived, and this ground has not been; it has been briefed and argued by both sides.

We doubt whether there is a substantive difference today between the standard for judging the lawfulness of a merger challenged under section 1 of the Sherman Act and the standard for judging the same merger challenged under section 7 of the Clayton Act. It is true that the operative language of the two provisions is different and that some of the old decisions (old by antitrust standards anyway) speak as if that should make a difference. A transaction violates section 1 of the Sherman Act if it restrains trade; it violates the Clayton Act if its effect may be substantially to lessen competition. But both statutory formulas require, and have received, judicial interpretation; and the interpretations have, after three quarters of a century, converged. 2 Areeda & Turner, Antitrust Law, ¶ 304 (1978); 4 id., ¶ 906, at p. 22.

* * *

Even if we are wrong that the standards under section 1 of the Sherman Act and section 7 of the Clayton Act have converged, and even if we are right that the teaching of Lexington Bank that a large horizontal merger (we mean of course large relative to its market) violates section 1 has been superseded, and even if the consequence of all this is that the old Columbia Steel decision remains canonical for mergers challenged under section 1, the defendants are still in deep trouble. The Court in Columbia Steel thought that a merger which created a 24 percent firm was not anticompetitive in the unusual conditions of the industry [United States v. Columbia Steel, 334 U.S. 495, 68 S.Ct. 1107, 92 L.Ed. 1533 (1948)], here we have a far larger merger and, as we shall see, such unusual conditions as may be present in the hospital industry reinforce rather than undermine the inference naturally to be drawn from the defendants' combined market share.

But all this is provided the district court's market definition is accepted. The "market" is the denominator of the fraction the numerator of which is the output of the defendants or some other select group of firms; the denominator is given by the output of the suppliers to which a group of customers can turn for their requirements of a particular product. Market share is the fraction of that output that is controlled by a particular supplier or particular suppliers whose market power we wish to assess. The higher the aggregate market share of a small number of suppliers, the easier it is for them to increase price above the competitive level without losing so much business to other suppliers as to make the price increase unprofitable; this is the power we call market power.

The district judge estimated the combined market share of the parties to the merger (hospitals of roughly equal size—the two largest in Rockford) at between 64 and 72 percent, depending on whether beds, admissions, or patient days are used as the measure of output. And he estimated the combined market share of the three largest hospitals in Rockford after the merger at 90 percent. Three firms having 90 percent of the market can raise prices with relatively little fear that the fringe of competitors will be able to defeat the attempt by expanding their own output to serve customers of the three large firms. An example will show why. To take away 10 percent of the customers of the three large firms in our hypothetical case, thus reducing those firms' aggregate market share from 90 percent to 81 percent, the fringe firms would have to increase their own output by 90 percent (from 10 to 19 percent of the market). This would take a while, surely, and would force up their costs, perhaps steeply—the fact they are so small suggests that they would incur sharply rising costs in trying almost to double their output, and that it is this prospect which keeps them small. So the three large firms could collude to raise price (within limits of course) above the competitive level without incurring the additional transaction costs and risk of exposure that would result from their trying to coordinate their actions with that of their small competitors.

This analysis, however, collapses if customers can turn to suppliers who (or products that) have been excluded from the market. The market defined by the district judge consists of the provision of inpatient services by acute-care hospitals in Rockford and its hinterland. The defendants point out correctly that a growing number of services provided by acute-care hospitals are also available from nonhospital providers. But the force of the point eludes us. If a firm has a monopoly of product X, the fact that it produces another product, Y, for which the firm faces competition is irrelevant to its monopoly unless the prices of X and Y are linked. For many services provided by acute-care hospitals, there is no competition from other sorts of provider. If you need a kidney transplant, or a mastectomy, or if you have a stroke or a heart attack or a gunshot wound, you will go (or be taken) to an acute-care hospital for inpatient treatment. The fact that for other services you have a choice between inpatient care at such a hospital and outpatient care elsewhere places no check on the prices of the services we have listed, for their prices are not linked to the prices of services that are not substitutes or complements. If you need your hip replaced, you can't decide to have chemotherapy instead because it's available on an outpatient basis at a lower price. Nor are the prices of hip replacement and chemotherapy linked. The defendants' counsel correctly noted that diet soft drinks sold to diabetics are not a relevant product market, but that is because the manufacturers cannot separate their diabetic customers from their other customers and charge the former a higher price. Hospitals can and do distinguish between the patient who wants a coronary bypass and the patient who wants a wart removed from his foot; these services are not in the same product market merely because they have a common provider. The defendants do not argue for the broader market on the basis of substitutability in supply—that is, the ability of a provider of outpatient services to switch to inpatient services should the price of the latter rise as a result of collusive pricing, making such services more profitable.

The more difficult issue is the geographical market. The defendants offered evidence, which the judge accepted, that their service area is a ten-county area of northern Illinois and southern Wisconsin centered on Rockford. Medicare records the address of all hospital patients, so it was possible to determine the zip codes from which the defendants draw their patients. The district judge noticed that 87 percent of the defendants' patients come from an area surrounding Rockford and consisting of the rest of Winnebago County (the county in which Rockford is located) and pieces of several other counties; the remaining patients are widely scattered. The defendants accept the area picked out by the district judge as a reasonable approximation of their service area (though not of the relevant market). There are four other acute-care hospitals in that area. Their output (as measured, we said, by beds, admissions, or patient days, all of which are highly correlated) plus that of the defendants is the market that the judge used to estimate the defendants' market share.

The defendants point out correctly that the hospitals in the defendants' service area may not exhaust the alternatives open to the residents of that area. Maybe a lot of people who live in Rockford, or if not in Rockford then at the edge of the Rockford hospitals' service area at the farthest possible distance from Rockford that is still within that area, use hospitals outside the area. Maybe—but the record shows that the six hospitals in the defendants' service area, plus a hospital in Beloit just north of the service area, account for 83 percent of the hospitalizations of residents of the service area, and that 90 percent of Rockford residents who are hospitalized are hospitalized in Rockford itself. For highly exotic or highly elective hospital treatment, patients will sometimes travel long distances, of course. But for the most part hospital services are local. People want to be hospitalized near their families and homes, in hospitals in which their own—local—doctors have hospital privileges. There are good hospitals in Rockford, and they succeed in attracting most of the hospital patients not only from Rockford itself but from the surrounding area delineated by the district judge. The exclusion of the Beloit hospital from the market was not adequately explained, but apparently does not affect the figures materially.

It is always possible to take pot shots at a market definition (we have just taken one), and the defendants do so with vigor and panache. Their own proposal, however, is ridiculous—a ten-county area in which it is assumed (without any evidence and contrary to common sense) that Rockford residents, or third-party payors, will be searching out small, obscure hospitals in remote rural areas if the prices charged by the hospitals in Rockford rise above competitive levels. Forced to choose between two imperfect market definitions, the defendants' and the district judge's (the latter a considerable expansion of the government's tiny proposed market), and bound to review the judge's determination under the deferential "clearly erroneous" standard, we choose the less imperfect, the district judge's.

The defendants' immense shares in a reasonably defined market create a presumption of illegality. Of course many factors other than the number and size distribution of firms affect the propensity to collude, but here as in Hospital Corporation of America, a factually similar case, most of them strengthen rather than weaken the inference of market power from market shares. Regulatory limitations on entry into the hospital industry increase the propensity to collude by preventing (or at least delaying and increasing the cost of) entry by new competitors to take advantage of an increase in prices. And neither generally nor in this instance does the existence of regulation work an implied repeal of the antitrust laws. The excess capacity that is part of the motivation for the regulatory limitations is itself an incentive to collude, although excess capacity in the competitive fringe reduces the feasibility of collusion—but concerning that excess capacity there is no evidence in the record. The urgencies of medical care and the prevalence of third-party (insurance or governmental) payment no doubt dilute price sensitivity, but that this weakens—rather than strengthens— the importance of encouraging competition is far from obvious.

We would not repeat any more of what we said in Hospital Corporation but for the emphasis that the defendants place on their status as nonprofit corporations. This status, they argue, removes any ground for concern that they might seek to maximize profits through avoidance of price or service competition. If this is correct, the Supreme Court was wrong in National Collegiate Athletic Ass'n v. Board of Regents, 468 U.S. 85, 100 n. 22, 104 S.Ct. 2948, 2960 n. 22, 82 L.Ed.2d 70 (1984), to reject an implicit exemption of nonprofit enterprises from the antitrust laws. We are aware of no evidence—and the defendants present none, only argument—that nonprofit suppliers of goods or services are more likely to compete vigorously than profit-making suppliers. Most people do not like to compete, and will seek ways of avoiding competition by agreement tacit or explicit, depending of course on the costs of agreeing. The ideology of nonprofit enterprise is cooperative rather than competitive. If the managers of nonprofit enterprises are less likely to strain after that last penny of profit, they may be less prone to engage in profit-maximizing collusion but by the same token less prone to engage in profit-maximizing competition. Hospital Corporation of America v. FTC, supra, 807 F.2d at 1390–91.

The question cannot be resolved a priori, and once the government showed that the merger would create a firm having a market share approaching, perhaps exceeding, a common threshold of monopoly power— two-thirds (United States v. Aluminum Co. of America, 148 F.2d 416, 424 (2d Cir.1945) (L. Hand, J.))—it behooved the defendants to present evidence that the normal inference to be drawn from such a market share would mislead.

It is regrettable that antitrust cases are decided on the basis of theoretical guesses as to what particular market-structure characteristics portend for competition, but to place on the government an insuperable burden of proof is not the answer. We would like to see more effort put into studying the actual effect of concentration on price in the hospital industry as in other industries. If the government is right in these cases, then, other things being equal, hospital prices should be higher in markets with fewer hospitals. This is a studiable hypothesis, by modern methods of multivariate statistical analysis, and some studies have been conducted correlating prices and concentration in the hospital industry. Kopit & McCann, Toward a Definitive Antitrust Standard for Nonprofit Hospital Mergers, 13 Journal of Health Politics, Policy & Law 635, 645–46 and n. 30 (1988) (discussing studies); Blackstone & Fuhr, Hospital Mergers and Antitrust: An Economic Analysis, 14 id. at 383 (1989); Dranove, Shanley & Simon, Is Health Care Competition Wasteful? No! (U.Chi.Grad.Sch.Bus., March 1, 1990). Unfortunately, this literature is at an early and inconclusive stage, and the government is not required to await the maturation of the relevant scholarship in order to establish a prima facie case. The principles of civil procedure do not require that the plaintiff make an airtight case, only that his case satisfy some minimum threshold of persuasiveness and be better than the defendant's case. The government showed large market shares in a plausibly defined market in an industry more prone than many to collusion. The defendants responded with conjectures about the motives of nonprofits, and other will o' the wisps, that the district judge was free to reject, and did. The judge's findings establish a violation of section 1 under the standards of Columbia Steel, and the judgment must therefore be affirmed without our needing to decide whether the district judge was correct in holding that section 7 does reach mergers between nonprofit corporations.

The defendants press upon us a recent, not-to-be published (and therefore nonprecedential) opinion by the Fourth Circuit, United States v. Carilion Health System, 892 F.2d 1042 (4th Cir.1989), affirming a decision in favor of the defendants in a hospital-merger case much like this one. 707 F.Supp. 840 (W.D.Va.1989). The discussion in the Fourth Circuit's opinion is brief, indeed perfunctory, consisting as it does very largely of a conclusion that the district court's findings were not clearly erroneous; in any event the court did not want its decision to have a precedential effect. As for the discussion by the district court in Carilion, we find it unpersuasive as well as inconsistent with our analysis in Hospital Corporation of America—a case cited by neither the district court nor the court of appeals in Carilion.

AFFIRMED.

NOTES AND QUESTIONS

1. In a case involving antitrust scrutiny, what is the impact if a court selects a wider geographical market? What are the possible harms to competition when hospitals merge?

2. If payments to hospitals are fixed by federal statute under the Prospective Pricing System, hospitals cannot obtain higher prices directly through cooperation. How then might they collude?

3. *An Economic Justification for Applying Antitrust Law to Nonprofits.* In a recent article, Antitrust in the Not–For–Profit Sector, 52 J.L. & Econ. 1 (2009), Professor Tomas Philipson and Judge Richard Posner argue that under plausible assumptions and with possible exceptions, the same incentives to restrain trade exist in the nonprofit as in the for-profit sector. They maintain that the main efficiency rationale for applying antitrust law to for-profit firms—that it reduces or eliminates the deadweight loss associated with market power—is equally applicable to nonprofit firms. Even when producers care about the welfare of consumers rather than just about their own profits and even though as a result the quantity and quality of output may be greater for a nonprofit than for a for-profit firm, the effects of competition and the incentive to change that behavior through collusion, and the adverse social consequences that flow from that change, are similar for the two types of firms.

Altruistic motives may result in lower prices but may also raise markups relative to competitive levels because altruistic firms benefit from exploiting market power. They show that this is true even when altruism would lead nonprofits to set price below cost in situations where there is no competition. The authors use as an example the collusive behavior in violation of antitrust law demonstrated by the Ivy League in U.S. v. Brown University (see infra p. 1038) where the sales (tuition) revenues of the universities were below their operating costs (they priced below average cost of educating students). Because promoting competition turns out to be socially valuable regardless of the particular objectives of producers, the fact that antitrust law does not distinguish between the two sectors is efficient. They claim that antitrust law may have greater beneficial effects on efficiency when it is enforced against firms that seek to promote the welfare of their consumers. Their argument for uniform antitrust treatment of the two sectors extends to exemptions from antitrust law as well.

4. *United States v. North Dakota Hospital Association.* In United States v. North Dakota Hospital Association, 640 F.Supp. 1028 (D.N.D. 1986), the United States brought a civil antitrust action against the North Dakota Hospital Association and 14 nonprofit North Dakota hospitals charging that the defendants violated the antitrust laws by agreeing among themselves to deny the Indian Health Service a contractual price discount. The Indian Health Service (IHS), an agency of the United States Department of Health and Human Services, is responsible for providing medical and hospital care to eligible Native Americans. Because IHS facilities were insufficient to meet the health care needs of Native Americans, traditional health care was provided on a contract or open market basis at private IHS selected North Dakota hospitals. The North Dakota Hospital Association (NDHA), a nonprofit corporation, is a trade association for hospitals and nursing homes in North Dakota. The defendant nonprofit hospitals provided hospital services to IHS patients and were reimbursed. Prior to 1983

IHS contracted with the defendant hospitals to reimburse on a cost paid basis. Since certain costs actually incurred were excluded from "reasonable costs," medicare reimbursement necessarily was less than the hospital's actual costs. In 1982 IHS proposed a new medical reimbursement formula. After a series of negotiations, the defendant hospitals indicated that they would not give discounts to IHS on medical services for Indian health care cases. The hospitals continued to provide health services up to a $10,000 limitation.

The government alleged that the agreement among the hospitals to adhere to their existing policies against voluntarily giving discounts by denying the request of Indian Health Services for medicaid reimbursement rates was an unreasonable restraint of trade under § 1 of the Sherman Act. The court found the jurisdictional requirement of the Sherman Act was met by the linkage with interstate commerce in the revenues from out of state third party payers, purchases from out of state vendors, and treatment of patients who travelled across state lines. It held that there was direct evidence of an express agreement between the defendant hospitals against voluntarily giving discounts by denying IHS's request for medicaid reimbursement rates. This constituted an unreasonable restraint on trade. The United States claimed that the considered activities fell within the category of restraints labelled *per se* price fixing. Though the defendants refused to accept the medicaid reimbursement methodology in the IHS contract, they did agree to accept the $10,000 per admission limitation. Therefore, the hospitals did not fall squarely within the price fixing mold. The court declined to apply *per se* rule analysis. Because the hospitals continued to treat IHS patients though they did not have a contract with the agency, the $10,000 limitation resulted in the hospitals' granting IHS discounts. Nevertheless, the court found that the defendants' agreement was an unreasonable restraint of trade which forestalled all potential competition concerning Medicaid rates for IHS contracts. The anticompetitive harm of the agreement outweighed the procompetitive benefits because it suppressed competition.

The court observed that because the defendant hospitals were nonprofit charitable institutions with operating margins only a few percentage points above their costs, the new medicaid cost based reimbursement method reimbursed hospitals at levels below their actual costs. This caused private third party payers and patients to pay more to make up the difference, thus shifting the cost of the discount from one payor to another. The purpose of the agreement between the hospitals was to prevent shifting costs of the medicaid discount on to other patients and payers. Though this was laudable, the anticompetitive harm outweighed the procompetitive benefits. "Antitrust law does not permit this court to consider whether defendants' agreement, although anticompetitive, is in the public interest because it was intended to prevent one consumer of their services from receiving a benefit at the expense of all other consumers." Id. at 1039.

5. *Recent Antitrust Challenges to Nonprofit Hospital Mergers.* The nationwide consolidation of hospitals and the competitive threat of for-

profit chains have caused some nonprofit hospitals to merge. The government has challenged many of these combinations on antitrust grounds, but the courts have not been receptive. In contrast to the views of Judge Posner in *Rockford Memorial*, they have assumed that the hospitals' nonprofit status or community-oriented interests of the hospitals' boards would resist anti-competitive behavior to raise prices despite newly acquired market power. See F.T.C. v. Butterworth Health Corporation, 946 F.Supp. 1285 (W.D.Mich.1996), aff'd per curiam, 121 F.3d 708 (6th Cir. 1997). In F.T.C. v. Freeman Hospital, 911 F.Supp. 1213 (W.D.Mo.1995), aff'd, 69 F.3d 260 (8th Cir.1995), the court said at 1222–23:

> The FTC essentially ignores the relevance of the merging hospitals' status as nonprofit entities. However, there is an economic basis for seriously questioning the assumption that nonprofit status is a distinction that does not matter. This is not to say that nonprofit organizations are inherently more altruistic than their for-profit counterparts. To the contrary, nonprofits generally have an incentive to maximize profits whenever practical, just like private sector organizations. However, by simply doing what is in their own economic best interest, certain nonprofit organizations ensure a competitive outcome, regardless of market structure.
>
> Arguably, a private nonprofit hospital that is sponsored and directed by the local community is similar to a consumer cooperative. It is highly unlikely that a cooperative will arbitrarily raise prices merely to earn higher profits because the owners of such an organization are also its consumers. See Henry B. Hansmann, The Role of Nonprofit Enterprise, 89 Yale L.J. 835, 889 (1980). Similarly, if a nonprofit organization is controlled by the very people who depend on it for service, there is no rational economic incentive for such an organization to raise its prices to the monopoly level even if it has the power to do so. William J. Lynk, Property Rights and the Presumptions of Merger Analysis, Antitrust Bulletin, 363, 377 (1994). In the hospital context, this rationale applies to nonprofit hospitals whose boards are effectively controlled by persons representing the interests of hospital consumers or other groups that desire competitively-priced hospital services.
>
> To determine if this theory is applicable in a given context, it is necessary to evaluate who controls the hospitals. Local businesses have an interest in competitively-priced hospital services, because they pay those prices through the cost of their employees' hospitalization. Physicians also have an interest in maintaining competitive prices at the hospitals where they practice because higher prices drive patients to alternative hospitals, thus causing a reduction in the physicians' patient volume.
>
> As of March 1, 1995, the combined Freeman–Oak Hill Board of Trustees was composed of eighteen business and community leaders from the southwest Missouri area who serve without compensation. Eight Trustees are owners or employees of local businesses and another four are retired owners or employees of local businesses. Five

Trustees are local physicians who practice at Freeman and or Oak Hill and one Trustee is a Freeman administrator. Thus, the vast majority of the combined Board of Trustees is comprised of persons who indirectly represent the interests of hospital consumers. Consequently, it would not be in these individual Board member's best economic interest to permit prices to be raised beyond a normal competitive level. Interestingly, John Hale, Chairman of the Tri–State Health Care Coalition, a group of twenty Joplin area employers formed in 1993 to seek lower prices for health care, made a similar observation when he was asked about the future prices of the consolidated entity.

But see United States v. Mercy Health Services, 902 F.Supp. 968 (N.D.Iowa 1995) (judgment for hospitals, but nonprofit status could not be used as a defense because one of the nonprofit hospitals operated in a fashion similar to a for-profit corporation) and United States v. Long Island Jewish Med. Center, 983 F.Supp. 121, 146 (E.D.N.Y.1997).

6. *Do Mergers Involving Nonprofit Hospitals Raise Health Care Costs?* Freeman Hospital and F.T.C. v. Butterworth both relied on the research of William J. Lynk, who concluded that nonprofit hospitals have a lower association between higher market share and higher prices than for-profit hospitals. See William J. Lynk, Nonprofit Hospital Mergers and the Exercise of Market Power, 38 J.L. & Econ. 437 (1995).

Recent research has undermined these conclusions and found that in concentrated markets, all types of nonprofit hospitals exercised market power in the form of higher prices. See David Dranove & Richard Ludwick, Competition and Pricing by Nonprofit Hospitals: A Reassessment of Lynk's Analysis, 18 J. Health Econ. 87, 97 (1999). In July 2004 the Federal Trade Commission and the Department of Justice issued a report, "Improving Health Care: A Dose of Competition", which noted: "several panelists maintained that the best available empirical evidence indicated no significant differences between the pricing behavior of for-profit and nonprofit hospitals." Dep't of Justice & the Fed. Trade Comm'n, Improving Health Care: A Dose of Competition 31 (2004), available at www.ftc.gov/reports/healthcare/040723healthcarerpt.pdf. The report added: "[r]ecent empirical studies of pricing behavior paint a fairly consistent picture." One study found that there was no significant difference in how for-profit and non-profit hospitals exerted market power; for-profits generally had higher prices in 1986, but nonprofits increased their prices faster from 1986 to 1994. Id. at 32. See also John D. Colombo, The Role of Tax Exemption in a Competitive Health Care Market, 31 J.Health Pol., Pol'y & L. 623 (2006) (if nonprofit status does not result in differential financial behavior and if competition will end the ability of hospitals to cross subsidize free care for the poor as the FTC/DOJ report speculates, is there any reason to retain tax exemption for nonprofit hospitals?); Thomas L. Greaney, Antitrust and Hospital Mergers: Does the Nonprofit Form Affect Competitive Substance?, 31 J. Health Pol., Pol'y & L. 511 (2006) (the social function of the nonprofit hospital has a subtle influence on merger litigation and the social and political context is never far from the surface); Gary J. Young et. al.,

Community Control and Pricing Patterns of Nonprofit Hospitals: An Antitrust Analysis, 25 J. Health Pol.,Pol'y & L. 1051, 1073 (2000) (arguing that even nonprofit hospitals, which would be expected to be the least profit-oriented, tend to raise prices after a merger).

7. *Unwinding Nonprofit Mergers.* The challenges to Professor Lynk's hypothesis that nonprofits have no incentives to raise their prices to the monopoly level, even if they have the power to do so, have not gone unnoticed by the government. In a complaint filed in February 2004, the Federal Trade Commission sought to unwind a previously approved merger in 2000 of two nonprofit hospitals, Evanston Northwestern Healthcare Corp.(ENH) and Highland Park Hospital, on the ground that the hospitals engaged in anti-competitive actions in violation of § 7 of the Clayton Act.

The FTC alleged Evanston Northwestern took over Highland Park, and used its post-merger market power to impose price increases on insurers and employers ranging from 40 to 190 percent. By looking back after the merger was completed, the FTC, which had lost seven straight challenges to hospital mergers in the 1990s, attempted a new approach, examining the actual effect of concentration on price. In a 239–page decision, In the Matter of Evanston Northwestern Healthcare Corporation, 2005 WL 2845790, F.T.C., Oct. 20, 2005 (NO. 9315), the FTC Chief Administrative Law Judge concluded that contemporaneous and post-acquisition evidence established that ENH exercised its enhanced post-merger market power to obtain price increases significantly above its pre-merger prices and substantially larger than price increases obtained by other comparison hospitals. As a result of the elimination of Highland Park as a competitor, ENH was able to convert existing price methodologies to managed care organizations to much more favorable post-merger terms than either Evanston or Highland Park could have achieved alone. The evidence further showed that ENH in 2002 and 2003, continued to unilaterally raise rates, which significantly increased the prices paid by managed care organizations for ENH services. The court ordered full divestiture of Highland Park from ENH.

In August 2007, the Federal Trade Commissioners unanimously found that the merged entity violated section 7 of the Clayton Act by creating a highly concentrated market, increasing prices and harming consumers. However, the Commission vacated the Administrative Law Judge's divestment order, noting that divestiture after a long period of time is more difficult with a greater risk of unforeseen costs and failure. It imposed an injunction that required Evanston Northwestern to negotiate its hospital contracts separately without sharing information among its hospitals and giving payors the option of renegotiating existing contracts. The Commissioners stated "ENH's [Evanston Northwestern Healthcare] non-profit status did not affect its efforts to raise prices after the merger, and * * * does not suffice to rebut complaint counsel's evidence of anticompetitive effects." In re Northwestern Healthcare Corp., 2007 WL 2286195 (No. 9315, August 6, 2007).

8. *For Further Reading*. Judith C. Appelbaum & Jill C. Morrison, Hospital Mergers and the Threat to Women's Reproductive Health Services: Applying the Antitrust Laws, 26 NYU Rev. L. & Soc. Change 1 (2000/2001) (focuses on mergers with religiously affiliated hospitals); Jennifer R. Conners, A Critical Misdiagnosis: How Courts Underestimate the Anticompetitive Implications of Hospital Mergers, 91 Calif. L. Rev. 543 (2003); Nicole Harrell Duke, Hospital Mergers Versus Consumers: An Antitrust Analysis, 30 U. Balt. L. Rev. 75 (2000); Barry R. Furrow, Sandra H. Johnson, Timothy S. Jost & Robert L. Schwartz, Health Law, Ch. 10 (2000); David L. Glazer, Comment: Clayton Act Scrutiny of Nonprofit Hospital Mergers: The Wrong Rx for Ailing Institutions, 66 Wash L. Rev. 1041 (1991); Thomas L. Greaney, Night Landings on an Aircraft Carrier: Hospital Mergers and Antitrust Law, 23 Am. J.L. & Med. 191 (1997); Peter J. Hammer & William M. Sage, Antitrust, Health Care Quality and the Courts, 102 Colum. L. Rev. 545 (2002); Tomas J. Philipson & Richard A. Posner, Antitrust in the Not–For–Profit Sector, 52 J. L. & Econ. 1 (2009); Barak D. Richman, Antitrust and Nonprofit Hospital Mergers: A Return to Basics, 156 U. Pa. L. Rev. 121 (2007).

C. EDUCATION

INTRODUCTORY NOTE

Many university activities and aspects of higher education are potential targets of antitrust scrutiny including the accrediting process, athletics, financial aid and tuition pricing, information exchange and sharing, joint ventures for research or commercial purposes, medical centers and programs, and purely proprietary functions in which colleges and universities compete with traditional businesses. Douglas R. Richmond, Antitrust and Higher Education: An Overview, 61 U.Mo.K.C. L. Rev. 417, 446 (1993).

The courts initially deferred to educational institutions in matters with possible antitrust overtones. In Marjorie Webster Junior College v. Middle States Association, 432 F.2d 650 (D.C.Cir.1970), cert. denied 400 U.S. 965, 91 S.Ct. 367 (1970), the Middle States Association, a nonprofit accrediting association dedicated to improving quality in institutions of higher learning, refused to evaluate Marjorie Webster Junior College for accreditation because it was a proprietary institution. The college brought suit to compel its consideration, alleging a violation of the Sherman Act. The court held that the Sherman Act's proscriptions did not extend to the "non-commercial aspects of the liberal arts." Id. at 654. Therefore, the refusal to accredit an institution absent an intent or purpose to affect the commercial aspects of the profession did not constitute commerce. The court also found that denial of accreditation was not fatal to operating a successful junior college. In light of subsequent Supreme Court decisions involving professional associations such as Goldfarb, supra and Arizona v. Maricopa County Medical Society, 457 U.S. 332, 102 S.Ct. 2466 (1982), *Marjorie Webster* is a doubtful precedent. In recent years, the courts have addressed antitrust issues in a variety of other educational settings.

1.   *Regulation of College Television Appearances.* The National Collegiate Athletic Association (NCAA) is a private, voluntary association consisting of over 1,000 members including colleges, athletic conferences, and educational associations whose mission is to promote and regulate intercollegiate athletics. Since 1951 the NCAA had controlled televised college football by limiting the number of games broadcast and restricting universities' annual television appearances. No NCAA member was permitted to make any sale of television rights except in accordance with the NCAA plan. The purposes of the NCAA television restrictions were to reduce the impact of television on live game attendance, to expand television coverage to as many schools as possible, and to provide coverage of college games to the public to the extent compatible with the other objectives.

NCAA member schools with major football programs formed the College Football Association (CFA) to promote the interest of football and to obtain a greater voice in the formulation of football television policy than allowed by the NCAA. The CFA then negotiated a contract with the National Broadcasting Company (NBC) that liberalized the number of television appearances. In response the NCAA announced it would take disciplinary action against any CFA member who complied with the CFA–NBC contact. The Universities of Oklahoma and Georgia, both CFA members, filed suit.

In NCAA v. Board of Regents, 468 U.S. 85, 104 S.Ct. 2948 (1984), the Supreme Court held that the NCAA's television plan violated § 1 of the Sherman Act. Although horizontal price fixing and output limitations are ordinarily condemned as a matter of law under the *per se* approach because the probability that such practices are anticompetitive is so high, the court applied the rule of reason, as some horizontal restraints on competition were essential if the product was to be available at all. Id. 468 U.S. at 101, 104 S.Ct. at 2960. Since the NCAA's television plan restrained price and output, it had a significant potential for anticompetitive effects without sufficient offsetting procompetitive justifications. The college football market had been restrained by the NCAA's fixing the price for particular broadcasts. Its exclusive network contracts were the equivalent of a group boycott of all other potential broadcasters, and the NCAA's threat of sanctions of members constituted a threatened boycott against potential competitors. The NCAA plan placed an artificial limit on the amount of televised college football. In a footnote the court stated that there was no doubt that "the sweeping language" of § 1 of the Sherman Act applied to nonprofit entities and questioned the NCAA's nonprofit character as the organization and its member institutions was organized to maximize revenues. Id. at n. 22.

2.   *Regulation of Athletic Eligibility and the Use of Agents.* Bradford Gaines, a football player at Vanderbilt, declared himself eligible for the National Football League Draft in April 1990, after his junior year. He was not selected by any team. At the time NCAA rules provided that an athlete

lost his amateur status when he entered a professional draft or signed an agreement with an agent. Therefore, Gaines became ineligible to participate in collegiate athletics his senior year. He sued alleging that the NCAA engaged in an unlawful exercise of monopoly power in violation of § 2 of the Sherman Act. In Gaines v. NCAA, 746 F.Supp. 738 (M.D.Tenn.1990) the court distinguished between the NCAA's restrictions on the televising of college football games at issue in *Board of Regents*, which were commercial rules, and its attempt to maintain a discernible line between amateurism and professionalism by enforcing eligibility rules, which were noncommercial in nature. The eligibility rules, the court concluded, were rooted in the NCAA's concern for the protection of amateur athletics and would not be subject to antitrust scrutiny and, in any event, there was a legitimate business justification for the rules at issue.

NCAA eligibility rules also have been upheld under § 1 of the Sherman Act on the ground that the "no-agent" and "no draft" rules have procompetitive effects because they promote the integrity and quality of athletics, encourage competition and the educational pursuits of student-athletes, and limit commercializing influences from destroying the distinctive product of college football. Banks v. NCAA, 977 F.2d 1081 (7th Cir.1992), cert. denied, 508 U.S. 908, 113 S.Ct. 2336 (1993). Accord: Smith v. NCAA, 139 F.3d 180 (3d Cir.1998).

Do these decisions reflect a realistic view of big-time college sports? Is the ideal of amateurism outmoded in the highly commercial environment of Division I athletics? Aren't the no draft, no agent rules restraints of trade in the market for the skills of student-athletes? See Note, Sherman Act Invalidation of the NCAA Amateurism Rules, 105 Harv. L. Rev. 1299 (1992) (the no-draft, no-agent, and limited compensation rules are agreements among NCAA member institutions to prevent price competition for student athletes and to boycott illegally athletes who attempt to pursue careers in professional sports before their eligibility expires). The NCAA changed its no-draft rules in 1994.

3. *Student–Athlete Access to Professional Sports: National Football League Eligibility Rules as an Antitrust Violation.* The National Football League, a section 501(c)(6) organization, limits eligibility for its NFL entry draft to players who are three full college football seasons removed from high school graduation. Student-athlete Maurice Clarett, a former Ohio State football player, sought to participate in the NFL draft after one season of college football and but two years after his high school graduation. He was precluded from doing so because of the NFL's rules on draft eligibility. Clarett filed suit alleging that the NFL's draft rules were an unreasonable restraint of trade on the market for players' services in violation of section 1 of the Sherman Act and section 4 of the Clayton Act. The district court granted summary judgment to Clarett, finding *inter alia* the eligibility rules were blatantly anti-competitive. The Second Circuit reversed. Clarett v. National Football League, 369 F.3d 124 (2d Cir. 2004).

Unlike college football players, professionals are bound by a collective bargaining agreement. The eligibility rules were not part of it, but they are mentioned in the NFL Constitution. In order to accommodate collective bargaining between and among labor and employees, certain concerted activity, which would otherwise be prohibited, is beyond the reach of the antitrust laws. This has been classified into two types of exemptions: statutory, derived from the language of antitrust laws; and non-statutory, which is inferred from labor statutes. The court found that the non-statutory labor exemption defeated Clarett's claim. To permit antitrust suits against sports leagues on the ground that their concerted action would impose a restraint upon the labor market would seriously undermine fundamental principles of federal labor polices embodied in the labor laws promoting collective bargaining. The terms and conditions of Clarett's employment were committed to the collective bargaining table and reserved to the NFL and its players union.

4. *Regulation of Coaches' Salaries.* During the 1980s the NCAA became concerned over the steadily rising expense of maintaining competitive athletic programs. One problem was the costs associated with part-time assistant coaches. The NCAA initially imposed salary restrictions on part-time assistants, but athletic departments circumvented these compensation limits. In 1991 the NCAA implemented a bylaw amendment that limited Division I basketball coaching staffs to four members—one head coach, two assistant coaches, and one entry level coach called a "restricted-earnings coach." The NCAA limited restricted-earnings coaches' annual compensation to $16,000. A group of restricted-earnings coaches challenged the rule as a violation of § 1 of the Sherman Act.

The Tenth Circuit affirmed the district court, which had granted summary judgment in favor of the coaches on the issue of liability and issued a permanent injunction against promulgation or reenactment of the rule. Law v. National Collegiate Athletic Association, 134 F.3d 1010 (10th Cir.1998). The court applied the "quick look" rule of reason to hold that the agreement of NCAA members to limit the price which NCAA members had to pay for services of the restricted-earnings coach was an illegal restraint of trade through impermissible horizontal price fixing. The Court found that the rule would not create more balanced competition by barring teams from hiring four experienced coaches because schools could subvert the entry-level goal: cost cutting was not a defense under the antitrust laws, and there was no indication that the rule would assist a competitive balance. On remand in May 1998, a jury awarded more than $66 million in triple damages to the class of restricted-earnings coaches. The case was settled for $54.5 million.

5. *Proprietary Activities of Educational Institutions.* Other areas of potential antitrust liability arise where colleges and universities compete or collude with profit-seeking enterprises. Educational institutions compete with businesses with their bookstores, food services, computer sales, and housing. In Sunshine Books v. Temple Univ., 697 F.2d 90 (3d Cir.1982), a private book seller alleged that Temple University attempted by means of predatory pricing to monopolize sale of undergraduate textbooks to students. The Third Circuit, vacating the district court's grant of summary

judgment, held that the book sellers' submissions on questions of payroll allocation raised a genuine issue of material fact with respect to the University's cost against which the prices were to be measured.

In American Nat'l Bank & Trust Co. of Chicago v. Board of Regents for Regency Universities, 607 F.Supp. 845 (N.D.Ill.1984), the owners of a private dormitory adjacent to the Northern Illinois University campus claimed that certain university housing policies violated Sections 1 and 2 of the Sherman Act. The university required freshmen under the age of 21 not residing with their parents to live in one of the university residence halls so long as space remained available. The plaintiffs alleged that the board of regents intentionally delayed informing incoming freshmen about the availability of permanent space and implemented "temporary" housing, whereby students were housed in non-dormitory rooms indefinitely. As a result, they argued, the university violated its own parietal rules by continuing to impose the residence requirement even though space was not available. Thus, students were housed in non-dormitory rooms, precluding the private residence hall from entering the market and renting to students. The court denied defendant's motion for summary judgment. See also Campus Center Discount Den, Inc. v. Miami U., 114 F.3d 1186 (6th Cir.1997).

Colleges may enter into joint ventures with other businesses that engage in behavior prohibited by the antitrust laws. For example, university medical centers may be charged with conspiring with other hospitals. See Nurse Midwifery Associates v. Hibbett, 918 F.2d 605 (6th Cir.1990), cert. denied 502 U.S. 952, 112 S.Ct. 406 (1991) (Vanderbilt University Medical Center prevailed on motion for summary judgment against charge it conspired to prevent nurse midwives from competing with Nashville obstetricians).

6. *For Further Reading.* Jeffrey C. Sun & Philip T.K. Daniel, The Sherman Act Antitrust Provisions and Collegiate Action: Should There Be a Continued Exception for the Business of the University, 25 J.C. & U.L. 451 (1999); Sarah M. Konsky, An Antitrust Challenge to the NCAA Transfer Rules, 70 U.Chi.L.Rev. 1581 (2003); John D. Colombo, The NCAA, Tax Exemption, and College Athletics, 2010 U.Ill.L.Rev. 109; Gregory M. Krakau, Monopoly and Other Children's Games: NCAA's Antitrust Suit Woes Threaten Its Existence, 61 Ohio St.L.J. 399 (2000); Douglas R. Richmond, Antitrust & Higher Education: An Overview, 61 U.Mo. K.C.L.Rev. 417 (1993).

United States v. Brown University

United States Court of Appeals, Third Circuit, 1993.
5 F.3d 658.

■ Cowen, Circuit Judge:

[In 1958, MIT and the eight Ivy League schools formed the "Ivy Overlap Group" to collectively determine the amount of financial aid to award to students who had been accepted by more than one of their institutions and requested financial aid. The presidents of these institutions also shared information on tuition, budgets, salary increments, and other data. The Ivy Overlap Group agreed that financial aid only should be awarded after it was determined that family resources were inadequate to meet a student's educational expenses. In other words, financial aid was awarded solely on the basis of demonstrated need. Merit-based aid was prohibited.

The schools jointly developed and applied a uniform needs analysis for assessing family contributions. Each school determined the amount of tuition a particular student and her family would pay. The names of students were compiled in rosters by Student Aid Services, a for-profit corporation owned by the administrators of the overlap schools. The financial aid officials of the schools would meet and discuss the family contribution of each student that appeared on the roster of more than one school. The differing amounts of family contribution were averaged or a consensus was achieved so that the student was awarded the same amount of financial aid by each institution. The purpose of the overlap agreement was to neutralize the effect of financial aid so that applicants would choose a college for non-financial reasons.

On May 22, 1991, the Antitrust Division of the Department of Justice filed a complaint against M.I.T. and the eight Ivy League schools alleging that the institutions colluded by agreeing to award financial aid exclusively on the basis of need, agreeing to utilize a common formula to calculate need, and collectively setting each commonly admitted students' family contribution toward the price of tuition in violation of § 1 of the Sherman Antitrust Act. The Ivy League schools quickly settled, but MIT refused. The district court found that the Overlap Group's conduct constituted trade or commerce under § 1. Characterizing the Overlap Agreement as setting a selective discount off the price of educational services that constituted price fixing, the court issued a broad permanent injunction against such conduct. U.S. v. Brown Univ., 805 F.Supp. 288 (E.D.Pa.1992). MIT appealed. Eds.]

II.   TRADE OR COMMERCE

As a threshold matter, we must decide whether section one of the Sherman Act applies to the challenged conduct—MIT's agreement with the other Overlap institutions to award financial aid only to needy students and to set the amount of family contribution from commonly admitted students. Section one, by its terms, does not apply to all conspiracies, but only to those which restrain "trade or commerce." 15 U.S.C. § 1. MIT characterizes its conduct as disbursing charitable funds to achieve the twin objectives of advancing equality of access to higher education and promoting socio-economic and racial diversity within the nation's most elite universities. This alleged pure charity, MIT argues, does not implicate trade or commerce, and is thus exempt from antitrust scrutiny.

It is axiomatic that section one of the Sherman Act regulates only transactions that are commercial in nature. Congress, however, intended this statute to embrace the widest array of conduct possible. Section one's scope thus reaches the activities of nonprofit organizations, including institutions of higher learning. * * * Nonprofit organizations are not beyond the purview of the Sherman Act, because the absence of profit is no guarantee that an entity will act in the best interest of consumers.

Although nonprofit organizations are not entitled to a class exemption from the Sherman Act, when they perform acts that are the antithesis of commercial activity, they are immune from antitrust regulation. This immunity, however, is narrowly circumscribed. It does not extend to commercial transactions with a "public-service aspect." Courts classify a transaction as commercial or noncommercial based on the nature of the conduct in light of the totality of surrounding circumstances.

The exchange of money for services, even by a nonprofit organization, is a quintessential commercial transaction. Therefore, the payment of tuition in return for educational services constitutes commerce. MIT concedes as much by acknowledging that its determination of the full tuition amount is a commercial decision.

We thus come to the crux of the issue—is providing financial assistance solely to needy students a selective reduction or "discount" from the full tuition amount, or a charitable gift? If this financial aid is a component of the process of setting tuition prices, it is commerce. If it is pure charity, it is not.

When MIT admits an affluent student, that student must pay approximately $25,000 annually (tuition plus room, board and incidental expenses) if he or she wishes to enroll at MIT. If MIT accepts a needy student and calculates that it will extend $10,000 in financial aid to that student, the student must pay approximately $15,000 to attend MIT. The student certainly is not free to take the $10,000 and apply it toward attendance at a different college. The assistance package is only available in conjunction with a complementary payment of approximately $15,000 to MIT. The amount of financial aid not only impacts, but directly determines the amount that a needy student must pay to receive an education at MIT. The financial aid therefore is part of the commercial process of setting tuition.

MIT suggests that providing aid exclusively to needy students and setting the amount of that aid is not commercial because the price needy students are charged is substantially below the marginal cost of supplying a year of education to an undergraduate student. Because profit maximizing companies would not engage in such economically abnormal behavior, MIT concludes that such activity must be noncommercial. MIT's concession, however, that setting the full tuition amount is a commercial decision subject to antitrust scrutiny undermines this argument. The full tuition figure, like the varying amounts charged to needy students, is significantly below MIT's marginal cost. Therefore, whether the price charged for educational services is below marginal cost is not probative of the commercial or noncommercial nature of the methodology utilized to determine financial aid packages.

The fact that MIT is not obligated to provide any financial aid does not transform that aid into charity. Similarly, discounting the price of educational services for needy students is not charity when a university receives tangible benefits in exchange. Regardless of whether MIT's motive is altruism, self-enhancement or a combination of the two, MIT benefits from providing financial aid. MIT admits that it competes with other Overlap members for outstanding students. By distributing aid, MIT enables exceptional students to attend its school who otherwise could not afford to attend. The resulting expansion in MIT's pool of exceptional applicants increases the quality of MIT's student body. MIT then enjoys enhanced prestige by virtue of its ability to attract a greater portion of the "cream of the crop." The Supreme Court has recognized that nonprofit organizations derive significant benefit from increased prestige and influence. Although MIT could fill its class with students able to pay the full tuition, the caliber of its student body, and consequently the institution's reputation, obviously would suffer. Overlap affords MIT the benefit of an overrepresentation of high caliber students, with the concomitant institutional prestige, without forcing MIT to be responsive to market forces in terms of its tuition costs. By immunizing itself through the Overlap from competition for students based on a price/quality ratio, MIT achieves certain institutional benefits at a bargain.

Our holding that the Overlap Agreement clearly implicates trade or commerce is consistent with Marjorie Webster Junior College, Inc. v. Middle States Ass'n of Colleges and Secondary Schools, Inc., 432 F.2d 650 (D.C.Cir.1970), upon which MIT heavily relies. * * *

The *Marjorie Webster* court focused primarily on intent because the nature of the conduct in that case was distinctly noncommercial. The MSA [Middle States Association] received no payment or other benefit for evaluating institutions and deciding whether to accredit them. In contrast to the Overlap Agreement, there was no exchange of money for services or the setting of a price. We agree that the Sherman Act does not apply to "the noncommercial aspects of the liberal arts." MIT's conduct, however, presents the opposite side of the coin—the commercial aspects of the liberal arts. Like the district court, we "can conceive of few aspects of higher education that are more commercial than the price charged to students." The *Marjorie Webster* court even acknowledged that if the MSA engaged in commercial activity, "antitrust policy would presumably be applicable."

We hold that financial assistance to students is part and parcel of the process of setting tuition and thus a commercial transaction. Although MIT's status as a nonprofit educational organization and its advancement of congressionally-recognized and important social welfare goals does not remove its conduct from the realm of trade or commerce, these factors will influence whether this conduct violates the Sherman Act.

III. RESTRAINT OF TRADE

Section one of the Sherman Act provides that "[e]very contract, combination in the form of trust or otherwise, or conspiracy, in restraint of trade or commerce among the several states * * * is declared to be illegal." Courts long ago realized that literal application of section one would render virtually every business arrangement unlawful. "Every agreement concerning trade, every regulation of trade, restrains. To bind, to restrain, is of their very essence." Because even beneficial business contracts or combinations restrain trade to some degree, section one has been interpreted to prohibit only those contracts or combinations that are "unreasonably restrictive of competitive conditions."

Three general standards have emerged for determining whether a business combination unreasonably restrains trade under section one. Most restraints are analyzed under the traditional "rule of reason." The rule of reason requires the fact-finder to "weigh all of the circumstances of a case in deciding whether a restrictive practice should be prohibited as imposing an unreasonable restraint on competition." The plaintiff bears an initial burden under the rule of reason of showing that the alleged combination or agreement produced adverse, anti-competitive effects within the relevant product and geographic markets. The plaintiff may satisfy this burden by proving the existence of actual anticompetitive effects, such as reduction of output, increase in price, or deterioration in quality of goods or services. Such proof is often impossible to make, however, due to the difficulty of isolating the market effects of challenged conduct. 7 P. Areeda, Antitrust Law ¶ 1503, at 376 (1986). Accordingly, courts typically allow proof of the defendant's "market power" instead. Market power, the ability to raise prices above those that would prevail in a competitive market, is essentially a surrogate for detrimental effects.

If a plaintiff meets his initial burden of adducing adequate evidence of market power or actual anti-competitive effects, the burden shifts to the defendant to show that the challenged conduct promotes a sufficiently pro-competitive objective. A restraint on competition cannot be justified solely on the basis of social welfare concerns. To rebut, the plaintiff must demonstrate that the restraint is not reasonably necessary to achieve the stated objective.

While the rule of reason typically mandates an elaborate inquiry into the reasonableness of a challenged business practice, there are certain agreements or practices which because of their pernicious effect on competition and lack of any redeeming virtue are conclusively presumed to be unreasonable. Such "plainly anticompetitive" agreements or practices are deemed to be "illegal per se." "Business certainty and litigation efficiency" are the principal salutary effects of per se rules. Such rules tend to provide guidance to the business community and to minimize the burdens on litigants and the judicial system of the more complex rule-of-reason trials.

In addition to the traditional rule of reason and the per se rule, courts sometimes apply what amounts to an abbreviated or "quick look" rule of reason analysis. The abbreviated rule of reason is an intermediate standard. It applies in cases where per se condemnation is inappropriate, but where "no elaborate industry analysis is required to demonstrate the anticompetitive character" of an inherently suspect restraint. Because competitive harm is presumed, the defendant must promulgate "some competitive justification" for the restraint, "even in the absence of detailed market analysis" indicating actual profit maximization or increased costs to the consumer resulting from the restraint. If no legitimate justifications are set forth, the presumption of adverse competitive impact prevails and "the court condemns the practice without ado." If the defendant offers sound procompetitive justifications, however, the court must proceed to weigh the overall reasonableness of the restraint using a full-scale rule of reason analysis.

In the present case the district court applied the abbreviated rule of reason analysis. * * *

[The Court concluded that full rule of reason analysis was required to consider whether Overlap violated the Sherman Antitrust Act. Eds.]

* * *

The rationale for treating professional organizations differently is that they tend to vary somewhat from this economic model.

MIT does not dispute that the stated purpose of Overlap is to eliminate price competition for talented students among member institutions. Indeed, the intent to eliminate price competition among the Overlap schools for commonly admitted students appears on the face of the Agreement itself. In addition to agreeing to offer financial aid solely on the basis of need and to develop a common system of needs analysis, the Overlap members agreed to meet each spring to compare data and to conform one another's aid packages to the greatest possible extent. Because the Overlap Agreement aims to restrain "competitive bidding" and deprive prospective students of "the ability to utilize and compare prices" in selecting among schools, it is anticompetitive "on its face." Price is "the central nervous system of the economy," and "[t]he heart of our national economic policy long has been faith in the value of competition". We therefore agree that Overlap initially "requires some competitive justification even in the absence of a detailed market analysis."

MIT's principal counterargument is that an abbreviated rule of reason analysis is appropriate only where economic harm to consumers may fairly be presumed; and such harm may be presumed only when evidence establishes that "the challenged practice, unlike Overlap, manifestly has an adverse effect on price, output, or quality." As the Division aptly points out, however, if an abbreviated rule of reason analysis always required a clear evidentiary showing of a detrimental effect on price, output, or quality, it would no longer be abbreviated. This is because proof of actual adverse effects generally will require the elaborate, threshold industry analysis that an abbreviated inquiry is designed to obviate.

MIT's position also is contradicted by Supreme Court precedent. Without any mention of actual effects on price, output, or quality, the Court in

Professional Engineers required the association of engineers to affirmatively defend an ethics rule prohibiting members from discussing fees with prospective customers prior to being selected for a project. The Court reasoned that the "anticompetitive character" of the agreement could be presumed because the ban on competitive bidding, like price fixing, "impede[d] the ordinary give and take of the market place." Similarly, the Court in Indiana Dentists held that collectively withholding x-rays from patients' insurers was "likely enough to disrupt the proper functioning of the price-setting mechanism of the market that it may be condemned even absent proof that it resulted in higher prices or * * * the purchase of higher priced services, than would occur in its absence."

Since the Overlap Agreement is a price fixing mechanism impeding the ordinary functioning of the free market, MIT is obliged to provide justification for the arrangement. In NCAA, the Supreme Court credited the district court's findings that the NCAA's television agreements actually increased prices and restricted output. "Price is higher and output lower than they would otherwise be, and both are unresponsive to consumer preference." According to the Court, "these hallmarks of anticompetitive behavior place[d] upon [the NCAA] a heavy burden of establishing an affirmative defense."

The district court did not make any conclusive findings with regard to these "hallmark" consequences of price fixing in the present case. First, the district court did not find, and we do not understand the Division to suggest, that Overlap has caused or is even likely to cause any reduction of output. Second, while the parties sharply dispute the effect of Overlap on the price of education at the member colleges, the district court expressed doubt as to whether price effects could be determined to a reasonable degree of economic certainty. The court therefore assumed without deciding that the cooperation among the schools had no aggregate effect on the price of an MIT education. Thus, while MIT bears the burden of establishing an affirmative justification for Overlap, the absence of any finding of adverse effects such as higher price or lower output is relevant, albeit not dispositive, when the district court considers whether MIT has met this burden. Nevertheless, the absence or inconclusivity of a finding of actual adverse effects does not mitigate MIT's burden to justify price fixing with some procompetitive virtue, or with a showing of Overlap's reasonable necessity to its institutional purpose, because actual dollar amount effects do not necessarily reflect the harm to competition which Congress intended to eliminate in enacting the Sherman Act. * * *

At trial, MIT maintained that Overlap had the following procompetitive effects: (1) it improved the quality of the educational program at the Overlap schools; (2) it increased consumer choice by making an Overlap education more accessible to a greater number of students; and (3) it promoted competition for students among Overlap schools in areas other than price. The district court rejected each of these alleged competitive virtues, summarily concluding that they amounted to no more than noneconomic social welfare justifications.

On appeal, MIT first contends that by promoting socio-economic diversity at member institutions, Overlap improved the quality of the education offered by the schools and therefore enhanced the consumer appeal of an Overlap education. The Supreme Court has recognized improvement in the quality of a product or service that enhances the public's desire for that product or service as one possible procompetitive virtue. The district court itself noted that it cannot be denied "that cultural and economic diversity contributes to the quality of education and enhances the vitality of student life." Albeit in a different context, the Supreme Court also has recognized that "the atmosphere of 'speculation, experiment and creation'—so essential to the quality of higher education—is widely believed to be promoted by a diverse student body." Regents of the Univ. of California v. Bakke, 438 U.S. 265, 312, 98 S.Ct. 2733, 2760, 57 L.Ed.2d 750 (1978) (opinion of Powell, J.) (use of race as a factor in medical school admissions survives equal protection challenge).

MIT also contends that by increasing the financial aid available to needy students, Overlap provided some students who otherwise would not have been able to afford an Overlap education the opportunity to have one. In this respect, MIT argues, Overlap enhanced consumer choice. The policy of allocating financial aid solely on the basis of demonstrated need has two obvious consequences. First, available resources are spread among more needy students than would be the case if some students received aid in excess of their need. Second, as a consequence of the fact that more students receive the aid they require, the number of students able to afford an Overlap education is maximized. In short, removing financial obstacles for the greatest number of talented but needy students increases educational access, thereby widening consumer choice. Enhancement of consumer choice is a traditional objective of the antitrust laws and has also been acknowledged as a procompetitive benefit.

Finally, MIT argues that by eliminating price competition among participating schools, Overlap channelled competition into areas such as curriculum, campus activities, and student-faculty interaction. As the Division correctly notes, however, any competition that survives a horizontal price restraint naturally will focus on attributes other than price. This is not the kind of procompetitive virtue contemplated under the Act, but rather one mere consequence of limiting price competition.

MIT next claims that beyond ignoring the procompetitive effects of Overlap, the district court erroneously refused to consider compelling social welfare justifications. MIT argues that by enabling member schools to maintain a steadfast policy of need-blind admissions and full need-based aid, Overlap promoted the social ideal of equality of educational access and opportunity.

Congress has sought to promote the same ideal of equality of educational access and opportunity for more than twenty-five years. Testimony at trial established that a primary objective of federal financial aid policy is to promote "horizontal equity" and "vertical equity." In other words, [f]ederal financial aid policy aims to ensure that similarly situated students are treated the same regardless of which institution, or aid officer within that institution, reviews their applications, and that students with less financial need do not receive more aid than those students with more financial need. The federal government seeks to effectuate these goals through programs that distribute financial aid exclusively on the basis of need.

As the evidence attested, MIT has sought to promote similar social and educational policy objectives by limiting financial aid to those with demonstrated need, although the district court found that the Ivy Needs Analysis Methodology differed significantly from the Congressional Methodology. The Overlap Agreement states: Member institutions agree that the primary purpose of a college financial aid program for all students is to provide financial assistance to students who without such aid would be unable to attend that institution. Financial aid should only be awarded after it is determined that family resources are inadequate to meet the student's educational expenses, and such aid should not exceed the difference between educational expenses and family resources. * * * Although the percentage of American minorities comprising MIT's student body has dramatically risen over the last three decades, which MIT attributes to the Overlap policy, the Ivy Methodology for performing a student needs analysis was ironically less generous to needy students in certain key ways than the Congressional Methodology. The district court noted three main areas in which the Ivy Methodology departed from the Congressional Methodology, including the way in which the Overlap apportions family income when multiple siblings attend college simultaneously, the requirements of separate payment from non-custodial parents where there is a divorce or separation, and the way Overlap treats capital losses, depreciation losses, and losses from secondary business which are reported on the parents' tax returns. Despite these discrepancies, the facts certainly attest that MIT has widened the access of certain minorities to its educational institution, whether or not the Overlap was mainly responsible for or necessary to that result. MIT maintains Overlap's virtual necessity to its continuing commitment to widening its access to needy minority students.

The district court was not persuaded by the alleged social welfare values proffered for Overlap because it believed the Supreme Court's decisions in Professional Engineers and Indiana Dentists required a persuasive procompetitive justification, or a showing of necessity, neither of which it believed that MIT demonstrated. In Professional Engineers, the engineers maintained that an ethics rule banning competitive bidding was reasonable because price competition for projects would induce engineers to offer their services at unsustainably low prices and compensate by cutting corners on the quality of their work. Because consumers in most instances award contracts to the lowest bidder, regardless of quality, competitive bidding "would be dangerous to the public health, safety and welfare." The Court flatly rejected the engineers' "public safety" argument, viewing it as nothing more than an attempt to impose "[their own] views of the costs and benefits of competition on the entire marketplace." The Court explained that "the Rule of Reason does not support a defense based on the assumption that competition itself is unreasonable."

In Indiana Dentists, where a group of dentists agreed to withhold x-rays from patients' insurers, the dentists association argued that certain noncompetitive "quality of care" effects of the agreement were relevant to the Court's analysis under the rule of reason. According to the Court, [t]he gist of the claim is that x-rays, standing alone, are not adequate bases for diagnosis of dental problems or for the formulation of an acceptable course of treatment. Accordingly * * * there is a danger that [insurers] will erroneously decline to pay for treatment that is in fact in the interest of the patient, and that the patient will as a result be deprived of fully adequate care. Unconvinced, the Court explained that "[p]recisely such a justification for withholding information from customers was rejected as illegitimate in the [Professional Engineers] case." The Court continued: The argument is, in essence, that an unrestrained market in which consumers are given access to the information they believe to be relevant to their choices will lead them to make unwise and even dangerous choices. Such an argument amounts to "nothing less than a frontal assault on the basic policy of the Sherman Act."

Both the public safety justification rejected by the Supreme Court in Professional Engineers and the public health justification rejected by the Court in Indiana Dentists were based on the defendants' faulty premise that consumer choices made under competitive market conditions are "unwise" or "dangerous." Here MIT argues that participation in the Overlap arrangement provided some consumers, the needy, with additional choices which an entirely free market would deny them. The facts and arguments before us may suggest some significant areas of distinction from those in Professional Engineers and Indiana Dentists in that MIT is asserting that Overlap not only serves a social benefit, but actually enhances consumer choice. Overlap is not an attempt to withhold a particular desirable service from customers, as was the professional combination in Indiana Dentists, but rather it purports only to seek to extend a service to qualified students who are financially "needy" and would not otherwise be able to afford the high cost of education at MIT. Further, while Overlap resembles the ban on competitive bidding at issue in Professional Engineers, MIT alleges that Overlap enhances competition by broadening the socio-economic sphere of its potential student body. Thus, rather than suppress competition, Overlap may in fact merely regulate competition in order to enhance it, while also deriving certain social benefits. If the rule of reason analysis leads to this conclusion, then indeed Overlap will be beyond the scope of the prohibitions of the Sherman Act.

We note the unfortunate fact that financial aid resources are limited even at the Ivy League schools. A trade-off may need to be made between providing some financial aid to a large number of the most needy students or allowing the free market to bestow the limited financial aid on the very few most talented who may not need financial aid to attain their academic goals. Under such circumstances, if this trade-off is proven to be worthy in terms of obtaining a more diverse student body (or other legitimate institutional goals), the limitation on the choices of the most talented students might not be so egregious as to trigger the obvious concerns which led the Court to reject the "public interest" justifications in *Professional Engineers* and *Indiana Dentists*. However, we leave it for the district court to decide whether full funding of need may be continued on an individual institutional basis, absent Overlap, whether tuition could be lowered as a way to compete for qualified "needy" students, or whether there are other imaginable creative alternatives to implement MIT's professed social welfare goal.

We note too, however, that another aspect of the agreements condemned in *Professional Engineers* and *Indiana Dentists* was that those agreements embodied a strong economic self-interest of the parties to them. In *Professional Engineers*, the undisputed objective of the ban on competitive bidding was to maintain higher prices for engineering services than a free competitive market would sustain. The engineers' public safety justification "rest[ed] on the assumption that the agreement [would] tend to maintain price level; if it had no such effect, it would not serve its intended purpose." Likewise, the Court in *Indiana Dentists* characterized the dentists' agreement to withhold x-rays as an "attempt to thwart" the goal of "choosing the least expensive adequate course of dental treatment." Though not singled out by the Court in these two cases, the nature of the agreements made any public interest argument greatly suspect. To the extent that economic self-interest or revenue maximization is operative in Overlap, it too renders MIT's public interest justification suspect. * * *

In the case sub judice, the quest for economic self-interest is professed to be absent, as it is alleged that the Overlap agreement was intended, not to obtain an economic profit in the form of greater revenue for the participating schools, but rather to benefit talented but needy prospective students who otherwise could not attend the school of their choice.

The nature of higher education, and the asserted procompetitive and pro-consumer features of the Overlap, convince us that a full rule of reason analysis is in order here. It may be that institutions of higher education "require that a particular practice, which could properly be viewed as a violation of the Sherman Act in another context, be treated differently."

It is most desirable that schools achieve equality of educational access and opportunity in order that more people enjoy the benefits of a worthy higher education. There is no doubt, too, that enhancing the quality of our educational system redounds to the general good. To the extent that higher education endeavors to foster vitality of the mind, to promote free exchange between bodies of thought and truths, and better communication among a broad spectrum of individuals, as well as prepares individuals for the intellectual demands of responsible citizenship, it is a common good that should be extended to as wide a range of individuals from as broad a range of socio-economic backgrounds as possible. It is with this in mind that the Overlap Agreement should be submitted to the rule of reason scrutiny under the Sherman Act.

We conclude that the district court was obliged to more fully investigate the procompetitive and noneconomic justifications proffered by MIT than it did when it performed the truncated rule of reason analysis. Accordingly, we will remand this case to the district court with instructions to evaluate Overlap using the full-scale rule of reason analysis outlined above.

The final step of the rule of reason involves determining whether the challenged agreement is necessary to achieve its purported goals. The district court alternatively rejected MIT's social welfare justifications because it "questioned" whether Overlap was necessary to achieve egalitarian educational access. Even if an anticompetitive restraint is intended to achieve a legitimate objective, the restraint only survives a rule of reason analysis if it is reasonably necessary to achieve the legitimate objectives proffered by the defendant. To determine if a restraint is reasonably necessary, courts must examine first whether the restraint furthers the legitimate objectives, and then whether comparable benefits could be achieved through a substantially less restrictive alternative. Once a defendant demonstrates that its conduct promotes a legitimate goal, the plaintiff, in order to prevail, bears the burden of proving that there exists a viable less restrictive alternative.

The district court "questioned" whether the Overlap Agreement was "a necessary ingredient" to achieve the social welfare objectives offered by MIT. The district court implicitly concluded, and we agree, that to some extent the Overlap Agreement promoted equality of access to higher education and economic and cultural diversity. It thus turned directly to the second inquiry—whether a substantially less restrictive alternative, the free market coupled with MIT's institutional resolve, could achieve the same benefits. In a conclusory statement, the court found "no evidence supporting MIT's fatalistic prediction that the end of the Ivy Overlap Group necessarily would sound the death knell of need-blind admissions or need-based aid." Although the district court acknowledged that the end of Overlap could herald the end of full need-based aid at MIT, it also observed that this was not an inevitability if indeed MIT counted full need-based aid among its priority institutional goals.

On remand if the district court, under a full scale rule of reason analysis, finds that MIT has proffered a persuasive justification for the Overlap Agreement, then the Antitrust Division of the Justice Department, the plaintiff in this case, must prove that a reasonable less restrictive alternative exists. The district court should consider, if and when the issue arises, whether the Antitrust Division has shown, by a preponderance of the evidence, that another viable option, perhaps the free market, can achieve the same benefits as Overlap.

IV. CONCLUSION

For the foregoing reasons, we will reverse the judgment of the district court and remand for further proceedings consistent with this opinion.

[The dissenting opinion of Judge Weis is omitted. Eds.]

NOTES AND QUESTIONS

1. *Implications of Financial Aid.* Why do schools offer financial aid to students? Why did MIT and the other schools join the Overlap Group? What will be the impact to schools if they have to compete for students on the basis of financial aid awards?

2. *Price Fixing or Cross-subsidization?* Does the decision adequately account for the market environment in which nonprofit institutions operate? Was the collusive behavior among the Overlap Group the same as normal price fixing or is it an attempt at cross-subsidization, that is, to transfer dollars from students with higher income parents who otherwise would receive non-need based aid to other students? Arguably, the Overlap Agreement did not cause nor was it intended to cause any reduction in output, i.e. financial aid. On remand, if the district court had found under a rule of reason analysis that MIT had offered a persuasive justification for Overlap, what would the burden on the government be? On the last page of its decision, the Third Circuit instructed the district court to consider MIT's non-economic justifications. Is there a valid basis for distinguishing between valid and invalid noncommercial objectives or noneconomic and economic effects?

3. *Congressional Action.* Before the district court's decision, Congress passed the Higher Education Amendments of 1992, Pub. L. No. 102–325, § 1544, 106 Stat. 448, which permitted universities to distribute financial aid solely on the basis of need and to adopt common standards for assessing financial need. However, the legislation prohibited institutions from discussing the "financial aid award to a specific common applicant for financial aid." The district court was able to ignore the legislation because the statute stated " * * * nothing in this section shall * * * affect any antitrust litigation pending." Id.

4. *Settlement.* In December 1993 the Justice Department and MIT settled the lawsuit. The settlement restored several collaborative aspects of the Overlap process. Cooperating schools collectively could set financial aid policies and share certain information submitted to them by common applicants. However, they could not compare individual aid packages. The institutions must use a third party to monitor their activities and assure that the schools are adhering to the agreed upon policies. The practical effect of the agreement was small as the other members of Overlap were not part of the settlement. The agreement required participating schools to adhere to a "blind admissions" policy meaning that ability to pay could not be a factor in the admissions decision, and the school would meet the full financial needs of all admitted students, something only the wealthiest schools could promise. The settlement also prohibited colleges from agreeing or exchanging information about prospective tuition rates or faculty salaries. See Scott Jaschik, Antitrust Case Closed, Chron. Higher Educ., Jan. 5, 1994, at A24.

5. *For Further Reading.* The *Brown University* case created a cottage industry of law review comment. Among the useful contributions are:

Donald Robert Carlson & George Bobrinskoy Shepherd, Cartel on Campus: The Economics and Law of Academic Institutions' Financial Aid Price–Fixing, 71 Or. L. Rev. 563 (1992); Richard Morrison, Price Fixing Among Elite Colleges and Universities, 59 U. Chi. L. Rev. 807 (1992); Steven R. Salbu, Building a Moat Around the Ivory Tower: Pricing Policy in the Business of Higher Education, 75 Marq. L. Rev. 293 (1992); Mark D. Selwyn, Higher Education Under Fire: The New Target of Antitrust, 26 Colum. J. L. & Soc. Probs. 117 (1992); Srikanth Srinivasan, Note: College Financial Aid and Antitrust: Applying the Sherman Act to Collaborative Nonprofit Activity, 46 Stan. L. Rev. 919 (1994).

PROBLEMS

1. If MIT and the Ivy League schools had agreed on tuition, would the Third Circuit have applied the *per se* rule?

2. Would the antitrust laws apply to two philanthropists who "divided the market" by agreeing that one would care for the homeless on the east side of town while the other did so on the west side? See Phillip Areeda & Herbert Hovenkamp, Antitrust Law 261a (3d ed. 2006).

3. The Valley Harvest Coalition consists of a group of food kitchens in Metropolitan Valley that provides meals to individuals according to their ability to pay. Too many of the patrons with sufficient incomes to dine elsewhere are consuming the Coalition's meals leaving fewer meals for the truly needy. The Coalition agrees to grant discounts based upon the patron's income if any, and to prohibit persons above certain income levels from purchasing meals. How would the court in *Brown University* have handled this agreement? See Srikanth Srinivasan, Note: College Financial Aid and Antitrust: Applying the Sherman Act to Collaborative Nonprofit Activity, 46 Stan. L. Rev. 919, 953–54 (1994).

4. Sturdley College is a small coeducational school in bucolic Gowanus, Kansas. It provides residential services including housing in dormitories, meals and social meeting facilities to matriculated students. Approximately 87 percent of the student body resides in residential facilities owned and controlled by Sturdley, but the figure has been declining and dormitory vacancies have increased. Four fraternities provide housing, food and social activities. Because of the need to get to class easily, very few students live off campus. Sturdley desires to have all students reside on campus to improve their social life, particularly women who are not eligible for fraternities and had no sorority alternative. The College also wishes to emphasize its academic image and downplay its reputation as a "party school."

Sturdley's trustees have approved a regulation requiring all students to reside in college-owned facilities and participate in the meal plan. The College then offered to purchase the fraternity buildings at a price that the fraternities consider to be substantially below market. The fraternities allege that the College has violated the Sherman Act. What result?

D.   DAMAGES FOR ANTITRUST LIABILITY

Clayton Act § 4.

American Society of Mechanical Engineers, Inc. v. Hydrolevel Corporation

Supreme Court of the United States, 1982.
456 U.S. 556, 102 S.Ct. 1935.

■ JUSTICE BLACKMUN delivered the opinion of the Court.

[The American Society of Mechanical Engineers (ASME), a nonprofit membership corporation with over 90,000 members drawn from all fields of mechanical engineering, promulgates codes for areas of engineering and industry. Much of its work is done through volunteers from industry and government. The codes, while only advisory, have a powerful economic influence, many of them being incorporated by reference in federal regulations and state and local laws. The Hydrolevel Corporation marketed a safety device for use in water boilers and secured a customer that previously had purchased the competing product of McDonnell & Miller, Inc. (M & M). One of M & M's officials, a vice president (James), was vice chairman of ASME's subcommittee that drafted, revised, and interpreted the segment of petitioner's code governing the safety device in question. Subsequently, he and other M & M officials met with the subcommittee's chairman (Hardin). As a result, M & M sent a letter to the Society asking whether a safety device with a feature such as one contained in Hydrolevel's product satisfied the pertinent code requirements. The letter was referred to Hardin, as chairman of the subcommittee, and ultimately an "unofficial response" was issued, prepared by Hardin but mailed on ASME's stationery over the signature of one of ASME's full-time employees. The response in effect declared Hydrolevel's product unsafe. Thereafter, M & M's salesmen used the subcommittee's response to discourage customers from buying Hydrolevel's product. Hydrolevel subsequently sought a correction from ASME of the unofficial response, but continued to suffer market resistance after the pertinent committee replied. After James' part in the drafting of the original letter of inquiry became public, Hydrolevel filed suit in Federal District Court against the ASME (and others who settled), alleging violation of the Sherman Act. The trial court rejected Hydrolevel's request for jury instructions that ASME could be held liable for its agents' conduct if they acted within the scope of their apparent authority. Instead, the jury was instructed that ASME could be held liable only if it had ratified its agents' actions or if the agents had acted in pursuit of petitioner's interests. The jury, nonetheless, returned a verdict for Hydrolevel. The Court of Appeals affirmed, concluding that ASME could be held liable if its agents had acted within the scope of their apparent authority, and that thus the charge was more favorable to ASME than the law required. The

Supreme Court affirmed, finding that ASME was civilly liable under the antitrust laws if its agents acted with apparent authority.[3] Eds.]

* * *

B

We hold that the apparent authority theory is consistent with the congressional intent to encourage competition. ASME wields great power in the Nation's economy. Its codes and standards influence the policies of numerous States and cities, and, as has been said about "so-called voluntary standards" generally, its interpretations of its guidelines "may result in economic prosperity or economic failure, for a number of businesses of all sizes throughout the country," as well as entire segments of an industry. ASME can be said to be "in reality an extra-governmental agency, which prescribes rules for the regulation and restraint of interstate commerce." When it cloaks its subcommittee officials with the authority of its reputation, ASME permits those agents to affect the destinies of businesses and thus gives them the power to frustrate competition in the marketplace.

The facts of this case dramatically illustrate the power of ASME's agents to restrain competition. M & M instigated the submission of a single inquiry to an ASME subcommittee. For its efforts, M & M secured a mere "unofficial" response authored by a single ASME subcommittee chairman. Yet the force of ASME's reputation is so great that M & M was able to use that one "unofficial" response to injure seriously the business of a competitor.

Furthermore, a standard-setting organization like ASME can be rife with opportunities for anticompetitive activity. Many of ASME's officials are associated with members of the industries regulated by ASME's codes. Although, undoubtedly, most serve ASME without concern for the interests of their corporate employers, some may well view their positions with ASME, at least in part, as an opportunity to benefit their employers. When the great influence of ASME's reputation is placed at their disposal, the less altruistic of ASME's agents have an opportunity to harm their employers' competitors through manipulation of ASME's codes. * * *

A principal purpose of the antitrust private cause of action, see 15 U.S.C. 15, is, of course, to deter anticompetitive practices. It is true that imposing liability on ASME's agents themselves will have some deterrent effect, because they will know that if they violate the antitrust laws through their participation in ASME, they risk the consequences of personal civil liability. But if, in addition, ASME is civilly liable for the antitrust violations of its agents acting with apparent authority, it is much more

---

3. Apparent authority looks to what the third party (potential purchasers of Hydrolevel's safety device) reasonably believes about the relationship between the principal (ASME) and the agent (the full-time employee, who signed the letter prepared by Hardin, and mailed on ASME stationary). Under apparent authority the principal in some way holds out the agent as possessing certain authority and the third party reasonably believes the agent has such authority. See Restatement (Third) of Agency § 2.03. Eds.

likely that similar antitrust violations will not occur in the future. "[P]ressure [will be] brought on [the organization] to see to it that [its] agents abide by the law." United States v. A & P Trucking Co., 358 U.S. 121, 126, 79 S.Ct. 203, 207. Only ASME can take systematic steps to make improper conduct on the part of all its agents unlikely, and the possibility of civil liability will inevitably be a powerful incentive for ASME to take those steps. Thus, a rule that imposes liability on the standard-setting organization—which is best situated to prevent antitrust violations through the abuse of its reputation—is most faithful to the congressional intent that the private right of action deter antitrust violations. * * *

* * * Whether they intend to benefit ASME or not, ASME's agents exercise economic power because they act with the force of the Society's reputation behind them. And, whether they act in part to benefit ASME or solely to benefit themselves or their employers, ASME's agents can have the same anticompetitive effects on the marketplace. The anticompetitive practices of ASME's agents are repugnant to the antitrust laws even if the agents act without any intent to aid ASME, and ASME should be encouraged to eliminate the anticompetitive practices of all its agents acting with apparent authority, especially those who use their positions in ASME solely for their own benefit or the benefit of their employers.

C

Finally, ASME makes two additional arguments in an attempt to avoid antitrust liability. It characterizes treble damages for antitrust violations as punitive, and urges that under traditional agency law the courts do not employ apparent authority to impose punitive damages upon a principal for the acts of its agents. It is true that antitrust treble damages were designed in part to punish past violations of the antitrust laws. But treble damages were also designed to deter future antitrust violations. Moreover, the antitrust private action was created primarily as a remedy for the victims of antitrust violations. Treble damages "make the remedy meaningful by counter-balancing 'the difficulty of maintaining a private suit' " under the antitrust laws. Since treble damages serve as a means of deterring antitrust violations and of compensating victims, it is in accord with both the purposes of the antitrust laws and principles of agency law to hold ASME liable for the acts of agents committed with apparent authority. See Restatement § 217C, Comment c, p. 474 (rule limiting principal's liability for punitive damages does not apply to special statutes giving triple damages).

In addition, ASME contends it should not bear the risk of loss for antitrust violations committed by its agents acting with apparent authority because it is a nonprofit organization, not a business seeking profit. But it is beyond debate that nonprofit organizations can be held liable under the antitrust laws. Although ASME may not operate for profit, it does derive benefits from its codes, including the fees the Society receives for its code-related publications and services, the prestige the codes brings to the Society, the influence they permit ASME to wield, and the aid the standards provide the profession of mechanical engineering. Since the antitrust violation in this case could not have occurred without ASME's codes and ASME's method of administering them, it is not unfitting that ASME be liable for the damages arising from that violation. Furthermore, as shown above, ASME is in the best position to take precautions that will prevent future antitrust violations. Thus, the fact that ASME is a nonprofit organization does not weaken the force of the antitrust and agency principles that indicate that ASME should be liable for Hydrolevel's antitrust injuries.

III

We need not delineate today the outer boundaries of the antitrust liability of standard-setting organizations for the actions of their agents committed with apparent authority. There is no doubt here that Hardin acted within his apparent authority when he answered an inquiry about ASME's Boiler and Pressure Vessel Code as the chairman of the relevant ASME subcommittee. And in this case, we do not face a challenge to a good-faith interpretation of an ASME code reasonably supported by health or safety considerations. See Silver v. New York Stock Exchange, 373 U.S. 341, 83 S.Ct. 1246 (1963). We have no difficulty in finding that this set of facts falls well within the scope of ASME's liability on an apparent authority theory.

When ASME's agents act in its name, they are able to affect the lives of large numbers of people and the competitive fortunes of businesses throughout the country. By holding ASME liable under the antitrust laws for the antitrust violations of its agents committed with apparent authority, we recognize the important role of ASME and its agents in the economy, and we help to ensure that standard-setting organizations will act with care when they permit their agents to speak for them. We thus make it less likely that competitive challengers like Hydrolevel will be hindered by agents of organizations like ASME in the future.

The judgment of the Court of Appeals is affirmed.

So ordered.

[The concurring judgment of CHIEF JUSTICE BURGER is omitted. Eds.]

[The dissenting judgment of Justice Powell, with whom Justices White and Rehnquist joined, is omitted. The dissent feared the rationale of the majority, based on the concept of apparent authority, would impose a potentially crippling burden of treble damages on a broad spectrum of nonprofits, even though the organization never ratified, authorized or derived benefit from the act of the agent. In the dissenters' view, this was an unprecedented expansion of antitrust liability that threatened over deterrence and injustice to nonprofit organizations. Eds.]

NOTES AND QUESTIONS

1. *Standard Setting Organizations.* Trade associations like ASME encourage product standardization through standard setting which assists

consumer safety and reduces cost. ASME standards virtually have the force of law because they are incorporated into federal and state regulations by reference. As the court points out, there are many opportunities for anticompetitive conduct.

2.   Did the court base liability on an anticompetitive policy decision by ASME? Are trade associations such as ASME similar to bar or other professional associations? Are the treble damages punishment for past violations or designed to deter future ones? Note that although the liability here was imposed on the organization, the individuals also could have been sued.

3.   The theory of the majority is that private standard-setting organizations such as ASME will oversee their members more carefully to ensure they do not engage in anti-competitive activities. What supervisory measures could a standard-setting organization introduce to avoid ASME's situation? Does the decision place an insuperable burden on organizations that rely on volunteers?

INDEX

1057

†